THE OXFORD HANDBOOK OF

RHETORICAL STUDIES

THE OXFORD HANDBOOK OF

RHETORICAL STUDIES

Edited by

MICHAEL J. MacDONALD

OXFORD
UNIVERSITY PRESS

OXFORD
UNIVERSITY PRESS

Oxford University Press is a department of the University of Oxford. It furthers
the University's objective of excellence in research, scholarship, and education
by publishing worldwide. Oxford is a registered trade mark of Oxford University
Press in the UK and certain other countries.

Published in the United States of America by Oxford University Press
198 Madison Avenue, New York, NY 10016, United States of America.

Library of Congress Cataloging- in- Publication Data
Names: MacDonald, Michael John, editor.
Title: The Oxford handbook of rhetorical studies / edited by Michael J. MacDonald.
Description: Oxford University Press : New York, NY, 2017. |
Includes bibliographical references and index.
Identifiers: LCCN 2016056248 | ISBN 9780199731596 (hardback) |
ISBN 9780190681845 (updf) | ISBN 9780199984626 (online resource)
Subjects: LCSH: Rhetoric—History and criticism—Handbooks, manuals, etc.
Classification: LCC P301 .O95 2017 | DDC 808.009—dc23
LC record available at https://lccn.loc.gov/2016056248

1 3 5 7 9 8 6 4 2

Printed by Sheridan Books, Inc., United States of America

For my parents,
Shirley Marguerite MacDonald and Donald Kenneth MacDonald

And for my wife,
Carrie Anne Perce

Acknowledgments

I have incurred many debts in the course of editing this handbook. I would like to begin by extending my heartfelt thanks to the 60 contributors whose hard work, professionalism, and generosity of spirit have made this volume possible. I would also like to thank James I. Porter for commenting on an earlier draft of the proposal for this volume. I owe a special debt of gratitude to Stefan Vranka, Executive Editor, Oxford University Press, for his expert guidance over the years it took to organize and edit this volume. I would also like to acknowledge the reviewers and editorial staff at Oxford University Press for their advice and scrupulous copyediting, as well as my friend Jonathan Doering for his editorial assistance with the bibliographies. I am grateful to the Department of English Language and Literature at the University of Waterloo for its support for this project, and to all my colleagues, especially those working in the field of rhetoric: Fraser Easton, Beth Coleman, Frankie Condon, Jay Dolmage, Kenneth Graham, Randy Harris, Ken Hirschkop, Murray McArthur, Kevin McGuirk, Andrew McMurry, Aimée Morrison, Marcel O'Gorman, and Neil Randall. Conversations with these colleagues have shaped and reshaped my understanding of rhetoric over the years. I must also express my gratitude to several of my teachers for their long-standing support and intellectual companionship: Frederick Dolan, Avital Ronell, Judith Butler, Jonathan Culler, and Barbara Cassin. Finally, I would like to acknowledge two masters of the *ars rhetorica* to whom I am especially grateful: my mother, Shirley MacDonald, and my wife, Carrie Perce.

Contents

PART V: EARLY MODERN AND ENLIGHTENMENT RHETORIC

PART VI: MODERN AND CONTEMPORARY RHETORIC

List of Contributors

Rhiannon Ash, Fellow and Tutor, Department of Classics, Merton College, University of Oxford

Shadi Bartsch, Helen A. Regenstein Distinguished Service Professor, Department of Classics, University of Chicago

Ian Bogost, Ivan Allen College Distinguished Chair in Media Studies, Professor of Interactive Computing, Georgia Institute of Technology

Karlyn Kohrs Campbell, Professor, Department of Communication Studies, University of Minnesota

Chris Carey, Professor, Department of Greek and Latin, University College London

Barbara Cassin, Directrice of Research, Centre Nationale de la Recherche Scientifique, Directrice, Centre Léon Robin de recherches sur la pensée antique, University of Paris IV-Sorbonne

Gilbert Chaitin, Professor Emeritus of French and Comparative Literature, Indiana University

Lorraine Code, Distinguished Research Professor Emerita of Philosophy and Social and Political Thought, Department of Philosophy, York University

Joy Connolly, Professor, Department of Classics, New York University

Catherine Conybeare, Professor, Department of Greek, Latin, and Classical Studies, Bryn Mawr College

Rita Copeland, Sheli Z. and Burton X. Rosenberg Professor of Humanities, Professor of Classical Studies, English, and Comparative Literature, University of Pennsylvania

Virginia Cox, Professor, Department of Italian Studies, New York University

Jonathan Culler, Class of 1916 Professor of English and Comparative Literature, Cornell University

William J. Dominik, Emeritus Professor, Department of Classics, University of Otago

Richard Doyle, Liberal Arts Research Professor, Department of English, Pennsylvania State University

Jody Enders, Distinguished Professor of French, Department of French and Italian, University of California at Santa Barbara

Richard Leo Enos, Lillian Radford Chair of Rhetoric and Composition, Department of English, Texas Christian University

Lynn Enterline, Nancy Perot Mulford Professor of English, Department of English, Vanderbilt University

Michael Gagarin, James R. Dougherty, Jr. Centennial Professor Emeritus, Department of Classics, University of Texas at Austin

Eugene Garver, Regents Professor of Philosophy Emeritus, Department of Philosophy, Saint John's University

Cheryl Glenn, Liberal Arts Research Professor of English and Women's Studies, Director, Program in Writing and Rhetoric, Pennsylvania State University

Peter Goodrich, Professor of Law, Director, Law and Humanities, Benjamin N. Cardozo School of Law, Yeshiva University

Paul Goring, Professor, Department of Language and Literature, Norwegian University of Science and Technology

Angus Gowland, Reader in Intellectual History, Department of History, University College London

Erik Gunderson, Associate Professor, Department of Classics, University of Toronto

Thomas Habinek, Professor, Department of Classics, Director, Society of Fellows in the Humanities, University of Southern California

Jon Hall, Professor, Department of Classics, University of Otago

Edward M. Harris, Emeritus Professor, Department of Classics and Ancient History, Durham University, Honorary Professorial Fellow, Department of Classics, Archaeology and Ancient History, University of Edinburgh

Malcolm Heath, Professor of Greek Language and Literature, School of Languages, Cultures and Societies, University of Leeds

Lorna Hutson, Merton Professor of English Literature, Merton College, University of Oxford

Kathleen Hall Jamieson, Elizabeth Ware Packard Professor of Communication, Annenberg School of Communication, University of Pennsylvania

David Kaufer, Paul C. Mellon Professor of Rhetoric and English, Department of English, Carnegie Mellon University

Arthur F. Kinney, Thomas W. Copeland Professor of Literary History, Department of English, University of Massachusetts, Amherst

Robert Kirkbride, Associate Professor of Architecture and Product Design, Parsons School of Design

Elizabeth Losh, Director, Culture, Art, and Technology Program, Sixth College, University of California at San Diego

Andrea A. Lunsford, Louise Hewlett Nixon Professor of English, Stanford University

Michael J. MacDonald, Associate Professor, Department of English Language and Literature, University of Waterloo

Russ McDonald, Professor of English Literature, Department of English and Comparative Literature, Goldsmiths, University of London

Andrew McMurry, Associate Professor, Department of English Language and Literature, University of Waterloo

Peter Mack, Professor, Department of English and Comparative Literary Studies, University of Warwick

Paul Allen Miller, Carolina Distinguished Professor of Classics and Comparative Literature, University of South Carolina

Jean Dietz Moss, Professor Emerita, Department of English, The Catholic University of America

Andrew Norris, Associate Professor, Department of Political Science, University of California at Santa Barbara

Daphne O'Regan, Associate Clinical Professor of Law, Co-Director, Legal Writing Program, College of Law, Michigan State University

Laurent Pernot, Professor, Department of Greek Language and Literature, University of Strasbourg

Heinrich Plett, Professor Emeritus, Department of English, University of Essen

Stanley E. Porter, President and Dean, Professor of New Testament, Roy A. Hope Chair in Christian Worldview, McMaster Divinity College

Adam Potkay, William R. Kenan Professor of Humanities, Department of English, College of William and Mary

Angela G. Ray, Associate Professor, Department of Communication Studies, Northwestern University

Wayne A. Rebhorn, Celanese Centennial Professor, Department of English, University of Texas

Jill Ross, Associate Professor, Centre for Comparative Literature and Centre for Medieval Studies, University of Toronto

Jacqueline Jones Royster, Ivan Allen Jr. Chair in Liberal Arts and Technology, Professor, School of Literature, Media, and Communication, Georgia Institute of Technology

Edward Schiappa, John E. Burchard Professor of Humanities, Department of Comparative Media Studies/Writing, Massachusetts Institute of Technology

Catherine Steel, Professor of Classics, School of Humanities, University of Glasgow

Caroline van Eck, Professor, Department of History of Art, University of Cambridge

Frans H. van Eemeren, Professor Emeritus, Department of Speech Communication, Argumentation Theory and Rhetoric, University of Amsterdam, Director, International Institute of Pragma-Dialectics, Zhejiang University

Theo van Leeuwen, Professor, Department of Language and Communication, University of Southern Denmark

Jeffrey Walker, Professor, Department of Rhetoric and Writing, University of Texas at Austin

Peter Walmsley, Professor, Department of English and Cultural Studies, McMaster University

Arthur E. Walzer, Professor, Department of Communication Studies, University of Minnesota

John O. Ward, Honorary Associate, Centre for Medieval Studies, University of Sydney

Ruth Webb, Professor of Greek Language and Literature, University of Lille 3

Danielle Wetzel, Teaching Professor, Department of English, Carnegie Mellon University

Paul Woodruff, Darrell K. Royal Professor in Ethics and American Society, Department of Philosophy, University of Texas at Austin

Harvey Yunis, Andrew W. Mellon Professor of Humanities and Classical Studies, Rice University

Timeline[1]

CE

42   Hortensia, "Speech to the Triumvirs"

50   Longinus, *On the Sublime*

50   Aelius Theon, *Progymnasmata*

60   Philodemus, *On Rhetoric*

93   Quintilian, *Institutio oratoria*

97   Tacitus, *Dialogue on Oratory*

100   Suetonius, *De grammaticis et rhetoribus*

150   Aelius Aristides, *On Rhetoric: Against Plato*

190   Hermogenes, *On Issues, Progymnasmata, De inventione*

225   Apsines, *Rhetorica*

230   Athenaeus, *Deipnosophistes*

235   Philostratus, *Lives of the Sophists*

250   Demetrius, *On Style*

250   Diogenes Laertius, *Lives of Eminent Philosophers*

250   Menander Rhetor, *On Epideictic*

300   Aelius Donatus, *Ars minor, Ars major*

335   Marius Victorinus, *Commentary on the "De inventione"*

350   Libanius, *Types of Letters*

350   Julius Victor, *Art of Rhetoric*

365   Sulpitius Victor, *Oratorium institutionum praecepta*

395   Eunapius, *Lives of the Sophists*

398   Augustine, *Confessions*

399   Aphthonius, *Progymnasmata*

420   Martianus Capella, *De nuptiis Philologiae et Mercurii*

426   Augustine, *On Christian Doctrine*

450   Fortunatianus, *Artes rhetoricae*

520   Priscian, *Fundamentals Adapted from Hermogenes, Institutiones grammaticae*

523   Boethius, *De topicis differentiis, An Overview of the Structure of Rhetoric*

562   Cassiodorus, *Institutiones*

625   Isidore of Seville, *Etymologiae*

710   Bede, *De schematibus et tropis*

794   Alcuin, *Disputatio de rhetorica et de virtutibus*

817   Rabanus Maurus, *De institutione clericorum*

995   Notker Labeo, *Nova rhetorica*

1087 Alberic of Monte Cassino, *Flowers of Rhetoric*

1115 Hugh of Bologna, *Rationes dictandi prosaice*

1120 Hugh of St. Victor, *Didascalicon*

1135 Anonymous of Bologna, *Principles of Letter Writing*

1135 Thierry of Chartres, *Commentary on the "De Inventione," Commentary on "Rhetorica ad Herennium"*

1159 John of Salisbury, *Metalogicon*

1210 Geoffrey of Vinsauf, *Poetria nova*

1210 Thomas of Salisbury, *Summa de arte praedicandi*
1228 William of Auvergne, *De arte praedicandi*
1233 John of Garland, *Parisiana poetria*
1260 Brunetto Latini, *Rettorica*
1272 Giles of Rome, *Commentary on Aristotle's "Rhetoric"*
1320 Robert de Basevorn, *The Form of Preaching*
1340 Alain de Lille, *Compendium on the Art of Preaching*
1404 Christine de Pizan, *The Book of the City of Ladies*
1436 Margery Kempe, *The Book of Margery Kempe*
1440 George of Trebizond, *Five Books on Rhetoric*
1440 Lorenzo Valla, *The Refinements of the Latin Language*
1483 Rudolf Agricola, *Three Books Concerning Dialectical Invention*
1485 Giovanni Pico della Mirandola, *Letter to Ermolao Barbaro*
1511 Desiderius Erasmus, *De ratione studii*
1512 Desiderius Erasmus, *De copia*
1521 Philip Melanchthon, *Elementorum rhetorices libri duo*
1523 Philip Melanchthon, *The Praise of Eloquence*
1524 Leonard Cox, *The Arte or Craft of Rhethoryke*
1528 Desiderius Erasmus, *Ciceronianus*
1531 Juan Luis Vives, *On Teaching the Disciplines*
1533 Petrus Mosellanus, *De schematibus et tropis*
1543 Johannes Susenbrotus, *Epitome troporum ac schematum*
1544 Omer Talon, *Rhetorica*
1546 Sperone Speroni, *Dialogue on Rhetoric*
1550 Richard Sherry, *A Treatise of Schemes and Tropes*
1551 Thomas Wilson, *The Rule of Reason*
1553 Thomas Wilson, *The Art of Rhetoric*
1555 Peter Ramus, *Dialectique*
1555 Richard Sherry, *A Treatise of the Figures of Grammar and Rhetorike*
1560 Cypriano Soares, *De arte rhetorica*
1564 Richard Rainolde, *The Foundacion of Rhetorike*
1567 Rudolphus Agricola, *De inventione dialectica*
1573 John Rainolds, *Oxford Lectures on Aristotle's "Rhetoric"*
1575 Jacques Amyot, *An Epitome of Royal Eloquence*
1576 Johann Sturm, *De elocutione*
1577 Gabriel Harvey, *Rhetor*
1577 Henry Peacham, *The Garden of Eloquence*
1579 Sir Philip Sidney, *An Apology for Poetry*
1584 Dudley Fenner, *The Artes of Logicke and Rhethorike*
1586 Angel Day, *The English Secretary*
1588 Abraham Fraunce, *The Arcadian Rhetoric*
1589 George Puttenham, *The Arte of English Poesie*
1598 Charles Butler, *Rhetoricae libri duo*

1599   John Hoskins, *Directions for Speech and Style*
1605   Francis Bacon, *The Advancement of Learning*
1607   Bartholomeus Keckermann, *Systema rhetorica*
1619   Nicholas Caussin, *De eloquentia sacra et humana*
1620   Francis Bacon, *The New Organon*
1621   Gerard Vossius, *Rhetorices contractae*
1637   Thomas Hobbes, *Art of Rhetorique*
1644   John Bulwer, *Chirologia*, *Chironomia*
1657   John Smith, *The Mysterie of Rhetorique Unvail'd*
1666   Margaret Fell, *Women's Speaking Justified, Proved and Allowed by the Scriptures*
1671   René Rapin, *Réflexions sur l'usage de l'eloquence de ce temps*
1675   Michel Le Faucheur, *Traitté de l'action de l'orateur*
1676   Bernard Lamy, *De l'art de parler*
1682   Obadiah Walker, *Some Instructions Concerning the Art of Oratory*
1687   Dominique Bouhours, *La manière de bien penser dans les ouvrages d'esprit*
1694   Mary Astell, *A Serious Proposal to the Ladies*
1709   Giambattista Vico, *On the Study Methods of our Time*
1711   Giambattista Vico, *Institutiones oratoriae*
1718   François Fénelon, *Dialogues on Eloquence*
1728   Claude Buffier, *Traité de l'éloquence*
1728   John Henley, *Oratory Transactions*
1728   Charles Rollin, *Traité des études: De la manière d'enseigner et d'étudier les Belles Lettres*
1729   César Du Marsais, *Des tropes*
1748   John Mason, *Essay on Elocution*
1755   John Holmes, *The Art of Rhetoric Made Easy*
1759   John Lawson, *Lectures Concerning Oratory*
1759   John Ward, *A System of Oratory*
1762   James Burgh, *The Art of Speaking*
1762   Henry Home, Lord Kames, *Elements of Criticism*
1762   Thomas Sheridan, *A Course of Lectures on Elocution*
1763   Adam Smith, *Lectures on Rhetoric and Belles Lettres*
1773   John Herries, *The Elements of Speech*
1776   George Campbell, *Philosophy of Rhetoric*
1781   Joseph Priestley, *A Course of Lectures on Oratory and Criticism*
1781   John Walker, *Elements of Elocution*
1783   Hugh Blair, *Lectures on Rhetoric and Belles Lettres*
1806   Gilbert Austin, *Chironomia*
1827   Samuel Newman, *Practical System of Rhetoric*
1828   Richard Whateley, *Elements of Rhetoric*
1844   Alexander Jamieson, *Grammar of Rhetoric and Polite Literature*
1850   Henry Day, *Elements of the Art of Rhetoric*
1863   Carolus Halm, ed., *Rhetores latini minores*

1866 Alexander Bain, *English Composition and Rhetoric*

1870 John Hart, *A Manual of Composition and Rhetoric*

1873 Friedrich Nietzsche, "On Truth and Lies in the Extra-Moral Sense," *Lecture Notes on Rhetoric*

1877 David Hill, *The Science of Rhetoric*

1878 Adams Hill, *The Principles of Rhetoric*

1900 Gertrude Buck, "The Present Status of Rhetorical Theory"

1900 John Genung, *Working Principles of Rhetoric*

1931 Kenneth Burke, *Counterstatement*

1936 I. A. Richards, *The Philosophy of Rhetoric*

1945 Kenneth Burke, *A Grammar of Motives*

1948 Richard Weaver, *Ideas Have Consequences*

1950 Kenneth Burke, *A Rhetoric of Motives*

1951 Marshall McLuhan, *The Mechanical Bride*

1953 Jacques Lacan, "The Function and Field of Speech in the Unconscious"

1953 Richard Weaver, *The Ethics of Rhetoric*

1957 Roland Barthes, *Mythologies*

1958 Chaïm Perelman and Lucie Olbrechts-Tyteca, *The New Rhetoric: A Treatise on Argumentation*

1959 Stephen Toulmin, *The Uses of Argument*

1960 Hans-Georg Gadamer, *Truth and Method*

1961 Wayne Booth, *The Rhetoric of Fiction*

1962 Marshall McLuhan, *The Gutenberg Galaxy*

1964 Marshall McLuhan, *Understanding Media*

NOTE

1. This timeline is limited to key works of rhetorical theory and ends around 1960. Texts about rhetoric begin to proliferate after this date. Dates for many ancient and medieval works remain a matter of conjecture and should therefore be treated as approximations. More bibliographical information—more than 1,000 books, chapters, and articles—can be found in the references section at the end of each chapter.

INTRODUCTION

MICHAEL J. MACDONALD

Oratory is a greater thing, and has its sources in more arts and branches of study, than people suppose.

—Cicero, *De oratore*

I therefore propose that there be contrived with all convenient dispatch, at public expense, a Rhetorical Chest of Drawers ... divided into *loci* or *places*, being repositories for matter and argument.

—Alexander Pope, *The Art of Sinking in Poetry*

INTRODUCTION

Aims and Organization

IF a big book is a "big evil" (*megalōi kakōi*), as the Roman poet Callimachus contends, then a portly handbook devoted to rhetorical studies would appear to be a big evil indeed.[1] After all, rhetoric, if it is still a vital art, is widely viewed in Platonic terms as an "evil craft" (Plato, *Laws* 937e) of verbal artifice and deception that makes the unjust argument appear just and beguiles the mind with "a kind of evil persuasion" (Gorgias, *Encomium of Helen* 14; trans. Kennedy).[2] Nevertheless, one of the most remarkable trends in the humanities and social sciences in the last four decades has been the resurgence of interest in the history, theory, and practice of rhetoric as an object of serious scholarly inquiry. Far from vanishing into the "cemetery of human realities" (Gasset [1932] 1993: 117) or, at best, surviving like a Nietzschean "concept-mummy" (*Begriffs-Mumie*), rhetoric has enjoyed something of a renaissance in the twentieth century, both as a subject of research and as a field of practice.[3] To begin with, new methods of textual and historical analysis, from feminism and semiotics to psychoanalysis and New Historicism, have energized the field of rhetorical studies by advancing new (and often critical) interpretations of canonical texts and, more broadly, of the Greco-Roman rhetorical tradition and its "empire of the word" (Irigaray 1991: 109). In addition, new approaches to rhetorical theory have expanded the domain of rhetoric to include everything from the sophistic logic operating in dreams and unconscious desire (Lacan 1977) to the bio-rhetorical strategies of plants and nonhuman animals (Kennedy 1998). Finally, new media and information technologies have engendered novel forms of rhetorical practice, such as the persuasive design of computational games (Bogost 2007) and the use of digitized words and images as weapons of immaterial war (Defense Science Board 1999).[4] As a consequence, virtually every field and historical period of rhetoric has become a subject of intensive research and teaching in disciplines across the humanities and social sciences. The vibrancy of rhetorical studies as an international, transdisciplinary endeavor is reflected in the growing number of scholarly organizations devoted to rhetoric, each with its own system of journals, institutes, and conferences.[5] In an age of global digital data networks and "viral" communication, rhetoric, it seems, is once again "contagious" and "communicable" (Nietzsche [1872–3] 1989: 213).

Featuring 60 commissioned chapters by leading rhetoric experts from 12 countries, *The Oxford Handbook of Rhetorical Studies* is designed to offer students and scholars an accessible but sophisticated one-volume introduction to the multidisciplinary field of rhetorical studies. Aimed at readers approaching rhetoric for the first time, the *Handbook* traces the history of Western rhetoric from ancient Greece and Rome through the Renaissance to the present day and surveys the role of rhetoric in more than 30 academic disciplines and fields of social practice. This double structure—a chronological history with thematically interlocking chapters—allows the *Handbook* to be read serially, by historical period, as well as topically, by subject matter. Read as a history of rhetoric in the European tradition (the diachronic "journey"),[6] for example, the *Handbook* offers chapters on ancient Greek rhetoric (11), ancient Roman rhetoric (13), medieval rhetoric (5), Renaissance rhetoric (8), early modern and Enlightenment rhetoric (7), and modern and contemporary rhetoric (16). Approached as a survey of rhetoric across disciplines and fields of social practice (the synchronic "network"), the *Handbook* provides chapters on law (4), politics (7), historiography (2), science (3), education (3), poetry and literature (4), poetics and literary criticism (5), theater and performance (4), philosophy (4), sophistics (3), feminism and Critical Race Theory (3), and art and architecture (3), as well as introductory framing chapters (5) and others on rhetoric and homiletics, the elocutionary movement, argumentation, psychoanalysis, deconstruction, semiotics, composition, social epistemology, environment, and digital media.[7] This organization is designed to help readers chart the historical mutations and redeployments of rhetoric while exploring the manifold connections between rhetoric and other disciplines and cultural fields. It also reflects two primary objectives of the *Handbook*: first, to provide readers with an engaging and reasonably comprehensive one-volume introduction to the history and theory of rhetoric in the European and North American context and, second, to explore the intersections between rhetoric and other disciplines and social fields, including new sites of rhetorical theory and practice that emerge in the twentieth century.

To reach as broad a readership as possible, I have structured the *Handbook* around established academic disciplines and commissioned chapters that provide the basic information expected of a handbook—coverage of important texts, concepts, authors, problems, and scholarly debates—while still trying to pose challenging questions and present new arguments about the history, theory, and practice of rhetoric. More specifically, I envision four groups of readers who may find this handbook particularly useful, whether in print or digital format:[8] undergraduate and graduate students confronting rhetoric for the first time and searching for a map to the historical and theoretical "maze" (Fortunatianus, *Artis rhetoricae libri tres* 1) of rhetorical study; university instructors seeking a one-volume introduction to rhetorical studies for lectures and use in the classroom; advanced scholars of rhetoric searching for historical context and new points of departure for research projects; and scholars in disciplines across the humanities and social sciences looking for points of entry into the field of rhetoric. With this broad readership in mind, I have also incorporated a number of other features to make the *Handbook* useful and accessible, including: (1) detailed descriptions of all 60 chapters; (2) a timeline of key texts in the history of rhetorical theory; (3) translations of all passages in Greek, Latin, French, and other languages; (4) extensive cross-referencing between chapters to help readers navigate the book thematically; (5) repetition of basic Greek and Latin rhetorical terms across all chapters; (6) complete titles for ancient and medieval texts rather than the abbreviations customary in Classics; (7) a dual dating system to indicate the original publication date of older texts (e.g., "Puttenham [1589] 2007"); (8) suggestions for further reading at the end of most chapters; and (9) a glossary of more than 300 Greek and Latin rhetorical terms, many illustrated with examples—*florilegia*, or "flowers of reading"—culled from the plays of William Shakespeare. My hope is that these pedagogical features will make the *Handbook* a handy introduction to rhetorical studies for students and scholars in Classics, English, rhetoric, drama, comparative literature, communication, media studies, philosophy, political science, and other adjacent disciplines.

Although the chapters in this volume are arranged chronologically, the *Handbook* does not unfold a teleological narrative that traces the evolution—or devolution—of a fixed, unitary "classical" rhetorical tradition over the arc of centuries.[9] The conceptual lexicon of Greek rhetoric is historically contingent; there is no transhistorical essence of rhetoric, and the categories of Greco-Roman rhetorical theory do not "map easily" onto the verbal practices of other cultures (see Schiappa, ch. 1).[10] In fact, the image of rhetoric that emerges in this volume is not that of a monolithic cultural institution that is "immutable, impassive, and virtually immortal" (Barthes [1970] 1994: 15) but that of a protean, chameleonic art whose identity, purpose, and significance are contested in every period—beginning with the Greek word *rhētorikē* itself. And despite its heft, this handbook does not pretend to offer a comprehensive account of the history of rhetoric or the field of rhetorical studies. Even if this were a desirable goal, no book or series of books could hope to provide a *speculum*, or panoptic survey, of the realm of rhetoric, even in one historical epoch: the "empire" of Greco-Roman rhetoric, as Roland Barthes calls it, is so vast in historical and geographical scope that it has "digested regimes, religions, and civilizations" ([1970] 1994: 15). In terms of geography, for example, the *Handbook* is limited to the study of rhetoric in Europe and North America. In terms of history, entire centuries disappear, while countless major authors go missing, to say nothing of marginalized and subaltern authors and the verbal practices and traditions of other cultures. Gaps and lacunae abound in every period, especially in the modern and contemporary section, which lacks contributions on postcolonial rhetoric, disability rhetoric, comparative rhetoric, queer rhetoric, and countless other burgeoning areas of inquiry. Borgesian editorial fantasies aside, even a stout handbook must be highly selective: a "Rhetorical Chest of Drawers" can have only so many "repositories for matter and argument" (Pope 1883: 82). What *The Oxford Handbook of Rhetorical Studies* seeks to provide is a selective overview of current directions in rhetorical studies as practiced by preeminent scholars from across Europe, Great Britain, and North America—both established and emerging, many of them women (25)—working in different fields and periods in the history and theory of rhetoric.

Defining Rhetoric

"Competition over the correct definition of rhetoric," observes Friedrich Nietzsche in his *Description of Rhetoric* (1872–3), "goes on throughout the whole of antiquity, and specifically among philosophers and orators" ([1872–3] 1989: 5). Rhetoric defies definition in part because of the elusiveness of its subject matter (the contingent world of signifying practices and their effects)[11] and in part because definition itself is a rhetorical act that imposes a point of view on its subject and may even call it into being (Burke 1966; Lacan 1977). The English word "rhetoric" stems from the Greek *rhētorikē*, which means the art of the public speaker (*rhētor*) or politician. Ironically, however, the word *rhētorikē* itself may be a rhetorical artifact: Plato appears to have coined *rhētorikē* in his *Gorgias* (387 BCE) to narrow the scope of the sophistic art of *logos* (*technē logon*) and to counterpose rhetoric to Socratic dialectic (*dialektikē*) as the true science of discourse (Cole 1991; Schiappa 1999). In addition to inaugurating the war between philosophy and sophistry (*polemon* is the first word of the dialogue), Plato's virtuosic rhetorical performance in the *Gorgias* brings "rhetoric" into being and at the same time mounts its most decisive critique, one that resonates today: besides being the mere "producer of persuasion" (*peithous apa demiourgos*) (453a2), rhetoric is flattery, display, quibbling, sophistry, captious reasoning, deception, empty verbiage, and demagoguery.[12] After the *Gorgias* and its reduction of rhetoric to cookery in the soul (the sophist is a mere *saucier* of speeches), competing definitions of rhetoric begin to proliferate, starting with Plato's later dialogue, *Phaedrus* (370 BCE): the art of leading souls to true knowledge by means of dialogue and dialectic (Socrates's *psychagōgia*); the faculty of discovering the means of persuasion on any subject (Aristotle); speaking well (the Stoic *eu legein*); knowing how to speak well (Quintilian's *bene dicendi scientia*); discovering and communicating the truths of Scripture (Augustine); speaking well on civil questions (Rabanus Maurus); applying reason and imagination to move the will (Francis Bacon); producing belief and action by means of symbols (Kenneth Burke); the art of practical reasoning and non-formal argumentation (Chaïm Perelman); the study of the tropological dimensions of literary and philosophical language (Paul de Man); speaking as/by women (Luce Irigaray's *parler femmes/par [les] femmes*). As these examples suggest, competition over the definition of rhetoric begins in antiquity and continues throughout its history to the present day.

A further difficulty in defining rhetoric is that the meaning of the English word "rhetoric," like the Greek word *logos*, encompasses both the art of rhetoric and its products (e.g., persuasion, speeches, texts, advertisements, etc.). As a consequence, the terms "rhetoric" and "rhetorical" are today used to describe a baffling array of practices and artifacts, so much so that it is perhaps more appropriate to speak of "rhetorics" than rhetoric. Moreover, if the history of rhetoric since the eighteenth century has been one of gradual atrophy (Vickers 1988), disintegration (Lyotard 1984), and restriction to matters of style and figuration (Genette 1982),[13] recent decades have witnessed a remarkable expansion of what Chaïm Perelman calls the "realm of rhetoric" (*l'empire rhétorique*) (1982: 153). Kenneth Burke, for example, amplifies rhetoric to include all "symbolic action" (1966: 15) and dissolves the distinction between semantics and pragmatics ("Wherever there is 'meaning,' there is 'persuasion'" [1969: 172]), while George Kennedy contends that human rhetoric—defined, nebulously enough, as the "energy inherent in communication"—is one species of a universal genus of "bio-rhetoric" (1992: 2) that traces its origins not to the *Wunder-Ursprung* of "classical" Greek culture but to the earliest stages of the evolutionary trajectory of living systems. And although structuralism contributed to the modern dismantling of rhetoric by emphasizing language as system (*langue*) over discourse as performance (*parole*), it also renewed interest in the tropes and figures as core properties of language itself and, through semiology, the "study of the life of signs within society" (Saussure 1959: 16), extended the range of rhetorical objects to embrace the whole universe of signs and signifying practices—the semiosphere.[14] The sheer variety of artifacts and practices discussed in the present volume testifies to the multifaceted nature of rhetoric as a concept and a field of study: computational games, legal cases, speeches, plays, buildings, advertisements, astronomy treatises, bodies, statuary, feminist manifestos, novels, botanical atlases, music, parliamentary rolls, poems, propaganda, memory theaters, gestures, philosophical dialogues, sermons, presidential messages, medieval *summae*, farces, paintings, architectural ornament, thermodynamics, and countless others. In keeping with the expansive sense of the rhetorical that develops over the course of the 60 chapters that comprise this handbook, I shall define rhetoric (nebulously enough) as the art of effective composition and persuasion in speech, writing, and other media.

In light of the historical and disciplinary scope of the book in your hands (or on your screen), the best way to introduce this volume—and the field of rhetorical studies—is by providing an overview of the chapters and their arguments. Although the *Handbook* proceeds in chronological order, chapters in each historical period are organized into thematic clusters that move from rhetoric as politics and social practice (law, science, education, etc.) to rhetoric as literature and aesthetic theory (poetry, criticism,

architecture, etc.). In the foregoing I also organize the chapter summaries thematically to provide a topical survey or "snapshot" of the volume as a whole. These topics include: (1) introductory chapters; (2) rhetoric and law; (3) rhetoric and politics;
(4) rhetoric and historiography; (5) rhetoric and education; (6) rhetoric and philosophy; (7) sophistics, declamation, and homiletics; (8) rhetoric, theater, and performance;
(9) rhetoric, poetry, and literature; (10) rhetoric, poetics, and literary criticism; (11) rhetoric, art, and architecture; (12) rhetoric and science; (13) rhetoric, feminism, and Critical
Race Theory; and (14) contemporary developments.

THEMATIC OVERVIEW OF CHAPTERS

Introductory Chapters

Most sections of this handbook are framed by an introductory chapter that offers an
overview of rhetoric in the period to contextualize the chapters that follow. Edward
Schiappa (ch. 1: "The Development of Greek Rhetoric") introduces Part I by surveying
ancient Greek rhetoric from the fifth century BCE to the Hellenistic period. Focusing on
the "linguistic task" (Havelock 1983: 7) of the early writers on rhetoric, Schiappa argues
that the emergence of rhetoric as a discipline was "coterminous" with the development
of a technical vocabulary to conceptualize what would come to be known as rhetorical
theory and pedagogy. Beginning with the sophists and their investigation of language,
argument, and persuasion (the art of *logos*), this process of "disciplining" rhetoric culminates in the theorizing of Plato and Aristotle (as noted previously, *rhētorikē* itself
may be a Platonic neologism). In addition to tracing the origins and development of
rhetoric in the classical period, Schiappa outlines advances in rhetorical theory during
the Hellenistic era, including the intensive study of style, the emergence of *stasis* (issue)
theory as a method of legal analysis, and the codification of the 14 rhetorical exercises
known as the *progymnasmata*.

In his introductory survey of ancient Roman rhetoric that opens Part II of the
Handbook, William J. Dominik (ch. 12: "The Development of Roman Rhetoric")
argues that while Roman rhetoric is often treated as an adumbration of Greek models
and doctrines, another useful approach is to focus on the uniquely Roman "cultural
dynamic" that shaped Latin rhetorical theory and practice. In addition to Romanizing
Greek terms and employing Latin literary and legal examples, theorists strove to create a native Latin rhetoric that reflected its agrarian roots and reinforced elite male
Roman attitudes toward national, class, and gender identity. This attention to the sin-
gularities of the Roman social context also leads Dominik to challenge the scholarly
consensus that rhetoric degenerated under the Empire: law courts remained arenas
of rhetorical activity; genres such as epic, lyric, historiography, and the novel flourished; and declamation—often maligned for its lurid, improbable themes—emerged

as a vital cultural practice intimately connected to the "social and political realities" of Roman life.

John O. Ward (ch. 25: "The Development of Medieval Rhetoric") introduces Part III by charting the history of medieval rhetoric from the fourth century CE to the Renaissance. Emphasizing the practical orientation of rhetoric in the Middle Ages, Ward argues that teachers "kept alive" the repertoire of ancient rhetoric as an archive of knowledge for improving oral and written communication in the context of Christian culture. Ward details some of the principal trends in medieval rhetoric, including the role of declamation in schoolroom training, the rise of ecclesiastical rhetoric, the close link between rhetoric, grammar, and dialectic (the *trivium*), and the production of rhetoric manuals tailored to emerging "niche markets" in medieval society. In addition, Ward introduces a previously unknown rhetoric textbook discovered in a fourteenth-century manuscript in Bruges, Belgium: a *summa* that represents a breakthrough in the medieval "digestion" of classical rhetoric and prefigures the encompassing vision of rhetoric elaborated by the Renaissance humanists.

Rhetoric also exercised a decisive influence over European culture during the Renaissance: understood in its broad, humanist sense as a system of interpretation, composition, persuasion, and performance, rhetoric "structured the culture of the age" (Trousdale 2002: 631). In his introduction to Part IV, Heinrich Plett (ch. 30: "Rhetoric and Humanism") provides a history of humanist rhetoric from its inception in quattrocento Italy to its decline in the seventeenth century. In addition to outlining the causes for the resurgence of interest in rhetoric in the Renaissance, such as the unearthing of ancient rhetoric treatises, the advent of the printing press, and the wide dissemination of vernacular rhetoric manuals, Plett sheds new light on the "intermedial" aspects of Renaissance rhetoric by sketching out the relationship between the pictorial arts and the memory arts, the role of visual rhetoric in *Rederijker* plays in Dutch and Belgian chambers of rhetoric, and the use of rhetorical concepts to theorize and interpret nonverbal arts (including *Klangrede* or "musical eloquence"). The renaissance of rhetoric in the sixteenth century, Plett concludes, serves as a reminder that history is punctuated by declines and revivals of rhetoric, with the last several decades bearing witness to another *renovatio rhetorica*.

One such renovated rhetoric that emerged in eighteenth-century Britain was the "New Rhetoric" of Joseph Priestley and George Campbell. Arthur E. Walzer (ch. 41: "Origins of British Enlightenment Rhetoric") introduces a series of chapters on Enlightenment rhetoric by arguing that while the New Rhetoric departed from the Ciceronian tradition of rhetoric as civic persuasion by recasting rhetorical theory in psychological terms, it also developed in close dialogue with ancient rhetorical theory, especially in its use of "vivacity" (*enargeia*) to explain how sense impressions produce belief. In addition to showing how the New Rhetoric, like empiricist philosophy, drew on classical rhetoric for its epistemology, Walzer shows how Adam Smith and Hugh Blair turn to the French tradition of belles lettres to shift the focus of rhetoric from composition to criticism and to formulate a general theory of discourse that accounts for literature, history, philosophy, and other genres. The belletristic emphasis on literacy and vernacular literature,

Walzer suggests, also served an important sociocultural purpose—that of fashioning the modern, polite man of taste and sensibility.

Rhetoric and Law

Another cluster of essays in this volume explores the relationship between rhetoric and law. Focusing on the "mutual influence" of law on rhetoric and rhetoric on law in ancient Greece, Michael Gagarin (ch. 2) argues that a legal context was crucial for the development of rhetoric in Sicily in the mid-fifth century BCE, for the rhetorical innovations of the sophists, and for the critical assessments of rhetoric by Plato and Aristotle. In the absence of lawyers and professional judges, Gagarin argues, the persuasive skill of litigants before large, popular juries often decided the outcome of trials, and for this reason sophists and legal speechwriters (*logographoi*) devised rhetorical tactics and techniques—modes of narrative exposition, methods for creating character, and arguments from probability (*eikos*)—for composing effective forensic speeches. Arguing that rhetoric was not a perversion of justice (as Plato charges) but an essential component of legal argument that enabled Athens to sustain the rule of law, Gagarin analyzes these strategies of forensic persuasion in action through a reading of "On the Killing of Eratosthenes," showing how Lysias employs narrative, direct speech, vivid detail, and literary allusion to construct a plausible defense for the murder.

Roman law, like Greek law, was an intensely rhetorical field, though in ways that reflect the Roman fusion of legal and political matters and the adversarial, theatrical nature of forensic oratory as a weapon of intra-elite male rivalry—"lucrative and blood-soaked eloquence" (Tacitus, *Dialogus de oratoribus* 12). Tracing the history of Roman law from pre-Ciceronian advocates to the beginning of the Empire, Richard Leo Enos (ch. 13) argues that Roman legal rhetoric was not only a "dynamic activity" in interpreting, arguing, and making law but also a source of political power: laws themselves were the product of political debate, and winning cases was a way for the *advocatus* to secure favor and influence public affairs. Moving from politics to aesthetics, Enos also spells out the literate and literary elements of Roman judicial rhetoric, including the written text as the locus of juridical authority, the circulation of model trial speeches for study and emulation, and the publication of revised trial speeches as forensic fiction or "rhetorical literature."

Rhetorical training in early modern England, as in Rome, was oriented toward the law: the humanist pedagogical program was designed to produce lawyers. As Lorna Hutson (ch. 32) points out in her chapter on rhetoric and early modern law, however, many scholars maintain that humanist rhetoric exerted little influence over legal developments in sixteenth-century England. Hutson contests this view by arguing that the humanist emphasis on topical invention blurred the boundary between rhetoric and dialectic in ways that had important consequences for Anglo-American law. Focusing on the interaction of rhetorical and dialectical "habits of mind" in humanist legal thought, Hutson shows how this "reformed" dialectic absorbs rhetorical techniques such as topical invention, *stasis* theory, narrative, metaphor, appeals to emotion, and even arguments from etymology. To illustrate how rhetoric influenced the "reasoned decisions" of courts and, with them, the law itself, Hutson performs a close reading of this "mixed terminology" of rhetoric and dialectic at work in *Calvin's Case* (1608).

Finally, in his chapter on rhetoric and modern law, Peter Goodrich (ch. 48) contends that digital media and the pervasive role of images in society—the emergence of the "videosphere"—have transformed the practice of law and renewed interest in the rhetorical dimensions of legal advocacy. After noting that modern legal rhetoric is a "homeless" discipline that evolved in conjunction with semiotics, literary theory, and hermeneutics, Goodrich argues that the virtualization of the law by digital cameras, the Internet, and other tele-technologies has shifted the arena of legal argument from page to screen, democratized the law by erasing the boundary or "bar" between the courtroom and the public sphere, and inspired a curriculum devoted to new "technologies of lawyering," especially the invention, arrangement, and delivery of persuasive images. The virtual life of forensic rhetoric supports Goodrich's more general historical claim about the expanding jurisdiction of rhetoric and its emblematic motto, *Rhetorica non moritur*: rhetoric does not die—it "morphs" and mutates under the pressure of changing social demands and new media technologies.

Rhetoric and Politics

The next set of chapters in this handbook is devoted to rhetoric and politics. Rhetoric is not only a method for composing effective discourse but also an art of thinking and acting in the temporal, contingent sphere of opinion and probable knowledge. For this reason, rhetoric, as an art of judgment and prudential reasoning concerned with matters of opinion and persuasion (rather than logical or scientific demonstration), has always been closely associated with politics and political theory. A major impetus for the development of rhetoric in ancient Greece, for example, was the emergence of a political system in which citizens participated directly in deliberations about matters concerning the welfare of the *polis*. Edward M. Harris (ch. 3) contends that the practice of political rhetoric in ancient Athens was in many ways determined by the democratic institutions of the city, above all by the deliberative procedures of the Assembly (*ecclēsia*), the main forum for political speech. Unlike modern "aggregative" politics, Harris argues, ancient Greek politics was "integrative" and therefore concerned not with the interests of individuals, factions, or parties but with the common good of citizens. This democratic orientation, Harris contends, gave shape to many of the persuasive strategies of deliberative rhetoric, such as invoking traditional values, establishing one's moral integrity, addressing the whole body of citizens, focusing on what is advantageous to the *polis*, and avoiding the sophistic stratagems used in legal rhetoric.

Joy Connolly (ch. 14), in her chapter on rhetoric and politics in ancient Rome, argues that oratory played a central role in the civic operations of the Republic and in the history of republican political theory from Tacitus to Jürgen Habermas. Focusing on the "constitutive tensions" between the senatorial order and the masses at the center of Roman political rhetoric, Connolly argues that while the orator exploits myth, ritual, religion, and eloquence to dominate the *plebs*, public speaking was nevertheless an act of "terrifying uncertainty" for political elites because power in Rome rested on popular opinion. Oratory was thus a mechanism of social control as well as a "creator of community." For this reason, Cicero's treatises approach politics not only in terms of laws and institutions but also as volatile, precarious relations among citizens who render judgments grounded in common sense (*sensus communis*) and shared moral values. In its probing of the aesthetic, pluralistic, and contestatory aspects of politics, Connolly concludes, Roman rhetoric remains relevant to politics and political thought today.

In her chapter on rhetoric and medieval politics, Virginia Cox (ch. 26) challenges the scholarly consensus that medieval European culture was generally unconcerned with politics as a forum for rhetorical practice. Far from being a "desert" for political rhetoric, Cox argues, the Middle Ages elaborated a robust art of deliberative eloquence that was often "nonclassical" in form and couched in theological language that conceals its political aims from the modern reader. Focusing on the practice of parliamentary rhetoric in England and Catalonia-Aragon, Cox develops a "working model" to account for the distinctive features of medieval political rhetoric, including the role of female mystics in politics and diplomacy, the fusion of secular and sacred in political argument, the importance of delivery (*actio*) in political epistolography (letters were read aloud), and the proto-modern "spectacularization" of politics by means of ritual and multimedia.

The political systems of European nations during the Renaissance differed from the generally republican—and thus highly rhetorical—systems of ancient Greece and Rome: they were mostly absolutist monarchies ruled by kings, queens, and princes. Wayne A. Rebhorn (ch. 31), in his chapter on rhetoric and politics, explores the conflict between republican and monarchic models of political rhetoric in the Renaissance. Although most rhetoricians viewed the *ars rhetorica* as an instrument of absolutist power and authority,[15] Rebhorn argues that the democratic potential of rhetoric was nevertheless evident in many areas of society: in the popularity of vernacular rhetoric manuals, in the emphasis on controversy in schoolroom training, which cultivated a sense of truth (and politics) as a matter of dialogue and argument, and in the subversive power of rhetoric itself, which enabled a skilled speaker of any class to triumph over "royal eloquence" in a verbal contest. Rebhorn's account of the tension between republican and absolutist approaches to political rhetoric illuminates the ambiguous legacy of Cicero in the period—"a Janus-faced Cicero for a Janus-faced Renaissance."

Angus Gowland (ch. 38) examines the relationship between rhetoric and politics in the early modern period, devoting particular attention to the impact and legacy of Renaissance humanism. After delineating the social context for the genesis of humanist political rhetoric in late medieval Italy, Gowland elucidates the rhetorical thought of Niccolò Machiavelli and Leonardo Bruni, two political thinkers for whom civic eloquence is the foundation—and potentially the destruction—of republican polities. In addition to showing how the rhetorical theory of Machiavelli and Bruni informed humanistic theories of government, especially in discussions of counsel and exhortations to princely virtue, Gowland analyzes Thomas Hobbes's critical reappraisal of rhetoric in the era of absolutist monarchies and charts the decline of rhetoric with the rise of natural law, modern political economy, and representative forms of government.

Finally, in his chapter on rhetoric and modern political theory, Andrew Norris (ch. 49) explores Hannah Arendt's response to the anti-rhetorical tradition initiated by Plato's *Gorgias*, which portrays deliberative rhetoric as a practice of coercion and deception that traffics in mere opinion and appearance (*doxa*). According to Norris, ancient Greek rhetoric holds a central place in Arendt's "politics of opinion" and its agonistic, perspectival approach to democratic political life: political action is above all public speech, and for this reason rhetoric—the art of public persuasion—is the highest and most truly political art. As Norris demonstrates, Arendt rejects Plato's account of opinion as mere subjective belief. Stressing the political dimension of *doxa* as the outcome of argument and persuasion in the shared space of political appearances (the *agōn* of the *agora*), Norris shows that Arendt's recuperation of Aristotelian judgment and the politics of opinion situates rhetoric at the heart of modern democratic politics.

Rhetoric and Historiography

The tension between the objective reporting of historical events and their rhetorical representation was already a source of anxiety for ancient historiographers. As Lucian observes in "How to Write History" (166 CE), the boundary dividing rhetoric and historiography is not a "narrow isthmus" but a "mighty wall" (62; trans. Kilburn). Nevertheless, as Chris Carey (ch. 4) argues in his chapter on rhetoric and historiography in ancient Greece, the writing of history in any era has an ineradicable rhetorical dimension: in addition to persuading the audience of the truthfulness of their account (*historia*) of events, historians must employ a general "narrative rhetoric" that controls the selection of events, orders the narrative, and focalizes the point of view on the action. Ranging across works by Herodotus, Thucydides, and Polybius, Carey contends that the agonistic, performative milieu of Greek historiography—works of history were recited in public—accounts for its polemical tone and explains why historians often blur the generic boundaries between historical presentation (*apodeixis*) and rhetorical display (*epideixis*) in their use of stylistic devices, invented speeches, and arguments from probability.

Much as Carey shows that rhetoric was an essential component of Greek historiography, Rhiannon Ash (ch. 15), in her analysis of the "creative fusion" of rhetoric and history writing in Rome, argues that the rhetorical aspects of Roman historiography are not simply stylistic ornaments but a means of adding depth and significance to an author's interpretation of history. Taking us into the "rhetorical workshop" of the Roman historiographers, Ash demonstrates how Livy, Tacitus, and Polybius exploit wordplay, narrative, vivid description, invented speeches, and arguments drawn from judicial oratory to bring historical events to life through the rhetorical "expansion of the past." These rhetorical strategies, Ash suggests, also served an important persuasive purpose: history writing in Rome was oriented toward the future and therefore sought to influence the beliefs and conduct of its audience.

Rhetoric and Education

Another group of chapters in this volume is concerned with rhetoric and education. Rhetoric formed the core of the educational curriculum in ancient Greece and Rome and remained central to education in Europe throughout the Middle Ages, sustained in part by a program of teaching grounded in Cicero's *De inventione* and the pseudo-Ciceronian *Rhetorica ad Herennium* that persisted in the Latin West from late antiquity through the seventeenth century. In his chapter on rhetoric and pedagogy in ancient Greece from Homeric times to the Hellenistic era, Malcolm Heath (ch. 5) argues that formal instruction in rhetoric began with the sophists, who refined terminology, developed *stasis* theory, classified the structural components of a speech and their functions, and composed model speeches to be "quarried" by students. Heath devotes particular attention to the *Rhetoric to Alexander*, showing how this neglected work extends sophistic theory by linking rhetoric and judgment and treating genres of rhetoric in pragmatic terms as ways of doing things with words (exhorting, dissuading, praising, etc.). Noting that rhetorical theory develops in tandem with teaching practice, Heath argues that innovations in the Hellenistic era, especially the emphasis on declamatory exercise and the expansion of the conceptual domain of rhetoric with the idea of "intellection" (*noēsis*), established a pedagogical framework that later rhetoricians tinkered with but "never dismantled."

Catherine Steel (ch. 16), in her chapter on rhetoric and pedagogy in ancient Rome, argues that instructors retooled Greek systems of rhetoric to meet the demands of Roman political practice, which made public speaking an unavoidable obligation on elites. After examining the early Roman anxiety about the subversive influence of Greek rhetoric, Steel argues that the variety of Cicero's works on rhetoric—ranging from basic instructional manuals (*De inventione*) and elaborate theoretical investigations (*De oratore*) to a history of Roman eloquence (*Brutus*) and detailed technical discussions (*De partitione oratoria*)—makes them sure guides to the complexities of rhetorical theory, practice, and education in the late Republic. In addition to explicating most of the key features of Cicero's approach to oratory, Steel argues that all of his works on rhetoric display a commitment to pedagogy and a belief that oratory as civil science (*civilis ratio*) is essential to republican political life.

In the Renaissance, rhetoric took on new prominence in university education alongside dialectic, which had dominated European universities since the thirteenth century. Queen Elizabeth I—a monarch tutored in Greek and Latin rhetoric by leading humanists—even decreed in a statute (1570) that rhetoric would take precedence over mathematics in the curriculum at Oxford and Cambridge. In his contribution on rhetoric and pedagogy in the Renaissance, Peter Mack (ch. 33) investigates the role of rhetoric in the curricula of universities and grammar schools across Europe. Although the history of Renaissance rhetoric is a "history of textbooks," Mack contends, these textbooks only make sense in relation to the syllabuses in which they were taught. Ranging across schools in Italy, Germany, France, and England, Mack therefore offers a comparative survey of syllabuses and curricula that reveals some important "undercurrents" in rhetorical education across Europe, including the integration of reading and writing, the emergence of humanist logic and its emphasis on topical reasoning, and the teaching of Latin grammar through the rhetorical analysis of ancient literary texts. Mack concludes by calling for more "local studies" of statutes, syllabuses, and textbooks to deepen our understanding of the material practice of rhetorical training in specific countries and historical periods.

Rhetoric and Philosophy

Another sequence of chapters in the *Handbook* is devoted to the relationship between rhetoric and philosophy, which goes back to the beginnings of both disciplines: we have "found the philosopher," observes Plato's Eleatic Stranger, "while we were looking for the sophist" (*Sophist* 253c; trans. Fowler).[16] Harvey Yunis (ch. 9: "Plato's Rhetoric in Theory and Practice") approaches Plato's complex account of rhetoric by distinguishing two phases in the Socratic dialogues. The first, critical phase (exemplified by the *Gorgias*) casts sophistic rhetoric as a mere simulacrum of political science, because it caters to the irrational desires of the democratic masses (the sophist is a "pastry cook"). The second, constructive phase (the *Phaedrus*), Yunis argues, defines rhetoric as the leading of souls (*psychagōgia*) and elaborates a "universal art of discourse" grounded in true knowledge, governed by rational principles of composition, and oriented toward the well-being of the audience. Throughout the chapter, Yunis sheds light on Plato's own rhetorical practice by illustrating how the dialogues mobilize sophistic devices and strategies—from myth, humor, and imagery to analogy, vivid description, and contrasting arguments— to convince readers of the preeminence of philosophy.

Eugene Garver (ch. 10: "Aristotle's Rhetoric in Theory and Practice") argues that Aristotle's *Rhetoric*, for all its apparent familiarity, remains a "slippery" book marked by ambiguity and contradiction: rhetoric can be both sophistic deception and ethical persuasion. According to Garver, while rhetoric is constrained by factors outside the art, such as the demand for fidelity to facts and the goal of persuading an audience, it has its own internal standards that are irreducible to logic, politics, or expediency—its "relative autonomy." In addition to elucidating the political dimensions of Aristotelian rhetoric, including its power to prove opposites and its affinities with judgment, deliberation, and practical wisdom, Garver contends that the ultimate aim of the *Rhetoric* is to "make *logos*—discourse or argument—ethical."

In her contribution on rhetoric and Stoic philosophy, Shadi Bartsch (ch. 17) examines the conflict between the ends of rhetoric and the precepts of Stoicism in the Roman context. Although the Stoics maintained that philosophical discourse must be stripped of ornament and appeal to the emotions, Bartsch argues that later Roman Stoics were willing to exploit rhetoric to achieve the aims of Stoicism. Focusing on the "metamorphosis" of Stoic rhetoric in the work of Seneca the Younger, Bartsch shows how Seneca's use of paradox, epigram, vivid imagery, antithesis, and parataxis—a major influence on Renaissance drama and poetry—departs from Stoicism's ideal of a "rhetoric degree zero." According to Bartsch, Seneca forges a new model of philosophical rhetoric that utilizes figurative language, epistolary exchange, the dialogue form, and the medium of the published text to teach, persuade, and discover truth in the Stoic tradition.

Finally, Adam Potkay (ch. 42), in his chapter on rhetoric and Enlightenment philosophy, disputes the scholarly consensus that eighteenth-century philosophy rejected rhetoric as an art of deception and that the New Rhetoric itself ratified this critique by emphasizing plainness, perspicuity, and probable arguments. Far from abandoning rhetoric, Potkay argues, empiricist philosophers weave tropes and figures into their philosophical writing and, more fundamentally, into their science of mind: empiricism treats perception and belief as rhetorical processes that rely on persuasion, vivid representations, and tropological substitutions such as metaphor and metonymy. Throughout the chapter, Potkay explicates the "intertwining" of rhetoric and philosophy in the eighteenth century by showing how figuration and persuasion lie at the theoretical core of the empiricist theory of knowledge.[17]

Sophistics, Declamation, and Homiletics

Another group of chapters in this volume is devoted to sophistics and its constellation of related practices, especially in the Greco-Roman rhetorical culture of the imperial period. For all its veneration of speech, antiquity also passed down a fear of the *logos* and its potential effects—a "logophobia" (Foucault 1972: 229). This logophobia converges on the art of rhetoric and, more specifically, on the figure of the sophist. In her chapter on rhetoric and sophistics in ancient Greece, Barbara Cassin (ch. 11) contends that "rhetoric" is in fact a philosophical creation designed to neutralize the sophists' discursive practices and their unsettling effects: beginning with Plato's *Gorgias* and culminating in Aristotle's *Metaphysics*, ontology "invented" rhetoric to master the temporal dimensions of speech by "spatializing" time in discourse. According to Cassin, while ontology reduces time to space by means of places (*topoi* and the "rhetoric of space"), sophistic "logology" affirms the temporal condition of discourse and asserts the priority of *logos* over Being—*kairos* and the "rhetoric of time." In addition to defining the essential traits of this sophistic rhetoric of time, including paradox, reversible arguments, *ex tempore* invention, and the play of signifiers, Cassin argues that logology reached its apex during the Second Sophistic, when rhetoric and poetics coalesced into a "general rhetoric" that gave rise to a multiplicity of new genres of discourse, including biography, doxography, hagiography, and the novel.

A topic that has moved from the margins to the center of rhetorical studies in the last four decades is the Second Sophistic (100–300 CE), the Greek literary, educational, and social movement that spread across the Roman world of the Empire. Laurent Pernot (ch. 20) argues that the Second Sophistic did not represent a decline in oratory but rather a "redeployment" of Greek rhetoric that not only refined epideictic eloquence but also contributed to the novel, poetry, biography, historiography, and aesthetics and art criticism. As lawyers, politicians, and imperial administrators, the rhetors of the Second Sophistic also forged a new "alliance" of power and knowledge under the Empire. According to Pernot, the fascination with Attic Greek culture among imperial sophists was less nostalgia than a reaffirmation of Greek identity in the teeth of Roman power. In fact, by extending their *paideia* across the Roman world, the sophists performed a "rhetorical appropriation of the Empire" and established what Pernot calls a "new world order" of Greek rhetoric.

Another seemingly marginal rhetorical practice that has received increased scholarly attention in recent years is the art of declamation. Originally a sophistic invention that flourished in the Hellenistic period and into late antiquity (and beyond), declamation is the public performance of a fictitious speech, often impersonating figures from history and mythology. Erik Gunderson (ch. 21: "Rhetoric and Declamation") argues that declamation not only prepared orators for legal and political careers but also promoted literary invention and thought experiments that "unleash" the rhetorical imagination on hypothetical objects, topics, and scenarios. For this reason, Gunderson argues, declamation, with its artificial yet telling depictions of familial, social, and political relationships, became a forum for searching explorations of the Roman value system. Closely linked to fiction and theater, declamation fused the ludic and serious in a genre of display oratory that was a key component of rhetorical education as well as an institution through which Greco-Roman culture investigated its most intractable problems.

Finally, in her chapter on rhetoric and homiletics, Catherine Conybeare (ch. 24: "Augustine's Rhetoric in Theory and Practice") reassesses the relationship between Augustine of Hippo and the Latin rhetorical tradition he apparently disavowed. Despite his rejection of pagan rhetoric in the *Confessions* and elsewhere, Conybeare argues, Augustine never abandoned the precepts of Latin eloquence, especially the duty of the orator to teach (*docere*), delight (*delectare*), and move (*movere*) the audience. As Conybeare shows, however, in his advice to preachers Augustine subordinates this Ciceronian triad to the demands of conveying the word of God to a nascent Christian culture—moral rectitude and deep knowledge of the Bible could also be effective means of persuasion in the art of preaching (*ars praedicandi*). Moving from theory to practice, Conybeare examines Augustine's homiletic rhetoric in action through a close reading of a sermon, showing how Augustine fuses the ideal and the pragmatic in a forceful preaching style that uses parataxis, biblical quotation, direct address, and fictional dialogue to influence his audience.

Rhetoric, Theater, and Performance

Another series of chapters in the *Handbook* is concerned with the role of rhetoric in drama and performance. In his chapter on rhetoric and Greek tragedy, Paul Woodruff (ch. 7) analyzes the interplay between rhetoric and tragic theater in fifth-century BCE Athens. Drawing on plays by Aeschylus, Sophocles, and Euripides, Woodruff contends that tragedies were composed for a rhetorically sophisticated Athenian audience that took pleasure in "verbal pyrotechnics" such as artfully wrought set-speeches, intricate line-on-line dialogue (*stichomythia*), and the marshaling of arguments. According to Woodruff, tragedy also dramatizes techniques of forensic rhetoric—especially arguments from probability and paired antithetical speeches (*agōnes*)—that confront spectators with a plurality of contradictory but persuasive points of view. Thus, while tragic plots often foreground the deceptive cunning of sophistic rhetoric (embodied by Odysseus *polymēchanos*), they also dramatize its political virtues: arguing both sides of an issue, for example, fosters the capacity for compassion or "knowledge-with" (*syngnomosyne*) at the heart of tragic pity and democratic politics.

Daphne O'Regan (ch. 8) examines the dialogue between sophistic rhetoric and Old Comedy through a reading of Aristophanes's bitter farce *The Clouds*. After outlining the parallels between rhetoric and the institution of comic theater, including an audience of voting citizens and a public, agonistic context, O'Regan argues that playwrights "mined" sophistic teachings for comic material, especially Gorgias's claim that rhetoric enslaves its audience. According to O'Regan, however, *The Clouds* stages a failure of rhetoric: speech becomes hot air (thunder, nonsense, flatulence), and persuasion yields to violence when disgruntled students torch the Socratic school for sophistry (the "Thinkery"). This failure of persuasion, O'Regan suggests, reveals an "unsuspected fragility" of speech. Sophistic rhetoric, with its focus on the speaker and the dynastic power of persuasion as a "great tyrant" (*dynastes megas*) (Gorgias, *Encomium of Helen* 8), evades the question of audience and a prior, more "delicate negotiation"—the agreement to listen.

The flatulent farcing of Aristophanes's sophistic "speech cooks" played an important role in the history of comic theater well into the Middle Ages. Bringing up the rear of the medieval section, Jody Enders (ch. 29: "Rhetoric and Comedy") turns to an anonymous fifteenth-century French text—*The Farce of the Fart*—to begin plumbing a neglected feature of the rhetorical tradition: humor. Focusing on the theatrical farces of the late medieval French lawyers and legal apprentices known as the Society of the Basoche, who staged raunchy, fictional trials in real courtrooms, Enders argues that comedy is deeply imbricated in legal rhetoric, declamation, delivery—and in the law itself. The forensic travesties of the Basochiens reveal many points of intersection between law, theater, and rhetoric, including the body as performance medium, judicial rhetoric as popular entertainment, and parallels between trials and theatrical farces ("This trial is a farce!"). When medieval rhetoricians theorized and practiced comedy, Enders concludes, they not only mobilized a "pan-European" system of forensic argument but also staged a "rhetorical response to injustice."

In his chapter on rhetoric and Renaissance drama, Russ McDonald (ch. 36) investigates the role rhetoric played in the rise of Elizabethan commercial theater in the final decades of the sixteenth century. Focusing on Thomas Kyd, Christopher Marlowe, and William Shakespeare, McDonald argues that the exercises at the core of the grammar school curriculum in Latin rhetoric—imitation, impersonation, reverse translation, and identification of tropes, figures, and schemes—set the stage for the "repurposing" of classical rhetoric by English dramatists. In addition to acquainting students with elements of style, these exercises introduced principles of composition and argument, including patterns of logical reasoning and strategies for arguing both sides of a question (*argumentum in utramque partem*), that playwrights would use to create their imaginary worlds. As McDonald notes, the ambivalent nature of rhetoric itself often takes center stage in Renaissance comedy and tragedy, thus forcing the audience to reflect on the ethics of persuasion and the humanist idealization of the *ars rhetorica*.

In the rhetorical tradition that shaped the early modern discourse on rhetoric, verbal eloquence went hand in hand with physical eloquence. Oratory, like acting, is an embodied, public performance art whose rules were codified by the art of rhetorical delivery (*actio*), the "regulation of voice [*vocis*], countenance [*vultus*], and gesture [*gestus*]" (*Rhetorica ad Herennium* 1.3; trans. Caplan). In the final chapter on rhetoric, theater, and performance, Paul Goring (ch. 44: "The Elocutionary Movement in Britain") surveys the rhetorical treatises and cultural practices that constituted the elocutionary movement, a trend in eighteenth-century Britain (and France) that sought to resuscitate the dead art of rhetorical delivery for the good of the nation—English speakers had frozen into "speaking statues." Ranging across works by Hugh Blair, Thomas Sheridan, Gilbert Austin, and Michel Le Faucheur, Goring situates the elocutionary movement in relation to other schools of rhetorical thought in the period (neoclassical, belletristic, and the New Rhetoric) and details how elocutionary ideas were disseminated to popular audiences through print culture, public lectures, and animated demonstrations of *actio* in action.

Rhetoric, Poetry, and Literature

In recent years scholars have begun to reassess the influence of rhetorical education on Latin poetry, drama, and literature. In his chapter on rhetoric and epic, Jon Hall (ch. 18) measures the impact of rhetorical training—especially drilling in declamation—on the stylistic evolution of Latin epic poetry. Focusing on the verse epics of Virgil (*Aeneid*), Ovid (*Metamorphoses*), and Lucan (*Civil War*), Hall argues that declamatory performance fostered in Roman students a flair for the extravagant use of rhetorical tropes, figures, and schemes as well as mannerisms such as hyperbole, antithesis, paradox, and *sententiae* (pithy sayings). The ubiquity of these rhetorical devices and gestures in the poems, Hall suggests, points to a complex interaction between rhetoric and Latin epic composition that produced a new subgenre noteworthy for its "baroque grandeur"—the rhetorical epic.

Rhetorical training and declamatory exercise also left their mark on Greek and Latin lyric poetry. Jonathan Culler (ch. 19: "Rhetoric and Lyric Address") explores the functioning of address in lyrics by Pindar, Sappho, and Catullus. Although classicists generally contrast the ancient lyric's direct address to an audience with the solipsistic, meditative character of modern lyrics, Culler argues that apostrophe in ancient lyric poetry is in fact seldom direct. Instead, direct address in the ancient lyric functions— as it does in modern lyrics—to produce a structure of "triangulation," creating effects of immediacy and affecting the temporality of the lyric by placing us in the lyric present "where things happen." For this reason, Culler maintains, the rhetorical structure of apostrophic address in the Greek and Latin lyric offers a corrective to the models of the dramatic monologue and subjective expression inherited from nineteenth-century poetics and literary theory.

In her chapter on rhetoric and fiction in late antiquity, Ruth Webb (ch. 22) explores the zones of contact between rhetoric and the novel in the imperial period. Drawing on works by Apuleius, Petronius, and other Greek and Roman novelists, Webb argues that the impact of rhetoric on the composition of novels is visible not only in embedded speeches and courtroom disputes but also in more general techniques of storytelling such as character portrayal (*ēthopoēia*) and vivid, lively narration (*enargeia*). As Webb points out, however, rhetoric was not only a toolbox of techniques for inventing novel-istic worlds but also a means of investigating the relationship between fiction and reality itself: rhetoric and literature alike strive to depict coherent worlds, and it is to manuals of legal rhetoric that ancient novelists turned for theories of verisimilitude in narrative.

In recent decades feminist scholars have drawn attention to rhetorical educa-tion as a crucial site for the construction of gender identity. From antiquity through the Renaissance, training in rhetoric was an integral component of a sex-gender sys-tem (de Lauretis 1987: 5) that turned boys into men through a "calisthenics of man-hood" (Gleason 1995: xxii).[18] Lynn Enterline (ch. 39: "Rhetoric and Gender in British Literature") examines the interconnections between early modern rhetorical theory, educational training in Latin rhetoric, and literary representations that designate fig-ures, texts, genres, and bodies as male, female, and/or "epicene" (of common gender). Historicizing Jacques Lacan's concept of the symbolic order, Enterline analyzes the translation of Latin rhetorical training into vernacular literary practice in works by William Shakespeare, John Webster, and George Gascoigne. According to Enterline, grammar school training in Latin eloquence through declamation, delivery ("body-language games"), and the impersonation of fictitious characters—many of them female—made rhetoric a key mechanism in the social reproduction of gender and the training up of English "gentlemen."

Rhetoric, Poetics, and Literary Criticism

Thanks in part to the Romantic movement, rhetoric and poetry are today viewed as rad-ically different genres of discourse: rhetoric is a public, practical art of civic persuasion, while poetry is a solitary, aesthetic art of self-expression, perhaps even "the spontaneous overflow of powerful feelings . . . recollected in tranquility" (Wordsworth 2013: 98). In his chapter on rhetoric and poetics from Theognis to Aristotle, however, Jeffrey Walker (ch. 6) argues that the modern division between rhetoric and poetry was foreign to

Greek thought. Poetry emerged from archaic, oral-traditional forms of epideictic rhetoric that treat the poem as a "rhetorical act" that aims at persuasion. For this reason, Walker maintains, poetry as persuasive *epideixis* had the important social function of reinforcing the collective beliefs that ground legal and political deliberation. Walker contrasts this rhetorical view of poetry with Aristotle's later (and historically dominant) approach to poetry as *mimēsis* and allegory, which treats the poem as a hermeneutic object whose secret meanings must be deciphered.

The Platonic depiction of rhetoric as a feminine art of deceptive ornamentation and cosmetology (the adorning of *logos*) runs through antiquity into the Middle Ages. In her chapter on rhetoric and medieval poetics, Jill Ross (ch. 28) examines the formative influence of Horace's *Ars poetica* on textual culture in the Middle Ages, especially its negative precepts of composition that brandish the figure of the "monstrous feminine" as a warning to the male poet. Ranging across works by Boethius, Matthew of Vendôme, Geoffrey of Vinsauf, and others, Ross contends that medieval writers sought to avoid the feminine poetic vices that render texts seductive and transgressive, especially ornate style, textual gaps and seams, and the hybrid inventions associated with the Sirens. As Ross demonstrates, Horace's rules for exercising rational, masculine control over verbal *materia* informed many aspects of medieval poetics and rhetoric, including the perils and pleasures of the text in its material embodiment, the tension between the inventions of an author and the interventions of the compiler, and the liaison between rhetorical deception and feminine sexuality in exegeses of the Fall.

Although ancient rhetoric was primarily concerned with composition and performance, literary criticism and hermeneutics were also part of its remit. Rita Copeland (ch. 27), in her chapter on rhetoric and medieval literary criticism, examines the application of rhetorical thought to the interpretation of Scripture and fictional texts. Engaging closely with Cicero's works on forensic oratory, Copeland demonstrates the critical importance of rhetoric for medieval theorists and exegetes such as Augustine, Dante Alighieri, and Geoffrey of Vinsauf. Beginning with Augustine's rhetorical model of Scriptural exegesis, medieval hermeneutics adapted methods of rhetorical invention—*stasis* theory, topical analysis, the Ciceronian system of *circumstantiae*, and the distinction between letter and spirit—to the analysis of literary and religious texts. In addition to showing how rhetoric was assimilated to hermeneutics in the Middle Ages, Copeland demonstrates the relevance of theories of arrangement (*dispositio*) to the analysis of narrative structure and elucidates how rhetorical approaches to genre, style, and figurative language were translated into interpretative contexts.

In his contribution on rhetoric and poetics during the Renaissance, Arthur F. Kinney (ch. 35) argues that classical rhetoric provided the theoretical and practical foundation for poetics throughout quattrocento Europe. While the basic technique in both spheres was imitation of classical models, Kinney contends that literary mimesis was in fact a creative exercise in "rewriting" that employed rhetorical devices and methods of discovery—tropes, figures, and schemes, abundant style (*copia*), and places (*loci*) of invention—to compose new works from a plurality of "original" texts. This practice of rhetorical (re)invention evolved into an aesthetics of the marvelous (*maraviglia*) that sought to inspire wonder and admiration in readers. In addition to demonstrating the centrality of rhetorical *inventio* to Renaissance poetics, Kinney shows how schoolroom exercises in composition and performance provided techniques for fashioning fictional universes in drama, poetry, and literature.

In the final essay on rhetoric, poetics, and literary criticism, Stanley E. Porter (ch. 51: "Rhetoric and New Testament Studies") offers a survey of the methods of rhetorical criticism of the New Testament that have emerged in recent decades. After taking "socio-rhetorical" criticism to task for failing to understand the context for the composition and reception of the New Testament (few of its authors—or readers—were trained in rhetoric), Porter reviews a range of more fruitful critical approaches to the books of the New Testament, including text linguistics, formal and stylistic analysis, and rhetorical criticism of speeches. Discourse analysis, argues Porter, offers the most promising interpretive "matrix" for understanding the New Testament because it goes beyond the limited theoretical framework of classical rhetoric and makes use of the full array of contemporary methods of analyzing language and discourse.

Rhetoric, Art, and Architecture

The cover image of the *Handbook*, a sixteenth-century engraving by Virgil Solis (the third in his triptych on the *trivium*), portrays the ascendancy of rhetoric over grammar ("A B C") and dialectic ("Vs"), which are reduced to cowering *putti* at the borders of the tableau. This image of Rhetorica as queen of the sciences emblematizes the fact that rhetoric developed in dialogue and competition with other discourses and disciplines, including the visual and pictorial arts. In his contribution on analogies between music and the visual arts in ancient rhetorical theory, Thomas Habinek (ch. 23: "Rhetoric, Music, and the Arts") contends that rhetorical concepts such as propriety (*decorum*), ornamentation (*ornatus*), and vividness (*evidentia*) can be understood only in relation to their use in music, painting, sculpture, and other arts. Focusing on Isocrates's *Evagoras*, Cicero's *De oratore*, and Quintilian's *Institutio oratoria*, Habinek argues that these analogies reflect specific historical rivalries among the arts as well as a shared understanding of human cognition as embodied and externalized, whether in sound, paint, or marble. Latin rhetorical theory thus articulates a theory of "embodied cognition" that aligns rhetoric, music, and the arts against Platonism and its separation of body and mind, a theory that provides the groundwork for later defenses of the arts and accounts for the enduring importance of ancient rhetoric in new eras and contexts.

Rhetoric is a creative, productive art, and the system of five rhetorical arts—invention, arrangement, style, memory, and delivery—furnished artists with a suite of tools for creating persuasive artifacts in many different media and signifying modes, including painting. In her chapter on rhetoric and the visual arts, Caroline van Eck (ch. 37) sketches the main trends in the theory and practice of persuasion in painting during the Renaissance. Focusing on paintings by Masaccio, Caravaggio, and Titian, van Eck shows that rhetoric—the "only complete theory of communication" in the period—provided the conceptual framework for theorizing and interpreting works of visual art. More importantly, the verbal strategies developed in rhetoric offered painters a palette of visual strategies, including copious style, vivid representation, effective composition (*dispositio*), and eloquent gesture and facial expression (*actio*). These strategies of persuasive design, van Eck argues, delight, instruct, and move viewers by drawing them into the fictive world of the painting and its story or subject matter (*historia*).

Rhetoric also furnished the blueprint for architecture and architectural theory in the early modern period. Robert Kirkbride (ch. 40: "Rhetoric and Architecture") contends that architecture provided early modern thinkers with models for constructing speeches as well as for edifying the self and the community, from figurative structures as placeholders for memory (palaces, theaters, and cathedrals) to architectural ornaments as vehicles for private meditation and public persuasion (icons, emblems, and allegorical frescoes). Focusing on the dovetailing of rhetoric and architecture, Kirkbride demonstrates how Vitruvius and Leon Battista Alberti build on architectural concepts and analogies developed by Cicero and Quintilian, including composition, ornamental styling, and analogies between bodies, orations, and buildings. Moving from theory to practice, Kirkbride shows how professional architects employed a range of rhetorical skills over the course of a construction project, from eloquence, argument, and practical wisdom to visual persuasion by means of sketchbooks and illustrated codices designed to attract investors.

Rhetoric and Science

If one of the principal reasons for the modern decline of rhetoric was the advent of scientific positivism and its emphasis on certitude, apodictic proof, and language as a neutral (and neuter) medium of representation, in the twentieth century rhetoric exacted its "terrible belated revenge" (Eagleton 1981: 108) on science. In her chapter on rhetoric and science in the Renaissance, Jean Dietz Moss (ch. 34) argues that while modern scientists attempt to expunge rhetoric and emotion from their writing, early modern scientists such as Nicholas Copernicus, Galileo Galilei, and Johannes Kepler crafted eloquent, emotionally charged descriptions of their discoveries. Moss shows how these astronomers turned to rhetorical methods of discovery (invention using *topoi*), demonstration (enthymemes, examples), and style (analogies, vivid description) to convey the import and emotional impact of their findings. The eloquent, impassioned language these scientists use to describe celestial phenomena—comets, lunar mountains, moons of Jupiter—reflects the natural reasoning and "sensitive qualities" of human beings and thus calls into question the modern aversion to rhetoric and emotion in scientific prose.

Peter Walmsley (ch. 43), in his contribution on rhetoric and science during the Enlightenment, exposes the "rhetorical prehistory" of modern scientific objectivity by tracing its origins to the eighteenth-century rejection of classical eloquence in favor of the "close, naked, and natural" (Sprat 1667: 112) style proper to modern scientific discourse. Focusing on the "textual performance" of science in two landmark English works, Hans Sloane's *Voyage to Jamaica* (a botanical taxonomy) and Joseph Priestley's *Observations on Different Kinds of Air* (a narrative of chemistry experiments), Walmsley contends that the scientific revolution also initiated a "rhetorical revolution" as natural philosophers developed new genres to communicate their discoveries (illustrated atlases), strove to create audiences for their work by exploiting new modes of publicity (print), and embodied the ideals of industry and objectivity that have come to characterize the modern "scientific persona" (*ēthos*).

Finally, in his chapter on rhetoric and contemporary science, Richard Doyle (ch. 59) argues that rhetoric plays an integral role in the production and circulation of scientific knowledge. According to Doyle, while scientists employ all available means of invention and persuasion, from writing and images to diagrams and simulations, the tension between the scientific quest for objective knowledge and its tools is growing more acute as new "technologies of attention"—smart phones, networked computers, and open-source software—extend the practice of science beyond universities and laboratories. Focusing on the concept of entropy and the growing "noösphere," or realm of collective intelligence, Doyle develops thermodynamics as a heuristic model for understanding the "intertwingling" of rhetoric and science and applies this model to several examples, including the biblical narrative of the Tower of Babel, the chromatic strategies of pollinating plants, and the "tropic and entropic" aspects of information.

Rhetoric, Feminism, and Critical Race Theory

If the rhetorical tradition wields a unique historical power, it is in part because rhetoric lays down the laws that govern the order of discourse in general. As a metalanguage, or the "talk about talking" (*dicendo dicere*), as Cicero puts it in *De oratore* (24.112), rhetoric shapes the economy of discourse and with it the morphology of knowledge itself. Scholars in feminism and gender studies, however, have challenged the codes and laws handed down by the Greco-Roman rhetorical tradition, beginning with one of its founding prescriptions: rhetoric is reserved for men and the virile eloquence of the "good man skilled in speaking" (*vir bonus, dicendi peritus*) (Cato the Elder). Angela G. Ray (ch. 45: "Rhetoric and Feminism in the Nineteenth-Century United States") argues that accounts of nineteenth-century US feminist rhetoric have been shaped by the goals and rhetorical practices of twentieth-century feminism. Concentrating on the disciplinary contexts for the production of early studies of women's public advocacy, Ray employs the concept of "feminine style" as a model for analyzing the current state of feminist scholarship. As a strategic adaptation to differential power relations (rather than an "essence"), feminine style crystallizes several features of women's discursive practice, including the use of dialogue, testimony, affective arguments, inductive structure, and personal narrative. Drawing lessons for future scholarship from this disciplinary history, Ray surveys emerging trends in rhetoric and gender studies, including projects of historical recovery, reconceptualizations of gender and identity, and analysis of a wider range of rhetorical artifacts and practices by women.

Much as Ray provides a genealogy of twentieth-century feminist rhetoric, Cheryl Glenn and Andrea A. Lunsford (ch. 46) trace the relationship of rhetoric to first-, second-, and third-wave feminist movements to show how rhetoric and feminism have come to establish an "interanimating" relationship. In describing these "shifting currents," Glenn and Lunsford explore the tactics and strategies by which feminist rhetoricians seek to enact social, academic, and political change. These strategies include the "resistant rereading" of traditional texts, concepts, and categories; recovering works and performances by female authors; and examining artifacts and practices by women that are seldom viewed as rhetorical, such as dance, silence, cookbooks, etiquette manuals, journals, and parlor rhetorics. Glenn and Lunsford demonstrate that scholars have been "riding the waves" of feminisms as they develop rhetorical theories and practices that do justice to the experiences of women and other subaltern groups.

Finally, Jacqueline Jones Royster (ch. 47), in her chapter on rhetoric and race in the United States, approaches rhetoric and race as intricately connected forms of symbolic action that function within specific "ecosystems" defined by social, political, and cultural hierarchies. Noting that race is not a biological phenotype but a social, cultural, and ideological construction (not to mention a "performance"), Royster adopts two interpretative strategies—globalization and "critical imagination"—to create a pluralist, comparative method for analyzing rhetorical practices in non-Western contexts. This method situates race and rhetoric in a simultaneously local and global context and thereby explains how models of rhetoric and race "migrate" across historical and geographical borders. This global, ecological approach, Royster suggests, promises to yield a more nuanced understanding of race rhetorics in the United States and beyond.

Contemporary Developments

The final and longest section of the *Handbook* is devoted to other contemporary developments in the field of rhetorical studies.

Rhetoric and Presidential Politics

In their chapter on the US presidency as a rhetorical institution, Karlyn Kohrs Campbell and Kathleen Hall Jamieson (ch. 50) contend that the public's understanding of the presidency is shaped by genres of rhetoric that have been conventionalized by this office over the course of its history. Approaching these genres of presidential discourse—pardon messages, impeachment rhetoric, war rhetoric, national eulogies, and others—as forms of rhetorical action, Campbell and Jamieson argue that a generic perspective illuminates the manifold ways presidential power is augmented or diminished as a result of rhetorical performance: while the institutional function of each genre remains constant, individual presidents, for better (as with Abraham Lincoln) or for worse (as with Gerald Ford), give each exercise of a genre their unique "rhetorical signature."

Rhetoric and Argumentation

Frans H. van Eemeren (ch. 52) maintains that argumentation theory is a "hybrid" discipline because it requires a multidisciplinary approach that incorporates both descriptive and normative insights into its account of argumentative practice. Modern scholars of argumentation, van Eemeren argues, rely either on a dialectical perspective that stresses the reasonableness of argumentation or on a rhetorical perspective that emphasizes its effectiveness. Both perspectives are indebted to Aristotle, but in modern argumentation theory the reciprocity between rhetoric and dialectic—captured in Aristotle's term "counterpart" (*antistrophos*)—has broken down. The emerging field of pragma-dialectics, van Eemeren suggests, restores the ancient complementarity of rhetoric and dialectics with the concept of "strategic maneuvering," which accounts for the ways argumentative "moves" balance the pursuit of rhetorical effectiveness with the need for dialectical reasonableness in resolving disputes.

Rhetoric and Semiotics

Theo van Leeuwen (ch. 53) examines the interconnections between rhetoric and semiotics by comparing the contributions of the Paris school of structuralist semiotics and the Sydney school of social semiotics inspired by the work of Michael Halliday. After showing how Roland Barthes engaged with rhetoric in his analysis of the mythemes of French popular culture, van Leeuwen argues that the social-semiotic approach to genre can be understood as a modern theory of rhetorical arrangement (*dispositio*). In addition to breaking down the division between syntax and pragmatics, van Leeuwen argues, social semiotics approaches genres not as sclerotic linguistic templates but as strategies for social action and persuasion that may be realized in multiple media and signifying modes: social semiotics provides a method for analyzing speech acts as well as "visual acts" and "multimodal acts" with designs on an audience.

Rhetoric and Psychoanalysis

In his contribution on rhetoric and psychoanalysis, Gilbert Chaitin (ch. 54) contends that Jacques Lacan elaborated his linguistic theory of the unconscious and his approach to the analytic situation on the basis of rhetorical theory. Focusing on the role of figuration in Lacan's claim that the unconscious is structured like a language, Chaitin shows how Lacan, building on structural linguistics, asserts the homology between Sigmund Freud's primary processes of the unconscious—condensation (*Verdichtung*) and displacement (*Verschiebung*)—and the tropes of metaphor and metonymy. In addition to delineating the role of tropes and figures in the psychic economy, Chaitin clarifies the role of persuasion in analytic practice and shows how Lacan ascribes a rhetorical function to many of the fundamental concepts of psychoanalysis, from jokes, dreams, and symptoms to desire, repression, and transference.

Rhetoric and Deconstruction

Paul Allen Miller (ch. 55) explores the nexus between rhetoric and deconstruction through a reading of Jacques Derrida's infamous interpretation of Plato's *Phaedrus*.

Although rhetoric, especially in its sophistic guise, is contrasted with philosophy throughout the Platonic dialogues, according to Miller Derrida's reading of the opposition between speech and writing in "Plato's Pharmacy" shows that Plato himself deconstructs the opposition between rhetoric and philosophy through his use of Socratic irony. Focusing on the practice of writing—defined by the equivocal Greek term *pharmakon* (Gk. cure, poison)—as the deconstructive "hinge" of Derrida's analysis, Miller shows how Socrates outplays the sophists at their own rhetorical game by deploying myth, fiction, allegory, and imitation as "necessary supplements" to the dialectical quest for truth. Socrates's appropriation of sophistic techniques, Miller suggests, reveals that rhetoric and philosophy are not opposed practices but instead depend on each other: truth emerges in the "ironic, tropic movement of their interrelation."

Rhetoric, Composition, Design

In their chapter on contemporary approaches to the teaching of writing, David Kaufer and Danielle Wetzel (ch. 56) describe the foundations of a "design" approach to writing as it has emerged from the confluence of ancient and modern traditions in composition studies. According to Kaufer and Wetzel, the proliferation of writing outside the classroom, especially in digital spaces, has created the need for a "new paradigm" in writing instruction. While traditional approaches to composition emphasize correctness, language standards, and the authority of the instructor, a design approach stresses the cultivation of forethought, the writer's accountability for decision-making, and sustained attention to the way words on the page construct worlds of meaning and experience for the reader. A design approach, Kaufer and Wetzel argue, thus provides a new theoretical model for composition studies by reconfiguring the writing classroom as a design studio in which students learn to be "designers of the reading experience."

Rhetoric and Social Epistemology

Lorraine Code (ch. 57) elucidates how the emerging field of social epistemology challenges some of the fundamental assumptions of Anglo-American science and its "epistemic imaginary," beginning with the belief that legitimate knowledge transcends rhetoric and social persuasion. Taking as her point of departure the work of marine biologist Rachel Carson, Code argues that scholars are beginning to carve out a new rhetoric of social epistemology in the "closed rhetorical spaces" of normal science, which confers legitimacy only on knowledge that is asocial, universal, and disembodied. According to Code, this rhetoric of social epistemology is characterized by its respect for particularity, openness to testimonial evidence, awareness of the importance of trust in the creation of knowledge, and rejection of impersonal propositions in favor of the language of everyday discourse. Closely allied with feminism, antiracism, and postcolonialism, the rhetoric of social epistemology also recognizes the situated nature of knowledge and seeks to persuade in the name of "epistemic justice."

Rhetoric and Environment

In his contribution on the vexing relationship between rhetorical studies and the environmental "problematic," Andrew McMurry (ch. 58) argues that rhetoric fails to account for the consequences of its anthropocentrism, which makes man the measure of things and compels rhetoricians to frame biophysical emergencies as matters of human (mis)communication: rhetoric represents environmental crises such as toxification, global warming, and resource depletion as discursive, rhetorical crises. For this reason, rhetorical inquiry must begin accounting for the "thing-world" or "environmental Real" beyond language and symbol systems. McMurry therefore advances the concept of "rhetorical environmentality," which calls for a critique of the anthropocentrism of the Western rhetorical tradition, a broader conception of nonhuman rhetorical agency, and a theorization of the environmental conditioning of all rhetorical situations.

Rhetoric and Digital Media

In the final chapter of the *Handbook*, Ian Bogost and Elizabeth Losh (ch. 60) provide an overview of the emerging field of computational rhetoric. After charting the evolution of computational rhetoric in the disciplines of cybernetics, computer science, and media theory, Bogost and Losh survey contemporary approaches to "digital rhetoric," devoting particular attention to new rhetorical practices made possible by the unique technical affordances of the computer, such as multimodal composition, human-computer interaction, and computational gaming. These "procedural rhetorics," Bogost and Losh maintain, indicate that rhetorical studies has the potential to enrich our understanding of software and hardware systems and how these "rhetoric engines" involve persuasive practice as much as engineering practice.

CONCLUSION

Taken together, the chapters that comprise *The Oxford Handbook of Rhetorical Studies* show that rhetoric is not only a body of precepts for stylish, effective communication in speech, writing, and other media but also a social process embedded in manifold areas of culture, a process that both mirrors and engenders the society in which it operates. "Rhetoric, like any other field of activity," observes William J. Dominik, "is constructed socially, politically and cognitively in ways that reflect, express and extend—through its rules, structures, processes and values—the culture that produces it" (1997: 11). As a consequence, the portrait of rhetoric that emerges in this handbook is not that of a static, homogeneous institution that is "triumphant and moribund" (Barthes [1970] 1994: 43) but that of a dynamic, multifaceted art whose nature, ends, and importance are fiercely debated in every period of its history. It is my hope that the following chapters provide readers with a historical context for the contemporary study of rhetoric as well as a sense of the dynamism and complexity of rhetoric as a pragmatic, inventive, and critical art that operates in myriad academic disciplines and fields of social practice.

Notes

1. Callimachus composed short poems and epigrams: "A big book is like a big evil" (*to mega biblion ison* ... *tōi megalōi kakōi*; fr. 465 [Pfeiffer]). His laconic style influenced Ezra Pound, who invokes the poet in the first words of *Homage to Sextus Propertius*: "Shades of Callimachus, Coan ghosts of Philetus " (1957: 78).

2. Despite her jewels, flowers, and ball of twine (for erotic spellbinding), Peithō, the Greek goddess of persuasion and seduction, is also the attendant of Bia (violence) and the "over-mastering child of designing Destruction" (Aeschylus, *Agamemnon* 385–6; trans. Weir Smyth).

3. Although the systems of classical rhetoric have been gradually dismantled since the eighteenth century, modernity, according to John Bender and David Wellbery, is nevertheless characterized by the "universality of the rhetorical condition" (1990: 33): rhetoric is the "general condition" (38) of knowledge and action in the modern world.

4. It is not surprising that military planners are discovering the efficacy of rhetorical persuasion as an instrument of national power and authority. Rhetoric, after all, is the original psychotechnology, the first systematic attempt to manipulate the soul (*psychē*) by means of an art (*technē*) of discourse (*logos*). Today persuasive information—not just data, signals, and their vectors of transmission but knowledge that *becomes power*—is recognized as a medium of military power and a core element of American grand strategy.

5. These organizations include the International Society for the History of Rhetoric, the Rhetoric Society of America, the American Society for the History of Rhetoric, the Rhetoric Society of Europe, the Canadian Society for the Study of Rhetoric, the African Association for Rhetoric, the Latin American Rhetoric Association, the Nordic Network for the History of Rhetoric, and many others.

6. I borrow the terms "journey" and "network" from Roland Barthes's "The Old Rhetoric: An *aide-mémoire*," which also underscores the need for a new "history of rhetoric (as research, as book, as teaching) ... broadened by new ways of thinking (linguistics, semiology, historical science, psychoanalysis, Marxism)" ([1970] 1994: 92). The present volume is designed (in part) to meet this need.

7. Ironically, it is the modern disintegration of rhetoric and its dispersal across disciplines that have revitalized the field (see the excellent introduction in Bender and Wellbery [1990]), at the same time creating the need for synoptic works that provide a historical and theoretical context for current research in rhetoric.

8. The *Handbook* is also available via digital subscription at *Oxford Handbooks Online: Scholarly Research Reviews* (http://www.oxfordhandbooks.com). Digital subscription is another way to make this volume accessible for use in the classroom as a "teaching machine" (McLuhan 1962: 145): the portability of the digital version makes it a true handbook, or *manualis*—it is ready to hand on a cellular phone, tablet, or laptop computer.

9. I also use periodizing terms such as "medieval" and "Renaissance" not to designate a zeitgeist but as heuristic devices—familiar signs on a temporal map—to help orient readers in the immense historical field of rhetoric.

10. References to chapters in the present volume are indicated by the author's name and chapter number, with no publication date (e.g., "Cassin, ch. 11").

11. A basic definition of rhetoric, for example, is "the art of persuasion." Yet persuasion is the result of rhetoric, not the art itself. As Nietzsche puts it, the "effect [persuasion] is not the

essence of the thing, and furthermore, persuasion [*Ueberreden*] does not always take place even with the best orator" ([1872–3] 1989: 5).

12. The rhetoric of anti-rhetoric is often the most eloquent and, of course, ironic. John Locke, for example, resorts to a gendered simile to ban the "artificial and figurative application of words" from philosophical discourse: "Eloquence [is] like the fair sex. . . . And 'tis in vain to find fault with those arts of deceiving, wherein men find pleasure to be deceived" ([1689] 1975: 508).

13. The modern reduction of rhetoric to style began in the seventeenth century when the French humanist and logician Peter Ramus severed invention (*inventio*) and arrangement (*dispositio*) from the body of rhetoric and grafted these arts onto logic, thus leaving rhetoric with style (*elocutio*), memory (*memoria*), and delivery (*actio*).

14. In addition, in the field of media studies Marshall McLuhan opened a new phase in the "real war" between rhetoric and dialectic (logic) by rejecting the Shannon-Weaver model of communication and its "dialectical approach" to technology in favor of a rhetorical approach that views media not simply as data and their transport mechanisms but as "shaping causes" with powerful effects on psychic and social life: the message of the medium is not "transportation" (dialectic) but "transformation" (rhetoric) (1987: 256).

15. Even elements of style were viewed as weapons—ornament is armament (*orna* can also be a synonym for *arma*, "military gear"), a means of defending oneself and attacking adversaries. Literary and pictorial allegories of rhetoric in the Middle Ages and Renaissance therefore portray Lady Rhetorica armed with a sword, ornamented shield, breastplate, and helmet. Feminist scholars, however, have recently criticized such representations. Luce Irigaray, for instance, argues that when women enter the "net" or "grid" of the symbolic and imaginary orders, they find themselves petrified into "statues" and "buried beneath stylized figures" (Irigaray 1985: 144). Rhetorica herself embodies the "corpselike beauty" of these feminine figures: "How could she articulate any sound from beneath this cheap chivalric finery?" (143). For this reason, Irigaray argues, women must "cut through those layers of ornamental style, that decorative sepulcher, where even her breath is lost" (143).

16. Although the sophist looks like the philosopher, for Socrates it is a different kind of animal. The sophist resembles the philosopher as the "wolf" resembles the "dog"—the "wildest to the tamest" (see Plato, *Sophist* 230e–1b). The sophist is a wolf in dog's clothing.

17. In the working notes to his 1841 dissertation on the atomism of Democritus and Epicurus, Karl Marx describes the emergence of the sophists as the "Shrovetide" (1967: 50) of ancient Greek philosophy. With the sophistic revolution, metaphysics does "penance" for its flight from the world and returns to the "mundane siren" of the physical universe and the social cosmos of the *polis*. One reason for the renewed interest in rhetoric in the twentieth century has been a similar turn from philosophy as *theoria* toward *praxis*, especially discursive practice: the reversal of Platonism and the restitution of the sophists (Friedrich Nietzsche); the destruction of ontology and the turn toward poetic thinking (Martin Heidegger); the deconstruction of metaphysics and the practice of writing as *dissémination* (Jacques Derrida); the critique of psychoanalytic theory and the task of writing the body (Hélène Cixous); the critique of modern metanarratives of legitimation and the analysis of language games and phrase regimens (Jean-François Lyotard); and other linguistic turns and returns.

18. As a mode of public self-presentation, rhetorical delivery was an important signifier of class and gender hierarchy. The Roman orator, for example, was taught to avoid the uncultivated gestures of "day labourers" (11.3.203) and the effeminate histrionics of "stage actors"

or *histriones* ("aping the elegances of the stage") (*Rhetorica ad Herennium* 11.3.184; trans. Caplan).

REFERENCES

Barthes, Roland. (1970) 1994. "The Old Rhetoric: An *aide-mémoire.*" In *The Semiotic Challenge,* translated by Richard Howard, 11–95. Berkeley: University of California Press.

Bender, John, and David E. Wellbery. 1990. *The Ends of Rhetoric: History, Theory, Practice.* Stanford, CA: Stanford University Press.

Bogost, Ian. 2007. *Persuasive Games: The Expressive Power of Videogames.* Cambridge, MA: MIT Press.

Burke, Kenneth. 1966. *Language as Symbolic Action: Essays on Life, Literature, and Method.* Berkeley: University of California Press.

Burke, Kenneth. 1969. *A Rhetoric of Motives.* Berkeley: University of California Press.

Cole, Thomas. 1991. *The Origins of Rhetoric in Ancient Greece.* Baltimore, MD: Johns Hopkins University Press.

de Lauretis, Teresa. 1987. *Technologies of Gender: Essays on Theory, Film, and Fiction.* Bloomington: Indiana University Press.

Defense Science Board. 1999. *The Creation and Dissemination of all Forms of Information in Support of Psychological Operations (PSYOP) in Times of Military Conflict.* Washington, DC: Office of the Under Secretary of Defense for Acquisition and Technology.

Dominik, William J. 1997. *Roman Eloquence: Rhetoric in Society and Literature.* London: Routledge.

Eagleton, Terry. 1981. *Walter Benjamin, or Towards a Revolutionary Criticism.* London: Verso.

Foucault, Michel. 1972. *The Archaeology of Knowledge.* Translated by A. M. Sheridan Smith. New York: Pantheon.

Gasset, José Ortega y. (1932) 1993. *The Revolt of the Masses.* New York: W. W. Norton.

Genette, Gérard. 1982. *Figures of Literary Discourse.* New York: Columbia University Press.

Gleason, Maud W. 1995. *Making Men: Sophists and Self-Presentation in Ancient Rome.* Princeton, NJ: Princeton University Press.

Havelock, Eric. 1983. "The Linguistic Task of the Presocratics." In *Language and Thought in Early Greek Philosophy,* edited by Kevin Robb, 7–82. LaSalle, IL: Hegeler Institute.

Irigaray, Luce. 1985. *Speculum: Of the Other Woman.* Translated by Gillian C. Gill. Ithaca, NY: Cornell University Press.

Irigaray, Luce. 1991. *Marine Lover of Friedrich Nietzsche.* Translated by Gillian C. Gill. New York: Oxford University Press.

Kennedy, George A. 1992. "A Hoot in the Dark: The Evolution of General Rhetoric." *Philosophy & Rhetoric* 25.1: 1–21.

Kennedy, George A. 1998. *Comparative Rhetoric.* New York: Oxford University Press.

Lacan, Jacques. 1977. *The Four Fundamental Concepts of Psychoanalysis.* Translated by Alan Sheridan. New York: W. W. Norton.

Locke, John. 1975. *An Essay Concerning Human Understanding.* Edited by Peter H. Nidditch. Oxford: Oxford University Press.

Lyotard, Jean-François. 1984. *The Postmodern Condition: A Report on Knowledge.* Translated by Geoff Bennington and Brian Massumi. Minneapolis: University of Minnesota Press.

McLuhan, Marshall. 1962. *The Gutenberg Galaxy: The Making of Typographic Man*. Toronto: University of Toronto Press.

McLuhan, Marshall. 1987. *Letters of Marshall McLuhan*. Edited by Matie Molinaro, Corinne McLuhan, and William Toye. Toronto: Oxford University Press.

Marx, Karl. 1967. *Writings of the Young Marx on Philosophy and Society*. Translated by Loyd Easton and Kurt Guddat. New York: Anchor.

Nietzsche, Friedrich. (1872–1873) 1989. *Friedrich Nietzsche on Rhetoric and Language*. Translated by Sander Gilman, Carole Blair, and David J. Parent. New York: Oxford University Press.

Perelman, Chaïm. 1982. *The Realm of Rhetoric*. Translated by William Kluback. Notre Dame, IN: University of Notre Dame Press.

Pope, Alexander. 1883. *The Art of Sinking in Poetry*. In *The Works of Jonathan Swift*, vol. 13, edited by Walter Scott, 24–92. London: Bickers.

Pound, Ezra. 1957. *Selected Poems of Ezra Pound*. New York: New Directions.

Puttenham, George. (1589) 2007. *The Art of English Poesy*. Edited by Wayne A. Rebhorn and Frank Whigham. Ithaca, NY: Cornell University Press.

Saussure, Ferdinand de. 1959. *Course in General Linguistics*. Translated by Wade Baskin. New York: Fontana/ Collins.

Schiappa, Edward. 1999. *The Beginnings of Rhetorical Theory in Classical Greece*. New Haven, CT: Yale University Press.

Sprat, Thomas. 1667. *The History of the Royal Society of London*. London: J. Martyn.

Trousdale, Marion. 2002. "Rhetoric." In *A Companion to English Renaissance Literature and Culture*, edited by Michael Hattaway, 623–634. Oxford: Blackwell Publishing.

Vickers, Brian. 1988. *In Defence of Rhetoric*. Oxford: Oxford University Press.

Wordsworth, William, and Samuel Taylor Coleridge. 2013. *Lyrical Ballads: 1798 and 1802*. Edited by Fiona Stafford. New York: Oxford University Press.

PART I

ANCIENT GREEK RHETORIC

CHAPTER 1

....

THE DEVELOPMENT OF
GREEK RHETORIC

....

EDWARD SCHIAPPA

INTRODUCTION

....

ONE way to understand the development of classical Greek rhetoric is to trace the evolution of how people we would now call rhetorical theorists and teachers have used the word "rhetoric" to describe specific human activities. Putting my theoretical cards on the table, I begin by claiming that rhetoric does not have an essence, a nature, or a single correct definition to discover, but the *word* "rhetoric" has a history that we can describe. Indeed, I believe that the history of the development of Greek rhetoric is coterminous with the development of a specialized vocabulary deployed to describe and organize activities we recognize now as rhetorical theory, pedagogy, and practice.

The English word "rhetoric" comes from the Greek *rhētorikē*, which means art or skill of the *rhētōr*. The word *rhētōr* or "orator" originally referred to politicians who put forth motions in public settings such as the courts or Assembly, though eventually "orator" came to the point that it could refer to any public speaker. It is important to understand the origins of the word "rhetoric" because, over time, the word has been used in an almost endless variety of ways. In the pages of Ian Worthington's (2007) *A Companion to Greek Rhetoric*, for example, one can discern the word "rhetoric" or "rhetorical" being used to denote a wide range of phenomena, including oratory, parts of speech, prose genres, figurative language, performance, pedagogical practices, discourse, the strategic use of language, persuasion, and various theories of discourse, language, or persuasion.

Thus, for the purposes of this chapter, I wish to stipulate that Greek rhetoric refers to the emerging and evolving "discipline" that theorizes and teaches an art of oral and written composition and performance aimed at influencing audiences. Such a definition differentiates rhetoric from the products of such theorizing and instruction, namely, written or spoken oratory (*rhētoreia*). Although it is certainly common to refer to such products as "rhetoric," I avoid doing so to minimize the chance of confusion and to stress that the history of the development of rhetoric qua discipline is not as easily mapped onto the history of the development of oratory as is often imagined.

Thomas Cole begins his noteworthy book, *The Origins of Rhetoric in Ancient Greece*, by defining "rhetoric" as a speaker's or writer's self-conscious manipulation of a medium with a view to ensuring her/his message "as favorable a reception as possible on the part of the particular audience being addressed" (Cole 1991: ix). Although Cole and I agree that the "birth" of rhetoric as a discipline is properly dated to the early fourth century BCE and in particular to the writings of Plato, I respectfully dissent from Cole's formulation for two reasons. First, I am not as convinced as he is that one can distinguish between naturally occurring "eloquence" (ix) or "verbal virtuosity" (ix) on one hand and self-conscious manipulation on the other. As a result, I see evidence of such self-conscious artistry in Greek poetry, prose, and drama long before the appearance of rhetoric as a discipline; thus I disagree with Cole's generalization that "Greek literature before Plato is largely 'arhetorical' in character" (x). Second, my particular interests as a historian are more with rhetorical theory and pedagogy than with oratorical practice. Indeed, I reluctantly have come to the conclusion that rhetorical theory has much less of an effect on oratorical practice than we would like to believe. I would contend that self-conscious oratorical practice is as old as public speaking, but the same cannot be said of attempts to theorize and teach a discrete art of the rhetor.

Historical and comparative research support two generalizations about the practice of speaking in public to influence audiences, namely, that such practices emerge in virtually all cultures and that once they do, certain norms and traditions can be identified and potentially taught to others. Nonetheless, such research also underscores the fact that these norms and traditions cannot be translated into the vocabulary of the Greco-Roman rhetorical tradition without considerable distortion. Maurice Bloch's (1975) impressive collection, *Political Language and Oratory in Traditional Society*, provides a series of fascinating anthropological studies of what we would call oratorical practices in cultures in East and Southern Africa, Polynesia, Melanesia, and Madagascar. George A. Kennedy's (1998) *Comparative Rhetoric* describes a wide range of rhetorical practices found in Aboriginal Australian, North American Indian, and other nonliterate cultures, along with ancient literate societies in the Near East, China, India, Greece, and Rome.

The vocabulary used by these cultures to describe their practices is, not surprisingly, quite diverse and does not map easily across cultures. The Tikopian *fono* is not the same as Athenian Assembly meetings, even if both can be described loosely as gatherings for speech-making. Chinese *bian* is not the same thing as Greek *rhētorikē* or *peithō* (Wang 2004: 175–6). Xing Lu's account of Chinese "rhetorical" terms from the fifth to the third century BCE nicely illustrates the difficulties in using Western (English) terminology to make sense of ancient Chinese discourse; as she puts it, "The use of the word *rhetoric* in Western studies to describe and interpret persuasive discourse in ancient China" will miss the denotative and connotative nuances of the "original Chinese terms embedded within ancient Chinese texts" (1998: 70). Similarly, Robert T. Oliver's influential work on communication in ancient India and China argues that the most fruitful route for scholars is to "attempt to assess the rhetorical theories of Asia on their own terms—to go with them wherever they may take us, regardless of whether this may be close to or far from the kinds of rhetoric with which Westerners are familiar" (1971: 261).

The terms of art that emerge in different cultures to describe the practice of speaking in public to influence audiences should be thought of as identifying contingent categories or relevant kinds of activities that are salient to a particular community rather than universal categories or "natural" kinds that describe essential attributes of language and speech-making (Schiappa 2003a: 70–2; Timmerman and Schiappa 2010). The point here is both philosophical and historiographical. From a philosophical standpoint, most (though not all) philosophers have abandoned a worldview that embraces timeless essences (Schiappa 2003a: 38–42). "Rhetoric" is the name of a category that is used in some but not all cultures and some but not all time periods of human history, and used in a highly variable manner when it *is* used. But there is no timeless essence of rhetoric, and no God's-Eye View of what rhetoric "really is." Furthermore, from a historiographical standpoint, we do a disservice to the differences produced in various cultures and times by attempting to reduce them to a unified (typically Greek) set of categories and terms, which is both bad history and bad manners (Schiappa 1999: 166–8).

To be sure, one can argue by analogy that culture x's concept or practice of y functions in a similar manner to the Greco-Roman concept or practice of z, and the persistent temptation to trace contemporary ideas back to Greco-Roman "roots" is likely to continue. Even in the more focused historical topic of Greek rhetorical theory, many scholars deploy the vocabulary of rhetorical theory advanced by Aristotle to describe nascent or implicit theories of rhetoric based on ancient authors' discursive practices or comments about persuasion and language use that can be culled from the authors' texts, including Homer (Karp 1977; Roisman 2007), Hesiod (Kirby 1990; Clay 2007), Aristophanes (Hubbard 2007; Major 2013), the sophists Gorgias (Consigny 2001; McComiskey 2002) and Protagoras (Schiappa 2003b), and the dramatists Aeschylus, Sophocles, and Euripides (Sansone 2012; see Woodruff, ch. 7; O'Regan, ch. 8). While such accounts undoubtedly deepen our understanding of classical Greek thought, I want to emphasize the importance of naming the subject called rhetoric for its eventual "disciplinization."

ENTER THE SOPHISTS

The rise of literacy and conceptual thinking (what we now call theorizing and analysis) is associated closely with the Greek Enlightenment of the fifth century BCE. An integral part of the Greek Enlightenment was an intense interest in the workings of language, argument, and persuasion. It is with good reason that many associated disciplines— including philosophy, philology, linguistics, anthropology, and rhetoric—trace their origins to this period. Nonetheless, understanding the origins of such endeavors requires us to respect the difficulty of developing the vocabulary that constituted such disciplines; that is, to respect the language required to make such disciplines recognizable and objects of further analysis and refinement. As Eric Havelock notes, retrospectively imposing a disciplinary vocabulary that developed later "subtly distorts the story of early Greek thought by presenting it as an intellectual game dealing with problems already given and present to the mind, rather than groping after a new language in which the existence of such problems will slowly emerge, as language emancipates itself from the oral-poetic tradition" (1983: 57).

Prior to the fifth century BCE, young men learned how to give public speeches primarily through imitation and informal tutoring. Not surprisingly, public speaking was an important part of Greek political life that can be found even in the oldest surviving texts of Western history—Homer's *Iliad* and *Odyssey*. The earliest extensive prose texts of the historians Herodotus and Thucydides similarly contain many examples of speeches made in private and public contexts to attempt to persuade audiences to act or believe in particular ways (Stadter 1973; Fox and Livingstone 2007; see Carey, ch. 4). From its beginning, Greek drama also portrayed characters engaging in verbal efforts to argue and persuade that, with hindsight, clearly can be described as rhetorical (Sansone 2012).

During the fifth century, the first efforts toward formal "higher education" emerged and the ability to think and speak well was clearly a central concern. The traditional story of the origins of the discipline of rhetoric claims that the art was invented by Corax and Tisias when, in 467 BCE, tyrants ruling Syracuse were overthrown and there was a sudden need for the ability to speak well in public to participate in the new democracy or to present cases before the courts. Corax, and in some accounts Tisias, devised simple techniques for presenting arguments in speeches that they taught to students for money. While most and possibly all of the Corax and Tisias story is mythical (Schiappa 1999: 30–47), it is clear that in the latter half of the fifth century there emerged a new class of itinerant professional educators whose training sought to prepare young men for success in the life of politics. These educators are often referred to as sophists, a term that at the time simply meant a person of wisdom.

Precisely what and how the sophists taught remains a matter of contention, as we have very few surviving texts or descriptions that date to their era. Indeed, who we should label as a sophist is still controversial, though five names appear on virtually all lists: Protagoras, Gorgias, Hippias, Prodicus, and Antiphon. Some scholars have argued that the commonalities among the sophists produced a distinct school of thought that could be termed "sophistic rhetoric" (see, however, Schiappa 1999, 2003b). Based on Plato's largely unflattering descriptions of the sophists, for centuries sophistic rhetoric was understood as teaching the strategic, manipulative, and deceptive use of argument and oratory to achieve political success, regardless of the truth. In its most corrupt form sophistic rhetoric was described as aiming to make the worse argument appear the better. Such an account is influenced by Aristophanes's play, *The Clouds* (ca. 420 BCE) (see O'Regan, ch. 8). Although Aristophanes does not use the word *rhētorikē*, he presents the sophists (represented by Socrates) as part of a newfangled approach to education that champions attaining one's ends through clever, even if specious, reasoning.

The conflict between tradition and sophistic education is personified in *The Clouds* in a debate between the Stronger and Weaker Logoi. *Logoi* is the plural of *logos*, which may be translated in this context as "speech," "account," or—more to Aristophanes's purpose—a way of life. Aristophanes may have named the two Logoi after a statement attributed to Protagoras in which he claimed to teach how to make the weaker argument stronger. Protagoras probably meant how to make the best case one can for one's position, but it is not difficult to see how his statement could be described as representing an amoral relativism to which Aristophanes, and later Plato, would object (Schiappa 2003b: 103–16).

A number of scholars have sought to recuperate the notion of sophistic rhetoric. Classicists, rhetoric scholars, and philosophers have argued that there was nothing wrong with teaching practical argumentation and, in fact, in a democracy the teaching of such skills is necessary and laudable. Such scholars point out that the accounts of Plato and Aristophanes are inconsistent with other evidence, including the surviving texts and fragments of the sophists themselves. A case can be made that the sophists were not amoral relativists and that their texts contributed to fifth-century intellectual debates that most would now call philosophical. Prodicus of Ceos, for example, had a well-documented interest in word meanings that presaged Socrates's interest in definition, and he authored a speech known as the "Choice of Heracles" that promoted traditional Greek values.

Some scholars stress the philosophical interests of the sophists even further by noting similarities between more recent philosophical developments, such as pragmatism or postmodernism, and ideas that can be found in the fragments of Protagoras or Gorgias (Mailloux 1995; Consigny 2001). "Neosophistic rhetoric" is the name given to a contemporary strand of rhetorical theory that is contrasted to competing understandings of rhetoric derived from Plato or Aristotle (Schiappa 2003b: 64–85).

The concept and label "sophistic rhetoric" has been criticized on the grounds that it elides the differences among individual sophists and fails to reflect the fact that the sophists' teaching was broader than rhetoric. The "sophistic" text named *Dissoi Logoi*, dated to about 400 BCE, advocates what can be called omnicompetence: an ability to produce true and compelling discourse about topics of public concern in a variety of contexts. The unknown author states that "it belongs to the same man and to the same skill to be able to hold dialogue succinctly, to understand the truth of things, to plead one's court-cases correctly, to be able to make popular speeches, to understand argument skills, and to teach about the nature of all things—how they are [their condition] and how they came to be" (*Dissoi Logoi* 8.1; trans. Schiappa 1999: 74). Unquestionably, had such a paragraph been written 50 years later, words like *rhētorikē*, *dialektikē*, and *philosophia* would be used to describe the range of competencies described. The significance of this passage is that we see no incompatibility between what would later be called rhetoric and philosophy, between persuasion and truth-seeking. Indeed, the sentiments are consistent with what Plato portrays Socrates as advocating in *Phaedrus* as part of what would later be called philosophical rhetoric: "A man must know the truth about all the particular things of which he speaks or writes, and be able to define everything separately" (277b; trans. Fowler).

At the same time, it is clear that some sophists were interested in what would later be called the art of rhetoric. Antiphon wrote lengthy examples of arguments for both sides of hypothetical court trials. Speeches written by Gorgias and Prodicus appear to have been models that students may have studied. Protagoras apparently claimed to teach students the skills needed to participate in political life and give counsel in political decision-making, which would include the ability to argue in public. Most sophists expressed an explicit interest in *logos*, which can be best understood as "reasoned discourse."

Rhetoric in the Fourth Century

The earliest surviving use of the word *rhētorikē* is in Plato's dialogue, *Gorgias*, which appeared about 387 BCE. It has been conjectured that Plato coined the word, along with words for other verbal arts, including dialectic (*dialektikē*), antilogic (*antilogikē*), and eristic (*eristikē*). Plato may have done so to distinguish his approach to education, which he called philosophy (*philosophia*), from that of his chief rival, Isocrates, who had started a school not long before Plato opened his Academy (Schiappa 1999: 14–29, 2003b: 39–63). The exact dating of the word *rhētorikē* cannot be decided with certainty because we cannot know if the term "rhetoric" was in use orally prior to Plato or in texts that we no longer possess, but it certainly is the case that the term cannot be found before the early fourth century BCE and that it becomes increasingly common as the century progresses.

By the middle of the fourth century BCE, full-length textbooks on rhetoric had been written by Aristotle and an uncertain author (possibly Anaximenes) of the book called *Rhetoric to Alexander*. The transition can be described as a move from a broad and implicitly "predisciplinary" approach to argumentation, critical thinking, and public speaking to an explicit, disciplinary approach that finds its fullest expression in Aristotle's *Rhetoric*.

Although it appears that the word *rhētorikē* became well known in the fourth century, not all teachers embraced it. In fact, the first person to begin a "secondary" school with a fixed location was Isocrates, who described the education he provided as *philosophia* and, as far as we know, never used the word *rhētorikē* in his writings. Isocrates's *philosophia*, as described chiefly in *Against the Sophists* and *Antidosis*, can be understood as the cultivation of practical wisdom through the production of ethical civic discourse. He and his students produced written orations that they would analyze and critique for both form and content. Isocrates was not an active public speaker, but many of his written speeches were copied and widely distributed; indeed, some scholars contend that his essays, such as *Areopagiticus*, *Panathenaicus*, *Panegyricus*, and *Philip*, influenced some of the politics of his time.

Although Isocrates's model of teaching oratory proved highly successful, Plato's vocabulary and account of rhetoric also proved to be influential. In Plato's *Gorgias*, Socrates is portrayed as arguing that rhetoric is not a true art (or *technē*) but rather a knack, not unlike "cookery," that is picked up through practice and is aimed at flattery rather than truth. This critique of rhetoric cast a long shadow in the history of the discipline and is one to which many subsequent theorists felt a need to respond. In Plato's *Phaedrus*, the position of Socrates appears to be that an ethical and philosophical rhetoric is possible if closely aligned with dialectic. A number of other dialogues by Plato include examples of, and comments about, speech-making, including the *Symposium*, *Menexenus*, and *Apology*. Plato's texts are, of course, in dialogue form and depict imagined conversations, so it is difficult to identify a definitive Platonic theory with confidence; but it is fair to say that historically Plato has been read as hostile to or at least suspicious of rhetoric and was concerned about its misuse (see Yunis, ch. 9; Cassin, ch. 11; Miller, ch. 55).

The fullest account of rhetoric from the classical era appears in Aristotle's *Rhetoric*. Aristotle argues that rhetoric is indeed a genuine art that can be approached systematically and taught in order to help speakers find what he called the available means of persuasion. He claims that there are three, and only three, *pisteis* or "forms of persuasion": the speaker's self-presentation as credible and trustworthy (typically glossed as the speaker's *ēthos*), the logical argument presented (*logos*), and the emotional effect a speech elicits from the audience (*pathos*). Aristotle contends that there are three kinds of speech-making, each with its own distinct goals, audiences, and rules: deliberative (*symbouleutikon*) speeches for the legislative Assembly are arguments about what course of future action would be most advantageous; judicial (*dikanikon*) speeches are given in the law courts to determine past facts and seek justice; and epideictic (*epideiktikon*) speeches praise or blame people, actions, or qualities, with a focus on the present, such as a funeral oration (*epitaphios logos*) that praises fallen soldiers for their bravery and encourages the audience to carry on bravely, or a speech (*enkōmion*) that praises the greatness of a person's deeds. In the first two species of speeches the audience is described as having to make a decision, whereas epideictic speeches are typically ceremonial addresses where the audience merely observes the performance (see Garver, ch. 10).

Aristotle draws a distinction between artistic and nonartistic means of persuasion: nonartistic forms are direct kinds of evidence (facts, witness testimony, written documents, and laws) that the speaker uses but does not create, whereas artistic forms of persuasion are those the speaker invents, including inductive arguments (argument by example) and deductive arguments, which Aristotle calls enthymemes, that draw a conclusion from explicit or implicit premises. In rhetoric the speaker must argue about what is probable rather than what is certain, since there is no need to engage in persuasion when the subject matter can be determined with certainty. Although the subject matter of oratory may vary, Aristotle believes he has described a universal art because all speeches must rely on a shared and finite number of argument strategies he calls "topics" (*topoi*). Book 3 of Aristotle's treatise discusses the style and arrangement of speeches; virtually all scholars agree it was written separately and added to what we now call Aristotle's *Rhetoric*.

From Aristotle's perspective, the art of rhetoric is primarily about finding (*heuresis*) the most effective argumentative strategies one can in any individual case. This fundamentally "heuristic" approach is evident also in the other major rhetorical textbook that survives from the fourth century, the *Rhetoric to Alexander*. The *Rhetoric to Alexander* begins by identifying seven particular kinds of speech: exhortation, dissuasion, praise, blame, accusation, defense, and examination. Although the conceptual vocabularies of Aristotle's *Rhetoric* and the *Rhetoric to Alexander* differ as much as they overlap, both books intend to offer students a guide to inventing arguments and crafting public speeches. Traditionally, the *Rhetoric to Alexander* has not received the respect that Aristotle's *Rhetoric* has, but recently its reputation has improved. Scholars note that both books share a theoretical commitment to defining key terms and advancing an understanding of persuasion that links argumentative effectiveness with rationality (see van Eemeren, ch. 52). The vocabulary, definitions, and syntax suggest a late- fourth-century BCE text that takes a conceptual approach that is more philosophical than any other texts about rhetoric in the fifth or fourth century besides those of Plato and Aristotle (Timmerman and Schiappa 2010). Although Aristotle spends more time explicitly discussing the philosophical status of rhetoric, it is unlikely such concerns would have interested practitioners. Indeed, the *Rhetoric to Alexander* would not have survived had it not been found of value by practicing students of oratory.

GREEK RHETORIC IN THE POSTCLASSICAL ERA

By the end of the fourth century BCE, rhetoric was a well-established discipline of study. Three further developments in Greek rhetoric are particularly noteworthy. The first is the careful study of style. Critical observations concerning different approaches to prose and poetic composition styles can be found as early as Aristophanes, but Aristotle's *Rhetoric* and the *Rhetoric to Alexander* are the earliest surviving examples of sustained analysis. Aristotle's student Theophrastus reportedly authored a text called *On Style*, now lost, that advanced Aristotle's analysis by describing specific virtues of style, including using correct Greek, clarity, propriety, and appropriate ornament. He may have written also about three different kinds of style—plain, grand, and "mixed." Similarly, the later author Demetrius composed a treatise named *On Style* (date unknown) that provides an eight-part taxonomy of styles, four of which are desirable (plain, elevated, elegant, and forceful) and four undesirable (arid, frigid, affected, and unpleasant).

As the power of Rome grew, many elements of Greek culture were absorbed into Roman culture, including an appreciation of rhetoric (see Dominik, ch. 12). Dionysius of Halicarnassus wrote in Greek for a mostly Roman audience, and a number of his works were concerned with rhetoric. These include *On the Ancient Orators*, about four of the most famous Greek speech writers: Lysias, Isocrates, Isaeus, and Demosthenes. He also wrote in favor of a more modest or plain style of oratory, known as Atticism, which he favored over what he saw as the excesses of Asianism. Just how detailed analyses of style could become is evident in the text known as *On the Sublime* (author unknown), estimated to have been written in the third century CE. This work is wholly devoted to the thorough analysis of one stylistic virtue, which the author calls sublimity (*hypsos*). It is a remarkable text that remains valuable not only for its insights about literary style but also as a source of quoted passages that we would not have without it.

The second noteworthy postclassical development in rhetoric is known as *stasis* theory. Style and arrangement are recurring issues for students of rhetoric because all speakers must make artistic choices about how to present their ideas. But where do their ideas come from? Aristotle's answer was *topoi*, topics or "places" where argument strategies could be found. *Stasis* theory was another attempt to provide students with a set of conceptual categories to generate legal arguments by identifying the key elements involved in a dispute. The invention of *stasis* theory is typically credited to Hermagoras of Temnos in the second century BCE, though his writings have not survived. The most enduring and popular approach to *stasis* theory can be described as asking a series of questions: "Did he do it?" is a question of fact that identifies a conjectural point of *stasis*; "What did he do?" is a question that identifies a definitional point of *stasis*; "How do we characterize what he did?" is a question that identifies a qualitative point of *stasis* (that is, was the action good or bad, justified or not, etc.); and "Is this the appropriate venue?" raises a jurisdictional point of *stasis*. Later Latin texts by Cicero and the *Rhetorica ad Herennium* (author unknown) make it clear that Roman rhetorical pedagogy was influenced by *stasis* theory. An additional Greek work on *stasis* was written by Hermogenes of Tarsus, a gifted orator of the second century CE who advanced a far more complex approach in his *On Staseis*. Hermogenes also authored *On Invention*, the scope of which appears to be quite broad, covering most elements of speech-making, along with a text titled *On Ideas of Style*, which enumerates a taxonomy of seven stylistic virtues.

A third important postclassical development in rhetoric is the emergence of the *progymnasmata*. The *progymnasmata* were a graduated sequence of rhetorical exercises that become increasingly difficult and sophisticated, requiring ever greater skill and knowledge. Hermogenes, Theon, and Aphthonius are authors credited with devising this pedagogical strategy. Aphthonius's 14 steps are fable, narrative, anecdote, proverb, refutation, confirmation, commonplaces, encomium, invective, comparison, personification, description, thesis (logical examination), and deliberation (defend or attack a law). The *progymnasmata* have been described as one of the most influential teaching methods to arise from the rhetorical tradition and variations of these exercises are still used today (see Heath, ch. 5).

Along with philosophy, rhetoric is one of classical Greece's most enduring legacies throughout Western history; Aristotle's *Rhetoric*, in particular, has been one of the most influential texts from Greek antiquity. Rhetoric was a central part of Western education from the classical Greek era until the late nineteenth century. Understood as the theory and pedagogy of persuasive speaking and argument, Greek rhetoric involved issues that arguably are as vital today as they were in the fifth century BCE.

References

Bloch, Maurice, ed. 1975. *Political Language and Oratory in Traditional Society*. London: Academic Press.

Clay, Jenny Strauss. 2007. "Hesiod's Rhetorical Art." In *A Companion to Greek Rhetoric*, edited by Ian Worthington, 447–457. Oxford: Blackwell.

Cole, Thomas. 1991. *The Origins of Rhetoric in Ancient Greece*. Baltimore, MD: Johns Hopkins University Press.

Consigny, Scott. 2001. *Gorgias, Sophist and Artist*. Columbia: University of South Carolina Press.

Fox, Matthew, and Niall Livingstone. 2007. "Rhetoric and Historiography." In *A Companion to Greek Rhetoric*, edited by Ian Worthington, 542–561. Oxford: Blackwell.

Havelock, Eric. 1983. "The Linguistic Task of the Presocratics." In *Language and Thought in Early Greek Philosophy*, edited by Kevin Robb, 7–82. LaSalle, IL: Hegeler Institute.

Hubbard, Thomas K. 2007. "Attic Comedy and the Development of Theoretical Rhetoric." In *A Companion to Greek Rhetoric*, edited by Ian Worthington, 490–508. Oxford: Blackwell.

Karp, Andrew J. 1977. "Homeric Origins of Ancient Rhetoric." *Arethusa* 10: 237–258.

Kennedy, George A. 1998. *Comparative Rhetoric: An Historical and Cross-Cultural Introduction*. New York: Oxford University Press.

Kirby, John T. 1990. "Rhetoric and Poetics in Hesiod." *Ramus* 21 no. 1: 34–60.

Lu, Xing. 1998. *Rhetoric in Ancient China, Fifth to Third Century B.C.E.* Columbia: University of South Carolina Press.

Mailloux, Steven, ed. 1995. *Rhetoric, Sophistry, Pragmatism*. Cambridge: Cambridge University Press.

Major, Wilfred E. 2013. *The Court of Comedy: Aristophanes, Rhetoric, and Democracy in Fifth-Century Athens*. Columbus: Ohio State University Press.

McComiskey, Bruce. 2002. *Gorgias and the New Sophistic Rhetoric*. Carbondale: Southern Illinois University Press.

Oliver, Robert T. 1971. *Communication and Culture in Ancient India and China*. Syracuse, NY: Syracuse University Press.

Roisman, Hanna M. 2007. "Right Rhetoric in Homer." In *A Companion to Greek Rhetoric*, edited by Ian Worthington, 429–446. Oxford: Blackwell.

Sansone, David. 2012. *Greek Drama and the Invention of Rhetoric*. Chichester: Wiley-Blackwell.

Schiappa, Edward. 1999. *The Beginnings of Rhetorical Theory in Classical Greece*. New Haven, CT: Yale University Press.

Schiappa, Edward. 2003a. *Defining Reality: Definitions and the Politics of Meaning*. Carbondale: Southern Illinois University Press.

Schiappa, Edward. 2003b. *Protagoras and Logos: A Study in Greek Philosophy and Rhetoric*. 2nd ed. Columbia: University of South Carolina Press.

Stadter, Philip A., ed. 1973. *Speeches in Thucydides*. Chapel Hill: University of North Carolina Press.

Timmerman, David, and Edward Schiappa. 2010. *Classical Greek Rhetorical Theory and the Disciplining of Discourse*. Cambridge: Cambridge University Press.

Wang, Bo. 2004. "A Survey of Research in Asian Rhetoric." *Rhetoric Review* 23 no. 2: 171–181.

Worthington, Ian, ed. 2007. *A Companion to Greek Rhetoric*. Oxford: Blackwell.

....

CHAPTER 2

RHETORIC AND LAW

....

MICHAEL GAGARIN

THE relationship between law and rhetoric in ancient Greece was intimate, complex, and controversial. To begin with, law played a leading role in the development of oratory from the earliest times and in the study of rhetoric from its beginnings, traditionally assigned to Corax and Tisias in fifth-century Sicily. Law also continued to exert a strong influence on both Plato's and Aristotle's view of rhetoric, as different as these were, and on rhetorical theory and practice in Hellenistic and Roman times. Second, oratory was a fundamental component of Greek law from the time of Homer to the fourth century BCE, when the rhetorical ability of litigants—or of their logographers (speechwriters)—significantly influenced the nature and outcome of litigation in ways familiar from the US common law system (see Sickinger 2007). And third, whereas the Athenian legal system gave rhetoric an essential role, Plato condemns rhetoric in both *Gorgias* and *Laws* in large part because of its corrupting role in litigation. Plato's position has remained the dominant one among legal scholars down to the present day, although many scholars now argue that rhetoric is an inescapable component of any legal system (Goodrich 1998; Amsterdam and Bruner 2000). In this chapter I shall consider each of these aspects of the relationship between law and rhetoric to shed light on the ambivalent attitudes toward rhetoric and law in Athens and, ultimately, in modern American culture (see Goodrich, ch. 48).

THE ROLE OF LAW IN RHETORIC

....

According to traditional accounts, rhetoric was "invented" in Sicily by Corax and his pupil, Tisias, after the overthrow of the tyrants in the middle of the fifth century BCE. The restoration of democracy and its institutions, the Assembly and the popular courts, gave those who could speak well a clear advantage, and Corax and Tisias therefore began teaching the art of rhetoric to men who wanted to influence public policy or win a legal case. This story links the birth of rhetoric to the rise of democracy in ancient Greece, but when examined more closely it becomes clear that the primary venue for the development of rhetoric were the law courts (Kennedy 1963: 18; cf. Hinks 1940: 62–3; Carey 1996). The best-attested example of early rhetorical theory, attributed to both Corax and Tisias, is a legal case concerning a fight between a strong man and a weak man (see Plato, *Phaedrus* 273a–c; Aristotle, *Rhetoric* 2.24.11, 1402a; Gagarin 2007: 31–3). The case involves not only an argument from *eikos* (probability or likelihood) but also a new "reverse *eikos*" argument: "Because I, a strong man, am more likely to have started the fight, it is, in fact, not likely that I did so because I knew I would immediately be accused of starting it." The reliability of this account of the birth of rhetoric has recently been challenged, so it is best not to rely on it in detail (see Schiappa 1990, 1999; Cole 1991a, 1991b). But since arguments from *eikos* play an important role in forensic speeches a generation later, it is reasonable to conclude that this type of argument was in the air in the mid-fifth century whether or not Corax or Tisias had a hand in its development.

The second half of the fifth century saw continuing discussion of speech and argument (two meanings of *logos*) among the sophists, whose most important figure with regard to *logos* was another Sicilian, Gorgias of Leontini. His best-known work, *Helen*, is called an encomium (*enkōmion*) and is thus often categorized as epideictic rhetoric, but it is also explicitly a quasi-legal defense of Helen and thus as much forensic as epideictic. Gorgias's *Palamedes*, his other surviving speech (besides the fragment of an *epitaphios logos* or funeral oration), is also an example of forensic rhetoric and consists largely of arguments from probability. Gorgias's other main work, *On Non-Being*, preserved in commentaries by Aristotle and Sextus Empiricus, is a philosophical, not rhetorical, work that examines problems of being, knowledge, and language that preoccupied the Ionian and Eleatic philosophers. Another sophist, Antiphon, also contributed much in the area of *logos* and legal discourse: his *Tetralogies*—each with four speeches (two on each side) from a hypothetical homicide case—are exercises in forensic argumentation, and the first *Tetralogy* is devoted entirely to *eikos* arguments, including a reverse *eikos* argument (2.2.3).

Besides the argument from probability, the major contribution by a sophist to the development of rhetoric was Protagoras's method of training students to "make the weaker argument stronger" (not "make the weaker argument *the* stronger," as it is often mistranslated [see Gagarin 2002: 24–6]). Protagoras taught that one should try to make a weak argument as strong as possible, not that one should always make a weak argument prevail over a stronger one. Although Protagoras probably incorporated this argumentative strategy in his teaching in legitimate ways, it was often misconstrued, intentionally or not, as teaching the ability to make any argument prevail, no matter how weak, untrue, or unjust. We see this most clearly in Aristophanes's *Clouds* (423 BCE), in which the leading character, Strepsiades, wants to learn the "unjust argument" (*adikos logos*) so that he can escape his creditors. The "sophistic" arguments he learns turn out to be absurd (the play, after all, is a parody), but they reinforce the popular idea that the sophists taught clever speaking without regard for truth or justice. The play also confirms the impression that sophistic rhetoric was primarily used in court by defendants who were guilty but managed to persuade the jury otherwise (see O'Regan, ch. 8).

All of these sources, whether they are promoting or denigrating rhetoric, make clear that in the middle and second half of the fifth century the study of rhetoric—or better, *logos*—was primarily directed at forensic argument. This same focus is evident in the fourth century, when the art of logography reached its peak. The Athenian legal system was structured so that the outcome of cases depended almost entirely on the pleadings of the litigants; skill in speaking was thus highly desirable for anyone facing litigation. And although the same could be said for anyone wishing to influence debate in the Assembly, it appears that many more Athenians were involved in litigation than spoke in the Assembly. The craft of logography, moreover, was developed entirely as a service for those engaged in litigation; it was not practiced in the areas of deliberative or epideictic oratory. The only deliberative speeches that survive today were written by the author himself to deliver in the Assembly—we know of no one composing a speech for someone else to deliver there.

In practicing their craft, these logographers developed rhetorical tactics, techniques, and arguments that were influential in the study of rhetoric. Lysias, for example, became a master of a simple yet vivid narrative style that became a model for imitation by rhetoric teachers in Hellenistic and Roman times. Other forensic speakers, especially Demosthenes, also developed prose styles that influenced later rhetoric. Lysias also pioneered the art of creating character (*ēthos*), which probably influenced the discussion of *ēthos* by Aristotle and others. And Antiphon, Isaeus, and others created forms and methods of argument that similarly influenced the study of rhetoric. Thus, the Athenian art of forensic oratory, which was developed to address the needs of litigants in court, provided models of style and argument for later rhetoricians to draw on in their work.

On the negative side, forensic oratory also provided the target for Plato's attack on rhetoric, best known from *Gorgias*, although it is already evident in *Apology*, in which he has Socrates deny that he possesses any expertise in speaking (17a–8a). In *Gorgias*, Socrates gets Gorgias to agree that he teaches the craft (*technē*) of rhetoric, which is the "producer of persuasion" (*peithous apa demiourgos*), and then gets him to specify that it is persuasion "in jury courts and in other crowds . . . about things that are just and unjust" (Plato, *Gorgias* 453a). Gorgias admits that rhetoric is not concerned with truth or justice, that it works best in speaking to a large, ignorant crowd, and that the speaker himself is concerned only with what will be most likely to persuade this audience (448a–59b). This rejection of rhetoric as a perversion of justice continues in *Laws*, in which Plato prescribes severe penalties for anyone who employs rhetoric to avoid justice or help others avoid justice (937e–8c). In fact, the only place Plato does not discuss rhetoric primarily in the context of legal discourse is at the end of *Phaedrus*, where he holds out the possibility of a good rhetoric grounded in dialectic and philosophical knowledge (276a–8e) (see Yunis, ch. 9).

Plato's pupil, Aristotle, took a more constructive approach in *Rhetoric*, the most comprehensive and influential Greek treatise on the subject. Aristotle begins by dividing rhetoric into three kinds: deliberative (*symbouleutikon*), judicial (*dikanikon*), and epideictic (*epideiktikon*). But although much of Aristotle's work is applicable to all three branches, his chapters on forensic rhetoric (1.10–5) are the longest, and many of his other arguments, such as his arguments about *ēthos*, are also directed primarily at forensic rhetoric. The *ēthos* of one's opponent, for example, is a concern only in forensic argument. The other major figure in fourth-century rhetoric is Isocrates, even though he avoids using the term *rhētorikē* and insists that what he teaches is *philosophia*. Isocrates's philosophy manifested itself as a public discourse about the common good, and his views had a profound influence on education in antiquity. Yet although one of his greatest works, *Antidosis*, is cast as a forensic speech, forensic discourse had little overall influence on Isocrates's thinking. Moreover, the sophists, whom he seems to equate with logographers, are frequently cast as villains whose sole interest lies in winning legal cases—a convenient foil against which Isocrates elaborates his own practice of philosophy.

Finally, in the Hellenistic period, although certain topics applicable to all three branches of rhetoric, such as style (*lexis*), continued to occupy theorists, the main advance in rhetorical theory was the elaboration of *stasis* theory in the work of Hermagoras and his followers (see Kennedy 1963: 304–18). This theory, which divides and subdivides legal cases according to the "issue" (e.g., fact, legal definition, jurisdiction), was developed for and used primarily in judicial rhetoric (see Heath, ch. 5). As all of these examples indicate, Greek rhetoric, while not entirely confined to the legal sphere, developed primarily to serve forensic needs, and for this reason forensic concerns were the most powerful influence on rhetorical theory in ancient Greece.

THE ROLE OF RHETORIC IN LAW

Just as rhetorical theory drew inspiration from law and forensic discourse, oratory and rhetoric were fundamental to Greek law. Our earliest glimpse of a Greek trial comes in a scene on Achilles's shield depicting two litigants pleading before a group of judges who compete to "speak the straightest judgment" (Homer, *Iliad* 18.497–508). In *Theogony* Hesiod also praises the eloquence of the good judge, on whose "tongue the Muses pour sweet honey and soothing words flow from his mouth" (83–4). In the archaic period, written laws increasingly provided fixed rules to guide the outcome of litigation, thereby gradually reducing the discretion of judges to a simple decision for one or the other litigant; trials, however, continued to consist largely in litigants pleading their cases before a judge or group of judges (see Gagarin 2008).

In Athens, besides the procedure of deciding trials almost entirely on the basis of the litigants' pleas, a democratically inspired hostility to legal expertise ensured that trials were conducted by officials with no professional training and little authority over the proceedings. Verdicts were in the hands of large popular juries who voted without formal deliberation and could not be held accountable for their decisions. There were no judges (in the modern sense), no jurists, and no lawyers. A group of Exegetes had some authority in religious matters, and their opinions could sometimes be cited in court (e.g., Demosthenes 47.68–70), but they had no legal authority. Trials were supervised by officials selected annually, by lot, with the assistance of clerks. These officials had some control over the filing of cases, ensuring that proposed litigation met certain formal requirements, but had no authority to determine the outcome of cases. A litigant's single speech had to carry the full weight of his case (although certain cases, including homicide, permitted a second, rebuttal speech), and skill in persuasive speaking was therefore essential for success. Such a system fostered the growth of experts in speech writing, the *logographoi*, though they operated behind the scenes, composing speeches for a litigant to memorize and deliver himself rather than appearing in court on the litigant's behalf like a Roman *advocatus* or modern lawyer (see Enos, ch. 13). Whether litigants delivered their own speech or one written by a logographer, however, they had to persuade a large group of jurors (*dikastai*), and for this task rhetorical skill was essential.

The important role of rhetoric in forensic discourse does not, however, mean that Athenian litigation had no concern for the law, the facts, or the truth, as Plato concluded. On the contrary, one of the consistent messages proclaimed by litigants concerned the importance of adhering to the laws of the city. Nonetheless, rhetoric was also essential to the successful presentation of a case, as we may see by examining a specific example. Lysias's "On the Killing of Eratosthenes" was written by Lysias for a client named Euphiletus, accused of murdering a certain Eratosthenes. Euphiletus argues that the killing was justified because he found Eratosthenes in bed with his wife. His case requires the use of rhetoric in two ways: first, he must give a plausible account of the facts that will persuade the jurors that he did indeed find Eratosthenes in bed with his wife and that Eratosthenes was there because he had seduced his wife; and second, he must also show that the law not only allowed but also *required* someone to kill an adulterer found in bed with his wife.

For the first task, Euphiletus presents witness testimony that he found Eratosthenes in bed with his wife and killed him on the spot, but he has no witnesses to the alleged seduction of his wife. He must therefore present to the jury a plausible account (*logos*) of facts for which he has no hard evidence, and this requires the rhetorical skill of a storyteller. Among the more obvious rhetorical techniques that help convey the impression of truth in Euphiletus's account are the inclusion of small, memorable details and vivid use of direct speech, while the incorporation of stereotypical characters familiar from comedy would have lent plausibility to his account (Porter 1997; Gagarin 2003). Telling a story in such a case is not a rhetorical diversion but is fundamental to litigation, since even when the facts are known they take on meaning only in the context of a story. The same is true in the American legal system, in which trial lawyers on both sides strive to make their accounts of the facts (*narratio*) as plausible as possible. They face more constraints than Athenian litigants, of course, but the essential task of a trial lawyer is similar to that of a logographer. The Athenians, however, were more accepting of the role rhetorical persuasion played in their law than we are today.

Euphiletus's second task is to persuade the jurors that the law requires that an adulterer caught in bed with someone else's wife be put to death. This, too, requires rhetorical skill. He begins to make the case as he describes the climactic moment: "He [Eratosthenes] admitted his guilt, and begged and entreated me not to kill him but to accept compensation. I replied, 'It is not I who will kill you, but the law of the city. You have broken that law and have had less regard for it than for your own pleasure. You have preferred to commit this crime against my wife and my children rather than behaving responsibly and obeying the laws.' So it was, gentlemen, that this man met the fate which the laws prescribe for those who behave like that" (Lysias, "On the Killing of Eratosthenes" 1.25–7). Shortly thereafter, to prove his point, Euphiletus has the actual law read aloud to the jury: "If someone kills a person unintentionally in an athletic contest, or seizing him on the highway, or unknowingly in battle, or after finding him next to his wife or mother or sister or daughter or concubine kept for producing free children, he shall not be exiled as a killer on account of this."

Now, this law does not in fact prescribe death as the penalty for adultery; it is a law about circumstances in which people will not be punished for killing. We know from its language, moreover, that it is an old law, probably enacted by Draco more than two centuries earlier. Thus, even though the law was probably still technically valid, it is likely that by Lysias's time killing an adulterer was thought to be excessively severe by most Athenians. Other evidence we have, including other forensic speeches and the comedies of Aristophanes, mention various penalties for adultery but not the death penalty, and it had probably been some time since an adulterer was killed on the spot like this. Thus, many, perhaps most, jurors probably did not think an adulterer caught in the act should be killed; on the other hand, there may not have been any other clear penalty for adultery either. It is likely that one type of prosecution, the *graphē moicheias*, left it up to the jury in a second vote (*timēsis*) to decide the punishment in case of conviction (see Todd 2007).

If in fact there was no single statute governing adultery but rather a variety of statutes could apply in different circumstances, jurors would have to decide the proper punishment for adultery on a case-by-case basis. They would thus have had to judge Euphiletus's act of homicide on the basis of the evidence he presented about the laws on adultery and within the context of the events he had just finished narrating. From this perspective, many might have agreed with his claim that the killing was justified, for he has told a very effective story. Note especially his words to Eratosthenes as he is about to kill him: "It is not I who will kill you, but the law of the city. You have broken that law and have had less regard for it than for your own pleasure. You have preferred to commit this crime against my wife and my children rather than behaving responsibly and obeying the laws" (Lysias, "On the Killing of Eratosthenes" 1.25–7). This is not the ordinary language of everyday speech; it is rather the speech of a judge explaining to a convicted man why he must be punished. Whether or not Euphiletus actually spoke these words does not matter. The vividness of the scene and the formal, judicial quality of Euphiletus's pronouncement, followed by the reading out of the law in its archaic language, would certainly have encouraged the jurors to think that Euphiletus was presenting them with an official judicial explanation of the law.

Of course, the prosecution also gave a speech. However, it has not survived, and we do not know how they might have argued and sought to persuade. Whatever their precise arguments, the jury would then have been left to choose between competing stories (*logoi*), not only about the facts of the case but also about the law itself. And since no impartial authority existed who could tell them definitively what the law on adultery was, as a judge would do in our system, the jurors would have to determine for themselves the meaning of the laws presented to them and their relevance to the case. And to guide their judgment, they had only the two speeches they had just heard, perhaps supplemented by anything they may have heard in previous cases and by their own knowledge, if any, of other cases of adultery.

This use of rhetoric to persuade the jury of the meaning or applicability of a law is not unlike arguments made today to a trial judge or to the judge or judges on appeals courts. There the arguments of the lawyers on either side, which often include a discussion of legislative intent, are not so different from those used in Athens. In other words, both in constructing a plausible account of the facts and in explaining the meaning and applicability of a law, Athenian litigants and logographers employed the art of rhetoric in similar ways and toward similar ends as lawyers do today (see Hutson, ch. 32; Goodrich, ch. 48). The main difference is that in contemporary law a professional judge has the final authority in both areas: the judge decides on the admissibility and relevance of factual evidence and renders authoritative decisions about the meaning and applicability of laws. The Athenians left both tasks in the hands of jurors who lacked special training in the law.

The Relationship between Law and Rhetoric

The intimate relationship between rhetoric and law in ancient Greece raises important questions, still with us today, about the nature and meaning of their interaction. Plato viewed rhetoric as little more than a tool for persuading an audience regardless of the truth or justice of a case. In *Laws*, for example, he proposes an elaborate set of legal prescriptions for an ideal city, which include instructions for devising a legal system in which rhetoric would have a minimal role. Plato's ideal legal system requires a small number of experienced judges who hear the litigants' pleadings and then deliberate for two days before deciding a case; when they do reach a decision (*krisis*), they must cast their votes openly and can even be prosecuted for casting an unjust vote (Plato, *Laws* 767d–8d, 855d–6a). As for the pleadings of litigants, Plato accepts that they are a necessary feature of any legal system and are thus a good thing, but "a certain evil craft [*technē*], concealing itself behind a fine name, brings these fine things into disrepute, claiming that there exists a means by which someone bringing suits and pleading against another can win whether his case is just or not. This craft is a gift, moreover, that is available to anyone who pays." Plato is referring to rhetoric, of course, and he proceeds both to banish it from the judicial process and to set severe penalties for anyone caught using it (937e–8c).

Now, Plato's banishment of rhetoric from the pleadings of litigants presupposes that rhetoric is something separate from speech, an accessory or stylistic ornament that can be added to or subtracted from speech without altering its content (see Cole 1991a: 12–4): litigants can continue to plead in Plato's ideal court, but they need to do so without resorting to rhetoric. But this simplistic view of speech as a conveyor of content that is separable from whatever style may be used to convey it has long been discredited by philosophers of language, though it may still hold sway in the popular view of rhetoric (Cole 1991a: 18–22). Socrates may disclaim rhetorical ability, but his speech in *Apology* is widely recognized as a tour de force of rhetorical skill. Like all litigants' pleadings, Socrates's defense speech is necessarily rhetorical because rhetoric is inherent in speaking. The question, then, is not whether a speaker uses rhetoric but whether he uses it skillfully or not. Similarly, with regard to law, it is not whether rhetoric is present (it is, though its importance may vary) but whether, like the Athenians, one accepts its role or, like Plato, tries to deny it, to the point of banishing it from the *polis*.

Of course, rhetoric (or more specifically, rhetoric in law) was not the only Athenian institution Plato rejected. In *Republic* he criticizes democracy as a political system, arguing that the government should be in the hands of the educated few rather than the unruly masses. Plato was not alone in this latter view, but Athens nonetheless remained a democracy throughout the fifth and fourth centuries (except for two brief oligarchic coups brought about largely by the strain of the Peloponnesian War) until Athens's military defeat at the hands of Philip and Alexander.

To maintain its democracy Athens also maintained a democratic legal system in which, as in its political system, ultimate authority (*kratos*) rested with the people (*dēmos*). In law this authority was manifested in the use of large popular juries rather than legal professionals. Jurors' decisions were based entirely on the pleadings of litigants, giving rhetoric a larger role than it has in most other legal systems. Thus, the importance of rhetoric in Athenian law was closely related to the democratic nature of the Athenian legal system, and it is hardly surprising that Plato rejected both or that the Athenians valued both. The question for modern scholars is: How do we assess this intimate relationship between rhetoric and law? Do we accept Plato's analysis and condemn Athenian law as perverted by the influence of rhetoric to the point that it could not fulfill its proper function of achieving justice? Do we perhaps praise Athenian law for deciding cases using rhetorically influenced, nonlegal criteria such as social status? Or, as I would argue, does the crucial role of rhetoric still allow—and perhaps even help—the Athenian legal system to promote the rule of law?

In general, the Athenians gave litigants broad leeway in bringing cases and constructing their pleas. A plaintiff could often choose among several different procedures and select whatever particular actions he wished to specify in his formal complaint. The complaint was subject to acceptance by the official in charge of that type of case, but rarely was a complaint rejected or even returned for modification before being allowed to proceed. In his pleading, too, a litigant or his *logographos* enjoyed the freedom to say what he wanted. Athens did, however, impose one constraint on the proceedings: litigants had to stick to the issue in dispute. Although no formal means of enforcing this rule existed, jurors could express their displeasure at anyone straying from the issue, and litigants seem to have largely abided by the rule.

Nonetheless, however strictly litigants may have stuck to the issue, their pleadings were considerably more rhetorical than modern law either allows or recognizes as legitimate, and this must in some ways have diminished the legal system's ability to promote truth, justice, and the rule of law. In other ways, however, rhetoric worked to promote the rule of law. As we have seen in Lysias's defense of Euphiletus, because the laws concerning adultery did not prescribe one clear punishment, rhetoric was essential in guiding the jurors in their determination of what the law on adultery was for that particular case. The question for these jurors was: Do the laws cited by Euphiletus support his defense of justified homicide? In the United States a judge would decide this question based on the arguments of both lawyers, each of whom would support their position by citing one or more of the laws concerning adultery, explaining why they are relevant to the case at hand, and perhaps appealing to the legislators' intentions in crafting the law. A judge will normally make the decision seem inevitable, even though the process itself makes clear that there is a case to be made on both sides and that the judge could have reached the opposite opinion (and, of course, an appeals court might be split on the decision).

In Athens, this entire process took place in front of a jury of several hundred ordinary citizens. The litigants' pleadings may have been more rhetorical than they are today, but this was arguably necessary because Athenian jurors did not have professional expertise in legal matters and thus had a greater need to be educated. But this is a difference of degree, not kind. The American system may produce justice more often (though there is no clear proof of this), but the Athenian legal system was certainly more democratic. Furthermore, the Athenians clearly liked it that way, for they did nothing (beyond the rule of relevance) to restrict litigants' pleadings (Lanni 2006).

In sum, when questions arose about the meaning or applicability of a law, the ancient Athenians left these questions to the jury to decide. Such a system of broad, public decision-making necessarily resulted in a greater reliance on the art of rhetoric. For the majority of Athenians, it was not only acceptable but also desirable that law should be in the hands of the people, and should accordingly be subject to the influence of rhetoric. But the ultimate source of authority in their system was still the laws.

REFERENCES

Amsterdam, Anthony G., and Jerome Bruner. 2000. *Minding the Law: How Courts Rely on Storytelling, and How Their Stories Change the Ways We Understand the Law—and Ourselves.* Cambridge, MA: Harvard University Press.

Carey, Christopher. 1996. "Nomos in Rhetoric and Oratory." *Journal of Hellenic Studies* 116: 33–46.

Cole, Thomas. 1991a. *The Origins of Rhetoric in Ancient Greece.* Baltimore, MA: Johns Hopkins University Press.

Cole, Thomas. 1991b. "Who was Corax?" *Illinois Classical Studies* 16: 65–84.

Gagarin, Michael. 2002. *Antiphon the Athenian: Law and Oratory in the Age of the Sophists.* Austin: University of Texas Press.

Gagarin, Michael. 2003. "Telling Stories in Athenian Law." *Transactions of the American Philological Association* 133: 197–207.

Gagarin, Michael. 2007. "Background and Origins: Oratory and Rhetoric before the Sophists." In *A Companion to Greek Rhetoric*, edited by Ian Worthington, 27–36. Oxford: Wiley-Blackwell.

Gagarin, Michael. 2008. *Writing Greek Law.* Cambridge: Cambridge University Press.

Goodrich, Peter. 1998. "Law by Other Means." *Cardozo Studies in Law and Literature* 10 no. 2: 111–116.

Hinks, D. A. 1940. "Tisias and Corax and the Invention of Rhetoric." *Classical Quarterly* 34: 61–69.

Kennedy, George A. 1963. *The Art of Persuasion in Greece.* Princeton, NJ: Princeton University Press.

Lanni, Adriaan M. 2006. *Law and Justice in the Courts of Classical Athens.* Cambridge: Cambridge University Press.

Porter, John R. 1997. "Adultery by the Book: Lysias 1 (*On the Murder of Eratosthenes*) and Comic *Diegesis.*" *Echos du Monde Classique* 40: 421–453.

Schiappa, Edward. 1990. "Did Plato Coin *Rhētorikē*?" *American Journal of Philology* 111: 457–470.

Schiappa, Edward. 1999. *The Beginnings of Rhetorical Theory in Classical Greece.* New Haven, CT: Yale University Press.

Sickinger, James P. 2007. "Rhetoric and the Law." In *A Companion to Greek Rhetoric*, edited by Ian Worthington, 286–302. Oxford: Blackwell.

Todd, Stephen C. 2007. *A Commentary on Lysias: Speeches 1–11.* Oxford: Oxford University Press.

....

CHAPTER 3

RHETORIC AND POLITICS

....

EDWARD M. HARRIS

In the modern world, political speech can take many forms. There are party platforms, manifestos, campaign speeches at political rallies and conventions, addresses to political bodies like Congress or Parliament, speeches on public holidays, editorials in newspapers, books outlining political programs, and advertisements on television for political candidates and causes. These media can use different techniques of persuasion, ranging from the brief slogan or sound bite to lengthy reports complete with documents and statistics (see Campbell and Jamieson, ch. 50). In classical Athens and most other Greek city-states, there was one main forum for political speech, the Assembly, in which all citizens had the right to participate, make proposals, and vote on laws and decrees about public affairs. One finds many examples of speeches delivered in the Assembly in the histories of Thucydides and Xenophon. Thucydides implies that the speeches in his work are not verbatim transcriptions of what was said but were an attempt to capture the general thrust of what was said and "what was required in the given situation" (*The Peloponnesian War* 1.22). Scholars have endlessly debated the meaning of this statement, but there is no reason to doubt that speakers in Thucydides use the kinds of arguments one would have normally heard in the Assembly (see Carey, ch. 4; Badian 1992). There are also 16 speeches written for delivery in the Assembly attributed to Demosthenes, but one of these was probably written by Hegesippus ([Demosthenes] 7) and another two are spurious ones (11, 17), which leaves 13 genuine speeches (1–6, 8–10, 13–16). Some scholars have argued that these were actually political pamphlets not intended for oral delivery, but it is more likely that they are attempts to recreate the kind of speech one would have heard in the Assembly (Adams 1912; Tuplin 1998). *On the Peace*, attributed to Andocides, is a forgery composed in the Hellenistic period (Harris 2000).

To understand political rhetoric in classical Greece it is necessary to study the basic procedures of the Greek Assembly. The Greeks divided the functions of the state into three main parts. First, there was the deliberative part, which included the Council and Assembly, the judicial, and the magistrates (Aristotle, *Politics* 1297b35–8a3; Harris 2006: 29–40). The function of the Council and Assembly was to decide about matters pertaining to the entire community as opposed to the courts, which resolved disputes involving individuals (Thucydides, *The Peloponnesian War* 2.37.1). The Council and Assembly combined the functions of the legislature and the executive in modern states; magistrates in a Greek city had very narrow jurisdictions defined by law and normally took orders from the Assembly. The Greek city-state did not delegate power to representatives; all citizens voted directly on proposals made in the Council and debated in the Assembly. This was possible because the city-state was relatively small; Athens probably had about 30,000 adult male citizens in the fourth century BCE, and most other cities had far fewer (Hansen 1991: 92–3). Even though all citizens had the right to attend the Assembly, there were probably around 6,000 citizens attending most meetings in the fourth century BCE. Because the Assembly in Athens had to decide so much business, it held 40 regular meetings a year and could convene extra meetings in emergencies (Harris 2006: 81–120). In democratic cities such as Athens, many offices were filled by lot, and officials served only for a year and could not hold most offices twice. This meant that the average citizen had experience in public office and was relatively well informed about public affairs.

One did not have to join a political party and get elected to office to speak in the Assembly. The only qualifications for making a proposal in the Assembly at Athens were certain moral standards: first, one should have shown respect for one's parents and provided them food and shelter; second, one should have performed one's military service; third, one should not have squandered one's patrimony; and fourth, one should not have been a prostitute (Aeschines 1.28–32). Although the Athenians had respect for expertise, especially in military matters, the most important qualification was moral integrity. There was a strong belief that if an individual acted virtuously in private life, he could be trusted to give good advice in public life (Aeschines 1.30; Sophocles, *Antigone* 661–2). There were political groups in classical Athens, but they tended to be small collections of friends who cooperated for limited purposes and might not last for more than a few years (Hansen 1991: 277–89). There were no parties united by ideology and claiming to represent the interests of a particular group. Speakers in the Assembly therefore did not promote an aristocratic or progressive agenda or speak only to their own supporters but tried to address the people as a whole and to appeal to their common interests and their shared belief in democracy. To use the terminology of modern political theory, politics in Athens and other Greek city-states was "integrative" rather than "aggregative." Leaders did not mobilize partisan support to win election to office and then bargain behind closed doors with other leaders, each pursuing the self-interest of his constituents. Instead, speakers in the Assembly attempted to discover through deliberation in open discussion "the general welfare within a context of shared social values" (March and Olsen 1989: 118). For speakers in the Assembly "the public interest becomes an ethical criterion and a spur to conscience and deliberation, a stimulus to a process for imagining a sense of public purpose and public morality, rather than negotiating a bargain in the name of self-interest" (127). Pericles justifies his right to direct public policy by asserting his devotion to the public good, his personal integrity, and his ability to assess the city's needs (Thucydides, *The Peloponnesian War* 2.60). When Nicias calls on the older men in the Assembly to oppose the young men who are in favor of war,

Alcibiades rebukes him for being divisive and urges both groups to work together. He reminds the Assembly that the Athenians are strongest when all groups cooperate (6.12–3, 18). In Demosthenes's opinion, it is a disaster when the Athenians conduct politics in small groups of 300 following a politician and a general, with the rest divided among them; instead, "all should join together in deliberating, speaking and taking action for the common good" (2.29–30).

Speeches were therefore not designed to gain power for politicians at elections so that they could control the government. To gain the support of the Assembly, speakers had to address everyone, not just their supporters. They had to portray themselves as statesmen who aimed to benefit all citizens. For instance, Demosthenes in the *Fourth Philippic* says that he attempts to protect the interests of the rich and the poor (Demosthenes, *Fourth Philippic* 10.37–45). On one hand, he underlines the importance of protecting the property rights of the wealthy against unjust confiscation. On the other, he supports distributions of money to average citizens through the Theoric Fund to promote political stability. When trying to rouse the Athenians to oppose Philip's aggression, Demosthenes stresses that all Athenians, both the wealthy and average citizens, must do their duty (2.30–1, 3.33–6).

That is not to say that political views were never divided by class interests (*Hellenica Oxyrhynchia* 9.2–3; Aristophanes, *Assemblywomen* 197–8). Yet even when they were, speakers try to avoid drawing attention to such conflicts. When speakers appeal to political beliefs, they invoke traditional values held by the vast majority of citizens. In the *Second Philippic* Demosthenes recalls how he warned the Messenians that states governed by law should keep their distance from tyrants and that mistrust is the best defense against their attacks (6.21, 24). In the *Second Olynthiac* Demosthenes depicts Philip as a typical tyrant, who surrounds himself with flatterers and cannot tolerate men who are seasoned warriors or object to his drunkenness and wild parties (2.17–9). One finds a similar warning against tyrants in a speech made by Athenagoras at Syracuse under the democracy (Thucydides, *The Peloponnesian War* 6.38). Speakers in Athens never question the basic tenets of democracy. They may criticize specific laws or practices but never the system as a whole. Demosthenes berates the Athenians for deliberating after they act rather than before but never denies the right of the Assembly to decide major questions of public policy (5.2).

All proposals had to be discussed first in the Council, which set the agenda for the Assembly. The Council could either recommend a proposal for approval by the Assembly or put an item on the agenda for discussion without endorsing it (Hansen 1991: 255–6). As a result, speeches in the Assembly were normally aimed at persuading citizens either to accept or reject a specific proposal. Although a speaker might address general issues, the main task of the public speaker was to persuade the Assembly to take action on a decree to be implemented in the immediate future. For instance, Pericles's speech in 431 ends with an order to give the Spartan ambassadors who have come to Athens a specific response to their demands (Thucydides, *The Peloponnesian War* 1.144). Demosthenes often ends his speeches with specific proposals. In *On the Peace* he recommends that the Athenians not start a war over Delphi (5.24–5). And at the end of the *Third Philippic* Demosthenes makes several concrete proposals: embassies should be sent to the Peloponnese, Rhodes, Chios, and the Great King, and funds should be provided for the troops in the Chersonnese (9.71–3).

One of the reasons that we have far fewer speeches written for delivery in the Assembly than those for the law courts may be the different procedures followed in each venue. The accuser in court had to present his charges in a written indictment (*enklēma*) to an official before the trial (Harris 2012). At the trial he knew that he would speak first for an uninterrupted period and would have to confine himself to proving the charges in his indictment. The defendant for his part knew that he would have an equal amount of time and have to reply to the charges. The person who spoke in the Assembly would have known what items the Council had placed on the agenda but could not anticipate the arguments his opponents might use (Trevett 1996: 433–4). He could also not predict when he would speak. There was a rule requiring that the eldest speak first and the rest in order of seniority, but it had fallen into abeyance by the middle of the fourth century (Aeschines 3.2). For this reason there was little sense in preparing a written text in advance and committing it to memory. It is not surprising, therefore, that Isocrates associates written oratory with the courts and unwritten with the Assembly (*Panathenaicus* 12.29, 271; cf. Plato, *Phaedrus* 261b, 257–8). Alcidamas also appears to imply that it made little sense to write speeches for the Assembly (*Peri Sophiston* 2.11). Plutarch reports that Demosthenes wrote out his speeches for the Assembly because he was not good at extemporaneous delivery, which implies that his practice was unusual (*Demosthenes* 11).

To win the trust of citizens in the Assembly, speakers would often criticize the people. When the Athenians were considering sending an embassy to negotiate peace with Sparta in 429, Pericles took them to task for their inconsistency and lack of resolve (Thucydides, *The Peloponnesian War* 2.61). Cleon says the Athenians are ill-suited to govern an empire because their peaceful life at home makes them incapable of seeing foreign plots against them (3.37.1). He accuses them of making decisions on the basis of elegant speeches rather than facing the obvious facts (3.38). Even foreign ambassadors might criticize an Assembly. When speaking to the Spartans, the Athenian Autocles faults them for not respecting the freedom of the Greeks and for setting up tyrannies (*Hellenica Oxyrhynchia* 6.3.7). Criticism of the narrow pursuit of self-interest is a way of showing one's moral integrity and devotion to the public good. Conversely, speakers would allege that their opponents were flattering and appealing to their desire for pleasure without concern for their best interests in the long term.

Speakers use different types of arguments to persuade the Assembly, but the most common is an appeal to the public interest. When the Corcyrean embassy addressed the Athenian Assembly in 435, they stressed the advantages they would gain from an alliance, in particular their large fleet and their ability to block supplies from Italy and Sicily to the Peloponnese (Thucydides, *The Peloponnesian War* 1.33, 36). King Archidamus attempted to stop the Spartans from going to war against Athens by enumerating the advantages of their opponents: a large fleet, many allies paying tribute, and vast reserves of money. Even if the Spartans invade their land, the Athenians can still import supplies from abroad (1.80–2). Speaking before ambassadors from the Sicilian cities at Gela in 424, Hermocrates advised them to settle their differences and agree not to seek allies from abroad because this was in their collective interest (4.59–64). In *On the Megalopolitans*, Demosthenes argues that Athenian interests require that there be a balance of power between the Spartans and the Thebans (16). On one hand, they should maintain their alliance with the Messenians to restrain Spartan aggression in the Peloponnese. On the other, they should insist that the Messenians abandon their alliance with the Thebans to check the expansion of the latter's power. Some of the appeals to self-interest can be quite blunt: Brasidas told the people of Acanthus that if they did not become allies of the Spartans he would ravage their land (Thucydides, *The Peloponnesian War* 4.87). When Hermocrates tried to convince the people of Camarina to take their side against the Athenians, he threatened them with reprisals if they stayed neutral (6.80).

Speakers also remind their audiences of favors they have done in the past. When an Athenian embassy attempted to dissuade the Spartans from going to war in 433, they reminded them about their contributions to victory in the Persian Wars, which assured the freedom and safety of all the Greeks (Thucydides, *The Peloponnesian War* 1.73–4). Similarly, the Corinthians attempted to convince the Athenians not to conclude an alliance with their enemies, the Corcyreans, by recalling how they had once given the Athenians 20 ships in their war against Aegina and had prevented the Spartans from sending support to the Samians during their revolt (1.41). And when asking for an alliance in 370, the Spartans reminded the Athenians how they drove out the tyrants in the sixth century and supported the decision to have the Athenians lead the alliance against Persia (Xenophon, *Historia Graeca* 6.5.33).

Speakers often encourage citizens to live up to their glorious past. When encouraging the Athenians to stand up to the Spartans in 431, Pericles reminds them of how their fathers abandoned Attica to resist the Persians (Thucydides, *The Peloponnesian War* 1.144). To persuade the Spartans to lead the Peloponnesians against the Athenians, the Corinthians call on them to maintain the greatness handed down to them by their ancestors (1.72). In response to their arguments, King Archidamus says that it is more important for the Spartans to imitate the prudence of their ancestors and not rush into war before they are ready (1.85.1). In *On the Freedom of the Rhodians* Demosthenes urges the Athenians to defend Rhodes and Cos because their ancestors won honor and glory by fighting for them in the past (15.27–8). In *On the Navy-Boards* Demosthenes calls on the Athenians to live up to their fathers' achievements (14.41). In the *Second Olynthiac* he tells them that they should protect the Greeks against Philip's injustices just as they did against the Spartans (2.24). And in the *Third Olynthiac* Demosthenes reminds the Athenians how their ancestors ruled the Greeks, brought more than 10,000 talents to the Acropolis, made the Great King their subject, and erected many trophies for their victories on land and sea (3.24–30). Some speakers, however, warn that one should be careful in making such appeals to the past glory of Athens. Isocrates thus advises the Athenians to imitate their ancestors who defeated the Persians, not those who fought the Spartans in the Decelean War (*On the Peace* 8.36–8; cf. 8.79–85). Similarly, Aeschines argues that the Athenians should follow the example of their ancestors who maintained peace and not those who embarked on wars of aggression (2.74–5).

Even though speakers always try to show that their proposals serve the public interest, they often pay attention to questions of justice and international law. When ambassadors from Corcyra asked the Athenians to conclude an alliance, they stressed that the alliance would not violate the treaty between Athens and Sparta because the treaty allows neutral states to become the allies of either side (Thucydides, *The Peloponnesian War* 1.35). The Corinthians replied that an alliance between Corcyra and Athens would violate the spirit of the treaty between Athens and Sparta because it would bring Athens into conflict with one of Sparta's allies (1.40). The Corinthians also insisted on their rights as a mother city to discipline one of their colonies (1.38). The Athenians clearly considered these arguments because they voted to conclude only a defensive alliance with Corcyra to avoid the appearance of aggression against an ally of Sparta (1.44). The debates at Sparta and Athens leading up to the outbreak of the Peloponnesian War also paid close attention to the terms of the Thirty Years' peace between Athens and Sparta. Sparta's allies claimed that the Athenians had violated their promise to respect the freedom and autonomy of the Greeks (1.67). The Athenians defended their powers over their allies on the basis of their role in defeating the Persians (1.73–4) and rejected charges that they were infringing the rights of their allies (1.77). When they refused to yield to Spartan demands, they cited the clause of the treaty that required both sides to arbitrate their differences (1.78, 140).

In modern states, politicians debate major issues of foreign policy but leave matters of strategy and tactics in the hands of professional soldiers. The US Congress, for instance, can declare war, approve funds for the armed forces, or approve treaties with foreign powers but does not involve itself in the details of military campaigns even though it may exercise general oversight. There is also a strict division between the civilian authorities and the military; generals are not elected to office as senators or representatives in the United States or as members of Parliament in the United Kingdom. Such a distinction did not exist in classical Athens and most other Greek city-states. Generals were elected in the Assembly and could make proposals about military campaigns directly to the people (see Aristotle, *Constitution of the Athenians* 61; Demosthenes 4.26). All the major leaders of the fifth century were generals: Themistocles, Aristides, Cimon, Pericles, Nicias, and Alcibiades. Herodotus reports that in 480 Themistocles made his proposal to evacuate Athens and to fight the Persians at sea in the Assembly and received the people's approval (*Histories* 7.142–4). When in 429 Pericles favored continuing the war against Sparta, he made his proposal in the Assembly. The debate about the Sicilian expedition and the resources to be allocated for it also took place in the Assembly (Thucydides, *The Peloponnesian War* 6.20–3). When Nicias made his request for additional support for the Athenian troops fighting Syracuse, he wrote a letter to the Athenians and appealed directly to the Assembly (7.11–5). Military decisions thus occupied a prominent place in political discourse.

This pattern continued in the fourth century: Conon, Timotheus, and Phocion led the armed forces and spoke in the Assembly. Even though Demosthenes never served as general, many of his speeches contain specific proposals about military campaigns. In the *First Philippic*, for example, Demosthenes urges the Athenians to send against Philip 2,000 soldiers, of which 500 are to be Athenian citizens, the rest mercenaries, 200 cavalry with the same proportion of citizens and mercenaries, and special ships to transport the horses (Demosthenes, *First Philippic* 4.21–2). The citizens are to serve for a fixed period, and in relays 10 fast triremes will escort the expedition to northern Greece. Demosthenes also calculates the exact costs of the expedition (40 talents for the triremes, 40 talents for the soldiers, and 12 talents for the cavalry) and specifies from which accounts the money is to be paid (4.28–9). The force should be permanent and have winter quarters on Lemnos, Thasos, Skiathos, and other islands in the region (4.32).

Another important topic of deliberative rhetoric in the Assembly was public finance. Even though the administration of public funds was handled by officials, major decisions lay in the hands of the Assembly. To justify his optimism about victory in the war against Sparta, Pericles gave a detailed account of Athenian finances to the Assembly (Thucydides, *The Peloponnesian War* 2.13). In *On the Navy-Boards*, Demosthenes puts forward a detailed reform of naval finances (14.16–23). He proposes increasing those eligible to pay for triremes from 1,200 to 2,000, placing them in 20 navy-boards, creating 20 squadrons of 15 ships, and assigning each to one navy-board. There follow proposals about naval equipment and the organization of the dockyards.

In contrast to most modern states, there was no separation between church and state in Athens and other communities in ancient Greece (Harris 2006: 41–80). The discussion of religious business had a regular place on the agenda of the Assembly (Aristotle, *Constitution of the Athenians* 43.6), and the Assembly elected priests as well as secular officials (54.6). When the Persian army was approaching Attica in 480, the Assembly voted to consult the Delphic oracle. When the oracle said the Athenians should place their trust in the "wooden walls," speakers in the Assembly debated about the meaning of this ambiguous phrase and Apollo's intentions (Herodotus, *Histories* 7.142–4). Speakers in Thucydides rarely mention the gods, but this probably reflects the historian's skepticism about the value of oracles and divination, not normal practice in the Assembly. Yet Thucydides reports that in 415 the predictions made by seers and oracle mongers played a major role in convincing the Athenians to launch the Sicilian expedition (*The Peloponnesian War* 8.1). In fact, Aristophanes parodies the use of oracles by politicians in his *Knights*. Many of the decrees preserved on stone concern religious matters. For instance, in 352 the Assembly voted to consult the Delphic oracle about whether or not to cultivate the Sacred Orgas on the border of Attica (*Inscriptiones Graecae* ii^2 204). Religion was also important in the Spartan Assembly. In 371 BCE the Athenian ambassador Callias reminded the Spartans how his ancestor Triptolemus taught their ancestors the mystic rites of Demeter and Kore (Xenophon, *Historia Graeca* 6.3.6). Anaximenes in his *Rhetoric to Alexander* lists the discussion of finances for sacrifices as one of the main topics of deliberative oratory (2.3–12, 1423a8–4a8).

The Athenians made a strict distinction between the kind of speech to be delivered in the Assembly and those given in the courts or at public festivals. Both Aristotle and the author of the *Rhetorica ad Alexandrum* (1.1, 1421b1) divide oratory into three types: the judicial (*dikanikon*), the deliberative (*demegorikon* or *symbouleutikon*), and the epideictic (*epideiktikon*). Aristotle describes the basic characteristics of each type of speech in the first book of the *Rhetoric* (Aristotle, *Rhetoric* 1.3.1–7, 1358a–9b). A deliberative speech aims either to exhort or dissuade and concerns the future because the speaker discusses future events. The goal of this kind of speech is to show that a certain course of action is going to be either advantageous (*to sympheron*) or harmful (*blaberon*). The audience for this kind of speech is the member of an assembly. A speaker may introduce considerations of justice, but they should be subordinate to the main issue of advantage. In the law court, there is either an accusation or a defense. This kind of speech concerns the past because the accusation and the defense examine what has been done. The goal of the speaker is to prove that an action is just or unjust (see Gagarin, ch. 2). The audience for this speech is the judge. The aim of the epideictic speech is to praise or to blame. This kind of speech generally looks to the present and praises or blames existing qualities but may also glance at the past and future. The audience of the epideictic speech consists of spectators (*theatai*) who are concerned with the speaker's ability (1.3.2, 1358b).

The speeches of Cleon and Diodotus in the debate about the punishment for Mytilene in 427 reveal a keen awareness of the differences between political speeches delivered in the Assembly and those given in other venues. Cleon attacks his opponents for delivering an epideictic speech in the Assembly. He claims that his opponents act like sophists who revel in paradoxes (Thucydides, *The Peloponnesian War* 3.38.2). Just like sophists in epideictic contests, they try to disprove what appears to be common sense (3.38.5). Cleon blames the Athenians for setting up these contests (*agōnes*) and for acting like spectators rather than citizens who are deliberating (3.38.4, 7). Speakers should concentrate on what is good for Athens rather than showing off their intelligence (3.37.5).

But Cleon falls into the trap of delivering a court speech in the Assembly. He treats the people of Mytilene like defendants who are guilty (Thucydides, *The Peloponnesian War* 3.38.1, 39.1, 6). He uses the language of punishment (3.39.6, 40.5, 7). Instead of speaking about what is best for Athens, he stresses the importance of maintaining the laws and enforcing them (3.37.3). Like an accuser in court, Cleon tells the Athenians they must act on their anger and that the Mytilenians deserve no pity (3.37.2, 38.1, 40.2). He also attacks the motives of those defending the Mytilenians and insinuates that they have been bribed (3.38.2, 42.3, 43.1). The Mytilenians have acted deliberately and were not forced to revolt because of Athenian oppression (3.39.2). Cleon ends his speech by asking the Athenians to punish the Mytilenians and to make an example of them (3.40.7; cf. Demosthenes 19.343, 21.227, 22.68).

As his opponent Diodotus points out, these kinds of arguments were out of place in the Assembly. The duty of the speaker is to look to the future and consider what will be best for the Athenians, not to dwell on the past and determine whether the Mytilenians are guilty or not (Thucydides, *The Peloponnesian War* 3.42.1, 44.3). The Athenians are not in a law court but are deliberating in the Assembly (3.44.4). Diodotus objects to any talk about anger or pity, which may be appropriate to a law court but has no place in the Assembly (3.42.1, 48.1). Even though Aristotle did not formulate general rules about deliberative rhetoric until the late fourth century, the debate about Mytilene shows that speakers understood the basic differences between the main genres of oratory and the standard practices associated with each genre.

Diodotus also accuses Cleon of violating the implicit etiquette of speaking in the Assembly: one might criticize the arguments of one's opponents, but it was wrong to question their integrity by suggesting that they have taken bribes (Thucydides, *The Peloponnesian War* 3.42). Because speakers were supposed to address issues of public concern, they were expected to refrain from personal attacks on their opponents. Diodotus notes that such charges have a corrosive effect on public debate and discourage men with good ideas from making proposals in the Assembly (3.42–3). In his own deliberative speeches Demosthenes never mentions his opponents by name (with one exception at 10.70). This stands in stark contrast to his personal attacks on Aeschines in his court speeches. This sense of etiquette required in the Assembly is also evident in Thucydides's account of a debate at Syracuse in 415 when Hermocrates attempted to warn his fellow citizens of the imminent invasion of Sicily by the Athenians (6.33–4). When Athenagoras expressed skepticism about the news of the invasion, he also accused Hermocrates of plotting to overthrow the democracy and place his supporters in power (6.38–9). This personal attack provoked an immediate rebuke from one of the generals, who reminded him that the Assembly was no place for slandering the character of other speakers (6.41).

Even though the Assembly of the Greek city-state was the main forum for political speech, one might also make speeches at one of the Panhellenic sanctuaries (Olympia, Delphi, Nemea, and Isthmia) during the festivals that met there every four years on a rotating basis. These speeches address the Greeks in general and stress their common interests and traditions. Diodorus (*Bibliotheke Historike* 14.109) reports that Lysias delivered a speech at the Olympic games of 388 BCE, and Dionysius of Halicarnassus preserves a fragment of this speech. Lysias begins by recalling the founding of the games by Heracles, who put down tyrants and encouraged the Greeks to meet in a spirit of concord and friendship. He urges the Greeks to set aside their quarrels and unite against the tyrants Dionysius of Syracuse and the barbarian king of Persia. As in Assembly speeches, Lysias calls on the Greeks to imitate their ancestors who defeated the Persians. He ends by calling on the Spartans, the leading power in Greece at the time, to save Greece as they had done in the past. Isocrates's *Panegyricus* is a literary composition that was too long to have been delivered before a live audience, but it obviously reflects the kinds of topics one might expect to hear at a Panhellenic festival. Isocrates's aim is to promote the claim of Athens to lead the Greeks against the barbarians. He cites their founding of the Eleusinian Mysteries (Isocrates, *Panegyricus* 28–33), their colonies (34–7), their reputation for the rule of law (38–40), promotion of trade (41–2), festivals (43–6), support for intellectual activity (43–6), and their help for the oppressed (51–3). He then compares the way the Athenians ruled the Greeks for their benefit with Spartan methods (100–78). The *Panegyricus* often crosses the boundary between deliberative and epideictic oratory, yet it illustrates the different approach a speaker would take when addressing a Panhellenic audience. Here the stress is on shared moral and cultural values, and cold calculations of political interest are absent. The practice of rhetoric in ancient Greece was thus shaped by the political institutions of the city-state and played a crucial role in politics.

REFERENCES

Adams, Charles Darwin. 1912. "Are the Political 'Speeches' of Demosthenes to Be Regarded as Political Pamphlets?" *Transactions and Proceedings of the American Philological Association* 43: 5–22.

Badian, Ernst. 1992. "Thucydides on Rendering Speeches." *Athenaeum* 80: 187–190.

Hansen, Mogens. 1991. *The Athenian Democracy in the Age of Demosthenes*. Oxford: Oxford University Press.

Harris, Edward M. 2000. "The Authenticity of Andocides' *De Pace*: A Subversive Essay." In *Polis and Politics: Studies in Ancient Greek History*, edited by P. Flensted-Jensen, T. H. Nielsen, and L. Rubinstein, 479–506. Copenhagen: Museum Tusculanum Press.

Harris, Edward M. 2006. *Democracy and the Rule of Law in Classical Athens: Essays on Law, Society, and Politics*. Cambridge: Cambridge University Press.

Harris, Edward M. 2012. "The Plaint in Athenian Law and Legal Procedure." In *Legal Documents in the Ancient World*, edited by Michele Faraguna, 143–162. Trieste: EUT Edizioni Università di Trieste.

March, James G., and Johan P. Olsen. 1989. *Rediscovering Institutions: The Organizational Basis of Politics*. New York: Free Press.

Trevett, Jeremy. 1996. "Did Demosthenes Publish His Deliberative Speeches?" *Hermes* 124: 425–441.

Tuplin, Christopher. 1998. "Demosthenes' *Olynthiacs* and the Character of the Demegoric Corpus." *Historia* 47: 276–320.

CHAPTER 4

RHETORIC AND HISTORIOGRAPHY

CHRIS CAREY

IN a sense, all narrative, including the telling of history, is governed by a rhetoric, since a narrator needs to persuade his audience of the veracity of his story. Objectivity in narrative, whether in Homer or in Thucydides, is an aspect of the presentation, not of the psychology of the historical author or narrator. This larger narrative rhetoric includes and, if done well, integrates the different components (speech, action) that make up the narrative. It finds expression in the selection of incidents to report out of the wealth of material that clamors for inclusion; in the narrative structure (the ordering, juxtaposition, and separation of events narrated); in implied or explicit focalization (the perspective from which an action is viewed); in verbal echoes (between narrative moments, between speeches, and between speech and action); and in judgments offered in the text with greater or lesser frequency. This is no truer of ancient than of subsequent historiography, including modern. But Greek historiography emerged in a world in which—despite the existence of a growing book market—most texts were experienced in oral, public performance. Its origin in performance intermittently makes the ancient historian's text rhetorical in a way that goes beyond the need for persuasive presentation. Herodotus, the earliest historian whose work survives, introduces his *Histories* with the words: "This is the presentation [*apodeixis*] of the enquiry [*historie*, in his Ionian dialect] of Herodotus of Halicarnassus . . ." As recent scholarship has observed, *apodeixis* (presentation) easily slides into *epideixis* (display); later tradition makes Herodotus give his history as lectures, and Herodotus himself seems to hint at this when he pauses in his account of the democracies set up by Persia in the aftermath of the failed revolt by the Greek cities in (what is now) coastal Turkey (Herodotus, *Histories* 6.43.14). He stops the narrative to justify his earlier account of the constitutional debate between the conspirators who brought Darius to the throne of Persia in the late sixth century BCE (3.80.6) and to respond to expressions of disbelief he had encountered. In a single, complete published text like a modern historical work this makes little sense; it makes perfect sense, however, in a narrative experienced in installments like a Charles Dickens novel. The role of performance is attested negatively in a passing dismissal by Thucydides in his history of the Peloponnesian War between Athens and Sparta, though he leaves unclear whether he is spurning performance or acknowledging the limited audience for his text: "For oral presentation [lit. hearing] it will perhaps appear rather unappealing because of its lack of stories. But it will suffice that all who wish to observe the actuality of what took place, and will according to human experience [or human nature, *to anthropinon*] at some point take place again in the same or a similar way, find it useful. It is written as a lasting possession rather than a competition piece for immediate hearing" (*The Peloponnesian War* 1.22.4).

This performative background is perhaps responsible for the antagonistic tone Herodotus occasionally adopts, as when he takes issue with Ionian views on the division of the world into continents (*Histories* 2.15–6). This combative tone was a feature Herodotus inherited from his immediate predecessors. Hecataeus of Miletus, for example, opened his work with a much-quoted statement: "Hecataeus of Miletus speaks as follows: I write this as I believe it to be true; for the accounts of the Greeks are many and risible, in my opinion." More strikingly, this argumentative (in the literal sense) strand in Greek historiography finds expression in set-piece arguments whose focus on magnifying praise is reminiscent of epideictic or "display" oratory (as it was to be labeled in the fourth century BCE), which Aristotle associates particularly with praise (*epainos*) and blame (*psogos*) (*Rhetoric* 1358b). Herodotus's digression in praise of the Athenians in book 7 is an example of this, where he argues for the potentially unpopular thesis that Athens saved Greece from the Persian invader, beginning with a detail that finds echoes both in the Athenian funeral oration as represented by Thucydides (*The Peloponnesian War* 2.45.1) and in archaic praise poetry, namely, the resentment (*phthonos*) that praise inevitably arouses: "And here I am compelled by necessity to declare an opinion which in the eyes of most men would seem to be invidious, but nevertheless I will not abstain from saying that which I see evidently to be the truth. If the Athenians had been seized with fear of the danger which threatened them and had left their land, or again, without leaving their land, had stayed and given themselves up to Xerxes, none would have made any attempt by sea to oppose the king" (Herodotus, *Histories* 139.1–2; trans. Macauley). Herodotus's emphasis on praise is also present in his insistence on the importance of his theme: "Not all these expeditions [the Greek–barbarian conflicts culminating in the Trojan War] nor the others which have taken place were equal to this single one. For what race of Asia did Xerxes not bring against Greece? What river did not run dry from being drunk, except for the great ones?" (7.21).

This is not dispassionate statement but engaged argument. Herodotus's remarkable hyperbole places the Persian Wars not just above all individual interethnic wars in scale but suggests that they outweigh all previous conflicts combined ("not all of these nor the others which have taken place added"). The hyperbole is reinforced by a series of rhetorical questions stressing the superlative nature of the subject in the manner of epideictic oratory (cf. Gorgias, frag. 6 [*Funeral Oration*]; Lysias 2.34, 40, 54 [*Funeral Oration*]; Hyperides, *Funeral Oration* 6, 10, 12). Even his final concession—that all the rivers were drunk dry except the big ones—does not so much tone down as enhance the claim of magnitude: only the biggest rivers could cope.

The agonistic tone becomes part of the stock-in-trade of the historian. It is visible in Thucydides's rejection of a more entertaining manner (previously described) and his dismissive suggestion that other narrators are more interested in their immediate audience than in the lasting value of their work. It appears fleetingly in Thucydides's comment that he includes the 50 years between the Persian Wars and the Peloponnesian War because this interval has been neglected, except for a cursory treatment by Hellanicus (*The Peloponnesian War* 1.97.2). It is striking that the only time Thucydides names a predecessor it is to condemn them; similarly, though Herodotus deals generously with his great predecessor Hecataeus as a participant in historical events (*Histories* 5.36.2, 125–6), he is acerbic in his treatment of him as a historian (2.143.1–2, 5.137). By the Hellenistic period, the number of predecessors available individually or collectively for adverse comment had grown considerably.

The readiness to slip into sustained argument that we found in Herodotus is, if anything, more pronounced in Thucydides, despite the latter's preference for a less prominent narrative persona. Thucydides matches Herodotus's hyperbolic claims for his theme in stressing the significance of the Peloponnesian War:

> The greatest achievement of former times was the Persian War; yet even this was speedily decided in two battles by sea and two by land. But the Peloponnesian War was a protracted struggle, and attended by calamities such as Hellas had never known within a like period of time. Never were so many cities captured and depopulated—some by barbarians, others by Hellenes themselves fighting against one another; and several of them after their capture were repeopled by strangers. Never were exile and slaughter more frequent, whether in the war or brought about by civil strife. And traditions which had often been current before, but rarely verified by fact, were now no longer doubted. For there were earthquakes unparalleled in their extent and fury, and eclipses of the sun more numerous than are recorded to have happened in any former age; there were also in some places great droughts causing famines, and lastly the plague which did immense harm and destroyed numbers of the people. (Thucydides, *The Peloponnesian War* 1.23.1–3; trans. Jowett)

Here, surprisingly for a writer who pointedly focuses on human acts and motivations, even the natural world is dragooned into the service of his rhetoric of the superlative. But the epideictic mode is equally pronounced in his treatment of the successors to Pericles in book 2 (65), with its sustained antithesis between statesmen and political opportunists, and in the chapters on *stasis* (civil strife) in book 3 (82–3). The claim that one's theme outdoes all preceding subjects is a *topos* that establishes itself in the tradition. Polybius is even more overtly rhetorical. He opens his *Histories* with a figure of thought (*praeteritio*, "omission," "I shall/need not say") taken from legal and political oratory:

> If it were the case that the praise of history had been passed over by former chroniclers, it would perhaps have been necessary for me to urge the choice and special study of accounts of this sort, on the ground that there is no more accessible means men can have of improvement than the knowledge of past events. But since my

predecessors have not used this argument intermittently nor to a limited degree but have all begun and ended, so to speak, by asserting that the study of history is the truest education and a training for political life, and that the most vivid and the only method of learning to bear with dignity the vicissitudes of fortune is to recall the catastrophes of others, it is evident that no one need think it his duty to repeat what has been said by many, and said well. Least of all me; for the surprising nature of the events which I have undertaken to narrate is in itself sufficient to challenge and stimulate the attention of every one, old or young, to the study of my work . . .

Polybius here takes Thucydides's taut *to anthropinon* (human experience, human nature) and turns it into a sustained argument for the value of history; he retains all the superlatives we find in Herodotus and Thucydides but also adds the special element of *to paradoxon*, itself a concept familiar to rhetorical theory as a means of stimulating audience attention, here applied to the unparalleled rise of Rome.

At issue here, as recent writers have stressed, is authority. Ultimately, the approach has its origins in the precepts of the rhetorician. For Aristotle, *ēthos* (character) is one of the three basic elements—along with emotional appeal (*pathos*) and argument (*logos*)—that create belief (*pistis*) (Aristotle, *Rhetoric* 1356a). In this Aristotle is simply codifying a practice whose value had long been recognized by Greek speakers and writers. The credibility of the historian is an important part of the credibility of his theme, which is most effectively established not in the absolute but by means of antithesis. The claim of importance for the topic is again an approach recognized by rhetoric. People pay attention to what is significant (1415b) and dismiss what is insignificant, so one must argue that what one has to say is significant. This, of course, is still an opening ploy in most academic books, which rarely invite the reader to reflect on the insignificance of their theme or the limited nature of their contribution.

There is another, more overt way that rhetoric and historiography converge: in the role of speech embedded in narrative. The aforementioned opening of Herodotus's *Histories* continues: ". . . so that what took place may not vanish from mankind with time [or "what was done by men may not vanish with time"] nor the great and wondrous achievements displayed some by Greeks and some by non-Greeks [*barbaroi*] lose their glory, including the reason why they went to war with each other." This much discussed statement stands at a crossroads in European culture. The emphasis on understanding causation places it in a direct line with Thucydides, Edward Gibbon, George Grote, and Eric Hobsbawm. But the determination to preserve the glory (*kleos*) of great deeds and achievements looks back to archaic epic. This affiliation with epic is manifested in Herodotus's language and theme but most noticeably (and importantly) in the ubiquitous presence in his work of speeches purporting to record public debates and private conversations. In a world in which the term *historie* (*historia*) meant "inquiry" rather than "narrative of past events," in which most artistic literature, spoken or written, had been in verse and prose genres yet to be mapped out, the porous boundaries between prose *historie* and archaic verse epic may have seemed natural to Herodotus. Epic had also in this respect influenced the elegiac precursors of Greek historiography. But the decision to include speeches on the scale we find in Herodotus reflects a very specific epic model: Homer. We learn from Aristotle that the Homeric epics made more use of direct speech than other epics of the archaic period (*Rhetoric* 1460a). Herodotus chose not epic in general but the more dramatic Homeric manner in particular (see Hall, ch. 18). This choice had profound implications for the development of European historiography. The inclusion of extended speeches remained a core feature of historiography not just in Greece but also in Rome and then Byzantium; it was taken up by the historians of Western Europe in the Middle Ages and the Renaissance; and it had not quite died out in England by the time of the Civil War (1642–51). The role of generic tradition means that as *historie* becomes historiography, any serious historian includes speeches in his work (see Ash, ch. 15).

The reasons for this are partly aesthetic. The distinction between scholarly research and art is a modern invention. A narrative without speeches is dry and unappealing. But there is another important reason for the use of speeches: political culture throughout Greece relied heavily on sustained formal speech in public contexts (see Harris, ch. 3). Although modern discussion inevitably focuses on classical Athens—partly because our knowledge of Athens (limited as it is) is greater than for any other state and partly because the city was a magnet for teachers of rhetoric—it is a mistake to focus exclusively either on democracy or on Athens. The teachers themselves came from all over Greece: Gorgias from Leontini in Sicily; Hippias from Elis; Protagoras from Abdera; Thrasymachus from Chalcedon. Although Athens imported sophists, they were produced elsewhere, evidently in political cultures that also found space for debate and persuasion. They also traveled, which indicates that Athens was not the only market for rhetoric (see Schiappa, ch. 1). When Herodotus and Thucydides describe decision-making in Sparta or Thebes, whether or not they record speeches, they envisage the public exchange of opinions. Debate was not exclusive to democracy. Herodotus's oligarchic Thebans (*Histories* 5.79–80), when confronted with a puzzling response from the oracle of Apollo at Delphi, behave exactly like his democratic Athenians (7.142): they call a meeting and argue about the interpretation. All Greek legal and political systems to some degree depended on oratory. The same applied to interstate dealings. When the Athenians sent ambassadors to Macedonia in 346 BCE to negotiate a peace treaty, each of the 10 emissaries in turn delivered a formal speech. Philip listened patiently and then replied, taking account of all the speeches he had heard (Aeschines, *On the Embassy* 2.22–38). Politics at the *polis* or supra-*polis* level was based on oratory. Any attempt to reach beyond the dry narrative of events into psychology or policy without simple assertion of motives needed speeches. This, however, created a problem for a genre that claimed to present a factual account of the past. Few of the speeches that were delivered in any context in the ancient world were ever archived. Thus, the historian is compelled either to omit speeches or to fill the lacunae in his evidence—that is, to invent (*heuriskein*). And that is precisely what Herodotus and his successors did for the next two millennia.

Nevertheless, I have oversimplified matters in presenting fictionalization simply as a strategy foisted on the historian by the lack of documentation, for some original speeches did in fact survive. We have a very revealing counterexample in a speech by

Claudius that was found at Lyon (*Corpus Inscriptionum Latinarum* xiii [1668]). This inscribed text corresponds to one of his speeches reported in Tacitus (*Annals* 11.23–4). Tacitus must have had access to a text of this speech. Yet apart from other changes determined by his view of Claudius, he elects to recast it in his own style. The same must also have been true for Polybius, at least on occasion. A revision in the narrator's own words is preferable to an original. It is here that the status of historiography as literature, not merely reportage of research, supervenes. It is questionable whether any ancient historian would have felt it appropriate to incorporate a speech, either in its entirety or as a collection of edited highlights, into his narrative in the original words of the speaker. Polybius, while insisting (in an echo of Thucydides) more than once on the duty to report what was actually (*kat' aletheian*) said (*Historiae* 36.1.7, 2.56.10), also frankly acknowledges that the style (*lexis*) is his own (29.12.10). The most that access to the original wording of the text would have offered the ancient historiographer is the opportunity to improve the accuracy of the arguments included. To incorporate the original would have compromised the stylistic integrity of the narrative without adding significantly to the text as body of knowledge and coherent story.

It is also a mistake to see generic tradition as something imposed on the individual writer. Literary genres are shaped and reshaped by the expectations that occupy the space between and around writers and audiences. Speeches persist in historiography because that is what writers and readers think history is about. Polybius, for example, is severely critical of Timaeus for the level of free invention in his speeches (*Historiae* 12.25.5), but it is the scale of the intervention rather than the fact of its presence that offends him.

Herodotus himself, the starting point of our inquiry, shows little awareness of the problem of accuracy in speech reporting. His passing defense of his account of the constitutional debate (previously discussed) is unusual in this respect, and it relates to a single incident, not his overall strategy. Otherwise, however, the speeches he reports are offered as factual accounts; he invariably uses *tade* (this, these words) to introduce his speeches, even those for which there can have been no source (such as the private conversation between King Candaules and his bodyguard, Gyges, inviting him to see Candaules's wife naked and the subsequent exchange in which Candaules's angry wife persuades Gyges to kill him). The general problem is recognized by Herodotus's successors, however. It exercised Thucydides, who, unlike Herodotus, is at great pains to justify his historical method. Thucydides makes a distinction between acts (*erga*) and speeches (*logoi*). Of the latter he says:

> As to the speeches which were made either in the approach to or during the war, it was difficult for me in relation to what I heard, and for others who reported them to me from any other occasion, to recollect the actuality of what was said. I have set out the speeches as I myself believe each speaker would have said what was needed in relation to each occasion, while keeping as nearly as I could to the general sense of what was actually said. As to the events of the war, I did not see fit to write them down from any chance information, nor according to my own opinion; I have described

events where I was present myself or learned of from others by careful and precise enquiry. (Thucydides, *The Peloponnesian War* 1.22.1–2)

Thucydides's method for events is relatively straightforward: he relies on autopsy (*autopsia*, "seeing with one's own eyes") wherever possible (though this leaves unanswered the question whether he compared his memories with others to guarantee accuracy) and on multiple interviews for events he did not witness. For speeches, Thucydides describes a balancing act. He tries to stay as close as possible to the general tenor[1] of what was said, but given the problems of recovery he supplements this on the basis of three criteria: first, the way that each speaker would have spoken; second, the historical context; and third, what was required (*ta deonta*) under the circumstances. The first must include features such as known or perceived character, affiliation, and views (e.g., the lofty Periclean idealism). It does not include style, since Thucydides's characters use the same dense style, but it can include tone, manner, or personality (e.g., the aristocratic arrogance of an Alcibiades or the intimidating bluster of a Cleon). The second gives us the occasion (peace and war, alliance) and chronological context (imperialism before the war versus imperialism at bay after the revolt of Mytilene). The third is closely related to the second: the speech is created from "what had to be said" (trans. Dover; cf. 1.70.8 = "what had to be done"). Evidently Thucydides was satisfied with this formulation, but every detail has been scrutinized and scholars have taken dramatically different positions on the historicity of the speeches as a collection and as individuals. Not least of the difficulties is the presentation of sources and methods as constant, when in fact access to and quality of information must have varied. What interests me here, however, is the explicit statement of invention. This is not pure fiction, since there is always some (variable but for us unrecoverable) factual basis. But fiction it is. The effect of all of this is to make the historian in part a speechwriter for his characters. Often, in fact, he is the speechwriter for more than one character. This is a technique Thucydides and Herodotus could have observed at work in the teaching of the major sophists of the day. Protagoras, for example, famously claimed to be able to teach his pupils to argue a case from opposing directions (*antilogiae*). This technique is exemplified in the *Tetralogies* of the politician and speechwriter Antiphon, which presents a series of matching speeches for prosecution and defense in fictive homicide cases and whose outlines are designed to teach students to advance opposing arguments drawn from the same factual base. Thucydides, unlike Antiphon, is writing about real people and events, but the activity is very similar.

There is of course an easy slide from "what they had to say" to "what they should have said." Thucydides was aware of this risk, as his insistence on the factors that govern his rhetorical reconstructions demonstrates. But he was evidently as confident in this as in other areas that he could get it right. To understand his confidence we need to bear in mind the cultural context. The fifth century was an era of systematization, and technical proficiency in speaking was an important, if not the most important, part of this cultural process. Lurking behind Thucydides's claim to reconstruct events and speeches is a concept that became a mainstay of fifth- and fourth-century oratory: *eikos*, or probability.

Essentially, the concept of *eikos* involves arguing from general trends in human behavior to specific cases. Though inevitably reductive, since improbabilities do occur, it has a firm basis in fact and a strong appeal to common sense because it invites hearers to interpret a situation against the background of their cumulative experience. Not for nothing does Aristotle in the *Poetics* prefer impossible probabilities to improbable possibilities in plot construction (1460a). This mode of argument is especially at home in the forensic rhetoric (*genos dikanikon*) of the law courts, where it helps to compensate for a universal lacuna in Greek legal practice: no Greek state had an independent body responsible for investigating and pursuing offenses, and there was no means of scientific proof; therefore, any evidence was necessarily circumstantial. Argument from probability offered a reasonable means of filling this gap in knowledge (see Gagarin, ch. 2). It is also relevant to political debate, to the extent that the future is inevitably predicted on the basis of the past, however imperfectly understood. Although we naturally focus on probability, and indeed rhetoric more generally, as a verbal tool, it is more than just a matter of words. It rests on the belief that human nature is a constant and that it is subject to rules that are susceptible to empirical observation, what Thucydides calls *to anthropinon* (human experience, human nature). This is as much psychology, sociology, and political history as logic or verbal skill. And since speech acts, like other acts, are subject to rules of probability, *eikos* offered a useful tool for reconstructing debate. But more than that, Thucydides did not invent the idea of fitting argument to context; fifth-century rhetoric worked on the basis of set arguments to be used (sometimes with verbatim repetition of an authoritative model) at certain places and in certain situations. Subsequent ages refined the rules of persuasive speech but retained the conviction that specific contexts invite and sometimes demand specific arguments. On this basis it becomes possible to predict with a degree of confidence—and by extension reconstruct retrospectively—what a speaker will say. For Thucydides *ta deonta* probably seemed far less subjective than it does to us, especially since his formulation (which emphasizes necessity) precludes by implication arguments that are merely feasible. Thucydides is unusual in addressing this meta-historiographical problem head-on in this way. His successors are generally silent on the subject. Evidently they felt that Thucydides had provided all the justification needed.

As well as furnishing modes of argument, rhetoric also provided the historian with stylistic devices (the so-called *schēmata lexeos*, "figures of speech"). Just as certain contexts attract certain arguments, so the need to persuade more generally attracts a style needed to present arguments forcefully. By the Hellenistic period some writers at least saw the fictive speech as an opportunity for rhetorical display (*epideixis*), and Polybius protests vigorously against this practice (*Historiae* 12.25a–b, 25i–6a). Though less overtly pyrotechnic, the impact of rhetoric on speeches in historical narrative is a phenomenon visible from the beginning. Space prevents a fuller discussion, but the following example from Herodotus should show how early developments in rhetoric affect speeches in the historians: "Son of Darius, have you then plainly among the Persians renounced your expedition, and treated my words as of no account, as though you had heard them from a nobody? Rest assured that, if you do not lead out your army at once, this will be the outcome for you: as you became great and mighty in a short time, so in a moment will you be brought low again" (*Historiae* 7.14). The punch line in the last sentence displays the love of antithesis underlined by carefully balanced clauses typical of fifth-century rhetoric. The speaker is the superhuman figure in the dream that presses Xerxes to invade Europe to his ruin. Herodotus's apparitions, well briefed in contemporary developments in rhetorical style, know how to combine rhetorical balance with stylistic variation.

FURTHER READING

For Homer and objectivity, see especially Irene de Jong (1987) and Scott Richardson (1990). For Herodotus in his intellectual (and rhetorical) environment, see Rosalind Thomas (2000). For authorial authority in ancient historiography, see John Marincola (1997). For speeches in ancient historians in general, see Marincola (2008). Cecil Wooten (1974) offers a discussion of Polybius on speeches and speeches in Polybius. The bibliography on speeches in Thucydides is vast; for Thucydides on speeches (especially on 1.22), a valuable starting point is Simon Hornblower (1999).

NOTE

1. Like every other detail in this dense programmatic statement, the phrase used here, *he xympasa gnome*, has attracted much discussion. Since I take it that he cannot mean "the avowed purpose" (e.g., execute the Mytilenian/Melian males), it must mean something like "the overall tenor," that is, the (kinds of) arguments used, where recoverable.

REFERENCES

de Jong, Irene. 1987. *Narrators and Focalizers: The Presentation of the Story in the "Iliad."* Amsterdam: B.R. Grüner.

Hornblower, Simon. 1999. *A Commentary on Thucydides.* Vol. 1. Oxford: Oxford University Press.

Marincola, John. 1997. *Authority and Tradition in Ancient Historiography.* Cambridge: Cambridge University Press.

Marincola, John. 2008. "Speeches in Classical Historiography." In *A Companion to Greek and Roman Historiography*, vol. 1, edited by John Marincola, 118–132. Oxford: Blackwell.

Richardson, Scott. 1990. *The Homeric Narrator.* Nashville, TN: Vanderbilt University Press.

Thomas, Rosalind. 2000. *Herodotus in Context: Ethnography, Science and the Art of Persuasion.* Cambridge: Cambridge University Press.

Wooten, Cecil. 1974. "The Speeches in Polybius: An Insight into the Nature of Hellenistic Oratory." *American Journal of Philology* 95: 235–251.

CHAPTER 5

··

RHETORIC AND PEDAGOGY

··

MALCOLM HEATH

We use language to influence other people's beliefs, attitudes, and decisions—in short, to persuade. Since some people are more consistently successful in this than others, and experience is one of the factors that contribute to success, it is clear that skill in the persuasive use of language can in some measure be learned. Can it also be taught? The assumption that it can is present in the very earliest stages of the Greek literary tradition. In the *Iliad*, Achilles's father, Peleus, assigns his son a tutor, Phoenix, tasked "to teach you all these things, to make you a speaker of words and a doer of deeds" (Homer, *Iliad* 9.440–3). Achilles later acknowledges his failure to master one-half of the curriculum: "I, a man without equal . . . in war, though there are others better skilled at debate" (18.105). Achilles's self-assessment is realistic: his mishandling of the assembly in *Iliad* 1 has had catastrophic consequences. The fact that he had been tutored makes his failure less excusable than that of Odysseus's son, Telemachus, a young man who grew up without paternal oversight in a community in which normal political life was in abeyance (his mother remarks on his inexperience in the *Odyssey* [4.818]). When he convenes an assembly to challenge the position of a powerful clique, it is not surprising that the outcome is a humiliating failure (Heitman 2005: 14–28).

These two cases illustrate situations in which success or failure in persuasion have significant public consequences, and in which the teachability of effective speech carries the greatest premium. Greeks accordingly came to associate rhetoric paradigmatically with the use of language to persuade in certain kinds of public dispute. Deliberative disputes may be directly concerned with the welfare of a whole community, though the outcome will also affect the disputants' public standing. Individual status, property, or life are directly at stake in judicial disputes. There are, however, also contexts requiring skilled public speech in which it would be a faux pas to treat a proposition as open to dispute. If you are welcoming a visiting dignitary, for example, it would be inappropriate to argue that he is an important person whose presence is an honor and a delight; you must take that for granted and exhibit the (putatively) acknowledged fact. No deliberative or judicial decision is demanded of the audience, but your words will, if successful, make certain facts more salient to those already inclined to accept them. Even here, then, language is used to influence attitudes.

The classification of speeches into deliberative, judicial, and ceremonial (epideictic) kinds constructed in the previous paragraph is so familiar that it may seem self-evident. As we shall see, however, other ways of conceptualizing the domain of rhetoric remained current at least to the end of the fourth century BCE. This provides a simple reminder of two essential features of the Greek rhetorical tradition. First, it was in constant evolution: according canonical status to any particular theorization or theorist (Aristotle, for example, or Cicero or Quintilian) inevitably falsifies the historical reality. And second, rhetorical pedagogy and its evolution were inseparably connected with the evolution of theoretical codifications of rhetoric (Heath 2009a). It is characteristic of the Greek rhetorical tradition that teachers enhanced their pedagogy by providing pupils with a guiding framework based on explicit categorizations and principles abstracted from the untidy complexities of successful practice. Aristotle's *Rhetoric* begins by recognizing that rhetoric, like reasoning, is something with which everyone has some acquaintance; the function of art (*technē*) is to transform spontaneous or habitual persuasion into a methodical practice by determining the factors that explain success (1.1, 1354a1–11). Speaking of arts in general, he distinguishes experts who can give an explanation of successful practice from skilled practitioners whose ability to achieve success is based on experience and is relatively inarticulate. The former have more prestige and are better able to teach (Aristotle, *Metaphysics* 1.1, 980b25–30). But Aristotle does not deny that practical success, which depends on judgment of individual cases, may owe more to experience than to theoretical generalization (1.1, 981a12–24). Although the rejection of theory was an eccentric minority view (e.g., Quintilian, *Institutio oratoria* 2.11, with Heath 2009a: 71), Greek rhetoricians never questioned, and usually emphasized, the importance of tacit procedural insight to successful persuasion.

How early did the theoretical tendency become established? In Plato's *Phaedrus*, Socrates refers to the handbooks on rhetoric that Nestor and Odysseus wrote in their spare time during the Trojan War (261b–c). Phaedrus sees a reference to more recent figures behind this playful anachronism. In reality, Homeric education would not have dealt in theoretical abstractions. The closest we come to seeing Phoenix acting as teacher is in *Iliad* 9, where he is a member of the delegation sent to persuade Achilles to rejoin the fighting. Advising Achilles how to behave in a crisis limits Phoenix's options: there is, for example, no opportunity to expose Achilles to live models, to demonstrate techniques, or to rehearse his pupil and give "feedback." But he can tell stories that provide Achilles with models to emulate or avoid, and he can offer situation-specific instructions supported by general injunctions ("You should not have a heart that does not forgive"). Such seemingly universal imperatives always presuppose an assessment of the specific situation, and Phoenix also draws his pupil's attention to circumstances that make the recommended assessment appropriate to the situation. One function of rhetorical theory in later times will be to help students bridge the gap between universal precepts and particular situations.

When we turn to the sophists of the late fifth and early fourth centuries BCE we are on only slightly firmer ground. The diversity of the intellectual interests of the sophistic movement (Kerferd 1981; Ford 2001) makes it unrealistic to suppose that rhetoric was a primary concern of every sophist—though even contemporaries could make the misleading generalization that sophists in general were experts in making people "clever at speaking" (Plato, *Protagoras* 312d). But Gorgias certainly undertook to make people clever at speaking about the most important human affairs—that is, capable of persuading by speech in courts and deliberative bodies (Plato, *Gorgias* 448e–9e, 451d, 452d–e, 454b, *Meno* 95c). According to Aristotle, Gorgias's teaching consisted of supplying his pupils with speeches to be learned by heart. This, he complains, provided the pupils with products of the art of rhetoric but not with the art itself. Aristotle scornfully compares this technique to teaching someone to avoid sore feet by providing them with lots of different shoes: a need has been met, but no expertise has been imparted (*Sophistical Refutations* 34, 183b36–4a8). Texts such as Gorgias's *Encomium of Helen* and *Defense of Palamedes* are likely to have been written as such exemplars (Cole 1991a: 71–94); the uncomfortable density of their stylistic and argumentative devices suggests that they were designed as concentrated repositories of techniques to be quarried rather than faithfully reproduced. The example of Plato's Phaedrus, who has borrowed and memorized a speech by Lysias (*Phaedrus* 228d–e), provides further attestation for this pattern of teaching.

Gorgias is mentioned in Plato's *Phaedrus* as asserting the superiority of probabilities (*eikota*) to truth and the capacity of rhetoric to make small things seem large and vice versa (267a). Since such claims (relevant to advertising the power of persuasive speech, as in the *Encomium of Helen*) would be more convincingly supported by demonstration than by theory, Plato's evidence is consistent with Aristotle's characterization of Gorgias's teaching methods. Plato here pairs Gorgias with an earlier rhetorician, Tisias. This shadowy figure must be approached with extreme caution (Cole 1991b). According to some later sources, Tisias and his teacher, Corax, founded the art of rhetoric and in doing so anticipated theoretical doctrines not otherwise attested until a much later date. This "evidence" is thoroughly unreliable: it is compromised by the persistent tendency of doxographic traditions to fill evidential voids by conjecture (a tendency that still flourishes in the modern literature on sophistic rhetoric). The earliest stratum of surviving evidence is a safer guide. There are two references to Tisias in *Phaedrus*, both associating him with arguments from probability (267a, 273a–e), defined as "what most people think" (267a). Aristotle mentions Tisias as one of the earliest contributors to the development of rhetoric (*Sophistical Refutations* 34, 183b302) and reports that arguments from probability were the sole content of the art of Corax (*Rhetoric* 2.24, 1402a18). Corax ("Crow") is likely to be a nickname, and it has been plausibly suggested that Tisias and Corax are in fact one person (Cole 1991b: 80–3). Plato provides evidence that a written text by Tisias was available for Phaedrus to study (*Phaedrus* 273a), but all that we can infer about that text is that it was about arguments from probability and included examples.

We return to the more secure ground of extant texts with Antiphon's *Tetralogies*, sets of speeches (dating perhaps to the latter part of the fifth century) illustrating how to argue each side of three imaginary homicide cases. These are demonstration texts with an interesting difference (Innes 1991). Each of the three cases requires a different defense: denying the homicide, maintaining that it was accidental, and claiming justification. The complete set therefore provides not only an illustrative repository of technical means of persuasion but also a systematic overview of different kinds of dispute that may arise from a legal charge and the way each party should approach them (see Gagarin, ch. 2). This is the aspect of rhetoric that would, in later times, be elaborately theorized in successive versions of the theory of issue (*stasis*). The *Tetralogies* themselves do no more than illustrate: they convey no explicit theory. But it is hard to imagine that someone capable of constructing this package of examples would be unable to supplement the texts with at least a minimal articulation of their underlying framework ("If the defendant disputes the alleged facts, then this is how the case should be argued . . .").

Another kind of demonstration text took the form not of a complete speech but of a collection of variants on a single part of a speech. An extant example of this genre is the collection of proems attributed to Demosthenes, but others are known to have existed. Antiphon is credited with collections of proems and epilogues (*Suda* AI325); the *Art of Rhetoric* attributed to him (*Suda* M1310) is likely to have comprised these collections of examples rather than explicit theoretical exposition. Thrasymachus, one of the rhetoricians mentioned in *Phaedrus*, is credited with another collection of proems (Athenaeus, *Deipnosophistae* 10, 416a); a lengthy quotation in Dionysius of Halicarnassus (*Demosthenes* 3) is probably one of these model proems (Yunis 1997). In another collection, Thrasymachus demonstrated ways of appealing for pity (Aristotle, *Rhetoric* 3.1, 1404a14–5). In this case, the examples illustrate not one part of a speech but one persuasive technique. Tisias's work on arguments from probability is likely to have been of this kind.

Although such collections teach by providing examples, they are also evidence of some movement in a theoretical direction. The fact that certain parts of a speech and certain persuasive techniques have been isolated and explicitly identified presupposes a conception, however rudimentary, of the normative structure of a speech and of its various functions. Plato's *Phaedrus* again provides corroboration. The context of the second reference to Gorgias is a brief catalog of the kinds of thing that can be learned from "the books written on the art of speeches" (266d–7d). This catalog shows unmistakable signs of the emergent analytical and theoretical tendencies in rhetoric. Its frame adumbrates what would later become a standard account of the structure of a speech (proem, narrative, supporting arguments, and recapitulation), though the analysis is not yet fully explicit and the terminology remains unstable. Arguments are classified as witness statements, inferential arguments from evidence (*tekmēria*), and arguments from probability (*eikota*). Socrates also mentions more refined distinctions among techniques (confirmation and supplementary confirmation; refutation and supplementary refutation; covert allusion and oblique praise) and a variety of contributions concerned with diction and style, as well as Thrasymachus's techniques for invective and for achieving emotional effects (arousing and assuaging anger or pity). Though teachers may still have been working primarily through demonstration, the proliferation of terminological refinements at which Socrates pokes gentle fun makes it certain that analytical frameworks were under development. A teaching practice based on demonstrations accompanied by explanatory comment is not the same as one based on theoretical precepts illustrated by examples, but the boundary is easily crossed.

The frustrating fact remains that the available evidence does not provide a secure basis for more than the vaguest conjectures about how early sophistic rhetorical pedagogy would have worked in practice. Isocrates raises hopes of more substantial insights. His writings contain passages reflecting on his own pedagogical practice and contrasting it with that of other teachers of "political speeches." This contrast reminds us that we cannot assume uniformity in teaching practice: Isocrates may be an unrepresentative figure from whom we cannot generalize. On the other hand, we should not take Isocrates's word on trust: when he speaks of rivals in the context of self-promoting polemics, he has an incentive to exaggerate differences. There may, then, be an element of caricature when he criticizes teachers of political speeches for failing to recognize the importance of experience and natural talent: they treat speaking as if it were the same as spelling—that is, as if it were governed by a set of fixed rules that could be applied across all situations. Isocrates insists that creativity is an essential component of the art of public speech, since no speaker gains by saying just what has been said already: the key is to say something that others have not thought of, while still speaking appropriately on the subject. Speech needs to fit the specific occasion (*kairos*), to be appropriate, and to be innovative (Isocrates, *Against the Sophists* 9–13). For this reason, Isocrates affirms the necessity of talent and experience. Indeed, they are sometimes sufficient: many have become effective speakers and politicians without formal training (14). Training can enhance such people's skill and resourcefulness; the success they achieve unsystematically becomes more directly accessible (15). The parallel with Aristotle's conception of rhetoric as the transformation of spontaneous or habitual persuasion into a methodical practice is clear.

A sketch of Isocrates's own model of rhetorical training follows (*Against the Sophists* 16). One part is to learn the *ideai* of speech, the basic forms from which all speeches are constructed. This is comparatively easy, given genuinely expert tuition; what is harder is selecting the *ideai* for any given subject and then combining and arranging them. This must be done in a way that fits the specific occasion, and the whole speech must be appropriately elaborated in thought and expression. The student's contribution is intensive study, which is fruitless without a "courageous and imaginative soul"; he must learn the *eidē* (species) of speech and practice their uses (*khrēseis*). The teacher's contribution is to give an accurate and comprehensive exposition of these basics and, for the more advanced aspects, to present himself as an exemplar (*paradeigma*) on which students can pattern themselves by imitation. Imitation here clearly does not mean merely repeating or adapting the teacher's demonstrations: it is not the surface of the text that the student must emulate but its underlying, and necessarily creative, art. The pattern that emerges is a two-stage program: the student first assimilates the exposition of basic theory and then models his practice on the master's demonstrations (cf. *Antidosis* 183). We might expect the master to provide some feedback on the student's efforts, but there is no positive evidence of this, and we should not necessarily assume it: we know of later teachers who disdained giving feedback (Seneca, *Controversiae* 9.2.23).

Isocrates mentions the *ideai* or *eidē* of speech without elucidation. The so-called *Rhetoric to Alexander* may help. This is the earliest surviving technical handbook, written in the decades 340–300 BCE. It was transmitted under Aristotle's name, together with the fake dedicatory preface that gave it its traditional title; its real author is uncertain, but Anaximenes of Lampsacus is a plausible conjecture. The dominance of Aristotelian and later conceptions of rhetoric has been an obstacle to understanding this text. Indeed, this was already the case in later antiquity: readers who took the familiar trichotomy of kinds of speech—deliberative, judicial, ceremonial—for granted were perplexed by this treatise's different classification (the opening sentence, which asserts the trichotomy, is probably a later addition, an attempt to tame the unfamiliar). In fact, the author works with seven species (*eidē*), the capacities and uses (*khrēseis*) of which he undertakes to enumerate. These species are not kinds of speech but kinds of things that can *be done* in speeches (exhortation, dissuasion, praise, blame, attack, defense, and investigation), and they are distributed in various combinations across three contexts of speech: courts, public addresses, and private discussions (*homiliai*). After he has completed a piecemeal discussion of these *eidē* (*Rhetoric to Alexander* 1–28), the author turns in the second part of the treatise to how they should be arranged in the body of a complete speech (28–38). The parallel to Isocrates's reference to *eidē* and to their uses, combinations, and arrangement is unmistakable, though Isocrates's vague and expansive use of *ideai* in other contexts makes it hard to pin down the significance of the parallel. The *Rhetoric to Alexander* is certainly not reproducing Isocratean theory, but both appear to be drawing on a shared, pre-Aristotelian rhetorical tradition.

In one respect, the *Rhetoric to Alexander* is likely to be more representative of that tradition than Isocrates. The inclusion of private discussions within rhetoric's domain may seem surprising, but it is consistent with other evidence for sophistic theory (Plato, *Phaedrus* 261a, *Sophist* 222c; Alcidamas, *Peri Sophiston* 9). Even Gorgias, whose promotional emphasis on "the most important human affairs" (i.e., judicial and deliberative debates) has already been noted, is represented as illustrating the power of his rhetorical art from his experience with persuasion in private contexts (Plato, *Gorgias* 456a–b). This is consistent with Protagoras's claim to teach how to deliberate well (*euboulia*) in household as well as civic matters (Plato, *Protagoras* 318e–9a; cf. *Meno* 91a–b, *Republic* 10, 600c–d; Xenophon, *Memorabilia* 1.2.64). Isocrates, too, is concerned with *euboulia*: rhetorical speech is the outward expression of good deliberation, since the proofs we use to persuade others and those by which we ourselves are convinced in our own reflections are the same (*Antidosis* 255–7 = *Nicocles* 7–9). But Isocrates almost completely effaces the private dimension: he says only that rhetorical training may, as a side effect, improve performance in private *homiliai* for those who choose not to enter public life (*Antidosis* 204; cf. 99, 285). Isocrates also departs from the earlier sophistic tradition in disparaging judicial oratory to concentrate on public affairs. This narrowing of focus has a moral dimension. Gorgias's claim to make people clever speakers was accompanied by ridicule of the claims of some other sophists to teach virtue (Plato, *Meno* 95c; cf. *Gorgias* 456d–7c for the moral neutrality of Gorgias's rhetorical teaching). Isocrates, too, dismisses claims to be able to educate in virtue. But he argues, even so, that learning to speak well and persuasively will nevertheless produce moral improvement (*Antidosis* 274), primarily on the grounds that persuasiveness depends on having internalized the values of those one aims to persuade (276–80). (Plato would agree, of course, but deplores the values that the politician must internalize to be persuasive in existing societies.) This position would have been harder to maintain if judicial oratory had not been excluded: the sometimes dishonest tactics recommended in the *Rhetoric to Alexander* indicate a more purely instrumental, less morally engaged, conception of rhetorical education (the tactical dishonesties of law court oratory are a persistent worry in ancient discussions of rhetoric: e.g., Quintilian, *Institutio oratoria* 2.17.26–9, 4.5.5, 12.1.33–45; Heath 2009b: 151–3).

The link between rhetoric and *euboulia* makes sense, since any argument you can use to defend a position in public is—unless you know it to be flawed—also a reason for holding that position yourself, and any argument you know to be flawed is a potential liability in defending that position publicly. The persuasive force of tactical manipulations is limited, even in judicial contexts: only the use of substantively good arguments can guard against the risk of canny audiences seeing through, and intelligent opponents pointing out, the merely specious. In the Hellenistic and Roman periods, when cases were heard by elite magistrates who had been trained in rhetoric and knew the tactical tricks, the premium on substantively good argument would be even greater. An effective regime of rhetorical training must therefore include procedures for identifying the objectively strong resources for arguing a given case (on both sides, since each party's strengths are weaknesses on the other side and vice versa).

At this point we should pause to consider what range of skills successful practitioners of persuasive speech need. Obviously, one must be able to speak fluently and coherently. But speaking presupposes that you have something to say: the first and fundamental requirement is thus the ability to find what, in any given situation, is worth saying (Gk. *heuresis*; L. *inventio*). Once you have found it, you must be able to put your material into coherent and intelligible order (Gk. *taxis*; L. *dispositio*) and express it well (Gk. *lexis*, *phrasis*; L. *elocutio*). But these preparations will be wasted if, when the time comes, you cannot remember what you intended to say (Gk. *mnēmē*; L. *memoria*) or cannot present it effectively in performance (Gk. *hypokrisis*; L. *actio*). This catalog of skills reconstructs another important element of ancient rhetorical theory—the five parts of oratory: invention, disposition, expression, memory, and delivery. But this, too, was not a timeless canon: the theory developed gradually in the Hellenistic period, after Aristotle and before Cicero, and by the end of the second century CE it had broken down, in part for pedagogical reasons. Fundamental to the discovery of good arguments is the ability to identify a relevant and effective way of handling the particular kind of question in dispute: a disputed question of fact, for example, requires different treatment from a dispute about the justification of an admitted fact (the point implicit in Antiphon's *Tetralogies*). But it makes little sense to treat under the single heading of invention both the mapping out of a global argumentative strategy and the detailed implementation of that strategy, which must vary between the parts of a speech according to their different functions. This problem, which defeated the authors of Hellenistic and Roman handbooks, was eventually solved by separating out the preliminary analysis under the heading of "intellection" (*noēsis*). The scope of invention was then narrowed to the parts of a speech but at the same time expanded to embrace questions of style and tactical organization that arise within the different parts.

This change in rhetorical theory implies a corresponding change in teaching practice, for which we have relatively plentiful evidence. The innovations of the second and early third centuries CE established a new framework that later rhetoricians modified and elaborated but never dismantled (Heath 2004: 3–89). These innovations therefore mark a watershed in the availability of evidence. The innovations rendered earlier texts obsolete, and in an essentially practical discipline like rhetoric the obsolete is likely to be discarded. Consequently, very little rhetorical literature survives from before the second century CE, but from the second century onward the literature is abundant. Moreover, much of that literature is closely connected to pedagogical practice: handbooks that expound the content of rhetorical teaching; texts composed for, or even in, the classroom (lectures might be written up by teachers or written down by students or stenographers); demonstration texts; and diverse texts that explicitly or allusively comment on or describe elements of classroom practice. Though many gaps and uncertainties remain, it now becomes possible to give a circumstantial account of the practice of rhetorical pedagogy.

The theoretical texts of the period help us to establish a series of stages in rhetorical pedagogy. Beginners worked on a graded series of introductory exercises that familiarized them with a number of techniques that would need to be combined in a complete speech (e.g., telling a story, criticizing or defending a narrative's plausibility, arguing a general thesis). Students would then proceed to the more advanced exercise (the Latin term *declamatio* may give a misleading impression of its primary point: the Greek name, *meletē*, means simply "exercise"), in which they were given a hypothetical scenario and asked to speak on one or the other side of a judicial or deliberative dispute arising from it (Russell 1983; see Pernot, ch. 20; Gunderson, ch. 21). To prepare them to tackle these advanced exercises, students were taught *stasis* theory (issue theory), which distinguished between different kinds of dispute (the number of issues had now stabilized at 13) and provided a division for each: that is, an ordered set of heads of argument that established a default strategy for handling each kind of dispute. Given a theme for declamation, the student had first to identify the issue and then apply the division to the particular case, using its circumstances to give concrete content to the abstract template (Heath 1995, 2007). Issue theory was the main component of intellection (*noēsis*). Invention (*heuresis*) then showed students how to frame the argumentative strategy of the division in the structure of a complete speech, providing schemes for unfolding particular lines of argument in detail (Heath 1997) but also, as already noted, touching on points of verbal expression (*hermēneia*). Some attention was given to fluency and flexibility in expression at earlier stages: beginners might be asked to repeat an exercise using a series of different grammatical structures; at a higher level, paraphrase of existing texts provided a more demanding exercise. But intensive cultivation of stylistic excellence was reserved for the most advanced stage of the program, which was based on the analysis and deployment of the components of different kinds of style (Wooten 1987).

Theory is not autonomous. At each stage, theoretical exposition prepares the way for the practical exercises fundamental to the acquisition of a practical skill. What is learned through precept must be transformed into a habitual, internalized skill, and it is practice that effects this transformation. The demand for constant and intensive practice on the part of students of rhetoric was a commonplace; when Galen, for example, insists on the importance of practice in studying medicine, he turns to the rhetoric student's workload to illustrate his point (*De placitis Hippocratis et Platonis* 2.3.16, 9.2.31). The rhetoric teacher's workload could also be heavy, since the student's constant practice needed to be supported by individual feedback—a chore that, as noted earlier, some of the most eminent teachers disdained.

Precepts also, as Quintilian says, need to be illustrated by a constant and diverse diet of examples (*Institutio oratoria* 7.10.5–9). The teacher's demonstrations therefore provided a further form of support for the student's practical exercises; public displays by expert rhetorical performers would give added variety, as would visits to the courts to observe professional advocates (specialists in rhetoric, not law) in action (see Enos, ch. 13). Reading exemplary speeches by the classical orators was also important: although the teacher's "living voice" is essential, since it demonstrates speech in action with greater immediacy, it cannot convey everything there is to be learned from a masterpiece by Demosthenes (Quintilian, *Institutio oratoria* 2.2.8, 2.5.16). These would be studied in class, with the teacher providing a commentary that might also be the vehicle for advanced theoretical instruction (Heath 2004: 184–213), but private study was yet another addition to the rhetoric student's heavy workload.

The pattern of teaching and learning that emerged in the second century CE marked the culmination of a long history of experiment and innovation in rhetorical pedagogy. One noteworthy feature is its flexibility: it creates a plurality of exit points. A student who had, for example, practiced the introductory exercises and learned the art of division would be equipped for basic advocacy. He could analyze a case, pinpoint the nature of the dispute, and identify a range of relevant argumentative resources. Missing out on the study of invention and advanced style would not disadvantage him in low-level courts, where any attempt to make a lengthy speech, elaborately structured and elegantly expressed, was likely to be preempted by the interventions of a magistrate with a heavy caseload and a great deal of latitude in the conduct of hearings. It would be primarily in more elite social strata that an advocate would benefit from displaying his stylistic virtuosity, his command of classical Attic linguistic norms, and his familiarity with the inheritance of classical culture. Since contemporary society had a need for trained practitioners at a variety of social and professional levels, the flexibility of this teaching pattern was entirely appropriate. Change in rhetorical theory is symptomatic of change in teaching practice; but changes in teaching practice were themselves sensitive to changing social demands for the skills pedagogy fosters (see Steel, ch. 16; Mack, ch. 33; Kaufer and Wetzel, ch. 56). Rhetoric, as a practical discipline, must be responsive to its social and cultural environment. But rhetoric, in turn, contributed to the shaping of the larger social and cultural environment of which it was part: rhetorical teaching was one of the influences that created the elite culture whose expectations students of rhetoric had to learn to meet.

FURTHER READING

There is no satisfactory account of Greek rhetorical education in the classical period. The task may be impossible in view of the sparse and problematic nature of the evidence. But useful starting points include Cole (1991) on the origins of rhetoric, Kennedy (2007) on early handbooks, Goebel (1989) on arguments from probability, and Livingstone (1998) on Isocrates. The evidence for later antiquity is far more abundant and in recent years has emerged from comparative neglect. Heath (2004) quarries the technical literature; Cribiore (2007) focuses on Libanius, the most successful fourth-century teacher of Greek rhetoric, and Cribiore (2001) builds on her excellent introduction to the educational context.

REFERENCES

Cole, Thomas. 1991a. *The Origins of Rhetoric in Ancient Greece*. Baltimore, MA: Johns Hopkins University Press.

Cole, Thomas. 1991b. "Who Was Corax?" *Illinois Classical Studies* 16: 65–84.

Cribiore, Raffaella. 2001. *Gymnastics of the Mind: Greek Education in Hellenistic and Roman Egypt*. Princeton, NJ: Princeton University Press.

Cribiore, Raffaella. 2007. *The School of Libanius in Late Antique Antioch*. Princeton, NJ: Princeton University Press.

Ford, Andrew. 2001. "Sophists Without Rhetoric: The Arts of Speech in Fifth-Century Athens." In *Education in Greek and Roman Antiquity*, edited by Yun Lee Too, 85–109. Leiden: Brill.

Goebel, George H. 1989. "Probability in the Earliest Rhetorical Theory." *Mnemosyne* 42: 41–53.

Heath, Malcolm. 1995. *Hermogenes on Issues: Strategies of Argument in Later Greek Rhetoric*. Oxford: Clarendon.

Heath, Malcolm. 1997. "Invention." In *A Handbook of Classical Rhetoric in the Hellenistic Period, 330 B.C.–A.D. 400*, edited by Stanley E. Porter, 89–119. Leiden: Brill.

Heath, Malcolm. 2004. *Menander: A Rhetor in Context*. Oxford: Oxford University Press.

Heath, Malcolm. 2007. "Teaching Rhetorical Argument Today." In *Logos: Rational Argument in Classical Rhetoric*, edited by Jonathan Powell, 105–122. London: Institute of Classical Studies.

Heath, Malcolm. 2009a. "Codifications of Rhetoric." In *The Cambridge Companion to Ancient Rhetoric*, edited by Erik Gunderson, 59–73. Cambridge: Cambridge University Press.

Heath, Malcolm. 2009b. "Platonists and the Teaching of Rhetoric in Late Antiquity." In *Late Antique Epistemology: Other Ways to Truth*, edited by Panayiota Vassilopoulou and Stephen R. L. Clark, 143–159. London: Palgrave Macmillan.

Heitman, Richard. 2005. *Taking Her Seriously: Penelope and the Plot of Homer's "Odyssey."* Ann Arbor: University of Michigan Press.

Innes, Doreen. 1991. "Gorgias, Antiphon and Sophistopolis." *Argumentation* 5: 221–231.

Kennedy, George. 2007. "The Earliest Rhetorical Handbooks." In *Aristotle on Rhetoric: A Theory of Civic Discourse*, 2nd ed., 293–306. New York: Oxford University Press.

Kerferd, George B. 1981. *The Sophistic Movement.* Cambridge: Cambridge University Press.

Livingstone, Niall. 1998. "The Voice of Isocrates and the Dissemination of Cultural Power." In *Pedagogy and Power: Rhetorics of Classical Learning*, edited by Yun Lee Too and Niall Livingstone, 263–281. Cambridge: Cambridge University Press.

Russell, Donald A. 1983. *Greek Declamation.* Cambridge: Cambridge University Press.

Yunis, Harvey. 1997. "Thrasymachus B1: Discord, not Diplomacy." *Classical Philology* 92: 58–66.

Wooten, Cecil W. 1987. *Hermogenes on Types of Style.* Chapel Hill: University of North Carolina Press.

CHAPTER 6

··

RHETORIC AND POETICS

··

JEFFREY WALKER

If anyone says that poetry is panegyric discourse in meter, I can't say that
he is mistaken.

—Hermogenes, *On Types of Style*

ARCHAIC ATTITUDES
··

CONSIDER the following verses from the *Theognidea*: "Listen to me, child, and discipline
your wits: I'll tell / A tale not unpersuasive nor uncharming to your heart. / But set your
mind to gather what I say: there's no necessity / To do what's not according to your will"
(1235–8). The *Theognidea*, a collection of epigrammatic poems ascribed to the sixth-
century BCE poet Theognis, belongs to the archaic period of Greek culture (eighth to
mid-fifth centuries BCE). No one yet has written a "poetics," in the sense of a systematic
theory or treatise (a *technē*), or for that matter a "rhetoric." Indeed, the terms poetry
(*poiēsis, poiētikē*) and rhetoric (*rhētorikē*) do not yet exist: the usual terms are song
(*aoidē, mousikē*) and speech (*logos*), meaning discourse composed in verse and meant
usually to be sung (or chanted or intoned in a stylized way) and discourse composed in
prose and meant to be spoken (Gentili 1988: 3; Cole 1991: 2; Schiappa 1991: 40–9).

In this passage from Theognis the poet/speaker speaks to a teenaged boy, Kyrnos
Polypaides, the main addressee of the *Theognidea*. Possibly Kyrnos is a son of the rising class of *nouveaux riches* who, in the sixth century, were crowding in upon, displac-
ing, and mixing with the old nobility across much of the Greek world (see Figueira 1985;
Morris 1996). Possibly Kyrnos is the child of what Theognis would consider a "mixed"
marriage between a baseborn (but rich) father and a highborn (but poor) mother. That
sort of thing shocks Theognis. But whatever the case may be, Kyrnos is the new crudity
that owns the future, slouching toward his destiny, handsome and unworthy: "O child,
you've grown up beautiful [*kalos*] in form, / But placed upon your head is a mighty crown
of ignorances" (Theognis, *Theognidea* 1259–60). So Theognis has a few "persuasive" and
"charming" things that he wants to say to Kyrnos and to his wider audience as well.

What Theognis offers Kyrnos may sound like a pederastic proposition—and may be one—but that is unlikely here, except as a figure for the politics of association in Theognis's faction-riven city of Megara. At stake is with whom young Kyrnos will associate, how he will be educated, what character (*ēthos*) and practical intelligence (*phronēsis*) he will develop, and what it takes to properly rule. "Tale" in my translation renders *mythos*: not myth in the classical or modern sense but in the archaic sense of speech, word, or story—in general, a telling of some sort. Theognis's use of *mythos* here suggests the moral, political, and philosophical advice to which most of the *Theognidea* is devoted: the gnomic sayings (*gnōmai*) Isocrates will later describe as *chrē zēn*, "useful for living" (*To Nicocles* 3).

This useful telling, then, is to be persuasive (*peithos*) and charming (*charis*) to Kyrnos's heart (*kardia*)—a locution that figures persuasion as a soul-guiding enchantment (*psychagōgia*) producing emotional and bodily effects as well as rational conviction, much as Gorgias of Leontini will describe it about a century later in *Encomium of Helen* (8–10, 14) or as Plato will define rhetoric in the *Phaedrus* (261a). For his part, Kyrnos is to discipline (*damazein*, "rein in") his wits (*phrēn*, "practical intelligence") and set his mind to gather what Theognis says (*synein epos*, "understand the poem"). And on the basis of this understanding Kyrnos is to judge and respond, be persuaded or not persuaded, since "there is no necessity to do what's not according to your will." Will here translates *thymos*, more properly "heart" in the sense of the spirited part of the psyche from which emotions, wishes, and intentions arise (as in "my heart tells me to do this"). Kyrnos, then, is under no compulsion to do what Theognis advises if, having understood the telling, his *thymos* finds it unpersuasive or uncongenial. Kyrnos is free to disagree, to walk away, to do as he wishes. So, too, is the wider audience of Theognis's poetry.

The relationship between Theognis and Kyrnos, the rhetorical transaction in which they are involved, represents the traditional understanding of the relation between poet and audience in archaic Greek culture. The poem is a *rhetorical act*. The poet's role is to offer persuasion. The audience's role is to respond, to be persuaded or not, to approve, dispute, or simply reject what the poet says. This way of understanding poetry persisted, as old tradition, into what we now call the classical age and formed the background for its theorizing.

EPIDEICTIC SONG, PRACTICAL SPEECH

Archaic Greek culture regarded both song and speech as modalities of what we call rhetoric: the art or practice of persuasive discourse, or as Kenneth Burke puts it, "The use of language as a symbolic means of inducing cooperation in beings that by nature respond to symbols" (1950: 43). Simply stated, the modern distinction between poetry and rhetoric as somehow antithetical—the one aesthetic and expressive, the other practical and persuasive—was foreign to archaic Greek thought. Both song and speech were understood to express ideas and attitudes *persuasively*, and aesthetic appeal was part of the suasory force of both.

More particularly, archaic thought identified song and speech, respectively, with what one strand of the classical tradition would call epideictic rhetoric (*to epideiktikon*) and practical rhetoric (*to pragmatikon*). As Aristotle observes in *Rhetoric* (1.3.1–3), the key distinction is the kind of setting in which the discourse is performed and the role of the audience. Practical rhetoric leads to specific actions (*praxeis, pragmata*) and is presented to audiences acting as judges (*kritai*) empowered to take or reject the action recommended. The classical examples of this genre of rhetoric are dicanic (judicial) discourse in a court of law and symbouleutic (advisory) discourse in a deliberative assembly or council convened to vote on a proposal. Epideictic rhetoric, in contrast, does not lead to specific actions but is a display (*epideixis*) typically presented in ritual, ceremonial, festal, symposiastic, paideutic, or entertainment settings (e.g., a theater). Here the audience of spectators (*theōroi*) will not vote on the matter in question but will simply observe (*theōrein*) the performance, respond and consider, applaud or not applaud, and go away. Further, in primarily oral societies like archaic Greece, epideictic discourse is meant to be memorable and repeatable: it encodes the community's important lore in an aesthetically impressive, recitable form. Epideictic rhetoric speaks the language of timeless ancestral wisdoms.

The *persuasive* function of epideictic discourse lies in its traditional orientation toward praise (*epainos*) and blame (*psogos*), or what Burke calls "persuasion to attitude." An attitude is an "incipient action" or predisposition to act in certain ways when action is called for. Notably, Burke further aligns "persuasion to attitude" with poetic discourse and "pure persuasion" (1950: 50–1, 70–3, 267–94): persuasion for its own sake, the game of putting ideas in question to see what can be argued, as an antidote to ideological rigidity. What this means is that epideictic rhetoric, along with archaic epideictic song, is not (as is often thought) limited to the conservative function of celebrating and intensifying existing values and beliefs. The poet/singer offers the audience a charmingly persuasive telling so that they may praise what the telling praises, blame what it blames, love and hate what it loves and hates, affirm what it affirms, question what it questions, and so on—or talk back. By responding in this way to epideictic suasion, the audience rehearses its commitment or opposition to the values and beliefs offered for its embrace. Epideictic rhetoric thereby cultivates the communal attitudes—the ideological and emotional commitments—that will constitute the available grounds for deliberation and decision in specific practical situations. Viewed this way, epideictic discourse, or song in the archaic world, can be understood, as Chaïm Perelman (1969: 47–51) suggests, as the central or primary form of rhetoric.

THE PROLIFERATION OF PROSE EPIDEICTIC IN THE CLASSICAL AGE

In the archaic period, song or poetry was the main medium of epideictic rhetoric, while speech was the main medium of practical rhetoric. This traditional arrangement may have been a function of the primarily oral character of archaic Greek culture. Indeed, it seems to be an almost universal characteristic of the oral-traditional societies studied by anthropologists in modern times: speech for practical business-talk, song for epideictic (see Bloch 1975; Ong 1982). (There are exceptions to this pattern, of course, and the two can interpenetrate; we should think of sliding scales rather than completely distinct categories.)

After the Greek archaic period (the later fifth century BCE onward), however, the functions of epideictic song were gradually taken over by new genres of epideictic prose, which now stood alongside or replaced the older genres. Hesiodic lore-poetry gave way to "philosophical" kinds of prose like that of the pre-Socratics and early sophists, though some philosophers (e.g., Parmenides, Xenophanes, and Empedocles) continued to frame their new philosophies in verse. Homeric narrative gave way to history, though epic poems continued to be written; lyric poetry and ritual song gave way to the prose encomium and its variants, such as the funeral oration (*epitaphios logos*). Aristotle notes in *Poetics* (1.7–10) the emergence of a new kind of prose poetry in the late-fifth and early-fourth century prose mimes of Xenarchus and Sophron and the fourth-century Socratic dialogues of Plato and Xenophon. (Ancient mime [*mimos*] was popular skit theater, consisting of brief and usually comedic dramas or dramatic monologues.) Prose mimes, too, were probably the model for another novelty: the early sophistic declamation—the display performance (*epideixis*) of an imaginary speech—exemplified by Gorgias's *Defense of Palamedes* and *Encomium of Helen*, Antiphon's *Tetralogies*, and Alcidamas's *Odysseus* (Walker 2005).

In the later second century CE we find Hermogenes of Tarsus dividing the realm of rhetoric into *politikos logos* (practical civic discourse) and *panēgyrikos logos* (epideictic discourse), the latter including poetry, history, and philosophy as well as civic panegyric such as the public funeral oration (*On Types of Style* 2.9–12). Menander Rhetor's treatise on the various genres of epideictic rhetoric, probably composed in the later third century CE (Heath 2004), included "hymns to the gods"—an ancient form of religious epideictic still piously performed in song—as well as such things as the imperial panegyric (an annual speech celebrating the emperor's deeds), speeches of formal greeting and farewell, the funeral oration, praise of cities, the birthday speech, the wedding speech, the epinician speech in praise of victorious athletes (which performed exactly the function of Pindar's victory odes), and many others (see Russell and Wilson 1981). The second-century CE sophist Aelius Aristides, for his part, invented the prose hymn, which he defended as more natural and suitable to the praise of a god (*To Sarapis* 1–14), and in his *To Plato: In Defense of Rhetoric* Aristides whimsically refers to the traditional Muses of poetry as "the old ladies" (394). The category of epideictic rhetoric, in short, came to include everything that we might call literary prose as well as all types of poetry as an ancient subdivision (see Cassin, ch. 11; Pernot, ch. 20).

This gradual shift toward epideictic prose seems closely related to the emergence of literacy in Greek culture, which began as early as the eighth century BCE and seems to have reached critical mass in the fifth, when literacy training and the study of written texts (as opposed to memorizing and singing songs) became a normal and fundamental part of

Greek education (*paideia*). It was not an absolute shift: oral performance remained the chief medium for both epideictic and practical discourse. Nevertheless, the written document increasingly became a familiar medium of communication. The *Oxyrhynchus Papyri*, comprising thousands of fragmentary documents from Greco-Roman Egypt, shows literate activity for various purposes and at various levels of skill, ranging from sales contracts, school exercises, and private letters to administrative records, official correspondence, and copies of high-literary texts. More importantly, writing was an instrument for preserving texts: it conferred on any recorded text the perceived permanence and repeatability that had been identified with song. Even a practical oration could be written down, refined, and performed later as an *epideixis*: the audience could not decide the (already decided) case, but they could approve or disapprove, admire or detest, and form attitudes, thus playing the role of an audience in a theater. In this way, even literary representations of practical oratory—polished versions of real speeches as well as imaginary declamations—became part of the realm of epideictic literature (Perelman 1984; see Enos, ch. 13).

There was, in short, from the fifth century BCE onward no longer a compelling reason to compose epideictic discourse only or primarily in verse, other than piety, tradition, or the aesthetico-rhetorical appeal of the echo of antiquity (and the feeling of being contemporaneous with the glorious past)—or, of course, the sheer aesthetic appeal of poetic form. The traditional distinction between epideictic song and practical speech had broken down; now there could be epideictic speech and writing. And from this breakdown arose the new modes of epideictic prose that would become the "modern" literature of the classical age. Meanwhile, poetry remained the name for epideictic discourse composed in verse.

THE PERSISTENCE OF THE ARCHAIC PARADIGM

Traces of the archaic understanding of epideictic and practical suasion, and of poetry and speech (or prose), persisted in the classical rhetorical tradition. Consider, for example, the commonplace notion that poetry preceded prose. If one takes this statement as a claim about the history of language (as did eighteenth-century linguistic theory), it seems ridiculous. But taken as a claim about *the evolution of rhetoric*, it makes more sense. As the first-century geographer Strabo puts it, echoing the Stoic view, "Artistic prose is an imitation of poetic discourse; for poetic artistry came first into the world and was esteemed, and then came [the early pre-Socratic prose writers] Cadmus [of Miletus], Pherecydes, Hecataeus, and their followers, imitating poetry but loosening the meter and keeping the other poetic qualities" (*Geography* 1.2.6). Perhaps, as Burke (1966: 34, 37) suggests, such notions of temporal priority (evolution or "entelechy") are better understood as metaphors for *logical* priority: epideictic is the primary form of rhetoric, and poetry is the primary form of epideictic. As the Second Sophistic rhetorician Hermogenes of Tarsus puts it, "All poetry is, without a doubt, a panegyric affair [*panēgyrikon pragma*], and is the most panegyric of all discourses" (*On Types of Style* 2.10, in Rabe 1913: 389).

But perhaps, again, it is not a matter of either temporal or logical priority but of *developmental* priority. This notion is clearly reflected in the classical curriculum. At the pre-rhetorical stage of grammar (literacy training), students began by reading poetry, above all Homer's *Odyssey* and *Iliad*, followed by other canonical poets. They "disciplined their wits" to understand the poets and recite them properly and observed various grammatical, rhetorical, and poetic features of the text: poetic diction, obscure words and dialects, inflected forms, syntactic structures, tropes and figures, forms of verse, schemes of arrangement, elements of allegory, and so on. The students then moved on to canonical prose writers: historians, philosophers (or philosophic dialogues), and eventually the orators.

Rhetorical training itself had two main stages: first, the *progymnasmata*, or preliminary exercises, in which students practiced basic rhetorical forms; and second, advanced training in practical rhetoric by means of declamation exercises (speeches on fictive cases) in which the basic forms were to be creatively recombined. The *progymnasmata* consisted of a fairly standardized sequence of exercises, starting with the maxim (the pithy saying), *chreia* (the edifying anecdote), fable, and (factual) narrative and continuing through more complex exercises in disputation (refutation and confirmation), encomium, description, comparison, *ēthopoēia* (the speech in character), commonplace (the amplification of a general proposition), thesis (proof of a general proposition), and the proposal of a law (see Heath, ch. 5). These exercises were preparatory to training in practical civic discourse, but they also laid the foundations for the primary epideictic genres recognized in antiquity or in some cases (e.g., the encomium) simply *were* epideictic genres. The encomium, maxim, *chreia*, fable, and *ēthopoēia* exercised the student in prose equivalents of lyric, gnomic, narrative, and dramatic poetry and *would be* poetry if composed in verse. Narrative and description were the main constituents of history writing, while disputation, the commonplace (Gk. *topos koinos*; L. *locus communis*), and the thesis trained students in basic philosophical argument. The proposal of a law was a bridge to declamation but still involved a general principle (the proposed law). Comparison was a means of amplifying one's point in any genre (x is even better, or even worse, than y). And so on. The point is that the *progymnasmata* prepared the student for advanced training in practical rhetoric by providing foundational training in the major forms of epideictic rhetoric. Even the declamation, as an *imaginary speech* for a fictive case, could be regarded as epideictic—and indeed was during the Second Sophistic period (second to fourth centuries CE), when Aristides, Fronto, Polemo, and other sophists regularly performed virtuosic "concert" declamations before large audiences (see Gunderson, ch. 21).

How long students of rhetoric stayed at each level is unclear, but they probably spent one to two years practicing the *progymnasmata* and then another year or two (and possibly more) doing declamation. Isocrates said that most of his students stayed with him for three or four years (*Antidosis* 87). This seems to have been the normal pattern for the rest of antiquity, though some students left the rhetorician's school after just a year or two, usually for financial or personal reasons (Cribiore 2001, 2007). Among those who stayed for the full four years, most did not pursue oratorical careers—did not try cases in the courts or engage in politics—but remained in private life, in various capacities, where their trained sophistication in artful speech and argument gave them some distinction. For many students the *progymnasmata* provided all the rhetorical training they would ever need and were a sufficient foundation for those who aimed at a literary career in poetry, history, philosophy, prose panegyrics, encomia, fictional narratives, and other genres of discourse (see Heath, ch. 5).

Finally, there is the almost constant reference to poetry in the teaching of prose style, and especially prose rhythm, from early to late antiquity. We see it in Aristotle's *Rhetoric*, Dionysius of Halicarnassus's *On the Composition of Words*, Hermogenes's *On Types of Style*, Demetrius's *On Style*, Longinus's *On the Sublime*, and other texts—including texts in the Latin tradition (especially Cicero's *Orator*, which reflects Greek doctrines). In every case, prose rhythm is analyzed in terms of the metrical feet that compose it, with remarks on how it resembles and differs from poetry: the prose writer should compose in rhythmic cadences that incorporate a medley of poetic meters, but the rhythm should not be strictly *in* meter. Poetry thus provided the ancient student of rhetoric with the reference point for learning the art of style (Gk. *lexis*; L. *elocutio*).

In short, epideictic discourse—the old-fashioned poetic genres as well as the newer prose epideictic genres—remained the core of the classical rhetorical tradition, not only as logically or theoretically prior to practical civic discourse but also as developmentally prior in rhetorical education. The educated person was steeped in epideictic rhetoric, including (and starting from) poetry, and to this general training in epideictic was added, for some, approximately two more years of work in declamation.

Aristotle and the Narrowing Path of Poetry

Aristotle's *Poetics* is the single most influential statement on poetics in the Western tradition of literary theory. Yet it is also the most eccentric, perhaps because of Aristotle's effort to work out, in new terms, the blurred relation between poetry/song and epideictic (as well as practical) speech. On one hand, Aristotle focuses on discourses that were in fact composed in verse and performed to musical accompaniment, such as drama (tragedy and comedy) and epic (Homeric narrative). He considers these to have evolved from primitive forms of song performed at festivals, such as encomia, hymns, invectives, and satyr-songs (Aristotle, *Poetics* 4.7–21). On the other hand, he denies the common view that verse or song is the defining feature of poetic discourse. Taking an essentially theatrical view of poetry, Aristotle focuses instead on the *mimēsis* (imitation, representation) of human action (1.1–12), by which he means the representation—and preferably the acting-out—of a *mythos*, a story or fable. (The archaic meaning of *mythos* as speech had faded out by Aristotle's day.) Thus, as he famously maintains, the philosophical poetry of Empedocles is not really poetry at all but physics (natural-scientific theory) set to verse, while prose mimes and Socratic dialogues may well be a kind of poetry in prose.

Aristotle's position makes it questionable whether lyric poems that are essentially speeches in verse can be regarded as "poetry" at all—unless, perhaps, they can be viewed as dramatic monologues excerpted from some background story. Aristotle does not cite a single lyric poet or poem in the *Poetics*, though he cites them repeatedly in the *Rhetoric*. Apparently speeches in verse are rhetoric but not poetry, while storytelling and drama are poetry. (But not rhetoric? A further problem is that Aristotle thinks of rhetoric primarily as practical civic discourse and hence implicitly limits epideictic rhetoric to civic ceremonies like the state funeral oration.) Clearly Solon's political-philosophical elegies are not true poetry by Aristotle's standards. Likewise, the works of Hesiod, Theognis, and any number of other nonnarrative poetries may not count as poetry. On the other hand, it is not clear that a declamation like Gorgias's *Defense of Palamedes* (which certainly is a dramatic monologue) should not be classified as poetry, especially in view of its resemblance to prose mime. Even in a practical oration there is *mimēsis* in the orator's self-presentation, as Aristotle recognizes, if obliquely (see *Rhetoric* 2.1.2–7). In short, Aristotle's categories divide up the field of discourse in ways that are often problematic.

Nevertheless, by later antiquity we find that poetry, while still defined essentially as verse, also tends to be conceptualized—at least in schoolhouse theory, if not in practice—in terms of *mimēsis* and *mythos*, dramatistic representation and narrative fabulation. Thus, Hermogenes can define poetry as "panegyric discourse in meter" (as in the epigraph to this chapter) but still say, in the same passage, things like this:

> Since poetry is an imitation of all things, he who best imitates in artistic language [*lexis*] orators making public speeches and singers singing panegyrics ... and all other characters and actions, that man is the best poet.... [And that is Homer]....
> Typical of poetry, apart from all other literature [*logos*], is meter, both as conventionally understood and as perceived by the naked ear itself. And all mythical subject matters are especially typical of poetry, such as the legends of Cronos and the Titans and the Giants and Zeus ... [or] how Tiresias was changed from man to woman ... [or] how far Achilles jumped.... In general poetry indulges in marvelous tales that are impossible and incredible. (*On Types of Style* 2.10, in Rabe 1913: 389–92; trans. partially based on Wooten 1987: 115–6)

Poetry is thus "panegyric in verse" but also, and more narrowly, an ancient form of it that characteristically deals in "marvelous tales."

The notion of poetry as fable leads also to the notion of poetry as *allegorical* fable. This line of thought surfaces as early as fifth-century BCE Homeric interpretation and develops in the grammatical tradition (see Lamberton 1986; Lamberton and Keaney 1992; Irvine 1994). It is observable, too, in Aristotle.

From one point of view, Aristotle does seem to recognize the rhetorical dimensions of poetry, and not only through his oft-cited statement that the speeches in a drama belong to the art of rhetoric (which, incidentally, implies that they are not poetry) (Aristotle, *Poetics* 6.22, 19.1–6). Most notably, he defines tragedy as a mimesis of events that arouse "pity and fear" (*eleos kai phobos*) in the audience (6.1–4). This implies a persuasive effect. Further, in stressing that this emotional effect is produced through the story—even a bare summary of the plot (14.1–4)—Aristotle further observes that the story must be *probable* (*eikos*) to be effective (9.1–2) and that a "persuasive impossibility" is better than an "unpersuasive possibility" (24.19–20). Finally, there is Aristotle's famous assertion that poetry is "more philosophical" than history because, through its probabilistic rather than realistic narration, it portrays philosophical "universals" or general truths (*ta katholou*; 9.3). Thus, by putting these remarks together, one can arrive at a notion of poetry as a form of argument by example (the particular plot) that achieves persuasiveness through probability and leads the audience to a recognition of the general truths that it embodies while also producing an emotional response to that truth (pity and fear in tragedy). From this point of view, then, poetry is a form of philosophical epideictic that argues a general thesis through the presentation of a probable (if impossible) exemplar story and calls for an attitude in response.

Aristotle, however, also undercuts this view. People, as he says, enjoy watching a poetic imitation because they "learn something" from it. One experiences a flash of recognition—"this is that" (*houtos ekeinos*; Aristotle, *Poetics* 4.1–6). But while everyone is capable of this intellectual pleasure to some degree, those who are not philosophers have a meager capacity for it. Further, he says, if the spectator has not "seen" the thing before, he will not experience this flash of recognition but will enjoy, instead, things like the "workmanship" or the "colors" of the production (4.6), features that Aristotle generally considers superficial and "accessory" to the central poetic pleasure. From this viewpoint, then, the philosophical pleasure of poetry consists of discovering in it a pleasing representation of general truths one already knows, while *hoi polloi* will thrill to spectacle and music, swordfights and costumes, and the like.

This approach, which came to dominate the study of poetry in the grammatical schools, tended to make of poetry a hermeneutic object: the student's role was not to *respond* as much as to *decode* or translate allegorically, discovering the proper *hyponoia* (the "under-thought" or subtext) "hidden" beneath the surface story. Perhaps the most notable example of this tendency was the Neoplatonic reading of Homer's *Odyssey* as an allegory of the soul's return to unity with the One. A handbook titled *The Life and Poetry of Homer*, written by an unknown grammarian and misattributed to Plutarch, discusses Homer's biography, the linguistic and formal features of his poetry, and the various philosophical lessons that his poetry contains—including lessons, such as the Stoic theory of emotion, of which Homer could not have been aware. This point is raised in the closing remarks as proof of Homer's greatness (Keaney and Lamberton 1996)!

The actual Plutarch, in *How the Young Man Should Study Poetry* (collected in *Moralia*), is more sensible but likewise stresses the use of poetry as an introduction to philosophy (*prōtophilosophia*). The young man is to be rendered impervious to poetry's drug-like persuasive charms (especially its sensory and emotional appeal) and taught to recognize the philosophical teachings that it represents by means of fable. Poetry, in short, is philosophical fabulation for minds too young or simple for the rigors of philosophy itself: poetry is the sugar coating on the serious pill of doctrine.

We have, then, two main ancient views of poetry that interpenetrate but are nevertheless distinguishable in theory. On one hand, and more broadly, poetry is an old-fashioned mode of epideictic rhetoric—any kind of it—composed in verse or song. Verse/song is the defining feature. Direct argument in verse, as in Solon's political elegies, is poetry, as are Hesiod's and Homer's epics. On the other hand, and more narrowly, poetry is philosophical fabulation (allegory), which conventionally is composed in verse but need not be. The defining feature is *mimēsis*, representation, and especially allegorical representation. In the former view, poetry is a rhetorical (persuasive) act, and the audience's role is to respond; in the latter view, the poem is a hermeneutic object, and the audience's role is to decode and decipher. The former, broader view of poetry accounts most fully for actual poetic practice from early to late antiquity. But it is the latter, narrower view of poetry that will survive into modernity as the main thread in Western literary theory and criticism.

FURTHER READING

Albert Lord's (1960) *The Singer of Tales* and Walter Ong's (1982) *Orality and Literacy* are foundational texts for the study of pre-literate song and speech practices. Bruno Gentili's (1988) *Poetry and Its Public in Ancient Greece* is an exceptionally insightful examination of the public and civic functions of ancient poetry, as are Thomas Figueira and Gregory Nagy's (1985) *Theognis of Megara* and Leslie Kurke's (1991) *The Traffic in Praise*. See also W. R. Johnson's (1982) *The Idea of Lyric*. Finally, several of the arguments presented in this chapter are developed at greater length in my *Rhetoric and Poetics in Antiquity* (2000).

REFERENCES

Bloch, Maurice, ed. 1975. *Political Language and Oratory in Traditional Society*. New York: Academic Press.

Burke, Kenneth. 1950. *A Rhetoric of Motives*. Berkeley: University of California Press.

Burke, Kenneth. 1966. "Poetics in Particular, Language in General." In *Language as Symbolic Action*, 25–43. Berkeley: University of California Press.

Cole, Thomas. 1991. *The Origins of Rhetoric in Ancient Greece*. Baltimore, MA: Johns Hopkins University Press.

Cribiore, Raffaella. 2001. *Gymnastics of the Mind: Greek Education in Hellenistic and Roman Egypt*. Princeton, NJ: Princeton University Press.

Cribiore, Raffaella. 2007. *The School of Libanius in Late Antique Antioch*. Princeton, NJ: Princeton University Press.

Figueira, Thomas, and Gregory Nagy, eds. 1985. *Theognis of Megara: Poetry and the* Polis. Baltimore, MA: Johns Hopkins University Press.

Figueira, Thomas. 1985. "The *Theognidea* and Megarian Society." In *Theognis of Megara: Poetry and the* Polis, edited by Thomas Figueira and Gregory Nagy, 112–158. Baltimore, MA: Johns Hopkins University Press.

Gentili, Bruno. 1988. *Poetry and Its Public in Ancient Greece, from Homer to the Fifth Century*. Translated by Thomas Cole. Baltimore, MA: Johns Hopkins University Press.

Heath, Malcolm. 2004. *Menander: A Rhetor in Context*. Oxford: Oxford University Press.

Irvine, Martin. 1994. *The Making of Textual Culture:* Grammatica *and Literary Theory, 350–1100*. Cambridge: Cambridge University Press.

Johnson, W. R. 1982. *The Idea of Lyric: Lyric Modes in Ancient and Modern Poetry*. Berkeley: University of California Press.

Keaney, J. J., and Robert Lamberton, eds. and trans. 1996. *[Plutarch]: Essay on the Life and Poetry of Homer*. American Philological Association: American Classical Studies no. 40. Atlanta, GA: Scholars Press.

Kurke, Leslie. 1991. *The Traffic in Praise: Pindar and the Poetics of Social Economy*. Ithaca, NY: Cornell University Press.

Lamberton, Robert. 1986. *Homer the Theologian: Neoplatonist Allegorical Reading and the Growth of the Epic Tradition*. Berkeley: University of California Press.

Lamberton, Robert, and John J. Keaney, eds. 1992. *Homer's Ancient Readers: The Hermeneutics of Greek Epic's Earliest Exegetes*. Princeton, NJ: Princeton University Press.

Lord, Albert B. 1960. *The Singer of Tales*, 2nd ed. Edited by Stephen Mitchell and Gregory Nagy. Cambridge, MA: Harvard University Press.

Morris, Ian. 1996. "The Strong Principle of Equality and the Archaic Origins of Greek Democracy." In *Dēmokratia: A Conversation on Democracies, Ancient and Modern*, edited by Josiah Ober and Charles Hedrick, 19–48. Princeton, NJ: Princeton University Press.

Nagy, Gregory. 1985. "Theognis and Megara: A Poet's Vision of His City." In *Theognis of Megara: Poetry and the* Polis, edited by Thomas Figueira and Gregory Nagy, 22–81. Baltimore, MA: Johns Hopkins University Press.

Ong, Walter. 1982. *Orality and Literacy: The Technologizing of the Word*. London: Methuen.

Perelman, Chaïm, and Lucie Olbrechts-Tyteca. 1969. *The New Rhetoric: A Theory of Argumentation*. Translated by John Wilkinson and Purcell Weaver. Notre Dame, IN: Notre Dame University Press.

Perelman, Chaïm. 1984. "Rhetoric and Politics." *Philosophy & Rhetoric* 17.3: 129–134.

Rabe, Hugo, ed. 1913. *Hermogenis Opera*. Leipzig: Tuebner.

Russell, D. A., and N. G. Wilson, trans. 1981. *Menander Rhetor*. Oxford: Oxford University Press.

Schiappa, Edward. 1991. *Protagoras and* Logos: *A Study in Greek Philosophy and Rhetoric*. Columbia: University of South Carolina Press.

Walker, Jeffrey. 2000. *Rhetoric and Poetics in Antiquity*. New York: Oxford University Press.

Walker, Jeffrey. 2005. "Mime, Comedy, Sophistry: Speculations on the Origins of Rhetoric." *Advances in the History of Rhetoric* 8: 199–210.

Wooten, Cecil, trans. 1987. *Hermogenes' "On Types of Style."* Chapel Hill: University of North Carolina Press.

CHAPTER 7

....

RHETORIC AND TRAGEDY

....

PAUL WOODRUFF

FIFTH-CENTURY Athenian tragedy was more concerned with rhetoric than drama has been since the Renaissance. Many scenes turn on attempts by one character to persuade another. Formal set-piece speeches abound in this genre, as do formal contests of speeches, especially in the format of a trial. As the teaching of rhetoric advances in the fifth century, we find tragic characters making more use of formal rhetorical devices, and, at the same time, we find increasing suspicion directed at clever rhetoric on the part of all concerned.

Nevertheless, audiences evidently loved to witness speaking contests, and we can infer from the frequency of such contests in tragic plays that rhetoric had a central role in entertainment. Some people learned to speak artfully because they hoped the art would prevail in court or assembly, but they also practiced the art so they might delight private audiences. Indeed, artful speaking carries a paradox: when audiences recognize speakers as artful, they generally discount the arguments, although they take pleasure in displays of expertise and explore ideas through the artful display of balanced speeches (Gagarin 2001).

An artful way of beginning a speech is to disclaim all training or experience in public speaking. Plato has Socrates begin his defense speech in the *Apology* with a comment on the elegance of the prosecution's speech, contrasting it with his own ignorance of the language used in court (17a–8a6). Indeed, ancient Greek speakers used the word "artlessly" (*atechnos*) most often to mean "to tell the truth." Thus, in the *Hippolytus* by Euripides, the young hero begins his defense as follows:

> I don't know how to speak pretty words to a crowd;
> I am more clever among a few people my own age.
> That is my assigned fate. Those who are worthless among the wise
> Show more cultivation speaking to the crowd. (986–9)

This is a standard way for practiced orators to diffuse the bad odor of rhetoric; Hippolytus is truly unpracticed in rhetoric, but the speech he will give is a highly polished one, one to delight an audience thirsting for rhetorical display. Successful rhetoric in tragedy, however, is often quite plain. Audiences brought up on Homer expected the plainest speaking to be the most effective; in the embassy scene of Homer's *Iliad* (book 9), Ajax's blunt speech outweighs the fabled artfulness of Odysseus. The fame of this scene in the fifth century made Odysseus come to represent the archetype of the dishonest demagogue; as such, he plays a major role in many of the later tragedies. At the same time, the scene illustrated the importance of a speaker's character. Good character, as in the case of Ajax, easily trumps the rhetorical skill of an Odysseus, and this theme, too, is often sounded in Greek tragedy.

Rhetoric typically tunes a speech to a particular audience—a forensic speech to a jury or a political one to the Assembly. But tragedy addresses speeches simultaneously to multiple audiences. Hippolytus's defense speech is aimed at his father, who is judge and jury. But we shall see that the speech is framed for a crowd: Hippolytus addresses the chorus, and the poet, through him, addresses the audience. Often the chorus stands in for the audience and provides a model for audience response, but sometimes a speech is designed to elicit a different response from one audience than from another. In Ajax's great speech, we shall see that the chorus hears one thing and the audience another. This is the poet's intention, for it enlivens the scene with dramatic irony.

Defining Rhetoric in Tragedy

Rhetoric was probably not defined as such at the time Athenian tragic poetry was first composed. Professional teachers of a wide range of subjects began to visit Athens around the time the tragedies were produced; among their subjects was the art of words (probably not yet known as rhetoric), which became highly popular. By the end of the fifth century, the art of words affected the way virtually every tragic play was written. At some point, probably after Plato attacked it in the fourth century, the art of words taught by these traveling teachers became known as rhetoric, and its teachers became known as sophists (Cole 1991).

Broadly speaking, rhetoric is found wherever words are in use. In this chapter, however, I will use the term for two more specific uses of words—to persuade and to display artfulness. The two uses overlap. Persuasive speech may use art, but it tends to be most effective when its artfulness is not apparent to the listener. Artfulness may be intended to persuade, but it may also be intended to entertain or to educate. A contest (*agōn*) in the art of words is entertaining quite apart from any persuasive effect either side may have, as verbal gymnastics are a delight in themselves. Such a contest may also be educational for both hearers and participants, if it helps them appreciate both sides of a complex issue.

Under artful speech, I include any use of words showing that the speaker has studied the *technē* (art or skill) of words as taught by the teachers who became known as sophists. Under persuasive speech, I include any use of words intended to persuade, whether or not it succeeds and whether or not it is artful. Set-piece speeches and formal contests are obvious cases. Less obvious, but sometimes more effective, are exchanges known as *stichomythia*, in which speakers trade rapid-fire single lines like volleys in table tennis; such exchanges may drive the speakers further apart, but they may also bring them together.

PERSUASION

Persuasion in tragedy is contrasted both with force and deception. When tragic characters act under persuasion, the audience sees them as acting voluntarily—even when their actions are destined by the gods. Philoctetes, in the play by Sophocles that bears his name, is destined to join the Greek army at Troy, but Zeus has apparently arranged matters so that he goes voluntarily, persuaded by his friend Heracles, and neither tricked nor trapped by Odysseus. Similarly, in Sophocles's *Oedipus at Colonus*, we see Oedipus choosing to take actions that lead to his destiny while refusing to be persuaded by his enemies to change course.

Because of its contrast with force, persuasion is endemic to democracy: a tyrant has no need to persuade his people; he has power and force on his side, as does Zeus in the opening of the *Prometheus Bound* (probably a late play of Aeschylus). But power and force do not change anyone's mind, as Prometheus vividly demonstrates. Successful persuasion, however, changes people's minds in a context of freedom. Persuasion is also natural to the theater. Theater represents actions, as Aristotle rightly noted (*Poetics* 6), and actions entail choice. Prometheus did not choose to lie bound to the rock, but once bound he engages in a string of verbal actions that show how free his mind remains. A typical tragic plot is an arrangement of actions—mostly verbal—through which characters influence each other.

The oldest play we have, Aeschylus's *Suppliant Maidens*, opens with a sequence of persuasions; first the suppliants persuade the king of Argos, in a rapid-fire dialogue, that they can prove their descent from Argive stock. Then the king goes off to persuade his people; as he leaves, the king says, "May persuasion go with me" (Aeschylus, *Suppliant Maidens* 523), and evidently it does, because the people vote by a decisive majority to accept the refugees. This vote will save the lives of the suppliants; persuasion on matters such as citizen rights could be a matter of life or death in the democratic culture of Athens—an importance the poet here projects onto his mythical Argos.

Persuasion is no less important in a monarchy, as we learn from the *Agamemnon* when Clytemnestra persuades Agamemnon to tread on weavings that ought to be reserved for gods. First we hear an exchange of speeches, which present the positions of the two sides but leave the situation unchanged (Aeschylus, *Agamemnon* 895–930). Then, in lightning-fast dialogue (931–44), Clytemnestra wins her case through analogy:

If Priam had won the war, he would have done this, so why not you? Clytemnestra ends the exchange with this line, which underscores the contrast between persuasion and force: "Be persuaded; you rule but you can willingly yield to me" (944).

Both of these early successes in persuasion are in the form of *stichomythia*—an exchange of single lines in which a question is asked and answered or a keyword or concept is served and volleyed. For example:

> CLYTEMNESTRA. What do you *suppose* Priam would do if he had won?
> AGAMEMNON. He would have stepped on the tapestry I *suppose*.
> CLYTEMNESTRA. So do not now have respect for blame from *human beings*.
> AGAMEMNON. But the clamor of the *people* has great power.
>
> (Aeschylus, *Agamemnon* 935–8; emphasis added)

Other playwrights use the device in scenes of attempted or successful persuasion. In Euripides's *Hecuba*, the Trojan queen uses *stichomythia* to persuade her enemy to enter the tent where she will take vengeance on him (990–1018).

In Sophocles's *Antigone*, however, *stichomythia* drives characters apart as they become more firmly entrenched in opposition. The opening scene, a line-on-line exchange between Antigone and Ismene, drives a wedge between the sisters as Antigone makes a rhetorical case (Bers 1994: 185–6). Later, Creon debates with the prophet Tiresias and ends with the line, "You'll never collect your fee; I am not changing my mind" (Sophocles, *Antigone* 1048–63). But he will change his mind after Tiresias's set-piece speech followed by the endorsement of the Chorus.

Set-piece speeches are a common feature of Greek tragedy. They often use the art of speaking as taught by the traveling teachers later known as sophists, but, as we shall see, set speeches often fail to persuade. Character is often more decisive than skill in tragedy. In *Antigone*, Creon does not trust his son because he is young, in love, and buffeted by irrational emotion, and the Chorus agrees with him (Sophocles, *Antigone* 756, 781–805). Later, Creon distrusts Tiresias because of his general distrust of prophets, who, he believes, are easily bribed (1045–7). But he trusts the Chorus for the wisdom he expects them to have in virtue of their character as older citizens (162–9, 1091–9).

PAIRED SPEECHES (*AGŌNES*)

Most often, set-piece speeches come in pairs, arranged as for a trial or contest (*agōn*). The first great trial scene in the history of Western theater is in Aeschylus's *Eumenides* (*Furies*). Here the furies deliver their argument through cross-examination by *stichomythia*, while Apollo's defense takes the form of a speech (583–673). Evidently the arguments are equally powerful, because the jury divides evenly and the issue must be resolved by Athena's vote. A generation later, Sophocles gives us a balanced pair of speeches between Creon and his son in *Antigone*; the two speeches are the same length and use similar types of argument (639–723).

Euripides builds a number of his plays around contests in forensic style. His *Trojan Women* presents the trial of Helen; here the defense speaks first, and then Hecuba prosecutes successfully, appealing to *eikos*, what is likely (914–1032). In *Andromache*, we have trial-like contests between Hermione and Andromache (147–231) as well as between Peleus and Menelaus (590–690). The *Hecuba* puts Polymestor and Hecuba both on trial, simultaneously over his crime against her and her vengeance against him. This time the arguments are not balanced, and Agamemnon, serving as judge, delivers a verdict in favor of Hecuba (1132–237). In the *Hippolytus*, Theseus is both prosecutor and judge for the trial of his own son and fails to be moved by the boy's stirring formal defense speech (936–1035).

Such contests in Euripides often illustrate the weakness of rhetoric. Hecuba wins her case against Helen in *Trojan Women*, but that will make no difference in the long run; Helen is too beautiful to ride home in a boat with Menelaus and not win forgiveness without argument. As for Hippolytus, no eloquence could save him, for all his innocence, because a jealous goddess has clouded his father's mind with anger.

The paired speeches of tragedy are often of more or less the same length (Lloyd 1992: 5–6), just as the lengths of speeches at trials in Athens were regulated by the water clock. Paired speeches are also often balanced in argument as well, equally strong, so that the contest between them serves not to decide the issue but to expose different views clearly to the audience, as in the case of Creon and Haemon in *Antigone* (Sophocles, *Antigone* 639–723). The arguments on both sides are similar in style and strength; the Chorus, acting as jury, declares that both sides spoke well and should listen to each other (724–5 with 681–2). That is good advice to give the citizen audience of a democracy. Athenian history shows what mistakes are made when one side does not hear from the other, as happened when the antiwar party gave up the debate as the Assembly decided to make disastrous war on Syracuse (Thucydides, *The Peloponnesian War* 6.19; cf. 7.48).

Thucydides's *The Peloponnesian War* is structured as a prose tragedy, with ineffective formal debates, proud overreaching by both sides, and disastrous outcomes for all concerned. Although the Spartans heard a finely argued four-part debate before going to war with Athens (Thucydides, *The Peloponnesian War* 1.68–86), their decision to go to war was based not on the reasons stated in the speeches but on the fear they felt of Athenian expansion (1.88). Their king, Archidamus, had truly predicted trouble—rather like Tiresias in the stage tragedies—but he was not heard, and the Spartans set a course for an expensive defeat in the first phase of the war. Thucydides writes the speeches not to explain events but to lay out the different ways the parties justified their actions to themselves and each other and, at the same time, to foreshadow the disastrous future (see Carey, ch. 4). As it is in history, told by a tragic historian, so it is on stage, shown by a tragic poet. Writers introduce paired speeches not so much to move the action of the play or story as to entertain and instruct through the exposure of different well-argued points of view.

ARTFUL SPEAKING

Artful speech tends to begin formally with a gambit designed to deflect suspicion of artfulness, as we have seen in the case of Hippolytus. Artful speech of the period often uses arguments based on what is likely or reasonable to believe (*eikos*), an appeal that was fashionable in the law courts as well as on the stage (Gagarin 1994; see Gagarin, ch. 2). In Euripides's *Alcestis*, Alcestis uses a formal speech to persuade her husband not to remarry after her death, using the argument that a stepmother would be likely to harm their children.

In forensic contexts, the appeal to *eikos* is not so successful. In the absence of clear evidence, a defendant is taught to plead the unlikeliness of his guilt. In effect, he asks, "Why would I do a thing like that?" He canvasses various possible explanations and shows that all are unlikely. An elegant example is the defense speech of Creon, in Sophocles's *Oedipus Tyrannus*, against the charge that he has plotted to take power from Oedipus and set himself up as tyrant. He argues that his privileges as brother in the royal house are all that anyone would reasonably want; it is therefore unlikely that he would want to trade those privileges for the burdens and fears of tyranny (Sophocles, *Oedipus Tyrannus* 583–615). He ends his speech with a string of gnomic proverbs, also a staple of artful speech. Although the chorus is moved, Oedipus is not convinced; only the power of his wife, Jocasta, will deter him from punishing Creon. Artful speaking fails.

Hippolytus, in Euripides's play of that name, is accused of abusing his young stepmother, Phaedra, on the basis of her suicide note, although it was she who made advances to him. He has sworn to Phaedra that he will not reveal her secret. True to his oath, he has no recourse but to appeal first to his chaste character and then, if that is not convincing, to what is likely. He asks, in effect: "Why would I do this? She is not the most beautiful of women. Would I have done it in order to seize power by marrying the queen?" And here he advances an argument that mirrors Creon's: it is more sensible to enjoy the second rank, without the danger of kingship. Therefore, he implies, it is unlikely I would have done that of which I am accused.

The structure of the speech also illustrates an artful method: the piling or layering of argument on argument. If one argument does not persuade you, try this one. An artful speaker may use a variety of hypotheses, as Gorgias does in his famous encomium of Helen, all of which point toward innocence. The effect of piling arguments in this way is not so much persuasive as it is impressive; it shows the power and range of the speaker, and Hippolytus does that. He ends his defense by taking a powerful oath sparkling with the verbal fireworks taught by sophists—rhymes, rhythms, and repetitions that resound in the ear of the audience.

Hippolytus faced stiff headwinds: the goddess Aphrodite was against him. But the play seems to show that he would have lost in any case. Artful speech almost never succeeds in tragedy or in real life. The best defense speech Thucydides had ever known failed to save the life of Antiphon, the Athenian sophist and orator (*The Peloponnesian War* 8.68). Hippolytus's defense speech (Euripides, *Hippolytus* 983–1035) illustrates most of the techniques taught by professionals like Antiphon: formal opening, layering of argument, *eikos*, and verbal pyrotechnics (Hesk 2000: 286–7). Like Creon, however, he persuades the chorus but leaves the king as angry as before. Hippolytus will die because the art of speaking has failed to dispel anger.

Reflections on Rhetoric and Rhetoricians

Athenian audiences were of two minds about rhetoric. They knew that, as an alternative to force, persuasion is essential to democracy as well as to the harmony that any successful city-state requires. At the same time, they felt that rhetoric is dangerous: in the Assembly it can lead to bad policy, while in court it can convict an innocent person or exonerate a guilty one. In an argument with his brother Menelaus, Agamemnon voices a sentiment that Athenian audiences would applaud: "A tongue that's clever [*sophos*] is hateful" (Euripides, *Iphigenia at Aulis* 333). And after Jason delivers a speech in justification of his second marriage, Medea begins her answer with an attack on his kind of rhetoric:

> I think anyone who, while being unjust, has a talent
> For speaking cleverly deserves the greatest punishment,
> For by bragging that he can cloak injustice with his tongue
> He leads himself to dare any wrongdoing. But he is not all that clever.
>
> (Euripides, *Medea* 580–4)

By the last line she means that she has seen through his cloak of rhetoric, and she foreshadows here the dreadful punishment she will bring upon him.

Attitudes to rhetoric coalesce in the tragic period around the figure of Odysseus. Known as clever and deceptive from the Homeric epics, Odysseus comes to embody the rhetorical cleverness that Athenian audiences and their poets loved to hate. In Euripides's plays, Odysseus is the sort of crowd-pleasing speaker who can lead an assembly to vote for an evil course of action. He has "a shifty nature with the crowd" and is "the sweet-worded people-pleaser" who swings the vote of the Greek army to sacrificing the life of Hecuba's daughter, Polyxena (*Iphigenia at Aulis* 526, *Hecuba* 131–40 [cf. 256–7]). He is also the politician who talks the army into voting for the death of Hector's son, Astyanax (Euripides, *Trojan Women* 721). With his "double-talking tongue" he turns friends into enemies, as Hecuba complains (286–7; cf. 1224–5).

But Odysseus's rhetoric is not all bad. Sophocles shows its good side in his *Ajax* and its questionable side in his *Philoctetes*. The *Ajax*, probably an early play, begins after

Odysseus has won a contest over Ajax for possession of the armor of Achilles, which was to go to the best soldier of the Greeks. Ajax felt he should have won in virtue of his huge size and strength, along with his bravery, loyalty, and success on the battlefield. But the army had held the contest in trial format, with a jury that voted for Odysseus after hearing speeches on both sides. Ajax was convinced that Odysseus won by trickery, calling him a "smooth fox" (Sophocles, *Ajax* 103), and Ajax's brother suspects that the jury's vote was fixed (1135–6). Athenian audiences probably felt, as Ajax did, that a contest of words was the wrong way to settle this question of valor and that Odysseus had used tricky rhetoric to win a prize that belonged rightfully to someone else. But all of that is before the play opens.

The play itself deals with the consequences of Ajax's rage over the outcome of the contest. He attempts to kill King Agamemnon and the wily Odysseus, but a god foils him. Now doubly ashamed, he sees only one way to save his honor—suicide. His wife and soldiers also see this and watch him closely. But in his hour of need Ajax finds himself master of Odysseus's art of speaking and delivers a brilliant speech with the sort of double meaning that audiences loved (Sophocles, *Ajax* 646–92); indeed, it is the finest example of double-meaning rhetoric in the surviving plays of Sophocles. The *audience* hears that Ajax is determined to take his life, but his *wife* and friends take his words in another sense and are overjoyed to set their fears aside (693). They let Ajax go unwatched, and he dies on his own sword.

Odysseus in this play is a sympathetic character. He shows his compassion for Ajax in the prologue, even though Ajax has tried to kill him (Sophocles, *Ajax* 121–6). Now, after Ajax's death, he steps in to save Ajax's honor from another threat. As one who has attempted to take the king's life, he is subject to the most severe penalty—the dishonoring of his body through nonburial. But Odysseus speaks persuasively for compassion and wins over the king (1332–73).

The play strikes some scholars as broken-backed, with a new plot developing after the death of Ajax. But we can read the entire play as a single-thread commentary on Odysseus's victory by rhetoric in the contest. The play shows that rhetoric is indeed more powerful than valor on the battlefield. Even Ajax needed rhetoric to evade the suicide watch, and even Ajax needed Odysseus to use rhetoric to save him from the ultimate dishonor. In this play, Odysseus deserved to win, although according to the prevailing view in Greece at the time he did not.

From an ethical standpoint, the play associates compassion with rhetoric through the figure of Odysseus, who is a champion of compassion and a master of rhetoric. Indeed, compassion and rhetoric are connected; the students of rhetoric—especially if they have Protagoras for a teacher—learn to argue both sides of an issue, and therefore they learn to understand views other than their own. Rhetorical training in ancient Greece often put students into the imagined situations of others, so that ancient audiences would not have been surprised to see Odysseus's verbal acuity linked to a capacity for compassion (see Heath, ch. 5; Webb, ch. 22).

Understanding is at the root of compassion as represented in ancient Greek tragic plays. The word for it is *syngnomosyne* (knowledge-with); it is a distinctly human virtue not exercised by the gods, because it requires one to imagine oneself in the situation of another human being (Sophocles, *Women of Trachis* 1264–9). When Odysseus shows compassion for Ajax, the goddess Athena markedly does not (Sophocles, *Ajax* 118–26). He knows that he is vulnerable (as the goddess is not), and he has sharpened his imagination for the suffering of others along with his verbal acuity.

By contrast, Odysseus sides with the gods in Sophocles's *Philoctetes*, one of his last plays. Here he shows no compassion and is perhaps less attractive, although he is working overtime for the benefit of the army. The plot turns on the problem of persuading the archer Philoctetes to rejoin the army at Troy after being marooned by the army in a deserted place for nine years. Odysseus is given the mission, and the son of Achilles, Neoptolemus, is assigned to assist him.

As a persuasive speaker, Odysseus faces a monstrous challenge in this play. Philoctetes is wounded in body and soul, absolutely determined never to join the army again. He is also consumed with hatred for Odysseus, who had persuaded the army to maroon him in the first place. It was to meet this challenge that the Greek leadership teamed Odysseus with Achilles's son, Neoptolemus. Achilles is as famous for honesty as Odysseus is famous for devious rhetoric, and everyone, including the youth, assumes that Neoptolemus has inherited his father's perfect honesty. So Odysseus's first task will be to teach an honest youth to be devious, while leaving him with the appearance of honesty.

Neoptolemus has just reached military age. Under the tutelage of the wily Odysseus, he would have reminded an Athenian audience of their own young sons who flocked to learn rhetoric at the feet of the sophists. What Odysseus offers the youth looks like the sort of education Aristophanes attacks in *The Clouds*, which promises to teach young people how to win arguments for false causes, clearing a family of debts, for example, that they deserve to pay (see O'Regan, ch. 8). If Odysseus succeeds, then his lies will come through the mouth of a youth believed to be honest. Good character and knavery will be united in successful persuasion.

Only persuasion will do in this case. Philoctetes is armed with the bow of Heracles, an unconquerable weapon that is destined to win the war at Troy but meanwhile allows Philoctetes to defend himself against any force the Greeks might use against him. In any case, Zeus's destiny requires that Philoctetes go of his own volition, freely persuaded. The plot therefore sets up a test case for persuasion against heavy odds. Philoctetes is determined to resist, but he is up against a masterly wordsmith who will deliver his message through an artless young man. If any rhetoric can win the day, it would be skillful words delivered by a man of flawless character. Odysseus teaches the young man to suspend his honest character for a day and deliver a whopping lie. He does not teach artful speaking to the young man—that would undermine the value of his character. All he teaches him is the necessity of lying.

And lie the young man does, right up through the last scene, when he is still maintaining that Odysseus stole his father's armor (Woodruff 2012: 137; cf. Buxton 1982: 124). In the end, however, it will not be lies that win the day; it will be friendship. Philoctetes's one true friend, Heracles, will appear as if he were *deus ex machina*, but although Heracles had risen to divine status on his death, it is not his divinity that brings Philoctetes to trust him. After all, the gods of the Greeks can be as mendacious as Odysseus. But Heracles would never lie to his trusted friend.

Persuasion (*peithō*) is one thing; Odysseus's deception is another—a trick (*dolos*). The play ends with a true case of persuasion, and we are left to wonder whether tricking Philoctetes into returning would have met the need. Probably not: persuasion aims to build harmony, deception does not do so in the long run. Once he realized he had been tricked, Philoctetes would not be a willing soldier in an army he deems hostile to himself. He is armed with the most effective weapon of all, he is angry, and he is dangerous. Sophocles suggests the point but does not make it explicit: genuine persuasion excludes the use of lies. The true persuader, his audience believed, needs no art, but only the truth to tell and a character worthy of trust.

Further Reading

Buxton (1982) offers a fine overview of plays and scenes that make persuasion central. Bers (1994) provides a clear introduction and detailed discussions of rhetoric in the *Agamemnon* and *Antigone*. Halliwell (1997) shows how the rhetoric of tragic characters changes as they move from public personae to private recognitions of their tragic status; he also explores the rhetoric of characters in conflict. McDonald's (2007) essay is illuminating and comprehensive, covering fragments and fourth-century tragedy as well as the canon that has survived. Goldhill (1997) provides sophisticated discussions of rhetoric in several of the previously discussed plays, notably the *Philoctetes*.

References

Bers, Victor. 1994. "Tragedy and Rhetoric." In *Persuasion: Greek Rhetoric in Action*, edited by Ian Worthington, 176–195. London: Routledge.

Buxton, R. G. A. 1982. *Persuasion in Greek Tragedy: A Study of* Peitho. Cambridge: Cambridge University Press.

Cole, Thomas. 1991. *The Origins of Rhetoric in Ancient Greece*. Baltimore, MA: Johns Hopkins University Press.

Gagarin, Michael. 1994. "Probability and Persuasion: Plato and Early Greek Rhetoric." In *Persuasion: Greek Rhetoric in Action*, edited by Ian Worthington, 46–68. London: Routledge.

Gagarin, Michael. 2001. "Did the Sophists Aim to Persuade?" *Rhetorica* 19: 275–291.

Goldhill, Simon. 1997. "The Language of Tragedy: Rhetoric and Communication." In *The Cambridge Companion to Greek Tragedy*, edited by P. E. Easterling, 127–150. Cambridge: Cambridge University Press.

Halliwell, Stephen. 1997. "Between Public and Private: Tragedy and the Athenian Experience of Rhetoric." In *Greek Tragedy and the Historian*, edited by Christopher Pelling, 121–141. Oxford: Clarendon Press.

Hesk, Jon. 2000. *Deception and Democracy in Classical Athens*. Cambridge: Cambridge University Press.

Lloyd, Michael. 1992. *The Agon in Euripides*. Oxford: Clarendon Press.

McDonald, Marianne. 2007. "Rhetoric and Tragedy: Weapons of Mass Persuasion." In *A Companion to Greek Rhetoric*, edited by Ian Worthington, 473–485. Oxford: Blackwell.

Woodruff, Paul. 2012. "The *Philoctetes* of Sophocles." In *A Companion to Sophocles*, edited by Kirk Ormand, 126–140. Hoboken, NJ: Wiley-Blackwell.

CHAPTER 8

....

RHETORIC AND OLD COMEDY

....

DAPHNE O'REGAN

By the last quarter of the fifth century BCE, sophistic speculation and persuasive practice, and varying reactions to it, seemed to be everywhere in Athens—Assembly, courts, street corners, homes, and, of course, the stage—and comedians were mining this marked feature of contemporary life. Contemporary comedies were familiar with rhetorical technique, and sophists and their patrons were part of the comic repertoire (Hubbard 1997, 2007; Carey 2000; Storey 2003: 179, 197, 321–7).

Three comedies staged at the Great Dionysia of 423 BCE showcased conflicting approaches to the new sophistic intelligentsia and the art of skillful speech, including comedy. Ameipsias's *Konnos* featured a chorus of thinkers, Socrates, and Konnos, Socrates's music teacher. However, Ameipsias, like most comic dramatists, muted the sophists' novelty by integrating them into the generic crowd of social parasites or "non-productive intellectuals who aspire to influence in society" (Carey 2000: 422, 426, 429–30; Storey 2003: 193). In response to Aristophanes's insulting jokes the year before, Cratinus staged himself and his art, "Comedy," as a married couple threatened by his affair with the floozy, "Drunkenness." Cratinus's play emphasized his self-portrayal as an Archilochean poet inspired by wine to pour out irresistible streams of poetry (*Pytine* 128; Biles 2002: 172–6; Bakola 2008: 11–20). Although his play was innovative in topic and perhaps form (Revermann 2006b: 95–106), association with Aeschylus and notions of divine inspiration branded Cratinus as representing a traditional paradigm of skillful speech and its claim to benefit the city (Bakola 2010: 25–9).

Aristophanes's entry, the first version of *The Clouds*, shared subject matter with his competitors—Socrates and artful speech, including comedy—but Aristophanes's engagement with the sophistic intelligentsia and their rhetoric was unique (Carey 2000: 430). The year before, he created a new theatrical form—the demagogue comedy—when he devoted the entire *Knights* to an attack on Cleon, leader of Athens, and the rhetoric widely believed to be the basis of his political power. Further, in contrast to his rivals, Aristophanes was building a comic persona notoriously intrigued by the latest intellectual innovations and, in particular, those of Euripides, a dramatist closely associated with the sophists and their novel theories (*Testimonia* 3, 4, in

Kassell and Austin 1998; Biles 2002; Bakola 2008). A famous neologism by Cratinus, "Euripidaristophanizing," played off this approach, implying that for the sophisticated theatergoer who enjoyed hyper-subtlety Euripides and Aristophanes seemed one and the same (Cratinus, *Pytine* 342, in Kassell and Austin 1998). Such association with Euripides signaled affiliation with "cultural, social, and political innovation and subversion" (Bakola 2010: 66). The *Clouds* continued Aristophanes's project. Although the plot is lost, it probably staged the power of sophistic theory and persuasive practice, ending with the triumph of an avant-garde son over a traditional father (Dover 1968: lxxx). Aristophanes's comic innovation reflected his subject matter. Modeling sophistic claims for the power of rhetoric and underlining a similar claim for the potency of his own wit, the first *Clouds* seems to have abandoned traditional elements of Old Comedy—slapstick violence, screams, movement, dangling phallus, and lewd dancing—in favor of verbal humor alone (Aristophanes, *Clouds* 537). Like its subject, play and playwright are *sophos* (522) and *sophizethai* ("clever or subtle," echoing *sophistēs*, or "sophist"; 547), replete with novel ideas and clever images that require equally clever spectators (520). Thus, Aristophanes hoped to exploit the common ground between comedy and sophistic practice to win.

Comic drama and the art of persuasive speaking had deep roots in the democratic *polis* (Pseudo-Xenophanes, *Constitution of the Athenians* 2.18; Plato, *Gorgias* 502; Poulakos 1995: 13–5; Henderson 1998; Yunis 1998). Most obviously, they shared an audience—a varying subset of the people of Athens—and a competitive context: the audience, or their representatives, would choose the victor. To prevail, speakers and poets relied on similar rhetorical techniques to produce verbal pleasure (*tērpsis*). As Gorgias famously observed in *Helen*, in a world of opinion (*doxa*) words sway the soul, and the most persuasive speaker therefore commands allegiance and action. The power of speech was closely tied to techniques of composition (meter, elaborate figures, and word choice), innovative ideas, and emotional appeals that would stun the hearers and impress their souls (DK [= Diels and Kranz 1969] 82 A 1.2, 2, 4, 32, B 5a, 15, 16; 83 A 5; 84 A 10; 85 A 1, 12, 13, B 6). The *Helen* explicitly ties this model of verbal power to the experience of poetry, including drama, as well as astronomical, political, and philosophical debate (DK 82 B 11.9, 13).

Although Gorgias links the deception (*apatē*) inherent in rhetoric and tragic drama (DK 82 B 23; Segal 1962), the sophists were also closely linked with comedy and mockery. Plato's *Euthydemus* represents reactions to sophistic displays as including laughter and applause provoked by witty sallies and decisive points (267b7, 303b2). Aristotle's analysis of wit, metaphor, and simile in the *Rhetoric* leaves no doubt of the overlap between comedy and use of jokes to diminish an opponent or shore up a position (1406b, 1412, 1413a). Tradition preserves jokes by others (DK 80 A 25; 82 A 15, 23, 24; 85 A 5), but humor seems to have been particularly associated with Gorgias. His art of rhetoric famously advised speakers "to destroy the seriousness of the opposite parties by laughter and the humor by seriousness" (DK 82 B 12), and this advice is the heart of Aristotle's brief discussion of jokes in *Rhetoric* (1419b). Ancient and modern commentators also find Gorgias's use of language to be playful, in keeping with his identification of *Helen* as a *paignion*, a jocular game (DK 82 B 11.21). Not surprisingly, the sophists' humor seems to have been highly verbal, employing, like their other persuasive strategies, neologisms, changes of register, puns, comic inversion, personifications, and manipulation of myth (Schiappa 1999: 90–1; Consigny 2001: 177–83). Of course, these are also the verbal resources of the comic stage (see Enders, ch. 29).

Topical comedy and persuasive speech also rely on timely exploitation of the immediate context, or *kairos*. Tradition records that Protagoras first wrote about its power (DK 80 A 1); Gorgias also discussed *kairos* as the opportune moment for persuasion (DK 82 A 1, 12a, B 13). Context and audience shape speech in any competitive situation in which participants are judged on a single performance. But *kairos* and invention play a particularly important role when speech aims to fashion a new world, whether comic, speculative, or political (see Cassin, ch. 11). Creators of new norms, be they adultery or a separate peace, cannot rely on the familiar. Like the extemporaneous jokes of the sophists, which turned mockery back against its speaker to win over the audience and earn praise, not blame (DK 80 A 25), topical Old Comedy emerged from the exigencies of the moment. Virtuosic display of kairotic invention underlay sophistic claims to speak *ex tempore* on any topic (DK 82 A 1a; 85 A 8; Poulakos 1995: 29–31). The same value prompted the common charges of plagiarism exchanged among comic poets (e.g., *Clouds* 545; Heath 1990: 151–2; Slater 1999: 363).

Comedy and sophistic speculation and persuasion also shared a programmatic reliance on man as a human animal focused on the appetites, food, and sex. Comic ugliness—padded costume, distorted mask, prominent phallus, robust and obscene language—provided generic branding, allowing comedy to appropriate "any character as its own" (Henderson 1991, 1993; Revermann 2006b: 147, 149; Robson 2006: 70–94) and exploit the resulting discrepancies and bodily humor. The sophists' natural man likewise functioned as a sort of trademark, providing arguments from the opposition of culture (*nomos*) and nature (*physis*) in many arenas. Further, comic drama and sophistic argumentation required similar mental gymnastics. Ian Ruffell argues that comedy, unlike tragedy, "demands the manipulation of abstract and general concepts, requiring a great deal of cognitive work which is linked through work across the comic episodes" (Ruffell 2008: 51). The interplay of comic particulars and broad concepts across contexts resolves into the "surprising or implausible that is at the heart of this sort of humour" (53). Sophistic argument relies on similar moves: the audience's ability and desire to follow the manipulation of categories and particulars to end up at something new.

Thus, Aristophanes's first *Clouds* was perfect for the Athenians, whom the Thucydidean Cleon famously charged with attending the Assembly as if spectators of a sophistic display (*epideixis*), addicted to innovative verbal technique and overcome by the pleasure of hearing clever, beautiful discourse (see Woodruff, ch. 7). These slaves of novelty approved speeches about public affairs not for their content but for their style and technical execution (Thucydides, *The Peloponnesian War* 3.36). Such an audience should have delivered a smash victory for Aristophanes. Instead, his *Clouds* came in third. Whatever the real reasons, Aristophanes blames the spectators: they were too boorish to appreciate his innovative, rhetorically sophisticated play (*Clouds* 524; *Wasps* 104).

The first *Clouds'* defeat revealed an unsuspected fragility of speech, a profound gap between verbal resources and what is actually required to win. The revised, second *Clouds* (the version that survives) is Aristophanes's response to this problem. In this play, an ordinary Athenian, Strepsiades, attempts to harness the power of sophistic persuasion to avoid paying the debts of his son, Pheidippides. Strepsiades enters Socrates's school of sophistry (the "Thinkery," *phrontistērion*), fails his lessons, enrolls his son instead, violently drives away the creditors, and is in turn beaten by the newly sophistic Pheidippides. Persuaded by his son that beating one's father is just, Strepsiades becomes enraged when Pheidippides offers to prove that beating one's mother is also just. He ends the play by burning the school, Socrates, and his students. The play features a chorus of female clouds and common structural conventions of Old Comedy, including a debate or *agōn* between the old, stronger, just argument and the new, weaker, unjust argument (which the weaker argument seems to win) as well as direct address to the audience by the chorus, both as clouds and as "Aristophanes," who takes the stage to denounce the defeat of his first *Clouds*. Although not all differences between the first and second *Clouds* are known, the debate between the arguments, the discussion of the first *Clouds*, and the violent ending are new (Dover 1968: lxxx). Thus, our *Clouds* stages the failure of *logos*, not its triumph, in a comedy replete with the generic violence and vulgarity missing in the first version.

The revised *Clouds* exploits the resources of comedy to stage the corrosive interaction of sophistic theory and natural/comic man. From the first (94–199), Aristophanes's sophists—the "sage souls" (*psychon sophon*) Socrates and his students—enact the philosophical detachment from the body that is traditionally a precondition of the life of the mind. Socrates's students starve as they pursue their studies. Socrates explains his own entrance, dangling on high in a basket, as an attempt to escape the pull of earthly forces that rule the body and cheat the mind of its discoveries: "I tread the air and scrutinize the sun" (Aristophanes, *Clouds* 225; trans. Henderson). His signature interest, investigation of the heavens, has yielded a striking insight into cosmology: the sky is a fiery oven lid over the earth. The subsequent lesson on thunder—revealed to be not the voice of Zeus but the noise of clouds propelled by natural forces—makes Socrates's atheism explicit. "Whirl? That's a new one on me," confesses Strepsiades, "that there's no Zeus and instead whirl [*dinos*] is ruling at this point" (380). The orientation is familiar. Gorgias, Protagoras, and others offended contemporaries when their celestial investigations replaced the divine with natural causes and forces. The curriculum of the Thinkery comically retraces that of Pericles, who was believed to owe his rhetorical prowess to Anaxagoras (nicknamed *Nous*, "Mind"), the philosopher who liberated Pericles from religious fears by teaching him that the sun was a hot rock and thunder the sound of clouds banging together (Plutarch, *Life of Pericles* 4). The disappearance of the divine is paralleled by an equally significant change in man: congruent with their oven world, men are mere coals, subject to the universal laws of nature (O'Regan 1992: 27–9).

Comedy, as well as (parodic) philosophy, shapes the introduction of the sophists in the *Clouds*. All characters, including the sage souls, sport the comic costume, emphasizing belly and phallus; lessons about sophistic, natural man are to be delivered by a comic one. Juxtaposition of the sage souls' philosophical orientation and their costumes invokes traditional mockery of pretentious intellectuals who think, quite wrongly, that they have left the body behind (Carey 2000: 428). Thales was ridiculed by his servant girl when, while looking up at the stars, he fell down a well (Plato, *Theaetetus* 74a2). Eupolis castigated Protagoras for putting on false airs about the heavens but eating from the earth, and leveled a similar charge against Socrates (DK 80 A 11; Eupolis 157, 386, in Kassell and Austin 1998; Storey 2003: 184–8). Our Socrates reenacts the fate of Thales in an even more absurd form: he is cheated of a celestial discovery when lizard shit falls from the roof onto his upturned face. "He was investigating the moon's paths and revolutions," a pupil tells Strepsiades, "and then, down from the roof, at night, a lizard shat [*katachezo*] while he was gaping upward " (Aristophanes, *Clouds* 171–3). Signature sophistic discoveries, oven world and coal men, have a comic genesis as well. Cratinus mocked Hippon for a similar theory, and the joke was recycled by Aristophanes in *Birds* (1000 [*scholium*]; Dover 1968: 96). In *Clouds* (97) a conspicuous comic pun, already familiar from *Acharnians* (336), transforms *anthropoi* (men) into *anthrakes* (coals) (O'Regan 1992: 29–30).

This is the comic and sophistic background for what Strepsiades needs: the ability to win any argument, whether just or unjust (Aristophanes, *Clouds* 98). His phrasing transparently refers to Protagoras's famous claim to make the weaker into the stronger argument in a world where only man remains to measure value and confer meaning (DK 80 B 1, 4, 6). Strepsiades's identification of the weaker with the unjust argument comically deforms Protagoras's original formula and underlines the role of skill in the outcome of debate. Strepsiades's goal—to learn the unjust argument that repays nothing—is the antithesis of a traditional Greek definition of justice: "To say true things and to return whatever someone should take" (Plato, *Republic* 331d). The project and Strepsiades's probable success as a comic hero, however unsavory, echo contemporary controversy about sophistic speech and confirm its tremendous power (O'Regan 1992: 31–3).

But Strepsiades's phrasing invokes another familiar image crucial to the interplay of sophistic rhetoric and contemporary comedy in ancient Athens: what Strepsiades desires and the chorus proffers are the tactics of a verbal brawl ("tongue warfare," *glotte polemizon*; 417; cf. 316–21), reflecting the programmatic imagery that advertised claims about the power of sophistic rhetoric and its revolutionary potential. The image may have originated with Protagoras's seminal works, *Kataballontes Logoi* (*Overthrowing Arguments*) and *Peri Pales* (*On Wrestling*), which featured arguments to overcome the arguments of experts in different fields (DK 80 A 1, B 8; Poulakos 1995: 32–8). As Gorgias's *Helen* makes even clearer, this image both analogizes *logos* to force (DK 82 B 11.6) and asserts its superiority in achieving the speaker's goals. As the Platonic Gorgias points out, "Persuasion differs much from the other arts—for it makes all things slaves to itself willingly, but not through force, and is by far the best of all the arts" (*Philebus* 58a6). A famous comic image from 417 BCE likening Pericles's persuasive power to a winner in a race (Eupolis 102, in Kassell and Austin 1998; Storey 2003: 114) clarifies the implications of this view of rhetoric: skillful speech replaces traditional elite competition as a source of pride and admiration, providing a new vehicle for the display of heroic virtues (DK 82 B 8, 19) and a unique avenue to political power and its spoils. Pericles's words drive his listeners like an aristocratic charioteer drives his horses. In the process, however, listeners are reduced to animals, bewitched and goaded at the will of another.

Not surprisingly, this view of persuasion as compulsion struck at the heart of democratic ideology by turning one of its central mechanisms—public debate—into a form of tyranny (Plato, *Gorgias* 456c; Euripides, *Hecuba* 814). Plato mockingly compares the all-powerful word in the Assembly to a dagger, carrying no more moral value and the same utility (*Gorgias* 469c8). A well-known joke by Pericles's political rival, Thucydides, illustrates the reach of martial imagery as commentary on Athenian affairs. Asked by a Spartan king whether he or Pericles was the better wrestler, Thucydides punned on Protagoras's *kataballontes logoi* to explain his political situation: "I overthrow [*kataballein*] him wrestling, he sophistically refutes that he has fallen, prevails, and persuades the onlookers" (Plutarch, *Life of Pericles* 8). Physical might has been eclipsed by verbal cleverness (*deinotes*). With words alone Pericles reverses the outcome of the contest by persuading the spectators of what is not true. Ethics aside, the point is clear (O'Regan 1992: 11–7).

Pericles was commonly known as the "Olympian" in part because of his powerful speech (DK 80 B 9). Comedy satirized the new divinity's words as lightning and thunder enacting his will on Earth (Plutarch, *Life of Pericles* 8; Cratinus, *Nemesis* 73, 326, *Cheirons* 258; Telecleides 18, 47, 48; Aristophanes, *Acharnians* 530–1). The same image applied to juries (Aristophanes, *Wasps* 620) and demagogues (671, *Knights* 626–9). But this thunder was conflated with other matters: flatulence and shit. The characteristic comic move from high to low, divine to human animal, mind to body, reworked sophistic claims by linking speech (*logos*) and the stomach (*gaster*), long a symbol for the appetites that shape lies and deceptions (Hesiod, *Theogony* 26; Homer, *Odyssey* 14.122, 18.52; Worman 2008: 62–120). The resulting overlay of mouth and anus drove a famous comic riddle that asserted equivalence of a babbling sophistic asshole, farting its own wind, and the demagogue Callistratus (Eubulos 106.1–4, in Kassel and Austin 1998). Similarly, in the *Knights'* violently negative picture of contemporary political rhetoric, political speakers' mouths and assholes are indistinguishable. The *Clouds'* innovation is to further overlay the comic vision with a sophistic "theoretical" justification. As Strepsiades learns from his first lessons, in a world governed by natural forces and inhabited by natural men, the thunder of the cloud goddesses—divinities of nature and of sophistic rhetoric—is best understood by reference not to Zeus but to the rumble of a stomach overly full of soup (Aristophanes, *Clouds* 383). Typical sophistic evidence from language is given a comic twist with a pun (394) on "thunder" (*brontē*) and "fart" (*pordē*). Such sounds betray only the pressure of natural forces, whether working on clouds, insects, or men. Lightning, a traditional punishment for perjury, is assimilated to the same model: it is like the spitting of an overcooked sausage that burns the inattentive cook. Skill, not transgression, determines "punishment" in this new world (O'Regan 1992: 56–60).

The collapse of the traditional *logos/gaster* antithesis is a stinging comic rebuke of the optimism of the sage souls, who traditionally phrased their devotion to intellectual achievement as a necessary renunciation of *gaster* and all it represents (Xenophon, *Memorabilia* 1.6). The situation is comically practical—life on Earth means that Socrates's students will be defined by the (comic) body and its needs—but it is also sophistically theoretical, for even emblematic sophistic speakers fall within this comic paradigm. Strepsiades illustrates the problem when, after being ordered into a flea-infested bed to cogitate something to escape his debts, he emerges, in good comic fashion, with his phallus (*pēos*) in hand. His solution enacts the premise of Gorgias's *Helen*. That glorious manifesto of the power of *logos*—exonerating the maligned Helen—turns out to be an argument for the unavoidability of adultery. In our *Clouds*, the same topic provides the weaker *logos* with its victory over its more traditional rival. Action and speech are driven by comic, natural needs—above all, the need for sex. The process also transforms rhetorical tools in ways that have a rich comic and philosophical history. The verbal pleasure that Gorgias made central to the power of *logos* cannot withstand competition with natural pleasures common to sophistic theory and comic vision. The *Knights* staged successful persuasion as corruption—providing edible sweets, not verbal ones. The same underlying image—cooking up a speech—edifies Strepsiades's initial lessons. The resulting degradation of speaker and listener also transforms *kairos* into mere pandering. Success rides on the speaker's ability to adapt to an audience whose needs and desires of the moment must be deduced and gratified. The apparently dominating *logos* and its speakers are, in fact, enslaved to listeners (O'Regan 1992: 61–4).

But any notion of verbal power—even a redefined one—cannot survive the last scenes of the *Clouds*, for the common comic strategy of staging metaphor initiates an even more fundamental reversal. The force of technical persuasion is read backward to reveal not words but violence as the preferred "persuasive" strategy of comic, natural man. The process begins with Strepsiades. In a generic scene in which the comic hero repulses his enemies, he compels his creditor to leave. But not with words. For the creditor, an ordinary man, does not feel any need to listen to persuasive speech; he ignores Strepsiades's arguments, even credible ones. In turn, Strepsiades, too, deserts speech. He drives the creditor from the stage, threatening to goad him in the ass like a horse (1297, in Dover 1968; O'Regan 1992: 111–3). This comic Pericles is not persuading with the tongue. Nor does the situation improve with Pheidippides, the full-fledged sophist. In a dispute over poets, he demonstrates the preeminence of Euripides not by analyzing his verse but by kicking and choking his father. Only when Strepsiades runs outside screaming for help does Pheidippides deploy his alternative tool: arguing that father beating is just by appealing to the laws of nature. The natural substitution of violence for persuasion in this new comic, sophistic world culminates in the burning of Socrates's school by the enraged Strepsiades, who explicitly rejects a trial for the sage souls. Brutal comic puns and repetitions from the beginning of the play assimilate Strepsiades's violent blows to the subtleties that wrestle in sophistic debates, while choking screams signal that Socrates and his students have become the human coals they had postulated: "Alas, suffering wretch, I'm choking to death! . . . And I, ill-fated, am being burnt up!" (Aristophanes, *Clouds* 1504–5). This new ending treats the audience to Protagoras's overthrowing arguments in a more literal way (1495–6; O'Regan 1992: 114–25). What had seemed the theoretical context for the triumph of sophistic rhetoric is now revealed as the practical context of its destruction. Yet the news for Aristophanic comedy is hardly good. The revised ending also provides the slapstick humor that Aristophanes identified as missing in the failed version of *Clouds*, the same laughter that has greeted the burying of unwelcome *logos* in blows since the Greek army's guffaws at Odysseus's beating of Thersites. This comedy, akin to food, shitting, and sex (Aristophanes, *Birds* 785–96), marks the grimmest joke of our *Clouds*: sophistic and comic "truths" agree on a natural man who makes rhetoric irrelevant.

The breakdown of the power of speech on stage is a step beyond what critics see as the project of the *Clouds* and many of Aristophanes's other plays: cautionary spectacles about the perils of persuasive discourse. The charge that the Athenians were more or less willing dupes was common in the theater, Assembly, and courts—and it had a salutary role, providing for "Athens's democratic citizenry some important interpretive equipment with which they could enter their rhetoric-based and 'logocentric' institutions" (Hesk 2002: 247–74; cf. Henderson 1991; Hubbard 1997, 2007; Slater 2002: 236–7; Worthington 2007: 264–5). Nor did Aristophanes exempt his comedy from analysis of "the fictive, constructed and potentially misleading quality of the democracy's political, legal and dramatic rhetorics" (274). Hesk identifies this rhetoric of anti-rhetoric and deception as "unsettling" (274). It was that and more. Strepsiades's decision—motivated by self-interest, fear of overpowering verbal skill, and freedom from legal and social restraint—to close his ears and silence speech strikes at the heart of democratic Athens. For Athenian political ideology made the city and speech mutually supportive. The gift of speech made possible man's escape from bestial violence, while, in turn, *logos* required a privileged position whose enforcement can differ (divine intervention, just kings, the laws, democratic institutions, or the comic chorus) but without which speech is powerless and the democratic city would cease to exist.

The privileged position of speech in ancient Greek comedy (and democratic politics) cannot be taken for granted; it is a staple of rhetorical theory that speech must create its audience. Comic poets were vulnerable (Halliwell 1991: 296), well aware of the necessity of creating a bond with their audience (Revermann 2006b: 159–62, 171–5), and open about the project of educating the audience (e.g., Aristophanes, *Wasps* 54, *Frogs*; Foley 2008: 20–1). However, the difficulty of securing a hearing is largely elided in surviving sophistic reasoning. Civic, democratic institutions and the metaphor of persuasion as force obscure the delicate negotiation of this necessary first step. The exclusive focus on the speaker means that even *tērpsis* (verbal pleasure) and *kairos* (opportunity of the moment) are conceptualized not as means of fostering mutuality but as strategies of domination.

Protagoras may have acknowledged the fragility of language; in a dubious fragment he concedes the existence of fools who do not appreciate the glories of the tongue (DK 80 B 12). Yet if Plato's *Protagoras* is accurate, he glanced at the problem only to push it away. The Platonic Protagoras's account of the origin of human society assumes early man's command of language but marks it as insufficient: men continued to injure each other and live at the mercy of wild animals. It required Zeus to implant justice (*dikē*) and respect (*aidōs*) in everyone before the bonds of *philia* and ordering of cities could emerge to provide safety from beasts of prey (Plato, *Protagoras* 322c). Justice, the city, and man's safety depend not on a preexisting ability to talk but on the ability *to listen*, prompted not by self-interest but by respect for the speaker. These civilizing qualities, foundational to the *polis*, are innate yet not entirely natural, part of human reality yet a late addition to the human, speaking animal. Protagoras's notorious agnosticism (DK 80 B 4) means that his choice of mechanism—divine intervention—pushes the problem of listening, like the existence of the gods, outside the realm of productive investigation. The agreement to listen and be persuaded, if the right words can be found, is a precondition of his teachable art, not part of his curriculum.

Protagoras's alternative, social explanation for justice and the political art clarifies the situation. Universal teaching occurs in the family and the city at large through punishment of those heedless of parents, teachers, the rulers, and laws (Plato, *Protagoras* 323c). Protagoras claims to be part of this process (328b), but his instruction offers something a little different. His students progress toward the aristocratic standard familiar since Homer (328b). Through rhetorical skill, a student can become a civic Achilles, the most capable and powerful man in the city in doing and in speaking (319a). A receptive audience is a given.

A similar dynamic is apparent in Gorgias. When the Platonic Gorgias celebrates the ability of persuasive rhetoric to create willing slaves, he glances at the voluntary nature of listening and agreeing to be persuaded. Yet his *Helen*'s famous explanation of the power of persuasion exonerates Helen from blame for adultery because of a shared, innate human ignorance and susceptibility to the charms of speech (DK 82 B 11.8). Less clear is why she ever began to listen to Paris's seductive words in the first place. *Ēros*, which might have explained her willing attention, instead acts as an alternative compulsive force and a foil for the power of *logos* (DK 82 B 11.15). Yet Gorgias, too, acknowledges the problem of listening while never letting it color his account of technical persuasion. He concedes that drama, which, like all skillful speech, relies on deception, does not exert its spell over everyone. The wiser spectator coexists with another, less wise one who remains oblivious to the power of the word (DK 82 B 23).

The less wise spectator is also immune to much else, like Philocleon in *Wasps*, a juror deaf to arguments about guilt and innocence before always voting to convict, and like the chorus in *Acharnians*, who wish to stone Dikaiopolis before hearing him defend himself. This "less wise" spectator may, like Strepsiades, fear the power of speech, or, like the first *Clouds*' audience, find no reason to listen if it means foregoing other pleasures. Yet our *Clouds* stages a solution to this problem. Among ordinary people, emotional bonds may secure a hearing even for speech that one does not wish to hear. Filial love prompts a reluctant Pheidippides to listen to his father's plans and enter the Thinkery. Strepsiades attends to an argument for the justice of father beating because the speaker is his son, whose childhood tears must be repaid (Aristophanes, *Clouds* 860, 1435). Likewise the chorus, speaking as Aristophanes, promotes a familial relationship with the spectators to encourage them to listen to and prefer his comedy (530–6). That such arguments are standard rhetorical strategies underlines, rather than diminishes, their pertinence. Protagoras and Aristophanes agree: for less wise souls, an emotional underpinning sustains the reciprocity necessary for *logos* to display its power.

Comedy is a particularly appropriate vehicle for this insight because laughter, the fundamental comic pleasure of natural man, nourishes the bonds that secure listeners for something more. This mechanism was clear to Gorgias, Aristophanes, and, it seems, even the audience as they laughed. In *Wasps*, Philocleon identifies advocates' ingratiating jokes as an enjoyable prerequisite of jury service (567; Ruffell 2008: 50; Sommerstein 2009: 111). Verbal persuasion may work on the individual soul, but shared laughter— even if provoked for different reasons in a stratified audience (Revermann 2006a)— knits together individual listeners and binds the speaker and audience, at times through exclusionary mockery but more often through shared pleasure (Slater 1999: 361; Robson 2006: 81–7, 92–3). Rhetorical jokes, comic drama, and the institution of the comic competition nurture more and more widely the fundamental social agreement that makes possible both the democratic city and the art of skillful speech: the agreement to listen.

References

Bakola, Emmanuela. 2008. "The Drunk, the Reformer, and the Teacher: Agonistic Poetics and the Construction of Persona in the Comic Poets of the Fifth Century." *Proceedings of the Cambridge Philological Society* 54: 1–29.

Bakola, Emmanuela. 2010. *Cratinus and the Art of Comedy*. New York: Oxford University Press.

Biles, Zachary P. 2002. "Intertextual Biography in the Rivalry of Cratinus and Aristophanes." *American Journal of Philology* 123: 169–204.

Carey, Christopher. 2000. "Old Comedy and the Sophists." In *The Rivals of Aristophanes*, edited by David Harvey and John Wilkins, 419–438. London: Duckworth and The Classical Press of Wales.

Consigny, Scott. 2001. *Gorgias*. Columbia: University of South Carolina Press.

Diels, Hermann, and Walther Kranz, eds. 1969. *Die Fragmente der Vorsokratiker*. Vol. 2. Dublin: Weidmann.

Dover, Kenneth J., ed. 1968. *Aristophanes: "Clouds."* London: Oxford University Press.

Foley, Helene. 2008. "Generic Boundaries in Late Fifth-Century Athens." In *Performance, Iconography, Reception: Studies in Honour of Oliver Taplin*, edited by Martin Revermann and Peter Wilson, 15–36. Oxford: Oxford University Press.

Halliwell, Stephen. 1991. "The Uses of Laughter in Greek Culture." *Classical Quarterly* 41 no. 2: 279–296.

Heath, Malcolm. 1990. "Aristophanes and his Rivals." *Greece & Rome* 37 no. 2: 143–158.

Henderson, Jeffrey. 1991. *The Maculate Muse: Obscene Language in Attic Comedy*. New Haven, CT: Yale University Press.

Henderson, Jeffrey. 1993. "Comic Hero Versus Political Elite." In *Tragedy, Comedy, and the Polis*, edited by Alan Sommerstein, 307–319. Bari: Levante editori.

Henderson, Jeffrey. 1998. "Attic Old Comedy, Frank Speech, and Democracy." In *Democracy, Empire, and the Arts in Fifth-Century Athens*, edited by Deborah Boedeker and Kurt Raaflaub, 255–273. Cambridge, MA: Harvard University Press.

Henderson, Jeffrey, ed. and trans. 1998–2007. *Aristophanes*. 5 vols. Cambridge, MA: Harvard University Press.

Hesk, Jon. 2002. *Deception and Democracy in Classical Athens*. Cambridge: Cambridge University Press.

Hubbard, Thomas K. 1997. "Utopianism and the Sophistic City." In *The City as Comedy*, edited by Gregory Dobrov, 23–50. Chapel Hill: University of North Carolina Press.

Hubbard, Thomas K. 2007. "Attic Comedy and the Development of Theoretical Rhetoric." In *A Companion to Greek Rhetoric*, edited by Ian Worthington, 490–508. Oxford: Blackwell.

Kassell, Rudolf, and Colin Austin, eds. 1998. *Poetae Comici Graeci*. 7 vols. Berlin: Walter de Gruyter.

O'Regan, Daphne. 1992. *Rhetoric, Comedy, and the Violence of Language in Aristophanes' "Clouds."* New York: Oxford University Press.

Poulakos, John. 1995. *Sophistical Rhetoric in Classical Greece*. Columbia: University of South Carolina Press.

Revermann, Martin. 2006a. "The Competence of Theatre Audiences in Fifth- and Fourth-Century Athens." *Journal of Hellenic Studies* 126: 99–124.

Revermann, Martin. 2006b. *Comic Business*. New York: Oxford University Press.

Robson, James. 2006. *Humour, Obscenity and Aristophanes*. Tübingen: Narr.

Ruffell, Ian. 2008. "Audience and Emotion in the Reception of Greek Drama." In *Performance, Iconography, Reception: Studies in Honour of Oliver Taplin*, edited by Martin Revermann and Peter Wilson, 37–58. Oxford: Oxford University Press.

Schiappa, Edward. 1999. *The Beginnings of Rhetorical Theory in Classical Greece*. New Haven, CT: Yale University Press.

Segal, Charles. 1962. "Gorgias and the Psychology of the *Logos*." *Harvard Studies in Classical Philology* 66: 99–155.

Slater, Niall. 1999. "Making the Aristophanic Audience." *American Journal of Philology* 120 no. 3: 351–368.

Slater, Niall. 2002. *Spectator Politics*. Philadelphia: University of Pennsylvania Press.

Sommerstein, Alan. 2009. *Talking About Laughter*. Oxford: Oxford University Press.

Storey, Ian. 2003. *Eupolis*. Oxford: Oxford University Press.

Worthington, Ian. 2007. "Rhetoric and Politics in Classical Greece: Rise of the *Rhētores*." In *A Companion to Greek Rhetoric*, edited by Ian Worthington, 255–271. Oxford: Blackwell.

Worman, Nancy. 2008. *Abusive Mouths in Classical Athens*. Cambridge: Cambridge University Press.

Yunis, Harvey. 1998. "The Constraints of Democracy and the Rise of the Art of Rhetoric." In *Democracy, Empire, and the Arts in Fifth-Century Athens*, edited by Deborah Boedeker and Kurt Raaflaub, 223–240. Cambridge, MA: Harvard University Press.

CHAPTER 9

PLATO'S RHETORIC IN THEORY AND PRACTICE

HARVEY YUNIS

PLATO both wrote about rhetoric—the art of persuasive discourse—and practiced it. In regard to his writing about rhetoric, one must recognize that his dialogues do not constitute treatises in which the author addresses readers directly. Thus, one cannot simply read off Plato's views on rhetoric from these texts, even though rhetoric is a significant concern in several dialogues and one of the main topics in the *Gorgias* and *Phaedrus*. This chapter forgoes the ticklish problem of how to read and interpret Plato's dialogues and instead seeks to explicate the arguments about rhetoric made by Socrates and his interlocutors. Yet rhetoric differs from most other topics that arise in Plato's dialogues, insofar as one can compare his arguments about rhetoric with his actual rhetorical practice. Here there is a further twist: it sometimes happens that Plato's characters, not least Socrates, present ideas on rhetoric while speaking rhetorically. For example, Socrates, addressing his judicial audience in the famous opening of the *Apology* (17a–8a), warns them of the prosecutors' deceptive rhetoric and proclaims that he has rejected such rhetoric in favor of truthfulness. Since Socrates's artifice throughout the speech is plain, the effect is complex: a rhetoric that aims at making the truth as evident as possible to the audience within the allotted time. A writer and thinker of the very first rank, Plato is in control of his medium, his message, and the manner in which the two interact (de Strycker and Slings 1994: 27–40; Blondell 2002: 1–52; Michelini 2003).

An Athenian, Plato was born ca. 425 BCE and died ca. 348/347, which puts him squarely at the time and place when rhetoric began to emerge as a self-conscious discipline. Plato was instrumental in this process, which was competitive among those concerned and entangled with political and intellectual controversies of the day (Cole 1991; Yunis 1998). Hence, Plato's writing on rhetoric is critical and constructive, in both cases contributing to rhetoric's formation as a discipline (see Schiappa, ch. 1). The critical phase takes aim at sophistic rhetoric, that is, the techniques and doctrines of persuasion elaborated by the sophists of the preceding generation, such as Gorgias of Leontini, Protagoras of Abdera, and Thrasymachus of Chalcedon (see Cassin, ch. 11). The sophists' works have mostly been lost; our knowledge of the sophists depends largely on Plato's representation of them, which is hardly objective, and on comments and quotations in other, later writers. The sophists seem to have staked a claim to rhetorical "art" (*technē*) even though they did not, as far as we know, articulate what such a claim entails (Kerferd 1981; Pernot 2005: 10–23). As used in this chapter, the term "sophistic rhetoric" covers the range of rhetorical theories put forward by or ascribed to the sophists. This usage follows Plato's, to whom the differences among the sophists' rhetorical theories were trivial (*Phaedrus* 266d–9d). For Plato, what all forms of sophistic rhetoric have in common—and what renders them all futile—is the notion that a speaker can persuade by art without knowledge of the subject of his discourse.

In his corpus of dialogues Plato presents two major arguments intended to reveal the failure of sophistic rhetoric. First, in the *Gorgias* Plato argues that sophistic rhetoric preys on certain weaknesses of human nature and, as employed by politicians (such as Pericles and the fictive, Alcibiades-like Callicles of the *Gorgias*) in Athens' mass democratic institutions, harms both speakers and audiences. A kind of flattery (*kolakeia*), it merely caters to the irrational desires of mass audiences. Second, in the *Phaedrus* Plato argues that sophistic rhetoric does not produce, or even reasonably aim at, persuasion, which is after all the goal of the art. Because of these political and artistic failures sophistic rhetoric is, despite its pretensions, no art at all. Plato's response (and innovation) is to propose an alternative vision of rhetorical art. To aid philosophy's legitimate, universally beneficial political and ethical goals, Plato outlines in the *Phaedrus* an effective, useful, rational rhetoric that would, in his account, reliably produce persuasion and thus warrant recognition as an art. The attempt to make rhetoric into a genuinely artistic enterprise also reveals the manner in which Plato's true rhetoric reflects his understanding of reality and the human soul.

This chapter first examines Plato's argument against sophistic rhetoric in the *Gorgias* and then considers his innovative, philosophically useful rhetoric in the *Phaedrus*. The chapter concludes with a brief look at Plato's own rhetorical practices, which are evident in the political program of the *Republic* and *Laws* and in his manner of composing philosophical dialogues addressed to his contemporary reading public.

GORGIAS: POLITICAL CRITIQUE OF SOPHISTIC RHETORIC

The *Gorgias* establishes a connection between sophistic rhetoric and the unbridled pursuit of power in Athens' democratic institutions. At issue are not linguistic and discursive strategies of persuasion but the question of whether the sophistically schooled *rhētōr* advances the interests of his audience of fellow citizens by delivering the guidance they need for their welfare but otherwise lack (Yunis 1996: 117–71).

Plato opens the dialogue by indicating his view of Gorgianic rhetoric even before the argument proper begins (*Gorgias* 447a–9a). Gorgias and his sophistic protégé, Polus, are comfortable only when they use their customary epideictic style of discourse, which aims at impressing audiences with displays of verbal dexterity with little or no import. They are reluctant to accommodate themselves to Socrates's customary dialectical form of discourse, which eschews display (*epideixis*) and employs question-and-answer to test arguments and enhance understanding. Socrates's ironic humor at the expense of Gorgias and Polus clearly implies that these sophists labor, to their own detriment, under misconceptions about the value of their epideictic discourse. Plato commonly uses satire in tandem with argument in the creation of literary fictions that serve his philosophical objectives, a practice that is conspicuous in the *Ion, Euthydemus*, and *Protagoras* (Dalfen 1985–6).

Despite Gorgias's difficulty with Socrates's mode of discourse, the conversation moves forward, and Gorgias is led to state his views clearly. The art he teaches, which is called "rhetoric" (Plato, *Gorgias* 449a), is "the greatest good because it brings men freedom for themselves and rule over others in their own *polis*" (452d). Rhetoric is "the ability to persuade by speech the judges in court, the councilmen in the Council, the assembly-men in the Assembly, and those in any gathering which is a political gathering" (452e). Gorgias is thereby recognizing, and seeking to exploit, the crucial role that public speaking played in classical Athenian democracy, which endured from about the 460s until its demise under Macedonian supremacy after 322 BCE (see Harris, ch. 3). In Athens' democratic institutions, chiefly the Assembly and the courts, power was exercised by large numbers of anonymous citizens listening to open public debate and then voting in mass decision-making audiences. The ability to persuade these audiences, especially in competition with other politicians also seeking to persuade, became the prime political skill. At this time Athens was also the largest Greek *polis* and for most of this time the head of a maritime empire that vastly increased the stakes in domestic political debates. Hence, rhetoric was a weapon that no Athenian politician could afford to omit from his arsenal. For instance, Thucydides famously asserts that under Pericles "the democracy existed in name but in fact it was rule by the first citizen [i.e., Pericles]" (Thucydides, *The Peloponnesian War* 2.65.9). Athens' political institutions were fully democratic during Pericles's time, but he dominated them, as Thucydides demonstrates in the speeches he attributes to Pericles (1.140–4, 2.35–46, 2.60–4), with his skill in public speaking (Ober 1989; Hansen 1991; Yunis 1996: 59–86). Polus adds that rhetoric, as taught by Gorgias, makes the skilled rhetorician comparable to a tyrant in the ability to satisfy his own desires without limit (Plato, *Gorgias* 466b–c).

The conjunction of rhetoric and power in Athenian democracy put the skills taught by Gorgias in high demand. Callicles, portrayed as an ambitious politician intent on achieving mastery in Athens' democratic institutions for his own aggrandizement, is an eager customer of Gorgias's sophistic wares. To Socrates this situation is a disaster. He offers a theory of human nature according to which determining what is good for human beings, both individually and collectively and with regard to both body and soul, is a matter of expertise, and administering what is good for human beings normally entails pain for the recipients (Plato, *Gorgias* 476a–9e, 500a–2d). The *dēmos* are ignorant of their true needs and therefore require the expert guidance that actually serves their interests, yet the teachers of sophistic rhetoric and the politicians who use it possess no such expertise. Rather, they persuade their audiences by supplying them with things the audiences find pleasurable, such as "harbors and dockyards and walls and revenues and similar rubbish" (519a), even though such things will inevitably harm them. At the same time, they neglect justice, moderation, piety, and the other virtues essential to a city's well-being (502d–3a). The expertise of such speakers, such as it is, lies merely in predicting the moods and humors of "the great beast," as Socrates refers to the *dēmos* in the *Republic* (493b–c). But since there is nothing rational about this beast, sophistic rhetoric is not a matter of systematic choices based on underlying rational phenomena. On the contrary, sophistic rhetoric is merely an imitation or counterfeit image of the true political art that actually benefits citizens, much as cosmetics, by creating the mere appearance of health and beauty, imitates the true medical art that actually heals the body (Plato, *Gorgias* 464b–5d).

Socrates belittles Callicles, and the entire crop of fifth-century Athenian politicians who led Athens to unprecedented wealth and power at home and abroad, by describing sophistic rhetoric in democratic conditions as a kind of competitive flattery that demeans the speakers even as it harms the audience (Plato, *Gorgias* 502e–5b, 513a–c). Since democratic deliberation is a contest among flatterers to see who can gratify the audience with the most pleasure, the political expert (namely, the philosopher) has no chance of communicating his advice in this environment and therefore withdraws. In an analogy that alludes to Socrates's conviction in an Athenian popular court (in 399), he offers the example of a physician (Socrates himself) who is prosecuted by a pastry cook (a politician using sophistic rhetoric) before a jury of children (the Athenian *dēmos*) (522a). The physician would be unable to defend the harsh medical treatment that he correctly prescribes the children when the pastry cook offers them sweet cakes and cookies instead. The physician/political expert is silenced, and the children/*dēmos* suffer by having their worst and most destructive inclinations catered to by the self-aggrandizing cook/politician.

For Plato, then, sophistic rhetoric is a harmful kind of political discourse that thrives in democracy. Both democracy and sophistic rhetoric must therefore be eliminated if society is to flourish. From this point it is a direct line to the political principles of the *Republic*, in which philosopher-kings wield authority not because of the consent of the governed but because of their political expertise, which they reliably use on behalf of the entire *polis*, the silent, anonymous masses included.

PHAEDRUS: THE ART
OF PSYCHAGOGIC RHETORIC

Whereas the *Gorgias* focuses on sophistic rhetoric as a form of political discourse, especially with regard to its tendency to obstruct the transfer of political wisdom from concerned expert to uninformed *dēmos*, the *Phaedrus* removes rhetoric from the strictly political domain and focuses on rhetoric as the discursive means of producing persuasion in any context. Plato thereby seeks principles for making rhetoric a rational, systematic enterprise. He also thereby provides the philosopher with the means of addressing nonphilosophers and inculcating, for their own good, philosophical ideas and values.

Just past the midpoint of the *Phaedrus*, after Socrates has finished delivering his brilliant second speech on Eros (passionate love, desire), Socrates and Phaedrus undertake to investigate what constitutes good discourse (Plato, *Phaedrus* 257b–8e). Socrates begins with the claim that the speaker of good discourse must have knowledge (*epistēmē*) of the subject of the discourse. He supports this claim with an argument that recalls (and alludes to) the argument against sophistic rhetoric in the *Gorgias*, namely, that good discourse must provide its recipient with the knowledge he needs for his welfare but otherwise lacks (259e–61a). Phaedrus rejects this claim because, he says, good speakers can *persuade* audiences without such knowledge so long as they know what the audience believes about the subject of the discourse (259e–60a). This view, in fact, is the common basis of sophistic accounts of persuasion. Yet instead of repudiating persuasion for the political reasons laid out in the *Gorgias*, Socrates embraces the challenge posed by sophistic rhetoric, and he and Phaedrus then examine how persuasion can be achieved by art. Maintaining his claim that knowledge is necessary for good discourse, Socrates argues not that a speaker must have knowledge of his subject to deliver good advice (his task in the *Gorgias*) but that a speaker will be effective at persuading his audience if and only if he has knowledge of his subject matter.

Plato's account of rhetoric follows from the kind of persuasion he wants rhetoric to accomplish, which differs in quality from the persuasion sought by sophists and democratic politicians. Socrates offers the following definition: "Must not the art of rhetoric, as a whole, be a kind of leading-of-the-soul [*psychagōgia*] through speeches, not only in law courts and all other meetings of the *dēmos* but also in private ones, it being the same art in regard to small issues and great ones and a thing deserving of no more respect, at least in its proper use, when it concerns serious issues than when it concerns trivial ones?" (Plato, *Phaedrus* 261a–b). Socrates continues a few lines later: "So the art of arguing opposing sides of a case [*antilogike*] not only concerns law courts and speeches in the assembly, but, it seems, a single art concerning all things that are said, if it exists, would be this art [rhetoric]" (261e). These crucial sentences are explained in the following paragraphs.

First, to describe the task of his newly conceived art of rhetoric, Plato borrows a word—*psychagōgia*—that originally referred to the raising of (dead) souls by ritual or magical means. Depriving *psychagōgia* of all ritual or magical meaning, Socrates turns rhetoric into an art that uses discourse to influence human beings to go in a particular direction (Yunis 2011: 183). If sophists such as Gorgias, democratic politicians such as Callicles, and speechwriters such as Lysias (Plato's target in the *Phaedrus*) flatter to win the approval of large audiences, particularly when competing with others seeking the same, Plato seeks to persuade individual human beings (in his parlance, "souls") to make certain choices and to pursue certain ends, or, in the sense of *psychagōgia*, to lead them in one direction rather than another.

Second, Plato removes rhetoric from the purely political realm specified by Gorgias (*Gorgias* 452e, previously quoted) and expands its range to include all discourse, regardless of occasion, genre, subject matter, or audience. The universal scope of Plato's rhetoric is based on his view that no discourse is neutral in its effects on the soul and that a person may therefore be affected for good or ill by any discourse (*Phaedrus* 241d–3e; cf. *Protagoras* 314a–b). Plato thus opposes the sophists' tendency to understand rhetoric as a tool for manipulating the beliefs of the masses and for wielding power in the political institutions of the city. Further, by rejecting the strictly politico-legal scope of rhetoric and moving toward a universal art of discourse, Plato removes from consideration the problem identified in the *Gorgias*, namely, the inevitable futility of the expert's discourse in a competitive democratic setting. The account of rhetoric in the *Phaedrus* shifts the focus away from the approval of (irrational) mass audiences toward the form and content of the speaker's discourse and the receptive properties of its intended audience. These are factors that in Plato's view can be systematically examined and that provide a systematic basis for artistic choices. The rhetorical art elaborated in the *Phaedrus* has nothing to say about the manner in which the success of a discourse may be affected by contingent features of the rhetorical situation, such as competing speakers, the wild impulses of audiences, or the effect of the discourse on audiences other than those intended by the speaker or author. Such features lie outside the art. Thus, when Aristotle defines rhetoric as "the ability to observe in each case *the available means* of persuasion" (*Rhetoric* 1355b25–6; emphasis added) and thereby limits rhetoric to features that a speaker or author can control, he is following the lead of Plato's *Phaedrus*.

Socrates begins his account of psychagogic rhetoric by making good on his claim that persuasion by art requires knowledge of the subject matter of the discourse: only such knowledge provides the speaker with the means to create a persuasive, nonflattering *argument* on the subject (Plato, *Phaedrus* 261e–2c). Such an argument moves the auditor step by step from the view he or she holds at the outset to the view the speaker wants the auditor to hold at the end. It is a process of consecutive reasoning in which each element must have its proper place for the whole to have the desired effect. Now, a rhetorical argument of this kind may well be a deceptive one, as Socrates clearly states (261e).[1] Thus, Socrates embraces rhetoric's traditional ability to speak persuasively on either side of an issue, which Plato calls *antilogike* (261d). Socrates maintains that both of his speeches on Eros (one condemning, one praising) provide examples of true rhetorical art (262c–d), though only the second of these speeches—the so-called palinode named after the poem by Stesichorus—provides the advice that actually serves the interests of its auditor. Yet both speeches contain compelling arguments that begin by defining Eros and proceed by consecutive steps to their respective, but opposed, conclusions. It is the very potency of the argument of Socrates's first speech that makes it necessary for him to compose the palinode as a response to the first speech (241d–3e). We are made aware at the beginning of the dialogue (227c), and reminded later (257a), that Socrates is an expert in erotic matters, so his speeches on Eros are composed by someone with expert knowledge of the subject matter, just as Plato's rhetorical theory requires.

By way of contrast, as soon as Socrates hears Lysias's speech on Eros he criticizes it for lacking a compelling argument (Plato, *Phaedrus* 235e–6a). Lysias's speech, composed by Plato for the dialogue, functions as an example of Gorgianic verbal display; it makes no effort to persuade the young man to whom it is addressed and stakes its claim to rhetorical excellence entirely on its cleverness (*deinotes*). The audience for which it was composed consisted of rhetorical enthusiasts interested more in verbal games than in the mechanisms of how real people are actually persuaded, in real circumstances, to do something. To highlight the absence of argument in Lysias's speech, Socrates later compares it to an epitaph for Midas, in which the four lines can stand in any order without altering the effect of the whole (264c–e). Plato thereby raises—for the first time in Greek literature—the idea of design in artistic composition and invents a term for this idea: "logographic necessity" or, more informatively, "necessity in the composition of discourse" (264b). Design means that every element in an artistic composition, down to the smallest detail, is devised for a particular place in the discourse with a view to advancing the purpose of the discourse as a whole. Plato also uses the metaphor of organic unity for this concept (a discourse must be akin to a "living organism" [264c]), which reflects his view of natural organisms as complex, teleologically structured unities (cf. *Timaeus*). In speeches that possess design there is a compelling reason, related to the persuasive goal of the speech, for the elements of the discourse to be what they are and to be set out in a particular order. There is also a compelling quality to the persuasion that is produced when discourses are artfully designed (271b) (see Kaufer and Wetzel, ch. 56).

Socrates introduces two intellectual disciplines—dialectic and psychology—that must inform rhetoric if it is to be constituted as a proper art. Dialectic provides the speaker with the requisite knowledge of his subject matter, which in turn enables the speaker to create rhetorically effective arguments (Plato, *Phaedrus* 265d–6c). Dialectic consists of two movements of thought. The first, collection (*synagōgē*), is the process of bringing together related phenomena under a single general form, enabling the speaker to define his subject clearly. A clear definition, formulated by the speaker with his persuasive goal in mind, is the first step in breaking down the auditor's resistance to the speaker's proposition and preparing him to accept it (263d–e). The second movement of thought, division (*diairesis*), is the process of dividing the general form into subclasses according to natural criteria. Thanks to this double process of definition and classification, the speaker is able to say pertinent things about his subject, in particular, things that make the subject look good or bad according to the speaker's needs. A rhetorical argument is not the direct or raw presentation, as it were, of a dialectical argument, nor does rhetorical argument derive its persuasiveness from the logical force of a dialectical argument. Rather, dialectic merely provides the material for rhetorical argument that the speaker then casts in a form that suits the particular audience (Yunis 2009).

Psychagogic rhetoric also requires psychology because persuasion takes place in the soul, or *psychē* (Plato, *Phaedrus* 270b). Individual human souls are not unique; each belongs to one of the large (but finite) number of types of soul (248d–e, 252c–3c). Socrates presents an outline of what psychological training for rhetorical art would consist in. In addition to conveying knowledge of the nature and types of soul, training in psychology enables the student of rhetoric to recognize what type of soul any particular human being possesses and on that basis to create a speech that will persuade that person, in a face-to-face encounter, to hold a particular view (269d–72a). By making persuasion contingent on matching particular forms of speech to a person's soul, Plato creates the basis for the use of style and the practice of expressing content in different forms with a view to effectiveness. Form in rhetoric is not a matter of display, as it is for Lysias and the sophists, but is strictly functional with regard to persuading particular auditors. Socrates anticipated this point when he explained that the palinode was cast in poetic form for the sake of its effect on Phaedrus (257a).

Plato was innovating when he based the art of rhetoric on dialectic and psychology (see Chaitin, ch. 54). Each of the two disciplines responds to a crucial failure in the persuasive capabilities of sophistic rhetoric. A sophistic speaker, ignorant of the subject of his discourse but schooled in his auditor's beliefs (*doxai*) about the subject, can do no more than persuade the auditor to accept something that, by virtue of his existing beliefs, he is already inclined to accept. *Psychagōgia*, however, is a more demanding persuasive task. It requires the speaker to be able to replace the auditor's current beliefs (which may be conventional) with entirely new ones, ones that might even be sufficiently transformative to make him pursue philosophy. Dialectic provides the speaker with the knowledge to produce arguments with that psychagogic power, as Socrates illustrates in his analysis of the palinode that had precisely this effect on Phaedrus (Plato, *Phaedrus* 265b–6b). Further, although Socrates ridicules the techniques and formulae that fill the sophists' rhetoric manuals (*technai*), such as emotional appeals, probability arguments, and imagistic diction, as mere stimuli that sophists deploy ad hoc to produce given responses (266d–9d), rhetorical psychology allows all formal elements—including the sophists' linguistic and argumentative techniques—to be organized to produce a precise persuasive effect in the auditor's psyche. Since the art of psychagogic rhetoric entails mastering dialectic and psychology in addition to expertise in language and discourse, it is an immense and daunting undertaking. But for the Platonic Socrates there is no shortcut to the true art of *rhētorikē* (272b–3e).

PLATO'S RHETORIC IN PRACTICE

Plato's rhetorical efforts can be assigned to one of two broad categories, though in both cases he uses rhetoric for the same reason and with the same purpose. Plato's situation parallels that of Gorgias's brother, the physician, who, unable to persuade his patients to undergo the painful but beneficial treatment he prescribes, looks to Gorgias to take over the job of persuasion (*Gorgias* 456a–7c). The need for persuasive ability over and above expert knowledge is a basic requirement for Plato's conception of philosophy, especially if philosophy is to have any effect in the world, where it is forced to communicate with the ignorant masses if it is to benefit them. In Plato's case, the patient is humanity as a whole: there is no hope of progress until and unless politics and education come under the guidance of philosophy (Plato, *Republic* 473c–d), but people are unwilling— the few philosophers excepted—to accept that truth and its practical consequences. Philosophy's worldly burden, symbolized by the philosopher's return to the cave (519c– 21a), is therefore to persuade nonphilosophical citizens to accept philosophical rule and to instill in them—to the extent possible—philosophical understanding and values. This burden falls to rhetoric.

The first category of Platonic rhetoric includes the formal mechanisms of Plato's political thought with which philosophers encourage citizens to accept philosophical rule and educate them in the values that maintain the rule of *philosophia*. This category includes the program of early childhood education of the guardian class described in the *Republic* (376c–402c), the philosopher's speech in the *Republic* intended to persuade the assembled mass of future citizens to accept philosophical rule on its merits (499d–502a), and the legal preambles of the *Laws* (718b–23d), which are deliberative speeches that add persuasion to the compulsion of the law proper (Yunis 1996: 167–71, 211–36; Burnyeat 1999: 217–22, 236–63).

The second category is more intriguing than the formal mechanisms of Platonic political rhetoric because it is even more innovative. These are Plato's writings them- selves, viewed as rhetorical compositions in the service of philosophy (see Cassin, ch. 11; Miller, ch. 55). Virtually all the dialogues of Plato's early and middle periods, in which Socrates engages with nonphilosophical interlocutors on questions of broad interest, contain material aimed at nonphilosophical readers whose reception of philosophy is enhanced by discourse shaped to their needs and abilities.[2] The most potent example is the *Republic*, in which Plato makes the same case to his readers—it always pays to be just under all circumstances—that Socrates makes to Glaucon and Adimantus. The argument on justice (*dikē*) that constitutes the core of the work is conveyed to the inter- locutors, and thus to readers, by means of the most concentrated use of rhetorical art in Plato's corpus. Beyond the liveliness and vivid realism evident in all the Platonic writ- ings, the *Republic* employs such memorable rhetorical devices as the analogy of city and soul, the simile of the divided line, the image of the cave, and the concluding myth of Er to efface difficulties of the core argument, enliven it, and make it easier to understand (Yunis 2007).

Both the rhetorical mechanisms of Plato's explicit political theory and the rhetorical elements of the dialogues embody the principles of the rhetorical art described in the *Phaedrus*. Like the auditors of the dialectically based, deceptive persuasion described in the *Phaedrus* (261e), recipients of Plato's rhetorical discourses who are resistant to his message must be moved to accept a new belief in place of an old one.[3] Such movement of the soul—*psychagōgia*—is the very purpose of the rhetorical endeavor in question. In each case, Plato's rhetorical discourse contains an argument that is pertinent to the audi- tor's situation and constructed with material about the matter at hand arrived at through dialectic. The discourse is delivered in a setting controlled by the speaker with no com- peting speakers. Sometimes Plato exploits rhetoric's antilogical capability in a manner similar to Socrates's opposed speeches on Eros in the *Phaedrus*. Recall, for example,

Callicles's diatribe against philosophy in the *Gorgias* (482c–6c), Protagoras's speech on virtue in the *Protagoras* (320c–8c), and the speeches of Glaucon and Adimantus on the futility of justice in the *Republic* (358e–67e). Plato composed these brilliant speeches against the positions he ultimately wants to defend for the sake of making his overall discourse more compelling. The rhetorical features of Plato's dialogues are therefore highly effective, but the artistry extends only to the combination of form and content in relation to the intended audience. Whether or not auditors or readers are actually persuaded is a contingent matter that lies beyond the art.

Notes

1. Deceptiveness of the kind presented in this passage is in itself morally neutral; moral evaluation pertains to its use (Murray 1988). Socrates later makes clear (273e–4a) that the good man uses deceptive rhetoric only for good purposes.
2. The dialogues of Plato's late period—*Theaetetus, Parmenides, Sophist, Statesman, Philebus, Timaeus*, and *Laws*—are mostly technical and apparently aimed at students of philosophy (Yunis 2007: 9–15).
3. The "noble lie" of the *Republic* (414c–5d) exemplifies this deceptive rhetoric. The noble lie is false with respect to its form (a myth about the origins of the just city's inhabitants) but true with respect to its content (the relative capabilities of the city's inhabitants). It is the mythological form that makes the content persuasive.

References

Blondell, Ruby. 2002. *The Play of Character in Plato's Dialogues*. Cambridge: Cambridge University Press.

Burnyeat, Myles. 1999. "Culture and Society in Plato's *Republic*." *Tanner Lectures in Human Values* 20: 215–324.

Cole, Thomas. 1991. *The Origins of Rhetoric in Ancient Greece*. Baltimore, MD: Johns Hopkins University Press.

Dalfen, Joachim. 1985–1986. "Literarische Fiktion-Funktion von Literatur: Zum 'Lysiastext' in Platons *Phaidros*." *Grazer Beiträge* 12–13: 101–130.

Hansen, Mogens H. 1991. *The Athenian Democracy in the Age of Demosthenes: Structure, Principles, and Ideology*. Oxford: Blackwell.

Kerferd, George B. 1981. *The Sophistic Movement*. Cambridge: Cambridge University Press.

Michelini, Ann N., ed. 2003. *Plato as Author: The Rhetoric of Philosophy*. Cincinnati Classical Studies 8. Leiden: Brill.

Murray, James S. 1988. "Disputation, Deception, and Dialectic: Plato on the True Rhetoric (*Phaedrus* 261–266)." *Philosophy & Rhetoric* 21 no. 4: 279–289.

Ober, Josiah. 1989. *Mass and Elite in Democratic Athens: Rhetoric, Ideology, and the Power of the People*. Princeton, NJ: Princeton University Press.

Pernot, Laurent. 2005. *Rhetoric in Antiquity*. Translated by W. E. Higgins. Washington, DC: Catholic University of America Press.

Strycker, Emile de, and Simon R. Slings. 1994. *Plato's "Apology of Socrates": A Literary and Philosophical Study with a Running Commentary*. Leiden: Brill.

Yunis, Harvey. 1996. *Taming Democracy: Models of Political Rhetoric in Classical Athens*. Ithaca, NY: Cornell University Press.

Yunis, Harvey. 1998. "The Constraints of Democracy and the Rise of the Art of Rhetoric." In *Democracy, Empire, and the Arts in Fifth-Century Athens*, edited by Deborah Boedeker and Kurt Raaflaub, 223–240. Cambridge, MA: Harvard University Press.

Yunis, Harvey. 2007. "The Protreptic Rhetoric of the *Republic*." In *The Cambridge Companion to Plato's Republic*, edited by G. R. F. Ferrari, 1–26. Cambridge: Cambridge University Press.

Yunis, Harvey. 2009. "Dialectic and the Purpose of Rhetoric in Plato's *Phaedrus*." *Proceedings of the Boston Area Colloquium in Ancient Philosophy* 24: 229–248.

Yunis, Harvey, ed. 2011. *Plato: "Phaedrus."* Cambridge: Cambridge University Press.

CHAPTER 10

··

ARISTOTLE'S RHETORIC IN THEORY AND PRACTICE

··

EUGENE GARVER

ARISTOTLE'S *Rhetoric* is a very slippery book. It is very hard to hold it down for long, and especially hard to try to hold all of it at the same time. Aristotle never tells us how to read the *Rhetoric*, what to expect from it, or what he is trying to accomplish. At times his picture of rhetoric is so restricted to reasoning to the exclusion of emotion, style, and indeed any consideration of an audience, that his description seems to be an idealization with no relation to persuasion as it is actually practiced. At other times, he seems to veer to the other extreme, offering cynical advice about how to win an argument without regard for the truth, the interest of the audience, or any ethical considerations. Sometimes it looks like Aristotle tells us what audiences typically believe rather than what is true; at other times, he criticizes what most people think and offers his own account instead. Truth is naturally more persuasive than what is false (*Rhetoric* 1.1, 1355a31–3), but people are ready to believe anything (see Grimaldi 1980, 1988).

To navigate through Aristotle's argument in the *Rhetoric*, I suggest that we turn to his programmatic statement at the beginning of the fourth book of the *Politics*:

> In all arts and sciences which embrace the whole of any subject, and do not come into being in a fragmentary way, it is the province of a single art or science to consider all that appertains to a single subject. For example, the art of gymnastic considers not only (1) the suitableness of different modes of training to different bodies, but (2) what sort is absolutely the best (for the absolutely best must suit that which is by nature best and best furnished with the means of life), and also (3) what common form of training is adapted to the great majority of men. And if a man does not desire the best habit of body, or the greatest skill in gymnastics, which might be attained by him, still (4) the trainer or the teacher of gymnastic should be able to impart any lower degree of either. The same principle equally holds in medicine and shipbuilding, and the making of clothes, and in the arts generally. (*Politics* 4.1, 1288b10–9)

In the *Politics*, this enumeration of four jobs for a complete treatment of a subject results in four separate examinations of the best constitution, with "best" having four meanings, ultimately related to the four causes: (1) the best suitable to different civic bodies; (2) the best absolutely, which he also calls the best "according to our prayers"; (3) the best constitution that would pretty well suit any group of citizens; and (4) the best under the extreme circumstances in which the city has to worry so much about stability and civil war that the best constitution becomes the one that simply holds the city together and does not even aspire to justice or virtue (see Garver 1994, 2011). The *Rhetoric*, I suggest, aims at the same completeness but does not separate the four projects. The frustrating range of attitudes toward rhetoric with which I began is matched by the range of projects in the *Politics*.

To begin with, at the one extreme, the best rhetoric does not even look like rhetoric—just state the facts without embellishment; the orator establishes what happens, and the judges decide whether there was a crime and how serious it was (Aristotle, *Rhetoric* 1.1, 1354a26–8). In the same way, most of what we think of as politics, especially its competitive and contested side, is absent from the state under the ideal constitution elaborated in *Politics* 7 and 8. In that state, the business of politics is nothing but ethical education.

Second, *Politics* 4 shows how constitutions can be framed to suit, for example, cities with disproportionately powerful oligarchies or great masses of poor people, or how to take advantage of those states with a large and reliable middle class. In the same way, *Rhetoric* 1.8 shows how which arguments will be effective depends on the existing constitution, and *Rhetoric* 2.12–7 does the same for different particular audiences. More importantly, in the *Politics* each of the six different constitutions—monarchy, aristocracy, polity, democracy, oligarchy, and tyranny—presents its own characteristic problems, because each has its own particular purpose and vision of justice. Similarly, *Rhetoric* 1 treats the different arguments suitable for each of the three kinds of rhetoric—deliberative, judicial, and epideictic—because each of these has its own end or *telos*: advantage, justice, and the good, respectively. As Aristotle puts it, "Rhetoric has three distinct ends in view, one for each of its three kinds" (*Rhetoric* 1.1, 1358b21).

Third, just as the US Constitution was not designed to suit any particular class of people, not creditors or debtors, farmers, merchants, or slave-holders, the latter chapters of *Politics* 4 display the options a legislator can choose from in constructing a constitutional framework that allows citizens to pursue the best lives they can. Parallel to that, the *Rhetoric* offers a way of argument that would be useful in facing most audiences, even though it might not be perfect for any. The enthymeme, the rhetorical syllogism that Aristotle styles the "body of persuasion" (*sōma tēs pisteōs*; *Rhetoric* 1.1, 1354a14), can be dressed in a variety of ways for different audiences, but it provides a single structure of reasoning suitable for persuading audiences in general.

Finally, someone might have to use rhetoric in a situation so constrained that he or she has to limit him or herself to concerns about winning the particular case at hand, to the exclusion of any considerations of truth. The *Politics* is at its most cynical-sounding and most prescriptive when, as in books 5 and 6, the statesman is limited to aiming at stability rather than at living well, the overall purpose of politics. In exactly the same way, the *Rhetoric* is at its most cynical-sounding and most prescriptive when persuasion becomes detached from any relation to truth or practical wisdom.

At the end of this section I explain why the *Politics* treats these four tasks separately while the *Rhetoric* makes them inseparable. But I first want to point to one more similarity. The *Politics* has to consider both correct and corrupt constitutions—correct constitutions aim at living well, corrupt ones merely at living and thus at more limited ends such as wealth, honor, or freedom—but it contains no single demarcation between them; the criterion for identifying correct constitutions varies with the meaning of "best" (*aristos*). In the same way, it belongs to the single faculty (*dynamis*) of rhetoric to understand both real and apparent enthymemes (1.1, 1355b15), but the *Rhetoric* contains no single way of distinguishing what lies within the art of rhetoric from what lies outside, or between real and apparent enthymemes, both of which fall within its scope. There are things that lie outside the scope of rhetoric by being too "high," such as scientific teaching; too "low," as are appeals to the emotions, which can corrupt the audience; or simply other alternatives to rhetorical persuasion, such as the "nonartistic proofs" (*atechnoi pisteis*), statements of witnesses, and the evidence of written laws and contracts, which simply have to be produced, not woven into an argument.

An enthymeme is a rhetorical proof (*apodeixis*), a kind of syllogism (*syllogismos tis*) (Aristotle, *Rhetoric* 1.1, 1355a8). It is central to rhetoric under all four understandings, but the meaning of enthymeme and of rationality expand and contract as the meaning of "best" shifts. There are some techniques that would never be part of the art of rhetoric, regardless of how corrupt the audience. For example, wearing a Halloween costume while the opposing litigant is speaking is a distraction and not a relevant consideration in any legal system—such an act can never produce true conviction: "Opinion [*doxa*] requires conviction [*pistis*], and so in turn being persuaded [*pepeisthai*], and therefore reason [*logos*]" (Aristotle, *De Anima* 3.3, 428a19–24). Those exclusions from rhetoric have their political counterpart: there are some people, such as women, children, and slaves, who would never be citizens in any Greek *polis*, no matter how democratic. On the other hand, whether other appeals are appropriate or not depends on the kind of inquiry and the meaning of the "best." In the ideal *polis*, the one that Aristotle says we might pray for and dream about, citizen-farmers are replaced by farm laborers who are slaves. The closer a *polis* approximates the ideal, the smaller will be the number of citizens relative to the whole population. In a similar way, the rhetoric of an ideal situation not only limits rhetoric to argument but narrows argument to exclude purely emotional appeals. The better the *polis*, the more strict the criteria for being a citizen. The better the rhetorical situation, the more restricted will be the sense of argument or reasoning appropriate.

One could separate different statements according to which of the four projects outlined in *Politics* 4.1 corresponds to some particular part of the *Rhetoric* and thus generate a simpler consistency of four attitudes toward the practice of rhetoric. Because rhetoric, like dialectic, is a power to prove opposites—"rhetoric and dialectic alone of the arts prove opposites" (*Rhetoric* 1.1, 1365a35)—Aristotle does not separate the four projects outlined in the *Politics*. There will always be normative standards outside the faculties of rhetoric and dialectic because a faculty for opposites needs an external good, while politics answers to nothing outside itself. The *Rhetoric* has a permanent ambiguity because Aristotle does not treat these four tasks separately, as he does in the *Politics*.

Rhetoric and dialectic, as faculties without definite subject matter, are always in a sense inferior to science and to actual politics and ethics. But in another sense, they have their own integrity. Dialectic differs from demonstrative reasoning because it is based on generally accepted opinions (Aristotle, *Topics* 1.1, 100a20, b18). And yet dialectic "is useful in connection with the ultimate principles of each science; for it is impossible to discuss them on the basis of the principles peculiar to the science in question . . . and it is necessary to deal with them through the generally accepted opinions on each point" (1.2, 101a36–b2). Rhetoric, too, will base its arguments on common opinion but at times lead to understanding of truths beyond opinion.

The complex connections between rhetoric and both dialectic and politics generate three ways in which rhetoric is accountable to things outside itself. First, good laws should leave as little as possible to judgment and hence to rhetoric: "Friendliness and hostility and individual self-interest are often involved, so that judges are no longer able to see the truth adequately, but their private pleasure or grief casts a shadow on their judgment" (Aristotle, *Rhetoric* 1.1, 1345b10–1). Even so, the art of rhetoric is not trying to be science or law but not quite making it because of the pressures of time and the need for decision. Good rhetoric has its own standards and should not simply try to approximate science, as many public figures today try to imitate the supposed certainties of economics. Second, the speaker following the art of rhetoric will not always be victorious, but not because the art was not good enough. The art of rhetoric includes arguments that logic would judge invalid. Nevertheless, the standards for rhetorical argument are not inferior to those of logic—they are different. Because of the connections between argument and character, *logos* and *ēthos*, in rhetoric arguments can fail by being too strong as well as too weak. And third, rhetoric is not speech trying to be the expression of virtue yet not quite making it either. Rhetoric "assumes the character of [slips into the garb of] politics, and those who claim to possess it, partly from ignorance, partly from boastfulness, partly from other human weaknesses, do the same" (1.2, 1356a27–30). Aristotelian rhetoric has responsibilities toward a reality, an audience, and a constellation of ethical virtues, none of which rhetoric itself creates. While rhetoric has these three responsibilities, it also has its own standards of success and excellence. The excitement of reading the *Rhetoric* lies in seeing how Aristotle can bring this off.

Pistis, the central idea in the *Rhetoric*, can be rightly translated as proof, argument, reasoning, persuasion, belief, trust, faith, credit, conviction, and confidence. The credit in Aristotle's *Rhetoric* is similar to the credit of paper money in the United States between 1933 and 1971, where money was not redeemable in gold but not quite left to float free from gold altogether. Before 1933, printed money could be exchanged for gold. Every note represented a particular fraction of an ounce of gold. Since 1971, however, there has been no connection at all between paper money and gold; the worth of a dollar bill depends simply on what people think it is worth. Money is credible simply because people have faith that it is credible, a kind of self-reinforcing credibility that can lead to inflation because of its lack of grounding in gold. The relation between gold and paper money in the intervening years is more complicated. The value of the dollar was fixed in relation to gold—actually, the price of gold was fixed in dollars, which is a complication relevant to my analogy—but individuals could not exchange their paper money for gold. There was a relation between money and gold—not a simple relation of redemption but a more complicated relation of representation and interpretation. It is easy to conceive of rhetoric either as having nothing at all to do with truth, nor with persuading a particular audience, nor with ethics, like money after 1971, or as reducible to knowing and expressing the truth, or to speaking ethically, like paper money before 1933. It is difficult to maintain these tenuous and intermittent ties to knowable reality, to satisfying an audience, and to practical wisdom, as the *Rhetoric* does. These are three different meanings for William James's idea of the "cash value" of an idea. We can fit our words to the world, create the world through our words, or negotiate back and forth between world and word, recognizing that neither is determinate and neither fully under our control.

The *Rhetoric* is the difficult book it is because its ability to erect its own standards is constrained or guided in three distinct dimensions: a fidelity to the facts, the goal of persuading a given audience, and some kind of moral responsibility. Through persuasion, rhetoric makes the indeterminate—indeterminate facts, an audience that has not yet decided, and practical wisdom that has to decide what is the best thing to do—determinate because it leads to a judgment about what to do, what has happened, or what we value. Where things are already defined, there is nothing for rhetoric to do other than persuade the ignorant and frightened patient to take his or her medicine. Making deliberation central, most noble, and most civic (*kallionos kai politikōteras*) (1.1, 1355a8) is one of the most original contributions of the *Rhetoric*; it allows Aristotle to tie rhetoric to all three external guides without those guides being constraints. When any of these is determinate of what to think, say, and do, there is no room for rhetoric. Aristotle places deliberative rhetoric, not forensic or epideictic, at the center of his art to make the art fit for practice by citizens, not experts.

Rhetoric has what I call relative autonomy because none of these three guides is determinate enough to be a sufficient constraint to make rhetoric unnecessary. Rhetoric has permeable boundaries, boundaries that Aristotle points out in the course of his argument but never draws together, as I am doing here. Rhetorical argument has to be faithful to the facts, but we deliberate about an indeterminate future. The rhetorician aims at persuading an audience, but an audience that, like everyone, has not decided until it has to decide. Finally, the judgment of the *phronimos*, the person of practical wisdom, is the ultimate standard of ethics. Aristotelian ethics has few categorical rules—adultery is his example of something that is never right; we might use torture as our example—and to act virtuously is to act as the virtuous person would act, leaving a lot of room for deliberation. In all three dimensions, something external to the act of persuasion keeps rhetoric on course but with a lot of room for success and failure. Here there is an analogy to the *Topics*, which limits itself to problems and theses "where doubt might be felt by the kind of person who requires to be argued with and does not need castigation or lack perception. For those who feel doubt whether or not the gods ought to be honored and parents loved, need castigation" (1.11, 105a4–7).

The ideas of relative autonomy and permeable boundaries make manageable the other great problem in reading the *Rhetoric*. Anyone reading the *Rhetoric* has to wonder whether Aristotle is saying what he thinks is true or whether he is reporting on what most people think. One has to wonder, too, whether the orator is supposed to know what is true or should base his or her arguments on what the audience believes, and whether the tactics he explores in the *Rhetoric* are simply things known to work, or respond to a higher standard. Let us take just three examples. First, the definition of happiness in *Rhetoric* 1.5 looks very different from the definition of happiness at *Ethics* 1.13; Aristotle himself calls the definition of pleasure in *Rhetoric* "neither unclear nor precise" (1.11, 1369b31–2), a description that fits reputable opinions (*endoxa*), not scientific knowledge. Second, the definitions of the emotions in *Rhetoric* 2.2–11 seem to be what in the *De Anima* he calls dialectical rather than scientific definitions and so by scientific standards are incomplete, although easier to understand and use. And third, in *Rhetoric* 2.14 Aristotle says that those in the prime of life, by avoiding the extreme characters of young and old people, are virtuous, making virtue the outcome of a natural aging process rather than the more rigorous ethical development outlined in the *Ethics*. The definitions of happiness and the emotions, and the account of the ethical characters of the different ages of man, seem to accord more with what most people, and so most audiences an orator is going to try to persuade, think, and not what Aristotle's own scientific thinking would say.

There is worse. There are times when Aristotle seems to put speakers on their best behavior and encourages legislators to make sure that speakers behave, and other times when Aristotle gives quite cynical-sounding advice about how to play to an audience's weakness. At the beginning of the *Rhetoric*, Aristotle notes that handbooks of rhetoric that neglect the enthymeme devote their attention to matters outside the subject; for the arousing of prejudice, compassion, anger, and similar emotions has no connection with the matter at hand but is directed only at the judge: "It is wrong to warp the judge's feelings, to arouse him to anger, jealousy, or compassion, which would be like making the rule crooked which one intended to use. Besides, it is evident that the only business of the litigator is to prove that the fact in question is or is not so, that it has happened or not; whether it is important or unimportant, just or unjust . . . is a matter which the judge himself has to decide; it is not the business of the disputants to instruct him" (1.1, 1354a24–31).

The rest of the *Rhetoric* seems completely to betray this program. The reader learns how to create anger and other emotions and to show whether something is important or not, just or not. Book 3 begins apologetically: "We must pay attention to style, not as being right, but necessary; for, as a matter of right, one should aim at nothing more in a speech than how to avoid exciting pain or pleasure. For justice should consist in fighting the case with the facts alone, so that everything else that is beside demonstration [*apodeixis*] is superfluous; nevertheless . . . it is of great importance owing to the corruption of the hearer" (Aristotle, *Rhetoric* 3.1, 1404a1–8). But the investigation of the emotions and other expansions of rhetoric beyond just showing what happened are introduced without apology.

These apparent oscillations come from Aristotle's need to treat the four kinds of "best" together, rather than separating them as in the *Politics*. The guiding limits are worth a look in a little more detail. Just as we saw earlier that the enthymeme and hence the rational side of persuasion could range from reasoning to the exclusion of emotion all the way to a manipulative exploitation of an audience's opinions, so the three guiding boundaries provide a great deal of flexibility in rhetoric's relation to an external reality, to the audience, and to ethical responsibility. Hence my analogy to monetary credit.

First, rhetoric is not science. The rhetorician is not a teacher: "Rhetoric does not include technical knowledge of any particular, defined kind of thing" (Aristotle, *Rhetoric* 1.2, 1355b33–4). For Aristotle, "Rhetoric is partly dialectic . . . for neither of them is identifiable with knowledge of any specific subject, but they are distinct abilities of supplying arguments [*logoi*]" (1.2, 1358a24–6). But Aristotle's art of rhetoric has enough contact with reality to stop it from being "empty rhetoric," an art of words and manipulation (which he identifies with the sophists). The speaker has to know what he is talking about. Outside the three kinds of rhetoric and their ties to political functions, it is not clear that the knowledgeable speaker is more persuasive. The sophist Gorgias, for example, claims that he is more successful than his physician brother at getting patients to take their medicine, but within the politically anchored three genres, the power of mere words and rhetorical display is not so clear.

When the rhetorician inadvertently has an accurate grasp of the truth, he or she is no longer practicing rhetoric but some science: "In proportion as anyone endeavors to make of dialectic and rhetoric, not what they are, faculties, but sciences, to that extent he will, without knowing it, destroy their real character, by crossing over into the domain of sciences, whose subjects are certain definite things [*pragmata*], not merely words [*logoi*]" (Aristotle, *Rhetoric* 1.4, 1359b12–8; see 1.2, 1358a1–28). Perhaps the clearest example is the emergence of the frequency theory of probability, which made certain forms of deliberation otiose (see Hacking 1975). Most of rhetoric's arguments concern probabilities (*eikos*) and signs (*sēmeia*), but occasionally there are necessary signs (*tekmēria*): if a woman has milk, she has given birth. While the rhetorician must find the materials of persuasion, sometimes witnesses and written laws and documents can settle matters without persuasion. Rhetorical power makes no one any wiser (1.2, 1356a32–4). Yet it does help us to make better decisions.

Therefore the question arises: While rhetoric is subordinate to politics, as particular decisions are subordinate to laws, does the rhetorician have to know as much as the politician? The answer is a qualified "yes." Rhetoric is the "offshoot" of both politics and dialectic. And so I pose the parallel question: Does the rhetorician know as much logic and dialectic as the dialectician? In both politics and dialectic, the rhetorician's knowledge is less precise and less systematic but no less expansive. Too much precision would convert a civic art into a professional one.

Second, rhetoric aims at persuading an audience. Aristotle's rhetorician will not do just anything to persuade an audience. Aristotle's rhetorician is not a panderer: "We shall fully possess the method when we are in a position similar to that in which we are with regard to rhetoric and medicine and other such powers [*dynameis*]; that is to say, when we carry out our purpose with every available means [*ek ton endechomenon*]. For neither will the rhetorician seek to persuade nor the physician to heal by every expedient [*ek pantos tropou*]; but if he omits none of the available means [*ton endechomenon*], we shall say that he possesses the science adequately" (Aristotle, *Topics* 1.3, 101b5–10). Yet, while the rhetorician does not simply tell the people what they want to hear, it is the persuasive connection to audience that prevents rhetoric from becoming poetics. What is persuasive is what is persuasive to someone (1.2, 1356b24): no one would ever say that what is logical is logical to someone. Beliefs belong to people in the way that knowledge is no one's property. We not only want our beliefs to be true; we need for them to be ours.

Persuasion is a rational act of someone saying something to someone. Aristotle therefore infers that there are three sources of *pistis*, conviction, or persuasion: the character (*ēthos*) of the speaker, the frame of mind or emotions (*pathē*) of the audience, and the speech (*logos*) itself (*Rhetoric* 1.2, 1356a1–3). (Always bear in mind that *logos* can mean either speech or thought.) The useful and the harmful, the just and the unjust, the noble and the base are not the subject of rhetoric, as they are for many other thinkers, because rhetoric, like dialectic, has no determinate subject. Rather, they are the *ends* of its three genres. The three kinds of rhetoric are different ways of aiming at a judgment and a decision (*krisis*). Other kinds of speech, such as philosophy, might go on indefinitely, but any instance of persuasion imagines an end to speaking and the beginning of action. Rhetoric leads to judgment.

Only by making deliberation (*symboulē*) the focus of attention can Aristotle say the following without being foolish or naive: "That which is true and better is naturally always easier to prove and more convincing" (*aei talēthē kai ta beltiō tēi physei eusyllogistotera kai pithanōtera hōs eipein*; *Rhetoric* 1.1, 1355a31–3). In *On Liberty*, John Stuart Mill calls the idea that truth will eventually triumph over error a "pleasant falsehood." Fortunately, this is not Aristotle's meaning. On the contrary, it is striking how little of the *Rhetoric* looks at rhetoric as a competitive activity. In deliberation, the audience has an interest in getting things right and is therefore not easily distracted by the attractions of error. On any important decision "we deliberate together because we do not trust [*apistountes*] ourselves" (Aristotle, *Nicomachean Ethics* 3.3, 1112b10–1). While rhetoric is in a sense inferior to scientific reasoning—we deliberate when we cannot calculate, and dispute when we cannot measure—collective decision making is not inferior to the deliberations of an individual, even a virtuous individual. Therefore the opportunities and dangers of emotional appeals are greater in judicial than in deliberative rhetoric, and the emotions Aristotle considers in *Rhetoric* 2.2–11 are especially useful in changing the audience's opinion about the parties in a lawsuit. "That which is true and better" is not so clearly easier to prove and more persuasive than its opposite in judicial rhetoric, and epideictic rhetoric entertains by praising fictional and impossible people and situations.

Third, there are important affinities between rhetoric and *phronēsis*, but being able to persuade is no proof of virtue. Both rhetoric and practical wisdom take it on themselves to think about matters where there is no science available: "We call people intelligent [*phronimous*] about some [restricted area] whenever they calculate well to promote some excellent end, in an area where there is no art [*technē*]" (Aristotle, *Nicomachean Ethics* 6.5, 1140a28–30). As Aristotle puts it in book 1 of the *Rhetoric*, the "function of rhetoric is to deal with things about which we deliberate, but for which we have no *technē*" (1.2.12, 1357a6). *Phronēsis*, that is, is a virtue for deliberating about things for which there is no *technē*; rhetoric is a faculty for deliberating about things for which there is no *technē*. Yet rhetorical excellence is not identical to *phronēsis*. Rhetoric differs from politics because, like dialectic, it is a capacity for proving opposites. Justice, by contrast, is a virtue, a habit of acting justly, not a power of acting either justly or unjustly: "What is true of sciences and capacities is not true of states [*hexeis*, the genus of virtue]. For while one and the same capacity or science seems to have contrary activities [*energeiai*, "realizations"], a state that is a contrary has no contrary activities" (Aristotle, *Nicomachean Ethics* 5.1, 1129a13–5).

The autonomy of rhetoric appropriately reaches its extreme point with *ēthos*, which is for Aristotle "almost the controlling factor in persuasion" (*schedon kuriōtatēn pistin*; Aristotle, *Rhetoric* 1.2, 1356a12–3). Paradoxically, while *ēthos* might be the most powerful kind of proof, there is no section of the *Rhetoric* devoted exclusively to *ēthos*, as there is to *pathos* (2.2–11) and to *logos* in several senses of the term. Nevertheless, "this confidence [*pistis*] must be due to the speech [*logos*] itself, not to any preconceived idea of the speaker's character" (1.2, 1356a8). Twice Aristotle uses the expression, "making *logos*—discourse or argument—ethical" (2.18, 1391b, 1392a). Making our arguments ethical could be taken as the overall purpose of rhetoric.

Aristotle's *Rhetoric* is hard to understand as a whole because his project is so ambitious. Like the art of rhetoric itself, it does not speak to our natural expectations—not quite theory, not quite practical advice. If this is a rhetorical art to be practiced by citizens, Aristotle cannot tell his audience anything esoteric or technical. He merely shows the place of persuasive activity in a political and full life.

REFERENCES

Garver, Eugene. 1994. *Aristotle's "Rhetoric": An Art of Character*. Chicago, IL: University of Chicago Press.

Garver, Eugene. 2011. *Living Well and Living Together*. Chicago, IL: University of Chicago Press.

Grimaldi, William. 1980. *Aristotle, "Rhetoric" I: A Commentary*. New York: Fordham University Press.

Grimaldi, William. 1988. *Aristotle, "Rhetoric" II: A Commentary*. New York: Fordham University Press.

Hacking, Ian. 1975. *The Emergence of Probability*. Cambridge: Cambridge University Press.

CHAPTER 11

....

RHETORIC AND SOPHISTICS

....

BARBARA CASSIN

WHEN we, as patient scholars, read about the beginnings of rhetoric, we always learn that it begins, like any *technē*, by a practice improving upon chance. We can trust Roland Barthes's (1970) *L'ancienne rhétorique, aide mémoire*, George Kennedy's (1963) *The Art of Persuasion in Greece*, and even John Poulakos's (1995) more recent *Sophistical Rhetoric in Classical Greece* when they say that rhetoric began, more or less, with the sophists (see Schiappa, ch. 1). Its origins may lie with Corax and Tisias's attempts to help their Sicilian co-citizens win their lawsuits against the two tyrants Hiero and Gelo and to recover their properties (the beginnings of forensic speech); or with the embassy of Gorgias, who attempted to convince the Athenians not to make war on Sicily (deliberative speech); or with Gorgias's depiction in a public speech of Helen as an innocent woman (epideictic speech); or with the many foreign teachers and lawgivers who traveled from city to city. Credible or not, these are all very good stories. What clearly emerges from all of these accounts, however, is that rhetoric comes into existence very early and that the practice and training of the sophists is one of the earliest manifestations of its existence.

In this widely held view, the sophists are orators and rhetoricians, both described by a single Greek word: *rhētores*. Since, however, they are only beginners, they are not very good ones. They are "not yet," just as "phlogiston" is not yet oxygen. Aristotle says this in a very Maoist way at the end of the *Sophistical Refutations*: "The teaching which they gave to their pupils was rapid but unsystematic; for they conceived they could train their pupils by imparting to them not an art but the results of an art, just as if one should claim to be about to communicate knowledge for the prevention of pain in the feet and then were not to teach the cobbler's art and the means of providing suitable foot-gear, but were to offer a selection of various kinds of shoes; for he has helped to supply his need but has not imparted an art to him" (34, 184a2–10; trans. E. S. Forster). To give someone a few fish is not the same thing as teaching him how to fish. Of course, one has to know how to fish before one can teach it, and these early rhetoricians were not yet good enough to understand that.

But this description is a very biased one. In fact, it is a pure Platonico-Aristotelian description, that is, a strictly philosophical one, even if Barthes or Kennedy or Poulakos is not aware of it. And it matters because it makes a difference. My claim in this chapter is that rhetoric is a philosophical invention, an attempt to tame *logos*, in particular the sophist's *logos* and its effects. The creation of rhetoric by philosophy is itself the very first "rhetorical turn": in other words, the first rhetorical turn is in fact a philosophical turn. More specifically, on the basis of a close reading of Plato's *Gorgias*, I contend that ontology invented rhetoric to domesticate—to spatialize—time in discourse. Through rhetoric time is modeled as and reduced to space: a discourse is primarily an organism that unfolds (it has a "plan") and is articulated (for Plato one has to know how to "divide it up"). From a narrow perspective, it is woven out of tropes and metaphors (here again one can hear space being spoken of). In short, it is a question of shifting from the thread to-be-followed and the capture of the *kairos*, the point of time, to the *topos* and the *topoi*, the places of crafted speech. So if there is a sophistic particularity of rhetoric, a strictly sophistical *inventio* of rhetoric and within rhetoric, it would entail identifying something like a rhetoric of time, which would be to rhetorics of space as sophistic discursivity is to Platonico-Aristotelian ontology. It will come as no surprise that this distinction between space and time coincides with the distinction often made between rhetorics of the statement (*l'énoncé*) and rhetorics of enunciation (*l'énonciation*).

IMPROVISATION AND RHETORICS OF TIME

My point of departure is the eponymous text of the Second Sophistic, the very beginning of Philostratus's *Lives of the Sophists* (Anderson 1986, 1993). There may be differences between the old sophistic, the "philosophizing rhetoric" founded by Gorgias, and the Second Sophistic, which is actually just as ancient since its patron is Aeschines but it practices *hypotyposis* and history. However, the founding fathers have at least one feature in common upon which Philostratus discourses at length (Philostratus, *Lives of the Sophists* 482–4): they improvise. While reviewing all possible inventors of improvised eloquence, Philostratus concludes that Aeschines "must have engaged in the greatest number of improvisations" but that it is Gorgias who "began" this practice (482). Improvisation has such an important place in the *Lives of the Sophists* that one could ask whether it alone is not *a* or *the* defining characteristic of sophistics. It is Polemon, a veritable Sarah Bernhardt, who staged the most mediatized dramatizations of this feature in imperial sophistics (537). Improvisation, which is well named *ex tempore* (from the time, at the moment), is a key element that sums up an entire series of features of sophistic *logos* (see Gunderson, ch. 21).

The generic trait of rhetorics of time is that discourse, in its to-be-followed, is not projected as a closed totality, an organic whole (*holon*) to be dissected according to a plan and its articulations. It is not even a *pan* (piece) but rather a *panta*, a plurality of singular emissions that are necessarily in succession: hence the evident link stigmatized in Plato's *Theaetetus* and in Aristotle's *Metaphysics* (book *Gamma*) between the *panta rhei* ("everything flows") and Heracliteanism, if not atomism. What I propose, after Novalis, to call logology—being is an effect of saying—is in fact a chronology: time is the acting or efficient principle of discourse. This gives rise to a series of differential characteristics to be classified.

First, the present, and in particular the present of enunciation as produced by the latter, is included in the chain and cannot form an exception to it. There is no residual presence of the present, nor is there any place for a metalanguage. This is the source of the contradictions and inversions—in short, the entire sophistic paradoxology. The anecdotal paradigm is the well-known dispute between Protagoras and his pupil Euathles: "It is said that once, when he asked his student Euathles for his fees, the latter responded: 'But I haven't won any victories yet! [*oudepō . . . nenikēsa*; pluperfect].' 'Well,' says Protagoras, 'if I win [*all' egō men an nikēsō*; future], because it's I who will have won [*ego enikēsa*; aorist], you will have to pay me [*labein me dein*; present]; and if it's you, because it is you [*ean de su, hoti su*; verbs omitted]'" (Diogenes Laertius, *Lives of Eminent Philosophers* 9.56 [= DK 80 A 1]).[1] This is the very model of judicial eloquence; it can be found at work in a paradigmatic manner in Antiphon's *Tetralogies*. What fictionalizes the fact or the case is the immersion of the *logos* in time, in particular in the time of enunciation of the defense speech (first accusation and then first defense, second accusation and then second defense), such that every argument is apt to turn into its contrary the following moment. It is important to understand here that it is not a matter of proving that, given any argument, a counterargument can be produced, as in the *Dissoi Logoi*, but that every argument turns into its own contrary as soon as it is enunciated *because* it has been enunciated. (The more suspect he is, the guiltier he is; no: he is innocent. The less witnesses there are, the more innocent he is; no: he is guilty.) This follows the model of the *kataballontes* (reversing or catastrophe arguments) that Protagoras is said to have invented (see Gagarin, ch. 2).

This movement is brought to a halt by spatialization, by the *hama* of the principle of noncontradiction: the "at the same time as" that produces the spread-out vision of the *tota simul* and stops the to-be-followed by means of the co-presence of residual presents. This is the correct reading of the work of book *Gamma* of the *Metaphysics*; it opens up the space of writing, of formalization, of truth "tables" via the simple efficacy of the *syn*: *syl-logismos*, or, transposed into the Stoic world, *syn-ēmmenon*.

Second, sense, in turn, is created as the enunciation goes along, not only (as we have seen) at the level of argumentation and of the arrangement of phrases but also at the level of syntax, of the arrangement of words. This is what Gorgias's *Treatise of Non-Being* alerts us to with its exploitation of the slippery nature of any proposition of identity: "Non-being is . . . [therefore it exists] . . . non-being [here again it does not exist]." This is precisely what is blocked by the spatialization of syntax as established after Plato's *Sophist* in Aristotle's *Categories* and *On Interpretation*, in which subject and predicate are constructed as nonnegotiable places.

At this point, one could reflect upon the difference between languages: Are there both temporal and spatial languages? Perhaps Greek is a temporal language in that it presents a series of flexible unities, while German could be a spatial language through the verb being posed at the end of sentences, thus delimiting a *holon*. One could also reflect on the difference in styles: Aristotle forever Germanizing Plato's language; the Attic orators fabricating "periods" in which the phrase is given in its entirety (its greatness, like that of the city, is *eusynopton*: it "can be embraced in a single regard" [*Rhetoric* 3.9, 1409b1]) and in which the meaning is completed and delimited—until Dionysius of Halicarnassus deperiodizes the phrase by working on it via ascent and descent, substituting a kind of circumflex at the level of style.

Third, at the level of the words themselves, the focus is on the sounds and the signifiers: hence the privilege of the voice (*bombos*, *phōnē*) and rhetorical delivery (*actio*), on one hand, as Philostratus endlessly insists; and, on the other hand, the privilege of homonymy, carried by sounds, silences, inflections, accents, and tonalities, as can be seen in any *Sophistical Refutations* from Aristotle to Galen's (Cassin 1986). Joined to the quickness of the instant, this gives rise to the joke, also heavily emphasized by Philostratus (*Lives of the Sophists* 483). The spatial strategy—distinguishing and fixing meanings—is a response to this, as is the return to sender, which at least marks the place of the respondent when a definition is lacking and when dialectic must replace any critique.

This kind of focus generates certain kinds of figures. This was my starting point. "Gorgianize," the word Philostratus invented (*Lives of the Sophists* 493), says a lot, both by its phonic power alone and by its construction around a proper name. With his sonorous figures, Gorgias gives prose both meter and music. This is why Aristotle accused him of having a "poetical style" (*poietikē ... lexis*) and of not having understood that "the style of *logos* is different to that of poetry" (*Rhetoric* 3.1, 1404a24–9; cf. 1406b9, 1408b20). The *Suda* says that Gorgias gave rhetoric its "phrastic" and attributes to him use of more or less all figures (tropes, metaphors, allegories, *hypallages*, catachreses, *hyperbatons*). The properly Gorgianesque figures, however, are—or at least would have to be according to my overly systematic perspective—first of all those audible or sonorous figures in which an enumeration is completed: "And doubling [*anadiplōsesi*] and repetitions [*epanalēpses*] and returns [*apostrophais*] and correspondences [*parisōsesin*]." In any case, it is these figures that Diodorus retains when he describes the surprise of the Athenian philologists hearing Gorgias and his "extraordinary" figures for the first time: "And antitheses [*antithetois*] and isocolons [*isokolois*] and parisons [*parisōsin*] and homeoteleutons [*homoioteleutois*]" (*Suda* = DK 82 A 2 [2: 272]; Diodorus, *Historical Library* 12.53 = DK 82 A 4 [2: 273]).[2] This is why the *Encomium of Helen* can be really heard and properly understood only in Greek: the repetition of alliterations that, as Pierre de Ronsard says of the source, "wanders in whispering" (*ho smikrotatōi sōmati kai aphanestatōi theiotata erga apotelei*), a succession of sounds to describe the nature of the *logos* and testify to her dynasty (Gorgias, *Encomium of Helen*, sec. 8).

Our spatial tropes are opposed to the Gorgianesque tropes. Metaphor and metonymy are two ways of doing panoptical geometry by establishing an analogy of proportion ("The evening is the old age of the day") or by counting the part for the whole (the sail for the boat): it is always a question of "seeing the same," integrating the scene of the world and producing its well-ordered graph.

And fourth, in the end, it is *ex tempore* eloquence that is the primal manifestation of the rhetoric of time. Philostratus searched, literally, for the person in whom "the waves of improvised speeches found their source" (*skhediōn . . . pēgas logōn . . . ek . . . rhuēnai;* *Lives of the Sophists* 482): the metaphorics of time is evidently a metaphorics of flux, of waves. The time of discourse and the time of becoming are the perspectives from which the alignment of sophistics with Heracliteanism appears to be correct; "everything flows" in the world of those who speak. But what has not yet been understood is how *ex tempore* is said in Greek: *skhedioi logoi* (improvised speeches), *skhediazein* (improvise). The adverb and the adjective indicate proximity, whether it be spatial (that of two war-riors in close combat) or temporal (the approach of death as well as the unexpectedness of an event). *Skhedia*, for example, is the word used by Zeus in book 5 of Homer's *Odyssey* to designate the "stout binding" (*epi skhediēs polydesmou* [33] of the ties as numerous as those that bind Ulysses himself to the mast when he passes the Sirens) in that conjunc-tion of spatial adjustment and precariousness, of temporal immediacy, that makes up the approximative essence of the "raft" Ulysses fabricates to escape his love for Calypso. Improvised discourses are the rafts upon which man embarks along the course of time. Philostratus thus continues (as I gloss him):

> It's Gorgias who was at the origin of improvisation: advancing into the theatre at Athens he had the audacity [*etharrēsen*, from *tharsos*, the "bravery" and "bold-ness" of the Homeric hero; it also designates "recklessness" and "impudence," all the more so because everything is happening in full view of the public, in the the-ater] to say: "Propose!" [*proballete*, "throw first," is juridical terminology referring to the leveling of accusations: with *pro-* one secures the beginning, never the out-come], and he was the first to take such a risk without flinching [*to kinduneuma touto . . . anephthegxato*: "he articulated," and since the *phtoggoi* characterize voice as a set of sounds, accents, and articulations that are specific to man for Aristotle, what he articulated is the "danger" linked to the uncertainty of chance and, as Pierre Chantraine notices, to the "cast of the dice"], showing by this, on the one hand, that he knew everything [*endeiknumenos dēpou panta men eidenai*: Gorgias incar-nates the Philostratean definition of the old sophistic, which lays out, in contrast to *philo-sophia*, its omniscience; this is exactly why philosophy has always held sophis-tics to be the mere appearance of wisdom], and, on the other hand, that he would speak about everything by allowing himself to be lead by opportunity [*ephieis tōi kairōi*]. (482)

Here we find ourselves in the crux of the matter: led by Philostratus to the emergence of the *kairos*.

Kairos and Topos

The *kairos* of *kairos* is already instructive. Gorgias, Philostratus supposes, had had enough of Prodicus's hoary chestnut about the young Hercules caught between vice and virtue at the crossroads, an oft-repeated fable he took with him from town to town with success and money—a "stale turn" (*heōla*, from *heōs*, the "dawn," the "morning," characterizes yesterday's food, such as stale bread, for example). "Allow oneself to be taken up by the *kairos*" frames the tale of Prodicus's grand tour: this is the reaction of sophistics to hackneyed moralism.

On the basis of the Hippocratic corpus, on one hand, and Pindaric poetry, on the other, *kairos*, one of the most untranslatable of Greek words, is certainly specific to sophistic temporality. I will underline several of its pertinent features for the rhetoric of time. First of all, why is *kairos* dangerous? Like the Zen instant of archery, *kairos* is the moment of the opening of possibilities: that of the "crisis" for the doctor, the decision between cure and death; that of the unleashed arrow for the Pindaric or tragic archer, between hit and miss. *Kairos*, as distinct from *skopos* (the goal, the bull's-eye at the center), names, for R. B. Onians, the point at which "a weapon could penetrate in a fatal manner" (1951: 344): what is at stake is the arrow as destiny, striking the heart. It is the name of the goal inasmuch as the goal depends entirely upon the instant, the name of place inasmuch as place is entirely temporalized: one can understand how the Latin *tempus* means not only "time" but also "temple"; in considering the *kairos* we glimpse how temple, time, and religious temple belong to the same family of words from the Greek *temnō* (to cut) (on the possible etymologies, see Trédé 1992, ch. 1). With *kairos* it is a question of both opening and cutting: precisely at the "weak point of the armor," as in *The Iliad* (e.g., 4: 185–7), at the joint, in the "opportune moment," inasmuch as both "port" and "door" (*porte*) are heard.

Onians's superb hypothesis, which Bernard Gallet (1990) retains, fleshing it out and rendering it far more precise through the study of texts and drawings, is that *kair'os* ("the correct point that hits the goal," as Chantraine says [1968–80: 2: 480]) and *kaīros* ("the 'rope' that fixes the end of the warp to the loom"—Chantraine again, who is not hostile to this assimilation) "were originally the same" (Onians 1951: 346). For Onians, *kairos* is the name of the spacing, of the void, of the opening created by the warps of fabric. Gallet shows that it is not in fact the opening itself but more exactly that of the "regulating braid," which, like a comb, "separates the threads of the chain by keeping them parallel such that they do not become tangled" (Gallet 1990: 22), tying them together at the same time. This braid thus regulates both the vertical and the horizontal order of the insertion of the weft by marking out the work zone; it is sometimes paired with an apparatus installed at the top of the loom "that maintains the summit of the entire work" (93).[3] Pindar uses the term in this manner, by syllepsis, both in the literal and the figural sense, to refer to the "procedure of weaving themes together" (94, 357). Within the articulation of the *kairos*—and articulation should be understood in all of its senses in English: *kairon ei phthegxaio*, "if it is articulated," "if it is stated," "*kairos*"—words are both shot off and woven (Pindar, *Pythian Odes* 1.81).

This brief inquiry allows us to understand the relationship between *kairos* (the time of the moment) and *telos* (purpose). *Kairos* is *autotelic*: it contains its own purpose within itself. It is the moment in which *poiēsis* and *technē* (characterized by the exteriority between the *ergon*, the work, and its end, and also caricatured by the worst of architects—unlike the bees—possessing an idea of the house that he constructs), at the height of their inventiveness, approach *praxis*, approach a divine interiorization of purpose. But perhaps this is not yet radical enough; perhaps one should go so far as to say that *kairos* is *poros* (passage). One could economize on *telos* and the idea of purpose; hence, the monotonous, secondhand ends ascribed to anyone who lets himself be led by the *kairos* or by the sophists in general: money, success, victory. It would also underline the relation between *kairos* and singularity: with *kairos* one is engulfed in a particular case, and there is nothing apart from the case; all invention is singular because it is perfectly adapted. It is Aristotle, picking up the Platonic critiques at the beginning of the *Meno* (from the "swarm of virtues" to a "beautiful cooking pot, a beautiful woman, a beautiful lyre"), who demands generality precisely against such a conception; he demands that instead of presenting pairs of shoes, one should teach the art of shoemaking.

It is exactly on these two points that the two rhetorics of time and space—of *kairos* and of *topos*—are most clearly distinguished. As Jacques Brunschwig points out in the preface to his translation of the *Topics*, "The place is a machine for making premises *on the basis of a given conclusion*" (2003: xxxix; emphasis added): with *topos* we have the *telos* and all we have to do is follow the predetermined route, whereas with *ex tempore* we have the autotelic opening of the beginning. As for the singular, Brunschwig cites the sole Aristotelian definition of place, "commonplace is that embracing a large number of particular kinds of enthymemes" (*Rhetoric* 2.26, 1403a17), thus showing that "the same commonplace should be able to deal with many different propositions, and one should be able to deal with the same proposition via many different commonplaces" (Brunschwig 2003: xl). In short, there are no cases save those taken on a general, or a topical, level. Accordingly, as both Barthes and Brunschwig observe in the same terms, commonplace is no longer definable save through an extravagant series of spatial metaphors: mold, seam, matrix, circle, sphere, region, well, arsenal, reservoir, headquarters, storehouse, treasure (not to forget the most surprising metaphor, which hints at the *Theaetetus*'s "dovecote" but superimposes some *kairos*: George Ross's "pigeonhole" [Brunschwig 2003: xxxix, n. 3]; Barthes 1970: 206). This is where the kinship between a *logos* that harvests the real and a *topos* that harvests arguments falls apart.

These two conceptions of rhetoric, based on two conceptions of the *logos* and two different comprehensions of time, can also be laid out in a table 11.1:

Table 11.1 The Space of Saving and the Time of Spending

Rhetorics of space	Rhetorics of time
Logos	
space	time
saving	spending
plan	improvisation
organism, articulations	course
hierarchy of *syn-* (syllogism, syntax)	inversion
	(continued)

Table 11.1 Continued	
Rhetorics of space	Rhetorics of time
hama of noncontradiction	paradoxology
statement	enunciation
meaning	signifier, homonymy
periodization	joke, witticism
visual figures (metaphors)	sonorous figures (alliterations)
stock of *topoi*	opening of the *kairos*
Time	
spatial time (movement, size)	temporal time
physical, cosmic (totalized)	logical (involves the raft)
Past–present–future	now
presence of the present	performance

This table depicts the difference between ontology and what I have termed *logology*. To conclude this chapter, I shall sketch a *hypotyposis* of this contrast, portraying its ideal type with the help of a few citations.

The ontological paradigm can be easily identified in a number of Martin Heidegger's texts. It should not be forgotten that it is presented, in one of its clearest and most fully developed expressions, as an interpretation of the Heraclitean *logos*, which is also at work in the exegesis of Protagoras's famous phrase on man as a measure. "Phenomena" are *onta*, time is spatialized into presence, and the power of speech into a space of savings:

Who would want to deny that in the language of the Greeks from early on *legein* means to talk, say or tell? However, just as early and even more originally and therefore already in the previously cited meaning—it means what our similarly sounding *legen* means: to lay down and lay before. In *legen* a "bringing together" prevails, the Latin *legere . . . How does the proper sense of* legein, *to lay, come to mean saying and talking?* In order to find the foothold for an answer, we need to reflect on what actually lies in *legein* as laying. To *lay* (*legen*) means "to bring to lie." Thus, to *lay* is at the same time to place one thing beside another, to lay them together. To *lay* is to gather (*lesen*). The *lesen* better known to us, namely the *reading* of something written, remains but one sort of gathering, in the sense of bringing-together-into-lying-before, although it is the predominant sort. The gleaning (*Aehren-lese*) at harvest time gathers fruit from the soil. The gathering of the vintage (*Trauben-lese*) involves picking grapes from the vine . . . But *gathering* is more than mere amassing.

To *gathering* belongs a collecting that brings under shelter. Accommodation governs the sheltering; accommodation is governed in turn by safekeeping. That "something extra" which makes gathering more than a jumbling together that snatches things up is not something only added afterwards. Even less is it the conclusion of the gathering, coming last. *The safekeeping that brings something in has already determined the first steps of the gathering and arranged everything that follows.* If we are blind to everything but the sequence of steps, then the collecting follows the picking and gleaning, the bringing under shelter follows the collecting, until finally everything is accommodated in bins and storage rooms. This gives rise to the illusion that preservation and safekeeping have nothing to do with gathering. Yet what would become of a vintage (*eine Lese*) which has not been gathered (*gezogen*) with an eye to the fundamental matter (*Zug*) of its being sheltered? *The Sheltering (Bergen) comes first in the essential formation of the vintage.* (Heidegger [1951] 1985: 61; emphasis added)

To speak, for ontology, is thus to gather together and save.

Faced with this position, logology should take as its motto Aelius Aristides's phrase: "Speeches march with the same pace as time [*hoi logoi tōi khronōi symprobainousin*]" (Aelius Aristides, *Against Plato, in Defense of Rhetoric* 408; trans. Behr). Being contemporary with time is being from one moment to the next immediately there: what characterizes the present is not its persevering presence but its transition; discourse, explicitly tied to the *kairos*, to the "opportunity," to the propitious "occasion" seized by the orator, "immediately hits a bull's-eye" (408). "Immediately" is *parakhrēma* in Greek: the adverb, which hypostatizes the locution *para to khrēma*, "available for use," says a little more. It's a question of what is there, ready to hand, with the utility of a utensil available for any occasion, like those "riches" (*khrēmata*) that are so precious yet surpassed by the *logos*. This is the most surprising characteristic of the *logos*: its sempiternal immediacy makes it inexhaustible. Ordinary riches, those that are cumulative and accumulable, are doubly tied to use: they use up the earth that produces them (410), and they diminish when they are spent (409). On the contrary, "The possession and power of discourse is not spent when one uses it" (*para tēn khrēsin*; 409). In other words, real wealth lies in always having the *logos* ready to hand, in being an orator. Not only is discourse not used up when it is spent, but it also increases (410). A more banal transposition is possible: in the terms of a capitalist economy, spending is profitable; in terms of linguistics, competency increases with performance, and it is certainly not by chance that these two models happen to be superimposable. We should insist on this point because in Aristides's oeuvre there is a thematization (and for the first and perhaps the only time related explicitly to its proper object, the *logos*) of one of the most original problematics of sophistics: that of being, not as gathering and collection but as expenditure and consummation. Sophistry plays time against space: this engages, in a formidably precise analogy, one interpretation of being (and in saying an interpretation "of being" I recognize he won) against another, expenditure against accumulation; one interpretation of the *logos* against another: *logos* dis-courses, *logos* extends; the choice of a prevalence, that of *logos* over being (being is thought in terms of *logos*) or that of being over *logos* (*logos* is thought in terms of being). Finally, it implies a choice between two models of time: the coursing of discourse versus the presence of the present that ends by turning the ex-sistant into the "shepherd of being."

A contemporary echo of the sophistic model can be found in an "essay on general economy" for which "the expense (the consumption) of riches [is], in relation to production, the primary object" (Bataille 1989: 12). This echo—admittedly shot through with a no doubt one-sided reading of the valorizations that can be developed on the basis of Friedrich Nietzsche or Sigmund Freud—may well have its dated and unpleasant aspects. However, Georges Bataille does allow one to clearly situate the terms of the opposition. On the side of restricted economy one has the thing, accumulation, useful or commercial exchange, ordinary life; whereas on the side of general economy one has energy and its squandering (the sun, luxury, sex, potlatch, the gift, sacrifice). With the systematization of both economies—which always comes down to the triumph of the first—one cannot, Bataille says, avoid "giving the principles of 'general economy' a fairly ambiguous foundation: this is because squandering energy is always the contrary of a *thing*, but it only enters into consideration inasmuch as it is registered in *the order of things*, as transformed into a *thing*" (89, n. 1).

Literature and Philosophy: A *Mimēsis* of the Second Order

One last remark to conclude this discussion of Philostratus's *Lives of the Sophists*, with which we began: it is as though the difference between the old philosophizing sophistics (Gorgias) and the second, historicizing sophistics (that of Aeschines) was subsumed under the generic unity of improvised discourse. Thus, one finds excellence defined as fluency of expression (*tous xun euroiai hermēneuontas*; Philostratus, *Lives of the Sophists* 484): this confers upon the best philosophers the status of sophist. From this standpoint what Philostratus essentially does is blur boundaries: the boundaries between what, at the end of the entire process, appear to be "genres," "characters," "tendencies": philosophy, history, rhetoric, and literature are unified in sophistics, which is to say, in discursive practices. Philostratus also blurs the boundaries between epochs: the very essence of *paideia* and cultural *mimēsis*, joined to the passion he has for his own great men and his own modernity, undoes chronology in an aesthetic and "kairic" manner.[4] As such, one genuinely enters another world in which philosophy is no longer (or no longer only, or no longer primarily) the generator of signposts, criteria, names, meanings, epochs, temporality: taking sophistics into consideration gives one the means to examine the difference between philosophy and literature.

I believe that with the triumph of sophistical rhetoric in the Second Sophistic one can even say that one has entered into literature. How does one write outside these two great patented genres when one is neither a poet nor a philosopher? An abundant and unstable inventiveness unfolded over more than two centuries, throughout that late and genial antiquity, in a kind of melting pot born from rhetorical exercises, such that progressively and from a retrospective point of view new genres emerged, genres so profoundly transformed that the very genre of genre came into question: biography, autobiography, hagiography, doxography, historiography, literary criticism, and, finally, the novel (see Hall, ch. 18; Pernot, ch. 20; Webb, ch. 22).

What does it mean to say that one enters into "literature"? No doubt it is anachronistic and imprudent, even if unavoidable, to use a term forged across the Latin world but whose concept was stabilized only in the second half of the eighteenth century (the year 1759 saw the publication of Gotthold Lessing's *Briefe die neueste Literatur betreffend*, and 1800 saw that of Madame de Staël's *De la littérature*). However, Philippe Lacoue-Labarthe and Jean-Luc Nancy are quite right in noting that "when it is determined and established, the concept of literature—whatever it covers in its most general sense—tends to designate by predilection 'literature itself' as what imposes itself as the beyond (the truth, the critique, or the dissolution) of what ancient poetics and rhetoric had constituted as the genres of the written or spoken thing" (Lacoue-Labarthe and Nancy 1975: 149). They then specify that literature consequently "tends to fundamentally designate the novel, especially as the latter is understood by romanticism" (149). It is quite striking to see how this definition and diagnostic based on German romanticism agrees with that proposed by Barthes, but on the basis of antiquity. In his article on ancient rhetoric, Barthes insists on the fact that Aristotle's rhetoric is defined in opposition to poetics and that all the authors who recognize such an opposition could be ranked on the side of Aristotelian rhetoric: "This will end when this opposition is neutralized, when rhetoric and poetics fuse, when rhetoric becomes a poetic *tekhnē* of creation" (Barthes 1970: 178). Barthes then adds, "This fusion is crucial since it lies at the very origin of the idea of literature" (179).

Inventio is thus no longer simply one of the five parts of rhetoric (before or besides *dispositio*, *elocutio*, *memoria*, and *actio*) but rather forms the characteristic or essence of rhetoric as open rhetoric. This fusion in literature, characterized by a "poetic" rhetoric, in the sense of "productive," is certainly what is at stake in the Second Sophistic. The Second Sophistic is constantly characterized by its *mimēsis rhētorikē*—what Jacques Bompaire (1958) and B. P. Reardon (1971) propose to translate as "literary culture." *Mimēsis rhētorikē* is the appropriation by imitation—which is developed throughout the entire *cursus* in those schools in which the director was a sophist—of all the works of classical antiquity: poetry, philosophy, history, rhetoric strictly speaking, and, with it, political deliberation. All of this is thus absorbed as species of a quasi-universal genre constituted by general rhetoric placed under the sophistic aegis, via the same movement that Philostratus baptized the Second Sophistic (as we saw). The striking feature of this mimetic rhetoric is clearly its innovative nature: it is inventive and creative. The most violently new of all the new "genres" is of course the one that will become literature par excellence: the novel (see Webb, ch. 22).

But one should not mistake the meaning of this inventiveness. Although I grant, as Bompaire does, great importance to *mimēsis rhētorikē*, the position I adopt is nevertheless completely opposed to his. In *Lucien écrivain*, the subtitle of which is "Imitation and Creation," Bompaire insists on the historical continuity and logical compatibility of what he calls, with Eduard Stemplinger's categories, "philosophical imitation" and "rhetorical imitation." For example, Bompaire argues that "the imitation of books is only a particular case of the imitation of the world" (Bompaire 1958: 26; see Stemplinger 1912).

In my opinion this kind of evaluation leads to a rehabilitation of literary *mimēsis* as philosophically and literarily insufficient as those "rehabilitations" of sophistics that turn the latter into a complement of philosophy. This kind of evaluation is determined by a quite recognizable ethics, one that is foreign, or rather contrary, to the phenomenon in question: "Many excesses have been committed in its name [*mimēsis* in literary history] ... But if it is well managed in its technical detail and great and lofty in spirit, imitation does not dishonour ancient literature" (91). These evaluations concern style as well as content, and the least little detail: "Let's simply recall that Aristotle mocks Gorgias's reflex as the victim of a passing swallow, the reflex of an amateur pedant in mythology" (47). To take the occasion, upon being hit by swallow shit [*caca d'hirondelle*], to exclaim, "Shame on you, Philomela!" is solely pompous or "tragic" in the name of the separation of poetics and rhetoric (Aristotle, *Rhetoric* 3.3, 1406b15–9). From the standpoint of general rhetoric, of sophistics, of literature, the difference between "the evening is the old age of the day" and Gorgias's exaggerated figure is absolutely pertinent. It could even symbolize the difference between a first-order *mimēsis* of nature and a second-order *mimēsis* of culture. On one hand, art imitates nature and perfects it: with Aristotle's *Poetics* it becomes possible to describe carrion (4, 1448b6–19). On the other hand, it is "only" a matter of *logos*, of *mimēsis* transited [*transie*] by reference, according to the most ironic mode of the palimpsest. Again: ontology and phenomenology against logology.

That one enters, with this, into "literature" is also the sign, once and for all, that Platonico-Aristotelian philosophy has won—hence the natural, appropriate, and thus unavoidable character of Bompaire's judgment. One cannot escape the imperious conclusion: even if rhetoric and sophistics triumph upon the scene of the world, become the mistresses of the ears of youth, of the ears of princes and crowds, it is philosophy that will have chosen the ground: their terrain as literature, not as philosophy, and quite precisely as nonphilosophy. Aristotle's metaphysical gesture excluding "he who speaks for the pleasure of speaking" from the community of rational beings has repercussions: literature as such is projected into an elsewhere [*un ailleurs*]. Philosophy can quite easily treat it as an object and draw up its aesthetic rules; no doubt it is also obliged to recall, at least from time to time, beyond the wealth, risks, and inversions of the discursive regimes that Plato tries out, that it is itself a discourse, and to reflect upon the styles that suit it. But a "writer," orator, or novelist, for his part, does not have, as such and philosophically, the right to believe himself to be a philosopher. And this, regularly but not without contestation, commotion, and exceptions (obviously Nietzsche), persists to this day: Jacques Derrida will not have been doctor *honoris causa* at the University of Cambridge. (Translated by Oliver Feltham.)

Notes

1. Diogenes has just said that Protagoras is "the first to have distinguished *mere kronou*," the "parts of time" (which is always understood as "the tense of verbs"), "and to have exposed the dynamic of the *kairos*" (Philostratus, *Lives of Eminent Philosophers* 52).

2. Charles Sears Baldwin concludes his overview of the *Lives of the Sophists* by expanding space and time still further: "The same 'Gorgian figures' are learned by St. Augustine in Latin Africa, by St. Gregory of Nazianzus in the Greek East, and by the pagan Libanius. Greco-Roman rhetoric was as pervasive as Roman law and almost as constant" (1959: 9).

3. Gallet identifies and then verifies, in an admirable fashion, the four technical functions that produce a semantic descendance: as "guiding or main thread," *kairos* is a "take," an "influence," a "control"; as the "regulating thread" that limits the breadth of the loom determining the zone of weaving, it is a "rule," a "good order," a "precise measure," a "brevity," and an "advantage"; as "interwoven thread" encountering each of the warp's threads at a right angle, it is a "conjunction," a "conjuncture," an "occasion," a "propitious moment"; and as "separating thread" between the lap of odd threads and that of even threads, it is a "choice," a "separation," a "judgment," and a "decision" (1990: 65).

4. The difference between the two sophistics is certainly at work in the composition of the treatise because the second section of the first book deals with the old sophistic, from Gorgias (ch. 9) to Isocrates (ch. 17), while the third section and all of the third book deal with the Second Sophistic. But the sophists of the Second Sophistic do not stop imitating Gorgias (Proclus of Naucratis [Philostratus, *Lives of the Sophists* 604]; Scopelian [518]). Besides, the place of Aeschines (ch. 18) clearly demonstrates the ambiguity of the classification. He follows Isocrates, who is chronologically the last of the ancients. He precedes Nicetes of Smyrna, who flourishes at the end of the first century CE; logically the latter is the first of these "moderns" who go up until Claudius Aelianus at the end of the third century. One can see how chronologically twisted the sequence is: it resembles a collage, a precipitate of the ancient and the modern, that skips four centuries without leaving a trace and ignores those who elsewhere count among the greats.

References

Anderson, Graham. 1986. *Philostratus: Biography and Belles Lettres in the Second Century A.D.* London: Croom Helm.

Anderson, Graham. 1993. *The Second Sophistic: A Cultural Phenomenon in the Roman Empire.* London: Routledge.

Aristotle. 2003. *"Topiques." Tome I: livres I–IV.* Translated by Jacques Brunschwig. Paris: Belles Lettres.

Baldwin, Charles Sears. 1959. *Medieval Rhetoric and Poetic (to 1400).* Gloucester, MA: Smith.

Barthes, Roland. 1970. *L'ancienne rhétorique. Aide-mémoire. Communications* 16.

Barthes, Roland. (1970) 1994. "The Old Rhetoric: An *aide-mémoire.*" In *The Semiotic Challenge,* translated by Richard Howard, 11–95. Berkeley: University of California Press.

Bataille, Georges. 1989. *The Accursed Share.* Vol. 1, *Consumption.* Translated by Robert Hurley. New York: Zone Books.

Bompaire, Jacques. 1958. *Lucien écrivain.* Paris: De Boccard.

Cassin, Barbara, ed. 1986. *Positions de la sophistique.* Paris: Vrin.

Chantraine, Pierre, ed. 1968–1980. *Dictionnaire étymologique de la langue grecque.* 4 vols. Paris: Klincksieck.

Gallet, Bernard. 1990. *Recherches sur* kairos *et l'ambiguïté dans la poésie de Pindare.* Bordeaux: Presses universitaires de Bordeaux.

Heidegger, Martin. (1951) 1985. *Early Greek Thinking.* Translated by David Farrell Krell. New York: Harper Collins.

Kennedy, George A. 1963. *The Art of Persuasion in Greece*. Princeton, NJ: Princeton University Press.

Lacoue-Labarthe, Philippe, and Jean-Luc Nancy. 1975. "Le dialogue des genres." *Poétique* 21 no. 1: 148–157.

Onians, Richard Broxton. 1951. *The Origins of European Thought*. Cambridge: Cambridge University Press.

Poulakos, John. 1995. *Sophistical Rhetoric in Classical Greece*. Columbia: University of South Carolina Press.

Reardon, Bryan P. 1971. *Courants littéraires grecs des IIe et IIIe siècles après J.-C.* Paris: Les Belles Lettres.

Stemplinger, Eduard. 1912. *Das Plagiat in der griechischen Literatur*. Leipzig: Teubner.

Trédé, Monique. 1992. Kairos: *l'à-propos et l'occasion: Le mot et la notion d'Homère à la fin du IVe siècle avant J.-C.* Paris: Klincksieck.

PART II

ANCIENT ROMAN RHETORIC

CHAPTER 12

THE DEVELOPMENT OF ROMAN RHETORIC

WILLIAM J. DOMINIK

ROMAN rhetoric is as much a reflection of the natural process of cultural and political change as it is an expression of its theoretical and practical development from its Greek origins. Although rhetoric at its most basic level at Rome involved the act of speaking and at a more academic level was governed by a complex set of rules, it is best considered as part of a larger cultural process. A positive account of the development of Roman rhetoric may seem difficult to extract from the sources because of the theme of secondariness and decline that runs through the narrative of its evolution. But the Roman conception of rhetoric from the very beginning looked back ideologically to the native, rustic rhetoric that lay as its ultimate source in practical terms. Therefore a constructive approach involves not only a consideration of the ways Roman rhetoric evolved from the Greek but also how it made its mark upon the discipline so that it became an academic exercise and cultural phenomenon distinctive in its own right. The development of Roman rhetoric reflected established values of the male elite class even as its theory and practice helped to shape in important ways cultural attitudes toward national, class, and gender identity.

As the cornerstone of the Roman educational system, rhetoric played an important role in providing the young male elite at Rome with the training and experience necessary to defend and maintain their position in the public arena (see Steel, ch. 16). The practice of rhetoric in public meetings (*contiones*), law courts, Senate, Forum, and public funerals and halls was as much a mark of social privilege as it was a reflection of the political and social power of the patrician class. The public assemblies provided adult male citizens with the opportunity to hone their rhetorical skills for legislative and electoral purposes in a sometimes boisterous environment (on mass oratory, see Morstein-Marx 2004). But the pinnacle of Roman rhetoric seems to have been achieved in the Senate even though its prescribed and unwritten rules, social hierarchy, and political alliances predetermined, if not constrained, its use by highly skilled practitioners.

In reality only a relatively small number of the male elite class were able to speak at the public assemblies and in the Senate. In the public assemblies only those who had

been elected or invited could speak, while in the Senate even those who had the privilege of speaking did so according to their social rank and seniority. When the Senate
increased in size during the first century BCE, with some of the new members coming from provincial towns and from the equestrian, mainly nonsenatorial, class, it
remained a body of status and privilege distinguished by the exercise of rhetoric. It was
probably the law courts that provided the greatest number of opportunities for those
members of the upper classes who were intent upon making a name for themselves (see
Enos, ch. 13). The political advancement of a figure like Cicero, who in 63 BCE became
the first man in over 30 years to become a *novus homo* (new man) when he was elected
consul (cf. Cicero, *De lege agraria* 2.3), owed much to the rhetorical and oratorical skills
that he had acquired and displayed in his successful defense of prominent clients in the
courts.

EARLY STAGES

The earliest extant reference to rhetoric in Roman literature appears in Ennius's *Annals*
(308; Skutsch 1985: 96), a work that appeared just before or after the beginning of the
second century BCE. Cicero notes that the reference to Suada is the Roman counterpart
of Peithō, the Greek goddess of persuasion (*Brutus* 59). The reference in Ennius appears
about the same time Suetonius observes that rhetoric made its presence known in Rome
(*De rhetoribus* 1). Cicero, the most influential Roman rhetorician and orator of the
Republic, observes that formal rhetoric was originally unknown to the Romans but that
they achieved success as the result of their own talent and efforts; eventually, according
to Cicero, contact with Greek orators and teachers inspired Romans to develop their
skills through the study of formal rhetoric (*De oratore* 1.4.14). From the rhetorical treatises it seems that the two principal avenues of entry for Greek rhetoric into Rome were
via scholars familiar with rhetoric who came to Rome from Greece and Magna Graecia
as teachers and via Romans who traveled for the purpose of study to Greece, especially
Athens and Rhodes, and then returned to Rome. Despite the influx of Greek rhetorical
ideas into Rome, Cicero suggests that the Romans utilized rhetoric in the public setting according to the whims of individual orators without recourse to a systematized
form of rhetoric. This usage reflects rhetoric in its original form as a means of persuasion or celebration in the public sphere. In the early stages of its formal development,
however, Roman rhetoric was essentially Greek rhetoric adapted to the Roman environment, principally the law courts and public assemblies, though it always involved more
than just public speaking. While rhetoric appeared increasingly to function as a legal
instrument whose objective was concerned with persuasion, the political environment
assumed an important role in its expansion during the Republic (see Connolly, ch. 14).

One of the defining features of Roman society was its adaptability to and adaptation
of the ideas and practices of other cultures, as Caesar observes (Sallust, *Bellum Catilinae*
51.37–8). This was the case even when a culture like that of the Greeks was viewed with

suspicion and intolerance, as exemplified in the attitude of Marcus Porcius Cato: "Since that race will give us their culture, it will corrupt everything" (*quandoque ista gens suas litteras dabit, omnia corrumpet*; Pliny, *Naturalis historia* 29.14). The elder Cato himself reveals a familiarity with Greek culture and traces of knowledge of Greek rhetoric in his writings. This ambivalence toward things Greek applied particularly to Greek rhetoric in the early stages of the development of Roman rhetoric. During this period it seems that Rome resented and resisted Greek rhetoric even as it was absorbing its system and rules, as suggested in Cato's own debt to Greek rhetoric evident in the extant fragments of his speech, *Oratio pro Rhodiensibus* (Aulus Gellius, *Noctes Atticae* 6.3; Leeman 1963: 43–9). This process of assimilation invigorated the discipline of rhetoric and helped to transform Roman culture.

POLITICS OF GREEK RHETORIC AT ROME

The increasing presence of Greek rhetoric in Rome and its growing influence in the second century BCE is apparent from the decree that expelled the rhetoricians from Rome in 161 BCE along with the philosophers (Suetonius, *De grammaticis* 25), who were instrumental in the teaching of rhetoric. The reason for the rhetoricians' expulsion is difficult to ascertain, but it was perhaps due to the relative sophistication and effectiveness of Greek techniques in comparison with Roman rhetoric as embodied in the contemporary figure of the elder Cato, who stood both for rustic simplicity and anti-Hellenic sentiment. But the ban of the rhetoricians may also have had something to do with the concern felt by the senatorial elite over the use of rhetoric by outsiders who were beginning to forge careers that were perceived as a threat to the established political order. Although Cato, as a censor, may have been one of the voices behind the decree, he was a distinguished orator himself (cf. Cicero, *Brutus* 60, 65) and was knowledgeable about rhetoric. According to Quintilian, "Marcus Cato was the first Roman . . . to handle this topic" (*Romanorum primus . . . condidit aliqua in hanc materiam M. Cato*; *Institutio oratoria* 3.1.19), which may refer to a discussion of the sort evident in these surviving fragments of Cato: "The orator is a *vir bonus* who is skilled in speaking" (*orator est . . . vir bonus, dicendi peritus*; Quintilian, *Institutio oratoria* 12.1.1); "Grasp the subject matter; the words will follow" (*rem tene, verba sequentur*; Cato, *Libri ad filium*; Julius Victor 17, in Halm 1863: 374). While Cato's definition of *vir bonus* ("a good man") alludes to the moral conduct and skills expected of an elite male Roman, his advice to the orator, which stresses that speech follows naturally from having knowledge of the topic under discussion, suggests that the simplicity of the speech act is to be valued over the complex rules that governed formal rhetoric. Cato's concept of the Roman orator involved more than simply the ability to speak well: gender and status (*vir*) were closely linked with rhetorical competence, which emphasized the unique role of the male elite class in the social and political hierarchy of Rome. Simply put, rhetoric in Roman hands involved the exercise and maintenance of civic power by this small, privileged class.

It is possible to regard a figure such as Cato, who relied upon practical experience instead of formal training in rhetoric, as representing a crude stage in the development of Latin style and therefore as being deficient in comparison with later orators. Romans were uncertain what to make of the styles of different generations of orators but had the tendency themselves to regard early orators as primitive and less sophisticated. Cicero's assessment of Cato is an illustration of this tendency, but even he acknowledges that Cato's antiquated expression was appropriate for his own time (*Brutus* 68). As suggested in Cicero's observation, a more constructive approach is to consider style to be a reflection of a particular set of linguistic and cultural circumstances at work. Early Roman rhetoric attempted to assert its independence from Greek rhetoric in regard to style even at an early stage of development. In particular, Cato's approach is exemplary of the native Latin rhetoric that strove for its own effects rather than merely to adopt the models of the Greek rhetorical system (Sciarrino 2007). For Cato Roman rhetoric was as much about attitude and practicality as it was about formal theory and technique. He valued brevity, simplicity, and forcefulness, qualities that mirrored the Attic style of the Greeks, which may seem ironic given the derogatory comments made by him about Greek culture and rhetoric. Asianism, a florid style so called because it was thought to have originated in Asia Minor (Quintilian, *Institutio oratoria* 12.10.16–22), was viewed as excessive and therefore antithetical to the Roman character and sensibility.

Whatever the true motivation of the decree in 161 BCE may have been in respect of the rhetoricians, it was not able to stem for long the tide of Greek rhetoric in Rome, as suggested by the fact that Greek rhetoricians rather than Cato gained supremacy in the years following the ban. At first it seems that the Greek teachers of rhetoric reemerged in the private homes of elite Roman families (cf. Cicero, *Brutus* 27.104) and then gradually regained a foothold in the public setting. Famous rhetoricians such as Diophanes of Mytilene and Menelaus of Marathus, teachers of Tiberius Gracchus and Gaius Gracchus, respectively, taught rhetoric to both patricians and plebeians by using handbooks that made the subject comprehensible to those who had a moderate level of education. By the beginning of the first century rhetoric was a permanent fixture in Rome.

POLITICS OF ROMAN RHETORIC

While the earlier banishment of rhetoricians from Rome may be attributable partly to prejudice against Greek rhetoric, it is apparent that the sentiment toward rhetoric, especially Greek rhetoric, had changed markedly by the turn of the first century BCE. This changed sentiment is evident in two seemingly contradictory developments. The first was the composition of a Roman *commentarium* (notebook; Cicero, *De oratore* 1.48.208) or *libellus* (little book; 1.47.206) of rhetoric by the orator Marcus Antonius between 102 and 92 BCE. Judging from Cicero's account and the comments of Quintilian, this book appears to have been a compilation of notes and suggestions derived from Antonius's oratorical activity at Rome, including his practical experience in the law courts, rather than an actual rhetorical treatise; in addition, it seems to have been drawn from the Peripatetic and Academic philosophy he encountered in Athens (cf. Cicero, *De oratore* 1.8.82–20.93). While the sources convey the impression that rhetoric had become fully entrenched in Roman society by this time, it had been dominated by Greek rhetoricians. Antonius's *commentarium* was a reflection of the natural appeal of rhetoric to a Roman mind-set as well as an attempt to popularize it in Rome. This notebook was also a reflection of the increased confidence among Roman practitioners of rhetoric and an attempt to adapt it to prevailing social and political conditions.

The second development occurred in 92 BCE when Licinius Crassus and Domitius Ahenobarbus, the censors for this year, promulgated an edict disapproving of the Latin rhetoricians (Suetonius, *Rhetorica* 1). Crassus, a leader among the *optimates*, provides us in Cicero's *De oratore* with a cultural reason for the attempted suppression of the Latin rhetoricians by remarking that they lacked the education and sophistication of their Greek counterparts (3.24.93–5). Political motives were also evident, as may have been the case with the earlier ban of rhetoricians in 161 BCE. The decree in 92 BCE may have originated principally with Crassus, as his character suggests in *De oratore*, where there is no mention of Ahenobarbus, and may have been intended in part to protect the interests of the elite classes by blocking the path of political and social advancement to other classes. Plotius Gallus, who supposedly was the first rhetorician to teach in Latin (Cicero, *Epistula ad Marcum Titinium*; cf. Suetonius, *De rhetoribus* 2), was admired by Gaius Marius (Cicero, *Pro archia* 9.20). Greek culture and language were associated with the elite classes at Rome, with which Crassus identified and to which Marius was indifferent and even opposed to in Greek culture (Sallust, *Bellum jugurthinum* 85.32; Plutarch, *Marius* 2.2; Valerius Maximus, *Facta et dicta memorabilia* 2.2.3). Although Cicero (*Pro archia* 9.19) and some modern scholars (e.g., Clarke 1996: 12) have suggested that Marius's opposition was a reflection of his own ignorance or lack of cultural refinement, the privileging of Roman rhetoric itself was a way of asserting Roman superiority, a notion with which Marius would have concurred, judging from the comments of Plutarch (*Marius* 2.2) and Valerius Maximus (*Facta et dicta memorabilia* 2.2.3; cf. 2.2.2).

The decree may also reflect the political tensions that existed between Rome and her Italian allies that led to the outbreak of the Social War in 91 BCE. According to this scenario, the Latin rhetoricians and their schools would have been viewed as the means by which the allies obtained the skills necessary to push their case for a larger voice in public affairs at Rome. Regardless of the precise reasons for the edict in 92 BCE, it is apparent that the practice of rhetoric was seldom far removed from the political arena during the Republic.

RESHAPING GREEK RHETORIC

The censors' edict does not seem to have had a long-standing effect, however, judging by the appearance of two handbooks of rhetoric that emerged soon afterward. The earliest extant Roman rhetorical treatise is Cicero's *De inventione*, which may have appeared around 87/6 BCE or a little afterward; this dating is based on Cicero's own remark that the *De inventione* was composed in his youth (*De oratore* 1.1.5), which was probably in 88 BCE at the age of 18 after he had studied philosophy under Philon of Larissa in Rome (cf. Cicero, *Epistulae ad familiares* 13.1, *Tusculanae disputationes* 2.3). The *De inventione* was followed around the same time, possibly 86–2 or even later, by the *Rhetorica ad Herennium*, of uncertain authorship, which is the first complete rhetorical treatise in Latin to survive. Both of these works are derived from scholastic activity and a common Greek source that probably developed on the island of Rhodes, an important rhetorical center, and provide a glimpse of the state of rhetoric at Rome in the first couple of decades of the first century BCE. These early handbooks follow in the tradition of Greek rhetorical doctrine, specifically Anaximenes's *Rhetorica ad Alexandrum*, the sole extant pre-Aristotelian manual of rhetoric; Aristotle's *Rhetorica*; and the work of Hermagoras of Temnos.

Nonetheless, the beginnings of an independent Roman spirit and Roman ideas about rhetorical education can be detected in the *De inventione*, which possibly signals an attempt on the part of Cicero to establish his reputation as a Roman rhetorician in an environment dominated by Greek rhetorical treatises, and especially the more sophisticated *Rhetorica ad Herennium*. The *Rhetorica ad Herennium* not only conceives the idea of a Roman rhetoric based on correct Latinity (4.12.17) but also places an emphasis upon clarity, simplicity, and practicality in contrast to the complex, subtle, and theoretical nature of the Greek rhetorical system (cf. 1.1.1). Despite the ambivalent relationship between rhetoric and philosophy, much Roman rhetorical doctrine was influenced by Greek philosophy, as is evident in these texts (e.g., Cicero, *De inventione* 2.3.8; *Rhetorica ad Herennium* 2.11.16, 2.21.34, 3.2.3, 4.17.24) and as Crassus in *De oratore* relates to Antonius (3.15.56–8.68), whose own doctrine of *status*, the determination of the issue under dispute, is indicative of such influence (cf. Quintilian, *Institutio oratoria* 3.6.45; Montefusco 1986: 36–47, 197–203).

The system (*technē*) of rhetoric conveyed in these handbooks, which bear the clear marks of the philosophical and cultural content of Greek rhetoric, suggests that it had arrived in Rome in a comprehensive and sophisticated form. However, the description and analysis of rhetorical rules and doctrines in these early Roman manuals bear evidence of some simplification of the complex Greek system of rhetorical rules and doctrines. At the same time, a reflexive, rhetorically self-conscious approach is apparent, especially in the Romanization of Greek rhetorical terms and the use of exempla from Roman (as opposed to Greek) literature, history, and politics; this approach is also apparent in the treatment of such matters as style and the arrangement of subject matter in comparison with the Greek system. Despite the growing confidence of Roman rhetoricians evident in the appearance of their own manuals, they contain inconsistencies, uncertainties, and cautious remarks. Antonius did not finish his *commentarium* (Quintilian, *Institutio oratoria* 3.1.19), which Cicero viewed as being a slight work (*Brutus* 163); nor did Cicero, who repudiated his early *commentariola* (short treatises) in the later *De oratore* (1.2.5). The unknown author of the *Rhetorica ad Herennium* remarks that he is writing his work for his friend and relation Gaius Herennius (1.1.1, 4.56.69), which may suggest that it was not intended principally for a wider readership.

Other treatises soon followed, notably Cicero's *De oratore* and *Partitiones oratoriae*, which were composed in the 50s BCE. These were in turn followed by Cicero's *Brutus* and *Orator*, composed in 46 BCE, in which the orator placed great emphasis on stylistic and linguistic matters in his polemic against the Atticists. Cicero's own prose style seems to be a reflection of the views he espouses in these works and represents a notable departure from the native Roman style cultivated by Cato and other early rhetoricians (cf. Leeman 1963: 182–4). By the end of the first century CE, Roman rhetoric had developed its own systematic body of knowledge sufficiently to enable Quintilian to produce the most comprehensive handbook of rhetoric yet to appear: his *Institutio oratoria*.

From the beginning Roman rhetoric was much more than the mere systematization of Greek rhetoric. A Roman cultural dynamic and perspective pervaded even the earliest treatises because rhetoric assumed a significant role in the construction of an elite male identity. On a practical level the influence of rhetoric was felt especially in the political and judicial spheres, which were closely linked (see Enos, ch. 13; Connolly, ch. 14). Political power in republican Rome was concentrated in the Senate, the seat of the central government, and rhetorical activity in this restricted council at Rome took place among a small, elite group of senators. It was not until the latter part of the second century BCE, after the reforms of the Gracchi, that formal rhetoric appears to have assumed a larger role in Roman society. The popularization of the law depended in part on removing the courts from the power of senators, who were accustomed to dominating the judicial landscape and controlling its proceedings. This political development was reinforced in the judicial sphere, where Roman law became entrenched as a codified system, a process that seems to have begun with the *De usurpationibus* by Appius Claudius Caecus, censor in 312 BCE, and to have been continued by Quintus Mucius Scaevola and Servius Sulpicius Rufus into the first century BCE (cf. Bauman 1983: 21–66, 340–421, 1985: 4–65). The widespread use of rhetoric at Rome began with the great political trials when the introduction and rapid growth of prosecution on the popular level, that is, by accusers from outside the leading families at Rome, gave rise to much litigation (cf. David 1992: 281–310, esp. 286). The establishment in 149 BCE and growth of *quaestiones perpetuae* (standing jury courts) provided a legal mechanism by which leading citizens and politicians could institute criminal proceedings against another party (Cloud 1994: 491–530). Lawyers were senators and former magistrates and, as patrons of clients, were involved in criminal and civil cases. The bond between *patroni* and *clientes*, which dominated the Roman social fabric, naturally extended to the judicial arena in which patrons defended the rights of their clients and were supported in turn by them.

SYSTEMATIZING RHETORICAL EDUCATION

A picture of the system of rhetorical education in the early part of the first century can be constructed from the early rhetorical handbooks. At this stage there was no formal system of education in which students would progress from one level of competence to the next level. The role of the rhetor was not clearly defined, and, as Suetonius notes, each taught according to his training and his inclination (Suetonius, *De rhetoribus* 1). Although the methods of individual *rhetores* varied, the essential aims of the training remained the same: a thorough familiarization with the principles, rules, and definitions of the Greco-Roman rhetorical system. In addition to acquiring a knowledge of this system, a student would be expected to become proficient in speaking through the practice of preliminary exercises known as *progymnasmata*, which were intended mainly to enable students to learn to express the same idea in various ways. Suetonius describes how these exercises involved not only explaining speeches in regard to their figures, stories, and fables but also composing narratives, translating Greek works, praising and blaming notable men, arguing two sides of a given question, and defending or refuting the credibility of myths (1).

These aforementioned exercises were intended to provide a basic preparation for the more advanced exercises to follow. But even during the early part of the first century BCE it seems these elementary exercises already were under pressure from the more advanced exercises that dealt more directly with (or were seen to be more relevant to) the issues raised in the public assemblies and cases of the law courts. Many of these cases presumably were used as exercises in the schools. Indeed, Crassus in *De oratore* stresses not only the value of real-life training and practical experience (3.10.74) but also the importance of debating issues that resemble those of actual cases brought before the court (1.33.149), while he and other speakers allude to a number of cases similar to those of the assemblies and law courts (e.g., 1.57.244, 2.24.100, 2.30.132).

Some of the cases cited in *De inventione* (e.g., 1.6.8, 2.23.72–32.98, 2.51.153–4), *Rhetorica ad Herennium* (e.g., 1.11.19, 1.15.25), and *De oratore* (e.g., 2.15.116, 2.16.67, 3.28.109, 3.29.112–7) are a philosophical exercise of the type known as a *thesis* or *quaestio*. In this type of exercise the speaker is required to argue between two or more possible courses of action (cf. *Rhetorica ad Herennium* 3.2.2). Some topics deal with natural themes (e.g., what the shape of the world is [*De inventione* 1.6.8]) or abstract themes (e.g., whether virtue should be desired for its intrinsic value or for some benefit it brings [*De oratore* 3.29.112]); others treat issues of social life and mores (e.g., whether it is the duty of a good man occasionally to tell a lie [3.29.113]) as well as law and politics (e.g., whether right is the interest of the majority [3.29.115]). Some of the topics are from Greek and Roman history (e.g., *De inventione* 2.26.78–30.94; *Rhetorica ad Herennium* 1.15.25; *De oratore* 3.28.109), while the majority have no specific historical or geographical context (e.g., *De inventione* 2.24.72–6.78).

When a case was given a specific speaker, the exercise was classed as a *hypothesis* or *suasoria* (deliberation; *Institutio oratoria* 3.5.11) and was designed to train the speaker who would give advice in a public meeting. This type of exercise required the speaker to assume the perspective of a famous historical or mythological figure and to deliberate on the course of action to be taken in response to a dilemma or to dispense advice to this figure. Such questions dealing with Carthage cited in the aforementioned works of Cicero include whether any harm would come to the Roman state if Carthage was to be left unscathed (*De inventione* 1.8.11); whether an army should be sent to Macedonia against

Philip to support Roman allies or left in Italy to confront Hannibal (1.12.17); whether it is better to destroy Carthage or leave her standing (*Rhetorica ad Herennium* 3.2.2; cf. *De inventione* 1.12.17); and whether Hannibal, when recalled from Italy to Carthage, should remain in Italy, return to Carthage, or invade Egypt and capture Alexandria (*Rhetorica ad Herennium* 3.2.2).

Another type of exercise was the *controversia* (disputation), a forensic exercise that consists of a statement of one or more laws—sometimes related to contemporary Roman law—followed by the circumstances of a fictitious case in which the speaker argued one side or the other. Antonius cites one such example in Cicero's *De oratore*: "The law forbids a foreigner to mount the wall; he mounts the wall, repels the enemy, and is prosecuted" (*lex peregrinum vetat in murum ascendere; ascendit; hostes repulit; accusatur*; 2.24.100). This exercise shows that the *controversia* itself was already in existence in 91 BCE, the dramatic date of the *De oratore*, or at least by 55 BCE, the date of its composition (Clarke 1996: 17–8).

THE PHENOMENON OF DECLAMATION

The altered political conditions of the Empire naturally influenced the direction of public rhetoric (Dominik 1997: 59–66, 2007: 332–4). While the public assemblies seem to have diminished considerably in importance as a venue for the orator during the Empire, opportunities for speaking still existed in the Senate and especially the law courts; in addition, orators turned increasingly to the public halls in order to display their talents. In this setting, rhetoric functioned as a social pastime where orators practiced declamation—the *suasoria* and *controversia*—for intellectual fame and enjoyment (see Gunderson, ch. 21). During the Empire, declamation became associated with showmanship and exhibitionism (cf. Pliny, *Epistulae* 2.14; Quintilian, *Institutio oratoria* 2.10), but even during the Republic a figure such as Cicero strove for persuasive and emotional effects that depended upon a theatrical mode of delivery (Hall 2007).

There is little to distinguish the themes of these exercises from those practiced in the Republic. Examples of declamatory exercises of the late Republic and early Empire survive in the elder Seneca's *Controversiae* and *Suasoriae*, pseudo-Quintilian's *Declamationes majores* and *Declamationes minores*, and the *Declamationes* of Calpurnius Flaccus. Subjects from Seneca's *Suasoriae* include a historical figure such as Alexander (e.g., 1, 4) and a mythological character such as Agamemnon (e.g., 3). As can be seen in Seneca's *Controversiae*, the atmosphere was often violent and spectacular and featured such stock characters as the tyrant (e.g., 1.7, 2.5, 3.6, 4.7, 5.8), the pirate (e.g., 1.6, 1.7, 3.3, 7.1, 7.4), the parricide (e.g., 3.2, 5.4, 7.1, 7.3, 7.5), and the wicked stepmother (e.g., 7.1, 7.5, 7.6, 9.5, 9.6). The *practice* of declamation, despite criticism by various characters in Roman literature of its themes being removed from practical oratory (cf. Seneca, *Controversiae* 3, *praeface* 8–18; Petronius, *Satyricon* 1–4; Tacitus, *Dialogus de oratoribus* 35.4–5; Juvenal, *Saturae* 10.166–7), was intimately linked to the social and political realities of the Roman world. As exemplified in the aforementioned character types, the world of declamation both reflected and was reinforced by social and political problems of Rome involving autocracy, conspiracy, piracy, brigandage, slavery, family disputes, and violence, all of which were the subject of actual cases in the courtroom. On an acculturative level declamation played an especially important role in reaffirming the status of the budding male elite and in inculcating respect for masculine roles, norms, and values over those of the rest of society, such as stereotyped feminine roles and values.

Modern scholars (e.g., Caplan 1944: 162–73), following in the path of ancient critics (e.g., Maternus in Tacitus, *Dialogus de oratoribus* 29.1–35.5), generally condemn the schools that gave rise to public declamation. But it is apparent that the rhetoricians Seneca (*Controversiae* 2, *praeface* 3–4), Quintilian (*Institutio oratoria* 2.10.1–2, 10.5.14), and the younger Pliny (*Epistulae* 2.3.5–6) hold a high opinion of the utility of declamation in general and its role in rhetorical training. Declamation was valued in the schools because it provided the rhetorical training necessary for social and political advancement at Rome. The exercises, which fostered mental agility and required the ability to engage in clever argument, not only had the advantage of providing practice on broader (though still restricted) themes and more extreme situations than were found in real cases but also permitted practitioners to use expression more elaborate than that normally employed in a courtroom or public meeting (cf. Quintilian, *Institutio oratoria* 2.10.5–7). By dealing with complex and difficult themes, students learned to develop persuasive arguments and to manipulate legal technicalities so that actual cases would seem easy by comparison.

THE ALLEGED DECLINE

The major rhetorician of the Empire is Quintilian, whose *Institutio oratoria* is the largest extant manual on Roman rhetoric. For an orator to have spoken well (*bene dixisse*) meant to Quintilian speaking according to the rules of rhetoric (Quintilian, *Institutio oratoria* 2.17.25). The size of his treatise reflects both the confidence of Roman rhetoricians and the sophistication of their rhetorical system at the end of the first century CE. This handbook not only provides an overview of the Roman system of rhetoric during the imperial period but also discusses some of the more controversial subjects among rhetoricians, including the idea of a decline in oratory (10.1.80; cf. 2.4.41). Indeed the notion of such a decline is a *locus communis* among writers of the first century CE (Velleius Paterculus, *Historiae Romanae* 1.16–8; Seneca, *Controversiae* 1, *praeface* 6–7; Petronius, *Satyricon* 1–4, 88, 118; Persius 1.15–8, 32–6, 121; Pliny, *Naturalis historia* 14.2–6; Tacitus, *Dialogus de oratoribus* 25.3–6.8, 27.1–3, 28.1–35.5; Juvenal, *Saturae* 1.1–4, 1.12–4, 7.105–49; Longinus, *De sublimitate* 44), though it had appeared as early as Cicero (*De officiis* 2.67) in the previous century, and many modern critics have followed suit by arguing for the same idea (e.g., Williams 1978; Clarke 1996: 100–8). After the early part of the second century the notion of a decline seems virtually to disappear.

The younger Pliny's own career and reflections upon the state of rhetoric in his *Epistulae* provide important evidence about the thriving practice of oratory during the Empire and therefore serve as a valuable counterbalance to Roman and modern views of a decline in oratory (Dominik 2007). Over a period of three decades Pliny refers to numerous speeches delivered in the Forum (Pliny, *Epistulae* 5.8.8), the centumviral court (e.g., 2.11.14, 4.16.1–3, 6.33.1–11), Senate houses, and criminal courts (e.g., 3.9.1–37, 5.20.1–7, 6.5.1–7), which demonstrates the large number of venues and opportunities available to orators in the late first and early second centuries CE. Despite Pliny's own comments (3.20.10, 8.14.8–9, *Panegyricus* 76.3–4) that the Senate diminished in importance as a venue for political debate under the emperor, it is apparent from his own career that important cases were still debated in the Senate (e.g., *Epistulae* 2.11.2, 17, 7.33); in addition, the Senate continued to serve as a forum for minor proceedings dealing with legislation, the conferment of honors, and routine matters. The continuing evolution of rhetoric in the Empire is best viewed as a process of adaptation and shifting emphasis rather than secondariness and decline.

A host of other famous rhetoricians at the time appear in the works of the imperial rhetoricians. Quintilian mentions a number of rhetoricians who served as exemplars of contemporary oratory (*Institutio oratoria* 10.1.118–21): Domitius Afer; Julius Africanus; Galerius Trachalus; Vibius Crispus; and Julius Secundus. These same orators are mentioned in the works of Tacitus (*Dialogus de oratoribus* 1–3, 13.3–4, 15.3, 23.6, *Annales* 14.19, *Historiae* 1.90), who himself was known as an eloquent and distinguished speaker with many students (Pliny, *Epistulae* 2.1.6, 2.11.17, 4.13.10, 9.23.3). He and the younger Pliny were the leading orators at the turn of the second century CE when they prosecuted Marius Priscus, proconsul of Africa, for corruption (2.11). Pliny mentions dozens of speakers in his *Epistulae* who were prominent in the courts, Senate, and public halls of his own day. One of Pliny's most significant speeches, the *Panegyricus*, which was a celebration of Trajan's accomplishments, was delivered before the Senate in 100 CE and published sometime afterward; this speech, the earliest extant Latin panegyric, was the result of an amalgam of social and political factors unique to the imperial ruler cult.

Other Developments

The development of Roman rhetoric can be seen in Latin literature not only in regard to its role in the formation of literary genres such as epic, historiography, novel, and lyric poetry but also in its influence on particular writers such as Virgil, Lucan, Livy, Tacitus, Petronius, Apuleius, Catullus, and Horace (see Hall, ch. 18; Culler, ch. 19; Webb, ch. 22). These and other writers employ rhetoric to achieve certain effects consistent with their literary program, but the representation of Roman identity and values in their works can be attributed in part to the use of rhetorical models, devices, and strategies.

Later in the second century CE—during the age of the Antonines—a movement known as the Second Sophistic flourished, though it seems to have been mainly a Greek phenomenon (see Pernot, ch. 20). Two of the features of this movement were an attempt to revert to the style and diction of Attic Greek of the fourth century BCE and an increased emphasis on epideictic, which emerges from a reading of the letters of Fronto, the only extant Latin writer on rhetorical theory from this age. The rhetorical treatises of later Roman writers on rhetoric after the second century are represented in Carolus Halm's *Rhetores Latini minores* (1863).

Rhetoric as a Cultural Process

Roman rhetoric was both an academic exercise and a cultural phenomenon. Becoming well versed with the rules of the rhetorical system was only the first step in the process of becoming an orator. The development of Roman rhetoric involved a mutual process in which rhetoric, with its diverse origins and diverse forms (both Greek and Roman), helped to shape cultural and civic life at Rome; in turn various cultural forces helped to shape the form and practice of Roman rhetoric. The acculturative function of rhetoric cannot be overestimated, for it was in the schools, courts, public assemblies, and public halls that aspiring orators learned the modes of self-presentation and rhetorical skills expected of the elite classes. Rhetoric and oratory were the means by which the elite publicly defined their status, attained fame and prestige, empowered themselves, defended their position, met their social obligations, and transmitted their values within Roman society. The high esteem in which rhetoric was held and its vibrancy are evident in both the republican and imperial periods, during which the art of rhetoric dominated the social and political landscape of Rome.

References

Bauman, Richard A. 1983. *Lawyers in Roman Republican Politics: A Study of the Roman Jurists in Their Political Setting, 316–82 BC*. Munich: C.H. Beck.

Bauman, Richard A. 1985. *Lawyers in Roman Transitional Politics: A Study of the Roman Jurists in Their Political Setting in the Late Republic and Triumvirate*. Munich: C.H. Beck.

Caplan, Harry. 1944. "The Decay of Eloquence at Rome in the First Century." In *Studies in Speech and Drama: In Honor of Alexander M. Drummond*, edited by Herbert A. Wichelns, Donald C. Bryant, Barnard Hewitt, and Karl R. Wallace, 295–325. Ithaca, NY: Cornell University Press.

Clarke, M. L. 1996. *Rhetoric at Rome: A Historical Survey*, 3rd ed. Revised by D. H. Berry. London: Routledge.

Cloud, Duncan. 1994. "The Constitution and Public Criminal Law." In *The Cambridge Ancient History*, vol. 9 of *The Last Age of the Roman Republic, 146–43 B.C.*, edited by J. A. Crook, Andrew Lintott, and Elizabeth Rawson, 491–530. Cambridge: Cambridge University Press.

David, Jean-Michel. 1992. *Le patronat judiciaire au dernier siècle de la république romaine*. Rome: École française de Rome.

Dominik, William J. 1997. "The Style Is the Man: Seneca, Tacitus, and Quintilian's Canon." In *Roman Eloquence: Rhetoric in Society and Literature*, edited by William J. Dominik, 50–68. London: Routledge.

Dominik, William J. 2007. "Tacitus and Pliny on Oratory." In *A Companion to Roman Rhetoric*, edited by William J. Dominik and Jon Hall, 323–338. Malden, MA: Blackwell.

Dominik, William J., and Gualtiero Calboli. 1997. "Introduction: The Roman *Suada*." In *Roman Eloquence: Rhetoric in Society and Literature*, edited by William J. Dominik, 3–12. London: Routledge.

Hall, Jon. 2007. "Oratorical Delivery and the Emotions: Theory and Practice." In *A Companion to Roman Rhetoric*, edited by William J. Dominik and Jon Hall, 218–234. Malden, MA: Blackwell.

Halm, Carolus, ed. 1863. *Rhetores Latini Minores*. Leipzig: Teubner.

Leeman, Anton D. 1963. Orationis Ratio: *The Stylistic Theories and Practice of the Roman Orators, Historians and Philosophers*. 2 vols. Amsterdam: Adolf M. Hakkert.

Montefusco, Lucia Calboli. 1986. *La dottrina degli "status" nella retorica greca e romana*. Hildesheim: Olms-Weidmann.

Morstein-Marx, Robert. 2004. *Mass Oratory and Political Power in the Late Roman Republic*. Cambridge: Cambridge University Press.

Sciarrino, Enrica. 2007. "Roman Oratory Before Cicero: The Elder Cato and Gaius Gracchus." In *A Companion to Roman Rhetoric*, edited by William J. Dominik and Jon Hall, 54–66. Malden, MA: Blackwell.

Skutsch, Otto, ed. 1985. *The "Annals" of Quintus Ennius*. Oxford: Oxford University Press.

Williams, Gordon. 1978. *Change and Decline: Roman Literature in the Early Roman Empire*. Berkeley: University of California Press.

CHAPTER 13

....

RHETORIC AND LAW

....

RICHARD LEO ENos

FROM one perspective, the corpus of Roman law (*lex*) is stable, extensive, and substantive. From city to Republic to Empire, the sheer number of surviving laws is both amazing and daunting, making it readily apparent that Romans, whether secular or sacred, had a proclivity to "legalize" and regularize every mode of behavior in their culture. This disposition is apparent from the earliest origins of the Twelve Tables to its final manifestation in the Code of Justinian. The formalization of procedures, the distinctions between civil and criminal law, and the codification of laws that would reach its height of sophistication in the early Roman Empire were already under development in the Roman Republic. In addition to being a period of rapid legal development, especially in the refinement of judicial procedures, the Republic was also a period in which law was an intensely rhetorical activity.

In the normal operations of the Republic, the creation and interpretation of laws for the adjudication of discrete acts involved oral argument and deliberation. From the procedures of deliberation in the courts and the Senate (*Curia*) it quickly became obvious to Romans that training in rhetoric could facilitate both legal reasoning and effective argument and persuasion in the sphere of public policy. Legal activity in Rome was therefore inextricably bound up with politics. Many prominent Romans were both advocates and politicians, and their influence shaped much of the law and politics of the Republic. The "influences" that led to stable, inscribed laws were often the consequence of extensive argument, deliberation, and, on occasion, warfare.

One of the most influential of these Roman orator-politicians was Marcus Tullius Cicero (106–43 BCE). It is through our extensive knowledge of Cicero that we are able to understand the relationship between law and rhetoric in the Republic. Because of his enormous talent and extensive learning, Cicero became a person of influence in the courts of Rome. We know so much about Cicero from his extant speeches, letters, and rhetorical treatises that we have come to regard him as the first Roman whose brilliance as an advocate made him a source of political power in the Republic. Cicero, however, was not the only prominent advocate, and much of what he learned came from his knowledge of the great legal minds that preceded him in forensic rhetoric. For example,

Lucius Licinius Crassus and Marcus Antonius, the two prominent characters in *De oratore*, Cicero's masterpiece on the role of rhetoric in the Republic, both excelled as advocates and politicians.

Cicero's expertise in rhetoric also reveals that Roman law was both an oral and literate activity (Enos 1988). More specifically, when literacy facilitates oral rhetoric, literate advocates gain an advantage in argument over nonliterate orators. Roman rhetoric, both oral and literate, was thus a dynamic activity in interpreting, arguing, and making law as well as a source of political power in the Republic. Roman law may appear to be little more than a set of formalized rules that may be studied in their abstract, codified form, but from a perspective that is more sensitive to the social and cultural nature of laws, these social dicta are the result of a cultural dynamic that is not evident in the laws themselves. If we understand the development of Roman law as the consequence of social and cultural values that were deliberated and often vigorously contested, then we can see the important place rhetoric held in this civic activity. The importance of rhetoric to political and legal affairs is further evident in the rhetoric manuals themselves. For example, the treatment of legal argument dominates the *Rhetorica ad Herennium* (ca. 86–2 BCE), our earliest surviving Roman rhetoric manual (*ratio*). The first two of the four books of this text are devoted to judicial rhetoric and invention. However, this "Roman" rhetoric manual is clearly an appropriation of earlier Greek rhetoric (Caplan 1970; Enos 2005). To understand the impact of rhetoric on Roman law, we must therefore first understand its rudimentary origins and its Hellenic and Hellenistic antecedents (Enos 2008; see Gagarin, ch. 2).

Pre-Ciceronian Advocates

There is little doubt that Cicero held many of his predecessors and contemporaries in high esteem. His *Brutus* testifies to the high standards of eloquence attained by earlier *advocati*. His characterization of influential legal thinkers and political leaders as dialogue-participants is invariably laudatory. While his contributions to rhetoric and law became a standard of excellence for his own period and for much of rhetoric's history in the Latin-speaking West, Cicero saw himself as the beneficiary of a long and distinguished tradition of Roman forensic oratory. Like others of his generation, Cicero rooted his rhetorical practice in a careful scrutiny of prominent advocates. Cicero differs from his contemporaries, however, in his sensitive observation of their strengths and weaknesses, and his ability to capitalize on these observations was markedly different from other Roman advocates.

As a reading of *Brutus* reveals, there were no fewer than 200 prominent orators in the five generations that preceded Cicero. The age of pre-Ciceronian forensic rhetoric corresponds to the pre-classical age of Roman law; that is, the systematization and stabilization of law and society characteristic of the Augustan Principate (and of the early Empire in general) were already underway before the age of Cicero (Crook 1967: 8–9).

Yet prior to the age of Augustus—and even prior to the age of Cicero—the provinces of law and politics were far less discrete. The courts were the arena for the structuring and maintaining of Roman values, but they also served as a forum for the public artic-ulation of political positions. Cicero's own career—and no doubt the careers of many *advocati* before him—clearly reveals how proficiency in forensic rhetoric could lead to success in political affairs. In studying jurisprudence with the Augur, Quintus Mucius Scaevola, and in following in the steps of Quintus Hortensius Hortalus, Cicero was tak-ing the common course of synthesizing the precepts and emulating the style of success-ful advocates. Lacking advanced procedures for rhetorical training, the only source for a practical education in forensic oratory was the study of model cases and successful advocates—an education in legal theory and practice that often took the form of men-tor–apprentice relationships (Tacitus, *Dialogus de oratoribus* 34; Cicero, *Tusculanae disputationes* 1.7, *Brutus* 205; Plutarch, *Vitae parallelae: Cicero* 2, 3; Suetonius, *De rhetoribus*1).

Unfortunately, direct evidence of legal rhetoric from Cicero's predecessors is lim-ited. There is no doubt that Lucius Licinius Crassus (the principal character in *De ora-tore*) was Cicero's model advocate. However, copies of Crassus's legal arguments were rare artifacts even in Cicero's time, as he indicates in *Orator*: "There are very few ora-tions of Crassus's and none are forensic orations" (132). Today, our evidence is even slimmer; only fragments of Crassus's speeches survive, and the major sources for his style of argument are Cicero's *Brutus* and *De oratore* (cf. *Oratorum Romanorum frag-menta* 237–59). Cicero's lament over the inaccessibility of written copies of Crassus's legal arguments is revealing: it indicates that copies of legal speeches were avail-able and treated as models for serious study and imitation. However, their distribu-tion was limited, even for an advocate as revered as Crassus. Cicero's sensitivity to the importance of written texts—their diverse and enduring value—is thus readily apparent.

As Plutarch suggests, the best example of these pre-Ciceronian advocates is Cato the Elder (Plutarch, *Vitae parallelae: Cato major*; Bonner 1977: 10–4). Although wealthy and respected, Cato took such an interest in his son's education that he not only monitored it closely but also taught the younger Cato the principles of law. In this early period, much of education, and legal training in particular, took place in a mentor–apprentice rela-tionship in which aspiring advocates would follow and observe prominent advocates in the courts (the *tirocinia fori*). Cicero's own *De amicitia* begins with an anecdote about how he tried to arrive at the Forum early in order to learn legal argument and persua-sion from the best advocates. One of the limitations of this early legal training, however, was the absence of Greek rhetorical theory and exemplars. Cato the Elder, for example, resisted teaching Greek rhetorical models to his son (Bonner 1977: 12). His attitude was not unrepresentative of the way many early Romans viewed with suspicion the ever-increasing popularity of Greek culture and *paideia* in Roman society. Yet the refined methods of analysis, argument, and composition elaborated by the Greeks over the cen-turies could not be ignored, and despite objections Greek rhetoric began to influence Roman legal rhetoric (see Dominik, ch. 12).

HELLENIC INFLUENCES ON
ROMAN FORENSIC RHETORIC

Much to the dismay of pristine patricians, Roman legal practice developed under the influence of Hellenic, and particularly Athenian, rhetoric. As Aristotle's *Rhetoric* makes clear, forensic rhetoric was a major force in the civic operations of Athens. To that end, much of the Roman appropriation of Athenian rhetoric was carried out for the sake of law and *res publica*, and the emphasis on forensic rhetoric facilitated, and perhaps even induced, the emerging role of the *advocatus* in the Republic. Although classical Athens had no complementary concept of the *advocatus*, since each Athenian male citizen presented his case in person, sophists did develop detailed and effective manuals (*technai*) on forensic argument and persuasion. Argument with an emphasis on political and legal deliberation became a feature of Greek declamation to such an extent that formal rhetorical study prepared male citizens for legal deliberation as well as civic affairs (Russell 1983). This importance even filtered down to the educational training of young Romans (Bonner 1949, 1977). Exercises in *declamatio* sharpened minds by forcing students to compose speeches on contentious moral and political issues (*suasoriae*) as well as on legal issues (*controversiae*) (see Gunderson, ch. 21). Further, Athenian litigants cultivated the art of logography (our "ghost writing"), a practice by which sophists wrote arguments for clients to memorize and deliver in courts. Over time, Romans moved from appropriating Greek rhetoric to developing their own uniquely "Roman" rhetoric for their political and legal systems. The culmination of this development came about in the early Empire with Quintilian's *Institutio oratoria*. Drawing on his experience as a former advocate and established teacher of rhetoric, Quintilian provided a coherent, systematic, and comprehensive outline of education from childhood to maturity that was intended to cultivate leaders to serve the Roman state.

THE POWER OF RHETORIC IN
THE ROMAN COURTS

The courts of the Roman Republic were deeply influenced by political and social forces. Almost 50 years before Cicero's birth, the tribune Lucius Calpurnius Piso Fugi secured the enactment of his *Lex Pecuniis Repetundis* in 149 BCE, which firmly established a court for extortion cases (*questio*). The standing commission for this court was entrusted to the Senate, which was greatly influenced by the class of patricians (*nobiles*). Two decades later, however, the famous popular leader Gaius Gracchus sponsored his *Lex Judiciaria*, which shifted control of the courts away from the Senate to the wealthiest non-patricians (*equites*). This transfer of power between social classes intensified the already strained relations between the patrician-dominated Senate and the *equites*, a (sometimes) volatile condition that lasted well into the Republic. Such tumultuous events meant that forensic orators faced a constantly changing audience and that each trial was presented under ever-changing social constraints.

It would be difficult to overstate the political forces that influenced Roman law and rhetoric (see Connolly, ch. 14). Even during Cicero's childhood the courts were being manipulated by party politics. Quintus Servilius Caepio, consul in 196 BCE, passed a compromise law that provided for juries composed of senators and *equites*. About 101 BCE, the orator Gaius Servius Glaucia helped to enact a law restoring the *repetundae* (extortion) court and the quaestorship to the *equites*. Further reforms were attempts to elevate 300 *equites* to the Senate by Livius Drusus (91 BCE) and by the tribune Marcus Silvanus Platius, who introduced a *Lex Judiciaria* that promoted mixed rather than exclusively equestrian juries (89 BCE). Certainly, efforts at reform were made, but such changes openly dramatized the political and social implications of legal argument. One of the most significant reforms of the courts came when Sulla's conservative revolution and legislative programs restored power to the 600 members of the Senate by promoting *equites* who supported him. Sulla delegated all public procedures for judicial investigations (*quaestiones*) to the senators. The reforms of Sulla gave the Senate exclusive right to supply juries and control at least seven permanent *quaestiones* that covered all major crimes: murder and poisoning, forgery, extortion, treason, electoral bribery, peculation, and assault.

Later reforms, however, modified Sulla's conservative reform of the courts. Lucius Aurelius Cotta (*praetor* in 70 BCE) tempered Sulla's legal reforms by passing the *Lex Aurelia Judiciaria*, which allowed juries of criminal courts to consist of an equal number of senators, *equites*, and *tribuni aerarii* by creating three panels or *decuriae* of 300 members each (Jones 1972: 87). The *tribuni aerarii* were citizens whose property qualifications were immediately below the equestrian order, and their affiliation was with the *equites* rather than the patrician-dominated senatorial order. The *tribuni aerarii* were temporarily suppressed by Julius Caesar, but while an active force their support of the *equites* provided a two-thirds domination of the courts over the patricians of the Senate, which violated the spirit (if not the letter) of the Sullan reforms. During Cicero's legal career, factions of the Senate and *equites* continued to struggle for domination of the courts, which each group recognized as a source of political power.

The impact of politics on the courts often resulted in judicial corruption. The oligarchic control of the courts by patricians minimized the voice of the populace, and since the leading political offices were dominated by *nobiles*, politics blended unchecked with legal affairs. A clear example of such corruption came in Cicero's youthful defense of Sextus Roscius in 80 BCE. In fact, Cicero remarked that he was virtually the only advocate courageous enough to risk Sulla's displeasure by undertaking the defense (*Pro Roscio Amerino* 5; Aulus Gellius, *Noctes Atticae* 15.28). The primary reason for the unpopularity of the case was the prosecution being offered by a colleague of Sulla, who was then in his second consulship. The fear of the jurors that a verdict against one of Sulla's men could be taken personally by Sulla was so strong that Cicero had to devote part of his case to reminding the jurors of their obligations to justice (*Pro Roscio Amerino* 8). In spite of intimidation by the prosecution, Cicero won the case by carefully incriminating Sulla's men while praising Sulla himself (6, 127, 131).

By the time of Cicero's prosecution of proconsul Gaius Verres in 70 BCE, the corruption of the senatorial courts had become public knowledge. Rather than a political constraint, Cicero exploited the well-established corruption of the courts as a point of argument and, in doing so, demonstrated the interplay of law and politics in rhetorical deliberation. Cicero urged the senators to invoke their power and "blot out and remove the disgrace and infamy taken on by this order through the years" or else risk men continuing to believe that "a completely different order [equestrian] for judging matters ought to be sought" (Cicero, *In Verrem* 1.49). Cicero's purpose was to have his senatorial jurors believe that the entire revamping of the courts hinged on the outcome of this trial, and he even emphasized that Pompey and the *populares* already had enough force to change the jury, since it would determine "whether in the case of this man it can be established that a very criminal and very wealthy individual can be condemned by a senatorial court" (1.47). Clearly, control of the courts was hotly contested because the law itself was widely recognized as an instrument of political power and control. This control was often articulated as a plea for a return to the rule of law and justice in Rome.

ORAL AND LITERATE LEGAL RHETORIC: IMMEDIATE EQUITY AND LONG-TERM JUSTICE

Oral rhetoric could be used efficiently and effectively in the courts. But while proficiency in oral discourse could earn immediate victories and a word-of-mouth reputation, no artifacts of talent would endure beyond the moment to sustain a reputation. Revising forensic speeches for publication after trials provided stable and enduring evidence that could continually enhance a Roman's reputation as a champion of justice. After the current interest surrounding a trial and issues waned, the published orations remained popular both as legal accounts of trials and as commentaries on social and political conditions. In time, such forensic compositions changed as the political context changed, so that the "essays" came to be viewed less as legal documents and more as literary vehicles for social commentary and political advancement. In effect, the forensic rhetoric created for arguing and resolving specific legal controversies evolved to become lasting statements of epideictic rhetoric that provided commentaries about questions of value and morality that transcended the particulars of any single trial. Arguing for the value of justice became the locus of legal preparation.

The superiority of Cicero's literate skills enabled him to bring to the courts modes of thought and expression that are less easily attained by orality alone. Written texts of legal arguments were important to the study of successful advocates. Cicero's comments reveal that copies of speeches were common sources for study but were not always available in any systematic way. In one instance, for example, Cicero boasted to his brother, Quintus, that no one would read his opponent's speech but that schoolboys would commit his own orations to memory (*Epistulae ad Quintum fratrem* 3.1.11). Written texts frequently incorporated techniques to capture the liveliness and familiarity of oral communication. Proficiency in such writing skills goes beyond mere description, requiring sensitivity to effective oral presentation and knowledge of how to translate speech into writing.

Cicero's speeches composed after the trial were separate literary efforts. They exhibit the features of Roman oratory, but these speeches are in fact stylized, often dramatized, literary accounts. These published legal arguments are not fiction, for they do reflect actual events, but it is fair to consider them as rhetorical interpretations of events. That is, Cicero's oral arguments were indeed acts of rhetoric in the sense that the appeals were made not only to the jurors but also to the populace, who read his post-trial accounts. Legal speeches published as compositions became "rhetorical" literature, aesthetically contrived works that do not respond to the particular situations they appear to address but function as broader social statements concerning law, justice, and politics. The legal and literary practice of using rhetoric to transcend the exigencies of the moment for a more enduring social influence was also practiced in other Roman disciplines. Historians such as Livy, for example, often took actual events and dramatized them by putting speeches into the mouths of historical figures (see Ash, ch. 15). The line between chronicling historical events and creating mimetic discourse was not drawn as clearly in ancient Rome as it is today (see Carey, ch. 5; Ash, ch. 15).

THE LEGAL AUDIENCE

Our knowledge of the advocates of the Roman Republic is enhanced by understanding their audiences, for all forensic rhetoric is directed to audiences that make judgments based upon the cogency and persuasiveness of arguments. One would imagine that technical mastery of law would be a dominant feature of forensic rhetoric, but in the Republic we see a far different picture. Jurisprudential reasoning was doubtlessly valued, but what actually secured judgments in Roman litigation was popular approval (see Connolly, ch. 14). Roman jurors were not the only ones in attendance at major cases. Romans considered legal trials in the Forum as a form of public performance, and it was not uncommon to have large, vociferous crowds in attendance. Further, as Stanley Bonner (1977: 326) observes, the Latin equivalent to the phrase, "Silence in court!" was often drowned out by clamor and clatter during the proceedings. This raucous behavior of audiences did not diminish even in the early Empire. On one occasion, an advocate had to shout his argument so loudly to be heard that, when he finished, audiences hearing other cases in adjacent chambers applauded his mastery of rhetoric (Carcopino 1970: 188)!

Of course, certain advocates during the Republic emphasized the more technical elements of jurisprudence. Cicero realized how difficult it was for an advocate to develop the breadth of practical rhetoric necessary for popular support and, at the same time, to become an expert in jurisprudence (*De officiis* 2.67). Cicero believed that advocates who focused on jurisprudence often restricted themselves to a narrow interpretation of the principles of law. Less "technical" advocates such as Crassus, Antonius, and Hortensius aroused their jurors through a blend of wisdom and eloquence (*sapientia et eloquentia*). In fact, Cicero is quite direct on this point: "For who will ever doubt that in our State eloquence always held first priority in peaceful matters, and jurisprudence second? Since obviously, in the first place, there is a great deal of favor, glory, and protection; in the second, there is the instruction of prosecutors and bail-bond suits. Jurisprudence indeed often seeks aid from eloquence itself and, in fact, when opposed, can hardly defend its own sphere and aims" (*Orator* 141). Cicero believed that successful forensic advocates were gifted with more natural ability (*ingenium*) than legal education (*doctrina*) and that the role of giving legal advice was practical but trivial compared with other aspects of rhetoric (*Orator* 143, *De legibus* 1.14). In *De oratore*, for example, Crassus and Antonius mock technical rhetoric as irrelevant in cases where the law goes beyond legal minutiae and as being inferior to more effective devices such as wit and charm (1.234–43). Cicero decries skill in legal science in *Pro Murena*, even though he demonstrates his mastery of jurisprudence in *Pro Caecina* (69) and elsewhere. In essence, Cicero believed that knowledge of legal science and dialectic (along with high moral standards) was desirable but should be made only subtly apparent to listeners—probably because such traits held less appeal than the theatrics of forensic *rhetores*. It is likely that Cicero's published orations allowed him to introduce dramatic clashes that may never have been so lively in court. Sensitivity to the desires of audiences, whether listeners or readers, is a trait no one questions in Cicero, and his legal rhetoric often served as a point of departure for literary compositions that emphasize dramatic vitality over technical accuracy for his growing readership.

CONCLUSION

An analysis of the relationship between rhetoric and law in the Roman Republic reveals five points of significance. To begin with, there was no single formula for success in the courts of the Republic, no one particular rhetorical style that was most effective. In fact, seeking the perfect advocate would only blind the inquirer to the manifold sources of success and inspiration advocates such as Cicero recognized and emulated in their rhetorical practice. Second, the standards for effective advocacy were drawn primarily from popular judgment. Cicero may have had more personal respect (or dislike) for a particular advocate than the public, but he never contradicted public opinion completely:

Cicero's criteria for success were derived from the needs of the audience. Cicero may have isolated and explained the particular qualities that made an advocate successful, but his praise and analysis were *ex post facto*; they were predicated on an advocate already establishing himself with the people and jurors. In other words, for Cicero, the cogency of legal argument is determined not by static, abstract laws but by the audiences of the moment. Third, because success depended on the audience, it was important for advocates to present a style and appearance favored by listeners. Occasionally, an advocate faced a conflict wherein the jurors looked for technical arguments and the populace for emotive appeals and histrionics, but even in this situation the effectiveness of the advocate was often measured by his ability to secure the favor of as many parts of the audience as possible. Fourth, Romans associated certain traits with successful advocates: the ability to master the technical precepts of rhetoric, including the canon of memory (*memoria*); natural talent; the presentation of a positive and forceful image of *auctoritas*; zeal and industry; proficiency in reasoning; and an awareness and application of ethics. And fifth, writing had a profound effect on oral argument and on the law itself in ancient Rome. Writing helped to shift the codification of law away from the oral memory of those in power, who often interpreted meaning as they wished. In this way, written legal codes became a way of preserving and stabilizing the law itself. In addition, writing served as an aid to memory in the composition of oral arguments and a means of preserving speeches for teaching and for posthumous fame. Writing also helped to transform forensic rhetoric into non-mimetic, epideictic literature: long after the immediate exigencies of a trial had passed, the written texts of the arguments endured as powerful expressions of Roman values. Finally, writing was used in the formulation of oral arguments when compositions were written out and memorized for public delivery, while transcripts of legal arguments served a heuristic function as models for study by aspiring orators. Cicero and other advocates thus extended the uses of writing to create new ways of conceptualizing discourse and, after the trial, to help recreate legal speeches as eloquent works of imaginative literature.

Forensic rhetoric was a source of political power in ancient Rome. Young Romans who secured legal victories for influential clients achieved public offices. Cicero, a *novus homo* lacking noble birth, military talent, and wealth, concentrated his efforts in forensic rhetoric and gained enough success to secure the consulship in 63 BCE. Over the course of his long career as a legal and political orator—which paralleled a transitional era in the Roman courts that spanned from Sulla to Caesar—Cicero developed lofty and highly influential arguments about the value of rhetoric in civic affairs. For Cicero, rhetoric is a civilizing force that distinguishes man from animal, binds a society together, and helps maintain its tranquility (rhetoric alone cannot create a peaceful state out of discord). Rhetoric, through systematic argument, counterargument, and deliberation, also helps to discover and balance justice and equity. Cicero also maintained that justice was not an end in itself but a practical instrument for preserving the stability of society (as well as a means of gaining popular favor for the advocate). However, as the Republic gave way to the Empire and the rule of Augustus, rhetoric also underwent a transformation: cut off from legal and political matters (*res publica*), rhetoric retreated into the sphere of education and literature. In some ways rhetoric and law continued to thrive in the Empire, but the political element of legal rhetoric changed as dramatically as did the government of Rome itself (see Pernot, ch. 20). Cicero's works were used no longer as practical tools for political advancement in a free society but as literate guidelines for state propagandists such as Virgil, Horace, and Livy (Enos 2008: 182). Nevertheless, the impact Cicero had on rhetoric and law in Rome, and the standards he established, were the fruits of a long tradition of Greco-Roman rhetoric that continues to inform legal theory and practice today (see Hutson, ch. 32; Goodrich, ch. 48).

REFERENCES

Bonner, Stanley F. 1977. *Education in Ancient Rome*. Berkeley: University of California Press.

Bonner, Stanley F. 1949. *Roman Declamation in the Late Republic and Early Empire*. Liverpool: Liverpool University Press.

Caplan, Harry. 1970. "Introduction to the *Rhetorica ad Herennium*." In *Of Eloquence: Studies in Ancient and Medieval Rhetoric*, edited by Anne King and Helen North, 1–25. Ithaca, NY: Cornell University Press.

Carcopino, Jerome. 1970. *Daily Life in Ancient Rome*. Edited by Henry T. Rowell, translated by E. O. Lorimer. New Haven, CT: Yale University Press.

Crook, J. A. 1967. *Law and Life of Rome*. London: Thames and Hudson.

Enos, Richard Leo. 1988. *The Literate Mode of Cicero's Legal Rhetoric*. Carbondale: Southern Illinois University Press.

Enos, Richard Leo. 2005. "*Rhetorica ad Herennium*." In *Classical Rhetorics and Rhetoricians: Critical Studies and Sources*, edited by Michelle Ballif and Michael Moran, 331–338. Westport, CT: Praeger.

Enos, Richard Leo. 2008. *Roman Rhetoric: Revolution and the Greek Influence*. Revised and expanded edition. Anderson, SC: Parlor Press.

Jones, A. H. M. 1972. *The Criminal Courts of the Roman Republic and Principate*. Edited by J. A. Crook. Oxford: Basil Blackwell.

Oratorum Romanorum Fragmenta. 1953. Edited by Henrica Malcovati. Vol. 1. Textus. Torino: G.B. Paravia.

Russell, D. A. 1983. *Greek Declamation*. Cambridge: Cambridge University Press.

CHAPTER 14

RHETORIC AND POLITICS

JOY CONNOLLY

EARLY in his history of Rome, Livy describes the withdrawal of the army from the city to protest the failure of the patricians to resolve the plebeians' suffering at the hands of moneylenders (Livy, *The History of Rome* 2.31–2). The Senate panicked, and Menenius Agrippa, a senator of plebeian descent, ventured to the soldiers' campsite on the Sacred Mount. The fable he famously told compares the Roman people to a body where the plebs are the limbs, disgusted with the service they are compelled to render to the belly, the Senate. Refusing to bring the belly nourishment, the limbs weaken, and they realize that the belly, as the governing power of the body, deserves their collective labor. The fable, Livy says, "changed everyone's mind" (*flexisse mentes hominum*; 2.32.12): the soldiers ended the secession and the Senate established protection for the plebs through the office of the tribunate, which went on to play a key role in political life.

Menenius's speech exposes constitutive tensions in Roman politics that in recent decades have become the locus of renewed debate. Few agree with Fergus Millar's conclusion that the Republic deserves the name "democracy" (1998: 225). But to call Rome an oligarchy risks dismissing (among other factors) the prominence of public speaking in the operation of republican politics and in the Romans' understanding of its legitimacy. Elected magistrates, especially tribunes of the people, addressed citizens on legislation and other issues in meetings (*contiones*) held in the Forum and other public spaces, while senators gave speeches of advice to one another inside the Curia. Forensic speaking, which occurred in outdoor venues frequented by crowds, was an established method for men aspiring to public life to gain popular recognition and votes. Ceremonial occasions like funerals and triumphs provided opportunities for elites to celebrate their accomplishments and family history.

What political ends did these speeches serve? On one hand, Livy's story suggests that oratory is an instrument (in some conditions the primary instrument) used by the Senate to rule the people. It is this view Quintilian has in mind when he uses Menenius as an example of how to sway "country types" (*Institutio oratoria* 5.11.19) and the uneducated by entertaining them with stories. Historically, the elected magistrate is indeed the embodiment of political authority, and as the Empire grew, the sameness and predictability of the legal system exerted a powerful cohesive function across every province, a reassuring "promise of social order" (Ando 2000: 48). In Rome itself, speakers from ancient noble families could and did claim to be literally descended from divinities and ancient heroes, their speaking bodies imitating the grand statues in which the Empire took artifactual shape in urban public space. In the lived experience of Roman politics, economic, religious, legal, and political authority thus intersected and supported one another, made visible and audible through common patterns of stance and gesture and familiar patterns of speech (Connolly 2007: 54). Cicero and Quintilian are keenly alert to the skills and the opportunities for self-distinction that rhetorical training grants to men engaged in the intraelite competition for ruling power. In this context, the audience possesses little political significance beyond its service as a marker of elite popularity and prestige. "I want all my triumphs, the ornaments of my office, the memorials of my glory, the symbols of praise to be built and founded in your hearts," Cicero declares (*In Catilinam* 3.26; trans. mine). Wealth, honor, and fame accrue even to the moderately successful orator (Quintilian, *Institutio oratoria* 12.11.29). From this perspective, republican politics may be described as the rule of the senatorial order, composed of well-off men born into established families and trained for public life, exploiting ritual occasions to dominate a *populus* habituated to obedience (Flaig 2003: 13–6).

On the other hand, however, the tale of Menenius also represents oratory as a moment of risky exposure for the speaker, impossible to predict or fully control, where in order to succeed the speaker must persuade by gaining his audience's attention and assent, thus determining action on both sides: here, the soldiers return peacefully; the patricians set up the tribunate. Without communication that is capable of "changing minds," to use Livy's phrase, it is impossible to share divergent understandings of the world. Without shared understanding, collective thinking and acting are beyond reach. Framed in these terms, artful speech emerges as the core practice of Roman politics, cohesive yet dynamic, its power to dominate always balanced by the importance of popular approval.

Along this line of thought, Jacques Rancière, in his reading of Livy, argues that behind the obvious moral of inequality in Menenius's fable lies another, standing in tension with the first: a moral about equality that is inherent "in the very act of composing" a narrative (1995: 82). Acts of narrative are based on the assumption of the existence of a relation of equal exchange. Menenius based his journey to the Sacred Mount on the assumption that for the impasse between the haves and the have-nots to be resolved, he could speak and his audience could listen. The hierarchy of the relationship of a single patrician to the plebeians is thus replaced by a different relationship, that of narrator to listeners, a relationship whose egalitarian elements are enacted in the course of storytelling itself. This relationship is a grounding principle in the work of Jürgen Habermas and others, who view rhetoric as a "figurative language of conversational and public coherence" (Farrell 1993: 273).

Cicero shares Rancière's interest in the equality of intelligences, if not Rancière's commitment to democratic equality. No other thinker so strikingly embodies the tensions of Roman politics. Cicero aims to sway his listeners (*ducere animos*, as Quintilian describes Menenius) when he argues a case in the law court or offers an opinion in the

Senate or Forum. His conviction that eloquence grants power to the speaker underlies his overdetermined effort to argue that eloquence is equivalent to virtue throughout his magisterial dialogue, *De oratore*, and, indirectly, in his writings about politics and ethics (e.g., *De republica* 1.3–4, *De officiis* 1.114; see Quintilian, *Institutio oratoria* 2.20.1–10). In some contexts this power seems equivalent to pure manipulation: this explains Cicero's labeling the people as the "dregs" of the city in private letters to eminent friends (e.g., *Ad Atticum* 1.16.11; see Morstein-Marx 2004: 121–2) and his belief that the *boni*, the class of people with the most wealth, deserve the deciding voice in republican politics (*De republica* 2.40). Cicero frequently seeks to enhance his personal *auctoritas* and *dignitas* by appealing to popular religion and myth. In the Third Catilinarian, one of his few con-tional orations, he associates himself with the commanding persona of Romulus and arranges for a statue of Jupiter to be erected in time to create a dramatic backdrop for his exhortation (*In Catilinam* 3.2; see further Vasaly 1993: 54, 81).

In Cicero's rhetorical and philosophical writings, a more nuanced, creative, and ambi-tious portrait of oratory emerges. There Cicero defines politics not as the possession of power but as persuasive communication, which arises from the common capacity of human beings to convey meaning to one another. His celebratory account of the found-ing of the political community in his first treatise, *De inventione*, draws on Isocrates in its claim that a wise man first used the power of eloquence to bring men together out of the wilderness and establish laws (1.5). If the crowd of primitives in this image are silent witnesses to a single man speaking, that crowd nonetheless retains the agentic capacity of approval or rejection. This capacity is key to Cicero's understanding of political action and legitimacy.

Cicero's later work elaborates this view. In *De oratore*, which Cicero wrote in 55 BCE after his consulship and the Catilinarian uprising, the senators Crassus and Antonius explore oratory's dual function as the instrument of command and the creator of com-munity. They revisit the questions from Plato's *Gorgias*: Is rhetoric an art or a knack? Does it require natural talent? What is the scope of the knowledge the orator needs? Crassus describes the orator's practice as engagement in a serial contest that holds gath-erings of human beings together (*tenere hominum coetus*; Cicero, *De oratore* 1.30) and retains them in their civil state (*retinere homines in civitate*; 1.32). In the act of turning men toward one another (*converti*), eloquent words substitute for weapons and defenses (*arma, tectus*) in the ongoing struggles of the law court and public assembly that main-tain the conditions under which the state can survive (1.33). In a climactic passage that will be emblematic of early modern European views of the role of speech in politics, Crassus says he is seeking as his ideal orator not some narrow-minded legalist but "a man" (*vir*) who is "a high priest" or "master" (*antistes*) of the divine art of persuasion, who with words alone can "expose to the hatred of the citizens the crime and trickery of the guilty" (1.202), and who can guide the *populus*, kindling their fury against wicked men and soothing them when they are angry at good men.

In his dialogue, *De republica*, completed in 51 BCE, Cicero configures the Republic as a state whose structure and dynamic flow mimic the real-life contests of oratory. In the second book, Scipio Aemilianus describes Rome as having been founded through serial conflicts between the Senate and the people rather than, as in Greek city-states or Platonic philosophy, from the once-and-for-all constituting action of a single man or a single governing idea. Here speech does not exclusively serve the interests of the dominant order. Cicero notes that it can both calm and inflame class antagonism, and it is easily mobilized to attack the privileged (*De republica* 1.5–10). Clashes between Senate and people frame the dramatic setting of the dialogue, which occurs during the violent era of struggle between the populist Gracchi brothers and their senatorial opponents, and in his preface Cicero links this era to the current day. The framing suggests that the Republic is permanently constituted through agonistic contest mediated by the reconstituting power of persuasive speech.

Starting with the early first-century BCE treatise, *Rhetorica ad Herennium*, the earliest surviving handbook in Latin, public speech occurs in the context of the contest. Sallust's histories, which include populist speeches by both tribunes and conspirators, also represent speech as the heart of contestatory political action in the Republic. For the contest to play out properly, prejudgments are illegal and outcomes unpredictable. A Cicero may make tendentious arguments and ridiculous exaggerations successfully in one speech because of his celebrity or the reputation of his opponents, but in the next he may face a greater celebrity, a Hortensius, or the crowd may choose to laugh at his exaggerations, or he may suffer stage fright, or a show of force may scare him into silence. In *De oratore*, Antonius and Crassus agree that this is what makes the speech a site of terrifying uncertainty even for the experienced, skillful orator (1.120–1).

To avoid disaster, the speaker must connect: making a connection with the audience—and making the connection feel real—rests at the core of Roman rhetoricians' conception of the political. The *Rhetorica ad Herennium* and Cicero's treatises and dialogues seek to train the orator to develop skills in representing character and using commonplaces (*communes loci*) that establish lines of communication and identification between elite speaker and mass audience. Giving pleasure to the audience is seen as crucial, but the orator's effort in this area is not reducible to motivations of condescension or deceit. Pleasure is one important way to gain assent in the dialogic relationship between speaker and audience: the author of *Rhetorica ad Herennium* says that the orator's task (*officium*) is "to speak . . . with the agreement of his listeners," adding the important phrase, "as far as this is in his power to do" (*dicere . . . cum adsensione auditorum quoad eius fieri poterit*; *Rhetorica ad Herennium* 1.2.1). Avoiding arrogance and other signs that the audience might view as premeditated trickery (e.g., 1.4.5, 1.10.17) transforms the oration into a common theater of collective experience, where the public staging of different players' unequal portions of power to determine the course of events puts the legitimacy of the order to the test.

Illustrative of this complex dynamic is an episode in Livy's history from the second century BCE, when a tribune summoned Scipio Africanus to trial in the people's assembly. Ignoring the charges, Scipio delivered a lively speech recounting his services to the Empire, and the assembly postponed judgment to a later date that turned out to be the anniversary of his great victory over Hannibal. Scipio ultimately managed to rescript his trial before the people as the people's celebration of his accomplishments (Livy, *The*

History of Rome 2.31–238.51). Like other figures in Livy, Cicero's *Brutus*, and Valerius Maximus's *Memorable Deeds and Sayings*, Scipio uses the occasion of conflict between himself and a magistrate supposed to be working in the people's interest both to preserve his own authority and to create an opportunity for the people to celebrate membership in the Empire. Through the proximity to Scipio afforded by his speech, the people take vicarious pleasure in his victories and in the material goods of imperial conquest.

Pride in (and anxiety about) the extent and sway of the Empire and the military power that created it appear to have been constants in Roman popular discourse from the second century onward (Leigh 2004: 42–56). Other constants discernible from their use in *contiones* and forensic speeches were the people's liberty, their rights of protection against a historically overbearing Senate, the obligations of the senators to the people, the spread of moral corruption since the expansion of the Empire, and the cultural superiority of Rome. For politicians who sought popular support, whether throughout their careers or (like Cicero) only at times of crisis, these themes worked not to harden "party lines" but as the basic building blocks of communication with the *plebs* (Morstein-Marx 2004: 217, ch. 7).

Part of Scipio Africanus's success lay in the sheer impact of his presence, that is, in his *ēthos*, his character, which was amplified by his review of his achievements before the assembly. One of the three formal parts of rhetoric along with *logos* and *pathos*, *ēthos*, or the presentation of character, is central in Roman oratory and rhetorical discourse because it transforms political values and propositions into moral ones. More precisely, it reconfigures matters of political judgment such as policy disputes, legal cases, and factional conflict into matters of moral judgment (see Connolly 2007: 47–64). The character of the orator, his past achievements and those of his family, and his commitment to the virtue and security of the *res publica* become as important as evidence or logical argument. This held true in the law courts as well, where speakers sought to uphold justice not as an abstract value but "for the good of the Roman people as a whole" (Riggsby 1999: 157).

Playing out in different ways in the *contio* and the law court, the moralization of political judgment places the citizen mass on an ostensibly equal footing with the senatorial order. Consequently, more is at stake in Roman oratory than appealing to common beliefs and values. Praising traditional notions of manly youth and maligning lust and lack of self-control in speeches like the *Pro Caelio* and the Second Philippic, attacking uncontrolled greed (*In Verrem*), celebrating the Empire (*Pro Balbo, Pro Archia, De lege Manilia*), and other moralistic commonplaces replaced political and legal argument with the pleasures of moral agreement, blurring the standards of personal judgment with the political consensus of the whole *res publica*. With *ēthos* a central object of concern for the audience, oratory helped create a moral consensus whose reassuring attractions helped compensate for citizens' awareness of inequality and dependency. The paternalistic, traditional bent of moralist language provided a point of identification between the citizen mass and the senatorial order. Because it underlines what unites all free adult male heads of families, appealing to citizens' moral capacity as a spontaneous sign of moral equality lends an egalitarian feel to a society riven by structural inequalities of wealth and privilege.

Rhetorical discourse finds a second strand of commonality and equality across the Republic in aesthetic perception. For Cicero and Quintilian, the orator's ability to "guide" the people depends on a prior and primary intersubjective relationship between orator and audience that rests in the *sensus communis* of emotion and taste. If this relationship cannot properly be described as equal in the modern political sense, it may be best called a common field of perception and judgment. This notion is key to understanding Cicero's vision of rhetoric's legitimizing power in the Republic: the common denominator shared by all citizens—as well as certain groups outside the borderline of citizenship—is the capacity to feel emotions and to render judgments of taste. When assessing rhythm and pronunciation and other aspects of artifice, the orator must recognize that the entire audience, including the uneducated mass (the *vulgus imperitorum*), is capable of making good judgments thanks to this common sense (*communibus sensibus*) (Cicero, De oratore 3.195; cf. 2.68). So the orator must reach out to his audience in all its diversity and "taste" their experiences:

> For the faculty of speaking should not be plain and bare, but sprinkled and adorned with a certain pleasurable variety of things [*aspersa atque distincta multarum rerum iucunda quadam varietate*]. It should be the good orator's part to have heard much, to have seen much, to have gone over many subjects in his spirit and mind, and still others in his reading; though not so as to have taken possession of them as his own, but rather to have taken sips of them, like things belonging to others [*neque ea, ut sua, possedisse; sed, ut aliena, libasse*]. . . . He ought to penetrate the very veins [*oportet venas*] of each type, age, and class, and of those before whom he speaks or is going to speak; he must taste their minds and senses [*mentes sensusque degustet*]. (1.218, 222–3)

Sensus communis is a kind of extra sense by which the speaker does not possess or dominate but temporarily experiences the thoughts, feelings, and sensations of others.

Cicero's claims about *sensus communis* bear out a point made several times in *De republica*, namely, that the idea of a regime without multiplicity founded by a single man or based on a single principle is alien to politics properly understood. The singular regime is, of course, the ideal *politeia* of Plato's *Republic*, also rejected by Aristotle, who defends a mixed regime in his *Politics* (see Garver, ch. 10). Like the city of Rome from its founding to its early history, Cicero's rhetorical community is plural, mixed, and antagonistic. Consequently, those who wish to address the community are bound to think in the plural and muster a variety of arguments, styles, and vocabularies. This is why Crassus insists that there is no limited field of knowledge for rhetoric: it is the whole of human life, diverse and ever changing (*De oratore* 3.55).

The speaker himself must reflect this diversity. Vladimir Lenin defined politics as that which is concerned with the question, "Who, whom?": Who is doing what to whom, with what agency, with what authority, for what interests, and for what benefit? This formulation seeks to turn the question of political theory away from abstract analyses of the good or the just toward actors in the polity. Roman rhetoric goes deeper, as it were, calling into question the very identity of the "who" and the "whom." In the action of speech, identity is not fixed within the bounds of the self but enacted in the space between selves. *Ēthos*, it turns out, is not a fixed quantity but a fluid performance whose flow of energies is shaped by the relation between speaker and audience.

In the action of speech, as he appeals to the *sensus communis*, the orator is no longer fully only himself. This is a key claim in Cicero's *De oratore* and Quintilian's *Institutio oratoria*: that when the good orator speaks as an advocate for someone, he comes authentically to feel what that person feels, he views the world from their perspective, and he transmits that feeling and perspective to his listeners—even more effectively than the person or group on whose behalf he speaks. Quintilian praises the effect of an orator capable of compelling a judge "to grow angry, to favor, to hate, to pity" by first feeling himself what he wishes his listener to feel (Quintilian, *Institutio oratoria* 6.2.5–6, 26–8; trans. mine). Actors awaken pity for their fictitious characters, and by so much the more, in real cases, have the power to "set feelings afire" (6.1.35). In *De oratore* Antonius tells Crassus:

> No, by god, I never sought in the course of speaking to arouse grief, compassion, resentment, or hatred in the minds of the jury, unless I myself was moved to feel the same feelings I prompted in them. . . . Lest this seem too grand and miraculous, that a man should be so often made furious or wretched or beaten up by every sort of motion in the soul, the force [of language] is so great that there is no need for simulation and trickery: the very nature of speech [*orationis*] . . . moves the speaker even more profoundly than his listeners. (2.189, 191–2; trans. mine)

We glimpse the beginning of the formation of a normative notion of civic identity here, as responsive, mutable, and manifold.

Hannah Arendt is well known for her claims that speech involves a special kind of action: the action of disclosure (see Norris, ch. 49). Every utterance, she says, answers the question, Who? When men speak, they "show who they are . . . they reveal actively their unique personal identities and thus make their appearance in the human world" (Arendt 1998: 178–9). But Antonius's outburst about identity questions the assumption that underpins Arendt's claims about the revelatory nature of speech. In his account, the orator engaged in forensic argument speaks from and with another's identity, even as he retains and banks on his own *ēthos* to strengthen his act of advocacy. In this passage we are much closer to the kind of thinking Arendt calls "representative." Representative speech is not a blind adoption of "the actual views of those who stand somewhere else"; nor is it "empathy, as though I tried to be or to feel like somebody else"; nor is it a matter of "counting noses and joining a majority" (Arendt 1977: 241). It is the sign of an "enlarged mentality," a concept Arendt draws from Immanuel Kant's *Critique of Judgment*, which consists in "being and thinking in my own identity where actually I am not" (241).

The picture of what the orator does with his audience, in Cicero's and Quintilian's view, is not one of power being exercised *over* but of a relationship *between*. Arendt uses the notion of a table to describe the practice of living in common: "To live together in the world means essentially that a world of things is between those who have it in common, as a table is located between those who sit around it; the world, like every in-between, relates and separates men at the same time" (1998: 52). Like Arendt's table, the Roman orator fills the space between people with himself, and invites them, too, to join the space between.

The rhetoricians' seemingly contradictory acknowledgment that artifice is an irreducible element of artful speech and, at the same time, that there is no artifice involved in the speaker's performance of another's emotions, illuminates a third aspect of Roman rhetoric's political dimension. In his argument against unilateralism and singularity in political constitutions, Jacques Rancière appeals to the tradition of thinking about mixed constitutions. He argues that the perpetually self-correcting action of the mixed constitution represents a community in a state of constant change, in the course of which it embraces various points of view and "makes itself unlike itself," in a sort of "self-dissimulation" (Rancière 1995: 42). Where some dismiss politics as nothing more than the "illusion" of life in common (as Socrates comes close to doing in Plato's *Gorgias* when he compares sophistic speech to cosmetics and gourmet cookery), the process of self-dissimulation suggests that politics is precisely the "art or artifice of life in common" (43). Rancière concludes that for Aristotle, civic friendship is the artifice that actualizes his ideal of political life. For Cicero and Quintilian, the identification of and with an audience's interests, the impersonation of another's emotions, and the appeal to aesthetic perception—taken all together, the blurring of the boundaries between speaker and listener—are the artful activities that make life in common possible.

Cicero most ambitiously explores the possibilities for this kind of being and thinking in an alien identity in a speech he delivered not in the law court but in the Senate house, which has survived under the title of a defense speech, the *Pro Marcello* (see Connolly 2011). In 46 BCE, the civil war between Caesar and Pompey had just ended and Caesar was continuing his policy of *clementia*, guaranteeing the safety and reintegration of the partisans of Pompey. Marcellus, an ex-consul and committed Pompeian, for months refused Caesar's offer, maintaining self-imposed exile on the island of Lesbos. After repeated pleas from his brother, Cicero, and others, he finally agreed to return to Rome. With Marcellus expected to arrive any day (though in fact he was murdered before reaching Rome) Cicero breaks "a long silence" to praise Caesar for his clemency (*Pro Marcello* 1). The speech as a whole is an impassioned plea for the necessity of speech to politics. It mounts an apology for Caesar on the grounds of security: as Cicero later comments, "Under the rule of Caesar, we came into the Senate not as free men, but safe, at least" (*Philippics* 13.18). As Cicero represents him here, Caesar deserves praise because he has preserved a space for speech, even if, at the moment Cicero utters the *Pro Marcello*, speech is constrained, forced, literally unfree. This repetitive and self-critical speech may be understood as a programmatic demonstration of the orator's capacity to occupy and speak from a position of apology for autocratic rule that his audience knows is not actually his own, but which at the same time is and must be his because of the reality of the conditions of power. This is a position of subjection, which Cicero simultaneously embraces and ironically resists by ardently inhabiting the position of the still-resistant Marcellus.

In an important sense there is no authentic "Cicero" in the *Pro Marcello*. Nor in the Catilinarians, in which Cicero attacks the dissident Catiline in the paranoid authoritarian voice of the traditional antipopulist Roman noble. Nor in the Verrines, where he takes the part of abused and exploited Sicilian provincials. In the first book of *De oratore*, Antonius half-jokingly chides Crassus for his theatrically self-abnegating strategy in a famous speech: "Did you really mean to call yourself, and us, slaves?" (1.226). If, on one level, Antonius is making the obvious point that orators must assume different roles when they take on different cases, the politically significant point here is that Cicero embraces fluidity of identity as a model of political subjectivity, not because he is in love with blurring identity for its own sake but because he grasps the need to cultivate multiplicity in the political and legal *agōn*. As Eleanor Leach (1999: 147) observes, the world composed by the symbolic vocabulary of Roman *ēthos* is a fragmented world where wholeness exists only in the imagination.

One might object that politics is not limited to performance: it involves judgments and decisions to act in certain ways. The Roman rhetoricians appear to be subordinating morals, reason, and truth to aesthetic potentiality. This is Plato's argument in the *Gorgias*: if the orator speaks about things he knows nothing about, defends guilty parties, and depends on emotion and sensation as well as evidence and reason, he works in the space of appearance, not truth. What anchors the scene of politics? How is it possible to make evaluative distinctions between good and bad political actors?

For Cicero and Quintilian, norms emerge from practice rather than being externally imposed upon it. They rely on the audience's and the orator's sense of propriety as the guide for judgment. This response (unsatisfying by many standards) emerges in an important exchange in the first book of *De oratore*. The young Sulpicius presses Crassus to identify the areas the aspiring orator must study: Do they include law and the military arts? Crassus replies that he has designed his wide-ranging and ambitious account of the orator's intellectual formation to suit Sulpicius's potential—not only his innate talent and zeal (*ingenium studiumque*) but his outward appearance (*species*), which meets the all-important standard of *decorum* (*ut ne dedeceat*; Cicero, *De oratore* 1.131). Relaunched, the dialogue begins in earnest with the four fundamental precepts of communication: correct Latinity, clarity, ornament, and propriety (1.144).

Tacitus's *Dialogus de oratoribus*, whose characters debate the state of oratory in 75 CE, grants a decisive role to the audience in determining aesthetic criteria and sees taste as intimately related to changing moral and political conditions (Levene 2004: 175–6, 186–7). Nostalgic for Cicero's era, Messala suggests that aspiring orators of the past learned as much from the audiences as from exemplary speakers (Tacitus, *Dialogus de oratoribus* 34.4; see also 19.2–5). Maternus ascribes the decline of oratory to the emergence of autocratic rule, which has altered aesthetic and moral standards at the same time (36.1–41.5).

Both interlocutors agree that conditions for oratory differ significantly from those in Cicero's lifetime. The first speaker, Aper, emphasizes (and the younger Pliny's letters and *Panegyricus* agree) that orators continue to plead cases in the law courts, speak in the Senate, and deliver orations on public occasions. Maternus responds that with an autocrat ruling Rome, the freedom, risks, and rewards of republican politics—and thus of oratory—have fallen into decay (Barnes 1986). Republican chaos produced great eloquence; autocracy constrains and limits. In keeping with Maternus's summation, Tacitus's *Annals* and *Histories* represent politics as a game with predetermined players in which the unpredictability of republican dynamics is replaced by the unpredictability of the emperors' psychological state and personal relationships.

The central question for Tacitus, as for the agents in his histories, is legitimacy: On what basis does a particular person rule? This explains his choice to begin the *Annals* not with the victory of Octavian over Antony or Octavian's consolidation of power under the name Augustus but with the accession of his heir, Tiberius, who had to replace Augustus's claim to legitimacy as the restorer of the Republic with a new narrative about security.

Like Tacitus, political theorists since the nineteenth century have treated politics as primarily a matter of legitimacy, and they evaluate regimes, constitutions, laws, and processes by this measure. More recently, the revival of Carl Schmitt and the popularity of John Rawls and Giorgio Agamben have reinstalled legitimacy (and exceptions to it and suspensions of it) at the center of political thought. This development dovetails with the preoccupations of New Historicism-influenced studies of the role of literature and art in the formation and operation of authority and legitimacy. These studies ask: Whose voice has a claim to power and whose does not? How do the fields of art and literature, law and economics, education and science, reinforce the dominant order's claim to legitimacy? How do they resist?

Roman rhetorical discourse thinks politics from a different starting point. It sees the creation and sustaining of collective enterprises from law and elections to war- and treaty-making as action, the action of speaking for persuasive purposes in the context of a collective involved in decision-making about its past (in the law court) and its future (in the assembly or the Senate). It does not theorize rule or legitimacy. As Cicero and Quintilian regularly note in their references to the brothers Gracchi and other populist politicians, the potential for oratory to legitimize power in the status quo is matched by its power to undermine the status quo (see Rebhorn, ch. 31).

Cicero produced his work on rhetoric during years of bloody civil strife that were the result of competition among rich, powerful Romans mostly belonging to the senatorial class—competition that for centuries had been the customary pursuit of the elite and the driving force behind the conquest of new provinces, but that by the end of the second century BCE had become a profoundly destabilizing force in domestic politics. A crucial instrument for men to compete with peers in the Senate and to win over supporters in public, oratory gained new importance at times of civil unrest. This is the background to Cicero's idealizing construction of rhetoric as a form of political thought and to Tacitus's nostalgic memory of rhetoric's dynamism. Its concentration on action, antagonism, connections forged among citizens, and the role of aesthetic perception in civic collective experience make rhetoric a source of provocation even today.

References

Ando, Clifford. 2000. *Imperial Ideology and Provincial Loyalty in the Roman Empire.* Berkeley: University of California Press.

Arendt, Hannah. 1977. *Between Past and Future: Eight Exercises in Political Thought*. New York: Penguin.

Arendt, Hannah. 1998. *The Human Condition*. Chicago, IL: University of Chicago Press.

Barnes, T. D. 1986. "The Significance of Tacitus' *Dialogus de oratoribus*." *Harvard Studies in Classical Philology* 90: 225–244.

Connolly, Joy. 2007. *The State of Speech: Rhetoric and Political Thought in Ancient Rome*. Princeton, NJ: Princeton University Press.

Connolly, Joy. 2011. "Fantastical Realism in Cicero's Postwar Panegyric." In Dicere Laudes*: Elogio, Comunicazione, Creazione del Consenso*, edited by Gianpaolo Urso, 161–179. Pisa: ETS.

Farrell, Thomas B. 1993. *Norms of Rhetorical Culture*. New Haven, CT: Yale University Press.

Flaig, Egon. 2003. *Ritualisierte Politik: Zeichen, Gesten, und Herrschaft im alten Rom*. Göttingen: Vandenhoeck & Ruprecht.

Leach, Eleanor. 1999. "Ciceronian 'Bi-Marcus': Correspondence with M. Terentius Varro and L. Papirius Paetus in 46 B.C.E." *Transactions of the American Philological Association* 129: 139–179.

Leigh, Matthew. 2004. *Comedy and the Rise of Rome*. Oxford: Oxford University Press.

Levene, D. S. 2004. "Tacitus' *Dialogus* as Literary History." *Transactions of the American Philological Association* 134: 157–200.

Millar, Fergus. 1998. *The Crowd in Rome in the Late Republic*. Ann Arbor: University of Michigan Press.

Morstein-Marx, Robert. 2004. *Mass Oratory and Political Power in the Late Roman Republic*. Cambridge: Cambridge University Press.

Rancière, Jacques. 1995. *On the Shores of Politics*. London: Verso.

Riggsby, Andrew. 1999. *Crime and Community in Ciceronian Rome*. Austin: University of Texas Press.

Vasaly, Ann. 1993. *Representations: Images of the World in Ciceronian Oratory*. Berkeley: University of California Press.

CHAPTER 15

·····

RHETORIC AND
HISTORIOGRAPHY

·····

RHIANNON ASH

ORATORY and historiography were intricately meshed together in Roman society from
an early stage. Thus, Suetonius (ca. 69–122 CE) says that "the early debates [*controver-siae*] used to be derived either from works of history . . . or from some actual event that
had happened to occur recently" (*On Teachers of Grammar and Rhetoric* 25.5). Against
this backdrop, Cicero makes his friend Atticus say that writing history is "a task singularly well-suited to the orator" (*On the Laws* 1.5). Certainly, illustrative examples from
history are frequently embedded in many speeches of Cicero, who expects his listeners
to have at their fingertips the relevant historical knowledge to grasp this material with
dexterity (see van der Blom 2010: 65–147). Indeed, such historical examples are almost
a kind of shorthand for an orator, who can succinctly highlight a historical figure or
event in his speech to draw a suggestive analogy with his current case and to provoke an
emotional response. In addition, many practitioners of history were themselves distinguished orators. Cato the Elder (234–149 BCE) was equally renowned as an orator and
as the writer of one of the earliest historical narratives in Latin, the now fragmentary
Origins. Not only did he operate successfully in both spheres—history and oratory—
but he also included versions of his own speeches in his historical narratives (see Aulus
Gellius, *Attic Nights* 6.3, 13.25.15; Cicero, *De oratore* 1.227). Under the Empire, another
such ambidextrous figure is Tacitus (56/7–115/6 CE), a renowned orator who wrote the
Dialogue about Orators (a discussion set in the 70s CE surveying the state of oratory)
before going on to produce historical narratives, the *Histories* and *Annals*. In short, the
relationship between the writing of history and the professional practice of oratory both
in the law courts and the Senate was very much a two-way street.

   As a consequence, Roman historiography, shaped and enlivened by the rhetorical
skills of its talented practitioners, is a very different beast from its modern counterpart.
This aspect of Roman historical writing has at times created unease in its later reception.
The fundamental concern for modern audiences is how far rhetorical embellishment
compromises the reliability of written records of the past. Does the tendency of Roman

historians to use creative *inventio* really mean that we can trust everything (or even anything) that they tell us? Does the fact that some Roman historians had carved out careers both as professional orators and as historians vitiate the value of their written accounts as evidence because the rhetorical element "pollutes" the trustworthiness of their history? Such questions go right to the heart of the essentially rhetorical nature of Roman historiography. These concerns are compounded when dealing with a historian such as Livy, who wrote under Augustus and produced an extraordinary narrative of Roman history, *From the Foundation of the City*, which covers from 753 BCE down to 9 BCE in 142 books (now fragmentary). In this work, Livy not only wrote about the distant past but also deliberately did so in a monumentalizing format demanding that he cover the same events narrated by previous historians, but on a much grander scale. This is a phenomenon known as the "expansion of the past" and involves fleshing out the basic skeleton of historical events with additional material (e.g., speeches and debates, grandiose descriptions of battles and sieges). The need to do this is particularly acute when narrating early Roman history, for which written records were scant or nonexistent. Even Livy himself expresses frustration about the lack of written sources available to him as evidence for the earliest period of Roman history before the Gauls sacked Rome in 387 BCE, and he likens the process of writing about such material to seeing places only with difficulty over a great distance. In a second preface here, he optimistically heralds the subsequent narrative as an opportunity to write more clearly and accurately about his subject matter, beginning again "as if from the stalk" (Livy, *From the Foundation of the City* 6.1). The agricultural metaphor he uses here is typical of the vivid use of Latin by historical writers (and orators).

What is crucial to highlight, however, is that this creative rhetorical impulse also characterizes ancient historical narratives relaying events of the not-so-distant past. Thus, when Tacitus, for example, lays out what happened after the death of Augustus in 14 CE, he describes the emperor's widow, Livia, artfully orchestrating the situation in such a way as to conceal her husband's death until arrangements had been set in place to secure the succession of her son (Augustus's stepson), Tiberius: "For Livia had cordoned off the house and street with fierce guards, and from time to time favourable news was published until, after provision for what the occasion demanded, a single report carried the simultaneous announcement that Augustus had passed away and that Nero [i.e., Tiberius] was in control of affairs" (*Annals* 1.5.4). So far, so good—until we think back to Livy's version of events surrounding the death of the fifth king of Rome, Tarquinius Priscus, mortally wounded in an attack. His wife, Tanaquil, orders the palace to be closed (Livy, *From the Foundation of the City* 1.41.1), makes encouraging announcements about the king's health (1.41.5) and sets up her son (Tarquinius's stepson), Servius Tullius, to carry out the king's duties on a "temporary" basis, even though he is already dead (1.41.7). If one reads the two passages from Tacitus and Livy side by side, it becomes clear that Tacitus has narrated the death of Augustus (14 CE) using creative embellishment in such a way as to align it with Livy's description of the death of Tarquinius Priscus (traditionally 579 BCE), as Ronald Martin (1955) illustrates. This sort of practice can be explained away as symptomatic of an author adding some rhetorical color to elusive events, but that is to ignore the wider interpretative significance of such artistry. Tacitus here is using the shadow of the regal period implicitly to ask some fundamental political questions about the imperial system. Is the Principate, despite retaining some traditional mechanisms from the Republic (established in 509 BCE) such as the consulship and the Senate, really just a thinly disguised reincarnation of the pre-republican dynastic system that operated during the period when Rome was ruled by kings (753–509 BCE)? Is the palatable fiction that Augustus had "restored the Republic" actually worse than the openly autocratic dynastic system of the regal period? The rhetorical nature of ancient historical writing can and should encourage such collaborative reading strategies. However, whereas a modern historian might draw the comparison explicitly, Tacitus instead hints at the connection through suggestive literary and linguistic echoes in his own account.

It should be clear by now that concerns about the truth value of ancient historical narratives prompted by the genre's rhetorical nature can be viewed more positively than some pessimistic modern readings suppose. If we choose to work *with* the nature of ancient historiography and to read collaboratively, then the value of these accounts is restored. The rhetorical element, rather than being an inconvenient distraction needing to be shaved off to get at the kernel of truth hidden beneath the surface, can often add meaning and depth to an author's historical interpretation. However, even when that was not the case, the rhetorical element of these accounts is still valuable: an engagingly written historical narrative retains the interest of an audience and enhances pleasure. On the level of individual words and phrases, engagement and surprise can be triggered by a creative neologism, a paradoxical turn of phrase, or a suggestive allusion to another author (whether historian or poet); and on the level of more elaborate scenes, the minutiae of an author's style can combine to create spectacular purple passages, such as a gripping battle narrative or an emotive death scene (see Hall, ch. 18). The rhetorical element adds enjoyment to these historical narratives, and that pleasure in turn serves as a vehicle to serve the historian's moralizing agenda. In this connection, we should not forget that Roman historical narratives would often be read out in public to an invited audience at a *recitatio*, an ideal setting for a historian to show off his rhetorical powers and to engage his listeners emotionally and intellectually (see Dominik, ch. 12).

With these preliminaries in mind, the first section of this chapter elucidates how the rhetorical element adds impact to historiography on the level of its building blocks, such as in an author's creative choices of vocabulary and in his use of metaphor and wordplay. Then we will consider some more elaborate scenes before moving on to some general conclusions.

THE BUILDING BLOCKS

In the ancient world, a historian's stylistic choices had important consequences. Just as the ideal orator is cast as the *vir bonus, dicendi peritus*, the "good man skilled at speaking"

(Quintilian, *Institutio oratoria* 12.1.1), so too by implication is the ideal historian, who essentially deploys his rhetorical skills (or is meant to deploy them) for the benefit of the Roman state. In stylistic terms, Roman historiography operates across a broad spectrum of Latinity, resulting in an incredibly flexible and diverse genre. Yet regardless of the distinctive Latin styles adopted by individual historians, all practitioners of history were meant to be morally robust and independent men who constructed their narratives to illuminate for their audience bad conduct to avoid and good conduct to imitate (Livy, *From the Foundation of the City*, preface 10; Tacitus, *Annals* 3.65). A historian whose moralizing voice was particularly strong, such as Sallust, was always vulnerable to attack (whatever the reality of his life). Thus, the pseudo-Ciceronian *Invective against Sallust* denounces in colorful and imaginative detail the gulf between the historian's lofty words and his grubby life, and similarly, the freedman Lenaeus, furious at Sallust for describing Pompey the Great as "fair on the outside, shameless within," gives the historian a dose of his own medicine in a lampoon, calling him "a pansy, a greedy-guts, a waste of space, a barfly" (Suetonius, *On the Grammarians* 15.2). If historians in Roman society served as moral arbiters, then they themselves had to live up to the high standards they set for others. In this connection, it is a distinctive feature of the genre that one of its most significant early practitioners, Cato the Elder, served in public life as "censor" of Roman public life, a formal role that was inextricably bound up with the moralizing tone of his historical writings (see Carawan 1990; Cicero, *De senectute* 42; Plutarch, *Cato the Elder* 17–9.4). Subsequently, any historian who used Latin that was evocative of Cato the Elder was not just making a stylistic choice but was also aligning himself with a robust moralizing voice from the past to add weight to his own persona.

Historians such as Sallust and Tacitus are natural stylistic allies, successors to Cato the Elder, and themselves writers who deliberately use an artificial style of Latin that self-consciously sets them out of kilter with their immediate chronological context. They are verbal necromancers, bringing back to life items of vocabulary that had fallen out of ordinary use. This practice did not always meet with a warm reception. Asinius Pollio, for instance, criticizes the works of Sallust as being "sullied by an excessive affectation of archaic diction" (Suetonius, *On Teachers of Grammar and Rhetoric* 10.2). Similarly, Quintilian (*Institutio oratoria* 8.3.29) cites an anonymous epigram ridiculing Sallust for stealing items of vocabulary from Cato the Elder, and the emperor Augustus criticizes Antony for adopting a perverse style recalling Sallust's excerption of words from Cato's *Origins* (Suetonius, *Augustus* 86.3). Yet, as a way to mark an author's distance from a corrupt contemporary world, an archaizing style of Latin had cumulative impact (see Levene 2000). One small example is in choosing between the Latin synonyms *claritudo* and *claritas*, words both meaning "distinction." Where Cicero (and later Livy) had preferred *claritas*, Sallust instead chooses the archaizing alternative *claritudo*, "a Sallustian favourite" (Martin and Woodman 1989: 108). In this he was followed by Tacitus, particularly in his final work, the *Annals*, where *claritudo* (31 times) almost entirely ousts *claritas* (two times). There is also Sallust's tendency to choose resonant archaizing alternatives such as *lubido* for *libido* (lust). In a literary milieu in which historical works were regularly read aloud to audiences, these touches would have resonated and stood out.

Thus, when the (now fragmentary) republican historian Claudius Quadrigarius (first century BCE) describes the moment when the victorious Roman, Manlius Torquatus, snatches as a trophy the bloodstained torque that had adorned the neck of his dead Gallic opponent, he memorably describes it as *sanguinulenta* ("blood-drenched," in a fragment preserved verbatim in Aulus Gellius [*Attic Nights* 9.13.19]). This thunderous, polysyllabic adjective draws attention to the gruesome trophy that eloquently symbolizes Roman victory over the turbulent forces of barbarian brutality. At the same time, it reminds us of the levels of violence to which Romans sometimes had to resort in order to preserve the balance of their own civilized world. It is striking, too, that the adjective was not favored by later historians, even by Livy when he was recasting this famous single combat in his own history (Livy, *From the Foundation of the City* 7.9.6–10.14). In a creative shift, he instead describes the torque as *respersum cruore* ("scattered with blood") (7.10.11). Perhaps *sanguinulenta* sounded too archaic, or else he wanted to mark his own creativity by innovating. These two descriptions in Claudius Quadrigarius and Livy are also distinctive for showing the dynamics of the expansion of the past at work. Quadrigarius's narrative (219 words) is expanded by Livy to 352 words, partly by making much greater use of direct speech, by including an epic-flavor arming scene, and by directing the focus more extensively on the fluctuating emotions of the spectators. Modern scholars have understandably paid close attention to these two passages for what they reveal about the historian's rhetorical "workshop" (von Albrecht 1989: 86–101; Oakley 1998: 113–48).

One area where Roman historians overlap considerably with the orators is in their fondness for expressively metaphorical language, whether in the form of isolated instances or multiple, interlinked metaphors peppered over a section of narrative. Roland Mayer suggests that "the Romans felt metaphorical usages of their language more strongly than we do in ours, and commonly qualified any novel departure" (2001: 102), and it is clear that the historians regularly exploited such sensitivity. Livy, for instance, describes an attack by Valerius Corvus, *cum . . . velut indagine dissipatos Samnites ageret* ("when [the cavalry] drove the scattered Samnites *as if by a cordon of hunters*") (*From the Foundation of the City* 7.37.14; emphasis added). Here Livy uses a metaphor (qualified with *velut*) suggesting a ring of huntsmen encircling their quarry, casting the Samnites as beasts, which diminishes any potential sympathy for them. This sort of technique—bestializing the enemy—is memorably deployed in Cicero's invective, *Against Piso*, in which he cumulatively unleashes pejorative animalistic metaphors against his target, including *belua* ("beast"; 1, 8), *pecus* ("sheep"; 19), *maialis* ("gelded boar"; 19), and *volturius* ("vulture"; 38). We can also compare Livy's metaphor with another example, this time in a speech delivered by Cornelius Cossus in which he exhorts Manlius Capitolinus "to dislodge from their secret booty men who are brooding over the public treasures" (*istos incubantes publicis thesauris ex praeda clandestina evolvas*; *From the Foundation of the City* 6.15.5). As Christina Kraus suggests of *incubantes*, "the image is of a great serpent guarding its hoard," while the verb *evolvas* "continues the image of patrician snakiness" (1994: 181–2). Perhaps because the imagery is included in a speech, Livy refrains from qualifying his animal metaphor here with an "as it were."

Roman historians can also use metaphor in more elaborate and interlocking ways over a stretch of narrative. For example, Christopher Krebs (2008) argues that Sallust, in the preface to his *War against Catiline*, purposefully incorporates multiple metaphors involving travel, roads, and crossroads partly as a reflection of his own decision to turn away from the traditional *cursus honorum* toward the writing of history. In a different context, A. J. Woodman (2006) demonstrates how the pervasive metaphors of madness and medicine run through Tacitus's account of the mutinies that broke out in Pannonia and Germany in 14 BCE after Augustus's death (*Annals* 1.15–49). What these instances suggest is a partnership between language and core meaning, as authors economically and expressively build up sequences of metaphor that reinforce and add nuances to their historical arguments.

A particularly powerful weapon in the hands of a talented orator is humor. While one might perhaps not expect to detect much of this in a genre that took itself as seriously as historiography did, nonetheless it does exist, particularly in the form of wordplay and puns. For instance, historians could and did play creatively with proper names (see Woodman 1998: 222–8). Tacitus, for example, indulges in name-play when noting that with the arrival of the general Valens ("Strong"), the Vitellian party *convaluerunt* ("strengthened") (Tacitus, *Histories* 2.93.2). Such moments of wit provide some respite in an otherwise grim narrative of civil war. They also offer scope for Tacitean irony, in that here the general Valens, despite his name, turns out to be quite a weak creature. Just a few chapters later, after the Vitellian army has left Rome with his fellow general, Caecina, Valens sends word that the soldiers should await him on the road. Caecina, however, countermands this *praesens eoque validior* ("on the spot and therefore stronger") (2.100.2). Of all the Roman historians, Tacitus is certainly the most expressive, sustained, and accomplished artist of wordplay (Plass 1988).

All the same, despite the creative fusion between historiography and oratory, there were boundaries. For example, even when the historians are relaying speeches articulated by internal protagonists who were real orators, these men do not use Latin that reflects their own style but instead speak in the Latin of the historian. A particularly striking instance of this involves the two long speeches that form the climax of Sallust's *Catiline*, where Julius Caesar (*Catiline* 51) and Cato the Younger (52) present arguments in direct speech about what should be done with the Catilinarian conspirators. Although Caesar and Cato are orators in their own right, each with his idiosyncratic style, they both speak *Sallustian* Latin. As one critic sums up, "Nothing testifies more compellingly to the intricate unity of Sallust's verbal texture than its subordination, not to say erasure, of these two historical figures' distinctive and verifiable styles" (Sklenář 1998: 206). Modern scholars have been able to detect the odd expression and items of vocabulary, which appear only in speeches and are perhaps intended to recall the speaker's idiolect. For example, Vespasian's general, Licinius Mucianus (another accomplished orator), is twice made to use the phrase *clarus apud* ("well-known in the eyes of") in his speech (Tacitus, *Histories* 2.76.3, 2.77.1). The expression appears here only in extant Latin and therefore could reflect a linguistic affectation peculiar to Mucianus, but the speech itself is conspicuously in Tacitus's historical style (see Woodman 2010). In this connection, it is particularly striking that in his *Dialogue about Orators* Tacitus adopts a style that can be called neo-Ciceronian: here in his selection of vocabulary, sentence structure, word order, striving for balance, and rhythmical closure to periods, Tacitus evokes Ciceronian Latin (Mayer 2001: 27–31). Yet his style in his historical works, the *Histories* and *Annals*, is markedly different. This contrast demonstrates how authors could self-consciously develop a style appropriate to the genre in which they were writing. Pliny the Younger reminds us of this point in letter 5.8, in which he suggests how the appropriate Latin styles for a historical narrative and forensic oratory had significant differences, even if we should be cautious about taking this assertion at face value. After all, in this letter he is apparently refusing to write a historical narrative, so it was in his interests to play up the stylistic differences (Ash 2003; Woodman 2012).

Oratory in Motion

Oratory and historical writing also overlap in broader areas involving methodology and modes of argumentation. For example, Livy offers an intriguing and famous digression near the start of book 9 of *From the Foundation of the City*, speculating about what would have happened if Alexander had directed his campaigns westward (and faced the Romans) rather than eastward. In so doing, Livy halts the linear chronological progression of his narrative and engages in a burst of counterfactual speculation. Ruth Morello makes an intriguing observation in connection with the Alexander digression, which she says "fits neatly into . . . a strong tradition of counterfactual speculation both in public oratory and in historiography" (2002: 65). What this highlights is that historians and forensic orators often faced the same challenges in presenting plausible reconstructions of events they themselves had not witnessed (see Carey, ch. 4). In essence, they were obliged to ask similar questions about their evidence. Why did events happen in this way? What would have happened at any given point if an individual had taken one course of action rather than another? What would an individual gain from a particular result, and how might they have been involved in securing that outcome? Questions of motive, opportunity, and plausibility are common both to a historian analyzing a set of past events and to an orator pitching his legal case (see Gagarin, ch. 2; Enos, ch. 13; Hutson, ch. 32).

We can consider here an illuminating pair of examples. In 80 BCE Cicero, in one of his earliest cases, took on the defense of Sextus Roscius, who was accused of murdering his wealthy father, a citizen of Ameria. In responding to the prosecution's case, Cicero engages with the question, *cui bono* ("Who would benefit from the death of Roscius senior?"), and on this basis proceeds to identify alternative suspects for the murder, namely, two relatives of the defendant, Roscius Magnus and Roscius Capito. A large section of the speech (*On Behalf of Roscius* 83–123) is dedicated to a counter accusation of this pair. Yet Cicero also pursues a line of argument based on his defendant's character, challenging the prosecution to demonstrate that Roscius as a person would have been capable of parricide. He asks the prosecutor, Erucius: "Surely you should show the remarkable audacity of the man who is accused, his wild way, his brutal nature, his life dedicated to all vices and crimes, and in short a character depraved, abandoned, and utterly ruined?" (Cicero, *On Behalf of Roscius* 38). The argument is based on the likely conduct suggested by Roscius's individual character (*probabile ex vita*), which (Cicero argues) fails to manifest the traits necessary as a prerequisite to killing his father. As well as pursuing this strategy involving personality, Cicero bolsters this argument with a logical analysis of the family relationship between father and son: "Let us ask what great vices there might have been in an only son because of which he was displeasing to his father. Yet it is clear that there were none. So, was the father out of his mind, seeing that he hated without reason the son whom he had begotten? Yet the father was an utterly steadfast man. Consequently, it is already clear indeed that if the father was not out of his mind, nor the son a reprobate, then neither did the father have any reason to hate his son, nor did the son have any reason to commit a crime" (41). Cicero here goes on the offensive by setting a dilemma for the prosecution, whose arguments depend on establishing a serious character flaw in either the father or the son. Since neither father nor son manifests the prerequisite of madness or depravity, Cicero implies that the necessary conclusion is that the prosecution case is flawed.

Let us compare here another murder case, this time from a historical narrative. A central event for Tacitus's narrative of the year 23 CE is the death by poisoning of Drusus, the only son of the incumbent emperor, Tiberius. This death had a fundamental impact on the succession and elevated the ambitious praetorian prefect Sejanus to an unprecedentedly powerful role in the state. Now, Tacitus is clear from the start that Sejanus is the man who orchestrated the plot to kill Drusus, but he also feels obliged to record a rumor that in addition implicates Tiberius. According to the rumor, Sejanus warns Tiberius that his son Drusus intends to poison him and that he should therefore avoid the first drink offered to him by his son at a particular dinner. Tiberius allegedly heeds this advice but then hands the cup instead to Drusus, who drinks it in ignorance that it really has been poisoned. Tacitus at this point intervenes robustly to refute the whole story: "What man of average prudence—still less Tiberius, practiced as he was in great affairs—would have offered extermination to a son unheard, and that too with his own hand and no recourse to repentance? Would he not rather have racked the server of the poison, searched out its initiator, and finally, given the innate hesitancy and delay with which he treated even outsiders, treated his one and only son, who had been discovered in no outrage, with the same?" (*Annals* 4.11.1).

Tacitus's compelling questions here pursue very similar lines of argument to Cicero in his defense of Roscius. We can see that Tacitus puts the spotlight not only on Tiberius's prudent and cautious character as an individual but also on the family relationship between father and son. In the first question, Tacitus reminds us that Tiberius is a meticulous man, experienced and intelligent, and thus it is completely implausible that he would have killed his son without further investigation. In the second question, he enumerates in the subjunctive mood what Tiberius as a father of an only son would naturally have done instead. Woodman and Martin analyze this episode, suggesting that

Tacitus "has handled a typically exciting declamatory *topic* in a typically declamatory *manner*" (1989: 124) (see Pernot, ch. 20; Gunderson, ch. 21). Although oratory had certainly changed and developed between the time of Cicero and Tacitus (as Tacitus himself makes clear in his *Dialogue about Orators*), these two examples from a forensic speech and from a historical narrative show how the writers can revert to similar lines of argument to prove their point.

It is clear that in the Roman world there was potentially much scope for cross-fertilization between various kinds of oratory, whether deliberative, forensic, or declamatory, and the writing of history. In some cases, talented and ambidextrous practitioners turned their hand to both activities simultaneously, so that the professional orator directed skills learned in that sphere toward creating lively historical narratives. Orators and historians therefore often had similar concerns regarding their respective audiences. Entertainment was on the agenda in both spheres as a means to an end: in the courtroom, a lawyer needed to keep the jurors engaged with the case for the benefit of his client, while a historian had to convince his audience to keep reading (or listening) until the end so as to secure the credibility of his own distinctive version of events. In historiography, there are also *internal* audiences within the text who have to be convinced or dissuaded from taking or supporting a particular course of action (see Levene 2006). The art of persuasion was a crucial element of both oratory and history, and paradoxical though it may seem both activities were strongly rooted in the present and in the future: forensic oratory was designed to win a case and secure the defendant's future participation in affairs of state, while history was conceived not simply as a record of the past but as a way to influence contemporary conduct. As we have seen, the two disciplines inform and inspire one another in extraordinarily fruitful ways.

Further Reading

The fundamental study of the rhetorical nature of ancient historical writing is Woodman (1988), which considers both Greek and Latin historians, while Woodman (2008) robustly defends his earlier stance. Plass (1988) is an engaging study of wit and wordplay in historiography, particularly in Tacitus. There are useful studies of speeches in historiography in Berry and Erskine (2010).

References

Ash, Rhiannon. 2003. "*Aliud est enim epistulam, aliud historiam . . . scribere* (*Ep.* 6.16.22): Pliny the Historian?" *Arethusa* 36 no. 2: 211–225.

Berry, Dominic, and Andrew Erskine, eds. 2010. *Form and Function in Roman Oratory*. Cambridge: Cambridge University Press.

Carawan, Edwin. 1990. "Cato's Speech Against L. Flamininus: Livy 39.42–3." *Classical Journal* 85: 316–329.

Kraus, Christina. 1994. *Livy "Ab Urbe Condita" VI*. Cambridge: Cambridge University Press.

Krebs, Christopher. 2008. "The Imagery of 'The Way' in the Proem to Sallust's *Bellum Catilinae* 1–4." *American Journal of Philology* 129: 581–594.

Levene, David. 2000. "Sallust's *Catiline* and Cato the Censor." *Classical Quarterly* 50 no. 1: 170–191.

Levene, David. 2006. "History, Metahistory, and Audience Response in Livy 45." *Classical Antiquity* 25: 73–108.

Martin, Ronald. 1955. "Tacitus and the Death of Augustus." *Classical Quarterly* 5: 123–128.

Martin, Ronald, and Anthony Woodman, eds. 1989. *Tacitus "Annals" IV*. Cambridge: Cambridge University Press.

Mayer, Roland, ed. 2001. *Tacitus "Dialogus de Oratoribus."* Cambridge: Cambridge University Press.

Morello, Ruth. 2002. "Livy's Alexander Digression (9.17–19): Counterfactuals and Apologetics." *Journal of Roman Studies* 92: 62–85.

Oakley, Stephen. 1998. *A Commentary on Livy Books VI–X*. Vol. 2, *Books VII–VIII*. Oxford: Oxford University Press.

Plass, Paul. 1988. *Wit and the Writing of History: The Rhetoric of Historiography in Imperial Rome*. Madison: University of Wisconsin Press.

Sklenář, Robert. 1998. "*La République des Signes*: Caesar, Cato, and the Language of Sallustian Morality." *Transactions of the American Philological Association* 128: 205–220.

van der Blom, Henriette. 2010. *Cicero's Role Models: The Political Strategy of a Newcomer*. Oxford: Oxford University Press.

Von Albrecht, Michael. 1989. *Masters of Roman Prose from Cato to Apuleius*. Translated by Neil Adkin. Leeds: Francis Cairns.

Woodman, Anthony. 1988. *Rhetoric in Classical Historiography*. London: Croom Helm.

Woodman, Anthony. 1998. *Tacitus Reviewed*. Oxford: Oxford University Press.

Woodman, Anthony. 2006. "Mutiny and Madness: Tacitus *Annals* 1.16–49." *Arethusa* 39 no. 2: 303–329.

Woodman, Anthony. 2008. "Cicero on Historiography: *De oratore* 2.51–64." *Classical Journal* 104 no. 1: 23–31.

Woodman, Anthony. 2010. "*Aliena Facundia*: Seneca in Tacitus." In *Form and Function in Roman Oratory*, edited by Dominic Berry and Andrew Erskine, 294–307. Cambridge: Cambridge University Press.

Woodman, Anthony. 2012. "Pliny on Writing History, *Epistles* 5.8." In *From Poetry to History: Selected Papers*, edited by Anthony Woodman, 223–242. Oxford: Oxford University Press.

CHAPTER 16

RHETORIC AND PEDAGOGY

CATHERINE STEEL

RHETORIC has its origins in the belief that effective public speaking involves skills that can be taught (see Habinek 2005: 38–59; Connolly 2009). The Romans were, with some exceptions and a great deal of debate, adherents to this belief and enthusiastic students of what they could learn from Greek-speaking teachers of rhetoric (see Heath, ch. 5). Their exploration of the pedagogical implications of rhetoric provided fresh stimulus to Greek rhetoricians in the first and second centuries BCE and generated treatises and handbooks in Latin that were highly influential in preserving the tradition of classical rhetoric in post-classical Western Europe. Nevertheless, the history of Roman rhetoric is not simply one of the development of Greek rhetoric in the context of a Mediterranean-wide empire (see Dominik, ch. 12). Public speech had a different function at Rome than it did at Athens and other Greek city-states. This difference profoundly affected how public speaking was taught at Rome and the ways teachers and practitioners attempted to understand and control the art of rhetoric.

A good place to start exploring the peculiarities of the Roman context and their implications for the pedagogy of rhetoric is an Athenian embassy sent to Rome in 156–5 BCE (Cicero, *De oratore* 2.155, *Tusculanae disputationes* 4.5, *Academica* 2.137; Aulus Gellius, *Noctes Atticae* 6.14.8–10; Plutarch, *Cato Major* 22). The purpose of this embassy was to persuade the Romans to reduce or remit a large fine that had been imposed on Athens as punishment for its pillaging of Oropus during a border dispute (Habicht 1997: 264–7). The Athenians sent, as ambassadors, leaders of their philosophical schools: Carneades the Academic, Diogenes the Stoic, and Critolaus the Peripatetic. While they were waiting to present their case to the Senate, these philosophers delivered a number of well-attended public lectures. According to Aulus Gellius, the speeches that made the deepest impression on the historical record are the pair Carneades presented, on successive days, on the topic of justice, the first advocating justice, the second refuting his arguments of the previous day (Walbank 1965: 12–3). It was Carneades's speeches, according to Plutarch, that alarmed the elder Cato and provoked him to ask the Senate to reach a decision on the Oropus fine as quickly as possible and let the ambassadors leave "so that these men may devote themselves again to their leisure and converse with the sons of the

Greeks, and the young men of Rome pay attention, as before, to the laws and the magistrates" (*Cato Major* 22.7).

Precisely what aspects of justice Carneades's speeches may have handled and their relationship to the developing debate at Rome over the administration and purpose of its Empire are much disputed; so, too, is the relationship between Carneades's views and Cicero's treatment of them in *De republica* (Ferrary 1988: 351–63; Glucker 2001; Fitzpatrick 2010: 8–9). Whether or not Carneades lectured the Romans on the nature of their rule, the content of his speeches and their demonstration of how to argue contradictory theses (what the Greeks called *dissoi logoi* and *antilogiae*) may alone explain the stir he caused. Yet it is also worth noting that the ancient evidence stresses the quality of Carneades's eloquence as a factor in explaining his impact. In Plutarch's account, Carneades attracts his listeners through his skill in speaking as well as their enthusiasm for philosophy, and Cato is concerned by the speeches because he fears that young men will, under the influence of Carneades's eloquence, come to value oratory more highly than military activity. Gellius's detailed account of the embassy (one of the few to consider all three philosophers) is presented as an example supporting his argument about the three kinds of speech (*genera dicendi*): each of the three philosophers exemplified a different kind of speech (*Noctes Atticae* 6.14.10). In short, the Athenians attracted interest not simply because they offered examples of philosophical argument but also because these arguments were expressed in persuasive speech.

The Athenian embassy of 156–5 BCE provides evidence of the desire at Rome to experience eloquent speech. But the way the anecdote is told, particularly in Plutarch's biography of the elder Cato, also shows that not all Romans felt this enthusiasm. Cato's opposition, in Plutarch, results from anxiety that the knowledge and skills the Athenians offer will change Romans, and particularly young Roman men, for the worse. There is a danger that the pursuit of oratory and philosophy will displace traditional Roman interests in war, law, and government. Greeks may engage with the subjects that the philosophers treat; Romans should not. Cato's position exemplifies one aspect of Rome's engagement with the ideas and skills it borrowed from Greece: the fear that this engagement was incompatible with essential features of Roman character and identity (see Bartsch, ch. 17). This is why, five years before the embassy from Athens, the urban *praetor* was already being instructed to ensure that there were no philosophers or rhetoricians in Rome (Aulus Gellius, *Noctes Atticae* 15.11.1).

Enthusiasm for eloquence nevertheless triumphed over fear of its deleterious effects. An important reason for this triumph lies in the nature of Roman political life: power in the Republic, at least the power that depended on the tenure of magistracies and the membership of the Senate, was in practice in the hands of small, highly competitive elite (see Connolly, ch. 14). These men acquired power as individuals via elections in which all adult male citizens could vote. There were no formal political parties; alliances between individual politicians existed, certainly, and might influence elections, but candidates relied, as they presented themselves to the electorate, primarily upon their reputation, combined with their record of bestowing favors and their perceived capacity to keep the *beneficia* coming (see Lintott 1999; Yakobson 1999; North 2006; Tatum 2013). Public speech played an important part in the creation of reputation and obligations. Successful defense advocacy put the acquitted under a major obligation, which could be exchanged for their electoral support and that of their friends. Speeches to the people as a whole at public meetings (*contiones*) offered the opportunity to establish a relationship with the people, but this tactic needed careful handling, since a blatant populist stance could alienate the wealthy and backfire in elections for the most senior magistracies, where the organization of citizens into voting units favored property owners. Recent scholarship has begun to clarify the complex, shifting relationship between appeals to the people, individual political careers, and political programs; and the term *popularis* could cover a wide range of behaviors and stances. At the same time, the people's access to a politician's views was limited to his public actions and words. While modern students with access to Cicero's letters find in his stance as a *popularis* politician only hypocrisy, Roman citizens in 63 BCE, familiar only with Marcus Tullius Cicero the advocate and supporter of Pompeius, would have a rather different view (see Morstein-Marx 2004: 207–30).

In this political environment, speaking effectively was a valuable skill. But effectiveness was not identical to technical ability: diligence also mattered. Cicero's dialogue on the history of oratory at Rome, *Brutus*, contains many examples of men whom he lists as orators but whose ability as speakers he doubts (Steel 2003). A particularly striking example is his analysis of the consul C. Scribonius Curio: he "was counted close to the very best on account of the excellence of his language" despite being slow in finding arguments, careless in arranging them, hopelessly forgetful, and so eccentric in his style of delivery as to be the butt of memorable witticisms (Cicero, *Brutus* 216–20; see Wisse 2013). Curio's profile indicates that oratory demanded a wide range of different kinds of skills. Consequently, there were many different routes to improvement as an orator and, for the politician who intended to use public speech to advance his career, many opportunities to improve through training.

On an individual level, initial exposure to rhetoric came as part of the pattern of education provided for the children of the elite (see Bonner 1977; Kaster 1995; Morgan 1998). Instruction by *grammatici* in the use of language was followed by training in rhetoric, which developed skills by making students compose and perform practice speeches. Down to the end of the second century BCE, this instruction was in Greek; outlines of a debate about Latin as a language of instruction can be found in the censors' edict of 92, which censured the "Latin rhetors" (Suetonius, *De grammaticis et rhetoribus* 25.2; Kaster 1995), and in Cicero's recollection of how he was advised by his mentors to avoid rhetorical instruction in Latin (Cicero, *Brutus* 3.93). Although the elder Cato and Antonius (consul in 99 BCE) wrote about oratory in Latin, there is no evidence of systematic textbooks on rhetoric in Latin before the first decades of the first century BCE and the composition of the anonymous treatise, *Rhetorica ad Herennium*, and Cicero's *De inventione*. The similarities between these treatises point to a common origin (see Corbeill 2002). But the works are not identical, and the differences demonstrate Cicero's interest in the purpose of rhetorical education even at the start of his career.

Both the date and the purpose of Cicero's *De inventione* remain unclear. Cicero's only reference to it is in *De oratore*, in which he describes it as a work composed "when I was a boy or rather a young man" (*pueris aut adulescentulis nobis*; 1.5). In *De oratore* Cicero rejects what he said in *De inventione* as "unfinished and unsophisticated" (*incohata ac rudia*), a book unworthy of the figure he had become by the time of the composition of *De oratore* in 55 BCE. And it is certainly the case that the rhetorical content of *De inventione* is not original: the similarities with the material in *Rhetorica ad Herennium* are close and extensive. Nonetheless, *De inventione* raises some difficult questions. The first concerns its audience: For whom does Cicero write? He does not identify an addressee or addressees, in contrast not only to his later treatises but also to the author of *Rhetorica ad Herennium*, who begins by addressing Gaius Herennius and his desire to learn the art of rhetoric (*de ratione dicendi, rhetoricam*). The absence of an addressee obscures the work's pedagogical impulse. A second question is that of purpose. The opening chapters of the first book sketch the development of human society and the role of persuasive speech in creating civilized communities in a way that sets up an ambitious framework for rhetoric's scope and moral responsibility. Cicero takes over 1,500 words to reach his first definition of terms. A comparison with *Rhetorica ad Herennium* is instructive: the anonymous author uses a mere 169 words to introduce his treatise, identify an addressee, establish his authority by rejecting other approaches to the subject, and offer a piece of encouraging practical advice (namely, to supplement reading with plenty of speaking). Despite uncertainty about its date of composition, intended audience, and place and purpose in Cicero's developing public profile, *De inventione* does reveal three qualities that recur throughout his writings on oratory: a commitment to a systematic technical basis for effective public persuasion; an interest in communicating this technical system to others; and the conviction that effective public persuasion is an essential part of civilized communities.

After *De inventione* Cicero's prose, for nearly 30 years, consisted of letters and speeches. It is only after his consulship, in the face of the danger he had created for himself by his actions as consul, that Cicero returned to prose treatises with an account (now lost) of his consulship, and only after his return from exile that he began the next surviving prose treatise, *De oratore*. This work is the product of a time of deep personal disappointment for Cicero, as he contemplated his failure to secure a position as a leading influential consular. However, the Roman state was functioning more or less as it had done since Sulla, and *De oratore* could therefore set itself up, realistically, as a practical contribution to contemporary statecraft.

At the heart of *De oratore* is the tension between ambitious claims for the civic function of oratory and, conversely, apprehension about the potential of speech to be a disruptive force in political life (see Enos, ch. 13; Connolly, ch. 14). Indeed, the work's purpose lies in its attempt to resolve this tension through the figure of the ideal orator, the fully formed statesman whose ability to lead is based both on his rhetorical skill and his moral commitment to the *res publica*. *De oratore* is concerned not only with defining this figure in terms of the skills he will possess and the ways he will use those skills but also with teaching others to aspire toward Cicero's model of oratory.

The pedagogical method Cicero adopts in this work differs markedly from that of *De inventione. De oratore* is not a textbook. While its overall structure can be identified, it is in many ways an unsystematic work that, at the level of the paragraph, constantly defies readers' expectations. Central to its apparently unsystematic structure is the fact that it is a report of a conversation between specific people at a specific time. Book 1 begins with a conversation between Cicero and his brother, during which Cicero identifies, through references to current public crises, the moment at which he is writing. He then offers Quintus his recollection of an old conversation from which he "can find out what the most distinguished and eloquent of men thought about the whole art of speaking [*de omni ratione dicendi*]" (Cicero, *De oratore* 1.4). The issue at stake is then defined a little more precisely: Cicero and his brother disagree about the role of acquired knowledge (*ars*), on one hand, and innate talent (*ingenium*), developed through practice, on the other, with Marcus supporting the former and Quintus the latter.

It will emerge that this contrast between *ars* and *ingenium* is represented in the reported conversation by Lucius Crassus and Marcus Antonius, respectively. Before the reader is introduced to these figures, however, Cicero offers three further arguments. The first is that oratory is the most difficult of all *artes* to master. The evidence for this is the low number of orators compared with the much higher number who have excelled in other branches of knowledge, both practical (war and statesmanship) and theoretical (philosophy, mathematics, poetry, and the study of language). We may wish to take issue with Cicero's claim about the rarity of orators, but his point underpins an important claim: being an orator consists of more than simply speaking in public. If this were not the case, Cicero's argument could immediately be refuted by pointing to the realities of Roman political life. The criteria for classifying the true orator haunt Cicero's mature treatises on oratory, with the answer varying from the remote ideal of *De oratore* to the inclusiveness of the later *Brutus*.

The second of Cicero's prefatory arguments is that mastering oratory demands an exceptionally wide range of skills. More specifically, oratory requires extensive factual knowledge, wide linguistic competence, knowledge of human emotions, charm and humor, free-born competency, quick-wittedness, historical knowledge, legal knowledge, effective delivery, and a powerful memory (among other skills) (Cicero, *De oratore* 1.17, 18). This is why so few orators have existed: "Let us stop wondering," Cicero concludes, "at the small number of eloquent men" (1.19). There is certainly a connection between this repertoire of skills and the traditional five tasks of the orator (*oratoris opera*): invention (*inventio*), arrangement (*dispositio*), style (*elocutio*), memory (*memoria*), and delivery (*actio*). But the match is not exact, and Cicero implies that the process of invention depends on a much wider range of knowledge than what is normally encompassed under *inventio* in rhetorical training. In *De oratore* the demand for extensive knowledge is crucial both to Cicero's rejection of Quintus's claim about talent and practice and to his own distinction between the true orator and the orator trained in precepts and rhetorical handbooks. Cicero's third opening argument follows from the second, since it consists in rejecting the elementary precepts offered by Greek rhetoricians and *dicendi artifices*: "I shall not draw upon any list of instructions from our early, long distant, education, but from ideas discussed, so I understand, among our most eloquent and distinguished men" (1.23). Cicero's dismissal is respectful but unvarnished.

There is no need for him to provide that kind of material because it is available to all. He can, however, contribute by discussing Romans whose oratorical skills have been acknowledged by other Romans.

Yet Cicero does not abandon traditional rhetorical instruction entirely in *De oratore*. The five tasks of the orator—invention, arrangement, style, memory, and delivery—structure the account of oratory in books 1 and 3, even if the reader's perception of this structure is complicated by excursuses and by the varying levels of attention devoted to each task. The first book, however, concentrates on the nature of the orator, and consequently on his training, with a sustained defense of the conception of a broadly educated orator against challenges to both the relevance and practicability of this lofty model of oratory. Systematic instruction comes after basic definitional issues. The discussion of rhetorical training in book 1 makes this point clear. Over the course of a mere eight chapters (1.138–45), Crassus develops the chief tenets of the Ciceronian system: oratory concerns persuasive speech; speeches concern the general or the particular; speeches deal with a particular identifiable issue (status-theory); there are three kinds of oratory, namely, the deliberative (*genus deliberativum*), forensic (*genus judiciale*), and ceremonial (*genus demonstrativum*); speeches consist of an introduction (*exordium*), a narrative (*narratio*), an identification of the point at issue (*divisio*), an argument in favor (*confirmatio*), a refutation (*refutatio*) of the opposition, and a conclusion (*peroratio*); style must be correct, clear, ornate, and appropriate (*decor*); and there are precise rules for memorizing and delivering speeches. These "well-worn rules which everyone knows" (*ista omnium communia et contrita praecepta*; 1.137) are useful, Crassus acknowledges, but they are the product of observing fine orators, not a means of producing them: "Eloquence is not the offspring of the art, but the art of eloquence" (*sic esse non eloquentiam ex artificio, sed artificium ex eloquentia natum*; Cicero, *De oratore* 1.146).

The structure of *De oratore* thus reinforces the point that, while useful, traditional rhetorical instruction (exemplified by *De inventione*) cannot on its own produce orators. But Cicero's dialogue is also an extended demonstration that orators *are* indeed the product of training; although *ingenium* is an essential ingredient in the mix, it does not, *pace* Quintus, suffice on its own. Pedagogy matters: without the right kind of education, there can be no orators. Moreover, the civic concerns of *De inventione* remain. The right kind of education will produce morally as well as technically good orators, and good men are needed to protect the *res publica*. Crassus starts his exposition from this point: oratory matters because orators are essential to free communities. "In my opinion, on the control and wisdom of the ideal orator depend not only his own status, but also the safety of many private individuals and of the whole *res publica*. For that reason, young men, press on, as you are doing, and devote yourself to the discipline which you are studying, in order to be an honour to yourselves, a benefit to your friends, and a reward for the *res publica*" (Cicero, *De oratore* 1.30–4). As the work continues, it becomes apparent that Cicero is attempting to break down the early distinction between statesmen and orators: the orator is the man who should guide the state. As Elaine Fantham puts it, "The agenda behind Cicero's impersonation of Crassus is to fuse the concept of orator with that of statesman by the cumulative effect of a series of persuasive definitions" (2004: 313).

Much of *De oratore*—those long stretches of technical exposition that tend to get over-looked by scholars in favor of its conceptually rich opening and bridging passages—is a practical demonstration of these ideas about oratory: careful, useful technical informa-tion expressed in clear, elegant language and embedded in a Roman context. Cicero can write *De oratore* only because he has the skills and knowledge he claims an orator needs; indeed, according to Crassus's pedagogical model, composing *De oratore* contributes to Cicero's own skills as an orator, since writing is the best teacher of speaking (1.150). In addition, Cicero's decision to present his ideas in the form of an extended conversation set in 91 BCE, over 30 years prior to the time of its composition (55 BCE), adds a distinct flavor to *De oratore*'s pedagogical impulse.

As far as we know, *De oratore*'s complex dialogue form and historical setting are entirely new in Latin literature. Cicero's model is quite clearly Plato's dialogues, par-ticularly *Phaedrus* and *Republic*, and the relationship between these texts and *De ora-tore*—especially its careful adaptation of Greek eloquence to the norms of elite Roman culture—has been extensively discussed (Görler 1988; Zetzel 2003). It is, however, apparent that the setting and personnel of *De oratore* are far more elaborate than its con-tent requires, even to demonstrate the links with Plato. There are seven speaking charac-ters in *De oratore*: this is a superfluity, even allowing for convincing conversation, early departures, and late arrivals. Indeed, the profusion of characters at times obscures the clarity of exposition as the discussion winds its elaborate way between speakers and over days. The speakers in Cicero's dialogue nevertheless represent the best and brightest of Rome's intellectual and political talent, drawn from different generations and gathered together, unwitting, on the eve of disaster. Three are recent consuls. L. Licinius Crassus (consul in 95 BCE) was only days from his sudden death. Marcus Antonius (consul in 99), author of the aforementioned treatise on oratory, was assassinated in 87 on Marius's orders. Quintus Lutatius Catulus (consul in 102) fell victim to Marius in 87, forestalling execution by committing suicide. He is a late Alcibiadean arrival in *De oratore*, present only for the second day's discussion recounted in the second and third books. The older generation is represented by Crassus's father-in-law, Quintus Mucius Scaevola Augur (consul in 117). Scaevola is the Cephalus of the dialogue, leaving at the end of the first day, while Catulus's younger half-brother Gaius Julius Caesar Vopiscus (the only one of the dialogue's participants actually climbing the *cursus honorum* at the time), who arrives with Catulus, was murdered by the Marians in 87. Finally, there are two young men, Gaius Aurelius Cotta and Publius Sulpicius Rufus. Both appear to have been in their early thirties in 91, so they were not exactly student novices; indeed, Cotta had spoken in defense of his uncle, Rutilius, the previous year, and Sulpicius had been the prosecutor in the notorious Norbanus case, the central topic of book 2 of *De oratore*. Cotta is the only one of these figures to survive the dialogue by more than four years. He prospered in the Sullan and post-Sullan periods, reaching the consulship in 75 and pre-siding over the first modifications to Sulla's restrictions on the powers of the tribunate.

The cumulative effect of this cast is to emphasize the political catastrophe about to engulf Rome and, by implication, the need for oratory as a bulwark against disaster: this interpretation is preferable to an entirely pessimistic one, since Crassus is removed from events by fate—might things have been different had he not died?—and Cotta offers a brief glimmer of hope. There remains a point to oratory, even in times of crisis. The setting and characters of this dramatic dialogue also offer a picture of one model of oratorical instruction: conversation between men of different generations, in which experience can be juxtaposed with technical knowledge and expertise passed on to the younger generation (as in the *tirocinium fori* or rhetorical apprenticeship in the Forum). The characters of *De oratore* were men whom Cicero had encountered; when he came to Rome in the mid-90s his father used his connections to gain access for Cicero to the households of Crassus and of Scaevola. Like Sulpicius and Cotta, Cicero benefited from exposure to the practical authority and experience of these leading Roman statesmen as well as to the elementary technical instruction in rhetoric provided by Greek household intellectuals.

De oratore sets its content of personal conversation against its form of written instruction. How is the aspiring orator to *use* this work? Arguably, *De oratore* challenges the reader to navigate the binaries not only between *ingenium* and *ars* and speech and writing but also between system and exemplarity: rhetorical knowledge can be apprehended only by seeing skilled orators use this knowledge in practice.

In the final period of Cicero's writing (after the outbreak of civil war in 49) the focus of his pedagogical impulse shifts. In part this is because of the sheer volume of books he wrote during this period. But the experimentation in modes of communication, in ways of presenting material, is also even more intense than in Cicero's writing from the 50s. The rhetorical works offer us, in *Brutus*, a dialogue carefully located in time and space, with identified interlocutors (though one more slanted toward a single speaker's exposition than *De oratore*); treatises addressed to a single individual, in which Cicero speaks without breaks (*Orator*, to Brutus, and *Topica*, to Trebatius); an introduction to a pair of translations (*De optimo genere oratorum*); and a pedagogical conversation between Cicero and his adolescent son, Marcus (*De partitione oratoria*). *De partitione oratoria* is a dialogue, but one with much stricter rules than Cicero's other dialogues (the younger Cicero asks the questions, the older Cicero responds) and no suggestion of equality between the interlocutors: the work begins with the words, "I am keen, father, to have from you the Latin version of the instruction you have given me in Greek about the art of speaking" (1.1).

One interpretation of the difference between Cicero's pre- and post-civil war rhetorical treatises is that an interest in form has become an interest in content: whereas *De oratore* focuses—to the point of undermining its pedagogical usefulness—on the processes by which knowledge is created, tested, and shared, the works of the 40s concentrate on expounding a body of knowledge whose existence and validity is unchallenged. On this view, these later texts mark a return to the more straightforward pedagogic model of *De inventione*, now informed, of course, by Cicero's enormously enhanced experience and authority. Such an interpretation can be easily aligned with other trends in Cicero's works of this period: his withdrawal from active political engagement; the shift from speech to writing as his dominant mode of communication; and the concern, so obvious in the philosophical works, to create an authoritative and comprehensive corpus of texts.

But we can perhaps also complicate this picture of Cicero turning himself from politician into scholar. The rhetorical works of the 40s are deeply political, if only because they foreground the changed circumstances under which oratory is now practiced at Rome. Oratory is in the process of becoming, for specific reasons, a historical curiosity to be studied through written texts. Yet there is some engagement with the future, particularly in *De partitione oratoria*, because of its presentation of Marcus junior as a key interlocutor. Is his presence an encouragement to despair, inasmuch as all that Cicero senior can pass on to his son relating to rhetoric is a series of basic points and an encouragement to study philosophy? Or does the familial framework suggest that the teaching of rhetoric still remains of value?

Caesar's dictatorship thus posed a direct challenge to Cicero's engagement with oratory, but there are nonetheless important points of continuity in Cicero as a teacher of rhetoric. He systematically presents oratory as a skill for which theoretical knowledge is essential. Quintus's belief in talent and practice alone is not tenable, nor, by implication, is exposure to the rhetorical practice of one's seniors enough. This is a consistent message, even though the content of Cicero's theoretical prescription changes and develops over time, drawing in an increasing range of knowledge and skills and demanding ever greater levels of theoretical understanding. There is also a sustained commitment to rhetoric as a skill that matters to the well-ordered state. It is by concentrating on these aspects of Cicero's rhetorical works that we can best address the paradox of *De oratore* to which I alluded: its idealization of personal contact and oral communication in a written, instructional text. Writing supports the development and transmission of systematic knowledge, and examples of individuals using that systematic knowledge link learning rhetoric to learning how to be a good man who benefits his community. Rhetoric's dangerous tendency toward amorality is thus controlled by its embeddedness in social and political practice.

Cicero was not a writer of textbooks, and his writings are not the obvious place to start learning about ancient rhetoric as a system or a practice. But pedagogy nonetheless underpins all of his rhetorical writings. Rhetoric makes oratory teachable, and oratory is essential to the civic state. And since the moral character of orators directly affects the *res publica*, rhetoric, for Cicero, should concern all good men.

REFERENCES

Connolly, Joy. 2009. "The Politics of Rhetorical Education." In *The Cambridge Companion to Ancient Rhetoric*, edited by Erik Gunderson, 126–141. Cambridge: Cambridge University Press.

Corbeill, Anthony. 2002. "Rhetorical Education in Cicero's Youth." In *Brill's Companion to Cicero: Oratory and Rhetoric*, edited by James May, 23–48. Leiden: Brill.

Bonner, Stanley F. 1977. *Education in Ancient Rome: From the Elder Cato to the Younger Pliny.* London: Metheun.

Fantham, Elaine. 2004. *The Roman World of Cicero's "De Oratore."* Oxford: Oxford University Press.

Ferrary, Jean-Louis. 1988. *Philhellénisme et impérialisme: aspects idéologiques de la conquête romaine du monde hellénistique, de la seconde guerre de Macédoine à la guerre contre Mithridate*. Rome: École Française de Rome.

Fitzpatrick, Matthew. 2010. "Carneades and the Conceit of Rome: Transhistorical Approaches to Imperialism." *Greece & Rome* 57: 1–20.

Glucker, John. 2001. "Carneades in Rome—Some Unsolved Problems." In *Cicero's Republic*, edited by Jonathan Powell and John North, 57–82. London: Institute of Classical Studies.

Görler, Woldemar. 1988. "From Athens to Tusculum: Gleaning the Background of Cicero's *De oratore*." *Rhetorica* 6: 215–235.

Habicht, Christian. 1997. *Athens from Alexander to Anthony*. Cambridge, MA: Harvard University Press.

Habinek, Thomas. 2005. *Ancient Rhetoric and Oratory*. Oxford: Blackwell.

Kaster, Robert. 1995. *C. Suetonius Tranquillus: "De Grammaticis et Rhetoribus."* Oxford: Clarendon.

Lintott, Andrew. 1999. *The Constitution of the Roman Republic*. Oxford: Clarendon.

Morgan, Teresa. 1998. *Literate Education in the Hellenistic and Roman Worlds*. Cambridge: Cambridge University Press.

Morstein-Marx, Robert. 2004. *Mass Oratory and Political Power in the Late Roman Republic*. Cambridge: Cambridge University Press.

North, John. 2006. "The Constitution of the Roman Republic." In *A Companion to the Roman Republic*, edited by Nathan Rosenstein and Robert Morstein-Marx, 256–277. Oxford: Blackwell.

Steel, Catherine. 2003. "Cicero's *Brutus*: The End of Oratory and the Beginning of History?" *Bulletin of the Institute of Classical Studies* 46: 195–211.

Tatum, Jeffrey. 2013. "Campaign Rhetoric." In *Community and Communication: Oratory and Politics in Republican Rome*, edited by Catherine Steel and Henriette van der Blom, 133–151. Oxford: Oxford University Press.

Walbank, Frank. 1965. "Political Morality and the Friends of Scipio." *Journal of Roman Studies* 55: 1–16.

Wisse, Jaap. 2013. "The Bad Orator: Between Clumsy Delivery and Political Danger." In *Community and Communication: Oratory and Politics in Republican Rome*, edited by Catherine Steel and Henriette van der Blom, 163–195. Oxford: Oxford University Press.

Yakobson, Alexander. 1999. *Elections and Electioneering in Rome: A Study in the Political System of the Late Republic*. Stuttgart: Franz Steiner Verlag.

Zetzel, James. 2003. "Plato with Pillows: Cicero on the Uses of Greek Culture." In *Myth, History and Culture in Republican Rome. Studies in Honour of T. P. Wiseman*, edited by David Braund and Christopher Gill, 119–138. Exeter: University of Exeter Press.

CHAPTER 17

......

RHETORIC AND STOIC PHILOSOPHY

......

SHADI BARTSCH

In 92 bce the ex-consul Publius Rutilius Rufus, back in Rome after a year administering the Roman province of Asia, was indicted on charges of corruption and extortion in office. If our ancient sources are to be believed, Rutilius was in fact a man of impeccable character and morals, one of the few who had reined in the abuses of the equestrian tax collectors of that province (Cicero, *In Verrem* 2.2.27; Plutarch, *Life of Pompey* 37.3). But it seems he made a fatal mistake at his trial: as a Stoic, he was determined to adhere to Stoicism's principles on the use of rhetoric and as a result had produced a speech of self-defense so jejune and devoid of appeals to emotion that he was convicted despite his evident innocence and was assessed a huge fine. To protest this injustice he went into voluntary exile, taking up residence, ironically enough, in the very province he had supposedly plundered. This miscarriage of justice invited parallels to Plato's Socrates: like Socrates, Rutilius had refused to render himself a "suppliant" to the jury, and he had met with a similar defeat (Cicero, *De oratore* 1.227–33; cf. Quintilian, *Institutio oratoria* 9.1.13; on Rutilius, see Hendrickson 1933).

Cicero tells this story in his *De oratore*, downplaying the political machinations behind the conviction to play up the problem of the Stoic perspective on rhetoric (Colish 1985; Atherton 1988; Lévy 2000; Stem 2005; Aubert 2008; Kennerly 2010; Inabinet 2011). Abjuring any appeal to the emotions was the trademark of Stoic criticism of Roman oratory, a stance in sharp opposition to Cicero's general praise of such dramatics and his endorsement of *movere* (to move) as one of the three tasks of the orator (*De oratore* 2.115). When in his dialogue, *Brutus*, the *successful* Stoic practitioners of rhetoric are enumerated, there is only one to be found: Cato the Younger, whose success (Cicero claims) is precisely due to the fact that he learned Stoicism from the Stoics but oratory from the masters of speech (*Brutus* 118–9; cf. *Paradoxa Stoicorum* 1, *Pro Murena* 74). The Stoics, by contrast, fail at convincing. Their attention to what Cicero terms "syllogisms with the efficacy of pin-pricks" rendered their teachings on the power of virtue incapable of converting people even to the truth, since logic cannot triumph over belief: "Even those who agree are unchanged in their hearts and go away in the same state as when they came" (*De finibus* 7).

Cicero is speaking from a biased position. However, the general shape of this debate on appropriate forms of persuasion has a genealogy at least as old as Plato, and the relationship between rhetoric and philosophy, or more broadly of language to truth, was an issue for all three major philosophical schools influential at Rome: the Epicureans, Stoics, and Cynics. Despite the early interest in Epicureanism during the Republic, however, it was Stoicism through whose prism these issues were most sharply delineated in the first centuries BCE and CE—as Cicero's own attention makes clear. In part this was precisely because many of the other principles of Stoicism were already widely accepted and disseminated at Rome; in its emphasis on self-mastery, for example, it appealed to native sentiment, as did the Stoic emphasis on the content rather than the form of public oratory (cf. Cato's famous advice to his son to "grasp the subject matter, and the words will follow" [*rem tene, verba sequentur*; Julius Victor 17, in Halm 1863: 374], adopted and modified by a whole troop of epigones). But the Stoic view of the human emotions was the most uncompromising among the Hellenistic philosophies and hence was the most problematic in terms of a rhetoric aimed at persuasion via stimulation of the passions as well as the mind. As the early Stoic Zeno of Citium put it, emotion "is a commotion of the soul alien to right reason and contrary to nature," and as such it could hardly be the target of a properly Stoic orator (Cicero, *Tusculanae disputationes* 4.6).

Stoic rhetoric placed particular emphasis on certain features of a philosophically oriented communication: the transmittal of truth; the maintenance of ethical tenets; the refusal to warp judgment with appeals to emotion; and, concomitantly, the use of a style that was as close as possible to the actual fact (*res ipsa*) of the matter. However, according to the negative characterizations of Cicero and others, Stoicism's focus on truth and accuracy and its suspicion of rhetorical adornment resulted in aridity. As Cicero famously commented, it was true that Cleanthes wrote an art of rhetoric, as did Chrysippus; however, these texts were required reading only for those who were bent on being mute (*De finibus* 4.7)! Thus, when Crassus in the *De oratore* evaluates each of the main Hellenistic philosophical schools to see which one is most appropriate for the orator, he reserves his most scathing words for the Stoics.[1] Their language is dry, choppy, obscure, unsuited to oratory; they have no way of reaching their audience; they avoid periodicity and hypotaxis (characteristics of Cicero's own style); and they use words such as *honor*, *disgrace*, *reward*, and *punishment* as philosophical terms rather than in their common, everyday sense (*De oratore* 3.66; cf. 2.159, *De finibus* 5.74).

Cicero's criticism, however, is complicated for us by the fact that he takes little trouble to distinguish between Stoic rhetoric and Stoic dialectic, methods that were distinct in the early days of the school but that had come to resemble each other enough that he could criticize both in one breath. Greek Stoic dialectic seems to have had its origins in the same question-and-response form as Platonic dialectic, both having as their goal the discovery (or defense) of philosophical truths in the live interchange between two interlocutors.[2] Rhetorical language, by contrast, was used in an unbroken narrative, as is appropriate for a speaker addressing an assembly on matters of policy or law (Diogenes Laertius, *Lives of Eminent Philosophers* 7.42; Seneca, *Epistulae morales* 40).[3] It was this distinction that Zeno famously represented by contrasting a clenched fist to an open palm (*Stoicorum veterum fragmenta* 1.75 = Quintilian, *Institutio oratoria* 2.20.7).[4] Thus, the Stoic distinction between dialectic and rhetoric did not pertain to style (both were uncluttered by ornament or periphrasis), truth value (both reflected Stoic principles and epistemology), or manner of persuasion (neither was to appeal to the emotions of the audience). Both, too, were classified under logic, or *to logikon* (Diogenes Laertius, *Lives of Eminent Philosophers* 7.41; Seneca, *Epistulae morales* 89.17), and treated as sciences that assisted a right understanding of the world.[5] All of this makes sense in light of the Stoic view that appearances are generally reliable and that a natural link exists between the rational use of language and the order of the universe, with the former, *logos*, serving as a vehicle for the expression of the latter, *kosmos* (see Protopapas-Marinelli 2002; see Habinek, ch. 23).

With the passage of time, however, the Stoic school came to emphasize the logical and syllogistic aspect of dialectic over its dialogic quality, so that by Cicero's day in first-century BCE Rome the Latin term *dialecticus* is mostly used in the derogatory sense of "quibbler" or "logical hair-splitter," and "dialectic" refers to the short, syllogistically linked sentences of the logician himself. Given that the single Stoic addition to the four virtues of style listed by the Peripatetic philosopher Theophrastus (correct usage, clarity, propriety, and ornament) was that of brevity (Cicero, *Orator* 79–80; Diogenes Laertius, *Lives of Eminent Philosophers* 7.59), and taking into account their aversion to tropes, periodicity, and appeals to emotion, critics of the school seem to have characterized both their rhetoric and their dialectic as unpalatable for regular audiences. To hear Cicero tell the tale, even the virtues they endorsed were absent from their speech: clarity suffered from the obscuring force of exaggerated brevity; correctness fell victim to neologisms; and the style was not appropriate to the audience (*De oratore* 2.159–60; cf. *Brutus* 118–9).[6] Yet elsewhere Cicero himself, when not pushing his agenda, could find a Stoic style useful in its resemblance to the humble or Attic level of discourse, whose goal of *docere* (to teach) was appropriate for philosophical topics broached in public life (*De officiis* 1.3; cf. Kennerly 2010).

In their approach to rhetoric, the Greek Stoics were at least in part responding to Plato's attack on the art in his *Gorgias*. Here Plato had anointed philosophical dialectic as the good counterpart to a maleficent and deceptive rhetoric,[7] suggesting that dialectic was comparable to medicine in its curative properties—dialectic benefiting the soul, medicine the body—while rhetoric was akin to fancy cuisine in that both of them appealed to the wrong appetites and ultimately harmed the soul and the body rather than healed them (see Yunis, ch. 9). This quarrel between philosophy and rhetoric was, in fact, the same split for which Cicero would later hold Socrates accountable in the *De oratore* (3.59–61), a work that undertook to patch up the rift by making the consummate orator a philosopher as well. In inheriting this framework, Cicero and the other critics were therefore distorting the actual Stoic stance, which was to assign to both dialectic and rhetoric the job of leading the listener to knowledge, though by different (formal) means. The Stoics' new categorization may not have had much practical effect, and it was far less influential a form of training than the standard Aristotelian view of rhetoric as the art of finding the available means of persuasion. It also narrowed down the possibility for excellence in oratory, inasmuch as it limited this outcome to the wise man alone. But neither did Cicero have any better luck with his view that the training of the philosopher should be subsumed under that of the orator in an ideal world in which *eloquentia* was the master form of knowledge (*De oratore* 3.20).[8]

As we have seen, the efficacy of the Stoic orator in a civic context like that of Rome was severely delimited by this set of prescriptions. One need think only of Rutilius to see how such a stance suffered in the maelstrom of republican political life at Rome. We would have similarly poor results if we looked to the imperial court of the first century CE, where several senators of Stoic persuasion had the courage to stand up to Nero, and after him Domitian, and paid for this demonstration of principle with their lives. We hear next to nothing about the sort of rhetoric favored by these figures. Thrasea Paetus's resistance to Nero for the most part took the form of silence and withdrawal (Dio Cassius, *Roman History* 62.15.2; cf. Tacitus, *Annales* 14.12, 16.22)—as with Seneca after 62 CE. Likewise, Tacitus's account of Helvidius Priscus's confrontation, under Vespasian, with the evil *delator* (informant) Eprius Marcellus once again shows the Stoic foiled by Marcellus's (non-Stoic) eloquence and reduced to silence by imperial rebuke (Tacitus, *Dialogus de oratoribus* 5.7, *Historiae* 4.44.1). It might seem, then, that Stoic rhetoric at Rome lived mainly in theory and died a self-inflicted death—and to the extent that it had ceased to command much interest in its Rutilian manifestation, this would be true.

However, to focus narrowly on the theory and practice of Stoic rhetoric as it was inherited by Cicero and his fellows in the late Republic at Rome, or to consider only the lack of influence of Stoic senators who sought to curb imperial license, would be to overlook the significant metamorphosis of this rhetoric in the hands of the statesman, philosopher, orator, and playwright Seneca the Younger. It is a metamorphosis that has not always been accorded its due—a byproduct of Seneca's problematic status as a representative of Stoicism. Most obviously, Seneca's own writing style does not map well onto the kind of rhetoric that Rutilius Rufus represented. Although certain of its features could be labeled "Stoic," on the whole its attention to metaphor, *sententia*, and epigrammatic point has earned it, from the time of Quintilian onward, a series of uncomplimentary characterizations. Nor, of course, did the imperial court of the first century CE offer genuine opportunity for oratorical practice, whether political or forensic; Seneca's most famous speech was one he wrote for Nero in 59 CE, a composition with which Nero tried to exculpate his matricide to the Senate. Moreover, Seneca's Stoicism, both in his own day and subsequently, was believed to be compromised by his tremendous personal wealth and his prominent position as advisor to Emperor Nero. These are facts that Seneca himself tried to address in several of his essays, where he reminds his readers that he is no perfected Stoic wise man but a *proficiens*, a student on the path to wisdom.

However, while Seneca cannot lay claim to a Rutilian severity, his development of a species of philosophical rhetoric in early imperial Rome offered a new model for how the philosopher could speak—or at least write—persuasively for a nonspecialist audience. To start with stylistic issues, Quintilian makes clear that his antipathy to Seneca's style reflects an antipathy to the tastes of the day, and much of his concern is directed toward the widespread influence Seneca seems to have had among the younger generation. Quintilian's criticism of Seneca's style and influence reflects his preference for the periodic Ciceronian oratory that he taught in his own rhetorical school and that he sought to elevate over the post-classical tastes of the day (see Dominik 1997). Potential Stoic features that are singled out are Seneca's preference for shorter sentences, the lapidary quality of his prose, his avoidance of periodicity, and the preference for parataxis over hypotaxis—qualities that led Caligula to characterize Seneca's writing as "sand without lime" (Suetonius, *Caligula* 53.2). Even Seneca's attention to prose rhythm has a Stoic precedent in Cleanthes's observation that moral observations in meter have greater impact upon the hearer (*Epistulae morales* 108.10). But Quintilian also objects to markedly non-Stoic features of Seneca's rhetoric: his fondness for epigram, his indulgence in vices (*vitiae*) of style, and his incorrect usages (*Institutio oratoria* 10.1.125–31). And indeed, Seneca's silver Latin idiolect is not always linguistically orthodox, nor do his colloquialisms meet the usual standards for literary propriety. (His *Moral Epistles*, for example, is the only place in our literary sources where we come across the word for the profession of "armpit-hair plucker," or *alapilus* [56.2]!) Generally he is too intent on the impact of epigrammatic point and paradox, antithesis, poetic color, vivid imagery, and metaphor to qualify for the stripped-down quality of Rutilius's rhetoric degree zero (on Seneca's style, see Smiley 1919; Leeman 1963; Currie 1966; Coleman 1974; Motto 1975; Setaioli 2000; Albrecht 2004).

In Quintilian, this style earned Seneca the charge that his writing was *corruptus* and *fractus* (broken, spineless), terms with strong connotations of ethical and sexual deviance (*Institutio oratoria* 1.10.125; cf. 1.10.31). The language of criticism here is not per se unusual; it was common to use such laden terms to characterize matters we would conceive of as literary, and in epistle 114 Seneca himself is unrelenting in linking Maecenas's literary tastes to his sexual mores. In linking Seneca's style to the pleasure of his readers, however, Quintilian identifies a particularly vexing problem for a Stoic philosopher–rhetorician. Whether or not Seneca actually thinks that it is defensible to arouse any emotion in his audience remains a fraught issue in the scholarship (Atherton 1988; Armisen-Marchetti 1989: 46–52). However, even the most cursory reading of his *opera* suggests that he was open to the idea: the repeated descriptions of such fearsome things as torture, for example, are presumably there to help the reader habituate himself to his initially fearful response, while Seneca himself seems to suggest that we should be moved: eloquence, he says, should inspire in us a passion for its subject—though not for eloquence itself (*Epistulae morales* 52.14; cf. Traina 1987, ch. 2).

Yet Seneca himself insists, stoically enough, on the necessity of a direct and uncomplicated relationship between things and words, between the reality of the world and the language used to describe it. He correspondingly presents himself as sticking as closely as possible to the subject matter rather than engaging in rhetorical divagation: his *verba* (words) do not convey a misleading allure to the *res* (things) they describe, like dressed up items in a shop-window (Seneca, *Epistulae morales* 33.3; cf. 40.4, 52.14, 75.5, 115.1; Wilson 2007). On several occasions he cautions the student of philosophy who merely wishes to listen to fine speeches (20.2); it is the beauty of the subject matter, not the sound of empty words, that should seize the true listener and stir him to action (108.7). Similarly, one's language will reflect one's true character: fancy verbiage is a sign of the soul gone astray. As Seneca stipulates in the famous letter 114, "The nature of a man's ability cannot be of one sort and that of his soul another. If his soul is healthy, composed, serious, and restrained, his talent also is self-controlled and sober. But when the soul has been infected, the latter catches the disease as well" (114.3). This fault is due sometimes to the man and sometimes to his epoch. But in any case, it is clear that a philosopher will speak plainly and soberly—and walk the same way (cf. 40.14)!

Seneca's most significant innovations in his philosophical letters and dialogues extend well beyond the question of style. Most important here are those features of his prose writing that mimic the function of dialogue—in particular, his use of first- and second-person verbs, especially in the letters, in which he is constantly addressing his correspondent, Lucilius, and thus also his readers. His exhortations to Lucilius to work on his soul, to practice "reflections upon misfortune" (*meditatio malorum*), and to give the correct value to "indifferents" are exhortations with equal value to an imperfect audience in any era. Lucilius and other interlocutors will even seem to respond, voicing concerns and protests in reaction to what he is saying: "'It is difficult,' you say, 'to win over your mind to a scorn for life.' But don't you see how it is scorned already for frivolous reasons?" (Seneca, *Epistulae morales* 4.4). This style mimics conversation, and not surprisingly Seneca tells us that it is conversation rather than lectures that make a man learn, and whose words are most effective (e.g., 38.1): lectures go in one ear and out the other. We might surmise, then, that these "conversations" with absent interlocutors and with us are his way of replicating the philosophical method whose benefit is greatest (Wilson 2007; Hine 2010).[9] Like Cicero, Seneca was no friend to the (presumably Stoic) "dialecticians" of his own day, who have little to contribute to such genuinely philosophical topics as how one ought to help one's fellow man, or what in life is desirable, or how to calm the soul (*Epistulae morales* 45.5–8, 48, 108.12; cf. 65.15).[10] But in his conversational form we may recognize the distant heir of the original Stoic dialectic as well as the heir to the dialogue form favored by Plato, Xenophon, and other philosophers. His epistolary writing accordingly represents a return to dialogue in its broader sense and in a way is far more philosophically significant than Cicero's stylized production of purported dialogues between Roman noblemen in which each produces extended lecture-like narratives.

A final, nontraditional element in Seneca's philosophical rhetoric is the extensive use of figural language as a tool to help the reader conceptualize philosophical concepts. We have already briefly considered ornament as productive of pleasure; metaphor in particular was associated with this response in the reader (see Quintilian, *Institutio oratoria* 9.1.21).[11] Seneca exploits this pleasure but also gives metaphor a cognitive role to play in the teaching of philosophy. This usage is necessary "not for the same reason as poets use [figures], but in order that they may provide crutches for our weakness, so as to lead both the speaker and the hearer to the actual fact at issue" (Seneca, *Epistulae morales* 59.6). His intention in using metaphor, then, may be to lead readers to a state in which such unorthodox aids to philosophical self-improvement will be superfluous (Armisen-Marchetti

1989; Bartsch 2009). For the sake of pedagogical clarity, he is even willing to employ metaphorical explanations that are not consonant with Stoic orthodoxy—for example, describing the soul as encased in the body when trying to show that only the latter, and not the former, is vulnerable to attack (see Albrecht 2004: 24–33 for a discussion of Seneca's pedagogy). Reaching his readers and changing them, not observing orthodoxy, is the most important value for Seneca. Here finally we have a response, a century later, to those damning words of Cicero: "Even those who agree are unchanged in their hearts and go away in the same state as when they came" (*De finibus* 4.7).

Given his epoch, Seneca's radical practice represents the final transition of a failed Stoic rhetoric from the public and oral sphere of the city to the comparatively private medium of the published text. (Even the Stoic emperor Marcus Aurelius, who presumably would have been persuasive even as a Stoic orator, wrote private, reflective, and dialogic entries in a journal.) The Stoic sage was originally charged with participating in political life, a theme that Cicero's Cato picks up when he comments that the wise man should want to help in the governance of the state (*De finibus* 3.68; for the Greek sources, see *Stoicorum veterum fragmenta* 3.611; Diogenes Laertius, *Lives of Eminent Philosophers* 7.121; Atherton 1988; Kennerly 2010). If the Stoic would-be politician was hampered in the Republic by inherited notions of linguistic propriety and restraint (and a consequent inability to sway the crowds), under the emperors of the first century CE the restricted opportunities for oratory—outside the play world of declamation—would prove equally problematic (see Gunderson, ch. 21; cf. Pernot, ch. 20). Oratory, then, undergoes an inward turn in the search for a new and apolitical source of legitimacy, taking the reasoning self as its subject and seeking to work metamorphosis in this limited playing field—and in its readers.

FURTHER READING

Albert von Albrecht's (2004) *Wort und Wandlung: Senecas Lebenskunst* is an excellent study of Seneca's belief in the transformative power of language for self-improvement. Sophie Aubert's (2008) article, "Cicéron et la parole stoïcienne: polémique autour de la dialectique," provides a useful discussion of the distinction between Stoic rhetoric and dialectic, with special attention to Cicero's criticism. Luca Castagnoli's (2010) "How Dialectical Was Stoic Dialectic?" explores the meaning of the term *dialectic* in its Greek philosophical context. In "Self-Scrutiny and Self-Transformation in Seneca's Letters," Catharine Edwards (1997) examines the inward turn of the authorial self of the letters. Finally, Marcus Wilson's (2007) "Rhetoric and the Younger Seneca" is an illuminating essay on how the epistolary form helped Seneca to avoid the polarization of rhetoric and philosophy.

NOTES

1. The Epicureans, like the Stoics, are criticized for the public use of a technical ethical language at odds with their goal of pleasure, but their rhetoric is expansive rather than compressed (Cicero, *De finibus* 2.45).

2. In response to Daniel Babut's 2005 argument that Stoic dialectic was used solely to defend the truths that the Stoics already knew were true, see Aubert 2008, who argues for its heuristic function as well. On Stoic dialectic more generally, see also Castagnoli 2010, Gourinat 2000, and Long 2001.

3. As is clearly recognized by Sophie Aubert (2008: 68). Atherton's conclusion that the Stoics actually had a single style for both rhetoric and dialectic seems to me untenable.

4. Zeno used this simile, as Luca Castagnoli surmises, not only "to illustrate the difference between dialectical brachylogy and rhetorical macrology but also, perhaps, the 'agonistic' nature of *dialektike*" (2010: 160).

5. The Stoics even included under the heading of dialectic, rather than rhetoric, the usually rhetorical topics of style, diction, correctness of usage, and tropes and figures (cf. Diogenes Laertius, *Lives of Eminent Philosophers* 7.41).

6. Not that concessions were never made: Plutarch, for example, claims that Chrysippus spoke with passion (*De Stoicorum repugnantiis* 10), while Seneca notes that Cleanthes praised the effect of interjected verses (*Epistulae morales* 108.10). Cicero even has Cato admit that "when one is speaking about grander topics, the ideas themselves seize upon their expression, and thus the style becomes both more impressive and indeed more distinguished" (*De finibus* 3.19). See Armisen-Marchetti 1989: 39.

7. This is a view Aristotle repeats, without the moral judgment, at the beginning of his *Rhetoric*.

8. When Cicero argued for the unification of philosophical and oratorical learning, he proposed that *eloquentia* represented the sum of all knowledge (*De oratore* 3.20; Inabinet 2011); this ideal is inherited by Quintilian (see Walzer 2003). When Seneca explicitly addresses rhetoric, he instead calls it a propaedeutic to philosophy (*Epistulae morales* 88.20).

9. Desmond Costa (1995: 112) suggests that Seneca was composing in a style meant to be heard.

10. Miriam Griffin (2007) suggests that as the reader of the letters makes progress so too the frequency of dialectical argument in the letters increases.

11. It is worth noting that philosophical attitudes toward this figure varied. Aristotle, for example, gave it a cognitive role to play as a stimulant to the recognition of similarities and thus as a mechanism in the acquisition of knowledge (*Rhetoric* 3.10, 1410b14). Epicurus, on the other hand, disdains ornament in favor of straight speaking: metaphors obscure the meaning of words (*Deperditorum librorum reliquiae* 31.14). For a discussion of the Stoics on tropes, see Barwick 1957: 88–111. It seems that metaphor, as a source of ambiguity, was to be avoided, even though the traditional lists of types of tropes are attributed to the Stoics.

References

Albrecht, Albert von. 2004. *Wort und Wandlung: Senecas Lebenskuns*t. *Mnemosyne Supplements* 252. Leiden: Brill.

Armisen-Marchetti, Mireille. 1989. *Sapientiae Facies: Étude sur les images de Sénèque.* Collection d'Études Anciennes 58. Paris: Les Belles Lettres.

Atherton, Catherine. 1988. "Hand over Fist: The Failure of Stoic Rhetoric." *Classical Quarterly* 38 no. 2: 392–427.

Aubert, Sophie. 2008. "Cicéron et la parole stoïcienne: polémique autour de la dialectique." *Revue de Métaphysique et de Morale* 57: 61–91.

Babut, Daniel. 2005. "Sur les polémiques des anciens Stoïciens." *Philosophie Antique* 5: 65–91.

Bartsch, Shadi. 2009. "Senecan Metaphors and Stoic Self-Instruction." In *Seneca and the Self*, edited by Shadi Bartsch and David Wray, 188–220. Cambridge: Cambridge University Press.

Barwick, Karl. 1957. *Probleme der stoischen Sprachlehre und Rhetorik*. Berlin: Akademie-Verlag.

Castagnoli, Luca. 2010. "How Dialectical Was Stoic Dialectic?" In *Ancient Models of Mind: Studies in Human and Divine Rationality*, edited by Andrea Nightingale and David Sedley, 153–179. Cambridge: Cambridge University Press.

Coleman, Robert. 1974. "The Artful Moralist: A Study of Seneca's Epistolary Style." *Classical Quarterly* 24 no. 2: 276–289.

Colish, Marcia L. 1985. *The Stoic Tradition from Antiquity to the Early Middle Ages*. Vol. 1, *Stoicism in Classical Latin Literature*. Leiden: Brill.

Costa, Desmond. 1995. "Rhetoric as a Protreptic Force in Seneca's Prose Works." In *Ethics and Rhetoric: Classical Essays for Donald Russell on His Seventy-Fifth Birthday*, edited by Doreen Innes, Harry Hine, and Christopher Pelling, 107–115. Oxford: Clarendon.

Currie, H. Mac L. 1966. "The Younger Seneca's Style: Some Observations." *Bulletin of the Institute for Classical Studies* 13 no. 1: 76–87.

Dominik, William J. 1997. "The Style Is the Man: Seneca, Tacitus, and Quintilian's Canon." In *Roman Eloquence: Rhetoric in Society and Literature*, edited by William J. Dominik, 50–68. Routledge: London.

Edwards, Catharine. 1997. "Self-Scrutiny and Self-Transformation in Seneca's Letters." *Greece and Rome* 44: 23–38.

Gourinat, Jean-Baptiste. 2000. *La dialectique des stoïciens*. Paris: Vrin.

Griffin, Miriam T. 2007. "Seneca's Pedagogic Strategy." In *Greek and Roman Philosophy 100 BC to 200 AD*, vol. 1, edited by Richard Sorabji and Robert W. Sharples, 89–113. BICS Supplement 94. London: Institute of Classical Studies.

Hendrickson, G. L. 1933. "The Memoirs of Rutilius Rufus." *Classical Philology* 28 no. 3: 153–175.

Hine, Harry. 2010. "Form and Function of Speech in the Prose Works of the Younger Seneca." In *Form and Function in Roman Oratory*, edited by D. H. Berry and Andrew Erskine, 208–224. Cambridge: Cambridge University Press.

Inabinet, Brandon. 2011. "The Stoicism of the Ideal Orator: Cicero's Hellenistic Ideal." *Advances in the History of Rhetoric* 14 no. 1: 14–31.

Kennerly, Michele. 2010. "*Sermo* and Stoic Sociality in Cicero's *De Officiis*." *Rhetorica* 28 no. 2: 119–137.

Leeman, Anton D. 1963. Orationis Ratio: *The Stylistic Theories and Practice of the Roman Orators, Historians and Philosophers*. 2 vols. Amsterdam: A.M. Hakkert.

Lévy, Carlos. 2000. "Cicéron critique de l'éloquence stoïcienne." In *Papers on Rhetoric*, vol. 3, edited by Lucia Calboli Montefusco, 127–144. Bologna: CLUEB.

Long, A. A. 2001. *Stoic Studies*. Berkeley: University of California Press.

Motto, Anna Lydia, and John R. Clark. 1975. "*Ingenium facile et copiosum*: Point and Counterpoint in Senecan Style." *Classical Bulletin* 52: 1–4.

Protopapas-Marinelli, Maria. 2002. *La rhétorique des stoïciens*. Paris: L'Harmattan.

Setaioli, Aldo. 2000. Facundus *Seneca: aspetti della lingua e dell'ideologia senecana*. Bologna: Pàtron.

Smiley, C. N. 1919. "Seneca and the Stoic Theory of Literary Style." *University of Wisconsin Studies in Language and Literature* 3 no. 3: 50–62.

Stem, Rex. 2005. "The First Eloquent Stoic: Cicero on Cato the Younger." *Classical Journal* 101 no. 1: 37–49.

Traina, Alfonso. 1987. *Lo stilo drammatico del filosofo Seneca*. Bologna: Pàtron.

Walzer, Arthur E. 2003. "Quintilian's *'Vir Bonus'* and the Stoic Wise Man." *Rhetoric Society Quarterly* 33 no. 4: 25–41.

Wilson, Marcus. 2007. "Rhetoric and the Younger Seneca." In *A Companion to Roman Rhetoric*, edited by William J. Dominik and Jon Hall, 425–438. Malden, MA: Wiley-Blackwell.

CHAPTER 18

....

RHETORIC AND EPIC

....

JON HALL

PERSUASIVE speech played a prominent part in the ancient epic tradition. The heroes in Homer's *Iliad* and *Odyssey* were men of words as well as men of war. It is no surprise, then, to find skillful oratory in the later Latin epics: as in other literary genres, Roman epic poets readily borrowed and adapted the conventions of their Greek predecessors (cf. Culler, ch. 19). As modern scholars have noted, however, the poetic aesthetic of Latin epic did not remain constant. In the generations following Virgil, the general approach to composition seems to have been strongly influenced by the declamatory exercises popular in the schools of this period. Indeed, this influence has been regarded as so significant that the term *rhetorical epic* is often used to describe this new style of poetry (see, e.g., Morford 1967: ix; Roche 2009: 47). As we shall see, this label has both merits and drawbacks.

SPEECHES IN HOMER AND VIRGIL

We should begin, however, at the beginning. There are many extended passages of direct speech in Homer's epics, a feature that reflects in part the orality of ancient Greek society. Most public and political business was conducted in face-to-face settings, where a facility with persuasive speech brought considerable advantages. In the *Iliad*, for example, we find Agamemnon in book 2 addressing at some length (with deceptive intent) an assembly of Greek forces (2.110–41); in book 9, Odysseus, Phoenix, and Ajax make concerted attempts to convince Achilles to return to the fray against the Trojans (9.225–306, 434–605, 624–42); and in book 22, Priam pleads with Achilles for the return of Hector's corpse (24.486–506). Yet Homer evidently also appreciated the artistic potential of speeches for depicting character and conflict. He uses debate and argument to reveal the motives of the protagonists and to articulate issues important to the action as a whole. Note, for example, the powerful speech of Achilles in book 9 (308–429), where we gain crucial insights into the ethical values and sense of grievance that drive the hero.

Likewise, Odysseus's skill in deceptive speech defines him in the *Odyssey* as a cunning and formidable leader (see Woodruff, ch. 7). Yet, as George Kennedy (1963: 26–40) shows, although the characters in Homer's epics are often linguistically accomplished and persuasively shrewd they have little interest in the subtleties of logical argument (cf. Kennedy 1957). They are effective speakers but do not use the full range of techniques developed in the following centuries by the sophists and later rhetoricians.

Virgil, by contrast, composed his *Aeneid* in a very different world. Rhetorical study had by this time become the central educational focus for members of Rome's elite. Nevertheless, the poem's main inspiration derives from the epic tradition, and its creative adaptation of Homeric motifs is one of the ways Virgil displays his erudition. In book 1 alone we find a soliloquy by Juno (1.37–49) that recalls that of Poseidon in the *Odyssey* (5.286–90); a speech of despair by Aeneas (1.94–101) modeled on that of Odysseus (*Odyssey* 5.299–312); and a request for hospitality by Aeneas to Dido (1.595–610), which alludes to that of Odysseus to Nausicaa (*Odyssey* 6.149–85). Virgil, however, brought to these scenes a far greater degree of rhetorical awareness than his Greek predecessors. The more extended speeches in particular are informed by a deep understanding of persuasive principles. One example will help to illustrate the degree of this rhetorical sophistication.

In book 11 Virgil depicts a debate at a council of Italians summoned by King Latinus to consider their ongoing conflict with Aeneas. One of the participants, Drances, is portrayed as a highly accomplished yet morally ambiguous orator, driven not so much by a concern for the public good as by envy at Turnus's prestige within the community (Virgil, *Aeneid* 11.336–7). His rhetorical cunning is evident first in his shrewd construction of *ēthos*. Drances presents himself as a staunch representative of popular sentiment, stubbornly refusing to be cowed by those in power: "No, I *will* speak, even though he makes violent, deadly threats against me" (*dicam equidem, licet arma mihi mortemque minetur*; 11.348). With this image of plain speaker established, he can then go on the attack and ridicule Turnus's martial incompetence, alliteratively depicting him as *fugae fidens* ("reliant on running away"; 11.351) and full of ineffective bluster (*caelum territat armis*; 11.351). He is careful, however, to show respect to King Latinus (*unum . . . unum, optime regum, adicias*; 11.352–3), even adopting a pose of humble suppliant toward the end of his speech (*en supplex venio*; 11.365).

This diplomatic self-effacement lays the groundwork for his masterstroke of manipulation. Deploying an elegantly ascending tricolon (*si . . . si . . . si*; Virgil, *Aeneid* 11.368–9), he challenges Turnus to face Aeneas in a duel (*aude atque adversum fidens fer pectus in hostem*; 11.370), complaining bitterly that otherwise the prince will get to enjoy a royal wife while the rank-and-file end up strewn across the battlefield, unburied and unmourned (*scilicet ut Turno contingat regia conjunx / nos animae viles, inhumata infletaque turba / sternamur campis*; 11.371–2). This artful speech produces exactly the response Drances wants: Turnus loses his temper and embarks upon an abusive rant. For all his sneering at Drances's reliance on words rather than action—*tibi copia fandi* (11.378), *verbis* (380), *eloquio* (383), *ventosa in lingua* (390)—the man is utterly outmaneuvered. Impetuous as ever, he rashly pledges to fight Aeneas alone (11.440–2), a decision that will cost him his life.

Virgil, then, understood well the art of verbal persuasion. For the purposes of this chapter, however, it is what he does *not* do in this episode that is perhaps most relevant. He depicts Drances as a clever manipulator, but not one interested in argument or arresting wordplay for their own sake. The rhetorical flourishes are present because the plot and the characterization demand them. In other words, Virgil does not flaunt his mastery of technique. As we shall see, in these respects his approach differs from that of Ovid and Lucan.

Schools of Declamation

For several generations of modern scholars, it was a plainly evident fact that both Ovid and Lucan were influenced significantly by their training in the schools of declamation. One critic, for example, asserts that "the main clue to the literary qualities of Silver Latin is to be found in education, and particularly in rhetorical education" (Wight Duff 1960: 20; cf. Fraenkel 1945: 1–8; Bonner 1949: 149–67; Morford 1967: 1–12). More recent studies, however, tend to underplay this association, not least because the influence of rhetoric is often regarded as antithetical to poetic inspiration (see Quintilian, *Institutio oratoria* 10.1.90; see Servius, *Ad Aeneidem* 1.382, for the supposed dichotomy between rhetoric and poetry). Yet the rise in popularity of the declamatory schools is a historical datum that cannot be casually discounted. Serious consideration needs to be given to the ways such training may have shaped the literary aesthetics of the time.

Declamation had been a feature of Greek education since at least the third century BCE, and Cicero certainly engaged extensively in such exercises—both in Latin and Greek—as part of his own oratorical training (*Brutus* 310). Nevertheless, it took some time for Rome to establish itself as a prominent center of learning that could support significant numbers of experts in Latin rhetoric. By the time of Ovid, however, public declamatory performance had become a regular feature of educational and intellectual life in the city (see Pernot, ch. 20; Gunderson, ch. 21). The elder Seneca, for example, writing around 38 CE, records the participation of over 100 individuals in such events during the course of his long life (Clarke 1996: 87; see also Seneca, *Controversiae* 1, preface 12; Sussman 1978: 1–17; Fairweather 1981: 104–31). Originally, such performances by teachers served a very specific pedagogical purpose, providing students with examples of rhetorical excellence to be analyzed and emulated. Older students, too, sometimes performed in front of parents and friends in order to demonstrate their educational accomplishments (see, e.g., Persius, *Satires* 3.47: *quae pater adductis sudans audiret amicis*). Over time, however, such events came to be regarded as significant literary occasions in their own right, attracting leading intellectual figures and sometimes extending beyond a single day (Bonner 1949: 49).

Not surprisingly, such occasions often turned into venues for competitive intellectual display. This agonistic element was fostered in the first place by the very nature of declamatory exercise. One speaker's treatment of a set theme implicitly offered itself for comparison with all the other versions that had preceded it. This recycling of material could produce, in the hands of mediocre students, the tiresome "reheated cabbage" (*crambe repetita*) that Juvenal condemns (*Satires* 7.154). But the more ambitious declaimer responded to this challenge with energetic imagination, attempting to find new and ingenious approaches to well-explored problems. The lively context of public performance further heightened this pursuit of novelty and brilliance. Already by Ovid's day, audiences were prone to overexuberant shows of admiration for a speaker's elegance in phrasing (see, e.g., Seneca, *Controversiae* 7.4.10: *cum scholastici maximo clamore laudarent*). This excitable atmosphere also characterized the schools in Quintilian's day, with students at times even jumping up from their seats (*Institutio oratoria* 2.2.12; cf. 8.5.13–4). It is understandable, then, if there was a temptation to play to the crowd and pursue immediate effect rather than intellectual profundity. Even Quintilian incorporates a competitive element into his pedagogical method (*Institutio oratoria* 1.2.24).

A good example of this phenomenon can be found in a *controversia* that Ovid himself declaimed (Seneca, *Controversiae* 2.2.8–9). The legal conundrum was as follows (2.2). A husband and wife took an oath that if anything should happen to one of them, the other would take his or her life. While on a trip abroad, the husband sends home a message reporting his death. The wife consequently attempts suicide but survives. She is instructed by her father to divorce her husband; she refuses and is consequently disinherited.

Although this scenario involves some rather improbable and melodramatic elements, its educational aim was sensible enough: to encourage students to debate the legal and moral issues surrounding inheritance and family duty. In his discussion, the elder Seneca notes that a particularly ingenious slant (or *color*) was given to the theme by the declaimer Romanius Hispo. His approach was to mitigate the apparent maliciousness of the husband's actions by arguing that the pair's initial oath had in fact been a lighthearted one (*jocosum*), typical of those made by lovers. It had thus been forgotten by the husband when he sent his message. Indeed, the intent of the note (Hispo claimed) was merely to test the wife's affections. Hispo's inventiveness, however, did not end there. He also asserted that the wife had perceived the truth of the situation and thus had deliberately failed in her suicide attempt in order to give the husband a fright and teach him a lesson (Seneca, *Controversiae* 2.2.7).

There is a cleverness here that Seneca evidently admires. Hispo engaged creatively with the motives of the two characters in order to come up with an ingenious line of pleading. We may wonder whether anyone would have been so bold as to attempt this kind of argument in the courts, but in the competitive environment of the schools, practical matters were not paramount. What mattered was intellectual vitality. Indeed, the declaimer's skill in devising a clever line of argument constitutes one of the elder Seneca's main focuses in his work, and we know, too, that Junius Otho published at least two books dedicated to the subject (see Seneca, *Controversiae* 1.3.11: *libros colorum edidit*; cf.

Sussman 1978: 41–3; Fairweather 1981: 166–78). Students were thus encouraged to cultivate and display their wit and invention.

These displays extended also to the sphere of linguistic style. Declaimers were judged
not only on their content but also on the elegance and cleverness of their phrasing.
Seneca, for example, quotes the following sentence from Papirius Fabianus's version of
the *controversia* just discussed: "A husband, since he loved his wife too much, was almost
a cause of danger to her. A wife, since she loved her husband too much, was almost a
cause of grief to him. A father, since he loved his daughter too much, disinherits her"
(*vir, dum nimis amat uxorem, paene causa periculi fuit; uxor, dum nimis amat virum,
paene causa luctus fuit; pater, dum nimis amat filiam, abdicat*; *Controversiae* 2.2.4). The
style is highly contrived: there is careful parallelism in grammatical structure with three
dum nimis- clauses in succession; each begins with a familial term in the nominative
case (*vir, uxor, pater*); and each term is matched by a contrasting one in the accusative
(*uxorem, virum, filiam*). This mannered writing is designed as much to draw attention
to its own cleverness as to achieve a specific persuasive goal. Certainly it was striking
enough for Seneca to commit it to memory, and we can imagine that it also prompted a
round of applause from the audience at the time of its delivery.

This interest in linguistic ingenuity manifested itself most strikingly in the fashion
for coining clever *sententiae*, pithy remarks that wittily encapsulate the essence of the
situation at hand. Such phrases often served a valuable rhetorical function in rounding
off an argument emphatically and memorably (Bonner 1966: 264–5), but in the schools
they also became an end in themselves—a proof of the declaimer's talent and brilliance.
The elder Seneca gives these flourishes special attention in his discussion of declamation
(*Controversiae* 1, preface 22), and their appeal continued through successive generations.
Indeed, Tacitus paints a scene of students excitedly passing on to their friends news of
the latest witty *sententiae* heard at some recital or other (*Dialogus de oratoribus* 20).

Declamatory training, then, fostered a literary aesthetic that placed great value on
verbal ingenuity. Moreover, its emphasis on live performance promoted a competitive
mentality that encouraged students to test and transgress prevailing artistic norms.
Ostentatious virtuosity won greater plaudits than measured restraint. On occasion,
as ancient critics noted, this febrile setting could lead to misbegotten absurdities (see
Seneca, *Controversiae* 1.4.12; Bonner 1966: 280–2). But it also promoted intellectual
vitality and inventiveness. It is within this cultural context that the epics of Ovid and
Lucan were composed.

OVID

The influence on Ovid of contemporary declamatory practice can be seen in one very
specific way in book 13 of his poem, *Metamorphoses*. Here Ovid depicts the famous dispute between Ajax and Ulysses over the armor of the slain Achilles. The subject had been
treated over the centuries by both epic and tragic poets (Hopkinson 2000: 10–6; see

Woodruff, ch. 7). However, we know that it also provided the theme of a *suasoria* in the schools of Ovid's day, and his presentation of the episode certainly calls to mind the declamation halls. He focuses almost entirely upon the speeches given by the two heroes and passes quickly over other elements of the episode. Moreover, the elder Seneca informs us that two lines from Ovid's version (13.121–2) were modeled closely on a remark made by the rhetor Porcius Latro in his declamation on the subject (*Controversiae* 2.2.8). Ovid thus playfully bends the generic conventions of his epic. From one perspective, the speeches of Ajax and Ulysses are entirely at home in this heroic world of myth and legend. At the same time, however, they thrust the reader into the intellectual milieu of Augustan Rome and its penchant for declamation. Indeed, by presenting skillful speeches on both sides of the theme, Ovid casts himself as a master rhetor—or, to be more precise perhaps, as an expert in a newly minted subgenre: verse declamation.

But the influence of rhetorical education on the poem extends beyond this allusion to declamatory practice. It appears more generally in Ovid's design and stylistic treatment of episodes throughout the poem. The series of monologues delivered by female characters in the course of books 7–10 provides an excellent example of his typical technique. Such monologues already had an established tradition in Roman epic. Catullus, for instance, in poem 64 (his so-called *epyllion* [little epic]) depicts Ariadne lamenting her fate as she is deserted by Theseus on a beach on Naxos (*Carmina* 64.132–201). And in book 4 of the *Aeneid* Virgil portrays Dido delivering similarly distraught soliloquies as she is abandoned by Aeneas (4.534–52, 590–629, 651–62). Ovid, however, develops this familiar convention in a distinctive way. In the first place, he selects heroines whose situations allow him to explore particularly unusual conflicts between passion and family duty. In book 8, for instance, Scylla debates whether to betray her father and city to the enemy prince with whom she is infatuated; in book 10, Myrrha wrestles with her desire to commit incest. As we have seen, such curious moral conundrums were staple fare in the schools, and, just as declaimers took pride in contriving clever arguments to support their case, so Ovid's heroines demonstrate a fiendish ability to manufacture justifications for their intended immoral acts.

The accumulation of several monologues is also significant. It suggests the influence of *ēthopoēia*—a rhetorical exercise that required students to assume the character of a fictional figure—rather than epic poetry or drama (see Bonner 1949: 53; Kenney 1996: 1–2). By adopting, in *Metamorphoses*, the persona of six different female characters in similar yet different situations (Medea at 7.11–71, Scylla at 8.44–80, Althaea at 8.478–511, Byblis at 9.474–516, Iphis at 9.726–63, and Myrrha at 10.320–55), Ovid contrives a declamatory tour de force. This sequence of soliloquies is aimed at an audience that appreciates not merely a single witty speech by itself but a series of them, in which similarities and differences can be compared and contrasted. This aesthetic principle is one that was arguably fostered by the schools, where emphasis was placed upon clever variations of familiar themes. Indeed, like a declaimer handling a set exercise, Ovid's compositional method is essentially episodic. In this poetic world, as in the imaginary world of the school exercise, there is little serious exploration of the long-term moral consequences of actions.

This declamatory influence extends to the stylistic sphere as well. For example, Myrrha's dilemma leads her to exclaim: "As the matter stands, because he is already mine, he is not mine" (*nunc, quia iam meus est, non est meus*; Ovid, *Metamorphoses* 10.339). This is a typically Ovidian paradox. The remark's ostensible illogicality can be resolved only once we understand its linguistic ambiguity: *meus* in the first phrase means "mine as a relative," in the second, "mine as a lover." This is the type of verbal wit that, as we have seen, was admired in the schools of declamation. Indeed, Ovid's innate wit or *ingenium* is a quality recognized by ancient critics as central to the character of his poetry (see Quintilian, *Institutio oratoria* 10.1.88; cf. 10.1.98; cf. Seneca, *Controversiae* 2.2.12, 9.5.17). There is a kind of intellectual showmanship here that is absent from Virgil.

This quality appears elsewhere in the *Metamorphoses*. In book 8, for example, Ovid relates the story of Erysichthon, son of Triopas, who falls victim to an insatiable hunger. Such is the man's craving for food that he calls for new feasts even as he is feasting (8.832), and the more food he sends down into his stomach the more he desires (*plusque cupit, quo plura suam demittit in alvum*; Ovid, *Metamorphoses* 8.834). This remarkable affliction culminates in yet another strikingly phrased paradox: "All food in him / is a cause of more food, and, through his eating, the space constantly becomes empty" (*cibus omnis in illo / causa cibi est, semperque locus fit inanis edendo*; 8.841–2). In this case, the phrasing portrays brilliantly the irrationality of Erysichthon's addict-like behavior. Nevertheless, although Ovid here presents a powerfully disturbing image of uncontrollable gluttony, the cleverness of his depiction distances the reader from Erysichthon's plight. Rather than exploit the scene for *pathos*, Ovid focuses on its logical contradictions and in doing so highlights his own verbal and conceptual cleverness. This tendency toward self-advertisement finds a ready parallel with the aesthetic of the declamatory schools, which, as Quintilian notes, were characterized by an element of ostentation and display (*quoniam autem [declamatio] aliquid in se habet epidicticon*; *Institutio oratoria* 2.10.12; cf. 2.10.10).

LUCAN

Similar elements appear in Lucan's epic poem, *Bellum civile* (or *Pharsalia*). Like Ovid, Lucan received an intensive training in rhetoric. His grandfather was the elder Seneca, who dedicated his work on declamation to Lucan's father, Mela (Seneca, *Controversiae* 1, preface 1). And, like Ovid, his poetry is characterized by a constant striving for linguistic or intellectual surprise—often with unsettling results. A passage from book 3 of the poem will help to illustrate the distinctive elements of this style.

In his account of the sea battle between Caesar's forces and those of the Massilians, Lucan describes the heroic actions of (unnamed) twin brothers (*stant gemini fratres, fecundae gloria matris*; Lucan, *Bellum civile* 3.603). Before relating these exploits, however, he draws attention to several contrasts. The twins, he notes, were born from the same womb yet experienced very different fates (a distinction sharpened by the juxtaposition of *eadem* and *variis* at 3.604). Thus, although they looked identical while alive, death ended up distinguishing one from the other (*discrevit mors saeva viros*; 3.608). This outcome in turn produced another unusual result. In most circumstances, a surviving son would bring his parents solace and support in later years; in this case, however, his presence only stirred up bitter memories of the dead twin (3.605–9). Lucan thus contrives to insert several antitheses into just a few lines. To a degree, these observations foreshadow the tragedy of coming events, yet his concern seems to lie as much in manufacturing rhetorical twists as in generating *pathos*. This quest for conceptual surprise also characterizes the rest of the passage, as Lucan goes on to describe the twins' adventures in battle.

The scene, as we might expect, contains a good deal of blood and gore. Graphic portrayals of battlefield violence had been a conventional feature of epic poetry since Homer's *Iliad*, one that Virgil himself had continued in the second half of the *Aeneid*. Yet Lucan's violence often contains a rhetorical flourish. If there is a wound, he will find a way of making it remarkable. In doing so, he shifts the emphasis away from the emotional consequences of the fighting and toward the intellectual conceit of its form (Wight Duff 1960: 20). He begins, for example, by depicting one of the twins bravely reaching out to grab hold of an enemy ship. As he does so, however, the sword of an enemy soldier slices through his arm. Since this blow is a heavy one from above (*gravis insuper ictus*; Lucan, *Bellum civile* 3.611), we might expect the amputated hand to fall into the sea. However, in Lucan's perverse and surprising world, instead of dropping limp and lifeless it remains fixed to that very place, growing stiff in death (3.612–3). Moreover, although such a mutilation would handicap most warriors, in the case of our heroic twin adversity only increases his courage (*crevit in adversis virtus*), and he renews the fight with his "strong left hand" (*forti laeva*)—a piquant inversion of the ancient warrior's usual preference when fighting.

But the carnage does not stop here. As the injured twin attempts to grab his useless hand, he suffers another wound. Again there is a twist: this blow removes not just his remaining hand but his whole arm (*haec quoque cum toto manus est abscisa lacerto*; Lucan, *Bellum civile* 3.617). Yet even this more drastic wound does not deter our warrior. Unable now to attack the enemy, his thoughts turn to defense, and, stepping in front of his brother, he valiantly turns himself into a literal human shield. This is a heroic act of brotherly love, but here, too, Lucan places emphasis less on its display of filial loyalty than on the curious reversal it involves. The armless twin, he notes, now "covers his brother's armor with his bare breast" (*fraterna pectore nudo / arma tegens*; 3.619–20). In normal circumstances, of course, a soldier's armor (*arma*) protects his own chest, but in this inverted scene Lucan makes the twin's bare chest protect his brother's accoutrements. The conceit has a certain intellectual appeal yet undercuts the scene's emotional potential.

The episode's climax adds yet another twist to this already bizarre scene. Our mutilated hero, pierced by spears, does find a way to inflict harm upon the enemy: he launches himself onto the Roman ship as a human missile, his body weight alone serving as his weapon (Lucan, *Bellum civile* 3.626). There is much in common here with the practices of the schools. The exploits of famous heroes in battle had been a stock feature of Greek declamation in preceding centuries, and these, too, had been characterized by a search for novelty in their descriptions of wounds and maiming (Bonner 1966: 281–4). We should not of course overlook the influence of the existing epic tradition, but Lucan in particular seems to have reveled in the tendency toward exuberance and experimentation produced by the declamatory environment.

This same tendency appears in perhaps the poem's most notorious episode—the attempted revivification of a corpse by the witch Erichtho. Lucan depicts the sorceress eagerly plunging her hands into the eyeballs of corpses and nibbling upon the yellowed fingernails of their withered hands (Lucan, *Bellum civile* 6.540–3). Elsewhere she breaks apart the head of a corpse, opens its closed mouth with her teeth, bites off the tip of its tongue, and uses this as a vessel for sending messages down to the underworld (6.565–8). For the critic Otto Due (1962: 68–75), this lurid fixation on the macabre is best explained as the result of the excesses that the poet had observed firsthand in Nero's court. His literary style, in other words, derives from the cultural, rather than educational, zeitgeist. Such an explanation is not implausible, but to deny the declamatory influence in such episodes is to risk distorting our view of Lucan's compositional methods.

New Directions?

Nevertheless, the label *rhetorical epic* remains a problematic one, for several reasons. In the first place, it can all too easily be used in a constraining sense to suggest that these poems consist of *nothing but* rhetoric. Numerous critics in recent decades have sought to demonstrate that this is simply not the case (in the case of Lucan, see Ahl 1976; Bramble 1982; Masters 1992; Leigh 1997). A second problem with the label is that it has at times been used pejoratively, as if to distinguish "true" epic from its later, corrupted counterpart (Ahl 1976: 60; cf. Bramble 1982: 533). Such divisions, however, are simplistic. Although, as we have seen, Ovid's *Metamorphoses* and Lucan's *Bellum civile* are both "rhetorical" in a sense, and both acquire a tone of "intellectual astringency" (Martindale 1976: 47) through their use of paradox, their epic creations remain very different. Ovid's depiction of a heroic world populated by vindictive gods and immoral mortals is wryly subversive and presented with a detached insouciance. Lucan's main mode of exposition, by contrast, is one of indignant moralizing.

Moreover, it is important not to ignore the creative—and poetic—potential inherent in rhetoric. At its best, Lucan's hyperbole provides a powerful means of conveying the terrible scale of the horrors provoked by civil war. When the poet describes (for example) the corpses of those slain at Praeneste as so densely packed that they can scarcely fall to the ground (*vix caede peracta / procumbunt dubiaque labant cervice*; Lucan, *Bellum civile* 2.203–4), he certainly relies heavily on rhetorical point. Indeed, this intellectual twist is developed yet further when we learn that these corpses even deal out death as their weight suffocates those beneath (2.205–6). Yet whatever the element of careful artifice, the scene also memorably suggests the disturbed nature of a universe in which even the fundamental laws of death and gravity seem to be in abeyance. Indeed, over the poem as a whole, Lucan's relentless pursuit of rhetorical virtuosity endows this pessimism with a baroque poetic grandeur. For those writing in the long shadow cast by the brilliance of Virgil's *Aeneid*, the intellectual vitality of declamatory performance provided a bold new palette from which to create different and provocative styles of epic.

FURTHER READING

For a useful survey of the speeches in Virgil's *Aeneid*, see Highet (1972). Bonner (1949) provides a detailed study of Roman declamation, together with some discussion (149–67) of its influence on Latin literature. Fraenkel (1945: 4–10) and Higham (1958) present helpful introductions to Ovid's rhetorical education and its relevance to his poetic style, while Bonner (1966) and Morford (1967) explore in depth Lucan's poetry and its declamatory aspects. For a recent survey of the main issues, see also Roche (2009: 47–51).

REFERENCES

Ahl, Frederick. 1976. *Lucan: An Introduction*. Ithaca, NY: Cornell University Press.

Bonner, Stanley F. 1949. *Roman Declamation in the Late Republic and Early Empire*. Liverpool: University Press of Liverpool.

Bonner, Stanley F. 1966. "Lucan and the Declamation Schools." *American Journal of Philology* 87: 257–289.

Bramble, John C. 1982. "Lucan." In *The Cambridge History of Classical Literature*, vol. 2, edited by Edward J. Kenney and Wendell V. Clausen, 533–557. Cambridge: Cambridge University Press.

Clarke, Martin L. 1996. *Rhetoric at Rome: A Historical Survey*. 3rd ed. Revised by D. H. Berry. London: Routledge.

Due, Otto S. 1962. "An Essay on Lucan." *Classica et Mediaevalia* 23: 68–132.

Fairweather, Janet. 1981. *Seneca the Elder*. Cambridge: Cambridge University Press.

Fraenkel, Hermann. 1945. *Ovid: A Poet Between Two Worlds*. Berkeley: University of California Press.

Higham, Thomas F. 1958. "Ovid and Rhetoric." In *Ovidiana: Recherches sur Ovide*, edited by N. I. Herescu, 32–48. Paris: Les Belles Lettres.

Highet, Gilbert. 1972. *The Speeches in Vergil's "Aeneid."* Princeton, NJ: Princeton University Press.

Hopkinson, Neil. 2000. *Ovid: "Metamorphoses" Book XIII*. Cambridge: Cambridge University Press.

Kennedy, George A. 1957. "The Ancient Dispute over Rhetoric in Homer." *American Journal of Philology* 78: 23–35.

Kennedy, George A. 1963. *The Art of Persuasion in Greece*. Princeton, NJ: Princeton University Press.

Kenney, Edward J. 1996. *Ovid: "Heroides" XVI–XXI*. Cambridge: Cambridge University Press.

Leigh, Matthew. 1997. *Lucan: Spectacle and Engagement*. Oxford: Clarendon.

Martindale, Charles A. 1976. "Paradox, Hyperbole and Literary Novelty in Lucan's *De Bello Civili*." *Bulletin of the Institute for Classical Studies* 23: 45–54.

Masters, Jamie. 1992. *Poetry and Civil War in Lucan's "Bellum Civile."* Cambridge: Cambridge University Press.

Morford, Mark. 1967. *The Poet Lucan: Studies in Rhetorical Epic*. New York: Barnes and Noble.

Roche, Paul A. 2009. *Lucan: "De Bello Civili" Book I*. Oxford: Oxford University Press.

Sussman, Lewis A. 1978. *The Elder Seneca*. Leiden: Brill.

Wight Duff, John. 1960. *A Literary History of Rome in the Silver Age*. 2d ed. Edited by A. M. Duff. London: Ernest Benn Limited.

CHAPTER 19

RHETORIC AND LYRIC ADDRESS

JONATHAN CULLER

Many years ago, when working on the figure of apostrophe in the Romantic lyric, I was surprised to discover that critics ignored this blatant and ubiquitous figure (e.g., "O wild West Wind, thou breath of Autumn's being!" "Tyger, tyger burning bright / In the forests of the night," "Thou still unravished bride of quietness"). When they could not ignore it, they treated it as a convention of no significance inherited from Greek and Latin poetry (see Culler 1981: 135–54).[1] George Shuster, whose book, *The English Ode from Milton to Keats*, treats poems in which the figure is endemic, writes in his introduction, "The element of address is of no especial significance, being merely a reflection of the classical influence. All the verse of antiquity was addressed to somebody, primarily because it was either sung or read and the traditions of song and recitation required that there be a recipient" (Shuster 1940: 11–2). Later he continues, "Virtually all the melic verse of antiquity was addressed to someone, primarily because the forms of ancient rhetoric and music required it . . . The Romantic poets were so close to the classical tradition that they accepted the element of address as a matter of course, and we of the present are so remote from it that it seems a thing established in its own right" (255).

Interested in exploring the functioning of what I took to be the crucial rhetorical device of apostrophe in post-Enlightenment poetry, I did not then concern myself with the suggestion that address was not significant in classical verse either but was merely a requirement of the forms of ancient rhetoric and music. Ralph Johnson's (1982) *The Idea of the Lyric*, however, revived my interest in this topic through its claim that address is crucial to the classical lyric.[2]

Lyric as inherited from the Greeks was sung to an audience, Johnson observes, so that there is a *you* as well as an *I*, a speaker, or a singer, talking to, singing to, another person or persons: "The rhetorical triangle of speaker, discourse, and hearer is the essential feature of the Greek lyric, of the Latin lyric that continued and refined the Greek tradition, and of the medieval and early modern European lyric that inherited and further refined the Graeco-Roman lyric tradition" (Johnson 1982: 34). This model of an *I* speaking to a *you*, he argues, remains central to the best lyric tradition, though the modern conceptions of the lyric have obscured this and have led us to imagine that the lyric in general is to be understood as the solipsistic meditation of an individual, expressing or working out personal feelings, if not the impersonal statement of someone unable to communicate. In the classical model, *I* and *you*, speaker and listener, are (according to Johnson) directly related to one another in a community; with the modern lyric, he writes, "the disintegration of pronominal form entails the disintegration of emotional content, for in lyric, too, form and content are interdependent" (13).

Johnson takes as his principal cases Horace and Catullus, the two most appreciated lyric poets of the classical canon for whom we possess a substantial lyric corpus. He contrasts poems addressed to another person or persons with what he calls, following T. S. Eliot, the "meditative poem, in which the poet talks to himself, or to no one in particular or, sometimes, calls on, apostrophizes, inanimate or non-human entities, abstractions, or the dead" (Johnson 1982: 3). Only 14 percent of Horace's poems and 9 percent of Catullus's are meditative in this sense (soliloquizing or apostrophizing), while 70 percent of Horace's and 87 percent of Catullus's are addressed to another person. The inverse proportion holds for modern poets: 70 percent of Stéphane Mallarmé's poems are meditative whereas only 25 percent are addressed to another person. It seems clear that second-person address is the classical norm.

There is something of a puzzle here for me. Apostrophe in modern lyric is explained as a classical inheritance. Looking back to the classical lyric to see how apostrophic address worked then, before it supposedly became an inherited convention without significance, I find that the one critic inclined to stress the importance of the element of address classifies apostrophe as belonging to a meditative mode characteristic of modern, alienated, solipsistic verse rather than to the conventions of the classical lyric. What to make of this? Are Johnson's contentions well-founded?

This contrast between the classical and the modern, as formulated by Johnson, revolves around the question of pronominal structures of lyric address. The first question might be whether there are indeed two radically different historical models. "Directness" seems to be a primary value for many scholars of Greek literature: they either presume that the poets, discovering the inner self, give direct, passionate expression to feelings of the moment, or, stressing the circumstances of direct address to an audience, presume that the archaic lyric was the cry of its occasion (*kairos*), sung to its audience as part of a public ceremony. Although there are many second-person pronouns in Greek and Latin lyrics, they very rarely designate a community the poet could be said to address directly. Even Pindar, whose public victory odes have the undeniable social, rhetorical function of assembling a community around its champions, seldom addresses the citizens of the city of the victor. His *epinikian* odes address the victors, numerous gods, Truth, Peace, my lyre, my song, and my soul, but of 45 odes only Nemean 2 addresses a collective group of people: "Celebrate him, O citizens, / in honor of Timodemos upon his glorious return, / and lead off with a sweetly melodious voice" (Pindar 1997: 2: 19). This surprising failure of Pindar's odes to address the audiences makes one wonder whether there may have been, unbeknownst to us, some generic rule against addressing the citizens, since otherwise it would seem such an obvious thing to do in odes of this sort. Might it be that precisely to facilitate the ease of re-performance in a wide variety of contexts, the odist declines to address a specific audience?[3]

Sappho's only complete poem is a complex invocation of Aphrodite in which the discourse addressed to Aphrodite quotes how the goddess herself on previous occasions had addressed Sappho: "What is it now? Who, O Sappho, is wronging you?" This remarkable poem is anything but simple and direct:

> Intricate, immortal Aphrodite, snare-weaver, child of Zeus, I implore you,
> do not tame my spirit, great lady, with pain and sorrow.
> But come to me now, if ever before you heard my voice from afar and,
> leaving your father's house, yoked golden chariot and came.
> Beautiful sparrows swiftly brought you over the dark earth, with a quick flutter of wings
> from the sky's height through the clean air. They were quick in coming.
> You, blessed goddess, a smile on your divine face, asked
> what did I suffer, once again this time,
> and why did I call, once again this time,
> and what did I in my frenzied heart most want to happen.
> Whom am I to persuade, once again this time,
> to lead to your affection. Who, O Sappho, does you wrong?
> For one who flees will soon pursue, one who rejects gifts will soon be making offers,
> and one who does not love will soon be loving, even against her will.
> Come to me even now, release me from these mean anxieties,
> and do what my heart wants done. You yourself be my ally.[4]

This poem is a prayer to the goddess, not in formal circumstance of worship but a request for aid.[5] It follows conventions of prayer in beginning with the attributes and parentage of the goddess and mentioning past occasions on which aid was forthcoming, but "the solemn conventions of prayer are set to the melodies of popular song, so that the meter itself seems to comment saucily on the matter. Worse yet, a final military image [*symmachos*, "ally in battle"] is marshaled in such a way as to make the whole performance appear to poke fun at masculine battle-prayers" (Burnett 1983: 245). But the representation of Aphrodite's past visits strikes a surprising note: not just that you have helped me in the past, but "a smile on your divine face, you asked what did I suffer this time [*deute*], and why did I call this time." The speaker's appeal represents past visits as already involving Aphrodite's wry allusion to still previous appeals and visits. Her smile accompanies the gentle mockery of the verses, signaling amusement rather than anger or exasperation in its "What, you are calling me again? What is it this time?"[6] Anne Carson writes of this key term *deute*, "the particle *de* marks a lively perception in the present moment: 'Look at that now!' The adverb *aūte* peers past the present moment to a pattern of repeated actions stretching behind it: 'Not for the first time!' *De* places you in time and emphasizes that placement: *now*. *Aūte* intercepts 'now' and binds it into a history of '*thens*'" (1986: 118). We are thus engaged in a structure of regress and repetition where, when called in the past, Aphrodite already responded, "what, not again!"

"who is doing you wrong?" and declared that past scenarios would repeat themselves: "If she flees, she shall soon pursue." With the proliferation, as in fun-house mirrors, of Aphrodites (the present addressee, the past addressee, the actor, and the temporary speaker) and of Sapphos (the present petitioner, the past addressee of the goddess, and the petitioner from yet prior past times mentioned in the goddess's past address), this poem is striking in the involutions generated through address within address.

The representation of Aphrodite's responses in the past, with the different steps of the journey underlining the favor granted (Aphrodite cannot just miraculously appear), is powerful and seductive, above all with the transition from Aphrodite's reported speech to direct discourse displaying for us the stakes of apostrophe: the wish, seldom realized in the later lyric, that entities addressed might in their turn respond. It is especially effective to present such a delicate, amused response as from the past, which carries more authority than a response reported in the present ("and then you come . . .") or imagined for the future ("then you will say . . .").

Most remarkable, however, is the way the combination of the insistence on repetition—*deute*—and the representation of speech creates the effect of an appearance by Aphrodite *in the present*, even though the poem claims to represent the appearance and the speech of past occasions. "This narration, which is ostensibly reminding the goddess of her previous acquiescence to the speaker's requests, is delivered apostrophically (as indeed the whole poem is delivered) in second-person address as if the goddess is already present and as if her swift journey down from heaven is happening now, in the moment of speaking" (Walker 2000: 244). As the goddess shifts into the present and future of "Who am I to persuade this time? Who, O Sappho, does you wrong?" we have Aphrodite present and speaking now in the moment of the poem's utterance. The speech event narrated happens not only then "but also 'now' and always, in every instance of the 'this time' in which the poem is performed" (244). And readers can scarcely ask, "But will she come and assist this time?" because we experience her speech as if she were already here, already fulfilling the request.

This poem is not the product of a ritual occasion (though it alludes to such rituals of invocation), nor is it by any means the direct cry of passion. The double consciousness, the intricate-mindedness that allows her to represent the amused chiding of the goddess, is a great strength of the poem, and it illustrates that the institution of lyric composition already, in Sappho's day, allows for a highly complex composition that is neither the direct expression of a subjectivity newly discovered nor the ritual expression of community values.

As for Horace and Catullus, on whom Johnson focuses, it is striking that they do not address the Roman people or other collectivities. In the first three books of Horace's *Odes*, 26 poems are addressed to historical individuals; 26 to unknown individuals, most of whom, with names regarded as conventional, were certainly not supposed to be known; 3 are addressed to unnamed *you*'s and thus could be assimilated to the category of unknown *you*'s; 17 are addressed to gods and goddesses, including the muses; only 9 are addressed to no one; and 6 are addressed to nonhuman addressees (the ship carrying Virgil, the ship of the Republic, his lyre, a tree on his estate, the Bandusian spring, and a wine jar).

This is certainly different from a modern collection of poems, but not, I submit, because the pronouns designate the true audience for the poems. Even the poems addressed to historical individuals seem designed to honor them (as a dedication would today) rather than to tell them something they need to know (though scholars have worked hard to imagine why a particular poem might have been addressed to a given historical individual). However, the real test case is all the poems addressed to people regarded as fictional (many of them given Greek names). What is going on here? Let us consider one of the most famous, most frequently translated odes:

> What slim youngster drenched in perfumes
> is hugging you now, Pyrrha, on a bed of roses
>   deep in your lovely cave? For whom
> are you tying up your blonde hair?
> You're so elegant and simple. Many's the time
> he'll weep at your faithlessness and the changing gods,
>   and be amazed at seas
>   roughened by black winds,
> but now in all innocence he enjoys your golden beauty
> and imagines you always available, always loveable,
>   not knowing about treacherous breezes—
>   I pity poor devils who have no experience of you
> and are dazzled by your radiance. As for me,
> the tablet on the temple wall announces
>   that I have dedicated my dripping clothes
>   to the god who rules the sea.

(Horace 1997: 30)

> *Quis multa gracilis te puer in rosa*
> *perfusus liquidis urget odoribus*
> *   grato, Pyrrha, sub antro?*
> *   cui flavam religas comam,*
>
> *simplex munditiis? heu, quotiens fidem*   5
> *mutatosque deos flebit, et aspera*
> *   nigris aequora ventis*
> *   emirabitur insolens,*
>
> *qui nunc te fruitur credulus aurea;*
> *qui semper vacuam, semper amabilem*   10
> *   sperat, nescius aurae*
> *   fallacis! miseri, quibus*
> *intemptata nites! me tabula sacer*
> *votiva paries indicat uvida*
> *   suspendisse potenti*   15
> *   vestimenta maris deo.*

(Horace, *Odes* 1.5)

The last lines refer to the practice of victims who have escaped shipwrecks dedicating their apparel to the god in thanks or to the retiree dedicating the tools of his trade to the god as he hangs them up. The speaker has survived the storms of the seas of love and is now retiring from the field.

The poem is addressed to Pyrrha, but we do not imagine her sitting in an audience to whom this is recited. Critics are therefore tempted to treat it as a dramatic monologue, a representation of a speaker "addressing Pyrrha, and as we read we gradually come to understand their story and their characters" (West 1995: 40). A way to understand the poem, then, would be to read it as the fictional representation of a real-world speech act of address and thus to try to reconstruct the situation of utterance, the relation of speaker and hearer to one another (with as much of their history as is relevant and inferable), and the aim or purpose of the speaker's utterance. To read the poem in this way certainly gives readers something to do; however, it involves a great deal of speculation, and many simple questions are hard to answer. Where does this speech act take place? And why would the speaker say this to Pyrrha? Is the speaker supposed to have stumbled upon Pyrrha in a cave, being amorously pressed by a gracile youth unknown to him? Presumably not (we don't imagine he interrupts the love scene to ask, "Who's this?"), but if we posit that he encounters Pyrrha elsewhere, in the street, for instance, it is hard to imagine the motivation for the question, "What slim youngster is pressing you now?" Or if we take this as a wittily hyperbolic version of, "So who are you seeing these days?" then it is hard to imagine the circumstances or rationale for the comments that follow, which would be better addressed to a young man. This is especially true, given the *order* of the comments about this young lover: one might imagine someone saying, "I'm sure he is dazzled by your radiance now, not realizing that the future will bring storms," but the converse—"Many's the time that he will weep at your faithlessness . . . though he is dazzled now"—seems much more like musing about the vicissitudes of love than an utterance to the woman on a specific occasion.

But if, attempting to preserve the situation of speaking to Pyrrha, we conceive of the situation as one in which the speaker, having put to Pyrrha the question about the identity of her latest paramour, slips into a meditative mode in which he muses about how the young man will feel later and what he must now feel, then we are already imagining some sort of separation from the alleged addressee, as though from lines 5 to 13 the speaker became lost in his own thoughts and forgot he was addressing Pyrrha. At the very least, thinking of these lines as addressed to Pyrrha makes the poem obscure rather than clarifies it, whereas if we think of the poem as a disquisition on the vicissitudes of love directed at an *imagined* Pyrrha, in the lyric present the poem makes much more sense. And the final lines come to emphasize for the reader the speaker's position as worldly-wise, not jealous of the youth who may have supplanted him (as one might suppose he was if the poem were really spoken to Pyrrha). The speaker announces that he is no longer engaged in such matters, which he can now view with wry amusement. This is the sort of poem that would have been recited to a male audience at a banquet, with an addressee imagined for rhetorical purposes rather than the object of a real-world speech act. Why not take the ode as an act of poetic address: writing that imagines the addressee

as it imagines the gracile youth, with his present excitement and his future disappoint-
ments, and whose act of addressing, precisely because it does not seem focused on the
referent of the pronoun, is more likely to attain the reader?

We could say, in fact, that the key question is: Whom is the poem seeking to persuade? In ancient Greece poetry was a form of epideictic discourse, a rhetorical transaction and instrument of ethical *paideia* (see Walker, ch. 6; Heath, ch. 5). The audience
was expected to make observations (*theōros*) about what is praiseworthy, worthy of
belief.[7] In Plato's *Protagoras*, where the protagonists discuss the arguments of a poem by
Simonides in order to reach conclusions about the world, everyone takes it for granted
that, as Protagoras says, the most important part of a man's *paideia* is to be capable concerning verses—capable of judging which sayings of poets have been rightly done and
to give reasons when questioned (339–47). (Socrates argues, against the traditional view,
that people ought to discuss dialectic rather than poetry.)

So whom does this poem seek to persuade, and of what? Not Pyrrha—she is not
addressed so as to be persuaded to act differently; her behavior is compared to the natural changeableness of the sea. More plausibly, the gracile youth, or rather, since he is not
addressed at all, but pitied, as one of many "*Miseri*," perhaps all those "poor devils" who
don't anticipate the storms that will come. Arguably the rhetorical intent of the poem
is "disapprobation, not of the beautiful *hetaira* [courtesan], but rather of the immature
lover" (Davis 1991: 225). He is naive and a slow learner, who will be disappointed many
times. The participants at a banquet would be treated to gentle mockery of the type of
the amorous beginner. Is it not the audience of the poem that is to be persuaded to adopt
the attitude that the speaking voice projects of knowledgeable wariness, accepting what
comes? Pyrrha is elegant and not to be shunned; the youth should enjoy himself now
but not get too involved, for reversals will occur, suffering will follow. There is a time for
everything, says the wise man, retiring from the amorous fray.

Now a few of Horace's odes *should* be read as dramatic monologues, where to make
sense of the poem we really do have to imagine a context of utterance and work out why
in these circumstances someone would say just this. But they are rare, whereas this sort
of structure—address to an unidentifiable *you* in a situation better left indeterminate—
is extremely common. This structure of triangulation, where a poet addresses a beloved
or other absent interlocutor as a way of addressing an audience, is a staple of the post-
classical lyric as well, from Petrarch on. The second-person address functions above
all to place the act of lyric speech in the lyric present and to accentuate the paradox of
poetry, which evokes immediacy while adopting a temporality of deferral. It repeats
itself for readers in a future not even imagined and articulates an attitude whose appropriateness future audiences of readers are to judge.

Let me turn now to one of those small number of odes addressed to something that
cannot be a listener and that, it seems to me, provides a guide to how lyric address works
that can apply to poems with personal addressees. This is another famous poem:

> O fountain of Bandusia, brighter than glass,
> well do you deserve an offering of sweet wine

and flowers, and tomorrow you will receive a kid
   with new horns bulging on his brow,
marking him out for love and war—
to no avail, since he will stain your cold stream
   with his red blood, this offspring
     of the amorous flock.
The cruel hour of the blazing Dog-star
cannot touch you. You give delicious
coldness to oxen weary of the plough
   and the straggling flock.
     You too will become a famous fountain
as I sing of the holm-oak
   above your cave in the rock
     where your waters leap down chattering.

(Horace 1997: 92)

O fons Bandusiae, splendidior vitro,
Dulci digne mero non sine floribus,
   Cras donaberis haedo,
     Cui frons turgida cornibus
Primis et venerem et proelia destinat;   5
Frustra: nam gelidos inficiet tibi
   Rubro sanguine rivos,
     Lascivi suboles gregis.
Te flagrantis atrox hora Caniculae
Nescit tangere, tu frigus amabile   10
   Fessis vomere tauris
     Praebes et pecori vago.
Fies nobilium tu quoque fontium,
Me dicente cavis impositam ilicem
   Saxis unde loquaces   15
     Lymphae desiliunt tuae.

(Horace, *Odes* 3.13)

The classical models of lyric genres have the virtue of encouraging us not to imagine lyric as the fictional imitation of real-world speech acts; they provide a panoply of poetic speech acts of praise, invocation, celebration, and complaint. This poem emphasizes its link with other rituals of ceremonious praise by announcing, in its praise of the spring or fountain, that tomorrow—presumably October 13, *Fontanilia* or the "Festival of Springs," when offerings of wine and flowers were thrown into the waters of springs— this spring will receive a special sacrifice of young goat. Gregson Davis argues that the "presumed reference to an obscure festival" has distracted attention from the fact that wine, flowers, and young animals are the crucial elements of "the banqueting apparatus": "In fine, Horace's *fons* is to be honored with the irreducible tokens of convivial poetry" (1991: 128). In any case, the poem's separation from "tomorrow's" event, in which wine, flowers, and kid will honor the spring, stresses that this hymn of praise is not the fictional representation of some other sort of speech act. It performatively sets out to accomplish what it declares: that this spring will become a famous spring, like the springs of the Muses in Greece (Arethusa, Hippocrene, or Dirce)—and it has succeeded.[8] Although no one knows where this spring is or even whether there is any such spring, it is famous and the sacrifice of the kid is repeatedly enacted. The apparently gratuitous celebration of his budding horns—"marking him out for love and war"—confers value for the reader that is swiftly sacrificed, as we are compelled to imagine him killed off: he is marked for love and war "to no avail, since he will stain your cold stream with his red blood."[9]

The spring will not hear this praise, which is directed to us despite the vocative and second-person verbs, but it makes a difference that the poem is addressed to the spring rather than simply praising it. Consider what happens if we rewrite to remove the second-person address:

> The spring of Bandusia is brighter than glass;
> and well deserves an offering of sweet wine
>   and flowers, and tomorrow it will receive a kid
>   with new horns bulging on his brow,
> marking him out for love and war—
> to no avail, since he will stain its cold stream
>   with his red blood, this offspring
>   of the amorous flock.
> The cruel hour of the blazing Dog-star
> cannot touch this spring. It gives delicious
>   coldness to oxen weary of the plough
>   and the straggling flock.
> It too will become a famous fountain
> as I sing of the holm-oak
>   above its cave in the rock
>   where its waters leap down chattering.

The changes are minimal. They do not destroy the poem, but they do substantially change its character. It becomes resolutely descriptive from the outset rather than invocatory, and the *dicente* ("as I sing") at the end comes as more of an afterthought than a continuation and climax of a performativity. The fact that the spring is addressed constitutes it as potentially responsive: "By addressing the spring as *splendidior vitro*, 'more brilliant (not 'translucent') than glass,' the speaker constitutes the spring as an object that throws back his own voice just as it does the light, so that the final syllable of *vitro* echoes the 'O' of the apostrophe and the two polysyllabic choriambs in the middle of the line fill out the mirroring ABBA structure . . . the 'O' that is the pure voice of encounter is thrown back at the speaker" (Fitzgerald 1989: 98).[10]

One notable loss in my transmutation of the poem is "*your* chattering waters," which makes the poem conclude with attribution of speech *loquaces*—to a *you*. What is lost is not just the possibility that the spring becomes something more than an object, something raised to a different plane, with a life of its own, but "the reciprocity between the speaking of the poet and the prattling of the spring" (Fitzgerald 1989: 99), as if the spring's natural response were made verbal by the poetic address. What is thus lost, above all, is a sense of lyric as a ritualistic performance: conjuring, endowing, acting. In a modern poem, this comes with the risk of preciousness and pretentiousness: invocation seems too markedly poetical, though Kenneth Koch (2000), in a daring book of apostrophic poems, *New Addresses*, attempts to make it altogether more quotidian.[11] For Horace, imagining addressing a spring seems eminently possible, a regular lyric strategy. It enables him, as Fitzgerald puts it, "to explore the nature of the relationship with various forms of otherness in which pleasure is implicated, and most particularly, with that poetic otherness that appears against the solidity of solidly constructed statement and narrative" (1989: 101).

I would argue that there is continuity between address of this sort and address to named individuals and not, as Johnson maintains, a discontinuity separating the solipsistic and meditative from the social and discursive. Let us consider a poem by Catullus, whose poetic addressees are generally taken to be real people. Catullus, as far as we know, is the first poet in Greek or Latin who appears to write about a particular love affair in depth in a related collection of poems. After him innumerable other poets found that they were irresistibly committed to loving a figure like Lesbia and recounting the ecstasy and suffering of devotion to one dominating mistress. His collection sets the stage for a coherent genre, the Latin love lyric, in which Propertius loves Cynthia, Tibellus loves Delia, and Ovid loves Corinna. And after Dante and Petrarch established the genre in a European vernacular, we have a continuing international tradition. Despite the fact that Lesbia is mentioned in only a small number of Catullus's poems, criticism has worked to construct a life and a love affair from them, annexing to the Lesbian affair all the poems that might possibly be addressed to that feminine beloved (only poems explicitly addressed to male lovers or to other named women have to be omitted).[12] Let us consider the most famous poem to Lesbia, Catullus 5, in which we seem to get a straightforward address to Lesbia: let us love!

> Let us live, my Lesbia, and love,
> And value all the talk of stricter
> Old men at a single penny.
> Suns can set and rise again;
> For us, once our brief light has set,
> There's one unending night for sleeping.
> Give me a thousand kisses, then a hundred,
> Then another thousand, then a second hundred,
> Then still another thousand, then a hundred;
> Then, when we've made many thousands,
> We'll muddle them so as not to know
> Or lest some villain overlook us
> Knowing the total of our kisses.

> (Catullus 1990: 7)

Vivamus, mea Lesbia, atque amemus,
Rumoresque senum severiorum
Omnes unius aestimemus assis.
Soles occidere et redire possunt:
Nobis, cum semel occidit brevis lux,
Nox est perpetua una dormienda.
Da mi basia mille, deinde centum,
Dein mille altera, dein secunda centum,
Deinde usque altera mille, deinde centum,
Dein, cum milia multa fecerimus,
Conturbabimus illa, ne sciamus,
Aut ne quis malus inuidere possit,
Cum tantum sciat esse basiorum.

(Catullus 5)

The *carpe diem* poem, to use Horace's phrase, is in principle addressed to the beloved to persuade her to prolong the moment and make love before time passes on. One critic writes that this poem is addressed to Lesbia as a "direct and passionate demand for love" (Fredricksmeyer 1970: 439), but if so it is an odd demand. If the speaker were really asking Lesbia for a thousand and then a hundred and then a thousand kisses, she might well respond, impatiently, "How many do you want then?": "You ask how many of your mega-kisses would satisfy me, Lesbia" (*Quaeris quot mihi basiationes / tuae, Lesbia, sint satis superque*; Catullus 1990: 7.1–2). Urging her to disregard the grumblings of the censorious and contrasting the sun's ability to rise again with our inability to wake from an unending sleep might carry some persuasive force. And "one unending night for sleeping" (*nox est perpetua una dormienda*) may hint at the possibility of spending that perpetual night in bed with unending kisses.

But the second part of the poem takes a quite different direction. Instead of calling for a night of love before it is too late, it multiplies kisses in a count that at first bespeaks haste but then promises to go on and on, as if there were all the time in the world for endless foreplay. This introduces a different temporality from that of the brief mortal span. One might think of it as the temporality of the lyric, where, as in John Keats's "Ode on a Grecian Urn," "More happy love" is "For ever warm and still to be enjoyed, / For ever panting and for ever young" (1978: 373), and no doubt forever kissing. But this is a condition achieved by the poem, as addressed to readers, not an aspect of a speech act addressed to a real lover.

The extravagant multiplication of kisses is, however, a provocation of the audience, because being carried away with passion, especially a passion for kisses, was a violation of norms of masculine behavior—unmanly. Catullus's poem 16 virulently attacks Furius and Aurelius, who register this criticism: "Because you've read of my many thousand kisses / you doubt my virility" (*Vos, quod milia multa basiorum / legistis, male me marem putatis*) (1990: 19).[13] There is the presumption that readers, like the "stricter," grumpy old men of poem 5, will be put off, and it is perhaps they who need to be seduced. Poem 16 provides good evidence that poems such as 5 are aimed at readers rather than the addressee: Catullus treats Furius and Aurelius and the hairy old men (*pilosi*) of 16 as the appropriate audience for the poems about kisses. The old men are erotically stimulated—seduced—while the former inappropriately infer the author's character from his verses. However, there is no suggestion that either were reading something aimed at a different audience.

In the second half of poem 5 the language of counting and calculation and the reflection thereon seems directed at readers, not at a lover. It is the readers who may be seduced by the poem's cleverness in continuing the language of calculation or appraisal (*aestimemus*), associated with the censorious, in asking for kisses, and then at the end proposing to muddle the count (*conturbabimus*) so the lovers don't end up counting their blessings, which would be bad luck, or allow the censorious the knowledge that would allow the evil eye to harm them. If we were at first tempted to keep track as the kisses mount, the ending confounds such attempts and casts a counting reader in the position of the censorious. Our moralizing or envy of the young is not worth a penny. "Precisely by the insolent absurdity of its poetic logic," writes Fitzgerald, "the poem takes readers in, compelling us to assign the valuation (*aestimatio*)" it claims to erode (1995: 150).

The opposition between the loving couple and the censorious, between life and death, structures the poem, as the question becomes where readers will position themselves. It is we, more than Lesbia, who need to be persuaded to seize the day, not count the kisses or try to hex the unmanly display of amorous youth.

The fiction of addressing a lover is a strategy in the challenging and persuading of readers. We might compare this to a poem of more delicate foreplay, by whose *incipit* Catullus's book was known in antiquity, *Passer* (sparrow). This poem addresses the sparrow ("my girl's darling") with whom she plays while the speaker would play with her ("When my own bright-eyed desire / Fancies some endearing fun"), but it ends by telling the sparrow that he wishes he could play with it, as she does, to "lighten the spirit's gloomy cares" (Catullus 1990: 3). Addressing the sparrow, especially in the opening poem following the dedication, is a deliberately precious way of performing the lover, flaunting one of the hyperbolic roles the speaker is willing to adopt—the devotee of lightness, kisses (*lepos, facetiae*).

Addressing the sparrow works much the same way as addressing Lesbia here. The key question is to what end is the rhetorical stance and procedure of the discourse constructed: to solicit the interest of a sparrow, persuade a lover, or challenge and perhaps persuade a reader, or at least induce a reader to readjust his or her hierarchy of values? Is it not for readers that the rhetoric is designed? The startling census of kisses, the flouting of behavioral norms, and the clever turning of the language of accounting against the attempt to hold lovers accountable all suggest a focus on readers rather than on a partner in love. As Paul Veyne observes of the Latin love elegy generally, "ces doux propos sont destinées à amuser le lecteur et non pas à faire sourire un destinataire; à Rome l'amoureux poète pose pour son publique et lui exhibe sa maitresse" (1983: 211).

Later in the tradition of love poetry, the inaccessibility of the beloved became such a strong conventional element that neither Beatrice nor Laura seems to be the actual addressee of poems ostensibly addressed to her; the poems become enactments of homage to an absent figure. Here in Catullus the lover is scarcely divine, but the structure of triangulation is similar: the speaker addresses the beloved, but for an audience, for whom the rhetorical strategies are conceived.

Rather than oppose the apostrophic to the social, as Johnson's scheme suggests, we might conclude that the lyric is rhetorical regardless of who it addresses. Address to named individuals functions in much the same way that address to a fountain does: it stages a voice performing for an audience by addressing someone or something. One might even say that the less likely it is that the person or thing addressed can be the "real" target of the discourse, the more address to that imagined addressee will facilitate the performance of poetic discourse, the more poetically functional that imagined address will be.

My argument in this chapter has been that direct address to the audience is *not* the preferred mode of Greek or Latin lyric and that to imagine otherwise is to delude oneself with a fallacious model or to indulge in a sleight of hand that takes the *you*'s of the poem for its audience. This mistake is particularly unfortunate because the rhetorical structure of Greek and Latin lyric does offer a model for thinking about lyric that is an important corrective to the two models of the dramatic monologue and of subjective expression we have inherited from the nineteenth century. However, we cannot use the classical model for that purpose if we imagine that it is one of direct address.

In "Logic, Rhetoric, and Poesis," William Batstone writes, "Lyric poetry really is about who and where we are as beings who continually say 'I' to ourselves or to 'you.' That, I think, is the result of allowing ancient lyric the rhetoric of its traditional pronouns, 'I speak to you'" (1993: 150). Ralph Johnson, although he may go wrong in other ways, is right to declare, "What is essential, then, to lyric, is rhetoric, and essential to this lyrical rhetoric . . . is the pronominal form and lyric identity, the dynamic configuration of lyrical pronouns that defines and vitalizes the situation of lyrical discourse" (1982: 23). And although the temptation to contrast the healthy classical lyric with its decadent modern descendants leads him to write as if the *you*'s addressed by lyric are its real addressees, his stress on the rhetorical situation of lyric enables us to recognize that ultimately this address is figurative, as in apostrophic address, and that what the poems accomplish by addressing all these *you*'s is to create a relation to the reader. Not, as Johnson appears to believe, because the *you* is a metaphor for the reader, but because the apostrophic address to *you* places us in the temporality of the lyric present where things happen.

Notes

1. Fortunately, apostrophe is no longer ignored.
2. I am grateful to a large number of classicists for discussing various points with me, raising questions after talks, or commenting on drafts of my writings on the classical lyric. I especially want to thank Fred Ahl, Alessandro Barchiesi, Gregson Davis, Ralph Johnson, Michele Lowrie, Hayden Pellicia, Pietro Pucci, and Michael Putnam.
3. I am grateful to Richard Neer for this suggestion. On the conventions of the Pindaric ode, see Bundy 1962.
4. Sappho no. 1, in Winkler (1990: 167–8; trans. modified). Although the Greek has no quotation marks, modern translators generally insert them to mark "Whom am I to persuade

. . . even against her will" as the speech of the goddess. Leaving them out captures the slide from indirect discourse to direct and the momentary ambiguity of who says, "Come to me even now." Winkler and Carson (1986) prefer the reading of some of the manuscripts that makes the opening word *poikilophron*, "having a mind that is dappled, variegated, complex," to the reading of most modern editors, *poikilothron*, either "ornately enthroned" (from *thronos*, "throne") or "with variegated embroidered flowers" (from *throna*, "embroidered flowers"). Intricate-mindedness does seem more pertinent to the poem, but Putnam (1960–1: 79–83) and Scheid and Svenbro (1994: 61–91) argue convincingly for *with embroidered cloak*, as a deliberate echo of Athena's *peplos poikilos*, "embroidered cloak" (Homer, *Iliad* 5), Andromache's *throna poikila* (*Iliad* 22), and of the embroidered love charms that Hera seeks from Aphrodite in the *Iliad* when Zeus is wandering.

5. "This is not a cult-song, an appeal for epiphany, recited ritual accompaniment on a formal occasion to honor Aphrodite: yet it is constructed in accordance with the principles of the cult-song" (Page 1955: 16). The best reading I have found, among many, is by Burnett (1983: 245–59).

6. I have adopted Nagy's translation of *deute* as "once again *this* time" (1996: 100), which underlines, as does Carson's "what (now again)" or "why (now again)," this element of repetition (see also Sappho 2002: 3).

7. See Walker (2000: 9, 149). Epideictic rhetoric, which, Walker argues, derives from archaic lyric, includes panegyric. And unlike pragmatic rhetoric, which is directed toward decision, epideictic rhetoric is directed to an audience that does not make decisions (*kritēs*) but forms opinions in response to the discourse, which thus "shapes and cultivates the basic codes of value and belief by which a society or culture lives" (Walker 2000: 154). This holds, he argues, for the audience of Thucydides, Plato, and Sappho. And of course Horace aspires to revive the Greek lyric tradition of Sappho and Alcaeus.

8. "The explicit performative *dicente* has the self-fulfilling effect of ennobling the addressee," with the result that "the scene of the utterance becomes certified as an authentic (albeit Roman) locus of lyric creativity" (Davis 1991: 127–8).

9. Fitzgerald (1989: 98–102) offers a brilliant reading of the sacrifice of the kid in relation to poetic pleasure, which is radically other than the ordinary pleasure offered by a cool spring in summer. The sacrifice is an unbalancing of the relation between speaker and spring, an excess that links the energy of the spring's waters to the energy of the kid's potential life, answered by the excess of the final section where the speaker promises fame above ordinary springs.

10. Fitzgerald insists, correctly, that "in order to approach the poem as a rhetorical action we will have to take seriously the fact that it is cast as an address. I will therefore avoid the strategy by which the poem is treated as a dramatic monologue that merely *conforms* to the ancient habit of addressing a poem to a person or thing" (1989: 98).

11. But address to Jewishness, to driving, to World War Two, and so on remains comic.

12. Fitzgerald (1995) and Wray (2001) are notable studies that do not take this approach.

13. Batstone, in a complex and ingenious reading, suggests that "the charge and the joke was that when Catullus asked for many thousand kisses he was taken (and mistaken) to be asking, like a *senex*, . . . for *fellatio*, and that this was a confession of masculine inadequacy" (1993: 168, n. 45). See Horace, Epode 8: "If that is what you want from my fastidious groin / your mouth has got some work to do" (*quod ut superbo provoces ab inguine / ore adlaborandum est tibi*) (1997: 12).

References

Batstone, William. 1993. "Logic, Rhetoric, and Poesis." *Helios* 20, no. 2: 43–72.

Bundy, Elroy. 1962. "*Studia Pindarica I & II.*" *University of California Publications in Classical Philology* 18, nos. 1–2: 1–92.

Burnett, Anne. 1983. *Three Archaic Poets: Archilochus, Alcaeus, Sappho*. London: Duckworth.

Carson, Anne. 1986. *Eros the Bittersweet*. Princeton, NJ: Princeton University Press.

Catullus. 1990. *Catullus, the Complete Poems*. Edited and translated by Guy Lee. Oxford: Oxford University Press.

Culler, Jonathan. 1981. "Apostrophe." In *The Pursuit of Signs*, 135–154. Ithaca, NY: Cornell University Press.

Davis, Gregson. 1991. *Polyhymnia, The Rhetoric of Horatian Lyric Discourse*. Berkeley: University of California Press.

Fitzgerald, William. 1989. "Horace, Pleasure, and the Text." *Arethusa* 22, no. 1: 98–102.

Fitzgerald, William. 1995. *Catullan Provocations*. Berkeley: University of California Press.

Fredricksmeyer, Ernest. 1970. "Observations on Catullus 5." *American Journal of Philology* 91: 431–445.

Horace. 1997. *The Complete Odes and Epodes*. Translated by David West. Oxford: Oxford University Press.

Johnson, W. R. 1982. *The Idea of the Lyric: Lyric Modes in Ancient and Modern Poetry*. Chicago, IL: University of Chicago Press.

Keats, John. 1978. *The Poems of John Keats*. Edited by Jack Stillinger. Cambridge, MA: Harvard University Press.

Koch, Kenneth. 2000. *New Addresses*. New York: Knopf.

Nagy, Gregory. 1996. *Poetry as Performance*. Cambridge: Cambridge University Press.

Page, Denys. 1955. *Sappho and Alcaeus: An Introduction to the Study of Ancient Lesbian Poetry*. Oxford: Oxford University Press.

Pindar. 1997. *Pindar*. Edited and translated by William Race. 2 vols. Loeb Classical Library. Cambridge, MA: Harvard University Press.

Putnam, Michael. 1960–1961. "Throna *and Sappho 1.1.*" *Classical Journal* 56: 79–83.

Quinn, Kenneth. 1980. *Horace, The Odes*. Translation and commentary by Kenneth Quinn. London: Macmillan.

Sappho. 2002. *If Not, Winter: Fragments of Sappho*. Translated by Anne Carson. New York: Random House.

Scheid, John, and Jesper Svenbro. 1994. "*Aphrodite poikilōthronos*: l'épithète, le manteau, les amants." In *Le Metier de Zeus. Mythe du tissage et du tissu dans le monde gréco-romain*, 61–91. Paris: La Découverte.

Shuster, George N. 1940. *The English Ode from Milton to Keats*. New York: Columbia University Press.

Veyne, Paul. 1983. *L'elegie érotique romaine: l'amour, la poésie, et l'occident*. Paris: Seuil.

Walker, Jeffrey. 2000. *Rhetoric and Poetics in Antiquity*. Oxford: Oxford University Press.

West, David. 1995. *Horace Odes I, "Carpe Diem."* Translation and commentary by David West. Oxford: Oxford University Press.

Winkler, John J. 1990. *The Constraints of Desire: The Anthropology of Sex and Gender in Ancient Greece*. London: Routledge.

Wray, David. 2001. *Catullus and the Poetics of Roman Manhood*. Cambridge: Cambridge University Press.

CHAPTER 20

RHETORIC AND THE GRECO-ROMAN SECOND SOPHISTIC

LAURENT PERNOT

THE so-called Second Sophistic was a literary and social movement in the Greek-speaking world of the Roman Empire during the first to the third centuries CE. The sophists who formed this movement were simultaneously professors of rhetoric, orators, lecturers, and politicians, and they were highly influential in their day. The appearance of the Second Sophistic in a section devoted to "Ancient Roman Rhetoric" prompts two initial observations. First, the Second Sophistic was principally Greek: if it concerns the Roman world, it is because the Roman Empire consisted of a mainly Greco-Roman community and because the sophists had particular ties to Rome. And second, as its name indicates, the Second Sophistic is focused on the notion of sophistic: if it concerns rhetoric, it is because rhetoric is essential to the definition of sophistic.

THE SECOND SOPHISTIC

The term Second Sophistic is understood with reference to the First Sophistic, which occurred in the fifth and fourth centuries BCE and had as representative figures Protagoras, Gorgias, Hippias, Antiphon, and others (see Cassin, ch. 11). Just as in the fifth to fourth centuries the Greek world experienced a flowering of sophists, so in the first three centuries (CE) of the Roman Empire a large number of men appeared with comparable characteristics. To distinguish the latter from the ancient sophists, the terms "new sophists," "New Sophistic," and "Second Sophistic" were employed (Menander Rhetor, *On Epideictic Orations* 2.411.32; Philostratus, *Lives of the Sophists*, preface [481], 1.18 [507]). The Greek word "sophist" (*sophistēs*) signified "professor of rhetoric" and "specialist in oratory." It was used in both positive and pejorative senses, somewhat like the word "intellectual" in modern languages.

The Second Sophistic was not an organized movement but a multitude of individual currents united by a common spirit, the shared practice of educational and intellectual institutions, and numerous personal contacts. No official list of the sophists of the Second Sophistic, therefore, exists: it is a phenomenon with shifting contours (Bowersock 1969; Anderson 1993; Pernot 2005: 128–201; Whitmarsh 2005).

Philostratus's *Lives of the Sophists* (230 CE) provides the best description of the Second Sophistic (see Wright 1921). It presents roughly 40 biographies of sophists from the imperial period, from Nicetes of Smyrna (second half of the first century CE) to Aspasius of Ravenna (beginning of the third century CE). Philostratus covers the careers of the sophists, their connections with their teachers, students, and colleagues, and the role they played in public life. He focuses especially on describing their teaching, depicting their oratorical style, and recalling their most memorable contributions. We possess today some works of about 10 of the 40 sophists: Polemo (Swain 2007); Herodes Atticus (Tobin 1997); Hermogenes (Heath 1995; Kennedy 2005; Patillon 2008); Aelius Aristides (Behr 1981–6; Pernot 1997); Hadrian of Tyre; Pollux of Naucratis; Rufus; Aelian; Apsines (Patillon 2001); and the sophist-philosophers Favorinus and Dio of Prusa, nicknamed Chrysostom or "golden-mouthed" (Cohoon and Crosby 1932–51; Jones 1978). Additional entries would include Lucian (Jones 1986; Mestre and Gómez 2010), who was close to the Second Sophistic in many ways but whom Philostratus does not mention, and Philostratus himself (Bowie and Elsner 2009). Besides the literary sources, archaeology, papyri, coinage, and, above all, inscriptions enhance our knowledge of the sophistic movement considerably.

The Second Sophistic was not a radical innovation but a gradual development within a specific political and social context. The Greek-speaking East, especially the province of Asia, exhausted at the end of the Roman Republic, recovered peace, comfort, and prestige under the Roman Empire. In this renaissance of the Greek world, which the imperial government fostered, the sophists played a central role: more numerous than ever, they became officials and enjoyed unprecedented oratorical and political authority. The second century, in particular, represented an apogee for the Empire in prosperity, security, and ease of communication. All of these elements were conducive to culture, especially the sophists' activity, which required stable institutions and opportunities for travel (the sophists were itinerant lecturers). The second century was also the time of philhellenic emperors (Hadrian, Antoninus Pius, Marcus Aurelius) who were admirably familiar with the Greek language and culture, respected Greek civilization, and encouraged the development of the Greek-speaking provinces by bestowing upon them economic and honorific privileges and supporting their intellectuals.

The principal centers of the Second Sophistic were Smyrna, Ephesus, and Athens. But these cities hardly accounted for all the rhetoric of the time, and we know of sophists plying their trade in many sorts of cities within Greece itself and in Asia Minor as well as in the provinces of Syria, Arabia, Egypt, at Rome and Naples, and in Gaul. The Second Sophistic enjoyed an extraordinary geographical extension. Yet what is remarkable is how it remained the same from one end of the Empire to the other. It benefited from the contemporary cohesion of the Greco-Roman world, a cohesion it reinforced in turn by disseminating its culture and values everywhere. Lucian's *Essays in Portraiture* (*Imagines*) offers a striking illustration: in this work written in Syrian Antioch, the author, a native of Samosata on the Euphrates, praises in Greek the Roman co-emperor Lucius Verus's "favorite" in Smyrna by using as his standard—this is the common denominator—the artists and poets of archaic and classical Greece and especially the rules of rhetoric.

In addition, the sophists formed networks, bound by kinship (there were sometimes father and son sophists) or by the master–disciple relationship. Such ties, which involved the handing down of a specific kind of experience and knowledge, including legacies of notes and libraries, contributed to the homogeneity of the milieu. They helped careers, too, as in the case of the sophist Hermocrates, who had as a drawing card in his oratorical performances the renown of his great-grandfather, the illustrious Polemo of Laodicea (Philostratus, *Lives of the Sophists* 2.25 [611]). In this way the Second Sophistic constituted a professional, social, and cultural environment, the largest that Greek antiquity had ever known. The principal center was no longer, as it had been in the past, classical Athens or Augustan Rome: the sophistic movement extended over the entire Empire.

The Sophists' Rhetorical Activity

Rhetorical activity is at the heart of the Second Sophistic (Kennedy 1972, 1983). The sophists were, above all, orators and professors of rhetoric. They held teaching chairs, imperially or municipally endowed, ran their own private schools, and surrounded themselves with students whom they principally taught the art of declamation. They gave classes, sometimes wrote theoretical treatises, and practiced the three genres of oratory (judicial, deliberative, and epideictic). They were often designated by the term *rhētōr* (professor of rhetoric, orator).

Rhetoric constituted the core of the ancient curriculum, alongside more specialized studies like philosophy, medicine, or law. It prepared students for bureaucratic, managerial, and political responsibilities (see Steel, ch. 16). The vast majority of the "movers and shakers" of the Empire studied rhetoric. This is where the sophists come in: they taught rhetoric at the advanced level (Russell 1983).

In the Greco-Roman world of the Empire, rhetorical instruction involved two courses of study. First came the "preparatory exercises" (*progymnasmata* in Greek, *praeexercitamenta* in Latin), which were short literary compositions required of school and university students. Next came exercises in "declamation" (*meletē* in Greek, literally "training," *declamatio* in Latin), a fictitious composition intended to train orators and supposed to resemble an oration that might have actually been delivered. At the time of the Second Sophistic, declamation was so highly regarded that it outgrew the strictly academic environment to become a literary genre, a public performance, and a popular entertainment (see Gunderson, ch. 21). Not only students practiced it; so did professors, including the most famous, orators, who used it to keep professionally in shape, and great leaders, including emperors, who regarded declamation as a high-level cultural recreation. The sophists regularly published their declamations.

Despite certain criticisms leveled at it, instruction in rhetoric had an undoubtedly formative value. It was an active pedagogical method that called upon the students' creativity by inviting them to compose speeches themselves (after having analyzed the works of the major authors), to invent details of a case, and to play multiple roles, as in the theater. The exercises were organized in a graduated series, whereby the students progressed from the simplest to the most difficult, from the more narrative types of exposition to those demanding the greatest argumentative effort. Thus, the *progymnasmata* offered an apprenticeship in the structures of discourse, achieved by means of exercises in creative writing (set within precise heuristic rules) and the oral and written handling of assorted texts (see Heath, ch. 5). The students gradually familiarized themselves with the different aspects of rhetoric: the "commonplaces" (*loci communes*) of thematic "discovery" (invention), outlines of argumentation (both to prove and disprove), the oration's structures and components, style, memorization, and oral delivery.

Instruction in rhetoric developed the aptitude for reasoning and taught how to make syntheses of complex and intricate issues. It fostered a deepening familiarity with the classics, aimed at perfecting language and imitating important writers. It developed and put into practice a linguistic, literary, legal, and historical culture. After this formation, students were equipped for the major literary, political, and administrative careers to which rhetoric led.

In addition to teaching rhetoric, the sophists also developed theories of rhetoric. The imperial age produced a great number of treatises on rhetoric in Greek and Latin. This was, first of all, a response to instructional needs, which required manuals and more in-depth works for the education of students and their teachers. In addition, research in the field of rhetoric developed in its own right, in a scientific and speculative manner, giving rise to ever more complex and refined analyses.

The treatises still preserved fall into three broad categories: preparatory exercise manuals (e.g., Aelius Theon, *Progymnasmata*); complete courses covering the entire field of rhetoric (e.g., Quintilian, *The Orator's Education*); and specialized treatises dealing with a specific oratorical genre (Menander Rhetor, *On Epideictic Orations*), with argumentation (Hermogenes, *On the Questions at Issue*), or with style (Hermogenes, *On Forms of Style*). Also to be included is the treatise *On the Sublime*, a high point of ancient literary criticism, by an unknown author traditionally called Pseudo-Longinus.

A third rhetorical activity of the sophists was public oratory. The Greek sophists of the imperial age had an important, and often lucrative, legal practice, pleading cases before local jurisdictions, before imperial representatives who handed down justice as the emperor's proxies (e.g., governors, legates), or before the imperial tribunal, where they defended their own interests or those of their city or province.

In the deliberative genre, sophists used their eloquence in the provinces, before cities' local councils, and before provincial assemblies. While major administrative, political, and military decisions rested with the central power, provincial assemblies composed of representatives from the province's cities were responsible for all sorts of important questions that local authorities preferred to handle among themselves without the intervention of Roman authority. Dio of Prusa's *Bithynian Discourses* (ca. 100 CE) provides a good example of deliberative rhetoric. It includes four orations on the topic of concord (*On Concord*), delivered in different cities of Bithynia, and 10 orations delivered before Prusa's political bodies (assembly or council) on various issues. These orations, representing only a fraction of Dio's public involvements during the period, demonstrate rhetoric's important role in municipal life.

Alongside the judicial and deliberative genres, the imperial age witnessed the rise of epideictic rhetoric (Pernot 1993, 1997). The name of this oratorical genre means "display" or "ceremony" (an *epideixis* is an exhibition, lecture, or oratorical demonstration), and the encomium (Greek *enkōmion*, Latin *laus*) traditionally defines its content. The different types of encomium include the encomium of the gods, or hymn (*hymnos*); the encomium of countries and cities; the encomium of human individuals; and, finally, the encomium of animals and inanimate objects and abstractions. Certain orations, combining encomia of an individual and of a city, were delivered on the occasion of journeys, whether to greet an arrival (e.g., a governor making his entry into a city) or to bid farewell upon a departure. Other orations, focused on the personal encomium, were presented at family events: marriages, birthdays, funerals, and so on. Panegyrics were delivered at religious festivals and, during the imperial period, contained praise of the festival and its patron god. In contrast, the mock encomium (*paradoxon enkōmion*) was a parody meant to amuse or invite reflection, as, for example, the encomium of a fly, of death, or of baldness (as in Synesius's rejoinder to Dio Chrysostom's "In Praise of Hair").

The new conditions created under the Empire, previously recalled, explain the importance of encomiastic rhetoric. Peace, prosperity, travel, multiplication of festivals, the rise of urban civilization, the increased role of local worthies and imperial bureaucrats, reverence toward the emperor: all of these developments offered new objects and new opportunities for the rhetorical encomium, making it more essential than ever. Rhetorical orations had to accompany every solemn occasion, whether religious, political, scholastic, domestic, or courtly (e.g., imperial or proconsular arrivals, victory celebrations, jubilees, foreign dignitaries). In each case the sophist was there: no beautiful celebration went without a beautiful oration.

Finally, it is crucial to emphasize that the sophists also worked in numerous literary genres and that rhetoric during the Second Sophistic left a noticeable mark on the rest of literature, especially poetry, the novel, history, and art appreciation, especially the aesthetics of *ekphrasis* (see Hall, ch. 18; Webb, ch. 22). Contacts between sophistic and philosophy were particularly important (Trapp 1997). In short, sophistic was bound up closely with the era's culture (Swain, Harrison, and Elsner 2007), and Fronto and Apuleius emulated it in the Latin world.

The Sophists' Social Prominence

Many sophists were scions of ancient, wealthy, and illustrious families and were therefore influential in many settings (Bowersock 1969; Bowie 1982). They were influential in their cities, where they performed official functions and were noted for their benefactions to the community. Sophists were also influential amid the Roman aristocracy, where they made use of networks of friends among senators, proconsuls, and other powerful individuals, themselves often hailing from the Greek region of the Empire. In addition, sophists were also powerful members in the imperial bureaucracy, where they held the posts *ab epistulis* (imperial secretary for Greek correspondence) and *advocatus fisci* (advocate for the treasury) and pursued successful careers as prefects, legates, procurators, and consuls. Finally, the sophists exercised influence over the emperor himself, before whom they led embassies and with whom the greatest among them—Dio of Prusa, Polemo, Herodes Atticus, Aelius Aristides—had personal ties.

This coupling of the sophists' profession and social influence is an interesting phenomenon in the history of rhetoric. To be sure, it was not necessary to be a sophist to succeed in the Roman Empire, and, conversely, there existed, alongside the sophistic stars described by Philostratus, numerous less socially prominent sophists. But there was a group of men, those most in the public eye, who united these two marks of accomplishment. Professional involvement with sophistic was thus neither a necessary nor sufficient condition to be a "player" in society, but sophistic and social influence went hand in hand. There is nothing surprising in this, inasmuch as rhetoric is what defines sophistic. A sophist was not a man of letters or a specialist in some technical skill cut off from the world. His realm was public speech—for the ancients, the very instrument of political and social life. The man who mastered speech, and who conveyed this mastery to others, was a model useful to the community and worthy of success. Through rhetoric, the sophist's art achieved the alliance of knowledge and power (Pernot 2003).

Issues of Interpretation

The Second Sophistic constitutes a lively field of research among scholars in the various branches of ancient studies. It is an area in which knowledge has made significant progress in recent decades, opening up new avenues of research and new ways of interpretation. One of these burgeoning areas of research is that of gender. Some recent works on Greco-Roman rhetoric have emphasized that the teaching of rhetoric participated in the division of roles between the sexes in society (Gleason 1995; Richlin 1997; Gunderson 2000). This teaching was meant for male students, since the orator's role was reserved for men. Consequently, the schools of rhetoric were tantamount to schools of manliness. They inculcated in young men a certain conception of what a man was supposed to be: the appropriate way for him to speak, to choose his ideas and words, to modulate his voice, to dress, to carry himself, and so forth. Rhetoric therefore reflected and contributed to maintaining the sexism that reigned in society, conveying and articulating the norms relative to manliness and the image made of it.

Another area of research concerns the tension between antiquarianism and self-affirmation. The Second Sophistic was founded on the concept of *paideia* (education, culture), encompassing the reading and explication of classic authors and study of the language, history, and aesthetic, intellectual, and ethical values of archaic and classical Greece: in short, an entire patrimony more than half a millennium old. *Paideia* led to *mimēsis* (imitation), consisting in using a language as similar as possible to that of the Attic Greek authors of the fifth and fourth centuries BCE (a phenomenon called Atticism) and in immersing oneself in the past (see Cassin, ch. 11). The veneration of the past was already criticized when it went too far. The philosopher Demonax, for example, berated an unknown author who wanted to be super Attic (*hyperattikōs*) by saying to him: "I asked you now, but you answer me as if I had asked in Agamemnon's day" (Lucian, *Demonax* 26; cf. *A Professor in Public Speaking* 18).

There was a time when scholarship portrayed the Second Sophistic as an antiquarian movement and the Greeks of the imperial age as seeking refuge in an idealized past. At first glance, Atticism and *mimēsis* can seem empty and artificial, and it explains why one spoke of anachronism and sterile obsession with an illustrious heritage. Today, however, most scholars think that the desire to assert Greek identity within the Roman Empire explains the Greeks' fixation on their past (Bowie 1970; Swain 1996; Goldhill 2001). Even as the Greek-speaking provinces submitted to Rome's political and military dominance, they demanded in return to be respected and recognized as Greeks. By affirming their culture, they asserted a claim: not a claim of independence (that was excluded) but a claim of respect and privileges. The Romans, for their part, accepted this claim because they were not putting their empire at risk and because Roman elites were bilingual and positively disposed to Greek culture. The Second Sophistic thus played an animating role in this self-affirmation of the Greeks at the heart of the Roman Empire. Indeed, the sophists were the spokesmen of Greek culture. With all their activity dependent on Greek language, literature, history, and political and ethical values, they represented and protected Greek identity in the face of Roman power. Viewed in this light, the Second Sophistic contributed to the equilibrium between Greeks and Romans within the Empire.

A third area of new scholarship on the Second Sophistic concerns the so-called decline of oratory. The famous analyses of Tacitus in *Dialogus de oratoribus* popularized a historical framework in which rhetoric allegedly lost its effectiveness and pertinence under the Empire. A decline ensued, owing principally to the new political conditions. Whereas previously, under the Republic, the stakes of public life elicited important orations, the imperial regime, by imposing order, deprived rhetoric of its most important topics and causes, leaving it nothing more to discuss. The Greek cities, deprived of their liberty by Roman military conquest, no longer had any possibility for independent initiative. Greek politicians wound up with an ability to act that was far inferior to what they had enjoyed previously, and as a consequence rhetoric lost its content.

However, the problematic of the "decline" of oratory and its implicit value judgment is probably not the best way to envisage the question. It would be more accurate to say that a mutation came about, a series of transformations, shifts in emphasis, and innovations that make up a different landscape (see Dominik, ch. 12). The Second Sophistic belongs precisely to this landscape.

On one hand, avenues remained open for political eloquence. As seen already, there were many occasions for judicial and deliberative speeches. Plutarch analyzed this situation in a treatise called *Advice on Public Life* (*Politika Paraggelmata*), in which he describes the places amenable to rhetoric in the Greek cities of the imperial age: public trials against adversaries, embassies to the emperor, civic institutional reforms (which required speeches before the council or assembly), and calls for concord (like the orations titled *On Concord* preserved among the works of Dio of Prusa and Aelius Aristides).

On the other hand, ceremonial oratory developed tremendously during the Second Sophistic. A poor relation in the classical period, obscure in the Hellenistic age, and still retiring at Rome, the epideictic genre triumphed in the Greek world of the first centuries CE. This development is quite the opposite of any occurrence of decline.

Epideictic oratory, consisting of the various types of encomia, was a way of functioning that affected all of society and needs to be recognized in all its complexity. It constituted, as speech governed by custom, an element of political, religious, familial, or social rituals. Encomia proclaimed honor and glory, and that was very important in ancient societies. Epideictic had a performative and ceremonial function. In addition, the content itself of rhetorical praise conveyed messages. It set forth models, and its principal aim was to reinforce public adherence to accepted and recognized values. Gods, cities, sovereigns, leading lights, institutions: it praised what everyone already respected or was thought to respect. Its function was constantly to reaffirm and recreate consensus around ruling values. The imperial age took encomium seriously. An official oration, governed by custom or by law, delivered most often by a commissioned orator speaking in the name of a group, was a social rite that affirmed the group's standards. Its ideological content consisted of ethical, political, and religious values expressed in beautiful language liberally enhanced with historical and cultural references.

Thus, in the field of rhetoric, as in some others, the Principate marked a mutation or, more precisely, a redeployment of oratorical forms across the *oikoumenē*. In this way the Greek world built for itself a rhetoric adapted to its new condition. It established a new world order of rhetoric.

Yet another promising field of investigation concerns the concept of figured speech (in Greek, *eskhēmatismenos logos*, in Latin, *figuratus sermo, figurata oratio*). The word "figure" does not refer here to the figures of style but to the form or mannered orientation given to a speech. Figured speech denotes cases in which the orator uses false appearances to disguise his intent, employing "double talk" to make his desired point obliquely. This was an important area of rhetoric that was studied by many Greek and Latin theorists, and it held a place in the training of orators in the form of figured declamation, an exercise in fictitious figured speech (cf. Quintilian, *The Orator's Education* 9.2.65–99; Hermogenes(?), *On Invention* 4.13, *On Method* 22; Pseudo-Dionysius of

Halicarnassus, *Rhetoric* 8–9; Apsines, *On Figured Problems*). Figured speech was quite fashionable in the schools of rhetoric during the Empire.

Given its importance, it seems legitimate to investigate the body of sophistic orations for texts demanding to be read as figured speeches, whether in the strictly technical sense of the term or more generally in the sense of speeches with false appearances or double meaning. Obviously, considerable prudence in interpretation is required, because subtexts, by definition, are difficult to discern and analyze (Pernot 2008).

Rhetorical discourses on tyrants provide a clear example. Two passages in the historian Cassius Dio show us the emperors Gaius Caligula and Domitian reading rhetorical texts on tyrants "figuratively": "[Gaius] banished Carrinas Secundus, an orator, for delivering a speech against tyrants as a rhetorical exercise"; "Maternus, a sophist, was put out of the way because in a practice speech he had said something against tyrants" (*Roman History* 59.20.6, 67.12.5). In both cases, the targeted speeches were academic exercises developing a theme against tyranny. They probably belonged to the so-called commonplace (*locus communis*) exercise in the *progymnasmata* that consisted of a tirade involving "amplification" or the "building up" of indignation, an exercise that could in fact have tyrants for its subject (Aelius Theon, *Progymnasmata* 106.8). Although the orator criticized tyrants in the abstract, without naming any names, he could be suspected of aiming at a particular case, in accordance with a rhetorical procedure that involved speaking "in general" (*katholou*) to avoid offending those being addressed (Tiberius Rhetor, *On the Figures of Demosthenes* 21). The two passages from Dio confirm, therefore, the possibility of political subtexts in rhetorical discourses.

Such subtexts appear to have been frequent during the Second Sophistic in Greek orations on Rome and Roman power and notably in encomia. Rhetorical speech was a refined, coded instrument that served not only to express enthusiastic loyalty but also to send veiled messages, to present requests, to negotiate, even to criticize, as some examples show. Thus, in Menander Rhetor's theory of the ambassadorial oration addressed to the emperor (*presbeutikos*), he advises the ambassador to praise the emperor not only to win the latter's goodwill but above all to remind him of his previous benefactions that he ought to feel bound to repeat in the present circumstances (*On Epideictic Orations* 2.423–4). Praise serves here to press a request.

Dio of Prusa's *Third Discourse on Kingship* begins with praise of Emperor Trajan (3–11), but the orator very quickly interrupts himself to develop a tirade against flattery (12–24). The speech then changes into a philosophical treatise on monarchy and the ideal ruler, with Trajan implicitly in mind. Thanks to these detours, the sophist-philosopher displays his reluctance to resort to rhetoric and suggests the impossibility of making an encomium of the emperor. By implication, Dio reminds Trajan (as he does in the other discourses on the topic of kingship [*On Kingship*]) that the emperor is not perfect, that he ought not to listen to flatterers, and that, on the contrary, he ought to improve himself, imitate good models, and profit from admonitions.

Glaring omissions characterize the oration, *In Praise of Rome*, by Aelius Aristides, whose purpose is to celebrate the city of Rome and its empire. He employs the technique of telling silence, whereby an orator says nothing explicit when confronting a well-known, awkward situation about which he does not have the right to speak and that he can mention only indirectly (Quintilian, *The Orator's Education* 9.2.67, 97; Hermogenes, *On Invention* 4.13; Apsines, *On Figured Problems* 27). First, Aristides chooses to consider only the current state of affairs, the present functioning of the Empire in the political realm, which in turn leads him to avoid resolutely all local color and all artistic, religious, mythological, and historical features. The only fact that interests the orator is the power Rome exerted over the Empire and, more specifically, Rome's relations with the Greek-speaking provinces, provinces to which he belonged. Thus, he imposes a Hellenocentric point of view, reducing Rome to just a governing power, to the neglect of everything else. Then, concerning Rome's empire, Aristides avoids speaking of the military and political process by which Rome succeeded in dominating the Greek world. Here again the speech displays a remarkable series of omissions. Since everyone knew the situation, Aristides prefers not to discuss it openly. Aristides tempers his praise, and he focuses on what he approves, namely, the material benefits of the Roman peace. As for the rest, he hints at his meaning, suggesting that Roman culture does not count for much in Greek eyes and that Roman dominance must be borne with resignation.

In general, all the sophistic speeches on Rome, beyond these particular instances, represent a Greek point of view about Rome. The orators addressed the fact of Rome in their own manner, with their own individual means: the Greek language, the Attic dialect, and the literary, mythological, and historical references of their *paideia*. This *interpretatio Graeca* demonstrates the desire of Greek orators to consider the fact of Rome through the structural categories of their own thought and to acclimate themselves to Rome by submitting it to their Greek standards. It was a rhetorical appropriation of the Empire.

When it comes to Greek rhetoric in the Roman Empire, then, one must not trust in appearances. Through the encomium a type of negotiation unfolded. The encomia of the sophists, written in Greek, by Greeks, in the name of Greek interests, proposed a proud and self-interested reading of the Empire's reality; they set down the terms of Hellenic adherence to Roman domination. On the question of the rapport between Greek-speaking elites and Roman authority, a tricky issue, rhetoric provided muffled forms of expression and ambiguous discourses in which expectations, bargaining terms, and cracks appeared beneath the surface of the most enthusiastic approval.

One might wonder what the Romans made of all this. Probably one should not overestimate the impact of Greek oratory on the Romans. To be sure, there were Romans educated in both languages and philhellenic emperors, but the Roman bureaucracy had other concerns and other priorities than Greek rhetoric. Rome tolerated talk.

A final interpretative issue involving the Second Sophistic concerns religious rhetoric. Religious oratory represented a considerable part of the sophists' rhetorical activity. The sophists delivered panegyrics and hymns at ceremonies. Polemo, for example, was invited by Emperor Hadrian to give the address for the inauguration of the temple of Olympian Zeus at Athens: "He fixed his gaze, as was his custom, on the thoughts that were already taking their place in his mind, and then flung himself into his speech, and delivered a long and admirable discourse from the base of the temple" (Philostratus, *Lives of the Sophists* 1.25 [533]). Speeches often began and ended with a prayer. In preparatory exercises and in actual orations, the sophists often narrated, criticized, and interpreted myths and rites.

In the rhetorical culture of the Empire, themes of religious philosophy (of Stoic and Platonic derivation) often appear in speeches, and there is a tendency to monotheism, based on demonology, and to sun worship and theosophy. Aristides famously compared Demosthenes to Hermes: "Demosthenes, who, I should say, came down to mankind as an image of a Hermes of oratory" (*In Defense of the Four* 663; cf. Pernot 2006: 129–75). By citing Demosthenes, Aristides was referring to rhetoric's classic model, the orator par excellence, as *paideia* and *mimēsis* defined it. But at the same time, by introducing Hermes Logios as a point of comparison, Aristides was exposing his example to a mystical conception of rhetoric and to hermeticism. That is why this comparison interested the authors of late antiquity, especially the Neoplatonists, who cited and recycled it frequently.

The works of Aristides offer the example of a lifetime's experience of a religion both personal and anxious, a demanding and mystic regimen that is forcefully expressed in the *Sacred Tales* and the *Hymns*. Aristides consecrated himself completely to the god Asclepius, from whom he received aid and support throughout his life. Nor was this devotion separate from his sophistic career. Aristides was not a religious devotee at one moment and a sophist at another. On the contrary, these two aspects were closely connected because the protection of Asclepius applied as much to Aristides's oratorical talent and public career as to his physical health.

The Second Sophistic witnessed intimate and exaggerated forms of devotion. Polemo of Laodicea frequented, like Aristides, Asclepius's sanctuary at Pergamum, and he dedicated there a statue to Demosthenes at the behest of the god received in a dream. The sophist Antiochos went to the sanctuary of Asclepius in his homeland, at Aigeai, and there conversed with the god day and night (Philostratus, *Lives of the Sophists* 2.4.1 [568]). Such instances permit us to see how the sophists, as sophists, could maintain special relationships with the gods.

From here to the divinely anointed is only a step. Some sophists introduced themselves as endowed with supernatural powers. Thus, the titles of certain works of Aristides, such as the *Sacred Tales* (*Hieroi Logoi*) and the *Oracular Sayings* (*Manteutoi*), transform the author into a sort of prophet or divine interpreter. The sophists Dionysius of Miletus and Hadrian of Tyre seemed magicians in the eyes of many, as did Apuleius (Philostratus, *Lives of the Sophists* 1.22.2 [523], 2.10.6 [590]; Apuleius, *Apologia*). The charm and fascination wrought by orations were likened to magical power. Aristides speaks of "drug" (*pharmakon*) and "enchantment" (*epōidē*) in this regard (*Panathenaic Oration* 330, *In Defense of Rhetoric* 412, *Against Those Who Burlesque the Mysteries* 26). Lucian compares persuasion to an invisible chain that holds distant listeners spellbound, their ears linked to the orator's tongue (*Heracles* 3, 5, *Zeus Rants* 45, *Icaromenippus* 3, *Scytha* 11). These examples show that the sophists tended to appropriate the image of the holy man, which gained currency in the imperial period and grew in importance during late antiquity (see Anderson 1994). This was a cultural and religious type represented by individuals who claimed to hold special relations with the gods and to be endowed with magical powers, and who traveled, won over admirers and devotees, and established cults. Such sorts were found equally among Jews, pagans, and Christians. The sophists, in their fashion, attached themselves to this model with their rhetoric.

As for the connections between the Second Sophistic and Christianity, one must not erect an impermeable barrier (Pernot 2002). The Second Sophistic was pagan, but it did not completely ignore Judaism and Christianity. The sophist Amphicles of Chalchis wrote invectives influenced by the Book of Deuteronomy, the sophist Rufinus met the martyr Pionius in Smyrna, and Pseudo-Longinus cites the Book of Genesis (*On the Sublime* 9.9). These texts betray the existence of sporadic exchanges—sometimes peaceful, sometimes hostile—between sophistic and Christianity (see Conybeare, ch. 24). Conversely, Tertullian has been called a Christian sophist.

These last observations reveal how far one must extend the notion of the Second Sophistic after the High Roman Empire. The crisis of the third century did not interrupt sophistic, as is sometimes believed. There were still sophists in the second half of the third century. And there were yet others afterward, so that one might speak of a continuation of the Second Sophistic or a Third Sophistic from the fourth century and beyond.

References

Anderson, Graham. 1993. *The Second Sophistic*. London: Routledge.

Anderson, Graham. 1994. *Sage, Saint and Sophist*. London: Routledge.

Behr, Charles. 1981–1986. *P. Aelius Aristides: The Complete Works*. 2 vols. Leiden: Brill.

Bowersock, Glen. 1969. *Greek Sophists in the Roman Empire*. Oxford: Clarendon.

Bowie, Ewen Lyall. 1970. "Greeks and Their Past in the Second Sophistic." In *Studies in Ancient Society*, edited by Moses Finley, 166–209. London: Routledge.

Bowie, Ewen Lyall. 1982. "The Importance of Sophists." In *Later Greek Literature*, edited by John J. Winkler and Gordon Williams, 29–59. Yale Classical Studies 27. Cambridge: Cambridge University Press.

Bowie, Ewen Lyall, and Jaś Elsner, eds. 2009. *Philostratus*. Cambridge: Cambridge University Press.

Cohoon, J. W., and H. L. Crosby. 1932–1951. *Dio Chrysostom*. 5 vols. Cambridge, MA: Harvard University Press.

Gleason, Maud W. 1995. *Making Men: Sophists and Self-Presentation in Ancient Rome*. Princeton, NJ: Princeton University Press.

Goldhill, Simon, ed. 2001. *Being Greek Under Rome: Cultural Identity, the Second Sophistic and the Development of Empire*. Cambridge: Cambridge University Press.

Gunderson, Erik. 2000. *Staging Masculinity: The Rhetoric of Performance in the Roman World*. Ann Arbor: University of Michigan Press.

Harris, William V., and Brooke Holmes, eds. 2008. *Aelius Aristides Between Greece, Rome, and the Gods*. Leiden: Brill.

Heath, Malcolm. 1995. *Hermogenes on Issues: Strategies of Argument in Later Greek Rhetoric*. Oxford: Clarendon.

Jones, Christopher P. 1978. *The Roman World of Dio Chrysostom*. Cambridge, MA: Harvard University Press.

Jones, Christopher P. 1986. *Culture and Society in Lucian*. Cambridge, MA: Harvard University Press.

Kennedy, George A. 1972. *The Art of Rhetoric in the Roman World: 300 B.C.–A.D. 300*. Princeton, NJ: Princeton University Press.

Kennedy, George A. 1983. *Greek Rhetoric Under Christian Emperors*. Princeton, NJ: Princeton University Press.

Kennedy, George A. 2005. *Invention and Method: Two Rhetorical Treatises from the Hermogenic Corpus*. Atlanta, GA: Society of Biblical Literature.

Mestre, Francesca, and Pilar Gómez, eds. 2010. *Lucian of Samosata*. Barcelona: Universitat de Barcelona.

Patillon, Michel. 2001. *Apsinès*. Paris: Belles Lettres.

Patillon, Michel. 2008. *Corpus rhetoricum* 1. Paris: Belles Lettres.

Pernot, Laurent. 1993. *La rhétorique de l'éloge dans le monde gréco-romain*. Paris: Etudes Augustiniennes.

Pernot, Laurent. 1997. *Éloges grecs de Rome*. Paris: Belles Lettres.

Pernot, Laurent. 2002. "Christianisme et sophistique." In *Papers on Rhetoric*, vol. 4, edited by Lucia Calboli Montefusco, 245–262. Rome: Herder Editrice.

Pernot, Laurent. 2003. "L'art du sophiste à l'époque romaine: entre savoir et pouvoir." In *Ars et ratio*, edited by Carlos Lévy et al., 126–142. Brussels: Latomus.

Pernot, Laurent. 2005. *Rhetoric in Antiquity*. Washington, DC: Catholic University of America Press.

Pernot, Laurent. 2006. *L'ombre du Tigre: Recherches sur la réception de Démosthène*. Naples: D'Auria.

Pernot, Laurent. 2008. "Les faux-semblants de la rhétorique grecque." In *République des lettres, république des arts*, edited by Christian Mouchel and Colette Nativel, 427–450. Geneva: Droz.

Richlin, Amy. 1997. "Gender and Rhetoric: Producing Manhood in the Schools." In William J. Dominik, *Roman Eloquence*, 90–110. London: Blackwell.

Russell, Donald A. 1983. *Greek Declamation*. Cambridge: Cambridge University Press.

Swain, Simon. 1996. *Hellenism and Empire*. Oxford: Clarendon.

Swain, Simon, Stephen Harrison, and Jaś Elsner, eds. 2007. *Severan Culture*. Cambridge: Cambridge University Press.

Tobin, Jennifer. 1997. *Herodes Attikos and the City of Athens*. Amsterdam: Gieben.

Trapp, Michael. 1997. *Maximus of Tyre: The Philosophical Orations*. Oxford: Clarendon.

Webb, Ruth. 2009. *Ekphrasis, Imagination, and Persuasion in Ancient Rhetorical Theory and Practice*. Farnham: Ashgate.

Whitmarsh, Tim. 2005. *The Second Sophistic*. Oxford: Oxford University Press.

Wright, Wilmer. 1921. *Philostratus and Eunapius: The Lives of the Sophists*. Cambridge, MA: Harvard University Press.

CHAPTER 21

···

RHETORIC AND
DECLAMATION

···

ERIK GUNDERSON

A declamation is a rhetorical performance whose imagined occasion differs from its concrete occasion. A premise is set, and then one speaks according to it: "A hero and an orator were seeking the consulate" (Calpurnius Flaccus, *Declamations* 47). What would the hero or the orator say? These imagined occasions varied. So did the concrete ones. Heterogeneity and internal contradiction are, in fact, qualities that suffuse the institution of declamation, lending it a protean "essence" that renders the genre easy to misunderstand and difficult to grasp. Let us attempt to answer basic questions about this genre before moving on to a few case studies.

The imagined case can evoke political or judicial oratory, but in practice it is always also a piece of display oratory (what the Greek rhetors called *epideixis*). The tidy division between the three canonical modes of rhetoric—forensic, deliberative, and ceremonial—drawn by ancient theorists breaks down here. The deliberative declamations tend to be derived from myth or history: "Alexander the Great considers whether or not to sail the Ocean" (Seneca the Elder, *Suasoriae* 1).[1] This premise makes a myth of history. Libanius writes an *Embassy of Menelaus*. A Greek hero from Homer addresses his Trojan foes: Do they care more about Paris's pleasure or their own safety (Libanius, *Declamation* 3.2.2)? Demosthenes proposes that the captives sent back by Philip after the Athenian defeat at Chaeronea should be barred from participating in public debates. This last example comes from a *Minor Declamations* attributed to Quintilian (338).[2] Despite, then, the gap between autocracy and democracy, Latin and Greek, Rome and Athens, the second century BCE and the second century CE, one is still ready to talk about and listen to such things. In fact, one seems to enjoy it.

More common are speeches that imagine a courtroom setting. The court can be mythological, historical, or purely abstract and lacking time, place, or proper names. Defend Orestes for matricide (Libanius, *Declamation* 6). Open anew the case against Socrates (1, 2). Accuse an old man of madness when he takes into the family the child his dead son conceived with a prostitute (Calpurnius Flaccus, *Declamations* 30). Cases that lack context are the norm. Time and place remain unspecified. The parties are generic (a demented father, a luxurious son, a war hero, a tyrant . . .), although the "genre" of this motley crew might well remind us of the ancient stage rather than the typical courtroom. The laws themselves are peculiar to declamation, and they diverge from actual Greco-Roman legislation (see Paoli 1953). Meanwhile, the speeches contain all of the familiar elements of "proper" oratory, such as an introduction (*exordium*), a narration (*narratio*), arguments (*probatio*), and a peroration (*peroratio*), but these elements have been deployed according to a new logic and adapted to a new occasion (see Sussman 1978; Fairweather 1981).

Actual events are in practice avoided. History tends to be remote and fantastical. Even the proximate is approached via allegory (see Mazzoli 2006). Rhetoric had long been asked to defend itself on a charge of frivolity and a dangerous detachment from actuality leveled by the philosophers. Plato's indictment of rhetoric in *Gorgias* is especially eloquent. Declamation offers an even better target for critics of the art: this is all about pleasure, and the community is not a better place for it. As with philosophy and rhetoric, an analogous debate breaks out concerning the relationship between canonical rhetoric and declamation: practical rhetoric both fends off and defines itself against declamatory rhetoric. It also finds itself drawn into a quasi-declamatory game in which rhetoric plays the stern father that would disown his wastrel son.

Who declaimed? The answer is fairly easy: everyone. Education in antiquity was always a rhetorical education (see Heath, ch. 5; Steel, ch. 16). And from the third century BCE on through to the Byzantine era, rhetorical education included a variety of declamatory as well as quasi-declamatory exercises (Gk. *progymnasmata, theseis, meletai*; L. *suasoriae, controversiae, declamationes*). If you received an education in Greek or Latin you had almost certainly both heard and composed declamations (Bonner 1949, 1977). These exercises came toward the end of rhetorical training; a student was asked to compose a complete speech only after being thoroughly introduced to the elements of oratory. And as Martin Bloomer (1992, 1997) shows, boys were rehearsing how to be Roman men in the fullest sense and not just acquiring a practical understanding of a craft.

Quintilian praises declamation as an educational tool (see *Institutes of Oratory* 2.10). His own back-to-Cicero project routinely evokes declamatory scenarios in the same breath as it adduces passages from Cicero.[3] The rhetorical articulation of Quintilian's *Institutes of Oratory* itself even smacks of the declamatory at choice moments (see Winterbottom 1975; Zinsmaier 2003). And of course, Cicero's own education had included declamation in Greek (see Corbeill 2002: 28–9).

But here is where an error in reasoning can creep in: declamation is a school exercise; therefore, declamation is both childish and for children. And what children! But reactionary grumbling is never the whole of the story. There are indeed a number of puerile possibilities. These possibilities are not, however, certainties. Let's face it: Philip of Macedon does not menace Athens every day of the week, nor does Milo murder Clodius with any regularity. In imperial Rome the occasions for stirring oratory are few, even if the would-be stirring orators are many.

Indeed, even if the occasions were more numerous, there would still be a surfeit of ora-tors, especially for deliberative oratory at Rome: impressing one's teachers does not yield a seat in the Senate. Declamation can represent for some the highest rung of the rhetori-cal ladder. Given the differential access to participation in public life in the ancient world, declamation offers a natural point of reinvestment for educational capital that finds its worldly opportunities to be constrained by various all-too-practical considerations.

As display oratory, then, declamation offered more than just a chance for a student to dis-play to his teacher his understanding of judicious arrangement (*dispositio*). It also afforded a means for producing and consuming rhetorical culture outside of the schoolroom, the courthouse, or the deliberative assembly. Assembled instead would be an appreciative crowd. And the question of the hour would be less the guilt or innocence of the accused than the genius of the speaker or speakers: "Declamations, at least those intended for a wider audience, required the skills of an actor. They were essentially dramatic monologues" (Russell 1996: 7). Perhaps this kind of oratory is even more fun than the real thing: these imaginary speeches can even "show up the limits of forensic rhetoric or, on the positive side, the creativity of [the declaimer's] own genre of show declamation" (Hömke 2009: 243).

When Cicero is worried that he can no longer speak his mind freely in public, he turns to declamation as an outlet: he ponders the declamatory motif of tyrannicide. Not, of course, that there are any tyrants in Rome (see Gunderson 2003: 104–10). In Tacitus's *Dialogue on Orators* (41) Messala wonders if imperial peace and tranquility have not killed off oratory: a doctor is superfluous among the healthy. Such musings give us one tradi-tional answer to the question of who declaimed: "The (rather sad) subjects of the imperial age."[4] What else would rhetoric look like under a Caligula or a Nero than some strange hothouse flower that could not live for a minute outside of its contrived environment? Doubtless there were substantial changes over time, and politics affects rhetoric, but this diagnosis is also a misdiagnosis. Some of the Roman elite at a certain point understood their own cultural history in those terms, but we need not share their malaise. The great mass of the educated had long been declaiming in both Greek and Latin, and it would continue to do so. As in politics, so in rhetoric: the Roman revolution mattered most to the old elites and to those contemporary voices who wished to tap into aristocratic nostal-gia as a means of evincing their own cultural distinction and superiority. One seldom cuts a poor figure when praising the classics and lamenting contemporary failings.

The cast of characters from Seneca the Elder contains in the background leading lights of politics and literature. The foreground is generally filled with a different sort of person: eloquent men who have come to Rome (often from Greece) to teach and to make a name for themselves.[5] In many cases, all one knows of these men is what Seneca tells us of them.

Who were these declaimers? Porcius Latro was a Spaniard and a professor of rheto-ric. Ovid is said to have versified some of his memorable sayings (*sententiae*). Cestius Pius was born in Smyrna, but he would go on to teach rhetoric at Rome in Latin. He wrote replies to Cicero's speeches, but he would not deign (or is it dare?) to give real ora-tions himself. Albucius Silus was from Cisalpine Gaul. He taught at Rome and was an advocate in a few cases, but with mixed success. He left Rome and returned home when he got old. Arellius Fuscus came to Rome from the Greek east. He opened a school but seems never to have been a practicing advocate. Ovid studied with him. Junius Gallio offers a story of a political rise and fall. It is not clear where he was born, but his fame as a declaimer and his personal eloquence win him Tiberius's favor and a seat in the Senate. Tacitus preserves one of his legislative proposals, an ill received bit of flattery that wins him expulsion from the Senate and exile (see *Annales* 6.3).

Declamations were given for more than 700 years throughout the Greco-Roman world, in schools, in public gatherings, in private homes. Different speakers at different times and in different places would, of course, speak differently. One perhaps cringed at a school exercise in the afternoon while looking forward to hearing that very evening the witty and self-conscious excesses of one's good friend. Let us make the transition, then, to the how and why of the declamatory art.

Creativity and imagination (*ingenium*) are key elements of the practice of declamation (see Hömke 2007). Both, however, are modulated by the limits prescribed by the fictive context and hypothetical occasion: a law has been broken; a prosecutor or defender is needed. Declamation encourages explicit reflection on precisely how to think through topics and to express oneself on them.[6] A great deal of commentary on how to properly construct a declamation attends the corpus of declamations. Seneca, for example, offers perhaps more commentary than declamation, while Libanius's declamations can have brief methodological comments before the declamation proper begins. And finally, despite the fantastical premises, the commentators quickly identify the thoroughly practical aspects of the case: this is a matter of the spirit of the law versus its letter, and in such circumstances one will . . .

Nevertheless, one need not only color within the lines. Wit and self-display are fundamental elements of declamation. Such features can (and did) lead to excesses. But, for the most part, a lot of excess comes prelicensed by the genre and the rhetorical occasion. The stern scowling of onlookers can be read as a pose struck by people who have their own vested interest in being taken seriously. That the scowling is a pose is itself made clear by the opening of Petronius's *Satyricon*: two (declamatory) scoundrels carp at declamation, and each thereby accredits himself in the other's eyes (Gunderson 2003: 9–12).

Declamatory training, if not declamation itself, cultivates the imagination. The genre can and should be connected to the various other creative endeavors of ancient authors: rhetoric, acting, and poetry are convergent cultural pursuits (Hömke 2009: 241; see Hall, ch. 18; Culler, ch. 19; Webb, ch. 22). Some declamations even stage declamation's own relationship to other cultural enterprises. In *Minor Declamations* 268, for example, an orator, a doctor, and a philosopher each lay claim to a paternal inheritance (Buffa Giolito 2002). Ancient historians frequently took themes set by their topic and ran with them. The excesses of Hellenistic historians are lamented today, and the narratives of Livy about periods of which he confessedly has no knowledge occasion misgivings (see Carey, ch. 4; Ash, ch. 15). But when Horatius kills his sister because she pines for his defeated foe and when their father defends the slaying, the theme and the articulation remind us of nothing so much as a declamation: core values find themselves in wordy conflict (see Livy, *Ab urbe condita* 1.24–6). We hear that some speakers liked to import ideas from the poets into their declamations (see Seneca, *Suasoriae* 3.5). Conversely, the poet Ovid used to declaim, and his own poems are redolent of a specific kind of rhetorical culture wherein one wittily plays the game of persuasion (see Seneca, *Controversiae* 2.2.8). The theme of two of the *Major Declamations* (14, 15) is an antilove potion, and the paired speeches can be read as a rhetorical fugue on an elegiac theme set by Catullus, *odi et amo*, "I hate, and I love" (Hömke 2002: 252–78). The melody's bass notes are provided by the *Lex Cornelia de sicariis et veneficis*, the law against poisoners. When Encolpius denounces the topics of declamations in the *Satyricon*, he fails to note that pirates are relatively uncommon in the declamatory corpus, yet they are a staple of the ancient novel, including, of course, the one in which he finds himself (see Webb, ch. 22). Indeed, the ancient novels are filled with debates on set themes in addition to improbable and morally difficult scenarios that are spun of the same stuff as declamations.[7]

The characters and scenarios of declamation also recall those of the so-called New Comedy (see Fantham 2004: 68–70). Fathers and sons, husbands and wives, restraint and luxury, rich and poor: this is the thematic stock and trade of the declamatory enterprise. And we find the same, although in different relative measure, on the stage. And here we can see an implicit ideology of the genre. Working through these issues with these characters in this way—that is what is important, even if the genre flags itself as "not to be taken seriously" and "a pure exercise of the imagination."

The declamatory tales of excess and transgression show a strong tendency to be obsessed with the reconciliation of the irreconcilable rather than despair in the face of the contradictory. One is striving to make a case for "the right" in a situation that is often very "wrong." A father and a son fight, but they fight over who is really living up to "paternal" values, the actual father or the son (see Gunderson 2003: 59–89; Fantham 2004). A rich man and a poor man are at loggerheads: In a world of unequals in which differential political privilege according to status is recognized as just, what will curb the excesses of the powerful or the dangerous spite of the subordinate?

A hero is allowed to make a wish: Can the exceptional desires of the exceptional individual be incorporated into the fabric of society? There is an imperial allegory here, but the theme also has a more general relevance. These hero cases are common in declamation: a war hero (*vir fortis*) is allowed to choose a reward (*optio*). His desire, however, is frequently transgressive: the man so vital to the state's preservation—and there are few signs that wars are fought for imperial expansion in this imagined universe—picks something that potentially upsets the very order he has safeguarded.

A hero moves to quash an adultery prosecution ([Quintilian], *Minor Declamations* 249, 310). A hero moves to quash a treason prosecution (87, 294). A madman breaks his bonds and fights bravely and asks to be restored to the community (295). A hero father fails to pick a reward; his wastrel son brings a charge of madness (367). A father and a son are both heroes: Who will get to make his wish (258)? A hero father seeks to avoid the obligation to kill his deserter son (315).[8] One notices a strong tendency to explore the relationship between two favorite topics or commonplaces (*loci communes*): the privileges of generations and the privileges of accomplishment.

The Master offers some commentary about handling the case of a man who had been accused of treason, convicted, and exiled, only to fight heroically during a war whose difficulties had necessitated a recall of exiles ([Quintilian], *Minor Declamations* 266). After a valiant effort on the battlefield, the exile asks that his treason case be retried. But one is not allowed to hear cases twice. This declamation has a lot in common with others, the Master says. And then he ticks off the familiar lines of argumentation that one will employ when speaking on behalf of this hero: the law does not make exceptions to the rewards one might choose, and it is just for a hero to choose what he wishes. Next will come the question of whether or not a hero can choose something against the law. Here one will say what one usually says (*solemus*): "No reward can be found which is not contrary to some law, and that is why the power of heroes is great: because it transcends all laws" (266.1). Next one looks at the conflicting laws and argues which is more advantageous for the state if one has to be suspended. Further, is it wrong to hear the same issue twice even in questions of public import?

The commentary from the teacher is instructing us how to move around in our own system of values. How can we use the putative spirit of the law against its letter? What sorts of distinctions and exceptions are already folded into the texture of the law? Where can we intervene to make space for our own case? And this case, even when seemingly (or even actually) transgressive, is nevertheless packaged as a defense of some agreed upon common ground. The trick is to find the points of general agreement amid a scenario that seems to be predicated on a tear in the fabric of things.

Another common theme of declamation is the conflict between rich and poor. The mere evocation of a distinction in wealth between two parties in a case works as an effective shorthand. They are typically figured as "natural" enemies: the poor man envies the rich man; the rich man is overbearing toward the poor man. Rather than evoke the vast array of such cases, it might be useful to examine the possibilities exploited within a single treatment of this theme. In pseudo-Quintilian's *Major Declamations* a rich man and a poor man had neighboring properties.[9] The rich man says the bees of the poor man are damaging his flowers. When the poor man does not move his hives, the rich man sprinkles poison on his flowers. The bees die. The poor man sues for damages.

The speech is presented in the character of the poor man and plays up the simple virtues of country life. Its colorful Latin style bespeaks a prose that is deeply engaged with the poetic tradition. Even a basic appreciation of the vocabulary and syntax of the piece requires a familiarity with the traditions of Roman verse. For example, the old man alludes to Virgil's *Georgics* when he uses *vitam fallere* for "(agreeably) passing (disagreeable) old age" ([Quintilian], *Major Declamations* 2.467). Only readers of Horace, Ovid, Virgil, and Valerius Flaccus will recognize such a use of this verb (see Krapinger 2005: 75). We have thus been transported into a bucolic land redolent of Virgil, one of the many rich gardens of verse from which this hard-working minor author has gathered material.[10] The bees themselves have flown straight out of Virgil's *Georgics*. There are also philosophical and ethical overtones to the presentation, but here, too, one can hear the poets: this little lot of land and his peace of mind were like a kingdom to him;

he had riches enough in wanting nothing more (see [Quintilian], *Major Declamations* 13.2).[11] Meanwhile, beekeeping enables a man who once dominated the land and wrested fertility from it—his images are quite militaristic throughout—to continue to enjoy martial valor by proxy: the bees also are a busy little army of agrarian worker-warriors.

The poor man makes himself as small as possible: he is old and frail. His land is worthless. Only his apiary is left to him. Conversely, the rich man swells up to fill the universe of the speech: it is only the two of them out there. The rich man bought up all of the countryside: these farms used to feed the citizenry, but they have all become the garden of a single rich man ([Quintilian], *Major Declamations* 13.2). One can almost hear allegory here: Nero's Golden House was criticized in a similar vein.[12] The rich man is called a tyrant. His desires are unchecked (*inpotentissime tyranne*; 13.4).

The narrative of the death of the bees is protracted and affecting. Here is the punch line: "Then for the first time I felt myself to be a pauper!" The "poverty" of his language and genius is flagged precisely where it is being overcome by his rhetorical riches (Cicero's *copia verborum*): "Who could possibly represent . . . ?" ([Quintilian], *Major Declamations* 13.6). A catalog of figurative language follows this declaration of the limits of representation (*figurare*). So we see that the speech is cunning and sly, ironic to its core. This is a chance to show off one's exuberant genius, the riches of one's education, the bounty of one's relationship to rhetorical technique. As the busy bee visits the neighbor's flowers, so this declamation visits poets, philosophers, and orators, taking now this and now that and converting the lot of it into a honeyed flow of words. Just try to call declamation the poor neighbor of forensic oratory.

We hear stirring phrases like, "You suffered a loss? There was the law, the forum, a judge, unless, of course, you are ashamed to lay a legal claim" ([Quintilian], *Major Declamations* 13.11). Words like "law," "forum," and "judge" ring out and sound good, but one pointedly need not ask any follow-up questions: Which version of Rome's Forum, exactly? The pauper continues by fantasizing about a class war: if this man gets away with it, then the servitude of the plebs beneath the dominion of the few is not far off (13.11). In Roman thought, as well as in reality, when political relations become figured as master–slave relations, bloodshed is in the offing. This declamation is no exception. We find a threat of retaliatory violence: if you make my life not worth living, then . . . This oblique and elided reference to murder as well as the fantasy of the enslavement of the poor to the rich conjures a nightmare. But—and this is the point—it is all just a dream: this is not really the case in this fictive state; this is not really the case in the real Rome; and, of course, this is all just fake—a declamation.

A nerve was touched? Almost, but also definitely, "no, not at all." It is absurd to take declamatory absurdities too seriously. Everything, that is, is always deniable, especially what seems most provocative. Moreover, there is a structuring irony to this whole case that forestalls the possibility of a full-scale revolutionary sensibility emerging from it: this is a baroque and privileged presentation of an often outlandish and a specifically literary countryside. This necessarily means that "class" is not going to be receiving especially sympathetic treatment: only the most educated can understand this farm, and an actual impoverished farmer would be baffled by what he hears. Indeed, the specific style, structure, and texture of the speech imply that the only interest one might have in poor men stems exclusively from one's zeal for bucolic poetry as a potential source of declamatory fun.[13]

The speech does much to remind us that it is merely a dream: "Maybe my passion seems to outstrip the raw material [*materia*] of the case, but we paupers must love what we have . . ." ([Quintilian], *Major Declamations* 13.15). Strictly speaking, this is about bees. But *materia* is a word that points to rhetoric itself. Poor though they may be in recognized cultural capital and in worldly influence, declaimers love what they have. And they know how to make the most of what little they have, as well as to insist on a real place in the state of letters for their productions.

We have just entered into a "superfluous" and colorful coda to the technical argument of the speech. But the superfluous is the essential in declamation, given that declamation is itself superfluous, as Cassius Severus once quipped (Seneca, *Controversiae* 3). We drift back into rhetorical art for its own sake: How can one praise bees enough? Bees are the very models of men; why do we not have a god of honey as we do one of wine, crops, and olive oil? One's aesthetic verdict at this moment will vary, but it is clear that expatiating on the virtues of those industrious little creatures is one of the chief interests of this author. He would be thrilled to be read along with Virgil.

As this chapter has demonstrated, declamation was a durable and widespread element of a highly rhetorical culture. It could be used and appropriated variously (see Pernot, ch. 20). And it was. Its lack of "seriousness" is, for the most part, embraced rather than lamented. It becomes a place for experimentation and exploration. Nevertheless, there are significant conservative structures built into the declamatory form itself as well as a constant policing of the community of speech by a critical, sophisticated audience. What one finds are less revolutionary thought experiments than meditations on the difficulties of living within the order of things as they stand. It might be fruitful to compare declamation with the treatment of the legal system in film and television. On one hand, these are manifestly fictions: a lawyer barely recognizes the laws, procedures, and modes of argumentation as applicable to his or her working life. Yet these fictions and inaccuracies are less problems than they are solutions to a problem. The relationship between the subject and the law can be explored much more freely and much more engagingly by means of these fictions. That some explorations are more serious than others is likewise beside the point. What matters instead is the manner in which the laws of genre interact with the law itself. The impossible and conflicted quality of subjectivity—both a citizen and a father—is acknowledged and then negotiated. As such, we find at the core of the declamatory art a sort of truth game. It is always possible to sneer at the "game" portion of such a formulation, but one should not lose sight of the other half of that pair.

FURTHER READING

Declamation has long been an area researched only by specialists. Even translations of the basic texts have been few, although the Latin corpus is now available in English almost in its entirety. One would do well to begin by reading some of the *Major Declamations* of pseudo-Quintilian (trans. Sussman), then a few *Minor Declamations* (trans. Shackleton Bailey), and next a bit of *The Elder Seneca* (trans. Winterbottom), especially the opening. One could likewise dip into Russell's (1996) *Libanius: Imaginary Speeches*. This should give a feel both for the genre and the way one talked about it. Bonner (1949), Sussman (1978), Fairweather (1981), and Gunderson (2003) offer general studies of declamation.

Notes

1. For a prolix description of imaginary advice speeches and how to produce them, see Quintilian, *Institutes of Oratory* 3.8.
2. One convention is to designate the author of these cases as "The Master" to disambiguate him from Quintilian. Despite a long-standing consensus against authenticity, however, the *Minor Declamations* are listed in library catalogs as being by Quintilian. Adding to the confusion: the *Major Declamations* are certainly not by Quintilian—they are by various hands from various dates—and they, too, were preserved under his name. These today have "[Quintilian]" listed as their author.
3. A striking example may be found in Quintilian's *Institutes of Oratory* 8.3.22: four passages from Cicero are cited in rapid succession and immediately followed by two from a famous declamation. The account of "quality" adduces Cicero's *Against Verres* (7.4.33) explicitly, but the discussion often reads like a mélange of real and imagined cases (7.4.35–7).
4. A recent treatment of the "imperial" quality of declamation can be found in Gall (2003).
5. The work of Robert Kaster (1988) is invaluable for an appreciation of the place of teachers in Roman society.
6. The corollary: declamation acculturates (see Bloomer 1997). It also offers schooling in gender (Richlin 1997).
7. Another cultural connection: declamation and logic (see Calboli 2007).
8. Betrayal, heroism, and family ties also appear in *Minor Declamations* (361, 375, 387).
9. Readers should consult Krapinger's (2005) translation and commentary on this case. Non-Anglophone readers of the *Major Declamations* will soon find themselves—after centuries of dearth—with an embarrassment of riches: a complete set of translations and commentaries is in the offing (see Stramaglia 2009).
10. A Virgilian parallel is adduced on virtually every page of Krapinger's commentary. Ovidian moments are also common. Horace and Propertius should likewise be consulted.
11. See Krapinger on this philosophical *topos*. And as Krapinger notes, *me latentem* in the next sentence recalls the Cynic injunction to "keep a low profile" (*lathe biosas*) (2005: 75).
12. See Pernot (2007) on political allusions in declamation. Declamation's air of unreality may be just that—so much air (cf. Gall 2003: 125–6).
13. Contrary to this clash between form and content, consider the insightful reading of Schneider (2009) that explicates the magical and incantatory quality of the rhetoric to be found in the pseudo-Quintilianic declamation about necromancy (*Major Declamations* 10).

References

Bloomer, W. Martin. 1992. *Valerius Maximus and the Rhetoric of the New Nobility*. Chapel Hill: University of North Carolina Press.

Bloomer, W. Martin. 1997. "Schooling in Persona: Imagination and Subordination in Roman Education." *Classical Antiquity* 16 no. 1: 57–78.

Bonner, Stanley F. 1949. *Roman Declamation in the Late Republic and Early Empire.* Liverpool: University Press of Liverpool.

Bonner, Stanley F. 1977. *Education in Ancient Rome: From the Elder Cato to the Younger Pliny.* Berkeley: University of California Press.

Buffa Giolito, Maria Franca. 2002. "*Contendunt orator, medicus, philosophus*: retorica giuridica/giudiziaria in Ps. Quintiliano, decl. min. 268." *Euphrosyne* 30: 89–100.

Calboli, Gualtiero. 2007. "Le declamazioni tra retorica, diritto, letteratura e logica." In *Papers on Rhetoric VIII*, edited by Lucia Calboli Montefusco, 29–56. Rome: Herder Editrice.

Corbeill, Anthony. 2002. "Rhetorical Education in Cicero's Youth." In *Brill's Companion to Cicero: Oratory and Rhetoric*, edited by James M. May, 23–48. Leiden: Brill.

Fairweather, Janet. 1981. *Seneca the Elder.* Cambridge: Cambridge University Press.

Fantham, Elaine. 2004. "Disowning and Dysfunction in the Declamatory Family." *Materiali e discussioni per l'analisi dei testi classici* 53: 65–82.

Gall, Dorothee. 2003. "Römische Rhetorik am Wendepunkt Untersuchungen zu Seneca pater und Dionysios von Halikarnassos." In *Studium declamatorium. Untersuchungen zu Schulübungen und Prunkreden von der Antike bis zur Neuzeit*, edited by Bianca-Jeanette Schröder and Jens-Peter Schröder, 107–126. Munich: Saur.

Gunderson, Erik. 2003. *Declamation, Paternity, and Roman Identity: Authority and the Rhetorical Self.* Cambridge: Cambridge University Press.

Hömke, Nicola. 2002. *Gesetzt den Fall, ein Geist erscheint: Komposition und Motivik der ps-quintilianischen Declamationes maiores X, XIV und XV.* Heidelberg: Winter.

Hömke, Nicola. 2007. "'Not to Win, But to Please': Roman Declamation Beyond Education." In *Papers on Rhetoric VIII*, edited by Lucia Calboli Montefusco, 103–127. Rome: Herder Editrice.

Hömke, Nicola. 2009. "The Declaimer's One-Man Show. Playing with Roles and Rules in the Pseudo-Quintilian *Declamationes maiores*." *Rhetorica* 27 no. 3: 240–255.

Kaster, Robert A. 1988. *Guardians of Language: The Grammarian and Society in Late Antiquity.* Berkeley: University of California Press.

Krapinger, Gernot. 2005. *Die Bienen des armen Mannes: Grössere Deklamationen, 13.* Cassino: Università degli studi di Cassino.

Mazzoli, Giancarlo. 2006. "La guerra civile nelle declamazioni di Seneca il Retore." *Ciceroniana* 12: 45–57.

Paoli, Ugo Enrico. 1953. "Droit attique et droit romain dans les rhéteurs latins." *Revue historique de droit français et étranger* 31: 175–199.

Pernot, Laurent. 2007. "Il non-detto della declamazione greco-romana: discorso figurato, sottintesi e allusioni politiche." In *Papers on Rhetoric VIII*, edited by Lucia Calboli Montefusco, 209–234. Rome: Herder Editrice.

Richlin, Amy. 1997. "Gender and Rhetoric: Producing Manhood in the Schools." In *Roman Eloquence: Rhetoric in Society and Literature*, edited by William J. Dominik, 90–110. London: Routledge.

Russell, D. A. 1996. *Libanius: Imaginary Speeches: A Selection of Declamations.* London: Duckworth.

Schneider, Catherine. 2009. "Le *Sepulcrum incantatum* du pseudo-Quintilien ou les sortilèges de la rhétorique." *Rhetorica* 27 no. 3: 312–331.

Stramaglia, Antonio. 2009. "An International Project on the Pseudo-Quintilianic *Declamationes Maiores.*" *Rhetorica* 27 no. 3: 237–239.

Sussman, Lewis A. 1978. *The Elder Seneca*. Leiden: Brill.

Winterbottom, Michael. 1975. "Quintilian and Rhetoric." In *Empire and Aftermath: Silver Latin II*, edited by Thomas Alan Dorey, 79–97. London: Routledge and Kegan Paul.

Zinsmaier, Thomas. 2003. "Quintilian als Deklamator. Die Topik des *parens superstes* im Proömium zu Buch VI der *Institutio oratoria*." In *Studium declamatorium. Untersuchungen zu Schulübungen und Prunkreden von der Antike bis zur Neuzeit*, edited by Bianca-Jeanette Schröder and Jens-Peter Schröder, 153–176. Munich: Saur.

CHAPTER 22

RHETORIC AND FICTION

RUTH WEBB

"Fiction," for speakers of modern English, is a relatively unproblematic term that often serves as the name for a literary genre, the novel.[1] We have fiction sections in our local bookshops and prizes for fiction, and we even define "factual" literature as being its opposite, nonfiction, as if the fictional were the definition of the literary (Genette 1993: 55, n. 3). In consequence, a great deal has been written about the nature and function of fiction, focusing on two questions in particular: how fictional literature creates worlds (Pavel 1986) and how we as readers respond to a work whose contents we know to be false (see Walton 1990; Schaeffer 1999). Rhetoric, by contrast, is the poor relative, maligned and misunderstood in popular discussions. In the period we are concerned with here, however, the relative status of rhetoric and fiction was very different. Rhetoric dominated the school curriculum, a myriad of treatises were devoted to it, whereas, despite the fact that several sophisticated works of fictional prose narrative were produced during the imperial period, there was practically no acknowledgment of their existence as a genre, still less any coherent attempt to theorize them.

Today, the two are not readily linked; to say that a work of fiction is "rhetorical" has a ring of mild reproach, implying at worst that it is overblown and pompous, at best that it is didactic in aim and in tone (although Wayne Booth's [1961] seminal work, *The Rhetoric of Fiction*, used the term to refer to the techniques used by authors to communicate with readers, a sense that does intersect in important ways with the domain of ancient rhetoric). In the ancient context, however, rhetorical training was not only the mainstay of the education system and a social rite of passage for male members of the elite, it was also the principal source of training in composition, imparting many skills that we would now associate with creative writing, such as organizing a story, representing character, settings, and actions, or manipulating levels of style. What is more, rhetoric—even serious rhetoric—made frequent use of what we could call fictions, as it still does today if we understand rhetoric to mean the full range of persuasive techniques available to a speaker (Danblon 2002).

It is not surprising, therefore, to find that the ancient works of extended prose fiction, which we customarily call novels, frequently use techniques that were taught in the rhetorical schools. The rhetoric of ancient fiction (in Booth's terms) was fully rhetorical. Indeed, certain techniques that could be considered central to literary fiction, such as the vivid evocation of scenes and characters, had their counterparts in ancient rhetoric in the techniques of vivid description (*enargeia, evidentia, hypotyposis*) and characterization (*ēthopoēia, fictio personae*) (on vivid description, see Webb 2009; on *ēthopoēia*, see Amato and Schamp 2005; on novelistic concepts of characterization derived from rhetoric, see de Temmerman 2010). These techniques aimed at making the listeners feel as if they were present at the events treated in the speech—the crime under discussion, the heroic deeds of the recipient of an encomium, or the exempla presented by the deliberative orator—or that they were in direct contact with a character, able to understand his or her feelings and motivations at a particular moment. These are just some of the fundamental techniques shared by rhetoric and fiction alike, illustrating the type of transferable skills taught by rhetoricians. The ancient novelists go further in acknowledging this intimate connection by referring openly to rhetorical practice in various ways. The most obvious of these is the inclusion of speeches, often involving formal argumentation, particularly in court cases (as in Chariton's novel, *Chaereas and Callirhoe* [5.4–8], Achilles Tatius's *Leucippe and Clitophon* [7.7–8.10], and even transposed to the pastoral setting of Longus's *Daphnis and Chloe* [2.15–6]) or pseudo-court cases (as in Petronius's *Satyricon* [107] and Apuleius's *Metamorphoses* [3.2–11]) (see Hock 1997; Puccini-Delbey 2006). Petronius's *Satyricon*, in particular, makes the allusion to contemporary rhetorical training explicit in the diatribe against the artificiality of schoolroom speechmaking (declamation) that comes at the beginning of the surviving fragments of the novel (1–4), in which we encounter the narrator, Encolpius, denouncing speeches on melodramatic themes such as pirates in chains, tyrants signing edicts, and the sacrifice of virgins: "I believe that our hapless youngsters are turned into total idiots in the schools of rhetoric, because their ears and eyes are trained not on everyday issues, but on pirates in chains on the sea-shore, or on tyrants signing edicts bidding sons decapitate their fathers, or on oracular responses in time of plague urging the sacrifice of three or more maidens. These are nothing but verbal gob-stoppers coated in honey, every word and every deed sprinkled with poppy-seed and sesame!" (1; trans. Walsh).

To some extent, these uses of rhetoric are linked to the social status of the male protagonists—mostly young men of good families—who would normally be the product of the rhetorical schools, a fact that is underlined in the use of school rhetoric almost in its pure form by Achilles Tatius's narrator-hero, Clitophon, and the increasing complexity of the rhetorical forms used as the novel progresses (Webb 2007; van Mal-Maeder 2007: 136–7). They also reflected, no doubt, the expectations of readers, with the result that we can see in some open allusions to rhetorical training a subtle form of communication between author and audience, as in the case of Longus's peasants with their rustic versions of the rhetoric familiar to sophisticated readers. Rhetorical performance also functions at the level of the story in that, in the case of a character like Chariton's Chaereas, the mastery of public speech he achieves by the end of the novel is just as much a sign of his maturation as are his military exploits (Webb 2007; de Temmerman 2009). The use of rhetoric by characters in the novel can therefore play a role in depicting the achievement of maturity that is a central feature of the Greek novels.

However, the contribution of rhetorical training to the ancient novel goes far beyond the inclusion of speeches and diatribes by the characters (Achilles Tatius's Clitophon is particularly prone to the latter) or set-piece descriptions by narrators. In terms of the story and characters, the similarity in theme between declamations, with their exotic stories of pirates, brigands, virgins, love, and sexual violence, and the ancient novels has long been noted and has recently been treated in depth by Danielle van Mal-Maeder (2007) (see Gunderson, ch. 21). The contribution of declamation was far greater than simply providing a stock of material (itself often inspired by earlier oratory, historiography, and poetry); it also ensured an intensive training in fictional composition and in the reception of fiction, encouraging students to think themselves into characters and situations and to imagine various perspectives—and thus possible arguments for and against—on a single scenario (see Hall, ch. 18). What is more, its confined and predictable stock of material, justified by the need for students to work with familiar themes illustrating a consistent set of values (the rich man is wicked, the poor man is virtuous), also constituted a model of a fictional universe.

Nor was it just in the special case of declamation that fiction played an important role. Barbara Cassin (1986, 1995) has underlined the importance of the conception of an autonomous realm of the "as if" in sophistic, including the Second Sophistic, which formed the background to most of the Greek novels (see Cassin, ch. 11). But rhetoric of all types can be said to deal in fiction in that it creates coherent worlds that are analogous to the real world of the audience. One consequence is that a story that is factually inaccurate but conforms to audience expectations of what usually happens will be more effective than one that is strictly true but less plausible (Quintilian, *Institutio oratoria* 4.2.34). The predominance of such verisimilitude or "likeness to truth" in rhetoric provoked the condemnation voiced by Plato's Socrates (e.g., *Phaedrus* 259e–60a). However, this affinity between rhetoric and fiction goes beyond the domain of storytelling to encompass the shared assumptions about the world and the social and cultural norms—themselves a form of fictional construction—on which the orator bases his communication with his audience (Perelman 1977; Danblon 2002) and which he in turn helps to reinforce.

In what follows, I will look briefly at some of the specific details of rhetorical training in antiquity that prepared for fictional composition and then examine the approach to a definition of fiction that we find in rhetorical contexts. To conclude, I will discuss some passages in the ancient novels in which rhetoric appears to be used to comment on and question the very nature of fictional creation.

RHETORIC AND NARRATIVE FICTION

The importance of likeness to truth in judicial narratives makes it possible to see them as works of narrative fiction in miniature, and it is clear that students of rhetoric in antiquity learned many storytelling skills when they were studying this aspect of rhetorical composition. The *progymnasmata* or elementary rhetorical exercises (Kennedy 2003) included two narrative forms: the *mythos* or Aesopic fable, which featured animal characters engaged in speech and action to illustrate a moral, and the *diēgēsis* or narration, which prepared students more directly for judicial narratives. In this latter *progymnasma*, they learned techniques of organizing material (the rhetorical *circumstantiae*: "who," "what," "when," "where," "why," and "how") that were then supplemented by the more advanced exercises in description and characterization (see Heath, ch. 5; Hutson, ch. 32). All this training developed skills that we can see in practice in the novels.

However, the aspects of rhetorical storytelling that are most closely linked to fiction in general and the novel in particular are the demands that rhetorical narratives be plausible or truth-like and that they involve the audience. Any rhetorical narrative will be a form of fiction in the sense that it is a coherent, truth-like construction, and the elementary stages of ancient rhetorical training developed an acute awareness of these qualities in various ways. The exercise of fable, for example, required the actions of the animal characters to be consistent with the characteristics of the beasts (monkeys are imitative, ants are industrious) and involved the retelling of the same story from different perspectives in a manner that demanded an imaginative engagement with the story (Bloomer 2011: 130). The example of narration offered by the first-century rhetorician, Theon, is drawn from Thucydides's *History of the Peloponnesian War* (the opening of book 2), and Theon's commentary (*Progymnasmata* 84.27–5.28) emphasizes the qualities of likeness to truth and plausibility (*eikos* and *pithanon*) in the historian's presentation of events (see Gagarin, ch. 2; Carey, ch. 4; Ash, ch. 16). Then, the twin exercises of confirmation and refutation encouraged students to criticize a verbal account on various grounds that sometimes appeal to the laws of nature (possibility) but often focus on internal consistency (coherence, lack of contradiction) or conformity to expectation (plausibility or verisimilitude). Students trained in this system would therefore be well aware of the need to respect these criteria and more particularly of the way in which internal consistency can be more important than strict adherence to fact in constructing a rhetorical narrative. That is to say, they were well aware of the fundamentals of the creation of fictional worlds and the broader social and cultural importance of fiction. This training was taken further by the practice of declamation (see Gunderson, ch. 21; Pernot, ch. 20). Despite their many coincidences and far-fetched plots, declamations do respect certain rules and, perhaps more telling still, play with the audience's expectations of the imaginary world they represent (see van Mal-Maeder 2013).

World creation is therefore as central to rhetoric as it is to the novel. If we move on to consider the audience's response to these fictional worlds, ancient rhetorical theory, as we have seen, was also concerned with the techniques that enabled the orator to entice the listener or reader into these worlds and to engage their imagination. Vividness was a necessary quality of judicial narrations, as Quintilian points out (*Institutio oratoria* 8.3.62). He also points out the importance of plausibility, or conformity to audience expectations, in achieving this powerful effect (6.2.31). The discussion that he includes within his analysis of the *narratio*, or statement of facts, in book 4 of the *Institutio oratoria* is particularly interesting because he brings up the question of the presentation of invented stories in judicial oratory. Contradicting other rhetoricians who claimed that one should hurry over aspects of the events that do not help the case and avoid drawing attention to them, Quintilian argues that in such cases it is particularly important to replace the inconvenient facts with an invented story presented with the *enargeia* necessary to make it appear evident to the listener (4.2.63–5). That is to say, if the orator is going to invent, it is essential that he do so in a manner that involves the listener. Given that these false stories, or false elements of stories, will necessarily belong to the category of the "credible," Quintilian points to the practice of drawing the audience into a false but truth-like story that is central to the project of fiction. The results of this training can be seen throughout the novels, but the openings of the Greek novels in particular make use of richly detailed scenes (twice presented in the special form of *ekphraseis* of works of art) and their attendant effects of focalization to draw the reader into their fictive worlds (see Longus, *Daphnis and Chloe*, prologue; Achilles Tatius, *Leucippe and Clitophon* 1.1–2; Heliodorus, *Aethiopica* 1.1–2; see also Webb 2007, 2009: 178–85).

The discussions in Quintilian and other theorists show that reflection on the relation of narratives to truth and on the nature of narratives that are like truth in contrast to those that are strictly true was integral to rhetorical theory. It is in this rhetorical context that we should probably place the threefold division of narratives into *historia* (true), *plasma* or *argumentum* (false but like truth, the closest that we come to an explicit definition of fiction in ancient texts), and *mythos* or *fabula* (impossible inventions such as Medea's winged chariot or various hybrid monsters and metamorphoses, a different sense of the term than that of the *progymnasmata*) that has been much discussed in relation to the ancient novel (Morgan 1993). This tripartite schema is found, with variations, in various rhetorical and grammatical treatises in Greek and Latin (Cicero, *De inventione* 1.27; *Rhetorica ad Herennium* 1.8.13; Nicolaus the Sophist, *Progymnasmata* 12.1.17–13.1.13). Even though the fullest discussion is found in Sextus Empiricus's contentious discussion of grammar (*Adversus mathematicos* 1.252–65) the logic behind it seems to reflect the needs of rhetoric (on the medieval afterlife of this schema, see Copeland, ch. 27). It was vitally important for the student of rhetoric to understand in principle the distinction between a story that was false and so unbelievable that it would never convince a judge or jury, a story that might not be strictly true but was sufficiently like the truth to be effective in a legal case, and, finally, the (ideal) case of a story that corresponded entirely to reality. The extreme cases chosen by the theorists to illustrate the category of *mythos* have the didactic virtue of clarifying the difference between the categories of the "impossible" (*adynaton*) and the merely "unlikely" or "lacking in credibility" (*apithanon*) that were used as heads in the critique of narratives in the exercises of *confirmatio* and *refutatio* mentioned above. (I have found in teaching the elementary exercises of narrative [*diēgēsis*, *narratio*], confirmation, and refutation that the difference between the categories of the possible and the likely or truth-like is one of the most frequent issues raised by students.) The category of *plasma*, moreover, is commonly illustrated by the plots of (New) comedies and mimes. These dramatic genres, with their everyday plots and characters, were also recommended by Quintilian (*Institutio oratoria* 4.2.53) as models for narrations in judicial oratory precisely because of their plausible chains of events (*ductus credibilis*).

As we have seen, then, fiction, in the sense of truth-like narratives and more, is central to rhetoric. The rhetorical schools of antiquity provided an intensive training in skills that could be put to use equally well in the composition of novels, but, as we have seen, there is also an essential affinity between rhetoric in general and the idea of fictional creation. Rhetoric provided far more than plots and characters or tricks to encourage the audience to immerse themselves in a fictional world. It represented the forum in which reflection on the very nature of fiction could be undertaken. It is not surprising, therefore, to find that allusions to rhetoric and rhetorical theory in the novels often seem to perform a metafictional function.

Rhetoric and Metafiction

As we have seen, Petronius's novel includes explicit discussions of declamation by the characters. The first of these is the critique of declamation at the beginning of the surviving sections of *Satyricon*. Here, the narrator and central character Encolpius rehearses common complaints about declamation, such as the remoteness of its invented themes to reality and the overblown presentation of declaimers. As several critics have pointed out, there is no need to see these remarks as an echo of Petronius's views, and, more significantly, Encolpius later finds himself in situations that are similar to the ones he mocks as unrealistic (van Mal-Maeder 2003, 2007; Laird 2008: 213). A further critique of declamation, with more relevance to questions of fictionality, occurs slightly later, placed this time in the mouth of the extravagant freedman Trimalchio, who interrupts Agamemnon's account of a declamation involving the stock theme of the rich man and the poor man to ask, "What is a poor man?" (see Gunderson, ch. 21). The irony of Trimalchio's claim of ignorance of poverty is clear, but what is more important is the remark that follows. Trimalchio goes on to dismiss the subject entirely by claiming that "if this happened, there is no dispute; if it didn't happen, it's nothing" (*Hoc, inquit, si factum est, controversia non est; si factum non est, nihil est*; Petronius, *Satyricon* 48; trans. mine). Trimalchio's response is striking in that it reflects the vocabulary of the schools in its use of the term *controversia*. Beyond his no-nonsense commentary on the utility of declamation as an exercise there is a further and deeper irony in his obstinate refusal to recognize any category other than truth (*factum*), in the absence of which there is simply nothing (*nihil*). The strict dichotomy espoused here by Trimalchio is at odds with the tripartite division we saw earlier (*historia, argumentum, fabula*), which allows a place for the truth-like, or the fictive, alongside truth and impossible lies. By refusing any place for the intermediate category of fiction, Trimalchio, a fictional character, rejects the very conditions that make possible his own existence.

If Petronius's characters speak openly about the practice of declamation, its presence in Apuleius's *Metamorphoses* is more subtle. The *Metamorphoses* is a novel that constantly questions the boundary between the categories of truth and lies, the credible and the incredible, that were central to the concerns of rhetoricians (see, e.g., Laird 1993; Puccini-Delbey 2006). The adventures recounted by the narrator take place in a world that resembles closely the real world that would have been familiar to the original readers (Millar 1981). But most of these meticulous evocations of bars, villas, and workshops are related through the eyes of a man transformed into an ass—precisely the kind of story of metamorphosis that was classified by the rhetoricians as an unbelievable *fabula*. One particular metafictional game is to be found at the very beginning of the book and forms part of the series of internal narrations that serve to establish the rules of the world that the narrator and thus the reader is entering into. The narrator tells us how, before his transformation, he met up with two travelers just as one of them was accusing the other of telling untrue tales (Apuleius, *Metamorphoses* 1.3). The tale in question is the story of Aristomenes, who recounts his encounter with an old friend named Socrates who claimed to have fallen victim to a seductive witch. The two men agreed to share a room at an inn, and during the night witches entered, slit Socrates's throat, pulled out his heart and disappeared. To his great surprise, Aristomenes found that Socrates was alive and well the next morning and they set off together, but as they were sitting by a stream (in an obvious allusion to the *locus amoenus* of Plato's *Phaedrus*) the wound in Socrates's throat opened up and he died. Aristomenes therefore had no choice but to bury his friend in a shallow grave (1.19).

   In itself, this traveler's tale raises questions about verisimilitude and truth. This latter, according to Aristomenes's version of events, is far from what is normally accepted, involving as it does witches in the night and a walking corpse. The paradox is raised explicitly by Aristomenes in his narration when he explains his thoughts as he lay in his bed after the witches' incursion, believing that he was alone in a locked room with a murder victim: "Who will think that my story is plausible [*verisimilia*] even though I am recounting the truth?" (*Cui videbor verisimilia dicere proferens vera?* [Apuleius, *Metamorphoses* 1.14; trans. mine]). In the world of Aristomenes's tale, a world that is soon to become that of Lucius, the normal rules of truth-likeness no longer apply, or no longer apply uniformly, for Aristomenes is acutely aware that the other inhabitants will leap to the most obvious conclusion, as the doorkeeper of the inn does when Aristomenes tries to flee in the night (1.15). One connection with rhetoric is quite simply his concern for verisimilitude, but the fact that the episode as a whole is close to a widespread declamation scenario suggests that the link runs deeper (see Cicero, *De inventione* 1.11, 1.92; *Rhetorica ad Herennium* 1.18, 1.27, 2.28–30; Quintilian, *Institutio oratoria* 4.2.13; Hermogenes, *Peri Staseon* 30.19–21). In the rhetoricians' example, a man is found burying a corpse in a lonely place. It is cited by Hermogenes as an example of conjecture (*stochasmos*) in which the signs are clear (a man burying a body) but the facts that lie behind those signs are less than clear: as Hermogenes explains, the man could be a murderer (the inference that Aristomenes fears) or a Good Samaritan showing due concern for the dead by giving a decent burial to a stranger. As if to point us directly toward this link, Aristomenes recounts how he imagined all the arguments against his version of events, just as a student attempting this declamation would have done (1.14).

Students of rhetoric were therefore thoroughly familiar with the scenario that Aristomenes claims to have experienced, so that, as readers, they would have realized immediately (as Lucius, the narrator and internal audience, fails to do despite his education) that this tale is a construction born of art. But there is more to the use of this problem by Apuleius. The school exercise would have required the pupils to work through a number of arguments based on probabilities reflecting the structure of what usually happens (one does not commit murder without a motive, for example). The choice of the declamation theme thus distances the reader, who recognizes its artifice, while simultaneously involving him in a reflection on the possible arguments and thus on the possible worlds in which they could be valid. In Aristomenes's case, the norms governing the definitions of plausibility have been suspended: the truth is an incredible *fabula* according to the usual rules, but within the world created by his narration it is a perfect example of *historia*, what happened. The fact that Aristomenes himself recognizes the problem and shares certain expectations about the world with Apuleius's readers makes him a particularly effective and unsettling guide into the world of the novel. By prompting us to envisage a case in which truth is stranger than normal rhetorical *plasma* he involves us actively in the creation of the fictional world of the novel. A rhetorical reading of Aristomenes's story, then, both emphasizes the ways in which it introduces questions of likeness to truth and draws the reader into an unsettling storyworld in which truth and plausibility do not necessarily coincide.

The two Roman novels, Petronius's *Satyricon* and Apuleius's *Metamorphoses*, are characterized by their contemporary settings. The ideal worlds of most of the Greek novels, by contrast, do not allow for such open discussion of contemporary rhetorical practice, even if the techniques of world and character making and of creating imaginative engagement are found throughout. The declamatory extravaganza that ends Achilles Tatius's novel (*Leucippe and Clitophon* 7.7–8.11) is, however, one example, even if the allusion to declamatory practice is implicit. As I have noted elsewhere (Webb 2007), the end of the trial, which is abruptly terminated and replaced by a trial by ordeal, sets up a gap between words and facts (or certain knowledge). I would like to return here to one particular aspect of the trial: the insistence by Clitophon's adversaries that his (false) admission of guilt regarding Leucippe's (false) murder means that he must be treated as a murderer even after Leucippe has been produced alive and well (7.16, 8.8). Clitophon's words, aided by their plausibility (he explains his motive for killing his former lover), their correspondence to the facts within the world of the novel, and his plain, apparently sincere style, serve to create a state of affairs that has its own reality. This is a perfect illustration of the power of rhetoric to create not just verbal representations of states of affairs but actually to *bring about* these states of affairs as fiction (the false claim to guilt) comes to be treated as fact (the judgment that Clitophon is a murderer) and almost leads to an irrevocable outcome (his execution). Within the world of the novel, the attachment of the definition "murderer" to Clitophon is eventually undone. However, Achilles Tatius's ludic play with the notions of truth and fiction points to a different and more serious connection between trials and fiction: the way in which the law can create its own fictions, imposing definitions on the world which have real effects on its workings (Danblon 2002: 73–92; see Hutson, ch. 32).

CONCLUSION

As van Mal-Maeder (2007: 116) has pointed out, we should not see the relationship between rhetoric and the novel in antiquity in terms of the contamination of one genre by another. Still less should we seek out any process of evolution that led inexorably from rhetorical exercises to the ancient novel. What we find is a far more diffuse and profound interaction between the two that makes rhetoric an integral part of fiction writing in antiquity and fiction an integral part of rhetoric in any period. In the case of ancient fiction, we can see how rhetoric, besides providing the basic tools of the trade, prepared both authors and audiences to enter into worlds that they knew to be untrue and provided the codes in which this complex process, and the status of the persons and events it created, could be discussed and questioned.

NOTE

1. The analysis of Schaeffer (2005) shows how varied the meanings of the term in fact are in modern usage.

REFERENCES

Amato, Eugenio, and Jacques Schamp, eds. 2005. Ethopoiia: La représentation de caractères entre fiction scolaire et réalité vivante à l'époque impériale et tardive. Salerno: Helios.

Bloomer, Martin. 2011. The School of Rome: Latin Studies and the Origins of Liberal Education. Berkeley: University of California Press.

Booth, Wayne C. 1961. The Rhetoric of Fiction. Chicago, IL: University of Chicago Press.

Cassin, Barbara. 1986. "Du faux, ou du mensonge à la fiction." In Le plaisir de parler, edited by Barbara Cassin, 3–29. Paris: Minuit.

Cassin, Barbara. 1995. L'Effet sophistique. Paris: Gallimard.

Danblon, Emmanuelle. 2002. Rhétorique et rationalité: Essai sur l'émergence de la critique et de la persuasion. Brussels: Université de Bruxelles.

de Temmerman, Koen. 2009. "Chaereas Revisited: Rhetorical Control in Chariton's 'Ideal' Novel Callirhoe." Classical Quarterly 59: 247–262.

de Temmerman, Koen. 2010. "Ancient Rhetoric as a Hermeneutical Tool for the Analysis of Characterization in Narrative Literature." Rhetorica 28: 23–51.

Genette, Gérard. 1993. Fiction and Diction. Translated by Catherine Porter. Ithaca, NY: Cornell University Press.

Hock, Ronald F. 1997. "The Rhetoric of Romance." In Handbook of Classical Rhetoric in the Hellenistic Period, edited by Stanley E. Porter, 445–465. Leiden: Brill.

Kennedy, George A. 2003. Progymnasmata: *Greek Textbooks of Prose Composition and Rhetoric*. Atlanta: Society of Biblical Literature.

Laird, Andrew. 1993. "Fiction, Bewitchment and Story Worlds: The Implications of Claims to Truth in Apuleius." In *Lies and Fiction in the Ancient World*, edited by C. Gill and T. P. Wiseman, 147–174. Exeter: Exeter University Press.

Laird, Andrew. 2008. "Approaching Style and Rhetoric." In *The Cambridge Companion to the Greek and Roman Novel*, edited by Tim Whitmarsh, 201–217. Cambridge: Cambridge University Press.

Millar, Fergus. 1981. "The World of *The Golden Ass*." *Journal of Roman Studies* 71: 63–75.

Morgan, John. 1993. "Make-believe and Make Believe: The Fictionality of the Greek Novels." In *Lies and Fiction in the Ancient World*, edited by C. Gill and T. P. Wiseman, 175–229. Exeter: Exeter University Press.

Pavel, Thomas. 1986. *Fictional Worlds*. Cambridge, MA: Harvard University Press.

Perelman, Chaïm. 1977. *L'Empire rhétorique: rhétorique et argumentation*. Paris: Vrin.

Puccini-Delbey, Géraldine. 2006. "Les discours dans les *Métamorphoses* d'Apulée: vérité ou mensonge ou faut-il croire celui qui parle." In *Discours et débats dans l'ancien roman*, edited by B. Pouderon and J. Peigney, 141–152. Lyon: Maison de l'Orient et de la Méditerranée.

Schaeffer, Jean-Marie. 1999. *Pourquoi la fiction?* Paris: Seuil.

Schaeffer, Jean-Marie. 2005. "Quelles vérités pour quelles fictions?" *L'Homme* 175–176: 19–36.

van Mal-Maeder, Danielle. 2003. "La mise en scène déclamatoire chez les romanciers latins." In *The Ancient Novel and Beyond*, edited by S. Panayotakis, M. Zimmerman, and W. Keulen, 345–355. Leiden: Brill.

van Mal-Maeder, Danielle. 2007. *La Fiction des déclamations*. Leiden: Brill.

van Mal-Maeder, Danielle. 2013. "Fiction et paradoxe dans les *Grandes déclamations* de Quintilien." In *Théories et pratiques de la fiction à l'époque imperiale*, edited by C. Bréchet, A. Videau, and R. Webb, 123–135. Paris: Picard.

Walton, Kendall. 1990. *Mimesis as Make-Believe: On the Foundations of the Representational Arts*. Cambridge, MA: Harvard University Press.

Webb, Ruth. 2007. "Rhetoric and the Novel: Sex, Lies and Sophistic." In *A Companion to Greek Rhetoric*, edited by Ian Worthington, 526–541. Oxford: Blackwell.

Webb, Ruth. 2009. *Ekphrasis, Imagination and Persuasion in Ancient Rhetorical Theory and Practice*. Farnham: Ashgate.

CHAPTER 23

RHETORIC, MUSIC, AND THE ARTS

THOMAS HABINEK

In his 1664 lecture before the Academy of Saint Luke in Rome, the Italian art theorist Giovan Pietro Bellori invoked Cicero's analogy between the sculpture of Phidias and his own rhetorical treatise to introduce a series of reflections on the role of intellection in artistic practice.[1] For Cicero, the claim that no matter how beautiful a sculpture or painting, we can always imagine something more beautiful still, serves as an apology in advance for the limitations of his own attempt to describe the ideal or perfect orator: no matter what he says or whom he points to, the *orator perfectus* will remain out of reach. For Bellori, the fact that the artist contemplates (and reproduces) a beauty that is not previously present in any single object makes his work superior to that of nature—and of Cicero. Indeed, the entirety of Bellori's lecture builds to the claim that "the Idea of eloquence yields to the Idea of painting" (*l'Idea dell' eloquenza cede tanto all' Idea della Pittura quanto la vista è più efficace delle parole*; [1672] 1976: 13; trans. Wohl 2005: 62): a neat way of concluding a speech addressed to painters and their patrons but also a declaration of rivalry between painting and eloquence and of the victory of the former over the latter. As a slight but significant misquotation of Cicero at the outset of the lecture allows him to suggest, the artist improves upon visible nature, while the writer, or rhetorician, is forever grasping after what is unseen, only to fall short.

Bellori's use of Cicero to privilege his own favored arts at the expense of eloquence was anticipated almost a century earlier by musicologist Gioseffo (Giuseppe) Zarlino, whose influential treatise, *Le Istitutioni Harmoniche* (1592), begins with a silent correction of the opening remarks of Crassus, the lead speaker in Cicero's *De oratore*. Zarlino echoes Crassus's account of the advantages linguistic competence gives humans over beasts and repeats his description of the early use of articulated voice (*voce articolata*) to organize scattered peoples into stable social institutions. However, instead of finding in this civilizing force a justification for the prestige of oratory, as does Crassus, Zarlino reports that the early heroes of linguistic culture "were called musicians, poets, or sages without distinction" (*senza differenza alcuna vennero nominati musici, poeti, e sapienti*; 1592: 1). Bellori seizes upon Cicero's admission of his own limitations as a writer to build a case for painting and sculpture; Zarlino reassigns the virtues of eloquence to music and poetry, the latter being for him a type of music. Just as Crassus and elsewhere Cicero, writing in his own person, will assert that oratory comprehends all other arts, Zarlino will insist that music embraces (*abbraccia*) all the disciplines, including oratory.

If Bellori and Zarlino were able to use the foundational texts of ancient rhetoric to assert the importance of painting, sculpture, and music, that is in part because the ancient rhetoricians themselves repeatedly turned to those arts to explain, justify, and clarify their own field of inquiry. As acute readers of the ancient, especially Latin, texts, writers like Bellori and Zarlino—to whom we might add Johannes Tinctoris, Nicolas Poussin, and others—are alert to the anxiety and equivocation that mark ancient rhetoric's relationship to other arts. Why should eloquence—as opposed to music or visual art—be considered the highest human achievement? If the orator, as Cicero and others contend, must have knowledge of all the subjects he treats, is the same not true of the painter, sculptor, even the musician? Especially in the Roman tradition, the orator is understood to be a creator of ornament who transforms, adorns, amplifies, and otherwise makes special both his subject matter and the linguistic medium (e.g., Cicero, *De oratore* 1.54, 3.104). Yet the very language used to describe this rhetorical capacity is drawn from the visual and musical arts: we learn of oratory's *decorum*, or comely appearance (Cicero, *Orator* 70); of *lumina*, or brilliant flashes of style (85, 134); of oratorical depiction, or *exprimo* (61); and of the creation of sheen (*nitor*) through the removal of squalor or caked-on dirt (115). The work of the writer/speaker "brings to light" (*illustre*, *illuminatio*; e.g., 120, 136) what is otherwise murky or invisible. He fashions language to "summon the appearance" of the object or event he describes (*evidentia*; cf. Quintilian, *Institutio oratoria* 6.2.32).

As for the musician, his work is understood to affect emotions and delight the ear in ways the rhetorician can only hope to match. To Antonius's rhetorical question in *De oratore*—"Can any music be composed that is sweeter than a well-balanced speech?" (*qui enim cantus moderata oratione dulcior inveniri potest?* [Cicero, *De oratore* 2.34; trans. Sutton and Rackham])—there is no self-evident answer, even in the context of Cicero's treatise, in which the claims for priority advanced by musicians (*musici*), philologists (*grammatici*), and mathematicians (*mathematici*) are noted but never explicitly refuted. Indeed, when Crassus takes up the issue of ornamentation he turns almost immediately to painting and singing to explain what he has in mind (*in picturis . . . in cantu*; 3.98). Music illustrates the advantages of variation in tone and cadence, and, most importantly, music supplies the principles of rhythm and modulation (*numerus, modus*; 3.174) that are to be mastered by the would-be orator—and that allow him, in turn, to maintain and direct the attention of his audience. Crassus's view corresponds to Cicero's own view, as the later *Orator* makes clear. Here Cicero's initial use of painting and sculpture as *comparanda* for special speech gives way to the fullest discussion of prose rhythm to survive among the major texts of the classical rhetorical tradition (Cicero, *Orator* 147–236). The musicality of fine prose contributes both to its ornamentation (*ornatum*, *ornandi*; 81, 113, 134, 172) and its cohesion (*apte*; 149, 170, 174).

The attention devoted to music and art across the classical rhetorical tradition reflects writers' interest in both the historical development (or perhaps better, prehistory) of eloquence and the current state of rhetoric. Oratory's evolution from within the broader sphere of song or special speech prompts a need for self-definition on the part of rhetorical theorists that comes to characterize their relationship with the visual arts as well. Prose is first attested at a later date than song and poetry in both the Greek and Latin traditions, a characteristic of the evidence that may in fact reflect historical reality: after all, poetry and song lend themselves to memorization, and hence codification, more readily than everyday speech and thus are more likely to be institutionalized as cultural practices, with their products canonized as authoritative (Nagy 1990; Sciarrino 2001; Habinek 2005a; see Walker, ch. 6). Prose, as a crafted but nonmusical mode of linguistic communication, enters the picture with the spread of writing. In both the Greek and Roman traditions prose is understood to be derivative of song, in effect song minus features such as regular meter and melody—*oratio soluta*, in Latin terminology. If this historical reconstruction is correct, then the rhetoricians' description of prose in terms that also apply to music and song represents not just a borrowing from a parallel, coexistent art but also a survival of an older way of discussing, transmitting, and exercising skills of communication within the new and narrower confines of prose. Thus, Aristotle understands the major prose styles (*lexis eiromene* and *lexis katestrammene*) as variants of the older lyric dithyramb and the musical dyad of strophe and antistrophe (*Rhetoric* 3.9, 1409a–b; cf. Cicero, *Orator* 183), while Cato the Elder, the founder of Latin literary prose, describes the work of the politician/writer as a distribution (*discriptio*) of social and linguistic prerogatives comparable to the musician's distribution of parts to a chorus or the clustering of words into metrical and melodic units (Sciarrino 2001). Cicero in particular draws heavily on the historical association of oratory with song, both in his theory and practice of prose rhythm and in key passages in his speeches that invoke archaic or sacral musical style. For example, the opening periods of his consular speech in defense of Murena are designed to echo the cadence and diction of traditional Roman prayers, called *carmina*, or songs (see Habinek 1985: 158–62, 2005b: 29–30).

The emergence of prose and accompanying spread of rhetorical theory and practice scarcely put an end to the cultural authority of music, despite what some ancient rhetoricians might have wished. Aristotle's attempt in the *Poetics* to tame the spectacular and affective aspects of tragedy valorizes drama to the extent that the latter defers to the orderly and dispassionate characteristics of prose (Ford 2002; Dupont 2007). But the effort would have been superfluous had not drama, as multimedia musical performance, continued to rouse and instruct Greek audiences (Hall and Wyles 2008). The Romans, too, were acutely aware of the overlapping roles of the orator and the actor/singer, with each using body and voice to communicate on behalf of others, negotiate social and political tensions, and, in the standard formulation, please (*delectare*), instruct (*docere*), and set in motion (*movere*) their respective audiences (Habinek 2005a: 94–104). In Tacitus's account of the reign of Nero, the young emperor's preference for musical performance is depicted as coming at the expense of oratorical competence (*Annals* 13.3.2–5, 14.16.1–3). The popularity that accrues to the singing emperor breaks the bond between eloquence and power on which aristocrats of a more conventional disposition had traditionally relied (Dupont 1985; Habinek 2005a: 94–103).

Ancient rhetoric's relationship with painting and statuary is likewise a mix of codependence and rivalry. Orators explicitly seek the effects of "presentification" (*enargeia* or *evidentia*) that recent scholarship has come to recognize as characteristic of a good deal of ancient art (Saïd 1987; Steiner 2001; Platt 2011). Visual art was considered successful to the extent that it made the viewer feel the presence of the object or person depicted, an effect that could, but need not, entail realistic modes of representation (see van Eck, ch. 37). So, too, the orator is urged to show (*ostendere*) rather than tell (*dicere*) the events he describes, to stir the emotions of the audience by making them "feel as though they are present at the actual occurrence" (Quintilian, *Institutio oratoria* 6.2.32; cf. Aristotle, *Rhetoric* 3.10.4–1.5, 1410b–2a on techniques of "bringing before the eyes" and "actualization"). To do so, the orator is encouraged to create a verbal portrait or *imago*—the very term used to refer to the material portraits (paintings, death masks) that he is pointedly advised not to parade through the courtroom (Quintilian, *Institutio oratoria* 6.1.32, 40, 49).

In his eulogy of the Cyprian ruler Evagoras, the Greek theorist Isocrates explicitly discusses the relative advantages of sculpture and oratory as ways of honoring the deceased and turning them into models for imitation. Not surprisingly, he prefers oratory, yet his speech is occasioned by a celebration at the physical monument of the dead king and thus serves as an *eikon* (his term) for the deceased leader's spirit, to match the *eikones*, or statues, of his body (Isocrates, *Evagoras* 1, 57, 73–7). As is well-known, Roman aristocratic funerals juxtapose the wearing of death masks of the ancestors with speeches celebrating their achievements. Such speeches explain the achievements of those whose waxen images are preserved and displayed, but it seems reasonable to suppose, with the Greek observer Polybius, that the impact of the laudatory addresses was intensified by the dramatic visual display of reanimated ancestors (*Historiae* 6.123). Here, too, shared terminology encompasses material and verbal artifacts. Words such as the Greek *eikon* and *enargeia* or the Latin *imago*, *evidentia*, *illuminatio*, *formare*, and *fingere* do double duty in rhetorical and artistic contexts by describing the ability of art and eloquence to shape reality to induce new thoughts, feelings, dispositions, and actions in the audience (see Quintilian, *Institutio oratoria* 6.2.1).

As with music, so too with art: the extent to which a practice is viewed as a rival to rather than a resource for eloquence varies with historical context. Isocrates asserts the priority of eloquence for commemoration because it can take the form of writing and thereby be transmitted to new and distant audiences—an important strategy at a time when he and others seek to mobilize a sense of shared Greekness, or Hellenicity, among scattered communities. But the relative fixity of statuary can be turned to its advantage, as when, for example, the Athenians of the first century BCE wait until their Roman patron Titus Pomponius Atticus leaves the city before placing statues of him (and Phidias) in their most sacred precincts (Cornelius Nepos, *Life of Atticus* 3.2). Present, he resisted all such honors; absent, there is little he can do about them. It seems typical of the emperor Augustus's talent for compromise that his Forum near the center of Rome highlights the relationship between visual and verbal encomia (*laudationes*): statues of Roman heroes were accompanied by inscriptions celebrating their achievements. In this way what had previously been a familial practice of honoring the dead becomes an important technique of civic validation. The program of the Augustan Forum may have been influenced by the success several decades earlier of Varro's *Imagines*, a portable text that combined visual and verbal images of leading Romans. The use of language to clarify and define the alleged meaning of visual representations allows speakers and writers to take advantage of the increasing use of visual communication in the mass culture of the Roman Empire while channeling its power to their own ends. Rhetoricians commenting on art, from the fictional Eumolpus of Petronius's *Satyricon* to the seductive speakers of Philostratus's *Eikones*, extend to new media the Aristotelian project of judging art by the protocols of "rational" thought.

Competition between art forms presupposes and reinforces a distinctive function for each. To focus on such competition—in ancient or modern times—is to beg the questions of whether and why human creativity must be organized, taught, and analyzed as it is. Are the skills of the sculptor or musician categorically different from those of the writer and public speaker? And, to pursue a similar train of thought, are the experiences enjoyed by individual or collective viewers and audiences of a fundamentally different nature, depending on the medium of representation? Ancient rhetorical treatises tend to presuppose boundaries between practitioners of the arts—a sculptor will never be a musician, just as an orator will never paint—but this presupposition is largely social in nature, a reflection of the convention that artists are (mere) craftsmen while speakers are higher-ranking free citizens: for an orator to paint would diminish his authority as an orator. Indeed, some orators did bring paintings into the courtroom, while others, such as Gaius Gracchus, relied on a trained musician to regulate the pitch and tempo of their speech (Cicero, *De oratore* 3.225; Plutarch, *Tiberius Gracchus* 2.4–5). However aberrant their actions might have seemed to some, they apparently believed that art, music, and eloquence could be mutually reinforcing, that the three together could accomplish the particular goals of one.

Indeed, from the standpoint of ancient writers on rhetoric, just as important as rivalry between the arts is recognition of their shared foundation in the structures of human cognition. Rhetoric, music, painting, and sculpture may work with different materials, but all constitute modes of acquiring and sharing knowledge that are both embodied and externalized. In classical antiquity, as in later periods, these arts collectively provide an alternative to philosophies that assert the autonomy of intellection or posit a transcendent realm of the knowable. Although their proponents may assert competing hierarchies of arts and artists, all artistic practices, including rhetoric and oratory, are understood to entail flesh-and-blood engagement with worldly objects. More recent tendencies to decouple language from embodiment may make the materiality of rhetorical production harder to recognize, but, as the numerous instances already cited in this chapter indicate, classical rhetoricians conceived of language as matter (*materia*) to be shaped, measured, and polished and believed that the orator, like the musician and the artist, effected physical changes in the audience through his own embodied interaction with the external world. As Ruth Webb (2009) notes in her study of rhetorical *ekphrasis*, the speaker seeks to transfer an image from his mind to that of each member of his audience (see Webb, ch. 22). The orator invokes in the audience an emotion that he feels and draws upon the physical resources of music and art to effect material changes in himself, his medium, and his listeners.

A key text for understanding classical rhetoric as a theory of embodied, externalized cognition is the third and final book of Cicero's *De oratore*. Although the announced topic of Crassus's lengthy discourse in this book is style (*elocutio*), one of the five standard subdivisions of rhetoric (along with *inventio*, *dispositio*, *memoria*, and *actio*), Crassus begins by proclaiming nothing less than the interconnected order of the universe: "In my own view, the great men of the past, having a wider mental grasp, had also a far deeper insight than our mind's eye can achieve, when they asserted that all this universe above us and below us is one single whole, and is held together by a single force and harmony of nature; for there exists no class of things which can stand by itself, severed from the rest, or which the rest can dispense with and yet be able to preserve their own force and everlasting existence" (Cicero, *De oratore* 3.20). Such claims ostensibly justify Crassus's refusal to consider style independent of subject matter, but their appearance at the outset points to the deeper significance of the book that follows. Indeed, just a few sections later Crassus again situates a fairly technical and local issue (Should we rank orators as a single group or according to specialized performance genres?) in a broad discussion of unity and interconnectedness, both within categories of natural objects and within single arts like (once again) sculpture, painting, poetry, and oratory (3.25–6). Again we can imagine particular reasons for introducing such broad claims; indeed, Crassus goes on to say that the principle of diversity within unity implies that his own remarks—even if limited to a particular type of style—are nonetheless relevant to style as a whole (3.37). However, the fact remains that Crassus, and through him Cicero (or vice versa), has proposed that thought, action, and sensation are all interconnected; that the universe as a whole is organized along the same lines as individual arts; and that "a marvelous agreement and harmony underlies all branches of knowledge" (3.21). The last claim alone helps us to understand the appeal of rhetorical theory—and of *De oratore* in particular—to proponents of other arts. Privileging painting or music need not entail an assault on eloquence if one understands that all three art forms depend upon and give access to the underlying order of the universe as processed through purposive human activity. Viewed from this perspective, the pursuit of art or music instead of eloquence is no different from practicing one oratorical style as opposed to another. As Crassus explains, his argument is valid no matter which genre it is applied to: art, music, and eloquence all make use of shared human faculties rooted "deep in the general sensibility" (3.195). All must be "accommodated to the human mind and sensorium" (*hominum sensibus et mentibus accommodata*; 1.54).

Crassus's theory of cognition carries with it both positive and negative entailments. On the positive side there is the validation of personal and cultural experience. How else does one acquire an art—and through it gain access to deeper knowledge of the ultimate "causes and consequences of things" (Cicero, *De oratore* 3.21)—than through study, practice, and imitation of one's predecessors? "What good will a man be in geometry if he has not studied it? Or in music? He will either have to hold his tongue or be set down as a positive lunatic" (3.79). *Consuetudo*, or custom, is a decisive factor in every phase of rhetorical creativity not because the orator is a hidebound traditionalist but because the accumulated experience (*usus*) of the community constitutes a potent form of knowledge. Thus, despite an expressed preference for maintaining a theoretical tone in his discourse, Crassus concedes the necessity of expatiating on his own biography, in which "public life was my education, and practical experience of the laws and institutions of the state and the custom of the country was my schoolmaster" (3.74). Cicero himself structures the entirety of *De oratore* as an homage to his main character, Crassus, whose death is announced at the outset of book 3, and to others of his generation of Roman statesmen. Practicing an art—here eloquence, but by extension music, painting, sculpture, and so on—becomes for Crassus a virtue and exercise of wisdom (*virtus, sapientia*; 3.65). As the Stoics might say, it is a way of aligning oneself with the natural order of the universe (and Crassus attributes the identification of eloquence with virtue to the Stoics alone among philosophers [cf. Quintilian, *Institutio oratoria* 2.15.20, 2.20.9–10]).

The real rivals to rhetoric, in Crassus's view, are not musicians and artists but philosophers—although again, with the exception of the Stoics. It was philosophers, in his view, who shattered the primordial unity of wisdom and eloquence (*sapienter sentiendi et ornate dicendi*; Cicero, *De oratore* 3.60) by retreating from the public sphere. Socrates comes in for particular criticism on the grounds that he stole the term philosophy, which ought to apply to comprehensive knowledge of everything that is good (*omnis rerum optimarum cognitio*; 3.60), and applied it instead to his own limited practice of eristic or dialectic. In a vivid image that reminds us of Crassus's commitment to embodiment, he charges the philosophers with "separating tongue from brain" (*discidium linguae atque cordis*; 3.61). And (in his account) this urge to create unnecessary distinctions has come to afflict other activities as well, with each art increasingly restricted in purview, and philosophy, even more so than other disciplines, proliferating into multiple competing sects and incompatible points of view (3.62–8). All the more reason for the orator to hold fast to the claim that "the most ornate speeches [*ornatissimae*] are those which take the widest range and which turn aside from the particular matter in dispute to engage in an explanation of the meaning of the general issue, so as to enable the audience to base their verdict . . . on a knowledge of the nature and character of the matter as a whole [*universa re*]" (3.120). Ornamentation—a practice that even the most parochial defender of rhetoric agrees is shared by music and art as well—turns out to be a means of bridging the gap between particular and universal that was first opened and is now sustained by philosophy.

From one perspective, Crassus's emphasis on unity of practice and on the value of generalizing discourse can be seen as a historically contingent lament for the Roman aristocracy's loss of totalizing authority in the face of rising specialization and rationalization of knowledge (see Wallace-Hadrill 1997). Crassus himself cites the example of earlier aristocrats who were masters of multiple fields of knowledge and shared their insights with all and sundry (*De oratore* 3.132–6). But the basis of his critique of the altered contemporary scene is as much intellectual and ethical as social, for he regards the rationalizing practices of Hellenistic Greece and late republican Rome as symptomatic of a turn from experience and as grounded—although he does not quite put it this way—in a dualist metaphysics that divorces the processes and products of cognition from those of the body.

Crassus's insistence on the interconnected nature of the entire universe and, by implication, the ontological equivalence of everything within it, helps us to understand Cicero's hesitation, expressed elsewhere in his own person, to single out one orator as ideal. Although he briefly mentions Plato in his discussion of ideals and ideation at the outset of *Orator* (the passage that so intrigued Bellori), in fact Cicero's understanding of "ideas" is quite different from the one advanced, more or less consistently, in the Platonic corpus. As John Dillon (1996) notes, the theory of ideas introduced in *Orator* is Platonic in name only. The ideas to which Cicero refers, whether of the gods in the case of Phidias's sculpture or of the perfect orator, as in his own exchange with Brutus, do not exist anywhere "except in the mind of the beholder . . . [they] derive their eternity and immutability not from their existence in a transcendent realm, but rather from the essential uniformity of the human intellect" (Dillon 1996: 94). In Cicero (as opposed to Plato) "the artist is not making a copy of a copy, but rather is in direct contact with the archetype, and in a way which is, it is suggested, uniquely open to him as an artist" (94)—even, we might add, if his art is the art of speaking.

Whether we call the view advanced by Cicero Stoic, Middle Platonist, Antiochan (after his teacher, Antiochus of Ascalon), or just Ciceronian, it clearly dovetails with the aims and practices of rhetoric broadly understood. The artist seeks to make present in the minds of others the contents of his own mind and does so through his own particular medium, whether paint, marble, melody, or words. He teaches—and pleases and moves—not by inducing a process of recollection (as does Socrates with the young slave in Plato's *Meno*) or inculcating first principles (like most ancient philosophers) but by studying and advancing the sequence of causes that knits together the entire universe, especially the minds (understood as physical entities) of mortal men. In line with Stoic epistemology, the vivid presentification that the orator, along with other artists, seeks to create, is taken as warrant for the truth of what he says (or paints or sings).

By the time Cicero's view of the artist as one who produces knowledge by materializing the relationship between general and particular and by exploring causation through the manipulation of substance reaches Bellori, it has been refracted through the Neoplatonic lens of Proclus and Plotinus (Panofsky 1968). Yet while Bellori, unlike Cicero, is willing to entertain the existence of a supreme, eternal intellect operating on a different ontological plane from humankind, he still agrees that the "exemplary causes" to which the artist refers are to be found "in the minds of artists, abiding without uncertainty perpetually most beautiful and most perfect" (2005: 57). For Bellori, it is the ability of artists to transform those causes into objects that accounts for artists' resemblance to "that first maker." For Cicero, the man who most fully exemplifies the work of the orator merits no less an epithet than *divinus*, or divine (Cicero, *De oratore* 3.6), an accolade granted elsewhere to Plato (for his eloquence; 1.49), to Sulpicius (1.131), and to Demosthenes (*De optimo genere oratorum* 17) (see Habinek 2005b: 25–37).

Rather than dismiss reference to the orator's divinity as mere hyperbole, we would do well to remember that for many in Cicero's audience—and perhaps for Cicero himself—the "gods" were nothing other than particular configurations or materializations of the universal life-spirit, the ordering reason of the cosmos. A human being could perfectly well be expected to approach divine status by performing extraordinary achievements in the common interest. In this context, Cicero's reference to the work of Phidias at the outset of *Orator*, echoed elsewhere in his writings (e.g., *De oratore* 2.73), in Quintilian (*Institutio oratoria* 12.10.9), in Plotinus (*Enneads* 5.8), and finally, for our purposes, in Bellori, is an ornament of literary or rhetorical style not in the contemporary sense of decoration or pleasing example but as Crassus understands it: as a means of linking particular to universal. The particular statue that Phidias has created manifests the divine force that is Zeus; the sculptor's unique artistic achievement instantiates a universal human capacity to think, see, feel, and understand what is beyond immediate sensation, to create from the contents of sensory experience, personal and cultural, an image to be shared with others, even an image of the greatest god. To call an orator divine is to say that his effect on the material world, broadly understood to include human bodies and minds, is comparable to that of a god. It connects his particular achievement with the more general order and harmony of the universe.

The rivalry between rhetoric, music, and the arts, like rhetoric itself, arose in the context of the ancient Mediterranean city-state. By calling attention to similarities and differences between the various arts, proponents of rhetoric sought to legitimize and privilege their own practices and products. But competition with philosophy, of both a social and an intellectual sort, forced a deeper reflection on the shared understanding of human nature—in particular, human cognition—that links the arts to one another and, in Cicero's view, to philosophy as well. Painting, sculpture, music, and eloquence presuppose an interconnectedness of mind and matter and facilitate intersubjective communication by manipulating the objects of the world and investigating the causal processes that lie behind them. Philosophy can contribute to this enterprise by articulating general principles to which particular events and objects are linked, but if it seeks to dominate the arts or force them to submit to its judgments it will fail. As Crassus puts it, the ideal orator will possess all the knowledge of the philosophers, but there is no reason to suppose that a philosopher will automatically know how to be eloquent (Cicero, *De oratore* 3.143).

Cicero's account of rhetoric as one of the arts, and the theory of embodied cognition he articulated in its defense, did not prevail in all quarters in antiquity. It is not even clear whether ancient proponents of music, painting, and sculpture grasped the implications of his theories or felt a need to. But the survival into the early modern period of treatises like *Orator*, *De oratore*, and Quintilian's *Institutio oratoria* provided an important resource for theorists and practitioners of other arts who were equally committed to the view of human nature and human cognition these texts contain (see van Eck, ch. 37; Kirkbride, ch. 40). As the social and political conditions that sustained classical oratory and rhetoric were altered beyond recognition, rhetoricians' insistence on the cognitive and, indeed, philosophical significance of eloquence, provided a powerful justification for pursuing music and the visual arts as well.

Note

1. I wish to thank Hector Reyes for directing me to the early modern uses of Cicero discussed in this chapter and for his comments on an earlier draft. Bellori's lecture was printed as the preface to his *Vite de' pittori, scultori e architetti moderni* (Rome 1672). For translation and discussion, see Wohl, Wohl, and Montanari (2005: 55–68). The relevant passage of Cicero is section 9 of *Orator*, a work written in 46 BCE in response to Brutus's request that Cicero describe the "insurpassable and perfect type of oratory" (*eloquentiae genus . . . summum et perfectissimum*; 3) and "portray the best orator" (*in summo oratore fingendo*; 7). See also Reyes 2009.

References

Bellori, Giovan Pietro. (1672) 1976. *Le vite de'pittori, scultori e architetti moderni*. Edited by E. Borea. Turin: Einaudi.

Bellori, Giovan Pietro. 2005. *The Lives of the Modern Painters, Sculptors, and Architects: A New Translation and Critical Edition*. Translated by Alice Sedgwick Wohl, notes by Hellmut Wohl, introduction by Tomaso Montanari. Cambridge: Cambridge University Press.

Dillon, John. 1996. *The Middle Platonists, 80 B.C. to A.D. 220*. Revised edition. Ithaca, NY: Cornell University Press.

Dupont, Florence. 1985. *L'acteur-roi, ou, Le théatre dans la Rome antique*. Paris: Société d'Edition "Les belles lettres."

Dupont, Florence. 2007. *Aristote ou le vampire du théâtre occidental*. Paris: Editions Flammarion.

Ford, Andrew. 2002. *The Origins of Criticism: Literary Culture and Poetic Theory in Classical Greece*. Princeton, NJ: Princeton University Press.

Habinek, Thomas. 1985. *The Colometry of Latin Prose*. California Studies in Classical Philology 25. Berkeley: University of California Press.

Habinek, Thomas. 2005a. *The World of Roman Song: From Ritualized Speech to Social Order*. Baltimore, MD: Johns Hopkins University Press.

Habinek, Thomas. 2005b. *Ancient Rhetoric and Oratory*. Malden, MA: Blackwell.

Hall, Edith, and Rosie Wyles, eds. 2008. *New Directions in Ancient Pantomime*. Oxford: Oxford University Press.

Nagy, Gregory. 1990. *Pindar's Homer: The Lyric Possession of an Epic Past*. Baltimore, MD: Johns Hopkins University Press.

Panofsky, Erwin. 1968. *Idea: A Concept in Art Theory*. Translated by Joseph J. S. Peake. New York: Harper and Row.

Platt, Verity. 2011. *Facing the Gods: Epiphany and Representation in Graeco-Roman Art, Literature and Religion*. Cambridge: Cambridge University Press.

Reyes, Hector. 2009. "The Rhetorical Frame of Poussin's Theory of the Modes." *Intellectual History Review* 19 no. 3: 287–302.

Saïd, Suzanne. 1987. "Deux noms de l'image en grec ancien: Idole et icône." *Comptes rendus de l'Académie des Inscriptions et Belles Lettres* 131 no. 2: 309–330.

Sciarrino, Enrica. 2001. *Cato the Censor and the Beginnings of Latin Prose: From Poetic Translation to Elite Transcription*. Columbus: Ohio State University Press.

Steiner, Deborah. 2001. *Images in Mind: Statues in Archaic and Classical Greek Literature and Thought*. Princeton, NJ: Princeton University Press.

Wallace-Hadrill, Andrew. 1997. "*Mutatio morum*: The Idea of a Cultural Revolution." In *The Roman Cultural Revolution*, edited by Thomas Habinek and Alessandro Schiesaro, 3–22. Cambridge: Cambridge University Press.

Webb, Ruth. 2009. *Ekphrasis, Imagination and Persuasion in Ancient Rhetorical Theory and Practice*. Farnham: Ashgate.

Zarlino, Gioseffo. 1592. *Le Istitutioni Harmoniche*. Venice: Pietro da Fino.

CHAPTER 24

AUGUSTINE'S RHETORIC IN THEORY AND PRACTICE

CATHERINE CONYBEARE

THE relationship of Augustine of Hippo (354–430 CE) to the tradition of classical rhetoric in which, as a young man from provincial North Africa, he once excelled, seems convoluted and contradictory. He grew up in a world in which proficiency in rhetoric was the best passport to success. Born to a modest background and dependent on patronage, educated in his small home town of Thagaste (modern Souk Ahras in Algeria) and then at Carthage, teacher at Carthage and then at Rome, his rhetorical powers were such that at the age of 30 he was promoted to public orator in the imperial city of Milan. Shortly thereafter a mysterious *dolor pectoris* forced a pause in his rhetorical duties; a period of reflection hastened a turn to committed Christianity and a return to North Africa. Although his initial aim seems to have been more contemplative, his talent for speaking was recognized by his ecclesiastical superiors, and he was made first a priest, with special dispensation to preach, and then bishop of Hippo Regius (modern Annaba in Algeria). Augustine preached some 4,000 sermons, of which about 800 survive; he never left North Africa again.

At first glance, this biographical narrative seems to tell a simple story. It is a story of urban center versus provincial periphery; of professional ambition versus Christian commitment; of rhetorical success versus humble homiletics. Augustine's school curriculum rested heavily on Cicero, along with Virgil, Terence, and Sallust; in eschewing his secular career, one might assume that he eschewed these authors as well. But the story is far more complicated. Certainly, Augustine developed a distinctive style for his preaching, which apparently owed little to the conventions of classical rhetoric. But toward the end of his life, after more than 30 years of delivering sermons, as he completed his popular work on Christian teaching (*De doctrina christiana*) with a section on "presenting what we have learnt," he still expounded his ideas with reference to Cicero's rhetorical treatises. Even the division between urban center and provincial periphery wavers and blurs. Augustine may, as a restless and ambitious young man, have envisaged a career for himself in the established metropolis of Rome, and certainly the nostalgic idea of Rome remained important to him; but by the late fourth century, Carthage was one of the wealthiest and most populous cities in the Empire, and even Hippo Regius, far from being a backwater, was a bustling port town. Augustine may have been aware of the deficiencies of North African pronunciation of Latin ("African ears do not distinguish between short and long vowels" [*De doctrina christiana* 4.65]), but he also placed himself conspicuously in a tradition of North African writers and speakers that ran back through Tertullian and Cyprian of Carthage to the decidedly non-Christian Apuleius. This chapter examines what is not a simple transition from rhetoric to homiletics but a complex interpenetration of the two, on which Augustine reflected intermittently throughout his life.

The *Confessions* is all too often read as if it contained transparent reporting of events in Augustine's life amid its prayers and theological reflection. The autobiographical passages, however, are selected and mediated according to the theological thrust of the argument. So it is not surprising that Augustine (writing around 397 CE, when he was already a bishop) emphasizes his rejection of the techniques of rhetoric and finds the *ars grammatica* ethically superior. His encapsulation of the moral hollowness of the accomplished rhetor is justly famous: "A man [*homo*] eagerly seeking a reputation for eloquence and prosecuting his enemy with implacable hatred in front of a man [*hominem*], a judge, with a crowd of men [*hominum*] standing around, is constantly alert lest he erroneously say, '*inter hominibus*' [it should be *inter homines*], and pays no attention to the fact that, in his fury, he might remove a man [*hominem*] from among men [*ex hominibus*]" (Augustine, *Confessions* 1.18.29; all translations from the Latin are my own). The determined lack of euphony in this passage, punctuated by the stolid repetition of *homo* in its different cases (the word *homo* being generally an unnecessary expansion in classicizing Latin), underscores Augustine's point: words are just playthings to the rhetor, empty signs to be elegantly rearranged. The rhetor does not pause to think of their referents, and hence, their moral significance. Augustine's misbegotten dedication of his first published work to the rhetor Hierius at Rome, whom he did not know, prompts a deeper reflection on the meaning of *homo* (J. J. O'Donnell calls it "complex and gnomic" [1992: 2: 252]): here Augustine focuses on the affective entanglements of *homines*, the way in which a *homo* may think he loves another whom he has not met, and the peculiarities and imperfections of human ties. He ends with the exclamation, "The actual man is a great mystery" (*grande profundum est ipse homo*; Augustine, *Confessions* 4.14.22). The dedication to Hierius might be traced to wishful loyalty to a man also from the outer reaches of the Empire who had succeeded at Rome: Augustine writes that "people were astounded that a marvelous speaker [*dictor mirabilis*] had emerged *from a Syrian man*, who was learned in Greek eloquence before Latin" (4.14.21).

Thus, in the *Confessions*, Augustine uses the figure of the rhetor to call attention to the moral failings of rhetoric: it fills the empty "vessels" of words with the "wine of error" (Augustine, *Confessions* 1.16.26) to engage and sway the affections of imperfect humans. The turning point comes when he meets Bishop Ambrose at Milan, himself an accomplished sometime rhetor and now a renowned preacher. Augustine goes to hear him preach, and "even though I wasn't concerned with learning what he was saying, but just listening to how he said it . . . there crept into my mind, along with the words that I loved, the content [*res*] that I was neglecting, *and I could not split them apart*" (5.14.24). Here, then, is the union of *verba* and *res* that Augustine has portrayed himself as unknowingly seeking; and it is effected, dramatically, through the interpretation of divine Scripture. It is worth noting here that the very style of the *Confessions*, suffused as it is with biblical language and cadences and repudiating the conventions of classical *clausulae* and euphony (Di Capua 1931; Burton 2007), ostentatiously enacts a union of *verba* and *res* that jolts the reader into an intense reflection on its content—moral, spiritual, and affective (Conybeare 2012a, 2012b).

Once we reach the point of Augustine's (re-)conversion in autumn 386, however, we can read his thoughts on rhetoric as they unfurl—for his first surviving works date to this era—and the picture becomes more nuanced. These works are philosophical dialogues on a Ciceronian model, composed while on retreat at a friend's villa at Cassiciacum: they portray him as simultaneously suspicious of the *mores* of the rhetorical schools (e.g., chiding his students for bickering about superficialities *causa gloriandi*, "for the sake of winning" [*De ordine* 1.10.29]) and yet attempting to reframe the liberal disciplines in a Christian mode (a programmatic speech occupies the greater part of *De ordine* 2; see Pollmann and Vessey 2005, especially Shanzer). Augustine puts on display in the so-called Cassiciacum dialogues his gradual realization that it will not do simply to Christianize his earlier patterns of thought and continue to speak—or write—in the same style to the same audience: he needs entirely to reinvent his discursive practices (Conybeare 2006). In this context, it is not surprising that his grand project to write Christian treatises on each of the disciplines soon foundered: only *De musica* is anything like complete, and while brief sets of notes for *De dialectica*, *De grammatica*, and *De rhetorica* are attributed to him, only the first of these may be genuinely from his hand (Jackson and Pinborg 1975). Augustine is now, he recognizes, committed to speaking to those who have had little or no access to education as well as to those trained in the schools. He first spells out this commitment in the preface to his commentary, *De genesi contra manichaeos*, composed around 391:

> If the Manichaeans were choosy about whom they deceived, I too would be choosy about the words in which I responded to them; but since they persecute with their error not only the learned but also those without a proper education . . . their folly has to be refuted not with elaborately polished speech [*ornato politoque sermone*], but with clear facts [*rebus manifestis*]. . . . [Christians educated in liberal learning] have kindly advised me not to depart from the ordinary way of speaking [*communem loquendi consuetudinem*], if I intend to drive out these most destructive errors from the minds of the uneducated. After all, this sort of ordinary, simple speech is understood by the educated as well, while the other sort is not understood by the uneducated. (Augustine, *De genesi contra manichaeos* 1.1.1)

Here are the principles of Augustine's preaching, already laid out: the commitment to aligning *sermo/verba* and *res*; the rejection of elaborate polishing in favor of clarity; the embrace of the uneducated; the appeal to *communis loquendi consuetudo*. Here, too, are the conditions under which his preaching emerged: the impassioned correction of doctrinal error, whether Manichaean, Donatist, or Pelagian (the confrontation of these "heresies" occurring more or less sequentially in Augustine's life), and the repeated asseveration of Christian truth. In Leslie Dossey's superb discussion of rural preaching in North Africa, she underscores the urgency of the preachers' project: "There was the danger . . . that if they failed to communicate, a preacher from the other sect would succeed" (2012: 171).

It is at this point in his life that Augustine himself began to preach, and in the next few years he would embark on an ambitious handbook for preaching, *De doctrina christiana*, as well as complete a much smaller and more limited treatise on the subject, *De catechizandis rudibus* (*On Catechizing the Uneducated*), addressed to a deacon in Carthage who had asked for help. This he begins with the humble assertion, "My preaching almost always dissatisfies me . . . because I want whoever hears me to understand everything that I do; and I feel that I'm not speaking in such a way as to effect that" (Augustine, *De catechizandis rudibus* 2.3). The problem is, he suggests, the difference between the flash of understanding and the slow, cumbersome process of speech—another theme that goes back to *De genesi contra manichaeos*, which suggests that before the Fall there was no need of language because God communicated directly into the hearts of his creation (*insinuatio*). But being resigned to language, Augustine is immensely attentive to context and audience—to whether he is dictating or addressing people directly, to their familiarity with the material and whether they agree with it. "And again, there is one *intentio* when one sits together pretty much in private, as if having a conversation, and another when a silent populace watches intently as one man gets up to speak from a raised place; and it makes a great difference whether few or many are present, educated or uneducated or a mixture of both, urban or rural or the two simultaneously" (15.23). Augustine completes *De catechizandis rudibus* with two sample sermons—a long and a short one!—designed to educate the person approaching baptism about the essential points of Christianity. Yet neither displays the characteristics of his mature preaching style, which I shall anatomize shortly: they remain more literary than oral.

The oddity of *De doctrina christiana* is not so much that some 30 years elapsed between its inception (around 396) and its completion but that its style and structure remain so consistent across the break that we would not be able to detect it had Augustine himself not revealed it in his *Retractationes* (2.4.1; Green 1995: xii; all references to *De doctrina christiana* follow Green's system of numeration). The first three books constitute an important treatment of biblical hermeneutics for the guidance of the preacher (Pollmann 1996; Eden 1990); it is the fourth and final book that concerns itself directly with the practice of preaching. By the time Augustine composed this book, it had been some 40 years since he had left his position as orator in Milan and some 35 since he had started to preach in North Africa. He refers dismissively to the "incredibly tangled and prickly disciplines" (*nodosissimae et spinosissimae disciplinae*; Augustine, *De doctrina christiana* 2.134) and to the "rhetorical precepts that I both learned and taught in worldly schools" (4.3). And yet, for all that we see many of his deepest Christian themes poignantly reiterated, the framework within which Augustine sets his thoughts on preaching is explicitly Ciceronian. The reduction of the *disciplinae* to their most useful essence is the work of *De doctrina christiana* 4—and, arguably, of the intervening years of Augustine's preaching.

Augustine begins *De doctrina christiana* (its preface was almost definitely composed first [Mayer 1974]) with a reassertion—notwithstanding the association of language with the Fall of man—of the value of interpersonal communication: "The human condition would be abject indeed if God seemed not to want to give his word to humankind through human beings," and love, "which binds people together in a knot of unity, would not have a way of pouring souls into each other and mingling them together, if humans could learn nothing through humans" (preface 13). There are five instances of the word *homines* in this short passage, vividly underscoring the point about the importance of human communication; the idea that God's word and its human avatars is given not *a hominibus* but *per homines* is first explored in one of Augustine's earliest works, his dialogue, *De magistro*, in which Christ is the *magister interior* who teaches *through* humans.

The early sections of *De doctrina christiana* 4 seem at first sight to waver between an argument for the intentional acquisition of technical skill in speaking—because otherwise those who teach falsehood will be more convincing (4.4, recalling *De genesi contra manichaeos*)—and the promotion of a more natural approach: infants learn to speak "by learning the speech of speakers" (*locutiones discendo loquentium*), so why shouldn't people learn to be eloquent "by reading and listening to and . . . imitating the eloquence of the eloquent" (*elocutiones eloquentium legendo et audiendo et . . . imitando*; Augustine, *De doctrina christiana* 4.12)? There are passages about the need for clarity in preaching (4.61) and the need for a preacher to be attentive to the response of the *avida multitudo* (4.67–8), which directly recall the pragmatic concerns of *De catechizandis rudibus*.

Yet the underlying structure, right from the beginning of the book, is supplied by a triad derived from Cicero's works on oratory. Although Cicero is never actually named, he is invoked as the *Romani auctor eloquii* before a verbatim quotation from the *Orator* (Augustine, *De doctrina christiana* 4.96); he is also *quidam eloquens* ("some eloquent man") who said that the eloquent speaker ought "to teach, to delight, to sway" his listeners (*ut doceat, ut delectet, ut flectat*; 4.74; cf. Cicero, *Orator* 69). We first detect the triad in its negative form when Augustine insists on the need for technical skill: while those purveying falsehoods speak well, "should our people tell the truth in such a manner that it's tedious to hear, impossible to understand, and altogether affords no incentive to believe?" (4.4; cf. Cicero, *De oratore* 2.80). But once the notion of improving eloquence by immersion amid the eloquent has been explored, and once Augustine has said that preachers will speak more wisely the deeper their understanding of the Bible (4.19), then the triad returns. Indeed, Augustine says specifically that simply teaching with clarity will not suffice; the speaker must also delight his listeners and, above all, prompt them to action: "And so our eloquent man will take care . . . to be heard with intelligence, pleasure, and obedience" (*Aget itaque noster iste eloquens . . . ut intellegenter, ut libenter, ut oboedienter audiatur*; 4.87).

This Ciceronian triad of teaching, delighting, and moving (the *officia oratoris*) then forms the basis for a discussion of the three levels of style—again, grounded in

Ciceronian ideals. Augustine observes earlier in the book that there is a specialized form of *eloquentia* for matters pertaining to the divine (*De doctrina christiana* 4.26) but then goes on to demonstrate that the Scriptures conform to more traditional notions of *eloquentia* as well. Later on, he returns to the theme with an analysis of a passage from Galatians, which he sums up with the remark that, although it has none of the formal characteristics of high style, it nevertheless conveys "the grand emotion with which we feel the speech boiling" (*grandis affectus quo eloquium fervere sentimus*; Augustine, *De doctrina christiana* 4.124). And yet he devotes a fair amount of space to commentary on the appropriate times at which to use each level of style—dubbed by him *grandis*, *temperatus*, and *summissus*—and observes that one should not overuse the grand style; he remarks on the *pondus*, gravity, of the grand style as opposed to the embellishment of the mixed (*temperatus*) style and the acuity of the humble (*summissus*) style (4.139). He clearly associates these three with the Ciceronian aims of speaking: the *grandis* moves, the *temperatus* delights, the *summissus* informs. But in the end (4.145–50) the three meld into each other, and what is left preeminent is the character of the speaker, "so that his way of life should be, as it were, an overflowing of eloquence" (*ut . . . sit eius quasi copia dicendi forma vivendi*; 4.159)—which is exactly the conclusion of *De ordine*, some 40 years before, when Augustine tells his mother that she does not need a formal education so long as she "remain[s] steadfast in her present life and character" (2.17.46). The final sentence of the work reflects the theme of the formation of character, the cultivation of the self, that is one of the ideals of rhetoric but is now transposed into a Christian key: Augustine thanks God that he has been able to expound "not the sort of person I am, but the sort of person who applies himself to sound—that is, Christian—teaching [*in doctrina sana, id est Christiana*] should be" (*De doctrina christiana* 4.166).

This mixture of the practical and the ideal is quintessentially Augustinian. Having found his own way to what he considered to be the truth, he would use every method at his disposal to draw others toward it as well. The passionate engagement of his audience was the only real test of success. In an atypical report on his own preaching (an attempt to dissuade the inhabitants of Caesarea in Mauretania from bloody and futile annual battles), he observes, "I didn't think I'd accomplished anything when I heard them applauding, only when I saw them weeping" (Augustine, *De doctrina christiana* 4.139). The techniques of the *ars rhetorica*, intellectual immersion in the Christian Scriptures, repeated exposure to gifted speakers, the simple communication of an exemplary life— all were pertinent to Augustine's theological project. If we look for a singular or doctrinaire approach, we will be disappointed. Augustine's stylistic pliability has generally been underappreciated (note, however, Burton 2012, an excellent essay on the subject). So, to my mind, has the consistency of his fundamental concerns throughout the 40-odd years of his extant writings. The imperfections of human language, and yet our obligation to use its imperfections so that Christ can teach through us and so that we can strive to be bound together *in nodo caritatis*—these are the basis of Augustine's thoughts on eloquence.

What, however, of Augustine's actual practice in his sermons? The sermons of late antiquity remain, as Averil Cameron observed more than 20 years ago, "the hidden iceberg of Christian discourse" (1991: 79). Hundreds of them remain to us—hundreds, indeed, of Augustine's alone—even though many thousands of them were preached. Recent writers have stressed the novelty and power lent by the sheer frequency with which Christian teachings were promulgated (Shaw 2011: 409–11; Dossey 2012, ch. 6) and the commitment to communicate with the broadest possible audience. Dossey concludes a case study with the observation, "To the amazement of a well-educated landlord, brutish rustic minds were beginning to understand reason. The sort of intellectual discourse previously reserved for the educated was being attempted on estates" (2012: 159). Moreover, it has recently been suggested by Hildegund Müller (2012) that the ongoing purpose of the sermons was not just to teach, or for that matter to reinforce a sense of community among the diverse range of listeners. Müller, building on Cameron, describes Augustine's use of the "homiletic situation . . . as a process of stylization, *even alienation*," in which he engages himself and his congregation in a "figurative mystery play" (Müller 2012: 302; emphasis added). This accounts, she argues, for the relative lack of reference to the external world in the sermons, and for their nature as "performative, quasi-sacramental ritual" (302). If correct, this characterization would place Augustine's homiletic practice in sharp contrast to the *mores* of forensic rhetoric: the notion of alienation is particularly startling.

The best way of examining Augustine's homiletic practice is to take a sliver from the putative iceberg itself and analyze a specific sermon. I have selected sermon 302 partly because, unlike many, it has the benefit of a relatively recent edition (Lambot 1950) but also because it makes a good test case for the idea of alienation—the creation within the basilica of a hermetic discursive environment—because it was in fact preached in the aftermath of a traumatic event. It was preached at Hippo in 412 on the feast day of Saint Laurence, August 10, shortly after a corrupt customs officer at the port of Hippo had been lynched in the city. We may suppose that Augustine's congregation was expecting guidance, reassurance, even exoneration. But this is a searing sermon to preach under the circumstances.

The sermon starts quietly and conventionally, with a statement of the occasion and an exhortation to follow Laurence: "Today is the solemn feast day of the blessed martyr Laurence. Sacred readings that befit this feast day have sounded out. We have heard, we have sung, we have intently listened to the gospel reading. So let us follow the footsteps of the martyrs by imitation, lest we celebrate their festivals in vain" (*Beati martyris Laurentii dies sollemnis hodiernus est. Huic sollemnitati sanctae lectiones congruae sonuerunt. Audivimus et cantavimus et evangelicam lectionem intentissime accepimus. Martyrum ergo vestigia imitando sectemur, ne sollemnitates eorum inaniter celebremus*). The short clauses, mostly paratactic; the rhythms of assonance and homophones; the clarity of focus—all set a measured tone (for further discussion of Augustine's prose rhythms, see Oberhelman 1991). Augustine continues with a reminder of successful petitions to Laurence—who obliges like a father (*pater*) giving small toys to his children—but directs his congregation to think of this as nugatory in comparison with the gifts to come. There is an extended and passionate comparison of the earthly and heavenly life, marked with hammering rhymes and stabbing questions:

Why must I describe what this brief life is like? We have experienced how wearisome and troubled it is; surrounded by temptations, full of fears; burning with desires, flattened with disasters; grievous in adversity, fearful in prosperity; rejoicing in rewards, tormented in losses. . . . What should we do? What action should we take? What should we say? What threatening goads, what hortatory fires should we apply to hard, lazy hearts, frozen with the ice of worldly stupidity, one day to strike away the earthly torpor and set them ablaze for eternity?

> *Qualis sit brevis haec vita, quid describere opus est? Experti sumus quam aerumnosa, quam querelosa; circumdata temptationibus, plena timoribus; ardens cupiditatibus, subdita casibus; in adversis dolens, in prosperis tremens; lucris exsultans, damnis excrucians. . . . Quid faciamus? Quid agamus? Quid dicamus? Quos comminationis aculeos, quos exhortationis ignes admoveamus cordibus duris et pigris, et terreni stuporis glacie congelatis, ut torporem mundi aliquando decutiant, et in aeterna inardescant?*

The earthly lot of the just and the unjust is equal; but *Christianus es*, "you are Christian" (Augustine habitually, and strikingly, addresses his congregation with the second-person singular [Comeau 1930]), and Christians look for rewards in heaven and do not fear death. But there are still lovers (*amatores*) of this foul, brief life: "What are you going to say, evil lover, perverted lover? What are you going to say to this beloved of yours? Talk, engage, flatter—if you can. What are you going to say? 'Your beauty led me on to that nakedness.' She shouts at you: 'I am foul, and you love me?' She shouts: 'I am hard, and you embrace me?' She shouts: 'I am flighty, and you are trying to follow me?'" (*Quid dicturus es male amator, perverse amator? quid dicturus es huic amatae tuae? Dic, alloquere, blandire, si potes. Quid dicturus es? Ad istam nuditatem me perduxit pulchritudo tua. Clamat tibi: Foeda sum, et tu amas? Clamat: Dura sum, et tu amplecteris? Clamat: Volatica sum, et tu sequi conaris?*).

At this point, Augustine has been speaking for about 15 minutes. We can imagine his congregation jumping guiltily at every feigned shout, at every reference to worldly misbehavior or moral gelidness. He has not yet alluded to the lynching, but he has begun to establish the terms in which he will address it. He returns to Laurence, "who suffered so many things that make one shudder to hear them" (another anxious moment for the listeners, perhaps: What is going to be put on display?). Gradually, Augustine works toward the burden of his sermon:

> Why are you raving against evil people? "Because they are evil," you say. *You are adding yourself to their number by raving against them.* . . . It is not enough that you should dislike such men, it is not enough: that is something which is expected of you. No one should say: "God knows that I didn't do it," "God knows that I didn't do it," "God knows that I didn't want it to happen." Look, you've said two things: both "I didn't do it," and "I didn't want it to happen." *It's still not enough.* It's not enough if you didn't want it to happen, if you didn't also prevent it [emphasis added].
>
> *Quid saevis in malos? Qui mali sunt, inquis. Addis te illis, saeviendo in illos. . . . parum est ut tales displiceant vobis, parum est: est aliquid quod de vobis exigendum est. Ne quis dicat: Et deus novit quia non feci, novit deus quia non feci, et deus novit quia*

nolui fieri. Ecce duas res dixisti: et non feci, et nolui fieri. Adhuc parum est. *Parum est prorsus si noluisti, si non etiam prohibuisti.*

The excoriating message is reinforced by one of Augustine's favorite homiletic devices, the vivid conversation with an invented but all-too-plausible interlocutor, a particularly dynamic form of *prosōpopoēia* (Comeau 1930: 7; Zwierlein 1978: 72–80; Dodaro 2009). Everyone is implicated in what happened; everyone shares the guilt; no one— Augustine develops the biblical reference (John 8:7)—can cast the first stone. Clearly, there is a rumble of protest: at one stage, Augustine interjects *fratres mei, obsecro vos*: "Brothers, please!" (Augustine's sermons were recorded by stenographers: one of the pleasures of reading them is that they retain such markers of their moment of delivery.) But Augustine presses on—the guilt of the community must be absolved by the community: "Each one in his own home, impel his son, his slave, his friend, his neighbour, his client, his inferior, not to do these things. . . . If one searches carefully, there is no house [in this city], in which there are not more Christians than pagans.—It's true, you're agreeing.—And so you see that there would not be evils, if the Christians did not wish it.—That is unanswerable" (. . . *unusquisque in domo sua filium suum, servum suum, amicum suum, vicinum suum, clientem suum, minorem suum, agite cum illis, ut ista non faciant. . . . si discutiatur diligenter, [in hac civitate] nulla domus invenitur, ubi non plures christiani sint quam pagani. Verum est, consentitis. Videtis ergo quia mala non fierent, si christiani noluissent. Non est quod respondeatur*).

In this address to the *patresfamilias* in his congregation, we see why—some 45 minutes earlier—Augustine had chosen to begin his sermon by reflecting on the gifts of a judicious father. We see why he reflected on Christian hope for eternity, on the temporal mingling of just and unjust, and on the Christian obligation to be virtuous even amid the reprobate. The repetition of the reflexive possessive *suum* drives home the obligations of his individual hearers to an entire network of people who are, in some sense, "their own." The sheer force of Augustine's sermon—logical, rhetorical, affective—is designed to ensure that his words do not remain in the basilica. They reach out into the world and accompany his congregation into their everyday life (the *res ipsae quotidianae* that he invokes early in the sermon).

This sermon is, of course, preached under conditions of exceptional anxiety. Certainly, Augustine's language—its sonorities, its repetitions, its urgent questions and contraposed answers—can be mesmerizing: I have quoted it at such length to try to give an impression of its power. Certainly, he is using his sermons to reinforce a sense of community. But it does not follow from this that his aim is to alienate them from the world. On the contrary: he is profoundly concerned to fire his audience to act, to continue the chain of communication. The novelty lies, perhaps, in the way in which he includes himself with his audience, for they are all, in the end, being taught by Christ, weaving together their imperfect words in an approximation of the perfect Word (*Logos*).

In the end, I wonder whether we have not been too focused on Augustine's supposedly vexed relationship with classical rhetoric. Augustine could still write in "Ciceronian style" (Burton 2012) when composing *De civitate dei* (412–27); for that matter, passages of *De doctrina christiana* itself are notably classicizing. For sermons, Augustine recommends using every resource at the preacher's disposal, as long as the congregation is both educated and moved, and he puts this into practice in his own homiletics. Rhetoric—or eloquence: despite efforts to distinguish the two (Mohrmann 1958), they are interchangeable—is, for Augustine, simply the *consuetudo loquendi*, the habit of communication.

FURTHER READING

The starting point for any newcomer to Augustine is Peter Brown's (2000) biography, which should be read in the second edition with its substantial epilogue. Book 4 of *De doctrina christiana* is reproduced in Enos and Thompson (2008), with text in both Latin and English, and a number of useful introductory essays. A recent selection of Augustine's sermons in a translation by Edmund Hill (2007) is readily available. Part 1 of Kaster (1988) is indispensable as an introduction to education in late antiquity. Cameron (1991) sets Christian rhetoric in a wider imperial context; its broad scope has yet to be superseded.

REFERENCES

Brown, Peter. 2000. *Augustine of Hippo: A Biography*. New edition, with epilogue. Berkeley: University of California Press.

Burton, Philip. 2007. *Language in the "Confessions" of Augustine*. Oxford: Oxford University Press.

Burton, Philip. 2012. "Augustine and Language." In *A Companion to Augustine*, edited by Mark Vessey, 113–124. Oxford: Wiley-Blackwell.

Cameron, Averil. 1991. *Christianity and the Rhetoric of Empire: The Development of Christian Discourse*. Berkeley: University of California Press.

Comeau, Marie. 1930. *La rhétorique de saint Augustin d'après les "Tractatus in Ioannem."* Paris: Boivin and Compagnie.

Conybeare, Catherine. 2006. *The Irrational Augustine*. Oxford: Oxford University Press.

Conybeare, Catherine. 2012a. "Beyond Word and Image. Aural Patterning in Augustine's *Confessions*." In *Envisioning Experience in Late Antiquity and the Middle Ages: Dynamic Patterns in Texts and Images*, edited by Giselle de Nie and Thomas F. X. Noble, 143–164. Farnham/Burlington: Ashgate.

Conybeare, Catherine. 2012b. "Reading the *Confessions*." In *A Companion to Augustine*, edited by Mark Vessey, 99–110. Oxford: Wiley-Blackwell.

Di Capua, F. 1931. "Il ritmo prosaico in san Agostino." In *Miscellanea Agostiniana: Testi e studi*, 2.607–764. Rome: Tipografia Poliglotta Vaticana.

Dodaro, Robert. 2009. "Augustine's Use of Parallel Dialogues in his Preaching on Nonviolence." In *Philological, Historical, and Theological Studies on Augustine's "Sermones ad Populum,"* edited by Gert Partoens, Anthony Dupont, and Mathijs Lamberigts, 327–344. Ministerium Sermonis. Turnhout: Brepols.

Dossey, Leslie. 2012. *Peasant and Empire in Christian North Africa*. Berkeley: University of California Press.

Eden, Kathy. 1990. "The Rhetorical Tradition and Augustinian Hermeneutics in *De Doctrina Christiana.*" *Rhetorica* 8: 45–63.

Enos, Richard Leo, Roger Thompson et al., eds. 2008. *The Rhetoric of St. Augustine of Hippo: "De Doctrina Christiana" and the Search for a Distinctly Christian Rhetoric*. Waco, TX: Baylor University Press.

Green, R. P. H. 1995. *Augustine "De Doctrina Christiana."* Oxford: Oxford University Press.

Hill, Edmund, trans., and Daniel E. Doyle, ann. 2007. *Saint Augustine: Essential Sermons*. Hyde Park, NY: New City Press.

Jackson, B. Darrell, trans., and Jan Pinborg, ed. 1975. *Augustine "De Dialectica."* Dordrecht/Boston: D. Reidel.

Kaster, Robert A. 1988. *Guardians of Language: The Grammarian and Society in Late Antiquity*. Berkeley: University of California Press.

Lambot, Cyrille, ed. 1950. *Sermones selecti duodeviginti*. Brussels: Aedibus Spectrum.

Mayer, C. 1974. "*Res per signa*: Der Grundgedanke des Prologs in Augustins Schrift *De Doctrina Christiana* und das Problem seiner Datierung." *Revue des Études Augustiniennes* 20: 100–112.

Miscellanea Agostiniana: Testi e studi. 1930–1931. 2 vols. Rome: Tipografia Poliglotta Vaticana.

Mohrmann, Christine. 1958. "Saint Augustine and the *Eloquentia.*" In *Études sur le latin des chrétiens*, 351–370. 2 vols. Rome: Edizioni di Storia e Letteratura.

Müller, Hildegund. 2012. "Preacher: Augustine and his Congregation." In *A Companion to Augustine*, edited by Mark Vessey, 297–309. Oxford: Wiley-Blackwell.

Oberhelman, Steven M. 1991. *Rhetoric and Homiletics in Fourth-Century Christian Literature. Prose Rhythm, Oratorical Style, and Preaching in the Works of Ambrose, Jerome, and Augustine*. Atlanta: Scholars Press.

O'Donnell, J. J. 1992. *Augustine "Confessions."* 3 vols. Oxford: Oxford University Press. http://www.stoa.org/hippo

Pollmann, Karla. 1996. Doctrina Christiana. *Untersuchungen zu den Anfängen der christlichen Hermeneutik unter besonderer Berücksichtigung von Augustinus, "De doctrina christiana."* Freiburg: Universitätsverlag Freiburg Schweiz.

Pollmann, Karla, and Mark Vessey. 2005. *Augustine and the Disciplines: From Cassiciacum to "Confessions."* Oxford: Oxford University Press.

Shanzer, Danuta. 2005. "Augustine's Disciplines. *Silent diutius Musae Varronis?*" In *Augustine and the Disciplines: From Cassiciacum to "Confessions,"* edited by Karla Pollman and Mark Vessey, 69–112. Oxford: Oxford University Press.

Shaw, Brent. 2011. *Sacred Violence: African Christians and Sectarian Hatred in the Age of Augustine*. Cambridge: Cambridge University Press.

Zwierlein, Otto. 1978. "Der Fall Roms in Spiegel der Kirchenväter." *Zeitschrift für Papyrologie und Epigraphik* 32: 45–80.

PART III

MEDIEVAL RHETORIC

CHAPTER 25

···

THE DEVELOPMENT OF
MEDIEVAL RHETORIC

···

JOHN O. WARD

THIS chapter takes as its subject "rhetoric" in the sense defined by Marius Victorinus, Saint Augustine's teacher and the author of a celebrated commentary on Cicero's *De inventione*. Defining the orator, the *sophista*, and the *rhētōr* in the introduction to his commentary, Victorinus tells us that the rhetor is the person *qui dat precepta artis*. In other words, the rhetor is not necessarily an orator or the teacher who sets exercises and trains in disputation but the teacher who passes on the "precepts of the art." In antiquity, of course, there presumably was such a class of teachers, despite the contempt with which Cicero treats the term.[1] Whether or not we can call great teachers such as Quintilian or even Victorinus rhetors, we must accept that insofar as they wrote treatises handing down the precepts of the art, they *were* rhetors. In this sense, of course, Cicero himself was a despised *rhētōr*, and his *De inventione* became the major textbook for medieval rhetorical teaching and study at least until the twelfth century, when it was replaced to a large extent by what contemporaries called the "second" rhetoric (*De inventione* being the first): the anonymous *Rhetorica ad Herennium*, which, despite a few queries, was accepted as a work of Cicero up to and even beyond the serious objections raised by Raffaelo Regio in 1492.

Before continuing with this story, it is necessary to counter any expectation that we are going to deal here with rhetoric as defined by Martin Camargo: "The art of producing spoken and/or written texts" (2010a: 174). Such an art, amply supplied with manuals and textbooks from the twelfth century onward, for example, and in particular the *Poetria nova* of Geoffrey of Vinsauf, which Camargo calls "the principal textbook on rhetorical composition for the later Middle Ages," was popularly taught all over Europe and concentrated on letter and verse composition. Camargo points out, however, that the teachers of this art "would not have called themselves 'rhetoricians.' The name to which most of them would have answered, at least in the context of their pedagogical activities, was 'grammar master'" (2009: 91). There was much overlap between rhetoric as taught in antiquity and grammar as taught under the heading of "producing spoken and/or written texts" in the Middle Ages. It is also being increasingly realized that the art of producing spoken and written texts in the medieval period included substantial practical or declamatory "performance-oriented" exercises (see Enders, ch. 29). Nevertheless, the full curriculum of classical rhetoric—invention (*inventio*), arrangement (*dispositio*), style (*elocutio*), memory (*memoria*), and delivery (*pronuntiatio* or *actio*)—was nevertheless not taught in the medieval and Renaissance periods except by way of commentary on *De inventione* and *Ad Herennium* or by way of texts substantially based upon these late Roman republican texts. This chapter therefore confines itself to the teaching of rhetoric in this latter sense and eschews the far broader and more widespread teaching of "the art of producing spoken and/or written texts," known as the *ars poetria*, the *ars dictaminis*, and the *ars predicandi* (the "applied" arts of rhetoric). It is true, of course, that at least one of the later Latin rhetoricians—C. Julius Victor's fourth-century *Ars rhetorica*—included a section on letter writing (*ars dictaminis*), but this, and the immediately preceding discussion of *de sermocinatione* ("on informal discourse, ranging from conversation in a gathering to oral disputation" [in Halm 1863: 446–89]), must be regarded as an exception to the general rule, such matters being not normally thought of as part of the ancient rhetorical curriculum[2] and therefore not dealt with in the medieval art derived from the ancient curriculum.

The History of Medieval Rhetorical Teaching to the Advent of the Italian Renaissance

Why medieval and early Renaissance rhetors chose the early works of Cicero to teach and comment upon, rather than such mature writings as his *De oratore* or Quintilian's *Institutes of Oratory* (known and to some extent used in the period), is explained by the utilitarian nature of the medieval interest in rhetoric, which was concerned with learning *from* and *using* the skills taught in these manuals rather than learning *of* and *about* them. Most readers of *De oratore* and the *Institutes of Oratory* will agree that they are profound, extensive, and diffuse works that are ill suited to the elementary classroom. At the same time, the study of *De inventione* and *Rhetorica ad Herennium* is in itself a remarkable phenomenon. We do not seek to learn of or from these works today because they are remote in time, studded with references and allusions we no longer understand, written in a language foreign to those in use today, and concern a subject no longer taught in our schools and academies, at least not in anything like the ancient form presented in these classical manuals. Nevertheless, despite the appearance from the twelfth century onward of rhetorical textbooks adapted to particular uses current in the later medieval period (the already mentioned arts of poetry and letter writing and manuals of preaching, for the most part, but not excluding manuals on the so-called *ars arengandi*, the art of addressing public assemblies and councils, of "haranguing"), the *De inventione* and *Ad Herennium* had a continuous pattern of basic teaching usage from the third or fourth to the sixteenth centuries of our era. Even in the Renaissance, humanists did not begin commenting on alternative sources of classical rhetorical theory, such as Cicero's *De oratore*, until the sixteenth century, and slightly earlier for Quintilian's *Institutes of Oratory*, though they never really compiled a full commentary on the latter text. Instead, they came early to write their own manuals and compilations of classical rhetorical theory. The continuous usage pattern for such basic texts as the *De inventione* and *Ad Herennium* required ever larger commentaries designed to explain and expound aspects of the art no longer familiar or suited to the worlds of the Middle Ages and Renaissance; such commentaries were compiled and survive in an overwhelming quantity today.

It was certainly not the case, however, that this pattern of usage was uniform and comprehensive or was found at all times and places in our period, and one of the reasons for this must have been that the user framework for the classical manuals was far removed from medieval and Renaissance user contexts. In other words, whether a medieval scholar chose to delve into the classical manuals depended on exceptional circumstances and motivations. Because routine teaching of classical rhetoric as it had flourished under the Roman Empire had faded from all school curricula by pre-Carolingian times, the rhetors we shall deal with in this chapter were not really rhetors. They were, instead, church intellectuals, usually cathedral-school masters holding a *benefice* (a portion of land or an assigned ecclesiastical income) that enabled them to teach persons designated for a clerical, ecclesiastical career. In Italy they may even at times have been laymen teaching for profit, but few medieval rhetors were very far from being churchmen or intellectuals of a broader stamp than "mere" rhetors. They usually taught rhetoric alongside grammar and dialectic, the other two arts of the *trivium* (the four arts of the *quadrivium* being astronomy, music, geometry, and arithmetic). The arts of the *trivium* and the *quadrivium* made up a preliminary educational system adhered to by youths in the schools and their teachers. Deriving from the liberal arts manuals of antiquity, it reached its formative pattern in Martianus Capella's *De nuptiis Mercurii et Philologiae*, written probably in the fourth century CE and containing an informative chapter on rhetoric.[3] The "liberal arts" curriculum was not, however, followed systematically and comprehensively, despite the appearance of unusual manuals such as Thierry of Chartres's *Heptateuchon* in the twelfth century. For the most part, training in some of the liberal arts preceded either departure to find a job (usually as a secretary, clergyman, or other office holder in church or court) or else graduation to the higher faculties of law, medicine, or theology.

The vicissitudes of the teaching of classical rhetorical theory in the medieval period are an interesting comment on the general intellectual history of the time. The broad tone of medieval teaching of the classical art of rhetoric was set in late antiquity, where the so-called *rhetores latini minores* (see Halm 1863) indicate the drift of rhetorical teaching down to the time of Augustine, himself a professional teacher of rhetoric who converted to Christianity and turned from precepts to "imitation" based on biblical *exempla* (see Conybeare, ch. 24). A brief look at Victorinus's commentary on *De inventione* will acquaint the reader with the principal features of these late ancient rhetorical treatises, one of which was already mentioned (Martianus's *De nuptiis*). A good summary of the gradual shift from courtroom to didactic contexts in the later Latin rhetoricians can be found in Rita Copeland and Ineka Sluiter's (2009: 104–6) introduction to their partial translation of Victorinus's commentary on the *De inventione*.

The earliest properly medieval rhetors were the encyclopedists Martianus, Cassiodorus, and Isidore of Seville, whose coverage of rhetoric varied from the cursory to the quite thorough (Halm 1863). The basic patterns were, of course, already set by earlier treatises, in particular *De inventione* and *Rhetorica ad Herennium*. Later *rhetores latini minores* such as Bede and Alcuin (Howell 1941) did not change these patterns much, apart from the source of *exempla* for the figures of speech and thought (the Bible instead of the poetic works of antiquity). Some regions depended upon grammatical treatises for their knowledge of rhetoric (e.g., England before the Norman conquest), and even in the heartland of classicism, the Carolingian Empire, major manuals dealt only scantily with rhetoric when compared with their treatment of grammar. The earliest attempts to expand the rhetorical curriculum took place in the Carolingian Renaissance, when the first attention to the *Ad Herennium* since late antiquity can be noticed (Taylor-Briggs 2006). From this time onward, despite an apparent contentment in the ninth century with the treatment of rhetoric to be found in Martianus, a growing number of manuscripts that have survived testify to the increasing study of the *De inventione*, a study that reaches a climax in the circle of Lawrence of Amalfi, teacher of the celebrated Pope Gregory VII, who reigned from 1073 to 1085. Lawrence's teaching showed considerable interest in the legal cases and theoretical illustrations to be found in *De inventione* and to a lesser extent in the *Ad Herennium*.

Gerbert of Rheims, later Pope Sylvester II (from 999 to 1003), who may be connected with the magnificent tricolumnar glossed *De inventione* of the early eleventh century (Bodleian Library, MS Laud Lat. 49), was much interested in what could be gained from classical rhetorical theory for the presentation of cases in the ecclesiastical law and jurisdiction of his day, and Anselm of Besate left behind a remarkable (and practical) declamatory rhetorical textbook that may reflect his teaching in northern Italy around the middle of the eleventh century. It was, however, a later figure who initiated a renaissance of rhetorical studies, based on *De inventione* and *Ad Herennium*: the commentator Menegaldus, who may be Manegold of Lautenbach, the celebrated papal propagandist and teacher of the liberal arts in Germany and France during the second half of the eleventh century.

One scholar saw the resort to ancient treatises on argument and persuasion (instead of inherited authoritative texts) in the eleventh century as a sign of an emerging scholarly community in which persuasion of equals replaced hierarchical assertions of authority. This renaissance of ancient texts was taken up, together with a number of anonymous writers, by a Rheims master, Odalricus; Abelard's teacher, William of Champeaux; Abelard; Thierry of Chartres; Petrus Helias; and Alan of Lille. All of these teachers of rhetoric put together our finest collection of original commentaries on the classical works to date. Possibly the last of these commentaries, an anonymous one that may exemplify teaching practices in Paris anywhere between the middle and the end of the twelfth century, shows unusual use of Quintilian's *Institutes of Oratory*. Although not used extensively in the commentary tradition, Quintilian's *Institutio oratoria* was known in the twelfth century (and at other times), and we still have an outstanding summary of the whole work, written by a monk, Stephen of Rouen, in the first half of the twelfth century (Ward 1995a).

The pattern of development of the art of rhetoric evidenced in these commentaries has received much commentary (Fredborg 1987). For reasons unknown to us, however, the impetus to study classical rhetorical theory waned in the second half of the twelfth century, possibly because rhetoric had been used to introduce students to Roman law, and in the second half of the twelfth century the teaching of Roman law reached a sufficient stage of maturity to render unnecessary the "introduction" that may have been provided by way of the *De inventione* and *Ad Herennium* (Taliadoros 2006; Brundage 2008). Further, in the second half of the twelfth century an independent art developed that dealt with rhetoric and canon law, the so-called *ecclesiastica rhetorica*. Although this was not a major art in terms of textbook production, its appearance indicates the overpowering urge of medieval teachers to develop instructional manuals closely suited to what they considered the niche markets of the day. Again, the study of dialectic, an introduction to which can be found in Cicero's *De inventione* and *Topica*, matured and came to depend on the study of the complete logical writings of Aristotle, supplemented with a growing volume of specialized commentaries. Finally, by the second half of the twelfth century, the "applied" or medieval arts of prose, sermon, and poetic composition had reached a measure of maturity in regard to manuals and textbooks, thus reducing, perhaps, the need for contemporaries to devote themselves to the classical manuals.

In the thirteenth century, at the emerging universities of the north, especially Paris, the study of classical rhetoric seems to have been largely reduced to the treatment of inventional topics to be found in Boethius's treatise, *On Different Topics* (*De topicis differentiis*) (Stump 1978). From a practical point of view, would-be secretaries seem to have been content with the growing number of available dictaminal or letter-writing manuals that put into acceptable form the etiquette of greeting and the modes of presenting requests and subject matter effectively, and the *Poetria nova* of Geoffrey of Vinsauf introduced them to the very important matter of style (Woods 2010; see Copeland, ch. 27). Ecclesiastical orators (preachers) had a growing volume of specialized manuals and handbooks prepared for them, dating from one of the earliest, Alan of Lille's 1340 *Compendium on the Art of Preaching* (Evans 1981).

It is possible that the study of classical rhetorical theory might have died out here if not for another renaissance: the intellectual ferment that developed in Dante's day at the University of Bologna, where canon and Roman law had long been favored subjects of study for laymen and clergy alike (see Cox, ch. 26). The reasons for this renaissance seem to be connected with the new forms of discourse and argumentation that developed in the maturing polities of the northern Italian cities, all the way from elite "democracies" like Dante's Florence to the succession of dictatorships seeking legitimacy in the more northerly towns (Ward 2001; Cox 2006; Milner 2006). This growing interest in speech-making and council debates created instructional needs that went beyond the letter-writing manuals that had reached a fine maturity in Bene da Firenze's *Candelabrum* (Camargo 2010a: 176–82) and seems to have resulted in a crescendo of commentaries on the *Ad Herennium* (and to a lesser extent on *De inventione*) that eventually merged with the Italian Renaissance proper, which gave another impetus to the study of classical rhetorical theory, this time enlarged by study of the works of Hermogenes, Cicero's *De oratore*, and Quintilian's *Institutes of Oratory* (Ward 1999).

Not all teaching of classical rhetorical theory and practice was done via commentaries on the *De inventione* and *Ad Herennium*, and the composition of independent textbooks or *summae* (summaries) based on, but *not* commentaries on, these ancient treatises has already been discussed. There are two such examples, one from the twelfth century and another from the early fourteenth century (perhaps). The latter example is examined in the next section. Although highly innovative in various ways, this treatise remained an isolated example of its type. One swallow, it seems, did not make a spring, and the author's innovations did not strike a chord with his contemporaries, who continued to bury themselves in commentaries on the *Ad Herennium* or else to devise new works dealing more intensively with aspects of rhetorical practice in their day. The author's work has survived only in one manuscript. No further copies were made of it, as far as we know.

The much copied gloss on the *Ad Herennium* of Guarino da Verona—one of the two or three greatest humanist teachers of the Renaissance, teaching in the main at Venice, Verona, and Ferrara during the first half of the fifteenth century—is a good example of teaching that stuck close to tradition, while the *Rhetoricorum libri quinque* of George of Trebizond, Guarino's near contemporary, is a good example of teaching that strove to incorporate new ancient sources and manners (Monfasani 1976, 1984; see Mack, ch. 33).[4]

Commentaries continued to be written on the *Ad Herennium* after Guarino's time, and they were to take the study of the subject back toward its classical basis. Quintilian's *Institutio oratoria* was subjected to close textual attention. In fact, the arguments against the Ciceronian authorship of the *Ad Herennium* derive from the observation that nowhere in the whole *Institutes of Oratory* does Quintilian cite this work: if it was written by Cicero himself, Quintilian would surely have known and cited it. The *De oratore* finally came into its own as the subject of commentary with the work of the sixteenth-century Jacques-Louis d'Estrebay. With this last work, the medieval rhetor was transformed into the Renaissance humanist and our story is done (see Plett, ch. 30).

One feature worth commenting on here, however, is the movement of classical rhetorical theory from the practical communication classroom to the classical studies classroom. Medieval rhetorical study had always been an intriguing combination of the practical and the theoretical. The classical sources of rhetorical theory had never died out and had remained close to the practical edge of those in charge of communicating effectively during their day, sometimes taught for themselves as one of the three ancient arts of thinking and speaking (grammar, rhetoric, and dialectic or logic) and sometimes inserted and redeveloped in new treatises designed to serve emerging oratorical and compositional contexts. With the Renaissance, however, classical rhetorical theory came to be studied more as an end in itself than as an aid to practical communication needs (which were increasingly moving into the vernacular in any case).

A FULL MEDIEVAL *SUMMA* OF THE RHETORICAL ART

To understand the full range of the teaching of classical rhetoric in the medieval period we need to note the fortune of treatises that, while incorporating much of what was to be found in *De inventione* and *Ad Herennium*, did not take the form of commentaries but of *summae* or manuals. One such *summa* of rhetoric—which has not yet been studied—is contained, uniquely, in MS Bruges (Bibliothèque de la Ville 553, s.xiv) alongside a twelfth-century *catena* gloss on *De inventione* (see Ward 1972: 2: 486–9; Cox and Ward 2006: 70–5) and *Somnium Pharaonis* by Jean de Limoges, a thirteenth-century dictaminal manual in the form of fictional letters between Joseph and the Pharaoh. Although the three texts in this manuscript are separate (they were not written at the same time), they were originally clearly separate booklets and were probably obtained in Paris during the monks' university studies there. On the monks' return to the abbey they had their booklets bound into a collected volume for ease of storage and, possibly, reference. The value of this Bruges manuscript is that almost nothing has survived of later thirteenth- and fourteenth-century classical rhetorical studies at the University of Paris, apart from teaching based upon Boethius's *De topicis differentiis* (Ward 1996a, 1997), so much so that scholars have denied the subject was even taught there. This little Bruges volume, which is as far as I can see unique, enables us to peer into that dark arena and throw a little light upon the rhetoric of the period.

The *summa* in question here is entirely unknown and begins, "The whole basis of philosophy is divided into three parts" (*Omnis philosophie ratio in tres partes dividitur*) (see Ward 1996b).[5] The work is clearly a full-scale textbook on rhetoric, widely informed by classical prose and poetry and using all major Latin sources: Quintilian, Cicero's *De oratore*, *De fato*, and *De inventione*, Boethius's *De topicis differentiis*, together with the *Ad Herennium*, and other works by Apuleius, Virgil, Claudian, Lucan, Horace, and Terence. The use of the *De oratore* and *Institutio oratoria* puts the *summa* later than the twelfth century, when no one (to my knowledge) used the *De oratore*. Yet it is not a commentary on *De inventione* or *Ad Herennium*. One novelty is the inclusion of humor from a wide variety of Latin sources (but principally *De oratore*), which is why the last sentence of the treatise suggests the possibility of treating the work as *de facetiis*, namely, a text belonging to the class of *facetiae*—witticisms and *bon mots* to sweeten all kinds of speeches (see *Ad Herennium* 1.6.10; Cicero, *De oratore* 2.54.216). This work is, however, far more than this[6] and may well be a fine product of rhetorical teaching at the University of Paris in the later thirteenth and fourteenth centuries.

The Bruges *summa* claims at the outset that all systematic philosophy is divided into three parts: the obscurity of nature, the subtlety of discourse (*disserendi subtilitatem*), and life and customs (*vitam et mores*). These are, of course, the "three philosophies" of Plato's division and medieval usage: natural or physical philosophy, rational philosophy, and ethical philosophy. The third, "life and customs," is bestowed upon the orator. This is most unusual, for rhetoric was normally thought to be part of rational philosophy (the second division here). The author, however, concentrates clearly at this stage upon oratory, rather than rhetoric, echoing the decided ambivalence displayed among the speakers in Cicero's *De oratore* about the relative merits of rhetorical precepts and oratorical practice (cf. 1.32.144): "Indeed the whole principle and law of speaking [*ratio jusque dicendi*] should be expressed in relation to arousing or calming the minds of those who are listening. For the speech of an orator is grave and elegant and is accommodated to the senses of humans." The author then elaborates in a remarkable *paeon* to oratory:

> For it is not the case that a suitable speech and a richness of language bring too small a reward (*Ad Her.* 1.1.1). For what is more remarkable, what is more amiable than to hold people's attention by speaking ornately, to attract their pleasures to drive them whither you will and to lead them from whence you will? Moreover, what is so royal, so noble, so magnificent as to be a help or to bring help to those imploring it and to protect innocence beset by the calumnies of informers? I consider it to be sufficiently great that a circumspect orator can stand out in court such that the case which he is handling [seems] more probable, truer and more genuine. In addressing meetings or in giving opinions the obligation of your speech is very much to persuade, so that, in short, it should seem that you have spoken most skillfully to all most learned minds. This is a faculty which is not just expedient on occasions, as are most of the others, but is always necessary: for which of the other [skills] colors its novelty by clothing it in its own ornament? For to define the universal force of oratory, in the words of Crassus, "he should be called an orator who can speak practically, fulsomely, accurately and elegantly about any matter at all that has to be explained in speech, bringing to it a certain dignified charm of action." (Trans. mine)

The author here proposes a fourfold division of the rhetorical art, each of which has its particular end: the first makes the crude orator learned (*erudiet*); the second makes the learned orator useful (*expediet*); the third advances the useful orator in his training (*provehet*); and the fourth places the useful orator in situations in which this utility can be put in the service of others (*proficiet*). The first part of the treatise assigns invention— locating topics of argument—to the three first parts of the rhetorical oration, namely, the introduction (*exordium*), narration (*narratio*), and division (*divisio*). The second part deals with invention as it applies to confirmation (*confirmatio*) and refutation (*refutatio/confutatio*), which are defined in the *Ad Herennium* thus: "By means of the division we make clear what matters are agreed upon and what are contested. Proof [*confirmatio*] is the presentation of our arguments, together with their corroboration. Refutation [*confutatio*] is the destruction of our adversaries' arguments" (9–11). The third part sets out in detail (*specificat*) the nature of invention as it applies to the types of issue (*constitutio*)—a major preoccupation in the medieval commentaries on *De inventione* and *Ad Herennium*—in the judicial kind of case and also as it applies to the epideictic and deliberative kinds of cases. Finally, the fourth part of the *summa* elaborates the arts of arrangement, pronunciation, memory, and style and also provides that eloquent system of introducing jests.

What, then, is to be made of this unique manuscript? In the first place, reconstruction of it is rendered difficult by the fact that we have at present no other copy of the text. We have no idea concerning the date and authorship of the work, except that it appears in a manuscript commonly dated to the fourteenth century and, from its use of the *De oratore*, must postdate the twelfth century by a considerable period. While following the rhetorical treatment of the *De inventione* and the *Ad Herennium*, like the various commentaries on these texts, the *summa* displays independence in not following the commentary format and in citing other materials (though not extensively), especially the *De oratore*, which had not been previously used in the rhetorical teaching tradition.

This author has indeed moved the whole study of classical rhetorical theory forward, in a manner that anticipates the breakthroughs characteristic of the Italian Renaissance. He clearly felt that burying material in dense commentaries on difficult and obscure works (e.g., *De inventione* and *Rhetorica ad Herennium*) had to cease and that rhetoric, as a key pathway to good oratory, must be simplified and brought out of its ancient straightjacket but kept in close conjunction with elements of the medieval teaching structure that had proved their worth over time: for example, the classification of dialectical argumentation; the division into extrinsic and intrinsic aspects of an art; the need to link wisdom and eloquence; and the need to keep in mind biblical and Christian contexts for rhetorical topics. The author's attempt to link rhetoric with practical oratory leads him to reintroduce the *De oratore* as a text for study into the rhetorical curriculum, a feature that takes us back to the Carolingian Lupus of Ferrières, who copied out for us the whole Harley manuscript of that ancient text. We would today support this revival of the *De oratore*, for this work is roundly recognized as antiquity's major contribution to oratorical practice and theory. Although much of his material is straight from the rhetorical textbook, our author keeps the focus upon oratory by using such circumlocutions as *oratoria narratio*, or "what ought to be useful for all of the rhetoric of the speech [*tocius orationis rethorice*]," or "to what the whole speech [*oratio*] must be brought down to" (when discussing, from the *De inventione*, terms such as *ratio*, *judicatio*, and *firmamentum*). Here, of course, he follows the *Ad Herennium* and the *De inventione*, whose authors do not hide the fact that these treatises are giving rules for forensic orators and orations, that is, speeches in court. The author of our *summa* has thus come closer to the Italian Renaissance by introducing a wider array of classical works and texts into his teaching. This, together with its summary of ancient rhetorical materials, its links to medieval contexts, and its disregard of the clutter of ancient legal (and other) references usually found in the old commentary format, indicates that the *summa* in the Bruges manuscript represents a remarkable advance in the digestion of classical rhetorical theory and its representation to contemporary audiences.

CONCLUSION

The combination of theoretical and practical, together with the elaborate development of new contexts for oral and written persuasion, remains the major impression that we take away from our study of medieval rhetoric. Treating the persuasive art as a unifying subject, spread across the entire face of European education, in a language invented by the ancient Romans and continually modified to suit new contemporary contexts, medieval teachers attempted a Herculean task, even more Herculean than if teachers today taught us continually to persuade using Elizabethan and Shakespearean discourse, language resources, and vocabulary. Effective communication was a sovereign and difficult art, and all the resources of teaching over time immemorial were marshaled to achieve a goal. Slowly but effectively, standards were raised, from one generation to the next. The Carolingian period, the twelfth century, and the age of Dante are landmark periods in which teachers groped back into the past to equip themselves and their pupils to more effectively grasp the principal ancient divisions of oratory, the extensive classifications of special language effects outlined in the ancient systems of style, and the essence of Aristotelian ideas about argument and persuasion—all of this in a language that had not been spoken on the streets of Europe for more than 1,000 years.

Nevertheless, we cannot say of the medieval period, as Marc Fumaroli says, for example, of sixteenth- and seventeenth-century France, that "France in this period was entirely dominated by the myth, civilizer and regenerator, of Latin eloquence" (1994: 34; trans. mine) and as we might say of the Roman world after Cicero. Latin eloquence in the medieval period had to jostle with many other elements of the ancient past as well as many new cultural elements: rhetoric was not the force that dominated all. European cultural life at that time was both too fragmented for that and focused on theological disputation and the arsenal of ancient dialectical or grammatical teaching that, in the medieval view, ministered most usefully to this subject. Leading intellectuals were trained in theological and dialectical disputation at the major European universities, and most advanced students were cajoled incessantly to compose and speak in Latin prose and verse that derived much sustenance from classical rhetorical theory. The formal study of classical rhetorical theory was thus put into contexts at the same time broader and more particularized than the contexts for ancient rhetorical theory and therefore hovered uncertainly between grammar, poetics, and dialectic, in a more spasmodic mode than was the case for these latter three arts.

Further, the message of medieval rhetorical study is not one for the textbooks of philology or our modern researchers into the classical past. The medieval study of these texts unearthed nothing about them that could not easily be deduced from the texts themselves. Medieval scholars and users of classical rhetorical theory suspected that the relationship between the "first" and the "second" rhetorics of "Cicero" (the *De inventione* and the *Rhetorica ad Herennium*) was an odd one, but they could not solve it. Nor, of course, can we today, though we, unlike medieval users, seem convinced that the latter work was *not* written by Cicero himself. However, we do not claim to learn anything of a practical nature from either text. We study them as artifacts of the classical past, and very minor ones at that, for we have numerous other works on rhetoric from the classical past to study, many of which were scarcely known or used in the Middle Ages. In the Middle Ages, however, the *De inventione* and the *Rhetorica ad Herennium* were thought of as good and accessible didactic texts, and together they proved that Cicero was a master teacher of rhetoric and that his rhetoric was essential to the art of stylish and effective communication. The medieval use of these texts shows that in the childhood of our own Western intellectual development, texts that were 1,000 years old could not be ignored or discarded. They had to be examined, taught, and used, put into verse even, turned into recitations, oral disputes, and staged oral demonstrations of technique but hardly ever translated into the vernaculars. The last age of the Roman world was a very long one.

What, in the end, then, is the message for today of any study of classical rhetorical theory and practice in the Middle Ages? It is a lesson, I suppose, that is only now coming home, as teachers of communication theory and practice in America discovered the resources of the classical past in the immediate post-war period, and as lawyers today are beginning to delve into the rhetorical past to find advice and tricks that may help them in the courtroom (see Goodrich, ch. 48). In the medieval period leading teachers and intellectuals were not blinded by the array of contemporary modes and points of access to communication practice and the tricks of the current technology trade; they were not blinded by the myriad textbooks on advertising that had profit for manufacturers and sellers as their only aim. They kept alive and explored the vast repertoire of the past as an invaluable repository of tips and advice for improving oral and written communication in their own day. They did not set the classics of the past up as monuments of a culture that had disappeared (the way we do in our academies today). They kept them open as texts that spoke continually to new generations of contemporaries (see Miller, Prosser, and Benson 1973). To do this, they had to keep alive a fluency in written (and perhaps also spoken) Latin, much as it must have existed as a phenomenon in Caesar's and Cicero's day, and they had to continually process, update, and digest the classic texts written in Cicero's Latin to place before leading students in their own classrooms the best of classical advice, for the communication theaters of their own day. This is definitely something to study and to contrast with our own approaches to such things today. What might we have lost that medieval communicators carefully kept in currency?

NOTES

1. Many passages could be cited here reflecting not only Cicero's speakers' views but also his own that the schools of the rhetors were a far cry from the eloquence of the bar and the marketplace. It is a curious irony that the medieval period learned its rhetoric and oratory from sources that Cicero himself condemned.

2. The absence of an ancient art of letter writing is certainly odd, given the great currency of the practice of letter writing.

3. Martianus begins with his usual elaborate allegory and has the female rhetoric address the student directly. She discusses in turn the nature of the rhetorical question (*thesis/hypothesis*); the parts of rhetoric ("matter, arrangement, diction, memory and delivery"); the "issues" (*constitutiones*) that determine the nature and shape of a case at law; the three types of speech (judicial, deliberative, demonstrative [epideictic]); the handling of the issues in judicial cases; deliberative and demonstrative oratory; the "direction" (*ductus*) of the case (i.e., "consistency in a particular approach, held throughout a case"—an unusual topic for rhetorical manuals); arguments and argumentation; arrangement (of arguments and of the material of a speech, or *dispositio*); style (*elocutio*); memory; delivery (*actio, pronuntiatio*); the parts of the speech (*exordium, narratio, digressio, propositio, partitio, argumentatio, epilogus*). The treatment is original and was not particularly popular in the Middle Ages, although the commentators on Martianus enjoyed some prosperity in the period following the Carolingian Renaissance (see Ward 1972).

4. Guarino's commentary, however, abandons much of the specialized terminology of the medieval commentary as well as the hermeneutic procedure known as *divisio*, which was "used at every point to render the text of Cicero amenable to systematic commentation" and to "structure every observation or comment on the text of Cicero" (Ward 1995b: 123–4).

5. I am using here, with a few modifications, a text and partial translation very kindly made available to me by my colleague, John Scott, who is preparing for publication an annotated edition and translation.

6. As the author intimates early in his treatise, "It is not a constant jocosity [*festivitas*] of language or a combination of witty sayings [*lepide propositionis*] that make an orator, but, as Cicero attests in his *On the Orator* (the *De oratore*), the sharpness of dialecticians, the opinions of philosophers, the language of poets, the memory of a lawyer's and the voice of a tragic actor that lead to an orator being heaped with all praise."

References

Brundage, James A. 2008. *The Medieval Origins of the Legal Profession: Canonists, Civilians, and Courts*. Chicago, IL: University of Chicago Press.

Camargo, Martin. 2009. "Grammar School Rhetoric: The Compendia of John Longe and John Miller." *New Medieval Literatures* 11: 91–112.

Camargo, Martin. 2010a. "Special Delivery: Were Medieval Letter Writers Trained in Performance?" In *Rhetoric Beyond Words: Delight and Persuasion in the Arts of the Middle Ages*, edited by Mary Carruthers, 173–189. Cambridge: Cambridge University Press.

Camargo, Martin. 2010b. "Introduction to the Revised Edition." In *Poetria Nova*. By Geoffrey of Vinsauf. Rev. ed. Translated by Margaret F. Nims, 4–18. Medieval Sources in Translation 49. Toronto: Pontifical Institute of Medieval Studies.

Copeland, Rita, and Ineke Sluiter, eds. 2009. *Medieval Grammar and Rhetoric: Language Arts and Literary Theory AD 300–1475*. Oxford: Oxford University Press.

Cox, Virginia. 2003. "Rhetoric and Humanism in Quattrocento Venice." *Renaissance Quarterly* 56 no. 3: 652–694.

Cox, Virginia. 2006. "Ciceronian Rhetoric in Late Medieval Italy: The Latin and Vernacular Traditions." In *The Rhetoric of Cicero in Its Medieval and Early Renaissance Commentary Tradition*, edited by Virginia Cox and John O. Ward, 109–143. Leiden: Brill.

Cox, Virginia, and John O. Ward, eds. 2006. *The Rhetoric of Cicero in Its Medieval and Early Renaissance Commentary Tradition*. Leiden: Brill.

Evans, Gillian, trans. 1981. *The Art of Preaching by Alan of Lille*. Cistercian Studies Series 23. Kalamazoo, MI: Cistercian Publications.

Fredborg, Karin Margareta. 1987. "The Scholastic Teaching of Rhetoric in the Middle Ages." *Cahiers de l'Institut du Moyen-Âge Grec et Latin* 55: 85–105.

Fumaroli, Marc. 1994. *L'Âge de l'éloquence: Rhétorique et* res literaria *de la Renaissance au seuil de l'époque classique*. Paris: Michel.

Halm, Carolus, ed. 1863. *Rhetores Latini Minores, ex codicibus maximam partem primum adhibitis*. Leipzig: Teubner.

Howell, Wilbur Samuel, ed. and trans. 1941. *The Rhetoric of Alcuin and Charlemagne*. Princeton, NJ: Princeton University Press.

Miller, Joseph M., Michael H. Prosser, and Thomas W. Benson, eds. and trans. 1973. *Readings in Medieval Rhetoric*. Bloomington: Indiana University Press.

Milner, Stephen J. 2006. "Communication, Consensus and Conflict: Rhetorical Precepts, the *ars concionandi* and Social Ordering in Late Medieval Italy." In *The Rhetoric of Cicero in Its Medieval and Early Renaissance Commentary Tradition*, edited by Virginia Cox and John O. Ward, 365–408. Leiden: Brill.

Monfasani, John. 1976. *George of Trebizond: A Biography and Study of his Rhetoric and Logic*. Columbia Studies in the Classical Tradition 1. Leiden: Brill.

Monfasani, John. 1984. Collectanea Trapezuntiana: *Texts, Documents, and Bibliographies of George of Trebizond*. Medieval and Renaissance Texts and Studies 25. Binghamton, NY: Renaissance Society of America.

Radding, Charles M. 1997. "Individuals Confront Tradition: Scholars in Eleventh- and Twelfth-Century Europe." *The European Legacy: Toward New Paradigms* 2 no. 8: 1313–1324.

Radding, Charles M., and Francis Newton. 2003. *Alberic of Monte Cassino and Berengar of Tours: Theology, Rhetoric, and Politics in the Eucharistic Controversy, 1078–1079*. New York: Columbia University Press.

Stump, Eleonore. 1978. *Boethius's "De topicis differentiis": Translated, with Notes and Essays on the Text*. Ithaca, NY: Cornell University Press.

Taliadoros, Jason. 2006. *Law and Theology in Twelfth-Century England: The Works of Master Vacarius (c. 1115/1120–c. 1200)*. Disputatio 10. Turnhout: Brepols.

Taylor-Briggs, Ruth. 2006. "Reading Between the Lines: The Textual History and Manuscript Transmission of Cicero's Rhetorical Works." In *The Rhetoric of Cicero in Its Medieval and Early Renaissance Commentary Tradition*, edited by Virginia Cox and John O. Ward, 77–108. Leiden: Brill.

Ward, John O. 1972. Artificiosa Eloquentia *in the Middle Ages: The Study of Cicero's "De inventione," the "Ad Herennium" and Quintilian's "De institutione oratoria" from the Early Middle Ages to the Thirteenth Century, with Special Reference to the Schools of Northern France*. 2 vols. PhD diss., University of Toronto.

Ward, John O. 1995a. "Quintilian and the Rhetorical Revolution of the Middle Ages." *Rhetorica* 13 no. 3: 231–284.

Ward, John O. 1995b. "The Lectures of Guarino da Verona on the *Rhetorica ad Herennium*: A Preliminary Discussion." In *Rhetoric and Pedagogy: Its History, Philosophy, and Practice; Essays in Honor of James J. Murphy*, edited by Winifred Bryan Horner and Michael Leff, 97–128. Mahwah, NJ: Erlbaum.

Ward, John O. 1996a. "Rhetoric in the Faculty of Arts at the Universities of Paris and Oxford in the Middle Ages: A Summary of the Evidence." *Archivum Latinitatis Medii Aevi* 54: 159–232.

Ward, John O. 1996b. "From Marginal Gloss to *Catena* Commentary: The Eleventh-Century Origins of a Rhetorical Teaching Tradition in the Medieval West." *Parergon* 13 no. 2: 109–120.

Ward, John O. 1997. "Rhetoric in the Faculty of Arts (Paris and Oxford): A Summary of the Evidence." In *L'enseignement des disciplines à la Faculté des arts (Paris et Oxford, XIIIe–XVe siècles)*, edited by Olga Weijers and Louis Holtz, 147–182. Turnhout: Brepols.

Ward, John O. 1998. "The *Catena* Commentaries on the Rhetoric of Cicero and Their Implications for Development of a Teaching Tradition in Rhetoric." *Studies in Medieval and Renaissance Teaching* 6 no. 2: 79–95.

Ward, John O. 1999. "Cicero and Quintilian." In *The Cambridge History of Literary Criticism*, vol. 3, *The Renaissance*, edited by Glyn P. Norton, 77–97. Cambridge: Cambridge University Press.

Ward, John O. 2001. "Rhetorical Theory and the Rise and Decline of *Dictamen* in the Middle Ages and Early Renaissance." *Rhetorica* 19 no. 2: 175–224.

Woods, Marjorie Curry. 2010. *Classroom Commentaries: Teaching the "Poetria nova" Across Medieval and Renaissance Europe*. Columbus: Ohio State University Press.

CHAPTER 26

RHETORIC AND POLITICS

VIRGINIA COX

A "major and vital part of civil science": so Cicero, in *De inventione*, defines "that rationalized eloquence they call rhetoric" (*artificiosa eloquentia quam rhetoricam vocant*; 1.6).[1] The Ciceronian notion of rhetoric as an element of civil science (*civilis ratio* or *civilis scientia*) was diligently echoed by numerous medieval commentators, within the tradition reconstructed by John O. Ward (1995). Yet what purchase did this political conception of rhetoric, so fundamental and intuitive for Cicero, truly have for his medieval readers? Among the many uses medieval Europe found for classical rhetoric in poetics, preaching, mnemonics, epistolography, and other fields, how significantly did politics endure as a living context for the deployment of the art?

Some definitions may be useful before essaying an answer to this question. Considerations of the role of rhetoric within politics have very often tended to limit their purview to republican polities on the classical model, in which oral deliberation has a privileged institutional role. George Kennedy's frequently cited distinction between "primary" and "secondary" rhetoric reflects this perspective. Primary rhetoric, for Kennedy, is oral and civic; "secondary" rhetoric is textual and literary. The former is characteristic of republican regimes, and the latter is characteristic of monarchic regimes. Without meaningful deliberative institutions to sustain it, such as we find in republics, rhetoric devolves from "persuasion to narration, from civic to personal contexts, and from speech to literature" (Kennedy 1999: 3)—essentially, that is, from a political to a depoliticized art.

How does medieval Europe fare in this analysis? Certainly, if we look to Cicero's Rome or Demosthenes's Athens for our paradigms of political rhetoric, it must be said that medieval Europe offers little that meets the prescription. General histories of rhetoric have correspondingly tended to characterize medieval Europe as overwhelmingly secondary in its rhetorical practices: focused on the textual rather than the oral, with the exception of preaching, and largely oblivious to political contexts. This perception was so widespread that a sustained tradition of scholarship focused on medieval political eloquence has emerged only in the past quarter-century (Artifoni 2007: 3, n. 5). Even now the record is patchy, in that most scholarship has focused on a few environments, notably northern Italy and the kingdom of Aragon. This chapter surveys findings to date in the field of medieval political rhetoric while expanding its geographic reach into England. At the same time, it revises Kennedy's classically derived notion of primary rhetoric, with the aim of evolving a working model of political rhetoric better tailored to medieval contexts.

Without doubt, the medieval site in which the conditions for primary rhetoric in Kennedy's sense were met most exactly was that of the city republics or *comuni* of northern Italy. Within these densely populated urban settings, with their rising commercial elites and precociously thriving document culture, a cult of political eloquence is already attested from the twelfth century, when we find contemporaries commenting wryly on the "Lombard" tendency to prolixity and verbal ceremony (Artifoni 2007: 3–5). From the early thirteenth century onward, manuals of speech instruction began to appear for communal officials whose role required oratorical competence. This tradition of speech training, sometimes termed the *ars arengandi*, expanded from the middle of the century, when the guild-based, mercantile movement known as the *popolo* came to power in key cities, including Florence and Bologna. Reflecting the guild origins of the movement, the regimes instituted by the *popolo* were notably deliberative in character, with government conducted through a complex system of councils and assemblies. To serve the needs of the new, relatively broad-based political class, a rich, mainly vernacular literature developed to teach the art of public speaking, some theoretical (Brunetto Latini's and Bono Giamboni's adaptations of Ciceronian rhetoric, from the 1260s), some exemplificatory (Matteo de' Libri's and Giovanni da Vignano's collections of model speeches from, respectively, ca. 1275 and ca. 1290).

The example of the Italian *comuni* would seem to bear out, at first appearance, the appropriateness of Kennedy's analysis. It is here, within these anomalously neoclassical, republican regimes, that we find the most self-conscious culture of political eloquence discernible in medieval Europe. It is here that secular oratory first flourishes and that Ciceronian rhetoric begins to be studied with a view to civic applications of a type that Cicero himself would have recognized.

Despite the markedly neoclassical character of the Italian *comuni*, however, the resemblance between the political-rhetorical culture they generated and that of Cicero's Rome is far from exact. One very significant difference, pointed up by Latini, is that written practices of political rhetoric loomed much larger in the Middle Ages than in antiquity: where Cicero's precepts deal only with oratory, Latini's encompass both speaking and writing (*dire* and *dettare*). This points to a first problem in transposing classical conceptions of political rhetoric to a medieval environment. Kennedy's equation of political-rhetorical cultures with orality and depoliticized secondary rhetorical cultures with writing is unsuited to a context like medieval Europe, in which a powerful and widely diffused tradition of political epistolography coincided with more local and precarious cultures of political speaking. It is revealing on this score that Latini, reaching for an example of a modern orator in his *Rettorica*, cites Frederick II's chancellor, Pier della Vigna, a man far better known for written than spoken eloquence (Copeland and Sluiter 2009: 758–9).

The need, in medieval contexts, to work from a model of political rhetoric that can encompass written as well as oral practices is all the more acute in that a distinction between the two is notoriously difficult to make in this period. It was habitual in medieval Europe for letters to be read aloud on delivery, a custom that inevitably blurred the lines between the written and oral. True to this ambiguity, Italian civic oratory appears to have drawn heavily on the nominally "written" *ars dictaminis* for its norms of arrangement (Artifoni 2007: 10–6), while public epistolography showed a concern with auditory effects that betrays its oratorical roots. The prevalence of the *cursus* in diplomatic missives illustrates this last point. First systematized within the papal chancery in the early years of the twelfth century, this was a regulated system of prose rhythm, envisaging a series of set patterns of accented and unaccented syllables to be used at the close of sentences. In combination with the insistent sound patterning supplied by rhetorical devices such as alliteration and anaphora (repetition of words at the beginning of clauses), the *cursus* served to enhance the "ear appeal," and hence the persuasive effect, of diplomatic prose while at the same time underlining rhetoric's otherness from everyday language and its status as "the special speech of the state" (Habinek 2004: vi). The oral quotient of diplomatic letters is so prominent that we can describe this species of *dictamen* more appropriately as a written-oral form than as a written one. Some such hybrid term may also be useful in categorizing other written political documents intended for oral delivery, such as royal proclamations in fourteenth-century England (Doig 1998).

If work on medieval political rhetoric demands a flexible understanding of the relationship between oral and written, it also requires a more flexible understanding of the role of rhetoric within different regimes than we find in some traditional narratives. While it is clear why a tradition evolved of associating meaningful practices of political rhetoric exclusively with republican regimes, this is unhelpful in the case of medieval Europe, where such regimes were extremely rare. Preferable in a medieval context to any formula limiting political rhetoric to republics is the rule of thumb that rhetoric comes to play a larger part in the public realm within regimes in which power is negotiable or contested. This includes republics almost by default but also monarchic and imperial regimes in which the ruler's power is challenged, whether domestically or externally. Latini's theoretical perspective can be useful again here, specifically his insistence on conflict (*tencione*), "tacit" or overt, as a defining property of rhetorical discourse (Copeland and Sluiter 2009: 775–6).

Keeping these considerations in mind, we might turn our attention to the practice of parliamentary speaking within the monarchic regimes of Europe, a subject that has been relatively under-investigated to date in rhetorical scholarship (see, however, Feuchter and Helmrath 2008). Across the course of the thirteenth and fourteenth centuries, throughout Europe parliaments were gradually transformed from occasional events into something resembling institutions—a particularly striking manifestation of the more general "politicization" of power apparent from the later twelfth century (Bisson 2009: 484–529). Rhetoric was both an agent in and a beneficiary of this politicizing process: an agent in that it served in negotiations between the crown and the increasingly assertive social groups below it; a beneficiary in that persuasive language came to enjoy an increasing salience as a signifier of rational, consensus-based government.

Exemplary evidence of these developments is offered in the records of the Aragonese-Catalan parliament, the only such institution whose rhetorical norms have come under close scrutiny to date. Two unusual features of this parliament account for the prominence it has attained within the history of rhetoric: the remarkable quality of the documentation, which from the early fourteenth century includes complete accounts of speeches; and the routine participation of the monarch in parliamentary oratory, an exceptional occurrence elsewhere (Cawsey 2002: 21, 145–6). These two features are, predictably, connected. The speeches most attentively documented are those of the monarchs, who customarily delivered the opening speech of the parliament (*praepositio*), although the responses of representatives of the clergy are sometimes also recorded at length. An interesting feature of the tradition is, indeed, the assiduousness with which Aragonese kings oversaw the transcription of their speeches, sometimes building this act of recording into parliamentary ritual by handing the text of their speech to a clerk at its close (36).

The Aragonese royal speeches are of exceptional interest formally as a record of medieval deliberative oratory, surpassing the documentation from Italy, where we have to rely mainly on chroniclers' reconstructions of debates and on model council speeches composed for didactic ends (Cox 1999: 260–2). Structurally, the Aragonese speeches rely on two models: some follow the essentially dictaminal *dispositio* of the Italian political *arenga*, while others take the form of a sermon, expanding on an initial biblical quotation or "theme" (Johnston 1992: 103–14). An interesting feature of the royal speeches is the self-consciousness with which the Aragonese monarchs enact their kingship performatively through eloquence, coming to embody the civilization-building "great and wise man" (*vir magnus et sapiens*) of Cicero's proem to *De inventione*. As Suzanne Cawsey (2002: 27–34) argues, eloquence, together with spiritual and military leadership, was regarded as a required competency in Aragonese rulers, and there is evidence that they were educated as thoroughly as preachers in this skill.

Although the English tradition of parliamentary speaking has not attracted the attention of historians of rhetoric to date, it offers interesting parallels with the Aragonese tradition, especially where the use of the sermon form is concerned. The early fourteenth-century treatise, *How to Hold a Parliament* (*Modus tenendi parliamentum*), envisages three opening speeches at parliament: a secular summons (*pronunciatio*) announcing the reasons for the parliament; a sermon preached by a distinguished cleric; and a reply by the king (Pronay and Taylor 1980: 71–2). In the course of the fourteenth century the first two speeches merged, giving birth to a new model of parliamentary sermon, delivered by the chancellor, combining general moral and political reflection with the more specific material required by the summons. The character of the speech as a sermon seems to have depended on the clerical status of the speaker: in the rare cases when a layman was chancellor, a straight secular *pronunciatio* was given instead.

Although the sermon-summons does not appear to have become a standard element in parliamentary procedure until the late 1370s, the first mention in the parliamentary rolls of a summons "en fourme de predication" dates from 1332, when it was delivered by John Stratford, bishop of Winchester. The context is an intriguing one, for only five years before this three bishops, including Stratford, are recorded in chronicles as delivering sermons in parliament justifying the deposition of Edward II (Haines 1986: 181–6). These speeches were highly political: Stratford's took as its theme "when the head is sick, the other limbs languish," while his colleague Walter Reynolds, archbishop of Canterbury, preached on the theme "the voice of the people is the voice of God." This suggests that the ritual form of the parliamentary sermon-summons may have had its roots in more ad hoc practices of political sermonizing, most visible at moments of high political tension. In this connection, it is interesting to note that the full recording of sermon-summonses in the parliamentary rolls commenced during the crisis following the "Good Parliament" of 1376, when the Commons, unprecedently, initiated impeachment proceedings against prominent members of the court. An extraparliamentary sermon delivered by Thomas Brinton, bishop of Rochester, at the time when this parliament was sitting is quite explicit on the duty of preachers to intervene in political debate (Wenzel 2008: 245–6).

The English parliamentary sermon, as it evolved from the later fourteenth century, was the equivalent of the Aragonese royal *praepositio* and was clearly comparable in length and erudition. Although the reporting in the rolls is often terse, stating only the sermon's initial theme and briefly summarizing its content, there are several instances in which speeches are recorded more fully. Especially vivid is the *reportatio* of the very first sermon to be reported at any length in the rolls, that delivered by Adam Houghton, bishop of Saint David's, at the "Bad Parliament" of January 1377. This records even normally ephemeral details such as the initial *salutatio*, "Lords and sirs" (*Seigneurs et sires*), and a wittily self-deprecating *captatio benevolentiae* in which the speaker begs his listeners' tolerance by citing 2 Corinthians 11:19 ("Ye suffer fools gladly, seeing ye yourselves are wise").[2] The English sermons were clearly rhetorically elaborated, and the recording clerks' comments sometimes reveal some degree of rhetorical connoisseurship. Henry Beaufort, in May 1413, is said to have spoken "wisely and prudently"; Edmund Stafford, in September 1402, "graciously and clearly"; Thomas Arundel, in February 1388, "wisely and eloquently"—a distinctly Ciceronian pairing. More specifically, chancellors are complimented for the copiousness and choiceness of their "citations and noteworthy sayings" (*auctoritees et notabilitees*) or their "arguments and citations" (*resons et aucthoritees*).

The English parliamentary sermons offer clear evidence that a self-consciously artful culture of political oratory existed in England, at least from the later fourteenth century. Despite their form, heavily influenced by the art of preaching (*ars praedicandi*), these speeches were distinctly political in content, bending their Scriptural sources with considerable ingenuity to fit the political needs of the day. Nor were their sources invariably Scriptural: Beaufort, in the early fifteenth century, cites Horace, Cicero, and the *Secretum secretorum*, while his successor as chancellor, Thomas Langley, compares Henry V to "the most valiant emperor Julius Caesar."[3] A further secularizing feature of the speeches is their reference to the classical deliberative topics of the honorable and expedient. Beaufort, for example, defines Henry's proposed expedition to France in 1415 as "convenient, honorable, and expedient (*profitable*)," while Simon Sudbury, in October 1377, argues the need for defense funding on the basis of "honor and advantage." This habit of referring to the deliberative topics is not limited to the opening sermons: Benjamin Thompson (2010: 82–3) remarks on the frequency of references to "profit" in the 1376 Good Parliament, though without noting their rhetorical source in classical discussions of deliberative oratory.

Although the rolls give little attention to the form of parliamentary oratory outside the special case of the opening sermon, it seems safe to assert that expertise in political speaking was not limited to clerical grandees. The fascinating account in the *Anonimalle Chronicle* of the election of Sir Peter de la Mare as speaker of the Commons during the Good Parliament portrays his eloquence as a key factor in his election. He is described as speaking "well and wisely and expertly [*en bone fourme*]" and as knowing how to articulate (*enfourmer*) his colleagues' arguments better than they were able to themselves (*Anonimalle Chronicle* 83). Also noted for his eloquence was Sir Arnald Savage, said by the chronicler Thomas Walsingham to have spoken at the parliament of January 1401 "so fluently [*diserte*], eloquently, and pleasingly [*graciose*] . . . that he deservedly won praise from all" (Walsingham 2003–11: 308). The roll for the parliament hardly does justice to Savage's eloquence in its terse accounts of his wranglings on taxation—the focus of Walsingham's praise—but it does, exceptionally, record at length his closing speech, which develops an extended comparison between parliament and the celebration of mass (item 47). The analogy is elegantly handled, and also remarkably assertive, in that it implicitly positions the Commons' closing address—which Savage makes analogous to the *Ite, missa est* and *Deo gratias* of the mass—as a ritually required component of parliament, parallel with the chancellor's initial summons.

How did medieval English political speakers acquire their rhetorical mastery, if not purely through practice and observation? In the case of the chancellors, university-educated and clerics by profession, familiarity with the *ars praedicandi* may be assumed. In the case of laymen the answer is less obvious, but some possible sources of instruction in secular oratory may be suggested. One is the chapter on rhetoric in Brunetto Latini's encyclopedic *Tresor*, a work that circulated widely in medieval Europe and, being written in French, was linguistically accessible to English readers. This is one of the principal theoretical sources that has been suggested in connection with the Aragonese-Catalan tradition of political speaking in this period: the Aragonese royal library contained two copies of the *Tresor*, and a translation of the rhetorical section into Catalan was produced in the early fourteenth century (Johnston 1992: 106; Cawsey 2002: 29). That Latini's treatment of rhetoric attracted some interest in late fourteenth-century England is attested by John Gower's *Confessio amantis* (ca. 1386–90), book 7 of which contains a lengthy, unacknowledged summary of this portion of the *Tresor*. Of particular interest from a political perspective is Gower's strikingly full summary of Latini's dramatic account, following Sallust, of the debates in the Roman Senate following the discovery of Catiline's conspiracy (lines 841–2, 1595–1629; in Copeland and Sluiter 2009). As Ann Astell notes (1999: 85–9), the passage in Gower demands to be related to events at the so-called Merciless Parliament of 1388, in which the Lords Appellant arraigned for treason numerous members of Richard II's court. Gower's use of Latini attests to the currency of the *Tresor* in circles close to those that interest us here; the poet was an acquaintance of the Commons speaker Arnald Savage, who was one of the executors of his will (see Galloway 2010: 299).[4]

In addition to Latini, who teaches political oratory directly, we should also take seriously the possibility that dictaminal training may have provided some preparation for aspiring political speakers. As was noted previously, public letters in this period were written for oral delivery, and Martin Camargo (2010) speculates that dictaminal education habitually incorporated some training in performance. Camargo (2012: 189–90) also identifies oral delivery as a particular focus of *ars dictaminis* teaching in late fourteenth-century and early fifteenth-century Oxford, with one treatise most unusually dedicating an entire chapter to this topic. Although dictaminal treatises did not embrace specialized teaching on political argument as did classical treatises on oratory, medieval dictaminal theory was not intended to be self-sufficient; rather, it was customarily studied alongside collections of model writings (*dictamina*) intended to exemplify its rules. If we examine the *dictamina* recommended by Oxford masters or that occur with *ars dictaminis* manuals within the manuscript tradition, it is not difficult to identify texts that would have lent themselves well to instruction in political argument, oral and written. Examples are the diplomatic letters of imperial and papal chancellors such as Pier della Vigna and Tomaso di Capua; Jean de Limoges's epistolary "mirror for princes," *Pharaoh's Dreams Moralized*; and Guido delle Colonne's epic, *History of the Destruction of Troy*, with its lengthy reportage of deliberative speeches, particularly suggestive where political speaking is concerned (Camargo 1994: 181).

Summarizing my argument to this point, there are strong grounds for thinking that politics was a more significant context for rhetorical practice in medieval Europe than has often been thought. This is the case even when we work with a relatively narrow understanding of political rhetoric as being limited to essentially deliberative practices and confined to the verbal medium. It is disputable, however, whether this is the conceptual framework best suited to capturing the complex nature of political persuasion, especially in a physically demonstrative and ritualistic culture like that of late medieval Europe. As classical rhetorical theorists themselves acknowledged, it is difficult in practice to draw a sharp distinction between deliberative rhetoric and epideictic, between the rhetoric of counsel and rational persuasion and the rhetoric of celebration and display. Classical theorists also recognized the reductiveness of confining an analysis of the mechanisms of persuasion to the purely verbal and gave much weight to the visual and gestural component of eloquence (*actio*). Following these hints, there seems a strong case for a richer notion of political rhetoric in the medieval period, one capable of encompassing the epideictic as well as the deliberative and extending its reach to the visual and ritual dimensions of persuasion.

A remarkable example of medieval political-rhetorical culture at its most exuberantly mixed is offered by the Anonimo Romano's chronicle of the career of the Roman revolutionary, Cola di Rienzo, who briefly held power in Rome in 1347 and 1354. Born into a humble family and qualified as a notary, Cola is portrayed by the Anonimo as rising to prominence partly as a result of Rome's tumultuous politics during the popes' absence in Avignon but chiefly as a result of his own rhetorical mastery. This is manifested in part through his excellence as a speaker; "suckled on the milk of eloquence from his youth" (Anonimo Romano 1981: 104), Cola is seen repeatedly throughout the narrative galvanizing the populace and seducing popes and diplomats with "dazzling orations" (*luculentissime dicerie*). One speech, mingling biblical and Livian allusions, leaves his listeners "gaping" and spontaneously rising to their feet (80). In addition to this verbal eloquence, Cola is also represented as a master of visual rhetoric, commissioning elaborate painted political allegories and orchestrating striking rituals, processions, and ceremonies. Even an activity as seemingly unpropitious as the composition and dispatch of diplomatic letters was subject to the same process of spectacularization. Cola used only a silver pen to compose his letters, the Anonimo tells us, and his couriers traveled unarmed, bearing only wooden, silver-coated wands (107–8, 118).

In addition to illustrating the complex interaction of the verbal, visual, and ritual within medieval political persuasion, the Anonimo's narration of Cola's career also helps alert us to a further characteristic of medieval political rhetoric: its powerful religious dimension. One of Cola's most complex multimedia events, orchestrated shortly prior to his accession, centered around a speech he delivered in the basilica of Saint John Lateran, in which he glossed an ancient bronze tablet inscribed with the *lex de imperio Vespasiani*, arguing from it that temporal power in Rome was ultimately vested in the *populus*, even during the imperial age (Anonimo Romano 1981: 108–9). While the content of the speech was essentially political, its effect must have depended powerfully on the sacrality of the setting. The Anonimo describes Cola's speech as a "fine vernacular sermon [*sermone*]" and talks of him ascending to a "pulpit" to speak.[5]

Although Cola's performance was characteristically idiosyncratic in its details, it was not unusual for a political speech to take place in an ecclesiastical setting. The Aragonese royal *praepositiones* were delivered in the cathedral of the town in which the parliament was held (Cawsey 2002: 144–5, 150–1), while Florentine political meetings habitually took place in the church of San Pier Scheraggio, prior to the construction of the Palazzo del Popolo in the early fourteenth century. Religious observances were also a part of parliamentary procedure; the Aragonese and English parliaments, for example, opened with a mass. Matthew Giancarlo describes the medieval English parliament as "a form of civic spiritual ritual" whose "ideological sanction" came in part from "a pentecostal model of apostolic assembly" (2007: 50). This quasi-sacramental character of parliamentary assemblies is made explicit in the opening speech to the parliament of October 1378, held in Saint Peter's Abbey, Gloucester, where the chancellor, Adam Houghton, cites Matthew 18:20 among his Scriptural authorities: "For where two or three are gathered together in my name, there am I in the midst of them." As we have seen, in 1401 Arnald Savage compared parliament to the celebration of mass.

The extent and character of the imbrication of political and religious discourses in medieval Europe is a topic far beyond the scope of this chapter, but a few points may usefully be made. Most centrally, of course, it must be stressed that it is anachronistic to distinguish between politics and religion in a culture that saw the hands of God, and the devil, at work in directing the events of the secular world. This is not to say that medieval thinkers were incapable of analyzing political affairs as contingent and determined by human agency and circumstantial factors (Shepard 1999: 161–73, 175–7), but this mode of analysis coexisted with alternative modes that drew on providential understandings of history, such as the one apparent in Henry Beaufort's speech to the 1416 English Parliament (*Gesta* 122–7), which interprets a recent event—Henry V's victory at Agincourt—as proof of a divine "sentence" against the French. Even the most apparently superficial gestures of religious *contaminatio* within secular oratory—the deployment of sermon models and of biblical quotations, the use of ecclesiastical spaces for secular debates—ultimately refer to this providential perspective, which folds secular politics into a greater, transcendent whole.

One important consequence of the religious dimension of political rhetoric is that much medieval discourse that may be described as functionally political does not resemble political discourse as we would recognize it today. Another is that medieval political orators—in the broad, written-oral sense envisaged by Latini—may not resemble the *vir bonus, dicendi peritus* of classical tradition very closely at all. One very striking innovation within medieval political discourse, only faintly anticipated in the classical world by the figure of the Sibyl, is the role that was played in it by religious women, especially visionaries, whether nuns like Hildegard of Bingen and Bridget of Sweden or tertiaries like Rose of Viterbo and Catherine of Siena. These women's language was primarily religious, to the extent that, in some cases, their modern reception has effectively depoliticized them as figures (Luongo 2006: 7–18). Any understanding of medieval politics that excludes a religious perspective must necessarily be lacking, however, as must any understanding of medieval political rhetoric that excludes the commonplaces of divine judgment, prophetic revelation, and satanic interference, or of Christ as lacerated by human ingratitude and worldliness, or of the need to remake society in the image of the city of God.

Catherine of Siena offers a particularly interesting example of the type of the late medieval politicized religious. Freer in her movements than a nun, during the War of the Eight Saints (1375–8), which pitted the papacy against a league of Italian states headed by Florence, she engaged in various diplomatic missions on behalf of the papacy, in addition to vigorously pursuing a letter campaign in support of papal policies. Despite their radical contrast in style, her colloquial, trenchant vernacular letters offered worthy opposition to the powerful Latin epistolary oratory of the Florentine chancellor, Coluccio Salutati. Although she was managed by the papacy sufficiently closely for F. Thomas Luongo to refer to her as a papal "agent" (2006: 203), Catherine's rhetoric drew much power from her self-presentation as a moral-political commentator *super partes* in the manner of the exiled Dante and the deracinated Petrarch, both of whom had preceded her in deploying the letter as a vehicle for political polemic. While this polemical use of the letter was not new in the fourteenth century (one great earlier exponent was Pier della Vigna, perhaps not fortuitously an ancestor of Catherine's papal "handler," Raymond of Capua), the appropriation of the epistolary medium by voices outside the chanceries may be seen as a relative novelty of the age.

To conclude, once we see medieval rhetoric on its own terms and not through the lens of classical models, there seems no good reason to regard medieval Europe as a desert for political rhetoric, as it has often been portrayed. On the contrary, the medieval tradition of political rhetoric emerges as a rich one and one of considerable importance in the history of political rhetoric generally. Structural novelties of this period such as the extensive deployment of written forms of political persuasion, the incorporation of religious discourses into political argument, and the presence of women as political commentators would all continue to shape post-medieval traditions of political rhetoric, even as the "reborn" rhetorical culture of humanism assumed a more classical form. What has traditionally been seen as a hiatus in the history of political eloquence may come instead to be seen as a pivotal moment in that history, with as strong a claim to the anticipation of modernity as the Renaissance has conventionally enjoyed.

FURTHER READING

Robinson (1978) remains the best study of the prototypical "pamphlet war" of the Middle Ages, which anticipated the thirteenth-century papal-imperial struggle analyzed by Shepard (1999). Milner (2006) offers an excellent survey of late medieval Italian political eloquence, especially read in conjunction with Cammorasano (1994), which takes in both visual and verbal forms of political "propaganda." Pryds (2000) is useful as a study of royal eloquence complementary to Cawsey (2002), while at the other end of the social hierarchy Cohn (2006: 193–201) has an intriguing discussion of medieval popular revolutionary oratory.

NOTES

1. All translations in this essay are mine. I am grateful to Andrew Galloway for helping orient my research on the English material in this essay, to Martin Camargo for sharing unpublished work with me, and to Rita Copeland for comments.
2. Other relatively fully recorded sermons include those of the parliaments of 1377 (October), 1378, 1399, 1414 (April), 1415, 1425, 1437, 1439, 1442, 1485, 1487, and 1504. Thomas Arundel's 1399 sermon following the deposition of Richard II (iii 423) is also recorded at length. A series of authorial drafts of parliamentary sermons survives from the 1480s (Watts 2002: 42), while *Gesta* (122–7) contains a detailed record of a sermon of 1416 recorded more briefly in the rolls. The language of recording is French down to 1425 and is Latin thereafter, but chancellors are described as speaking in English in 1363, 1365, and 1381 (on the use of English in parliament generally, see Dodd 2011: 253–66). Very little critical work exists on the English parliamentary sermons (see, however, Watts 2002; Genet 2005).
3. *Parliament Rolls*, January 1410 (pseudo-Aristotle); March 1416 (Horace); October 1416 (Cicero); May 1421 (Caesar). Classical references in the parliamentary sermons increase sharply from the 1480s.
4. Galloway also documents Savage's and perhaps Gower's acquaintance with the politically aware preacher Thomas Brinton, mentioned previously.

5. Although the connotations of *sermone* were not exclusively religious in medieval Italian, this seems the correct translation here: the Anonimo's usual term for a secular speech is *diceria*.

References

The Anonimalle Chronicle, 1333–1381. 1927. Edited by V. H. Galbraith. Manchester: University of Manchester Press.

Anonimo Romano. 1981. *Cronica.* Edited by Giuseppe Porta. Milan: Adelphi.

Artifoni, Enrico. 2007. "Una forma declamatoria di eloquenza politica nelle città comunali (secolo XIII): la concione." In *Papers on Rhetoric. VIII. Declamation*, edited by Lucia Calboli Montefusco, 1–27. Rome: Herder.

Astell, Ann W. 1999. *Political Allegory in Late Medieval England.* Ithaca, NY: Cornell University Press.

Bisson, Thomas N. 2009. *The Crisis of the Twelfth Century: Power, Lordship, and the Origins of European Government.* Princeton, NJ: Princeton University Press.

Camargo, Martin. 1994. "Beyond the *Libri Catoniani*: Models of Latin Prose Style at Oxford University ca. 1400." *Mediaeval Studies* 56: 165–187.

Camargo, Martin. 2010. "Special Delivery: Were Medieval Letter Writers Trained in Performance?" In *Rhetoric Beyond Words: Delight and Persuasion in the Arts of the Middle Ages*, edited by Mary Carruthers, 173–189. Cambridge: Cambridge University Press.

Camargo, Martin. 2012. "Chaucer and the Oxford Renaissance of Anglo-Latin Rhetoric." *Studies in the Age of Chaucer* 34: 173–207.

Cammorasano, Paolo, ed. 1994. *Le forme della propaganda politica nel Due e nel Trecento.* Rome: École Française de Rome.

Cawsey, Suzanne F. 2002. *Kingship and Propaganda: Royal Eloquence and the Crown of Aragon c. 1200–1450.* Oxford: Oxford University Press.

Cohn, Samuel. 2006. *Lust for Liberty: The Politics of Social Revolt in Medieval Europe, 1200–1425.* Cambridge, MA: Harvard University Press.

Copeland, Rita, and Ineke Sluiter, eds. 2009. *Medieval Grammar and Rhetoric: Language Arts and Literary Theory, AD 300–1475.* Oxford: Oxford University Press.

Cox, Virginia. 1999. "Ciceronian Rhetoric in Italy, 1260–1350." *Rhetorica* 17 no. 3: 239–288.

Dodd, Gwilym. 2011. "The Spread of English in the Records of Central Government, 1400–1430." In *Vernacularity in England and Wales, c. 1300–1500*, edited by Elizabeth Salter and Helen Wicker, 225–266. Turnhout: Brepols.

Doig, James A. 1998. "Political Propaganda and Royal Proclamations in Late Medieval England." *Historical Research* 71 no. 176: 253–280.

Feuchter, Jörg, and Johannes Helmrath. 2008. *Politische Redekultur in der Vormoderne: Die Oratorik europäischer Parlamente in Spätmittelalter und Früher Neuzeit.* Frankfurt: Campus.

Galloway, Andrew. 2010. "Reassessing Gower's Dream-Visions." In *John Gower, Trilingual Poet: Language, Translation and Tradition*, edited by Elisabeth Dutton, with John Himes and R. F. Yeager, 288–303. Cambridge: D.S. Brewer.

Genet, Jean-Philippe. 2005. "Paix et guerre dans les sermons parlementaires anglais (1362–1447)." In *Prêcher la paix et discipliner la société: Italie, France, Angleterre*, edited by Rosa Maria Dessi, 167–200. Turnhout: Brepols.

Gesta Henrici Quinti: The Deeds of Henry the Fifth. 1975. Edited and translated by Frank Taylor and John S. Roskell. Oxford: Clarendon.

Giancarlo, Matthew. 2007. *Parliament and Literature in Late Medieval England.* Cambridge: Cambridge University Press.

Given-Wilson, Chris, et al., eds. 2005. *The Parliament Rolls of Medieval England.* [CD-ROM]. Leicester: Scholarly Digital E   Gower, John. 2009. *Confessio amantis.* In *Medieval Grammar and Rhetoric: Language Arts and Literary Theory, AD 300–1475,* edited by Rita Copeland and Ineke Sluiter, 836–844. Oxford: Oxford University Press.

Habinek, Thomas. 2004. *Ancient Rhetoric and Oratory.* Oxford: Blackwell.

Haines, Roy Martin. 1986. *Archbishop John Stratford, Political Revolutionary and Champion of the Liberties of the English Church, ca. 1275/80–1348.* Toronto: Pontifical Institute of Mediaeval Studies.

Johnston, Mark. 1992. "Parliamentary Oratory in Medieval Aragon." *Rhetorica* 10 no. 2: 99–117.

Kennedy, George A. 1999. *Classical Rhetoric and Its Christian and Secular Tradition from Ancient to Modern Times,* 2d ed. Chapel Hill: University of North Carolina Press.

Latini, Brunetto. 1999. *Rettorica.* Translated by Justin Steinberg. In *Medieval Grammar and Rhetoric: Language Arts and Literary Theory, AD 300–1475,* edited by Rita Copeland and Ineke Sluiter, 757–779. Oxford: Oxford University Press.

Luongo, F. Thomas. 2006. *The Saintly Politics of Catherine of Siena.* Ithaca, NY: Cornell University Press.

Milner, Stephen J. 2006. "Communication, Consensus and Conflict: Rhetorical Precepts, the *ars concionandi* and Social Ordering in Late Medieval Italy." In *The Rhetoric of Cicero in Its Medieval and Renaissance Commentary Tradition,* edited by Virginia Cox and John O. Ward, 411–460. Leiden: Brill.

Pronay, Nicholas, and John Taylor, eds. 1980. *Parliamentary Texts of the Later Middle Ages.* Oxford: Clarendon.

Pryds, Darleen N. 2000. *The King Embodies the Word: Robert d'Anjou and the Politics of Preaching.* Leiden: Brill.

Robinson, I. S. 1978. *Authority and Resistance in the Investiture Contest: The Polemical Literature of the Late Eleventh Century.* Manchester: University of Manchester Press.

Shepard, Laurie. 1999. *Courting Power: Persuasion and Politics in the Early Thirteenth Century.* New York: Garland.

Thompson, Benjamin. 2010. "Performing Parliament in the *Rotuli Parliamentorum.*" In *Aspects of the Performative in Medieval Culture,* edited by Manuele Gragnolati and Almut Suerbaum, 61–97. Berlin: Walter de Gruyter.

Walsingham, Thomas. 2003–2011. *The St. Albans Chronicle: The "Chronica maiora" of Thomas Walsingham.* 2 vols. Edited by John Taylor et al. Oxford: Clarendon.

Ward, John O. 1995. *Ciceronian Rhetoric in Treatise, Scholion, and Commentary.* Turnhout: Brepols.

Watts, John. 2002. "'The Policie in Christian Remes': Bishop Russell's Parliamentary Sermons of 1483–84." In *Authority and Consent in Tudor England: Essays Presented to C. S. L. Davies,* edited by G. W. Bernard and S. J. Gunn, 33–59. Aldershot: Ashgate.

....

CHAPTER 27

RHETORIC AND LITERARY CRITICISM

....

RITA COPELAND

THE Middle Ages inherited most of its rhetorical orientations from antiquity, adapting ancient precepts to new purposes and developing new forms of rhetorical art. But in the long process of reception and revision, medieval rhetoric also preserved one of the most interesting ambiguities of classical rhetoric: the distinction between theoretical and compositional approaches to texts, which was really no distinction at all. Was the aim of literary criticism really different from that of textual composition? Certainly the task of the grammarian differed from the task of the rhetorician: the grammarian assessed the given text for its usages in order to teach an *orthopraxis*, while the rhetorician gave guidelines for generating future texts. But within the discipline of rhetoric itself, the distinction between criticism and composition was almost moot. Throughout its history, from antiquity onward, rhetoric was concerned with the dynamic relation between composer (speaker or writer), text (oral or written), and audience (hearer or reader), and for this reason rhetorical criticism will always be bound up with an application to composition, whether through poetics, hermeneutics, or other systems.

INVENTION AND HERMENEUTICS

....

Hermeneutics as a practice existed long before the codification of rhetoric. Through its roles in religion and the various schools of philosophy, hermeneutics developed alongside and independently of rhetoric through and beyond the Hellenistic period (Eden 1987; Struck 2004). But Roman rhetoric extended its powerful influence into adjacent discourses, putting its stamp on such fields as law, literature, translation, and interpretation. Thus, insofar as interpretation or hermeneutics was important to rhetoric, rhetoric defined it in its own image as an active mode of discovering and engaging meaning in a text, a law, or a system of thought. While the Middle Ages received various models of hermeneutical inquiry from the ancient schools of philosophy and theology, it had an especially prestigious advocate for the rhetorical model of hermeneutics as discovery or *inventio*: Saint Augustine. Augustine, brought up in the rhetorical culture of the late Roman Empire, pursued a career as both teacher of rhetoric and public orator (see Conybeare, ch. 24). On his conversion to Christianity in 387 CE he turned his back on his profession, denouncing it as merely the selling of words (*Confessions* 9.5), but he never gave up his rhetorical habits of thought. His *De doctrina christiana*, the first systematic Christian preaching rhetoric, divides its coverage into invention, the "means of discovering" (*modus inveniendi*), and delivery, the "means of setting forth" (*modus proferendi*) what has been discovered. But under the rubric of invention Augustine offers nothing less than an exhaustive Scriptural hermeneutics. Books 1–3 of *De doctrina christiana* turn the devices of rhetorical invention to the purpose of interpreting a text, Scripture, in which all truth has already been revealed: the work of rhetorical discovery is now to draw out the meaning contained in Scripture, harmonizing seeming ambiguities with the rule of charity (*caritas*), that is, love as a theological principle.

In Augustine's program, invention of argument is turned into the process of interpretation, of grasping and explaining the truths contained in writing. Here interpretation has all the dynamism of rhetorical invention. Scripture does not always yield its meaning easily: the text is shrouded in ambiguities and mysteries. The theological truths contained in Scripture are the matter or "things" (*res*) toward which all interpretation must be directed. This is comparable to the *materia* of the controversy in rhetoric, which the orator must grasp before he determines the shape of his argument. Moreover, since Scripture partakes of human language, those "things" are conveyed through signs, some of which are unknown and some ambiguous. The signs in each of these categories, in turn, can be either literal (*propria*), meaning just what they seem to mean once we have adequate information about them, or figurative (*translata*), which requires another level of hard investigation to determine just how the figure should be read. The "figurative" meaning of signs is conveyed in the manner of figurative language, in which a term is "transferred" (*translatum*) from its "proper" sense to another (improper or alien) sense, thus requiring a certain stylistic analysis familiar from the rhetorical canon of *elocutio* (style). But the figuration is not necessarily *in* the words themselves but in the very things to which the words refer. This exegetical process layers the techniques of rhetorical invention, with its substantive analysis of fact, definition, and quality, over the stylistic analysis of figurative language (*figurae verborum*).

Distinctions between the letter and the spirit of a text, which have their most obvious origins in Pauline doctrine denigrating the flesh in favor of the spirit, are also traceable to Ciceronian legal thought, which distinguished between a written document (a will, a law) and the intention (*voluntas* or *sententia*) of the writer. The controversies that may arise over the "letter" of the law or document and the intention behind it were the object of inventional strategy (Cicero, *De inventione* 1.13.17, 2.40.116–8.141; *Rhetorica ad Herennium* 1.11.19). Cicero advises the advocate to look for the writer's intention in the writer's own words, to present as evidence the writer's own expression of his desires rather than one's own inferences (*De inventione* 2.44.128). What this assumes, of course, is that the "spirit" of the author's intention, the *sententia*, can be reflected in, consonant with, the words: that the true "literal sense" is what the author intended. When Christian thought takes over this distinction, as in Augustine and later in Thomas Aquinas (*Summa theologica* qu. 1 art. 9–10), the writer's intention becomes a theological rather than a legal matter (Eden 1990: 59–63; Copeland 2006: 45–7). Here a verbal sign can be taken literally (*proprie*) to reveal or coincide with the spiritual sense—the *sententia* or intention—of the biblical text. Here we can see the correspondence with the rhetorical-legal tradition that informed Christian exegesis (see Porter, ch. 51). The influence of the rhetorical tradition that values the letter works in counterpoint with the Pauline tradition that gives privilege to spirit: sometimes, as in Augustine's hermeneutics and in later scholastic thought, the *sententia* or spirit of the author's intention is to be found in the letter itself.

While Christian exegetes following Augustine do not always borrow as explicitly from rhetorical doctrine, his program set the stage for medieval hermeneutics and theoretical approaches to reading. To cast the work of exegesis as the *modus inveniendi* was to turn it from a static response to the given text to an active reformulation of the text toward persuasive exposition (see Ross, ch. 28). Medieval "strong reading" can be said to have taken its motivation from the rhetorical culture of late antiquity. Direct evidence of strong reading motivated by rhetoric would include the transference of inventional devices to frame hermeneutical procedures. Medieval academic "prologues to the authors" (*accessus ad auctores*), that is, overviews written to accompany commentaries on authoritative texts, derived their formats, either closely or indirectly, from the rhetorical vocabulary of topical invention, the Ciceronian system of the "circumstances" (*circumstantiae*) or attributes of the person and the act (*De inventione* 1.24.34–8.43; Minnis 1984: 9–39; see Hutson, ch. 32). In assimilating inventional topics, medieval prologues took on the form of arguments to be discovered under such important questions as cause (the author's intention), manner or *modus* (literary method, form, or style), and means or faculties (plot or some literary conceit). The inventional *topica* invited a dynamic perspective on meaning and purpose. Exegetes were encouraged to devote particular attention to the question of the author's intention because this gave almost unlimited scope to the exegete's own "intention" as an active reader of the work, his own facility for rewriting the work, and his assumption of the authorial power to project an intention (however belatedly) for the work (Copeland 1991: 67–86). This found a particularly imaginative ground in approaches to the classical poets, where interpretative ambition might play out more freely against critical consensus than it would in the exegesis of sacred texts. The tradition of Ovid commentary and the moral and philosophical allegorizing of classical myth are especially striking products of this dynamic (Ghisalberti 1932; Demats 1973; Minnis, Scott, and Wallace 1983: 314–72; Possamai-Pérez 2006; see also following discussion of Virgil commentary). But this inventional outlook and its vocabulary also generated fresh approaches to Scriptural commentary, as we shall consider herein.

ARCHITECTONICS

Rhetorical theory had long provided the language—and the outlook—for addressing the architectonic principles of a work, for seeing the whole structure. The rhetorical canon of *dispositio* or arrangement is the part of rhetoric most obviously concerned with the structure of the work, with the harmonious ordering of beginning, middle, and end. Such advice is relevant to compositional strategy, but it could also take on a more general theoretical application. Form manifests thought, as Quintilian saw it (*Institutio oratoria* 7.1), and ordered form is a sign of ordered intellectual consideration.

This principle finds continuous expression in medieval theories of artificial and natural order. In the teaching of poetic composition, artificial order can be presented as the superior choice—it is more pleasant for the reader because more complex. This is a key teaching in the *Poetria nova* (ca. 1208–13) by Geoffrey of Vinsauf and in the *Parisiana poetria* (ca. 1231–5) by John of Garland. But this can also have a fascinating application to commentative strategies. Where a commentator wants to read allegorically against the grain of the text, but without violating an author's supposed intention, it is the plot that can be "resequenced," as it were, according to natural or artificial order, to reveal different contents. Probably the most celebrated example of this is the prologue to the commentary by Bernardus Silvestris (or attributed to him) on Virgil's *Aeneid*. Bernardus (or whoever wrote this commentary) argues that Virgil conducted two different levels of meaning throughout the *Aeneid* (Jones and Jones 1977: 1–2): Virgil designed his work to operate simultaneously through an artificial order (*ordo artificialis*), which is the traditional understanding of the *Aeneid* (it begins *in medias res* and loops backward in time to arrive again at present action in book 4), and through a natural order (*ordo naturalis*), through which Virgil reveals his philosophical purpose of tracing human life through birth and infancy (books 1 and 2), childhood (book 3), adolescent passions (book 4), and adulthood and wisdom (books 5 and 6).

But the canon of *inventio* also deals with the division and order of the parts of the speech: *exordium*, narration, partition, proof, refutation, and *peroratio*. The process of invention is specific to each part of the oration, for the case is understood and treated from different structural perspectives: insinuation in the *exordium*, fictive or historical enhancements in the narration, or topical invention (attributes of the person and the act) in the proof and refutation. This model of dividing up the oration into its parts was easily transferable to literary criticism. For example, the late antique commentator Tiberius Claudius Donatus read the *Aeneid* as a persuasive "speech" that falls into the five parts of the oration (see translated section in Copeland and Sluiter 2009: 141–7), and this principle of structural division could serve to illuminate the architecture of various books of Scripture, as in the richly imaginative analysis by the Benedictine monk Rupert of Deutz in the early twelfth century (Copeland and Sluiter 2009: 390–404).

GENRE CLASSIFICATIONS

Inventional teaching about narration (*narratio*), the second part of the oration, occasioned some of the most fruitful intersections with literary thought about plot and genre. In classical rhetoric, the narration, or statement of the facts of the case, need not confine itself to attested facts: the orator can amplify his account with narratives of remote history, with plausible fictions, or even with entirely fantastic narratives (Cicero, *De inventione* 1.19.27; *Rhetorica ad Herennium* 1.8.12–3). Early on, these three kinds of narratives—*historia* (remote history), *argumentum* (plausible or realistic fiction), and *fabula* (fantastic story)—came to represent distinctive genres of narrative (see Webb, ch. 22). Because they were obviously digressive, these forms of *narratio* were of limited use in court pleadings. But they were used in late classical oratorical training to help the student practice shaping a plot and thus present a coherent sequence of events. In addition, the triad *historia–argumentum–fabula* passed into medieval literary theory as a ubiquitous scheme for classifying genres according to the degree of truthfulness in content. It was cited by encyclopedists and poetic theorists from late antiquity through the late Middle Ages. The triad was progressively detached from its original rhetorical context, even as its application to literary criticism became stronger. As a way of identifying the matter of literary genres, the triad served to link formal questions of plot construction with the material content of poetry (degrees of verisimilitude) (Mehtonen 1996: 12–61; Copeland and Sluiter 2009: 43–4). Thus, in chapter 5 of his *Parisiana poetria* John of Garland (1974: 99–101) can invoke this generic model both as a means of expounding the narrative principles of given plots and as a set of rules that should not be violated when the student is composing his own material.

At its macro level, rhetoric already presents a theory of genres in its division of speaking into three genres: forensic, deliberative, and epideictic. This division into genres of oratory was first articulated by Aristotle and later elaborated in Ciceronian theory. While the Middle Ages had rather limited practical use for these generic distinctions (even by the time of Augustine, Roman oratory was almost completely epideictic), they were conserved as categories for literary commentary. Most famously, Cassiodorus used the genres of rhetoric as a template for his exposition of the Psalms (ca. 540). In his powerful reinterpretation of rhetoric, he recast the genres of rhetoric according to the spiritual functions he saw at work in the Psalms: the deliberative genre is for meditation and seeking instruction and thus characterizes the Psalms that appeal to those spiritual needs; the forensic genre corresponds to penitence; and the epideictic genre corresponds to the purposes of inspiration or revelation (Astell 1999). Cassiodorus's exposition of the Psalms was influential throughout the Middle Ages as an exegetical resource: in his reading, rhetorical doctrine illuminates a fundamental structural principle that holds the Psalms together as a coherent work.

Medieval thought about form and structure looked to method as much as to content or function. Here the Middle Ages also borrowed from rhetorical language, giving a sharp new inflection to the word *modus*. In the Ciceronian theory of topical invention, *modus* signifies the manner or method by which an act was committed. It is one of the attributes of the person and the act embedded in that system. We have already considered how the "circumstances" or attributes of the person and the act were assimilated to hermeneutics, where the vocabulary of topical invention was used to introduce a text as if it were an argument to be invented by the exegete. One of those topics used in prologues was *modus*, the "manner" in which the text was written. This would produce an answer about form, whether the work was written in verse or prose. In twelfth-century prologues, the topic *modus* was recast to give the commentator a wider remit: it became *modus agendi* or *modus tractandi*, which referred to the method or manner of the treatment of the material or the formal procedure encountered in the work. The new prologues also contained the topic *ordo libri*, or order of the book, which could be discussed under the previous topic of *modus agendi*. The new version of the topic *modus* invited more expansive discussion of form with a view to the didactic efficacy of the style. This could involve the relationship of the style to generic categories, such as the high style of tragedy or the low style of satire and comedy. It could also relate form to function or content, as in the prose and verse (*prosimetrum*) construction of Boethius's *Consolation of Philosophy*, which offers consolation by reasoning in prose and giving delight in verse. Discussions of *ordo libri* might cover the same ground as the rhetorical canon of *dispositio*, with attention to plot structure, including natural and artificial order. But because so many works under consideration were not literary fictions but doctrinal or philosophical treatises, or indeed books of the Bible, this category expanded to address other structural frameworks: division into chapters or the architecture of a whole argument that ascends from lower to higher kinds of proof.

In the language of thirteenth-century *accessus* to academic and theological works, the term *modus agendi* became *forma tractandi* (the form of treatment), and the term *ordo libri* became *forma tractatus* (form of the treatise). This distinction could produce profound apprehensions of form in its largest senses. We see a culminative version of this in the magnificent account of Dante's *Commedia* in a work that claims to be (and probably is) by Dante himself: his self-commentary on the *Commedia* in the *Epistle to Can Grande*. Dante introduces the *Commedia* through an *accessus* and uses the terms *forma tractatus* and *forma tractandi* to articulate the formal complexity of the whole work (see translation and background in Minnis, Scott, and Wallace 1983: 439–69; Minnis 1984: 119–22, 144–5).

Dante tells us that the *forma tractatus* (form of the treatise) is threefold, according to its three divisions: the first, which divides the whole into three canticles (the largest poetic divisions), that is, the three distinct poems, *Inferno*, *Purgatorio*, and *Paradiso*; the second, which divides each canticle into cantos; and the third, which divides each canto into rhymed verses, or *terza rima*. This scheme grasps the architecture of the *Commedia* in its integrated totality. Such integration, however, should not be read in post-Romantic terms as "organic form." Like classical rhetorical ideals of form, this formal architecture is the product of careful artifice; it is a well-ordered machine, comparable to an organic body only in the sense that a body is also a highly wrought mechanism that functions well if it achieves a certain purpose. The purposeful artifice that integrates the parts of the *Commedia* is always before us, never to recede into invisibility behind an illusion of natural form. The *Commedia* works because it is constructed, driven by an intellectual intention and a purpose of form.

Dante's explanation of the *forma tractandi* (form of the treatment) allows him to open another field of analysis, a hybrid of stylistic and generic considerations. Behind his definition of *forma tractandi* lies the earlier exegetical term *modus tractandi/modus agendi*, and behind that, a long rhetorical tradition of the term *modus* as the manner, method, but also state of mind in which an act was performed (see Cicero, *De inventione* 1.27.41). Dante tells us that the *forma tractandi* or "style" of the *Commedia* is of two sorts: its style is poetic, fictive, descriptive, digressive, and "transumptive" (strongly marked by figurative language); at the same time, its style is also one of definition, analysis, proof, refutation, and exemplification. These two kinds of style related to discussions among scholastic theologians of the previous century about the nature or *modus* of sacred Scripture as opposed to the *modus* of rational knowledge (*scientia*) devised by humans. According to the theologians of the thirteenth century, sacred Scripture represented a knowledge apart from the human-produced arts of reasoning. Scripture works through pious affect, and its "genres" (*modi*) are meant to work on us affectively, in the manner of literary or poetic genres: teaching (as in the Gospels), example (as in the historical books), exhortation (Solomon, the Epistles), revelation (the prophetic books), and prayer (Psalms). In other words, the *modi* of Scripture represent not only a manner of telling but also an emotional state of mind that is produced in the reader by the text. This descends from the range of meanings attached to the word *modus* in classical rhetoric, where it can designate a formal genre, a manner in which an act is performed, or the subject's state of mind during the act. The term *forma tractandi* in Dante's usage is already loaded with the history of the term *modus* (as in the forerunner term *modus tractandi*) and with the more recent history of an affective theory of Scriptural genres as opposed to the *modus* of the human, ratiocinative sciences. Dante is saying that the style of his *Commedia* is both poetic in the affective sense of Scriptural genres and ratiocinative in the manner of the human sciences of reasoning. Through the window of Dante's terminology as applied to his *Commedia* we see the long history of a theoretical vocabulary of form and method that carries with it an ever-expanding capacity to apprehend the force of style, genre, and narrative structure.

STYLISTIC ANALYSIS

From antiquity through the Middle Ages, analysis of style, that is, of the figures of speech and the tropes, was a realm shared between rhetoric and grammar (see Ward, ch. 25; Ross, ch. 28). The field was early on established in rhetorical theory, and it appears that Greek grammatical thought among the Stoics first borrowed some terminology and methods of analysis about verbal style from the Greek rhetoricians (Holtz 1979: 215–9). In the Latin West the earliest comprehensive codification of the figures and tropes is in the *Rhetorica ad Herennium*. It should be noted that Quintilian's *Institutio oratoria* was not known widely in the Middle Ages. Throughout the early Middle Ages the specifically rhetorical sources on style would have been limited to the late classical compendia of classical doctrine (see the late classical and early medieval manuals collected in Carolus Halm's *Rhetores latini minores* [1863]) or Cassiodorus's exposition of the Psalms. Only in the early twelfth century did the *Rhetorica ad Herennium* and its treatment of the figures and tropes begin to exert influence. But the primary resource on style, at least through the twelfth century, was grammatical in origin and intent: the tradition of Donatus's *Barbarismus*, which was the third book of his longer treatise on grammar, the *Ars major* (fourth century CE).

Grammatical and rhetorical traditions may have conveyed similar information about verbal style, but their orientations were different. Grammar is concerned with correct usage (*orthopraxis*), and from this perspective figures and tropes are seen as deviations from correctness that are permissible under certain conditions, for embellishment or necessity (Holtz 1981: 660–7; Copeland and Sluiter 2009: 96–9). The grammarians focused their analysis on the occurrence of deviation in a word or group of words. Rhetoric, on the other hand, sees verbal figuration from a macro perspective, as the entitlement of persuasive speech to greater power through adornment that will enhance the intellectual dimension of the discourse and elicit an affective response. Thus, the classical Latin rhetoricians treated this material not under the rubric of licensed departure from conventional usage but as a special canon of rhetoric, *elocutio* (style), aimed at expression as a conceptual whole. Style was understood by the rhetoricians as a fulfillment of the generative processes of invention and arrangement, a process that was not merely superficial but intrinsic to the integrity of the argument. From this sense that ornament is inherent in argumentation it is not far to the emergence of certain tropes as critical categories in themselves.

This is most famously the case with metaphor, which had passed from close analysis in Aristotelian rhetoric (*Rhetoric* 3.10.7, 1405, *Poetics* 21–2, 1457–9) to Stoic grammatical classification as a trope (that which effects a transmutation) and into Roman rhetorical thought, where it was treated among the embellishments of diction (*Rhetorica ad Herennium* 4.31.42–4.46). In some of the medieval arts of poetry (which were themselves hybrid products of grammar and rhetoric), metaphor is treated as a subspecies of "transumption" (*transumptio*) (Purcell 1987). The term goes back to Quintilian (*Institutio oratoria* 8.6.37), who equates it with the Greek *metalēpsis*. In medieval usage *transumptio* had come to designate a general method for moving across logical or ontological categories, such as animate to inanimate. Thus, transumption was more familiar, in the Middle Ages, from logic and theology (Dahan 1992; Rosier-Catach 1997). The classic example for philosophical analysis of language was "the fields smile," which can make no sense unless it is immediately understood as "transuming" from one category (the inanimate "fields") to another (the animate and human "smile"). In his *Poetria nova* Geoffrey of Vinsauf uses the notion of transumption to teach how to apply figurative language by "transferring" or "commingling" attributes (lines 765–1093, in Faral 1924; cf. John of Garland, *Parisiana poetria*, in Lawler 1974: 48–51). In his *Declaracio oracionis de beata Dorothea* (1369), Nicolaus Dybinus, master of grammar and rhetoric in Prague and Vienna, gives the most complete theoretical explanation of *transumptio*, elevating it to the status of the genus under which all the colors of rhetoric (*colores rhetorici*), including metaphor, are the various species. Dybinus invests the concept with the strongest methodological affinities with language philosophy (see background and partial translation in Copeland and Sluiter 2009: 821–33).

It is difficult to disentangle poetics from critical analysis, but in some rhetorical contexts we find a stronger analytical interest aimed at understanding. One example is in an early art of preaching, more or less contemporary with the arts of poetry: Thomas of Chobham's *Summa de arte praedicandi* (ca. 1220), which offers a sustained theoretical engagement with both rhetorical teaching and the rhetoric of Scripture. In introducing the Scriptural "modes of signifying" (*modi significandi*), Thomas returns to the Augustinian distinction between the significations of words and things, but in so doing he also accords greater scope than Augustine to the figurative power of the verbal sign itself. The theological truths of Scripture seem not only to reside in the things to which language refers but also to emerge from the "metaphorical" properties of words themselves:

> Some history is called "analogy," other history is called "metaphor" [*metaphora*]. Proper speech or proper reason is called analogy, that is, when an event is described according to the literal meaning of the words, as for example, Hannibal did battle with the Romans and defeated them. Metaphorical history is when something else is demonstrated through non-proper signification of words, as for example, "a thistle sent to a cedar tree" (4 Kings 14:9; 2 Chronicles 25:18), that is, the lowly to the high ... This non-proper signification has various names. It is known as "trope" [*tropus*], that is, a turning [*conversus*], as "tropology" [*tropologia*], that is, a turned speech [*conversus sermo*], as "metonymy" [*methonomia*], that is, a transumption, and as "metaphor," that is, a transformation [*transformatio*], because everywhere that speech is turned, transumed, or transformed from proper to non-proper signification, this is known as metaphor. Grammar and dialectic deal with analogy, because these arts govern words in their proper significations, in the meanings they are instituted to signify. The art of rhetoric deals with metaphor because rhetoric teaches how to transform words from their proper significations to non-proper meanings by various colors [of rhetoric]. (Trans. Copeland and Sluiter 2009: 617–8)

Thomas of Chobham's approach here recognizes that the capacities of rhetoric are necessarily inscribed in Scriptural meaning. To find the theological truth concealed in a statement is not like decoding figurative discourse: it is in fact to read figurative discourse and capture its inherent multiplicity.

CONCLUSION

Medieval literary criticism and literary theory are categories retrospectively applied by modern critics and historians. But medieval writers and readers thought systematically and hypercritically about texts and hermeneutical procedure in ways that we moderns can recognize. Such thinking was deeply infused with rhetorical learning, at times closely allied with the interests of the grammatical curriculum. One read correctly in order to write gracefully, or one read forcefully to lay the groundwork for one's own future compositions. That commentary on sacred and secular texts was elevated to the status of a master discourse could be said to be one of the greatest contributions of the Middle Ages to the history of rhetoric.

REFERENCES

Astell, Ann W. 1999. "Cassiodorus's Commentary on the Psalms as an *Ars rhetorica*." *Rhetorica* 17: 37–75.

Bernardus Silvestris. 1977. *Commentum quod dicitur Bernardi Silvestris super sex libros "Eneidos" Virgilii*. Edited by Julian Jones and Elizabeth Jones. Lincoln: University of Nebraska Press.

Copeland, Rita. 1991. *Rhetoric, Hermeneutics, and Translation in the Middle Ages: Academic Traditions and Vernacular Texts*. Cambridge: Cambridge University Press.

Copeland, Rita. 2006. "The Ciceronian Tradition and Medieval Literary Theory." In *The Rhetoric of Cicero in its Medieval and Early Renaissance Commentary Tradition*, edited by Virginia Cox and John O. Ward, 239–265. Leiden: Brill.

Copeland, Rita, and Ineke Sluiter, eds. 2009. *Medieval Grammar and Rhetoric: Language Arts and Literary Theory, AD 300–1475*. Oxford: Oxford University Press.

Dahan, Gilbert. 1992. "Saint Thomas d'Aquin et la métaphore. Rhétorique et herméneutique." *Medioevo* 18: 85–117.

Demats, Paule. 1973. Fabula. *Trois études de mythographie antique e médiévale*. Geneva: Droz.

Eden, Kathy. 1987. "Hermeneutics and the Ancient Rhetorical Tradition." *Rhetorica* 5: 59–86.

Eden, Kathy. 1990. "The Rhetorical Tradition and Augustinian Hermeneutics in *De doctrina christiana*." *Rhetorica* 8: 45–63.

Faral, Edmond. 1924. *Les Arts poétiques du XIIe et du XIIIe siècle*. Paris: Champion.

Ghisalberti, Fausto. 1932. "Arnolfo d'Orléans, un cultore di Ovidio nel secolo XII." *Memori del Reale Istituto lombardo di scienze e lettere* 24: 157–234.

Halm, Carolus. *Rhetores latini minores*. 1863. Leipzig: Teubner.

Holtz, Louis. 1979. "Grammairiens et rhéteurs romains en concurrence pour l'enseignement des figures de rhétorique." In *Colloque sur la rhétorique*, edited by R. Chevallier, 207–220. Paris: Les Belles Lettres.

Holtz, Louis. 1981. *Donat et la tradition de l'enseignement grammatical: étude sur "l'Ars" Donati et sa diffusion (IVe–IXe siècle) et édition critique*. Paris: CNRS.

John of Garland. 1974. *The "Parisiana poetria" of John of Garland*. Edited and translated by Traugott Lawler. New Haven, CT: Yale University Press.

Mehtonen, Päivi. 1996. *Old Concepts and New Poetics:* Historia, Argumentum, *and* Fabula *in the Twelfth- and Early Thirteenth-Century Latin Poetics of Fiction*. Helsinki: Societas Scientiarum Fennica.

Minnis, A. J. 1984. *Medieval Theory of Authorship: Scholastic Literary Attitudes in the Later Middle Ages*. London: Scolar Press.

Minnis A. J., and B. Scott, with D. Wallace, eds. 1983. *Medieval Literary Theory and Criticism c. 1100–c. 1375*. Oxford: Clarendon.

Possamai-Pérez, Marylène. 2006. *L'Ovide moralisé. Essai d'interprétation*. Paris: Champion.

Purcell, William M. 1987. "*Transumptio*: A Rhetorical Doctrine of the Thirteenth Century." *Rhetorica* 5: 369–410.

Rosier-Catach, Irène. 1997. "Prata rident." In *Langages et philosophie: hommage à Jean Jolivet*, edited by A. de Libera, A. Elamrani-Jamal, and A. Galonnier, 155–176. Paris: Vrin.

Struck, Peter. 2004. *Birth of the Symbol: Ancient Readers at the Limits of Their Texts*. Princeton, NJ: Princeton University Press.

CHAPTER 28

....

RHETORIC AND POETICS

....

JILL ROSS

Medieval poetics, as embodied in *artes poetriae* (arts of poetry), instructional manuals that teach the novice how to compose in both poetry and prose, has been described as the product of Ciceronian preceptive rhetoric (based especially on the *De inventione* and the pseudo-Ciceronian *Rhetorica ad Herennium*), of Quintilian's *Institutio oratoria*, and of the poetic precepts set out in Horace's *Ars poetica* (Copeland 1991: 160). As Rita Copeland and others have demonstrated, medieval poetic preceptive discourse is also a product of the discipline of grammar that, in its practice of *enarratio poetarum* (explanation of the poets), sought to teach composition by means of formal literary analysis and imitation of textual authority (158–74; see also Murphy 1974: 161–93). As a result of such a "'grammaticization' of rhetoric in the medieval *artes poetriae*" (Copeland 1991: 166), medieval poetics constructed invention not as the finding of new things to say by means of standard topics (*topica*) but rather as the intervention in an already existing, authoritative body of texts that the writer uses as material to be reworked through techniques of amplification, abbreviation, and ornamentation. Instead of producing persuasive speeches, the generative power of rhetoric is turned to the production of new texts out of old texts, texts that can come into existence once the writer has assimilated the traditional material (*materia*) by means of the formal and stylistic modes of analysis taught by grammar.

The idea that the production of poetry in medieval theory constitutes a process of reading and rewriting (Kelly 1969, 1999; Copeland 2006: 254) points to a fundamental tension between fragmentation and integration, a desire to produce a new composition out of the building blocks of past authorities, knowledge, and texts. This chapter details the role of Horace's *Ars poetica* in the development of a pragmatic, preceptive medieval poetics and explores how medieval rhetorical theory negotiated the fraught nature of poetic invention, a process in which all assembled parts ought to cohere. It also examines how the dire consequences anticipated by Horace's negative precepts of composition, ones that hold up the monstrous feminine as a warning, come to condition medieval generative poetics.

From the rhetorical "pre-exercises" (*praeexercitamina*) intended to develop habits of invention by focusing on the imitation and rewriting of small units of discourse (Kelly 1999: 82–5) to the more creative incorporation of larger compositional blocks into longer critical or poetic texts, the idea of medieval writing as rewriting informs much of the literary and rhetorical theory inherited by the Middle Ages from late antiquity (see Copeland, ch. 27). The process of creating a coherent whole out of preexisting disparate parts raised many issues of crucial theoretical importance to all those engaged in the production and consumption of textual culture in the Middle Ages. One of the foremost questions that confronted medieval literary theory was how to calibrate the relationship of authors and texts when the text may range from a clunky grab bag of the work of others cobbled together by a compiler to an artfully wrought intervention in an established textual tradition. By the thirteenth century, theological commentary carefully distinguishes between the assertive activity of an *auctor* (canonical author) whose agency carries with it the weight of literary and moral authority, and the iterative role of the *compilator* (compiler) whose repetition of the words of others enables him to avoid responsibility for the effects his text may have upon the reader (Minnis, Scott, and Wallace 1998: 99–112). This scholastic conceptualization of the different shadings of authorship is enacted in medieval poetic theory and practice, where authors may choose to assume *auctoritas* (authority) or to shift the burden of responsibility to the moral choices of the reader by styling themselves as mere "reporters" of the words of others (100–2, 192–203).

The oblique relationship between the compiler and his text is also colored by the negative associations inherent in the history of the word *compilatio*. As Neil Hathaway's (1989) study of the history of the word has amply demonstrated, the connotations of plagiarism and plundering the work of others common in the classical period did not entirely lose their force in the medieval usage of *compilatio*. While the notion of compiling as the misappropriation of textual authority becomes more muted by the twelfth century, some writers chose, for strategic reasons, to exploit the potential for deception that compiling entails. Compilers and translators of authoritative Latin texts into the vernacular deceptively displaced the authority of Latinity by feigning respect for the authority and integrity of their source, thereby masking the cultural power and privilege claimed by their own vernacular compilations: "The power of the *compilator* lies in the way that he can retreat behind the *ipsissima verba* of the texts and conceal the very control that he exerts as orchestrator of *auctoritates*" (Copeland 1991: 118). What Copeland recognizes is that rather than a simple reiteration of words and texts, the act of compiling can be fundamentally creative—a gesture whose rhetorical power compels the respect of the reader.

The fraught nature of poetic *inventio* as an act of compiling is captured in the opening images of Horace's *Ars poetica*, where the consequences of the poet's inability to master his verbal material is likened to the painter's, potter's, or sculptor's failure to produce artifacts that are harmonious, balanced, coherent, and beautiful, the results of which include the possibility of producing a poetic monstrosity whose grotesque nature is bound up with its potentially feminine unruliness (see Purcell 1996). Horace's discussion of the artificially constructed nature of a poem in terms of a hybrid monster whose feminized alterity must be repressed and controlled by the imposition of masculinized poetic mastery and coherence is constitutive of medieval preceptive theory that advocates literary production as a seamless interweaving of disparate parts. Horace's *Ars poetica* articulates an ideal of poetic integrity and coherence that would become a fundamental precept in medieval poetics, whose dependence on Horatian theory is indisputable (Kelly 1999: 87–9, 97–102; Copeland and Sluiter 2009: 41, 547–8). Horace first expresses the principles of poetic coherence in negative terms, in the body of a female monster or in the artist's flawed product, terms that Horace exploits as a means of linking the successful poet with a socially sanctioned notion of masculinity. Medieval poetic theory appropriated and adapted Horace's imagery of integrity along with its implied construction of gender.

Horace begins his *Art of Poetry* with advice about the rhetorical necessity of creating a poem that is consistent in content, structure, style, and tone. The obvious and elementary nature of this advice has given rise to debate about the nature and purpose of his *Ars poetica*. Medieval commentators explained the simplistic opening of Horace's text by emphasizing Horace's role as teacher to the wealthy sons of the Piso family, at whose request Horace set out the basic tenets of poetic composition by exemplifying the errors that a would-be poet ought to avoid and then presenting more positive precepts. Modern critics have also been hard-pressed to account for the structure of a text that veers from a tendentious and sophomoric beginning to an ending that casts the poet as a tragic, almost unhinged outcast (Brink 1971; Golden 2000).

The description of poetic vices (*Ars poetica* 1–37) one should flee in the quest for perfection of form is as much an exercise in poetic and rhetorical self-fashioning as it is a lesson in the obvious. Horace, lacking the social and political clout of his patrons, the Pisos, uses his *Ars poetica* to construct an identity and rhetorical *ēthos* that provide him with an authority and mastery rooted in his poetic vocation. The images Horace uses in his representation of poetic transgression all exploit connotations of gender in a calculated effort to represent himself as master poet sharing in the dominance and control essential to the power and prestige of Roman manhood (Oliensis 1998: 198–214).

Horace's poem opens with the famous image of the monstrous result of a lack of artistic control: "If a painter wished to join a human head to a horse's neck and plaster all kinds of feathers on limbs gathered from all over, so that a woman beautiful on top ended foully in a black fish—let in for a viewing, could you hold back a laugh, my friends?" (*Ars poetica* 1–5). This laughably grotesque monstrosity figures the vice of poetic incoherence by combining the hybrid natures of a centaur and a mermaid-like Scylla whose feminine nature stamps the image as a whole and therefore functions as the pivot between "form and deformation, outside and inside, surface and depth, fair beginnings and foul endings" (Oliensis 1998: 200). The homosocial laughter on the part of Horace and his audience points to the conventional expectation that the male artist, whether his medium is the binding meter of poetry, the flowers of rhetorical artifice, or the colors of the painter, is expected to be in firm, rational control over his *materia* and rhetorical performance in the same way that he must rule over the appetites of his carnal nature through a corporeal mastery that can be read in his gestures, dress, gait, and voice (see Gleason 1995; Williams 1999). A failure to establish control over one's artistic material or one's body results in a deformation of nature evinced both by the violation of the boundaries between the human and animal worlds in the form of the hybrid she-monster and by the blurring of the lines of demarcation between the masculine and the feminine that is a sign of a depraved, indecorous effeminacy.

Horace conflates poetic ineptitude with questionable manhood when he offers the example of a craftsman who, while excelling at certain parts of his creation, is unable to turn out a wholly perfect, beautiful figure: "Near the Aemilian School, there is a craftsman who in bronze will mould nails and imitate soft hair, but is unhappy in the total result, because he cannot represent a whole figure" (*Ars poetica* 32–5). The sculptor's neglect of the power and musculature of the body in favor of the more inessential, frivolous parts would seem to be associated with an unbecoming feminine concern with cosmetics and grooming, an accusation leveled at rhetoricians by Plato and even by Quintilian. According to both ancient and medieval commentators (Zechmeister 1877: 4; Friis-Jensen 1990: 343), the Aemilian School was a gladiatorial school, and the subject of the statue was taken to be that of a gladiator, the epitome of Roman hyper-masculinity (Wiedemann 1992: 34–8). Horace's use of the word *mollis* ("soft") in reference to the statue's hair would certainly have resonated with his Roman audience, so attuned to the inflections of gender. The association of a man with *mollitia* was a standard means of impugning masculinity (Williams 1999: 127–32). Horace's subsequent remark distinguishing himself from such a craftsman makes clear that for Horace, to be like such a man would be to assume the position of a passive receptor of the admiring gaze of others and to share in a misdirected sexuality: "Now if I wanted to write something, I should no more wish to be like him than to live with my nose turned crooked, though admired for my black eyes and black hair" (*Ars poetica* 35–7). The *nasus pravus* ("crooked nose") is a sign of questionable manhood because *nasus* is sometimes a metaphor for the penis.

While Horace makes clear that the poet should be man enough to dominate his *materia*, he represents the act of artistic creation as fraught with danger for the unsuspecting poet or artist whose will may be overwhelmed by the voluptuous insistence of his subject matter. The resistance of an ideally passive *materia* to the control of the artist is as much of an issue as the artist's flawed masculinity. Horace warns the poet against inserting showy purple patches that would mar the integrity of the poem by dazzling the eye of the reader: "Works with noble beginnings and grand promises often have one or two purple patches so stitched on as to glitter far and wide . . . For such things there is a place, but not just now" (*Ars poetica* 14–9). Instead of creating poetic unity, the purple patches call attention to the seams between themselves and the rest of the poem. It is as if the *materia* itself were directing the creative process, thereby subverting the control of the maker, a subversion that also betokens a perversion of nature.

Immediately following the vice of alien purple patches, Horace turns to the examples of the painter who is supposed to depict a sailor swimming away from a shipwreck but who ends up drawing a cypress instead (*Ars poetica* 19–21) and of the potter who begins to mold a wine jar on the wheel but ultimately produces only a small pitcher (21–3). In both cases, the *artifex* lacks the proper will and desire to do what is required. The paint-er's *materia* is foisted upon him through whim, and the potter's will has been entirely coopted by the process of creation, by the mechanics of the wheel itself, which has usurped the unbridled power of creation over the theoretically inert, passive clay. Both painter and potter are unmanned by the creative act.

Patristic theology saw a similar correspondence between the allure of rhetorical art-istry and the deformation of the masculine will, which, interestingly enough, is also referred to metaphorically in terms of incoherent or physically torn textual (both ver-bal and textile) products. The moral as well as the aesthetic implications of incoherence come together in Christian exegeses of the Fall, the primal scene in which the conse-quences of linking rhetoric, sexuality, and deception are figured as patched-together garments. In both Ambrosian and Augustinian exegetical writing on the Fall, the per-suasion effected by the Satanic serpent on Eve, and Eve's subsequent verbal conquest of Adam's will, are represented as seduction by means of sweet, pleasurable words. Ambrose calls the serpent's deceptive, contrived speech an "agglutination" (Ambrose, *De paradiso* 13.61, in Jager 1993: 124), a composition made up of parts stuck incongru-ously together. Once Adam and Eve have fallen victim to verbal blandishment, their lack of moral integrity is made plain in the ineptly sewn garments of fig leaves whose patched-together quality mirrors the dangerous deception of rhetorically wrought lan-guage and the concomitant awakening of carnal appetite: "Whoever ... violates the command of God has become naked and despoiled, a reproach to himself. He wants to cover himself with fig leaves, sewing together, as it were, insubstantial and shady words which he interweaves word after word with patched-together lies in order to make a veil for his genitals and to cover his own awareness of his deed" (13.65, in Jager 1993: 126). This nexus of deceptive language, improperly sewn garments, and corruption of the will by carnal appetite meshes with Horatian imagery of poetic incoherence, which implies a similar abandonment of reason and will to the dangerous, overpowering sensuality of poetic *materia*. While Horace constructs the unruly nature of poetry as feminine in opposition to the masculine authority of the poet, the Church Fathers conflate the feminine dangerousness of ornate discourse with a theological principle of evil, thereby turning verbal arts like poetry and rhetoric into practices fraught with social, political, and psycho-social tension as well as real moral and soteriological consequences (see Jager 1993: 99–142).

Medieval readers of Horace's *Ars poetica* were aware of both the moral and aesthetic significance of improper composition. Extant in hundreds of manuscripts, the *Ars poet-ica* was the most widely read of Horace's texts, and was one of the canonical texts used in the teaching of grammar in the arts course since the late tenth century (see Olsen 1982–9; Villa 1994). Horace's *Art of Poetry* became the object of numerous commentaries and was a crucial influence in the formation of medieval poetic theory in the twelfth and thirteenth centuries (Friis-Jensen 1995). Indeed, a full-scale anonymous commentary on the *Ars poetica* from the twelfth century, known as the *Materia* commentary after its *incipit*, may even be considered as the first new art of poetry (Friis-Jensen 1990: 319). What did medieval readers make of Horace's highly charged imagery of poetic rectitude and mastery? The *Materia* commentary begins with an introductory section (*accessus*) in which Horace's graphic condemnation of poetic ineptitude forms the basis of a systematization of six poetic vices to be avoided: incongruous arrangement of parts; incongruous digression; obscure brevity; incongruous variation of style; incongruous change of subject matter; and incongruous imperfection of a work (partial translation in Copeland and Sluiter 2009: 552–6). The commentary not only defines and explains the basis for each vice but also attempts to provide the poet with the knowledge and technique for transforming each vice into a virtue. For example, the discussion of "incongruous digression," based upon Horace's condemnation of purple patches, advises that a poet may insert an element that seems to stray from the topic but that, if it usefully clarifies a character's motivation or circumstances in the narrative, may be considered to promote coherence (Friis-Jensen 1990: 336). Such a patch is "inwoven" (*intextus*) rather than "sewn on" (*assutus*), as Horace describes (*Ars poetica* 341). What is striking about the *Materia* commentary is the repetitious insistence on coherence, integrity, simplicity, and unity, which can be seen as an attempt to defang the specter of poetic monstrosity through the exercise of an authorial control that is so perfect that any potential vice becomes a virtue.

Other medieval commentaries on Horace's *Ars poetica* confront this anxiety about poetic and rhetorical transgression in a more forthright manner. The twelfth-century *Anonymous turicensis* provides a fuller explanation of Horace's image of hybrid, monstrous composition. In explaining why Horace chose to make his monster female, the commentator argues that "[Horace] said *woman* rather than man, because nature beautified women more than men" (Hajdu 1993: 246; trans. mine). After acknowledging the ornamental attraction of the feminine, he adds: "If anyone were to object that pleasure, and not laughter, is engendered from such a picture, we will respond that the work of the painter, sculptor, caster or writer is not delightful, is not artful, unless nature is in agreement. Artifice should imitate nature" (246). Here the commentator betrays an awareness of the power of the incongruous, fish-tailed female monster to provoke pleasure, and he attempts to preclude such a possibility by making desire incompatible with any deviation from nature. Conrad of Hirsau's *Dialogue on the Authors* makes explicit the link between the supervenient pleasure derived from Horace's hybrid female and the very essence of poetry: "*Poetria* or *poetrida* is a woman who is eager for verse. The poet [Horace] is thought to have chosen this title because he displays the beginning of his work as a woman who is beautiful on top. He wishes her to be understood as the *materia* [subject matter] in which are found or from which arise the ideas [*sententiae*] that perfect the whole body of the work by means of the congruent ordering of arguments [*rationes*]" (in Minnis, Scott, and Wallace 1998: 55; trans. modified). Conrad's explanation of the opening image of Horace's *Art of Poetry* also sidesteps the unsettling implications of the feminine monster for the exercise of poetic mastery by privileging only the beautiful part of the hybrid, the woman's head, which is aligned with the beginning of the work as the source of both the corporeal *materia* and the rationally ordered ideas that are necessary for the perfect textual body. In other words, Conrad subordinates the ugly, threatening body to the head, the seat of reason and coherent beauty.

The personification of poetry as a woman whose carnality constitutes a threat to the male poet can be further viewed as central to the medieval reception of Horace's *Ars poetica* through a more visual approach to the manuscript evidence. Beginning in the twelfth century, texts of Horace's *Ars poetica* began to carry illustrations. Many twelfth- and thirteenth-century manuscripts display Horace's hybrid monster entwined either in the members of the initial letter "H" or in the margin beside it. What is most striking about these representations is not their fidelity to Horace's textual description but their adoption of the conventions used to depict monstrous female hybrids. Many of the illustrations depict the she-monster with wings and bird-like feet in addition to the fish tail indicated in Horace's text (Villa 1988). Such depictions are virtually indistinguishable from visual representations of the Siren, which began in twelfth-century iconography to include a fish tail as the most prominent marker of identity rather than the earlier attribute of a bird-like lower body (Faral 1953).

The identification of the Sirens' sensual song with harmoniously beautiful verbal seduction brings us back to poetry. In Greek genealogical accounts of the Sirens, the Muses were considered to be the mothers of the Sirens, a connection reinforced by the view that each of the three Sirens produces melody in her own manner: by voice, lyre, or flute (see Servius, *Commentarius in Vergilii Aenidos libros*, in Faral 1953: 440). The meretricious nature of such poetic harmony, made explicit by the repeated commonplace that identifies Sirens as whores (440), reduces those who delight in the verbal arts to the status of powerless prey. The late twelfth-/early thirteenth-century *Book of Beasts* likens the victims of Sirens, who are first entranced and then destroyed, to those who are undone by pleasure derived from more literary pursuits: "Those who take pleasure in the delights of this world, in spectacles and the sensuality of the theatre, those who are corrupted by tragedies and comedies, as if lulled into a deep sleep, become prey for their enemies" (Latin in Faral 1953: 498; trans. mine). Boethius becomes the paradigmatic victim of the Middle Ages, whose captivity by the "sweet poison" of the Muses of poetry is decried by Lady Philosophy, who banishes them with a tart insult: "Get out, you Sirens; your sweetness leads to death. Leave him to be cured and made strong by *my* Muses" (Boethius, *The Consolation of Philosophy*, bk. 1, prose. 1.9–11; trans. Green 1962: 5). The opposition between the harlot-like status of the Muses and Lady Philosophy's integrity is established by means of a textile metaphor in the Boethian text. Philosophy's clothing, perfectly integral (*indissolubilis*) in its *materia* and woven by her own hands out of very fine threads, stands as a metaphor for her physical and moral integrity and suggests that the poetic, siren-like Muses would lack any such corporeal and moral perfection in light of their association with both harlotry and hybridity (bk. 1, prose. 1.3–6). That medieval readers of Horace were acutely aware of the flawed, whorish, monstrous nature of both Sirens and poetic texts is made crystal clear in a fourteenth-century Italian manuscript of Horace's *Ars poetica* in which, preceding the text, a long-haired Siren with both fish's tail and falcon's feet bears the title *Camena*, the poetic Muse (Villa 1988: 196, fig. 11).

The specter of this poetic Siren haunts the preceptive arts of poetry that began to appear in the twelfth century. By espousing Horace's ideal of poetic mastery and textual integrity expressed in the medieval Horatian commentaries, they hoped to keep the beautiful, seductive Siren of poetic composition at bay. However, despite the efforts of theorists like Matthew of Vendôme (ca. 1175) and Geoffrey of Vinsauf (ca. 1215) to confine poetic production to the coherent, chaste text, the fissures of the feminine hybrid text, with all the connotations of verbal seduction drawn from both classical tradition and Christian exegeses of the role of deceptive rhetorical language and textual raggedness in the Fall, cannot be easily sutured. Instead of engaging directly with the possibility of a feminine, monstrous text, Matthew and Geoffrey warn against producing poems that are like garments riddled with holes or lined with obvious seams. For Matthew, the creation of a harmonious, seamless poem implies the appropriate exercise of the male poet's patriarchal control over his linguistic behavior: "For expressions are like handmaidens and tribute payers who yield to the poetic *paterfamilias* and since his authority prevails over analogy, no poet should presume to transgress what poetic usage permits; rather, he should place words properly so that the meter's wantonness should appear more decent since it comes from a proper positioning of words" (Matthew of Vendôme, *Ars versificatoria* 4.26, in Faral 1962: 186–7; trans. mine). According to Matthew, the poet's role is to preside over the union of words. Correct poetic and linguistic behavior is predicated on the masculine, authoritative control of sexual conduct. The poet who cannot control the joining of word to word or of words to *sententia* produces a gaping, ragged poem that testifies to his poetic impotence: "Let those who patch together rags be excluded from the reading of this work. For although there are many who are called versifiers, indeed there are few excellent ones. Certain individuals, leaning on the word, strive more for the number of verses than for elegance, and subversively turn out ragged poetry which casts shade by its trunk and not by its leaves" (prol. 7, in Faral 1962: 110). The reference to the barren tree comes from Lucan's *Pharsalia* (1.140), where it is used to cast Pompey in the role of the slack, weak, sterile man of yesterday, in contrast to the vigor and virility of the young Caesar. For Matthew, then, the powerful, manly poet is the one who can marshal his *materia* and turn out an integral poem.

This imperative toward integrity and mastery also shares in the anxiety expressed by Horace about the seductive, deceptive monstrosity that is both result and cause of the unmanning of poets. Alberic of Monte Cassino, writing in the eleventh century about how to compose letters (the *ars dictaminis*), is aware that the feminine nature of poetic (and rhetorical) *materia* presents problems for any composer. Alberic advocates textual integrity and cautions against "abrupt transitions," which he likens to "barking out a story stitched with shreds and patches [*panniculis obgannies consutum*]" (Alberic of Monte Cassino, *Flores rhetorici* 2.5.35; trans. Dronke 1984: 19). A lack of integrity in the text results from a lack of correspondence between the body of the subject matter and the verbal covering woven by the writer: "Meaning [should] proceed with her own body, not torn by foul adulterous copulation: her own inner beauty will be enough to make her radiant" (11.5.36). The torn, ragged text is the sign of a disjunction between word and thing, a tear that carries with it the burden of eroticized deception issuing from the bodies and mouths of Eve and the Sirens.

What happens, however, if the poet gets so caught up in the desire for surface beauty and adornment that, like Horace's potter, he loses control over both matter and form and produces a work that is monstrous and truly capable of seduction? For Geoffrey, this possibility is all too real. He cautions poets about the meretricious nature of words that gad about with brazenly painted faces: "First examine the mind of a word, and only then its face; do not trust the adornment of its face" (Geoffrey of Vinsauf, *Poetria nova* 739–40, in Faral 1962: 220). The disjunction between base *materia* and deceptively beautiful linguistic ornament is so feared because, as Geoffrey admits, the hybrid status of such a gap is the essence of fiction: "If internal ornament is not in harmony with external, reason becomes tainted. Adorning the face of a word is painting a sordid picture: it is a false thing, its beauty fictitious [*forma ficta*]; the word is a whitewashed wall and a hypocrite, pretending to be something whereas it is nothing. Its fair form conceals its deformity; it makes a brave show, but has nothing within" (741–7). The mention of hypocrisy is consonant with the jarring monstrosity alluded to in the opening lines of Horace's *Ars poetica*. In the medieval cultural imagination, hypocrisy was a perfect example of the moral failings of the hybrid. Alan of Lille, in his *Art of Preaching*, uses monstrous hybrid figures graced with the deceptively beautiful faces of young girls to refer to heretics, slanderers, and those sunk in dissolute, carnal living (19, 35, 78, 113). Like Horace's hybrid monster that is beautiful only on top, like the Siren whose alluring voice and face distract her victims from her ugly tail hidden below the water, Geoffrey's representation of poetic fiction betrays the same anxiety that poetry is an absence, a hole into which the male poet will be seduced.

Geoffrey, however, unlike his Horatian master, has managed to keep the Siren at bay. Despite Horace's initial warnings, the seduction of the poet is evident in Horace's own text. The structure of the *Ars poetica* has been a source of critical controversy, with readers attempting to impose unity upon it by positing a tripartite structure of poem, poetry, and poet, based on a supposed Neoptolemaic source, or a bipartite structure that follows the obvious shift in tone, seriousness, and depth (Golden 2000). One critic has recently suggested that the *Ars poetica* exemplifies the vices that it ridicules: the "poet who begins the *Ars* by penning the monster in ends by letting it out of its cage" (Oliensis 1998: 223), with the final image of the poem—in which the mad poet himself becomes a grotesque, hybrid figure—combining the metaphor of a leech with the simile of a bear (215). Medieval readers of Horace also sensed a bifurcation in the text, divided between advice about what poets should *not* do, followed by positive precepts. However, it was Geoffrey of Vinsauf's *Poetria nova* that seems to have embodied the Horatian ideal of masterful integrity, for medieval commentators repeatedly praise Geoffrey's text for performing the art it expounds: *de arte* (about the art) as well as *ex arte* (produced out of the art) (Woods 1985: 1.50). Unlike the deceptively beautiful hypocrite, Geoffrey's text does what it says.

The admonitions of Horace and medieval theorists of poetry (and rhetoric) about the corporeal integrity of the text fix the writer in a masculine subject position from which he must participate in the social drama of gender by taming the monstrous, uncontrollable, and violent potential of fragmentation. The latent pleasure offered by the ragged, monstrous text to both writer and reader makes medieval rhetoric and poetics compelling sites for the exploration of medieval subjectivity and desire. Medieval vernacular poets, shaped by their deep engagement with basic rhetorical and poetic texts and commentaries that formed the core of their acquisition of literacy, quickly learned how to exploit and play with the subversive possibilities of the ragged, hybrid text, a text whose essence is that of poetry itself.

References

Alan of Lille. 1981. *The Art of Preaching.* Translated by Gillian R. Evans. Kalamazoo, MI: Cistercian Publications.

Alberic of Monte Cassino. 1938. *Flores rhetorici.* Edited by D. Mauro Iguanez and Henry M. Willard. *Miscellanea Cassinense* 14: 33–59.

Ambrose. 1836. *De paradiso.* Vol. 1 of *Opera Omnia,* edited by D. A. B. Caillou and D. M. N. S. Guillon. Paris: Parent Desbarres.

Boethius. 1962. *The Consolation of Philosophy.* Translated by Richard Green. Indianapolis, IN: Bobbs-Merrill.

Brink, Charles Oscar. 1971. *Horace on Poetry: The "Ars Poetica."* Cambridge: Cambridge University Press.

Copeland, Rita. 1991. *Rhetoric, Hermeneutics and Translation in the Middle Ages: Academic Traditions and Vernacular Texts.* Cambridge: Cambridge University Press.

Copeland, Rita. 2006. "The Ciceronian Rhetorical Tradition and Medieval Literary Theory." In *The Rhetoric of Cicero in Its Medieval and Early Renaissance Commentary Tradition,* edited by Virginia Cox and John O. Ward, 239–265. Leiden: Brill.

Copeland, Rita, and Ineke Sluiter, eds. 2009. *Medieval Grammar and Rhetoric: Language Arts and Literary Theory, AD 300–1475.* Oxford: Oxford University Press.

Dronke, Peter. 1984. *The Medieval Poet and His World.* Rome: Edizione di Storia e Letteratura.

Faral, Edmond. 1953. "La queue des poissons des sirènes." *Romania* 74: 433–506.

Faral, Edmond. 1962. *Les Arts poétiques du XIIe et du XIIIe siècle.* Paris: Champion.

Friis-Jensen, Karsten. 1990. "The *Ars Poetica* in Twelfth-Century France: The Horace of Matthew of Vendôme, Geoffrey of Vinsauf, and John of Garland." *Cahiers de l'Institut du Moyen-Age Grec et Latin* 60: 319–388.

Friis-Jensen, Karsten. 1995. "Horace and the Early Writers of the Arts of Poetry." In *Sprachtheorien in Spätantike und Mittelalter,* edited by Sten Ebbeson, 360–401. Tübingen: Gunter Narr.

Geoffrey of Vinsauf. 1962. *Poetria nova.* In *Les arts poétiques du XIIe et du XIIIe siècle: Recherches sur la technique littéraire au moyen age,* edited by Edmond Faral, 194–262. Paris: Champion.

Geoffrey of Vinsauf. 1967. *"Poetria nova" of Geoffrey of Vinsauf.* Translated by Margaret F. Nims. Toronto: Pontifical Institute of Mediaeval Studies.

Gleason, Maud W. 1995. *Making Men: Sophists and Self-Presentation in Ancient Rome.* Princeton, NJ: Princeton University Press.

Golden, Leon. 2000. "*Ars* and *Artifex* in the *Ars Poetica:* Revisiting the Question of Structure." *Syllecta Classica* 11: 141–161.

Hajdu, Istvan. 1993. "Ein Zurcher Kommentar aus den 12. Jahrhundert zur *Ars poetica* des Horaz." *Cahiers de l'Institut du Moyen-Age Grec et Latin* 63: 231–293.

Hathaway, Neil. 1989. "*Compilatio:* From Plagiarism to Compiling." *Viator* 20: 19–44.

Horace. 1956. *Horace: Satires, Epistles, "Ars Poetica."* Edited and translated by H. Rushton Fairclough. Cambridge, MA: Harvard University Press.

Jager, Eric. 1993. *The Tempter's Voice: Language and the Fall in Medieval Literature*. Ithaca, NY: Cornell University Press.

Kelly, Douglas. 1969. "Theory of Composition in Medieval Narrative Poetry and Geoffrey of Vinsauf's *Poetria Nova*." *Mediaeval Studies* 31: 117–148.

Kelly, Douglas. 1999. *The Conspiracy of Allusion: Description, Rewriting, and Authorship from Macrobius to Medieval Romance*. Leiden: Brill.

Matthew of Vendôme. 1962. *Ars versificatoria*. In *Les arts poétiques du XIIe et XIIIe siècle: Recherches et documents sur la technique littéraire au moyen age*, edited by Edmond Faral, 109–193. Paris: Champion.

Minnis, Alastair J., Brian Scott, and David Wallace, eds. 1998. *Medieval Literary Theory and Criticism, c. 1100–c. 1375: The Commentary Tradition*. Revised edition. Oxford: Clarendon.

Murphy, James J. 1974. *Rhetoric in the Middle Ages: A History of Rhetorical Theory from St. Augustine to the Renaissance*. Berkeley: University of California Press.

Oliensis, Ellen. 1998. *Horace and the Rhetoric of Authority*. Cambridge: Cambridge University Press.

Olsen, Birger Munk. 1982–1989. *L'étude des auteurs classiques latins aux XIe et XIIe siècles*. 3 vols. Paris: Editions du Centre National de la Recherche Scientifique.

Purcell, William M. 1996. *"Ars poetriae": Rhetorical and Grammatical Invention at the Margin of Literacy*. Columbia: University of South Carolina Press.

Villa, Claudia. 1988. "'Ut poesis pictura': Appunti iconografici sui codici dell'*Ars poetica*." *Aevum* 62: 186–197.

Villa, Claudia. 1994. "I manoscritti di Orazio." *Aevum* 66 (1992): 95–135; *Aevum* 67 (1993): 55–103; *Aevum* 68 (1994): 117–146.

Wiedemann, Thomas. 1992. *Emperors and Gladiators*. London: Routledge.

Williams, Craig. 1999. *Roman Homosexuality: Ideologies of Masculinity in Classical Antiquity*. New York: Oxford University Press.

Woods, Marjorie Curry. 1985. *An Early Commentary on the "Poetria Nova" of Geoffrey of Vinsauf*. New York: Garland.

Zechmeister, Joseph, ed. 1877. *Scholia Vindobonensia ad Horatii "Artem Poeticam."* Vienna: Geroldum Filium Bibliopolam.

CHAPTER 29

....

RHETORIC AND COMEDY

....

JODY ENDERS

IN the anonymous fifteenth-century play known as *The Farce of the Fart* (*La Farce nou-velle et fort joyeuse du Pect*), Jehannette has "polluted" her clean house by farting, so husband Hubert hauls her ass to court. The cause of action? Begging the reader's pardon, it is whether marital property extends to the asshole. From one and the same unethical attorney representing both parties, here is the illustrious forensic rhetoric launched on Hubert's behalf: "But here is what he offers in his own defense. He says that there is no proof whatsoever that he ever married his wife's asshole. He further alleges that, if an asshole produces filth, then it's all perfectly clear: it follows that he is to assume no role or responsibility in that whatsoever" (Enders 2011: 81).[1] The turning point in the trial occurs when Hubert denies ever having taken possession of the malodorous body part in question, to which Jehannette interjects with proof from their wedding night: "How's this for a piece of evidence . . . ? My asshole was the first place he took me" (82). The pre-siding judge rejects Hubert's doltish protestations that it was so dark that he couldn't see which end was up and rules that, inasmuch as Hubert sodomized his wife, he married *all of her* and, ergo, must share and share alike in all that her asshole produces, including farts: "Inasmuch as you hold title to the asshole that laid the fart, then it follows that you were the one who laid it. That is clear and compelling proof. What's good for the goose is good for the gander. And, therefore, I rule that you must acknowledge having done it. That is my verdict" (82).

And that, ladies and gentlemen, is the world of medieval farce: raucous, rowdy, bawdy, obscene, satirical, sexist, violent, troubling, troublingly funny, and, above all, highly juridical. One of scores of such dramatic offerings, *The Farce of the Fart* is legal rhetoric at its most playful and theatrical. Or perhaps it is better to say that it is playful and theatrical rhetoric at its most legalistic. Either way, chiasmic phrasing suits the phe-nomenon quite well, as in the "rhetoric of comedy" and the "comedy of rhetoric." There was a powerful kinship between rhetoric, law, theater, and comedy in the Middle Ages, and that kinship is the focus of this chapter.

Be it medieval, modern, or postmodern, theater represents a privileged site at which the forensic, deliberative, and epideictic genres of classical rhetoric came together as communities explored, in performance, the *koinoi topoi*, or common topics, of their eras. Notwithstanding centuries of polemic against theatricality, the once meritorious, enacted, embodied art of rhetoric—ever concerned with the persuasion of judges and governments—constitutes an unbroken tradition by means of which legal systems marshaled powerfully cathartic emotions through any number of dramatic deliveries. Whatever scholarly doubts may endure as to what Aristotle truly meant by "catharsis" when he urged that tragedians proceed "not through narrating the thing, but through pity and fear expressed by the deeds, in that way purging and relieving all such violent disturbances of the soul" (*Poetics* 1449b; trans. Fyfe), one thing seems clear: thanks to forensic rhetoric, the law allows communities to bear witness to the ultimate catharsis of setting the world to right and, at least for some, of seeing justice done. In medieval France, it is equally clear that anger against injustice was frequently expressed in comic form. When spectators of any era laugh until they cry, their purgative tears are produced by the same tear ducts that are stimulated by tragedy. These are matters related to the history of rhetoric that are best addressed by a critical engagement with its long history: a history that, in turn, sheds new light on the notorious verbal and bodily excesses of farce. More precisely, thanks to delivery (Gk. *hypokrisis*; L. *actio*, *pronuntiatio*), these are also matters related to the intellect, affect, and politics of performance that enlivened invention, arrangement, style, and memory in fascinating ways that remain underexplored. When medieval rhetors classified the five rhetorical canons, they rehearsed a Pan-European model for legal argument (*inventio*), corporeal structure (*dispositio*), comic style (*elocutio*), and performances well remembered (*memoria*) because legal argument had been incarnated by actants with great theatrical flair (*actio*).

On one hand, the forensic rhetorical genre had long served as the locus at which the master theories of rhetoric were codified and articulated, so it is not surprising to see legal rhetoric so prominently displayed in the work of learned medieval writers. On the other hand, ever since Quintilian's counsel that effective advocates (*actores*) were to "draw a parallel from the stage" (*Institutio oratoria* 6.1.26; trans. Butler), forensic delivery has constituted a veritable program for dramatic conception, performance, and reception. Thanks to such proto-dramatic components as theatrical space, costume, staging, ritual conflict, audience participation, spectacle, dialogue, action, and, most importantly, impersonation (*ēthopoēia* or *prosōpopoēia*), dramatic rhetoric was regularly transformed into rhetorical drama (see Enders 1992, chs. 1 and 2). In short, Johan Huizinga was right about the interplay of "Play and Law" (1955, ch. 4), as was Howard Graham Harvey when he claimed that "the preparation and trial of a case in the courtroom is essentially a dramatic art" (1941: 19). Even today, a plethora of televised police dramas or gavel-to-gavel coverage of sensational trials amply confirms that the mise en scène of the specialized vocabulary and structures of forensic rhetoric has never waned as popular spectacle (see Goodrich, ch. 48).

After a brief recapitulation of the critical problems surrounding the use of rhetoric as an approach to medieval literature, we turn first to the rhetorico-theatrical influence of the Basoche, a French society of legal apprentices who were as (in)famous for their courtroom antics as for their oratory, authorship, and performance of numerous farces.

(It is believed, for instance, that *The Farce of the Fart* was authored by a Basochien.) Next, a quick perusal of rhetorico-legal sources reveals serious political issues underlying the veritable explosion of fifteenth- and sixteenth-century courtroom histrionics. Even when rhetorical questions of *actio* are treated under the rubric of style (*elocutio*), such exemplary rhetors as Matthew of Vendôme (born ca. 1130), Geoffrey of Vinsauf (fl. 1200), an anonymous twelfth-century commentator of Horace's *Ars poetica*, and the jurist Guillaume Du Breuil (ca. 1280–1344) all paved the way for the humor, sexuality, and even the anger that would come to inform Basochial theatrics as a comically rhetorical response to social injustice. Nor can those issues be readily resolved merely by invoking the critical commonplace that authors frequently critique their governments by means of the alleged veil of satire. Rather, as we shall see in the sexually charged language with which the Basochiens advertised a performance of 1634, the history of rhetoric sets the stage for an enhanced understanding—if never quite an acceptance—of the always "politically incorrect" humor of a farcical, forensic theatricality that is, literally, *barely* legal.

LAWYERS LAUGHING OUT LOUD

In contrast to its cousins from across the English Channel,[2] medieval French theater is peppered with trial scenes: tort cases, lawsuits, contested wills, and contracts in dispute, whether these unfold in an official courtroom, a marketplace, or in a domestic space in which husbands and wives, masters and servants, merchants and marks negotiate and renegotiate their social contracts. Lawyers are everywhere. They are onstage and behind the scenes; they are roaming about the countryside, eavesdropping on the altercations between husbands and wives; they are ever ensuring that minor domestic disputes reach the courtroom. In a word, they are litigating their proverbial asses off, their very body parts of a piece with the history of rhetoric itself. Despite a general scholarly reticence to posit the availability of Plato in medieval Europe prior to the Renaissance, such a jurist as Du Breuil describes rhetorical arrangement in corporeal terms that might have come straight out of the *Phaedrus*. In that dialogue, Socrates recommended that "any discourse ought to be constructed like a living creature, with its own body, as it were; it must not lack either head or feet; it must have a middle and extremities so composed as to suit each other and the whole work" (Plato, *Phaedrus* 264c; trans. Hackforth). In the French language, oratorical "body parts" are not only "extremities" but *membres*, the term that denotes arms, legs, and virile *members*. Says Du Breuil in the *Style du Parlement de Paris*: "Item, one must divide the legal matter into its constitutive parts [*membres*] in order to remember it better and the better to engage in hot yet subtle legal pursuit" (*Item diviser par membres la matière de ces causes pour la mectre mieux en mémoire et poursuir plus chaudement et subtillement*) (1877: 61–2).[3]

Fortunately, literary scholars can no longer simply dismiss all things rhetorical as annoying, uninteresting, nonliterary, and even offensive excursuses into pedantry.

Given the popularity of such excursuses, one can but wonder: Pedantic to whom? For example, admiration abounds for Guillaume de Machaut's bona fide rhetoric of courtly love in the fourteenth-century *Remède de Fortune*, in which an almost personified "Rhetoric makes the lover write in verse and meter, and compose poems that are diversified and in varied meters" (*Retorique versefier / Fait l'amant et metrefier, / Et si fait faire jolis vers / Nouveaux et de metres divers*) (lines 147–50; trans. Kelly 1978: 11–2). And no critic has seemed particularly ruffled by the Virgin Mary's retrieval of a signed, sealed, delivered, and redelivered legal contract between the Devil and a fallen priest in Rutebeuf's fourteenth-century *Miracle de Théophile*. But one does not find similar appreciation for the highly legalistic, rhetorically deft literary tribunals of the fifteenth century, notwithstanding Ernst Robert Curtius's early declaration that antiquity "had rhetoric for a general theory of literature" ([1953] 1973: 71), James J. Murphy's (1981: 3) assertion that rhetoric is where any study of modern Western communication theory begins, or George Kennedy's emphasis on the *letteraturizzazione* by which rhetoric shifts focus "from persuasion to narration, from civic to personal contexts, and from discourse to literature, including poetry" (1980: 5). Even Adolphe Fabre, who authored several important works on the Basoche, condemned much of so-called serious drama as "stuffed . . . with legal terms, formulas, procedures, and juridical definitions" (Fabre 1882: 55). Deploying an erotic metaphor of "monstrous coupling" that would do any farce proud, he objected that the Basochiens had "prostituted the muse by delivering her (as it were) to the caresses of the legal process and to contact with parliamentary style" (37–8). Yet when Arnoul Gréban opened his fifteenth-century *Mystère de la Passion* with a celestial trial, teeming with *stasis* theory, as to whether humankind should be redeemed when the Devil was not (Enders 1992: 171–82), his complex rhetorical ratiocinations were as forensically serious as those of rectal possession were comical in *The Farce of the Fart*. The endurance of a false critical dichotomy between the comic and the serious has hardly helped matters, but it is surely unreasonable to deem one and the same forensic rhetorical structure distasteful in some literatures and delicious in others or, more misguidedly still, distasteful in both. Furthermore, inasmuch as rhetorical *actio* and theatrical performance have the power to alter any mood through body language, intonation, and the like, who is to say that farcical litigation about a fart could not be extremely serious? Or, conversely, that serious litigation about the Redemption could not be farcical, especially in light of excellent studies on liturgical and hagiographical parody (Bayless 1996, chs. 3 and 6; Le Goff 1997: 50–1)?

Let's face it: medieval rhetorical treatises are not exactly light reading. But postmedieval students, teachers, and scholars have a peculiar tendency to assume (subconsciously at best and pretentiously at worst) that just because a text is written in Latin, Old English, Middle French, or Old High German, the author, rhetorician, playwright, or chronicler must be taken oh-so-seriously. What we find esoteric nowadays was not necessarily esoteric during the Middle Ages. Medieval rhetoric could be *funny*. Certainly its practitioners routinely satirized and ridiculed it in farce. They had a sense of humor about it, and so should we. Indeed, we do no service to the past by refusing to reckon with its laughter. As Mikhail Bakhtin once cautioned, "To ignore or to underestimate the laughing people of the Middle Ages . . . distorts the picture of European culture's historic development" ([1965] 1984: 6). Even if our own inquiry begins simply with "*What's so funny?*" the quest for answers promises to deepen our understanding of the transcendence of rhetoric and humor alike, neither of which can be understood independently of the thespian lawyers of the Basoche. When it comes to pondering the key social questions of justice and injustice—the bread and butter of the rhetorical tradition—the unsubtle farce offers up, with surprising subtlety, an ethical universe that demands ethical reflection, even though such reflection might well seem very far away from what everybody involved seems to be doing: laughing.

Barely Legal

According to Harvey (1941: 8–22), the Society of the Basoche was founded in 1303 and flourished between 1450 and 1550, at one point boasting as many as 10,000 members practicing their legal trade. The lawyers-in-training came together officially on Wednesday and Saturday afternoons, with one of those sessions apparently reserved for fictional cases (*causes fictives*). This was a tradition as old as the mock encomium of Greco-Roman antiquity and as new as the moot courts that spring up in contemporary law schools (to say nothing of rowdy, tension-releasing, end-of-the-year revues). Just as, in Roman declamatory practice, students agreed upon "some subject, real or fictitious," and then took "different sides, debating it as would be done in the courts" (Quintilian, *Institutio oratoria* 6.4.21), the same held true for the real or fictitious cases litigated by the Basochiens. Inside a real courtroom, bailiffs came forward to announce the case with solemnity, prosecutors prosecuted, defendants defended, audiences listened and joined in, a court clerk took notes, and judges withdrew to deliberate their verdicts and impose sentences, all creating a certain commingling of the rhetorically theatrical *cause fictive* and the actual court cases that the Basochiens were empowered to litigate (Harvey 1941: 10–20; Bouhaïk-Gironès 2007: 256–70). There is evidence, moreover, of bona fide theatrical collaborations outside the courtroom, notably, by the mid-fourteenth century, in the Passion plays (Harvey 1941: 24) and in the *causes grasses* or mock trials performed during Carnival (as in Mardi Gras). Wherever the Basochiens performed, their bailiwick was the petty dispute: failure to pay debts for books, food, or linen; punishment for fistfights or disorderly conduct (18–20). Frivolous though such minor judicial matters might appear, they are no more so than the countless civil actions that flood today's small claims courts; they are no less entertaining than such American televised offerings as *Judge Judy* or *The People's Court*. Consider the motley crew of litigants who brought their cases before the Basochial court: tailors, bakers, linen suppliers, barkeeps, and deadbeat students. Add cobblers to the mix, and the cast of characters resembles that of any farce. That realization, it seems, was not lost on the Basochiens, who incarnate the ageless popular expression, "That trial is a *farce!*" Lest the reader fear that I exaggerate the comic possibilities, consider now, from among hundreds of anonymous fifteenth- and sixteenth-century French farces, a few cases in point.

In the *Farce of the Washtub* (*Farce du Cuvier*), a husband discovers a legal loophole in the contract he has earlier signed with his wife (under duress), in which he guaranteed that he would perform all the household chores. When the legal tables are turned as she drowns in the washtub, he deadpans to each of her repeated pleas for help that "it's not on his list." In *Poor Bastards* (*Farce nouvelle et fort joyeuse à cinq personnages, c'est à sçavoir les Batars de Caulx*), three essentially disinherited children battle with their foolish and selfish older brother, Henry, for their own—and their mother's—rightful legacy (which includes such a stunningly generous provision for mom as all the bread she can eat). In *Less than Ravishing* (*Farce nouvelle à cinq personnages, c'est asçavoir la Mère, la Fille, le Témoin, L'Amoureux, et l'Official*), the adjudication of a rape case is played for laughs, a tradition that may well have been nurtured by medieval schoolboys' habitual training in the rape narratives of Ovid (Woods 1996: 56–61; see Enterline, ch. 39). In *Back Pay* (*Farce nouvelle très bonne et fort joyeuse des femmes qui demandent les arrérages de leurs maris*), a young and nubile wife sues her poor-performing husband for failure to grant the sexual entitlements to which she is due. In *Not Gettin' Any* (*Farce nouvelle très bonne et fort joyeuse du Marié qui ne peult fournir à l'appoinctement de sa femme*), it is an incensed mother who prepares to drag her new son-in-law into court because, after an entire year, he has yet to do his marital duty by his wife.[4] And, in the rightly beloved *Pathelin*, an exasperated judge shrieks his frustration, all in proper legal form, that litigation about stolen sheep has mutated into babble about stolen cloth. In fact, for as much as the *Pathelin* has been studied, medievalists have yet to make the connection between its acquisitive barristers and the desiderata of such rhetors as Du Breuil. Abstract notions of justice, ethics, or morality be damned! Du Breuil's lawyer was to create a pleasing physical demeanor, the better to camouflage his true intentions from his clients (*ne dire son intencion à son client*), whom he was to select based on their ability to pay (Enders 2011: 61). And so on.

For much of this, we have the Basoche to thank, as evidenced by our *pièce de résistance*, a culmination of sorts of two centuries' worth of mock trials played for laughs. From the following advertisement for a *cause grasse* in 1634, the reader will quickly intuit why matters of *bienséance* have prevented this historical artifact from penetrating canonical histories of rhetoric:

> In this particular case, you will see eloquence in the flesh, stripped to the bone[r], totally naked: alive, male, and virile [*On void dans ceste cause l'éloquence paroistre toute nue, en chair et en os, vive, masle et hardie*]. . . . In the exordium [*l'exorde*], you insinuate yourself into the listener's mind by means of something that strikes the senses; the statement of facts [*la narration*] is always about some kind of abused tart or some kind of mark that you take for all he's worth. . . . The intention of the litigators is always to stimulate the audience's laughter, not their empathy [*commisération*]: indeed, *who wouldn't laugh at the judges alone of this momentous trial, practically pissing themselves trying to hold back their laughter with all their might?* Or at

the lawyers who have the honor of litigating there, speaking gravely and seriously of the most ridiculous things in the world? (Harvey 1941: 22; emphasis added)

To put it all in perspective, this was precisely the kind of thing liable to revive the old Platonic objection that comic representations literally nourished "sex and anger, and all the appetites and pains and pleasures of the soul which we say accompany all our actions . . . when what we ought to do is to dry them up" (*Republic* 606c–d; trans. Shorey). A grotesque Basochien would likely say that sex and anger were social lubricants, that rhetorical *dispositio* was a naturally sexual, comic disposition, and that it was all enacted bodily through *actio* (if not always stripped bare). The root of the problem was barely legal: a very real anger against injustice.

Medieval courtrooms—fictitious or real—were clearly dramatic stages upon which communities grappled time and time again with the powerful and motivating emotion of anger (Rosenwein 1998). For example, in his list of dos and don'ts for attorneys endeavoring to create pleasing personae before the Parisian Parliament, Du Breuil was emphatic that anger was to be avoided at all costs. Even when legal adversaries attacked one another with satire or jests—Du Breuil's verb is *truffer*, a much used synonym for *farcer*—the ideal jurist was to exercise the very degree of control that is relaxed by farce. More indulgent of joking than of blatant insults, such a jurist was to

> refrain and moderate the movement of his heart and mind, lest, for a few words or other reasons, he be moved to anger, rage, or dissent [*ire, courroux ou discencion*]. . . . And if the opposing party or his lawyer were to say anything offensive or reproachful, *either obliquely or in jest* [*en truffant*], he must point this out courteously and without becoming indignant or blaming the court or others present. . . . But if the insults are made openly and clearly, then vigorously and just as openly must he point this out, and respond and defend himself reasonably, *without being moved to anger*—lest he lose his train of thought or the slightest degree of control [*sans soy à ire esmouvoir, affin qu'il ne perde son propos*]. (Du Breuil 1877: 61–2; emphasis added)

For Du Breuil, anger was the enemy of reason and, for the Basochiens, frustration with the legal system was an inspiration for farce, which provided countless outlets for anger, if never truly free rein. After all, trials, political theater, and plays were public events subject to censorship and could lead to the prosecution, imprisonment, and even execution of those involved (Enders 1992: 149–55). But there can be no denying the proximity, anointed by the rhetorical tradition, of laughter to rage.

Perhaps Matthew of Vendôme said it best in his *Ars versificatoria* (ca. 1175). When commenting on the possible slippage of anger into comic performance, he cites Horace: "The character of words ought to conform to the facial expression of the persons speaking and to their inner fortune; for 'somber words suit the sad face; *threatening words, the angry; jesting words, the light-hearted*; words of sober import, the serious. . . . If the words do not correspond to the fortunes of the speaker, *all the Romans will laugh in derision.*' But this seems to have *special reference to the manner of recitation*" (trans.

Copeland and Sluiter 2009: 563; emphasis added). Although Matthew's nominal subject is style, right he was about that "manner of recitation," otherwise known as delivery. In fact, the rhetorical stylistics of the performance of character lend new meaning to the infamous looseness and dissolution once signaled by Horace and reprised by an anonymous medieval commentator (ca. 1150) (see Ross, ch. 28). If the low, middle, and grand rhetorical styles (*humilis*, *mediocris*, and *altus*) were linked, respectively, to comedy, satire, and tragedy, of special note is the "corresponding fault" of the middle style, which is typically attributed to farce: that of "drifting and of being loose [*fluctuans et dissolutum*]" (trans. Copeland and Sluiter 2009: 554–5). Finding fault with farce has never been a problem, nor has finding anger in rhetorical performance, as did Geoffrey of Vinsauf in his anger-infused discussion of delivery in the twelfth-century *Poetria nova*. Geoffrey's impassioned orator was to "arise a voice full of gall, a face enraged, and turbulent gestures" in that "anger [*ira*], the begetter of flaming rage and the mother of fury, is kindled by the bellows and *poisons the heart and bowels*. It stirs one with bellows, *burns in flame, excites with fury*" (1971: 125; emphasis added). Any reader of farce is quick to spot Gallo's bowels (not present in all translations), be it in the anal sex of *The Farce of the Fart* or the endless discussions of the proverbial *merde* in *Shit for Brains* (Enders 2011: 252–78). Be that as it may, in the searing evacuations of farce we must be careful not to miss those flames of rage. Medieval actants are "bellowing," all right. We need only look and listen.

On one hand, medieval theatrical "farcing around" with the law captures the silly grandiloquence that has dogged rhetoric since the days of the sophists, anticipating the dialectical turn that some legal rhetorics would eventually take, as in *Pasquier, ou Dialogue des advocats du Parlement de Paris*, by Antoine Loisel (1536–1617). In a setting reminiscent of Plato or Alcuin, Loisel appears as the protagonist in a dialogue, intent on seeking wisdom from the great teacher, Pasquier. Only when pressed does Pasquier confess his "frank opinion" that Cicero got it "entirely backward" (*au rebours*) or, as a Basochien would have said, "ass-backward": "In sum, in my lawyer, I desire the contrary of what Cicero requires of his orator, which is eloquence in the first place, seconded by a bit of legal knowledge [*qui est l'eloquence en premier lieu, et puis quelque science de droict*]" (see Pasquier 1844: 122–5). Instead, Pasquier believes that judgment and principle trump "great or long speeches" and that his lawyer must "above all be knowledgeable in the law and in its practice, and passably eloquent, more of a dialectician than a rhetor [*sçavant en droict et en pratique, et mediocrement eloquent, plus dialecticien que rheteur*]."

On the other hand, the aforementioned farces incarnate precisely what incensed the fifteenth-century French jurist Thomas Basin at the same time that it delighted the authors and audiences of farce: namely, the "contagious influence" of the omnipresent lawyer who "gnaws at, stalks, and exhausts the very essence of . . . the people—somewhat, and even too litigious already by nature—[who] are taken in and caught up in judicial actions and in disputes, ever more numerous and almost infinite" (1974: 262–3). For Basin, such contagion had a great deal to do with the forensic theatrics that had become distracting enough to compromise the orderly exposition of trial logic. Thus, in his modest *Proposal for Juridical Reform* of 1455—a crucial document in the history of literacy—Basin advocated that litigation be conducted *in writing only* (*ex scripto*). His colleagues were to "strip the pomp [*pompa divellere*] from their oral trials and forensic oratory" instead of "declaim[ing] them in a holiday atmosphere and style of pleading [*cum illa placitandi festivitate declamari*]" (Basin 1859: 4: 50–1). Needless to say, Basin's proposal did not carry the day, but his effort to cast the interdependence of rhetoric and theater as an enmity still endures. Such efforts invariably fail because, try as rhetoricians might to divest *hypokrisis* of *hypocrisy*, they can never divest *actio* of the physical *action* of performance. In the final analysis, for as long as we downplay the paramountcy of delivery as a performance medium, we shall continue to be denied access to the power of comedy as a social—and also antisocial—rhetorical response to injustice. Rage, rage, against the dying of the guffaw.

NOTES

1. All translations from French are my own unless otherwise indicated. Middle French has no fixed orthography so its spellings often look curious or incorrect to readers of modern French. I regularize and modernize the spelling of *ie* as *je*, etc.
2. The Basoche has more in common with the civic-minded rhetoricians (*Rederijkers*) of the Low Countries (Kramer 1996; see Plett, ch. 30).
3. The French translation of the *Stilus Curie Parlamenti Stilus* (begun in ca. 1329) dates from the end of the fourteenth century or the first half of the fifteenth century (xlviii).
4. These are provisional titles for my new translations in progress.

REFERENCES

Bakhtin, Mikhail. (1965) 1984. *Rabelais and His World*. Translated by Hélène Iswolsky. Bloomington: Indiana University Press.

Basin, Thomas. 1974. *Apologie ou plaidoyer pour moi-même*. Edited by Charles Samaran and Georgette de Groër. Paris: Belles Lettres.

Basin, Thomas. 1859. *Histoire des règnes de Charles VII et de Louis XI*. Edited by J. Quicherat. 4 vols. Paris: Renouard.

Bayless, Martha. 1996. *Parody in the Middle Ages: The Latin Tradition*. Ann Arbor: University of Michigan Press.

Bouhaïk-Gironès, Marie. 2007. *Les Clercs de la Basoche et le théâtre comique (Paris, 1420–1550)*. Paris: Champion.

Copeland, Rita, and Ingrid Sluiter, eds. 2009. *Medieval Grammar and Rhetoric: Language Arts and Literary Theory, A.D. 300–1475*. Oxford: Oxford University Press.

Curtius, Ernst Robert. (1953) 1973. *European Literature and the Latin Middle Ages*. Translated by Willard R. Trask. Bollingen 36. Princeton, NJ: Princeton University Press.

Du Breuil, Guillaume. 1877. *Style du Parlement de Paris*. Edited by Henri Lot. Paris: Gouverneur.

Enders, Jody. 1992. *Rhetoric and the Origins of Medieval Drama*. Rhetoric and Society 1. Ithaca, NY: Cornell University Press.

Enders, Jody, ed. and trans. 2011. *The Farce of the Fart and Other Ribaldries: Twelve Medieval French Plays in Modern English*. The Middle Ages Series. Philadelphia: University of Pennsylvania Press.

Fabre, Adolphe. 1882. *Les Clercs du Palais: La Farce et Cry de la Bazoche*. Vienne: Savigné.

Geoffrey of Vinsauf. 1971. *Poetria Nova*. In *The Poetria Nova and Its Sources in Early Rhetorical Doctrine*. Translated by Ernest Gallo. The Hague: Mouton.

Harvey, Howard Graham. 1941. *The Theatre of the Basoche*. Cambridge, MA: Harvard University Press.

Huizinga, Johan. 1955. Homo Ludens: *A Study of the Play Element in Culture*. Translated by R. F. C. Hull. Boston: Beacon.

Kelly, Douglas. 1978. *Medieval Imagination: Rhetoric and the Poetry of Courtly Love*. Madison: University of Wisconsin Press.

Kennedy, George A. 1980. *Classical Rhetoric and Its Christian and Secular Tradition from Ancient to Modern Times*. Chapel Hill: University of North Carolina Press.

Kramer, Femke. 1996. "*Rederijkers* on Stage: A Closer Look at 'Meta-theatrical' Sources." *Research Opportunities in Renaissance Drama* 35: 97–109.

Le Goff, Jacques. 1997. "Laughter in the Middle Ages." In *A Cultural History of Humour From Antiquity to the Present Day*, edited by Jan Bremmer and Herman Roodenburg, 40–53. Cambridge: Polity Press.

Loisel, Antoine. 1844. *Pasquier, ou Dialogue des advocats du Parlement de Paris*. Paris: Videcoq.

Murphy, James J. 1981. *Rhetoric in the Middle Ages: A History of Rhetorical Theory from Saint Augustine to the Renaissance*. Berkeley: University of California Press.

Rosenwein, Barbara, ed. 1998. *Anger's Past: The Social Uses of an Emotion in the Middle Ages*. Ithaca, NY: Cornell University Press.

Woods, Marjorie Curry. 1996. "Rape and the Pedagogical Rhetoric of Sexual Violence." In *Criticism and Dissent in the Middle Ages*, edited by Rita Copeland, 56–86. Cambridge: Cambridge University Press.

PART IV

RENAISSANCE RHETORIC

CHAPTER 30

RHETORIC AND HUMANISM

HEINRICH PLETT

HUMANISM is the essential intellectual, scholarly, and cultural movement of the European Renaissance (Kristeller 1961, 1964, 1965; Grassi 2001), a period that extends approximately from 1300 to 1600 CE. Rhetoric formed an important part of this movement from the very beginning. According to the humanists, true eloquence could arise only out of a harmonious union between wisdom and eloquence. The ideological basis of humanist rhetoric is the *ratio–oratio* principle, namely, that the unity of reason and rhetoric is the presupposition of an ideal or truly humanist society (cf. Cicero, *De inventione* 1.1–3). To achieve that social *telos*, humanist education is based on the *studia humanitatis*, comprising the studies of grammar, rhetoric, poetry, history, and moral philosophy (Seigel 1968; Kallendorf 2002).

THE DEVELOPMENT OF HUMANIST RHETORIC

Humanist rhetoric originated as a result of the rediscovery of the manuscripts of ancient rhetoric: the speeches of Cicero (e.g., *Pro Archia poeta*) and his correspondence with Atticus, by Petrarch (1304–74); Cicero's *Familiar Epistles*, by Coluccio Salutati (1331–1406); the complete text of Cicero's *De oratore* in a manuscript also containing his *Brutus* and *Orator*, by Gerardo Landriani, cardinal of Lodi (1437–45), in 1421; and the integral text of Quintilian's *Institutio oratoria*, at the monastery of St. Gall, by the Florentine humanist Poggio Bracciolini (1380–1459), a papal secretary on his way to the Council of Constance (1415). A decade before Bracciolini discovered Asconius's commentary on Cicero's orations, Antonio Loschi (1365–1441) published his *Inquisitio super XI orationes Ciceronis* (1392–6). Although as a rhetorician Cicero was not unknown in the Middle Ages, his fame derived mainly from the rather unimaginative technical treatise, *De inventione*, and the spurious *Rhetorica ad Herennium* attributed to him. Now Cicero's image changed, and he became known as the witty writer of charming conversations composed in an elegant Latin style. Moreover, Cicero now emerged as the author of theoretical writings on rhetoric and simultaneously as its practitioner as a lawyer and statesman, thus uniting the qualities of both the *vita contemplativa* and the *vita activa* (see Kahn 1985).

A further stage in the revival of ancient rhetoric is marked by the printing of these rediscovered Latin and Greek manuscripts, which made it possible to disseminate knowledge of these texts throughout Europe. Thus, Cicero's *De oratore* was published as a single edition at Subiaco (ca. 1465), Rome (1468), Venice (ca. 1470), and Milan (1477) and went through at least eighteen more editions up to the 1696 Oxford edition. The important collection of the *Rhetores Graeci* appeared with the Aldine press at Venice from 1508 to 1509 in two folio volumes. The sheer quantity of these texts by Greek rhetoricians who today are known only to specialists testifies to the immense interest and even enthusiasm aroused by the rediscovery of this previous cultural *terra incognita*. The *Rhetores Graeci* contained the stylistic theory of Hermogenes of Tarsus (about 200 CE), the *Rhetoric* and *Poetics* of Aristotle, a treatise on prose composition by Dionysius of Halicarnassus (ca. 60 BCE to after 7 BCE), and Pseudo-Demetrius's stylistic treatise, *De elocutione*. This selection of treatises from the *editio Aldina* shows that the humanists were above all interested in the (literary) stylistics of the classical tradition.

A third stage of this revival of rhetoric came about thanks to deficiencies in the knowledge of classical languages. Translation of basic classical texts into the vernacular was required to render them accessible to those readers who, in Ben Jonson's famous dictum about his great rival, William Shakespeare, knew "small Latine & lesse Greeke." First, however, the poor knowledge of Greek among the humanists meant that the relevant Greek texts had to be translated into Latin, the language of the learned international *Respublica literaria*. Thus, Aristotle's *Rhetoric* was translated by the Greek scholar and philosopher George of Trebizond (1395–1473) and published in Paris (1475?) and Lyon (1541). In his *Rhetoricorum libri quinque* (*Five Books on Rhetoric*) of 1433 (printed in 1471 and 1538), the same author was the first to combine Greek and Latin sources to constitute a new theoretical approach to the discipline. The Italian poet Annibale Caro (1507–66) translated Aristotle's *Rhetoric* under the title RETTORICA/D'ARISTOTILE/FATTA IN LINGVA/TOSCANA/*DAL COMMENDATORE*/ANNIBAL CARO./Con Priuilegio./ IN VENETIA,/Al segno della Salamandra, MDLXX. Italian translations of Aristotle's *Rhetoric* and *Poetics* were produced by Bernardo Segni (1504–58) in 1549 under the title *Rettorica, et Poetica d'Aristotele Tradotte di Greco in lingua vulgare Fiorentina da Bernardo Segni Gentl'huomo, & Accademico Fiorentino*. A notable English specimen is the translation of *The Three Orations in Favour of the Olynthians* of Demosthenes (London, 1570), whom the translator Thomas Wilson (1524–81), diplomat and privy councillor under Queen Elizabeth I, calls "chiefe orator among the Grecians."

The fourth stage of the rhetorical revival of the classics was the hermeneutic procedure of producing annotations and commentaries. Of foremost importance are the glosses and commentaries on Cicero's works, which in their turn display several stages of erudition and complexity. Such an enriched knowledge of Cicero's works led to the creation of a specific norm of Neo-Latin style associated with the term "Ciceronianism." The compulsory force emanating from this stylistic habit at times sparked fierce controversies (cf. Sabbadini 1886), in which the "arch-humanist" Desiderius Erasmus of Rotterdam (1467–1536) also became involved. The orientation in this "master-code" had a predecessor in the Atticist movement of classical rhetoric (Wilamowitz-Moellendorf 1968).

A new phase in the reception of classical rhetoric in the age of humanism is the conception and formulation of new rhetorical treatises, partly in Neo-Latin and partly in a vernacular language. Many of these served as textbooks for grammar schools and universities, institutions in which Latin grammar and rhetoric had been taught since late antiquity (see Mack, ch. 33). An important humanist author of Neo-Latin treatises was Philipp Melanchthon (1497–1560). His rhetoric first appeared in 1519 in Wittenberg under the title *Philippi Melanchthonis de rhetorica libri tres*. It follows the Ciceronian schema of the five *officia oratoris* (*inventio, dispositio, elocutio, memoria, pronuntiatio/actio*), of which the latter did not receive full treatment. But its innovative additions also include chapters on hermeneutics (*De enarratorio genere* ["On the Genre of Expounding"]), commenting (*De commentandi ratione*), and sermons (*De sacris concionibus*). A characteristic feature that pervades the work is its emphasis on dialectic, the study of which is recommended time and again. This treatise was composed as a textbook for the University of Tübingen, where Melanchthon taught as one of the first professors of rhetoric. It is therefore not surprising that a second version of the same textbook (1521) bears the programmatic title, *Institutiones rhetoricae* (*Rhetorical Instructions*). Its overall disposition is, with minor changes, patterned on the author's *Rhetorica*, but the section on style (*elocutio*) is very much enlarged and in keeping with the humanists' predominant interest in style. In this respect, Erasmus's *De duplici copia rerum ac verborum* (*On the Twofold Copiousness of Things and Words*) (1512) can be regarded as the most important rhetorical textbook of humanism (cf. Baldwin 1956; Sloane 1997). Originally commissioned by the English humanist John Colet (1467–1519) for St. Paul's School, it quickly found its way into most countries of Renaissance Europe. In 1536 M. Veltkirchius published an elaborately annotated edition of this work. In the same year, Petrus Mosellanus's (i.e., Peter Schade's [1493–1524]) *Tabulae de schematibus et tropis* (*Tables of Schemes and Tropes*) was also published. Both works contributed to the rising fame of Erasmus's *De copia*. Consisting of detailed explications of the figures of speech as well as rich illustrations, *De copia* occupies an intermediate position between a rhetorical theory of precepts and a practical compendium of examples. Like Erasmus's work, many treatises on figurative rhetoric were conceived as secondary education textbooks to train students in the writing of stylistically elegant compositions. Their structure is almost always the same (Plett 1994, 2004, 2010; Adamson, Alexander, and Ettenhuber 2007). A brief general outline of the virtues of style and its three levels (high, middle, low) is followed by a broad treatment of the tropes and figures. *The Garden of Eloquence* (1577, 1593) by Henry Peacham (1546–1634) is a prime example of this general type. In contrast to the extensive rhetorical textbook that contains Cicero's fivefold schema of invention, disposition, elocution, memory, and delivery, the French humanist and philosopher Petrus Ramus (i.e., Pierre de la Ramée [1515–72]), a severe critic of Aristotle and his rhetoric, reduced this number and allocated *inventio* and *dispositio* to dialectic, while *elocutio* and *actio/pronuntiatio* remained in the realm of rhetoric. Ramist rhetoricians regularly dissected the corpus of stylistic schemes into neat dichotomies and arranged them in logically conclusive hierarchical *stemmata* that facilitated their memorization (Howell 1961; Ong 2004). A remarkable feature of Ramist treatises is their employment of classical literary examples to illustrate the stylistic categories, as in *The Arcadian Rhetoric* (ca. 1588) by the Englishman Abraham Fraunce (1558–93?). The overall reduction of rhetoric to style led to a widespread misconception of a curtailed rhetoric that is still alive today (see Goodrich, ch. 48).

The next phase in the development of humanist rhetoric originates in the seventeenth century or Baroque Age. Compared with the Renaissance, rhetoric now mostly assumes an encyclopedic character. Striving for utmost completeness, the treatises now include classical sources and sections of contemporary treatises along with learned annotations and commentaries. One of the first rhetorical encyclopedias is the *Thesaurus rhetoricae* (1599) by the Venetian nobleman and senator Giovanni Battista Bernardi. The *Thesaurus rhetoricae* claims to present the entire rhetorical discipline together with all the sources available in print; for this reason a long list of authors consulted, complete with publication years and printing locations, precedes the thesaurus proper. Further encyclopedic rhetorical manuals were compiled by Dutch scholars such as Gerardus Johannes Vossius (1577–1649), a classical scholar and theologian at Leiden University and Amsterdam's Athenaeum Illustre, and Daniel Heinsius (1580–1655), also a professor at Leiden. Vossius's rhetoric manuals claim to explain the whole range of rhetorical categories by including extensive commentaries, ample cross-references to other rhetorical treatises (both classical and contemporary), as well as a large number of marginal references and glosses (see Moss 1996, 2006). Among the Protestant humanists, Johann Heinrich Alsted (1588–1638) created encyclopedic works on rhetoric for the recently founded Protestant Academia Nassauensis at Herborn. Of the Jesuit scholars in the Baroque Age, Nicolas Caussin (1583–1651) excelled with his publication of a large folio on rhetoric titled ELOQVENTIÆ SACRÆ ET HVMANÆ PARALLELA. LIBRI XVI. Auctore P. NICOLAO CAVSSINO Trecensi è Societate IESV. *FLEXIÆ*, [...], 16XIX. Dedicated to the French King Louis XIII, this work extends over sixteen books that minutely describe the entire available knowledge of rhetoric. It includes references to practically all Greek and Latin rhetoricians, sophists, and philologists, whose names appear in a long list prefixed to this encyclopedic work. Perhaps book 8 (*De affectibus*) deserves the greatest attention, because the Jesuits in general laid special emphasis on strategies *de propaganda fide*, a principle they enacted in affective orations, plays, paintings, and musical compositions (e.g., "oratorios").

To conclude this account of the historical development of humanist rhetoric, it is worth noting the special case of the Chambers of Rhetoric, which were founded and administered by guilds in Flanders, Brabant, Zeeland, and Holland (now Belgium and the Netherlands) with the purpose of cultivating and patronizing the creation of rhetorically elaborated poetry and plays (Koopmans et al. 1995). While they here were called *Rederijkers*, similar developments took place in northern France and southern Germany, where orator-poets were named *rhétoriqueurs* or, in Nuremberg, *Meistersinger*. In the Low Countries the large and wealthy cities such as Amsterdam and Antwerp competed with each other for the coveted "crown" for poetry. These competitions took the form of magnificent spectacles. Particularly striking in the staging of *Rederijker* plays was their sumptuous scenography. Often the stage was divided into several segments with allegorical figures on display. The statue of a personified Rhetorica enthroned on the upper stage usually surmounted this elaborate structure. A famous treatise devoted to this remarkable rhetorical art is *De const van rhetoriken* (1555) by Matthijs de Castelein (1485/9–1530). As these rhetorical spectacles suggest, intermediality is an invention of the Renaissance, when rhetoric expanded its range of applications and served as a semiotic construct for the theory and practice of nonverbal media. Such concepts as *inventio* and *decorum* were transferred from rhetoric to pictorial theory (Leon Battista Alberti, Franciscus Junius) and contributed to raising this former *ars mechanica* to the level of an *ars liberalis* (see van Eck, ch. 37; Kirkbride, ch. 40). In musical theory and practice an analogous transfer of rhetorical categories took place, of which Joachim Burmeister's *Musica poetica* (1600) provides ample testimony. The tradition of rhetoricizing music continued well into the eighteenth century, when the *Klangrede* or "musical eloquence" was still practiced by Johann Sebastian Bach (1685–1750) and George Frideric Handel (1685–1759).

The Practice of Humanist Rhetoric

Rhetoric as a system originally consisted of five stages of composing an oration. According to the Ciceronian view, these stages include *inventio*, or the discovery of subject matter; *dispositio*, the arrangement of this material; *elocutio*, its linguistic ornamentation; *memoria*, its memorization; and *pronuntiatio/actio*, its appropriate delivery in pronunciation, mimicry, and gesture. The Ciceronian view—a normative model for most humanist treatises—comprises the entire range of these stages. Whenever one of them was separated from the rest, it achieved autonomy as a theory of invention with a predecessor in Cicero's *De inventione* and an affinity with dialectics, or as a theory of style, of memory, or of delivery. *Dispositio*, from the beginning the least elaborated part of the rhetorical system, never attained such independence.

The Ciceronian *quinque partes artis* served as a pattern for various types of humanist oratory. One of these, judicial oratory, gained importance because many humanists had studied law at university (e.g., Bologna) and served as chancellors or secretaries to princes, republican authorities (e.g., the doges of Venice), or spiritual leaders (bishops, cardinals, popes). Rhetorical qualities for the clergy concentrated on the *ars praedicandi* or pulpit oratory, which was not a humanist invention in its own right but harked back to medieval predecessors. While this kind of rhetoric is mainly an oral one, an exclusively written branch was the *ars epistolica* or art of letter writing, as set forth in numerous theoretical treatises or practical manuals with model letters. This branch of rhetoric also has a medieval predecessor, the *ars dictaminis*, a creation of Alberic of Monte Cassino (fl. 1065–88), which proved necessary and useful for a wide range of administrative purposes. The art of drafting official letters or documents had not disappeared in the early Middle Ages; it was kept alive by notaries and royal clerks as a rigorously practical art, taught by the imitation of standard types and collections of forms, with no freedom or spontaneity of expression. This written practice continued in Italy and elsewhere in Europe during the early modern age but was supplemented by a new epistolary form: the private letter (Poster and Mitchell 2007). Inspired by Cicero's recently rediscovered *Epistulae ad familiares*, the private letter often served as a medium for the lively exchange of ideas among the humanists (Erasmus, Juan Luis Vives, Conrad Celtes, and Justus Lipsius, among others). On the whole, it can be stated that both the *ars praedicandi* and the *ars epistolica* adopted the five-part schema popularized by Cicero, although letter writing, of course, did not require sections on memory and delivery.

One part of rhetoric that did gain a certain autonomy was *memoria*. The classical art of memory was practiced in a primarily oral culture in which communicative interaction took place between individuals or groups of individuals. Renaissance *memoria*, however, emerges in an age of growing concern with the written and, in the wake of the Gutenberg "galaxy," the printed word. From around 1500, the art of *memoria* developed into an *ars multiplicativa*, for it increasingly addressed a larger number of people and, in the best of cases, a mass reading public. In ancient rhetoric the art of *memoria* consists of places (*loci*) and images (*imagines*), with the former serving a structuring and the latter a visualizing function. To remember words and arguments, orators associated them with images and stowed these *imagines* away in a memory architecture: in antiquity, in a patrician villa; in the Middle Ages, in a church or an abbey; in the Renaissance, in treasure-houses, temples, and theaters (e.g., *L'Idea del Teatro* [1550] of Giulio Camillo [1480–1544]) (see Kirkbride, ch. 40). The range of architectural manifestations of the *ars memoria* can be illustrated by two memory buildings: the late medieval Castle of Knowledge with Grammar holding the key to its entrance in Gregor Reisch's *Margarita Philosophica* (1583), and the elegant classicist Memory House on the title page of Johann-Heinrich Döbelius's *Collegium mnemonicum* (1707). Numerous illustrations, also of a nonarchitectural kind (e.g., zodiacs, the human body), can be found in many Renaissance treatises, such as Heaven and Hell in Cosmas Rossellius's *Thesaurus artificiosae memoriae* (1527) and the abbey in Johannes Romberch's *Congestorium artificiosae memoriae* (1533). Modern printing techniques of woodcutting and copperplate engraving made for three distinctive features of Renaissance memory architecture: visual objectivity, increase in diversity, and a far greater dissemination among the learned *litterati*. The affiliation of the memory places with the visual arts became a fact acknowledged (though sometimes grudgingly) by the Renaissance humanists. The fifteenth century invented the emblem, to be followed by the Ignatian theory of meditation, with its deeply rhetorical *compositio loci*—both of which were in the course of time absorbed by mnemonic theory and practice. Thus, the art of memory (Yates 1966) developed into an interdisciplinary activity that sometimes makes it difficult to attribute the proper hermeneutic function to the painted or printed icon.

Concerning the professions practiced by humanists, they were in the first place educators, theorists, and reformers of secondary modern education, initially in Italy, later in Germany and England. Concentrating on the *studia humanitatis* and the traditional *trivium* of grammar, rhetoric, and logic, with the addition of classical languages (Latin, Greek) and literatures, the humanist pedagogues developed innovative curricula and founded new grammar schools to implement them (see Mack, ch. 33). Early Italian humanists like Guarino da Verona (1374–1460) and Vittorino da Feltre (1378–1446), in whose schools a careful study of classical Latin as well as an attentive reading of the major classical authors was obligatory, attracted students from across Europe. In London, St. Paul's School, a humanist foundation of Colet established in cooperation with Erasmus, could boast of pupils that later attained prominent academic, social, and political positions. Humanists held positions as public orators at universities (e.g., George Herbert in Cambridge), as ambassadors (see Hans Holbein's "Double Portrait") and chancellors (Leonardo Bruni [ca. 1370–1444] in Florence), or in the higher ranks of the clergy (Enea Silvio Piccolomini [1405–64], later Pope Pius II [1458–64]). They also served in a broad spectrum of functions at the courts of greater or lesser dynasties in Europe. Rhetoric even proved a necessary art for military leaders to possess. In *The Art of War* (*Dell'Arte della Guerra*), for example, Niccolò Machiavelli (1469–1527) urged commanders to be trained in making public speeches (*parlare publicamente*) because an army may "come to grief if the captain does not know or does not undertake to speak to it. For such speech takes away fear, fires souls, increases determination, uncovers snares, promises rewards, points out dangers, and the way to escape them, reproves, entreats, threatens, fills again with hope, praises, condemns, and does all those things by which human passions are allayed or incited" (quoted in Gray 1963: 504–5).

Thus, the image of the orator's power reveals the humanistic optimism about the effectiveness of the word, particularly when used in the combination of *oratio* and *ratio*. This symbiosis of reason and eloquence is sometimes represented in mythological figures, especially Hercules Gallicus. As one of the founders of civilization, the figure of Hercules occurs in numerous texts, both literary and nonliterary, as well as in iconographic representations of the Renaissance. In Andrea Alciato's *Emblematum libellus* (1562), for example, Hercules Gallicus is portrayed, under the motto "Eloquence superior to strength" (*Eloquentia fortitudine praestantior*), as being armed with weapons but also with a "tongue [that] has light chains passing through it, which are attached to men's pierced ears, and by them he draws them unresisting along . . . even the hardest of hearts the skilled speaker [*Eloquio pollens*] can lead where he will" (Emblem 93). Another example of this iconography of eloquence is the *Imagini delli dei de gl'antichi* (1556) by Vincenzo Cartari (born ca. 1500): "Image of Hercules with the French by them held the god of eloquence [*Dio della eloquenza*], and of exercise, what by some is also held of Mercury, and this image signifies force and military discipline, especially in old captains and perfect orators [*consumati oratori*]." The illustration added to this ekphrastic motto shows an old, bald man with a club in his left hand and a bow in his right, both martial weapons. However, an extraordinary feature is a number of chains issuing out of his mouth that are tied to the ears of aggressive soldiers, who are thus held in check by the force of eloquence. In France the political implementation of the Hercules mythologeme begins with King Henri IV and seems to have been an established tradition ever since. Cardinal Richelieu, for instance, was celebrated by the painter and engraver Claude Vignon (1593–1670) as Hercules triumphant, this time equipped not with the golden chains of eloquence but with the traditional club and crowned with laurel, standing in a luscious landscape and triumphing over monsters lying at his feet.

In Italy many humanists succeeded in professional careers. Salutati, who had been a papal secretary, was appointed chancellor of Florence in 1375. In 1410 he was succeeded by the humanist Leonardo Bruni (ca. 1370–1444), author of *Laudatio Florentinae urbis* ("Praise of the City of Florence" [1403–4]), a panegyric modeled after Aelius Aristides's *Panathenaic Oration*. The Florentine humanist and lawyer Francesco Guicciardini (1483–1540), who, with *Storie fiorentine* (1508–10), wrote the first history of Florence (Struever 1970), enjoyed a long career in papal administration, in the course of which he was appointed successively governor of Parma and Bologna. Enea Silvio Piccolomini (1405–58), secretary and ambassador to several rulers, was author of a humanist Neo-Latin treatise on poetry and a romance titled *The Tale of the Two Lovers*, for which he was crowned imperial poet laureate in 1442. He later preferred an ecclesiastical career, which led to his election to the papacy in 1458. He is known in the history of the Roman Catholic Church as Pope Pius II.

Ferry Carondolet (1473–1528) entered upon a different career. Probably working at Rome as ambassador for the emperor Maximilian and Margaret of Austria, he made the acquaintance of the artist Sebastiano del Piombo, who painted his portrait. In this portrait he is represented as a man of superior stature and social status composing and sending dispatches. The beholder is expected to look up to the orator (Blow 2002). By contrast, in his obviously submissive posture, the secretary to his right, a minor figure and represented as such, typifies the subordinate status of this profession in early cinquecento Italy.

In England the best-known political career of a humanist is obviously that of the humanist and lawyer Sir Thomas More (1478–1535). As the author of the fictive *Utopia* (1516), which became the prototype of a literary genre, and a number of political treatises and pamphlets, he was an expert of theoretical statesmanship. But this situation changed when he was appointed lord chancellor by King Henry VIII in 1529. As a faithful member of the Catholic Church, he refused to acknowledge Henry as head of the Anglican Church. In 1532 he therefore resigned from all his functions and was sentenced to death.

Humanist rhetoric reached its highest and lasting climax not in statesmanship but in poetry. William Shakespeare (1564–1616) is the paragon of an author whose work demonstrates the perfectibility of rhetoric in the verbal arts. Rhetoric here appears in a threefold manner: as *demonstrare artem*, or the display of rhetorical art (represented by Brutus and Othello); as *celare artem*, or concealment of rhetorical art (Mark Antony and Iago); and as *negare artem*, or negation of rhetorical art (Desdemona, Coriolanus, and Cordelia). Taken together, these dramatic figures represent the entire cosmos of Shakespeare's rhetoric—and perhaps of rhetoric as such.

The end of humanist rhetoric can be traced to more than one cause. But whether its decline is attributed to the disintegration of the *quinque partes artis* into separate, independent disciplines initiated by Ramism (Sloane 1985) or to the beginning of the age of rationalism, of which René Descartes (1596–1650) and the Port-Royalists give testimony (Howell 1956), humanist rhetoric nevertheless does not disappear completely from the realm of the *artes*. On the contrary, it remains an undercurrent of further cultural developments, to reemerge whenever there is a demand for a *renovatio rhetorica*. Thus, the last renaissance of rhetoric, which revives the achievements of the age of humanism, began four decades ago and continues today.

References

Adamson, Sylvia, Gavin Alexander, and Katrin Ettenhuber, eds. 2007. *Renaissance Figures of Speech*. Cambridge: Cambridge University Press.

Baldwin, Thomas Whitfield. 1956. *William Shakspere's "Small Latine & Lesse Greeke."* 2 vols. Urbana: University of Illinois Press.

Blow, Douglas. 2002. *Doctors, Ambassadors, Secretaries: Humanism and Professions in Renaissance Italy*. Chicago, IL: University of Chicago Press.

Grassi, Ernesto. 2001. *Rhetoric as Philosophy: The Humanist Tradition*. Carbondale: Southern Illinois University Press.

Gray, Hannah H. 1963. "Renaissance Humanism: The Pursuit of Eloquence." *Journal of the History of Ideas* 24: 497–514.

Howell, Wilbur Samuel. 1956. *Logic and Rhetoric in England, 1500–1700*. Princeton, NJ: Princeton University Press.

Kahn, Victoria. 1985. *Prudence and Skepticism in the Renaissance*. Ithaca, NY: Cornell University Press.

Kallendorf, Craig, ed. 2002. *Humanist Educational Treatises*. Cambridge, MA: Harvard University Press.

Koopmans, Jelle, et al., eds. 1995. *Rhetoric-Rhétoriqueurs-Rederijkers. Proceedings of a Colloquium, Amsterdam 10–13 November 1993*. Amsterdam: Royal Netherlands Academy of Arts and Sciences.

Kristeller, Paul Oskar. 1961. *Renaissance Thought: The Classic, Scholastic and Humanist Strains*. New York: Harper.

Kristeller, Paul Oskar. 1964. *Eight Philosophers of the Renaissance*. Stanford, CA: Stanford University Press.

Kristeller, Paul Oskar. 1965. *Renaissance Thought II: Papers on Humanism and the Arts*. New York: Harper.

Leff, Michael. 2003. "Tradition and Agency in Humanistic Rhetoric." *Philosophy & Rhetoric* 36 no. 2: 135–147.

Moss, Ann. 1996. *Printed Commonplace Books and the Structuring of Renaissance Thought*. Oxford: Oxford University Press.

Moss, Ann. 2006. *Humanism and the Culture of Renaissance Europe*. Cambridge: Cambridge University Press.

Ong, Walter J. 2004. *Ramus, Method, and the Decay of Dialogue: From the Art of Discourse to the Art of Reason*. Chicago, IL: University of Chicago Press.

Plett, Heinrich F., ed. 1994. *Renaissance–Rhetorik/Renaissance Rhetoric*. Berlin: W. de Gruyter.

Plett, Heinrich F., ed. 2004. *Rhetoric and Renaissance Culture*. Berlin: W. de Gruyter.

Plett, Heinrich F., ed. 2010. *Literary Rhetoric: Concepts–Structures–Analyses*. Leiden: Brill.

Poster, Carol, and Linda C. Mitchell, eds. 2007. *Letter-Writing Manuals and Instruction from Antiquity to the Present: Historical and Bibliographical Studies*. Columbia: University of South Carolina Press.

Sabbadini, Remigio. 1886. *Storia del Ciceronianismo e di altri questioni letterarie nell'età de la Rinaccenza*. Turin: Loescher.

Seigel, Jerrold E. 1968. *Rhetoric and Philosophy in Renaissance Humanism: The Union of Eloquence and Wisdom, Petrarch to Valla*. Princeton, NJ: Princeton University Press.

Sloane, Thomas O. 1985. *Donne, Milton and the End of Humanist Rhetoric*. Berkeley: University of California Press.

Sloane, Thomas O. 1997. *On the Contrary: The Protocol of Traditional Rhetoric*. Washington, DC: Catholic University of America Press.

Struever, Nancy. 1970. *The Language of History in the Renaissance: Rhetoric and Historical Consciousness in Florentine Humanism*. Princeton, NJ: Princeton University Press.

Wilamowitz-Moellendorf, Ulrich von. 1968. "Asianismus und Atticismus." In *Rhetorika: Schriften zur aristotelischen und hellenistischen Rhetorik*, edited by Rudolf Stark, 350–401. Hildesheim: Olms.

Yates, Frances A. 1966. *The Art of Memory*. London: Routledge and Paul.

CHAPTER 31

RHETORIC AND POLITICS

WAYNE A. REBHORN

ALTHOUGH many ancient rhetoricians shaped the rhetoric of the European Renaissance, no one was quite as important as Cicero. Students in grammar schools began their education by learning Latin from his familiar letters, after which they absorbed moral lessons from essays such as *De officiis* (*On Duties*) and strategies for composing orations from his speeches. Moreover, the rhetoricians who taught them and who composed hundreds of manuals, stylistic guides, and treatises on their art lifted key ideas, arguments, and even phrasing directly from such works as Cicero's *De oratore* (*On the Orator*), *De inventione* (*On Invention*), and the pseudo-Ciceronian *Rhetorica ad Herennium*. The great French scholar Marc Fumaroli sums it up nicely: the Renaissance should be called the *aetas ciceroniana*, the "Age of Cicero" (1980: 40).

Cicero was actively involved in the public life of the Roman Republic, and for this reason his rhetoric, not surprisingly, was intensely political (see Connolly, ch. 14). In his most important theoretical statement, his *De oratore*, for example, he focuses almost exclusively on forensic rhetoric (the rhetoric of the law courts) and deliberative rhetoric (the rhetoric of political debate), limiting epideictic rhetoric (speeches of praise and blame) to just two brief sections in his lengthy work. It is not just that Cicero is writing about what he knows—he is writing about what he values. To master rhetoric in the Renaissance thus meant not just to study Cicero and the rhetoric manuals he inspired but also to encounter a thinker for whom rhetoric was a matter of politics and its close cousin, the law (see Enos, ch. 13).

In general, Ciceronian rhetoric is republican, oratory being imagined as a contest like gladiatorial combat or actual warfare. In *De oratore* Cicero's spokesman Crassus declares that when the orator's preliminary training, "like that for the games" (Cicero, *De oratore* 1.32.147), is done, he must then be led "into action, into the dust and uproar, into the camp and the fighting-line of public debate" (1.34.157; trans. Sutton and Rackham). The orator's diction is compared to "a weapon" (3.54.206), and even humor involves combat, as when "a word is snatched from an antagonist and used to hurl a shaft at the assailant himself" (2.63.255). For Cicero, oratory is warfare carried on by other means.

What is surprising, coming from the republican Cicero, is his occasional recourse to metaphors that associate oratory with monarchical rule. At one point in *De oratore*, he invokes the authority of the poet Pacuvius, who describes eloquent speech as the "soul-bending sovereign [*regina*, literally "queen"] of all things" (Cicero, *De oratore* 2.44.187). Perhaps Cicero is drawn to such a metaphor because he repeatedly presents eloquence in terms of its powerful hold over the audience it rules. In a passage frequently repeated by Renaissance rhetoricians, he celebrates the ability of eloquence to help suppliants, raise up those who have been cast down, free people from peril, and so on, asking—rhetorically—what other art is "so kingly [*regium*], so worthy of the free [*liberale*]?" (1.8.32). The republican Cicero was, of course, a *liberalis*, a free man with the right to participate in the political activities of the Roman state, but when he thinks of the orator's power he describes it paradoxically as worthy of both free men and kings. The Cicero inherited by the Renaissance was thus a Janus-faced figure when it came to politics. One face offered a free republican rhetor engaged in combat with other rhetors; the other face made him a ruler who controlled an audience. Cicero gives republican rhetoric greater prominence in his works, to be sure, but the regal rhetoric that is there as well would be taken up by Renaissance rhetoricians with more enthusiasm than Cicero ever intended. The result is that the politics of Renaissance rhetoric can be defined as something like a debate or a dialogue between these two conflicting political models.

Strikingly, the vast majority of rhetoric treatises and manuals, stylistic guides, and other works written on the subject in the European Renaissance insist that rhetoric is the art of ruling others, thus reflecting the second face one finds in Cicero, who praised eloquence as the *regina* or queen of all things. As I have argued in *The Emperor of Men's Minds* (1995), the English minister Henry Peacham's formulation in his *Garden of Eloquence*—the orator is the "emperor of men's minds and affections"—is repeated by one rhetorician after another as defining the art (in Rebhorn 2000: 226). The orator they imagine dominates his audience of subjects by means of his verbal skill, getting them to do his bidding, paradoxically, of their own free will. The political model here is not republicanism but monarchy. Indeed, it comes close to the absolutist fantasy of so many Renaissance princes: the regal rhetor rules alone, with everyone else his subject. Indeed, the auditor is made into the regal rhetor's subject precisely in the act of being subjected by rhetoric.

This vision of rhetoric is clearly influenced by the fact that the vast majority of the European Renaissance states were dukedoms, monarchies, and empires. Many rhetoricians revealingly proclaimed that rhetoric was essential for the rulers of the ancient world, declaring that Philip of Macedonia, Alexander the Great, and Julius Caesar were all distinguished orators. Writing in the early fifteenth century, for example, the Italian friar Antonio da Rho claims that Rome conquered the entire world "no less by eloquence than by arms" (in Müllner 1970: 165). Much later, in his 1589 *Art of English Poesy*, George Puttenham declares that "Julius Caesar, the first emperor and a most noble captain, was . . . the most eloquent orator of his time" ([1589] 2007: 108). Guillaume du Vair, the French lawyer and Stoic philosopher, notes in his *On French Eloquence* that "the greatest men in all of Greece and the entire Roman Empire were those who were the most meticulous in the practice of eloquence" (in Rebhorn 2000: 253). Despite living in the Venetian Republic, Raphael Regius does not associate rhetoric with republican liberty but with rule and dominion, praising Cicero for having reigned in Rome as the most eloquent man of his age. And the Englishman Walter Haddon concurs, naming Cicero the "king" of Rome (1567: 5), as does the German Heinrich Cornelius Agrippa: "Cicero was called by many the king of Rome ... ruling all things through his eloquence" (*On the Uncertainty and Vanity of the Arts and Sciences*, ch. 6, in Rebhorn 2000: 80).

Renaissance rhetoricians do not see rhetoric merely as the art of ruling in the ancient world, however. Speaking of sixteenth-century Italy, the Paduan professor Giason Denores begins his short rhetorical treatise with the statement that the art is especially suited to those "who legitimately have occasion to rule and govern cities" (1970: 103), and Luigi Carbone, who taught theology at Perugia in the sixteenth century, proclaimed it the monarchical art par excellence (see Fumaroli 1980: 183). Writing during the Puritan Interregnum in England, Sir Balthazar Gerbiers claims that "well speaking in a Princes mouth, is that which above all other things captivates the hearts and affections of his Subjects" (1650: 5).

The identification of rhetoric with ruling is underscored by the fact that the dedications rhetoricians composed for their treatises were aimed at members of the ruling class, especially in England and France. Richard Rainolde's *Foundacion of Rhetorike* (1563) was addressed to Elizabeth's favorite, Robert Dudley; Henry Peacham's *Garden of Eloquence* (1593) to John Puckering, Lord Keeper of the Great Seal; and Angel Day's *The English Secretary* (1599) to Edward de Vere, Earl of Oxford. Although Puttenham's *Art of English Poesy* was dedicated to Elizabeth's principal adviser, Robert Cecil, Lord Burghley, the book was really aimed at "our Sovereign Lady the Queen" ([1589] 2007: 90). Similarly, across the Channel, Jean Brèche dedicated his rhetoric manual (1544) to François I, and no less than two treatises on the subject were composed for Henry III: Germain Forget's *French Rhetoric Expressly Composed for Henry III* (1580–3) and Jacques Amyot's *Epitome of Royal Eloquence, Composed for Henry III, King of France* (ca. 1570–80). For all these rhetoricians, and for so many more, rhetoric was the royal art par excellence.

This does not mean that the other face of Ciceronian rhetoric, the republican face, went missing, although it is remarkable how few Renaissance writers directly identify rhetoric that way. The Spanish humanist Juan Luis Vives is one of the exceptions. In his monumental *Twenty Books on Education* (1531), he includes a section on what he sees as the causes of the corruption of the arts. He begins the book on rhetoric by claiming that although eloquence is the most important rudder of society it has almost no role to play in states where one man or an oligarchy rules, whereas in a democratic state "the power of speech has enormous influence in everything" (Vives, *On the Causes of the Corruption of the Arts*, bk. 4, in Rebhorn 2000: 83). Vives describes how rhetoric was first cultivated in Sicily after its people had thrown out the tyrants who once ruled over them, and, following Aristotle and Quintilian, he traces the history of the art from Sicily to Athens and Rhodes and eventually to Rome, commenting on how its scope broadened from legal concerns until it embraced the goal of moving people's minds in public meetings and the Senate house. In such city-states, the orator's audience was composed of "intelligent, quick-witted, unrestrained, and excitable people," and because of his skill with speech, in those places "the orator was lord" (84).

Subscribing to the historical view that oratory declined in Rome after Augustus—the view of Tacitus in his *Dialogus de oratoribus* (*Dialogue on Orators*)—Vives argues that the art was rendered irrelevant when everything was reduced to the rule of one man, turning public speaking into little more than a show to amuse crowds of slave-like auditors (Vives, *On the Causes of the Corruption of the Arts*, bk. 4, in Rebhorn 2000: 87–8). The Middle Ages offered only religious harangues of an inferior style, and despite the recent revival of ancient culture (for which Vives praises fifteenth-century Italian humanists) there has been no real revival of public speaking, only speeches of praise and canine attacks in which style trumps content because auditors, once smart and attentive, are now "stupid, slow, distracted, rude, and ignorant" (90). For Vives, the past glory of oratory is unmistakably identified with the rough-and-tumble politics of democratic states such as Athens and Rome.

Vives was an independent thinker not just for identifying rhetoric with republicanism but also for embracing the fundamental disorderliness of democratic states. Most rhetoricians in both antiquity and the Renaissance subscribed to some version of the myth of the orator-civilizer, which was transmitted to the Renaissance primarily through Cicero's *De inventione*. According to this myth, human beings in their natural state wandered like animals and remained unrestrained by law or discipline until orators persuaded them to band together and form a civil society. Vives, however, stresses that in the great democracies the people were "quick-witted, unrestrained, and excitable," that Athens was a "hot-blooded and excitable city-state," and that the inhabitants of Rhodes, Sicily, and Rome were not only "endowed with shrewd intelligence" but also "unsettled, ambitious, and puffed up by the air of liberty" (*On the Causes of the Corruption of the Arts*, bk. 4, in Rebhorn 2000: 84). While Vives is not known as a political thinker, he seems remarkably close to Niccolò Machiavelli here, whose *Discourses* identified the vitality of the Roman Republic precisely with the constant internal strife and disorderliness of the state. In the Renaissance, a period in which political order was generally valued, Vives's celebration of republican rhetoric and the disorder it entailed could not fail to put him at odds with almost everyone.

Vives's celebration of republican rhetoric was anticipated by the Greek émigré to Italy George of Trebizond. At some point during the 1430s, in a Latin oration in praise of eloquence that he delivered in Venice, George identified the key part of rhetoric, invention (the finding out of one's arguments), with "politics itself," and insisted that this "most flourishing republic is steered by eloquence alone" (*An Oration in Praise of Eloquence*, in Rebhorn 2000: 33–4). Moreover, Vives's vision of republican rhetoric was shared, after a fashion, by the sixteenth-century Italian writer Sperone Speroni. In his unfinished *Dialogue on Rhetoric* (published in 1546), Speroni views rhetoric as being essential for participation in civic life, which involves "speaking well for the benefit of people's property, persons, and honor" (in Rebhorn 2000: 112). "Speaking well" is crucial here, for Speroni has an aestheticized view of rhetoric that emphasizes the ability of words to give pleasure. Rhetoric thus looks very much like poetry, for pleasure is the goal of both arts and is imagined as being the product of style or ornamentation. Speroni's emphasis on aesthetic pleasure leads him to award the palm to epideictic oratory, which provides pleasure through praise or blame, rather than to forensic oratory, which seeks to persuade, or to deliberative oratory, which aims at teaching. Although Speroni does not assign rhetoric a political function in a republican state, he actually does something more radical: he imagines his orator as achieving social and political advancement sheerly through his rhetorical skill, no matter what sort of state he lives in.

At one point in his dialogue, Speroni has his principal speaker imagine a hypothetical orator who comes out of nowhere and gains fame, power, and influence simply through his command of language. This orator "will exercise his eloquence constantly with his pen and employ epideictic rhetoric to praise and blame others. And by doing this . . . in a short while he will be feared and esteemed not only by his peers, but by lords and kings" (Speroni, *Dialogue on Rhetoric*, in Rebhorn 2000: 123). Speroni's principal speaker has been creating a riddle about this "hypothetical orator," but one of his interlocutors figures it out: "If I don't miss the resemblance, this eloquent man of yours is . . . Aretino" (123).

Pietro Aretino (1492–1556) was a renowned *littérateur* who gained fame and fortune through his writing, and he represents a perfect example of the self-fashioning that many scholars think of as defining the Renaissance. Aretino was the illegitimate son of a shoemaker and a prostitute, lacked a humanist education in Latin, but still managed to compose brilliant satires in the vernacular. His works made him enemies and attracted patrons as he moved about Italy until finally, in 1527, he settled permanently in Venice, from which he hurled his barbs at people throughout Europe, being paid, for example, by the Holy Roman emperor Charles V to attack the French king Francis I—and vice versa. His success led the epic poet Ludovico Ariosto to call him "the scourge of princes, the divine Pietro Aretino" (*il flagello / de' principi, il divin Pietro Aretino*) (1962: 45.14.3–4). In his essay, "On the Vanity of Words," Michel de Montaigne objects to the way language is used to "puff up" people and things and takes exception to the fact that the Italians bestowed the epithet "divine" on Aretino (in Rebhorn 2000: 221), but it seems clear, Montaigne's skepticism aside, that in the rough-and-tumble arena of the republic of letters an Aretino could take on princes and beat them—scourging them with the whip of his tongue—at the game they were all playing.

If few Renaissance writers on rhetoric shared the more radical, "republican" views articulated by George of Trebizond, Vives, and, in his different way, Speroni, that does not mean that people throughout the period failed to connect the art to republicanism. One powerful thesis argued by scholars such as Hans Baron, Quentin Skinner, Eugenio Garin, Paul Oskar Kristeller, and Jerrold Seigel is that rhetoric developed as a discipline in northern Italy during the thirteenth century, precisely at a time when various city-states had thrown off the yoke of imperial rule and become self-governing communes (see Cox, ch. 26). A new interest in public speaking stimulated a new appreciation for the rhetoric of antiquity and, in particular, that of Cicero, thus identifying the art with republicanism. Those scholars then see the gradual disappearance of republican governments in Italy during the course of the fifteenth and sixteenth centuries as sounding the death knell for rhetoric as well, accepting something like the Tacitean view that once the power of the state rested with a single ruler, rhetoric became irrelevant. Or rather, rhetoric could still play a role, but a limited one: in the law courts, in the occasional parliamentary debate, and, as epideictic (the least political form, according to Cicero), in the ruler's court.

This thesis about the rise and fall of rhetoric is too simple (see Rebhorn 1995). First, rhetoric's potential for debate and discussion—including debate about politics—was preserved in the very act of teaching the art to students. Second, a rhetoric that possessed potentially republican overtones was still recognizable in the sixteenth and seventeenth centuries throughout Europe, if not in most of the works celebrating its power then in those that criticized it. Finally, the thesis is wrong because the very act of writing and publishing rhetoric treatises and manuals could make the art available to anyone who could read. Ironically, rhetoric thus had the potential to open up utopian vistas of republican equality even when authors writing about it sought to define it as the art of princes.

First, the very teaching of rhetoric presented it throughout the Renaissance as an instrument of debate, and debate always had the potential to become political. In particular, more advanced students of rhetoric were trained to produce orations, usually on hypothetical propositions, which they were to attack or defend from different points of view. This was the famous *argumentum in utramque partem*, argument on each side (of a case), which was implicitly based on the ontological and epistemological assumptions common to a rhetorical understanding of the world, namely, that since truth was unknowable every question was a matter of opinion and could be argued from more than one perspective. Such rhetorical education helps to explain the proliferation of dialogues in the Renaissance. Thomas More casts his *Utopia*, for example, in the form of a dialogue, and for all of his loyal service to Henry VIII he assigns Utopia a republican form of government. And Baldassare Castiglione's widely influential *Book of the Courtier* is also cast as a dialogue, and in its fourth, and most serious, book allows its characters to debate whether a monarchy or a republic is the best form of government. Although monarchy seems to win, the connection of dialogue—and hence of the rhetorical deployment of arguments on both sides of an issue—with republicanism could not be stronger.

A close identification of rhetoric with republicanism can also be found in those writers who attacked it while defending the (usually monarchical) status quo. The German writer on the occult, Heinrich Cornelius Agrippa, for example, savaged rhetoric in his *On the Uncertainty and Vanity of the Arts and Sciences* (1531). Agrippa sees the art of rhetoric as fomenting sedition and leading to the destruction of the state, and while he does not specifically denounce it for advancing a republican agenda he does associate rhetoric with the disorder that characterized the republics of Athens and Rome, condemning republican orators such as "Brutus, Crassus, the Gracchi, Cato, Cicero, and Demosthenes" (*On the Uncertainty and Vanity of the Arts and Sciences*, ch. 6, in Rebhorn 2000: 79). Similarly, the Milanese rhetoric teacher Anton Maria de' Conti also has one of the characters in his *Dialogue on Eloquence* (ca. 1555) accuse rhetoric of being a source of sedition, blaming the Gracchi for the tumults of the Roman Republic and Pisistratus for those of Athens (in Rebhorn 2000: 144). John Jewel, who taught at Oxford and was one of the chief defenders of the English Church, also denounces eloquence as leading to sedition and the destruction of states, naming Demosthenes and Cicero along with the Gracchi, Brutus, and Cassius as the chief offenders (*Oration against Rhetoric*, in Rebhorn 2000: 168–9). Some scholars think that Jewel's *Oration Against Rhetoric* (ca. 1544–52) was ironic, but in all these cases the critics of rhetoric were articulating negative views about the art that must have resonated widely in the period.

Indeed, Montaigne expresses such a view in his "On the Vanity of Words." Rhetoric, he says, "is a tool invented to manipulate and stir up a mob and an unruly populace, a tool that is employed only in sick states, like medicine; in states, such as those of Athens, Rhodes, and Rome, where the crowd, the ignorant, where all the people had power over all things, and where things were in perpetual tempest, there the orators flooded in" (Montaigne, "On the Vanity of Words," in Rebhorn 2000: 219–20). Here Montaigne has taken Vives's vision of republican rhetoric and turned his judgment upside down: rhetoric still finds its natural home in the tempestuous world of democratic debate—which is exactly what is wrong with it. Montaigne acknowledges that a few orators, including Pompey, Caesar, and Crassus, gained fame and power through their eloquence, but these men are his villains, not his heroes.

Some critics of rhetoric condemned it for producing sedition and political chaos in their own time. In his *On the Uncertainty and Vanity of the Arts and Sciences*, Agrippa, for instance, blames rhetoric for having led people in antiquity and the Middle Ages to interpret Sacred Scripture incorrectly, and asks: "Who are the leaders of the German heresies, which, although they all started from Luther alone, are so numerous today that almost every single city has its own peculiar brand? Aren't the authors of these heresies the most articulate men?" (in Rebhorn 2000: 81). Like Agrippa, in *The Advancement of Learning* Francis Bacon also attacks Luther, blaming him (inaccurately) for having, essentially, created the Renaissance in that he valued words (*verba*) more than matter (*res*) and thus caused ancient authors "generally to be read and revolved" once again (in Rebhorn 2000: 266). In a later passage of this work, Bacon grudgingly accepts the usefulness of rhetoric because it is capable of moving the people's imagination and making it conform to (the orator's) reason, but he clearly thinks the world would be better off without the art of eloquence and the social discord it causes. In addition, the English Civil War was said by those with Royalist sympathies, such as Thomas Sprat, author of *History of the Royal Society* (1667), to have resulted from the passionate oratory that was used to stir up religious enthusiasm among the masses and to create sectarian violence. Sprat thus concludes that "*eloquence* ought to be banish'd out of all *civil Societies*, as a thing fatal to Peace and good Manners" ([1667] 1958: 111). Finally, Thomas Hobbes, who wrote *Leviathan* to defend the English monarchy, argued in the introduction to his translation of Thucydides's *The Peloponnesian War* (1629) that the rhetoric employed in the public assemblies of republics was responsible for leading to sedition and civil war.

Most of the treatises celebrating regal rhetoric were dedicated to noble or royal patrons who, supposedly, needed no instruction because they were already masters of the art. This, however, raises the question: If the dedicatee was not the real audience for the treatise, then who was? The answer has to be: anyone who was capable of reading. This answer opens up a utopian possibility that actually undermines, or at least complicates, the authors' insistence on the regal nature of rhetoric. For the ruler who is defined as such by his rhetorical ability may well not be identical with the actual figure who sits on the throne. Indeed, many of the readers of the rhetoric treatises and manuals in the Renaissance were doubtless men "on the make." Puttenham, in a telling formulation, captures the essence of the ambition involved. Although his book envisages the queen as his primary reader, Puttenham also addresses it to those whom it would pull "from the cart to the school, and from thence to the court" ([1589] 2007: 378), eventually advancing them to serve the queen herself. Such a fantasy-driven mission statement seeks to respect the traditional social hierarchy—one goes from the peasant's cart to the school, to the court, to the queen—but the social mobility involved essentially threatened the very principle of hierarchy. The fact that one can gain preeminence through language, rather than by inheriting one's social position, thus unintentionally summons up a utopian image of the oratorical contests of a republican society in which the eloquent are the ones who come out on top.

I want to end this chapter with two examples of the way rhetoric in the Renaissance could tend toward a kind of utopian republicanism even in the work of an ardent monarchist. Perhaps the most elevated vision of regal rhetoric in the period is contained in Jacques Amyot's *An Epitome of Royal Eloquence*, written for Henry III of France but not published until the nineteenth century. Amyot divides oratory into two kinds, the hard and the soft. The first is for such things as public speeches, which kings seldom have to deliver. By contrast, the other kind is more essential for him, finding its place in more conversational settings, as when he speaks with his courtiers. Amyot supplies several examples of how rulers manage people in such situations by putting them down, thus revealing how rhetoric could still be political even in the courts. Nevertheless, some of Amyot's examples are more complicated—and subversive—than he may have intended. For instance, at one point he tells an anecdote about how Augustus, the ultimate ruler, wittily put down a man who bore an uncanny physical resemblance to him. With malicious irony, Augustus asked the man if his mother had ever been in Rome. The man replied—just as maliciously?—that his mother had never been there, but his father had. The joke is thus on Augustus. What we see in this exchange is that even the greatest of emperors can be bested by an ordinary individual in a verbal contest. Amyot does go on to praise Augustus for not responding to the joke with anger, but the damage has been done: when emperors engage in rhetorical contests, there is no guarantee the "real" one will win.

There is another anecdote in Amyot's book that also undermines the political preeminence of the ruler-as-orator even as it seeks to reinforce it. In discussing the sorts of words the ruler is to use, Amyot declares that they should be "good French words, and not foreign ones," a case he then supports with the example of the emperor Tiberius, who once objected to the use of the word *strena* for "New Year's gift" because *strena* was a Sabine and not a Latin word. A lawyer named Capito rose to defend *strena*, saying that even if it was not good Latin it would become so "if that were pleasing to Caesar," at which point a grammarian stood up and declared, "No, no, Caesar, you have the power to give the right of citizenship and naturalization papers to men, but you cannot naturalize a word" (Amyot, *An Epitome of Royal Eloquence*, ch. 13, in Rebhorn 2000: 137). Although Amyot wants to present Tiberius as the defender of the principle of using one's native language, his anecdote actually shows that even absolute rulers are forced to operate within the constraints of the linguistic system.

This anecdote from Amyot is not, of course, an endorsement of republicanism per se, but it does offer the reader a vision of royal eloquence as being itself subordinate to a system of rules. Moreover, it assigns the final word not to the emperor but to the socially inferior, indeed unnamed, grammarian who triumphs over the lawyer who speaks for unlimited monarchical power. In this mini-contest between the high and the low, the low wins. Thus, Amyot actually winds up, at least in such passages, undermining the vision of royal eloquence his treatise aims to advance. His work would endorse the Ciceronian vision of eloquence as the queen of Rome, but it also offers us glimpses of a more republican rhetoric in which the real "ruler" is the best speaker, no matter his political status.

Renaissance writers may have sought to keep these two sides of Cicero's political rhetoric separate from one another, occasionally defending the messy give-and-take of republican debate but more typically celebrating the power of kingly eloquence. But in this final anecdote—as in so many other ways—we can see that no matter how hard Renaissance rhetoricians sought to keep the two faces of Cicero's political rhetoric distinct from one another, the closer one actually looks at the discourse, the more difficult it becomes to keep those faces apart. Thomas Sloane argues that the defining feature of Renaissance humanism—and thus, in a way, of the Renaissance itself—was its insistence on *controversia*, controversy, not just in rhetorical training but in practically every sphere of intellectual, social, and political life. For Sloane, the allegorical figure that summed it all up for the period was the two-faced Janus, the "Roman god of doors and gates . . . [who] suggests multiple, even incongruous perspectives" (1985: 57) on things. Thus, although we would agree with Fumaroli that the Renaissance might indeed be called the age of Cicero, it may be called the *aetas ciceroniana* only if we remember that the Renaissance Cicero was the source of both a monarchical and a republican view of rhetoric—a Janus-faced Cicero for a Janus-faced Renaissance.

FURTHER READING

Building on the work of important scholars writing since the Second World War who have made us see the central importance of rhetoric in the European Renaissance, Victoria Kahn's (1985) *Rhetoric, Prudence, and Skepticism in the Renaissance* is a brilliant exploration of the connections among rhetoric, prudence, and skepticism in Renaissance thought and the crucial role they played in humanism and in such writers as Erasmus, Montaigne, and Hobbes. Equally important, Patricia Parker's (1987) *Literary Fat Ladies: Rhetoric, Gender, Property*, though ranging well beyond the Renaissance, is a groundbreaking interpretation of the gendered nature of Renaissance rhetoric and of the literature and culture associated with it. Wayne A. Rebhorn's (1995) *The Emperor of Men's Minds: Literature and the Renaissance Discourse of Rhetoric* offers a reading of the politics of Renaissance rhetoric that complicates received scholarly views and connects the art directly to the literature of the period that is presented as modeling—and thereby evaluating and critiquing—it. By contrast, Peter Mack's (2002) *Elizabethan Rhetoric: Theory and Practice* is a more conservative study that is nevertheless essential, not only offering a detailed overview of rhetoric in the English Renaissance but also analyzing the important roles it played more generally in the culture. Finally, although centered on *Othello*, Joel Altman's (2010) *The Improbability of "Othello": Rhetorical Anthropology and Shakespearean Selfhood* illuminates with enormous subtlety the ways that rhetoric shaped Shakespearean—and Renaissance—epistemology, characters, and social interactions.

REFERENCES

Altman, Joel. 2010. *The Improbability of "Othello": Rhetorical Anthropology and Shakespearean Selfhood*. Chicago, IL: University of Chicago Press.

Ariosto, Ludovico. 1962. *Orlando furioso*. Edited by Remo Ceserani. 2 vols. Turin: Unione Tipografico Editrice Torinese.

Denores, Giason. 1970. "Breve Trattato dell'Oratore." In *Trattati di poetica e retorica del Cinquecento*, edited by Bernard Weinberg, 3: 101–134. Bari: Laterza.

Fumaroli, Marc. 1980. *L'âge de l'éloquence: Rhétorique et* res literaria *de la Renaissance au seuil de l'époque classique*. Geneva: Droz.

Gerbiers, Balthazar. 1650. *The Art of Well Speaking: A Lecture*. London: Printed for Robert Ibbitson.

Haddon, Walter. 1567. *De laudibus eloquentiae*. In *Lucubrationes passim collectae*, edited by Thomas Hatcher, 1–9. London: William Seres I.

Kahn, Victoria. 1985. *Rhetoric, Prudence, and Skepticism in the Renaissance*. Princeton, NJ: Princeton University Press.

Mack, Peter. 2002. *Elizabethan Rhetoric: Theory and Practice*. Cambridge: Cambridge University Press.

Müllner, Karl, ed. (1899) 1970. *Reden und Briefe italienischer Humanisten*. Munich: Wilhelm Fink.

Parker, Patricia. 1987. *Literary Fat Ladies: Rhetoric, Gender, Property*. London: Methuen.

Puttenham, George. (1589) 2007. *The Art of English Poesy: A Critical Edition*. Edited by Frank Whigham and Wayne A. Rebhorn. Ithaca, NY: Cornell University Press.

Rebhorn, Wayne A. 1995. *The Emperor of Men's Minds: Literature and the Renaissance Discourse of Rhetoric*. Ithaca, NY: Cornell University Press.

Rebhorn, Wayne A., ed. 2000. *Renaissance Debates on Rhetoric*. Ithaca, NY: Cornell University Press.

Sloane, Thomas O. 1985. *Donne, Milton, and the End of Humanist Rhetoric*. Berkeley: University of California Press.

Sprat, Thomas. (1667) 1958. *History of the Royal Society*. Edited by Jackson I. Cope and Harold Whitmore Jones. Reprint. St. Louis, MO: Washington University Press.

CHAPTER 32

RHETORIC AND LAW

LORNA HUTSON

In the final act of Ben Jonson's *The Devil is an Ass* (1616), the justice of peace, Sir Paul Eitherside, is faced with an apparent case of demonic possession, allegedly brought about as part of the conspiracy of a pair of adulterous lovers to defraud a cuckolded husband, Squire Fitzdotterel, of his land. As it happens, the demonic possession is a fake. The foolish Fitzdotterel (who has not really been cuckolded, either) is actually the dupe of his ostensible friends and advocates, Merecraft and Everill, who have persuaded him to feign the signs of diabolic possession in order to recover his estate. Justice Eitherside is apparently taken in by Fitzdotterel's foaming, gnashing, and wallowing about on his bed: "The proofs are pregnant," he concludes, ready to indict the conspirators (Jonson [1616] 1996: 5.8.77).

Since G. L. Kitteredge's (1911) discovery of the horrific Leicester case of 1616 in which, on the evidence of an unstable teenage boy, a justice of the common pleas sentenced nine women to be hanged, critics have plausibly interpreted Justice Eitherside as a satire on the credulity of common lawyers in the prosecution of witchcraft. In the context of a discussion of law and rhetoric, however, I want to propose that Jonson's Justice Eitherside is less a critique of judicial susceptibility to theatrical performance ("How the Devil can act!" observes Gilthead [Jonson [[1616]] 1996: 5.8.78]) than a critical illustration of the seventeenth-century common lawyer's immersion in certain rhetorical and dialectical habits of mind. For although those gathered around Fitzdotterel's bedside seem wholly taken in by the measly props and histrionics of old exorcism cases, it is not so much Fitzdotterel's performance as the circumstances of the framing forensic narrative that persuade Sir Paul. The justice first comes on stage in the midst of listening to an allegation: "THE JUSTICE *comes out wondering, and the rest informing him*" (5.8). The "rest" are the fraudsters, Merecraft and Everill, whose plan to persuade Fitzdotterel to deed his land to one of them has just gone badly wrong because Fitzdotterel, taken in by another of their scams, inadvertently deeded the land to his wife's admirer, Wittipol, who (for other reasons) was disguised as a Spanish noblewoman. Seeing that Wittipol and his friend Manly now hold the deeds to Fitzdotterel's estate, Merecraft and Everill come up with the scheme to claim, as they tell Fitzdotterel, that "you were / Not *compos mentis* when you made your feoffment" (5.4.11–2) by arguing that Wittipol, Manly, and Mistress Fitzdotterel all conspired to bewitch the husband in order to transfer his estate to his wife and her lover: "This, sir," Merecraft and Everill chorus, "will move in a court of equity / For it is more than manifest this was / A plot o' your wife's to get your land" (5.4.13–6). In the tangle of all this, what Jonson wants us to see is that Merecraft and Everill's fraudulent account of what has happened carries more motivational credibility and coherence—more likeness to truth—than the absurd and apparently random series of events the audience has witnessed in the previous four acts of the play. Wittipol may have drawn back from adultery with Mistress Fitzdotterel, but he did make a pass at her; moreover, without any obvious motive, he decided to prance about in drag as a Spanish lady. He seems, in other words, to warrant the allegations of adulterous conspiracy that Merecraft and Everill invoke against him. When Manly protests against Sir Paul's suspicions, he begs the justice to hear their defense: "We are not afraid / Either of law or trial; let us be / Examined what our ends were, what the means / To work by; and the possibility of those means. / Do not conclude against us ere you hear us" (5.8.94–7). Sir Paul replies, with pointed absurdity: "I will not hear you, yet I will conclude / Out of the circumstances" (5.8.98–9).

What were these "circumstances" out of which Justice Eitherside claims to conclude his judgment? The term might not seem to be one of art, but as I will explain more fully in the course of this chapter, "circumstances," along with "accidents," constitute a technical category of Renaissance rhetoric and dialectic (see Moss, ch. 34). "Accidents of person" and "circumstances of the thing [*res*]" are among the *loci argumentorum*, the topics (*topica*) or places (*loci*) where arguments are "found" (Cicero, *Topica*, para. 8; Quintilian, *Institutio oratoria* 5.10.20–2). Although they are only one strand in a much broader tradition of rhetorical and dialectical invention, accidents and circumstances occupy "a central position in the history of argumentation," offering, of all the topics, "the clearest artistic principles for constructing arguments" (Leff 1983: 25). At their simplest, circumstances were the topics that made a deed intelligible and able to be narrated and proved, and included "motive, time, place, opportunity, means, method and the like" (*causa tempus locus occasio instrumentum modus et cetera*), as Quintilian lists them (*Institutio oratoria* 5.10.23; trans. mine). When "THE JUSTICE *comes out wondering, and the rest informing him*," it is immediately evident that the legal "information" being given to him is structured according to these topics of argument. We hear Merecraft in the midst of his account of the conspiracy: "Sir, they had given him potions / That did enamour him of the counterfeit lady," and then Everill chimes in, "*Just to the time o' delivery o' the deed—*," after which Merecraft concludes the causal-temporal sequence: "And then the witchcraft 'gan to appear, for straight / He fell into his fit" (Jonson [1616] 1996: 5.8.2–6; emphasis added). According to Richard Bernard's 1627 *Guide to Grand Jury Men*, those evaluating cases of apparent demonic possession should "weigh seriously the occasion, of entering into the fits, with all circumstances, before whom, at what time, in what place" (1627: 38), so as not to be too credulous of witchcraft. Jonson, conversely, shows how easily circumstantial invention prompts us to find (that is, to *invent*) motives, explanations, and causes, including supernatural ones: Everill's argument of time (*tempus*)—which implicitly offers the appearance of Fitzdotterel's symptoms of demonic possession as the motive (*causa*) of his otherwise inexplicable deeding of land to the inexplicably disguised Wittipol—works to persuade Sir Paul Eitherside of the palpable existence of an adulterous plot: "This was the notablest conspiracy / That e'er I heard of" (Jonson [1616] 1996: 5.8.1). Thus Sir Paul's conclusion "out of the circumstances" is not quite as ludicrous or gullible as it might seem, nor is Sir Paul "treated contumeliously by Jonson" (Kitteredge 1911: 202).

It might seem perverse to open a discussion of law and rhetoric in Renaissance England with the fictional example of Jonson's Justice Eitherside. Yet the fictional example has the advantage of showing how irresistibly persuasive and affecting the suggestions of causality are that inhere not in the substance but in the *topical form* of arguments. And it will be the contention of this chapter that it was in the sphere of topics logic, or dialectical invention, that humanist rhetoric had a transformative effect on the arguments made in English law courts in the course of the sixteenth and seventeenth centuries (see Plett, ch. 30). For dialectical invention, as conceived by the humanists, was not remote from rhetoric: Lisa Jardine's study of changes in the Cambridge arts curriculum from the 1520s through the seventeenth century shows how, in this period, dialectic came to absorb oratory, so that "the arts course as a whole" came to be "characterized as *dialectical*" (1974: 44). Dialectic, as Peter Mack defines it, "concentrates on techniques of argument," while rhetoric "explores a variety of verbal, emotional and persuasive means," but in this period "the two subjects have to be studied together" (1993: 2; see Mack, ch. 33). Indeed, the reformed dialectic represented by Rudolph Agricola's *De inventione dialectica*, which subtracted much of the technical apparatus of scholastic logic and incorporated such traditionally rhetorical material as status theory (the theory of identifying the central question or issue at stake in a legal dispute), the parts of an oration, techniques for arousing emotion, and even principles for the composition of persuasive narratives, came to affect even grammar school syllabi. Not only are there "close parallels" between parts of Desiderius Erasmus's *De copia* and Agricola's *De inventione dialectica*, but the commentary appended to later sixteenth-century editions of *De copia* refers the reader to dialectical equivalents of such rhetorical techniques of *copia* as "*enargeia*" (ch. 5), "circumstances" (ch. 8), and "proofs and arguments" (ch. 11) (Mack 1993: 305–11; Erasmus 1573, fols. 127, 133v–4, 144, 149r–v).

Despite the work of R. S. Schoeck (1953, 1983), D. S. Bland (1967), Louis Knafla (1969), and Wilfred Prest (1977) on the presence and effects of rhetorical and dialectical studies at the Inns of Court, accounts of the relationship of rhetoric and law in the Renaissance, particularly with regard to the English legal context, may seem to deter any exploration of the impact of humanistic rhetoric on the actual development of law (see Goodrich, ch. 48). Thus while Schoeck notes that Sir Thomas Elyot describes the moots, or educational exercises of the Inns of Court, as a "shadowe" or likeness of "the auncient rhetorike" (1953: 113), he concludes, with Brian Vickers, that "the whole question of rhetoric's influence on legal oratory does not seem to have excited the interest of legal historians" (1983: 281). More recently, Hans Hohmann's account of the relationship between Ciceronian rhetoric and law in medieval and Renaissance Europe argues, with a similar tentativeness, that it was "a less than enthusiastic encounter on both sides" (Hohmann 2006: 194). Hohmann argues that disciplinary autonomy on the part of both rhetoricians and lawyers militated against the full engagement of Ciceronian rhetoric in legal practice, and that law eschewed identification with rhetorical argument on both sides of an issue (*in utramque partem*), seeking instead "methods that appeared to promise unequivocal, correct results rather than merely conflicting arguments on both sides of any given issue" (193–4). Hohmann's caution about the influence of Ciceronian rhetoric on medieval and Renaissance civil lawyers finds an echo in Sir John Baker's reluctance to ascribe developments in sixteenth-century common law to a humanist liberal education. Although he shows that the later sixteenth century saw the advent of law-reporting in the tradition of Edmund Plowden and Sir Edward Coke, a tradition that recorded the "full subtlety and range of reference" of arguments in court and helped produce a common law depending on "judicial decisions, interpreted in the context of the facts that gave rise to them" (Baker 1989: 40–2), Baker takes care not to ascribe any part of this transformation to the influence of humanist rhetoric or dialectic: English law was "manifestly not influenced by humanist scholarship in a narrow technical sense" (2003: 17).

Recent surveys from the history of rhetoric and of law seem, then, to be in consensus in arguing that the former had no great effect upon the latter in spite of the fact that there were, apparently, developments in the law that seem to be related to a more intricate and sophisticated sense of the textual form of argument. It may be worth suggesting, then, three reasons why the question of rhetoric's influence on law may still be a valid area for further research. First, the notion of "rhetoric" may have been too narrowly conceived. As the work of Jardine and Mack suggests, we need to be thinking, in the English context, not so much of Ciceronian rhetoric in all its purity, but in terms of a reformed dialectic that has absorbed both Cicero's and Quintilian's writings on rhetorical invention and that emphasizes *copia* and the discovery of arguments through topics or places. Second, we need to include, in our thinking about legal development, the effects of these techniques of topical invention, through criminal law, on the development of a law of proof and evidence, both on the Continent and in England. Third, in thinking about the transformation from "common learning" to the jurisprudence identified by Baker (that is, a new emphasis on the "reasoned decisions of courts as a source of law" [2003: 18]), we need to think about the way in which—as in my example of the fictional Everill's shaping of the circumstance of time into an argument of motivational causality—the impression of a "reason" on which to base a legal decision may be created by the *topical form* of dialectical invention.

First, then, why might it be helpful to rethink the question of rhetoric's influence on sixteenth-century common law in terms of rhetoric's absorption into a reformed dialectic that emphasizes invention, places of argument, and *copia*? One of the reasons that classical forensic rhetoric is often said not to influence the development of law and legal argument is that classical forensic rhetoric—identified with Cicero's *De inventione*, the pseudo-Ciceronian *Ad Herennium*, and Quintilian's *Institutio oratoria*—is largely concerned with criminal rather than civil cases, and hence with the *status conjecturalis* or "issue of fact" rather than with the "issue of law" (Hohmann 1996: 16–7). So, for example, in his *Topica*, addressed to the jurist Gaius Trebatius Testa, Cicero himself reports the jurisconsult Aulus Gallus saying, of a conjectural issue, "This has nothing to do with the law—it's Cicero's business" (*Nihil hoc ad jus; ad Ciceronem*; para. 141, 300–5), thus explicitly distinguishing the work of jurisconsults, like Trebatius, in forming legal arguments from that of rhetoricians, like himself, in inventing proofs of fact (Hohmann 1996: 16). Yet, as Tobias Reinhardt's (2003: 60–1) excellent edition of Cicero's *Topica* shows, the context of this quip is a text in which Cicero, as a rhetorician, is trying to help the jurist rationalize the grounds of legal decision-making. Reinhardt shows that while Cicero's earlier work, *De inventione*, was largely concerned with the invention of proofs in relation to a particular case—taking the sphere of rhetoric to be the "hypothesis" or definite question rather than the "thesis" or indefinite question—Cicero was also increasingly intrigued by "thetical rhetoric": that is, by a rhetoric concerned with identifying and arguing for and against a philosophically indefinite question (1–14). In the *Topica*, Cicero uses examples of specific legal cases, but shows Trebatius not only that these may be analyzed according to dialectical methods of division, definition, epistemology, and logic, but also that, in complex particular cases, what matters is the identification of the general, indefinite legal principle behind the question. The purpose of this activity was to enable the *responsa*, or opinions of the jurisconsults on given issues, to be grounded more rationally. Cicero was presenting Trebatius with a way of turning the reasoning behind legal decision-making in specific instances into abstract legal principles.

By the sixteenth century, in England Cicero's *Topica* had long been a feature of the *trivium* (the arts course) at the Universities of Oxford and Cambridge. As Jardine (1974) has shown, however, its framing intellectual context changed around the 1520s when Agricola's pioneering reformed dialectic, *De inventione dialectica* (1515), challenged the long didactic tradition centered on Peter of Spain's *Summulae logicales* (1246) and introduced a new *ars disserendi* (art of discourse) anchored in the study of literature and promoting the topics as places from which to invent arguments and discover how to speak *probabiliter* (plausibly) on any subject (Mack 1993: 168–73). Agricola's topic headings absorb and rearrange both those of Cicero's *Topica* and Quintilian's subordination of some of the Ciceronian topics to the status of arguments of confirmation and confutation (*Institutio oratoria* 5.54–87; Mack 1993: 134). Effectively, then, Agricola's arrangement seems to have loosened up the distinction between the rhetorical *circumstantiae* used to inquire into or construct the probability of particular issues of fact and the apparatus of predicables (categories of universal relation, such as genus, species, difference, property, accident) and predicaments (delimitations of an individual thing, such as quantity, quality, relation, location, time) used to ascertain the validity of propositions. Moreover, it seems that the popular dialectics used in Oxford and Cambridge from the 1530s all "openly affiliate[d] themselves to Agricola and Agricolan dialectic" (Jardine 1974: 53). Thus, although these dialectics apparently conform to a more traditional structure, presenting the technical apparatus of predicables and predicaments, they assume the presence of Agricola and preserve his emphasis on the places of copious invention as the backbone of dialectic. These important changes in the Oxford and Cambridge arts courses seemed to have coincided with, or been causally linked to, the advent of a new kind of student: the undergraduate destined for a professional life at court, in the law, or in the church, for whom the arts of reasoned and persuasive argument would be crucial.

One such manual of reformed dialectic, very popular at Trinity College, Cambridge (the college attended by Sir Edward Coke from 1567 to 1570), was John Seton's *Dialectica* (see Boyer 2003: 17). Seton offers his text as a simple treatment of Agricola's dialectic, schematically covering traditional material on terms and propositions, such as the predicables and predicaments, but, as Jardine notes, "There is no suggestion that this provides more than a convenient set of procedures for sifting and classifying material . . . and there is no philosophical discussion whatever" (Jardine 1974: 55). Dialectic is presented by Seton as a technical tool "not simply for debating exercises, but for all analysis of texts and spoken discourse," making it appear "that the rules of dialectic apply to narrative literature as well as to formal disputation" (55). That Coke used Seton's *Dialectica* in this way seems very likely. Not only was it one of the texts bought by John Whitgift for his pupils when he was master of Trinity, but Coke's own copy is listed, under "GRAMMAR, LODGICKE AND SCHOOLE BOOKS," in the catalog of his library at Holkham Hall. A copy of Quintilian's *Institutio oratoria* (Paris, 1541) features in the preceding section, "RHETORICKE" (Hassall 1950: 62). Coke is thus likely to have been familiar with Quintilian's presentation of the places of argument for proof as dominated by the accidents of person and circumstances of the thing (*causa tempus locus occasio instrumentum modus et cetera*) as well as with Seton's Agricolan presentation of dialectical predicables and predicaments as strategies for debate and textual analysis. As we shall see, he uses both sets of terminology in presenting the reasoned decisions of courts as the basis of common law.

Before examining Coke's legal uses of a mixed terminology of rhetorical and dialectical invention, however, we need to consider the question of rhetoric and dialectic's influence on the procedures of sixteenth-century English criminal trials, and the contribution of both to the emergence of Anglo-American standards of legal probability and the law of evidence. Here we are indebted to the groundbreaking work of the intellectual historian Barbara Shapiro. In books and articles from the 1980s to the present, Shapiro has examined the influence of rhetoric—especially the *loci argumentorum*, the places of invention—on the development of Anglo-American concepts of proof and "fact" in legal and scientific culture (Shapiro 1983, 1991, 2000; see also Giuliani 1969). Some of Shapiro's most important conclusions are summarized in an essential article titled "Classical Rhetoric and the English Law of Evidence" (2001). Where Bland, Schoeck, and others had mainly tried to explore the influence of classical rhetoric as *elocutio*, Shapiro saw that the crucial cross-fertilization was taking place less in *elocutio* than in *inventio*, and specifically where the classical tradition of rhetorical *inventio* enabled, through its doctrine of the formation of arguments of proof, the emergence of a legal discourse of evidential probability. Shapiro draws attention to the importance, in Cicero's *De inventione* and in Quintilian's *Institutio oratoria*, of the revival of the Aristotelian distinction between "artificial" (artistic) and "inartificial" proofs; of the importance, among artificial proofs, of signs and arguments of probability; and, finally, of the importance of the topics or places from which, with reference to the facts of the case in question, the signs and arguments of probability were to be drawn. Shapiro shows how Quintilian's identification of these *argumentorum loci* (*Institutio oratoria* 5.10.20) divided them into the accidents of persons and the circumstances of the thing after the manner of Cicero's *De inventione* and the *Rhetorica ad Herennium*, and she proceeds to demonstrate how these accidents and circumstances of person and thing gave rise to what became, in the Romano-canonical tradition on the Continent, the "fractional proofs" and "*indicia*" that helped to secure a conviction when there was doubt, while, in the English common law tradition, the same accidents and circumstances shaped the formal examination procedure of justices of peace, who were required to make inquiries into matters of suspicion (see Langbein 1974).

Shapiro's work represents a real breakthrough in understanding the contribution of classical rhetoric to the development of certain features of Anglo-American criminal law and procedure. Where earlier inquiries had sought evidence of rhetorical influence in the pleadings recorded in legal reports of cases, Shapiro (2001: 64–6) turns her attention to the justicing manuals written by William Lambarde, Richard Crompton, and Michael Dalton, among others, all of which incorporated Ciceronian topics of person and thing (including time, place, opportunity, means, and motive) as "causes of suspicion" that would enable a justice to evaluate the probabilities of an accusation. As well as these printed justicing manuals, manuscript notebooks kept by sixteenth- and seventeenth-century justices of the peace testify to the pervasive influence of these rhetorical topics on their methods of proceeding. In 1608 the Surrey justice Bostock Fuller recorded in his notebook examining "on bothe sydes" a case brought "on verye slyghte suspicion of ffelonye," which he decided "hathe noe probabilytye," while in his copy of *The Complete Justice* the Worcestershire justice Henry Townsend noted that Judge Popham's opinion that "a Justice of peace in furtherynce of Justice for the examination of a felon, may send for any to examine Circumstances to prove it" (Leveson-Gower 1888: 182; Bodleian MS Eng. Misc. e. 479, fol. 107r).

The justicing manuals examined by Shapiro use, in their discussions of pretrial examinations, the terminology of circumstances and the *status conjecturalis*. In *The Countrey Justice*, for example, Dalton speaks of the requirement that "Justices take due examination (of the offenders themselves, and also credible witnesses) as well concerning the facte it selfe, as the circumstances thereof" (1635: 22), while Lambarde glosses "the examination of an offence" as "the conjectural state of a cause" (1592: 218–9). If this terminology seems to derive exclusively from such rhetorical sources as *De inventione*, *Rhetorica ad Herennium*, and the *Institutio oratoria*, however, it is worth reminding ourselves how closely aligned these rhetorical *argumentorum loci* were with the dialectical topics of invention. For example, in his notes to chapter 8 of Erasmus's *De copia*—the chapter dealing with achieving *copia* by means of the circumstances of "*causa, locus, occasio, instrumentum, tempus, modus*"—Johannes Weltkirchius first observes that circumstances supply "an incredible wealth of arguments and ornaments," especially "rhetorical ones," and then goes on to note that Agricola calls circumstances "attachments of the thing" (*applicata rebus*) (Erasmus 1573, fols. 133v–4). Weltkirchius thus identifies the rhetorical circumstances of the thing—from which inferences might be drawn regarding a particular set of narrative facts under investigation—with the dialectical *applicata* as defined in Agricola's *De inventione dialectica*. Agricola's *applicata* correspond to what Cicero calls "adjuncts": they are "time, place and *connexa*," and, like the logical predicaments, they help to define a thing in a particular instantiation (Mack 1993: 165; Agricola [1539] 1967: 29, 92–105). Similarly, when glossing Erasmus's chapter on rhetorical *enargeia*, or vivid description, Weltkirchius derives *enargeia* "from that dialectical definition they call a description of accidents" (*ex Dial. praesertim illa quam accidentariam descriptionem vocant* [Erasmus 1573, fol. 127]), once again identifying a rhetorical effect with a dialectical mode of definition. Seton's *Dialectica* includes both formal accounts of dialectical definition as analytic tools and less rigorous procedures such as "*descriptio*," definition by etymology, and definition by metaphor (Jardine 1974: 56; Seton 1584, sig. I6v). It seems clear, then, that no hard and fast distinction can be made between the rhetorical circumstances from which arguments of suspicion regarding the alleged facts may be drawn and the dialectical topics from which various forms of definition by *applicata*, accidents, description, etymology, predicaments, or other means are discovered.

Finally, then, we come to the question of how rhetoric and dialectic might have contributed to the transformation from the common law as a generalized "doctrine" to the "new-found judicial positivism which laid emphasis on the reasoned decisions of courts as a primary source of law" (Baker 2003: 18). I will conclude with a minor but telling example of the blending of rhetorical and dialectical terminology to create a complex and emotive effect of reason from Coke's report on *Calvin's Case*, or the *Case of the Postnati* (1608). By all accounts, there could hardly be a case more illustrative of Baker's "new-found judicial positivism" than *Calvin's Case*, which, as Coke himself reported, "was one of the shortest and least that ever we argued in this court, yet . . . the longest and weightiest that was ever argued in any court . . . the least for the value . . . but the weightiest for the consequent, both for the present, and for all posterity" (2002: 4.6). At stake was the question of the legal status of James I's Scottish subjects in England: Were the Scots English subjects and possessed of English common law rights? Or were they aliens, subject only to their own law? Because the issue was not settled by debate in the Parliament of 1604, a suit was begun in the King's Bench to enable a judicial decision. The guardians of a Scottish child, Robert Calvin or Colville, born in Scotland after 1603, brought a suit claiming that Calvin had been unjustly disseized of his estate in Shoreditch. The defendants declared the plea invalid on the grounds that Calvin was an alien and could not inherit in England (Price 1997: 81).

Coke, Bacon, and Ellesmere, arguing for the plaintiff, had to consider that although the king was one person, the jurisdictions of the kingdoms were several. They also had to counter the powerful argument, resting on a legal fiction well established in the pages of Plowden's *Reports*, that the subject's allegiance is due not to the king's natural body but to the king as "politic body or capacity, so called, because it is framed by the policy of man" (Coke 2002: 4.17). This argument was reinforced by the defense's recourse to a maxim of the civil law to the effect that "when two jurisdictions run in a single person, it is equitable that they should be distinct" (*Quando duo jura . . . concurrunt in una persona, aequum est ac si essent in diversis*; 4.4–5). Not only, then, was "ligeance" (allegiance) argued to be due to "the King's several politic capacities of several kingdoms," but, because the king "hath several kingdoms by several titles and descents, there also are the ligeances several" (4.5).

In Coke's report, the arguments of his opponents are classified as belonging to four nouns in the case from which "all the said arguments and objections on the part of the defendants were drawn" (Coke 2002: 4). These nouns are: (1) *ligeantia* (allegiance); (2) *regna* (kingdoms); (3) *leges* (laws); and (4) *alienigena* (alien). Coke explains that in reporting the arguments, he aimed "to reduce the sum and effect of all to such a method as, upon consideration of all the arguments, the reporter himself thinketh to be fittest and clearest for the right understanding of the true reasons and causes of the judgement and resolution of the case in question" (4.7). As part of this method, he subdivides the four nouns from which all the defendants' arguments were drawn into further questions that would help to define them. It is at this point that his "method" seems to derive from both rhetoric and dialectic, for the topical questions that arise in relation to each noun seem to hover between the argumentative forms of predicament and circumstance.

Thus, concerning "ligeance," Coke offers various definitions, following Seton's *Dialectica*, where definition can include metaphor and arguments from etymology. Coke advances the metaphorical argument that "allegiance is the bond of faith" (*ligeantia est vinculum fidei*), as well as the etymological argument that "allegiance is the bandage or tie (*ligamentum*), that is, the *ligatio* (binding) of the *mens* (mind, disposition, heart) because the tie is the connection of all networks and junctures" (*ligeantia est ligamentum, quasi ligatio mentium, quia sicut ligamentum est connexioa r[e]ticulorum et juncturam*; Coke 2002: 4.8) (Knafla 1977: 229–30). Both of these arguments are emotive and vivid, tending to support the idea that allegiance, as a bond of faith, is anterior to law and policy, which munifies the plaintiff's argument against the defendants' contention that ligeances were distinguished by "the several politic capacities of the several kingdoms" (Coke 2002: 4.5).

Coke then goes on to identify four kinds of ligeances that are valid in English law: (1) natural; (2) by acquisition or denization; (3) *ligeanta localis*, when an alien, coming in amity, gains the king's protection; and (4) legal ligeance, which takes the form of the oath sworn in the Leet. This fourth category offered arguments against Scottish naturalization, for it was said that the Scots had another form of oath, and the English oath was thus an oath of loyalty to the laws of England (Knafla 1977: 235). To counter these arguments, Coke details the conditions of the oath, finding them to be five: (1) the time, which is indefinite ("from this day forward"); (2) the qualities of being "true and faithful"; (3) to whom the oath is sworn ("to our Sovereign Lord the King and his heirs"); (4) in what manner ("until the letting out of the last drop of our dear heart's blood"); and (5) where and in what places (2002: 4.11–2).

As Coke moves through these conditions, he calls them "circumstances," and, indeed, they seem like the topics of circumstance—*tempus, modus, locus*—that would identify the oath's particularity. He goes through the *circumstantiae* of time, quality, person, and manner and comes to the question of *where*: "Now we are come to (and almost past)," he writes, "the consideration of this circumstance, where natural ligeance should be due" (Coke 2002: 4.12). The question of *where*, of course, is crucial to what Francis Bacon called "the inward question, or state of the question" ([1859] 2011: 642), which turns on whether naturalization depends on the singularity of the king's person or the severality of territorially distinct kingdoms, two different *places*. At this point, however, Coke suddenly switches terminology and invokes the dialectical predicaments that do not so much identify the particularity of a thing or event as ascertain the validity of a proposition. By calling the question "Where?" a predicament, Coke implies that the idea of swearing allegiance to a country, rather than to a royal person, is a logical contradiction, an impossibility: "By that which hath been said," he continues, "it appeareth, that ligeance, and faith and truth, which are her members and parts, are qualities of the mind and soul of man, and cannot be circumscribed within the predicament of *ubi* [where] for that were to confound predicaments, and to go about to drive (an absurd and impossible thing) the predicament of quality into the predicament of *ubi*" (Coke 2002: 4.13). This formulation of Coke's—an effect of his method of reducing the arguments to topical heads—is by no means conclusive within the larger report of the arguments for the naturalization of James's Scottish subjects. It does, however, contribute to the emotional persuasiveness of the plaintiff's case. We know that it is not, in fact, absurd to suggest that allegiance might be locally distinct, but Coke's invocation of the terminology of dialectical invention lends an air of logic to what is actually more like a hyperbolic argument for the incommensurability of spiritual "faith and truth" and earthly locality: "So seeing that ligeance is a quality of mind, and not confined within any place" (4.16). It would be too much, to be sure, to ascribe the common law's new emphasis on reasoned decisions of courts as sources of law to the influence of humanist rhetoric and dialectic, but there is no doubt that in this, as in innumerable other instances in Coke's *Reports*, the impression of a "reason" on which to base a legal decision owes much to the topical form of rhetorical or dialectical *inventio*. To this extent, then, we may say that, during the sixteenth century in England, the practices of rhetoric and dialectic had considerable effect on legal procedure and development.

References

Agricola, Rodolphus. (1539) 1967. *De inventione dialectica lucubrationes*. Nieuwkoop: B. de Graaf.

Bacon, Francis. (1859) 2011. *The Works of Francis Bacon*. Vol. 7, *Literary and Professional Works 2*. Edited by James Spedding, Robert Leslie Ellis, and Douglas Denon Heath. Cambridge: Cambridge University Press.

Baker, John H. 1989. "Records, Reports, and the Origins of Case-Law in England." In *Judicial Records, Law Reports, and the Growth of Case Law*, edited by John H. Baker, 40–42. Berlin: Duncker and Humblot.

Baker, John H. 2003. *The Oxford History of the Laws of England*. Vol. 4, *1483–1558*. Oxford: Oxford University Press.

Bernard, Richard. 1627. *A Guide to Grand Jury Men*. London.

Bland, D. S. 1967. "Rhetoric and the Law Student in Sixteenth-Century England." *Studies in Philology* 53 no. 4: 498–508.

Boyer, Allen D. 2003. *Sir Edward Coke and the Elizabethan Age*. Stanford, CA: Stanford University Press.

Cicero, Marcus Tullius. 2003. *Topica*. Edited and translated by Tobias Reinhardt. Oxford: Oxford University Press.

Coke, Sir Edward. 2002. *The Reports of Sir Edward Coke in Thirteen Parts*. 6 vols. Union, NJ: Lawbook Exchange.

Dalton, Michael. 1635. *The Countrey Justice*. London.

Erasmus, Desiderius. 1573. *De duplici copia verborum ac rerum commentarii duo . . . cum commentariis M. Veltkirchii*. London.

Giuliani, Alessandro. 1969. "The Influence of Rhetoric on the Law of Evidence and Pleading." *Juridical Review* 62: 216–251.

Hassall, W. O., ed. 1950. *A Catalogue of the Library of Sir Edward Coke*. Preface by Samuel Thorne. New Haven, CT: Yale University Press.

Hohmann, Hanns. 1996. "Classical Rhetoric and Roman Law: Reflections on a Debate." *Rhetorik* 15: 15–41.

Hohmann, Hanns. 2006. "Ciceronian Rhetoric and the Law." In *The Rhetoric of Cicero in Its Medieval and Early Renaissance Commentary Tradition*, edited by Virginia Cox and John O. Ward, 193–207. Leiden: Brill.

Jardine, Lisa. 1974. "The Place of Dialectic Teaching in Sixteenth-Century Cambridge." *Studies in the Renaissance* 21: 31–64.

Jonson, Ben. (1616) 1996. *The Devil is an Ass*. Edited by Peter Happé. Manchester: University of Manchester Press.

Kitteredge, G. L. 1911. "King James I and *The Devil is an Ass*." *Modern Philology* 9 no. 2: 195–201.

Knafla, Louis. 1969. "The Law Studies of an Elizabethan Student." *Huntington Library Quarterly* 32: 221–240.

Knafla, Louis. 1977. *Law and Politics in Jacobean England: The Tracts of Lord Chancellor Ellesmere*. Cambridge: Cambridge University Press.

Lambarde, William. 1592. Eirenarcha; *or of the office of the Justices of the Peace*. London.

Langbein, John. 1974. *Prosecuting Crime in the Renaissance: England, Germany, France*. Cambridge, MA: Harvard University Press.

Leff, Michael C. 1983. "The Topics of Argumentative Invention in Latin Rhetorical Theory from Cicero to Boethius." *Rhetorica* 1 no. 1: 23–44.

Leveson-Gower, Granville. 1888. "Note Book of a Surrey Justice." In *Surrey Archaeological Collections Relating to the History and Antiquities of the County*, 9: 161–232. London: Surrey Archaeological Society.

Mack, Peter. 1993. *Renaissance Argument: Valla and Agricola in the Traditions of Rhetoric and Dialectic*. Leiden: Brill.

Prest, Wilfred. 1977. "The Dialectical Origins of Finch's Law." *Cambridge Law Journal* 36: 316–352.

Price, Polly J. 1997. "Natural Law and Birthright Citizenship in *Calvin's Case* (1608)." *Yale Journal of the Law and Humanities* 9: 73–145.

Schoeck, Richard. 1953. "Rhetoric and Law in Sixteenth Century England." *Studies in Philology* 50 no. 2: 110–127.

Schoeck, Richard. 1983. "Lawyers and Rhetoric in Sixteenth Century England." In *Renaissance Eloquence: Studies in the Theory and Practice of Renaissance Rhetoric*, edited by J. J. Murphy, 274–291. Berkeley: University of California Press.

Seton, John. 1584. *Dialectica . . . annotationibus Petri Cateri*. London.

Shapiro, Barbara J. 1983. *Probability and Certainty in Seventeenth-Century England: A Study of the Relationships Between Science, Religion, History, Law, and Literature*. Princeton, NJ: Princeton University Press.

Shapiro, Barbara J. 1991. *"Beyond Reasonable Doubt" and "Probable Cause": Historical Perspectives on the Anglo-American Law of Evidence*. Berkeley: University of California Press.

Shapiro, Barbara J. 2000. *A Culture of Fact: England, 1550–1700*. Ithaca, NY: Cornell University Press.

Shapiro, Barbara J. 2001. "Classical Rhetoric and the English Law of Evidence." In *Rhetoric and Law in Early Modern Europe*, edited by Victoria Kahn and Lorna Hutson, 54–72. New Haven, CT: Yale University Press.

Townsend, Henry. MS Eng. Misc. e. 479. Bodleian Library.

CHAPTER 33

RHETORIC AND PEDAGOGY

PETER MACK

RHETORIC textbooks were always written and almost always used as part of a wider program of education. To understand the way they are organized and the things they say or take for granted, we need to put them back, as far as we can, into the context of reading, composition exercises, and training in which they were taught. The difficulty in doing this arises partly from lack of evidence about what actually happened in classrooms and partly from the fact that textbooks written with one educational context in mind were often taught in a very different one. So, for example, a manual of Roman rhetoric that was intended as an introduction to the subject, in preparation for exercises in composition and an apprenticeship to a practicing orator, would later be treated as a complete work on the subject. This chapter focuses on local examples of the role that rhetoric played in school and university syllabuses in the Renaissance. The aim is first to give a small sample of the variety of different syllabuses that were doubtless taught across Europe and second to make a plea for many more local studies, which should be more thorough, thoughtful, and detailed than this selective survey. Ideally there is a need for a program of publication of documents, a series of studies of the reading, rhetoric teaching, and composition exercises of particular schools, and eventually for histories of rhetorical education for the different geographical regions of Europe. The history of Renaissance rhetoric that can be written today is inevitably a history of textbooks (Mack 2011: 1–10), but a true history of rhetoric must be based on understanding the teaching and learning that went on in the schools and universities. Eventually one should move on to analyze the impact that rhetorical training had on the writings of a particular society (which is what I attempt for a relatively well-documented society in *Elizabethan Rhetoric* [2002]).

Within the educational context, rhetoric had to compete with other subjects. While in the ancient world rhetoric was the dominant subject of higher education, for much of the Middle Ages universities were dominated by the study of Aristotelian logic and philosophy, leaving a much smaller space for rhetoric (see Heath, ch. 5; Steel, ch. 16; Ward, ch. 25). At the elementary level, medieval and Renaissance schools had to give priority to their pupils' need to learn Latin (and later also Greek) to gain access to the riches of learning. Renaissance educators introduced rhetorical principles early on in their reading of literature and in the letters and themes that they asked students to write. Toward the end of the grammar school or the beginning of the university syllabus, pupils would have read a textbook of the whole of rhetoric, usually *Rhetorica ad Herennium* or one of the modern textbooks by Philipp Melanchthon, Omer Talon, or Cyprian Soarez. In northern universities, studies of rhetoric would have been enriched by the humanist version of logic that they studied in the first few years. Renaissance education, as the following examples illustrate, benefited from connections among studies in grammar, rhetoric, and logic.

THE SCHOOLS OF GUARINO

Guarino da Verona (1374–1460) established schools in Verona (1418–29) and Ferrara (1429–60), for part of the time combining his teaching of pupils in his home with public duties as professor of rhetoric in the two cities. His practice of teaching is described in his letters and in Battista Guarini's *De ordine docendi et studendi* (1459). Battista divides his methodical account of Guarino's school into three stages: first, a focus on pronunciation and on learning the Latin accidence by heart (Garin 1958: 440–2; Grafton and Jardine 1986: 8–16; Kallendorf 2002: 268–71); second, the grammatical phase, emphasizing Latin and Greek language, literature, and knowledge about the classical world (Garin 1958: 446–58; Kallendorf 2002: 274–94); and third, the rhetorical stage.

The grammatical stage already includes some rhetorical emphases. Guarino recommends that pupils should collect together in their notebooks maxims on a particular topic. In their private reading they must ensure they have grasped the meaning and moral teaching of a passage before they gather the "flowers" of its expression. Myths and poetic fictions must be questioned carefully to establish their meaning and their appropriateness to a situation. Pupils should commit to memory whatever is adaptable to life and relates to virtue. Pupils will write letters and declamations based on their reading (Garin 1958: 458–62; Kallendorf 2002: 294–300).

At the rhetoric stage pupils will study *Rhetorica ad Herennium* (which Guarino, like his contemporaries, thought was by Cicero), "which sets out all parts of the subject fully and without excessive length," together with Cicero's speeches (Kallendorf 2002: 290–2). Later they can move on to Cicero's other rhetorical works and to Quintilian. All the works of Cicero are to be studied, particularly the moral philosophy of *De officiis* and the *Tusculan Disputations*. Pupils should also study logic, Aristotle's *Ethics*, and Plato's dialogues (Garin 1958: 458). Guarino's commentary on *Rhetorica ad Herennium* provides an exposition of the work's teaching and a detailed analysis of its language and style, treating it as a model as well as a manual of Latin eloquence (Cicero, *Rhetorica nova et vetus*; Ward 2006: 51–8, 61–3).

Guarino's school aimed to provide a wide-ranging education in classical literature and history, culminating in a thorough study of rhetoric, based on *Rhetorica ad Herennium*, but moving on to Cicero and Quintilian. Guarino analyzed Cicero's orations to demonstrate the operation of rhetorical doctrines in practice. Even at the grammatical stage the method of reading texts places an emphasis on style and on collecting vocabulary, maxims, and flowers of rhetoric. Guarino placed great emphasis on writing exercises and on Greek.

ITALIAN SCHOOLS AND UNIVERSITIES IN THE FIFTEENTH AND SIXTEENTH CENTURIES

Paul Grendler (1989) shows that early fifteenth-century Italian schools continued to use medieval grammar textbooks (especially the *Janua*, sometimes misleadingly called *Donatus*) but that these textbooks were gradually replaced. Robert Black argues that in Florentine Tuscany the humanist program did not cause significant change in lower-school Latin grammar teaching until the sixteenth century, but he accepts that the exercise of letter writing was introduced and that the range of classical authors studied widened (2001: 171–2, 238–74, 349–65; see also Black 2007).

Grendler suggests that sixteenth-century Italian Latin schools based their curriculum on a small group of grammar texts and intensive study of Virgil and Cicero. In grammar the principal text was Donatus's late classical *Ars minor*, supplemented or at times replaced by Guarino's *Regulae*, the *Janua*, and Nicollò Perotti's *Rudimenta grammatices* (Grendler 1989: 172–9, 188–94; see Percival 2004). Probably they began to practice letter writing as they began the study of Cicero's *Epistulae ad familiares*. Some of the grammar textbooks, among them Perotti's, included instructions on letter writing. Schools may also have used Latin phrasebooks like Stephanus Fliscus's *Synonyma sententiarum* (173, 210–2). Their principal rhetoric text was *Rhetorica ad Herennium*, which they studied alongside the works of Cicero, especially his letters (212–29). Some schools taught Geoffrey of Vinsauf's *Poetria nova* (ca. 1180) (Woods 2010: 51–2, 94–162). The pattern of grammar, letters, rhetoric, poetry, and history (sometimes represented by one text in each genre) seems to have been established at the end of the fifteenth century and continued into the sixteenth (Grendler 1989: 204–5).

Most Italian universities assumed that students' education in grammar and rhetoric would mainly have taken place before admission. The university programs concentrated on logic, philosophy, and the higher faculties (law, medicine, and theology), but in the late fifteenth and early sixteenth century universities gave relatively more attention to rhetoric, Latin literature, and Greek. Although the teachers of humanities were generally a small minority they were sometimes among the best-paid teachers in the university, suggesting that lectures on these subjects helped attract students to the university (Grendler 2002: 214–8). Texts lectured on by Paduan professors of Greek, Latin, and rhetoric (generally two people covered these roles) included Cicero's *Pro lege Manilia*, *Pro Milone*, *Pro Cluentio*, *Pro Rabirio*, and Aristotle's *Rhetoric* and *Poetics*. Florence and Rome employed more humanists and enjoyed a wider range of lectures on rhetoric (in

Florence Poliziano lectured on Quintilian in 1480–1 and on *Rhetorica ad Herennium* in 1481–2) and Latin and Greek literature (Poliziano later lectured on Hesiod, Virgil, Juvenal, Homer, and Aristotelian philosophy). It appears that, while lecturers in other subjects were expected to cover the set texts over a cycle of four years or so (258–9, 266), the lecturers in humanistic subjects were free to choose from the whole range of Latin and Greek literature. This may mean that in some universities there may have been no lectures on a rhetoric textbook for many years, but rhetorical approaches would generally have played a large part in the lectures given on orations or literary texts. Since there was generally no degree requirement in rhetoric or literature (172–8), students may have followed these courses as an adjunct to courses on material required for their degrees. There is little or no evidence in Italy for the influence of logic on rhetoric and vice versa that was usual in northern Europe in the sixteenth century (266). Grendler believes that humanism was in decline in Italian universities after 1575 (248).

In sixteenth-century Italian universities, then, an advanced classical rhetoric textbook, such as Quintilian's *Institutio oratoria*, Aristotle's *Rhetoric*, or Cicero's *De oratore*, could be taught in a particular year, but teaching in rhetoric was not reliably available. Pupils would have been expected to cover a wide-ranging course in Latin literature at the grammar school, including study of the tropes and figures, practice in writing Latin letters, and reading of *Rhetorica ad Herennium*.

THE UNIVERSITY OF PARIS IN THE EARLY AND MIDDLE SIXTEENTH CENTURY

The statutes in force in early sixteenth-century Paris ensured the dominance of Aristotelian logic over the arts course. The early Parisian humanists first sought the return to Aristotle's texts, in place of the late scholastic logic that had dominated in the fifteenth century. Then Jacques Lefèvre d'Etaples and others wrote introductions to the study of Aristotelian logic that observed humanist standards of Latinity. From around 1530 onward a group of younger teachers sought to enshrine the humanist idea of logic as the practical use of argument. This involved intensive study of Rudolph Agricola's *De inventione dialectica* and Philipp Melanchthon's works on rhetoric and dialectic (see Mack 1993, 2011). This study of humanist textbooks was reinforced by reading Cicero's orations with commentaries on their argumentative content by Johann Sturm, Bartholomaeus Latomus, Jacob Omphalius, and others. When Latomus was appointed *lecteur royal* in Latin eloquence, he began with a course on Horace's *Satires* and *Ars poetica*. The following year he taught Cicero's *Verrine Orations*. Later he turned his attention to Cicero's rhetorical works, including the *Partitiones oratoriae*. By the mid-1530s the teaching of logic in Paris was dominated by the humanist approach associated with Agricola. Cicero's *Orations* were studied as examples of dialectic in practice and serious teaching time was devoted to classical rhetoric (Meerhoff 2006: 306–24).

Petrus Ramus provides us with detailed accounts of his teaching innovations. He sought to combine rhetoric, dialectic, and literature in his university teaching. When he became head of the Collège des Presles in 1546, while he was still banned from teaching philosophy, he announced a program in which Talon would teach dialectic in the mornings and he would teach rhetoric in the afternoons (Ramus and Talon [1577] 1971: 295). Rhetoric and dialectic were presented as subjects that needed to be taught together to obtain a better understanding of classical literature (297–301). In his *Pro philosophica Parisiensis Academiae disciplina oratio* (1551) Ramus defends the teaching in his college against those who accuse him of not reading all the works of Aristotle required by the university statutes (Ramus and Talon [1577] 1971: 317–9). He asserts that the basis of all his teaching is the method of analysis followed by composition, once the basic precepts have been learned. Analysis involves showing the students the way the principles are used in literary texts. When the students understand how the rules work from their study of texts, they must then imitate those texts in writing of their own, which Ramus calls "genesis" (326–9). Pupils move on to rhetoric in the fourth year, learning the definitions and examples of the tropes and figures, observing them in use in Virgil, Homer, Cicero, and Demosthenes, and employing them in their own writing (330). Thus, rhetorical training is combined with the continued use of what was learned in grammar. The same principles apply to dialectic. It is not enough to learn the rules; they must be found in literary texts and practiced in students' own writing. Ramus finds illustrations for the topics of invention and the rules of judgment in the reading of Cicero, Demosthenes, Virgil, Homer, Plato, and Aristotle, and he expects his pupils to make use of dialectic in their own writing (331–6).

STRASBOURG 1538–81: JOHANN STURM'S PROGRAM

Sturm (1507–89) outlines the program for his school in *De literarum ludis recte aperiendis* (1538). His later advice to other schools and his letter collections indicate that he maintained the same program as long as he was rector of the school (Spitz and Tinsley 1995: 47). The aim of the program was to develop wise and eloquent piety. Nine years of boyhood education were to be followed by five years of advanced public lectures, covering history, philosophy, mathematics, Bible studies, and the principles of medicine and law. These public lectures were intended to give students a basis of general learning from which they could go on to attend one of the higher faculties (Law, Medicine, and Theology) at a university outside Strasbourg (85–6; Sturm [1538] 2007, sig. C4r–v). Rhetoric was one of the topics for the public lectures, and a substantial program in rhetoric was part of the nine-year course (Spitz and Tinsley 1995: 110–1; Sturm [1538] 2007, sigs. H1r–2r).

In the beginning three classes (named classes 9–7) pupils learned Latin grammar and read easier Latin texts. In the seventh class boys begin Latin composition in prose and poetry. They must be shown how to develop arguments and how to collect subject matter and model expressions from their reading. The teacher must point out words that belong to poetry and figures of speech. Their memory should be developed through learning by heart passages from Cicero and Virgil worthy of imitation. In reading through texts the teacher should point out customs, histories, moral teaching, rhetorical ornaments, and commonplaces (Spitz and Tinsley 1995: 88–93; Sturm [1538] 2007, sigs. D2r–E1v).

The sixth class extends their Latin reading, with more from the *Aeneid*, Catullus, and Horace, celebrated passages from Cicero and selections from Caesar and Terence. In their reading of Cicero attention should be given to effective argumentation, periodic sentences, and figures of speech. In the fifth class the boys begin Greek and extend their Latin reading. Alongside their composition exercises they begin to study the tropes and figures on the basis of the lists in *De oratore* and *Orator*. The rules for the ornaments should be explained on the basis of Hermogenes. Sturm believes that training in eloquent expression should come before invention (Spitz and Tinsley 1995: 93–6; Sturm [1538] 2007, sigs. E1v–3v).

In the fourth class pupils begin to read Latin and Greek side by side, comparing Homer with Virgil and Demosthenes with Cicero. They learn the elementary rules of rhetoric from the first book of *Rhetorica ad Herennium* before obtaining an overview of the whole subject from Cicero's *Partitiones oratoriae*. In this class they begin the formal analysis of the structure of orations and are taught to gather material from their reading into notebooks under headings. They are taught principles for the mental composition of orations, and they do exercises that resemble the ancient *progymnasmata* (Spitz and Tinsley 1995: 96–100; Sturm [1538] 2007, sigs. E4r–F3r).

In the later years when they are working more on dialectic and philosophy there is still considerable emphasis on aptness of expression and on ornamentation in both languages. There will be further study of Demosthenes and more work on the principles of dialectic. *Partitiones oratoriae* should be reread with commentary as a reminder of the whole of rhetoric. There must be more composition of orations, both in writing and mentally. Pupils should also study Cicero's *Orator*. Demosthenes and Homer will be read alongside Cicero's works on oratory (Spitz and Tinsley 1995: 101–3, [1538] 2007, sigs. F3r–4v). Sturm states that the most important of all works on rhetoric are Aristotle's *Rhetoric*, Cicero's *De oratore*, and Hermogenes's *On Types of Style* (Spitz and Tinsley 1995: 111; Sturm [1538] 2007, sigs. H1v–2r).

Sturm's plan accords great importance to Greek and keeps returning to four key authors: Cicero, Virgil, Homer, and Demosthenes. This selection reflects his emphasis on Latin writers' imitation of Greek. Rhetoric is introduced early in the program, starting with the tropes and figures, but is then maintained through classical works that offer an overview of the subject (*Rhetorica ad Herennium* and *Partitiones oratoriae*) and more specialized handling of particular aspects (Hermogenes and Cicero's *Topica* and *Orator*). The practical use of the rules of rhetoric and dialectic is explored by reading orations and dialogues alongside the textbooks. Perhaps surprisingly, the program makes no reference to letter writing or to the works of Desiderius Erasmus.

THE ELIZABETHAN GRAMMAR SCHOOL

Surviving statutes and teachers' manuals suggest that the Elizabethan grammar school program had three main aspects: first and foremost, acquiring the ability to read, write, and speak Latin; second, a course in Latin literature; and third, training in persuasive writing, particularly of letters and essays (which pupils and teachers usually call "themes") (Mack 2002: 12–4). Teachers were expected to draw attention to rhetorical features of the texts they read with their pupils, such as figures of speech, proverbs, and passages for imitation. School commentaries suggest that teachers also picked out ethical axioms and explained the moral teaching of the text or episode. In some schools pupils were taught to make commonplace books, recording especially striking phrases or narratives in their notebooks under particular ethical headings, such as justice, courage, peace, and treachery, so that the extracts were ready for pupils to reuse in their own compositions when a particular subject came up (14–24).

Latin composition began with letter writing, at first in imitation of Cicero's simpler letters to his wife and daughter from *Ad familiares* (14) but later using a letter-writing manual and taking subject matter from pupils' everyday life or their reading. Letter-writing manuals tend to provide recipes for the content and structure of a range of different kinds of letter (e.g., letters of encouragement, persuasion, request, advice, thanks, and consolation) together with suitable phrases, extracts from existing letters, and specially constructed examples. While much of the emphasis is on matter, order, and style, the manuals also consider the way a writer should address the recipient and the way the relationship between writer and recipient will influence what is appropriate both in content and in manner.

A second type of composition manual frequently mentioned in the English statutes is Aphthonius's *Progymnasmata* in Latin translation with Lorichius's commentary. This is a graded selection of 14 writing exercises that make use of material emphasized in reading (e.g., instructive narratives and moral axioms) and provide detailed instructions for producing materials that can become part of larger compositions (e.g., description, comparison, speech for a character) or form compositions in their own right (e.g., praise, thesis, proposal for a law). Several of the statutes mention Erasmus's highly successful textbook, *De copia*, which was first composed as a contribution to John Colet's founding of St. Paul's School. *De copia* suggests methods of enriching texts, based on figures of rhetoric and on dialectical techniques. It provides examples of many different ways of expressing a single idea (sometimes at comically great length: for example, 195 ways to say "your letter pleased me greatly") and gives instructions for descriptions and comparisons. Teachers' manuals suggest that many pupils would also have been provided with a list of the principal tropes and figures, perhaps one dictated by their teacher (Mack 2002: 24–47).

Rhetorical skills appear to have been at the heart of grammar school instruction, reinforced by the composition exercises and by the teachers' approach to reading texts.

Pupils would have learned about the figures of speech and about ways of constructing different types of letter and short composition, but they did not usually study the whole of rhetoric. Letter writing taught them something about audiences and about organization, but students did not receive training in topical invention, in status theory, or in the organization of the four-part oration. They seem to have studied fragments of rhetoric that were suited to the reading and writing they were doing rather than receiving the traditional full course in classical rhetoric.

OXFORD AND CAMBRIDGE IN THE LATE SIXTEENTH CENTURY

James McConica's studies of sixteenth-century Oxford suggest that alongside the requirements of the university statutes, pupils studied a wide variety of subjects, depending on their intentions and their tutors' interests (1986: 1–68, 645–732). While most arts students appear to have studied Latin literature, rhetoric, and dialectic, individuals also read widely in history, mathematics, physics, ethics, theology, and modern languages. The importance of literature and wider studies is suggested by the evidence of the small number of Oxford undergraduate booklists so far published (see Fehrenbach and Leedham-Green 1993–8). At Oxford the grammar course (lasting two terms of the 16 allocated to the B.A.) required Thomas Linacre's *Rudiments*, Virgil, Horace, or Cicero's *Epistles*. For rhetoric (four terms) the statutes mention Aristotle's *Rhetoric*, Cicero's rhetorical works, or his orations (Gibson 1931: 389–90). Sixteenth-century Oxford college statutes provide for lectures in humanity (usually involving Latin poetry, history, and rhetoric), Greek, and rhetoric. At Cambridge, where the first of the four years required for the B.A. was devoted to rhetoric, the texts specified by the statutes were Quintilian, Hermogenes, or any other book of Cicero's speeches (see University of Cambridge 1852).

The lists of books owned by members of the university who died in residence suggest a basic reading list in rhetoric at both universities that confirms what the statutes indicate. Cicero's *Orations* and his rhetorical works, especially the pseudo-Ciceronian *Rhetorica ad Herennium*, occur very frequently in the lists. Quintilian's *Institutio oratoria*, Cicero's *De oratore*, and Aristotle's *Rhetoric* are less frequent but still found very often. There is a small but significant number of copies of Hermogenes (Leedham-Green 1986). Our only known complete text for an Elizabethan lecture course in rhetoric, John Rainolds's lectures on Aristotle's *Rhetoric*, assumes that his audience understands the general syllabus of rhetoric and therefore concentrates on problems in Aristotle's division of the material and ethical approach (Green 1986). Ralph Cholmondeley's notebook (late 1570s) contains a complete set of notes on Cicero's *Partitiones oratoriae*, which looks like his record of a course of lectures, alongside notes on the structure, argument, figures, and content of some of Cicero's orations (Bodleian MS Latin misc. e.114).

The importance of dialectic within the university syllabus was reinforced by the obligation for students to participate regularly in disputations to graduate. There is some evidence of colleges requiring declamation as an internal exercise and of students and teachers making classical orations to introduce a disputation. From the booklists we note the continuing importance of letter-writing texts and *De copia*. Ciceronian textbooks of rhetoric were much studied, as were Cicero's orations, and Aristotle's *Rhetoric* was a significant presence. It thus appears that English university students undertook the complete course in classical rhetoric that they had lacked at school. They also appear to have followed the humanist dialectic syllabus, with its emphasis on topical invention (Mack 2002: 48–75).

GERMAN GRAMMAR SCHOOLS

Dilwyn Knox (1994: 63–80) treats Johannes Matthaeus's syllabus for the Latin school at Krems (1580) as a paradigm for late sixteenth-century Latin schools in Protestant Germany (Matthaeus 1581). As in other Protestant curricula, progress from one class to the next depended strictly on age (Matthaeus 1581, sigs. c7v–8r). At between six and seven boys entered the most elementary (fifth) class, in which they were taught writing (presumably they could already read German), the catechism, and Latin vocabulary and accidence. In the second class (entered at 11 or older) the pupils continued to improve their Latin, reading Virgil's *Eclogues*, Sturm's selection of Cicero's letters, and Sebastian Castalio's *Dialogues*. The second class was required to write Latin compositions and submit them to the teacher for correction every week (sig. b1r). Their compositions probably included letters (sig. b6v). The teachers were instructed to point out "metaphors and other tropes and the figures" when reading the set authors in this class (sig. b5r–v). In the highest class (aged 13 or older) the boys studied Melanchthon's dialectic and rhetoric, with the questions of Lucas Lossius. They read Virgil's *Aeneid*, Cicero's *Ad familiares*, *De officiis*, and some orations and Terence. They continued with the Greek New Testament and theological readings (sig. b1r–v). Their purpose in reading Cicero's orations was to understand the way the principles of rhetoric—invention, disposition, style, type of oration, status, parts of the peroration, and tropes and figures—worked in practice. Their reading of Cicero's letters was intended to provide useful phrases. In poetry they should study the rules of prosody and the use of the tropes and figures. They were expected to submit Latin prose compositions and poetry to their teacher every week and to begin composition in Greek (sigs. b1r–v, b4v–5r). In addition to writing letters and poems, more advanced pupils were expected to practice declamation and disputation (sig. b6v).

Knox contends that the pattern of reserving rhetoric for the highest class in a five-form school and teaching rhetoric and dialectic together was usual. It was also customary that modern textbooks (normally those of Melanchthon or ones based on his) would be used in place of the classical manuals. Some schools recommended a manual of tropes and figures for the second class. In a few schools, Erasmus's *De copia* was used as an aid to composition in one of the lower forms (Knox 1994: 64–5).

THE JESUIT *RATIO STUDIORUM*

The *Ratio studiorum* (1599) was the official book of instructions for all Jesuit academies in Europe and the expanding world. The final formulation of 1599 was based on over 30 years of experiment on similar lines. The complete course would take a student from the elementary stage to the equivalent of a degree in theology. The upper section comprised a three-year course in philosophy (principally logic, natural philosophy, and metaphysics but also including mathematics and ethics) and a four-year course in theology, based mainly on the works of St. Thomas Aquinas but also including Hebrew, Scripture, and training in the practicalities of serving a parish (Bianchi 2002: 86–90, 188–92, 196–200). The lower section had five grades: three levels of grammar, humanity, and rhetoric (98). In the earlier years the teacher is expected to point out some of the rhetorical features of the classical texts read. He will explain metaphors, myths, and any historical and cultural information that may be helpful. He will choose two or three phrases from the text as examples of elegant expression (292–4).

The fourth year, or humanities class, is intended to complete their knowledge of the properties and richness of the Latin language and prepare for rhetoric. They read the summary of rhetoric in Soarez's *De arte rhetorica libri tres*, with particular attention to the tropes and figures and to prose rhythm. They study the application of rhetoric by analyzing Cicero's *Pro lege Manilia*, *Pro Archia*, and *Pro Marcello*. The teacher is instructed to comment on the usage and etymology of individual words, to pick out elegant expressions and passages for imitation, and to show how the rules of rhetoric are observed in the speeches. Pupils are also trained to write Latin letters (Bianchi 2002: 278–88).

The aim of the fifth or rhetoric class is perfect eloquence in oratory and poetry. Pupils study the rhetorical works of Cicero, Cicero's speeches, Aristotle's *Rhetoric*, and, on occasion, his *Poetics*. For Latin style they are instructed to imitate Cicero alone. The teacher must explain each of the rules of rhetoric, citing the opinions of other rhetoricians where appropriate. He must give reasons for the rule and cite and explain examples from Latin literature illustrating the use of the rule in practice. Finally, he should show how the rule can be adapted to present-day circumstances, giving the most elegant examples possible. In reading texts points of invention, disposition, and style must be explained, as must the use of topics to persuade, embellish, and move. The teacher must pick out the tropes and figures of speech and give parallels from other authors both for the subject and the words employed. Finally, he must discuss the propriety, elegance, harmony, and variety of the words chosen (Bianchi 2002: 264–72).

For the pupils' monthly written orations the teacher must indicate the subjects, the parts, the topics to confirm and amplify the argument, the figures of speech to be employed, and, if appropriate, some passages from classical literature that can be imitated. Students will declaim once a month before their fellows and will take part in scenes from plays. Members of the Society must also practice public speaking to prepare them for lecturing and giving sermons (Bianchi 2002: 118, 236–40, 272–8). Although public speaking as such is not mentioned in the statutes relating to the courses in philosophy and theology, the general statutes for the higher courses insist on the necessity of pupils studying rhetoric before moving on to philosophy and theology (92, 116–8).

The Jesuit *Ratio studiorum* (plan of study) prescribes a wide range of classical texts. The teaching of a range of classical rhetoric textbooks is the capstone of the literary part of the course and an essential prerequisite for the philosophy and theology that follows. The instructions for commenting on authors and for pupils' compositions show the importance of a practical grasp of rhetoric even in the more grammatical part of the course. The direct reading of Aristotle and Cicero is prepared for, in the humanity year, by the study of Soarez's textbook of the whole of rhetoric, which summarizes their main ideas. The study of rhetorical theory must be reinforced by reading Cicero's speeches and writing orations and declamations.

CONCLUSION

Although teaching Latin grammar through the study of classical texts was the main aim of all the schools discussed in this survey, rhetoric played an important role in every school, typically either as the culmination of the linguistic training or as a constant undercurrent in the reading of texts. The teaching of rhetoric was always closely bound up both with practices of reading texts and with composition exercises. Rhetoric was thus a central feature of Renaissance education. But we have also observed considerable variety in the place of rhetoric within the curriculum, in the textbooks and doctrines actually studied, and in the framework of readings and exercises within which rhetoric was taught. To improve our understanding of Renaissance rhetoric, we need more studies of the role of rhetoric within the curriculum of individual schools and of the ways rhetorical principles were used in the practical life of the societies that those schools served.

FURTHER READING

Chomarat ([1981] 2002) is a clear and reliable discussion of the educational writings of Erasmus, the most influential textbook writer of the sixteenth century. Kallendorf (2002) is one of the key primary texts of Renaissance Italian educational theory, and it is clearly presented and well translated. For a thoroughly documented and groundbreaking study of what really happened in a Renaissance university and of its place in its society, see McConica (1986). Mack (2002) attempts to understand how the syllabus worked and what rhetorical training contributed to the ways people argued, persuaded, and made speeches in a particular society. Woods (2010) is a close study of the manuscripts of a centrally important medieval textbook, Geoffrey of Vinsauf's *Poetria nova*, showing how material evidence can be interpreted to throw light on the aspirations and practices of the classroom.

REFERENCES

Bianchi, Angelo, ed. 2002. *Ratio atque institutio studiorum Societatis Jesu.* Milan: Biblioteca Universale Rizzoli.

Black, Robert. 2001. *Humanism and Education in Medieval and Renaissance Italy.* Cambridge: Cambridge University Press.

Black, Robert. 2007. *Education and Society in Florentine Tuscany: Teachers, Pupils and Schools, c. 1250–1500.* Leiden: Brill.

Chomarat, Jacques. (1981) 2002. *Grammaire et Rhétorique chez Erasme.* 2 vols. Paris: Belles Lettres.

Fehrenbach, Robert J., and Elizabeth S. Leedham-Green, eds. 1993–1998. *Private Libraries in Renaissance England.* 5 vols. Binghamton, NY: Medieval and Renaissance Texts and Studies.

Garin, Eugenio, ed. 1958. *Il pensiero pedagogico dello Umanesimo.* Florence: Giuntine Sansoni.

Gibson, Strickland, ed. 1931. *Statuta antiqua universitatis oxoniensis.* Oxford: Clarendon.

Grafton, Anthony, and Lisa Jardine. 1986. *From Humanism to the Humanities.* London: Duckworth.

Green, Lawrence D. 1986. *John Rainolds's Oxford Lectures on Aristotle's "Rhetoric."* Newark, NJ: Associated University Presses.

Grendler, Paul. 1989. *Schooling in Renaissance Italy.* Baltimore, MD: Johns Hopkins University Press.

Grendler, Paul. 2002. *The Universities of the Italian Renaissance.* Baltimore, MD: Johns Hopkins University Press.

Kallendorf, Craig. 2002. *Humanist Educational Treatises.* Cambridge, MA: Harvard University Press.

Knox, Dilwyn. 1994. "Order, Reason and Oratory: Rhetoric in Protestant Latin Schools." In *Renaissance Rhetoric*, edited by Peter Mack, 63–80. Basingstoke: Palgrave Macmillan.

Leedham-Green, Elizabeth. 1986. *Books in Cambridge Inventories.* 2 vols. Cambridge: Cambridge University Press.

Mack, Peter. 1993. *Renaissance Argument: Valla and Agricola in the Traditions of Rhetoric and Dialectic.* Leiden: Brill.

Mack, Peter. 2002. *Elizabethan Rhetoric.* Cambridge: Cambridge University Press.

Mack, Peter. 2011. *A History of Renaissance Rhetoric 1380–1620.* Oxford: Oxford University Press.

Matthaeus, Johann. 1581. *Scholae Cremsensis in Austria descripta formula.* Viteberg.

McConica, James, ed. 1986. *The History of the University of Oxford, III, The Collegiate University.* Oxford: Oxford University Press.

Meerhoff, Kees. 2006. "Les lecteurs royeaux pour l'éloquence Latine." In *Histoire du Collège de France*, vol. 1, edited by André Tuilier, 293–352. Paris: Fayard.

Percival, W. Keith. 2004. *Studies in Renaissance Grammar.* Aldershot: Ashgate.

Ramus, Peter, and Omer Talon. (1577) 1971. *Collectaneae prefationes, epistolae, orations.* Paris. Reprinted as *Oeuvres diverses.* Geneva: Slatkine.

Spitz, Leonard W., and Barbara Sher Tinsley. 1995. *Johann Sturm on Education*. St. Louis, MO: Concordia Publishing House.

Sturm, Johann. (1538) 2007. *De literarum ludis recte aperiendis*. Strasbourg: Presses Universitaires de Strasbourg.

University of Cambridge. 1852. *Documents Relating to the University and Colleges of Cambridge*. 3 vols. London: Longman, Brown, Green, and Longmans.

Ward, John O. 2006. "The Medieval and Early Renaissance Study of Cicero's *De inventione* and the *Rhetorica ad Herennium*." In *The Rhetoric of Cicero in its Medieval and Early Renaissance Commentary Tradition*, edited by Virginia Cox and John O. Ward, 3–75. Leiden: Brill.

Woods, Marjorie Curry. 2010. *Classroom Commentaries: Teaching the "Poetria nova" across Medieval and Renaissance Europe*. Columbus: Ohio State University Press.

CHAPTER 34

RHETORIC AND SCIENCE

JEAN DIETZ MOSS

> It is not enough to understand a true proposition; one must also feel the truth of it.
>
> —Giacomo Leopardi, *Canti*

DESPITE what may seem unimaginable to many postmodern scholars, the central contention governing rhetoric and science in the early modern period was that objective truth exists. It was the pivotal point for declarations and arguments about nature. The methods of finding and defending it were inherited largely from Aristotle, interpreted by commentators, and taught as part of philosophy in the universities of the Middle Ages and Renaissance. They reigned relatively uncontested in academic culture until the early seventeenth century, when new discoveries and the rise of experimentation brought them into question. The logic of inquiry and truth-centered discourse—dialectic and demonstration—remained customary ideals even as sightings of comets, mountains on the moon, and satellites of Jupiter began to unsettle the reigning theory of the cosmos. The role of rhetoric, taught in tandem with logic and poetics, gained increasing scrutiny with the presentation of novel scientific contentions in print.

The great nineteenth-century Italian poet Giacomo Leopardi, without intending to do so, perspicuously offers (in our epigraph) a key to one of the sources of disruption: the ebullience evident in some of the most important scientific writings of the sixteenth and seventeenth centuries. This ebullience can be attributed both to the initial thrill of discovery—the "aha!" or "eureka!" of the experience—and to a desire to convey the import of that discovery. Surprisingly, as early as the twelfth century, Arab commentators on Aristotle's texts, Abu Nasr al-Farabi and Ibn Sina (Avicenna), had spoken of the emotional response attendant on intellectual discovery as a feeling of satisfaction (*qana ah*) (Black 1990: 102). In the twentieth century, R. G. Collingwood also drew attention to that initial impression when he noted that "*sensa* never comes uncharged with emotion" (1981: 163).[1]

Whether "seeing" through the light of the intellect or witnessing by means of instruments and experiments, these early modern scientists did not suppress their emotions in claiming validity for their discoveries.[2] Analogies, metaphors, and the *enargeia* of rhetorical figuration coalesce with astronomy, as Nicholas Copernicus speaks of the universe as a "most beautiful temple" and the sun as its "lamp" and governor of the "family of planets" ([1543] 1978: 22). Galileo Galilei's first telescopic view of the moon and the stars elicits even more vivid analogies: the moon's mountains, like the Earth's, are "shining with light" ([1610] 1989: 41) at sunrise; the Earth joins "the dance of the stars" (57). Johannes Kepler's writings also overflow with excitement. These authors seem to be nudging readers to feel with them the impact of what they have found. Rhetorical color flows effortlessly, given the observers' immersion in the culture of eloquence characteristic of the day. Early schooling in poetics and in rhetoric must be given credit for much of the grace and charm of their use of figurative language. Classical texts were thoroughly analyzed and imitated. But should that sensitivity to beauty emerge too freely in the mature author's scientific prose, he might suffer charges of insufficient concern for truth—for failing to honor the aim of elucidation over that of persuasion.

The conventions of rhetoric learned from childhood onward guided expression and presentation. Humanists had made available classical texts from Isocrates to Quintilian, but none could rival the popularity of Cicero's writings as keys to eloquence (see Rebhorn, ch. 31). Natural philosophers knew, however, that neither clever arguments nor reputation nor enthusiasm would suffice to convince their peers: proofs (*pisteis*) of scientific reasoning would be required to undergird their claims. Rhetoric could invite passionate belief, but it could also provoke passionate opposition. The import of Aristotle's observation in the *Rhetoric* (1.4.6, 1359b) that one leaves the realm of rhetoric behind when one enters deeply into a science may not have occurred to these astronomers, but it may explain the uneasiness of some scholastic readers who were anxious that the canons of philosophy be followed.[3]

THE DISCIPLINARY SCENE

Long before the development of the "new science" of the seventeenth century, science (*scientia*) or "perfect knowing" meant certain knowledge to philosophers in the speculative or theoretical sciences, whether they sought knowledge in metaphysics, mathematics, or natural philosophy. Following scholastic teaching, scholars believed that certainty could be achieved if one discerned the cause (*aitia*)—the explanatory factor—that made a thing be what it is. In the practical sciences of ethics and politics and in the arts, only probabilities or even possibilities, not certitude, could be expected. A natural philosopher, however, could claim to have certain knowledge if he were adept at employing induction and deduction to arrive at solid proof and displayed his finding in what was termed a "necessary demonstration." To convince others, his demonstration would need to expose the necessary and only cause of the effect observed.[4] He could do so in either a rigorous syllogism or in a looser narrative form, depending on the rhetorical genre and medium. A public forum or publication intended for a mixed audience of peers and other educated readers lent itself to a looser rhetorical formulation in the vernacular.

The sociologist and historian of science Stephen Shapin (1996: 5–6) notes the great differences between our present-day notions of science and those of the Renaissance, where necessary truths predominated. Alan Gross, rhetorician and professor of English, goes further than Shapin in his analysis. He sees the scientific breakthroughs of early modern astronomy as rhetorical magic. He does not treat the "eureka!" phenomenon or the philosophical formalism just discussed but, rather, the basis of knowledge claims, which he calls "rational persuasion": "Rhetorically, the creation of knowledge is a task beginning with self-persuasion and ending with the persuasion of others" (Gross 1990: 1).[5] Rhetoric pervades and encompasses science. Granting so much hegemony to rhetoric, as Gross does, may tempt us to ignore the work of later scientists who validated their forerunners' prescience. Indeed, a thorough study of the complex system of proof, which can be only sketched here, has led some scholars to attribute a greater truth-finding capacity to their methods. More importantly for our purposes in this chapter, such rhetorical imperialism prevents a fair engagement with the methodology used. Paradigms may shift, as Thomas Kuhn (1970) argues, but their formal and substantive force for natural philosophers in the period need not be denied. Similarly, John Pickstone conceptualizes the historical practices of science as "working knowledges" that combine "ways of knowing" and "ways of working" (2007: 494) that enable one to read and interpret cases. Rhetoric, for him, has a corresponding interpretative function.

In practice, natural philosophers of the early modern period often experienced difficulties in creating the demonstrations requisite for claiming certain knowledge. Finding the cause of effects, the usual starting point of the process, could require countless hours of study and still not yield answers. Dialectic, that part of Aristotelian logic treating invention and disputation, offered help. In such cases investigators could turn to a process of mental prompts formalized in dialectics as the topics (Gk. *topoi*; L. *loci*). It enabled them to interrogate phenomena with the concepts of genus, species, similarities, differences, properties and accidents, and further refinements of these (see Moss 1993, ch. 1). Such an exploration might yield only probable answers, and at times merely possible ones. Concomitantly, relevant respected opinions (*endoxa*) on the subject would be explored and aired before a tentative conclusion would be hazarded. Dialectical examinations appear not only in philosophical writings but also in political and literary texts dealing with puzzling questions (see Hutson, ch. 32).

As is frequently noted, however, humanist scholars tired of the hair-splitting teachings of dialectic inherited from the late Middle Ages and ejected dialectic from the arts curriculum, retaining poetics and rhetoric while adding history and moral philosophy. Nevertheless, other influential humanists protested the rejection of dialectical training, arguing that it left students without valuable preparation for analysis and debate.[6] Moreover, scholars such as Rudolf Agricola in the fifteenth century and Peter Ramus in the sixteenth, cognizant of those needs, began to publish texts treating dialectic or invention alone. In the practice of humanist oratory and in literature, a relaxed consideration of opposing authorities on questions of public interest replaced tighter dialectical reviews. Galileo himself ingeniously rehearsed dueling opinions by placing them in the mouths of lifelike characters in his *Dialogue Concerning the Two Chief World Systems* (1632).

Complicating this truth-centered methodology was the widely held belief of philosophers that distinct boundaries between disciplines should be respected. For example, astronomers, being mathematicians, would raise eyebrows were they to make pronouncements regarding the physical nature of objects in the heavens; they were expected to offer only mathematical models. When mathematical computations were applied to the physical world, the process would be termed an intermediate or mixed science, one removed from the natural world, like mathematics, but applied to it, like mathematical physics.[7]

The line between rhetoric and philosophy was considered as distinguishable as that between mathematics and natural philosophy. The question of whether rhetoric can be excised from discourse or whether it is a component of all language, so absorbing to modern scholars, did not trouble examiners of Galileo's *Dialogue*. The intrusion of rhetoric into scientific discourse was famously deplored by René Descartes and Thomas Hobbes and luminously addressed by Francis Bacon, whose directives for doing science without rhetoric were to become a mission for members of the Royal Society.

Most scholars who evaluated the claims of natural philosophers and astronomers in these early scientific arguments, however, were not troubled with the phenomenology of rhetoric but were concerned with its proper use. Thoroughly versed in the rhetorical canons of invention (*inventio*), arrangement (*dispositio*), and style (*elocutio*) as well as in the lore of scholastic philosophy and theology, they analyzed authors' reasoning, considered whether modifiers inflated a proof, and pondered whether analogies, metaphors, similes, and other tropes and figures of speech coerced a conclusion or simply clarified an issue. Arguments replete with rhetorical versions of induction and deduction—examples and enthymemes—were suspect if the former were not apt or sufficient and if the latter posed a shortcut to a conclusion that implied an untenable premise. As documents from interrogations before his trial disclose, Galileo's *Dialogue* was subjected to this kind of critique (see Finocchiaro 1989, ch. 9).

The revival of interest in rhetoric as a classical art in the mid-twentieth century has led to renewed analysis of rhetorical texts and practices of Renaissance rhetoric and science. Brian Vickers and others have focused their discussion on style as the dominant canon of the art in the period, particularly its epideictic *technē*. Vickers (1983) views Galileo's defense of Copernicanism in the *Dialogue* as an example of the epideictic rhetoric of praise and blame. That such an iconoclastic thinker as Galileo would be content with the rubric of only one kind of rhetorical argument is questionable. Instead, the full repertoire of logical and rhetorical stratagems seems to have been brought into play in that work. Scholars such as Walter Ong (1958), Lisa Jardine (1974), and Peter Mack (1993) have gone beyond discussions of *elocutio* to emphasize the period's concern with argumentation and particularly with *inventio*. In that vein, the application of rhetorical training to the work of early modern scientists has been refreshingly addressed by Jeanne Fahnestock. Her study of rhetorical figures—the "formal embodiment of certain ideational or persuasive functions" (Fahnestock 1999: 23)—treats with great insight their role in the creation and expression of science. The presence of *pathos* in scientific writing, however, has been regarded by most commentators as an inadvertent or even improper rhetorical intrusion. Perhaps contrarian scholars might give more attention to its positive and propulsive effects on science (see Walmsley, ch. 43; Code, ch. 57; Doyle, ch. 59).

Marcello Pera and other philosophers and historians of science have come to recognize the importance of the art of rhetoric in the early modern period. They have sought to restore a fuller understanding of the historical picture of the disciplinary scene, with special attention to the interplay between rhetoric and science. Pera writes of rhetoric's relation to "scientific dialectics" in significant historical cases. He "corrects" Aristotle, arguing that "rhetoric is not the counterpart of dialectics, rather it includes it" (Pera 1991: 35). Ernan McMullin also offers help in analyzing the role of rhetoric in science, whether it be ameliorative or negative. He suggests a way to exorcise ambiguities in judging the presence of "good," "pejorative," or "neutral" effects of rhetoric in science: distinguish its extra-logical or pejorative sense (P) from its logical-good argumentative use (L) and its neutral effect (N) in cases where persuasiveness predominates, whether through emotion, cogency of argument, or other nonepistemic elements (McMullin 1991: 60–1).

AUDIENCE AND RHETORICAL SCIENCE

As interest in the observations and contentions of philosophers and astronomers grew, and as printing made these views available to a wider public, authors expanded the format of argumentation, thus giving rhetorical persuasion a larger role. They retained the sinews of demonstration or dialectical argument in writing or speaking but unfolded their proofs in a discursive manner, as if in conversation with a cultured and erudite friend, paralleling the style of Renaissance letter writers. In popular presentations of scientific matters, clever enthymemes stood in for lengthy deductions and arresting examples for inductions. The livelier refutations of opposing opinions came sometimes studded with implicit ad hominem attacks and ludicrous illustrations of deficient reasoning. The writers anticipated wider audiences beyond academic philosophers, theologians, and prelates than in earlier centuries, a readership consisting of educated laymen and women from nobles to commoners.

The problems posed by the conventions of scientific discourse were magnified when astronomers published new explanations for the movements of the planets. Copernicus's hypothesis regarding the motion of the Earth was greeted with great skepticism by many because it transgressed theological tenets, overturned the regnant astronomical system, and, above all, defied common sense. Galileo's claims concerning the nature of the moon's surface and the movements of the satellites (or moons) of Jupiter were met with suspicion. The descriptions were astounding and rested on observations made with a novel instrument—a handmade spyglass. Even after his discoveries were witnessed by those fortunate enough to have access to one of these new instruments, the implications of his observations were hotly debated. Some did not even deign to look, dismissing the invention as impossibly flawed.

RHETORIC IN SCIENCE

Copernicus knew that his *De revolutionibus orbium coelestium* (1543) would encounter opposition, but he could not have guessed that a conservative interpretation would be inserted as a foreword to his work. This preemptive preface, written not by Copernicus but by Andreas Osiander, a Lutheran theologian, argues that all Copernicus intends is a mathematical model that seems to explain the phenomena of the motions of the cosmic orbs. The placement of Osiander's declaration was obviously a rhetorical intervention meant to ameliorate perceptions of the author's claims for those reluctant to countenance a theory that contradicts Scripture. Copernicus's own introductory matter contains an admixture of science and rhetoric that appears to argue strongly for a realist view. He received his education from progressive Aristotelians at the Jagiellonian University of Krakow who taught that mathematics could be applied to nature and yield valid demonstrations concerning the physical world (see Knoll 1978). Yet to demonstrate the movements of the Earth—that it rotated on its axis and revolved around the sun—would still require physical proofs that were not available to astronomers until the early nineteenth century (Copernicus [1543] 1978: 3–4).[8]

To placate those who might be scandalized by his work, Copernicus sought to disarm opposition with an apologetic dedication to Pope Paul III. Copernicus addresses the pope as one singularly endowed to protect his work, "for even in this very remote corner of the earth where I live you are considered the highest authority by virtue of the loftiness of your office and your love for all literature and astronomy too." Thus, he says, the pontiff can "easily suppress calumnious attacks, although as the proverb has it, there is no remedy for a backbite" (see Copernicus [1543] 1978: 5.32–6).

During this period of protest against Roman Catholic doctrines and practices, Copernicus, himself a Catholic and canon of the cathedral in Frauenburg, knew well that theologians as well as other astronomers had a strong stake in the validity of the Ptolemaic system. Trained in the liberal arts as well as the sciences before he pursued doctorates in canon law and medicine, Copernicus displays great rhetorical acumen in his attempt to enlist the good will of the pope when he says that he knows people will try to repudiate the contentions in his book, but he notes that "a philosopher's ideas are not subject to the judgment of ordinary persons" because he attempts "to seek the truth in all things" ([1543] 1978: 3–4). This statement alone would seem to support the view that he intended a physical as well as mathematical construct. He admits the gravity of his views by obliquely indicating the audience for whom he writes—philosophers, not common folk. The unstated assumption of the enthymeme remains: only other philosophers can suitably judge his work.

In passages that follow, Copernicus presents himself as hesitant to issue this work, knowing well the entropy of many philosophers when faced with something new and patently absurd to the senses. But drawing on his rhetorical *ēthos* as a faithful son of the Church, he mentions that only the encouragement of friends, among them a cardinal and a bishop, prompted him to bring to light his commentaries on the motions of the heavens, commentaries that had lain in darkness for nine years, as Horace had advised. Allusions to Horace's popular *Ars poetica* were sure to strike a resonant chord (see Ross, ch. 28).

His reason for seeking to publish *De revolutionibus*, Copernicus says, is his desire to correct the erroneous opinions of astronomers regarding the motions of the heavenly bodies. Using the *topos* of the relation of whole to part, he invokes the well-known advice of Horace to budding poets: they should not gather disproportionate elements like a mad artist who would paint a portrait by taking parts of the subject's anatomy from various animals and thus depict a monster instead of a man.[9] Just so have astronomers labored to create a picture of the heavens. But in their attempts to make observations and computations agree with an Earth-centered (geocentric) cosmos, they have combined ill-sorted parts, such as equants, epicycles, and eccentrics. This reworking of Horace's analogy provides a powerful illustration for his counterargument by recalling for readers a familiar classical text and by "setting before the eyes," as rhetoricians would phrase it, an apt critique of his predecessors' errors. His sun-centered (heliocentric) cosmos would reduce these additives in explaining the movements of the planets.

Knowing the reluctance of the Church to accept novel opinions in general (the Protestants, after all, were dubbed the *novatores*), he notes that his views actually are not novel. He invokes the authority of Cicero and Plutarch, who point out that ancient philosophers had argued that the Earth moves, as do the sun and the moon. Copernicus then attempts to finesse possible objections based on Scripture: "Perhaps there will be babblers who claim to be judges of astronomy although completely ignorant of the subject and, badly distorting some passage of Scripture to their purpose will dare to find fault with my undertaking. . . . I disregard them even to the extent of despising their criticism as unfounded" ([1543] 1978: 5.37–40). He ends his dedication in a more palliative register, voicing the pious hope that his system will provide a more reliable basis for computing the dates for holy days.

Copernicus begins book 1 with an *exordium* that includes an encomium for the study of astronomy, taking full advantage of the *topoi* of epideictic rhetoric. In the books that follow, as he delves more deeply into the astronomical evidence, he relies heavily on dialectical *topoi* backed by mathematical proofs as he refutes opposing opinions and supports his argument (see Moss 1993, ch. 2).

Whether Copernicus thought he had offered an actual demonstration has divided commentators. Cardinal Bellarmine was to tell Galileo that he thought Copernicus merely reasoned on the supposition of his computations, since no physical proof was presented. Galileo, however, thought Copernicus did demonstrate the motions of the Earth. Kepler also believed Copernicus had achieved a true demonstration. As Alexandre Koyré explains Kepler's view, Copernicus reasoned from effects to cause and found the one cause that necessitated the effects—a back-and-forth process called the *regressus* or "resolution and composition" (Koyré 1973: 133) (see Wallace 1972–4: 1: 140–9). The Harvard astronomer Owen Gingerich, on the other hand, thinks that Copernicus intended only what we would call an "explanation" (1981: 56), not a necessary demonstration, of the motions of the Earth. But regardless of one's view of Copernicus's intent, as Koyré (1973: 54) suggests, we should admire Copernicus even more because he had no physical proof and yet argued boldly for his views. The Polish astronomer obviously thought he had found the true explanation of the celestial phenomena observed, whether he actually demonstrated it or not. The rhetorical elements in his work press for attention to the mathematical support of the physical system. The response of the ecclesiastical authorities in 1620 was to order censorship of *De revolutionibus*. The wording of all assertions of proof was to be altered to make these merely hypothetical statements.

Galileo's revolutionary *Sidereus nuncius* (*The Sidereal Messenger*) of 1610 appeared 64 years after *De revolutionibus*. In this work we find a similar rhetorical ebullience and a similar effort to correct the astronomical record. Galileo begins with a dedication, replete with playful rhetoric designed to woo his patron, Cosimo de' Medici, and then moves on to serious description. But at various points in his account, rapture at seeing the moon, the Milky Way, and the planets so vastly enlarged leads him to passionate declarations regarding the implications of his discoveries.

Arguing from the topic of similarities, Galileo employs dialectical reasoning to persuasive effect when he claims on the basis of his observations with the telescope that there are mountains on the moon. He based his contention on observations made when only part of the surface of the moon was illuminated, the rest of it dark. He saw a jagged, irregular edge that changed over time as the light brought out bright spots and cast shadows similar to what one sees on Earth when the sun's rays catch mountain peaks and valleys. As with Copernicus, Galileo could come to no other satisfying explanation of these effects. He includes drawings to illustrate what he has seen. In the past, some observers had suggested that the moon's shadows appeared because the smooth surface of its face absorbed or reflected light differently.

Commentators on *Sidereus nuncius* often fail to see that comparison was an obligatory tool in approaching an unfamiliar phenomenon, not only in rhetoric but more importantly in this case also in dialectical analysis. The *topos* of similarities was used to help an investigator arrive at the causes of effects. Maurice Slawinsky, for example, faults Galileo for his overreliance on rhetoric in using analogies. Missing the presence of scientific dialectical reasoning, Slawinsky (1991: 95) is disappointed that Galileo uses analogies as a rhetorician might.

In further ruminations on his observations, the astonished Galileo denies that the moon generates light, arguing that not only does the sun illuminate the moon but also that at conjunction the Earth actually reflects the sun's light and shines it back on the moon. This phenomenon inspires a rhetorical question: "But what is so surprising about that? In an equal and grateful exchange the Earth pays back the Moon with light equal to that which she receives from the Moon almost all the time in the deepest darkness of the night" (Galileo [1610] 1989: 55). Here the *topos* of *decorum* or appropriateness—what is fitting—gracefully magnifies his claim. He goes on to describe the interaction of moon and sun in transmitting the sun's light during the phases of the moon when observed from Earth. At the end of the passage, he makes the significant announcement that in a forthcoming book he will "demonstrate" that the Earth moves, is brighter than the moon, and cannot "be excluded from the dance of the stars" (57). The Earth can no longer be viewed as "the dump heap of the filth and dregs of the universe, and we will confirm this with innumerable arguments from nature" (57). In these lines Galileo's mastery of rhetorical imagery releases the Earth from the ignominious position the Ptolemaic system has ascribed to it: the center of the universe that receives the detritus of the orbs that surround it. The comparative metaphor ennobles and energizes the Earth. This elegant and vivid depiction must have helped to persuade many who read it to believe Galileo's claims.

Galileo's reference to a forthcoming work that will provide demonstrations of heliocentrism proves to be the most portentous declaration in the book. That reference is, of course, to what would become the *Dialogue Concerning the Two Chief World Systems* (1632), the work that brought to an end his freedom to speak further on the subject or even to leave his villa at Arcetri.

It was these same satellites of Jupiter that Galileo had munificently dubbed the "Medicean stars" in his dedication to Cosimo in the hope of gaining a position at court in Florence. The discovery of the orbiting moons was revolutionary in Galileo's hands. He drew diagrams of their placement over a series of night viewings, providing telling evidence for his claim. The way he summarizes the implications leaves no doubt about his conviction. "We have an excellent and splendid argument," Galileo says, "that overcomes those who are reluctant to have the earth and its moon revolve around the sun annually. Here are four stars revolving around Jupiter, and these all together orbit the sun in 12 years" (Galileo [1632] 1953: 84–5). The qualifiers "excellent" and "splendid" transmit his triumphant feelings quite clearly. Galileo has trounced the opposition.

The *Sidereus nuncius* was an instant bestseller, indicating an eager readership, but its passionate arguments irritated rival astronomers in the service of the Church. That Galileo's observations were made with a new instrument (the telescope) not readily available to others gave credence to their rebuttals. More importantly, he had dared to contradict the widely accepted opinion that the heavenly orbs were immutable and immaculate.

The *Dialogue* contains many more clever dialectical and rhetorical arguments. It also purports to offer necessary demonstrations of the Copernican thesis. But this mixture of kinds of argumentation had the effect of multiplying the difficulties the ecclesiastical judges would find in the work. Had Galileo not claimed to offer demonstrations, restricting himself to dialectical and even rhetorical arguments, as the *Dialogue*'s preface promised, his judges might not have been as harsh. After several intense examinations by the Inquisitors, Galileo was moved to admit that he had been carried away by his own gifts of eloquence, asserting that "if I had to write out the same arguments now, there is no doubt I would weaken them in such a way that they could not appear to exhibit a force which they really and essentially lack" (quoted in Finocchiaro 1989: 278; see Moss and Wallace 2001: 11). The statement was certainly made under duress, for admitting an error in judgment does not seem characteristic of Galileo, but then again he may have simply acknowledged the effects of passionate belief.

The difficulties in assessing the immediate effects of rhetoric on the acceptance or rejection of the postulations of science are manifold. The authors, of course, would not have indulged their emotions had they not hoped to affect their readers as they themselves had been affected. Nevertheless, they expected their claims to be judged ultimately on the dialectical and demonstrative proofs presented. Contemporary responses to the work show that these were the grounds that engaged readers.

Gingerich's recent work reveals that Copernicus's *De revolutionibus*, far from being "the book that nobody read," as Arthur Koestler declared in *The Sleepwalkers*, had a remarkable circulation. Today the first edition of 1543 can be found in 24 countries (see Gingerich 2005, appendix 2). Among the more than 600 copies Gingerich examined in his census, he found many of these large tomes carefully annotated by readers mulling over the text; some of these contain ecstatic remarks that resonate with the author's enthusiasm. One is in verse. Surprisingly few books showed the dutiful application of the censorship ordered by the Church (67–8).

The reception of Galileo's work has been the subject of many studies. In his own day he was regarded as a persuasive speaker and convincing author. After *Sidereus nuncius* appeared, Galileo was hailed as a Columbus of the heavens—the analogy becomes a commonplace in the literature. Johan Faber, Florentine physician, says that Amerigo Vespucci and Christopher Columbus must step aside for the greatest explorer, Galileo; and John Wilkins of the Royal Society declares that Galileo's discoveries, like those of Columbus, must be acknowledged as equally real. But Kepler outstrips all of them when, overcome by the revelations in *Sidereus nuncius*, he pens a critique, quickly published in 1610 as *Dissertatio cum nuncio sidereo* (*Conversation with the Heavenly Messenger*). At the outset, he mentions that a friend had driven to his house to tell him of Galileo's discoveries. They were both so filled with excitement that his friend could hardly speak and he could barely hear. Kepler, who was mathematician to the Holy Roman emperor Rudolf II, borrowed the emperor's copy to read. Addressing Galileo, he says, "I yearned to discuss with you the many undisclosed treasures of Jehovah the creator, which He reveals to us one after another. For who is permitted to remain silent at the news of such momentous developments? Who is not filled with a surging love of God, pouring itself copiously forth through tongue and pen?" (Kepler [1610] 1965: 18). Kepler adds later, "Putting aside all misgivings, you turned directly to visual experimentation. And indeed by your discoveries you caused the sun of truth to rise, you routed all the ghosts of perplexity together with their mother, the night, and by your achievement you showed what could be done" (18). The book sold out immediately.

CONCLUSION

The forms of reasoning of Renaissance argument described in this chapter no longer explicitly enter scientific writings. Yet whether these forms were superimposed through a pious regard for classical philosophy or whether the canons might actually register basic characteristics of the process of reasoning remains an open question. George Lakoff and Mark Johnson (1980) argue that metaphors are "not decorative or rhetorical; they reflect the way their users think and perceive the world" (quoted in Otis 2010: 574, n. 8). Demonstration, dialectic, and rhetoric may also actually capture the inner dynamics of the mind at work.

Modern scientists since the Baconian era have tried assiduously to rid their scientific reports of emotional coloring, enthusiasm, and superfluous subjective commentary. While their writings may thus be more convincing, surely they move us much less. Regardless of our views concerning the ontology of method, in recognizing the presence of these formalities of reasoning in the written and spoken discourse of Renaissance science, we can appreciate the complexity of scientific investigation in this era as well as the difficulties of composing convincing scientific arguments.

FURTHER READING

James Langford (1971) offers an insightful explanation of the significance of Galileo's writings. William Wallace (1992) masterfully describes the debt of Galileo to Aristotelian logic. Maurice Finocchiaro (1989) provides the definitive account of Galileo's trial. Kepler's skills as astronomer and polemicist surface clearly in philosopher Nicholas Jardine's (1984) translation and commentary. Robert Westman's (2011) *The Copernican Question* magisterially describes the import of Copernicus's thesis for the early modern period.

NOTES

1. I discovered this quotation from Leopardi in Peter Campion's (2010) review of Jonathan Galassi's translation of the *Canti*. That quote led me to Leopardi's (1983) *Zibaldone di pensieri* (*Notebooks*), in which the poet comments extensively on reasoning and science. Collingwood investigates the interrelation between sense experience and emotion in *The Principles of Art*. Chapter 8 treats thinking and feeling.
2. Burgeoning studies in brain science today may be able to shed light on the cognitive-emotional connections noted. Daniel Gross (2006: 28–39) examines the import of recent studies of emotion and the brain for their relevance to rhetoric. He does not explore the relation of emotion to science.
3. Aristotle explains that rhetoric is a faculty of words, not a science of things. Translations of and commentaries on this work multiplied in the sixteenth century. A fuller discussion of the influence of Aristotle in the period appears in Moss and Wallace (2001).

4. Wallace describes this process in a number of texts. In the context of Renaissance science, see Wallace (1992: 74–9). See also Maclean (2002: 114–47).

5. Gross (1990) gives rhetoric the dominant role in the doing of science. He argues that the Copernican revolution was rhetorical and that the Polish astronomer was seduced by allegiance to method (see chapter 7 for his discussion of Copernicus).

6. Logic and rhetoric in the period are discussed at length in George Kennedy's (1980) magisterial *Classical Rhetoric and Its Christian and Secular Tradition from Ancient to Modern Times*.

7. Surprisingly, Albert Einstein also shared misgivings about the appropriate application of mathematics to nature, as Alastair Crombie (1952: 328) points out in *Augustine to Galileo*.

8. Jean Bernard Foucault's pendulum experiments demonstrated the Earth's rotation, and Friedrich Bessel showed that the Earth moved around the sun through stellar parallax.

9. Robert Westman (1987: 373) draws attention to the rhetorical and poetic power of what would have been a familiar image to readers.

References

Black, Deborah. 1990. *Logic and Aristotle's "Rhetoric" and "Poetics" in Medieval Arabic Philosophy*. Leiden: Brill.

Campion, Peter. 2010. "The Solitary Life." Review of *Canti* by Giacomo Leopardi, translated and annotated by Jonathan Golassi. *New York Times Book Review*, December 19, 10.

Collingwood, R. G. 1981. *The Principles of Art*. Oxford: Oxford University Press.

Copernicus, Nicholas. 1978. *On the Revolutions*. Translated by Edward Rosen, edited by Jerzy Dobrzycki. Baltimore, MD: Johns Hopkins University Press.

Crombie, Alastair. 1952. *Augustine to Galileo*. Cambridge, MA: Harvard University Press.

Fahnestock, Jeanne. 1999. *Rhetorical Figures in Science*. Oxford: Oxford University Press.

Finocchiaro, Maurice. 1989. *The Galileo Affair*. Berkeley: University of California Press.

Galilei, Galileo. (1610) 1989. *"Sidereus Nuncius" or The Sidereal Messenger*. Translation, introduction, conclusion, notes by Albert van Helden. Chicago, IL: University of Chicago Press.

Galilei, Galileo. (1632) 1953. *Dialogue on the Two Great World Systems*. Translated by Thomas Salusbury. Ed. Giorgio de Santillana. Chicago, IL: University of Chicago Press.

Gingerich, Owen. 1981. "The Censorship of Copernicus' *De revolutionibus*." *Annali dell'Istituto e Museo di Storia della Scienza di Firenze* 6 no. 2: 45–61.

Gingerich, Owen. 2005. *The Book Nobody Read: Chasing the Revolutions of Nicolaus Copernicus*. New York: Penguin.

Gross, Alan. 1990. *The Rhetoric of Science*. Cambridge, MA: Harvard University Press.

Gross, Daniel. 2006. *The Secret History of Emotion*. Chicago, IL: University of Chicago Press.

Jardine, Lisa. 1974. *Francis Bacon: Discovery and the Art of Discourse*. Cambridge: Cambridge University Press.

Jardine, Nicholas. 1984. *The Birth of History and Philosophy of Science: Kepler's "A Defence of Tycho against Ursus" with Essays on Its Provenance and Significance*. Cambridge: Cambridge University Press.

Kennedy, George A. 1980. *Classical Rhetoric and Its Christian and Secular Tradition from Ancient to Modern Times*. Chapel Hill: University of North Carolina Press.

Kepler, Johannes. (1610) 1965. *Conversation with Galileo's "Sidereal Messenger."* Translated by Edward Rosen. New York: Johnson.

Knoll, Paul W. 1978. "The Arts Faculty at the University of Cracow at the End of the Fifteenth Century." In *The Copernican Achievement*, edited by Robert S. Westman, 137–156. Berkeley: University of California Press.

Koyré, Alexandre. 1973. *The Astronomical Revolution*. Translated by R. E. W. Maddison. Ithaca, NY: Cornell University Press.

Kuhn, Thomas. 1970. *The Structure of Scientific Revolutions*. Chicago, IL: University of Chicago Press.

Lakoff, George, and Mark Johnson. 1980. *Metaphors We Live By*. Chicago, IL: University of Chicago Press.

Langford, James. 1971. *Galileo, Science, and the Church*. Ann Arbor: University of Michigan Press.

Leopardi, Giacomo. 1983. *Zibaldone di pensieri*. Edited by Anna Maria Moroni. Vol. 1. Oscar classici: 16. Milan: A. Mondadori.

Leopardi, Giacomo. 2003. *Selected Poems*. Translated by Thomas Bertin and Anne Paulucci. Bagehot Council. Smyrna, DE: Griffon House.

McMullin, Ernan. 1991. "Rhetoric and Theory Choice in Science." In *The Art of Scientific Rhetoric*, edited by Marcello Pera and William Shea, 55–76. Canton, OH: Science History Publications.

Mack, Peter. 1993. *Renaissance Argument: Valla and Agricola in the Traditions of Rhetoric and Dialectic*. Leiden: Brill.

Maclean, Ian. 2002. *Logic, Signs and Nature in the Renaissance*. Cambridge: Cambridge University Press.

Moss, Jean Dietz. 1993. *Novelties in the Heavens: Rhetoric and Science in the Copernican Question*. Chicago, IL: University of Chicago Press.

Moss, Jean Dietz, and William A. Wallace. 2001. *Rhetoric and Dialectic in the Time of Galileo*. Washington, DC: Catholic University of America Press.

Ong, Walter. 1958. *Ramus, Method, and the Decay of Dialogue*. Cambridge, MA: Harvard University Press.

Otis, Laura. 2010. "Science Surveys and Histories of Literature: Reflections on an Uneasy Kinship." *Isis* 101 no. 2: 570–577.

Pera, Marcello, and William R. Shea, eds. 1991. *The Art of Scientific Rhetoric*. Canton, OH: Science History Publications.

Pickstone, John V. 2007. "Working Knowledges." *Isis* 98 no. 3: 489–516.

Shapin, Stephen. 1996. *The Scientific Revolution*. Chicago, IL: University of Chicago Press.

Slawinski, Maurice. 1991. "Rhetoric and Science/Rhetoric of Science/Rhetoric as Science." In *Science, Culture and Popular Belief in Renaissance Europe*, edited by Stephen Pumfrey, Paolo L. Rossi, and Maurice Slawinski, 71–99. Manchester: Manchester University Press.

Vickers, Brian. 1983. "Epideictic Rhetoric in Galileo's *Dialogo*." *Annali dell'Istituto e Museo di Storia della Scienza di Firenze* 8: 69–102.

Wallace, William A. 1972–1974. *Causality and Scientific Explanation*. 2 vols. Ann Arbor: University of Michigan Press.

Wallace, William A. 1992. *Galileo's Logical Treatises: A Translation, with Notes and Commentary, of His "Appropriated Latin Questions on Aristotle's 'Posterior Analytics.'"* Boston Studies in the Philosophy of Science vol. 138. Dordrecht: Kluwer.

Westman, Robert S. 1987. "La Préface de Copernic au pape: esthétique humaniste et réforme de l'église." *History and Technology* 4: 365–384.

Westman, Robert S. 2011. *The Copernican Question*. Berkeley: University of California Press.

CHAPTER 35

··

RHETORIC AND POETICS

··

ARTHUR F. KINNEY

THE literary Renaissance began with the Italian poet laureate Francis Petrarch (1304–74), whose creative work grew directly out of his study of classical rhetoric. In a letter composed in his final year to the papal secretary Lucas de Penna, Petrarch recalls first reading Cicero as a young boy, although he could not remember whether this activity came from instinct or his father's encouragement. In an earlier letter (1539) to Giovanni Boccaccio, Petrarch notes that "I have read and re-read Virgil, Horace, Livy, Cicero, not once but a thousand times, not hastily but in repose, and I have pondered them with all the powers of my mind.... These writings I have so thoroughly absorbed and fixed, not only in my memory but in my very marrow, these have become so much a part of myself, that even though I should never read them again they would cling to my spirit, deep-rooted in its inmost recesses" (in Bishop 1966: 182–3). More broadly yet, in 1532 Petrarch confided to Lapo da Castiglionchio, a Florentine law professor, that both his imaginary and expository writing were direct consequences of studying classical and rhetorical treatises. Earlier in the quattrocento, Coluccio Salutati, chancellor of Florence from 1375 to 1406, argued that rhetoric and moral philosophy were indivisible because, comments Victoria Kahn, "it is in language that this moral dimension is most fully realized: language raises man above the animals and enables him to create a consensus and community, and language allows for the persuasion of the will to action. Accordingly, the poet and the orator do not perform a merely aesthetic function; rather, the aesthetic dimension is the pre-condition of the political" (1985: 39–40). Giovanni Pontano (1429–1503) would have agreed: both literary and rhetorical texts educate their readers by providing wise examples from the past. As these examples from Petrarch and Salutati indicate, rhetoric and poetics are blended in both the composition and the reception of texts.

In the cinquecento, Niccolò Machiavelli followed Petrarch's model. In 1513 he wrote his friend, Francesco Vettori, saying that "when evening comes . . . I go into my study . . . [and] enter into the ancient courts of ancient men and am welcomed by them kindly, and there I taste the food that alone is mine, and for which I was born; and there I am not ashamed to speak to them, to ask them the reasons for their actions; and they, in their humanity, answer me; and for four hours I feel no boredom, I dismiss every affliction,

I no longer fear poverty nor do I tremble at the thought of death: I become completely part of them" (quoted in Grafton 1999: 80; see Grafton 1991). The cinquecento further encouraged such study with a host of translations of ancient texts: Cicero's *Letters* and treatises (1536–7); Plato's *Lysis* and Xenophon's *Memorabilia* (both 1551); Demetrius's *On Style* (1562); Cicero's *Philippics* (1563); Aesop (1564); Catullus, Horace, Terence, and commentaries on Aristotle's *Rhetoric* (all 1548); Aristotle's *Poetics* (1560), *Politics* (1576), and *Nicomachean Ethics* (1584); and the fundamental rhetorical works of Cicero, *Orator* (1552) and *De oratore* (1587). A splendid folio edition of Livy (1555) was also instrumental in promoting classical texts on rhetoric. Guillaume Budé translated three Latin treatises of Plutarch (1502–5). Jacques Amyot translated Heliodorus (1547) with an important theoretical preface as well as Longus's *Daphnis and Chloe* (1559) and Plutarch's *Lives* and *Moralia*. Denis Lambin translated Aristotle's *Ethics* in 1558 and his *Politics* in 1567, Horace in 1561, Lucretius in 1564, and the whole of Cicero in 1556. Louis Le Roy translated Demosthenes's *Olynthiacs* and *Philippics*, Plato's *Timaeus*, *Phaedo*, *Symposium*, and *Republic*, Aristotle's *Politics*, and some treatises of Isocrates and Xenophon, while the Parisian printer Robert Estienne published the *editio princeps* of Eusebius (1544–6), Dionysius of Halicarnassus (1546–7), Dio Cassius in 1548, and Appian in 1551; subsequently, his son Henri printed an additional 58 Latin and 74 Greek authors, the *Thesaurus Graeci linguae*, and the great Stephanus edition of Plato in 1578. This movement to revive ancient texts, especially those dealing with rhetoric, spread rapidly throughout Europe: as many as 2,000 books of rhetoric were published between 1400 and 1700 (see Vickers 1988: 256).

"Along with grammar and the study of classical texts, rhetoric formed the staple component of a humanistic educational programme," Alison Thorne writes, "that by this time came to be ensconced throughout Western Europe. In this sense, it can be said to have functioned as a sort of *lingua franca*, capable of transcending cultural differences" (2000: 59) (see Plett, ch. 30; Rebhorn, ch. 31). It became the job of the schools, therefore, to teach rhetoric as fundamental to their curriculum. They did this by focusing on the *ars dissendi*, or the arts of speaking correctly, speaking well, and arguing well. The emphasis was on the verbal reasoning—the Aristotelian *pisteis*, or modes of persuasion—discussed at length in the rhetorical treatises of Cicero and in Quintilian's *Institutes of Oratory*. Cicero was central because his work promoted the rhetor as active citizen and effective lawmaker, combining speech and activity, precept and practice, and teaching how to persuade others to virtuous and serviceable ends. As Cicero puts it in book 1 of *De oratore*, a seminal text of Renaissance humanists, "Then at last must our Oratory be conducted out of this sheltered training-ground at home, right into action, into the dust and uproar, into the camp and the fighting-line of public debate.... We must also read the poets, acquaint ourselves with histories, study and peruse the masters and authors in every excellent art, and by way of practice praise, expound, emend, criticize, and confute them" (quoted in Kinney 1989: 12–3; trans. Sutton and Rackham). Quintilian also emphasized such ideas in his *Institutes of Oratory*, a redaction of Ciceronian rhetoric aimed at educators rather than the lawyers whom Cicero was addressing.

But during the fifteenth century new ideas about rhetoric and dialectic were provided by the Dutch scholar Rudolph Agricola (1444–85). He argued that to develop a persuasive argument the rhetor must first define the "seat" or basis of his argument. This seat (or *locus*) was the foundation for any argument invented through reasoning—inductive, deductive, or syllogistic. To aid in this, Agricola provided 24 classical places (L. *loci*; Gk. *topoi*) such as definition, genus, species, property, and whole and part. In book 2 he also notes that the best argument is classically ordered into four parts: *exordium* (an inviting beginning), *narratio* (a statement of the argument), *confirmatio* (assembled points of persuasion), and *peroratio* (conclusion). Following this formula, argues Agricola, the rhetor would have the most convincing case possible. Agricola's book 3 discusses issues of style (*elocutio*) and what he calls *affectus*—what impels the mind, evokes emotions, and employs ornamentation such as amplification or *copia*. A number of leading humanists—Desiderius Erasmus, Philipp Melanchthon, and Juan Luis Vives—were deeply influenced by his work, as were the poets Pierre de Ronsard and Joachim du Bellay. Agricola's reflections on the rhetorical aspects of dialectic also influenced humanists. Erasmus's *In Praise of Folly* (*Moriae encomium*) is a declamation that is inherently dialectical, for Folly's argument twists and turns upon itself, and the storytelling of Marguerite de Navarre's *Heptameron* and the conversations and debates of Baldassare Castiglione's *The Book of the Courtier* (*Il Cortegiano*) are also openly dialectical. François Rabelais's sprawling, untitled novel is thick with the ornamentation of *copia*. However, in holding the improbable alongside the well known, it is grounded on a dialectic of its own, as is Miguel de Cervantes's *Don Quixote*, with its dialogues between the Don and Sancho Panza. These fictive works are grounded on rhetorical practices as well as on the ideas of Agricola. Still, these works of art also address social and intellectual issues, illustrating what Daniel Shore finds in John Milton's fictive and poetic practice: "The point of rhetoric is not to describe the world but to change it" (2012: 13).

IMITATIO

Continental and English rhetoric and poetics therefore merged at the point of conceptualization as well as in practice; both are grounded in acts of imitation or the use of models in speaking and writing. The poet, observes George Puttenham in the *Arte of English Poesie* (1589), is "both a maker and a counterfeiter, and poesy an art not only of making, but also of imitation" (2007: 93–4). Ancient texts were increasingly read and translated in Europe in the cinquecento and, by the early sixteenth century, in England; as Chris Stamatakis remarks, "Reading is often heavily indebted to comparison and conflation of texts" (Stamatakis 2012: 49). Rarely were books consulted in isolation from one another. It was the age of the bookwheel, by which several books could be kept together on the same revolving reading stand for consultation back and forth, always one passage in terms of others, where the "point of the exercise . . . was to show off one's verbal finesse, matching or even departing from an anterior text" (49–50). Such readings developed from the manuscript practice of *collatio*, dominated by the Florentine humanist Angelo Poliziano (Grafton 1999: 45–75). This practice of reading, which naturally transformed into the practice of *imitatio*, is thus the writing of new texts (see Copeland, ch. 27; Ross, ch. 28). This practice of rewriting or "turning the word" spread quickly. Martin Luther, for example, applied it, "setting text against text … creating argument accretively" (Stamatakis 2012: 50). The English poet Thomas Wyatt noted that his own poetry often drew on Petrarch's examples.

But imitation was not only a matter of emulation or of comparison: it could also be a matter of rivalry. *Imitatio* was not mere copying but also an exercise in improving, combining, transforming, and *creating*. Wyatt, for instance, paraphrased Psalms, retranslated Petrarch, and even improved the passages of others in writing letters (Stamatakis 2012: 108, ch. 3). Nor need *imitatio* depend on a single source or text; it might rely instead on several prototypes. Pliny records of Flavius Arrianus that he learned to write best by combining Demosthenes, Licinius Calvus, and Cicero. What Pliny acknowledges, Cicero urges. In *De inventione* he refers to the painter Zeuxis, considered in his time the best of all artists because he chose many models so he could paint a composite of what was best in each. This, according to Cicero, is the way all artists, poets, and composers should proceed: "In a similar fashion when the inclination arose in my mind to write a text-book of rhetoric, I did not set before myself some one model which I thought necessary to reproduce in all details, of whatever sort they might seem to be, but after collecting all the works on the subject I excerpted what seemed the most suitable precepts from each, and so culled the flower of many minds" (*De inventione* 2.2; trans. Hubbell). In his lectures at Cambridge—the ones Edmund Spenser heard—Gabriel Harvey proposed that the best lesson of Cicero "may not be what Cicero himself writes but the practice of the best writers in every genre on every subject" (Mack 2010: 428). Harvey gives as examples Thomas More, Thomas Elyot, Roger Ascham, and John Jewel. Omer Talon, in his *Rhetorica*, draws on Homer, Virgil, Sir Philip Sidney, Guillaume du Bartas, Garcilaso de la Vega, and others for his precepts. Thus, the imitating artists, Quintilian says, ought not to make abstractions or, on the other hand, slavishly copy, but rather use a model both as instruction and as a source from which to diverge: "There is nothing harder than to produce an exact likeness, and nature herself has so far failed in this endeavor that there is always some difference which enables us to distinguish even the things which seem the most like and most equal to one another" (*Institutio oratoria* 10.2.10; trans. Butler).

Indeed, it is this very assimilation of many models that transforms them, making something new. And it is this new product, this new work of art, that is what the artist *creates*: a poem or painting in which multiple models have become sufficiently absorbed so as to coalesce into something different, each model receding and only the newly forged composite remaining. Thus, in *Il Cortegiano* Bembo argues that this transformation will lead to nothing short of mystical experience. Similarly, in Marguerite de Navarre's *Heptameron* Ocisolle argues that such acts of imitation, properly conceived, can lead to a reformation of the soul and spirit. Don Quixote, with his frenzied composite of Roldán and Amadis de Gaula, creates an unprecedented sense of knight errantry that, however foolish or mad it may at first appear, nevertheless becomes effective *because* of that new-ness: the Don's still-later transformation into the Knight of the Woeful Countenance, when he takes on his shoulders all the wrongdoings of the world, transforms him into a Man of Sorrows, a Christ-like divergence from a world of selfishness and deceit. As such enduring works of art illustrate, however, this divergence not only leads to discovery but also allows the original motivating texts to be seen as traces of the new work so that the reader can perceive the divergence and locate its meaning in the recognition of the transformation. The *significatio*, that is, lies precisely in charting where the divergence is and consequently how and why it is undertaken. Folly's tumbling catalog in Erasmus's *In Praise of Folly* does not hide its sources. Even more tellingly, the frozen words of Rabelais signify long before they become unfrozen and resume their past sounds. Jack Wilton, a character in Thomas Nashe's *The Unfortunate Traveller*, learns through the incongruity between model and adventure. And hovering behind all this remains Horace and his conviction that poetry results in instruction and pleasure: "'But,' you'll say, 'the right to take liberties of almost any kind has always been enjoyed by painters and poets alike.' I know that we poets do claim this licence, and in our turn we concede it to others, but not to the point of associating what is wild with what is tame or pairing snakes with birds or lambs with tigers" (quoted in Thorne 2000: 63) (see Ross, ch. 28).

Consequently, Aristotelian *mimēsis* was reconceived in the fifteenth century as *imitatio*, opening a range of resources. Daniello Bartoli argues that the poet, unlike the historian, could mingle fancy or fiction with fact because his perceptions did not need to be limited to what was—that is, what could be seen—but extended to incorporate what ought to be: what could be conceived. Francisco Robertelli, in his extensive *Aristotelis de arte poetica explicationes* (1548), agreed that rhetoricians and poets could invent material so long as it supported the imitation of reality, and he provides as evidence two case studies: Xenophon's ideal portrait of Cyrus and Cicero's ideal portrait of the orator. Girolamo Fracastoro argued that the poet should not be restricted to essential truths in imitating his sense of reality but instead adorn it in formal and aesthetic beauty, restricted only by his sense of *decorum*. Torquato Tasso, in his *Discorsi dell'arte poetica e del poema eroico*, proposes a heroic poetics that seeks some middle ground between Christian truth and poetic license, claiming that poetry should be characterized by novelty and surprise to create a sense of wonder, like the chimeras advocated by Sidney in his *Defence of Poesy*. Sidney's notion that poetic acts are formed within the "zodiac" of man's wits, while a startling new idea in England, actually draws on nearly a century of poetic theory on the Continent (see Olmsted 2008).

Spanish humanists followed the Italians in their reflections on *imitatio* and imagination. In his *De ratione dicendi* (1532), Vives studied the nature of language and the properties of words and suggested that their adaptation is what catches attention and ensures new meaning. Juan Huarte's *Examen de ingenios para las ciencias* (1575) opens with Galenic physiology, describing the humors of the rhetors' and poets' minds. He found that the brain was hot, moist, and dry, dividing its functions into three parts: cold and dry in combination produced understanding; heat alone activated the imagination; and moisture was responsible for memory. "From a good imagination," Huarte writes, "spring all the Arts and Sciences which consist in figure, correspondence, harmonie, and proportion: such are Poetrie, Eloquence, Musicke, and the skill of preaching: the practice of Phisicke, the Mathematicals, Astrologie, and the governing of a Commonwealth, the art of Warfare, Paynting, drawing, writing, reading" (quoted in Murphy 1983: 99). A century later, Baltasar Gracián would write in his *Agudeza y arte de ingenio* (1649) that the secret of forceful writing was a troping wit: "The clergyman will admire the nourishing conceits of St. Ambrose; the humanist the peppery ones of Martial. Here the philosopher will find Seneca's prudent sayings, the historian the rancorous ones of Tacitus, the orator, Pliny's keenness, and the poet, the brilliance of Ausonius. For whoever teaches is indebted everywhere. I took my examples from the languages in which I found them" (quoted in Murphy 1983: 101). For Gracián, poetry was grounded in the trope of metaphor.

Poetry should also produce *admiratio*. Antonio Minturno, in his *Ars poetica* (1564), argues that poetry should awaken wonder. Near the close of the fifteenth century, Francisco Patrizi's *Della poetica* (1586), popularly known as the *Deca ammirabile*, codified Minturno's sense of the wonderful. There are two sorts: one is the quality of the poem, arising from the divine enthusiasm of the poet, who rightly combines the credible with the incredible to produce the admirable (*mirabile*); the other is what is produced in the auditor or speaker, the extrinsic end of the poetry, *maraviglia*. As Patrizi remarks, "Not every poem will cause every mind to marvel, but they will be more marvelous to some than to others . . . But nevertheless the poet must always, as his proper function and as his proper end, strive to make marvelous every subject that he takes into his hands, no matter how the readers, who are not all alike, may take it" (quoted in Kinney 1989: 43). Thus, the understanding of *imitatio* in the cinquecento—progressing from a sense of modeling works on classical texts, through a sense of adding fiction, to increasing concern for the marvelous—can be charted in the parallel development of Continental humanist fiction. It progresses from the wit and wordplay of Erasmus in the *Moriae encomium* through the fictional embellishments of Castiglione's Urbino to the marvelous giants Don Quixote sees where Sancho Panza can find only windmills. This provides the theoretical basis for the popular development of prose and dramatic romance in the later sixteenth and earlier seventeenth centuries, such as Sidney's *Arcadia* and Thomas Lodge's *Rosalynde*. Robert Greene made a living by writing one prose romance after another, often carrying a block of his writing from one work to the next in an effort to develop an audience in England for his new sense of fiction. His work was inspired by Heliodorus's *Aethiopica*. Such works as *Philomela*, *Gwydonius*, and *Menaphon* reached their apex in *Pandosto*, Greene's most successful romance and the source of William Shakespeare's *The Winter's Tale*. Pandosto's reunion with his lost daughter Fawnia is transferred in Shakespeare to the marvelous in bringing the statue of Hermione back to life. All of Shakespeare's other romances—*Cymbeline*, *Pericles*, *The Tempest*—feature unexpected moments of wonder: "Admired Miranda! / Indeed, the top of admiration" (*The Tempest* 3.1.37–8). Francis Beaumont and John Fletcher followed this poetics for drama in tragicomedies such as *Philaster* and *A King and No King*. Such have become the poets' practice and imitation; as Jacques Pelletier du Mans notes in his *L'art poétique*, it was the poets' responsibility when imitating old things to compound them with something new, something beautiful, something novel.

RHETORICAL *TECHNĒ*

The line between classical rhetoric and a developing poetics was thus perilously thin. Both depended on "thynges likely." Both took up situations that were probable and persuasive; that is, they were persuasive because they were probable, and they were probable because they were persuasive. Grammar schools taught writing through forms of various kinds drawn from Aphthonius's *Progymnasmata*, including narrative, proverb, and commonplace (see Mack, ch. 34; Enterline, ch. 39). Rhetorical *technē* serves both rhetoric and poetics, including *prosōpopoēia*, or the recreation of historical persons, and *prosōpographia* or *topographia*, the recreation of place. Abraham Fraunce records in *The Arcadian Rhetoricke* (1588) that "prosopopoeia is a thynge of any person when in our speech we represent the person of anie, and make it speeke as though he were there presente," adding that it is "an excellent [rhetorical] figure much used of Poets wherein wee must diligentlie take heed" (sig. G2). Grammar schools found their models for teaching *prosōpopoēia* in the *suasoriae* of Seneca the Elder. In the first of Seneca's speeches, Alexander debates whether to sail the ocean, and the student must imagine himself as one of the sailors, as Alexander wishing to go on the voyage, or as Alexander's mother wishing to prevent his departure. In other exercises, the student is asked to take the part of a Spartan at Thermopylae, urging his companions to stand and fight the Persians or urging them to retreat. And in a third *progymnasma*, the speaker must take the part of Agamemnon telling Calchas why he refuses to sacrifice his daughter Iphigenia. Such speeches required the rhetorician to act as a poet. In developing such impersonations or *personae*, students were also asked to follow the ideas in book 2 of Aristotle's *Rhetoric*— the book translated by Sidney—and its discussions of *ēthos* and *pathos*. Aristotle defines *ēthos* as the character the speaker fabricates for himself; he defines *pathos* as a role the speaker suggests for his audience. Both employ *logos*, or a stylized speech resulting from the colorful choice of language and its undertones, as well as *eikos* (likelihood), or images to provide the portraits or issues with power and indelibility. Clearly poets understood these techniques because Erasmus displays them in his impersonation of Folly and Rabelais shows them in his imaging of giants.

In addition to these exercises, students of rhetoric during the Renaissance were also schooled in disputation, which rotated around three axes of thought drawn from ancient forensic oratory and its theory of issues (*staseis*): *An sit?* (Did it happen?); *Quid sit?* (How did it happen?); and *Quale sit?* (How do we interpret the act?). As with the *technē* of declamations, such rules helped create situations that are persuasive because they are probable (see Webb, ch. 22). In writing up their argumentative positions, students were asked to take one side or the other, and on occasion even both, so that they were always able to use language that is flexible and variable in its meaning and effects. Here is an exemplary declamatory theme from Seneca the Elder: "A girl who has been raped may choose either marriage to her ravisher without a dowry or his death. On a single night a man rapes two girls. One demands his death, the other marriage. Speeches for and against the man" (quoted in Kinney 1989: 25; trans. Winterbottom). James J. Murphy traces such rhetorical problems back to the very beginnings of rhetoric (around 476 BCE), when Corax, a resident of Syracuse, sued his pupil, Tisias, when the student refused to pay for his lessons:

> CORAX.   You must pay me if you win the case, because that would prove the worth of
> my lessons. If you lose the case you must pay me also, for the court will force you to
> do so. In either case you pay.
> TISIAS.   I will pay nothing, because if I lose the case it would prove that your
> instruction was worthless. If I win, however, the court will absolve me from paying.
> In either case I will not pay. (Quoted in Kinney 1989: 25; trans. Kennedy)

As Murphy wryly notes, "Tradition holds that the court postponed the decision indefinitely" (25).

Such declamatory *progymnasmata* emphasize plot, character, and situation through logomachy (contention) and teach students the art of antilogy, the ability to present either side of an argument with equal skill, conviction, and success (*argumentum in utramque partem*): "In showing that the same arguments can be used commenting on both sides of a question, and that the same text can be interpreted in different ways, these authors also address themselves to the contrary interpretations that their own texts are capable of eliciting" (Kahn 1985: 22). Thus, speeches that are presented as facts, true accounts, are actually hypotheses or propositions urged upon an audience: "Words are shown to be persuasive tools. Their meaning need not correspond to the truth; their use is dependent on the limited perspective and self-interested intentions of the speaker. In turn, critical reading requires an imaginative grasp of the author's purposes and designs on the reader [or auditor] coupled with the recognition that language is rhetorically constructed; it requires the ability to infer private motives and pretensions from public expression" (Shore 2012: 33). Eloquence was the outgrowth of Lucian's description of Gallic Hercules, a god who pulls crowds by a golden chain that connects his tongue to their ears: "Heracles . . . was a real man who achieved everything by eloquence and applied persuasion as his principal force" (Lucian [1913] 1961: 66–7). This story was promulgated by Cornelius Agrippa, du Bellay, and, in England, by Puttenham and Thomas Wilson (see Rhodes 1992).

Such a rhetorical basis for poetics relied on an art of triangulation in which the final meaning was determined by the audience. Works were made original and attractive by embellishments known as *copia*, drawing on Erasmus's sensationally popular *De copia* (printed 155 times between 1512 and 1580). "Readers of *De copia*," notes Peter Mack, "would learn both that every sentence involved a choice between many different ways of expressing an idea and a method of producing a densely complicated style" (Mack 2010: 423). Ways of varying and embellishing texts were available in book 3 of Wilson's *Art of Rhetoric*, Richard Sherry's *Treatise of Schemes and Tropes*, and Henry Peacham's

Garden of Eloquence (see Mack, ch. 33). These works in turn relied on book 4 of the pseudo-Ciceronian *Rhetorica ad Herennium*, Melanchthon, Peter Mosellanus's *Tabulae de schematibus et tropibus* (with 82 editions in the sixteenth century), and Joannes Susenbrotus's *Epitome troporum ac schematum* (29 editions). Rhetorical tropes such as "metaphor, metonymy, and irony," notes Mack, "generally describe ways in which a writer can give particular words new or extended meanings" (423; see Mack 1993). Rhetorical figures, on the other hand, encompass a "wide range of linguistic forms and approaches, from patterns of words (such as anaphora and climax), aspects of grammar (*zeugma* and *asyndeton*), patterns of sentence construction (*isocolon*), to ways of emphasizing material (such as *correctio*), ways of signaling emotion (such as *aposiopesis*), and attitudes you might take to an audience (such as *permissio* and *dubitatio*)" (424–5). Opposing views of place, for example, such as Athens and London in John Lyly's *Euphues and His England* (1580), Bourdeaux and Arden in Shakespeare's *As You Like It*, and Sicilia and Bohemia in *The Winter's Tale*, necessitated adjudication by the audience, which might prefer one place over another, be torn between them, reject both, or locate a new meaning by combining both. The interpretation of the audience, on which rests the meaning and significance of a work, is an issue Melanchthon raises in *Elementorum rhetorices libri duo* (1531), in which he defines what Kathy Eden claims is "the complementarity between composition and interpretation, between a rhetorical and literary reception" (1997: 79). Melanchthon is not so much concerned with speaking correctly as with prudently comprehending and evaluating what is said, and in the course of *Elementorum rhetorices* he argues for a contextual rather than literal sense of what is proposed. He is less concerned with the *verba*, what is said, than with the *hexis*, the mind-set of the author or speaker and the cultural matrices out of which he writes or speaks. Melanchthon advocates looking not at individual parts but at the whole of the work. In the rhetorical poetics of the cinquecento, meaning is determined by both the creator and the recipient.

This triangulation, a chief legacy of the Renaissance, sounds very familiar to us today, and forms an art whose permanence is arrived at by drawing on the rules and practices of rhetoric. These definitions and practices remain as fundamental now as when they were introduced in the days of Petrarch. Our poetics is quite possibly rhetoric's greatest gift.

FURTHER READING

Baldwin (1959) gives what is still considered the best general survey of the history and uses of rhetoric and poetics. Coussement-Boillot and Sukie (2007) write about the various ways silence becomes an extended medium of rhetoric. The current thinking on the way cognitive theory and rhetoric are interrelated is given in Lynne (2011). Mack (1994) is an anthology of essays on various facets of Renaissance rhetoric by many of its leading scholars. The best detailed history of the development of humanist rhetoric in England in the sixteenth century can be found in Pincombe (2001). Regarding the special uses and effects of rhetoric concerning women in the sixteenth and seventeenth centuries, see Richards and Thorne (2007).

References

Baldwin, C. S. 1959. *Renaissance Literary Theory and Practice: Classicism in the Rhetoric and Poetic of Italy, France, and England 1400–1600*. Edited by D. L. Clark. Gloucester, MA: Peter Smith.

Bishop, Morris. 1966. *Letters from Petrarch*. Bloomington: Indiana University Press.

Coussement-Boillot, Laetitia, and Christina Sukic, eds. 2007. *"Silent Rhetoric," "Dumb Eloquence": The Charity of Silence in Early Modern Literature*. Paris: Universitie Paris-Diderot.

Eden, Kathy. 1997. *Hermeneutics and the Rhetorical Tradition*. New Haven, NJ: Yale University Press.

Grafton, Anthony. 1991. *Defenders of the Text: The Traditions of Scholarship in an Age of Science*. Cambridge, MA: Harvard University Press.

Grafton, Anthony. 1999. "The Humanist as Reader." Translated by Lydia Cochrane. In *A History of Reading in the West*, edited by Guglielmo Cavallo and Roger Chartier, 179–210. Amherst: University of Massachusetts Press.

Kahn, Victoria. 1985. *Rhetoric, Prudence and Skepticism in the Renaissance*. Ithaca, NY: Cornell University Press.

Kinney, Arthur F. 1989. *Continental Humanist Poetics*. Amherst: University of Massachusetts Press.

Lucian. (1913) 1961. *Works*. Translated by A. M. Harmon. Cambridge, MA: Harvard University Press.

Lynne, Raphael. 2011. *Shakespeare, Rhetoric and Cognition*. Cambridge: Cambridge University Press.

Mack, Peter. 1993. *Renaissance Argument: Valla and Agricola in the Traditions of Rhetoric and Dialectic*. Leiden: Brill.

Mack, Peter, ed. 1994. *Renaissance Rhetoric*. New York: St. Martin's Press.

Mack, Peter. 2010. "Spenser and Rhetoric." In *The Oxford Handbook of Edmund Spenser*, edited by Richard A. McCabe, 420–437. Oxford: Oxford University Press.

Murphy, James J. 1983. *Renaissance Eloquence: Studies in the Theory and Practice of Renaissance Rhetoric*. Berkeley: University of California Press.

Olmsted, Wendy. 2008. *The Imperfect Friend: Emotion and Rhetoric in Sidney, Milton and Their Contexts*. Toronto, ON: University of Toronto Press.

Pincombe, Mike. 2001. *Elizabethan Humanism: Literature and Learning in the Later Sixteenth Century*. Edinburgh: Pearson Education Limited.

Puttenham, George. 2007. *The Art of English Poesy*. Edited by Frank Whigham and Wayne A. Rebhorn. Ithaca, NY: Cornell University Press.

Richards, Jennifer, and Alison Thorne. 2007. *Rhetoric, Women and Politics in Early Modern England*. London: Routledge.

Rhodes, Neil. 1992. *The Power of Eloquence in English Renaissance Literature*. New York: St. Martin's Press.

Shore, Daniel. 2012. *Milton and the Art of Rhetoric*. Cambridge: Cambridge University Press.

Stamatakis, Chris. 2012. *Sir Thomas Wyatt and the Rhetoric of Rewriting.* Cambridge: Cambridge University Press.

Thorne, Alison. 2000. *Vision and Rhetoric in Shakespeare: Looking through Language.* London: Macmillan.

Vickers, Brian. 1988. *In Defence of Rhetoric.* Oxford: Clarendon Press.

CHAPTER 36

··

RHETORIC AND THEATER

··

RUSS MCDONALD

EARLY in *The Taming of the Shrew*, shortly after arriving in Padua, Petruchio determines to woo the wealthy but unruly Katherine Minola. When his old friend Hortensio cautions against it, Petruchio's servant Grumio steps in to insist that her shrewishness poses no threat to his master:

> I pray you, sir, let him go while the humour lasts. O'my word, an she knew him as well as I do she would think scolding would do little good upon him: she may perhaps call him half a score knaves or so. Why, that's nothing; an he begin once he'll rail in his *rope-tricks*. I'll tell you what, sir, an she stand him but a little, he will throw a figure in her face and so disfigure her with it that she shall have no more eyes to see withal than a cat. (Shakespeare, *The Taming of the Shrew* 1.2.106–14; emphasis added)

Grumio's frequent confusion and liability to malapropism have led most editors to agree that "rope-tricks" is his misunderstanding of "rhet-tricks," or "rhetorics." At about the same time the satirist Thomas Nashe mocks Gabriel Harvey's "Paracelsian rope-rethorique," meaning something like "outrageous writing for which he deserves hanging" (1596: C₂), and "rhetoric" is supported by Grumio's troping on figure/disfigure. The sense, of course, is that Petruchio's verbal prowess will subdue her however wild she may be. Grumio's error is illuminating because it implies an attitude toward rhetoric both reductive and respectful, suggesting that the ancient art consists of nothing more than a collection of verbal tricks and, at the same time, that it grants the power of controlling others with words.

The subject of this chapter is rhetoric on the early modern English stage, and the collocation of those two topics immediately invokes Grumio's mixed assessment. For most of the sixteenth century, rhetoric in England was a dignified pursuit, if not entirely the province of pedants then certainly a subject limited to the realm of the educated, a native version of the august Greco-Latin discipline authorized especially by Cicero. The London stage, by contrast, was nothing if not popular, a public entertainment located squarely in the precincts of bear pits and brothels ("stewhouses") and open to all but the most abject members of society. If these characterizations of rhetoric and of theater are perhaps crude, they make the point that the two pursuits would seem unlikely partners. And yet the literary brilliance of Elizabethan drama is to a great degree attributable to the playwrights' repurposing of classical rhetoric for their own dramatic ends. Thomas Kyd, Christopher Marlowe, and especially William Shakespeare learned the lessons of the Roman rhetoricians and their Tudor progeny and, from about 1585, sold the products of that knowledge to an eager public. This chapter explores the vital role of rhetoric in the emergence of the greatest age of English drama. After a brief survey of rhetorical education in Tudor England, I look first at surfaces and then at subtexts, illustrating the ways that the Elizabethan playwrights employed the figures of rhetoric in the creation of their dramatic texts and then considering the ways in which, especially in the case of Shakespeare, their mastery of rhetoric led to a profound reevaluation of their own rhetorical instruments.

RHETORIC AND THE SCHOOLROOM

Rhetoric is one of the defining features of the European Renaissance, as many other chapters in this volume attest, and while it arrived later in England than on the Continent, its contribution to sixteenth-century intellectual and artistic life can scarcely be overestimated. The key to its saturation of the culture is the early modern English schoolroom (see Mack, ch. 33). Renaissance humanism, as Paul Oskar Kristeller estab-lished long ago, was an intellectual movement entirely dependent on grammar and rhet-oric (see Mack 2011: 10; see Plett, ch. 30), and the pedagogical system that took hold in early modern England was founded on the student's imitation of forms of expression taken from Cicero, Quintilian, and the pseudo-Ciceronian *Rhetorica ad Herennium*. Instruction in the Tudor grammar school was conducted in Latin, of course, and its pri-mary purpose was not the production of modern literature based on ancient models but the promotion of eloquence and prudence, talents that would help to create a liter-ate, civically responsible gentleman. Ancient rhetoric was the means to this end, and while differences emerged among the followers of Peter Ramus, Philipp Melanchthon, Rudolph Agricola and others, the introductory approach was similar throughout England, with pupils learning the obvious schemes and tropes in elementary Latin and proceeding to more sophisticated figures and texts. Richard Sherry's *Treatise of Schemes [and] Tropes* explains the accepted pedagogical method: "The common school-masters be wont in reading, to say unto their scholars: *Hic est figura*: and sometimes to ask them, *Per quam figuram?*" (1550: 7). After several years of such propaedeutic training, the stu-dent had gained access to the vast storehouse of ancient writing: Caesar, Cicero, Ovid, Terence, Plautus, Virgil, Livy and others supplied the expressive tools needed in creating original written work (Kahn 1985: 52–3; Vickers 1970: 48–52).

While acquiring the fundamental inventory of schemes, tropes, and figures, the Tudor schoolboy was also improving his Latin and absorbing the general principles of composition. Three important methods contributed to this program. The first was the system of double translation. Given a passage from Cicero or another approved ancient writer, the student translated the Latin into English. Then, after an hour or so, the master required the student to translate the passage again, this time rendering his own English version into Latin. The goal, of course, was to come as close to the original as possible. Roger Ascham, celebrated humanist and tutor to the young Queen Elizabeth, describes the conclusion in *The Schoolmaster*: "For then, the master shall have good occasion to say unto him: *N. Tullie* would have used such a word, not this; *Tullie* would have placed this word here, not there; would have used this case, this number, this person, this degree, this gender ... he would have ended the sentence with this verb, not with that noun or participle" (1570: 2). This method of translation may have done little for the imagination, but it certainly acquainted the student with the grammar, syntax, and rhetorical forms that the Renaissance humanists so revered in the writing of antiquity.

What did stimulate creativity was the technique known as *prosōpopoēia*, or the art of impersonation. From early in his education the grammar school boy was expected to devise speeches for types of characters, ranging from the roles of "master" and "scholar" in the lower forms to more ambitious personages as he grew older and more verbally adept. Assigned a literary or historical speaker—for example, Caesar, Mark Antony, or Dido—the student was obliged to compose a speech in that character's voice appropriate to the stipulated circumstances. As Lynn Enterline puts it, "The most advanced rhetorical exercises, based on Aphthonius's *Progymnasmata*, built on long inculcated practice ... boys were eventually set to imitate the *prosopopoeiae* of a series of emotional classical women—Hecuba, Niobe, Andromache, Medea, Cleopatra—as the basis for training in declamation" (2012: 83). The potentiality for dramatic amplification in such exercises is easily located.

A third practice was *argumentum in utramque partem*, in which the student was assigned a debating topic and required to write persuasively on the affirmative and the negative sides. Should a young man marry? Can regicide be justified? Which is preferable, the city or the country? Such an activity demanded imaginative exertion on the part of the student, an effort to place himself in the position of the debating opponent and thus to see both sides of the issue with absolute clarity. Certainly such imaginative training would profit the would-be dramatist, and whether or not the young William Shakespeare was an aspiring playwright when he attended the King Edward Grammar School in Stratford, he would later find the method useful in the creation of dramatic conflict. Joel Altman has demonstrated the influence of this pedagogical tactic on early Tudor imaginative writing, both dramatic and nondramatic:

> The habit of arguing *in utramque partem* permeated virtually all areas of intellectual life. . . . It had been deliberately cultivated by the humanists in the Tudor grammar school, an institution developed to produce men of firm moral conviction whose rhetorical skills would equip them for responsible public life. Here young boys were confirmed in Christian ethics and at the same time taught to look for at least two sides in every question—an ideological conflation that left its peculiar mark on much of the literature of the period. (1978: 34, 43)

The exercise of taking opposed positions obviously shaped such early modern forms as the dialogue (as in Baldassare Castiglione's *The Book of the Courtier*), the essay (especially those of Francis Bacon and Michel de Montaigne), and court and academic theater (plays by John Skelton and others). It also had a lasting influence on Shakespeare's capacity for putting himself in the mind of another person, the talent that John Keats calls "negative capability."

The discipline of rhetoric in England matured as the sixteenth century proceeded, adapting itself to multiple stimuli: the rise of the vernacular, the enrichment of the language from abroad, the contribution of print, and the abundance of writing undertaken in English. A major goal of the humanist rhetoricians was to domesticate the verbal system appropriated from the ancients, creating for adult consumers useful English equivalents of Cicero's *De oratore* or the *Rhetorica ad Herennium*. Some 20 of these handbooks were published and republished throughout the Tudor period. If the record of publication is taken as evidence, Thomas Wilson's voluminous *The Art of Rhetoric* was among the most successful of these guides, appearing in eight editions between 1553 and 1585. George Puttenham's *Art of English Poesy* (1589) is the text modern literary scholars favor, although its influence may have been more limited than we think given that it was never reprinted (Mack 2002: 76).

RHETORIC AND THE STAGE

After decades of humanist training and propaganda, playwrights began to apply their knowledge by exploiting the attractions of rhetorically enhanced speech shortly after the establishment of the permanent commercial playhouses in London in the last quarter of the sixteenth century. Highly decorated language came to be cherished, occupying the same category as elaborate jewelry, patterned fabric, or intricately organized knot gardens. Puttenham introduces the section titled "Of Ornament" with the following simile: "The ornament we speak of is given to it by figures and figurative speeches, which be the flowers, as it were, and colors that a poet setteth upon his language by art, as the embroiderer doth his stone and pearl or passements of gold upon the stuff of a princely garment, or as the excellent painter bestoweth the rich orient colors upon his table of portrait" (2007: 222). In short, the richness of enhanced dramatic speech became a kind of fashionable commodity newly available and thus highly desirable to the smart Elizabethan consumer. "Artful words," says a recent authority, "were the plumage of the new social elites, and those who could produce them in quantity and quality could find thousands of customers on the South Bank" (Watson 2012: 376).

As dramatic poets began to make such language available to the public, demand for it increased. One of the high-water marks of English theatrical rhetoric is also one of the most popular plays of the Elizabethan stage, Thomas Kyd's *The Spanish Tragedy*. This is Hieronimo's famous lament for his murdered son:

> O eyes, no eyes, but fountains fraught with tears!
> O life, no life, but lively form of death!

O world, no world, but mass of public wrongs,
Confused and filled with murder and misdeeds!
O sacred heavens, *if this unhallowed* deed,   5
If this inhuman and barbarous attempt,
If this incomparable murder thus
Of mine but now no more my son,
Shall *unrevealed* and *unrevenged* pass,
How should we term your dealings to be *just*   10
If you *unjustly* deal with those that in your *justice* trust?
The night, sad secretary to my moans,
With direful visions wake my vexed soul,
And with the wounds of my distressful son
Solicit me for notice of his death.   15
The ugly fiends do sally forth of hell,
And frame my steps to unfrequented paths,
And fear my heart with fierce inflamed thoughts.
The cloudy day my discontents records,
Early begins to register my dreams   20
And drive me forth to seek the murderer.
Eyes, life, world, heavens, hell, night and *day,*
See, search, show, send, some man, some mean, that may—
                                       (*A letter falleth*)
              (Kyd, *The Spanish Tragedy* 3.2.1–23; emphasis added)

In a play that laments the inadequacy of language to capture the pains of mortal experience—one of the last horrific gestures is Hieronimo's biting out his tongue to foil interrogation—the self-conscious, ostentatious manipulation of his verbal materials is one of Kyd's most potent instruments.

In both its organization as a lengthy formal lament and its self-conscious poetic particulars, the speech exhibits the writer's devotion to auricular and logical patterns, some of which I have indicated in the typography. As Jonas Barish maintains, compared to earlier examples of poetic drama, "the figures have ceased being mere aimless embroidery. . . . They now work actively to order the materials of the play" (1966: 66–7). The opening lines depend upon a tactic adapted from Petrarch by Sir Philip Sidney and other Elizabethan poets, the metaphoric revision of familiar nouns, associated here with disaster. The final couplet employs a figure that Puttenham calls "*Sinathrismus*, or the Heaping Figure": "If such earnest and hasty heaping up of speeches be made by way of recapitulation . . . then ye may give him more properly the name of the Collector or Recapitulator" (2007: 321–3). Between the showy opening and close, Kyd indulges in virtuosic play with repetition ("If this"), variation ("unrevealed and unrevenged"), oxymoron ("lively form of death"), and paronomasia ("just . . . unjustly . . . justice"). The public's delight in such extravagant rhetoric appears not only in the exceptional popularity of the play in its day but also in the way that the style was repeated, imitated, alluded to, and parodied for decades after its first appearance—for centuries, if we include T. S. Eliot's reference in *The Waste Land*.

Christopher Marlowe storms onto the London stage at the end of the 1580s, waving his rhetorical talent like a banner. When *Tamburlaine* was first performed, probably in 1587 at the Rose Playhouse, the charismatic Edward Alleyn greeted the crowd with a forecast of aural magic:

> *From jygging vaines of riming mother wits,*
> *And such conceits as clownage keepes in pay,*
> *Weele leade you to the stately tent of War:*
> *Where you shall heare the Scythian* Tamburlaine
> *Threatning the world with high astounding tearms . . .*

(Marlowe, Tamburlaine, Prologue, 1–5)

The diction of this Prologue—"jygging vaines," "riming," "conceits," "hear," "high astounding tearms"—attests to Marlowe's thinking of auditors rather than spectators. Throughout the drama he repeatedly stresses the power of artful language: "Thy words are swords," says Mycetes in the first scene, and the eloquence that the upstart Tamburlaine commands largely accounts for his triumphant career. In a famous confrontation words stand in for swords. As Tamburlaine and his enemy Bajazeth leave the stage to fight physically, their mistresses remain behind and enact verbally a surrogate version of the unseen struggle:

> ZABINA.   Base Concubine, must thou be plac'd by me
> That am the Empresse of the mighty Turke?
> ZENOCRATE.   Disdainful Turkesse and unreverend Bosse [large woman],
> Cal'st thou me Concubine, that am betroath'd
> Unto the great and mighty *Tamburlaine*?

(3.3.166–70)

This exchange, continuing for another 40 lines, is only one vivid instance of Marlowe's faith in the semiotic possibilities of poetic structures. Unlike Kyd, Marlowe makes little use of verbal repetition (Peet 1959: 150), but the tactics he does employ—the propulsive force of his iambic pentameter (what Ben Jonson called his "mighty line"), his skillful use of rhythmically beguiling names (Zenocrate, Usumcasane, Barabas, Mephistopheles), and his trick of ending a line with a colorful polysyllable ("And ride in triumph through Persepolis")—all manifest his impulse to transfer the schemes, tropes, and figures of an expanding language to the arena of the popular stage.

Among Marlowe's many auditors in the late 1580s and early 1590s, the most talented was William Shakespeare, twenty-something and new to London. Any consideration of Shakespeare's unparalleled command of rhetoric is aided by the inspired work of scholars who have recently devoted themselves to the topic. Patricia Parker (1987, 1996), for example, has analyzed such common figures as antimetabole, *geminatio*, and *hysteron prōteron*, revealing their ideological implications and demonstrating their structural and thematic contributions, while Wayne Rebhorn (1995) has placed the playwright more generally in the European rhetorical tradition. Several of the great deliberative speeches could be summoned to illustrate Shakespeare's understanding of the possibilities of rhetoric—for example, Brutus's "It must be by his death," Mark Antony's funeral oration, Macbeth's "If it were done when 'tis done," or Prospero's "Ye elves of hills"—and readers will have their own favorite examples. Instead, I shall illustrate his youthful discovery of the resources of rhetoric in a relatively unfamiliar sequence, the first tetralogy of histories: *King Henry VI, Parts One, Two*, and *Three*, and *Richard III*. And rather than excerpt a number of striking figures or tropes, I turn to a single scene from *3 Henry VI* that efficiently attests to Shakespeare's rhetorical enthusiasm.

Fleeing the battle at Towton (2.5), the feckless Henry VI ruminates on the horrors of war and desires relief from the burdens of sovereignty:

> This battle fares like to the morning's war,
> When dying clouds contend with growing light,
> What time the shepherd, blowing of his nails,
> Can neither call it perfect day nor night.
> Now sways it this way like a mighty sea
> Forced by the tide to combat with the wind,
> Now sways it that way like the selfsame sea
> Forced to retire by fury of the wind:
> Sometime the flood prevails, and then the wind;
> Now one the better, then another best—
> Both tugging to be victors, breast to breast,
> Yet neither conqueror nor conquered.
> So is the equal poise of this fell war.
> Here on this molehill will I sit me down.
> To whom God will, there be the victory.
> For Margaret my queen, and Clifford, too,
> Have chid me from the battle, swearing both
> They prosper best of all when I am thence.
> Would I were dead, if God's good will were so—
> For what is in this world but grief and woe?
> O God! Methinks it were a happy life
> To be no better than a homely swain.
> To sit upon a hill, as I do now;
> To carve out dials quaintly, point by point,
> Thereby to see the minutes how they run:
> How many makes the hour full complete,
> How many hours brings about the day,
> How many days will finish up the year,
> How many years a mortal man may live.
> When this is known, then to divide the times:
> So many hours must I tend my flock,
> So many hours must I take my rest;
> So many hours must I contemplate,
> So many hours must I sport myself,
> So many days my ewes have been with young,
> So many weeks ere the poor fools will ean,

So many years ere I shall shear the fleece.
So minutes, hours, days, months, and years,
Passed over to the end they were created,
Would bring white hairs unto a quiet grave.
Ah, what a life were this! How sweet! How lovely!

(Shakespeare, *3 Henry VI* 2.5.1–41)

This extended soliloquy (lengthy even with its last 12 lines omitted) takes the form of a pastoral fantasy. Beginning with the elaborately developed similes of the war, with vehicles of daybreak and then of sea and wind, the speech is replete with stiff repetitions, antitheses, chiasmus, extravagant anaphora, and another case of Puttenham's "Recapitulator" in line 38. Indeed the speech as a unit constitutes a rhetorical stroke in the rhythm of the drama, a reflective moment amidst the carnage of the battles.

Immediately following Henry's lament, the Folio presents one of the most memorable stage directions in the entire canon: "*Enter a Son that hath kill'd his father at one door, and a father that hath kill'd his son at another door*" (Shakespeare, *3 Henry VI* 2.5.54). With the stage design employed to highlight the symmetry, the speeches that develop the opposed familial catastrophes are also symmetrically organized, so that the pairing offers a visual summary of the struggle between York and Lancaster. Coming just after the soliloquy of the paralyzed king, at the center of the play, this series of actions epitomizes the central themes: the weak king whose failure to lead has generated widespread familial slaughter, a national version of the initial biblical crime, brother killing brother. Shakespeare underscores the horrors of the battle by modulating the three voices into a fugue and contriving a lamentable music in the verse:

KING HENRY.   Woe above woe! Grief more than common grief!
O that my death would stay these ruthful deeds!
O pity, pity, gentle heaven, pity!
The red rose and the white are on his face,
The fatal colours of our striving houses;
The one his purple blood right well resembles,
The other his pale cheeks, methinks, presenteth:
 If you contend, a thousand lives must wither.
FIRST SOLDIER.   How will my mother for a father's death
Take on with me and ne'er be satisfied!
SECOND SOLDIER.   How will my wife for slaughter of my son
Shed seas of tears and ne'er be satisfied!
KING HENRY.   How will the country for these woeful chances
Misthink the king and not be satisfied!
FIRST SOLDIER.   Was ever son so rued a father's death?
SECOND SOLDIER.   Was ever father so bemoaned his son?
KING HENRY.   Was ever king so grieved for subjects' woe?
Much is your sorrow; mine ten times so much.

(2.5.94–112)

The pair of soldiers' voices within the trio of king and combatants generates a complex music, doleful strains with antiphonal and succeeding responses. The assignment of anaphora to three speakers is accompanied by corresponding epistrophe, the ending of lines with identical words or phrases, so as to produce an effect known as syncope. The musical representation of civil war attests to Shakespeare's exploration of the multiple ways words can be made to work.

In these history plays rhetoric functions much as it does in *Tamburlaine*: the contest over control of language symbolically represents the struggle for sovereignty. In the climactic scene of *3 Henry VI*, the killing of the king, Richard of Gloucester figures the murder as a seizing of the floor (5.6.57–8):

> I'll hear no more. Die, prophet, in thy speech—
> *He stabs him*

Richard III, the play that follows hard upon this one, is dominated by a particular rhetorical turn, Puttenham's "*Antanaclasis*, or the Rebound" (2007: 292), in which one speaker seizes an adversary's verbal sign and twists its meaning:

> KING RICHARD.   You speak as if that I had slain my cousins.
> QUEEN ELIZABETH.   Cousins indeed, and by their uncle cozened
> Of comfort, kingdom, kindred, freedom, life.

> (Shakespeare, *Richard III* 4.4.222–4)

Rhetorical virtuosity is not, as this passage indicates, limited to Richard himself, although he is certainly master of the *ars rhetorica*. Rather, Shakespeare uses the verbal contest to stand for the competition for power that is his overarching concern.

Throughout the early histories such heavily patterned language is matched by what we might call theatrical rhetoric, visual configurations that structure the narrative, creating parallels and oppositions that impart meaning to the whole. The chiasmus of father killing son and son killing father is perhaps the clearest, but many such formations appear throughout the tetralogy. In *1 Henry VI* the entire struggle is prefigured in the Temple Garden scene (2.4), in which the followers of Lancaster and York pluck red and white roses to signify their allegiance. Often stage directions expose the author's mind in the act of arranging the theatrical picture: "*Flourish. Enter King Edward, Lady Grey, Pembroke, Stafford, Hastings. Four stand on one side and four on the other*" (Shakespeare, *3 Henry VI* 4.1.4–6). Visually, the molehill is used twice, once for York's murder and the second time for Henry's lament. The narrative also offers abundant pairs, the characterological equivalent of verbal parallels. In the center of *3 Henry VI*, when King Henry returns from Scotland in disguise, he is captured by two gamekeepers, an episode in which the dramatist has doubled the captors (the sources mention only a single keeper). Two paired women flank the newly crowned King Edward: the episode in which he stichomythically flirts with and marries Lady Grey is succeeded immediately by a scene with Lady Bona at Paris, where Warwick has arrived to make Edward's offer to the French king's sister. Warwick's ignorance of Edward's sudden marriage to Lady Grey humiliates him and prompts his defection from the York faction he has supported. In fact, "wind-changing Warwick" becomes something like a rhetorical figure himself, one whose repeated changing of sides represents a kind of semantic tergiversation. Finally, there are matching infanticides: in the first act, York's son Rutland is brutally stabbed by Clifford and the Lancastrian forces; in the last act, Henry's son Edward is brutally stabbed by the sons of York. Revenge itself, built into the narrative of this history play, presents a kind of parallel structure, in which emotions and actions are juxtaposed just as words and phrases are matched against one another in the dramatic dialogue.

Rhetoric and Interpretation

Although these striking examples of schemes, tropes, and figures illustrate the transit of classical rhetoric onto the English stage, the more profound influence of rhetoric on English drama is exerted by the practice of contradictory argumentation, the *argumentum in utramque partem*. As Victoria Kahn explains, "When the Renaissance humanist adopted the Aristotelian and Ciceronian rhetorical skills, he was not constrained by the same immediate concerns as is the orator in the forum or the law court. As a result he could actually present both cases and, in so doing, persuade the reader not to any specific action, but to the exercising of the prudential judgment that is required for all actions" (1985: 38–9) (see Hutson, ch. 32). Although this passage does not concern drama, it nonetheless describes the way that rhetoric functions on the Renaissance stage, and Shakespeare's plays offer the most discernible traces of this educational exercise. His almost obsessive attraction to antithesis derives from such rhetorical training, and delight in placing language, characters, and ideas in stark opposition and then further complicating the contrast is a major source of the famous Shakespearean thematic balance, the technique known as "complementarity" (Rabkin 1981: 113).

As Shakespeare gained confidence and experience, his treatment of the materials of rhetoric became considerably more sophisticated. The self-consciously artificial verbiage became less obvious, replaced by subtler configurations in poetry and prose. In some of the mature plays patterns or structures seem to have shaped entire works: Patricia Parker's (1996: 69–73) analysis of *geminatio*, or "the Doublet," in 2 *Henry IV* shows how the repetition of a word or phrase without interruption is pertinent to a story about the problems of royal succession, and George T. Wright (1981) has brilliantly explored the significance of hendiadys in *Hamlet*. The playwright's rhetorical energies seem to have gone underground, or at any rate he seems to have made them less visible. In the mature plays, characters who pride themselves on their rhetorical gifts are usually fools:

POLONIUS.   My liege, and madam, to expostulate
What majesty should be, what duty is,
Why day is day, night night, and time is time,
Were nothing but to waste night, day, and time.

(Shakespeare, *Hamlet* 2.2.87–90)

The great speakers—Hamlet, Brutus, Othello, Macbeth, Prospero—are all master rhetoricians, but their speeches display what Polonius would call the "soul" of rhetoric rather than its "outward flourishes."

This transition from an elementary to a sophisticated command of rhetoric raises finally the intimate connection, recognized by the humanist spokesmen, between rhetoric and interpretation. As Kahn points out in her survey of changing European attitudes toward the resources of rhetoric between about 1400 and 1700, the later humanists tended to emphasize the process of rhetorical endeavor rather than any particular persuasive end. Desiderius Erasmus, Montaigne, and Thomas Hobbes "are frequently less concerned with persuading us to action than with persuading us to consider the nature of persuasion itself. By emphasizing the problematic nature of interpretation, they force us to reflect on the relationship between interpretive and ethical practice, the practice of reading and practical reason" (Kahn 1985: 28). It is not too much to say that Shakespeare, in his passage from rhetorical apprentice to master, recapitulates exactly this cultural-historical movement. Knowing how the rope-tricks work does not diminish our pleasure in watching them.

FURTHER READING

Much valuable work on the importance of rhetoric to Elizabethan drama appeared in the middle decades of the twentieth century: Burke (1941), Joseph (1947), Lanham (1976), and some of the essays collected in Salmon and Burness (1987). The flight to contextual study characteristic of literary criticism from 1975 to the end of the century left little room for rhetorical analysis, but a few critics, such as Turner (1974), Elam (1984), Donawerth (1984), and Parker (1996) made fresh connections between the rhetorical tradition and Shakespeare especially. Useful studies from the last two decades include those of Anderson (1996), Platt (1999), McDonald (2001), and Altman (2010). Also see some of the essays in Adamson, Alexander, and Ettenhuber (2007).

REFERENCES

Adamson, Sylvia, Gavin Alexander, and Katrin Ettenhuber. 2007. *Renaissance Figures of Speech*. Cambridge: Cambridge University Press.

Altman, Joel. 1978. *The Tudor Play of Mind*. Berkeley: University of California Press.

Altman, Joel. 2010. *The Improbability of "Othello:" Rhetorical Anthropology and Shakespearean Selfhood*. Chicago, IL: University of Chicago Press.

Anderson, Judith. 1996. *Words That Matter: Linguistic Perception in Renaissance English*. Redwood City, CA: Stanford University Press.

Ascham, Roger. 1570. *The Schoolmaster*. London.

Barish, Jonas A. 1966. "*The Spanish Tragedy*, or the Pleasures and Perils of Rhetoric." In *Elizabethan Theatre*, 59–85. Stratford upon Avon Studies 9. London: Edward Arnold.

Burke, Kenneth. 1941. *The Philosophy of Literary Form*. Baton Rouge: Louisiana State University Press.

Donawerth, Jane. 1984. *Shakespeare and the Sixteenth-Century Study of Language*. Urbana: University of Illinois Press.

Elam, Keir. 1984. *Shakespeare's Universe of Discourse: Language Games in the Comedies.* Cambridge: Cambridge University Press.

Enterline, Lynn. 2012. *Shakespeare's Schoolroom: Rhetoric, Discipline, Emotion.* Philadelphia: University of Pennsylvania Press.

Joseph, Miriam. 1947. *Shakespeare's Use of the Arts of Language.* New York: Columbia University Press.

Kahn, Victoria. 1985. *Rhetoric, Prudence, and Skepticism in the Renaissance.* Ithaca, NY: Cornell University Press.

Lanham, Richard A. 1976. *Motives of Eloquence: Literary Rhetoric in the Renaissance.* New Haven, CT: Yale University Press.

Mack, Peter. 2002. *Elizabethan Rhetoric.* Cambridge: Cambridge University Press.

Mack, Peter. 2011. *A History of Renaissance Rhetoric, 1380–1620.* Oxford: Oxford University Press.

McDonald, Russ. 2001. *Shakespeare and the Arts of Language.* Oxford: Oxford University Press.

Nashe, Thomas. 1596. *Have With You to Saffron-Walden.* London.

Parker, Patricia. 1987. *Literary Fat Ladies: Rhetoric, Gender, Property.* London: Methuen.

Parker, Patricia. 1996. *Shakespeare From the Margins.* Chicago, IL: University of Chicago Press.

Peet, Donald. 1959. "The Rhetoric of *Tamburlaine*." *English Literary History* 26 no. 2: 137–155.

Platt, Peter G. 1999. "Shakespeare and Rhetorical Culture." In *A Companion to Shakespeare*, edited by David Scott Kastan, 277–296. Oxford: Blackwell.

Puttenham, George. 2007. *The Art of English Poesy.* Edited by Frank Whigham and Wayne A. Rebhorn. Ithaca, NY: Cornell University Press.

Rabkin, Norman. 1981. *Shakespeare and the Problem of Meaning.* Chicago, IL: University of Chicago Press.

Rebhorn, Wayne A. 1995. *The Emperor of Men's Minds.* Ithaca, NY: Cornell University Press.

Salmon, Vivian, and Edwina Burness. 1987. *A Reader in the Language of Shakespearean Drama.* Amsterdam: John Benjamins.

Sherry, Richard. 1550. *Treatise of Schemes [and] Tropes.* London.

Turner, Robert Y. 1974. *Shakespeare's Apprenticeship.* Chicago, IL: University of Chicago Press.

Vickers, Brian. 1970. *Classical Rhetoric and English Poetry.* London: Macmillan.

Watson, Robert. 2012. "Shakespeare's New Words." *Shakespeare Survey* 65: 358–377.

Wright, George T. 1981. "Hendiadys and *Hamlet*." *Publications of the Modern Language Association of America* 96 no. 2: 168–193.

CHAPTER 37

RHETORIC AND THE VISUAL ARTS

CAROLINE VAN ECK

CLASSICAL rhetoric informed practically all aspects of the visual arts in early modern Europe. It provided terms to discuss the arts and strategies of visual persuasion, but also the conceptual framework to analyze how works of art are created and act upon the viewer, and to formulate the first modern theories about art. That rhetoric could play such an important role has to do with the fact that by the early quattrocento, when humanists began to write about the arts, rhetoric was the only complete theory of human communication available—and art was conceived primarily in such terms. As Lodovico Dolce, the sixteenth-century Venetian art theorist and translator of Ovid's *Metamorphoses* and Cicero's *De oratore*, observed, "It is necessary that the figures move the soul of the viewers, perturbing some of them, making others cheerful, moving some to piety and others to disdain, in accordance with the nature of the story. Otherwise it will be thought that the painter has achieved nothing . . . as happens equally to the painter, historian and orator: that if things written or recited do not have this force, they lack also spirit and life" ([1557] 2000: 301).

But the importance rhetoric gave to visual means of persuasion also facilitated its role in the arts (see Habinek, ch. 23). Quintilian, for instance, comparing the persuasive power of gesture to that of images, observes that "gesture, which depends on various forms of movement, should have such power, when pictures, which are silent and motionless, penetrate into our innermost feelings with such power that at times they seem more eloquent than language itself" (*Institutio oratoria* 11.3.66–7; trans. Butler). The aims of oratory are to delight (*delectare*), instruct (*docere*), and move (*movere*), but some of the most powerful effects of persuasion are visual: speech literally *acts on* the public. The orator can establish an affective bond through the use of gesture and facial expression (*actio*, or rhetorical delivery). *Enargeia*, or vivid lifelikeness, suggests the experience of actually seeing what the orator describes (Webb 2009: 87–106; see Webb, ch. 22). Persuasion by visual means is therefore not a matter of simply presenting a speech in stone or paint, putting across a message visually that could have been put as well, or even better, in words. Instead, rhetoric always recognized the importance, power, and irreducible character of visual persuasion.

This chapter considers the roles rhetoric played in the practice and theory of visual persuasion in the visual arts of early modern Europe.[1] It takes as its starting point the fact that classical rhetoric, though originally developed for persuasive speech, always attached great importance to visual means of persuasion. The first section looks at rhetoric as a source of terms and concepts to discuss the arts. The second examines various strategies rhetoric offered for persuasive design, such as the creation of a common ground that allowed the viewer to identify with what a painting or statue showed, what early modern viewers, patrons, and artists alike considered to be the sine qua non of persuasion. The third part of the chapter looks at the concepts and competences informed by rhetoric that viewers brought to the analysis of art and, more particularly, to their understanding of visual persuasion, chief among them the concept of style. To conclude, I look at how spectatorship is shaped by the use of rhetoric in the arts.

Terms and Theories: Leon Battista Alberti on Painting

In the Florentine church of Santa Maria Novella, Masaccio painted a fresco of the Holy Trinity in 1426–8. Mary draws the beholder's attention to the crucified body of Jesus with a resigned gesture that accords with her expression of stoic forbearance, but somehow also translates it: her gesture and expression present the viewer with two coherent and complementary ways of expressing a complex emotion (Figure 37.1; Goffen 2002). She is alone among the figures depicted reaching out, literally, to make eye contact with the public. When the Florentine humanist, painter, and architect Leon Battista Alberti set out to write *De pictura* in 1435/6, the first early modern treatise on painting, he may very well have had Masaccio's fresco in mind when he advised the painter to include a witness—a figure who looks out of the picture at the spectators and draws them into what is happening (sec. 42). Gesture is used in painting to show emotions or interactions between the figures, or to address the viewer. Such use of gesture is one of the most straightforward instances of a rhetorical practice adopted by painters and developed by theorists as an instrument of persuasion. Where orators use apostrophe, turning from one topic or person to another, painters make their figures turn away from the pictorial space they inhabit toward the viewer.

Gesture thus provides a first bridge between rhetoric and painting in *De pictura*, but Alberti did not rest content with isolated borrowings from rhetoric. The entire structure of *De pictura* follows that of Quintilian's *Institutio oratoria*, discussing the basic principles or *elementa* in book 1, the art of painting itself in book 2, and the painter in book 3 (see *Institutio oratoria* 3.10.4–6; cf. D. Wright 1984). Painting is defined as consisting of outline or *circumscriptio* (*disegno* in Italian), composition (*compositio*), and reception of light

FIG. 37.1 Masaccio, *Trinity*, Santa Maria Novella, Florence, fresco, 1426–8 (Photo: public domain)

(*luminum receptio*), the varying colors of a surface resulting from the changing intensity of light. *Circumscriptio* and *compositio* are both terms that originate in classical rhetoric (cf. Cicero, *De oratore* 3.207, where *circumscriptio* means definition or, by extension, delineation). In rhetoric, *compositio* refers to the combination of words and clauses to form complex sentences; Alberti adapted the term to articulate how a pictorial composition or *historia* is made out of figures and objects (Scaglione 1972; Puttfarken 2000; Grafton 2003).

As Michael Baxandall has shown, when Alberti formulated criteria for the successful depiction of a *historia* he used a series of key terms employed in classical rhetoric for stylistic prescription and analysis:

> The *historia* you might justly praise and admire will be of a kind to show itself so pleasant and *ornata* with allurements that it long holds the eyes of the *doctus* and

indoctus beholder with a certain *voluptas* and *animi motus*. For the first thing to bring *voluptas* in a *historia* is precisely *copia* and *varietas* of things . . . in all things the mind is much delighted by *varietas* and *copia*. . . . I will declare that the *historia* is most *copiosa* in which there are mingled together in their places old men and men in their prime, youths, boys, mature women and maidens, young children, pet animals and puppy-dogs, small birds, horses, cattle, buildings and stretches of country; and I will praise all *copia* provided that it is appropriate [*conveniens*] to the event that is represented here. For it is usually the case that, when the beholder lingers over his examination, then the *copia* of the painter gains favour. But I should wish this *copia* to be *ornata* with a degree of *varietas*, and also *gravis* and *moderata* with *dignitas* and *verecundia*. (Alberti, *De pictura*, sec. 40; quoted in Baxandall 1971: 136)

Underlying this description of good painting are the three tasks of the orator: to instruct (implicit in the demand that paintings appeal to the educated and uneducated alike), to charm, and to move. Alberti offers detailed advice about charming and moving the viewer. *Copia* and *varietas* have well-circumscribed meanings in the rhetorical analysis of style: an abundance of subject matter and words, and diversity (on *copia* see Quintilian, *Institutio oratoria* 10.1.15 and book 8; on *varietas* see Cicero, *De inventione* 1.41.76 and Quintilian 2.8.8). Both are subordinated to *compositio*; if allowed free scope, a painting will become disorderly and disconnected (*dissolutus*), displaying only a loose connection between its parts (cf. Baxandall 1971: 136–7). *Convenientia* is related to *decorum*, which regulates the use of all stylistic means and strategies and ensures that what is said is in keeping with the subject, the occasion, and the public. *Copia* and *varietas* together bind the attention of the public by their pleasing fullness and variety. The latter is presented here as an absolute value. *Ornatus* and *convenientia* (appropriateness) were used by Cicero and Quintilian to characterize an effective style, one that manages to move the soul of the public, which is also the effect a properly represented *historia* achieves. To move the emotions of the spectator, Alberti recommends *verecundia* or truthfulness: "A *historia* will move spectators when the men painted in the picture outwardly demonstrate their own feelings [*animi motum*] as clearly as possible. Nature provides—and there is nothing to be found more rapacious of her like than she—that we mourn with the mourners, laugh with those who laugh, and grieve with the grief-stricken. Yet these feelings are known from movements of the body" (1972: 76–7 [sec. 41]). *Verecundia* helps to blur the boundary between the artificial space of the painting and the "real space" of the beholder by drawing on the human and cultural context shared by artists and their viewers. Alberti refers here mainly to the way persons and their emotions are represented. Their dress, gesture, and facial expression should give outward form to the emotions involved in what is depicted, but do so in such a manner that the spectator can identify with and feel the same emotions. Hence Alberti's suggestion to include a witness: a figure who looks out of the picture at the spectator and draws him or her into what is happening.

All these strategies to represent a *historia* in a moving and persuasive manner are determined by *compositio*, the central concept of *De pictura*. Aristotle gave its first systematic treatment in his *Rhetoric* (3.8–9, 1408b–10b), but Quintilian also discusses it quite extensively in *Institutio oratoria* (9.4). Writing in the early quattrocento, Cennino

Cennini had used the related terms *comporre* and *componire*, by which he probably meant the first actual drawing of a figure on a *tavola* or wall as opposed to preliminary sketching. He also associated it with poetical convention, comparing the poet's freedom to that of the painter in what is probably a misunderstanding of *ut pictura poesis* (Cennini 1933: 49–50). But Alberti gave it a new sense. In his definition of *compositio* he makes use of the fact that the Latin *membrum* can mean both "member of a body" and "part of a sentence": "Composition is the procedure in painting whereby the parts are composed together in the picture. . . . Parts of the *historia* are the bodies, part of the body is the member, and part of the member is the surface. The principal parts of the work are the surfaces, because from these come the members, from the members the bodies, from the bodies the *historia*, and finally the finished work of the painter" (Alberti 1972: 73 [sec. 35]). *Compositio*, in rhetoric a subdivision of *ornatus*, is the center of Alberti's conception of the pictorial representation of a *historia*, with *perspicuitas* as its basis and *decorum* as an all-embracing criterion. This is consistent with the three-part structure of *De pictura*. Linear perspective is presented in book 1 as one of the elements of the art of painting. Book 2 is about composition in keeping with *decorum*. This sense of *decorum* is something that the painter has to learn, and that is the subject of book 3. Linear perspective is the basic technique for painting a clear and well-organized *historia*; it is not only a pictorial technique to create the illusion of three-dimensional space on a flat surface but a narrative instrument as well, in that it helps the painter to impart visual hierarchy to the *historia* he depicts.

Although it is a small book, *De pictura* contains almost all applications of rhetoric to the visual arts that were to be made during the Renaissance and after: from Filarete's treatise on architecture of the 1430s to the seventeenth-century theories of Giovanni Pietro Bellori and Roger de Piles or the *Discourses* by Sir Joshua Reynolds, the last complete statement of classicist art theory (see Kirkbride, ch. 40).

Visual Persuasion

As we have seen, Lodovico Dolce urged painters to make their work so moving that it would act on the souls of their viewers. Like *ekphrasis*, vivid, lifelike paintings could enter the soul and recreate the experience of viewing what the painter had depicted. The psychological basis for such impact was imaginative identification by the viewers with the scene represented. The letters by the Venetian playwright and art critic Pietro Aretino, a great admirer of Titian, testify to such reactions. In his contemplation of Titian's *Ecce Homo* he describes how, in this painting of the *Cristo vivo e vero*, the thorns piercing Christ have become real thorns, and the blood they cause to flow becomes real blood. It is not the image that exhorts him to piety but the experience of seeing the pain constricting Christ's face. In a less familiar instance, the Florentine critic Francesco Bocchi described the viewers' reaction to Michelangelo's *Pietà*. After mentioning the powers of the artist to represent faces, characters, and emotions, he paid him the highest tribute the orator could give: no eloquence could praise his power to infuse dead marble with living grief and strike the viewers with piety and terror, filling their minds with memories of his bitter death (Bocchi 1978, folio 8).

Art could be so lifelike that it ceased to look like art. Visual persuasion became complete when the viewers felt they were in the presence of acting persons engaged in situations with which they could identify. Aretino (1997–2002: 1: 73) reported that when he and his friend Tribolo saw Titian's *Death of Saint Peter Martyr*, Tribolo reacted to the extreme vividness of the painting with fear and pity, as if he were present at the events depicted, not looking at an image of them, and claimed that the image stayed with him after he had left the church.

Pictures and statues could move the spectator through imaginative involvement. This was achieved by means of a series of pictorial strategies aimed at constructing a common ground. Through their use, the viewer could identify with what was depicted, sometimes in a relatively literal sense, as when linear perspective was used to suggest a continuum between the real space of the viewer and the virtual space of the painting. Painters could also suggest a common ground by using pictorial strategies that appealed to the viewer's imagination. One of the most powerful and subtle ways of achieving this is by making viewers feel they are not looking at an image but are part of the scene before their eyes. Many Renaissance paintings imply the presence of an external spectator: figures in the painting look out of the frame at the viewer, address him or her, and gesture at them to draw their attention.

Caravaggio's *Entombment* (Figure 37.2), now removed from its original setting above the altar in the Chiesa Nuova in Rome, presents one of the most dramatic uses

FIG. 37.2 Caravaggio, *Entombment*, Pinacoteca dei Musei Vaticani, oil on canvas, 1602–3 (Photo: Kunsthistorisch Instituut, Leiden University)

of this compositional device in Renaissance art. The dead weight of Christ's body is lowered over the slab of stone bordering the open tomb and out of the pictorial space into the space where the beholder is standing, suggesting that Christ's true resting place is in the heart of the believer (Langdon 1998: 241–7). Originally this painting was placed right behind the altar so that worshippers would immediately grasp that the adoration of the Host is in fact a bloodless reenactment of Christ's original sacrifice. But even in its present museum setting, the viewer is still compelled by the strong downward diagonal and outward direction of the composition to consider how the action of the figures affects him or her, and to react to it. Its composition both assumes the presence of a beholder and addresses him or her through the glance and gestures of the figures depicted; in this process the viewer is made to assume the role of a believer, an assistant at the grave, or a worshipper of the Host (for a reconstruction of the original setting and its liturgical meaning, see G. Wright 1978). The painting reenacts sacred history before the eyes of the viewer, recalling Cicero's praise of history as a "witness of the times" (*testis temporum*) and the "light of truth" (*lux veritatis*).

FIG. 37.3 Titian, *San Salvadore Annunciation*, Museo di Capodimonte, Naples, oil on canvas, 1557 (Photo: public domain)

When viewers describe the impact of paintings, they often mention that they are moved by their vivid lifelikeness to identify with the person or scene represented. They sometimes move beyond such accounts of direct emotional involvement and draw on the theater to analyze the persuasive power of images. Discerning observers like Aretino and Carlo Ridolfi, for example, thought of the work of Titian and Veronese in terms of theatrical representation. I have already quoted Aretino's description of the reaction of his friend Tribolo to *The Death of Saint Peter Martyr* in terms that clearly allude to the Aristotelian view of the impact of a tragedy on the audience. But this was not a unique instance. Titian's San Salvadore *Annunciation* (Figure 37.3) breaks with the Renaissance tradition of representing this event as a private encounter between Mary and the angel by giving it a dramatic staging that is very close to Aretino's description in his *Vita di Santa Maria*. There he wrote of the actors that they gesture as Titian would have painted them (Aretino 1539a: 152, 1539b: 63–75; cf. d'Elia 2005: 107). In the early seventeenth century Ridolfi called Veronese's *Feast in the House of Levi* a "majestic theatre" (*maestoso Teatro*) and described the action of Titian's *Crowning with Thorns* as taking place in a theater (1996: 91, 1919–24: 1: 315).

Interpretation

Classical rhetoric developed manifold strategies of persuasion, but it was also concerned with interpretation. It gave persuasive expression to thought, but this was not considered merely as a matter of finding the right formulation for some thought that had already been fully expressed in the speaker's mind (Quintilian, *Institutio oratoria* 9.1.19). It was an interpretative activity that shaped thought, not simply offered alternative wordings. The concept of style is perhaps the clearest case of rhetoric's double-sided potential. At the end of the *Institutio oratoria* Quintilian introduces a rhetorical concept that was to be most influential in art history: the concept of style (*elocutio*).[2] The ideal orator is the "good man skilled in speaking," Cato's *vir bonus, dicendi peritus*. But just as there is not one personality type that everybody agrees is the best orator, so there is not one single style of speaking that is most appropriate for every subject, occasion, or audience. To illustrate this point, Quintilian compares oratory to painting and sculpture, distinguishing various genera and species in an attempt to draw up a nonnormative classification of speaking styles. Here, for the first time in European art, styles of invention and elocution are used to devise a classification in terms of individual and group characteristics of art works, distinguishing, for instance, an Etruscan and an Athenian school. Quintilian then gives a brief history of painting, sculpture, and oratory that was to be mined by Renaissance authors looking for a critical vocabulary. His history of painting styles singles out aspects of composition and creative ability: talent and grace; the handling of color, line, light and shade, and roundness and solidity in the representation of the human body; and the capacity to take trouble over a painting or to depict imaginary scenes. He also sketched a development from the hardness of early beginnings through a less rigid style to the softness and beauty (*decor*) of Myron (12.1–12).

Although Quintilian did not use the term *stilus*, instead employing the biological concepts of genus and species when analyzing style, these discussions are the origin of that essential instrument of art-historical interpretation—the concept of style. All rhetorical instruction and practice is based, first, on the distinction between subject matter (*res*) and words (*verba*), and second, on the principle that speakers have a choice in how to formulate their subject matter. Modern art-historical discourse about style is based on this principle insofar as it uses style in the sense of a distinctive way in which a work of art is made: "There can be no question of style unless the speaker or writer has the possibility of choosing between alternative forms of expression" (Cicero, *Brutus* 100, *Orator* 71).

Style, however, would only become prominent as a classificatory tool in the eighteenth century, in the new academic discipline of art history as developed by Johann Winckelmann. In the preceding centuries much writing on the arts informed by rhetoric took as its starting point the doctrine of *ut pictura poesis*. Throughout the Renaissance, Horace's comparison of painting and poetry was used to legitimize the application of rhetoric to the visual arts (see Lee 1967; Gent 1981). But this comparison, unlike the rest of *The Art of Poetry*, which treats the writing of poetry, is also about how to understand art: how to read or listen to poetry, how to look at painting. "A poem," observes Horace, "is like a picture: one strikes your fancy more, the nearer you stand; another, the farther away. This courts the shade, that will wish to be seen in the light, and dreads not the critical insight of the judge. This pleased but once, that, though ten times called for, will always please" (*Ars poetica*, lines 361–5; trans. Fairclough). Horace was not the first to compare poetry and painting. The Greek sophist Simonides is the earliest author known to have done so, calling poetry a "resounding painting" (Plutarch, *Moralia* 346a–7d). And in Plutarch's *Moralia*, Simonides is quoted as saying that "poetry is articulate painting" (*phtheggomenēn tēn poiēsin*) and that painting is "inarticulate poetry" (*poiēsin sigosan*) (18a; see also Pseudo-Longinus, *On the Sublime* 25). But for both Simonides and Horace the common ground between painting and poetry is what the ancients considered to be the defining characteristic of humanity: the ability to speak, to articulate one's thought in a way that is comprehensible to others and can sway their thoughts and actions.

Painting was so often called mute or visible speech that this particular variety of *ut pictura poesis* became a commonplace in early modern Europe. Works of art were considered to speak not because of some inherently verbal or discursive characteristic but because they were so lively and vivid that they seemed to possess the distinctive feature of being alive—the ability to speak. And conversely, persuasive writing was able to conjure up moving and speaking images in the mind of the beholder, who was transformed into the spectator of a play set on a mental stage.

A record of a visit to a painting by Titian by the Neapolitan physician Bartolommeo Maranta illustrates the interpretative attitude fostered by rhetoric's close linking of invention and interpretation. Somewhere between 1559 and 1571 Maranta went with his friend Scipione Ammirato to see Titian's *Annunciation* at the Church of San Domenico Maggiore in Naples (Figure 37.3) (see van Eck 2007: 144–50). The text recording their conversation is an extended interpretation of one painting, which is in itself quite rare in the Italian Renaissance. Ammirato did not much like this painting: the face of the angel was too fat, it was not a good painterly decision to show it only in profile, and Titian had not understood the proportions of the figure of the angel very well. The opening gambit of Maranta's defense—yet another comparison between painters and poets—alludes to Horace's *poetis atque pictoribus aeque potestas*, the license that both groups of artists equally enjoy. But he gives this cliché an unexpected twist when he states that painters, like poets, are at liberty to vary not the plot or the situation they represent but the proportions, colors, and attitudes of the figures involved, just as the poet can vary the episodes in his plays. In the course of his defense, Maranta analyzes Titian's painting in great detail. His interpretation is based on the insight that subject matter and its representation should be distinguished: the subject, the sacred or mythological *historia*, is fixed, but the way in which it is represented pictorially can be varied. This reflects the fundamental rhetorical principle that *res* and *verba*, or theme, plot, or content, on one hand, and its representation, on the other, while in the end inseparable, should be distinguished in analyzing the painter's work, and that this distinction can be used as an instrument of interpretation. In other words, why did Titian choose to give this particular pictorial form to the theme of the Annunciation, and in what manner does it contribute to the overall persuasive effect of this painting?

To grasp the intentions of the painter, Maranta appeals to the similarity between painting and poetry. Painting offers silent metaphors, similes, figures of speech, and allegories with the help of paint, while poetry offers speaking metaphors using language and action. What can be said of one art may therefore be applied to the other. The supposed fatness of the angel, suggests Maranta, is not a defect of taste or design but a silent allegory of heavenly abundance, a visual sign of the "divine food, that is love, grace and splendor" (1971: 866) the angels enjoy in heaven.

Keeping in mind the distinction between *res* and *verba*, between *favola* and *episodi* in poetry and painting, helps to understand what Titian tried to achieve. In the course of answering some other points of Ammirato's critique, Maranta develops three criteria to judge painting that seeks to imitate human beauty: correct proportion (*debita proportione*), convenient or fitting liveliness of color (*debita quantità, convenevole vivacità di colore*), and a certain grace, which is called loveliness (*grazia*) or elegance (*leggiadria*). These are the qualities of the human form that painting sets out to imitate. But the painter also has to add disposition (*disposizione*), which is found in living bodies and which is needed in the composition of beauty. In nature it is part of *leggiadria*, but in painting it is a separate condition. Grace consists in the actions and movements of human bodies, but painting can only show one of these at a time, which must suffice to give a beautiful air to a painting and make it appear wonderful. *Disposizione* is therefore a matter of great discretion and judgment.

Fitting liveliness of color is a matter of handling light and shade. They convey wonderful vivacity because of the similarity between the angel's skin and human skin, and between its clothes and real fabrics, to such a degree that one does not seem to look at colors or dyed, painted canvas but at true and living human bodies. The hair of Titian's angel is of such a beautiful color, and painted with such expert shading, that it makes its head appear outside the frame, as if one could actually touch these locks.

Similarly, elegance or *leggiadria* is sent by God and gives life and persuasive power to painting. The painter copies it either from some living being, or it is composed by the painter after some mental image. The latter is more worthy of praise because it involves much more deliberation about clothes and character, depending on the mystery, story, or *istoria*, its time and place, and about persuasion or dissuasion, acceptance or denial, and their attendant emotions, such as fury, piety, peacefulness or rigidity, cheerfulness or sadness. These emotions and traits of character must be shown not only in the face of the figure but also in its attitudes, movements, and clothes.

Finally, Maranta's fifth critical term, disposition, is used in an analysis of the painting in terms of what is going on, of the emotional and narrative interaction between the depicted figures. This way of looking at painting ultimately goes back to the ekphrastic tradition (Alpers 1960; Carrier 1987; Land 1990; Rosand 1990; Goldhill 1994; Webb 2009). In Philostratus's *Imagines* the task of the painter—and the merit of painting—is to represent the characters and emotions of his figures, and to interpret the dramatic situation they find themselves in. By extension, the public becomes the spectator of these pictorial dramas:

> For he who is to be a true master of the art must have a good knowledge of human nature, he must be able to discern the signs of men's characters even when they are silent, and what is revealed in the state of the cheeks and the expression of the eyes and the character of the eyebrows and, to put the matter briefly, whatever has to do with the mind. If proficient in these matters he will grasp every trait and his hand will successfully interpret the individual story [*drama*] of each person. (Philostratus, *Imagines*, *proemium*; trans. Fairbanks)

Maranta's analysis could just as well have been the description of a scene in the theater: he describes the movement, gestures, clothes, and expressions of the figures, as well as what they are supposed to say to each other, not the pictorial means by which these are represented. This is not an Albertian analysis of *compositio* in terms of the way color, light, and outlines work together on the pictorial plane but a narrative analysis of the interaction between the figures, a way of establishing in what manner, in what kind of *episodi*, this particular plot or *istoria* has been narrated. All of these interpretative approaches will become key features of subsequent interpretations of art: in the *conférences* of the Académie Royale de Peinture, for instance, the distinction between invention, disposition, and elocution would often be the guiding feature of description and analysis (see, for instance, Merot 1996: 45–59 [on André Félibien] and 123 [on Sébastien Bourdon]).

THE RHETORICAL VIEWER

Maranta thus shows how the use of the rhetorical distinction between *res* and *verba*, coupled with *ut pictura poesis*, shaped the way viewers looked at art and discussed it, and also how it contributed to a very definite theatrical viewing attitude. But in the final reckoning it is the painting's *leggiadria*, its power to suggest the grace that only living beings possess, that truly affects the viewer. Painting therefore is like poetry not so much because it resembles the latter but because both seek to imitate life. Life, however, is taken in a very specific sense: that of character acting a plot, of human beings engaged in events and situations with which the spectator can identify (see van Eck and Bussels 2011). In giving in to the illusion of life, Renaissance viewers abandon the discursive, analytical, and interpretative potential suggested by the analogy between poetry and painting, exemplified by Alberti's comparison of the structure of the sentence with pictorial composition, in favor of close identification with what they see. They are no longer critics; they are spectators at a play. Spectators consider painting as a kind of theater, behave as if they are watching actors on a stage performing a play, feel themselves to be a public, and think about the effect of the spectacle on them in terms of theatrical effects. In this context it is interesting to note that according to Pliny the rivalry between the painters Zeuxis and Parrhasius was acted out in a theater: elocution becomes a staging of speech, just as action, its delivery, becomes a staging of the body.

NOTES

1. Although art historians still tend to consider Lee (1967) as the foundation of twentieth-century studies of the relations between rhetoric and the arts, the seminal work, based on a thorough knowledge of all aspects of rhetoric, was done by Baxandall (1971), Vickers (1988), and Fumaroli (1994). For a broader overview and bibliography see van Eck 2007.
2. On the history of art-historical concepts of style and their rhetorical origins see, for example, Hendrickson (1905) and Gombrich (1968). On the history of the art-historical concept of style see van Eck, McAllister, and van de Vall (1995).

REFERENCES

Alberti, Leon Battista. 1972. *On Painting and Sculpture.* Edited and translated by Cecil Grayson. London: Phaidon.

Alpers, Svetlana Leontief. 1960. "*Ekphrasis* and Aesthetic Attitudes in Vasari's *Lives.*" *Journal of the Warburg and Courtauld Institutes* 23: 190–215.

Aretino, Pietro. 1539a. *Vita di S. Maria.* Venice: Francesco Marcolini.

Aretino, Pietro. 1539b. *Humanità di Christo.* Venice: Francesco Marcolini.

Aretino, Pietro. 1997–2002. *Lettere sull'Arte.* Edited by P. Procaccioli. Rome: Salerno Editrice.

Baxandall, Michael. 1971. *Giotto and the Orators: Humanist Observers of Painting and the Discovery of Pictorial Composition.* Oxford: Oxford University Press.

Bocchi, Francesco. 1978. *Oratio Francisci Bocchij de laudibus Michaelisangeli Florentini Pictoris, Sculptoris, atque Architecti Nobilissimi.* British Library MS Egerton 1978 520 F, fol. 8.

Carrier, David. 1987. "Ekphrasis and Interpretation: Two Modes of Art History Writing." *British Journal of Aesthetics* 27: 20–31.

Cennini, Cennino. 1933. *The Craftsman's Handbook: The Italian "Il Libro dell'arte."* Translated by David V. Thompson, Jr. New York: Dover.

D'Elia, Una Roman. 2005. *The Poetics of Titian's Religious Paintings.* Cambridge: Cambridge University Press.

Dolce, Lodovico. (1557) 2000. "Dialogo della Pittura [. . .] intitulato l'Aretino." In *Dolce's "Aretino" and Venetian Art Theory of the Cinquecento*, edited by Mark W. Roskill, 84–196. Toronto: Renaissance Society of America.

Fumaroli, Marc. 1994. *L'école du silence: Le sentiment des images au XVIIe siècle.* Paris: Flammarion.

Gent, Lucy. 1981. *Picture and Poetry 1560–1620: Relations between Literature and the Visual Arts in the English Renaissance.* Leamington Spa: James Hall.

Goffen, Rona, ed. 2002. *Masaccio's "Trinity."* Cambridge: Cambridge University Press.

Goldhill, Simon, and Robin Osborne, eds. 1994. *Art and Text in Ancient Greek Culture.* Cambridge: Cambridge University Press.

Gombrich, Ernst H. 1968. *Art and Illusion: A Study in the Psychology of Pictorial Representation.* London: Phaidon.

Grafton, Anthony. 2003. "*Historia* and *Istoria*: Alberti's Terminology in Context." In *The Renaissance: Italy and Abroad*, edited by John Jeffries Martin, 199–214. London: Routledge.

Hendrickson, George L. 1905. "The Origins and Meaning of the Ancient Characters of Style." *American Journal of Philology* 26: 249–290.

Land, Norman E. 1990. "Titian's *Martyrdom of St. Peter Martyr* and the 'Limitations' of Ekphrastic Art Criticism." *Art History* 13: 293–317.

Langdon, Helen. 1998. *Caravaggio: A Life.* London: Chatto and Windus.

Lee, Rensselaer W. 1967. Ut Pictura Poesis: *The Humanistic Theory of Painting.* New York: Norton.

Maranta, Bartolommeo. 1971. "Discorso all'Ill.mo Sig. Ferrante Carrafa Marchese di Santo Lucido in Materia di Pittura nel quale si difende il quadro della Cappella del Sig. Cosmo Pinelli, fatto per Tiziano, da alcune opposizioni fattegli da alcune persone." In *Scritti d'Arte del Cinquecento*, vol. 1, edited by Paola Barocchi, 863–900. Milan and Naples: Ricciardi.

Merot, Alain, ed. 1996. *Les Conférences de l'Académie Royale de peinture et sculpture au XVIIe siècle.* Paris: École Nationale Supérieure des Beaux-Arts.

Puttfarken, Thomas. 2000. *The Discovery of Pictorial Composition: Theories of Visual Order in Painting, 1400–1800.* New Haven, CT: Yale University Press.

Ridolfi, Carlo. 1919–1924. *Le Maraviglie dell'Arte.* Edited by Detlev von Hadeln. Berlin: G. Grote.

Ridolfi, Carlo. 1996. *The Life of Titian.* Edited by Julia Conaway Bondanella, Peter Bondanella, Bruce Cole, and Jody Robin Shiffman. Translated by Julia Conaway Bondanella and Peter Bondanella. University Park: Pennsylvania State University Press.

Rosand, David. 1990. "*Ekphrasis* and the Generation of Images." *Arion* (3rd ser.) 1: 61–105.

Scaglione, Antonio. 1972. *The Classical Theory of Composition from Its Origins to the Present.* Chapel Hill: University of North Carolina Press.

van Eck, Caroline. 2007. *Classical Rhetoric and the Visual Arts in Early Modern Europe.* Cambridge: Cambridge University Press.

van Eck, Caroline, and Stijn Bussels, eds. 2011. "Theatricality in Early Modern Art and Architecture." *Art History* 33 no. 2: Special Issue.

van Eck, Caroline, James McAllister, and Renée van de Vall, eds. 1995. *The Concept of Style in Philosophy and the Arts*. Cambridge: Cambridge University Press.

Vickers, Brian. 1988. *In Defence of Rhetoric*. Oxford: Clarendon.

Webb, Ruth. 2009. *Ekphrasis, Imagination and Persuasion in Ancient Rhetorical Theory and Practice*. Farnham: Ashgate.

Wright, D. R. Edward. 1984. "Alberti's *De Pictura*: Its Literary Structure and Purpose." *Journal of the Warburg and Courtauld Institutes* 47: 52–71.

Wright, Georgia. 1978. "Caravaggio's *Entombment* Considered *in Situ*." *Art Bulletin* 60: 35–42.

PART V

··

EARLY MODERN AND ENLIGHTENMENT RHETORIC

··

....

CHAPTER 38

RHETORIC AND EARLY MODERN POLITICS

....

ANGUS GOWLAND

IN Europe from the fifteenth to the seventeenth centuries, it was more or less taken for granted by learned elites that rhetoric had great political significance, and indeed this period is the second era of European history (the first being that of the Roman Republic, from the third century BCE onward) in which a proficiency in rhetoric was widely considered to be a prerequisite for a political career. Like its medieval predecessor, early modern rhetoric was essentially classical, but from the late fourteenth century onward its social and political application was expanded and transformed. The agents of this transformation, with whom this chapter will be centrally concerned, were the humanists of the Italian and northern European Renaissance, scholars and pedagogues whose project to revive the literature and learning of classical culture had Latin eloquence at its core (see Ward, ch. 25; Cox, ch. 26).

A classical conception of the utility of rhetorical persuasion to political deliberation and governance is a commonplace of early modern rhetorical treatises and textbooks (e.g., Agricola [1515] 1539: 5–6; Melanchthon 1519: 9–10; Rainolde 1563: 1r–v). As in antiquity, however, the role of rhetoric in politics was contentious for political philosophers and historians, who postulated the detrimental as well as beneficial aspects of eloquence in both republics and monarchies. After a summary of the late medieval Italian background from which the humanistic conception of political rhetoric emerged, this chapter addresses the ways rhetoric was theorized as an element of republican and monarchical politics and, in general terms, relates its *fortuna* to some of the fundamental developments in early modern political thought.

RHETORIC IN THE ITALIAN CITY-STATES

....

The importance of rhetoric to Renaissance humanism was established in modern scholarship on the Italian city-states by the work of Paul Oskar Kristeller (1961: 92–119,

1979: 228–51). According to Kristeller, the majority of Italian humanists were professional rhetoricians, who practiced rhetoric as secretaries of princes or cities or taught it in universities and schools. The humanist study of rhetoric originated in part from the medieval arts of letter and prose composition, the *ars dictaminis* and *artes dictandi*, practiced throughout the peninsula, where *dictatores* had performed important legal and political roles—composing documents and letters as notaries, secretaries, and chancellors in the service of princes, popes, and cities. Teachers of *dictamen* also produced treatises and commentaries expounding an art that condensed the principles of classical rhetoric, principally of the forensic and deliberative genres, and applied them to administration and government.

Following the displacement of ruling elites by elective systems of government in the majority of the Italian city-states in the course of the twelfth century, the teaching of dictaminal rhetoric became tailored to a participatory and conciliar form of politics in which verbal debate and persuasive speech had an important role. At the same time, the exemplary topics and models propagated by the *ars dictaminis* came to incorporate the concerns of self-governing city communes, which were organized around the values of independence, liberty, and civic virtue. Training in dictaminal rhetoric became training in republican politics, practically and ideologically, and it acquired special significance when, in the later thirteenth century, systems of self-government came under pressure from chronic internal factionalism and the spread of hereditary *signori* across Italy (Skinner 1978: 1: 23–35).

Gradually, the abridgements of classical rhetorical theory propagated by the Italian *ars dictaminis* were supplanted by humanistic treatises and commentaries that engaged closely with Roman rhetorical works, especially those of Cicero (an early example is Antonio Loschi's *Inquisitio in XI orationes Ciceronis* [ca. 1395]). In the course of the fourteenth century, however, the progressive conversion of the Italian communes into principates—or, in the case of republics like Florence, socially restricted oligarchies— meant that when the classicizing influence of humanism was fully brought to bear on rhetoric, the political context for the *imitatio* of Roman culture had changed decisively. Adapting to civil life in principalities, early humanist rhetorical theory was primarily literary and philosophical, expressing a Ciceronian preoccupation with the moral status of the orator and focusing upon epideictic for ceremonial occasions.

Yet the political dimension of classical rhetoric would not be submerged for long. In 1402, the Venetian humanist Pierpaolo Vergerio criticized the sidelining of deliberative rhetoric by "princes and lords" who "want an opinion explained in few words and arguments brought nakedly into council" ([1402] 2002: 24–5). A little later, the Greek humanist George of Trebizond presented a Ciceronian vision of rhetoric as *civilis scientia* to train the leaders of the Venetian republic, where eloquence in the Senate and Great Council would be indispensable ([1433/4] 1538: 1–5; Monfasani 1976: 260, 294– 5). Similarly, although quattrocento Florence was effectively an oligarchy dominated by local elites, to humanist eyes its magistracies, councils, and consultative meetings made it an appropriate setting for civically orientated rhetoric. In humanistic writing based in both republics we witness the extension of classical rhetoric, in all three *genera*, into political discourse, and substantial meditations upon the nature and role of civil eloquence.

RHETORIC AND REPUBLICANISM: BRUNI AND MACHIAVELLI

The political thought of the Tuscan humanist Leonardo Bruni, chancellor of Florence in 1410–11 and again from 1427 until his death in 1444, has become highly controversial, mainly because of Bruni's role in the so-called civic humanism seen by Hans Baron (1966) as the key to the Florentine Renaissance and the republican ideals of liberty, equality, and participation. I am not directly concerned with the plausibility of Baron's thesis but with the rhetorical character of two of Bruni's epideictic speeches, the *Laudatio Florentinae urbis* and *Oratio in funere Johannis Stroze*. The first follows the *Panathenaicus* of Aelius Aristides and applies encomiastic topics to Florence (geography, climate, architecture, etc.) to celebrate its past, present, and future glory (Bruni [1403/4] 1978: 135–75; cf. Quintilian, *Institutio oratoria* 3.7.26). The oration for the funeral of Nanni degli Strozzi, who died fighting for the Florentines against the Milanese, follows the model of Pericles's funeral speech in Thucydides, extolling Florence as "one of the greatest and most illustrious" of cities before turning to the career of Nanni himself (Bruni [1428] 1987: 121–7).

Two features of these speeches have become central to the historiography of Renaissance republicanism. The first is their emphasis on liberty, justice, and equality as cherished principles at the heart of the Florentine constitution. According to the *Laudatio*, the republican origins of Florence as a Roman colony, founded before the imperial destruction of liberty and when Roman virtue and power were at their peak, have made Florentines into "the greatest enemies of tyrants" and enable them to "enjoy perfect freedom" (Bruni [1403/4] 1978: 149–51, 154). Correspondingly, the institutions of the republic produce its internal order in a Ciceronian fashion by maintaining liberty and justice, undergirded by equality before the law (168–9; cf. Cicero, *De re publica* 2.42.69, *De officiis* 1.13.41–14.42). In the oration for Strozzi, Bruni summarizes the interconnection of liberty, civic virtue, and self-government in the republic, which, in applying such values uniformly to "all the citizens," is "egalitarian in all respects" and so has what is properly termed "a 'popular' constitution" (Bruni [1428] 1987: 124–5). This *oratio* also expresses a negative conception of liberty as freedom from arbitrary power and an exclusivist critique of monarchy and aristocracy that gives legitimacy only to popular government (125).

The second important political theme elaborated in Bruni's speeches is imperialism. Composed when the power of the Florentine republic was nearing its peak in the Italian peninsula, the *Laudatio* presents the military strength of Florence, like its Roman forebear, as a central component of its civic greatness (Bruni [1403/4] 1978: 142, 144, 150,

155). The justification of republican imperialism in the Strozzi oration is notably more muted—appropriately in an era that witnessed the resurgence of Florence's rivals and would soon see the triumph of the Medici—but Bruni still praises "the citizens of this present age, who have extended the city's power even beyond what they inherited from their fathers" ([1428] 1987: 124; Hankins 2000: 145–59).

Despite the manifest republicanism of Bruni's speeches, for some scholars their rhetorical character undermines his sincerity, and certainly he was ambitious and ideologically flexible enough also to serve the papacy and admire a *condottiere* prince (Siegel 1966; Hankins 1995: 318–27). But even if we view these speeches as conventional Florentine propaganda repackaged to provide ideological cement for the grip of the governing elite, this does not mean that Bruni's rhetoric served only to provide him with eloquent cover for political careerism (cf. Siegel 1966: 25; Najemy 2000). Irrespective of their author's intentions, the speeches testify to the potential of classical humanist rhetoric for the effective and influential expression of a republican ideology with liberty, justice, and equality, in conjunction with imperial power, at its core (Pocock 2003: 59–60, 550; Skinner 1978: 1: 103).

Bruni's *Laudatio* and *Oratio* also exemplify the Ciceronian character of "civic humanist" rhetoric by illustrating the importance of public speech as a medium for political virtue. This is best revealed, however, by Bruni's exertions in another epideictic form, the *Historiae Florentini populi* (written between 1415/16 and 1442 but not published until 1476). Here he shows how, in the intrinsically conflictual politics of the republic, driven by "an ancient, even primeval struggle between the nobility and the common people" (Bruni [1476] 2001–7: 1: 349), public rhetoric has a crucially ameliorative role. Predictably in a work modeled on Livy, momentous decisions are debated by means of deliberative speeches addressed to meetings, councils, and informal gatherings of the citizen body. When Bruni signals approval, they typically have classical tripartite structures (*exordium-narratio-peroratio*) and are delivered by patriotic citizens, such as Teddhiao d'Aldebrando Adomari or Giano della Bella, who embody prudence, eloquence, and *auctoritas*: the element of rhetorical *ēthos* identified by Quintilian as essential to deliberative persuasion (1: 149–59, 361–71, 2: 487–503, 3: 83–91, 243–51; Quintilian, *Institutio oratoria* 1.6.1–2, 3.8.36). Bruni also underlines the agonistic character of Florentine civic rhetoric by presenting pairs of opposed *orationes*, marking public speech as a medium for the controlled expression and playing out of factional conflict (1: 261–77, 2: 61–9, 489–507).

Bruni's history, however, suggests that a flourishing republic requires the careful management of civic rhetoric. For Bruni, good government is dependent upon prudent counsel, which, we are told by an unidentified elderly citizen addressing the Florentine priorate in 1351, "requires . . . the widest consultation and a careful deliberation on the part of many persons," since "it is not honorable for a few to take decisions which affect many, nor is it safe for the decision-makers" (Bruni [1476] 2001–7: 2: 65). For such consultation to be effective, we are told by another speaker "of old-fashioned severity," there must be "freedom in giving counsel" to enable citizens to speak their mind (2: 325; cf. 1: 179). But history also teaches that such liberty should be kept within the bounds of moderation. If public speech is unrestrained, prudent counsel can be shouted down, and deliberation becomes reckless. When this happened with the revolt of the Ciompi in 1378, Bruni notes, it was only the persuasive speech of the virtuous standard-bearer, Michele di Lando, that restrained the mob "by advice, exhortation, and chastisement" (1: 159, 3: 9–11).

The necessity of tempering political liberty and freedom of speech with moderation and prudence is expressed most powerfully in Bruni's report of the oration given by Rinaldo Gianfigliazzi in the Palazzo Vecchio in 1399. Acknowledging the wisdom of the priors in consulting the citizen body about the imminent threat of Milan, Gianfigliazzi nevertheless criticizes unfettered freedom of speech and popular power and, in terms that anticipate later theories of "reason of state," counterpoises the utility of closed oligarchy in times of crisis. While traditional republican procedures of conciliar deliberation and wide consultation are cumbersome and expose wise counsellors to the risk of popular calumny, he warns, Florence's tyrannical enemy "does not wait upon the decree of the mob or the deliberations of the people" and is likely to strike first "while we are still pondering remedies." For Gianfigliazzi, the republic should rein in the "excessive license" of calumnious speech and appoint "vigilant persons in the state who have the power to act without being compelled to refer every single thing to the multitude and wait upon their decree," since "state affairs generally require swiftness and secrecy, things which are very much at odds with mass decision-making" ([1476] 2001–7: 3: 241–51). Ultimately, Bruni implies, restrictions upon traditional political and rhetorical freedom will be necessary to preserve the moderate liberty and prudential statesmanship vital to the continued existence of the Florentine state. In this history, the flourishing republic depends upon a series of delicate balancing acts that enable a number of potentially conflicting elements to coexist: between popular liberty and virtuous aristocratic leadership, freedom of speech and social dignity, prudential deliberation and swift decision-making, and consultation and secrecy.

The importance of the classical conception of civic rhetoric in Florentine republicanism is also attested by its most famous document, Niccolò Machiavelli's *Discorsi sopra la prima deca di Tito Livio* (completed in 1518/19 and published in 1531). For Machiavelli the history of the Roman Republic demonstrates the indispensability of public speech and rhetorical eloquence to the good of a state characterized by popular liberty and participation. As the behavior of the Roman plebs in Livy's *Ab urbe condita* illustrates, Machiavelli claims, the maintenance of social order and preservation of freedom require outlets for popular ambitions, either through deliberation in assemblies or informal protest and resistance (Machiavelli [1531] 1983: 114). Equally importantly, the civic eloquence that enables a wise and virtuous orator of the Ciceronian kind to persuade an assembled multitude is a crucial tool for mitigating the dangers of popular power. While Machiavelli maintains a positive valuation of the role of the *popolo* in upholding the common good because of their intrinsic interest in upholding freedom, he admits that their opinions are fallible. But a remedy exists: "The public platform on which some man of standing can get up, appeal to the crowd, and show that it is mistaken" (115). Although, as Cicero states, the populace is ignorant, it is also "capable of grasping the truth and readily yields when a man, worthy of confidence, lays the truth before it" (115).

For Machiavelli, the good judgment and persuadability of the populace give republics advantages over principates. When speakers of "equal skill" use deliberative rhetoric in the popular assemblies of republics, "very rarely does one find the populace failing to adopt the better view" (Machiavelli [1531] 1983: 255), and many examples from Roman history show that positive outcomes result when popular participation is combined with prudent and eloquent leadership. Princes, however, are notoriously subject to strong passions and easily persuaded to err. Even "a licentious and turbulent populace" can be "returned to the good path" (233–4) by a prudent orator, but "there is no one to talk to a bad prince, nor is there any remedy but the sword" (256). In fact, freedom of speech is itself partly responsible for the misguided blame of popular republics, since "of the populace anyone may speak ill without fear and openly," whereas "of princes people speak with the utmost trepidation and the utmost reserve" (257). In principates, political rhetoric is circumscribed by the coercive necessities of monarchical power, but republics function through the medium of public speech, which, when properly institutionalized, channels the sagacity of the citizen body and enables the state to respond effectively to the contingencies of political life.

In this republican vision, then, the common good is most reliably attained when citizens are able to discuss their interests freely and issue judgments in a public forum (Machiavelli [1531] 1983: 124–31); but Machiavelli was far from advocating modern "deliberative democracy" (Fontana et al. 2004). Social conflict, deception, and violence intertwine with formal, reasoned discussion in Machiavellian politics (113–5, 131–4, 141, 229, 526–7). Moreover the Ciceronian model of civic rhetoric is intrinsically fragile: although the people have good judgment in particulars, they are susceptible to demagoguery and manipulation by speakers with private ambition, easily deceived by "a false appearance of good," and prone to rashness and imprudence in times of crisis. If they lack trust in a leader capable of correcting their mistakes, Machiavelli warns, "it spells ruin, and necessarily so" (126, 197–8, 200–4, 238–42, 250–1). Most importantly, the utility of the institutions that enabled the Roman citizenry to propose and deliberate over laws was radically dependent upon their collective *virtù*. Permitting every citizen to speak for or against legislative proposals "was good so long as the citizens were good," he observes, but not when they had become "perverse," since then "only the powerful proposed laws, and this for the sake, not of their common liberties, but to augment their own power" (162). If the populace is corrupt, they will prove intractable even to a prudent and eloquent orator; then, the only solution is for the leader to resort to the "extraordinary" Machiavellian methods of "force and an appeal to arms," and in effect to transform the republic into a principate, which he can "dispose" according to his own designs (160–4).

RHETORIC AND PRINCELY GOVERNMENT

Since Roman antiquity it has been claimed that useful political rhetoric—the deliberative kind—thrives in the participatory and contentious environment found in republics, but withers away under monarchy, which is hospitable only to epideictic (Cicero, *Orator* 11.37, 13.42, *De oratore* 2.84.341; Tacitus, *Dialogus de oratoribus* 36, 44), a view that was often echoed by early modern commentators (Du Perron [1579] 2003: 135–6; Mulcaster 1581: 242–3; Montaigne [1595] 2007: 324–5). Humanist pedagogy, however, was designed for monarchies as well as republics. From Petrarch onward, humanists presented themselves as advisors to princes, composing letters, manuals of government and princely education, dialogues and treatises on monarchy, and encomia, all routinely permeated by classical rhetorical strategies tailored to the requirements of courtly discourse. Some, such as Jacques Amyot in his *Projet de l'éloquence royale* (written in the 1570s), encouraged princes to cultivate eloquence as the basis of virtuous and effective governance. The most common vehicle used in humanistic political thought about monarchy, however, was the medieval *speculum principis* genre, which humanists filled with deliberative *topoi*—the honorable, the expedient, and the necessary—to portray the virtuous prince and to discuss the role of rhetoric in prudent and free counsel.

Although formally laudatory, humanistic "mirror of princes" texts employed deliberative methods by exhorting their addressees to particular virtues or honorable courses of action, and by delivering implicit criticisms (cf. Aristotle, *Rhetoric* 1.9.36). This rhetorical strategy had been established by Seneca's *De clementia* (1.1.1–4), which describes the text as a mirror showing the prince how he is and ought to be (Stacey 2007: 23–72). In Petrarch's encomiastic letter of 1373 to Francesco da Carrara, the humanist makes it clear that his purpose is "to spur the prince on to greatness with the very stimulus of praise" (1978: 36); conversely, as Coluccio Salutati noted, if such praise is false, "it warns him that he has not been praised but rather told what he should do" ([1406] 1951: 68). According to Desiderius Erasmus, in the preface to his panegyric of Archduke Philip of Austria, the ostensible flattery of this literary form not only works as a "cover" for the exhortation and admonition of the prince but also reinforces obedience to monarchical rule by encouraging his subjects to hold him in "exceedingly high regard" ([1516] 1997: 114–6).

Humanist works on monarchy also exalted the rhetorical figure of freedom of speech (Colclough 2007), presenting it as the precondition for the frank, wise, and constant counsel required by rulers, and warning that its absence would generate one of the principal dangers to virtuous governance, namely flattery (Petrarch 1978: 36; Erasmus [1516] 1997: 54–8; Elyot 1531: 107v–8r, 154v–8v; Bacon [1624] 1985: 63–8). Some humanists, however, came to doubt the practicability and desirability of this ideal, and by extension their roles as advisors in princely courts. In *Utopia*, Thomas More dramatized the conflict between the civic duty of offering prudent and decorous counsel and the evident futility of dispensing wisdom in corrupt courts full of flatterers ([1516] 1989: 28–38, 110–1). The most striking departure from the traditional understanding of counsel, however, was made by Machiavelli in *Il Principe*. Warning his prince that "if anyone may speak frankly to you, respect for you will soon disappear," Machiavelli demarcates strictly between the powerful and active prince and his passive counsellors, who are excluded from anything resembling free deliberation. The prince "should never lack advice, but should have it when he wants it, not when others want to give it" (Machiavelli [1513] 1988: 81–2; Stacey 2007: 302–3).

RHETORIC AND ABSOLUTIST MONARCHY

From the later sixteenth century onward, the traditional humanistic understanding of monarchy, which drew heavily upon classical ethics to elaborate the duties and virtues of the ruler, was gradually being displaced by absolutist theory granting the monarch unquestionable power and preeminence. In part this was due to the spread of religious-political disorder across post-Reformation Europe, which prompted political theorists to reassess the relationship between sovereign power and its subjects drastically in favor of the former. The study of rhetoric remained central to learned humanistic culture, but the turn toward absolutism entailed a reconsideration of the political status of rhetoric, best seen in the works of two of the most influential theorists of absolutism: Jean Bodin and Thomas Hobbes.

For Bodin, writing *Les six livres de la république* in the midst of the French civil wars, the civic rhetoric extolled by previous generations of humanists had become a liability. "There is nothing which has greater power over souls," he observes, "than the art of speaking well" (Bodin 1576: 509; trans. mine); but whatever the potential benefits of rhetoric, it has commonly caused factionalism and sedition—especially when orators are granted excessive freedom of speech. Particularly treacherous, for Bodin, are the preachers "of our age," who have fomented spiritual disputes and encouraged rebellion "under the pretence of religion" (514–5). The history of political rhetoric, both ancient and modern, teaches that "a knife in the hand of a madman is scarcely as dangerous as eloquence in the mouth of a rebellious orator" (Bodin 1594: 764–5), above all when religious principles are in question.

For Bodin, the potentially destabilizing power of political rhetoric should be strictly bounded, and not be permitted to encroach upon the formal preeminence of absolute sovereignty. Although eloquence is useful in dealing with the ignorant in democratic assemblies, it has no place in the senates or councils of aristocracies or monarchies, where discourse should be truthful and unadorned by rhetorical manipulation (Bodin 1576: 300; cf. 514, 692). There is an unbridgeable division between advisory counsel and the command of the sovereign will; the freedom to be maintained is that of the ruler to ignore advice, which may be useful but is not indispensable (136–8, 284–5, 694; cf. Lipsius [1589] 2004: 430–3). The discourse that really counts in the Bodinian political universe—where "the principal mark of sovereign majesty and absolute power is the right to impose laws generally on all subjects without their consent"—communicates the will of the sovereign to his subjects, without interference or reply (140, 295).

The most vigorous early modern critique of the humanistic conception of civic rhetoric is found in the works of Thomas Hobbes. Hobbes was a humanistically trained rhetorical stylist, and translated Aristotle's *Rhetoric* into Latin and English, yet throughout his oeuvre eloquence is closely associated with the subversive tendencies inherent in popular government and republican ideology. This was partly due to his close engagement with Thucydides, whose meditations on the destabilizing effects of democratic rhetoric appeared directly applicable to Civil War England; Hobbes would always be in agreement with the Greek historian about democracy, a form of government disparaged in *The Elements of Law* as "no more than an aristocracy of orators, interrupted sometimes with the temporary monarchy of one orator" ([1650] 1994: 120). As he argues in *De cive*, deliberation in democracies is inherently flawed, exposing the *arcana imperii* to enemies and foreigners, permitting the trumping of prudential reasoning by eloquence, preferring the opinions of the many to the wisdom of the few, and provoking factional quarrels (Hobbes [1647] 1998: 119–20, 122–5). It is also, Hobbes notes in *Leviathan*, intrinsically seditious, since popular assemblies encourage those "whose interests are contrary to that of the Publique" to persuade others to adopt their views with passionate eloquence, effectively "setting ... the Common-wealth on fire, under pretence of Counselling it" (Hobbes [1651] 2012: 2: 408–10). In the same work, Hobbes extends his critique to the counsel given to monarchs, from which rhetoric must be expunged: in contrast to "the rigour of true reasoning" (2: 288), deceptive or emotionally manipulative rhetorical argumentation indicates that the counsellor "seeks his own benefit" and "not [that] of him that asketh it" (2: 398–402). Echoing Machiavelli and Bodin, he urges the ruler to receive prudent, unadorned counsel "of whom, when, and where he pleaseth," and "with as much secrecy, as he will" (2: 546–8).

What sets Hobbes's criticisms of political rhetoric apart from those of his predecessors is their explicit psychological and epistemological underpinning. For Hobbes, rhetorical speech does not make man better, but gives him "greater possibilities," particularly deceptions that short-circuit the process of understanding ([1658] 1972: 39–40). Drawing on classical conceptions of logic and rhetoric, he observes that while the former creates rational civil science, the end of the latter is persuasion, not truth; it is a product of the imagination, not reasoned judgment or scientific knowledge, employs metaphorical rather than correct speech, and is based upon the fluctuating terrain of "received opinions" rather than the solid ground of "true principles." The Ciceronian conjunction of wisdom and eloquence extolled by generations of humanists therefore has a dangerously oxymoronic tendency (Hobbes [1647] 1998: 9, 55–6, 139–40, [1650] 1994: 61–2, [1651] 2012: 2: 62, 70, 3: 1132; Skinner 2002: 3: 72–9, 87–141). In Hobbes's *De cive*, which mobilizes civil science in support of the monarchy against the parliamentary republicans, rhetoric is expelled from practical political deliberation and moral philosophy as a whole ([1647] 1998: 71–2, 123).

Hobbes admits in *Leviathan* that some form of eloquence will be required for the political implementation of rational arguments. But it must be shaped "by Education, and Discipline" to harmonize with reason and ensure that it is used "for adorning and preferring of Truth" rather than "Errour" (Hobbes [1651] 2012: 3: 1132–3). For Hobbes, England's troubles have been stirred up by "seditious Presbyterian Ministers, and ambitious ignorant Orators," who have been humanistically indoctrinated in the universities ("for the sake of Greek and Latin philosophy and eloquence") with rebellious opinions about democracy and religion. They have then disseminated these by rhetorical sophistry, producing a subversive, anti-Ciceronian union of "*stupidity* and *eloquence*" (Hobbes [1647] 1998: 138, 140–1, 146–7, [1650] 1994: 176–7, [1679] 2009: 252; Serjeantson

2006). His solution is a radical "Reformation of the Universities," which by teaching the "true Polyticks" of demonstrative civil science would lead "well principled Preachers" to inculcate the principles of duty and obedience to the civil law in the masses—thereby instantiating the rhetorical adornment of truth rather than error (Hobbes [1651] 2012: 3: 1097, 1140, [1679] 2009: 182–3, 199).

EPILOGUE

Although Hobbes did not see the precepts of *Leviathan* taught in the universities, as he had hoped ([1651] 2012: 3: 1140), on the larger issues he eventually got his way. As the influence of Renaissance humanism on learned European culture declined in the course of the seventeenth and eighteenth centuries, so too did the political significance of classical rhetoric. Debates about political deliberation and public speech would be central to the development of modern republicanism, but—with a few exceptions, as in the works of Jean-Jacques Rousseau—they became increasingly detached from the humanist vision of civic rhetoric; the model of absolutist monarchy, likewise, gave little scope for the exercise of eloquence in politics. In the dominant strains of political thought in the Enlightenment—in the works of Baruch Spinoza, Montesquieu, David Hume, Adam Smith, and their followers—the rhetoric of antiquity belonged to an era whose direct relevance was being rapidly undermined by the advent of modern commerce, political economy, and representative government. The modern study of politics was to be grounded in natural law and the newly formulated axioms of civil, moral, and economic science, rather than the study of Greek and Roman texts. Both classical rhetoric and politics were not to be imitated but evaluated, historically and critically. While not yet completely sidelined, they were on their way to becoming matters of antiquarian interest.

REFERENCES

Agricola, Rudolph. (1515) 1539. *De inventione dialectica libri tres.* Cologne: Johannes Gymnicus.
Bacon, Francis. (1624) 1985. *The Essayes or Counsels, Civill and Morall.* Edited by Michael Kiernan. Oxford: Clarendon.
Baron, Hans. 1966. *The Crisis of the Early Italian Renaissance.* Princeton, NJ: Princeton University Press.
Bodin, Jean. 1576. *Les six livres de la république.* Paris: Jacques du Puys.
Bodin, Jean. 1594. *De republica libri sex.* 3rd ed. Frankfurt: Peter Fischer.
Bruni, Leonardo. (1403/4) 1978. "Panegyric to the City of Florence." In *The Earthly Republic,* edited and translated by Benjamin Kohl and Ronald Witt, 135–175. Philadelphia: University of Pennsylvania Press.
Bruni, Leonardo. (1428) 1987. "Oration for the Funeral of Nanni Strozzi." In *The Humanism of Leonardo Bruni,* edited and translated by Gordon Griffiths, James Hankins, and David Thompson, 121–127. Binghamton, NY: Medieval and Renaissance Texts and Studies.

Bruni, Leonardo. (1476) 2001–2007. *History of the Florentine People*. Edited and translated by James Hankins. 3 vols. Cambridge, MA: Harvard University Press.

Colclough, David. 2007. *Freedom of Speech in Early Stuart England*. Cambridge: Cambridge University Press.

Du Perron, Jacques Davy. (1579) 2003. "Traité de l'éloquence." In *L'art de parler. Anthologie des manuels d'éloquence*, edited by Philippe-J. Salazar, 134–145. Paris: Klincksieck.

Elyot, Thomas. 1531. *The boke named the gouvernour*. London: Thomas Marsh.

Erasmus, Desiderius. (1516) 1997. *The Education of a Christian Prince, with the Panegyric for Archduke Philip of Austria*. Edited and translated by Lisa Jardine. Cambridge: Cambridge University Press.

Fontana, Benedetto, Cary J. Nederman, and Gary Remer, eds. 2004. *Talking Democracy: Historical Perspectives on Rhetoric and Democracy*. University Park: Pennsylvania State University Press.

Hankins, James. 1995. "The 'Baron Thesis' after Forty Years and Some Recent Studies of Leonardo Bruni." *Journal of the History of Ideas* 56 no. 2: 309–338.

Hankins, James. 2000. "Rhetoric, History, and Ideology: The Civic Panegyrics of Leonardo Bruni." In *Renaissance Civic Humanism*, edited by James Hankins, 143–178. Cambridge: Cambridge University Press.

Hobbes, Thomas. (1658) 1972. *Man and Citizen*. Translated by C. T. Wood, T. S. K. Scott-Craig, and B. Gert. New York: Doubleday Anchor.

Hobbes, Thomas. (1650) 1994. *The Elements of Law, Natural and Politic*. Edited by J. C. A. Gaskin. Oxford: Oxford University Press.

Hobbes, Thomas. (1647) 1998. *On the Citizen*. Edited and translated by Richard Tuck and Michael Silverthorne. Cambridge: Cambridge University Press.

Hobbes, Thomas. (1679) 2009. *Behemoth*. Edited by Paul Seaward. 2 vols. Oxford: Clarendon Press.

Hobbes, Thomas. (1651) 2012. *Leviathan*. Edited and translated by Noel Malcolm. 3 vols. Oxford: Clarendon Press.

Kristeller, Paul Oskar. 1961. *Renaissance Thought*. New York: Harper & Row.

Kristeller, Paul Oskar. 1979. *Renaissance Thought and its Sources*. New York: Columbia University Press.

Lipsius, Justus. (1589) 2004. Politica—*Six Books of Politics or Political Instruction*. Edited and translated by Jan Waszink. Assen: Royal Van Gorcum.

Machiavelli, Niccolò. (1531) 1983. *The Discourses*. Edited by Bernard Crick, translated by Leslie J. Walker and Brian Richardson. Harmondsworth: Penguin.

Machiavelli, Niccolò. (1513) 1988. *The Prince*. Edited by Quentin Skinner, translated by Russell Price. Cambridge: Cambridge University Press.

Melanchthon, Philipp. 1519. *De Rhetorica libri tres*. Basel: Johannes Froben.

Monfasani, John. 1976. *George of Trebizond: A Biography and a Study of his Rhetoric and Logic*. New York: Columbia University Press.

Montaigne, Michel de. (1595) 2007. *Les essais*. Edited by Jean Balsamo, Michel Magnien, and Catherine Magnien-Simonin. Paris: Gallimard.

More, Thomas. (1516) 1989. *Utopia*. Edited and translated by George M. Logan and Robert M. Adams. Cambridge: Cambridge University Press.

Mulcaster, Richard. 1581. *Positions wherein those primitive circumstances be examined, which are necessarie for the training up of children*. London: Thomas Vautrollier.

Najemy, John. 2000. "Civic Humanism and Florentine Politics." In *Renaissance Civic Humanism*, edited by James Hankins, 75–104. Cambridge: Cambridge University Press.

Petrarch, Francesco. 1978. "How a Ruler Ought to Govern His State." In *The Earthly Republic*, edited by B. G. Kohl and R. G. Witt, 35–78. Translated by B. G. Kohl. Philadelphia: University of Pennsylvania Press.

Pocock, J. G. A. 2003. *The Machiavellian Moment: Florentine Political Thought and the Atlantic Republican Tradition*. 2nd ed. Princeton, NJ: Princeton University Press.

Rainolde, Richard. 1563. *The Foundacion of Rhetorike*. London: John Kingston.

Salutati, Coluccio. (1406) 1951. *De laboribus Herculis*. Edited by B. L. Ullman. Zurich: Artemis-Verlag.

Serjeantson, Richard. 2006. "Hobbes, the Universities, and the History of Philosophy." In *The Philosopher in Early Modern Europe*, edited by Conal Condren, Stephen Gaukroger, and Ian Hunter, 113–139. Cambridge: Cambridge University Press.

Siegel, Jerrold E. 1966. "'Civic Humanism' or Ciceronian Rhetoric? The Culture of Petrarch and Bruni." *Past & Present* 34: 3–48.

Skinner, Quentin. 1978. *The Foundations of Modern Political Thought*. 2 vols. Cambridge: Cambridge University Press.

Skinner, Quentin. 2002. *Visions of Politics*. 3 vols. Cambridge: Cambridge University Press.

Stacey, Peter. 2007. *Roman Monarchy and the Renaissance Prince*. Cambridge: Cambridge University Press.

Trebizond, George of. (1433/4) 1538. *Rhetoricorum libri quinque*. Paris: Christian Wechel.

Vergerio, Pierpaolo. (1402) 2002. "The Character and Studies Befitting a Free-Born Youth." In *Humanist Educational Treatises*, edited and translated by Craig Kallendorf, 2–91. Cambridge, MA: Harvard University Press.

CHAPTER 39

RHETORIC AND GENDER IN BRITISH LITERATURE

LYNN ENTERLINE

RHETORIC, GENDER, POWER

ROLAND Barthes once observed that Augustan Rome saw a wholesale "conversion" of rhetoric into "poetic technique" (1970: 174). One might say much the same about early modern British poetry and drama—but with several differences that have important implications for the period's representations and experiences of gender. This chapter assesses the complex intermingling of rhetorical theory, educational training in Latin grammar and rhetoric, and literary representations that designate bodies, texts, genres, figures, and tropes as "male," "female," and/or "epicene." A tripartite rather than binary distinction for analyzing gender is appropriate to sixteenth-century British literature and culture for several reasons: it was a period marked by the highly self-conscious theatrical practice of transvestite performance on the commercial stage as well as in schools, and it was marked by labile fantasies stemming from Galen's still influential "one sex" model of human anatomy. But most important for my purposes here: from the point of view of humanist Latinity, which laid the groundwork for the explosion of rhetorical practice, theory, and experimentation in the period, English was not an inflected language. This meant that to all the authors examined in this essay, "English nouns are nearly all *de facto* epicene terms, of a common gender that cannot be distinguished as either male or female" (Mann 2012: 226).[1] In tracing the spectrum of gendered possibilities that attend rhetorical tropes and transactions in these texts, I keep two kinds of analysis in mind: the first derives from rhetoric's crucial place in psychoanalytic theory, the second from studies tracing the precise, historical nuance of Renaissance rhetorical practices (see Chaitin, ch. 54; Mack, ch. 33). Rarely thought comfortable allies, these two approaches nevertheless have the potential to produce a powerful dialectic for inquiry and analysis: the first allows one to pose feminist and queer questions about gender, desire, and power with respect to historically specific rhetorical habits; the second illuminates what is particularly "early modern" about the many fantasies about gendered bodies that permeate the period's literary experiments with ancient rhetoric.

Let me briefly sketch what I see as the critical potential of this combined approach for feminist and queer critique of rhetoric, gender, and literature in the period. Intrigued by Jacques Lacan's influential yet controversial proposition that much of Western culture is organized around a "phallic" symbolic order—that an asymmetrical distribution of power marked by pervasive fantasies about sexual difference inflects not only behavior but also modes of representation in cultures organized around father power—literary critics in the 1980s and 1990s began to consider what his speculations about such a hierarchical ordering of language and bodies might reveal about the cultural production of masculinity and femininity in early modern poetry and drama. And in so doing, many detected something like the failure of the "paternal function" in canonical texts such as *Hamlet*, *The Duchess of Malfi*, and *The Faerie Queene*. Moreover, this work resonated with Lacan's claim that a binary male/female distinction is a crude, reductive imposition of difference on speaking subjects—the "iron brand" of the "Law of the Father," which he delineates in its cost for individual subjects as well as in its failure to organize the polymorphous, labile field of possible dispositions and desires (Rose 1985; Garber 1987; Gregerson 1991; Enterline 1995; Halpern 1997).

The second mode of analysis guiding my account leans on Harry Berger Jr.'s suggestion that we modify—or better yet particularize—Lacan's abstract theory of "the symbolic" by shifting focus to investigate the historically specific "language games," "readymade community practices," and particular "social texts" (1997: 320–5) within which early modern poets, as well as their lyric personae and dramatic characters, represent themselves to themselves or to one another. The community practices and language games at issue in this chapter are those instilled by Latin training in humanist grammar schools, the institution within which so many of the period's male poets, dramatists, and lawyers acquired the rhetorical skill and knowledge of classical literature prominently on display in their vernacular texts (see Mack, ch. 33). If we bring together these different perspectives on the formative ideological power of symbolic practices, we see that the frequently gendered, at times highly eroticized and/or violent stories associated with rhetorical forms in early modern poetry and drama derive much of their aesthetic and emotional force precisely when drawing attention to the author's, or the text's, relationship to the eloquence of the classical past. At the same time, the rhetorically self-conscious texts discussed here draw on dominant notions of gender only to highlight significant contradictions within ostensibly hegemonic categories of identity and desire. That is, these literary texts shed light not merely on received hierarchies of gender embedded in the declared goals of early modern school training. Rather, they often put the primacy—indeed, the moral force and social efficacy—of father power in question. Indeed, their metarhetorical preoccupations frequently upend conventional assumptions about what counts as "male" or "female." Instead, they pose a restless question—"What is the difference?"—or suggest other, epicene possibilities. That is, like Lacan they suggest that a male/female binary distinction is, in fact, a reductive social script one must explain, historicize, and interpret, not assume.

William Shakespeare's *The Taming of the Shrew* and John Webster's *The Duchess of Malfi* share a commonplace, bawdy pun on "tale" and "tail" that captures the salience of Lacan's point with respect to early modern British culture, because it gives a sense of how thoroughly an idea of phallic supremacy informed early modern notions of rhetorical power and also how easily that supremacy can be called into question. In two famous dialogues—one comic, the other tragic—a gendered struggle for verbal, social, and sexual control brings the motivating principle of rhetorical training into focus: the orator's ability to persuade, or as Quintilian and Cicero would put it, to "move" (*movere*) an audience. Each stages a scene of persuasion in which a male speaker tries to win over a "female" auditor. In the first case, the goal is to persuade a woman to marry; in the second, not to marry. This means that both playwrights were working with a well-known topic for debate—persuading a young man to marry—only to change the audience's gender. It was a topic that, thanks to Desiderius Erasmus, became standard for Latin schoolboys who were learning to invent *in utramque partem* arguments (*uxor est ducenda, uxor non est ducenda* [Brinsley 1612: 184–5]).

In *The Taming of the Shrew* (1590–2), a comedy well known for pitting "the language of women" against "the order and authority of man" (Fineman 1985: 139) and for directly taking up the question of the efficacy of contemporary Latin education, the presumption of masculine verbal power—which the play repeatedly characterizes as a bid for "mastery"—quickly turns to farce. When Petruchio first appears on stage, a slapstick quarrel over his command, "knock me here," turns into a brawl between a "master" and the servant who either obtusely or deliberately misunderstands him. Later, a similar (rhetorically and comically resonant) equivalence between verbal power and physical force erupts again when Petruchio begins to woo Katharine. Their extended verbal scuffle begins with a familiar rhetorical term: *movere*. Petruchio says he has been "moved" to "woo thee for my wife"; Katharine counters, "Let him who mov'd you hither / Remove you hence" (Shakespeare, *The Taming of the Shrew* 2.1.194–6).[2] Their witty, punning dialogue reaches a climax with a lewd joke followed by a slap:

PETRUCHIO.   Come, come, you wasp, i'faith, you are too angry.
KATHARINE.   If I be waspish, best beware my sting.
PETRUCHIO.   My remedy is then to pluck it out.
KATHARINE.   Ay, if the fool could find it where it lies.
PETRUCHIO.   Who knows not where a wasp does wear his sting? In his tail.
KATHARINE.   In his tongue.
PETRUCHIO.   Whose tongue?
KATHARINE.   Yours, if you talk of tales, and so farewell.
PETRUCHIO.   What, with my tongue in your tail? Nay, come again, good Kate. I am a
    gentleman.
KATHARINE.   That I'll try. *She strikes him.* (2.1.209–19)

One might think that the slide from verbal to physical force signifies that Petruchio has won the day. But as I have argued elsewhere (Enterline 2012), much of the rest of the play

pulls against any such confidence in absolute rhetorical mastery. In this scene, the oppo-
sitional banter resumes almost immediately, and in the ensuing acts Petruchio follows
Katharine's example of the slap, using ever more vigorous, physically coercive measures
to win what many interpret as mere politic capitulation on her part—a capitulation that
is, of course, marked by Petruchio's claim to control her tongue (Crocker 2003; Mitchell
2009). On one level, the pun on tail/tale proposes a bodily figuration similar to the one
Lacan later theorizes as the Western tendency to represent language's slippage as phallic: Petruchio's quip makes the male member a figure for his victorious "tongue" as well
as for the "differential articulation" (Weber 2008: 62) that makes a sign system (and the
joke) possible. And yet their verbal squabble ends with his tongue in Katharine's "tail/
tale," which means that a female "part" is also at issue in the struggle for verbal and thus
social power. As tongues, tails, and tales shift from line to line, one is prompted to ask:
Which is hers, which his? In the hands of an author so very aware that his proper name,
"Will," signifies both male and female genitals,[3] their dialogue poses epicene possibilities, suggesting that an either–or question is hardly relevant. Perhaps the least one can
say is that the disagreement over "whose tongue" and whose "tale" is in question, or
dominant, puts a waspish "sting" not only in his words but in hers as well.

   The Duchess of Malfi (1612–3) is just as marked by its author's rhetorical education as
Shakespeare's comedy, not merely because of its classical allusions (Narcissus and Echo)
but also because of its continued recourse to moralizing *sententiae*, an important exercise in school rhetorical manuals and training.[4] For his part, Webster uses the tail/tale
pun to conflate a speaker's tongue, a story, and the penis, but he turns it into a far more
menacing display of "male" power. This time the phallus is blunt and visible—a father's
sword brandished onstage, a gesture that none too subtly proclaims that the paternal
member/law guarantees that male words of persuasion are (or should be) equivalent to a
weapon. Just before Ferdinand draws his father's sword, the Duchess's two brothers have
been cooperating to dissuade their widowed sister from marrying again, to little effect.
When they are both gone, the Duchess's only response is to ask, "Shall this move me?"
(Webster, *The Duchess of Malfi* 1.2.260)—a rhetorical question that signals the brothers'
aspiration for verbal efficacy and her resistance to it. Immediately following their joint
harangue, the cardinal leaves his sister and Ferdinand alone, at which point she wryly
comments: "I think this speech between you both was studied, it came so roundly off"
(1.2.249–50). He takes up the challenge to his *ex tempore* skill by making a threat:

> You are my sister,
> This was my father's poniard; do you see,
> I'll'd loath to see't look rusty, 'cause 'twas his. (1.2.249–51)

Charging her to abandon morally suspect evening entertainments, Ferdinand then
launches into his own version of Petruchio's dirty joke on the phallic power of discourse:

> FERDINAND.   And women like that part, which, like the lamprey,
> Hath nev'r a bone in't.

DUCHESS.   Fie, sir!
FERDINAND.   Nay,
I mean the tongue; variety of courtship;
What cannot a neat knave with a smooth tale
Make a woman believe? Farewell, lusty widow. (1.2.255–9)

Uttered under the sign of the paternal "poniard," whose power he claims as his own to regulate his sister's sexual conduct, the joke asserts Ferdinand's right to lay down family law. And it also allows him to compare discourse ("tale" and "tongue") to "that part" which "hath nev'r a bone in't"—a pun that, in being understood ("Fie, sir!"), marks his sister as a woman with sexual knowledge while insinuating that male tongues effectively conquer women.

Ferdinand may think he has had the last word, but the play proves otherwise. Apart from his sister's obdurate refusal to be "moved" (by either his "tale" or his "tail"), there are forms of resistance beyond her refusal to listen that defy his proposed equation between the "tongue" and a father's/son's "poniard." Ferdinand usurps their father's place, but his mode of declaring the paternal privilege of monitoring and controlling the family's sexual lives undermines the law even as he invokes it. As critics have been quick to note, Ferdinand's obsession with his "lusty" sister's sexuality—which even the cardinal calls a "wild tempest" and "intemperate noise" that flies "beyond the bounds of reason" (Webster, *The Duchess of Malfi* 2.5.47–54)—draws attention to the very desire that paternal law is supposed to make unspeakable. A brother's threat to polish the rust off his father's sword by using it on his sister eerily collapses the idea of paternal with fraternal incest. The law's failure is quickly followed by a series of images for other liminal predicaments that eradicate the hierarchical difference between male and female on which Ferdinand insists. Indeed, the tragedy abounds in neither–nor/both–and figures for boundary crossing: between the living and the dead (an echo "from the grave" that is either an omen or a mere "dead thing"), inside and outside ("a wolfe's skinne is hairy on the outside, mine on the inside"), self and other (the "familiar," the twin, the shadow, the eclipse), human and animal (the lycanthrope), human and vegetable (the mandrake), and male and female ("Excellent Hyena!" [2.5.39]; "Damn her; that body of hers / While that *my* blood ran pure in it, was more worth / Than that which thou wouldst comfort, call'd a soul" [4.1.119–20]).

MASCULINITY AND THE INSTITUTIONS OF RHETORICAL TRAINING

If we consider these two scenes of failed persuasion in light of the educational institution that promoted the idea of rhetoric's social power in order to make it the exclusive provenance of "gentlemen," further problems arise. In a period struggling to define the terms of national identity—and doing so in part by staking out claims for vernacular eloquence—writers were forced to contend with the ingrained cultural assumption, further entrenched by humanist schooling, that the language of fathers was Latin, not English. The Latin grammar school was designed to intervene in the social reproduction of eloquent masculinity; accordingly, humanists promoted a culturally pervasive set of associations around the differences and relations between English, the "mother," and Latin, the "father," tongue. In the words of one Tudor poet articulating his position on the art of making English verses, good poetry will catch the "natural or most common usuall pronunciation" in meter: "So would I wishe you to frame all sentences *in their mother phrase* and proper *Idioma*" (Gascoigne 1907: 470; emphasis added). Liberally sprinkling other Latin terms and figures throughout his treatise (i.e., "eschew straunge words, or *obsoleta & inusitata*" and "*Quot homines, tot Sententiae*" [469]), George Gascoigne shifts to the father tongue to lend authority to the pronouncements he is making about the mother tongue whose eloquence he wants to promote and refine. Informing rhetorical texts and literary theory, this gendered, parental division of labor emerged in educational practice as well: the figure of the parent was widely used to characterize Latin schoolmasters themselves as much as their language. Following Quintilian, a *magister* was represented in school texts as a "parent," predominantly as a "father," to his surrogate schoolboy "sons" (see Enterline 2012).

The rapid publication of vernacular rhetorical manuals in the sixteenth century indicates the immense collective effort that went into defining vernacular forms of eloquence capable of rivaling classical models.[5] Some of the anxieties attending this effort become apparent when Barnabe Googe praises contemporary English verse. Sounding as defensive as confident, Googe, in his "Epistle Dedicatory" to *The Zodiake of Life by Marcellus Palingenius* (London, 1565), writes that English poetry "is nowe so plenteously enriched wyth a number of eloquent writers, that in my fansy it is little inferior to . . . the auncient Romaines." Fraught with complications, linguistic as well as cultural, the struggle to define vernacular eloquence on the model of, yet distinct from, the classical past had considerable impact on figurations of gender. Perhaps one of the most significant points of stress for English poets and dramatists arose from the humanist attempt to inculcate ancient "Romaine" stories at the expense of vernacular ones, to establish a distinction between elite and popular discourse—the latter often being dismissed as the language of "nurses" and "old wives' fairy rubbish." And yet, as several feminist critics point out, hybrid texts such as *A Midsummer Night's Dream* and *The Faerie Queene* remind us that the proposed distinctions between male/female and classical/vernacular did not entirely take root in the minds of all grammar school initiates (Lamb 2000; Wall 2002; Mann 2012). In addition to such mixed texts, an index of resistance to the wholesale distinction between elite Latin masculinity and effeminate vernacular fairy stories surfaces in the name Shakespeare gives to a school-aged boy in *The Winter's Tale*: Mamillius. Declined as masculine, his name is an epicene variant of the Latin noun for "breast," *mamilla*, which was included in almost all bilingual school dictionaries. An example of *enallage*, a figure of speech not easily replicated in English, the young boy's name is literate, witty, and foreboding. The noun signals Mamillius's close connection to his mother's body; the change of case, his difference; and the figure itself, the difficulty

of keeping that difference stable. And in his last appearance on stage, Mamillius's epicene name reminds us that the failure to distinguish father from mother tongue could be
maddening:

> Give me the boy. I am glad you did not nurse him.
> Though he does bear some signs of me, yet you
> Have too much blood in him. (Shakespeare, *The Winter's Tale* 2.1.56–8)

Leontes intervenes to take Mamillius away precisely when he is telling vernacular "tales"
to ladies, and, like a proud schoolmaster, his mother praises his verbal skill—saying he is
"powerful good" at narrating "stories of sprites and goblins"—before Leontes puts a stop
to the story and their "vulgar" "female" conversation (see Enterline 2012, ch. 5).

As the scenes examined so far suggest, exactly how the culturally and institutionally
loaded distinction between a father and a mother tongue signified for individual writers is by no means as predictable as one might assume. That is, while the school's curriculum, texts, and instructional practices became increasingly standardized across the
country over the sixteenth and seventeenth centuries, the poetic and dramatic productions of former schoolboys indicate that individual reactions to early Latin training, and
the social distinctions implicit in it, varied considerably. One must read their texts on a
case-by-case basis, assessing not only the specific situation in which that text was written but also the interaction between the educational practices that made it possible and
what its tropes, figures, and situation of address suggest about individual reactions to
early experiences with classical rhetoric. In other words, I take as axiomatic that rhetorical training is a significant site from which to examine the shifting parameters of gendered and embodied experience in early modern England. But I also take as axiomatic
that while institutional practice placed certain limits on the field of possible representations and fantasies, it was by no means narrowly or predictably deterministic: the rhetorically self-conscious representations of eloquence in early modern poetry and drama
are often unstable, soliciting careful attention to personal engagements and investments
as well as the rapidly shifting terrain of social distinction in an increasingly volatile historical period.

So far this chapter has surveyed a few of many moments in which rhetoric's translation
into literature encouraged epicene figures that defy easy categorization. As critics are
well aware, Ovid is the Roman author who figures most prominently in such moments
of gender trouble. Elizabethan authors show a decided taste for Ovid's stories—a taste
one could begin to explain as the result of the intersection between literary history and
the grammar school curriculum. The highly erotic nature of Ovid's poetry remained a
bone of contention, and some of his texts were banned from the schools (particularly
the *Ars amatoria*, though Christopher Marlowe found that the *Amores* could also provoke the censors). Still, the *Metamorphoses* held a prominent place alongside the *Aeneid*
in most fifth- and sixth-form reading, as did the *Heroides*, because masters revered Ovid
for his wit and style. But it is important to remember that these texts were written by a
rhetorically savvy Roman poet who trained as a lawyer and became famous for his own

skill in the art of declamation (see Hall, ch. 18; Pernot, ch. 20; Gunderson, ch. 21). As I discuss below, humanist masters, commentators, and writers of textbooks were highly attuned to Ovid's metarhetorical reflections. And modern critics are increasingly aware that these reflections carry in them both political possibilities (a Roman declaimer's sense of rhetoric's retreat from any true public engagement under the Principate) as well as gendered ones (Ovid repeatedly dramatizes what it means to inhabit a body that speaks in stories that are as much about violence as desire).

Indeed, the sheer number of violated bodies associated with rhetorical predicaments in Ovid's poem suggests that, however unsettling it may seem, phantasms of "the body in bits and pieces" became part of the cultural high ground humanists were so assiduously trying to cultivate—and by that route, part of the warp and woof of early modern masculinity. From revenge tragedy to the lyric "anatomy"—*Titus Andronicus*'s "handle not the theme, to talk of hands," Adonis's "wounded flank," the wax hand Ferdinand hands to his sister, the numerous allusions to Ovid's stories of Actaeon, Orpheus, Daphne, and Philomela, or the countless beloveds blazoned on stage and in English sonnets—early modern texts suggest that many poets educated in humanist grammar schools connected the art of imitating figures and texts from the ancient past with bodily fragmentation. In this regard, institutional habits reinforced literary history: the school's discursive and disciplinary practices had no less potential than Ovid's epic for creating a culturally determined link between rhetoric, gender, and anxieties about the body's coherence and meaning. First, schoolmasters were assiduous in teaching the corporeal dimension of rhetoric known as *actio*—and here the proto-dramatic nature of school training becomes palpable, as teachers routinely described theatricals as excellent tools for teaching young orators how to achieve "eloquence of the body" (Folger MS V.a.a381: 98). Second, whether used in reality or merely as a warning, the spectacle of the master's birch is a ubiquitous presence in texts about the school as well as those used in it. As William Lily's *A Short Introduction of Grammar* declared, Latin was a language "well-beaten into" a student. In such a context, the performative dimension of oratory meant that even for those who achieved the desired end of bodily eloquence, success might well carry in it memories of an ongoing threat, if not always the event, of corporal punishment. Perhaps it was the early threat of the birch, not merely the ancient tendency to write about rhetorical "force" (*vis*), that encouraged the period's literary variations on the idea that words are the equivalent of weapons.

OVID AND THE ART OF "CROSS-VOICING"

Sixteenth-century writers extended the practice of theatrical cross-dressing to poetry, developing a tradition of what Elizabeth Harvey aptly calls "cross-voicing" (see Harvey 1995; Enterline 2000). In that tradition, Ovidian heroines make frequent appearances: Echo, Hecuba, Niobe, Ariadne, Medea, Philomela, and others form a virtual lexicon of "female voices" to whom writers in the period turned to capture vexing poetic, rhetorical, and political problems. George Sabinus's popular commentary on the *Metamorphoses*, clearly written for use in the schools, liberally glosses Ovid's verse with observations about his figures of speech, forms of argument, and emotional effect. His commentary is suggestive about the way the grammar school *habitus* might make fledgling orators keenly aware of the metarhetorical nature of Ovidian poetry. For example, Sabinus glosses Orpheus's performance in Hades not as a "song" but as an "oration" (*Orphei oratio*). And he directs readers to appreciate the verses in which the perlocutionary "*force* of his oration" makes even the Eumenides weep: *Observa quanta fuerit* vis *orationis Orphei* (Sabinus 1584: 382–3; emphasis added). More important for our purposes, Sabinus likes to point out how well "Ovid's female orators . . . deploy the gamut of 'masculine' argumentative tactics" (367; trans. mine).[6] For example, he interprets Medea's monologue, in which she deliberates whether or not to yield to her passion for Jason and betray her fatherland, as a *disputatio*. Sabinus praises her skill in the courtroom tactic of canvassing both sides of the issue: his commentary describes her as "debating what love, what reason would advocate" (*disputans quid amor, quid ratio suadeat*) (in McKinley 2001: 150). On his account, Medea first considers the line of reasoning about the debt one owes a parent, but in the end "pleads the opposite position to this argument" (*sed hic argumento opponit contrarium* [150]) and decides to follow Jason. Similarly, and in tandem with school exercises designed for boys to memorize and invent dialogues, Sabinus calls Scylla's last, desperate series of questions—"Where shall I go, deserted like this? To my country? It is defeated"—an "elegant dialogue" (*dialogismus elegans*) in which she "poses questions and answers herself" (Sabinus 1584: 298). Sabinus also uses the margins to flag "elegant" tropes and figures so that a reader might learn to imitate them: *hypallage, epiphonema, periphrasis*, apostrophe, and *hypotyposis* are among his favorites. But such pedagogical pointers occur with particular frequency in the margins of female speeches like Byblis's (and Medea's and Scylla's)—speeches that, as he puts it, depict the "emotion of a virgin captured by love" (367). And finally, with respect to Procne and Philomela, Sabinus explains that these sisters are "to be understood as Oratory and Poetry, which are nearly sisters" (*Oratoriam & Poeticam, quae prope sorores sint*). Why? Because Procne, the swallow, "is like the eloquence of the city, and those who practice eloquence in houses, in the senate, and the forum. Philomela is truly like the eloquence of the groves and the poets . . . who handle matters as different from legal disputes as can be imagined" (245). Different habitat, different matter, same parent: ancient rhetoric.

   The grammar school's discursive and disciplinary practices inculcated habits of speech that Berger might call the kind of "language games" and "readymade community practices" (1997: 325) that give a historically specific perspective on representation's formative power on experiences of gender. Alongside commentaries such as Sabinus's and Ovid's own tendency to inflect his stories of "bodies changing form" with meditations on the power and limitations of rhetoric, these language games provided an important framework for the way ancient texts would be read and interpreted. But remembering that poetry is the sister to oratory, which requires the corporeal discipline of *actio*, I think it is perhaps more accurate to call them "body-language games." Realized through daily repetition, much of which required public performance, grammar school training constituted an important mechanism for the social reproduction of gender, materializing conceptual categories into embodied experience.

Among the most influential—yet unpredictable—of the school's characteristic language games was that of impersonation (Enterline 2012). Across the curriculum in a variety of exercises, humanist masters made *prosōpopoēia*, the Greco-Roman practice of giving a voice to historical and legendary characters, central to rhetorical training (see McDonald, ch. 36). Young Latin scholars were required to adopt a series of personae over the course of their education: from *vulgaria*, which offered a (protolyric) series of first-person sentences for translation, to more advanced lessons in letter writing and inventing dialogues, schoolboys were often required to imitate the voices of others in ways that laid the groundwork for a range of literary genres. In addition, impersonation moved from the page to speeches delivered "without book" and finally to the stage. School theatricals, which many school bylaws required at least once a week, ensured that boys learned how to play both male and female parts. And finally, Aphthonius's *Progymnasmata* instilled a lesson in *ēthopoēia* (character-making) by asking would-be orators to memorize and then invent speeches according to the following formula: "What x would say on y occasion." These exemplary speeches were uttered by a familiar set of Ovidian women: Niobe, Hecuba, Andromache, Medea. Although Roman theorists like Quintilian were careful to warn against *prosōpopoēia*'s tendency to blur the line between oratory and acting— here we might remember the intriguing aside in *Hamlet* about Cicero's rival, Roscius, who "was an actor in Rome" (2.2.363–4)—the records of Tudor school practice show no such caution. Indeed, masters thought school theatricals were good training for orators, not just for improving memory but also for encouraging students to practice "eloquence of the body" along with that of the voice and tongue.

The school's many demands for impersonation meant that Ovid's own talent for cross-voiced *prosōpopoēia* found a perfect audience. Soon, many of his "female" voices lent a distinctive texture to the period's translation of rhetorical technique into poetic expression. Whether deriving from the school's disciplinary threat of flogging, from Ovid's own association between loss of verbal power and corporeal violence, or from the traumatic mythological/literary scenarios within which Aphthonius asked young orators to imagine what Hecuba or Niobe might say (the first describing her pain over the loss of her children and Troy, the second her grief "over the bodies of children, scattered about")—or all three—Ovid's emotional female characters emerge in the literary texts of former schoolboys in ways that associate rhetoric's techniques and emotional force with bodily violation. One of the most compelling of these impersonated voices is that of Philomela. Perhaps some students were struck by Sabinus's suggestion that the nightingale of poetry is oratory's sister. For others, the demand for eloquence that shaped their own struggle to attain status within the school community may have underlined the fact that Philomela's tongue, severed and "murmuring on the dark earth," was one of Ovid's surrogate figures for the trials of authorship. Indeed, the way that Tudor poets interpret the story of her severed tongue and her tapestry often anticipates what Lacan later describes as the condition of being subject of, as well as to, language.

Whether the inspiration was textual or institutional, or both, the nightingale of poetry became an influential figure in the period for male writers thinking about the vicissitudes of language, eloquence, and authorship. My last two examples illuminate the deep-seated connections I have been outlining among classical rhetoric, poetic technique, institutional training, epicene uncertainty, and fantasies of bodily pain and violation. In Shakespeare's *The Rape of Lucrece* (1596), Lucrece's apostrophes to Philomela and then to Hecuba echo the narrator's founding gesture of *prosōpopoēia*, by which I mean his evident desire to give a voice to a legendary character who, in Ovid's and Livy's treatments, has but few words to say. In Shakespeare's hands, Lucrece turns orator, or rather a rhetorically self-conscious speaker meditating on the power and limitations of speaking. His Lucrece holds "disputation with each thing she views" and worries, in turn, that her own story will become a "theme for disputation" in the future (Shakespeare, *The Rape of Lucrece* 820–1). During these reflections on rhetoric's power and limitations, the poem confronts us with a disturbing pun on legal "case" and "case" as female genitalia (see Mann 2012: 146–8). It occurs just when Lucrece complains that even assiduous school training would be no use to her:

> Out, idle words, servants to shallow fools,
> Unprofitable sounds, weak arbitrators!
> Busy yourselves in skill-contending schools,
> Debate where leisure serves with dull debaters;
> To trembling clients be you mediators:
> For me, I force not argument a straw,
> Since that my case is past the help of law. (1016–22)

The unhappy pun, much like the story of rape, relies on the crudest form of gender difference. But in Lucrece's apostrophes to Philomela and Hecuba something rather more like resemblance than difference emerges between this ancient character and her narrator. In fact, Lucrece becomes something of a surrogate, drawing attention to the very rhetorical problems Shakespeare's narrator faces. In her apostrophe to Philomela, she finds momentary relief in the act of classical imitation (Gk. *mimēsis*; L. *imitatio*). Hoping to "imitate thee well," Lucrece addresses Philomela as if they were singing a duet ("burthen-wise I'll hum on Tarquin still / While thou on Tereus descant'st better skill" [1137, 1133–4]). And in her address to Hecuba, Lucrece imagines herself a ventriloquist ("'Poor instrument,' quoth she, 'without a sound / I'll tune thy woes with my lamenting tongue'" [1464–5]). Each apostrophe revisits the narrator's inaugural gestures—*imitatio* and *prosōpopoēia*—and in so doing reveals something important about the difficulty of finding a voice to tell this story. Moreover, each posits a relationship of sympathy, perhaps even to the point of identification, between speaker and the victim to whom she or he would lend a tongue.[7] In short, each apostrophe reveals that Lucrece and her narrator share an intractable rhetorical problem: representing what Ovid's Philomela calls an "unspeakable" event (*nefas*).

In George Gascoigne's satire, *The Steel Glass with the Complaint of Philomene* (1575), yet another associative relay between poetry and rhetoric, institutional training and sexual violence, turns unexpectedly epicene. In *The Steel Glass*, Gascoigne's narrator styles himself, by turns, "an right Hermaphrodite" and the muse "Satyra." As Syrithe Pugh astutely observes, the oddly spelled name, Satyra, feminizes the narrator while reminding readers of the "widespread but false etymology" of satire from "satyr," which means that a decidedly "priapic" creature "peeps through" the persona's "modest female dress" (2009: 579). In *The Complaint*, the narrator attributes a voice to Philomela twice. The first occurs in a *prosōpopoēia* of the rape victim's last words to Tereus:

> *I will revenge* (quoth she)
> For here I will shake off shame,
> And wil (my selfe) bewray this facte
> Thereby to foile thy fame.
> Amidde the thickest throngs
> (If I have leave to go)
> *I will pronounce* this bloudie deed,
> And blotte thine honor so. (Gascoigne 1910: 190; emphasis added)

In these lines, revenge and effective speech are tantamount to the same thing. The second moment occurs when the narrator describes the metamorphosed nightingale's struggle to pronounce just a few syllables: "Tereu," "fye," "Jug," and finally, "Nemesis." Repeating these "notes" in his own voice as the basis for further invention, the narrator announces his presence ("I") only to speculate, in his own voice, what the nightingale might mean:

> Hir second note is *fye*,
> In Greeke and latine *phy*,
> In englis *fy*, and every tong
> That ever yet read I.
> Which word declares disdaine . . .
> Phy filthy lecher lewde,
> Phy false unto thy wife,
> Phy coward phy, (on womankinde)
> To use thy cruel knife. (200)

His anaphora of "phy" continues for another 12 lines, allowing the narrator to upbraid Tereus and to surmise what feelings these syllables express. As in Shakespeare's epyllion, Gascoigne's narrator and Philomela conduct a kind of duet. But theirs is based on shared sound—a syllable that unites the two and simultaneously implies that the sounds of "English" resemble, and are as worthy as, those "in Greeke and latine."

The nightingale's final word, "Nemesis," and Philomela's earlier call for "revenge" suggest something of the occasion that made Philomela's story appeal to Gascoigne: his quarrel with those who censored his early volume of poetry, *A Hundredth Sundry Flowers*, as scandalous. Pugh argues that he uses the banished Ovid as an exemplary figure for his own condition as censored, punished author. In particular, Gascoigne's self-portrait as a hermaphrodite alludes to Ovid's complaint in *Tristia ex ponto* that exile makes him like "one of the eunuch priests of Cybele" (1.1): as Pugh puts it, Ovid, "like Attis, has incurred the wrath of a vengeful god for transgressing a strict code of sexual morality" (Pugh 2009: 574). Pugh therefore concludes that Gascoigne, whose verse about adulterous love was condemned just as Ovid's had been, "found a model for the hermaphroditic *persona* in Ovid's exile poetry" (574) and is invoking his example to warn readers that satiric verse may yet be an effective form of revenge.

But in addition to Gascoigne's critique of overweening authorities, *The Complaint of Philomene* reveals something further, and more general still, about why Philomela's "lamenting tongue" might appeal to male poets trained by humanist schoolmasters. That is, when the narrator rings changes on the nightingale's single "notes," his lines contain what a former schoolboy would recognize as *pronuntiatio*, exercises also called "vociferation" and designed to promote an orator's skills of delivery. Indeed, when the narrator quotes the bird's third "note," he goes out of his way to invoke the learned Latin context of Ovidian "commentary":

> The next note to hir *phy*
> Is *Jug, jug, jug,* I gesse,
> That might I leave to latynists
> By learning to express.
> Some commentaries make
> About it much adoe:
> If it should only *Jugum* meane
> Or *Jugulator* too. (Gascoigne 1910: 201)

With respect to her first "note," the narrator produces an unexpected simile that summons a child's terror of the schoolroom. Philomela's lingual predicament provides a startling analogy between Ovid's rape victim and a schoolboy:

> And for hir foremost note,
> Tereu, Tereu, doth sing,
> Complaining stil upon the name
> Of that false Thracian king.
> Much like the childe at schole
> With Byrchen rodds sore beaten,
> If when he go to bed at night
> His maister chaunce to threaten
> In every dreame he starts,
> And (o good maister) cries,
> Even so this byrde upon that name,
> Hir foremost note replies. (199)

Clearly Ovid's biography provided a powerful precedent for the dangerous consequences of authorship. But his poetry also offered young Latinists countless examples of speakers undone by their own words. As Gascoigne's narrator points out, Tereus cuts out Philomela's tongue because her outcry, "I will pronounce this bloudie deede / And blotte thine honor so," "amazes" him and drives him into a "rage" (190). Carefully imitating the Ovidian original, which emphasizes the victim's potential verbal power, the narrator replicates Philomela making the (Orphic) claim that "the Woods, my words shal heare, / The holts, the hilles, the craggie rocks, / Shall witnesse with me beare" (190). For boys whose success or failure in the school community revolved around the daily performance of Latin eloquence, Ovid's narratives about the vicissitudes of speech offered memorable precedents for the aspirations and predicaments implicit in their own situation.

If Gascoigne draws on Ovid's exile poetry to hint, with plausible deniability, that satiric verse can achieve "revenge," his allusion to Philomela pulls in another direction, acknowledging a writer's potential vulnerability. The comparison suggests that, like Philomela's objections, words of protest uttered by a "childe at schole" fall on deaf ears. The significance attached to the master's birch in this simile is not merely situational; it is disciplinary and rhetorical. That is, Gascoigne's self-portrait on the frontispiece of *The Steel Glass* balances a sword on one side with pen and books on the other, an emblem that suggests that words and weapons are equivalent. But in the poem's sudden analogy between the plight of a student and that of Philomela, a fear surfaces that exercises in pronunciation, which were invented to enable a "child" to mount an effective defense, might miscarry. Philomela's precedent ominously suggests that even the most moving utterance can fail (or worse yet betray) its speaker.

The "Byrchen rodd" of a schoolmaster—who was usually represented as a "father" to his schoolboy "sons"—returns us to yet another early modern phallus wielded as weapon. But in this poem, as in *The Duchess of Malfi*, the paternal weapon undermines more than it shores up normative definitions of masculinity. In Ovid's story of Philomela, the "paternal metaphor" is already under considerable strain. Seeing Philomela sitting in her father's lap, the lustful Tereus wishes only that he were "in her father's place." Later, she helplessly calls out "her father's name" during a rape that, as Philomela protests, "confuses everything" from kinship relations to the symbolic order of names organizing those relations. In *The Complaint of Philomene*, the unexpected analogy between Tereus and a schoolmaster indicates that a father's punitive rod can misfire. Rather than ordering normative sexual and linguistic relations, Gascoigne's version of the birch calls the efficacy of rhetorical training into question—words meant to persuade change nothing—while at the same time feminizing the schoolboy as a master's sexual victim. The specter of the master's rod may "chaunce to threaten" in this poem. But Gascoigne's epicene, "hermaphroditical" rhetorical performance, with its continued oscillation between male and female, revenger and victim—as well as the rape fantasy connecting frightened schoolboy to Ovid's Philomela—tells us that for him the master's paternal weapon might not fix gendered identity, or the erotic dispositions thought to attend such identities, so much as cast the entire heteronormative presumption of either–or into doubt.

NOTES

1. Mann (2012) makes the compelling argument that vernacular rhetorical manuals illuminate the boundary anxieties implicit in the desire to elevate English eloquence to a level that would rival the classical past. The perceived limitations of English with respect to Latin—a language dependent on word order rather than inflection and with only minor distinctions of gender—mean that certain tropes (like *hyperbaton* and *enallage*) are untranslatable. As Mann points out, writers of rhetoric manuals as well as drama and poetry attempted to translate such tropes anyway, with fascinating results for representations of gender and sexuality.
2. All quotations are from *The Riverside Shakespeare* (Shakespeare 1974).
3. See sonnet 135: "Wilt thou, whose will is large and spacious,/Not once vouchsafe to hide my will in thine?"
4. Webster attended the Merchant Taylor's School. Boys would have practiced formulating proverbial expressions under the guidance of Aphthonius's *Progymnasmata*, which devotes an entire chapter to such "brief speeches." *Sententiae* are all over the play, particularly at the ends of scenes and acts.
5. Mann illustrates how English rhetoricians were "ever mindful of classical models," translating Greek and Latin figures into "an everyday English that could serve the ends of literary and national invention" (2012: 3).
6. Sabinus manages to turn even Byblis's story into an allegory about rhetoric. He comments that Gregory Nazianzen interpreted Chimera (the place of her metamorphosis) according to the threefold monster killed there as an allegorical sign for the "three divisions of rhetoric" (*Sic item rhetorica in tria divisa est genera, Judiciale, Deliberativum, & Demonstrativum*) (1584: 376).
7. I analyze the shifting terrain of gendered identifications in *Lucrece* more fully in *The Rhetoric of the Body* (Enterline 2000), ch. 4. Lucrece's apostrophe to Hecuba combines *prosōpopoēia* and *ekphrasis*, the former being part of what it means for the latter to be successful.

REFERENCES

Barthes, Roland. 1970. "L'ancienne rhetorique." *Communications* 16: 172–223.
Berger, Jr., Harry. 1997. *Making Trifles of Terrors: Redistributing Complicities in Shakespeare.* Stanford, CA: Stanford University Press.
Brinsley, John. 1612. Ludus literarius: *or the grammar schoole . . . intended for the helping of the younger sort of teachers.* London: Humphrey Lownes.
Crocker, Holly. 2003. "Affective Resistance: Performing Passivity and Playing A-Part in *The Taming of the Shrew*." *Shakespeare Quarterly* 54 no. 2: 142–159.
Enterline, Lynn. 1995. *Tears of Narcissus: Melancholia and Masculinity in Early Modern Writing.* Stanford, CA: Stanford University Press.
Enterline, Lynn. 2000. *The Rhetoric of the Body From Ovid to Shakespeare.* Cambridge: Cambridge University Press.
Enterline, Lynn. 2012. *Shakespeare's Schoolroom: Rhetoric, Discipline, Emotion.* Philadelphia: University of Pennsylvania Press.
Fineman, Joel. 1985. "The Turn of the Shrew." In *Shakespeare and the Question of Theory*, edited by Patricia Parker and Geoffrey Hartman, 138–159. New York: Methuen.

Garber, Marjorie. 1987. *Shakespeare's Ghost Writers: Literature as Uncanny Causality.* New York: Methuen.

Gascoigne, George. 1907. "Certayne notes of Instruction concerning the making of verse or ryme in English." In *The Complete Works of George Gascoigne*, vol. 1, edited by John William Cunliffe, 465–473. Cambridge: Cambridge University Press.

Gascoigne, George. 1910. *"The Steel Glass"* with the *"Complaint of Philomene."* In *The Complete Works of George Gascoigne*, vol. 2, edited by John William Cunliffe, 133–207. Cambridge: Cambridge University Press.

Googe, Barnabe. 1565. "Epistle Dedicatory." In *The Zodiake of Life by Marcellus Palingenius.* London.

Gregerson, Linda. 1991. "Protestant Erotics: Idolatry and Interpretation in Spenser's *Faerie Queene." ELH* 58 no. 1: 1–34.

Halpern, Richard. 1997. *Shakespeare among the Moderns.* Ithaca, NY: Cornell University Press.

Harvey, Elizabeth. 1995. *Ventriloquized Voices: Feminist Theory and English Renaissance Texts.* New York: Routledge.

Lamb, Mary Ellen. 2000. "Taken by Fairies: Fairy Practices and the Production of Popular Culture in *A Midsummer Night's Dream." Shakespeare Quarterly* 51 no. 3: 277–312.

Lily, William. 1557. *A Short Introduction of Grammar Generallie to be used, compiled and set forth, for the bringing up of all those that intend to attaine the knowledge of the Latin tongue.* London.

Mann, Jenny C. 2012. *Outlaw Rhetoric: Figuring Vernacular Eloquence in Shakespeare's England.* Ithaca, NY: Cornell University Press.

McKinley, Kathryn L. 2001. *Reading the Ovidian Heroine: "Metamorphoses" Commentaries, 1100–1618.* Leiden: Brill.

Mitchell, Marea. 2009. "Performing Sexual Politics in *The Taming of the Shrew."* In *The Taming of the Shrew*, edited by Dympna Callaghan, 237–247. New York: W.W. Norton.

Pugh, Syrithe. 2009. "Ovidian Reflections in Gascoigne's *Steel Glass."* In *The Oxford Handbook of Tudor Literature*, edited by Mike Pincombe and Cathy Shrank, 571–586. Oxford: Oxford University Press.

Rose, Jacqueline. 1985. "Introduction—II." In *Feminine Sexuality: Jacques Lacan and the Ecole Freudienne*, edited by Jacqueline Rose and Juliette Mitchell, 27–57. New York: W.W. Norton.

Sabinus, George. 1584. *Fabularum Ovidii Interpretatio, Ethica, Physica, et Historica.* Canterbury.

Shakespeare, William. 1974. *The Riverside Shakespeare.* Edited by G. Blakemore Evans. London: Houghton Mifflin.

Wall, Wendy. 2002. *Staging Domesticity: Household Work and English Identity in Early Modern Drama.* Cambridge: Cambridge University Press.

Weber, Samuel. 2008. *Return to Freud: Jacques Lacan's Dislocation of Psychoanalysis.* Cambridge: Cambridge University Press.

CHAPTER 40

RHETORIC AND ARCHITECTURE

ROBERT KIRKBRIDE

ARCHITECTURAL ornament is ubiquitous. Plentiful and diverse or reduced to a minimum, it is never *not* there. In the language of construction, moldings and reveals are akin to ligaments and grammatical conjunctions; they are material gestures, finishing the rough seams that emerge between trades as a building is assembled. Loquaciously, cryptically, or somewhere in between, ornament tells stories, conveying the client's aspirations, the architect's prudence and persuasiveness, and the fabricator's dexterity. Within these marginal and pragmatic origins, poetry has flourished. For at least two and a half millennia, architecture and its ornament has offered perches for the birds of thought, informing personal and cultural identity by equipping the mind with figurative structures and placeholders for memory. During the European Renaissance, architecture furnished an expanding range of rhetorical performance, private and public, by practices inlaid in pedagogy and the fabric of everyday experience. This chapter touches on pedagogical, professional, and poetic convergences of architecture and rhetoric and their joint contributions to shifting perceptions of truth and methods of inquiry.

Pedagogically, architecture and rhetoric intersected in *memoria*, considered by Renaissance humanists to be the foundation of learning and "mother of all arts" (Kirkbride 2008: 4.1.9).[1] Steeped in ancient and medieval practices, *memoria* drew from the material environment—cathedrals and palaces, gardens, frescoes, and birthing trays—to preserve ideas for vivid recollection. Through educational and ethical metaphors, architecture provided models for composing one's thoughts and oneself by a process of self-edification that was not a purely intellectual but an emotional, wholebody experience. As the cathedral provided a medieval mind with an "engine for prayer" (Carruthers 1998: 263), facilitating ritual and meditation, the Renaissance city furnished citizens with festivals and palaces that conveyed the imagination between public spectacle and private reflection (Figure 40.1).

The multisensory character of memory was pivotal to the reflexivity of architecture and rhetoric in Renaissance experience, underpinning ornament's capacity to transport

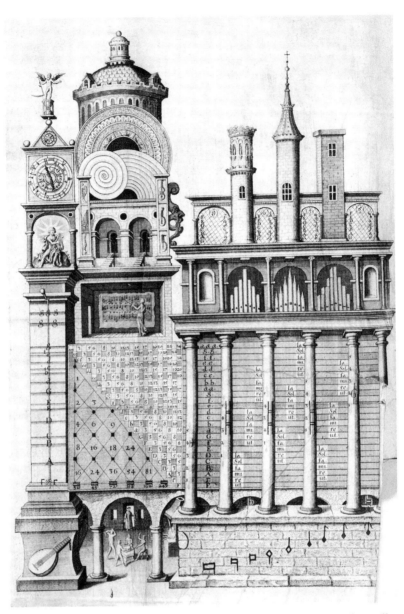

FIG. 40.1 Although memory palaces perished with the minds of their makers, illustrations such as Robert Fludd's "Temple of Music" (1621) reflect an accumulation of classical, medieval, and Renaissance rhetorical practices. Fludd's Temple facade offers a rebus of lessons on the origins and principles of music, fueling *ekphrasis* by a process described by Francesco Sansovino in 1562: "The preface of the oration is similar to the beautiful and rich entrance hall of a well-planned palace: as soon as it presents itself to the eyes of the beholders, they begin to discuss it and they pass judgment that the inside of the palace must be well decorated, composed with perfect architecture, with each part corresponding to the whole" (quoted in Bolzoni 2001: 193). "Temple of Music," from Robert Fludd, *Utriusque cosmic majoris scilicet et minoris metaphysica* (Oppenheim: Ære Johan-Theodori de Bry, typis Hieronymi Galleri, 1617), 1.160.

the imagination between the sensible and intelligible. While historical emphasis has been placed on the intertextualities of architecture and rhetoric, their interplay was not at all limited to an elite, literate audience. According to Leon Battista Alberti, the subject of a painting, its *historia*, should affect learned and unlearned alike, a view consistent with contemporary vernacular preaching ([1435] 1972: 75 [2.40]). "For the homily or sermon to achieve its aims," notes Lina Bolzoni, "it was essential that its contents should remain in people's minds, especially when most of them were illiterate. The homily's structure and its formal characteristics . . . [have] to be memorable in order to be easily recalled both by the preacher delivering it and by the public listening to it" (2004: 3).

In quattrocento Europe, predominantly an oral culture, stories were told by the listener's ear as much as the storyteller's voice. In Ambrogio Lorenzetti's allegorical frescoes on good and evil governance, frequently cited by Renaissance orators and preachers, the figure of Pax extends her ear to the observer as an ethical reminder to Siena's magistrates that peace demands attentive listening (Figure 40.2). Such a gesture epitomizes ornament's role in evoking the senses and mimetic behavior, a point central to Alberti's influential treatise, *On Painting*: "I like there to be someone in the *historia* who tells the spectators what is going on . . . [who] by his gestures invites you to laugh or weep with them" ([1435] 1972: 77 [2.42]) (see van Eck, ch. 37). More generally, it reflects Walter Ong's (1982: 34) observation that oral cultures rely on dialogue to sustain the logical analysis of complex problems. Inflected by audiovisual wordplay, including onomatopoeia, antithesis, and paronomasia, ornament enabled buildings to speak on multiple levels, energizing dialogical habits. The term *granata*, for example, connoted both pomegranates and grenades: when mingled in a room's ornament, ripe pomegranates (prosperity) and exploding grenades (military prowess) signified the common trope of the "prince who fights for peace," a fitting visual pun for a military captain's semiprivate meditation chamber (Kirkbride 2008: 6.2.32).[2] Such figurative nuances are often challenging to retrieve and easily flattened by ocularcentric research methods that focus on meaning rather than contextual uses. For this reason, Michael Baxandall's (1972) notion of a "period eye," which encourages study of the evanescent cultural customs underlying a work's appearance, might be expanded to include a "period ear." Or, considering the kinetics of cognition and roles of physical gesture in Renaissance rhetoric and artworks, a "period body" offers a more appropriate *esprit de corps* for historical research.

The reciprocity of speaker and audience influenced the form and content of an oration and the gestures of its delivery. In turn, this bodily eloquence shaped the decor of physical settings, which offered cues and conduits for narrative flow, enhancing the memories of speaker and audience. The emotional impact of an image—its capacity to move a viewer inwardly as well as outwardly—was central to its usefulness in visual and verbal figuration. Preachers composed complex yet memorable sermons colored with such potent imagery as the *memento mori* of Buonamico Buffalmacco's fresco, *The Triumph of Death*, in Pisa's Camposanto (1338). This style of vivid oration continued well into the Renaissance, with galvanizing effect. For his speeches in Siena's Piazza del Campo, the Franciscan preacher San Bernardino da Siena drew vibrant life from Lorenzetti's frescoes. His fire-and-brimstone delivery, accompanied by bonfires of the

FIG. 40.2 Facsimile detail of the *Allegory of Good Government*, after frescoes by Ambrogio Lorenzetti in the Sala dei Nove, Palazzo Pubblico, Siena (1338).

Source: © Robert Kirkbride

vanities, prefigured Girolamo Savonarola's forceful homilies in the 1490s, which held Florentine citizens spellbound by their attacks on wealth and material luxury, inducing such artists as Sandro Botticelli to pitch their own paintings into the blaze. The power of Savonarola's unadorned oratory was described by a contemporary admirer as "without pretense and artificiality: pure and uncomplicated, not reeking of the lamp-light and affectation . . . truly laconic . . . not elaborate but chaste, modest" (quoted in Godman 1998: 135). The Dominican friar's language inspired Martin Luther and Niccolò Machiavelli, who described his own treatise, *The Prince*, in similar terms: "I have not sought to adorn my work with long phrases or high-sounding words or any of those superficial attractions and ornaments with which many writers seek to embellish their material" (1961: 35). Machiavelli's scorn for "superficial attractions" reflects one side of a deep-seated social and spiritual ambivalence toward material luxury (Binski 2010: 14), whose pendulum swings characterized the contrasting ornaments of Reformation and Counter-Reformation architecture and rhetoric.

Austere or ostentatious, in a culture preoccupied with signs and portents as enter-tainment and self-preservation, emblems and gestures fueled intellectual and political commerce, imbuing clothing, artifacts, and buildings. Allegorical games, such as the "game of emblems" mentioned by Baldassare Castiglione at the outset of *The Book of the Courtier*, cultivated shared habits of poetic figuration (Bolzoni 2001: 83). Fluency in the gestures and ornaments of poetry, dance, music, and architecture inspired cinquecento handbooks on emblems, including Andrea Alciati's:

> As often as any one may wish to assign fulness to empty things, ornament to bare things, speech to dumb things, and reason to senseless things, he may from a little book of Emblems, as from an excellently well-prepared hand book, have what he may be able to impress upon the walls of houses, on windows of glass, on tapestry, on hangings, on tablets, vases, ensigns, seals, garments, the table, the couch, the arms, the sword, and lastly, furniture of every kind. ([1551] 1871: 6)

Across the Renaissance palace, emerging social behaviors and modes of rhetorical performance—including dining, governance, dance, and music—gave rise to new room types, furnishings, and decor. Taste testing, for example, was performed by *credenzieri* to prove (*far credere*) the safety of food and drink. Linked etymologically to faith and certainty of opinion, the modern *credenza* manifests the evolution of an idea from the act of tasting to the setting where the tasting occurred, and later to the sideboard in which dishes, goblets, cutlery, and other secret valuables were secured to prevent tam-pering (Pianigiani 1907: 1.365). Proof of another sort was displayed in the salon. In a republic such as Venice, where a complex process of debate and deliberation shaped the organs of state, the significance of mnemonic prowess and rhetorical dexterity was reflected in the decoration of the doge's palace. In the 1550s, Daniele Barbaro, translator and commentator on Vitruvius and former historian of the Serenissima, composed the iconographic program for the decoration of the Sala del Consiglio dei Dieci, executed by Paolo Veronese. Among principalities, where governing rights centered on dynastic claims, emphasis was placed on ceremonial panegyrics, encomia, and the propagandis-tic interplay of visual and verbal figures. The Salone dei Mesi of the Palazzo Schifanoia (1470), a site of dancing and festive celebration, offers one example: created in antic-ipation of the investiture of Borso d'Este as duke of Ferrara, the fresco cycle merged traditional allegories of *buon governo* with Neoplatonism and was composed to be read both horizontally, as a calendar of seasonal activities in d'Este's well-governed city, and vertically, ascending from worldly activities through a central band of zodiacal signs to a triumphal procession of pagan gods near the ceiling, with wagons drawn by a variety of fantastic creatures. According to Alberti, the *salon* derived from dancing (*saltare*) "because that was where the gaiety of weddings and banquets took place" ([1452] 1988: 119 [5.2], 383, n. 9). Gestures of dance were believed to reveal a soul's inner beauty, while belabored affectation drew ridicule. "A single step, a single unforced and graceful movement of the body," observed Castiglione, "at once demonstrates the skill of the dancer" (1929: 67). Jennifer Nevile elaborates: "Correct bearing, carriage, and manner of moving, engendered by years of dance training, were important social skills, the rules according to which courtiers were expected to move on the dance floor applied to every other part of their lives: a noble and temperate bearing helped to distinguish them from those who did not belong to the elite" (2004: 2).

Ornate semiprivate settings such as the *studioli* at Urbino (Figure 40.3) and Gubbio (Figure 40.5), two contemplation chambers designed for the Montefeltro dukes in the late quattrocento, embodied a weave of rhetorical practices. By *ekphrasis* and training in the *progymnasmata*, an educated observer digested a flow of emblematic tropes—eddies of encomia, proverbs, and poetry—that were composed to draw the eye and body around the rooms in spiraling rotation, from top to bottom and left to right. While the dukes and learned guests shared fundamental habits of reading and description, they were not the only means of navigation. Striking details of perspectival "truthfulness" demonstrated principles of Alberti's *verecundia* (van Eck 2007: 22), blurring boundaries of pictorial and real space. Uncanny optical phenomena, such as trompe l'oeil objects that "follow" observers across a room, nourished a belief that depicted space was an extension of physical space, stimulating empathy in the observer for the observed and introducing new narrative possibilities (Kirkbride 2008: Lute Anamorphosis).[3] By sharpening the ability to describe an artifact or event, *ekphrasis* opened spaces of interpretation among verbal, visual, and constructed environments. Renaissance observers were habituated to enter a painting, and characters depicted therein were believed to occupy the same space as the observers, enabling the imagination to move between states of being, perhaps as a dream within a dream, as popularized in *Hypnerotomachia Poliphili* (1499) and embodied by the garden follies at the Parco dei Mostri in Bomarzo (1552).

Intertextually, correspondences among Vitruvius's *De architectura* and the rhetorical treatises of Cicero and Quintilian resonated with early quattrocento humanists. While Poggio Bracciolini and his circle are often credited with resuscitating these works, a rounder view recognizes their long-standing influences (Binski 2010: 18). Through Saint Augustine and early church authorities, medieval pedagogy had absorbed memory structures from classical rhetoric (beehives, birdcages, and buildings), imbuing them with Christian doctrine to guide the mind's eye from the physical world to an idealized, heavenly city. Gregory the Great described this process: "First we put in place the foundations of literal meaning (*historia*); then through typological interpretation we build up the fabric of our mind in the walled city of faith; and at the end, through the

FIG. 40.3 Facsimile detail of the Urbino *studiolo* (1476), an emblem-filled chamber a few hundred feet from the evenings of dancing and figurative gamesmanship described by Castiglione. A triumphal arch in the east wall—the chamber's compositional target—evokes the ancient trope of the triumph, a popular theme for Renaissance architects, artists, and poets, influential to the papal *possesso* and celebratory processions (Kirkbride 2008: extended captions 20, 29).[1]

Source: © Robert Kirkbride

grace of our moral understanding, as though with added color, we clothe the building" (quoted in Carruthers 1998: 18; see Carruthers 2010). In a similar vein, Hugh of Saint Victor advised twelfth-century readers to construct in their hearts a meditational vehicle based on Noah's ark and to fill it with spiritual learning colored with experiences from daily life.

Bracciolini's reinfusion of Cicero, Quintilian, and Vitruvius nonetheless brought the ancient complementarity of architecture and rhetoric to new light. Where Cicero and Quintilian illustrated the art of rhetoric with analogies of construction, Vitruvius applied rhetorical schemes to describe the art of building. During the Renaissance, this reciprocity stimulated visual and verbal expression, expanding the tradition of *ut pictura poesis* by material *ekphrasis* (Carruthers 1998: 222) and *ut pictura architectura* (Payne 1999: 65). Architecture and its decor informed an oration's content (*inventio*), composition (*dispositio*), and ornamental styling (*elocutio*), along with the imaginary structures used to memorize the oration (*memoria*) and inspire the physical gestures of its delivery (*actio*). Two central texts for the subject at hand, *On Painting* (1435) and *On Building* (1452), each the first of its kind in the Renaissance, were authored by Leon Battista Alberti, whose erudition and experimentation inspired generations of architects. With his humanist colleagues, Alberti plumbed the writings of Vitruvius, Cicero, and Quintilian, seizing upon shared affinities of public speaking and building and the ancient notions of *politeia* and *res publica* they evoked to inspire contemporary citizens to emulate their Roman ancestors and invest their growing mercantile wealth in dignified residences and durable artifacts, as public displays of civic *virtù* (Goldthwaite 1993: 206).

Emerging from a period in which modesty and poverty were extolled, early quattrocento humanists stimulated interest in history and investment in the arts and the urban fabric by composing new treatises and buildings that reconstituted ancient customs from literary and architectural fragments. Like the ruins of Roman civilization, strewn across Europe, North Africa, and the Middle East, many classical texts had survived only in part, as translations of translations, palimpsests, and rumor. While humanists expanded the scope of inquiry to include such pagan and unorthodox authors as Lucretius, Lucian, and Pietro d'Abano, theirs was a pursuit of truth centered on *logos* and authoritative origins, performed as a search among texts and evidenced by philology and etymology. Bracciolini's *De varietate fortunae* (1431–48) described fortune's power to destroy human endeavor, precipitating archaeological examinations of the Roman Forum and compelling generations of architects to populate their sketchbooks and projects with imagery from their remains (Kirkbride 2008: 3.18)[4] (Figure 40.4).

Professionally, architects and rhetors were trained to move clients and audiences through spatial and narrative gestures and persuade by a range of visual and verbal compositional techniques. For architects this performance extended over the life of a project, precipitating drawings, models, written specifications, and contracts. Throughout construction, from initial client engagement to the site management of various contractors, securing authority was critical. Due to the range of material and rhetorical skills exercised in its practice, Vitruvius (1983: 7–8 [1.1.1–4]) had asserted that architecture was born

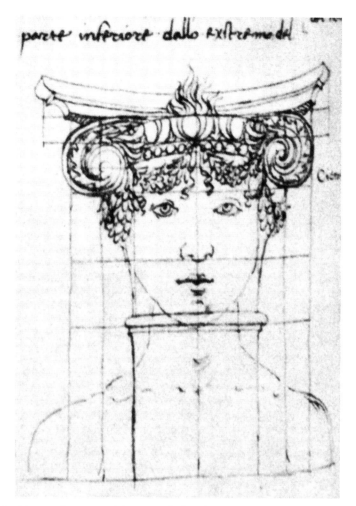

FIG. 40.4 Architectural opportunities expanded with growing economic prosperity and material investment, raising the profession's cultural standing and yielding greater diversity in patronage and projects. This was particularly true on the Italian peninsula, where an architect's activities often encompassed painting, sculpture, furniture, interiors and theatrical scenography, chapels and mausoleums, palaces and fortresses, and siege engines and catapults. In addition to worldly *praxis*, learned pursuits and field investigations fertilized the architect's imagination with historical precedents, informing design practice and bolstering credibility with patrons (van Eck 2007: 31). Francesco di Giorgio Martini's rendering of the invention of the Corinthian capital, based on book 4 of Vitruvius. Martini, *Trattati di architettura ingegneria e arte militare*, folio 33v (Milan: Il Polifilo, 1967).

Source: © Collection Centre Canadien d'Architecture/Canadian Centre for Architecture, Montréal

of fabrication (*fabrica*) and reasoned argument (*ratiocinatio*), and urged architects to be fluent in ornaments and their histories. Without such knowledge, he warned, the architect would remain a mason and never receive the honors due his efforts. Humanist architects such as Martini and Roberto Valturio followed suit, demonstrating their learned

FIG. 40.5 In the northeast corner of the Gubbio *studiolo*, designed by Martini, the word "INGENIOQUE" (innate talent or brilliance) appears in a poem encircling the chamber (Kirkbride 2008: extended caption 13).[2] Directly below, a trompe l'oeil cabinet displays a compass, hourglass, and cittern, instruments of measure and proportion. Behind them hangs a setsquare, counted by Vitruvius (1983: 1.1.4) among the architect's instruments. Used to calculate height and distance, the setsquare establishes right angles and its plumb bob indicates levelness. In addition to physical applications, the instrument was commonly used in basic memory training, appearing as a letter-shaped *aide-mémoire* for topics beginning with the letter A—*Alberti* or *Architettura*, for example. The image also offered a popular metaphor for adroit leadership and moral rectitude, as Castiglione mused: "The prince ought not only to be good, but also to make others good, like that square used by architects, which not only is straight and true itself, but also makes straight and true all things to which it is applied" (1929: 26). To a young prince such as Guidobaldo da Montefeltro, for whom the room was designed (Kirkbride 2008: 4.1),[3] the alignment of *ingenioque* and the measuring instruments emphasized that talent must be coupled with discipline and a willingness to learn, a combination that marked Cicero's ideal orator (*De oratore* 1.23), Vitruvius's "perfect craftsman" (1983: 1.1.3), and informed Martini's assertion that *ingenium* powers *inventio*, "without which it is impossible to be a good architect" (1967: 2.484).

Source: Photograph by author by permission of the Metropolitan Museum of Art of New York City, Rogers Fund, 1939 (39.153). Photo © Robert Kirkbride

expertise through sketchbooks and illustrated codices that were instrumental in persuading clients to invest in construction—a costly, dangerous, and highly political endeavor.

In his own discourse, Alberti dovetailed architecture and rhetoric: "I would have [an architect] take the same approach as one might toward the study of letters. Through his intellect he must *invent*, through experience *recognize*, through judgment *select*, through deliberation *compose*, and through skill *effect* whatever he undertakes" ([1452] 1988: 315 [9.10]; emphasis added), activities corresponding to *inventio, memoria, elocutio,*

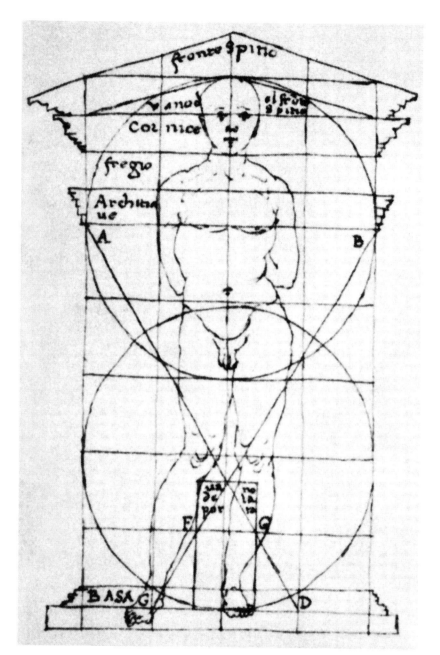

FIG. 40.6 Vitruvius aimed to constitute the corpus of the architectural discipline, construing architectural terms for the orders and ornaments from the human body. Martini reveled in the Hellenist architect's Greek and Latin ferruminations as a source of invention (Hersey 1988: 77). With the ruins of Rome in his sketchbooks and the renowned Urbino library at hand, Martini composed his sketchbook-treatise on architecture over many years, digesting Vitruvius with access to scholars and manuscripts on etymology and epigrams, including Niccolò Perotti's *Cornucopiae*. Drawing by Martini, in Martini, *Trattati di architettura ingegneria e arte militare*, folio 38v (Milan: Il Polifilo, 1967).

dispositio, and *actio*. Alina Payne characterizes Alberti's efforts as an elaboration on Cicero's definition of an orator as one who speaks ornately: "Only the learned architect/orator can build/speak ornately, and architecture and culture thus come together" (1999: 76). Composed in Ciceronian Latin, prior to sixteenth-century advances in the printed image, Alberti's *On Building* is a work of humanist ambition presented in scholastic attire (or, as Mario Carpo observes, "new wine in an old bottle" [2001: 120]).

As rhetorical skills calibrated audience, occasion, and setting, for Alberti and Vitruvius salubrious architecture tuned local inflections of climate, flora, and fauna with the cultural and personal habits of inhabitants. Where ancient Greeks and Romans were mindful of *kairos* and the *decorum* of rhetorical performance, likewise for the Renaissance the clothing of thoughts and buildings was evaluated according to appropriateness. A *degna casa* signified both a dignified palace *and* the family dwelling inside. But what signified dignified? The humanist archaeology of classical texts and ruins outfitted architects and patrons with examples of public and private spaces for rhetorical performance. Settings described by Vitruvius and Pliny and unearthed in the Roman Forum during the quattrocento offered exemplary guides. Designed to move observers, literally and figuratively, their spatial arrangements and ornament prepared a mind with tropes and figures that fed the imagination.

For Renaissance architects, "style" was not defined by historical categories—"baroque," "modernist," or others—that did not yet exist (Kirkbride 2008: 4.27; see Kirkbride 2010).[5] A language of ornamental taste and critique evolved from Quintilian's rendering of Aristotle's categories of genus and species, finding purchase in Alberti's writings and coming to flower in the first quarter of the following century, in the combinatorial *mescolanza* of Sebastiano Serlio's copiously illustrated treatises (Carpo 2001: 96; Payne 1999: 122). Ornament equipped a building to voice the character of its inhabitants. Vitruvius had transposed styles of oration, traditionally associated with geographical regions and their inhabitants, to the architectural orders of the column and capital: the direct and masculine Attic style became Doric; the flowery and feminine Asiatic became Ionic; and the style "between," Rhodian, became Corinthian. Joined by the Tuscan and composite styles, the five orders blossomed into the fugal subjects of Renaissance architectural theory and composition and became the crux of debates on rules for ornamentation (van Eck 2007: 31).

In emulation of Cicero, Quintilian, and Vitruvius, Renaissance orations and buildings were often described as harmoniously built bodies, a theme central to humanist architectural thought (Kirkbride 2008: 3.22)[6] (Figure 40.6). Alberti explicitly compares buildings and bodies: "Beauty is that reasoned harmony of all the parts within a body, so that nothing may be added, taken away or altered, but for the worse" ([1452] 1988: 156 [6.2]), a subtle play on the ancient adage that little could be added to Cicero's eloquence, where nothing could be subtracted from Demosthenes's. Antonio Piero del Averlino (Filarete) expanded the body/building metaphor in his *Trattato* (1464), attributing the conception of a building to a client father and an architect mother, who after nine months produces a wooden model; raised well, the model matures into a beautiful, full-grown building. Filarete, whose assumed name signified "lover of virtue" (*phil* + *arēte*), prepared his treatise as a Platonic dialogue centered on the discussion of an ideal city, Sforzinda. Named for Filarete's patron, Duke Francesco Sforza, the star-shaped city was an animated communal organism, manifesting Vitruvian principles of utility, endurance, and beauty. Among its pragmatic planning features, of particular note is the 10-story House of Vice and Virtue, supplied with a brothel at its base and an academy on its upper levels, an architectonic rendering of contemporary Neoplatonism. Akin to speculations on the ideal orator, the figure of the ideal city absorbed the Renaissance mind, from its roots in the City of God and the New Jerusalem to Thomas More's *Utopia* (1516), Vincenzo Scamozzi's plan for the city of Palmanova (founded in 1593), and Tommaso Campanella's *City of the Sun* (1623).

In their archaeological investigations, architects discovered discrepancies between Vitruvius's written accounts and quantifiable field evidence. While these inaccuracies did not trouble Alberti or Martini, who shared Cicero's enthusiasm for *ingenio* and *inventio*, they preoccupied cinquecento exegetes of Vitruvius like the Accademia della Virtù, whose members sought aesthetic rules (*licentia*) for the profession and its lettered clientele (Payne 1999: 15, 116). Such pursuits echoed unceasing debates over stylistic imitation and emulation in oratory. In response to Ciceronians such as Pietro Bembo, who advocated purity in historical examples, Desiderius Erasmus, in his *Ciceronianus* (1528), questioned strict imitation, referring to the compositional practices of an architect: "Does he, when preparing to build some great house, take all the details from a single building? Not at all, he selects from many what he finds to his taste. What is the reason then that we have devoted ourselves so religiously to Cicero alone?" ([1528] 1991: 82). An alternative compositional process was proposed by Bembo's Ciceronian colleague Giulio Camillo, whose bewitching treatise, *L'Idea del Teatro* (1543), describes a memory theater structured to give "*place* to the *materials* of eloquence, and to the artifice with which they clothe themselves, the different forms they take" (Bolzoni 2001: 140). Camillo's fabrication, a small wooden amphitheater filled with emblems and choice phrases extracted from the works of Cicero and Virgil, merged the geometries of a Vitruvian theater (Vitruvius 1983, bk. 5) with the combinatorial mechanics of mnemonic devices and settings (Figure 40.7A, B). While its workings are shrouded in metaphoric language, the chamber was conceived to operate on two levels. For initiated occupants, the chamber channeled divine wisdom, empowering the imagination; for those with less *ingenio*, the theater offered an apparatus for rhetorical training, by "an easy and straightforward pedagogy, accessible to all" (Carpo 1993: 167, n. 18). Written in the same year as the publication of Andreas Vesalius's anatomical studies and Nicholas Copernicus's heliocentric system, Camillo's treatise envisioned a site for dissecting the classical body of literature and composing new works from its elements, by endless permutation.

Across the Renaissance, architecture served as a rhetorical vehicle for inquiry and a material guide to *virtù*, evidenced by well-formed, well-reasoned arguments from Cato's "good man, speaking expertly." Buildings and decor embodied a belief that beauty was de facto a physiognomic sign of goodness, an alignment of ethics and aesthetics that often trumped empirical inquiry. With truth as *logos*, as a search among authoritative

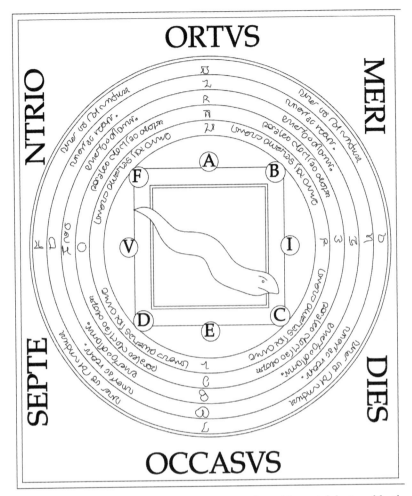

FIG. 40.7A, B Pedagogical exercises, ornate settings, and combinatorial devices, like the wheels devised by Alberti (*De cifris*, 1466) and included in Jacobus Publicius's *Ars memoriae* (1482), enhanced memory and composition. The vermiform volvelle of Publicius's memory wheel evoked the valve-like vermis in the brain, whose opening and closing was believed to control the flow of spirits among the mind's chambers, activating memory and cogitation. Although this role was disputed in the 1540s by Vesalius's anatomical research, the vermis continued to appear in mind-mapping diagrams into the following century (Kirkbride 2008: extended captions 8, 17).[4] However, a Renaissance mind was not limited to the brain, but included the heart, liver, and viscera, a biomechanical arrangement with architectural consequences: while circumambulating a chamber and interpreting its decor, the body's gestures circulated spirits throughout the body-mind, enabling an observer to decipher and forge new associations among the *res/verba* displayed. By habitual use, rooms like the Montefeltro *studioli* and their contents were transposed to an observer's mind, providing a portable memory chamber for decision-making in the field of action. Far from their palaces, the Montefeltro dukes could "enter" their memorized *studioli* as avatars and gyrate through them like the vermis in its wheel, opening and closing chambers in their minds while navigating the text and images displayed, echoing the gestures of illustrious men portrayed overhead, and construing and constructing arguments tuned with *logos*,

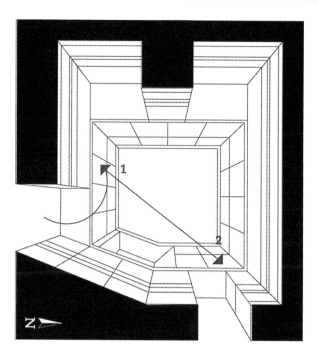

FIG. 40.7A, B Continued   *pathos*, and *ēthos* to the predicament at hand. Figure 7A. Facsimile of memory wheel drawn after Publicius, *Ars memoriae* (Venice: Ratdolt, 1482).

Source: © Robert Kirkbride.

Figure 7B. Worm's eye view of the Urbino *studiolo*, featuring two station points for decoding the patron's faithfulness (Kirkbride 2008: 6.6.69).

Source: © Robert Kirkbride

texts, *ratio* and *oratio* recombined form and content endlessly, as mise en abyme, spurring emblematic thought to generate space for further emblematic thought (Kirkbride 2008: 4.4.73).[7]

Following Columbus's westward voyage, however, predilection for reasoned argument was increasingly challenged by phenomena that did not quite fit into traditional categories. The hunt for knowledge veered from the word toward a world tremendously expanded, with the theater as a primary site of inquiry where knowledge was performed (Figure 40.8). Methods were recalibrated by entrepreneurial ambition to reveal the hidden secrets of nature (Eamon 1993: 281). In tandem with advances in printing, astronomy, and anatomical research, corroboration of visual documentation with empirical observation became increasingly central to inquiry, in architecture as in the sciences. Andrea Palladio, who examined the Roman forum with his patron in the 1540s, carefully noted in his *Four Books of Architecture* (1570), "I will set out the dimensions of each of [the orders] not so much in line with what Vitruvius teaches but according to what I have observed in ancient buildings" ([1570] 2002: 13 [1.12]).

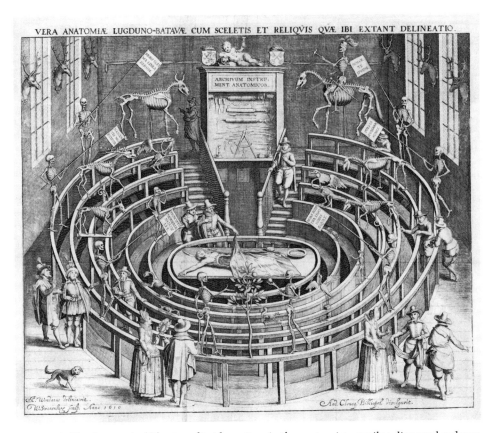

VERA ANATOMIÆ LUGDUNO-BATAVÆ CUM SCELETIS ET RELIQVIS QVÆ IBI EXTANT DELINEATIO.

FIG. 40.8 The Anatomical Theatre of Leiden, 1610. As the anatomist unveils a dissected cadaver, a skeletal Adam reaches for the apple held by a skeletal Eve in the foreground, demonstrating a coexistence of witnessing and believing that had inspired Camillo to exclaim, "Let's turn scholars into spectators" (Findlen 1994: 118).

Source: © Trustees of the British Museum

For the network of natural philosophers and amateur academies of science emerging in the cinquecento, rhetorical skills remained central to establishing credibility. At the heart of a restrained performance—specifically, the *ekphrasis* of a reproducible experiment, combining text and image—empirical methods took root in framing a new sort of truth, one affirmed by shared witness as distinct from inner *fantasia*, characterized by a delivery whose *enargeia* was vivid yet ornamentally and emotionally chaste (Eamon 1993: 338). This shift was, however, gradual: virtuoso collectors animated their idiosyncratic cabinets of curiosities with narratives that traversed empirical, spiritual, and propagandistic terrain with aplomb. In the frontispieces of their catalogs, they are often shown in the middle of performance, Albertian-fashion, pointing out a prized possession to guests and readers. In the engraving of the anatomical theater of Leiden such gestures abound, indicating that the site of inquiry has traveled from an ark carried within the heart to the realm of public consensus, where that heart is opened and its workings revealed for further interpretation.

NOTES

1. http://www.gutenberg-e.org/kirkbride/chapter4.html#s4.1.
2. http://www.gutenberg-e.org/kirkbride/chapter6.html#s6.2.
3. http://www.gutenberg-e.org/kirkbride/video/urbino_lute_anamorph_a.html.
4. http://www.gutenberg-e.org/kirkbride/chapter3.html.
5. http://www.gutenberg-e.org/kirkbride/chapter4.html#s4.2.
6. http://www.gutenberg-e.org/kirkbride/chapter3.html.
7. http://www.gutenberg-e.org/kirkbride/chapter4.html#s4.4.

FURTHER READING

In *The Gallery of Memory*, Lina Bolzoni (2001) expands Baxandall's notion of the "period eye" to consider multisensory and jocoserious dimensions of visual and verbal play. Mario Carpo's (2001) *Architecture in the Age of Printing* illuminates influences of the printing press on the codification and dissemination of architectural thought and practice, from Alberti's imageless text to Giacomo Vignola's virtually textless images. Through careful examination of Renaissance commentaries on Vitruvius, Alina Payne's (1999) *The Architectural Treatise in the Age of the Renaissance* addresses the complex roles of ornament in architectural discourses on style in an increasingly text-based culture. In *Classical Rhetoric and the Visual Arts in Early Modern Europe*, Caroline van Eck (2007) considers the impact of rhetoric on style and practices of visual persuasion in architecture and the decorative arts in early modernity. Focusing on the life of the model Renaissance man, Anthony Grafton's (2000) *Leon Battista Alberti* conveys the tensions inherent to reclaiming historical precedents and knitting them meaningfully into contemporary life.

REFERENCES

Alberti, Leon Battista. (1452) 1988. *On the Art of Building in Ten Books*. Translated by Joseph Rykwert, Neil Leach, and Robert Tavernor. Cambridge, MA: MIT Press.

Alberti, Leon Battista. (1435) 1972. *On Painting*. Translated by Cecil Grayson. New York: Penguin Books.

Alciati, Andrea. (1551) 1871. *Emblematum flumen abundans*. Edited by Henry Green. Manchester: A. Brothers. Facsimile reprint of the Lyons edition by Bonhomme.

Baxandall, Michael. 1972. *Painting and Experience in Fifteenth-Century Italy*. Oxford: Oxford University Press.

Binski, Paul. 2010. "Working by Words Alone." In *Rhetoric Beyond Words*, edited by Mary Carruthers, 14–51. Cambridge: Cambridge University Press.

Bolzoni, Lina. 2001. *The Gallery of Memory*. Toronto: University of Toronto Press.

Bolzoni, Lina. 2004. *The Web of Images: Vernacular Preaching from Its Origins to Saint Bernardino da Siena*. Translated by Carole Preston and Lisa Chien. Aldershot: Ashgate.

Carpo, Mario. 1993. *Metodo e ordini nella teoria architettonica dei primi moderni*. Geneva: Librairie Droz.

Carpo, Mario. 2001. *Architecture in the Age of Printing.* Cambridge, MA: MIT Press.

Carruthers, Mary. 1998. *The Craft of Thought: Meditation, Rhetoric, and the Making of Images, 400–1200.* Cambridge: Cambridge University Press.

Carruthers, Mary, ed. 2010. *Rhetoric Beyond Words.* Cambridge: Cambridge University Press.

Castiglione, Baldassare. 1929. *The Book of the Courtier.* Translated by Leonard Eckstein Opdycke. New York: Horace Liveright.

Eamon, William. 1993. *Science and the Secrets of Nature.* Princeton, NJ: Princeton University Press.

Erasmus, Desiderius. (1528) 1991. "Ciceronianus." In *Controversies Over Cicero*, edited and translated by Izora Scott, 19–130. Ann Arbor, MI: Hermagoras.

Findlen, Paula. 1994. *Possessing Nature.* Berkeley: University of California Press.

Godman, Peter. 1998. *From Poliziano to Machiavelli: Florentine Humanism in the High Renaissance.* Princeton, NJ: Princeton University Press.

Goldthwaite, Richard A. 1993. *Wealth and the Demand for Art in Italy, 1300–1600.* Baltimore, MD: Johns Hopkins University Press.

Grafton, Anthony. 2000. *Leon Battista Alberti.* Cambridge, MA: Harvard University Press.

Hersey, George. 1988. *The Lost Meaning of Classical Architecture.* Cambridge, MA: MIT Press.

Kirkbride, Robert. 2008. *Architecture and Memory.* New York: Columbia University Press. http://www.gutenberg-e.org/kirkbride/

Kirkbride, Robert, ed. 2010. "Geometries of Rhetoric." *Nexus Network Journal* 12 no. 3: Special Issue. http://www.nexusjournal.com/volume-12/number-3-november-2010.html.

Machiavelli, Niccolò. 1961. *The Prince.* Translated by George Bull. Harmondsworth: Penguin.

Martini, Francesco di Giorgio. 1967. *Trattati di architettura ingegneria e arte militare.* Edited by Corrado Maltese. Translated by Livia Maltese Degrasse. Milan: Edizioni Il Polifilo.

Nevile, Jennifer. 2004. *The Eloquent Body: Dance and Humanist Culture in Fifteenth-Century Italy.* Bloomington: Indiana University Press.

Ong, Walter J. 1982. *Orality and Literacy.* New York: Routledge.

Palladio, Andrea. (1570) 2002. *The Four Books on Architecture.* Translated by Robert Tavernor and Richard Schofield. Cambridge, MA: MIT Press.

Payne, Alina. 1999. *The Architectural Treatise in the Age of the Renaissance.* Cambridge: Cambridge University Press.

Pianigiani, Ottorino. 1907. *Vocabolario etimologico della lingua italiana.* Rome: Albrighi.

van Eck, Caroline. 2007. *Classical Rhetoric and the Visual Arts in Early Modern Europe.* Cambridge: Cambridge University Press.

Vitruvius. *On Architecture.* 1983. Translated by Frank Granger. Cambridge, MA: Harvard University Press.

CHAPTER 41

ORIGINS OF BRITISH ENLIGHTENMENT RHETORIC

ARTHUR E. WALZER

THE most important works in British rhetorical theory during the eighteenth century are those that Wilbur Samuel Howell, in his comprehensive *Logic and Rhetoric in the Eighteenth Century*, identified as the "new" rhetorics (1971: 441). Howell identifies two types of innovative work in this period. First are the rhetorics that had their origin in the new empiricist philosophy (see Potkay, ch. 42). These works offered a theoretical account of rhetoric in what we would today call psychological terms. A second type had its origin in an emerging French belles lettres tradition. This work shifted the focus of rhetoric from composing speeches to criticizing discourse, charging rhetoric with establishing criteria of excellence not only for oratory but for works of philosophy, history, and literature as well. There can be no doubt that the new rhetoric marked a significant departure from classical theory; scholars, however, have debated the degree and nature of this transformation of classical rhetoric and whether it was a welcome innovation or a radical wrong turn. This chapter, drawing on the now standard terminology first proposed by Douglas Ehninger (1952) in "Dominant Trends in English Rhetorical Thought, 1750–1800," considers first the "psychological-epistemological rhetoric" that developed from the merging of rhetorical theory with the new empirical philosophy of Francis Bacon, John Locke, and David Hume. The second section focuses on "belletristic rhetoric" that had its origin in French theories of aesthetics. More generally, this chapter assesses the nature and value of the eighteenth century's transformation of rhetorical theory from a theory grounded in the practice of rhetoric in the civic arena to a theory that attempted to explain in psychological and aesthetic terms our response to all types of discourse.

Psychological-Epistemological Theories

The two most important psychological-epistemological theories of rhetoric produced during the period are George Campbell's (1776) *Philosophy of Rhetoric* and Joseph Priestley's (1777) *Course of Lectures on Oratory and Criticism*. Both works draw on the new empiricism of Bacon, Locke, Hume, David Hartley, and others. Since Campbell's is more comprehensive, more methodologically self-conscious, and more influential, his work will be the focus of the first part of the chapter.

Campbell's *Philosophy of Rhetoric* is a significant departure from the Ciceronian tradition of rhetorical theory that dominated the Renaissance (see Rebhorn, ch. 31). His *Philosophy of Rhetoric* is not a *technē* in the sense that Cicero's *De inventione* is; Campbell does not provide advice on how to compose, memorize, and deliver an oration. His is a genuine theory: it offers an explanation in psychological (Campbell would say "pneumatological") terms of why and how language can please us, educate us, transport us, rivet our attention, and, especially, create belief and move us to action. Campbell signaled his intention to provide such an explanation by calling his work a "philosophy," which in his Enlightenment intellectual milieu meant that he would ground his account of rhetoric in the human sciences, specifically in the evolving science of the mind found in Bacon, Locke, Hume, and others. In his *Advancement of Learning* Bacon (1605), offered a taxonomy of the arts and sciences based on the particular faculty or faculties of the mind that a science or art engages. Campbell, invoking Bacon in the headnote to *Philosophy of Rhetoric*, draws on a similar faculty psychology for his framework, developing his taxonomy of the purposes of discourse on the basis of the mental faculty each species of discourse primarily addresses: discourse that intends to please (*delectare*) targets the imagination; discourse that intends to move (*movere*) seeks to engage the emotions; and discourse that would persuade (*persuadere*) must engage the will (as well as the understanding and the emotions) ([1776] 1998: 2–6). For Campbell, a theory of rhetoric would therefore explain how the faculties process language (and here he anticipates what is known today as "cognitive rhetoric"). For his explanation of how the mind arrives at belief, Campbell drew on Locke's (1690) *Essay Concerning Human Understanding* and Hume's *Treatise of Human Nature* (1739) and *An Enquiry Concerning Human Understanding* (1748).

Campbell is especially indebted to Hume. Hume argues that ideas that resemble sense impressions in their impact on the mind are more likely to be believed, and he employs a rhetorical vocabulary to make this point. Belief is "nothing but a more vivid, lively, forcible, firm, steady, conception of an object [or relationship], than what the imagination alone is ever able to attain. . . . It is evident that belief consists not in the peculiar nature or order of ideas, but in the manner of their conception, and in their *feeling* to the mind" (Hume [1748] 1988: 5.2; see also Hume [1739] 1984: 1.7). Insofar as Campbell would follow Hume, he would move away from Aristotle, for Hume emphasizes that the way we experience sense impressions and ideas, not a logical procedure such as the syllogism, determines belief.

Lloyd Bitzer, perhaps the foremost Campbell scholar, emphasized Hume's influence on Campbell's theory: "Vivacity, or the liveliness of ideas, became the dominant concept in Campbell's rhetoric" (1969: 140). According to Bitzer, Campbell had offered a new theory of rhetoric based on Hume's empirical epistemology, especially his notion of the crucial role of the "lively idea" in the construction of belief. But although Bitzer established his case with textual evidence from *Philosophy of Rhetoric*, critics, drawing more on Campbell's biography, were skeptical. Would Campbell, a respected member of the Scottish Kirk, embrace the philosophy of Hume, whose work the General Assembly had condemned in 1755 (Sefton 1987: 124)? Moreover, Campbell was a founding member of the Aberdeen Philosophical Society, whose members were among Hume's most persistent and effective critics (Ulman 1990: 25). Finally, Campbell (1762) himself had attacked Hume in his *Dissertation on Miracles*. Pointing to Campbell's profession, his associations, and his friends, a number of scholars denied Bitzer's conclusion (Cronkhite 1967; Mohrmann 1968; Bormann 1985) or qualified it (Bevilacqua 1964; Rasmussen 1974). All maintained that Campbell would have more likely sided with Hume's most effective contemporary critic, Thomas Reid, Campbell's colleague in the Aberdeen Philosophical Society.

The question of whether Campbell is influenced or not by Hume has implications for Campbell's rhetorical theory because of the important place it assigns to *vivacity*. If by vivacity Campbell does not mean Hume's "lively idea," how should we interpret this term? Dennis Bormann (1988) provides one answer. He maintains that Campbell's concept of vivacity was not only not derived from Hume but was unoriginal—merely "the old and traditional rhetorical-poetic doctrine of *enargeia*" (Bormann 1988: 46). *Enargeia* (in Latin, *evidentia*) is the term in ancient rhetoric for detailed verbal description intended to paint a picture in the mind of the listener. Is Campbell's theory truly innovative or not? After all, Campbell refers to Quintilian more often than Bacon, Locke, or Hume. Perhaps the idea that Campbell's rhetoric represents a radical departure from ancient rhetorical theory had been oversold.

If the issue rests on what vivacity means in Campbell's *Philosophy of Rhetoric*, the text supports both interpretations. At times, Campbell's use of such terms as "vivacity" and "resemblance" seems hardly different from the Latin equivalent in Cicero or Quintilian, as when he writes that "nothing contributes more to vivacity than striking resemblances in the imagery" (Campbell [1776] 1998: 73). But when Campbell writes that "by vivacity of expression, resemblance is attained, as far as language can contribute to the attainment" (285), he implies that vivid language creates belief because it resembles in its impact a sense impression—as Hume stated.

The compositional history of Campbell's *Philosophy of Rhetoric* helps explain the polysemous quality of its terminology. In his preface, Campbell explains that he composed his work over a period of 25 years (1750–75). Some sections were written as early as 1750, before Campbell read Hume critically in the Aberdeen Philosophical Society. Campbell's encounter with Hume, however, changed the psychology at the heart of his theory of rhetoric. Rather than revise his work, Campbell preferred to present *Philosophy of Rhetoric* as a "series of Essays closely connected with one another" ([1776] 1998: lxv), a description that suggests something less than a sustained argument (Walzer 2000: 222–3).

But had Campbell edited his work, it is not certain he would have changed how he used terms such as "vivacity" and "resemblance." Campbell's intention was not to choose a side in the quarrel between the ancients and the moderns but to use modern empirical philosophy to confirm what the ancients taught. In *Philosophy of Rhetoric*, Campbell maintains that this new philosophical approach would deepen, not replace, ancient rhetorical theory, and he provides a synoptic history of rhetoric to indicate the novelty of its contribution. In the first three historical stages, the ancients had created a technical vocabulary, a taxonomy of types of speeches, and methods of teaching. Now, in the fourth stage, Campbell would "arrive at that knowledge of human nature, which, besides its other advantages, adds both weight and evidence to all precedent discoveries and rules" ([1776] 1998: lxxiv). His intention was to draw on empirical epistemology to confirm what the ancients thought (Walzer 2003: 72–4). If in his work Hume's theory of rhetorical vivacity seemed consonant with the ancient concept of *enargeia*, well, that was the point, wasn't it?

The second area of disagreement among scholars—whether Campbell sides with Reid or Hume—is similarly best addressed when we recall that the *Philosophy of Rhetoric* was written not by a philosopher but by a Presbyterian minister with a keen interest in modern ideas. His impulse was not to identify conflicts or to create a rigorous philosophical system but to reconcile the old Christian faith with the new science. Campbell wanted to accept the implications of Hume's new ideas about the imagination for rhetoric but not its radical ontological and epistemological implications, which so disturbed traditional concepts of being and knowledge: "I will not say with a late subtle metaphysician [Hume] that 'Belief consisteth in the liveliness of our ideas.' That this doctrine is erroneous, it would be quite foreign to my purpose to attempt here to evince. Thus much however is indubitable, that belief commonly enlivens our ideas; and that the lively ideas have a stronger influence than faint ideas to induce belief" ([1776] 1998: 73). Campbell wants to adopt Hume's description of the imagination's operations but within the framework of his traditional allegiances.

Campbell found the philosophical basis for rejecting Hume's epistemology in Thomas Reid's concept of "common sense." In his *Inquiry into the Human Mind* Reid (1764), maintains that, contrary to the claims of Locke and Hume, the mind *does* have direct contact with sense data. Experiencing, believing, and judging are simultaneous, and this fact is the basis for the first principle of the cognitive process, what Reid calls common sense: the senses give the mind access to reality, not merely an idea of reality ([1764] 1970: 268). Campbell accepts Reid's ontology but also accepts an attenuated version of Hume's psychology: the imagination's response to a verbal presentation of an idea that strikes the mind with the vivacity of a sense impression is not the basis for belief but does increase the likelihood that it will be accepted and remembered.

Campbell's appropriation of Reid's theory of common sense for his theory of rhetoric has been identified by composition scholars as a representative example of Campbell's role in bringing an end to the civic tradition of rhetoric. These critics contrast Reid's concept of common sense, which is internal to the mind, with the classical concept of common sense as cultural opinions (*endoxa*). For Thomas P. Miller (1997: 216), this difference becomes a synecdoche for Campbell's putative role in moving the discipline of rhetoric away from a cultural context to a psychological context. Miller's criticism follows in the wake of similar scholarship in rhetoric and composition in the 1980s and 1990s. Composition scholars (Connors 1981; Berlin 1984; Crowley 1990) were unhappy with the expressive and formal approaches to writing instruction taken in many contemporary writing textbooks and often traced the emergence of such approaches to the shift in the eighteenth century away from civic rhetoric toward a psychological rhetoric. Campbell was judged to play a crucial role in this narrative of decline (see, e.g., Crowley 1990: 98–9, 145–6).

Since Campbell was part of the universalizing project of the Enlightenment, he was seeking to develop a theory that transcended culture. It is true, then, that in his theory rhetoric is divorced from its classical, civic context. It is not true, however, that Campbell breaks from classical rhetoric entirely. Quintilian and Cicero still figure prominently in the *Philosophy of Rhetoric*, though Campbell borrows the tenets that can be extricated from the civic, political context of ancient rhetoric as *civilis ratio* (see Connolly, ch. 14; Rebhorn, ch. 31). In the process of doing so, he produces a genuinely creative theoretical synthesis of ancient rhetoric and modern humanistic psychology.

BELLETRISTIC RHETORIC

As the term suggests, belletristic rhetoric has a French lineage. Although Bernard Lamy's (1676) *De l'art de parler* anticipated some of the changes that characterize belletristic rhetoric, the works most influential to the development of belletristic rhetoric in Britain were René Rapin's *Réflexions sur l'usage de l'eloquence de ce temps* (1671), Dominique Bouhours's *La manière de bien penser dans les ouvrages d'esprit* (1687), Francois de Fénelon's *Dialogues sur l'éloquence* (1718), and Charles Rollin's *Traité des études: De la manière d'enseigner et d'étudier les Belles Lettres* (1726–8). By the middle of the eighteenth century all were available in English translation (Warnick 1993: 15). These works expanded the province of rhetoric into belles lettres, a term that included history, philosophy, poetry, and oratory. They added to creating speeches an emphasis on developing students' critical abilities through the reading and analysis of all types of literature. In terms of rhetoric's formative ideal, Quintilian's ideal orator would share his place of privilege with the person of "taste" and "sensibility," for the venues for rhetoric would now include polite conversations in the coffeehouses and clubs of Edinburgh and London (Howell 1971: 503–35; Conley 1990: 194–202; Warnick 1993). These interventions of belletrism have been controversial—praised by some for giving vernacular literature and criticism central places in the liberal arts curriculum but criticized by others for uprooting rhetoric from its ancient legal and political traditions and transplanting it in the garden of self-improvement.

The alignment of belletristic rhetoric with polite learning served immediate social and political needs in Scotland, where it had its British origin. With the Act of Union in 1707, Scotland gave up its independent Parliament in exchange for promises of freer access to English markets. This loss of political independence made civic republicanism for many a matter of nostalgia. What was needed were citizens who could take advantage of the commercial and cultural potential the new alliance with England seemed to promise. Furthermore, the emphasis in the new belletristic rhetorics on criticism and critical literacy seemed appropriate to the emerging "age of print," when periodicals such as *The Spectator*, *The Tatler*, and *The Guardian* dominated English social life and *The Mirror* and *The Lounger* flourished in Scotland. The Ciceronian ideal of the orator who inspires a senate to nobly resist an encroaching tyranny seemed like a relic in an age in which agreeability greased the wheels of a commercial society and civic discourse took place not at the Forum but in the coffeehouse.

In Scotland, Adam Smith was the first to conceive of rhetoric in belletristic terms. Smith was invited to lecture on rhetoric at the University of Edinburgh in 1748 by Henry Home (Lord Kames), who, hoping to improve the accent and taste of Scots, negotiated for Smith a lectureship in rhetoric and belles lettres (Howell 1971: 542). Smith offered his lectures at Edinburgh until he left for a professorship in logic and rhetoric at Glasgow in 1751, where the lectures were offered until 1763 (Smith 1963: 536). Unfortunately, Smith's lectures were destroyed, on his orders, upon his death, along with other works he deemed not sufficiently edited for publication (536). Fortunately, in 1958 John M. Lothian discovered a student notebook of the lectures Smith delivered in 1762–3; Lothian edited and published these notes in 1963. Surviving in this form are 29 of the (probably) 30 lectures that Smith delivered.

Smith's *Lectures on Rhetoric and Belles Lettres* follows the French belletristic model. The first 11 are concerned with style and the rest with the species of composition, in which Smith analyzes oratory, poetry, and history writing as genres and illustrates each with critical analyses of model examples. The differences between Smith's belletristic rhetoric and the handbook tradition are obvious. Smith does not directly take up invention (*inventio*) as a heuristic (invention is *heuresis* in Greek), though his discussion of what is appropriate to particular genres would be of use to the writer as well as the critic. Instead, Smith focuses on style (*elocutio*) and arrangement (*dispositio*), canons that apply to both written and oral discourse, while ignoring entirely the uniquely oratorical canons of memory (*memoria*) and delivery (*pronuntiatio, actio*). Furthermore, Smith does not defer to the ancients, often questioning the relevance of civic rhetoric and its aristocratic *ēthos* to his and his students' civil, polite, egalitarian context.

As Stephen McKenna (2006) shows, the most important rhetorical concept in Smith's *Lectures on Rhetoric and Belles Lettres* is rhetorical "propriety," or what ancient rhetorical theorists called *to prēpon* (Greek) and *decorum* (Latin). Ironically, this ancient

rhetorical principle frequently becomes the basis for Smith's criticism of classical theorists. According to Smith, with regard to style, Cicero and Quintilian hold that in the
rhetorical figures and the high style "all the beauties of language, all that is noble, grand
and sublime, all that is passionate, tender, and moving is to be found" (Smith 1963: 25).
For Smith, however, the "case is far otherwise" (25). Smith maintains that no style has
an innate claim to superiority: excellence is a matter of appropriateness to time, place,
audience, and circumstance. Of course, Cicero and Quintilian make the same point;
however, since the ornate, passionate style is, in their view, the orator's highest achievement, Smith can be forgiven his exaggeration. As it turns out, however, Smith also has a
preferred style, though it is the antithesis of Cicero's: "But we may observe that the most
beautiful passages are generally the most simple"; or, more comprehensively, "When the
sentiment of the speaker is expressed in a neat, clear, plain and clever manner, and the
passion or affection he is possessed of and intends, by sympathy, to communicate to his
hearer, is plainly and cleverly hit off, then and then only the expression has all the force
and beauty that language can give it" (25).

The *Lectures on Rhetoric and Belles Lettres* follows the Isocratean tradition of rhetorical *paideia* in promoting a formative ideal, but it is not the politically engaged, aristocratic, ideal orator envisioned by Cicero and Quintilian. Instead, the ideal orator
of Smith's *Lectures on Rhetoric and Belles Lettres* is the agreeable gentleman. A man is
"agreable company" when "his sentiments appear to be naturally expressed, when the
passion or affection is properly conveyed and when their thoughts are so agreable and
naturall that we find ourselves inclined to give our assent to them" (Smith 1963: 55).
The twin faults in self-presentation and in writing are affectation and bluntness. Lord
Shaftesbury, the *bête noir* of the *Lectures on Rhetoric and Belles Lettres*, is guilty of the
first defect, but Smith also censures the "plain man," who proudly "pays no regard to
the common civilities and forms of good breeding" and delights in exposing the "stupidity of others" (36). Compassion "finds littl[e] room in [the plain man's] breast," who,
uncharitably, is apt to find "ill motives" behind an innocent mistake (37). Smith's ideal
is the "simple man": "always willing to please" (37) and "plainly . . . shew the goodness
of his heart" (37). This polite man of sensibility practices Christian humility and charity
("contempt never enters into his mind, he is more ready to think well than meanly both
of the parts and the conduct of others" [37–8]). Smith doubtless intends to bring a degree
of polish to unpretentious Scottish students by emphasizing sensibility, but in doing so
he also seeks to shape their manners and morals as well as their prose style. Concepts
such as propriety and sympathy, so essential to Smith's *Theory of Moral Sentiments*, are
prominent in the lectures in rhetoric (McKenna 2006). With his emphasis on unaffected
manners and a sensitivity to others, Smith would fashion an *ēthos* appropriate to his
Christian, democratic, egalitarian context that is strikingly different from the classical
rhetorical ideal.

Smith also faults classical rhetoric for its arbitrariness and lack of systematic-
ity. He dismisses stylistic rhetorics as "silly books" whose taxonomies produce
overlapping classes, and faults ancient rhetoric's exclusive focus on the three civic
types of discourse—legal, political, and epideictic—as an arbitrary and incomplete

categorization that endures merely from a "reverence for antiquity" (Smith 1963: 63). Consistent with the pervasive impulse of Enlightenment writers, Smith would make his subject more rational. In lecture 1, which begins his consideration of the different types of composition, Smith first separates the universe of discourse into three "species of composition": narrative, didactic, and persuasive. He identifies the materials, tone, organization, and style appropriate to each genre. He derives from each a controlling purpose; the controlling purpose of history writing, for example, is to narrate facts, not to prove. Propriety in this context means that the rhetorical variables that constitute a genre serve the particular species's purpose. Smith supplements his analysis of genres with illustrative examples from exemplary texts, often comparing the different ways notable writers or speakers handled the conventions of the genre. In this way, Smith cultivates his students' critical sensibilities, develops their taste, and strengthens their capacities as writers and public speakers.

Smith's lectures on rhetoric and belles lettres, though never published, were influential, largely because of the work of Hugh Blair, who attended Smith's course in Edinburgh in 1748 (Howell 1971: 538). Blair's (1783) *Lectures on Rhetoric and Belles Lettres* follows the French belletristic model, broadening the province of rhetoric to include history, philosophy, and literature and emphasizing criticism more than composition. The lectures also adopt Smith's view of the centrality of propriety and the *ēthos* of the plain man. There are differences, however: Blair takes up directly some heady topics that Smith deals with only indirectly, such as the nature of taste, of criticism, and of the sublime. Moreover, Blair devotes 10 lectures to classical rhetoric and, clearly more conflicted than Smith, presents his *Lectures on Rhetoric and Belles Lettres* as a marriage of the ancient and the modern (Walzer 2007: 25–34).

Although Blair follows Smith in making propriety the standard of stylistic eloquence, he departs from Smith in his unwillingness to characterize his view as a break with the classical tradition. According to Blair, classical rhetoric is still viable; the problem is that we have mistakenly associated ancient eloquence with specious reasoning or an impassioned, ornamented style. The defining measure of eloquence—ancient or otherwise—has never been and should never be one particular style. A close imitation of the actual qualities of Ciceronian style would be as "ridiculous" today as appearing in a modern courtroom in the "Toga of a Roman Lawyer" (Blair [1783] 2005: 304). In fact, Demosthenes and Cicero are models precisely because the style they chose was appropriate to their setting. True eloquence is ever "the Art of Speaking in such a manner as to attain the end for which we speak" (317). Blair confidently disassociates eloquence from the high style; what was once the paradigmatic "scene" of civic republicanism in Greece and Rome becomes in the *Lectures on Rhetoric and Belles Lettres* simply an example of stylistic appropriateness.

Similarly, Blair fosters an *ēthos* of sincerity appropriate to the culture of politeness, not the enactment of passion central to the Ciceronian high style. For Blair a speaker will be eloquent only "when he is in earnest, and uttering his own sentiments" ([1783] 2005: 290). In contrast, sincerity for Quintilian was, like honesty, helpful but not essential, since it could be feigned as an actor would. But Blair does not present this difference as a break with the ancients. On the contrary, he links his advice to be sincere to classical precedent by citing the Roman truism that the sentiments expressed should be "true voices from the depth of the heart" (*verae voces ab imo pectore*). We feel passionately only when we utter what we sincerely believe.

This pattern of affirming classical concepts while transforming their meaning characterizes Blair's treatment of the character and voice he would inculcate in his students. In lecture 34 Blair draws on the connection between virtuous character and oratorical success most famously captured in Cato the Elder's ideal (taken up by Quintilian) of the *vir bonus, dicendi peritus*: "In order to be a truly eloquent or persuasive Speaker, nothing is more necessary than to be a virtuous man. This was a favourite position among the antient Rhetoricians: '*Non posse Oratorem esse nisi virum bonum*'" (Blair [1783] 2005: 381). But Blair's notion of the character traits and voice of the good man is not Quintilian's. "Probity," "disinterestedness," and "candour" (384), which for Blair are linked to sincerity, are the key qualities a writer or speaker must project. These are not the traits of Cicero or Quintilian's masculinist, magnanimous, proud, impassioned patriot. But rather than acknowledge this difference, Blair attempts to merge the two: "Joined with the manly virtues, [the orator] should, at the same time, possess strong and tender sensibility to all the injuries, distresses, and sorrows of his fellow-creatures; a heart that can easily relent; that can readily enter into the circumstances of others, and can make their case his own" (383).

The belletristic transformation of British Enlightenment rhetoric that Smith, Blair, Lord Kames, and others ushered in has been controversial. The introduction of the critical study of vernacular literature into the rhetoric course that Scottish belletrism brought about became the basis for the professional study of English literature and the modern department of English (Court 1992; Crawford 1992; Miller 1997), a transformation praised by those who welcome a central place for vernacular literature in the liberal arts curriculum (Ferreira-Buckley 1998: 183). But others have lamented the concomitant marginalization of the civic tradition within the liberal arts (Miller 1997: 248). Belletrism has also been faulted for an emphasis on *English* literature that seems to some to have come at the expense of *Scottish* and *Irish* nativism (Beach 2001) and, with its emphasis on cultivating a London dialect, for promoting a Westminster linguistic imperialism (Crawford 1998). Some counter this charge by citing Blair's advocacy of Ossian (however misguided) as evidence of his effort to cultivate a proud Scottish identity. Whatever the ultimate effects of the changes belletrism ultimately brought about, Scottish rhetoricians in their time were motivated to improve their students' chances of success in an environment characterized by marked economic disparities between England and "North Britain."

It is not true, as some scholars allege, that eighteenth-century rhetoric represents a radical departure from classical rhetorical theory. At least in the theories of Campbell and Blair, the most important theorists in eighteenth-century Britain, Cicero and Quintilian remain authorities. Furthermore, as Lois Agnew (1998) argues, in Scotland belletrism was not conceived of as being distinct from the oral, civic tradition but as preparation for entry into civil society. Nor is it true that in the eighteenth century rhetoric abandons its formative social role for an individualistic one. Smith and Blair counter the individualism they feared by shaping, in Blair's case, a Christian gentleman and, in Smith's, a Stoic ethic (Agnew 1998). But eighteenth-century British rhetoric does indeed mark a break with the civic republicanism of ancient Greek and Roman rhetoric. For better or worse, Smith and Blair's emphasis on the *ēthos* of the plain man and on the temperate, restrained style is part of a larger, twofold transformation noted by cultural historians: the decline of a "heroic honor culture" and the emergence of a "civil" one (Becker 1988: ix), and the disappearance of the rhetorical, civic actor and the appearance of the unique, sincere person.

FURTHER READING

Wilbur Samuel Howell's (1971) magisterial *Eighteenth-Century British Logic and Rhetoric* is, for the completeness of its archival work and the detail of its summaries, still the point of departure for work in eighteenth-century British rhetoric, though most think Howell overstates the break between the new rhetorics and the classical tradition. Barbara Warnick's (1993) *The Sixth Canon: Belletristic Rhetorical Theory and Its French Antecedents* is a reliable overview of the French origins of British belletristic rhetoric. On Campbell, see the works by Lloyd Bitzer and Arthur Walzer in the bibliography. For Smith, see Stephen McKenna's (2006) *Adam Smith: The Rhetoric of Propriety*. There is no comprehensive study of Blair on rhetoric, though the introduction to the *Lectures on Rhetoric and Belles Lettres* (Ferreira-Buckley and Halloran 2005) is reliable and helpful. For an excellent recent bibliography of eighteenth-century rhetoric, see Ferreira-Buckley (2010).

REFERENCES

Agnew, Lois. 1998. "Civic Function of Taste: A Re-assessment of Hugh Blair's Theory of Taste." *Rhetoric Society Quarterly* 28 no. 2: 35–36.

Beach, Adam R. 2001. "The Creation of a Classical Language in the Eighteenth Century: Standardizing English, Cultural Imperialism, and the Future of the Literary Canon." *Texas Studies in Literature and Language* 43 no. 2: 117–141.

Becker, Marvin G. 1988. *Civility and Society in Western Europe, 1300–1600*. Bloomington: Indiana University Press.

Berlin, James. 1984. *Writing Instruction in Nineteenth-Century American Colleges*. Carbondale: Southern Illinois University Press.

Bevilacqua, Vincent. 1964. "Campbell, Priestley, and the Controversy Concerning Common Sense." *Southern Speech Journal* 30 no. 2: 79–88.

Bitzer, Lloyd F. 1969. "Hume's Philosophy in George Campbell's *Philosophy of Rhetoric*." *Philosophy & Rhetoric* 2 no. 3: 139–166.

Blair, Hugh. (1783) 2005. *Lectures on Rhetoric and Belles Lettres*. Carbondale: University of Illinois Press.

Bormann, Dennis R. 1985. "Some 'Common Sense' about Campbell, Hume, and Reid: The Extrinsic Evidence." *Quarterly Journal of Speech* 71 no. 4: 395–421.

Bormann, Dennis R. 1988. "George Campbell's *Cura Prima* on Eloquence—1758." *Quarterly Journal of Speech* 74 no. 1: 35–51.

Bouhours, Dominique. (1715) 1971. *La manière de bien penser dans les ouvrages d'esprit*. Paris: Brunet. Reprint. Brighton: University of Sussex.

Campbell, George. 1776. *A Dissertation on Miracles; containing an Examination of the Principles advanced by David Hume, Esq. in an "Essay on Miracles."* Glasgow: J. Mundell.

Campbell, George. (1776) 1998. *The Philosophy of Rhetoric*. 2nd ed. Edited by Lloyd Bitzer. Carbondale: Southern Illinois University Press.

Conley, Thomas. 1990. *Rhetoric in the European Tradition*. Chicago: University of Chicago Press.

Connors, Robert J. 1981. "The Rise and Fall of the Modes of Discourse." *College Composition and Communication* 32 no. 4: 444–456.

Court, Franklin E. 1992. *Institutionalizing English Literature: The Culture and Politics of Literary Study, 1750–1900*. Stanford, CA: Stanford University Press.

Crawford, Robert. 1992. *Devolving English Literature*. Oxford: Clarendon Press.

Crawford, Robert, ed. 1998. *The Scottish Invention of English Literature*. Cambridge: Cambridge University Press.

Cronkhite, Gary Lynn. 1967. "Intuition: Campbell's Escape from Scepticism." *Western Speech Journal* 31: 165–171.

Crowley, Sharon. 1990. *The Methodical Memory: Invention in Current-Traditional Rhetoric*. Carbondale: Southern Illinois University Press.

Ehninger, Douglas. 1952. "Dominant Trends in English Rhetorical Thought, 1750–1800." *Southern Speech Journal* 18: 3–12.

Fénelon, Francois de. (1718) 1951. *Dialogues on Eloquence*. Translated by Wilbur Samuel Howell. Princeton, NJ: Princeton University Press.

Ferreira-Buckley, Linda. 1998. "Scottish Rhetoric and the Formation of English Studies in Nineteenth-Century England." In *The Scottish Invention of English Literature*, edited by Robert Crawford, 180–206. Cambridge: Cambridge University Press.

Ferreira-Buckley, Linda. 2010. "The Eighteenth Century." In *The Present State of Scholarship in the History of Rhetoric: A Twenty-First Century Guide*, edited by Lynée Lewis Gaillet, with Winifred Bryan Horner, 114–151. Columbia: University of Missouri Press.

Ferreira-Buckley, Linda, and S. Michael Halloran, eds. 2005. *Lectures on Rhetoric and Belles Lettres*. Carbondale: Southern Illinois University Press.

Howell, Wilbur Samuel. 1971. *Eighteenth-Century British Logic and Rhetoric*. Princeton, NJ: Princeton University Press.

Hume, David. (1739) 1984. *A Treatise of Human Nature*. Edited by Ernest G. Mossner. London: Penguin Books.

Hume, David. (1748) 1988. *An Enquiry Concerning Human Understanding*. New York: Prometheus Books.

Lamy, Bernard. (1676) 1988. *La Rhétorique, ou, L'art de Parler*. Edited by Christine Noille-Glauzade. Paris: H. Champion.

Locke, John. (1690) 1894. *An Essay Concerning Human Understanding*. 2 vols. Edited by Alexander Campbell Fraser. New York: Dover.

McKenna, Stephen. 2006. *Adam Smith: The Rhetoric of Propriety*. Albany: State University of New York Press.

Miller, Thomas P. 1997. *The Formation of College English: Rhetoric and Belles Lettres in the British Cultural Provinces*. Pittsburgh, PA: University of Pittsburgh Press.

Mohrmann, G. P. 1968. "George Campbell: The Psychological Background." *Western Speech Journal* 32: 99–104.

Priestley, Joseph. (1777) 1965. *A Course of Lectures on Oratory and Criticism*. Edited by Vincent Bevilacqua and Richard Murphy. Carbondale: Southern Illinois University Press.

Rapin, René. 1731. *The Whole Critical Works of Mr. Rapin*. 2 vols. Translated by Basil Kennet, Mr. Rymer et al. London: Walthoe Wikin.

Rasmussen, Karen. 1974. "Inconsistency in Campbell's Rhetoric: Explanation and Implications." *Quarterly Journal of Speech* 60: 190–200.

Reid, Thomas. (1764) 1970. *An Inquiry into the Human Mind*. Edited by Timothy Duggan. Chicago: University of Chicago Press.

Rollin, Charles. 1764. *De La manière d'enseigner et d'étudier les Belles Lettres*. Paris: Chez la veuve Estienne.

Sefton, Henry. 1987. "David Hume and Principal George Campbell." In *Aberdeen and the Enlightenment: Proceedings of a Conference Held at the University of Aberdeen*, edited by Jennifer J. Carter and Joan H. Pittock, 123–128. Aberdeen: Aberdeen University Press.

Smith, Adam. 1963. *Lectures on Rhetoric and Belles Lettres*. Edited by John M. Lothian. Carbondale: Southern Illinois University Press.

Ulman, H. Lewis, ed. 1990. *Minutes of the Aberdeen Philosophical Society, 1758–1973*. Aberdeen: Aberdeen University Press.

Walzer, Arthur E. 2000. "On Reading George Campbell: 'Resemblance' and 'Vivacity' in the *Philosophy of Rhetoric*." *Rhetorica* 18: 321–342.

Walzer, Arthur E. 2003. *George Campbell: Rhetoric in the Age of Enlightenment*. Albany: State University of New York Press.

Walzer, Arthur E. 2007. "Blair's Ideal Orator: Civic Rhetoric and Christian Politeness in Lectures 25–34." *Rhetorica* 25: 269–295.

Warnick, Barbara. 1993. *The Sixth Canon: Belletristic Rhetorical Theory and Its French Antecedents*. Columbia: University of South Carolina Press.

CHAPTER 42

RHETORIC AND PHILOSOPHY

ADAM POTKAY

PHILOSOPHY rejected eloquence as an instrument of deceit and a source of error, and rhetoric accepted the standards of the new philosophy, placing a premium on perspicuity and probable arguments. That, at least, is the standard mid-twentieth century story about rhetoric and philosophy in the long eighteenth century that was developed by a cadre of rhetoric and communication professors (Vincent Bevilacqua, Lloyd Bitzer, Harold Harding, et al.) and culminated in Wilbur Samuel Howell's magisterial *Eighteenth-Century British Logic and Rhetoric* (1971). This generation of scholars revived interest in the lectures and treatises on rhetoric and belles lettres by Adam Smith, George Campbell, Lord Kames, Joseph Priestley, Hugh Blair, and others, in part by writing critical introductions to Southern Illinois University Press reprints of these authors' works (see Walzer, ch. 41). The achievement of the eighteenth-century "New Rhetoric," as Howell dubbed it, was to respond effectively to the criticisms of eloquence, and specifically of tropes, offered by philosophers from René Descartes and John Locke onward. Philosophers decried tropes, figures, and oratorical blandishment as deceptive, disruptive, and vulgar; rhetoricians, in response, downplayed the stylistic elements of classical rhetoric, emphasized clarity and order, and, taking up the philosophical mantle, demonstrated how literature and oratory reflect basic principles of the mind, particularly the association of ideas and the manner in which we acquire beliefs.

As we shall see, philosophers of the period did not always decry tropes—but when they did, they did so with gusto. Locke influentially expressed the case against figurative eloquence in his *An Essay Concerning Human Understanding*: "All the art of rhetoric, besides order and clearness, all the artificial and figurative application of words eloquence hath invented, are for nothing else but to insinuate wrong ideas, move the passions, and thereby mislead the judgment; and so indeed are a perfect cheat . . . [Tropes] are certainly, in all discourses that pretend to inform or instruct, wholly to be avoided" ([1689] 1975: 508).[1] Locke here draws on an anti-rhetorical animus that extends back, ultimately, to Plato's *Gorgias* and, more immediately, to Thomas Sprat's *History of the Royal Society* (1667). David Hume, in turn, complains of eloquence in the learned world: "'Tis not reason, which carries the prize, but eloquence; and no man needs ever despair of gaining proselytes to the most extravagant hypothesis, who has art enough to represent it in any favourable colours. The victory is not gained by the men at arms, who manage the pike and the sword; but by the trumpeters, drummers, and musicians of the army" ([1739–40] 1978: xiv).

With philosophers setting the tone, rhetoricians looked askance at tropes and figures, emphasized substance over style, and placed a premium on order and "perspicuity" (their favorite term). From the Latin *perspicuus*, "transparent," this term of art derives from Quintilian's *Institutio oratoria* (*nobis prima sit virtus perspicuitas*; 8.2.22). But for Locke, as for the rhetoricians who followed him, perspicuity takes on a more central role in eloquence than it had for the Romans: "The art of speaking well, consists chiefly in two things, viz. perspicuity, and right reasoning" (quoted in Howell 1971: 450). The notes we have from Adam Smith's lectures on rhetoric begin: "Perspicuity of style requires . . . that the expressions we use should be free from all ambiguity" ([1762–63] 1985: 3). George Campbell devotes four chapters to the topic (bk. 2, chs. 6–9). Hugh Blair, by far the era's most widely read rhetorician,[2] praises perspicuity as a "positive beauty," not merely a "freedom from defect": "We are pleased with an author . . . who frees us from all fatigue of searching for his meaning . . . whose style flows always like a limpid stream, where we see to the very bottom" ([1783] 1965: 1: 186 [lecture 10]). British rhetoric thus becomes concerned with clear-sightedness in part because of Locke's influence but also because of rhetorical developments on the Continent (see France 1972 on the Cartesian and post-Cartesian reforms of rhetoric in France).

What attracted Howell to the eighteenth-century New Rhetoric was twofold. First, he approved as properly modern its promotion of inductively probable arguments and a perspicuous style. Second, he saw it as assuming rhetoric's rightful status as a science not only of the oratorical arts but also of all modes of communication, including historical, philosophical, literary, and didactic discourses. In the New Rhetoric Howell saw the role rhetoric ought to be playing, even though it was not actually doing so, in the university of his own day. (Born in 1904, he served as professor of rhetoric and oratory at Princeton from 1952 to 1972.) He thought the New Rhetoric struck the right balance between a generative model of rhetoric (teaching people to write and speak) and an analytic model aimed at discovering the principles and assessing the merits of literature, modern as well as classical. (An alternative view of the New Rhetoric, which tended to emphasize belles lettres, would be to see it as a critical stage in the preponderance of an analytic model that would, by the later twentieth century, largely collapse rhetoric into literary theory.)

Howell's story about philosophy's challenge to rhetoric and the New Rhetoric's triumphant if short-lived response to it is fine as far as it goes, but it is not the full story. Complicating it are the following counter-stories, which have been elaborated in the scholarship of the past 30 years. First, empiricist philosophers, far from precluding eloquence, employ the tropes of rhetoric not only in their style but also, more fundamentally, in their very science of mind. In depicting perception and belief as processes involving transference and persuasion, they reveal philosophy's deep implication with rhetoric. Second, philosophers did not always denounce tropes; they could admire the figurative eloquence of earlier eras and even wish, at least half-heartedly, for its recur-rence. Third, philosophers and rhetoricians sought to account for the origins of tropes in their speculative histories of primitive culture. According to their quasi-anthropological analyses, tropes originally express false beliefs that a cultivated or "polite" audience has put behind them. However, the underlying passions (including fear and hope) that motivate irrational beliefs are ineradicable elements of human nature and as such con-tinue to actuate, if in a moderated way, the polite audience that philosophy and rhetoric jointly sought to fashion.

THE RHETORIC OF EMPIRICISM

Philosophy did not, for all its anti-rhetorical flourishes, simply reject rhetoric. Despite objections to rhetoric as a cause of error (Locke) or dissension (Sprat), or as an unnec-essary frill in discourses addressed to the understanding (Hume), philosophers none-theless employed analogies and metaphors. Locke's diatribe against figurative speech is itself figurative in its final flourish: "Eloquence [is] like the fair sex . . . And 'tis in vain to find fault with those arts of deceiving, wherein men find pleasure to be deceived" ([1689] 1975: 508). Thomas Leland responded, "Even Mr. Locke, that enemy to figurative speech, slides imperceptibly into those paths, from whence he is so solicitous to divert mankind" (1764: 18). It might be noted as well that Locke here animates his prose with well-placed alliteration and the figures of epistrophe and polyptoton. In a similar slide, Hume depicts eloquence as the mere musician of an army, rather than its real force, an analogy marshaled against the eloquence it exhibits.

More fundamentally, however, tropes or at least trope-like substitutions lie at the heart of empiricist epistemology itself.[3] As William Walker argues, "Although he con-demned as instruments of deceit the substitutions that define tropes, Locke was contin-ually describing them in his account of how the mind thinks and of the specific concepts that it produces" (1994: 158). Consider the mental activity by which a person transforms the retinal image of a flat circle into what is judged to be a round globe. Locke explains this process: "The judgment presently, by an habitual custom, alters the appearances into their causes: so that from that, which truly is variety of shadow or colour, collect-ing the figure, it makes it pass for a mark [or sign] of figure, and frames to its self the perception of a convex figure, and an uniform colour" ([1689] 1975: 145). Walker notes that Locke here describes a "form of substitution" in which "the idea of a sphere, an idea of judgment, takes the place of the idea of a circle, an idea of sensation," and that "the substitution of the *name* of a cause for the *name* of an effect is a metonymy" (1994: 157–8)—metonymy being the rhetorical term used by the philosopher Gottfried Leibniz in his commentary on this passage in his *New Essays on Human Understanding* (1704). Locke implicitly structures and Leibniz explicitly understands epistemological writing in terms of tropes.

For Locke, moreover (as later for Hume), the way beliefs arise in us is analogous to the way an orator persuades an audience. As Walker points out, Locke uses the term "persuasion" more or less interchangeably with "belief" and presents "ideas and words as material objects that strike the mind with different amounts of force and which compel or correspond with varying amounts of belief" (1994: 161). Hume develops Locke's analysis of belief in his *Treatise of Human Nature* (1739–40), where, in describing the impact of impressions or ideas upon the mind, he draws upon an idiom developed in classical rhetoric. For Hume the mind is struck with more or less force and liveliness, and a greater or lesser degree of belief ensues. This epistemological scene harkens back to *On the Sublime*, in which Longinus attributes physical "force" (*bia*) to sublime oratory (sec. 12); in Latin rhetorics, force (*vis*) is attributed to effective eloquence more generally (Cicero, *De oratore* 2.44.187). From Aristotle onward, good eloquence also possesses *energeia*, a term variously translated into English as "vigor," "animation," "actuality," or "viability."[4] Hume appears to have these rhetorical usages in mind when he grants perceptions the necessary "force" and "vivacity" to persuade the mind. According to Hume, direct sensory impressions always command belief, but for ideas to do so they must be vivified, either by our mental principles (e.g., associating causes and effects) or by artificial means such as eloquence. Having stated that "belief must please the imagination by means of the force and vivacity which attends it," Hume conversely argues that "belief not only gives vigor to the imagination, but that a vigorous and strong imagination is of all talents the most proper to secure belief and authority. 'Tis difficult for us to withhold our assent from what is painted out to us in all the colours of eloquence; and the vivacity produc'd by the fancy is in many cases greater than that which arises from custom and experience" ([1739–40] 1978: 122–3).

The roles Hume assigned to force and vivacity in the production of belief, as borrowings from rhetoric, were easily recuperated by the New Rhetoric, which borrowed generally from empiricist philosophy and, in Campbell's *Philosophy of Rhetoric*, specifically from Hume. Campbell follows Hume in holding that sense, memory, and imagination possess decreasing amounts of vivacity; thus, the orator's task is to find ways to enliven the ideas raised in the imagination to such a degree that they resemble the perceptions of the senses and the transcripts of the memory. As Campbell phrases it, the orator must "make the ideas he summons up in the imagination of his hearers, resemble, in luster and steadiness, those of sensation and remembrance" (Campbell [1776] 1963: 81). Luster or liveliness in communication derives chiefly from precise diction. Campbell illustrates this proposition by contrasting the vivacity of the biblical verse on the Egyptians that pursued Moses across the Red Sea—"They *sank* as *lead* in the mighty waters" (Exodus 15:10)—with the slackening effected by rendering the verse's key terms "more comprehensive or generical": "They *fell* as *metal*" (286). The "vivacity" (284) at which Campbell aimed was variously expressed by most if not all the rhetoricians and critics of the period: for example, Joseph Addison's "lively idea"[5]; Priestley's "vivid representation" ([1777] 1965: 79–115); and Lord Kames's "ideal presence" ([1785] 2005: 1: 66–77). All but Addison—himself an influence on Hume—engage with Hume's psychology of belief and of the passions.

But again, rhetoric can readily draw upon Hume's philosophy because of Hume's own debts to rhetoric. Even his famous account of sympathy as a mechanism of emotional sharing has rhetorical antecedents: "When I see the *effects* of passion in the voice and gesture of any person, my mind immediately passes from these effects to their causes [another metonymy], and forms such a lively idea of the passion, as is presently converted into the passion itself" (Hume [1739–40] 1978: 575–6). Hume's doctrine of sympathy corresponds to rhetorical descriptions of "action" (*actio*) or oratorical delivery (see Goring, ch. 44). In Cicero's *De oratore*, Crassus maintains that "action, which by its own powers displays the movements of the soul, affects all mankind, for the minds of all men are excited by the same emotions which they recognize in others, and indicate in themselves by the same tokens" (3.59; trans. Watson). Cicero's conception of a sympathetic identification between orator and audience is a commonplace of eighteenth-century rhetoric. According to Thomas Gordon's "Of Eloquence, considered philosophically" (*Cato's Letters* no. 104, 1722), "Nothing is so catching and communicative as the passions. The cast of an angry or a pleasant eye will beget anger, or pleasure: One man's anger, or sorrow, or joy, can make a whole assembly outrageous, or dejected, or merry" (Gordon 1995: 2: 735). This transmission of passion operates presemantically, and thus the orator's sound and gestures may win "the human sympathy in our souls"—but "how vastly prevailing must be their [united] force, when it comes arrayed and heightened by a swelling and irresistible tide of words . . . ?" (2: 738). It is no far cry from Gordon's to Hume's model of sympathetic exchange—or, as we shall see in the next section, from Gordon's to Hume's philosophical understanding of the power of eloquence.

Empiricist philosophy and rhetoric are, in conclusion, inherently intertwined, impossible to extricate from one another. Rhetorical tropes and persuasion are not just the "cheat" that Locke calls them; they also fundamentally inform the philosophers' accounts of how we perceive, how we share perceptions, and how we come to believe in their truth or reality.

The Nostalgia for Sublime Eloquence in a Polite Age

Some philosophers were not impervious to the flamboyant oratorical tropes of the past. Philosophers and rhetoricians alike expressed their admiration for a particular figurative style: the sublime style as configured in Longinus's *On the Sublime*. Hume, in his essay, "Of Eloquence" (1742), goes so far as to call for a revival in modern Britain of the "sublime and pathetic" eloquence of Demosthenes and Cicero. His preference, however, is for Demosthenes, of whom he concludes: "Could [Demosthenes's style] be copied, its success would be infallible over a modern assembly. It is rapid harmony, exactly adjusted to the sense: It is vehement reasoning, without any appearance of art: It is disdain, anger, boldness, freedom, involved in a continued stream of argument: And of all human productions, the orations of Demosthenes present to us the models, which approach the nearest to perfection" (Hume [1742] 1985: 105–6).

"Of Eloquence" is a pivotal essay, borrowing its terms of praise from both Longinus (sec. 34) and François Fénelon ([1717] 1787: 17–8) and in turn propelling a taste for the sublime in deliberative eloquence well into the nineteenth century via Blair's lectures on rhetoric, which crib most of Hume's essay in their discussion of political eloquence (see lectures 25–7).[6]

Howell judged "Of Eloquence" to be "curiously static, curiously unhistorical, and curiously antiquarian" (1971: 616). Yet the essay is less "static" than Howell claims. On the contrary, it is animated by ambivalence toward its topic that increases as Hume revises the piece for successive editions of his *Essays*. Hume never withdraws his praise of ancient eloquence, but he does suggest that it is part of an unrecoverable past, and one that we would not entirely want to recover. Hume's rousing call for the revival of eloquence has a bathetic ending. Directly after urging the modern orator to employ "the strongest figures and expressions" in extemporaneous speech, Hume stoops, unexpectedly, to conclude "that, even though our modern orators should not elevate their style or aspire to a rivalship with the ancient, yet there is, in most of their speeches, a material defect, which they might correct, without departing from that composed air of argument and reasoning to which they limit their ambition" (Hume 1985: 109–10). Hume proceeds to recommend greater "order and method" in public discourse. And in a 1768 addition to his essay, he distances himself from his earlier praise of the sublime figures of ancient eloquence, remarking of a *prosōpopoēia* in Cicero, "Should this sentiment even appear to us excessive, as perhaps it justly may, it will at least serve to give an idea of the style of ancient eloquence, where such swelling expressions were not rejected as wholly monstrous and gigantic" (101). Hume's earlier enthusiasm is superseded by a tone of wry detachment.

Hume is divided, finally, between the allure of ancient power and his respect for modern sociability and politeness, according to the standards of which figures such as those Demosthenes used and Longinus praised seem "monstrous" or "vulgar," suited to the best men of a different era but only to the worst classes now. Hume was probably influenced, between 1742 and his final revisions of 1768, by the rise in his native Scotland of the New Rhetoric, with its social function of training provincial youths in metropolitan modes of comportment and authority (see Walzer, ch. 41). Thus, Adam Smith informed his students at Glasgow, "The behaviour which is reckoned polite in England is a calm, composed, unpassionate serenity noways ruffled by passion" (Smith [1762–63] 1985: 198). This social *decorum* must inform polite communication, which should be deferential, perspicuous, and (at least relatively) unornamented. The tropes and figures that once animated eloquence now inhabit the less restrained precincts and lower orders of society. "There is nowhere more use made of figures," Smith explained, "than in the lowest and most vulgar conversation. The Billingsgate [London fish market] language is full of it" (34). Oliver Goldsmith, the Irish man of letters, chimes in: "It has been remarked, that the lower parts of mankind generally express themselves most figuratively, and that the tropes are found in the most ordinary forms of conversation" (1966: 1: 447).

The passionate tropes and figures, relegated to the lower ranks of society, did not cease to fascinate Enlightenment authors. They continued to exert a retrospective fascination, beckoning to polite authors from stages in mankind's past. For Hume—as, indeed, for Longinus—that past comprised the democratic and republican governments of an earlier Greece and Rome, where orators acted on the will as well as the understanding of deliberative assemblies. In the second half of the eighteenth century other fonts of sublime eloquence were identified: the Hebrew books of the Bible (particularly Job and Psalms) were ranked most sublime by, among others, Robert Lowth and Blair; Blair argued as well, along with Lord Kames, for the sublimity of the pseudo-ancient epics of Ossian, a supposed bard of the third century CE "translated" (in fact, largely constructed) by James Macpherson.[7] Tropes flourish in the earliest stages of mankind. Goldsmith merely states a commonplace when he writes that "barbarous nations speak in a style more affecting and figurative than others; they feel with passions unabated by judgment, and tropes and figures are the natural result of their sensations" (1966: 1: 169). As long as they remained in the past, the tropes and figures were still admirable.

THE ENLIGHTENMENT QUEST FOR THE ORIGINS OF TROPES

The consignment of tropes to the past—or, atavistically, to the lower ranks of present society—coincided with a philosophical search for their conjectural origins. How do tropes come into being? What is their basis in human nature? Cicero's account of tropes as necessitated by a deficiency of proper terms in early languages (*De oratore* 3.38; cf. Quintilian, *Institutio oratoria* 8.6.4–6) does not take up the root causes of tropes. These causes could be the fundamental processes of mind, particularly the association of ideas as it prominently featured in Kames and Priestley (Kallich 1970). But Enlightenment authors often trace figurative thinking back to traumas in a conjectural past and associate it with false beliefs.

For Jean-Jacques Rousseau, pressing danger gives rise to figurative language as a function of false belief:

> Upon meeting others, a savage man will initially be frightened. Because of his fear he sees the others as bigger and stronger than himself. He calls them *giants*. After many experiences, he recognizes these so-called giants are neither bigger nor stronger than he. . . . So he invents another name common to them and to him, such as the name *man*, for example, and leaves *giant* to the fictitious object that impressed him during his illusion. That is how the figurative word is born before the literal word, when our gaze is held in passionate fascination; and how it is that the first idea it conveys to us is not that of the truth. (1966: 12–3)

Rousseau thus turns on its head the traditional notion that figurative language "turns from" (the root of "trope") the literal words that preexist it. In his account, figurative language involves a transposition of ideas ("large fearsome creature" substituted for "creature like me"), not of words. Thus, his savage man, inhabiting a world that is presocial and full of surprises, thinks figuratively before he arrives at the proper or true name for what he sees.

Fear also figures prominently in stories that link the origin of tropes with that of religion. For Bernard Fontenelle in his "On the Origin of Fables" gods are the personified causes of nature's agitations: "To make sense of the thunder and the lightning, one represents god with a human face hurling arrows of fire on us" ([1724] 1968: 2: 390; trans. mine). In Giambattista Vico's *New Science* (1725, revised 1744) the origins of god, conscience, and speech (at least among the Gentiles) occur at the moment when a people see in the thundering sky an anthropomorphic presence and name it, in onomatopoeic echoes of the thunder, "Zeus" or "Jove." Deity-words are the first words of all languages; these ur-words arise, in rhetorical terms, as interjections and *prosōpopoēiae* (Vico [1725] 1968: 150).

The rhetorical origin of religion is more pronounced in Hume's *Natural History of Religion* (1757), which also explicitly distinguishes between the enlightened who think *in terms of* tropes and the ignorant who think *in* tropes. Hume writes as a connoisseur who admires "the frequency and beauty of the *prosopopoeia* in poetry, where trees, mountains and streams are personified," but who notes, with ironic understatement, that personification "may sometime enter into the real creed of the ignorant vulgar" ([1757] 1957: 29–30). The same tropes that the enlightened have catalogued for the purpose of rhetorical ornamentation enable the vulgar to posit reality. Thus polytheistic religions see gods in all the forces of nature, from sky to sea. So far Hume elaborates on an analysis of pagan religion familiar from Lucretius onward (*De rerum natura* 5.1161–1240). He turns toward more sensitive matter, however, in deriving monotheism (and thus, implicitly, Judeo-Christian religion) from an aggravation of the passions that accounts for all personification. While Thomas Hobbes as well as eighteenth-century deists held that monotheism, unlike the pagan religions, arose from man's rational speculation on the ultimate causes of the natural world, Hume, by contrast, maintains that monotheism merely issues from a more urgent fear, one that transfigures the original *prosōpopoēia* of religion into something much more than human. Monotheism is the product of the "eulogy or exaggeration"—we might say hyperbole—bestowed upon one god above all others at a moment when "men's fears or distresses become more urgent" and thus the god's favor or mercy more critical (Hume [1757] 1957: 42–3).

Hume and other Enlightenment philosophers, in imagining the passions appropriate for humans in different circumstances, historicize the "rhetoric of passions" that, as Daniel Gross (2006: 8, 114–30) observes, begins with Aristotle's social analysis of the passions in book 2 of the *Rhetoric*. Aristotle posited that, to excite and allay the passions of the audience, the orator must know the dominant passions of different conditions and stages of life, and the project of acquiring such knowledge continues into Hume and Smith. But in addition to this analysis of the passions in present-tense communities, we

ADAM POTKAY   543

find in Enlightenment authors a detailed analysis of how passions probably functioned in the past. Enlightenment mythography and conjectural history offer a psychopathology of irrational beliefs and unreflective figurative expressions: Jove, giant, one God. Enlightenment philosophy and rhetoric, if these two fields can here even be separated, give the passions both a conjectural history (How, in all probability, did primitive or natural men act and speak?) and, within the present, a class provenance (the uneducated "mob" is more likely to act and speak according to primitive or atavistic passions from which the gentleman distances himself). With the refinement of the passions, language progressed over the course of history, and developmentally within each individual, from "vivacity to accuracy; from the fire of poetic enthusiasm, to the coolness of philosophical precision" (Jamieson 1818: 31). But it has done so only for the polite of the present—indeed, it would seem, for those trained in the new philosophy and rhetoric.

Conclusion

We have returned, then, to where we began, with a version of the standard story in which philosophy rejected eloquence and rhetoric accepted philosophy. But we have seen, along the way, the degree to which "primitive" language and sublime eloquence remained objects of peculiar fascination, from the apostrophe of Demosthenes to the prose poems of Ossian. We have seen, too, how the language of philosophical precision is not devoid of tropological substitutions. Empiricist philosophy was itself informed by an analytic strand of ancient rhetoric in studying impressions and words that make an impact and more or less enforce belief. Thus, while beliefs consigned to past ages and vulgar peoples were marked as unreasonable, even reasonable beliefs were depicted in the text of empiricist philosophy as acquired not by reason but through forceful imprinting, in a manner analogous to that by which ancient orators swayed assemblies.

Notes

1. In my quotations from seventeenth- and eighteenth-century texts I have modernized typographical conventions and orthography.
2. Thomas Conley (1990: 220) notes that by 1873 Blair's *Lectures on Rhetoric and Belles Lettres* had gone into over 50 editions in Britain and America and had appeared on the Continent in German, French, Spanish, Italian, and Russian translations.
3. Literary critics galvanized by (if often critical of) the work of Paul de Man, particularly his essay, "The Epistemology of Metaphor" (1978), have variously explored the rhetoric of classical empiricism, chiefly in the writings of Locke, Berkeley, Hume, and Burke. See Richetti (1961), Law (1993), Potkay (1994), Walker (1994), Potkay (1995), and Thompson and Meeker (2007).
4. On *bia/vis* and *energeia* as rhetorical terms of art that influence Hume's epistemology, see Potkay (1990: 17–53); on the career of *energeia* from Aristotle to Campbell and beyond, see also Gross (2005: 36–43).

5. "Words, when well chosen, have so great a force in them that a description often gives us more lively ideas than the sight of things themselves" (*The Spectator* no. 416; in Steele and Addison 1892: 387).

6. On the influence of Hume and Blair on ideals of civic oratory in the early American republic, see Potkay (1999).

7. Lowth's (1787) lectures on Old Testament poetry, originally published in Latin in 1753, propound its sublimity in lectures 14–7 (1: 302–87); Blair ([1783] 1965), in lecture 4, touches upon the sublimity of the Scriptures (1: 57–62) and of Ossian (1: 65–6), though he treats the sublime of the latter throughout his 1763 *Critical Dissertation on the Poems of Ossian*. On Macpherson's Ossian poems as an attempted reconciliation of ancient eloquence and modern politeness, see Potkay (1994: 189–228).

FURTHER READING

Thomas Conley's (1990) *Rhetoric in the European Tradition* treats eighteenth-century rhetoric as a trans-European phenomenon and is sensitive toward, but finally skeptical of, its influence by the "new philosophy" of Descartes and Locke. Peter France's (1972) *Rhetoric and Truth in France: Descartes to Diderot* sketches the development of French rhetorical theory in the period while offering rhetorical analyses of select literary and philosophical texts. Daniel Gross's (2006) *The Secret History of Emotion: From Aristotle's "Rhetoric" to Modern Brain Science* offers an innovative view of the "rhetoric of emotions" from Aristotle's *Rhetoric* onward, with a particular emphasis on eighteenth-century philosophy and literature. Wilbur Samuel Howell's (1971) *Eighteenth-Century British Logic and Rhetoric* traces the career of rhetoric to its perfection in the New Rhetoric of Smith and Campbell, followed by its decline in the nineteenth and twentieth centuries. Although dated, it remains the standard study on its topic. Michael Moran's (1994) collection, *Eighteenth-Century British and American Rhetoric and Rhetoricians: Critical Studies and Sources*, features excellent chapters on Locke, Hume, Kames, Smith, Campbell, and Priestley. Adam Potkay's (1994) *The Fate of Eloquence in the Age of Hume* analyzes the tension in eighteenth-century philosophy and literature between the "ancient" taste for sublime eloquence and the "modern" preference for polite style. Finally, William Walker's (1994) *Locke, Literary Criticism, and Philosophy* is a masterful study of the rhetoric of empiricism.

REFERENCES

Blair, Hugh. (1783) 1965. *Lectures on Rhetoric and Belles Lettres*. Edited by Harold F. Harding. 2 vols. Carbondale: Southern Illinois University Press.

Campbell, George. (1776) 1963. *The Philosophy of Rhetoric*. Edited by Lloyd F. Bitzer. Carbondale: Southern Illinois University Press.

Conley, Thomas. 1990. *Rhetoric in the European Tradition*. Chicago: University of Chicago Press.

de Man, Paul. 1978. "The Epistemology of Metaphor." *Critical Inquiry* 5 no. 1: 13–30.

Fénelon, François de Salignac de La Mothe. (1717) 1787. *Dialogues sur L'Eloquence*. Paris: F. A. Didot.

Fontenelle, Bernard. (1818) 1968. "De l'origine des fables." In *Oeuvres Complètes*, edited by G.-B. Depping, 2: 388–393. 3 vols. Geneva: Slatkine.

France, Peter. 1972. *Rhetoric and Truth in France: Descartes to Diderot*. Oxford: Clarendon Press.

Goldsmith, Oliver. 1966. *Collected Works*. Edited by Arthur Friedman. 5 vols. Oxford: Clarendon.

Gordon, Thomas, and John Trenchard. 1995. *Cato's Letters: Or, Essays on Liberty, Civil and Religious*. Edited by Ronald Hamowy. 2 vols. Indianapolis, IN: Liberty Classics.

Gross, Alan G. 2005. "The Rhetorical Tradition." In *The Viability of the Rhetorical Tradition*, edited by Richard Graff et al., 31–45. Albany: State University of New York Press.

Gross, Daniel. 2006. *The Secret History of Emotion: From Aristotle's "Rhetoric" to Modern Brain Science*. Chicago, IL: University of Chicago Press.

Howell, Wilbur Samuel. 1971. *Eighteenth-Century British Logic and Rhetoric*. Princeton, NJ: Princeton University Press.

Hume, David. (1757) 1957. *The Natural History of Religion*. Edited by H. E. Root. Stanford, CA: Stanford University Press.

Hume, David. (1739–1740) 1978. *A Treatise of Human Nature*. Edited by L. A. Selby-Bigge and Peter H. Nidditch. Oxford: Clarendon.

Hume, David. 1985. *Essays: Moral, Political and Literary*. Edited by Eugene F. Miller. Indianapolis, IN: Liberty Classics.

Jamieson, Alexander. 1818. *A Grammar of Rhetoric and Polite Literature*. London: Printed for G. and W. B. Whittaker.

Kallich, Martin. 1970. *The Association of Ideas and Critical Theory in Eighteenth-Century England*. The Hague: Mouton.

Kames, Lord, and Henry Home. (1785) 2005. *Elements of Criticism*, 6th ed. Edited by Peter Jones. 2 vols. Indianapolis, IN: Liberty Classics.

Law, Jules David. 1993. *The Rhetoric of Empiricism: Language and Perception from Locke to I. A. Richards*. Ithaca, NY: Cornell University Press.

Leibniz, Gottfried. (1704) 1994. *New Essays on Human Understanding*. Cambridge: Cambridge University Press.

Leland, Thomas. 1764. *A Dissertation on the Principles of Human Eloquence*. London: Printed for W. Johnston.

Locke, John. 1975. *An Essay Concerning Human Understanding*. Edited by Peter H. Nidditch. Oxford: Oxford University Press.

Lowth, Robert. 1787. *Lectures on the Sacred Poetry of the Hebrews; Translated from the Latin of Right Rev. Robert Lowth, D. D.* Translated by G. Gregory. 2 vols. London: J. Johnson.

Moran, Michael. 1994. *Eighteenth-Century British and American Rhetoric and Rhetoricians: Critical Studies and Sources*. Westport, CT: Greenwood Press.

Potkay, Adam. 1990. "The Ideal of Eloquence in the Age of Hume." Ph.D. dissertation, Rutgers University.

Potkay, Adam. 1994. *The Fate of Eloquence in the Age of Hume*. Ithaca, NY: Cornell University Press.

Potkay, Adam. 1995. "Writing about Experience: Recent Books on Locke and Classical Empiricism." *Eighteenth-Century Life* 19 no. 2: 103–110.

Potkay, Adam. 1999. "Theorizing Civic Eloquence in the Early Republic: The Road from David Hume to John Quincy Adams." *Early American Literature* 34 no. 2: 147–170.

Priestley, Joseph. (1777) 1965. *A Course of Lectures on Oratory and Criticism*. Edited by Vincent M. Bevilacqua and Richard Murphy. Carbondale: Southern Illinois University Press.

Richetti, John. 1961. *Philosophical Writing: Locke, Berkeley, Hume*. Cambridge, MA: Harvard University Press.

Rousseau, Jean-Jacques. 1966. "Essay on the Origin of Languages." In *On the Origin of Language*, translated by John H. Moran and Alexander Gode, 1–83. Chicago, IL: University of Chicago Press.

Smith, Adam. (1762–1763) 1985. *Lectures on Rhetoric and Belles-Lettres*. Edited by J. C. Bryce. Indianapolis, IN: Liberty Classics.

Sprat, Thomas. 1983. *History of the Royal Society*. Edited by Jackson I. Cope and Harold Whitmore Jones. St. Louis, MO: Washington University Press.

Steele, Richard, and Joseph Addison. 1892. *Selections from "The Tatler" and "The Spectator."* Edited by Angus Ross. Harmondsworth: Penguin.

Thompson, Helen, and Natania Meeker, guest eds. 2007. *Empiricism, Substance, Narrative*. Special issue, *The Eighteenth Century: Theory and Interpretation* 48 no. 3.

Vico, Giambattista. (1725) 1968. *The New Science*. Translated by Thomas Goddard Bergin and Max Harold Fisch. Ithaca, NY: Cornell University Press.

Walker, William. 1994. *Locke, Literary Criticism, and Philosophy*. Cambridge: Cambridge University Press.

CHAPTER 43

··

RHETORIC AND SCIENCE

··

PETER WALMSLEY

The history of science has recently been galvanized by Lorraine Daston and Peter Galison's (2007) study of the emergence of objectivity in the nineteenth century. They argue that as the ideal of the creative subject emerged in Romantic aesthetic discourse, science countered with its opposite: the rigorously objective scientist who strove to eliminate the human and the imaginative from his or her work, who practiced "techniques of self-imposed selflessness" (Daston and Galison 2007: 203), and who aimed for a "new form of unprejudiced, unthinking, blind sight" (16). By contrast, earlier eighteenth-century science strove for "truth-to-nature" (58): a disciplined observation of the natural world that sought archetypal natural forms by winnowing out the accidental. Daston and Galison's compelling argument is preoccupied with the practice of research—how scientists see what lies before them and record it in their logbooks. However, it has rich implications for the rhetoric of science as well; their talk of objectivity as "a new epistemic virtue" (16) and their attention to the scientific self raise questions about ethics and scientific representation (see Code, ch. 57). This chapter seeks, in part, to build on what they observe of Enlightenment science by offering a rhetorical prehistory of objectivity. Where Daston and Galison propose a sea change between the authoritativeness of idealizing truth-to-nature and the selflessness of messy objectivity, I would suggest something more continuous: that objectivity has its roots in the diffidence and often chaotic formal rhetorical conventions of eighteenth-century scientific writing. In the process, it is important to reassert the centrality of rhetoric to the reimagining of natural philosophy in the late seventeenth and eighteenth centuries, showing how the new science's grappling with problems of representation eventually became transformative for rhetorical theory in the period. I will then consider the rhetoric of two influential and exemplary English scientific texts that participate in the performance of a new rhetoric to express natural philosophy's new values and practices: Hans Sloane's *Voyage to Jamaica* (1707–25) and Joseph Priestley's *Observations on Different Kinds of Air* (1772). Different as these texts are, one being a botanical catalog and the other an experimental narrative, they together share a response to what were, for science writers between 1660 and 1820, two core rhetorical challenges: the arrangement of materials (*dispositio*) and the establishment of the character of the author (*ēthos*).

PERSPICUITY

In the second book of his *History of the Royal Society* (1667), Thomas Sprat offers several examples of the wide-ranging research in which the Society is engaged and particularly of their commitment to histories of specific trades and manufactures. Among these is an anonymous report on "The History of the Generation and Ordering of Green Oysters, commonly called Colchester-Oysters." It describes how in May the dredgers gather the oyster spawn and bring it to the oyster beds in the creeks or, if they are farming green oysters, to the pits in the salt marshes. Sprat frames this account of the oyster fishery as being of obvious national importance, an opportunity for the improvement of a lucrative industry. The Royal Society's histories of trades reflect early modern aspirations for cross-fertilization between natural philosophy and the knowledge of the artisan: the scientist can learn about the properties of specific substances from the tradesperson, and the tradesperson can benefit from the scientist's more expansive understanding of the laws of nature. As Sprat puts it elsewhere, natural philosophy will only "attain to perfection, when either the *Mechanic* Laborers shall have *Philosophical heads*; or the Philosophers shall have *Mechanical hands*" (Sprat 1667: 397). Sprat stresses the scientist's respect for, and cautious transmission of, the skilled worker's embodied knowledge of his trade: the Society's Fellows "have begun to collect by the plainest Method, and from the plainest Information. They have fetch'd their Intelligence from the constant and unerring use of *experience'd Men* of the most unaffected, and most unartificial kinds of life" (257). Sprat's emphasis here is on what the scientist and the tradesperson share, a knowledge that is based on experience and a set of simple virtues—plainness, unaffectedness, industriousness. These virtues, practiced in the *History of the Royal Society*'s spare description of the Colchester oyster fishery, are fundamentally rhetorical, the virtues of a particular plain style that Sprat makes a hallmark of the new scientific method. Throughout the *History of the Royal Society* he advocates "a close, naked, and natural way of speaking" (112), repudiating the tropes and schemes of classical rhetoric as so much obfuscation, a preoccupation that has made the *History of the Royal Society* a locus classicus in the study of scientific style (Vickers 1986; Conley 1990: 168–9; Skouen 2011). He also, importantly, works to establish a social location for natural philosophy, claiming an allegiance between natural philosophy and commerce: the scientist and the tradesperson share a rich experience of the material world that they are committed to conveying in the most transparent language.

Sprat's famous articulation of the new science's dispensing with stylistic "fineness" in favor of "sound simplicity" (1667: 114) was taken up in the following century by learned writers of all stripes, including rhetorical theorists (see Walzer, ch. 41; Potkay, ch. 42). In this sense what has been called the scientific revolution demanded, and in many senses attained, a rhetorical revolution. In his influential *Essay Concerning Human Understanding*, physician and Fellow of the Royal Society John Locke blamed language for many systemic errors: "All the artificial and figurative application of Words Eloquence hath invented … are indeed perfect cheats" ([1689] 1975: 508). Indeed, book 3 of the *Essay Concerning Human Understanding* is dedicated to exploring the delusion of language whereby we commonly suppose that because we know a word we also have a clear and distinct idea to attend it, a delusion particularly dangerous when it comes to the names of substances used in scientific inquiry and communication.

By the second half of the eighteenth century, British rhetoricians seem to have embraced this position (Howell 1971). Where sixteenth- and seventeenth-century rhetorics were largely devoted to preserving the tropes and schemes of the ancients, eighteenth-century handbooks took an increasingly modern approach, a process culminating in books that could almost be described as anti-rhetorics, such as George Campbell's *Philosophy of Rhetoric* and Hugh Blair's *Lectures on Rhetoric and Belles Lettres*. The influence of Locke's hostility to scholastic essences, attack on eloquence, and general suspicion of language is everywhere evident in this process. Like Locke, Campbell is acutely aware that language has a dynamic of its own, independent of thought; writers, he observes, tend to keep writing despite a "total want of meaning," and for their part readers happily keep reading, oblivious to the "vacuity of thought" in the pages before them (Campbell [1776] 1963: 243–8). Campbell sees as the modern rhetorician's first ambition not elegance or novelty of expression but counteracting the imperfections of language, diligently pointing out the confusions that spring from using the same word in different senses, from overcomplicated or overlong sentence structures, from jargon and ambiguous reference, and from mixed and muddled metaphor (216, 222–5). Like the scientist, his priorities are to attain precision and specificity by exposing "the abuse of very general and abstract terms" (273). Similarly, Blair, who praises Locke's *Essay Concerning Human Understanding* as a model of "the greatest clearness and distinctness of Philosophical Style," aims "to explode false ornament, to direct attention more towards substance than show, to recommend good sense as the foundation of all good composition, and simplicity as essential to all true ornament" (1785: 1: 4).

While the *Lectures on Rhetoric and Belles Lettres* is interested in cultivating in its readers good taste and the appreciation of polite literature, Blair makes it clear that he has a new standard of beautiful writing: "We prefer a simple and natural, to an artificial and affected style" (Blair 1785: 1: 40). Blair and Campbell agree that the chief virtue of language is "perspicuity," defined by Blair as embracing "*Purity, Propriety,* and *Precision*" (1: 235), and both writers retain the literal, optical meaning of "transparency, or translucence." As Campbell puts it, "Though the impurity or the grossness of the medium will render the image obscure or indistinct, yet no purity in the medium will suffice for exhibiting a distinct and unvarying image of a confused and unsteady object" ([1776] 1963: 244). At its best, language is the optician's perfectly ground lens: a clear medium for conveying experience in all its crisp detail.

As Enlightenment rhetoric absorbed and ultimately endorsed natural philosophy's austere and suspicious attitudes toward language, science itself became increasingly conscious of its dependency on words and moved to embrace new modes of publicity and communication. Proponents of the renewed study of nature, such as Sprat and Robert Boyle, followed Francis Bacon in stressing the novelty of their mission. The quarrel of the ancients and moderns informed all aspects of European cultural and intellectual politics, and scientific writers consistently and self-consciously identified themselves as modern, repudiating ancient authority and advocating a more open dissemination of knowledge. From Bacon onward, the project of modern science was collective and cumulative; the amassing and organizing of nature's vast store of phenomena and the deploying of this knowledge for the general good demanded not just the labor of many hands but also a new openness and communicability. Apologists for the new science promoted its sociality—its reliance on networks of correspondence, on communal witnessing and replication, and on the meetings of the scientific societies that were springing up all over Europe, practices that Jürgen Habermas associates, in the political realm, with the formation of a bourgeois public sphere. Thus, despite the apparent suspicion of language, best embodied in the Royal Society's motto, *Nullius in verba* ("Take nobody's word for it"), linguistic exchange was central to this movement, and, as Steven Shapin and Simon Schaffer argue, the scientific book was a crucial new "literary technology" (1985: 25) in the process of both capturing and sharing new kinds of knowledge about the natural world. But how does Sprat's "sound simplicity" or Blair's "perspicuity" become translated into the practices of eighteenth-century scientific writing? What does it mean for such central rhetorical concerns as *dispositio* and *ēthos*?

DISPOSITIO

In classical rhetoric treatises *dispositio*, or the organization of an argument, received considerable attention. Aristotle, Quintilian, and Cicero, all drawing on models of political or forensic persuasion, stressed the careful selection of only the most salient arguments turned up during *inventio* and their strategic arrangement to lead the mind of the hearer to conviction. Even descriptive classical history, whether natural or human, did its best to adopt some of these formal conventions, shaping the materials of nature or of human conflict to support a larger interpretative agenda, to the proof of some formal or final causes. Bacon's call for a reimagined and distinctly modern natural history had radical formal consequences. As modeled by Bacon himself in his *Sylva sylvarum*, the *dispositio* of the new natural history should aim not for proof or synthesis but rather for inclusiveness: the text should mirror, in its structure, an omnivorous openness to nature as it presents itself to the senses, repudiating any rush to order or impulse to impose hypothetical structures on phenomena.

Sloane (1707–25) manages to include no fewer than three emergent natural history genres in his *Voyage to Jamaica*. The long, rambling introduction to volume 1 has two major movements: a scientific travel journal, describing his journey to Jamaica and offering a chorography of the island; and a physician's log of the various cases he treated on the island. This is followed by what would have been called an "atlas" of Jamaican plants: textual descriptions of individual species, and then 156 corresponding folio copper-plate engravings, advertised on the title page as being "as big as the Life." Volume 2, which appeared 18 years later, covers trees, all the fauna of Jamaica and some minerals as well, with 274 plates, and more importantly provides an exhaustive 98-page index for both volumes. Sloane's *Voyage to Jamaica* is thoroughly typical of the atlases of natural kinds produced in Europe in the Enlightenment in adopting a design that reflects the plenitude and randomness of the natural world, privileging the description of the discrete natural organism in what is, more than anything else, an open-ended catalog of the flora and fauna of Jamaica. Such a form takes incompleteness as a given, despite its considerable bulk; Sloane everywhere invites future additions: "I shall be extremely pleased to see my Observations of any kind rendered more perfect and usefull" (1707–25: 2: xviii). And he takes a self-consciously cavalier approach to recent attempts to establish more comprehensive taxonomic schemes, loosely borrowing from the systems of Augustus Rivinus and John Ray but largely unconcerned about the problems of classification they raise. The atlas is designed to focus our attention on the discrete specimen: suasive rhetoric's concern with the masterly organization of the parts into a whole is abandoned as the part—the species—comes to the fore and is appreciated in its absolute autonomy.

Here is a typical species description of the kind Sloane became famous for, an "invention" or the first account of a plant by a European observer:

> XXV. *Lysimachia lutea non papposa erecta minor, flore luteo pentapetalo, fructu caryophylloide. Cat. p. 85. Tab. 128. Fig. 2, 3.*
>
> This rises about ten inches high, from small fibers it sends out from its joints, into the neighbouring mud, thereby drawing its Nourishment. Its Stalk is green, round, succulent, smooth and brittle, on which are plac'd by a quarter of an Inch long red Foot-Stalks, several Inch long Leaves, half as broad in the middle where broadest, smooth and shining. *Ex alis foliorum* come the Flowers. They are pentapetalous, very large, yellow, and making a fine show. The Seed I did not observe, though by its Stalks and Flower it should be of kin to, if not a Purslane.
>
> It grows in Marshy places near Black River Bridge, *&c.* where water stands shallow most part of the year, among the Mud, into which it strikes its fibrous roots. (Sloane 1707–25: 1: 201)

What strikes the reader first is how circumstantial this account is, even in the highly elaborated polynomial. In contrast to ancient natural history—where, as Sloane says, the descriptions "were very dark and short" (2: xvii)—the modern atlas aims for a rhetoric of copiousness. The presiding structural principle is division, as Sloane is concerned to treat this plant as separate from all others, as the numbering of each description implies. Above all, he aims to offer as lively and sensuous an account of this plant as possible, an ekphrastic accounting for each part of the plant, their sizes, and relations.

Sloane struggles to render the visual in words, to replicate and flesh out in language the image in the engraving, which, though more precise in its rendering of form, is inevitably partial because it is colorless and shows only part of the plant at one phase of its life. He offers tactile as well as visual evidence, describing the smoothness and brittleness of the stalk, and he establishes its relations with its habitat, even naming one place on the island where it can be found. There is exemplary diffidence here, as Sloane concedes that he did not have a chance to see the plant in seed and that he is not really sure which family it might belong to. He calls it *lysimachia* or "loosestrife" but admits that it seems like a purslane (it is now classified as *ludwigia peploides* or floating primrose-willow). But his account shows an unquenchable curiosity as well, as he wonders at the fibers that extend from the stalk to the mud or appreciates the "fine show" of the blooms. The cumulative effect is anything but the impersonality of nineteenth-century scientific objectivity, which would purge the observation of the observer; rather, it presents a narrative of an actual lived and embodied encounter with nature, in which Sloane shows himself as the engaged and active witness.

Sloane's species account, with its cross-reference to the engraving of the plant, makes distinctive demands of its readers. Reading a natural history atlas is not linear but selective and active, moving between index, description, and plate, instantiating a web of relations between text, reader, and the world, thus making the atlas a site for "collective empiricism" (Daston and Galison 2007: 22). The *Voyage to Jamaica* is meant to serve not simply as a paper catalog of Caribbean flora and fauna but as a tool for confirming the identity of specimens. In the preface to volume 2, Sloane describes how his friend Henry Barham, a physician at Saint Jago in Jamaica, uses the *Voyage to Jamaica* to make crucial distinctions among local medicinal plants (1707–25: 2: viii). It also refers back, continually, to Sloane's own London museum of dried botanical specimens, where the curious reader could see for herself. His introductions to both volumes make it clear that his vast collections (the 800 specimens and seeds he brought back from Jamaica but also the many other botanical cabinets he has acquired since) are, with his field notes, the raw material from which the *Voyage to Jamaica* was created.

The randomness and circumstantiality of the natural history atlas are also features in the design of experimental narratives like Joseph Priestley's (1772) *Observations on Different Kinds of Air*. The scientific "trial," like the description of a plant or animal species, is always staged as a distinct performance: a discrete series of actions whose outcome is, importantly, unpredictable. The result is, again, a rhetorical form that is episodic and inclusive: the *Observations on Different Kinds of Air* fills 105 pages of the Royal Society's *Philosophical Transactions*—long for a communication in the journal— and though Priestley roughly divides the paper according to the different gases he has worked with, there is no orderly progression. His wayward pursuit of tentative hunches is marked by uncertainty and surprise. He opens by telling how happenstance and curiosity brought him to this research in the first place:

> Living for some time in the neighbourhood of a public brewery, I was induced to
> make a few experiments on this kind of air ["fixed air" or carbon dioxide], there

always being a large body of it, ready formed, upon the surface of the fermenting liquor, generally about nine inches, or a foot in depth. . . . A person, who is quite a stranger to the properties of this kind of air, would be agreeably amused with extinguishing lighted candles, or chips of wood in it, as it lies upon the surface of the fermenting liquor; for the smoke readily unites with this kind of air. . . . It is remarkable, that the upper surface of this smoke, floating in the fixed air, is smooth, and well defined; whereas the lower surface is exceedingly ragged, several parts hanging down to a considerable distance within the body of the fixed air, and sometimes in the form of balls, connected to the upper stratum by slender threads, as if they were suspended. . . . Making an agitation in this air, the surface of it, which still continues to be exactly defined, is thrown into the form of waves, which it is very amusing to look upon. (Priestley 1772: 149)

Like Sloane with his loosestrife, Priestley describes this scene in evocative detail, painting with words and so conveying a sense of wonder and delight at this novelty (see Moss, ch. 34). Of course Priestley opens with this more spectacular episode of fixed air rendered visible by smoke to draw us in and remind us that common air is, in fact, heterogeneous. But by foregrounding "amusement" and play he also reinforces his intellectual openness, suggesting that he follows nature's lead here. The following trials are clearly random. He shifts, for example, from experiments dissolving fixed air in various liquids to observing its effects on the lungs of animals; he holds a range of animals—butterflies, frogs, snails— over the brewing vat, evoking Robert Boyle's landmark air-pump trials with animals nearly a century before. Experiments that catch the observer off guard, that are "pleasing" (216) and "amaze and surprise" (212), are particularly valued. Nor does Priestley hesitate to describe the dead ends of his inquiries and the trials with unexpected results: indeed, the most profound discovery in the *Observations on Different Kinds of Air* is a matter of pure accident. Priestley shows himself unable to replicate some experiments on the effect of heat and cold on air by the Comte de Saluces: "Though this experiment failed, I flatter myself that I have accidentally hit upon a method of restoring air which has been injured by the burning of candles. . . . It is vegetation" (166). What follows is a long sequence of experiments in which Priestley pursues, cautiously, on this suspicion, moving slowly toward confidence. But phrases like "a considerable degree of uncertainty" (183) and "it is a doubt with me" (188) mark his prose throughout. With this tentative rhetoric the *Observations on Different Kinds of Air*, like Sloane's *Voyage to Jamaica*, projects an active and engaged readership: his detailed accounts of technique and his illustrations of his apparatus assume that the reader will attempt to replicate these experiments and even "pursue them farther than I have done" (249), replication by the scientific community being the ultimate proof of the validity of an outcome. He even provides guidance on keeping the mice necessary for an extensive course of experiments on animal respiration (249–50). So if the experimental narrative differs from the natural history atlas in having time as a structural principle, with the experimenter relating a sequence of scientific events, the genres are otherwise similar in adopting flexible and heuristic forms. Their *dispositio* convinces by being cumulative and inclusive rather than purposeful and complete, finding confirmation and closure only in the reader's own encounters with nature.

ĒTHOS

Classical rhetoric following Aristotle established *ēthos* as essential to convincing an audience: the speaker must convey a creditable character, one that is virtuous, knowledgeable, and well disposed to the audience. Late seventeenth-century science's repudiation of affective and metaphorical language meant that, for the scientist, displays of virtuous indignation or passages of exhortation were out of order. A new *ēthos* emerged, not yet the absence and utter selflessness of Victorian objectivity but certainly a step in that direction. The character performed by eighteenth-century science writers was invariably dispassionate and intellectually cautious, an honest witness to natural phenomena who is hesitant to jump to generalities and one who is, above all, industrious in the pursuit of nature. Of course the *ēthos* conveyed in language could build on the established public reputation of the speaker and thus presented a particular challenge to most natural philosophers venturing into print, most of whom lacked the preestablished social authority conferred by family, money, and land, or the kind of register of social place that attached to more traditional social roles, such as cleric or courtier (Shapin 1994). This was certainly an issue for Sloane and Priestley, both relative outsiders at the beginnings of their careers. To compensate, both used print strategically to create public identities, effectively publicizing themselves and, at the same time, working to define the persona of the new scientist in the public's mind.

Like so much of the natural philosophy written in the period, Sloane's *Voyage to Jamaica*, though visually sumptuous with its many illustrations, is a strikingly intimate and personal text, using the genre of the journal to narrate firsthand encounters with the natural, both in his initial travel and medical journals and, as we have seen, in the species accounts themselves. This autobiographical form permits the creation of an elaborate *ēthos*, as Sloane strives to perform and embody the scientific virtues promulgated by his mentors, Ray, Boyle, and Thomas Sydenham. Foremost among these virtues is disinterestedness, the ethical expression of the perspicuity that is the hallmark of scientific writing. In his preface to the *Voyage to Jamaica*, Sloane praises natural history for being free of the biases that distort civic and religious history, quoting Gabriel Naudé as saying "that he Acquiesc'd in Ecclesiastical History, Doubted the Civil, and Believ'd the Natural" (1707–25, preface B1v). Natural history is cast here as at once morally innocent yet genuinely progressive. Sloane frequently recurs to the social utility of his task and the enormous medical promise of tropical botany; this is a historical moment when quinine, from the bark of the west Andean cinchona tree, was one of the most valued and valuable medicines in the European pharmacopoeia. The work of natural history does not, however, depend on extraordinary expertise: its objects of study are a common legacy to humanity, accessible to the senses of all, and Sloane's only purpose is to capture them and set them in some order for future generations.

By this account the task is a lowly one: the painstaking but simple recording of the world. And Sloane stresses that the new natural history is a collective endeavor. He is but one worker among many, building on the bulk of botanical research that has gone before and consulting widely with Jamaicans in the field—of all races—about the local uses of plants. The text is strewn with gestures of humility: Sloane admits the faultiness of his text, both in his conjectures and his language, even "in the Observations themselves, which were generally written in haste, and by me, who know too well how unduly qualified I am for such an Undertaking" (Sloane 1707–25: 1: A2r). As both a botanist and physician, Sloane admits that he pronounces, in all cases, with "doubt and reluctancy" (2: xi), and indeed many of his medical case histories show cautious guesswork.

The extreme diffidence and humility of this *ēthos* is balanced, indeed quickened, with some spark of heroism, by an embrace of that most Protestant of virtues, industry. In the introduction to volume 1 he paints himself as restless, driven by a curiosity to see the world, dissatisfied by secondhand knowledge: "I was Young, and could not be so easy, if I had not the pleasure to see what I had heard much of." Like those fictional wayward men of science, Robinson Crusoe and Lemuel Gulliver, Sloane dramatizes his own intrepidity as he describes the danger and adventure of botanizing in a place where "the Heats and Rains are excessive . . . [the woods] often full of Serpents and other venomous Creatures . . . [and] very often full of run away Negros, who lye in Ambush to kill the Whites who come within their reach" (Sloane 1705–25: 2: xviii). The epigraph Sloane chooses for his title page, from Daniel 12, follows John Milton in finding biblical sanction for science's busy and needful stewardship of nature: "Many shall run to and fro, and Knowledge shall be increased." These displays of energy and industry are evident as he explains the delay in the publication of the second volume; anxious that the reader not think him "careless or negligent" (2: xiv), he describes how he was distracted by his burgeoning medical practice and the challenges of handling the many accessions to his museum. What the scientist lacks in certainty can be compensated for, it would seem, by labor.

Priestley, too, opens *Observations on Different Kinds of Air* with displays of diffidence: the observations are "very imperfect, and some of the courses of experiments are incomplete" (1772: 147). And while the text, even more than Sloane's *Voyage to Jamaica*, becomes very much a personal, even intimate narrative of one man's patient testing of nature, it also evokes a network of scientific collaborators with whom Priestley is in constant correspondence, including William Hey, Benjamin Franklin, and Sir John Pringle, and on whose approbation and further labors Priestley relies. Again, science is portrayed as a collective endeavor, moved slowly forward by the efforts of many hands and heads. And again, industry redeems the scientific life from its difficulty and uncertainty. Priestley, like Sloane, is tireless in his pursuit of "real knowledge": *Observations on Different Kinds of Air* records several hundred experiments, and alludes to the fact that many were replicated several times. Priestley portrays the embodied labor of experiment, foregrounding rather than hiding the gross materiality of his trials. Working with gases, at once invisible and hard to contain, presents him with innumerable challenges, and he strives to establish the purity of his gases, uncontaminated with "common air," by continually modifying and fussing over his apparatus. Priestley rejects corks and bladders as too porous and insists on using inverted glass vessels partially immersed in water or quicksilver as the only reliable seal. *Observations on Different Kinds of Air* makes clear that Priestley is not just staging and witnessing these experiments but is himself the operator, working with an apparatus that is a complex prosthesis linking his senses to the world. He is, par excellence, Sprat's philosopher with mechanical hands. Priestley's own body—busily at work in setting up his flasks and pipes; seeing, tasting, and smelling the products of his various trials; even producing oxygen-depleted air with his own lungs as needed—becomes part of the nature he is exploring. This valuation of physical work by the new science is captured in the full title of the *Philosophical Transactions*—"giving some account of the present Undertakings, Studies, and Labours, of the Ingenious, in many considerable parts to the world." In the realm of natural philosophy, labor is on a par with study in the quest for knowledge.

SCIENCE AND COMMERCE

In working to elucidate Sloane and Priestley's textual performances of science, I have been led by Daston and Galison's discussion of the importance of scientific *ēthos*, their sensitivity to how scientists inevitably engage with "normative codes of conduct that are bound up with a way of being in the world" (2007: 40) (see Doyle, ch. 59). Returning to Sprat's *History of the Royal Society* and its account of the Colchester oyster fishery, it is possible to see the beginnings of a very specific social location for the Enlightenment scientific persona. The commonalities of style and purpose that Sprat attributed to both science and trade in the 1660s increasingly became, over the course of the century that followed, taken for granted as natural philosophy became thoroughly entangled with two other distinctively modern cultural projects emerging at this moment: the development of a new credit economy and a global empire dependent on slavery. The scientific and financial revolutions were practically synchronous, and both offered visions of boundless expansion, of a mastery of the world through accumulation and accounting (Baucom 2005). As we have seen, scientific writing particularly sought to claim for the natural philosopher the merchant's virtues of industry and credibility, a transparency of which the double-entry ledger—so like the natural historian's atlas—is the public guarantee (Poovey 1998). And for their part, writers on trade were as keen as Sprat to advocate the virtues of the plain style. Daniel Defoe advises the tradesman to be "plain, concise, to the purpose; [with] no quaint expressions, no book-phrases, no flourishes" (1738: 1: 16) and Richard Steele admires the merchant's "natural unaffected Eloquence . . . [and] Perspicuity of Discourse" ([1711–2] 1965: 1: 10–1). Priestley's own life exemplified this perceived synergy between scientific and commercial interests; much of his work with gases aimed to develop a method of carbonating beverages, and he frequently advised his in-laws, Isaac and John Wilkinson, ironmasters and early industrialists. At the same time, colonial development depended on advances in navigation and agricultural technology, and it repaid the scientific community in turn with specimens of exotic flora and fauna, as Sloane's work perfectly exemplifies. Sloane eventually acquired, through marriage, a share of a Jamaica plantation, making him a slave owner and an importer of sugar through all the many years he served as president of the Royal Society. Both science and finance capital rapidly adopted a global perspective as colonial trade grew. In this process the scientist and the tradesman became uncanny twins, modeling together an exemplary modernity with their independence from traditional forms of social control and hierarchy and jointly laying claim to new worlds.

References

Baucom, Ian. 2005. *Specters of the Atlantic: Finance Capital, Slavery, and the Philosophy of History*. Durham, NC: Duke University Press.

Blair, Hugh. 1785. *Lectures on Rhetoric and Belles Lettres*. 2nd ed. 3 vols. London: W. Strahan et al.

Campbell, George. (1776) 1963. *The Philosophy of Rhetoric*. Edited by Lloyd F. Bitzer. Carbondale: Southern Illinois University Press.

Conley, Thomas M. 1990. *Rhetoric in the European Tradition*. Chicago, IL: University of Chicago Press.

Daston, Lorraine, and Peter Galison. 2007. *Objectivity*. New York: Zone.

Defoe, Daniel. 1738. *The Complete English Tradesman*. 4th ed. 2 vols. London: C. Rivington.

Howell, Wilbur Samuel. 1971. *Eighteenth-Century British Logic and Rhetoric*. Princeton, NJ: Princeton University Press.

Locke, John. (1689) 1975. *An Essay Concerning Human Understanding*. Edited by Peter H. Nidditch. Oxford: Clarendon.

Poovey, Mary. 1998. *A History of the Modern Fact: Problems of Knowledge in the Sciences of Wealth and Society*. Chicago, IL: University of Chicago Press.

Priestley, Joseph. 1772. *Observations on Different Kinds of Air. Philosophical Transactions* 62: 147–264.

Shapin, Steven. 1994. *A Social History of Truth*. Chicago, IL: University of Chicago Press.

Shapin, Steven, and Simon Schaffer. 1985. *Leviathan and the Air-Pump: Hobbes, Boyle, and the Experimental Life*. Princeton, NJ: Princeton University Press.

Sloane, Hans. 1707–1725. *A Voyage to the Islands of Madera, Barbados, Nieves, S. Christophers and Jamaica*. 2 vols. London: Printed by B. M. for the author.

Skouen, Tina. 2011. "Science versus Rhetoric? Sprat's *History of the Royal Society* Reconsidered." *Rhetorica* 29 no. 1: 23–52.

Sprat, Thomas. 1667. *The History of the Royal Society of London*. London: J. Martyn.

Steele, Richard, and Joseph Addison. (1711–1712) 1965. *The Spectator*. Edited by Donald F. Bond. 5 vols. Oxford: Clarendon.

Vickers, Brian. 1986. "The Royal Society and English Prose Style: A Reassessment." In *Rhetoric and the Pursuit of Truth: Language Change in the Seventeenth and Eighteenth Centuries*, edited by Brian Vickers and Nancy S. Struever, 3–76. Los Angeles, CA: Clark Memorial Library.

CHAPTER 44

THE ELOCUTIONARY MOVEMENT IN BRITAIN

PAUL GORING

AN oft-retold anecdote in the history of rhetoric concerns Demosthenes, the celebrated Athenian orator, and his response when questioned about his craft: "When being asked, What was the first point in Oratory? he answered, Delivery; and being asked, What was the second? and afterwards, What was the third? He still answered, Delivery." Mediated through classical works on rhetoric by Cicero, Quintilian, and others, this is Hugh Blair's retelling of the anecdote in his *Lectures on Rhetoric and Belles Lettres* (Blair [1783] 2005: 369). For Blair, Demosthenes was making a sound point. "Nothing is of more importance" than delivery, Blair avers: "The management of the voice and gesture, in Public Speaking ... is intimately connected with what is, or ought to be, the end of all Public Speaking, Persuasion; and therefore deserves the study of the most grave and serious Speakers" (368). Blair, a Scottish Presbyterian preacher and professor of rhetoric and belles lettres at the University of Edinburgh, was among many eighteenth-century writers who sought to provide instruction in how to speak effectively in public and who lent classical authority to their works by citing Demosthenes's boldly stated view. Thomas Sheridan, for example, included this anecdote in *British Education: Or, The Source of the Disorders of Great Britain* (1756), a hefty work that argues that a revival of the art of public speaking is the key to curing the woes of the British nation. In this work the story appears in a translation of a long passage from Quintilian's *Institutio oratoria* (11.3), with Sheridan preferring the term "elocution" to Blair's "delivery" (1756: 118–9). The anecdote had been used earlier by John Mason (1748), in the introduction to *An Essay on Elocution, or, Pronunciation*, a treatise offering guidance on how to cultivate effective oratorical skills, especially delivery. The term Mason puts into Demosthenes's mouth is "pronunciation," reflecting his use of Quintilian, who uses *pronuntiatio* at this point in *Institutio oratoria*. There were further retellings of this little tale. Taken together, they suggest that while there was no consensus regarding the principal term to render Demosthenes's point in English, this insight into Demosthenes's priorities as an orator—his emphasis upon the fifth canon of classical rhetoric: delivery (Gk. *hypokrisis*;

L. *actio, pronuntiatio*)—*had* become a commonplace in eighteenth-century British culture (see Monboddo 1773–92, especially 4: 280–1).[1]

The currency of this anecdote in the eighteenth century indicates an important strand of thought and activity in which matters concerning delivery—the use of the voice and body in public speaking—were prioritized over other elements of rhetoric. It is indicative of the emergence and growth of what has commonly been termed a British "elocutionary movement," a movement that focused first on improving the delivery of orators in traditional public fora (the pulpit, the senate, and the bar) but that later evolved to embrace, with reformist ambitions, speech practices beyond public oratory per se. Other issues addressed included, notably, the pronunciation of English in general, the idea of a standard pronunciation (Could the spoken language be "stabilized"?), protocols of speech for both men and women in settings less public than those of formal oratory, and how reading aloud should be conducted. Figures associated with this movement were concerned, then, with the use of language as a medium of live communication and with how this medium might best be cultivated; they sought to ease communication in the linguistically diverse nation of Britain and to imbue spoken English with standards of proper, polite eloquence. The extent to which elocutionists actually influenced the behavior of speakers is, of course, difficult to determine. Certainly they did not bring about the sea change in speaking habits some of them desired, but collectively they maintained the importance of effective delivery as an issue throughout the period.

Scholars have often seen the elocutionary movement as one of four fundamental constituents of the period's rhetoric, along with a neoclassical movement, exemplified by such works as John Ward's Ciceronian *A System of Oratory* (1759); a belletristic movement that developed and honed notions of taste and polite refinement; and a "New Rhetoric" that reconsidered classical traditions in the light of modern theories of human psychology, notably John Locke's thinking on how the mind develops ideas through association (see Howell 1971). Principal works of the last movement are George Campbell's *Philosophy of Rhetoric* (1776) and Joseph Priestley's *A Course of Lectures on Oratory and Criticism* (1777) (see Walzer, ch. 41; Potkay, ch. 42). There are many points of overlap between these four movements, and in practice few rhetoricians or rhetorical works can be neatly located within any one of them (e.g., classical precursors play a part in all these movements, not only the neoclassical). Taken together, these movements also *exclude* numerous areas of linguistic practice that many twenty-first century scholars choose to embrace within the broad field of "rhetoric."[2] The four-part division, in other words, is not immediately recognizable when one examines the vibrant, mixed culture of what we might now think of as eighteenth-century rhetorical activity, but it is not entirely redundant as a way into exploring the various matters that preoccupied the period's thinkers. Moreover, with its identification of an "elocutionary movement," it usefully highlights the serious attention being given to the business of delivery, even when this attention commonly appears mixed up with other concerns.

The focus on delivery in the eighteenth century can also be plotted within a broader, longer-term evolution of rhetorical theory, whereby issues of style came to dominate rhetoric's purview while content was increasingly seen to fall within other realms, notably the field of logic (or dialectic). Barbara Warnick (1993) explored the shift away from a classical conception of rhetoric, which encompasses both the discovery of knowledge (*inventio*) and the communication of knowledge (*actio*), toward a new understanding of rhetoric that gave precedence to delivery. One impetus for this shift, as Warnick points out, lay in the work of Peter Ramus, the sixteenth-century French scholar who "removed invention from rhetoric and left to the study and teaching of the art only style and delivery" (Warnick 1993: 129). Following Ramus—and despite the work of anti-Ramist rhetoricians—invention was "eclipsed as Enlightenment rhetoricians focused on stylistic management or conduct of a discourse" (129). But the encouragement of high standards of delivery in the eighteenth century was also fueled by factors beyond the sphere of rhetorical theory.

There were social and cultural reasons for the growing emphasis upon delivery, and elocutionists tended to cite these, rather than theoretical concerns, when they promoted the necessity of their work. Despite the rapid expansion of the print trade, oral communication remained vital to the general commerce of Britain. Levels of illiteracy were a factor here (in the middle of the eighteenth century about half of Britons could not read), but those empowered by literacy also remained dependent upon the medium of public speech: print did not significantly colonize traditional forums of speech, although it did supplement and modify them. "It is by speech," Sheridan declared as late as 1780, "that all affairs relative to the nation at large, or particular societies, are carried on. In the conduct of all affairs ecclesiastical and civil, in church, in parliament, courts of justice, county courts, grand and petty juries, vestries in parishes, are the powers of speech essentially requisite" (1780, preface n.p.). However, while such institutions depended on the spoken word, standards of oratory were regarded by many as deplorably low, and complaints had long been voiced that British orators lacked eloquence and were too reserved to engage their hearers. "Our Preachers stand stock-still in the Pulpit," wrote Joseph Addison in *The Spectator*, "and will not so much as move a Finger to set off the best Sermons in the World. We meet with the same speaking Statues at our Bars, and in all Publick Places of Debate" (in Bond 1965: 521). The same point was made by many commentators, some merely noting the situation and others seeking to redress it. Sheridan begins the first of his lectures in the *Course of Lectures on Elocution* (1762) by complaining of the "general inability to read, or speak, with propriety and grace in public," a failing that ran "thro the natives of the British dominions" and could be observed "in our senates and churches, on the bench and at the bar" ([1762] 1968: 1). Indeed, the figure of the dull orator droning on to a drowsy audience—the type of preacher depicted in William Hogarth's "The Sleeping Congregation" (1736)—became a recurring *topos* in eighteenth-century culture.

The bored audience in this *topos* suggests why effective delivery had become a serious issue. Not only matters of "propriety and grace," as Sheridan put it, were at stake when standards of delivery were scrutinized and found wanting, but ineffective delivery—speech that fails to *persuade*—was also held to endanger the social and political structure of Britain. A just cause in a law court might be lost through its artless presentation, a military officer lacking eloquence might fail to inspire his men, a sound political principle might be rejected if its proponents could not speak up for it, and an uninspiring preacher might fail to hold on to his congregation. This last possibility became a particular concern for the Anglican majority, not least because of the threat posed by alternative forums for worship—notably Methodism, which, from its beginnings in the 1740s, soon became renowned for the inspiring eloquence of its leaders. Vehement evangelical preachers such as George Whitefield could attract huge crowds with their rousing delivery. Many would attend simply out of curiosity, but significant numbers converted, and this ability among Methodist preachers to outshine typical Church of England clergy brought into sharp focus what a powerful tool effective public speaking could be. Methodists, like many earlier nonconformists, were regularly condemned as deranged "enthusiasts," but the effectiveness of their oratory was hard to deny. Indeed, Methodist preachers were sometimes held up as exemplars who, if studied with a critical and selective eye, could help to improve the practice of preachers in the religious mainstream. "Even Whitefield may be placed as a model to some of our young divines," Oliver Goldsmith suggests in an essay of 1760, if "to their own good sense" they join "his earnest manner of delivery" (1966: 154). The reserve of British speakers was seen by many to be a national trait. Addison, for example, was contrasting "Our Preachers" with those abroad when he censured the immobility of his countrymen, and it became common in elocutionary writing to draw comparisons between cold, stiff British delivery and the more exuberant—more *affective*—speech of nations like France and Italy. Sheridan worked with a consciousness that superior eloquence could be found on the Continent, as did the Scottish philosopher Adam Smith, who contrasted the general tendencies of French and English speakers in a lecture of 1763: "Foreigners observe that there is no nation in the world which use so little gesticulation in their conversation as the English. A Frenchman, in telling a story that was not of the least consequence . . . will use a thousand gestures and contortions of his face, whereas a well-bred Englishman will tell you one in which his life and fortune are concerned, without altering a muscle in his face" (1963: 192). At the same time as this native reserve was noted and criticized, it was also seen to be correctable by orators willing to study and practice the art of delivery. "It is certain," notes Addison, "that proper Gestures and vehement Exertions of the Voice cannot be too much studied by a Publick Orator" (in Bond 1965: 521). And this is where the elocutionists made their intervention: they offered guidance regarding what constituted good oratory along with instruction in how to achieve it.

This instruction took different forms. Public lectures were used by some elocutionists as a way of both explaining their ideas about good delivery and demonstrating them in the process of the performance. Sheridan, probably the most ardent and dedicated elocutionist of the century, toured England and Scotland with his lectures from the 1750s until around 1780, and he was welcomed north of the border not only for his teaching of the methods of public speaking but also for the training he could offer in English pronunciation to those seeking to thrive in the south (though he himself was Irish) (see Benzie 1972). Before Sheridan, John "Orator" Henley had, from the 1720s, run a preaching house in London that endured for some 30 years (see Midgley 1973). Henley was an eccentric but staunch devotee of the art of preaching, and he regularly included lectures on public speaking in the program of events at his Oratory. His primary objective in setting up the establishment was to bring renewed attention to "the beautiful, and long neglected science of rhetoric and elocution" (Henley 1727: 38), and he pursued this goal with lectures exploring and promoting the eloquent potential of both voice and body. Deeply influenced by classical rhetoric, Henley lectured on such topics as "The general Principles of Speaking," "The general Principles of Action," the "Antient History of Action," "The Action of the Eye and Features," "The Action of the Hands," and Quintilian's rules for effective speaking (Henley 1729: 1). Henley attracted a largely lower-class audience, and the Oratory came to be regarded by many as a curiosity in the world of popular entertainment rather than a reputable venue for serious pedagogy. Other public examinations of oratory were found in more securely established educational settings, such as Gresham College, home to the Royal Society, where John Ward delivered the lectures later published as *A System of Oratory* (1759), and the universities, particularly those in Scotland where Smith, Blair, and others lectured on rhetoric. The subject was also taught in smaller and shorter-lived institutions, such as the school devoted to elocution and public speaking set up in London by the Reverend Dr. John Trusler. Having gained a reputation for preaching, Trusler, according to his own account of this venture, succeeded in attracting "a great many pupils" (1806: 186), even though the school did not endure for long.

Clearly there were commercial as well as reformist motivations behind many of these enterprises: Sheridan and Henley were both concerned with attracting paying crowds for their lectures, and their careers in the field are a testimony to the public interest in oratory at the time. A further opportunity to capitalize on this interest lay in offering private tuition in oratory and elocution (an avenue explored by a number of the period's actors, such as Charles Macklin and James Love), and the print market, of course, offered yet another way of both making money and circulating elocutionary thought. Henley produced numerous publications in the course of his career, including many works on linguistic topics and numerous reports on the activities taking place at his Oratory, while Sheridan authored some of the period's most substantial and influential works on public speaking, notably *British Education, Lectures on Elocution*, and later his *Lectures on the Art of Reading* (1775), which sought to institute methods for reading aloud as part of the process of obtaining a "just delivery." In fact, elocutionary writing already constituted a fairly well-established field in the print market by the time Sheridan began making his own contributions in the 1750s.

The most important early intervention in this field, however, was not a native production but a translation of a seventeenth-century French treatise on public speaking by Michel Le Faucheur, a Protestant clergyman, originally from Geneva, who made his career in France. Le Faucheur's *Traitté de l'action de l'orateur, ou de la pronunciation et du geste* first appeared in 1657, shortly after the author's death, and there were several French editions of this work prior to its translation into Latin in 1690. Thereafter it was translated into English and published in London, probably in 1702, under the title *An Essay upon the Action of an Orator; As to his Pronunciation & Gesture. Useful both for Divines and Lawyers, and necessary for all Young Gentlemen, that study how to Speak well in Publick* (see Howell 1971: 165–8). It proved to be an influential work. There were two subsequent editions of the translation, the first appearing in 1727 as *The Art of Speaking in Publick*, a work inspired, in part, by the interest in oratory created by Henley (its full title includes "*Introduction relating to the Famous Mr. Henly's present Oratory*"). The third edition of the translation was published in 1750 as *An Essay upon Pronunciation and Gesture*. The translation of the *Traité* was also used as a source for a number of new works. Le Faucheur's teachings were condensed and repackaged in the popular anonymous pamphlet, *Some Rules for Speaking and Action; To be observed at the Bar, in the Pulpit, and the Senate, and by every one that Speaks in Publick* (1715). John Mason similarly drew upon Le Faucheur for his oft-reprinted *An Essay on Elocution; or Pronunciation* (1748), as did the Methodist leader John Wesley for a pamphlet offering *Directions concerning Pronunciation and Gesture* (1749). The *Traité* was also seen to have a pertinence to stage practice: in 1710 it was plundered to fill out a biography of the actor Thomas Betterton by Charles Gildon, whose *The Life of Mr. Thomas Betterton* includes a consideration of "The Action and Utterance of the Stage, Bar, and Pulpit." What doctrine of rhetorical delivery was being borrowed and adapted in these various publications?

Le Faucheur's *Traité* is grounded in the classical tradition of rhetorical theory and, more specifically, in Cicero's *De oratore* and Quintilian's *Institutio oratoria*. Importantly, however, its sole focus is the fifth and last element of rhetoric: delivery (*actio, pronuntiatio*). It is a substantial treatise that addresses how both pronunciation and gesture—"the very Life and Soul of Rhetorick"—can best be managed in order to reach the primary goal of oratory: persuasion (Le Faucheur 1702[?], preface n.p.). And this should be achieved, Le Faucheur argues, by appealing to the emotions (or "passions") of the audience: the power of the emotions makes composition—the building up of an argument through the steps of *inventio, dispositio*, and *elocutio*—less important than *actio*. Le Faucheur promotes a form of oratory constructed around natural sympathy, whereby a speaker should demonstrate his own emotional involvement in a topic by means of voice and gesture, following which similar feelings will be aroused in the audience. Orators, then, should do more than *perform* the signs of feeling. Like Stanislavskian method actors, they should actually *feel* the emotions they seek to convey: "The *Orator* ought first of all to form in himself a *strong Idea* of the *Subject* of his *Passion*; and the *Passion* itself will then certainly follow in course; ferment immediately into the *Eyes*, and affect both the *Sense* and the *Understanding* of his *Spectators* with the *same Tenderness*" (189).

The *Traité* can be seen as a celebration of the body's capacity to render emotions contagious: the passions "are wonderfully convey'd from *one person's Eyes* to *another's*," and the use of tears is particularly recommended as a means of creating "a *visible sympathy*" between speaker and audience (Le Faucheur 1702[?]: 189–90). At the same time, however, Le Faucheur is keen that orators should maintain a high degree of stateliness; they should impress their audiences "not only with their discourse and Style, but in some measure also by the decency of their *Speaking* and the Fineness of their *Action*" (18). So while we might see in Le Faucheur's emphasis upon the passions an early promotion of the emotionalism that would later be extolled in eighteenth-century sentimentalism, it should be noted that his doctrine also emphasizes restraint in the expression of emotion. A number of rigid rules, mostly derived from classical sources, are advanced with a view to upholding the dignity of the public speaker. Classical strictures concerning the use of the hands, for example, are reproduced: "You must make all your *Gestures* with the *right Hand*; and if you ever use the *left*, let it only be to accompany the *other*, and never lift it up so *high* as the *right* . . . to use an *Action* with the *left Hand* alone is a thing you must avoid for its *indecency*" (196–7). The general rule is to observe restraint: the voice should be controlled, while gestures "ought to be very moderate and modest; not bold, vast and extensive, nor indeed too frequent neither, which would make such a violent Agitation of the *Arms* and the *Hands* as would not become an *Orator*" (203). There is, then, a tension between affect and precept in Le Faucheur's doctrine of rhetorical delivery: a conflict between the advice to let expression flow as part of a physiological process originating in genuine feeling and the instruction that specific rules of art be followed to maintain somatic *decorum*. This tension appears in many later publications indebted to Le Faucheur, but some elocutionists challenged his approach to eloquence and, while upholding the importance of the appeal to the emotions, resisted the imposition of classical rules on an orator's performance.

Some later elocutionists followed the practice of delineating how particular passions should be expressed by means of voice and gesture, but they eschewed the classical model of "natural" eloquence. An example here is James Burgh, a Scot who set up an academy in London in 1747 and whose *The Art of Speaking* (1761) became one of the more popular elocutionary tracts of the later eighteenth century (see Moran 1994: 37). Burgh's work seeks to explain how numerous passions and states of mind affect the voice and body, and it includes many vignettes of highly dramatic emotional transport. "Grief, *sudden* and *violent*," for example, is expressed by "*beating the head; groveling on the ground; tearing of garments, hair*, and *flesh; screaming aloud, weeping, stamping* with the feet" (Burgh 1761: 16). It seems clear that Burgh took pleasure in writing such sensational passages, and that *The Art of Speaking* explores the language of the emotions at a histrionic level above what might actually be useful to an orator. Nonetheless, it is also clear from such passages that Burgh was operating with an idea of emotional eloquence that was liberated from the strictures found in the work of Le Faucheur and his followers.

Other elocutionists took a different approach and refrained altogether from outlining the particular ways in which emotions are communicated. If the language of the passions operates according to a natural process, they argued, then there is no need either to catalog its signs or to provide instruction in its articulation. This was the attitude of Sheridan. Regarding manufactured language, Sheridan did believe that the codification and prescription of norms and standards was both possible and desirable: he was a dedicated advocate of the study of English and a significant figure in the movement to standardize English pronunciation. His major contribution here (aside from teaching) was his *A General Dictionary of the English Language* (1780), which, unlike Samuel Johnson's dictionary, included a system of notation to indicate how words should be pronounced.

But with regard to the tones and gestures that would accompany these words in a public oration, Sheridan argues that an orator should "speak entirely from his feelings; and they will find much truer signs to manifest themselves by, than he could find for them" (Sheridan [1762] 1968: 121). He was unequivocal in his rejection of guidelines regarding the language of the passions, insisting that "no general practical rules . . . can be laid down in this respect" (118), and as a result his works contain few examples of the emotional language he regarded as the foundation of good oratory ("to move," he insists, "should be the first great object of every public speaker" [133]). Sheridan does require an orator to be "graceful," "refined," and "elegant," but aside from the injunction to feel and to follow nature he offers no explicit instruction.

Within the elocutionary movement, then, there were competing ideas about the nature of proper delivery and a wide range of approaches to the question of how delivery should be taught. None of these approaches can be said to have been rigorously scientific—something that was regarded as a failing by the last notable elocutionist of the period, the Reverend Gilbert Austin, an Irish clergyman, teacher, and the author of *Chironomia; Or A Treatise on Rhetorical Delivery* (1806). For Austin, who is generally held to represent the "culmination of the elocutionary movement" (see Miller 2001: 230), the first four parts of classical rhetoric had been well served by earlier scholars and educators, but his forerunners had achieved little regarding delivery: "It is a fact that we do not possess from the ancients, nor yet from the labours of our own countrymen, any sufficiently detailed and precise precepts for the *fifth* division of the art of rhetoric, namely, *rhetorical delivery*, called by the ancients *actio* and *pronunciation*" (1806: ix). Austin, unlike Sheridan, firmly believed that the nonverbal forms of expression used in delivery could be classified, described, and taught, and his *Chironomia* is an ambitious attempt to frame the eloquence of the body in a truly scientific system (see Spoel 1998). Although the work addresses the management of the voice, Austin was more concerned with the rhetoric of gesture, and he invents a complicated notation system for describing gestures: *Chironomia* features numerous diagrams illustrating different poses and the directions in which body parts should move to signify specific meanings and emotions. Austin's work thus offered an additional approach to what had been a problematic area of British cultural life for at least a century.

Austin's motivations, in fact, were remarkably similar to those of the earliest contributors to the elocutionary movement: the absence of a codified system of "rules for rhetorical delivery," he believed, was the "chief cause of the reproach of frigid indifference which is charged against our public speakers" (1806: x–xi). At the time Austin was working on his system a number of individuals had, of course, become famous for the extraordinary power of their oratory (e.g., parliamentarians William Pitt and Charles James Fox), but his remarks nevertheless point to the ongoing critique of "frigid" British speakers. It appears, then, that while the elocutionists inspired considerable interest in the topic of public speaking, their efforts did not have a major impact on the manner in which oratory was actually practiced: the "speaking Statues" described by Addison had not truly been brought to life.

NOTES

1. The commonplace status of the anecdote is suggested by its retelling in Gorges Edmund Howard's *A Collection of Apothegms and Maxims for the Good Conduct of Life* (1767): "Boldness in Civil business, is like pronunciation in the oratory of Demosthenes, the first, second, and third thing" (1767: 29). Terminological instability regarding delivery dates back to the ancient Latin texts on rhetoric, if not earlier: Quintilian, citing Cicero, states that *actio* and *pronuntiatio* can be used interchangeably to refer to voice and movement (*vocem atque motum*) (see *Institutio oratoria*, bk. 11). *Elocutio* in the classical schema refers to style rather than delivery.

2. Lynée Lewis Gaillet and Elizabeth Tasker describe the growth of what has come to be embraced by rhetorical studies: "Scholars have expanded the canon to include the voices of women, people of colour, civic rhetors, and activists—people who speak and write not only in the traditional classroom or from the pulpit but also on stage, in newspapers, and flyers, from the parlor, at grass-root meetings, in public squares, on reservations, in letters and essays, from recovered diaries and journals, in commission reports, and in autobiographies, etc. These recovered voices no longer represent addenda, codicils, and asides to the tradition but are . . . richly integrated" (2009: 78–9).

FURTHER READING

Brunström (2011) is a biography of the eighteenth century's most prominent elocutionist, with much to say about the significance attached to public speaking in the period. Goring (2005) examines eighteenth-century innovations in persuasive expression (particularly bodily expression) on the stage, in the novel, and in the elocutionary movement. Howell (1971) is a major survey of eighteenth-century writers on rhetoric with extensive coverage of the elocutionary movement (though a classicist agenda leads to the condemnation of many elocutionary works). Moran (1994) is a valuable multiauthored guide to all of the major—and many of the minor—figures who contributed to eighteenth-century rhetorical theory and practice. Finally, Shortland (1987) provides an informative article-length introduction to the elocutionary movement and its significance.

REFERENCES

Austin, Gilbert. 1806. *Chironomia; or a Treatise on Rhetorical Delivery*. London: T. Cadell and W. Davies.
Benzie, William. 1972. *The Dublin Orator: Thomas Sheridan's Influence on Eighteenth-Century Rhetoric and Belles Lettres*. Leeds: Scolar Press.
Blair, Hugh. (1783) 2005. *Lectures on Rhetoric and Belles Lettres*. Edited by Linda Ferreira-Buckley and S. Michael Halloran. Carbondale: Southern Illinois University Press.
Bond, Donald F., ed. 1965. *The Spectator*. Vol. 3. Oxford: Clarendon.
Brunström, Conrad. 2011. *Thomas Sheridan's Career and Influence: An Actor in Earnest*. Lewisburg, PA: Bucknell University Press.

Burgh, James. 1761. *The Art of Speaking*. London.

Gaillet, Lynée Lewis, and Elizabeth Tasker. 2009. "Recovering, Revisioning, and Regendering the History of 18th- and 19th-Century Rhetorical Theory and Practice." In *The SAGE Handbook of Rhetorical Studies*, edited by Andrea A. Lunsford, 67–84. Los Angeles, CA: SAGE.

Goldsmith, Oliver. 1966. *Collected Works of Oliver Goldsmith*. Vol. 3. Edited by A. Friedman. Oxford: Clarendon.

Goring, Paul. 2005. *The Rhetoric of Sensibility in Eighteenth-Century Culture*. Cambridge: Cambridge University Press.

Henley, John. 1727. *The Appeal of the Oratory to the First Ages of Christianity*. London.

Henley, John. 1729. *Oratory Transactions. No. II. To Be Occasionally Publish'd*. London.

Howard, Gorges Edmund. 1767. *A Collection of Apothegms and Maxims for the Good Conduct of Life*. London.

Howell, Wilbur Samuel. 1971. *Eighteenth-Century British Logic and Rhetoric*. Princeton, NJ: Princeton University Press.

Le Faucheur, Michel. 1702[?]. *An Essay upon the Action of an Orator*. London.

Mason, John. 1748. *An Essay on Elocution, or, Pronunciation*. London: M. Cooper.

Midgley, Graham. 1973. *The Life of Orator Henley*. Oxford: Clarendon Press.

Miller, Thomas P. 2001. "Eighteenth-Century Rhetoric." In *Encyclopedia of Rhetoric*, edited by Thomas O. Sloane, 227–237. Oxford: Oxford University Press.

Monboddo, James Burnet. 1773–1792. *Of the Origin and Progress of Language*. Vol. 4. Edinburgh: Bell.

Moran, Michael. 1994. *Eighteenth-Century British and American Rhetorics and Rhetoricians: Critical Studies and Sources*. Westport, CT: Greenwood Press.

Sheridan, Thomas. 1756. *British Education: Or, the Source of the Disorders of Great Britain*. London: R. and J. Dodsley.

Sheridan, Thomas. (1762) 1968. *A Course of Lectures on Elocution*. Menston: Scolar Press.

Sheridan, Thomas. 1775. *Lectures on the Art of Reading*. London.

Sheridan, Thomas. 1780. *A General Dictionary of the English Language*. Vol. 1. London.

Shortland, Michael. 1987. "Moving Speeches: Language and Elocution in Eighteenth-Century Britain." *History of European Ideas* 8: 639–653.

Smith, Adam. 1963. *Lectures on Rhetoric and Belles Lettres*. Edited by John M. Lothian. London: Nelson.

Spoel, Philippa M. 1998. "The Science of Bodily Rhetoric in Gilbert Austin's *Chironomia*." *Rhetoric Society Quarterly* 28 no. 4: 5–27.

Trusler, John. 1806. *Memoirs of the Life of the Rev. Dr. Trusler*. London.

Warnick, Barbara. 1993. *The Sixth Canon: Belletristic Rhetorical Theory and Its French Antecedents*. Columbia: University of South Carolina Press.

PART VI

MODERN AND CONTEMPORARY RHETORIC

CHAPTER 45

RHETORIC AND FEMINISM IN THE NINETEENTH-CENTURY UNITED STATES

ANGELA G. RAY

IN 1968 the women's liberation group New York Radical Women staged public demonstrations, including the Burial of Traditional Womanhood in January and the Miss America Protest in September. In June the group also published a short, typed journal titled *Notes from the First Year*. Alongside texts such as Anne Koedt's "Myth of the Vaginal Orgasm" and Katie Amatniek's "Funeral Oration for the Burial of Traditional Womanhood" was an essay by Shulamith Firestone called "Women's Rights Movement in the U.S." Firestone rejected characterizations of the nineteenth-century woman activist as a "granite-faced spinster obsessed with a vote" (Firestone 1968: 1). Castigating those who spread "superficial, slanted, or downright false" information about feminist history, she identified its consequences: "To be called a feminist has become an insult, so much so that a young woman intellectual, often radical in every other area, will deny vehemently that she is a feminist, will be ashamed to identify in any way with the early women's movement, calling it cop-out or reformist or demeaning it politically without knowing even the little that is circulated about it" (1). Firestone, like legions of activists before and after her, recommended education.

Drawing on the 1959 edition of historian Eleanor Flexner's *Century of Struggle*, Firestone laid claim to the "dynamite revolutionary potential" present in the women's movement from the beginning, noted its connections with abolition and labor activism, and outlined its lessons for radical women of the 1960s, many of whom had become politically active in the New Left. She summarized: "1. Never compromise basic principles for political expediency. 2. Agitation for specific freedoms is worthless without the preliminary raising of consciousness necessary to utilize these freedoms fully. 3. Put your own interests first, then proceed to make alliances with other oppressed groups. Demand a piece of that revolutionary pie before you put your life on the line" (Firestone

1968: 7). Asserting that "women's rights were never won," she urged her contemporaries to continue the fight on economic, social, cultural, and legal grounds.

Firestone's short essay not only sought to diminish the ignorance of activists of the 1960s about the heritage of US women but also recovered the experiences of earlier women as models and as cautionary tales to be applied in the present. She wrote in the informal idiom common to radical political movements of the 1960s, calling the anti-suffrage groups of the early twentieth century "a female front for big money interests" (Firestone 1968: 3), noting the close ties between "the Black Struggle and the Feminine Struggle" (2), and bemoaning women's routinized "shit jobs" (7) that fell far short of economic power. Rejecting the suppression of women's history and the lies told by institutional authorities, Firestone's essay led *Notes from the First Year* as an incendiary call to power through historical knowledge.

Firestone's essay dramatically shows that history is not neutral or benign, and that arguments about what was significant in the past—or even about what happened—are embedded in the dynamics of the moment when the historical narrative is generated. Appeals to the past are generated for rhetorical purposes, and the contexts of production and circulation of these appeals help to determine which aspects of the past are recovered and remembered. Whereas rhetorical scholarship is not equivalent to activist discourse, in that the audiences, purposes, and formal requirements differ markedly, it is still true that scholarly writing is rhetorical practice and that choices of subject, method, and conceptual framework are consequences of audiences, goals, and prior utterances. Firestone's essay, with its fervent commitment to a usable past, illustrates a resonant historical connection: how we understand nineteenth-century feminism is intimately intertwined with mid-twentieth-century feminism. Furthermore, Firestone's political lessons offer an analogical model for an evaluation of scholarship: What can we learn, what can we celebrate, and what can we do better? In this chapter I argue that by attending to the past we sharpen our understanding of how we came to know and how we might know more, or better, or differently, in the future.

READING NINETEENTH-CENTURY FEMINISM THROUGH A TWENTIETH-CENTURY LENS

Nineteenth-century US feminist rhetoric as an arena of scholarly inquiry exists as a consequence of twentieth-century feminism. This is displayed most vividly in terminology: the English word *feminism*, derived from the French *féminisme*, is idiosyncratic in a nineteenth-century context; the *Oxford English Dictionary* traces the term to 1895, and historian Nancy Cott (1987: 3–10) observes that it became common parlance in the United States only during the later woman suffrage campaigns of the 1910s. Thus, applying the label to nineteenth-century activism constitutes a political choice, a definitional argument for continuity in advocacy on behalf of women based on a theory of sex equality, a rejection of sex hierarchy, and an assumption that gender roles are culturally specific, not natural (Cott 1987: 3–10). Whereas an argument for continuity is not difficult to marshal, nineteenth-century activists did not refer to "feminism" but instead spoke of "woman's rights," "the woman question," or "the woman movement" and vigorously debated the scope of those terms.

Within the academic discipline of communication, several studies of nineteenth-century women's discourse predated the 1960s (Yoakam 1937, 1943; O'Connor 1954; Yoakam Twichell 1955). These studies simultaneously pioneered new terrain and employed well-established themes and methods of twentieth-century rhetorical inquiry. Demonstrating nineteenth-century women's capacity for public influence through means recognizable to and valued by their academic colleagues, Doris Yoakam and Lillian O'Connor recovered and promoted the public oratorical practice of nineteenth-century women activists such as Frances Wright, Maria Miller Stewart, Sarah and Angelina Grimké, Lucretia Mott, Sojourner Truth, and Susan B. Anthony. Performing scholarship according to the dominant paradigms of their day, Yoakam generated historical narratives of women's oratorical practice, and O'Connor presented biographical information on 27 women orators alongside assessments of pre-1860 speeches according to Aristotle's three modes of rhetorical proof: *ēthos*, *pathos*, and *logos*. Despite its nonthreatening presentation, this scholarship, like much early work in women's history, had little apparent influence on the study of US public discourse, which continued to be dominated by the study of male elite orators (Campbell 2006: 180). Ironically, this pattern replicated in a twentieth-century academic setting the laborious, oft-ignored nineteenth-century efforts for social change on behalf of sex equality in educational, legal, and political contexts.

In 1963 Wil Linkugel's critical essay about the suffrage advocacy of Anna Howard Shaw appeared in the *Quarterly Journal of Speech*, but substantive development in scholarship on nineteenth-century women's activism—and innovations in analytic methods suitable to the power dynamics of women's discourse—would await the seismic cultural shifts of mid-twentieth-century feminism.

The 1970s witnessed the introduction of collegiate courses on US feminist rhetoric (see Linkugel 1974; Foss 1978) as well as scholarly studies of contemporary feminism. Then, during the last three decades of the twentieth century, the study of nineteenth-century women's advocacy developed as a respected, identifiable area of inquiry owing in great measure to the scholarship and teaching of Karlyn Kohrs Campbell. Campbell, a former colleague of Linkugel's, has produced numerous foundational essays on feminist discourse. In 1989 she published a groundbreaking two-volume classroom text, *Man Cannot Speak for Her*, which provides critical analysis and an anthology of texts of the nineteenth- and early twentieth-century woman's rights movement. The main title, a quotation from an 1848 lecture by Elizabeth Cady Stanton, asserts a distinctive feminist voice, and the subtitles of both volumes—*A Critical Study of Early Feminist Rhetoric* and *Key Texts of the Early Feminists*—lay claim to a feminist heritage by using the term and thus dramatizing continuities between prior rhetorical action and the historical moment of the reader's encounter. The authorial persona is an explicitly political one: "As a feminist, I . . ." (Campbell 1989: 1: 15). Soon after these volumes appeared, Campbell published an edited collection, *Women Public Speakers of the United States*, which provides biographical and bibliographic resources for scholars and students.

Although this scholarship remains continuous with disciplinary traditions in its emphasis on public advocacy, it notably departs from prior work by generating conceptual understandings of women's rhetorical practice that respond to its own characteristics and the social conditions under which women advocates labored. "Feminine style," as a theoretical model and an analytic category, has proven so influential that tracing its historical development can aid understanding of the current state of scholarship on rhetoric and feminism. Feminine style crystallizes a set of concepts about rhetorical performance and women's experience (see Glenn and Lunsford, ch. 46).

Campbell introduced the term feminine style in her "Style and Content in the Rhetoric of Early Afro-American Feminists" (1986), an essay about African American women speakers of the late nineteenth and early twentieth centuries. Here she characterized feminine style as "a mode of address that is consistent with traditional norms of femininity" and emphasized the ways "oppressed groups" respond to the "special conditions and experiences" of oppression (Campbell 1986: 440). Depicting the challenges faced by early women speakers generally while highlighting oppressions that rested unequally on black women, Campbell demonstrated a pronounced contrast between Ida B. Wells's 1892 anti-lynching speech, "Southern Horrors," and Mary Church Terrell's 1906 speech, "What It Means To Be Colored in the Capital of the United States." Campbell finds Wells's powerful indictment of attitudes that condoned lynching to have almost no stylistic markers indicating adaptations to conventions of femininity. In Church Terrell's speech, however, Campbell locates adaptations appropriate for empowering the "white, middle-class, largely female audience," such as reliance on personal experiences and anecdotes as well as implied rather than directly stated conclusions (442–3). This essay emphasized the discursive markers that Campbell called feminine style as a response to oppressive circumstances and at the same time demonstrated clearly that these discursive markers did not appear in all public speeches of women rhetors.

Although the term feminine style did not surface until her 1986 essay on early African American feminists, the concept is traceable in Campbell's earlier work. In "The Rhetoric of Women's Liberation: An Oxymoron" (1973), for example, Campbell characterizes key features of twentieth-century consciousness-raising in ways that would later be adapted as feminine style (Campbell 1973: 75). Campbell delineates the arguments and "stylistic strategies" (79) of the contemporary discourse of radical women's liberation. In addition to her key observation that social conventions meant that the attributes of the ideal rhetor—"self-reliance, self-confidence, and independence" (81)—were imagined to be masculine, Campbell identifies the dynamics of women's consciousness-raising groups and locates comparable features in publications by mid-twentieth-century feminists. She notes that "women's liberation is characterized by rhetorical interactions that emphasize affective proofs and personal testimony, participation and dialogue, self-revelation and self-criticism, the goal of autonomous decision making through self-persuasion," and the use of discursive strategies to challenge cultural commonplaces

(83; see also Campbell 1999). Some of these characteristics would resurface as feminine style, for Campbell's further study of earlier women rhetors yielded the insight that the features of women's liberation discourse that initially appeared extraordinary were in fact ubiquitous in much discourse produced by women speaking under conditions of oppression. Thus, contemporary experience produced questions and perceptions about the past.

In 1980 Campbell published "Stanton's 'The Solitude of Self': A Rationale for Feminism," an important analysis of Elizabeth Cady Stanton's 1892 address that emphasized its lyric qualities and unconventional logic. Although she did not then use the label feminine style, six years later she would write that her essay on "The Solitude of Self" showed "how 'feminine' style can be used effectively for male audiences" (Campbell 1986: 444, n. 25), highlighting a strategic response to the dynamics of gendered power. By this time Campbell was also publishing on rhetorical theories of genre, and her evolving scholarship on US women's rhetoric likewise emphasized commonalities of form. In "Femininity and Feminism: To Be or Not To Be a Woman" (1983), for example, she traced rhetorical form to argue that the nineteenth- and twentieth-century US women's movements constituted a single rhetorical movement. Drawing on the pioneering historical scholarship of Barbara Welter and Aileen Kraditor, Campbell notes the contradictions in ideology and argument in US feminist rhetoric that proceed from its emphasis on women's purportedly special features and on the qualities women share with men as part of humanity. Campbell argues that activist women rhetors often negotiated this tension through the use of recurring forms, including "personal tone, speaking as a peer, relying on examples, testimony, and enactment as evidence, inductive structure, and efforts to stimulate audience participation" (Campbell 1983: 106) (see Code, ch. 57). Such rhetorical forms had special value for disempowered audiences because they were a means of "transforming women into agents of social change." Again, however, Campbell observed that not all women's discourse followed this pattern, noting as a counterexample Susan B. Anthony's strictly logical defense of her allegedly illegal vote in 1872 (1983: 104–7; see also 1986: 445, n. 29).

The term feminine style made its first appearance three years later, characterized as a rhetorical adaptation to oppression. Then, in 1989, in volume 1 of *Man Cannot Speak for Her*, Campbell offered feminine style as a framework for understanding US women's reform rhetoric from the 1830s to 1920. Because this text has been used extensively in classrooms, it is likely that this is the description of feminine style that has been circulated most widely. In this work Campbell proposes that traditional processes of craft-learning may have made the style particularly well suited for women during the period studied. Although Campbell explicitly states that the form was not restricted to women rhetors, she also observes that "the acculturation of female speakers and audiences" made it particularly "congenial" (Campbell 1989: 1: 14) to persons socialized as feminine:

> If the process of craft-learning is applied to the rhetorical situation . . . it produces discourse with certain characteristics. Such discourse will be personal in tone . . . relying heavily on personal experience, anecdotes, and other examples. It will tend to

be structured inductively.... It will invite audience participation.... Audience members will be addressed as peers ... and efforts will be made to create identification with the experiences of the audience and those described by the speaker. The goal of such rhetoric is empowerment.... Given the traditional concept of womanhood, which emphasized passivity, submissiveness, and patience, persuading women that they could act was a precondition for other kinds of persuasive efforts. (1: 13)

Campbell mentions consciousness-raising as a close analogy, although here she stops short of a claim of equivalence.

Campbell thus introduced feminine style to explain the strategic adaptations that allowed some US women advocates of the nineteenth and early twentieth centuries to balance cultural expectations for public advocacy and the social norms of femininity. Communication scholars have used the concept productively, identifying it as a rhetorical strategy, a resource for political judgment, and a way of knowing. It has been applied across time and across cultures, and it continues to motivate scholarly publications and student projects. But widespread use has its disadvantages. As an unusual example of a conceptual model developed in feminist communication to achieve prominence, feminine style by the mid-1990s had become so ubiquitous that Bonnie J. Dow expressed her concern that it was becoming a "litmus test to which female rhetors are subjected" and, "even worse, a deductively applied framework that will be used to explain the discourse of female rhetors that could be better explored in some other way" (1995: 108).

Problems with feminine style derive from at least three sources. First, sometimes the use of the term as a rhetorical response to differential social power has become conflated with data from social scientific studies that describe interpersonal linguistic behaviors of contemporary men and women. A strategic response to cultural conventions of gender is thus transmuted into "how women talk." Second, perhaps because of the correlation in ordinary language between *female* and *feminine*, claims of essentialism persist, despite scholars' repeated assertions that this style is not natural to women. And third, the clearly delineated list of features that describe feminine style has undoubted appeal, and the ease of matching a list of attributes with a specific text has resulted both in simplistic observations about individual texts and in implausible claims about the presence of feminine style in a vast range of discourses, even those produced by the most powerful male elites, owing only to the presence of a single feature, such as personal anecdotes.

Now, more than a quarter century after the development of the term, does feminine style have continuing utility? Is it primarily important as a marker of a moment in the disciplinary history of communication, or does it remain productive of important insights? It is undoubtedly fundamental to the history of feminist studies in communication, and its development marks a sea change in perspectives on women's discourse because it drew theory from practice. It also demonstrates the ways the social critique, the revolutionary fervor, and the rage of mid-twentieth-century feminism generated new foci in interpreting US history.

Yet the constraints of an apparent essentialism combined with the too-easy reliance on a typology of features have led some to suggest that feminine style is ready for the academic dustbin. Certainly its application can result in overgeneralized observations and tedious delineations of textual attributes. But revisiting history—in this case the history of feminist rhetoric—can also uncover dynamic potential. Reconsidering feminine style from the perspective of the early twenty-first century may inspire ever more nuanced interpretations of nineteenth-century discourse. What are its lessons?

LESSONS

The first lesson is that concepts are historically situated. This is true in this case on two counts. First, feminine style derived from mid-twentieth-century discourses of feminist consciousness-raising and discourses of rhetorical inquiry. Thus, scholars have focused considerable attention on attributes like personal narrative, social critique, and gendered power within overt public advocacy. And second, because the nineteenth-century discourse for which feminine style offered fruitful explanations responded to ideologies of gender common in its own time, the concept meshed closely with the antebellum notions of "separate spheres" (a nineteenth-century term) and the cult of "true womanhood" (a twentieth-century description of nineteenth-century phenomena). These ideals had significant racial, class, regional, and religious dimensions, and feminine style is therefore especially helpful in illuminating the features of texts like Mott's "Discourse on Woman" (1849), which responded directly to the norms of gender articulated in a lyceum lecture by Richard Henry Dana, Sr. The concept of feminine style encourages focus on the attributes of gendered ideology and power, and hence it illuminates obstacles to argument and expression faced by many women rhetors.

Although certain features of gender norms can be traced across time and space, investigation of historical and cultural difference should counterbalance scholarly arguments for continuity. For example, historical study shows that the separate spheres ideology represented a backlash. Susan Zaeske (1995: 193), a scholar of rhetoric, demonstrates that the idea of the promiscuous audience, before whom a woman speaking was perceived to be immoral, dates from approximately the late 1820s, and historian Carolyn Eastman argues persuasively that in the late eighteenth century many Americans believed that in the new nation girls as well as boys should be capable of "polished, confident speech" (Eastman 2009: 54). Thus, some girls received training in oratory comparable to that of boys, and schoolgirls' speeches appeared in print (53–82; see also Kelley 2006). Studying parlor rhetorics, conduct manuals, and letter-writing guides of the post-Civil War era, Nan Johnson (2002) demonstrates the resilience of a separate spheres ideology for white middle-class women even in a period when such strictures seemed to be loosening. Such scholarship not only offers revised interpretations of the past but also underscores the temporally, geographically, and culturally situated conditions in which discourse is produced and circulated.

The second lesson is that rhetorical form matters. This disciplinary truism bears repeating. The concept of feminine style developed from studies of women's public speaking and, to a lesser extent, published writing. It developed from studies of persuasive efforts to change institutional norms and cultural beliefs, typically designed to empower disempowered persons to understand themselves as potentially influential or to encourage opponents to see substantive change as somehow desirable to them or less threatening than they imagined.

In the discipline of communication, the array of artifacts identified as rhetorical practice has multiplied exponentially since the mid-1960s, and the study of rhetoric and feminism in the nineteenth century has participated in this expansion of the object domain. Whereas women's discourse in organized political contexts persists as a major focus, communicative phenomena as diverse as visual images, dress and costuming, elocutionary textbooks, and quilts are now studied alongside speeches and published arguments (Campbell and Keremidchieva 2006: 187–90; Ray 2009: 530–1). Furthermore, meticulous studies such as Ronald J. Zboray and Mary Saracino Zboray's *Voices without Votes* (2010), a history of women's political involvement based on the diaries and letters of 448 women in antebellum New England, further challenge public and private as meaningful distinctions and revolutionize knowledge about the interests of ordinary women. As the objects of study change, so stylistic features alter. Indeed, the Zborays contrast the public feminine style with what they call a "diffident" style used in informal everyday communication. Women writing in diaries and letters, they note, "were not obliged to legitimate [their authority] directly," so they "could be more subtle" in laying claim to political investments and partisanship (Zboray and Zboray 2010: 13).

Finally, the third lesson of the history of feminine style is that cultural stereotypes of gender invite recognition and assessment. Uneasiness about the apparent essentialism of the term *feminine* in feminine style can prove productive. Certainly, scholars should resist reinforcing simplistic gendered binaries. Biological sex constitutes a continuum rather than a dichotomy; social norms of gender vary with race, socioeconomic status, sexuality, region, religion, and other variables; and scholarly generalizations about a group called US women have too frequently produced narratives limited to the experience of white, well-to-do, heterosexual northeastern Protestants (see Royster, ch. 47; Code, ch. 57). Challenging assumptions produces growth. Nonetheless, rhetoric scholars, who study cultural forms as they are expressed and experienced, do not have the luxury of destroying stereotypes by fiat. Rhetoric is more about perception than ontology. Scholars of the nineteenth-century United States must take stereotypes seriously to show how they function in rhetorical action. We must therefore also take seriously the language of gender duality, which generates and reinforces cultural expectations. The disciplinary heritage of feminine style already points contemporary scholars toward studies of gender, investigating how femininity and masculinity alike are explained, performed, and challenged at specific places by specific people at specific moments. Scholars of rhetoric and feminism create new interpretations of congressional debates over slavery, for example, by attending closely to their gendered elements (Zaeske 2009).

At the same time, theorizing feminine style as a strategic adaptation to the dynamics of gendered power implies that other rhetorical strategies respond to different dynamics. Although scholars increasingly recognize the multiplicity of experienced identities, especially as expectations of gender mesh with norms of race, class, and sexuality, and are beginning to take masculinity seriously as gender (and whiteness as race), it is less common, in studies of discourse produced by women, to question whether gender necessarily suggests the most important insights. Even discourse produced by nineteenth-century women whom we retrospectively define as "feminist" may have alternative stories to tell, not only about gender but also about, say, citizenship or nationalism or trajectories of public argument (see Eastman 2009: 180).

LOOKING TO THE PAST FOR THE FUTURE

Whereas in 1965 only one book and a handful of essays represented scholarship on nineteenth-century US women's rhetoric, a recent survey of rhetorical scholarship published between 1996 and 2007 on late nineteenth-century US public discourse finds that gender, commonly studied through women's advocacy for social change, was a primary interest, with such studies exceeding even studies of governmental institutions (Ray 2009: 532–4). Rhetorical scholarship on prewar discourse by and about women is similarly voluminous. Nineteenth-century women's rhetoric is a burgeoning area of study, and the sheer quantity of new materials recovered for investigation is prodigious. Recovery efforts proceed apace, often as part of graduate education. Just as the scholarly publications of Yoakam, O'Connor, and Linkugel developed from their dissertation projects, so twenty-first-century graduate students are wending their way back into the nineteenth century, simultaneously responding to the necessity of speaking in a language familiar to the academic fields in which they are studying and making choices based on their own interests and the concerns of their own historical moment.

Yet the term *feminist* in this context remains slippery. Although the term is relevant in many studies of nineteenth-century discourse—especially those that examine organized efforts for woman's rights or woman's suffrage—it often applies more easily to the scholars than to the discourse studied, as studies of discourse by and about women increasingly range well beyond movement practices. This does not mean that organized movements have been fully mined, of course—far from it. But the current scholarly trajectory appears to be toward ever-increasing pluralism in artifact selection and analytic approach.

There is much to celebrate about multiplicity, and exciting recovery projects regularly amend our understanding of nineteenth-century life. Yet balancing the centripetal forces of variety is the centrifugal force of common concerns. How are studies of nineteenth-century feminist rhetoric, or feminist studies of nineteenth-century rhetoric, linked? Are there shared questions or recurrent themes? Perhaps the continuing ubiquity of feminine style in rhetorical scholarship is testimony to the desire for such connections. Although I align myself with those who worry about the overuse of the list of features, I also find feminine style helpful for classroom use, primarily as a way of showcasing the *variety* of nineteenth-century women's rhetorical practices: "Place the following texts on a continuum, from greatest to least use of feminine style. . . . Explain your rankings and provide evidence from the texts to support them." As a scholar, I admire the revolutionary potential of the concept of feminine style in its own historical moment, and I read its history as inspiration. In looking to a disciplinary past, we take lessons from those who dared to listen to women's voices. They offer us nothing less than dynamite.

FURTHER READING

Campbell (2001) summarizes the concepts key to feminist rhetorical studies and provides a bibliography. Logan (1995) anthologizes key speeches by seven African American women. Ronald (2009) traces feminist rhetorical studies from the perspective of a scholar in an English Department. Royster (2000) provides critical analysis of women's essays and explains an Afra-feminist perspective. And Zaeske (2003) demonstrates the power of women's petitioning in the antislavery debates and in the generation of women's political consciousness.

REFERENCES

Campbell, Karlyn Kohrs. 1973. "The Rhetoric of Women's Liberation: An Oxymoron." *Quarterly Journal of Speech* 59 no. 1: 74–86.

Campbell, Karlyn Kohrs. 1980. "Stanton's 'The Solitude of Self': A Rationale for Feminism." *Quarterly Journal of Speech* 66 no. 3: 304–312.

Campbell, Karlyn Kohrs. 1983. "Femininity and Feminism: To Be or Not To Be a Woman." *Communication Quarterly* 31 no. 2: 101–108.

Campbell, Karlyn Kohrs. 1986. "Style and Content in the Rhetoric of Early Afro-American Feminists." *Quarterly Journal of Speech* 72 no. 4: 434–445.

Campbell, Karlyn Kohrs. 1989. *Man Cannot Speak for Her.* 2 vols. New York: Praeger.

Campbell, Karlyn Kohrs, ed. 1993–1994. *Women Public Speakers in the United States: A Bio-Critical Sourcebook.* 2 vols. Westport, CT: Greenwood.

Campbell, Karlyn Kohrs. 1999. "'The Rhetoric of Women's Liberation: An Oxymoron' Revisited." *Communication Studies* 50 no. 2: 138–142.

Campbell, Karlyn Kohrs. 2001. "Feminist Rhetoric." In *The Oxford Encyclopedia of Rhetoric*, edited by Thomas O. Sloane, 301–308. New York: Oxford University Press.

Campbell, Karlyn Kohrs. 2006. "Gender and Communication in Rhetorical Contexts: Introduction." In *The SAGE Handbook of Gender and Communication*, edited by Bonnie J. Dow and Julia T. Wood, 179–184. Thousand Oaks, CA: SAGE.

Campbell, Karlyn Kohrs, and Zornitsa Keremidchieva. 2006. "Gender and Public Address." In *The SAGE Handbook of Gender and Communication*, edited by Bonnie J. Dow and Julia T. Wood, 185–199. Thousand Oaks, CA: SAGE.

Cott, Nancy F. 1987. *The Grounding of Modern Feminism.* New Haven, CT: Yale University Press.

Dow, Bonnie J. 1995. "Feminism, Difference(s), and Rhetorical Studies." *Communication Studies* 46 no. 1–2: 106–117.

Eastman, Carolyn. 2009. *A Nation of Speechifiers: Making an American Public after the Revolution.* Chicago, IL: University of Chicago Press.

"Feminism." 1989. *Oxford English Dictionary*, 2nd ed. Oxford: Oxford University Press.

Firestone, Shulamith. 1968. "Women's Rights Movement in the U.S." In *Notes from the First Year*, 1–7. New York: New York Radical Women.

Foss, Sonja K. 1978. "Teaching Contemporary Feminist Rhetoric: An Illustrative Syllabus." *Communication Education* 27 no. 4: 328–335.

Johnson, Nan. 2002. *Gender and Rhetorical Space in American Life, 1866–1920.* Carbondale: Southern Illinois University Press.

Kelley, Mary. 2006. *Learning to Stand and Speak: Women, Education, and Public Life in America's Republic.* Chapel Hill: University of North Carolina Press.

Linkugel, Wil A. 1963. "The Woman Suffrage Argument of Anna Howard Shaw." *Quarterly Journal of Speech* 49 no. 2: 165–174.

Linkugel, Wil A. 1974. "The Rhetoric of American Feminism: A Social Movement Course." *Speech Teacher* 23 no. 2: 121–130.

Logan, Shirley Wilson, ed. 1995. *With Pen and Voice: A Critical Anthology of Nineteenth-Century African-American Women.* Carbondale: Southern Illinois University Press.

O'Connor, Lillian. 1954. *Pioneer Women Orators: Rhetoric in the Ante-Bellum Reform Movement.* New York: Columbia University Press.

Ray, Angela G. 2009. "Explosive Words and Glimmers of Hope: U.S. Public Discourse, 1860–1900." In *The SAGE Handbook of Rhetorical Studies*, edited by Andrea A. Lunsford, Kirt H. Wilson, and Rosa A. Eberly, 525–540. Thousand Oaks, CA: SAGE.

Ronald, Kate. 2009. "Feminist Perspectives on the History of Rhetoric." In *The SAGE Handbook of Rhetorical Studies*, edited by Andrea A. Lunsford, Kirt H. Wilson, and Rosa A. Eberly, 139–152. Thousand Oaks, CA: SAGE.

Royster, Jacqueline Jones. 2000. *Traces of a Stream: Literacy and Social Change among African American Women.* Pittsburgh, PA: University of Pittsburgh Press.

Yoakam, Doris G. 1937. "Pioneer Women Orators of America." *Quarterly Journal of Speech* 23 no. 2: 251–259.

Yoakam, Doris G. 1943. "Women's Introduction to the American Platform." In *A History and Criticism of American Public Address*, vol. 1, edited by William Norwood Brigance, 153–192. New York: McGraw.

Yoakam Twichell, Doris. 1955. "Susan B. Anthony." In *A History and Criticism of American Public Address*, vol. 3, edited by Marie Hochmuth, 97–132. New York: McGraw.

Zaeske, Susan. 1995. "The 'Promiscuous Audience' Controversy and the Emergence of the Early Woman's Rights Movement." *Quarterly Journal of Speech* 81 no. 2: 191–207.

Zaeske, Susan. 2003. *Signatures of Citizenship: Petitioning, Antislavery, and Women's Political Identity.* Chapel Hill: University of North Carolina Press.

Zaeske, Susan. 2009. "'The South Arose as One Man': Gender and Sectionalism in Antislavery Petition Debates, 1835–1845." *Rhetoric and Public Affairs* 12 no. 3: 341–368.

Zboray, Ronald J., and Mary Saracino Zboray. 2010. *Voices without Votes: Women and Politics in Antebellum New England.* Durham: University of New Hampshire Press.

CHAPTER 46

....

RHETORIC AND
FEMINISM

....

CHERYL GLENN AND
ANDREA A. LUNSFORD

Although they are
Only breath, words
which I command
are immortal.

—Sappho, Fragment 9

FOR millennia, rhetoric seemed to have no connection with women, much less feminism. Traditional histories of rhetoric by Thomas Conley, Edward Corbett, W. S. Howell, George Kennedy, and James J. Murphy make no mention of women's participation in or contributions to rhetorical history and practice. In fact, until the 1980s, rhetoric and feminism could easily be viewed as near opposites. With its roots in Western traditions of masculinist, agonistic, public, political discourse, rhetoric offered little room for the women who followed its practices and no recognition of the men and women who employed rhetoric in different ways, in different scenes, and toward different ends. Indeed, rhetoric's long-held focus on the crucial importance of persuasion, dominance, and winning served to discourage women (and other subaltern groups) from its study and practice.

Neglected as subjects of scholarly interest, women were nonetheless developing rhetorical practices and traditions all along, with evidence of their accomplishments appearing in the ancient compositions of Enheduanna (ca. 2300 BCE), Sappho (ca. 530 BCE), and Aspasia (ca. 450 BCE). But for thousands of years, such women-inflected practices, even those deployed by powerful, public women (Queen Elizabeth I [1533–1603] comes to mind), went unrecognized by men (from Aristotle through George Kennedy), who were all the while writing and recording the rhetorical tradition. Little wonder, then, that activists in the early waves of feminism focused on political concerns, giving scant consideration to rhetorical studies:

> This is my letter to the World
> That never wrote to Me.
>
> (Emily Dickinson, "This Is My Letter to the World")

RHETORIC AND THE FIRST WAVE: DIVING IN

Instead, American first-wave feminists concentrated on the right to vote, to participate fully as US citizens. In 1848, a small group of suffragists, including Elizabeth Cady Stanton and Lucretia Mott, gathered at the first Women's Rights Convention in Seneca Falls, New York (see Ray, ch. 45). There the women collaborated on their Declaration of Sentiments, listing 18 rights in the US Declaration of Independence that men—but not women—enjoyed, despite the fact that the US Constitution refers to "people" and "citizens," never specifying "men" or "women." Those rights, which would accord women equal treatment under US law, included speaking in public, testifying in court, preaching from a pulpit, pursuing education, and entering into professions—all rights that would afford them opportunities to display their rhetorical abilities. Women also sought to obtain civil existence after marriage, control wages and property, hold legal custody of children, earn wages equal to those of men doing the same jobs, and, of course, secure the vote. In 1920, 72 years later, US women finally won the right to vote, guaranteed by the Nineteenth Amendment: "The right of citizens of the United States to vote shall not be denied or abridged by the United States or by any State on account of sex." These first-wave feminists rallied around issues of voting rights for women, the abolition of slavery, and patriotism vis-à-vis both the Civil War and what would eventually be called World War I. Along the way, they continued to develop skills in speaking out and up on the lecture circuit, organizing public meetings, and composing and then gathering petitions (the only legal means of political expression open to women at the time). But despite the fact that each of these efforts constituted a rhetorical practice, these early feminists were not seen as orators, writers, or rhetors whose powerful public words and actions were worthy of attention, let alone further study. First-wave feminism (named retroactively, of course) is considered to have ended with the 1920 passage of the Nineteenth Amendment.

> I bring you these women.
> Listen.
> They speak, but their lives
> are under attack.
> They . . . are denied adjustment of status
> in the land of the free. In the home of the brave.
>
> (Margaret Randall, "Under Attack")

RHETORIC AND THE SECOND
WAVE: SWIMMING TOWARD EQUALITY

During the second wave of feminism (from the 1950s through the 1980s), activists were once again employing rhetorical power publicly; they did not, however, think of themselves as rhetors, nor were they recognized as such by others. Bella Abzug, Susan Brownmiller, Mary Daly, Andrea Dworkin, Marilyn French, Betty Friedan, Carolyn Heilbrun, Maxine Hong Kingston, Barbara Jordan, Audre Lorde, Adrienne Rich, Gloria Steinem, and many others were all writing and speaking publicly, politically, and persuasively, yet they were regularly ignored by the rhetoric community and vice versa.

Second-wave feminism proved to be a natural outgrowth of first-wave feminism as well as the Civil Rights, Black Power, Student, and Anti-Vietnam War movements. Second-wave feminism not only pressed for a brand of equality that went beyond women's right to vote but also addressed and resisted the male domination of contemporary political movements. Motivated by systemic power relations that continued to render women and other so-called minority groups subordinate, these feminists campaigned (taking to the page, the stage, the pulpit, the airwaves) on a Pro-Woman/Women's Liberation platform to promote women's right to participate fully and equally in cultural, political, legal, and personal affairs. "The personal is the political," coined by Carol Hanisch, became the movement's slogan, locating, as it did, the cultural expectations of any individual body (as marked by sex, race, culture, and socioeconomic status) within the infinite yet predictable network of power relations that reflected social values. Its clarion call would become materialist feminism, an insightful analysis of the material conditions that influence women's and men's daily lives and pursuits (or lack thereof). Because women—all women—endured the same constraints to their personal lives and bodies, their release depended on the power of collective action.

The publication of such feminist works as *The Dialectic of Sex: The Case for Feminist Revolution* (Firestone 1970); *The Feminine Mystique* (Friedan 1963); *Intercourse* (Dworkin 1987); *Our Bodies, Ourselves* (Boston Women's Health 1971); *Outrageous Acts and Everyday Rebellions* (Steinem 1983); *Pornography: Men Possessing Women* (Dworkin 1979); *Titters* (Stillman and Beatts 1976); *The Cancer Journals* (Lorde 1980); *This Bridge Called My Back* (Moraga and Anzaldúa 1981); *Toward a Recognition of Androgyny* (Heilbrun 1964); and many others all contributed to the rhetorical power of feminists and to transformative societal changes. Many men and women began to reconsider the sexual division of labor (work outside and inside the home); some women began receiving equal pay for equal work, often earning well-deserved promotions; women were admitted to graduate and professional schools in large numbers; and, most of all, women won the right to control their own bodies in terms of safety, reproduction, and sexuality. In addition to the anti-sexual assault and anti-domestic violence campaigns (again, the personal is political) that effected changes in social work and legal procedures, feminists pressed forward for reproductive rights. Oral contraceptives were available (not always readily) to married women in 1965 and to unmarried women in 1972. In 1973, the US Supreme Court's landmark *Roe v. Wade* decision was handed down, giving women the right to choose an abortion during the first trimester of pregnancy. (Like the pill, legal abortions were not always readily available either.) In addition, the cultural expectation of heterosexuality (heteronormativity) was rigorously questioned, opening up safe space for lesbian identity, which feminists and nonfeminists alike embraced.

Despite the cultural advances created by second-wave feminism, the movement was not an unmitigated success. The activists had not achieved a crucial goal, the passing of the Equal Rights Amendment, which Alice Paul had introduced in 1923. The amendment (which is yet to be seriously considered, much less passed) reads: "Equality of rights under the law shall not be denied or abridged by the United States or any state on account of sex." Moreover, the mostly unremitting focus of second-wave feminists on the concerns of white, middle-class, heterosexual women exasperated other women (nonwhite, working-poor, lesbian, bisexual, non-Western) who wanted (and needed) to participate in collective action. Despite second-wave's sincere gestures of inclusivity, these "other" women considered themselves and their issues neglected by an otherwise cooperative movement that could have easily leveraged those "other" concerns as rallying points. This difficult and deeply regrettable situation, illustrated perfectly in Audre Lorde's (1984) "Open Letter to Mary Daly," demonstrated once again the degree to which the personal *is* political.

Over the course of more than 150 years, then, US feminists have actively used public persuasive language—that is, rhetoric—to invite men and women into the movement, inform the public about sociocultural ills and possibilities, and persuade legislators to underscore equality under the law. Only when second-wave feminism sparked a scholarly interest in women's studies, however, did feminists officially stake a claim in academia, where they initiated women-centered courses in sociology, anthropology, linguistics, literature, law, medicine, and religion. Still, not until the advent of its third-wave did feminism and rhetoric finally commence a series of encounters that would result in a serious, mutually enhancing relationship.

Given the fact that even the male bastion of philosophy had begun to consider the contributions of women, rhetoric's turn to a similar inquiry was markedly late. But as more feminists took up studies of rhetoric (in English, speech communication, and linguistics departments), they began questioning its very foundations: Where are the women? How can their exclusion be accounted for? Are their contributions simply waiting to be found? These questions gained urgency between the second and third waves of feminism, so much so that by the mid-1980s academic feminists of many stripes began the arduous but necessary work of rethinking every feature of the Western rhetorical tradition, and doing so armed, at last, with feminist theory, methods, and practice.

> Poets, and poems, are not apolitical.
> Women and other radicals who choose
> venerable vessels for subversive use

affirm what Sophomore Survey often fails
to note: God and Anonymous are not white males.
"We always crafted language just as they did.
We have the use, and we reclaim the credit."

(Marilyn Hacker, "Introductory Lines")

RHETORIC AND THE THIRD WAVE: HANGING TEN

Among the first to respond to this call for change were Patricia Bizzell, Karlyn Kohrs Campbell, Lisa Ede, Cheryl Glenn, Shirley Wilson Logan, Andrea Lunsford, and Krista Ratcliffe, all of whom argue that feminist rhetoricians must pursue several means of bringing about social, academic, and political change, including resistant rereadings of canonical rhetoric treatises; recovering and recuperating female-authored texts and performances; constructing feminist theories and practices of rhetoric; and extrapolating theories from texts not usually thought of as rhetorical.

Focusing on these four goals gives us an opportunity to highlight some of the efforts that have been made to bring feminism and rhetoric into alliance with one another in the United States. The first goal—resistant rereadings of canonical rhetoric treatises and categories—has proved to be fundamental to achieving all the other feminist-rhetorical goals and, as such, has been carried out by scholars (too numerous to mention) in rhetoric and writing studies as they have produced various publications and presentations. For our part, we (initially with Ede) took on the challenge of rereading traditional rhetorical categories to articulate the unspoken relationships between rhetoric and feminism. To do just that, we began with the traditional rhetorical canons of invention, arrangement, style, memory, and delivery. We have continued to carry out our resistant reading of the rhetorical canons vis-à-vis then-underappreciated (if not disregarded altogether) feminist rhetorical displays.

Upon examining the canon of invention (*inventio*), for example, we have found women claiming the right to the arts and practices of invention conducted in nonrational ways (i.e., drawing on neither Aristotelian nor Platonic epistemologies). Audre Lorde reminds us that "as women, we have come to distrust that power which rises from our deepest and nonrational knowledge. We have been warned against it all our lives by the male [rhetorical] world, which values this depth of feeling enough to keep women around in order to exercise it in the service of men, but which fears this same depth too much to examine the possibilities of it within themselves" (1984: 53–4). Feminists like Lorde challenge this distinction between supposedly rational or logical and nonrational or intuitive invention, insisting that knowledge and wisdom come also from "nonrational" and private domains. In addition, feminists have sought to change what counts as knowledge in the first place. Why not go, they ask, to *topoi* other than the classical ones suggested by Aristotle? Instead of automatically moving into definition, comparison, relationship, circumstance, and testimony, why not go directly to "ephemera" that reveal the information we need? Why not go to household accounts, cookbooks, secondary references to women's compositions, journals, commonplace books—to books of memory of all kinds to "invent" our arguments?

In raising these challenges, feminism seeks to expand invention, link it to memory, and open it up to the use of new materials, to the intuitive, the experiential, the paralogical, the nonmainstream—as well as to the words/works of "others." We have noted, in this regard, the ways in which women have linked *inventio* to *memoria* to such great effect, as in the work of writers like Toni Morrison, who tells us that memory is "a form of willed creation" (1984: 385). In their writings, Alice Walker and Isabel Allende regularly weave together past, present, and future events that result not in "individualistic autobiographical searchings but in revelations of traditions, re-collections of disseminated identities . . . that are a modern version of the Pythagorean arts of memory: retrospection to gain a vision for the future" (Fischer 1986: 198). Walker's *In Search of Our Mothers' Gardens* and *The Temple of My Familiar* as well as Allende's *House of Spirits* and *The Sum of Our Days* provide spectacular cases in point.

Turning to the canon of *dispositio* or arrangement, we have chronicled a long list of feminist challenges and appropriations, all of which resist Aristotle's dictum that "a speech has two parts. You must state your case, and you must prove it" (*Rhetoric* 3.13, 1414a1; trans. Roberts and Bywater). Obvious feminist patterns range from Tillie Olsen's use of silences within her texts to the double-voiced discourse of Geneva Smitherman; the seemingly erratic line patterns of Emily Dickinson, who preferred to "tell it slant" rather than in a linear way; the conversational and circular movements of Margaret Fuller (whom Orestes Brownson insisted never had a "beginning, middle, or end" to anything she wrote); the *écriture féminine* of Hélène Cixous; and the autoplagiarisms of Kathy Acker that juxtapose materials from her own life with swatches from canonical literary texts (like *Don Quixote*) to such startling effect. Such texts resist the linearity of beginning, middle, and end, preferring to alternate warp and woof, to move in circular or spiral rhythms, to weave and dance rather than march in a straight line.

In terms of style or *elocutio*, we have found women busily stretching and reshaping stylistic possibilities, from Mary Daly, who invented a whole new feminist vocabulary (showcased in her *Intergalactic Wickedary*), to writers like Susan Griffin and Michelle Cliff, both of whom write in multiple voices, genres, and in often wrenchingly different or incompatible styles that include Cliff's attempts to "write in fire." We also find that style marks a borderland where conflicting ideological, cultural, and political forces important to both rhetoric and feminism contend. Gayatri Spivak's "Can the Subaltern Speak?" wonders, in essence, whether a style of any kind is even available to the subaltern. After all, as Lorde reminds us, "The master's tools will never dismantle the master's house" (1995: 110). And even if those whom Spivak refers to as the "subaltern" could speak, would anyone really hear them? And what might those listeners actually (be able to) do? In other words, for feminist experiments with style to "count" in the rhetorical tradition, a rhetor requires an audience who agrees to listen to and authorize her, maybe even be moved by her words. For these reasons, Spivak (1987) turns toward a kind of self-authorization, which she calls "strategic essentialism."

"Delivery, delivery, delivery"—Demosthenes's response when asked to name the three most important parts of rhetoric has never been more true than today. In fact, we have found delivery (*actio*), the fifth canon of rhetoric, to be of the greatest importance, given the opportunities afforded us by new technologies of communication, many of which are decoupled from traditional print texts (see Goring, ch. 44). In the United States, scholars are only now beginning to understand the full extent of repression resulting from the growing hegemony of writing, with the concomitant erasure of oral, performative, and embodied traditions of rhetoric. What became a thoroughly textualized rhetoric systematically erased rhetorical practices delivered in nonprint, nonverbal, embodied ways, practices often employed by women. The work of James Fredal (2006) has helped to illuminate the fallout from such a textualized rhetoric and to provide a historicized response to calls for a writing of the body. In the Western intellectual tradition, the body has always been marked as "feminine," the mind "masculine." Thus, removing validated rhetorical performance from the body and grounding it, instead, in mental activity and externalized textuality has been crucial to the obliteration of women's embodied performances as rhetorical. Yet, throughout Western rhetorical history, women have been denied access to endorsed mediums of delivery (forbidden to speak in public, preach, teach, and even learn); have been silenced (with torture, shunning, and other instruments of power); have been erased (consider the history of Sappho and Aspasia); or have been simply ignored as insignificant or worse (especially those who "spoke" through mystical visions, translations, letters, preaching, teaching, and performance) (see Cox, ch. 26).

Rethinking the rhetorical canons in this way has led us to see that other rhetorical categories could and should be rethought as well. In rereading the Western rhetorical tradition, for example, feminist rhetoricians can turn to the traditional *pisteis* or proofs of classical rhetoric (*ēthos*, *logos*, and *pathos*), which call out for reconsideration and recuperation from feminist perspectives. In addition, we can reexamine traditional concepts such as *kairos* and *metanoia* to see how feminist theory and methods can transform them in ways that will speak to the abilities, and the needs, of women and other disenfranchised groups who want and need to speak out even or especially when doing so is seen as inappropriate by those with the most power. Such groups may be particularly attuned to *metanoia*, to the change of heart relevant to any person who moves from an apolitical into any politicized stance (from suffrage and abolition to equal rights and peace, for example). In her coupling of *kairos* and *metanoia*, Kelly Myers (2011) explains how *metanoia* follows on the heels of *kairos* when the appropriate opportunity to speak up and out is missed. Carrying regret, *metanoia* can be paralyzing *or* transformative (as in the case of many newly politicized, newly transformed rhetors).

> Somewhere in the landscape past noon
> I shall leave a dark print

Of the me that I am
And who I am not

(Audre Lorde, "Prologue")

The resistant reading of canonical rhetorical texts, categories, and concepts continues to serve as a crucial element in all the other goals that feminist rhetoricians have set for themselves. Such resistant readings have been particularly useful in the work of recuperating erased or marginalized women's rhetorical works. After all, if women's rhetorical contributions are ever to be recognized, we must use criteria different from those that had excluded them in the first place. Because women never had the opportunity to speak or write as public, political, agonistic, aristocratic *men*, they were never considered to be rhetors. But once the definition of rhetoric was expanded to include private, collaborative, domestic, any-class *women*, rhetorical studies blossomed in terms of who and what rhetorical displays merited our study. Little wonder, then, that the last 25 years, in particular, have witnessed an outpouring of work on feminism and rhetoric. Glenn's *Rhetoric Retold: Regendering the Tradition from Antiquity through the Renaissance* (1997), Susan Jarratt's *Rereading the Sophists: Classical Rhetoric Refigured* (1991), Shirley Wilson Logan's *"We Are Coming": The Persuasive Discourse of Nineteenth-Century Black Women* (1999), Andrea Lunsford's *Reclaiming Rhetorica* (1995), Jacqueline Jones Royster's *Traces of a Stream: Literacy and Social Change among African American Women* (2000), and Kathleen Welch's *The Contemporary Reception of Classical Rhetoric* (1991) are all outstanding examples of such recovery and recuperation work (see Royster, ch. 47). This critical mass of scholarship paved the way not only for the inaugural Feminism(s) and Rhetoric(s) biennial conference (first held in 1997) but also for the development of a Southern Illinois University Press series, "Studies in Rhetoric and Feminism." It seems fair to say that if rhetorical studies once lagged behind in building on the insights of feminism, feminist scholars in the field have worked very hard to catch up and to ride the waves of feminism with vigor and determination.

In terms of the third goal we listed—of constructing feminist theories of rhetoric— feminist rhetoricians have proved to be both resourceful and successful. Perhaps the most unusual and striking effort to build a feminist theory of rhetoric has been carried out by Starhawk, whose *Truth or Dare: Encounters with Power, Authority, and Mystery* sets forth and staunchly defends a new-age rhetoric that finds its origins in theories of the Goddess and in the conviction that we must return to the most basic tenets of democracy—that is, people sitting together, in a public forum, searching for ways to make good decisions. In a recent posting to the *Washington Post* blog, Starhawk (2011) takes a look at the Occupy Wall Street movement and its goals, arguing that it "demonstrates a different model of organizing: emergent, decentralized, without a command and control structure." Such new models of organizing are part of the theory she seeks: a rhetoric founded on inherent human value and capable of accounting for thoroughly democratic, feminist performances. Starhawk is not alone in attempting to create feminist theories of rhetoric. In communication studies, Sonja Foss and Cindy Griffin (1995) work out the characteristics and strategies of what they call "invitational rhetoric," a rhetoric of mutual engagement, while in composition studies Susan Kates (2001) articulates an activist rhetoric, a pedagogical paradigm designed to prepare marginalized learners to take on social responsibility.

Over the last seven years, a group of feminist scholars have been working to articulate a concept of rhetoric adequate to explaining and valuing the rhetorical practices of women and other marginalized groups for the *Norton Anthology of Rhetoric and Writing*. Anthologies can be a powerful influence, and in this instance the editors hope for nothing less than reshaping the field of rhetoric and writing, first by refusing a separation of the language arts (reading, writing, speaking, and listening), second by refusing a separation of theory and practice, and finally by refusing to define rhetoric as a solely Western phenomenon. Thus, the anthology will include not only the "theory" of white male authors but also the rhetorical practices and performances of women and people of color—in speeches, pamphlets, manifestos, letters, and so on, drawn from a number of cultures.

A very recent move toward articulating a feminist conception of rhetoric is Jane Sutton's *The House of My Sojourn: Rhetoric, Women, and the Question of Authority* (2010), in which Sutton figures rhetoric as a house, one that has consistently denied entry to women. She demonstrates that even when women gained a toehold on some space in the house, they were never recognized as speaking or writing with real authority. (The Master's tools cannot dismantle the Master's house, after all.) Sutton mixes memoir, research report, photography, analysis, and metaphorical projection in demonstrating that building a new house of rhetoric from the foundation up will not be done easily and never by simply allowing time to pass. Instead, Sutton calls on feminist rhetors to begin using their feet—and their speech—to begin material and symbolic work on a new foundation, maybe not to a new house but to a "new standard of construction" altogether, in which women and men can participate "equally with authority" (2010: 144).

While alternative theories of rhetoric are still few and far between, scholars like Damián Baca are working to develop them. Baca's *Mestiz@ Scripts, Digital Migrations, and the Territories of Writing* (2008) provides an alternative history of writing in the Americas. Building on the insights of Anzaldúa, he draws on ritual dances, for instance, to show how their use of improvisation and embodied performance resists dominant narratives. Baca also employs the idea of a *mestiza* consciousness, which "promotes the resistant movement between diverging cultural practices" (2008: 5), particularly rhetorical practices. In addition, Jaime Mejía's expansive review essay illuminates the potential of newly recognized rhetorical theories and practices, shining a light into the "rather dark shadow of the Western tradition of rhetoric," which is not and has never been "everyone's rhetoric" (Mejía 2011: 147). He extols the scholarship and pedagogy that "acknowledge[s] and respect[s] the cultures and rhetorical strategies that our students of color bring with them," for when the opposite occurs (as it has for far too long) "we deprive ourselves of richer and deeper understandings of different cultures from around the world as well as from within our nation's borders" (149). Such new rhetorical theories hold the power to help each of us gain insight into the experiences, histories, hopes, and dreams of others (anyone other than ourselves, that is).

> Nothing moves in a straight line,
> But in arcs, epicycles, spirals and gyres.
> Nothing living grows in cubes, cones, or rhomboids,
> But we take a little here and we give a little there,
> And the wind blows right through us,
> And blows the apples off the tree, and hangs a red kite suddenly there,
> And a fox comes to bite the apples curiously,
> And we change.
> Or we die
> And then change.
> It is many as raindrops.
> It is one as rain.
> And we eat it, and it eats us.
> And fullness is never,
> And now.
>
> (Marge Piercy, "I Saw Her Dancing")

The last goal of feminist rhetoricians has been that of extrapolating rhetorical theories from other kinds of texts (i.e., not rhetorical manuals or treatises). Again, we can discern some progress, most notably in Foss, Foss, and Griffin's (1999) *Feminist Rhetorical Theories*, in which they examine the writings of Cheris Kramerae, bell hooks, Gloria Anzaldúa, Mary Daly, Starhawk, Paula Gunn Allen, Trinh Minh-ha, Sally Miller Gearhart, and Sonia Johnson, effectively arguing that each of these women's works (from sociolinguistic analyses and memoirs to theological treatises and religious critiques) can yield a distinctly feminist theory of rhetoric. In this groundbreaking text, Foss, Foss, and Griffin describe their own metanoic journey from a traditional to a feminist rhetoric, saying that "the three of us eventually came to see feminism as more than the effort to achieve equality for women with men: as the means to create a different kind of world characterized by different practices and values" (1999: 4). Their goal, like that of all feminist rhetoricians, is to use language in such a way as to create a world that is rounder, more humane, and more oriented toward both the present and the future. As Lorde admonishes us, "To refuse to participate in the shaping of our future is to give up. . . . And in order to do that we must allow each other our differences at the same time as we recognize our sameness" (1995: 141–2).

> I came to explore the wreck.
> The words are purposes.
> The words are maps.
> I came to see the damage that was done
> And the treasures that prevail.
>
> (Adrienne Rich, "Diving into the Wreck")

Rhetoric and Feminism Today: Riding the Waves into the Future

This summary demonstrates, we hope, that scholars of rhetoric and writing studies have been riding the waves of feminisms, struggling to resist, resee, and reshape the rhetorical tradition in ways that not only admit but also embrace and celebrate women and feminist understandings, understandings that we firmly believe are beneficial for all human beings. After all, feminist rhetorical principles of invitation, inclusion, and full representation give us access to alternative perspectives, the kind of knowledge that feeds our process of intellectual and moral growth.

Has this work been successful? Yes, but the advances remain modest at best. As we write this essay, women around the world are being beaten, raped, tortured, murdered, and otherwise violated apace. The World Health Organization asserts that violence against women—both intimate-partner violence and sexual violence against women—remains a major public health problem. The organization reports that, in the United States alone, an average of nine women are murdered every day, three by an intimate partner (National Organization for Women). Such physical violence, according to sociologist Carol Gilligan, exemplifies "the gendered universe of patriarchy" (2011: 19), a universe of oppression, injustice, and physical as well as verbal violence. We believe this violence is related to the age-old agonistic base of the rhetorical tradition, with its reliance on combat, on dominance, and on winner-takes-all. That this traditional understanding of rhetoric is still too often accepted without critique is now completely unacceptable.

Yet such violence also can serve, as it has over millennia, as the exigence for women to respond rhetorically, but in a markedly different and completely performative, embodied way. Consider the work that women perform on International Women's Day (March 8). All around the world—from Santa Fe, New Mexico to Cape Town, South Africa, and from Antarctica to Hiroshima, Japan—women celebrate the day with antiwar protests. They meet in groups large enough to create artistic shapes with their bodies, which they form into the international peace sign or into letters that spell out "PEACE," "PAZ," "NO WAR," or "WHY?" (Go to http://w.w.w.baringwitness.org to see what we mean.) One aspect of this performance that makes their protest newsworthy is the fact that they form these shapes with their *naked* bodies, with photographers on hand to document and then help them circulate their message. Another aspect that makes their protests so rhetorically important and powerful is their silence. Inspired by the tradition of worldwide nonviolent demonstrations, these women cast off the old paradigm of public, verbalized, well-armored aggression to inhabit, instead, a new paradigm of public silence in all its human vulnerability. They make the papers, the newscasts, the webpages, of course—as well as their shared point. No doubt, their purposeful nudity enhances their newsworthiness, but it is their purposeful *silence* that enhances their rhetoric of community.

Using silence to foster community effort is not new, even though it is rarely thought of in those terms. Ever since Lysistrata and the coalition of women from Sparta, Thebes, and Athens closed their bodies to their warring men, nonviolent, nonverbal protest has provided a vibrant alternative to verbal and physical combat. The Dalai Lama, Martin Luther King, Jr., Aung San Sui Kyi, Mahatma Gandhi, and many others have followed along that same pathway, closing their mouths in order to draw attention to their situations and invite understanding and exchange.

Given that our talkative Western culture pays such homage to speaking out, being heard, verbal prowess, eloquence, and persuasion, it comes as no surprise that positive, productive silence has long been overlooked as a source of rhetorical power. What we refer to here as positive silence (see Glenn 2004), Ratcliffe refers to as "rhetorical listening," which she defines as a "stance of openness that a person may choose to assume in relation to any person, text, or culture" (2005: xiii). Feminist rhetoricians are drawn to a stance of openness, which declares a vulnerability not unlike that of the naked antiwar protesters and antiwar journalists (see Lunsford and Rosenblatt 2011). The overarching purpose of productive silence and rhetorical listening, closely aligned rhetorical positions, is to transcend self-interested intent (long the preferred stance of rhetors). To do so is to anticipate the other person's interest—the first move toward mutual receptivity and understanding and a purposeful departure from the traditional rhetorical ideal of mastery over others.

Thus, positive silence and listening reveal the already existing grounds for feminist rhetorical negotiation. One person honors another person's desire to be heard by listening intently, delivering peaceful, silent presence, listening for the ideas and emotions of another, listening across a divide of cultural, experiential, or intellectual difference. Such offerings of reciprocity provide the ideal rhetorical engagement: rather than concentrating on one's own opportunity to talk or talk back, one attends to another person's position, anticipating the grounds for negotiation and collaboration (see Code, ch. 57).

We should note that in their use of silence women are creating a *performative rhetoric*, one that is not bound to written texts that for too long failed to address the gender-based violence rooted in a worldwide culture of denial of women's rights. We might point to Code Pink, a women-initiated grassroots network that has spread to 150 communities around the world; their work is grounded in the body, in performance, and in the ludic. Or we could note the work of Women in Black, inspired by the anti-apartheid Black Sash in South Africa and the Madres de la Plaza de Mayo in Argentina. Since 1988, this movement has spread across the globe, with large groups in the United Kingdom, the United States, Europe, South America, Australia, New Zealand, Canada, Bahrain, Egypt, India, Japan, Mexico, and Turkey. And we could cite Liberia's Women in White, the first Christian–Muslim alliance that grew into the Liberian Mass Action for Peace, a nonviolent women's movement that helped end Charles Taylor's dictatorship and the war there. In fall 2011, Ellen Johnson Sirleaf, the president of Liberia, Leymah Gbowee, a prominent Liberian peace activist, and Yemeni pro-democracy campaigner Tawakkol Karman were awarded the Nobel Peace Prize in recognition of their nonviolent struggle for women's safety and women's rights. For decades, they have performed a rhetoric of peace and justice.

> *A reasonable woman adapts to the world.*
> *An unreasonable woman makes the world adapt to her.*
> *What this world needs are more unreasonable women.*
>
> (Unreasonable Women of the Earth)

In short, feminists today are attempting to build an alternative to traditional agonistic rhetoric through their strategic use of speech, silence, and resistance guided by nonviolent principles, a thoroughly feminist rhetoric that can account for embodied, performed rhetorical practices. What will such a rhetoric entail? At the very least, it will focus not only on the written but also on the performed (whether virtual or "real"); not on linearity but on webbed connection and collaboration; not on consumers of knowledge, art, and craft but on active, mutually informing producers of the same; not on winning at all costs but on *understanding* and working together. Such a rhetoric and the multiple practices it will evoke, render, and embody can help women and men, disenfranchised and powerful alike, in the United States and everywhere, break the links between traditional rhetoric and dis/empowerment, between power and violence. Such a rhetoric of invitation, listening, and empathy can transform the rhetorical tradition from one of persuasion, control, and discipline (on the part of the rhetor) to one of inherent worth, equality, and empowered action (for rhetor and audience alike). Rhetors using such a rhetoric will be embodying and performing rhetoric in ways that will reject combat and dominance in favor of sharing perspectives, understandings, and power. These are the goals an interanimating connection between rhetoric and feminism can—and must—achieve. After all, feminists and traditionalists, the subaltern and powerful, men and women, are all the same species: we are all human beings, humans with an innate capacity for language and the ability to care about one another, to work together, to change, to respond to *kairos* and *metanoia*. The feminist rhetorical possibilities we offer support our belief that rhetoric is an endlessly pliable human art, one that always has the potential to be used toward *eudaimonia*, the greatest good for all of us human beings. Such feminist interventions into traditional rhetorical principles provide opportunities for new ways of being rhetorical, of showing respect, making commitments, sharing power, and distinguishing ourselves as human. Achieving these goals is the new—and ongoing—work of feminism and rhetoric.

REFERENCES

Acker, Kathy. 1986. *Don Quixote: A Novel*. New York: Grove Press.
Allende, Isabel. 1985. *The House of Spirits*. New York: Knopf.
Allende, Isabel. 2008. *The Sum of Our Days*. New York: Harper Collins.

Baca, Damián. 2008. *Mestiz@ Scripts, Digital Migrations, and the Territories of Writing.* New York: Palgrave.

Boston Women's Health Book Collective. 1971. *Our Bodies, Ourselves: A Book for and by Women.* Boston: Boston Women's Health Book Collective.

Brownson, Orestes. 1845. "Miss Fuller and Reformers." *Brownson's Quarterly Review* 7: 249–257.

Cixous, Hélène, and Catherine Clément. (1975) 1996. *Newly Born Woman.* London: Tauris.

Cliff, Michelle. 2009. *If I Could Write This in Fire.* Minneapolis: University of Minnesota Press.

Daly, Mary. 1989. *Websters' First New Intergalactic Wickedary of the English Language.* Boston, MA: Beacon.

Dickinson, Emily. 2010. "Tell all the truth but tell it slant." In *Dickinson: Selected Poems and Commentaries*, edited by Helen Vendler, 431. Cambridge, MA: Harvard University Press.

Dworkin, Andrea. 1979. *Pornography: Men Possessing Women.* New York: Putnam.

Dworkin, Andrea. 1987. *Intercourse.* New York: Free Press-Simon and Schuster.

Firestone, Shulamith. 1970. *The Dialectic of Sex: The Case for Feminist Revolution.* New York: William Morrow.

Fischer, Michael M. J. 1986. "Ethnicity and the Post-Modern Arts of Memory." In *Writing Culture: The Poetics and Politics of Ethnography*, edited by James Clifford and George E. Marcus, 194–233. Berkeley: University of California Press.

Foss, Karen A., Sonja K. Foss, and Cindy L. Griffin. 1999. *Feminist Rhetorical Theories.* Thousand Oaks, CA: SAGE.

Foss, Sonja K., and Cindy L. Griffin. 1995. "Beyond Persuasion: A Proposal for an Invitational Rhetoric." *Communication Monographs* 62: 2–18.

Fredal, James. 2006. *Rhetorical Action in Ancient Athens: Persuasive Artistry from Solon to Demosthenes.* Carbondale: Southern Illinois University Press.

Friedan, Betty. 1963. *The Feminine Mystique.* New York: Norton.

Fuller, Margaret. 1994. *The Portable Margaret Fuller.* Edited by Mary Kelley. New York: Viking.

Gilligan, Carol. 2011. *Joining the Resistance.* Cambridge: Polity.

Glenn, Cheryl. 1997. *Rhetoric Retold: Regendering the Tradition from Antiquity through the Renaissance.* Carbondale: Southern Illinois University Press.

Glenn, Cheryl. 2004. *Unspoken: A Rhetoric of Silence.* Carbondale: Southern Illinois University Press.

Hacker, Marilyn. 1955. "Introductory Lines." In *100 Great Poems by Women*, edited by Carolyn Kizer, 148–149. New York: Ecco-HarperCollins.

Hanisch, Carol. 1970. "The Personal Is Political." In *Notes from the Second Year: Women's Liberation*, edited by Shulamith Firestone and Anne Koedt, 76–78. New York: Radical Feminism.

Heilbrun, Carolyn. 1964. *Toward a Recognition of Androgyny.* New York: Knopf.

Jarratt, Susan C. 1991. *Rereading the Sophists: Classical Rhetoric Refigured.* Carbondale: Southern Illinois University Press.

Kates, Susan. 2001. *Activist Rhetorics and American Higher Education, 1885–1937.* Carbondale: Southern Illinois University Press.

Logan, Shirley Wilson. 1999. *"We Are Coming": The Persuasive Discourse of Nineteenth-Century Black Women.* Carbondale: Southern Illinois University Press.

Lorde, Audre. 1984. *Sister Outsider: Essays and Speeches.* Berkeley, CA: Crossing Press.

Lorde, Audre. 1980. *The Cancer Journals.* San Francisco, CA: Aunt Lute Books.

Lunsford, Andrea A., ed. 1995. *Reclaiming Rhetorica.* Pittsburgh, PA: University of Pittsburgh Press.

Lunsford, Andrea A., and Adam Rosenblatt. 2011. "'Down a Road and into an Awful Silence': Graphic Listening in Joe Sacco's Comics Journalism." In *Silence and Listening as Rhetorical Arts*, edited by Cheryl Glenn and Krista Ratcliffe, 130–146. Carbondale: Southern Illinois University Press.

Mejía, Jaime Armin. 2011. "Ethnic Rhetorics Revisited." *College Composition and Communication* 63 no. 1: 145–161.

Moraga, Cherríe, and Gloria E. Anzaldúa. 1981. *This Bridge Called My Back: Writings by Radical Women of Color*. Boston, MA: Persephone.

Morrison, Toni. 1984. "Memory, Creation, and Writing." *Thought* 59: 385–390.

Myers, Kelly. 2011. "*Metanoia* and the Transformation of Opportunity." *Rhetoric Society Quarterly* 48 no. 1: 1–18.

Myerson, Joel, ed. 1980. *Critical Essays on Margaret Fuller*. Boston, MA: G.K. Hall.

National Organization for Women. "Violence Against Women in the United States: Statistics." Accessed 2012. http://now.org/issues/violence/stats.html#endref1.

The Norton Anthology of Rhetoric and Writing. Edited by Andrea A. Lunsford, Susan Jarratt, Jacqueline Jones Royster, Robert Hariman, Tom Miller, and Jody Enders. New York: W.W. Norton & Company. Forthcoming.

Olsen, Tillie. (1965) 2003. *Silences*. New York: Feminist Press.

Piercy, Marge. 1988. "I Saw Her Dancing." In *Available Light*, 118–121. New York: Knopf.

Randall, Margaret. 1988. "Under Attack." In *Ain't I a Woman!* edited by Iloona Linthwaite, 99. New York: Peter Bedrick.

Ratcliffe, Krista. 2005. *Rhetorical Listening: Identification, Gender, Whiteness*. Carbondale: Southern Illinois University Press.

Rich, Adrienne. (1973) 1994. *Diving into the Wreck*. New York: W.W. Norton & Company.

Royster, Jacqueline Jones. 2000. *Traces of a Stream: Literacy and Social Change Among African American Women*. Pittsburgh, PA: University of Pittsburgh Press.

Smitherman, Geneva. 1977. *Talkin and Testifyin*. New York: Houghton Mifflin.

Spivak, Gayatri Chakravorty. 1987. "Subaltern Studies: Deconstructing Historiography." In *In Other Worlds: Essays in Cultural Politics*, 197–221. New York: Routledge.

Spivak, Gayatri Chakravorty. 1988. "Can the Subaltern Speak?" In *Marxism and the Interpretation of Culture*, edited by Cary Nelson and Lawrence Grossberg, 271–316. Urbana: University of Illinois Press.

Starhawk. 2011. "What Drives Occupy Wall Street?" *Washington Post*, October 20. http://www.washingtonpost.com/blogs/on-faith/post/faith-in-the-99-percent-what-drives-occupy-wall-street/2011/10/20/gIQAS2R3oL_blog.html.

Steinem, Gloria. 1983. *Outrageous Acts and Everyday Rebellions*. New York: New American Library.

Stillman, Deanne, and Anne P. Beatts, eds. 1976. *Titters: The First Collection of Humor by Women*. Springfield, OH: Collier.

Sutton, Jane. 2010. *The House of My Sojourn: Rhetoric, Women, and the Question of Authority*. Tuscaloosa: University of Alabama Press.

Walker, Alice. 1983. *In Search of Our Mothers' Gardens: Womanist Prose*. New York: Harcourt.

Walker, Alice. 1989. *The Temple of My Familiar*. New York: Harcourt.

Welch, Kathleen. 1991. *The Contemporary Reception of Classical Rhetoric: Appropriations of Ancient Discourse*. New York: Routledge.

CHAPTER 47

RHETORIC AND RACE IN THE UNITED STATES

JACQUELINE JONES ROYSTER

WHAT do we know about rhetoric and race? The most fundamental assertions in this chapter about these two terms draw attention not to rhetoric and race as separate, individual terms but to the ways these concepts intersect and generate insights about the implications of race in rhetorical performances and the impact of these performances on sociopersonal identities. One underlying claim is that rhetoric is a social practice, a perspective that rests on over 2,500 years of Western rhetorical scholarship, not to mention the rhetorical experiences in non-Western contexts about which scholars are now learning—China, Japan, India, Africa, the Middle East, Meso-America, and others. Another claim is that race is an idea that has ebbed and flowed over time as a product of complex sociopolitical human relationships, a point of view that rests on thousands of years of theory-making about human variety in the context of tribe, nation, and other geopolitical relationships over the generations of human societies.[1] Together, these two perspectives create a complex third viewpoint focused on the basic question of what happens at the convergence of the two phenomena: the points at which a sociocultural practice meets a sociopolitical concept.

Focusing on the crosscurrents of rhetoric and race rather than their center points calls for robust models of inquiry like the one I develop with Gesa Kirsch in *Feminist Rhetorical Practices: New Horizons for Rhetoric, Composition, and Literacy Studies* (Royster and Kirsch 2012). This model identifies four sets of data-gathering strategies for critical engagement, analysis, and interpretation: critical imagination, strategic contemplation, social circulation, and globalization. In this chapter I use primarily two of these strategies: critical imagination, which refers to using reflective, reflexive, dialectical, and dialogical strategies to build "high-definition" analytical matrices; and globalization, which focuses on connecting local practices and processes across geopolitical boundaries to interrogate continuities and discontinuities of them not as culture-bound or geography-bound experience but as *human* experience.

The analytical imperative is twofold. One task is to build a definitional matrix of these two terms as a local performance, taking into account both "biospheric and semiospheric implications,"[2] to create an ecologically grounded view of practices and processes in geopolitical space. In the United States, language users are persistently rendered as raced, gendered, acculturated, and otherwise socially and personally identified, and rhetorical performances are defined and interpretable within the currents and crosscurrents of these ecological relationships. A second task is to use this multidimensional, multidirectional matrix to look beyond the local American dynamic (defined iconically by rhetorics of race from the abolitionist and the civil rights movements) for connections to other performances in other contexts to tell a broader human story, not simply a story of African American oppression as a "peculiar" experience.[3] The goal with this type of data-gathering process is not to present tried and true answers but to gather evidence about how practices and processes related to rhetoric and race are grounded in experiences (e.g., social, political, economic, cultural, spatial) and to use this grounding to articulate a "plateau" or vantage point from which to interpret how such relationships endow both concepts with broader and deeper meaning and a clearer sense of sociopolitical value and consequence. With this type of inquiry we come full circle to the original task of accounting for what we know about rhetorical actions—as performances by human beings in space, time, and context—and what we know about performers of rhetoric, who are identifiable within the social hierarchies of race and other sociopersonal identities.

RHETORIC AND RACE IN AN AMERICAN ECOLOGICAL SYSTEM

Framing rhetoric ecologically magnifies the immemorial view of rhetoric as purposeful action and provides a springboard for interrogating even more dynamically core questions in Western rhetorical traditions: Who says what to whom? For what reasons and from what imperatives? For which occasions in which settings? Under what circumstances? Using which media, modes, and forms? With what effects and consequences? Likewise, this type of framing creates a similar positioning for race, not simply as a system for categorizing human phenotypes but as a critical factor in the processes by which we form sociopersonal identities.[4] In this scenario, race constitutes an analytical focal point through which we negotiate social, political, and cultural hierarchies; develop a sense of agency and authority in relation to these hierarchies; and use the sensibilities that emerge to direct decision-making, action, and the interpretation of action. Such analyses of race pay attention to the values, habits, and expectations of communities, accounting for the performance of identity (including rhetorical performances) within those communities. They interrogate the terms of engagement in sociopolitical hierarchies and the processes of sociopolitical action (including, again, rhetorical actions). Moreover, they critique the mechanisms by which various sociocultural binaries are established (for example) as valuable and not valuable, successful and failed, good and evil, and so forth.

From such perspectives, rhetoric and race are inevitably dynamic. As separate phenomena, they are each complex, but when they converge their complexity is magnified as they form a powerful, dynamic system. In the American context, this system becomes a lever for understanding the disconnections between the mythological beliefs of the nation in the value of truth, freedom, and justice and the extent to which these values have not been extended to all citizens, thus creating the need for the disempowered to use language eloquently to negotiate these dynamics and to pursue their quest for agency and authority, for power and possibility. Herein lies the raison d'être of "race rhetorics" in the United States.

This approach raises a twofold question. On one hand, the question is: When you look at rhetorical action through the lens of race, how does it inform and filter our view of what rhetoric is as a dynamic human endeavor? On the other, the companion question is: When you look at the performance of race through the lens of rhetoric, viewing race not as a phenotype but as a sociopolitical enactment, how does it inform and filter our view of what race is as a dynamic instantiation of ways of being and doing? A first response is that rhetoric and race are animated in context, nourish each other, and gain strength in their surrounding sociopolitical ecologies. As specific evidence of human engagement, rhetoric and race can be investigated, described, analyzed, and interpreted with an eye toward broadening and deepening our understanding of the nature, scope, and mechanisms by which we fashion who and how we are as human beings. This view of the symbolic potential of both rhetoric and race resonates well with Kenneth Burke's categorization of language (and by extension, race) as "symbolic action" (1966: 15).

Viewing rhetoric and race as entwined forms of symbolic action in an ecosystem offers a strategic opportunity to use such performances not so much as categories of being and doing but as points of reference, as analytics for understanding critical relationships between being (biospheric implications) and doing (semiospheric implications) (see Code, ch. 57; McMurry, ch. 58). In other words, in the United States race has constituted a dramatic mandate for activism and an empowering occasion (*kairos*) for rhetorical action. Likewise, rhetorical action has been an enactment of self-authorization for voice, vision, and agency by groups of nonauthorized peoples—those discriminated against by phenotype and other sociopersonal identities—as they find and invent strategies for exercising freedom, justice, and equality in a country in which these values form the national bedrock, despite persistent practices of discrimination and oppression.

Consider in this discussion Marilyn Cooper's view of ecosystems and writing, accompanied by an analogical glossing and re-interpretation:

> Systems are concrete. They are structures that can be investigated, described, altered; they are not postulated mental entities, not generalizations. Every individual writer [language user] is necessarily involved in these systems: for each writer [language user] and each instance of writing [the convergence of rhetoric and race] one can specify the domain of ideas activated and supplemented, the purposes that

stimulated the writing [the convergence] and that resulted from it, the interactions that took place as part of the writing [performance], the cultural norms that enabled and resulted from the writing [performance]. . . . But in the actual activity of writing [producing rhetorics of race]—as in the economy—the systems are entirely interwoven in their effects and manner of operation. The systems reflect the various ways writers [language users] connect with one another through writing [rhetorical practices]: through systems of ideas, of purposes, of interpersonal interactions, of cultural norms, of textual forms. (1986: 369)

Building on Cooper's theories, then, the convergence of rhetoric and race in the United States within a complex ecosystem can be defined as an operational matrix formed by the dynamic, interdependent interactions of citizens within a specific sociohistorical context. On this account, Americans function within biospheres and semiospheres that mark us all quite matter-of-factly by social status, political power (or the lack thereof), economic capacity, sociopersonal traits, and so forth, with phenotype, race, and ethnicity operating with considerable force in terms of the performance of identity and issues of representation. Further, as citizens we are situated in time and space in terms of power, prestige, agency, authority, and entitlement, not to mention covered, as it were, by the shadow of our slaveholding and imperialistic history.

Recognizing these interrelationships underscores the point that American rhetorics of race have emanated from the disjunction between the nation's belief in the fundamental values of freedom, justice, and equality as universal human rights and the application of these rights by means of civil law (i.e., the specific articulation of human rights as civil rights) in the *Constitution of the United States* (see Royster and Cochran 2011). Rhetorics of race emerged in the context of more than two centuries of slavery, another century of racist oppression, and yet another century of the remnants, effects, and consequences of slavery and racism. Rhetorics of race in the United States are closely linked with the African American experience. As a peculiarly racialized discourse, American rhetorics of race are connected historically to slavery as a "peculiar" institution in a nation defined by both its freedoms and trusteeship of global human rights and its peculiar lack of freedoms for certain groups.

Also important is that, despite critical disconnections, these rhetorics have functioned with tremendous iconic value and set the watermarks for rhetorical action as a sociopolitical practice more generally, in keeping with Toni Morrison's (1992) articulation of what it has meant in American culture to "play in the dark." Morrison's analysis sheds light on the ways race (and by extension its rhetorics) has constituted a backdrop against which a range of social, political, and cultural issues have played out. By proxy, rhetorics of race have provided lenses through which all sorts of other concerns can be clarified, critiqued, and interpreted metonymically, with the racialized lenses acknowledged occasionally, but not always. Sometimes, as Morrison suggests,

it is as if I had been looking at a fishbowl—the glide and flick of the golden scales, the green tip, the bolt of white careening back from the gills; the castles at the bottom, surrounded by pebbles and tiny, intricate fronds of green; the barely disturbed water, the flecks of waste and food, the tranquil bubbles traveling to the surface—and suddenly I saw the bowl, the structure that transparently (and invisibly) permits the ordered life it contains to exist in the larger world. (1992: 17)

A prime example from the nineteenth century of these iconic relationships is the rise of the women's suffrage movement within groups of women who had honed their habits of activism in the cause of abolitionism. Essentially, through their advocacy related to the abolition of slavery, white women activists of this generation were able to see far more dramatically and interpret with greater clarity the gendered implications of their own oppressed conditions (see Ray, ch. 45; Glenn and Lunsford, ch. 46). Over time, other dynamic cross-connections emerged as well, such as the interconnections at the turn of the nineteenth century and across the twentieth century between civil rights activism and workers' rights, as illustrated by Martin Luther King, Jr.'s linking of civil rights and resistance to the Vietnam War and his linking of civil rights and workers' rights during his last campaign in Memphis in 1968. Such stories of crosscurrents recur regularly throughout the history of the United States, but instead of permitting clear discursive linkages they have ushered in another dilemma.

On one hand, from a general perspective rhetorics of race have served metaphorically as leverage for sociopolitical action for many challenges to freedom, justice, and equality in American culture. One might argue, however, that the result of providing this leveraging service has been to cast the functioning of race as a specific system of processes and practices in shadow, positioning the system as a *generalization* (as Cooper explains in her discussion of ecosystems). As a generalization race can be set aside, functioning mainly as a point of departure for other concerns but having its own materiality as a key focal point for interrogation and analysis relegated to the periphery, muted in relative silence by the larger discourses.

On the other hand, inside the bubble of civil rights discourses lies a distinctive contrast. Rhetorics of race have flourished in peripheralized space in their capacity to interrogate systems and ecosystems of race directly and to provide leverage for resisting domination and oppression in all of its varieties. These rhetorics have emerged at the eye of sociopolitical storms in the negotiation of agency, authority, entitlement, and empowerment. From this perspective, rhetorics of race have a dual presence. Provocative insights about power, privilege, and human experience have come forth dynamically at this convergence, but simultaneously these insights have emerged within the ecologies that surround them. In American culture the deep desire to retain an international identity as the global champion of democracy and human rights provides strong incentives to treat American rhetorics of race as exceptional and peculiar, linked to slavery as a scar healed long ago and not systemically tied to our own ongoing national operations or to our master narratives of who and how we are.

One result is that while rhetorics of race are often recognized as eloquent and compelling—Sojourner Truth, Frederick Douglas, Martin Delaney, Martin Luther

King, Jr., Malcom X, and many others provide models—they are also positioned as "museum pieces" (Spitzack and Carter 1987) or serendipitous opportunities for appreciating days gone by, as exceptional cases or as entertainment rather than agents of action, sense-making, and decision-making. In this scenario, rhetorics of race are made peripheral to enterprises deemed by the national *mythos* to be more normal and valuable. Such positioning becomes visible, for example, in recent assertions that the United States, despite evidence to the contrary, is now "post-racial" and that rhetorics of race are therefore anachronistic, less salient, and less consequential.

Thus, despite some efforts to broaden the lenses of interrogation and interpretation in sociopolitical discourses, rhetorics of race are often situated within the narrow historical framework of American constructions of racialized experiences—"anti-slavery," "abolitionism," "civil rights," and "post-civil rights"—that isolate rhetorics of race (and other sociopersonal identities) from global struggles for human rights. By this schema, "civil rights" serves in the United States as a metonym for a troublesome conceptual space between human and civil rights and casts core relationships between the two focal points in shadow. In effect, then, when we talk about "rhetorics of *race*" in the United States we focus, more often than not, on discourses of "rights within the law" and the negotiation of power and authority within the purview of the nation. When we talk about "rhetorics of *human* rights," we tend to disassociate them from long-standing activist struggles for the just application of civil law in the land of the free and the home of the brave. Instead, we locate human rights as an international concern on one horizon and civil rights as a national concern on another.

Scholarly challenges in recent decades (in feminist studies, gender studies, postcolonial studies, cultural studies, and other fields) have included, therefore, a push to recognize, articulate, and interrogate the fluid, complex intersections of relationships embedded in the performance of race (see Glenn and Lunsford, ch. 46). These embedded relationships connect in the view that rights are endowed by human nature (i.e., the innate, natural rights of all human beings regardless of our human variety or geopolitical location). They connect also the growing multidimensional pool of evidence generated by these fluid relationships to more fully textured interpretations of the ways language users define, shape, and nourish arguments and rationalities related to freedom, justice, and empowerment, whether in national frameworks of racialized rhetorics or international frameworks of human rights.

Acknowledging this scholarly mandate underscores the significance of using a global framework in analyses to link local situations to the global landscape. From a local perspective, African American participants in rhetorics of race have indeed focused on their own immediate needs and desires, but they have not remained inside the ideological space of national issues in constructing their arguments and operational strategies. Instead, they have also looked across national borders to make vibrant connections between conditions at home and conditions elsewhere. This strategy is illustrated, for example, by the well-known connections between Martin Luther King, Jr. and Mohandas Gandhi in King's embracing of nonviolent resistance. Likewise, consider co-related situations of citizens from other nations who have enacted their own rhetorical work inside their own nation but also looked inside the borders of the United States for operational models. The fluidity of these interconnections from the inside out and the outside in speaks to the ways frameworks and strategies migrate across sites and situations, enriching the perspective that there are indeed global crosscurrents that underscore notions of human dignity and human rights. Viewed in this simultaneously local and global context, American rhetorics of race become one set of social practices; one exemplar of the ways practices have the capacity to become iconic and, in this case, to function symbolically in translating reality for others similarly challenged; and one focal point for understanding how models of rhetoric and race migrate in support of varying human needs. The bottom line is that working at the intersection of race and rhetoric offers provocative opportunities for understanding both concepts locally and globally as modes of human behavior.

THE RHETORIC OF RHETORICS OF RACE

Amid this type of ecological analysis there remains the question of what rhetorics of race in the United States have entailed. To repeat, we habitually talk about African American rhetorics as though they took shape and evolved only in a peculiar national vacuum defined by the politics of the enslavement of Africans, rather than also as part of the larger schema of global human rights discourses. By contrast, ecological analyses push us to situate both human rights and civil rights not as separate but as inexorably connected via quests around the world for autonomy, agency, and human dignity. This reframing clarifies the viewpoint. Despite the fact that rhetorics of race in the United States have evolved in the context of slavery and its historical legacies, these rhetorics stand on the bedrock of passionate human resistance to oppression, discrimination, and disenfranchisement and on the mandate to dismantle obstacles to the right of all human beings to freedom, justice, agency, authority, and full participation in sociopolitical arenas.

Regardless, then, of the silences and invisibilities that have surrounded rhetorics of race in American discourses, research across the disciplines on race, racial identity formation, and performances of race have been instructive in disrupting these patterns of disregard. This scholarship has enhanced our capacity to view, understand, and value the lives, conditions, and achievements of African Americans (and others caught in these matrices of sociopersonal identity). Race rhetorics have focused on garnering respect for humanity in all of its variety, establishing self-determination and self-governance, questioning assumptions of authority, agency, power, and so forth.

Researchers in literary and rhetorical studies have gathered an array of textual and contextual information to flesh out these complexities and actions. For example, in recent years several anthologies have documented expressive traditions in African American literature, including *The Norton Anthology of African American Literature* (Gates and McKay 1997), *The Prentice Hall Anthology of African American Literature* (Smith and Jones 2000), and *The Prentice Hall Anthology of African American Women's*

Literature (Lee 2006). Other researchers have created similar collections related to specific rhetorical traditions, including *With Pen and Voice: A Critical Anthology of Nineteenth-Century African-American Women* (Logan 1995), *African-American Orators: A Bio-Critical Sourcebook* (Leeman 1996), and *Lift Every Voice: African American Oratory, 1787–1900* (Foner and Branham 1998).[5]

When placed within an ecological framework (see Royster and Kirsch 2012), all of these volumes (and others) offer artifactual evidence from two critical perspectives that are particularly relevant to this discussion. Quite dramatically, they clarify the historical quest by African Americans for the right to voice, agency, authority, and empowerment in their resistance to oppressive sociopolitical environments. That is, these works constitute an archive of evidence about the convergence of rhetoric as a social practice and race as a sociopersonal identity. In addition, when we consider this scholarly work from a global perspective, the connections of these practices to a larger, more international enterprise come into sharp focus, especially in light of two documents that constitute a critical foundation for contemporary human rights discourses: *The Universal Declaration of Human Rights* (1948) and the *United Nations Declaration of the Rights of Indigenous Peoples* (2007). Understanding this interface between American civil rights discourses and international human rights discourses offers us a richer understanding of what happens when we use the lens of race to inform our view of what rhetoric is as a dynamic human endeavor.

RACE AS A SOCIAL CONSTRUCTION

When we use a rhetorical lens, enriched by critical imagination and globalization as perspectives for robust critical inquiry, some conclusions no longer seem so contentious. For example, stating that *race* is a social, cultural, political, and ideological construction, rather than a biological one, becomes a given, as does the assertion that the theory and practice of rhetoric is intricately intertwined with the politics of race and other embodiments of identity in sociopolitical contexts. Moreover, it becomes possible to argue, as I did in the previous section, that the imbrication of race and rhetoric is related to the garnering and exercise of agency, power, privilege, authority, and entitlement. In fact, the pressing need to argue for the existence, saliency, or importance of such dynamic realities thus becomes basic.

Generally, in the field of rhetorical history we accept the notion that agency and identity—the *who* of rhetorical performance—matter, often quite spectacularly. However, we need to go further in understanding how the study of rhetorical agency may be enhanced by an interrogation of human difference, with race being one key element of difference. Conversely, when we use race as a lens for analyzing rhetorical performance, it draws attention to the need to scrutinize the nuances of performance that occur when the sociopolitical identities of a person change. Shifting the analytical paradigm acknowledges in specific terms, rather than generalities, that the vision, voice, experiences, and perceptions of the rhetor matter in rhetorical decision-making, in audience reception, and in the potential for impact and consequence. Who is the "good man" (*vir bonus*) speaking? Is the speaker deemed credible by the audience? Given the audience's perception of the speaker's identity, is the discourse persuasive, capable of creating desired or unintended effects? And more.

The point to be emphasized in raising such questions at a lower level of generality is that in rhetorical studies today we are interested not simply in directing attention toward the speaker or writer but in bringing texture and materiality to this rhetor's identity. In doing so, of course, we operationalize deeper layers of the inquiry process that remain contentious and subject to negotiations related to the formation of identity, agency, and authority. Further, we signal the need to assess the variable means and mechanisms for expression and persuasion. Beyond these imperatives, there remains also a pressing need to document actual rhetorical performances across social, cultural, geographical, and chronological boundaries. The goal of such comparative inquiry is to create an ever-generative flow of well-textured evidence that expands and enriches our knowledge of rhetorical practices around the world and helps us develop more nuanced, fully rendered interpretations of these practices.

This comparative approach to rhetorical studies draws attention to critiques and theories that question, rather than accept, the terms, values, and expectations of rhetorical performance—handed down for more than two millennia—that reflect just one geopolitical experience: that of elite white males in the traditional public arenas of power.[6] The intersection of rhetoric and race, then, makes it clearer that rhetorical performances are embodied experiences, with African American rhetorics serving as an important exemplar for building knowledge and understanding.

If we begin interrogating rhetoric and race, as the previous discussion suggests we do, with the commonplace sense of rhetoric as a material, embodied experience, then it makes sense to view race as a specific dimension of a schema that functions kaleidoscopically. First, it centralizes rhetoric itself as a multidimensional and dynamic process rather than a static phenomenon that is essentially captured in time and space. This approach thus highlights the concept of race not as a simple, isolated, and peculiar factor to be acknowledged (or not) and then set aside but as a primary analytical point capable of dramatic effects, one that interweaves itself dynamically with other factors to create leverage for determining other types of dramatic effects and consequences.

Viewing rhetoric and race kaleidoscopically through robust inquiry strategies pushes us to attend to both the rhetorical situation and the rhetorical action itself, but with the twist of endowing these points of reference as fully as possible with materiality. Even when an inquiry focuses on long-standing interests in Western rhetorical traditions (who says what, to whom, within what contexts, under what circumstances, and to what ends), other dimensions of concern necessarily form and re-form around them. The effort is to devote careful attention to generating rich descriptions across all inquiry points, in keeping with Clifford Geertz's (1973) view of dense or "thick" qualitative inquiries. The goal of this commitment becomes to collect details of fact and description that bring a given analytical factor to life in bolder relief—visibly, audibly, materially.

As a consequence, questions emerge that go beyond the traditional limits of the Western rhetorical tradition: Who counts in the rhetorical engagement? What are the values and conditions that establish credibility? Who has or creates the agency and authority to speak? When? Where? Why? How? Who has or creates the agency and authority to listen? How? Why? Who is heard? By means of what sorts of media and mechanisms? What are the mandates and imperatives of the rhetorical occasion? What matters? To whom? How? Why? What are the effects and consequences of the act of speaking? The act of listening? The act of responding—or not responding? What contexts and frameworks make such questions intelligible? As questions are generated and reconsidered, bold and subtle dimensions of the analysis emerge and permit us to see concepts like rhetoric and race as functioning with broader and deeper consequence.

When we reconfigure rhetoric and race as analytical opportunities within a dynamic ecosystem, we pose specific questions about what sorts of historical framing optimizes the potential for creating new knowledge. One historical frame that has had particular saliency is the extent to which the quest for imperial control (including the use of slavery and other oppressive institutions in the United States) has hindered the aspirations of human beings—regardless of race, creed, color, or gender in a free, democratic, and just society—to operate in the world with agency and authority. In other words, how could a nation founded on the values of freedom, justice, and equality establish and sustain an institution that enslaves other human beings? This question highlights a glaring misalignment of beliefs, values, and practices. When human beings in such a context are hampered in their "natural" quest for agency and authority by oppressive conditions and the imperialistic desire for power, authority, and control, the situation itself creates a powerful exigency for the powerless to resist. In this context, the historical experiences of African Americans become exemplary: at the convergence of race and rhetoric, African Americans have used language eloquently to empower themselves, to negotiate sociopolitical dynamics, and to pursue their own quests for power and possibility.

CODA

If we shift analytical paradigms to interrogate rhetoric and race at their points of convergence, not just at their centers, we open new opportunities for understanding the biospheric and semiospheric implications of rhetoric as a social practice and of race as a sociopolitical idea. By using such pluralist and comparative frameworks to interrogate the dynamic interplay between these two concepts in a complex ecosystem, we enhance our capacity to think more imaginatively about rhetoric and race, two of our thorniest and most consequential human enterprises.

Notes

1. Theoretical and ideological renderings of race in social relationships have had a long and quite checkered past, as exemplified by views as old as the ancient Egyptians and Nubians, who created a sense of otherness by associating phenotypes with tribal and national identities (lighter-skinned Egyptians and darker-skinned Nubians); or the ancient Greeks, who understood the impact of environmental conditions on skin color and social practices but who considered non-Greeks "barbarians" unless they adopted Hellenic culture. This habit of "othering" came into particularly bold relief with the advent of the age of European exploration, discovery, and conquest and the rise of European imperialism and colonization. During this era there emerged far more negative renderings of human diversity, which gave rise, in turn, to centuries of worldwide racist domination and oppression by European societies. These negative renderings include classifications of humanity based on ideological interpretations of the biblical story of the three sons of Noah that cast Japhetic (Indo-European) peoples as morally superior to Semitic (Asiatic) and Hamitic (African) peoples; the creation of sociopolitical hierarchies that positioned Western Eurasian societies as preeminent civilizations; and debates about monogenism and polygenism, scientific racism, eugenics, and so on that continued well into the twentieth century and, in terms of residual impacts on belief systems, persist today. These types of negative views of human diversity have argued for biological and geographical distinctiveness and carried various overt and covert cautions about the chaos and corruptions of "race" mixing: cautions against the mixing of inferior bloodlines, phenotypical features, and cultural characteristics with the superior ones of the Western world, as well as cautions against permitting inclusive practices in terms of the sharing of power, privilege, and entitlements or the assumption of agency and authority as global human rights. In this chapter I fully acknowledge this long history and its profound consequences for our contemporary beliefs and practices, but I draw my conceptual framework from the equally long history of thought that views race as a sociocultural construction and human diversity as biologically insignificant (a fact confirmed by contemporary genetic research).

2. In *Natural Discourse: Toward Ecocomposition*, Sidney Dobrin and Christian Weisser suggest that human beings inhabit two spaces at once: one is "biospheric" and concerns conditions that support our physical existence; the other is "semiospheric" and concerns processes that shape our existence within biospheres and permit us to negotiate and make sense of them. Using this framework, they posit that these two spaces are interdependent and constitute an "inquiry of relationships" (Dobrin and Weisser 2002: 13), an argument that complements the approach taken in this chapter.

3. See Kenneth Stampp (1984), *The Peculiar Institution*, for a helpful discussion of slavery as a profoundly vexing social problem within a nation supposedly dedicated to freedom, justice, and equality.

4. A few examples of seminal scholarship that have shed light on the intersections of race and rhetoric from the huge body of work accumulated over the last century include Du Bois (1903), Myrdal (1944), Lorde (1984), Friere and Macedo (1987), Delgado and Stefanic (1987), Fairclough (1992), Gilroy (1993), Takaki (1993), Crenshaw (1995), Fine (1997), Logan (1999), and many more.

5. These contemporary anthologies, of course, were not the first. Here are five important examples among a substantial list of anthologizing efforts during the twentieth century: *The*

Negro Caravan (Brown, Davis, and Lee 1969); *Black Fire: An Anthology of Afro-American Writing* (Baraka and Neal 1968); *The Black Woman: An Anthology* (Bambara 1970); *Early Negro Writing 1760–1837* (Porter 1971); and *A History of Afro-American Literature, Volume I* (Jackson 1989). This list indicates the extent to which early anthologies of African American literature and rhetorical performances were prepared by African American scholars.

6. As an example of the importance of shifting perspectives away from the dominance of Western rhetorical traditions in rhetoric, composition, and literacy, see Royster and Kirsch's (2012) *Feminist Rhetorical Practices: New Directions in Rhetoric, Composition, and Literacy.* This volume assesses the globalizing impact of feminist rhetorical practices on studies in rhetoric, composition, and literacy and encourages these disciplines to continue opening up analyses to more inclusive practices by race, gender, class, geographical location, and other factors as we build a better, more deeply and broadly informed base of knowledge and understanding.

REFERENCES

Bambara, Toni Cade. 1970. *The Black Woman: An Anthology.* New York: New American Library.

Baraka, Amiri, and Larry Neal. (1968) 2007. *Black Fire: An Anthology of Afro-American Writing.* Baltimore, MD: Black Classic.

Brown, Sterling A., Arthur P. Davis, and Ulysses Lee. (1941) 1969. *The Negro Caravan.* New York: Arno/The New York Times.

Burke, Kenneth. 1966. *Language as Symbolic Action.* Berkeley: University of California Press.

Cooper, Marilyn M. 1986. "The Ecology of Writing." *College English* 48 no. 4: 364–375.

Crenshaw, Kimberlé, et al., eds. 1995. *Critical Race Theory: The Key Writings that Formed the Movement.* New York: New Press.

Delgado, Richard, and Jean Stefancic, eds. 1997. *Critical White Studies: Looking Behind the Mirror.* Philadelphia, PA: Temple University Press.

Dobrin, Sidney I., and Christian R. Weisser. 2002. *Natural Discourse: Toward Ecocomposition.* Albany: State University of New York Press.

Du Bois, William E. B. (1903) 1994. *The Souls of Black Folk.* New York: Gramercy Books.

Fairclough, Norman, ed. 1992. *Critical Language Awareness.* London: Longman.

Fine, Michelle, et al., eds. 1997. *Off White: Readings on Race, Power, and Society.* New York: Routledge.

Foner, Philip S., and Robert James Branham, eds. 1998. *Lift Every Voice: African-American Oratory, 1787–1900.* Tuscaloosa: University of Alabama Press.

Freire, Paulo, and Donaldo Macedo. 1987. *Literacy: Reading the Word and the World.* South Hadley, MA: Bergin and Garvey.

Gates, Henry Louis, Jr., and Nellie Y. McKay, general eds. 1997. *The Norton Anthology of African American Literature.* New York: W.W. Norton.

Geertz, Clifford. 1973. *The Interpretation of Cultures.* New York: Basic Books.

Gilroy, Paul. 1993. *The Black Atlantic: Modernity and Double Consciousness.* Cambridge, MA: Harvard University Press.

Jackson, Blyden, ed. 1989. *A History of Afro-American Literature: The Long Beginning, 1746–1985.* Vol. 1. Baton Rouge: Louisiana State University Press.

Lee, Valerie, ed. 2006. *The Prentice Hall Anthology of African American Women's Literature.* Upper Saddle River, NJ: Pearson/Prentice Hall.

Leeman, Richard W., ed. 1996. *African-American Orators: A Bio-Critical Sourcebook.* Westport, CT: Greenwood.

Logan, Shirley Wilson. 1995. *With Pen and Voice.* Carbondale: Southern Illinois University Press.

Logan, Shirley Wilson. 1999. *"We Are Coming": The Persuasive Discourse of Nineteenth-Century Black Women.* Carbondale: Southern Illinois University Press.

Lorde, Audre. 1984. *Sister Outsider.* Freedom, CA: Crossing Press.

Morrison, Toni. 1992. *Playing in the Dark: Whiteness and the Literary Imagination.* Cambridge, MA: Harvard University Press.

Myrdal, Gunnar. 1944. *An American Dilemma: The Negro Problem and Modern Democracy.* New York: Harper.

Porter, Dorothy, ed. 1971. *Early Negro Writing, 1760–1837.* Boston, MA: Beacon Press.

Royster, Jacqueline J., and Molly Cochran. 2011. "Human Rights and Civil Rights: The Advocacy and Activism of African American Women Writers." *Rhetoric Society Quarterly* 41 no. 3: 213–230.

Royster, Jacqueline J., and Gesa E. Kirsch. 2012. *Feminist Rhetorical Practices: New Directions for Rhetoric, Composition, and Literacy Studies.* Carbondale: Southern Illinois University Press.

Smith, Rochelle, and Sharon L. Jones, eds. 2000. *The Prentice Hall Anthology of African American Literature.* Upper Saddle River, NJ: Prentice Hall.

Spitzack, Carol, and Kathryn Carter. 1987. "Women in Communication Studies: A Typology for Revision." *Quarterly Journal of Speech* 73 no. 4: 401–423.

Stampp, Kenneth. (1956) 1984. *The Peculiar Institution: Slavery in the Ante-Bellum South.* New York: Vintage Books.

Takaki, Ronald. 1993. *A Different Mirror: A History of Multicultural America.* Boston, MA: Little, Brown.

United Nations Declaration on the Rights of Indigenous Peoples. United Nations. September 13, 2007. http://undesadspd.org/IndigenousPeoples/DeclarationontheRightsofIndigenousPeoples .aspx. Accessed October 10, 2011.

The Universal Declaration of Human Rights. United Nations. December 10, 1948. http://www. un.org/en/documents/udhr/index.shtml. Accessed October 10, 2011.

CHAPTER 48

RHETORIC AND LAW

PETER GOODRICH

THE motto for modern rhetoric, its emblematic expression, should be some version of the maxim, *Rhetorica non moritur*: "Rhetoric does not die." It subsists, it morphs, it shifts its ground and style. That this needs to be said, that some tracking of the divagations and changing colors of the rhetorical is necessary, results from the fact that rhetoric is not what it seems: it is a practice of dissimulation, it is protean in its relation to other disciplines. The English barrister George Puttenham put it well in announcing, in his discussion of "sensable figures altering and affecting the mind by alteration of sense or intendments," that one who does not know how to dissimulate does not know how to rule: *Qui nescit dissimulare nescit regnare* ([1589] 2007: 271) (see Rebhorn, ch. 31). Rhetoric in the modern tradition—and what better source could there be than a treatise from the Elizabethan Inns of Court?—is a paradoxical juridical enterprise. It offers the indeterminacy of images, figures of persuasion, false truths, noble lies, which are not the easiest of positions and perlocutions for lawyers to manipulate and defend.

My remit is modern rhetoric and law, and it should be noted, for reasons not unconnected with the aforementioned, that rhetoric has been placed on the defensive in this period. The history of rhetoric, modern authors inform us, has been that of a "generalized restraint" (Barthes 1970: 172), of the constriction of the discipline, its exile to the peripheries of the ornamental and incidental, the merely stylistic and logically nugatory.[1] This banishment of rhetoric has a long history, of course: it goes back to Plato and Aristotle, to the Church Fathers, to the Reformation iconoclasts, and to the Enlightenment. But it is the residue of such discomfort, the anxieties produced by witnessing the flowers of speech, the indeterminacy and play of legal rhetoric, that deserve noting. The various "new rhetorics," as with the modern "defense" of rhetoric, tend to start on a negative footing.[2] Whatever the generalized restraint, variously depicted in terms of the study of tropes and even master tropes alone, legal oratory and advocacy tend to the extreme. The first new rhetoric, *The Philosophy of Rhetoric* (1776), by the Scottish lawyer-turned-priest George Campbell, offers these salutary words: "At the bar, critical explications of dark and ambiguous statutes, quotations of precedents sometimes contradictory, and comment on jarring decisions and reports, often necessarily consume the great part of the speaker's time. Hence the mixture of a sort of metaphysics and verbal criticism, employed by lawyers in their pleadings, hath come to be distinguished by the name *chicane*" ([1776] 1963: 104).

That lawyers use verbal trickery, unnecessary quibbles, and figurative sleights of hand is not a promising start for the post-Enlightenment tradition of legal oratory. Staying momentarily among the Scottish philosophers, Adam Smith, in his *Lectures on Rhetoric and Belles Lettres* (1762), offers a vivid image of the abuse of speech in "ancient courts," where "orators managed the Courts of Judicature in the same manner as the managers of a play-house do the pit. They place some of their friends in different parts of the pit, and as they clap or hiss the performers the rest join in" (1963: 173). Rhetoric stacks the audience, plays to the jury, and cheats logic with chicanery and demagoguery. Chaïm Perelman, the Belgian lawyer and author of a more recent new rhetoric, similarly complains that the field of rhetoric has been unduly constrained by (in his case) a Cartesian logic that left modern logicians, philosophers, and lawyers "totally disinterested" in rhetoric (1969: 4–5) (see van Eemeren, ch. 52).[3] There is, then, in the long term of the modern tradition a virulent and polemical resistance to rhetoric that leaves it not so much constrained as shunned, homeless, without disciplinary support, everywhere and nowhere, a matter of just doing what needs to be done (Fish 1989).

It is my argument in this chapter that it is necessary to be conscious of the negative ground, the hostile environment, the diminutions and dismissals that surround rhetoric in the humanities, particularly in the field of jurisprudence. For this enmity is symptomatic, ironically, of the success of rhetoric, of its persistence as a covert operator and disciplinary chameleon whose sphere of application and ambit of influence is ever growing. The notion of resistance to rhetoric, widely repeated in contemporary accounts of the discipline, fails to appreciate Michel Foucault's observation that power generates resistance, and that resistance is consequently a symptom of being a threat: "Where there is power, there is resistance, and yet, or rather consequently, this resistance is never in a relation of exteriority to power" (1978: 95–6; see Reichman 2010). To resist is to be an agent of change, a potentiality and a novelty. This chapter develops this theme by retracing the hostility to rhetoric as a sign of its subsisting effects, and specifically of the contemporary expansion of its jurisdiction and, in our case, of its power to do justice in difficult times. I proceed in two stages. I argue first that rhetoric, as a discipline, is homeless. Ravit Reichman (2010) in her recent survey places rhetoric in the family of narrative. For James Boyd White (1973), literary scholar and cartographer of the contemporary legal imagination, it is a humanistic enterprise connected primarily to the classics and secondarily to literary criticism and poetics as devices for legal interpretation and for community building. For Richard Weisberg (1992) it is a part of "poethics," a neologism that signals, in a circuitous revival of the work of the seventeenth-century lawyer Antoine Furetière, that justice is a matter of linguistic felicity and poetic expression (White 1973, 1992; Sarat and Kearns 1994; Weisberg and Binder 2006). Others have viewed rhetoric and its incessant revivals as an avenue, variously, into legal culture, legal politics, gender, race, and law. The point is that rhetoric signals—no matter how strangely diverse the forms—the conjunction of law with other disciplines. It is perhaps even the master trope of what is often and sadly termed "law and . . . ," with the second term left blank either from indifference or for later, plural inscriptions.

It is another Belgian jurist, Benoît Frydman (2005: 15), who suggests that the return to rhetoric is a sign of a crisis of interpretation (see Derrida 1975: 232). Frydman politely refers to the American critical legal scholar Duncan Kennedy, but the interpretative turn was above all the product of a mix of French Freudianism and German hermeneutics, while the notion of rhetoric as a sign of crisis is more or less peculiar to him and marks my second argument, namely, that materiality determines consciousness. It is the emergence of new media, digital relay, and the virtual life of law that most immediately catapults rhetoric into the center of the interpretative stage. Film, television, YouTube, the Internet, and other tele-technologies have reopened the question of interpretation, of images and figures of truth, in their ever-novel forms. Moreover, the constraint of legal rhetoric is giving way to a little acknowledged and even less understood expansion in law's rhetorical uses and domains.

LAW AND . . . RHETORIC

The tacit art of exterior rhetoric teaches lawyers to evidence their higher calling and to enact their theological inspirations without actually stating them. The solemnity, the ceremonial, the robes, rites, and emblems of justice all speak to the order of honor, of acclamation, laudation, and, indeed, glory within which the silent staging of law loudly occurs. The old expression for external rhetoric—for all that is seen without voice—is *muta eloquentia*, which the German theorist of drama, Johann Engel, boldly calls the necessary context for the "illusions of the mimic world" (Siddons [1822] 2009: 31). Law enacts, and despite its denial of its own drama, despite its frequent historical bans upon theater, reported in the *Digest*, noted by Tacitus, repeated in the early Christian era and onward, the legal system has always been dependent upon the force of mimic persuasion (Dupont 1977, 2000; Goodrich 2001). It needs its devices, its modes of promulgation, its specialized registers and rites of social presence. These are the *arcana imperii*, the symbols of sovereignty hidden behind the spectacle of rule.

To understand law—why not say it again?—requires a head for the symbolic. Legal rhetoric, in the guise of teaching modesty and *decorum*, the closeting of emotion and the restraint of expression, is engaged in training the unconscious, in directing the bodily eyes of the subject to the proper forms of representation. This minimal yet crucial engagement of rhetoric with law (the training of the body, if you will) to do the work of the lawyer is inculcated silently, by example and tacit modes of expression and emulation. Unthought, repeated, preconscious, the unspoken rhetoric of law is that of reverence and constraint, a tendency to the choral and acclamatory as the proper general expression of observance and subservience. There is a recognized and legitimate mode of argument in relation to authority that requires—the emblems and portraits show it often enough—"line, square, and compass," rod, portrait, text and robe, bar and portent, as the props and mechanisms of the ceremonial dimensions of legal action. The textual hermeneutics of law, the rules of interpretation and of proper figuration in juristic argument, are therefore to be understood as symptoms of a much greater yet unannounced rhetorical project of capturing the visible, what is imagined, recognized, and what is seen.

Extant as a dissimulated utility and at best as good style, it is not surprising that a rhetorical tradition gauged to the essential transparency of appearance and of style—that is, to the nonrhetorical—will have a precarious and frequently denied relationship to law. There may be rules of method and maxims of construction, but the modern legal curriculum eschews any robust rhetorical analysis, let alone any critical acknowledgment of *lex gestus* and the other visibilities of rite and performance of law. These belong initially to the utopia of scholars grown old, to the sociology and social anthropology of law, to the *soixante-huitard* disciplines par excellence. There were studies of courtroom drama, the legal theater of the absurd in one analysis (Carlen 1974), *theatrum veritatis et justitiae* in another (Garapon 1985, 2001). The anarcho-Marxist text, *Images of Law*, coauthored by a self-proclaimed anarchist law professor and a Marxist sociologist, bore the image of a judicial wig with a blank face on the inside front cover. The American critical legal samizdat circular, *The Lizard*, was full of cartoons and playful performances of critical style, with law professors playing sociologists and gathering up the tools of a critique of the *melancholia juridica* that emblematizes the modern lawyer's style. Here, momentarily, a rhetorical analysis of law emerged again. There was a short-term encounter and even collusion between sociology and law, but it suffered from the beginning from problems of disciplinary status differences, often couched in conflicting epistemic projects and wildly distinct existential styles.

Allow me to put it bluntly: if legal rhetoric is the art of hiding law's rhetorical character, of dissimulating the persuasive function of legal performance and the staging of judgment, then sociology is not the discipline to work with. Sociology is the science of empirically exposing social practices as artifice and expression of interests; it is the dramatic opposite of the professional desire for covert modes of persuasion and unquestioned legitimacy. Let the sociologists do sociology, and that was pretty much what happened, with the Law and Society movement in the United States representing the interests of sociologists in engaging with law and often hoping to have some of the status of law rub off on their worthy but little-appreciated discipline. Law and society expressed an antinomy: law acted upon society, and society was thereby defined as the externality of law. It was the job of lawyers to keep society at bay—law and sociology could hardly be an acceptable institutional combination in such a context.

If there was to be any empirical study of law, it was to be that of the objects of legal regulation, of the market, of economic actors and actions defined in terms of ideal types, rational action, and pervasively hypothetical situations. There was no room for rhetoric in law and economics, probably because economics as practiced by lawyers was nothing more than rhetoric in the pejorative rather than technical sense. A desire for legitimating certain species of regulation and nonregulation through a veneer of market rationality and a smattering of scientific vocabulary helped to fuel this passing fashion for ecfactic calculus (see Goodrich 2007). As the conservative trend in the legal academy continues apace and recession constrains the borders of disciplines, the calls for economic analysis and empirical legal studies offer a rhetoric for the academy but for little else. Other than providing status credentials within the severely striated network of law schools, beyond the rather limited glamor and quiet success of the jurist-scholar, the adoption of briefly and laconically fashionable argots of research neither extends the purview of rhetorical analysis nor greatly affects the public realm of law and letters.

The "law and ..." disciplines, much derided by conservative jurists and generally lamented by nonlegal scholars as sorry attempts to provide a degree of intellectual credibility to trade-school activities, were not and are not the avenue for the advance of rhetoric in law. The "and" between the disciplines is disjunctive, unnecessary, and distracting. Easy prey. Weak thinking. There is no law and economics, but there are economic laws. So too with the most obvious home for forensic rhetoric in the legal academy, namely, law and literature. There are literary laws, modes of textual persuasion and action, juristic representations of character, community, and desire. There is no law "and" literature precisely because the separation alerts the lawyer and the audience alike to the mixing of genres and an apparent, stranger fiction in the realm of law. As one judge put it in a thoroughly literary case on copyright infringement by the author of *The Da Vinci Code*, "A judgment is not a work of fiction ... nor is it a piece of conjectural fact" (*Baigent v. Random House* [2006] EWHC 717; see Goodrich 2010). There is no explicit fiction, no invented narrative, little room, in short, for literary flourishes or rhetorical flowers in the scribblings of judges we politely call "judgments." It is, however, in striving to persuade, in building their argument and disposing of cases, that judges manipulate the symbols of law and wax rhetorical.

The rhetorical function of the modern legal judgment is to evidence the character of the judge as a rational actor and of the law as a rule-governed system. The judge should be a synecdoche for the law, and the decision (*ratio*) must appear persuasively concatenated from sources extrinsic to and independent of the judicial frame—the further the better. As one judge put it while struggling to find a way of dealing with contracts made on the Internet, "Promises become binding when there is a meeting of minds and consideration is exchanged. So it was at King's Bench in common law England; so it was under the common law in the American colonies; so it was through more than two centuries of jurisprudence in this country; and so it is today. Assent may be registered by a signature, a handshake, or a click of a mouse transmitted across the invisible ether of the Internet" (*Specht v. Netscape Communications Corporation*, 2002). In effect, the king has spoken, the centuries have dictated, and, most surprisingly, "the ether" transmits and submits. There is no escape from the narrative of inexorability, the imposition of precedence as respect for what is old. Judgment needs to evidence the exemplary quality of the law—the legal community—and persuade by indicating that the rules followed lead to desirable outcomes: they are just, they are efficient, they are realistic, they are right, effective, and acceptable. For such rhetoric to work it has to be a covert, closeted rhetoric, a manipulation of line, square, and compass. *Decorum* and *dignitas* reign. Not even Law and Literature can provide much of a home for rhetoric, offering rather (and only) the solace of exile, disciplinary and institutional separation from the battleground of agonistic advocacy and the new technologies of lawyering. "Law and . . ." trails off into indistinctness, amorphous academicism, fantasies of community and felicity that—while not being in themselves harmful—neither provide a home for forensic rhetoric nor have an impact directly within the epistemic field of law (see Goodrich 2009). If we are to find rhetoric in law, indeed an expanded legal rhetoric, then it is honor and dissimulation that have to be traced, the opacity of appearances and the play of images as they inexorably affect the computer-driven, Internet-wired, satellite-relayed practice of law today.

Advocacy in Images

The concept of a "literary criticism of law" (Binder and Weisberg 2006) sidelines the study of rhetoric to an academic periphery and, increasingly, to an outmoded technology of physical print. It is not only that law will generally and hierarchically claim to have precedence over its subdisciplines, be it anthropology, economics, literature, film, music, cultural studies, or others, but also that the notion that the canon of literary works—William Shakespeare, Herman Melville, Charles Dickens, Jane Austen, Mark Twain, and others—provides a common cultural referent as a *sensus communis* recognizable to the populace is antiquated. These works represent *vox Dei* rather than any more plural and plebeian *lex populi*. The skills of literary persuasion, the breadth of character, the virtues and ethical commitments that the literary inculcates are without question valuable and engaging, adaptive and manipulable in modern contexts, but the action is elsewhere. The future of legal rhetoric, the cutting edge of the art of persuasion in matters juridical, has migrated to the advocacy of the visual, and the techniques that now need to be studied and taught are increasingly related to the new media.

French mediologist Régis Debray (1992: 221–54, 1995, 1998, 2002) traces a trinity of "mediaspheres" in the history of Western scopic regimes. Each regime corresponds to a particular dominant form of conservation and transmission of knowledge. To each belongs a specific order and law carried by the material means of transmission that mediology separates and studies. *Ordo, lex, medium* is the maxim Debray uses to indicate the interdependence of culture, law, and media: the three "have to be thought together. A mediasphere . . . is an environment, an intellectual and moral climate; it is also an ethos, and therefore a State. A revolution in media always signals a climatic and ethical 'catastrophe' . . . a change in collective values propelled by the novel media" (1991: 322). The division between media epochs is schematic and fluid because each new regime incorporates and carries over much of the previous technology and matrices of transmission, but each regime is characterized by a novel configuration propelled by new modes of viewing.

The schema is illustrative and begins with the "logosphere," the religious era of the living word in which the scopic regime is that of idols. In the logosphere, image and writing are living things, magical modes of communication, opaque signs manipulated by ecclesiastical and charismatic leaders. Law is here theistic, imperial, and supernatural. Piety is the dominant mode of viewing and intercession the proper form of communication. In the second mediasphere, the "graphosphere," print is the revolutionary technology that inaugurates a new scopic regime predicated upon the artistic image and the linear mnemotechnics of the printed work. In this regime the sign becomes the object of experimentation, a symptom of causes and the expression of history. The visual is viewed as a source of illusion, something to be read through rather than relied upon, not least because it has an author and is in essence an invented simulation. In this regime, government becomes political and clerical administration accedes to professional governance. The third scopic regime, the "videosphere" with which we are now most crucially concerned, represents the conclusion of the trinity in digital relay. The new matrix—and here it is necessary to expand upon Debray's schema—is virtual, constantly in motion, and everywhere in play, ludic and ironic. Characterized by technics, driven by publicity, and expressed in the continuum of events perceived as spectacles and crises, the videosphere combines elements of the earlier scopic regimes in a multiplicity of new media relays. The screen becomes the medium, and the law increasingly gets transmitted through images.

The first point to make, as obvious as it is overlooked by most legal doctrine, is that law in the videosphere becomes infinitely more visible and hence more public. Cameras are virtually omnipresent across all the boundaries of what used to be public and private spheres: in every mobile phone, every computer, and on every street corner, let alone in most institutions, whether projecting or recording, on the dashboard of police cars, in taxicabs, and on buildings. Almost nothing goes unseen; cameras are always "rolling," and some website, feed, network, or relay will carry the "footage." Law has gone pop, merged with the multiple relays of images and become visible where it was once esoteric and hidden. In an elegant study of *lex populi* (law in popular film and fiction), William MacNeil makes the point in terms of a positive democratization of law: "The various media highlighted in this book not only reach a much larger audience than standard legal texts, but potentially, and even more democratically, they also help restore topics of jurisprudential import—justice, rights, ethics—to where they belong: not with the economists, not with the sociologists, not even with the philosophers, but rather with the community at large" (2007: 1–2). The popular replaces the professional, the specialist gives way to the generalist, and the page yields to the screen. Insofar as the argument is a quantitative one, it seems indisputable. The law transmits as image, goes on display, becomes film, "a particular kind of visual cultural representation," and it follows that "law as visual representation leads us beyond the rubric of law and film to a more expansive formulation for law on the screen, perhaps under the rubric of visual legal studies" (Sherwin 2010: 243). Jean Baudrillard's notion of the degree Xerox of culture has become a Photoshop-altered, picture-driven, film-friendly law.

Trained in texts, at common law, brought up on case reports and the minutiae of legislation, the advent of images as evidence and advocacy is both suspicious and at times threatening to the law: according to the courts, the trial must not be turned into farce, burlesque, or show business (*Standard Chartered PLC v. Price Waterhouse* 945 P.2d at 359 [1996]; Schwartz 2009). At a more theoretical level, the strict hierarchy and procedure of the courtroom, the various barriers that physically and conceptually separate court from world, should not be collapsed lest the rigor of law be turned into the lax theater of the tribunal (Vismann 2003). That said, and despite the continued though episodic resistance of a judicial generation that grew up before the current saturation of video media and relays to cameras in court, the new media are omnipresent, and it can only be a matter of time before the camera provides both the primary audience and the official record of proceedings. Familiarity will breed content. Advocacy by image—law's embracing of the videosphere—is the foreseeable future of forensic persuasion.

What then, practically, does this exodus from print to picture, from courtroom to video tribunal, from inside to outside, portend for the rhetoric of law? First, lawyers will require skill in the invention, ordering, and manipulation of images (an echo of the ancient *inventio, dispositio, elocutio* schema). Lawyers will require a facility in making, interpreting, and delivering images as if they were writing. Of course, the fact that images are used, that the argument presented is not only told but also shown, not simply stated but seen and understood, has roots in early modern law, in the emblem tradition, and in the linear depiction of law that came with print and printed woodcuts. Today, however, the legal recourse to images moves onto a different level. The pervasiveness of the media, the 24-hour news cycles, and the explosion of "reality"-based programming all suggest an enhanced role for images that is inexorable and therefore to be studied, developed, and incorporated into legal practice. Resistance continues, of course, and video links to witnesses are still challenged, although, intriguingly, because the courts want to see the person, witness the face-to-face confrontation, and so arrive at a decision on the basis of *in vivo* theater rather than televised testimony (*Coy v. Iowa*, 407 U.S. 1012 [1988]; *United States v. Yates*, 438 F.3rd 1307 [2006]; Sherwin 2011). The advancement of current camera technology, however, means that the artificial lens will soon see much more than the naked eye. Thus, if requiring presence remains the rule, it will be because it provides, ironically enough, the witness or litigant a degree of cover not available in front of high-definition cameras.

The second point, which is also a technical one, concerns the difference in mode of reasoning that advocacy by image entails. Punning on the distinction in legal method between *ratio decidendi*, the rule in the decision, and *obiter dicta*, things said along the way to judgment, I will offer a third term commensurate with images: *obiter depicta*, things *shown* in the course of coming to decision. The key factor is that to think, argue, and decide in images alters the medium and the character of legal decision-making. To think has of course always required first imagining—"inventing," in the argot of rhetorical theory—and images have always played a significant role in promulgating law and ensuring its legitimacy and jurisdiction. No mediasphere is autonomous or distinct from others, but the seismic shift of the videosphere comes in the quantity of images, the multiplicity of their relays, and the instantaneous, mobile quality of the pictures themselves. Thinking in images, interpreting, advocating, and judging in images is not the same as the linear argumentation of text-based reasoning. It is a different concatenation, a lateral and associative mode of connection based upon a very distinct organization and combination of visual elements using the various established lexicons of visual symbols and their known effects.

If the constrained advocate of early modern law spoke so as to produce effects upon auditor and judge, the avatar of the future lawyer shows to generate affects. It is important, however, to stress that much as pictures (including the rhetoric of gesture and dress) are "silent speech," the image cannot be conceived as being independent of words: "There is visibility that does not amount to an image; there are images which consist wholly in words. But the commonest regime of image is one that presents a relationship between the sayable and the visible, a relationship which plays on both the analogy *and* the dissemblance between them" (Rancière 2007: 7). There is a change in the relationship between word and image—between *syntagma* and *pictura*, in the early modern idiom— that can be understood both as a projection back to the early era of print in which texts were conceived as schema and image, as "ink divinitie" along the carefully compassed, squared, and ruled lines Hugh Blair evoked in his *Lectures on Rhetoric and Belles Lettres* (1788), and forward to a future of affective advocacy as juridical montage. In acknowledging the importance, indeed the centrality, of image and affect to the continuingly agonistic nature of the legal trial and of most transactional law, the self-conscious advent of law in the videosphere requires coming to terms with both the dissemblance of images and their creativity and power. It requires an openness to images—in the rhetorical sense of gesture, the extension of an open palm—and to the screen of a legality that is increasingly visible and accessible through new media and thus generating both *punctum* (affect) and *studium* (information) in a growing class and diversity of viewers.

The trajectory of expansion this chapter has traced from the constraint of Enlightenment legal rhetoric to the expansiveness of law in the videosphere portends— and this is my final point—significant changes in the way law is transacted. As noted earlier, the boundary between the inside and outside of the courtroom, and by extension of the discipline of law, is being erased. The breaching of the boundary—the bar—of the courtroom brings the world into the inner sanctum of legality and allows the advocate increasingly frequently to show what happened with pictures, with film, with animatrix and cartoon, with borrowed images or live footage. It is important to note that the root of this legal admission of images, specifically of film, lies in international war crimes tribunals and therefore implicitly suggests the lower threshold of evidentiary relevance in international law and a political impetus to advocacy by images, which is in its modern origin, at least, fairly directly war by other means (see Delage 2012). If film brings the world and its chaos of facts into the purview of the juridical, onto the screens in court, the camera also takes the court out into the world and its varied domains of *lex populi*.

The effects of the erasure of the boundaries between inside and outside, between the arcane ceremonies of professional law and the elided spaces of the public sphere, are several and growing. First, and to an increasing degree, law loses its thresholds. If, most emblematically, appearance in court, *in vivo* self-presentation and testimony, can be realized by video link, as will soon be the case in most jurisdictions, then the architectural distinctiveness of law—the columns and steps, the murals and portraits, the lists and ushers, the snarls of lawyers and clients that mark the ritual difference of law—will have been obliterated. The aura and atmosphere of law will change correspondingly along with its context, costumes, and rites. At a disciplinary level the becoming-virtual of law is already having similar boundary-breaking effects. In addition to adding *obiter depicta* to the curriculum in elements of law and so introducing a syllabus in visual advocacy, there is also the breakup of the hierarchy of legal texts, the dissipation and declassification of the authoritative collections that comes with the availability of almost all forms of law, statutes, and case reports on the Internet. It is tempting to argue that the text on screen becomes a figure, an image, but I will simply observe that the disciplinary boundaries as well as the typography and distinction of such texts are much less evident than was the case when print reigned in the realm of law. Harking back to that earlier era of gothic typeface, text and treatise, the relevant rhetorical maxim of interpretation for the populace was *ut pictura poesis,* "as in painting so in poetry": the poem was an image, it offered pictures. Today, in our futuristic context, as the image comes to lodge itself in the heart of law, legal rhetoric has finally to come out of the closet that Gilbert Austin suggested in 1806: "The matter and manner of the oration are both generally composed in the closet" ([1806] 1966: 445). We might also want to coin a comparable maxim and aspiration: advocacy in images brings poetry to law.

NOTES

1. Roland Barthes's thesis is taken up by Gérard Genette (1982) in "Rhetoric Restrained." Tzvetan Todorov (1982) also usefully rehearses much of the same history in *Theories of the Symbol.*
2. In his *In Defence of Rhetoric,* for example, Brian Vickers sets out to "remove the misapprehensions and prejudices that still affect our appreciation of rhetoric" (1988: 1).
3. Perelman's (1976) work on law, *Logique juridique: Nouvelle rhétorique,* awaits translation.

REFERENCES

Austin, Gilbert. (1806) 1966. *Chironomia, or a Treatise on Rhetorical Delivery.* Carbondale: Southern Illinois University Press.

Barthes, Roland. 1970. "L'ancienne rhétorique: aide-mémoire." *Communications* 16: 172–223.

Blair, Hugh. 1788. *Lectures on Rhetoric and Belles Lettres.* Basel: Tourneisen.

Binder, Guyora, and Robert Weisberg. 2006. *Literary Criticisms of Law.* Princeton, NJ: Princeton University Press.

Campbell, George. (1776) 1963. *The Philosophy of Rhetoric.* Carbondale: Southern Illinois University Press.

Carlen, Pat. 1974. *Magistrate's Justice.* Oxford: Martin Robertson.

Débray, Regis. 1991. *Cours de médiologie générale.* Paris: Gallimard.

Débray, Regis. 1992. *Vie et mort de l'image: Une histoire du regard en Occident.* Paris: Gallimard.

Débray, Regis. 1995. "The Three Ages of Looking." *Critical Inquiry* 21 no. 3: 529–555.

Débray, Regis. 1998. *Media Manifestos.* London: Verso.

Débray, Regis. 2002. *Transmitting Culture*. New York: Columbia University Press.

Delage, Christian. 2012. *Caught on Camera: Film in the Courtroom from the Nuremberg Trials to the Trials of the Khmer Rouge*. Philadelphia: University of Pennsylvania Press.

Derrida, Jacques. 1975. *The Postcard: From Socrates to Freud and Beyond*. Chicago, IL: University of Chicago Press.

Dupont, Florence. 1977. "La scène juridique." *Communications* 26: 62–77.

Dupont, Florence. 2000. *L'orateur sans visage: Essai sur l'acteur romain et son masque*. Paris: Presses Universitaires de France.

Fish, Stanley. 1989. *Doing What Comes Naturally: Change, Rhetoric, and the Practice of Theory in Literary and Legal Studies*. Durham, NC: Duke University Press.

Foucault, Michel. 1978. *The History of Sexuality: An Introduction*. New York: Random House.

Frydman, Benoît. 2005. *Le sens des lois*. Brussels: Bruylant.

Genette, Gérard. 1982. *Figures of Literary Discourse*. Oxford: Blackwell.

Garapon, Antoine. 1985. *L'âne portant des réliques*. Paris: Centurion.

Garapon, Antoine. 2001. *Bien Juger: Essai sur le rituel judiciaire*. Paris: Odile Jacob.

Goodrich, Peter. 2001. "Law." In *Encyclopedia of Rhetoric*, edited by Thomas O. Sloane, 417–426. New York: Oxford University Press.

Goodrich, Peter. 2007. "The New Casuistry." *Critical Inquiry* 33 no. 4: 673–709.

Goodrich, Peter. 2009. "Screening Law." *Law and Literature* 21 no. 1: 1–23.

Goodrich, Peter. 2010. "Legal Enigmas: Antonio de Nebrija, *The Da Vinci Code* and the Emendation of Law." *Oxford Journal of Legal Studies* 30 no. 1: 71–99.

Goodrich, Peter. 2013. *Legal Emblems and the Art of Law: Obiter Depicta as the Vision of Governance*. New York: Cambridge University Press.

MacNeil, William. 2007. Lex Populi: *The Jurisprudence of Popular Culture*. Palo Alto, CA: Stanford University Press.

Perelman, Chaïm, and Lucie Olbrechts-Tyteca. 1969. *The New Rhetoric: A Treatise on Argumentation*. Notre Dame, IN: University of Notre Dame Press.

Perelman, Chaïm, and Lucie Olbrechts-Tyteca. 1976. *Logique juridique: Nouvelle rhétorique*. Paris: Dalloz.

Puttenham, George. (1589) 2007. *The Art of English Poesy*. Ithaca, NY: Cornell University Press.

Rancière, Jacques. 2007. *The Future of the Image*. London: Verso.

Reichman, Ravit. 2010. "Narrative and Rhetoric." In *Law and the Humanities: An Introduction*, edited by Austin Sarat, Matthew Anderson, and Catherine Frank, 377–397. Cambridge: Cambridge University Press.

Sarat, Austin, and Thomas R. Kearns, eds. 1994. *The Rhetoric of Law*. Ann Arbor: University of Michigan Press.

Schwartz, Louis-Georges. 2009. *Mechanical Witness: A History of Motion Picture Evidence in U.S. Courts*. New York: Oxford University Press.

Sherwin, Richard. 2010. "Imagining Law as Film (Representation without Reference?)." In *Law and the Humanities: An Introduction*, edited by Austin Sarat, Matthew Anderson, and Catherine Frank, 241–268. New York: Cambridge University Press.

Sherwin, Richard. 2011. *Visualizing Law in the Age of the Digital Baroque*. London: Routledge.

Siddons, Henry. (1822) 2009. *Practical Illustrations of Rhetorical Gesture and Action Adapted to the English Drama. From a Work on the Subject by M. Engel*. London: Sherwood, Neely, and Jones.

Smith, Adam. 1963. *Lectures on Rhetoric and Belles Lettres*. Edinburgh: Thomas Nelson.

Todorov, Tzvetan. 1982. *Theories of the Symbol*. Oxford: Blackwell.

Vickers, Brian. 1988. *In Defence of Rhetoric*. Oxford: Oxford University Press.

Vismann, Cornelia. 2003. "Tele-Tribunals: Anatomy of a Medium." *Grey Room* 10: 5–21.

Weisberg, Richard. 1992. *Poethics and Other Strategies of Law and Literature*. New York: Columbia University Press.

White, James Boyd. 1973. *The Legal Imagination*. Chicago, IL: University of Chicago Press.

White, James Boyd. 1992. *Justice as Translation*. Chicago, IL: University of Chicago Press.

CHAPTER 49

RHETORIC AND POLITICAL THEORY

ANDREW NORRIS

> The whole business of rhetoric is to influence opinion/appearance [*doxan*].
>
> —Aristotle, *Rhetoric*

WITH very few exceptions, political theory is as hostile to rhetoric as politics itself is agreeable.[1] This hostility can be traced back to Plato, two of whose dialogues on politics are driven by Socrates's attempts to discredit the claims of master rhetoricians—Gorgias in the *Gorgias* and Thrasymachus in the *Republic*. In the earlier dialogue, Socrates argues that rhetoric's focus on successful persuasion restricts it to the appearance or opinion (*dokousin*) that is the object of the panderer rather than the expert (Plato, *Gorgias* 464a). Though "quite ignorant of the actual nature of good and bad or honor and dishonor or right and wrong, [the *rhētor* is] possessed of a power of persuasion which enables him, in spite of his ignorance, to appear [*dokeō*] to the ignorant wiser than those who know" (459d; trans. Hamilton and Emlyn-Jones). In both dialogues, Socrates draws the most damning implications from this rule of *doxa*. As a form of pandering akin to cookery and beauty culture, rhetoric is subject to the very forces it would manipulate: to be successful, the rhetor must appeal to the desires and opinions of his audience, appearing to them as he wishes only insofar as he shows them what they want to see (see Yunis, ch. 9). And since both speaker and audience are ignorant of the good, they will evaluate appearances on the basis of what pleases, what appears to be good, not what is healthy or conducive to a balanced life of self-awareness and reasoned judgment. Because the political rhetor possesses knowledge of how "to get the rule" and not knowledge of how to rule (Plato, *Republic* 488d), he inclines of necessity toward tyranny and the exercise of power rather than politics proper (Plato, *Gorgias* 521d); persuasion and force—the other way of "getting the rule"—are not contraries but species of a single genus. Hence Plato presents Gorgias as praising rhetoric on the grounds that it allows the rhetor to enslave those who know better than he (452e), while Callicles and Thrasymachus openly celebrate the life of the tyrant. The democratic rhetor whose appeals must be tailored to the opinions and desires of his audience can but resent this submission: persuasive dialogue only lightly veils the longing for a monologic dictation, as Callicles and Thrasymachus make plain when they choose sullen silence and perfunctory responses over Socratic *elenchus*. In the *Republic*'s typology of regimes and corresponding personality types, "the tyrannic man . . . is transformed out of the democratic man" (571a), at once his heir and his realization. The kinship between the two is manifest in their agreement that the satisfaction of desire is paramount and order of any sort an imposition. If an aristocratic political order is based on knowledge of the good and an oligarchic order is based on knowledge of what is valuable and hence at least calculable, tyranny and democracy together rest on nothing more than the shifting ground of opinion and appearance (cf. Harris, ch. 3). On this account, a rhetorical politics of *doxa* is in the end one of unreason and despair.

Taken as part of a wider critique of appearance, the terms of this Platonic account reverberate through modern philosophy, from René Descartes's destruction of his opinions as based on mere appearances to Immanuel Kant's phenomenal/noumenal distinction and the phenomenologies of Edmund Husserl and Martin Heidegger.[2] Taken as a more limited critique of political opinion as the modification of or response to appearance, their presence in modernity is similarly strong (see Rebhorn, ch. 31; Gowland, ch. 38). This might be surprising, given the almost wholesale abandonment of the Socratic ideal of a philosophical aristocracy. But the lack of the ideal alternative has not lessened the force of the criticism, and the majority of significant modern political philosophers continue to suspect the art of rhetoric of being, in John Locke's words, a "perfect cheat," "invented . . . for nothing else but to insinuate wrong *Ideas*, move the Passions, and thereby mislead the Judgment" (1991: 508; cf. Garsten 2006). As in Plato, this suspicion is bound up with a hostility toward democracy. Although democracy is today the coin of the political realm, it is only relatively recently that the term ceased to be a pejorative associated with the rule of the mob (Arblaster 2002). And, as is evident in the profusion of early twentieth-century critiques of "mass culture," such anxieties have hardly been left behind. While the democratic nature of modern republics like the United States is often wildly overstated (Lasch 1995; Dahl 2003), it remains true that the steady expansion of the franchise to include women and the working class has meant that politics must express and appeal to the opinions of huge numbers of disparate people, almost none of whom are expert in any relevant field. In the modern state each of their votes is given equal weight, regardless of the reasons for which it has been cast: a careful and learned study of the issues bears no more weight than the persuasive appeal of the talk show demagogue. The politics of *doxa* has if anything expanded its reach.

Walter Lippmann, still one of our most penetrating critics of public opinion, echoes Plato in his scathing account of its limitations. Where "specific opinions give rise to immediate executive acts" that involve performing specific tasks, the "general opinions" of the citizen regarding the actions of the state are "a vague and confusing medley, [and] action cannot be taken until these opinions have been factored down, canalized, compressed, and made uniform. The making of one general will . . . consists essentially in the use of symbols which assemble emotion after they have been detached from their ideas.

Because feelings are much less specific than ideas, and yet more poignant, the leader is able to make a homogeneous will out of a heterogeneous mass of desires" (Lippmann 2002: 36–8). In the end, the politics of democratic opinion is the rule of the leader; the private citizen's "sovereignty is a fiction" (4). "Democracy" is thus best run and managed by well-informed, sophisticated elites—people like Lippmann. Rhetoric may well be an important tool of management for such elites: Lippmann's enormously influential weekly columns in the *New Republic*, the *New York Herald Tribune*, and *Newsweek* are exemplary instances of "opinion formation." But rhetoric should play no part in the actual generation of policy and the conduct of government. Such a clean separation, however, is impossible to maintain: elites are chosen on the basis of the opinions of the *dēmos*, to whom they must appeal in speech and deed, rhetoric and action; and they remain subject to the blandishments of those who would influence them, among their advisors and at large. Again, Lippmann is exemplary, and the intensity of his hopeless search for "genuine" political leadership that would safely steer the polity through the shoals was matched only by the fervor of the flattery with which he hoped to lead such leaders (Steel 1999).

Responses to such critiques are of necessity complicated, for any complete response must address both theory and practice. No theoretical innovation can alone change the facts concerning matters such as the distinctive appeal and limitations of the various media involved in politics today (orchestrated mass rallies, websites, staged television "debates"), the oft-neglected responsibilities of the fourth estate, the dreadful state of public education in countries like the United States, or the resulting widespread susceptibility to organized propaganda. But, that said, the question of the nature and value of political opinion remains. The standard response to Platonic criticisms is to build upon Aristotelian conceptions of the practical wisdom of the statesman (*phronēsis*) and citizen (*synesis*) so as to demonstrate that political deliberation and judgment can steer a middle course between dialectic and pandering (Beiner 1983; Garsten 2006; Geuss 2010; see Garver, ch. 10). This is particularly true of the school of deliberative democracy influenced by Jürgen Habermas's distinction between instrumental action (like that of Plato's demagogues) and communicative action, which aims at reaching understanding, "the inherent *telos* of human speech" (1981: 287; see, e.g., Habermas 1998; Gutmann and Thompson 2004; Cohen 2009). But the direct defense of the rhetorical politics of opinion and appearance as such is the distinctive achievement of Hannah Arendt. While Arendt plays a central role in the development of both the neo-Aristotelian recuperation of political judgment and the Habermasian celebration of public, communicative action, she does so in the context of a broader reevaluation of the rhetorical politics of *doxa*. For Arendt, the political is not the realm of a *technē* such as that sought and claimed by Socrates but of the appearance of the citizen in deed and speech in a condition of plurality in which opinion is decisive.[3]

In *The Human Condition*, Arendt fleshes out her concept of the political through an idealized portrait of the ancient Greek *polis* as exemplified by Athens. The *polis* on Arendt's account was a second "order of existence" in which the citizen left behind what was "his own" and entered into "what is common" (Arendt 1958: 24). Arendt pointedly associates the *idion* of "one's own" with the privation of idiocy, on the grounds that the private is not an order of existence essentially characterized by action and speech (38). Action (*praxis*) and speech (*lexis*) are the only two activities considered by the Greeks to be political—or, as Arendt puts it in her German translation of *The Human Condition*, "eigentlich politisch" (1960: 29), actually or properly political. Of these two it is speech that is of central importance: "Speechless action would no longer be action" (Arendt 1958: 178). But if speech or rhetoric is what makes man political, the speech involved must be *public* speech if it is to be political. Whereas labor—the production of objects of consumption—and work—the production of enduring parts of the common world— can both in principle be performed in private, political action in speech, like dance, must appear in the presence of a plurality of judges: no audience, no dance performance, at best a rehearsal; likewise, no public community, no action in speech. And since action in speech is the expression or appearance of opinion, this is true of opinion as well. Hence Arendt argues that stateless persons are deprived of something "much more fundamental than freedom and justice. . . . They are deprived, not of the right to freedom, but of the right to action; not of the right to think whatever they please, but of the right to opinion" (1966: 296). To hold an opinion is to hold one publicly, as a citizen, and this requires a community or "world" of one's own in which one's words will be given a hearing. A *polis* is by definition such a community. Arendt (2003: 52) distinguishes between the authentic content (*eigentliche Inhalt*) or meaning (*Sinn*) of politics and the practical purpose (*Zweck*) of any given political act, and she argues that the meaning of politics is found in citizens managing their affairs by speaking with and persuading one another (*das Miteinander-Reden und das gegenseitige Sich-Überzeugen*) (39; on the distinction between *Sinn* and *Zweck*, cf. McDowell 1996: 70). Arendt writes of persuasion more than she does rhetoric, but it is plain that she identifies the two: for instance, in an important essay on the relation between philosophy and politics, Arendt defines "to persuade, *peithein*" as "the specifically political form of speech" (Arendt 2005: 7) and six pages later defines rhetoric as "the art of public speaking (and therefore the political art of speech)" (13). And she writes in praise of the Greeks that they "considered rhetoric, the art of persuasion, the highest, the truly political art" (7). Politics makes the sense (*Sinn*) it does because of its rhetorical nature. To construct a polity in which persuasion is absent or marginalized (as it is in the philosophical Callipolis of Plato's *Republic*) is to banish politics from the *polis* (Arendt 1968: 233).

Within the authentic political community, appearance does not veil reality; rather, "appearance—something that is being seen and heard by others as well as by ourselves— constitutes reality" (Arendt 1958: 50).[4] Reality in this sense is something quite distinct from objectivity: "The *reality* of the public realm relies on the simultaneous presence of innumerable perspectives and aspects in which the common world presents itself and for which no common measurement or denominator can ever be devised" (57). Whereas objects in pure geometrical space can be defined in a unitary set of measures, political actions require a plurality of judges, each of whom sees things *in her own way*: "This is the meaning of public life, compared to which even the richest and most satisfying family life can offer only the prolongation and multiplication of one's own position with its attendant aspects and perspectives. . . . Only where things can be seen by many in a variety of aspects without changing their identity, so that those who are gathered around them know they see sameness in utter diversity, can worldly reality truly and reliably appear" (57). Building upon the work of Karl Jaspers and Martin Heidegger, Arendt argues that this worldly reality is first and foremost a matter of opinion. On her account, in the Greek *polis* prior to the Platonic imposition of the notion of opinion as a lesser, incomplete form of knowledge, *doxa* named the individual's phenomenological or perspectival experience of the world:

> To Socrates, as to his fellow citizens, *doxa* was the formulation in speech of what *dokei moi*, that is, "of what appears to me." This *doxa* had as its topic not what Aristotle calls the *eikos*, the probable, the many *verisimilia* (as distinguished from the *unum verum*, the one truth, on the one hand, and the limitless falsehoods, the *falsa infinita*, on the other) but comprehended the world "as it opens itself up to me." It was not, therefore, subjective fantasy and arbitrariness, but was also not something absolute and valid for all. The assumption was that the world opens differently to every man according to his position in it; and that the "sameness" of the world, its commonness (*koinon*, as the Greeks would say, "common to all") or "objectivity" (as we would say from the subjective viewpoint of modern philosophy), resides in the fact that the same world opens up to everyone. (Arendt 2005: 14)

The public world is thus a perspectival matter: there is no "view from nowhere," in Thomas Nagel's (1986: 70) felicitous phrase. What is real in Arendt's sense of the term is always a view seen from a particular perspective. Even the most apparently "objective" view onto a thing—a blueprint, the measures of an object's weight and dimensions in space, a photograph—reveals its partiality in what it leaves out: the cost or meaning of the thing, its color, its relative size in relation to other objects, and so on.

Although Arendt does not develop the point as fully and explicitly as she might have, her reference to "subjective fantasy and arbitrariness" reminds us of what is too easily overlooked in such Nietzschean accounts: that one's perspective must actually be a perspective onto the thing in question. Not any "opinion" I happen to have will be an opinion in this sense. Consider the question of whether Iran in early 2009 was actively developing a nuclear weapons program and, if so, what ought to be done about it. No one at the time knew for sure the answer to this question. But it was a political matter upon which the world could hardly responsibly refrain from judgment. My opinion on this and related matters might reveal "the world as it opens itself up to me" in a variety of ways. If I were convinced that the Iranians are currently working hard to develop nuclear weapons, this might reflect my sense that Iran poses a standing threat to Israel and that Israel's defense is of overriding importance. If I felt that Iran needed to be threatened or attacked because it might be developing nuclear weapons, this might reflect my sense that order and decent behavior (in this case, *ex hypothesi*, not producing nuclear weapons) can only be produced by the threat of force. If I doubted that Iran were developing nuclear weapons, this might reflect my sense that the United States tends to exaggerate the threats that it faces in order to surreptitiously justify its power grabs, particularly in those parts of the world that produce large quantities of oil. And so on. The crucial point is that this sort of revelation of "the world as it opens itself up to me" is categorically distinct from a revelation of the world that is based upon actual observation of the matter at hand. All of the opinions that I have discussed thus far might be held by people who have given no sustained thought to the question, who have not actually looked at the germane reports and data, who know nothing of the history of the region, of the relevant behavior of Iran's political leaders, of the steps and time involved in the development of advanced weapons systems, and so on. Two such people whiling away the afternoon in a bar arguing about politics might well express their opinions about Israel, about authority and responsibility, and about American hegemony. But do they express opinions in anything but the most trivial sense about the question of whether Iran is developing nuclear weapons and what ought to be done or not done about it? It seems not, because these things can be revealed without any reference being made to Iran or nuclear weapons at all. One has only to discuss the war in Gaza, the American invasion of Iraq in 2003, or similarly unrelated issues to bring out precisely the same things. The possibility of an Iranian weapons program can "open itself up" only to those who look at it. Only by actually engaging the appearances and observing the matter at hand can one be said to have an opinion as opposed to a "subjective fantasy" regarding it. In the absence of this engagement with the facts of the matter, "freedom of opinion is a farce" and there is little hope that we shall indeed see "sameness in utter diversity" (Arendt 1968: 238).

The point here is not that one must be an expert to have a political opinion, least of all that an expert knows (best) the answers to any vexed political question such as this. As is, one hopes, obvious, the previous list of matters that should be considered by one actually holding an opinion on this matter is not exhaustive; no particular item on it is a necessary precondition for a *doxa* on this matter to emerge; such matters need to be weighed and interpreted, and such interpretations will bring out the larger "worldview" of the various individuals; and, finally, the amount of care one must devote to the consideration of such matters is not something that can be determined to a nicety, least of all in the absence of a discussion of the matter. Indeed, as we have seen, discussion of the matter is crucial for Arendt. One can have an opinion in her sense only when one has access to the political realm, only when others will hear and respond to that opinion. This is not only a matter of making oneself heard, as in contemporary debates concerning whether freedom of opinion requires at least some control of the media that allows access to large enough numbers of persons to make the expression of one's opinion more than an essentially private gesture. One must also have the ability to have one's opinion be challenged by others who have considered or seen the same matter from their own perspective, and are in a position to challenge one's claims. Arendt brings this out in a rather obscure discussion of how Socrates sought in his exchanges with his fellow Athenians "to find the truth in their *doxa*" (2005: 15). It is hardly obvious what this phrase might mean. Given Arendt's rejection of the position she associates with Plato, it cannot mean "helping the other to turn what is now mere opinion into actual knowledge of the truth." But then what room is there for any Socratic, "maieutic" help? One's *doxa* is what it is. As

Arendt puts it, there is "an inherent truth" to each opinion. If I have actually considered the matter, and not simply given voice to my prejudices or my thoughts on related matters, I have my *doxa*, and it is already as true as it is going to be. But this assumes that my *doxa* is in fact *mine*. Is this assumption warranted?

It seems clear on reflection that it is not. Consider a member of an oppressed minority group who has carefully considered the matter in question, and who is in a position to give voice effectively to her opinion. Meeting such criteria in no way guarantees that she will be seeing things from the actual perspective that she in fact occupies. It is a commonplace that a dominant or "hegemonic" culture is often (though not always) embraced by those it marginalizes and oppresses. Take the example of a young woman in a sexist culture that considers women as sexual objects. Looking in the bathroom mirror, she puts her makeup on or adjusts her hair, gauging the effect carefully. She judges the effect—judges herself—through the eyes of someone else—a callow young reader of *Maxim* magazine, for instance. In such a case, what seems to be her perspective is in reality the perspective of someone else. This "other" may not be a man, perhaps—it may rather be another woman or group of women who themselves have taken up such a perspective as their own. The important point is that it is not the young woman's own, and that such unexpected facts can most easily emerge in a situation in which one is describing what one thinks one sees to people who see things differently and are prepared to ask difficult and perhaps unwelcome questions concerning the nature of her beliefs and their implications. If such questions prod her toward adopting the viewpoint that is her own, they might be said to have brought out the truth in her *doxa*. Doing this might involve a period of disorientation in which she does not know quite how she looks at things. This is manifest in the Platonic texts that Arendt (rather ironically) relies upon in drawing the picture of Socrates as her anti-Plato. In these texts, Socrates's interlocutors regularly leave the discussion at a loss how to describe the virtues they and Socrates attempted to define, virtues they previously thought they understood and practiced quite well. Bringing out the truth in their *doxa* required that they pass through the confusion of throwing off the prejudice of custom and habit and look at the matter for themselves—then, as now, an unfamiliar exercise.

The confrontation between conflicting opinions in the public realm of speech and rhetorical persuasion not only allows for those holding those opinions to reflect on whether they are in fact committed to them. More fundamentally, it also allows for the opinions *as opinions* to be revealed. If I take my opinion regarding a political matter to be the obvious, uncontestable truth, I will not be aware of myself holding an opinion at all. If, say, patriarchy is experienced by me as part of the natural order of things, my approval of it is not so much an opinion I hold regarding it as it is a fact about the world that I (believe myself to) recognize, much as I recognize that warm clothing is a help in cold weather and wealth a blessing in any. It is only when I experience another's opinion of patriarchy—say, that it is irrational and degrading for all concerned—that I achieve the distance from patriarchy necessary to judge it and to have an opinion on it. And the more such opinions I (thoughtfully) encounter, the richer will be my understanding of patriarchy and myself as a citizen among others holding an opinion of it. This is the deeper, rhetorical sense of Arendt's claim that opinions are held not by human beings in private but by citizens in public. "Opinions," as she puts it in *On Revolution*, "are formed in a process of open discussion and public debate, and where no opportunity for the forming of opinions exists, there may be moods—moods of the masses and moods of individuals, the latter no less fickle and unreliable than the former—but no opinion" (Arendt 2006: 260-1). Or, as Arendt puts it in "Truth and Politics," "I form an opinion by considering a given issue from different viewpoints, by making present to my mind the standpoints of those who are absent; that is, I represent them. . . . The more people's standpoints I have present in my mind while I am pondering a given issue, the better I can imagine how I would feel and think if I were in their place, the stronger will be my capacity for representative thinking and the more valid my final conclusions, my opinion" (1968: 241). If Arendt appears here to conflate holding a valid opinion with holding an opinion as such, this is because an opinion, as an actual worldly relation with its object, already has some validity or "inherent truth." This validity is only increased when the opinion is confronted—through the *agōn* of public debate, argument, and persuasion—with other opinions that test it and expand its grasp of its multifaceted object. Arendt associates this greater validity with the shift from the citizen to the statesman who excels in political life and the art of rhetoric: "If we wanted to define, traditionally, the one outstanding view of the statesman, we could say that it consists in understanding the greatest possible number and variety of viewpoints . . . as these realities open themselves up to the various opinions of citizens; and, at the same time, in being able to communicate between the citizens and their opinions so that the commonness of the world becomes apparent" (2005: 18).

The worldly reality of political action, then, is one that is "opened up" by a plurality of opinions, each of which reflects an actual engagement with the matter at hand (I must witness *the deed*) and which can be more or less truthful in the sense of being one's own (*I* must witness the deed). Much as a work of art can accurately and precisely be described in a variety of terms—historical, formal, material, political, and so on—so a political act opens itself up to a variety of "readings," each of which brings out something that is there, in the act itself, and not just accidentally aroused in the subject observing the act. It is the talking about it from different perspectives in an agonistic, rhetorical context that brings out the various aspects of the thing in question: "There may be truths beyond speech, and they may be of great relevance to man in the singular. . . . Men in the plural, that is, men in so far as they live and move and act in this world, can experience meaningfulness only because they can talk with and make sense to each other and to themselves" (Arendt 1958: 4). Just as we interpret or make sense of a text by producing another text, so events in the world make sense to us insofar as we (can) express that meaning in words. "Action," as Arendt was fond of saying, "reveals itself fully only to the storyteller" (192). A particular linguistic utterance cannot mean just anything; its meaning is not a matter of subjective preference, like the preference for Coke or Canary wine over Pepsi. But neither is it rigidly constrained; what is meant is meaningful for a particular group of fellow speakers—a rhetorical community—in a particular situation or set of situations, each of whom has her own concerns and ideas within which what is said or written will appear as meaning what it does—which is to say, as meaningful *überhaupt*. Failing to mean something in *these* contexts to *these* people, the sentences lie there like messages in a bottle, to be wondered at but not understood by whoever might find them (Cavell 1969; Norris 2006).

As rhetoric or public speech appears to, and in the various opinions of, those to whom it is addressed, it is not to be judged by the unitary, abstract standard of veracity—though plainly judgments concerning truth and falsity will be reflected in those opinions—but by the standard of greatness or glory. In modern political theory, glory is most closely associated with Niccolò Machiavelli, who argues that enduring fame (*fama*) and glory (*gloria*) are more worthy and satisfying goals for an ambitious politician than the mere exercise of power in the present moment. For Arendt, glory is more closely tied to language and rhetoric; it is a matter of perceived excellence in "the specifically human way of answering, talking back and measuring up to whatever happened or was done" (Arendt 1958: 26). Not only is "most political action . . . transacted in words, but more fundamentally . . . finding the right words at the right moment, quite apart from the information or communication they may convey, is action" (26); glory is achieved when one is seen and heard as succeeding brilliantly in this in matters of great moment. As Arendt's allusions to *decorum* ("the right words") and *kairos* ("the right moment") suggest, this is a matter of rhetoric, of how one speaks and not simply of what one says: "The insight or judgment and with it the thought arise *from* the speech, and not the other way around" (1960: 29; trans. mine). "Thought is secondary to speech" (Arendt 1958: 25) not in the sense that great words do not convey information but in the sense that the greatness of the words is a matter of how they respond to a concrete situation, a rhetorical exigency, and not simply the information they convey. Simply saying "the only thing we have to fear is fear itself" conveys vividly the fact that fear makes a dangerous situation still more dangerous. But saying this is great only when these words are uttered in a situation such as Franklin Delano Roosevelt's first inaugural address in 1933 (see Campbell and Jamieson, ch. 50). Here, the right words spoken in the right way "talk back and measure up to what has happened or was done" so as to "illuminate" historical time (Arendt 1958: 43), bringing it to appearance in the polity.

This illumination and the *doxa* within which it appears is neither Socrates's political *technē* nor Lippmann's sovereignty. Indeed, it operates on another axis of political life altogether: not that of the rule of the city but that of the freedom of its citizens (Arendt 1958: 234–6). Unlike some "poststructuralists," such as Ernesto Laclau, Arendt rejects the Platonic alignment of force and persuasion, *bia* and *peithō* (Laclau 1996: 113–7): "To be political, to live in a *polis*, meant that everything was decided through words and persuasion and not through force and violence" (Arendt 1958: 26). Arendt's recuperation of *doxa* thus returns rhetoric and the rule of persuasion (*peitharchia*) to the central place in our political lives that it found, in different ways and to different extents, in the sophists, Isocrates, Aristotle, and Cicero. Here rhetoric is an integral part of "the good life" that citizens achieve only together (Aristotle, *Politics* 1252b29–30) (see Garver, ch. 10).[5]

NOTES

1. I do not differentiate here between political theory and political philosophy, as I find no interesting, consistent distinction between the terms in general practice, other than their age.
2. For the first, see Descartes 1968: 95–7. Even modern aesthetics is ambivalent toward appearance as such; witness Hegel: "Art liberates the true content of phenomena [*Erscheinungen*] from the pure appearance [*Schein*] and deception of this bad transitory world, and gives them a higher actuality" (1969: 22; trans. mine).
3. My discussion of Arendt here follows that of Norris 2013.
4. In *The Life of the Mind*, Arendt argues that in general "*Being and Appearing coincide*" (1978: 19). Space does not permit an evaluation of the relation between this ontological claim and those of her political theory.
5. My thanks to Stuart Gray, Michael MacDonald, and Tom Martin for their help with this chapter.

REFERENCES

Arblaster, Anthony. 2002. *Democracy*. Third Edition. Philadelphia, PA: Open University.

Arendt, Hannah. 1958. *The Human Condition*. Chicago, IL: University of Chicago Press.

Arendt, Hannah. 1960. Vita Activa *oder Vom tätigen Leben*. Munich: Piper.

Arendt, Hannah. 1966. *The Origins of Totalitarianism*. New York: Harcourt Brace Jovanovich.

Arendt, Hannah. 1968. "Truth and Politics." In *Between Past and Future: Eight Exercises in Political Thought*, 223–259. Harmondsworth: Penguin.

Arendt, Hannah. 1978. *The Life of the Mind*. New York: Harcourt Brace Jovanovich.

Arendt, Hannah. 2003. *Was ist Politik? Fragmente aus dem Nachlaß*. Edited by Ursula Ludz. Munich: Piper.

Arendt, Hannah. 2005. "Socrates." In *The Promise of Politics*, edited by Jerome Kohn, 5–39. New York: Schocken.

Arendt, Hannah. 2006. *On Revolution*. New York: Penguin.

Beiner, Ronald. 1983. *Political Judgment*. Chicago, IL: University of Chicago Press.

Cavell, Stanley. 1969. *Must We Mean What We Say?* Cambridge: Cambridge University Press.

Cohen, Joshua. 2009. *Philosophy, Politics, Democracy*. Cambridge, MA: Harvard University Press.

Dahl, Robert. 2003. *How Democratic is the American Constitution?* Second Edition. New Haven, CT: Yale University Press.

Descartes, René. 1968. *"Discourse on Method" and the "Meditations."* Translated by F. E. Sutcliffe. New York: Penguin.

Garsten, Bryan. 2006. *Saving Persuasion: A Defense of Rhetoric and Judgment*. Cambridge, MA: Harvard University Press.

Geuss, Raymond. 2010. *Politics and the Imagination*. Princeton, NJ: Princeton University Press.

Gutmann, Amy, and Dennis Thompson. 2004. *Why Deliberative Democracy?* Princeton, NJ: Princeton University Press.

Habermas, Jürgen. 1981. *The Theory of Communicative Action*, volume 1. Translated by Thomas McCarthy. Boston, MA: Beacon.

Habermas, Jürgen. 1998. *Between Facts and Norms: Contributions to a Discourse Theory of Law and Democracy*. Translated by Wilhelm Rehg. Cambridge, MA: MIT Press.

Hegel, Georg Wilhelm Friedrich. 1969. *Werke*. Vol. 13, *Vorlesungen über die Ästhetik*. Edited by Eva Moldenhauer and Karl Markus Michel. Theorie-Werkausgabe. Frankfurt: Suhrkamp Verlag.

Laclau, Ernesto. 1996. *Emancipation(s)*. New York: Verso.

Lasch, Christopher. 1995. *The Revolt of the Elites and the Betrayal of Democracy*. New York: Norton.

Lippmann, Walter. 2002. *The Phantom Public*. New York: Transaction.

Locke, John. 1991. *An Essay Concerning Human Understanding*. Oxford: Clarendon.

McDowell, John. 1996. *Mind and World*. Cambridge, MA: Harvard University Press.

Nagel, Thomas. 1986. *The View from Nowhere*. Oxford: Oxford University Press.

Norris, Andrew, ed. 2006. "Introduction." In *The Claim to Community: Essays on Stanley Cavell and Political Philosophy*, 1–18. Stanford, CA: Stanford University Press.

Norris, Andrew. 2013. "On Public Action: Rhetoric, Opinion, and Glory in Hannah Arendt's *The Human Condition*." *Critical Horizons* 14 no. 2: 200–224.

Steel, Ronald. 1999. *Walter Lippmann and the American Century*. New York: Transaction.

....

CHAPTER 50

RHETORIC AND PRESIDENTIAL POLITICS

....

KARLYN KOHRS CAMPBELL AND KATHLEEN HALL JAMIESON

RHETORICAL form responds in part to function. Confronted with the death of a loved one, for example, individuals respond to communal loss with rhetoric recognizable as eulogistic. Pericles's famous funeral oration (*epitaphios logos*) is a model of this rhetoric. He eulogized Athenian soldiers who fell in the first year of the Peloponnesian War and reconstituted the community by celebrating the Athenian values for which they fought and died. By inviting a rhetoric of stability and continuity, recurrent institutional functions elicit predictable patterns of rhetorical response. In the US presidency, these rhetorical patterns configure as genres. These genres of presidential rhetoric include the inaugural address, State of the Union address, war rhetoric, rhetoric to forestall and respond to impeachment, veto messages, farewells, and, more recently, national eulogies and de facto line item veto messages that assume the form of signing statements expressing reservations about legislation.

At the same time, the unique circumstances in which presidents craft these responses interact with their individual dispositions and skills to give each exercise of a genre its distinctive rhetorical signature. Because it focuses on explicating underlying rhetorical regularities, generic criticism is peculiarly suited to exploring the relationship between rhetorical action and the development and maintenance of such long-lived institutions as the US presidency.

This way of seeing focuses attention on variations in presidential power; on the relationship of presidential power to the performance of specific rhetorical functions; on the interdependence of and interplay among the branches of government; on the conditions that foster the expansion or contraction of executive power through symbolic action; and, finally, on the relationship between rhetoric and the performance of institutionally sustaining roles such as national priest, national voice, and commander in chief. In our view, rhetoric is a key part of the ways presidents exercise power, expand executive power, and establish precedents for its use by their successors. And importantly, the generically specifiable rhetoric through which presidents discharge central institutional functions may occur in predictable ways across many single instances of discourse.

THE RHETORICAL CONSTRUCTION OF THE PRESIDENCY THROUGH EXERCISE OF GENRES

In some important ways, what we know as the presidency is rhetorically constructed. For example, the US Constitution nowhere refers to "the presidency," only to the president or to the executive as one of the three branches of government. As we argue in *Presidents Creating the Presidency: Deeds Done in Words* (Campbell and Jamieson 2009), what we now understand as the presidency has come into being as a result of the actions of all presidents, a process in which rhetorical practices have been of particular importance. As it currently exists, the presidency is an amalgam of roles and practices shaped by what presidents have done. At any given moment, an awareness of these roles and capacities shapes the practices of the incumbent.

When ordinary citizens, journalists, scholars, and politicians refer to inaugural addresses, State of the Union addresses, veto messages, war rhetoric, and farewell addresses, they employ labels suggesting an implicit understanding that each type is somehow distinct, with identifiable features and functions. The discourses so cast can be viewed as genres defined by their pragmatic ends and typified by their substantive, stylistic, and strategic similarities. The rhetorical regularities exhibited by genres of presidential discourse permit critics to gain insight from examining them as a group.

A generic perspective on presidential rhetoric features those symbolic similarities that contribute to the institution's continuity and identity. It also offers a basis for highlighting the ways presidencies differ and for featuring unique contributions to the history and identity of this institution. An individual presidency—that of William Taft rather than John F. Kennedy, for example—gains some of its character from the ways a given executive chooses to exercise or not to exercise generic options. War rhetoric and veto messages, for example, are particularly sensitive indicators of a president's rhetorical initiative.

Rhetorical sensitivity and sophistication are at work in the ways individual presidents choose to exploit generic possibilities. Franklin Roosevelt, Kennedy, Richard Nixon, and Ronald Reagan, for example, were responsive to generic constraints and expectations in ways that Jimmy Carter and Gerald Ford were not. Some presidents excelled in some genres and were wanting in others. Although presidents are expected to recognize the limits of their office, Carter's inaugural statement that "your strength can compensate for my weakness, and your wisdom can help to minimize my mistakes" suggested executive inadequacy rather than appropriate humility. The 16 "I" statements in Nixon's first inaugural (e.g., "I have seen," "I know," "I speak from my own heart") caused the personal to complicate his assumption of the presidential role (Woolley and Peters 2011). Just two months after ascending to the presidency, Ford called a special joint session of Congress to urge action to reduce inflation. His speech was long and complex; he dramatized his concern with the slogan, "Whip Inflation Now," and promoted a WIN button to make his ideas memorable. Instead of eliciting congressional action, the slogan and button stimulated jokes on late-night talk shows and his proposals languished.

Genres of presidential rhetoric can be clustered into three broad categories, depending on the degree of freedom with which the president acts: genres in which the president acts unilaterally; genres that take exception, invite cooperation with the legislative branch, or assert the right of the executive to act in domains in which the Constitution gives another branch specific powers; and genres in which the Congress has greater control over the rhetorical situation than the president.

Genres in which the president acts unilaterally include the inaugural address, rhetoric delivered on ascending to the presidency following a death or resignation, and rhetoric in responding to crises or disasters in national eulogies, in issuing pardons, and in giving farewell addresses. In these genres the president engages in the creation of meaning unconstrained by the requirements, demands, or prerogatives of the other two branches of government. In each, the president has wide latitude to define the situation.

This is not the case in genres that take exception, invite cooperation with the legislative branch, or assert the right of the executive to act in domains in which the Constitution gives another branch specific powers. Whereas the State of the Union proposes, Congress disposes. The veto and de facto item veto explicitly respond to the rhetoric of the Congress embodied in legislation, and war rhetoric either invites congressional action in the form of a declaration of war or justifies presidential action in its absence.

In the final category of genre, Congress has the upper hand. When the president attempts to forestall or responds to impeachment, the Congress, which determines what is an impeachable offense, has greater control over the rhetorical situation than does the president. Farewell addresses symbolize continuity and change and as such are the counterpart of impeachment discourse. At these moments, as in inaugural addresses, pardons, and national eulogies, presidents are free from the constraints of the other branches of government, yet these addresses reflect the struggles among the co-equal branches and identify potential dangers threatening that relationship as well as the future of the nation.

GENRE AS RHETORICAL ACT

The functions that genres perform are not necessarily completed in a single act. We conceive of genres not as individual speeches but as rhetorical acts extended over time that carry out generic functions in many forms and venues and across a variety of speeches, press conferences, interviews, and rhetorical situations. In other words, rhetorical genres perform certain functions, but these functions can be incorporated into a variety of discourses. National eulogies, for example, often begin with immediate remarks after a disaster, continue with more extended remarks to the nation, come to fruition in a major speech, and then become a point of reference in addresses to Congress that build on them as a basis for legislation.

To understand the flexibility inherent in the concept of genre as rhetorical act, think of the path by which an individual becomes the president as a drama starting with a casting call and developing into a multi-act play. In dramatic terms, the primaries determine who has the talent and appeal to play a leading role; the general election determines who will play the lead. Throughout the primaries, candidates develop rhetorical skills by which they gain their party's nomination and that enable them to prevail in the general election campaign. Because the eyes of the nation are focused on the nomination acceptance speeches delivered at the national conventions, these become the rhetorical "kickoffs" for the fall campaign and as such forecast the central proposals the candidate, as president, would advance and the principles that would guide the aspirant in office. Typically, the nominee experiences a bump in national poll ratings after the acceptance address.

Act 1 of the presidential drama begins with the general election campaign, in which citizens act as critics of those who aspire to lead. During this period candidates must show themselves as presidential, even enacting various presidential roles, illustrated vividly by the simulated presidential oath in the conclusion of Kennedy's speech to the Houston Ministerial Association. The campaign is a dramatic test requiring a performer whose rhetoric can energize the groups that must be mobilized to do the vital work that enables victory.

At the same time, candidates must also reach out to unaffiliated and independent voters to show that they have the ability to "star on Broadway" and be president of all the people. Although candidates attempt to control the dynamics of the campaign, unexpected events may challenge them. In 2008, for example, Republican Party nominee John McCain and Democratic Party nominee Barack Obama were tested by the banking crisis and the Troubled Assets Relief Program proposed by President George W. Bush's secretary of the treasury, Henry Paulson. The rhetoric of the candidates can also be transformed by media coverage. This is illustrated, for example, by the ways minor verbal errors by presidential candidate Al Gore were magnified by journalists and became a theme influencing coverage of Gore throughout the 2000 campaign.

On election night (except under the most unusual circumstances), Act 1 concludes as the loser concedes and the winner declares victory, celebrating the work of dedicated supporters while effecting a subtle transition to speaking as the president-elect who can and should address the whole citizenry. Victory must simultaneously celebrate triumph over opponents and the democratic process by which national unity can emerge out of competition for the highest office. Thus, in his speech at Grant Park on the night of his election (November 4, 2008), Obama said:

> A little bit earlier this evening, I received an extraordinarily gracious call from Senator McCain. Senator McCain fought long and hard in this campaign. And he's

fought even longer and harder for the country that he loves. He has endured sacrifices for America that most of us cannot begin to imagine. We are better off for the
service rendered by this brave and selfless leader. I congratulate him; I congratulate
Governor Palin for all that they've achieved. And I look forward to working with
them to renew this nation's promise in the months ahead. (Woolley and Peters 2011)

As the paired concession and victory speeches move the country from a contest over
who will lead to embrace a democratically elected successor, a president remains in
office.

The presidential farewell is a rhetorical acknowledgment that a transition in power
is underway and a new leader waits in the wings. When Bush told the nation in a televised address on January 15, 2009, "For eight years, it has been my privilege to serve as
your President. . . . Tonight, with a thankful heart, I have asked for a final opportunity
to share some thoughts on the journey we have traveled together and the future of our
Nation" (Woolley and Peters 2011), he engaged in a rhetoric of divestiture as part of his
leave-taking of the presidency as surely as Obama was engaging in a ritual of investiture
and forecasting his presidency when, five days later, he began his inaugural address by
saying, "My fellow citizens: I stand here today humbled by the task before us, grateful for
the trust you have bestowed, mindful of the sacrifices borne by our ancestors. I thank
President Bush for his service to our nation" (Woolley and Peters 2011).

The presidential farewell occurs during the *entr'acte*, the interval between a nominee's victory in the general election and the inaugural moment when the president-elect
swears the oath of office. This is a liminal period in which the incumbent is beginning
the process of divestiture and the president-elect is beginning the process of investiture.
As such, the president-elect is neither candidate nor president; although he has no formal power, he may be pushed to support policies or take positions that may complicate
his term in office. This conflict clearly influenced the relationship between president-
elect Roosevelt and President Herbert Hoover, who refused to commit himself to
actions proposed by his predecessor, a conflict exacerbated by the long period between
election and inauguration. Similarly, Abraham Lincoln refused to speak between the
time of his election and his inauguration, fearing that any statement might be used to
provoke further division. If speeches are delivered in this period prior to the inaugural,
US audiences judge such performances to decide whether the successful candidate fits
comfortably in the new role of speaking for the nation.

Similarly, skillful planning for the transition by the president-elect reinforces the electoral victory. Of particular importance are the choices of appointees to administrative
and cabinet positions, for when nominees' credentials are flawed the president-elect's
judgment is called into question. These complications undermine the president-elect
and increase suspicions of partisan rather than presidential leadership in the future, as
is illustrated by Bill Clinton's difficulties in appointing an attorney general and Obama's
similar difficulties with Tom Daschle and Hilda Solis.

The election night victory speech of the declared winner is designed to divest him of
the role of candidate and invest him with the role of president-elect. As president-elect

he speaks for all the people in a unifying language and tone distinct from his campaign discourse. In the interim between winning and inauguration he must forego the campaigner's instinct to attack and contrast and instead move toward advocating a vision all can embrace. We hear nominee Obama making the transition to president-elect in the Grant Park speech when he says, "And to those Americans whose support I have yet to earn, I may not have won your vote tonight, but I hear your voices. I need your help. And I will be your president, too." He then articulates a shared vision:

> This is our time, to put our people back to work and open doors of opportunity for our kids; to restore prosperity and promote the cause of peace; to reclaim the American dream and reaffirm that fundamental truth, that, out of many, we are one; that while we breathe, we hope. And where we are met with cynicism and doubts and those who tell us that we can't, we will respond with that timeless creed that sums up the spirit of a people: Yes, we can. (Woolley and Peters 2011)

The campaigner whose 2008 slogan, "Yes we can," affirmed that "we" can win this election and carry out the promised agenda, has recast "Yes we can" as a shared commitment to a common vision, one that both McCain and Obama supporters could embrace.

Having assumed the role of unifying president-elect, any lapse into the role of campaigner anchored in a world of supporters and opponents risks undermining both presidential investiture and the capacity to deliver a rhetoric of unity in the name of a common purpose. Hence, in a speech the week before the inaugural address, Obama violated a generic rule of the rhetorical act required to carry him through the inaugural address when he shifted from a unifying rhetoric ("what gives me the greatest hope ... is you—Americans of every race and region and station who came here because you believe in what this country can be and because you want to help us get there") to a reprise of his stump speech: "It is the same thing that gave me hope from the day we began this campaign for the presidency nearly two years ago ... " (Woolley and Peters 2011).

Act 2 of this rhetorical drama begins with the inaugural address, the first major test of the presidency, an opportunity to reassure voters that they made the right choice, and an occasion for newly inaugurated presidents to show that they can inspire the nation to unite to solve current problems and that they have a clear sense of their presidential role and purpose.

GENRES THAT DEFINE THE PRESIDENCY

Presidential genres offer a lens through which the country understands both the presidency and an individual's exercise of its powers. Inaugural addresses maintain presidential stability insofar as each praises or blames, affirms traditional principles, heightens what is known and believed, uses elegant language, and focuses on the nation's eternal present while reconstituting "the people" who witness this ritual and invest this speaker with the presidency. Inaugurals adapt by drawing alternative strains from the past, by featuring different values and principles, and by recreating "the people" in diverse roles. The speeches of ascendant vice presidents reaffirm continuity at moments of unexpected and threatening change. An exemplar of this genre is Ford's memorable declaration that "our long national nightmare is over" after the resignation of Nixon.

National eulogies such as Lincoln's Gettysburg Address, Reagan's speech to the nation after the Space Shuttle *Challenger* explosion, Clinton's speech after the Oklahoma City bombing, and Bush's address at the National Cathedral after the terrorist attacks of September 11, 2001 reconstitute the citizenry after the national fabric has been torn by tragedy (Wilson 2006). This epideictic form of presidential eloquence mourns those lost while affirming national resolve and attesting to the resilience of the country and its ideals. A related epideictic form, namely, pardoning rhetoric, reaffirms the president as the symbolic head of state who acts in the public interest to preserve the public good while enabling the president to correct judicial errors that result from the passions stirred by specific events.

In delivering a farewell speech, as George Washington and Dwight Eisenhower did so memorably, a president sustains the office by attempting to bequeath a legacy to the nation. Because that legacy is a product of the person of the president and of the events of that presidency, it is grounded in historical particulars and uniquely reflects the persona of the individual president. As is the case with much of what we remember as eloquence, brief statements from these addresses have come to represent the addresses as a whole, with the warning against "permanent alliances with any portion of the foreign world" having the same function in Washington's farewell as the caution against the "military-industrial complex" has in Eisenhower's.

State of the Union addresses reaffirm continuity by displaying the president as symbolic head of state. They also respond to the discourse of past presidents and revivify and sustain the nation's identity. However, even as these messages address enduring national questions, the agendas they offer vary with the period in which they are presented and the specific circumstances in which presidents find themselves, as is illustrated by the Monroe Doctrine (proclaimed in 1823), which responded to the threat of Spanish recolonization in this hemisphere.

Veto messages affirm continuity and constancy insofar as they interdict legislation in a dispassionate document that employs the language of conservation of the government as an institution. By permitting presidents to develop lines of argument and present evidence appropriate to the particular case, these messages enable presidents to express their individual beliefs and to adapt to the specifics of legislation they oppose. A related genre, the de facto item veto embodied in a signing statement, asserts the president's power and obligation to defend the Constitution and the executive powers stipulated or implied by it. This peculiar message is simultaneously a form of intra- and interbranch communication in which the president defines the limits of legislative authority.

Presidential self-defense rhetoric is part of a dialectic about the limits of executive powers and the nature of the executive's obligations. In the process of considering impeachment, the elected representatives of the people ask whether the president has violated the oath of office. This mode of presidential rhetoric protects the office from congressional or judicial encroachment as debate emerges about how executive powers are to be understood and interpreted under the particular circumstances of a historical moment.

The functions of each genre remain constant, while the rhetorical means through which these can be performed vary. The genius of the founders resided in creating a framework that empowered presidents to exercise their rhetorical options as circumstances and their temperaments warranted. In most of these cases, the president can decide whether and when to issue discourse and what strategies to employ in accomplishing an end. Although it licenses rhetoric of pardoning and vetoing, the Constitution's rhetorical mandates are limited to swearing the oath of office and reporting from time to time on the state of the nation and recommending necessary and expedient legislation. Still, from the institution's inception, those elected to the nation's highest office have recognized the need for forms of rhetoric that the Constitution did not build into their job description. Oath taking, for example, has from the beginning been twinned with an inaugural address.

Except for specifying that the oath be sworn, the Constitution leaves the timing of rhetoric to the president. Article 2, section 3 of the Constitution specifies only that the president "shall from *time to time* give to Congress information of the State of the Union and recommend to their Consideration such measures as he shall judge necessary and expedient [emphasis added]." This flexibility of timing is evident as well because at any time, in any circumstance, a president can issue or withhold special messages, pardons, and invitations to declare war or authorize military action. When confronted with congressional action, a president can elect to respond with a veto or a de facto item veto or to remain silent. A president can opt to forego a national eulogy or formal farewell. In the use of these basic rhetorical genres, presidents signal the continuity of the institution; in their varying patterns of use, they show their individual dispositions and the adaptations through which presidents can respond to altered circumstances.

The Constitution offers the executive an array of rhetorical opportunities. The president can call Congress into special session, make recommendations that are necessary and expedient, act as commander in chief, veto legislation, and pardon. Some presidents grasp these grants of authority and deploy them in ways that increase presidential power. Others shy away from the exercise of discretionary powers and use those mandated only tentatively. In modern times, however, presidents have increasingly exploited and enlarged their powers through their use of rhetoric. The presidents who use these powers tend to take the initiative or to govern in times of crisis.

Although Article 2, section 3 of the Constitution grants the president authority "on extraordinary Occasions [to] convene both Houses," this is not a power presidents regularly use. When exercised, however, this act is rhetorical. By calling a special session, the president defines the situation as "extraordinary." Roosevelt, for example, communicated the urgency of the country's economic situation and his determination to act quickly on the promises made in his election campaign when he called Congress into special session and elicited quick passage of his banking legislation in March 1933.

Through time, presidents tried out lines of argument and developed new rhetorical forms; those conventionalized through use were added to the options available to a president contemplating invitations to investiture, pardoning, vetoing, reporting, recommending, responding to the threat of impeachment, seeking legitimation for assumption of the role of commander in chief, or bidding farewell. Injudicious choices of rhetorical forms and strategies disappeared as options. Over time, the presidency has therefore developed a corpus of tested genres signaling the boundaries and characteristics of the rhetoric through which key presidential functions are performed. Those who simply followed these formulas issued competent but sometimes cliché-ridden presidential discourse. Great presidents, however, enlarged the range of rhetorical possibilities by performing these functions while transcending the formulas, as Lincoln did in his second inaugural and Eisenhower did in his farewell speech.

CLUSTERS OF PRESIDENTIAL GENRES BASED ON PRESIDENTIAL POWER

From the perspective of rhetorical genre, the institutions of the US government constitute an experiment in rhetorical adaptation in which the initiatives of any one branch can be modified and refined by the reactions of the others and in which the flaws or idiosyncrasies of any one branch at any given time can be accommodated by action in the others. The moments that signal expansion and contraction of the executive often are marked by rhetoric. One early instance in which presidential power was expanded by rhetorical assertion occurred when the first vice president ascended to the presidency. John Tyler was notified that William Henry Harrison had died in a message addressed to "John Tyler, Vice-President of the United States" (Richardson 1909: 4: 22–3). The Constitution does not say that the vice president becomes the president upon being sworn in after the death of the president. Article 2, section 1 says only that if the office becomes vacant "the Powers and Duties . . . shall devolve on the Vice President." When Tyler's inaugural address was published, it was under his title as president. Similarly, he signed his papers "John Tyler, President of the United States" (see Binkley 1964: 225–6). In effect, he assumed the office as well as the powers and duties of the presidency by asserting that they were his.

The founders protected the country from miscreants and rhetorical bumblers by enabling the Congress and the Supreme Court to act as checks on presidential discourse. At one time or another, each is empowered to ask whether the president is discharging appropriately the executive powers specified in the Constitution. Presidents test the limits of their power rhetorically and are called to task by the rhetoric of the other branches. This process was adumbrated in Roosevelt's first inaugural address (March 4, 1933), in which he said, "I am prepared under my constitutional duty to recommend the measures that a stricken Nation . . . may require . . . But in the event . . . that the national emergency is still critical . . . I shall ask the Congress for the one remaining instrument to meet the crisis—broad Executive power to wage a war against the emergency" (Woolley and Peters 2011).

The checks and balances of our system not only control the distribution of power among the branches but also legitimize each branch in performing its functions. Regardless of its author, for example, the State of the Union message ensures that the Congress acknowledges the president's legislative prerogatives; the veto message ensures that Congress attends to presidential objections to a legislative initiative.

ROLES AND GENRES

When articulated by the president, each type of discourse becomes special. Only a president can issue an inaugural address after swearing the oath of office and becoming "the president." Only a president can issue a pardon and in so doing absolve a malefactor of a federal crime; only a president can state objections to a piece of legislation and thereby invite its reconsideration by Congress. The identity of the presidents as spokespersons fulfilling constitutional roles and exercising their executive power gives this discourse a distinctive character. Central among the roles available in the presidency are the roles of priest, national voice, and commander in chief.

The first role available to the president is that of national priest. The president takes on a priestly role in the inaugural by representing the country before God and praying for the nation, especially in the case of an ascendant vice president whose inaugural speech must vacate the office by appropriately memorializing the dead president before he can assume the office himself. Another example is the national eulogy, in which the president leads the nation in a commemorative service before setting forth the actions the government and the country will take to ensure that there is no recurrence of the tragedy that is the subject of this rhetoric. Finally, in the farewell speech the president draws on the moral leadership inherent in the role of priest to offer the country advice designed to ensure that it will survive into the future.

As national priest, the president is the custodian of national values, values embodied in the Constitution but extended beyond it to encompass what we have learned as a nation and memorialized in past presidential discourse. The national eulogy, for example, arises because national values have been attacked; those who have died incarnate them and become symbols of the nation. Likewise, in pardoning, the president, as national voice and priestly judge, recognizes those circumstances in which justice must be tempered by mercy.

The second role available to the president is that of national voice. "There is but one national voice in the country and that is the voice of the President," wrote Woodrow Wilson ([1883] 1956: 209). The president must be able to speak to and on behalf of the nation and beyond its partisan divisions. The Constitution assigns the president the distinctive role of assessing the state of the nation and the special authority to set priorities—to recommend necessary and expedient legislation. In vetoing, for example, the president speaks for the Constitution and for what is arguably best for the nation. And in times of national crisis, it is the presidential voice that is expected to comfort, counsel, and guide the nation in a response consistent with the national interest.

The third role available to the president is that of commander in chief. When military action is initiated, the president assumes a role described in Article 2, section 2 of the Constitution as "Commander in Chief of the Army and Navy of the United States and of the Militias of the several States, when called into the actual Service of the United States." That investiture occurs, first, when Congress enacts a declaration of war or passes a resolution authorizing military action, such as the Gulf of Tonkin Resolution or the congressional authorization of the 1991 Gulf War, and second, when the president mobilizes the nation to respond to attack or invasion. Roosevelt's invitation to declare war as a result of "a date which will live in infamy" is among the more famous entreaties to Congress. In this speech we hear the leader of both the nation and the armed forces rehearsing a role that the declaration of war will bestow.

This chapter has demonstrated that what we know as the presidency is constructed in part from our collective experience of the genres of discourse available to those who hold the nation's highest office. This optic entails the argument that institution-sustaining roles—including those of national priest, national voice, and commander in chief—are performed in part through rhetoric. A generic perspective's focus on recurrent responses to presidential functions thus offers crucial insight into the ways presidential power is enhanced or sacrificed as a result of rhetorical action.

References

Binkley, Wilfred E. 1964. *The Man in the White House: His Powers and Duties.* New York: Harper and Row.

Campbell, Karlyn Kohrs, and Kathleen Hall Jamieson. 2009. *Presidents Creating the Presidency: Deeds Done in Words.* Chicago, IL: University of Chicago Press.

Richardson, James D., ed. 1909. *A Compilation of the Messages and Papers of the Presidents, 1789–1908.* 11 vols. Washington, DC: Bureau of National Literature and Art.

Wilson, Douglas L. 2006. *Lincoln's Sword: The Presidency and the Power of Words.* New York: Vintage.

Wilson, Woodrow. (1883) 1956. *Congressional Government.* New York: Meridian Books.

Woolley, John, and Gerhardt Peters. 2011. *The American Presidency Project.* http://www.presidency.ucsb.edu/index_docs.php#axzz2htl4kMAk.

CHAPTER 51

....

RHETORIC AND NEW TESTAMENT STUDIES

....

STANLEY E. PORTER

RHETORICAL criticism has grown in interest and importance in New Testament studies over the last 30 or so years, to the point where it today constitutes a recognized form of New Testament criticism. Whereas before this time mention of the term rhetoric usually referred simply to the use of figures of speech or matters of style, with the growth of rhetorical study of the New Testament there has come to be a full-orbed exploration of the topic in a variety of dimensions. This includes most of the areas that fall within the purview of traditional rhetorical study, including the range of topics identified with invention, arrangement, and style (even if memory and delivery have generally been neglected), usually patterned after classical rhetoric and often invoking the classical handbooks but sometimes drawing upon modern theories of rhetoric and composition. As a result, important scholarly journals often publish articles of rhetorical criticism of portions of the New Testament, and there are even commentary series designated as rhetorical in perspective and approach. Nevertheless, despite growth in what has come to be called rhetorical criticism of the New Testament, questions remain as to what exactly such criticism entails, the strength of the theoretical foundations of this endeavor, and the significance of the interpretative results. This chapter pursues these topics in more detail. It first briefly surveys the development of rhetorical criticism of the New Testament, then examines and offers a critique of the major arguments surrounding the foundations for New Testament rhetorical criticism, and concludes by offering a way forward regarding rhetorical criticism and its place within the field of New Testament studies.

THE DEVELOPMENT OF RHETORICAL CRITICISM OF THE NEW TESTAMENT

Scholars occasionally refer to earlier rhetorical comments made about the New Testament such as by John Chrysostom (see Mitchell 2000) or Theodor Bezae the

Reformer and other early modern interpreters (see, e.g., Classen 2000) or to work by earlier classicists who have influenced New Testament studies such as Eduard Norden (1898) or Paul Wendland (1912). However, most robust contemporary rhetorical criticism of the New Testament is seen to emanate from the critical work of two scholars: the New Testament scholar Hans Dieter Betz (1979; cf. 1974–5) and especially his commentary on Galatians, and the classicist George Kennedy (1984) and his work on classical rhetoric applied to the New Testament. Betz's commentary opened the doors to examining the New Testament by means of rhetorical criticism, starting with the Pauline letters but extending to others as well. Following Betz's interpretative approach, organizational patterns and rhetorical conventions suggested by the rhetorical handbooks provided the basis for much of this form of rhetorical criticism. It was early on extended to other types of literature in the New Testament, following the approach of Kennedy, who sampled passages within the New Testament, from the Gospels to Revelation, and suggested their classical rhetorical features, especially species and organization.

Since that time rhetorical criticism has burgeoned and taken many different directions in studies of the New Testament. Besides those who question the applicability of classical rhetorical categories to the writings of the New Testament (see Porter 1993), two major types of rhetorical criticism have been rigorously pursued. The first type includes those who have thoroughly embraced widely varying forms of ancient rhetorical criticism as central and even fundamental to the New Testament interpretative task. This type of criticism often makes use of categories from classical rhetoric—including identification of species, types of invention and proofs, arrangement, and style—as a means of critically analyzing texts ranging in size from individual *pericopes* (e.g., a saying of Jesus, or even the Sermon on the Mount in Matthew 5–7) to entire books (e.g., a Pauline or other letter). These forms of rhetorical criticism have expanded beyond the Pauline letters first envisioned by Betz to encompass all of the subcorpora of the New Testament, including the Gospels, Acts, non-Pauline letters, and even the book of Revelation. Smaller studies are often found in individual essay collections or journal articles, while analyses of entire books are found in monographs or commentaries. These studies typically identify the species of rhetoric or its literary type (e.g., a *chreia* [maxim] from the *progymnasmata*) and then discuss its means of rhetorical argumentation, whether this involves arrangement, proofs, or other means. New Testament scholars who have pursued such work include Richard Longenecker, Duane Watson, and Ben Witherington, among many others. Concurrently with this development has been a second type of rhetorical criticism, which involves discussion of what has been variously termed general rhetoric, universal rhetoric, modern rhetoric, or the New Rhetoric, the kind of rhetorical practices originally grounded in classical rhetoric but adapted for modern rhetorical situations and discussed and exemplified in work by such nonbiblical literary and rhetorical scholars as I. A. Richards, Cleanth Brooks and Robert Penn Warren, Kenneth Burke, and Chaïm Perelman. The New Testament scholar Vernon Robbins (1996) has done the most important work in this area, developing what he calls "socio-rhetorical" criticism. However, despite a few New Testament scholars who utilize the interpretative resources of modern rhetoric, this area has remained relatively undeveloped in New

Testament rhetorical criticism compared with the number of works that draw upon classical rhetoric as their governing interpretative paradigm.

The Foundations for New Testament Rhetorical Criticism

The use of classical rhetoric to interpret the New Testament is founded upon a number of suppositions put forward by Betz and Kennedy and implicitly or explicitly reiterated by subsequent scholars. These suppositions can be succinctly summarized. Betz posits that the letter to the Galatians can be analyzed using categories from both ancient rhetoric and epistolography. In other words, the letter has a rhetorical body with epistolary prescript and postscript. As a result, he believes that Galatians conforms to the apologetic letter, represented by Plato's *Seventh Letter*, among others. Kennedy and others after him have extended the supposed basis for rhetorical analysis by the further suppositions that, even though rhetoric was only formally taught at the higher educational levels (in the rhetorical school by a rhetor) but not fully in the grammar school by the *grammateus* (even if there was some rudimentary exposure at that level), this was not a hindrance to New Testament authors becoming rhetors. Rhetoric was so pervasive in first-century CE Greco-Roman culture that Paul and other New Testament authors could have had access to it by their own reading of rhetorical handbooks or simply by observing rhetorical practice that was taking place around them. This same access would have been available to any writer of the New Testament, not just Paul. Witherington goes so far as to depict most first-century persons, whether educated or not, as "either producers or consumers of some kind of rhetoric" (Witherington 2009: 11). This leads him to conclude that most New Testament books are not the books they purport to be but are better described as "rhetorical speeches" (5). The result of such an approach has been a number of monographs and commentaries offering rhetorical analyses of New Testament books, especially of the Pauline epistles (though others also), in which they are seen to be in effect speeches in the form of gospel or epistle rather than gospel or epistle with rhetorical elements. The claim is also often made that this direct invocation of the categories of ancient rhetoric is to be preferred to the New Rhetoric, and even to other historically based forms of New Testament criticism, because such rhetorical analysis is itself a historical criticism that would have been recognized and practiced by those in the first century who first composed and heard read to them the individual books of the New Testament. Kennedy (1984: 12) goes so far as to claim that this rhetorical criticism provides access to the intentions of the original authors.

This justification for New Testament rhetorical criticism—despite its continuing appeal and functional warrant for continuing efforts of rhetorical analysis—is surprisingly lacking in substantial support. Betz offers no substantial argument for his use of the category of the apologetic letter (as a type of forensic rhetoric), apart from his ability to analyze the arrangement of Galatians. However, even here he is not successful. The parallels that he invokes are not germane or appropriate, for they either are not truly letters but treatises or speeches from the start or have been analyzed in different ways. Further, Betz's organizational analysis is problematic throughout. His use of *narratio* (Galatians 1:12–2:14) functions differently than in the examples he cites, a *probatio* (used to label Galatians 3–4) is not found in a forensic speech according to the rhetorical handbooks, and the *exhortatio* he posits for Galatians 5–6 is not found in forensic rhetoric (see Porter 2013). There is the additional problem that no substantive evidence exists of Paul partaking in rhetorical education, even if he was exposed to some elements of rhetoric in the grammar school. Becoming an accomplished rhetorician—as many advocates of New Testament rhetorical criticism claim that many if not most of the New Testament writers were—took specialized training, which was usually reserved for only a few elite men who had considerable financial means. Paul's secondary education was almost assuredly devoted to training in the law under Gamaliel in Jerusalem, where there may not even have been a rhetorical school at the time. In light of these factors, it is very difficult to posit, as do Kennedy and others, that rhetoric was so pervasive that most people of the time simply imbibed it with the air they breathed. To the contrary, to become an accomplished rhetor required specialized training and devotion of which most simply could not avail themselves, certainly not most of the writers of the New Testament.

There is the further, and perhaps more important, issue of whether the use of the species, arrangement, and invention of ancient rhetoric would have been used by the New Testament authors for the construction and interpretation of any of the books of the New Testament. As we have seen, it is unlikely that the writers of the New Testament can be considered rhetors. There is simply no evidence that they were trained in the specialized craft of rhetoric. Therefore, it is also unlikely that we can suppose that they used the technical skills of rhetoric in the creation of their works. The evidence indicates that training in rhetoric—that is, the creation of orations, even if rhetorical exercises may have been applicable to smaller units of rhetoric—was not applied to works apart from speeches. The early rhetorical handbooks do not include the types of writing found in the New Testament within their purview, including especially letter writing. One of few statements is found in Quintilian, who distinguishes between the style appropriate for an oration and a letter (*Institutio oratoria* 9.4.19–22). Cicero, who was both a rhetorician and an epistolographer, makes no reference to letter writing (and certainly not gospel writing!) in his works on rhetoric and thus distinguishes his and others' letter writing from rhetorical practice, as does Seneca, who states that he leaves the "foot-stomping" to rhetors (*Epistulae morales* 75.1–2). It is not until the fourth century in the writings of Julius Victor that letter writing is included with rhetoric, long after all of the books of the New Testament were written. There is the final problem that there is no evidence that the rhetorical handbooks served as guides to the analysis of speeches, to say nothing of other forms of literature. The rhetorical handbooks served as guides to instruct in the formation of the competent rhetor, providing a course of instruction in the means of invention, arrangement, style, memory, and delivery (see Heath, ch. 5; Steel, ch. 16). Rhetorical critics of the New Testament are (usually) asking us to believe that the handbooks provide a historically grounded guide to criticism of the New Testament documents. They may, of course, be used in this way, but one should not pretend this to be something the authors or original readers/hearers would have done or recognized. There is virtually no evidence that this is the case, and the mere positing of such a supposition or the ability of a modern interpreter to assert or argue for this on the basis of "successful" analysis of a New Testament document does not provide evidence otherwise. This can be seen in some so-called socio-rhetorical commentaries on various books of the New Testament that purport to combine modern sociological analysis with ancient rhetorical analysis, when in fact they seem to be for the most part examples of essentially traditional historical-critical commentaries in which the ancient works are often presented in the garb of classical rhetorical arrangement.

The final line of objection revolves around the literary character of the individual works of the New Testament. Not all rhetorical critics of the New Testament argue that, for example, the letters of the New Testament are actually rhetorical speeches. Some stratify their analysis, recognizing the epistolary element alongside rhetorical elements. Even for those who argue that the letters or any other books of the New Testament still function according to its literary type but are also examples of a piece of rhetoric, there is the problem of literary integrity. As noted previously, the examples suggested by Betz (1974–5, 1979) have been shown to be inadequate parallels, and even the use of categories of rhetorical *dispositio* within larger works, so-called examples of macro-rhetoric, cannot be justified on the basis of the ancient evidence.

Therefore, I think that much of the work in New Testament rhetorical analysis—apart from the actual analysis of speeches, such as the speeches (though abbreviated) in the book of Acts and possibly some of those in the gospels—is without justification or foundation insofar as it is purported to be a practice of the New Testament authors or first readers/hearers and understood by them as a contemporary interpretative tool.

RHETORICAL CRITICISM IN NEW TESTAMENT STUDIES: A WAY FORWARD

All of this does not mean that rhetorical criticism has no place in the study of the New Testament—only that it cannot be seen to provide better or more accurate readings of the ancient documents on the basis of their being closer to the original meaning of the author. Nevertheless, rhetorical criticism has, I believe, continuing potential for productive interpretative interaction with New Testament and related studies (see Conybeare, ch. 24). I will elucidate several types of criticism in roughly increasing order of importance.

To begin with, the rhetorical analysis of speeches is a useful way of approaching the New Testament. There are a number of purported speeches in the New Testament, especially by Paul in the book of Acts. There are also a number of speeches given by Jesus and others in the four gospels and Acts. However, on the basis of what has already been said—despite assertions to the contrary (e.g., Kennedy 1984: 39–63, on the Sermon on the Mount)—Jesus and most of the other speakers, such as Peter, were clearly and admittedly not trained rhetors, and their speeches, while they *can* be analyzed rhetorically, were not crafted by them as if they were. For that reason, analysis of these speeches through rhetorical means can at best reveal general principles of rhetoric commonly part of language usage but not technical rhetoric as practiced by rhetors. The same cannot necessarily be said of Paul's speeches in Acts. It is at least arguable that, in the book of Acts, we have records of speeches delivered by Paul, or at least speeches recorded that purport to present what Paul might have said on the occasion. The major difficulty in analyzing Paul's speeches is that they are apparently abbreviated for the occasion and therefore do not appear to be fully developed. There is the further difficulty that several of the speeches are interrupted, making it difficult to get a sense of the entire speech (if it were delivered). Nevertheless, even if that is the case, it is perhaps possible that Paul, on the basis of his grammatical education in practices of Greek rhetoric, such as the progymnasmatic exercises, constructed his speeches to persuade his audience and that they follow the arrangement of classical orations. There are eight speeches worth considering in this light: his missionary speeches, deliberative speeches designed to persuade toward belief (at Pisidian Antioch, Acts 13:16–41; at Lystra, Acts 14:15–7; on the Areopagus in Athens, Acts 17:22–31); his apologetic speeches, forensic speeches designed to defend his actions (before Jerusalem Jews, Acts 22:1–21; the procurator Felix, Acts 24:10–21; Herod Agrippa and others, Acts 26:2–23; Roman Jewish leaders, Acts 28:17–20); and his only speech before a Christian audience, his epideictic speech to the Miletan elders (Acts 20:18–35). These speeches are arranged in different ways. The deliberative speeches support their arguments through appeals to Jewish history, the Old Testament, or natural theological arguments. The forensic speeches all involve Paul's making a defense by invoking his personal history. A case can certainly be made that Paul is depicted as invoking classical techniques of invention and arrangement in creating these speeches (see Porter 2013). Such categories help us to understand the progression of his argument and the means by which it is made.

Another productive rhetorical approach is the analysis of style (Gk. *lexis*; L. *elocutio*). Before the resurgence in classical rhetorical studies of the New Testament, elements of style were often acknowledged in various of the New Testament writings. Style encompasses two areas. The first is levels of style, and the other is style as ornamentation. The ancients distinguished three or four levels of style, ranging from the grand or complicated style with its use of complex periods, the elegant or running style associated with narrative, and the loose or plain style of conversation—as well as possibly the forcible style characterized by short sentences, as in dialogue (see Porter 1997: 577). These categories are certainly valid in examining the writings of the New Testament, for they were known and used to describe other Greek writers of the time. In this regard, we find a range of levels of style represented in the New Testament, including multiple styles used by the same author at different times. For example, Paul arguably uses each at various times. Hebrews would be characterized as possibly achieving the grand style on

STANLEY E. PORTER 655

occasion, and certainly the elegant or running style, while the gospels typically display the running style and sometimes the plain style in their dialogues (the forceful style is in evidence in such passages as the contentious Romans 3:1–9).

The second area encompassed by style is what is often simply dismissed as ornamentation (see Porter 1997: 578–84; Rowe 1997). Scholars have long recognized that the New Testament has a variety of stylistic features that go beyond being simply ornamental. These include many if not most of the major tropes and figures used in ancient rhetoric. However, these do not represent macro-rhetoric but instead micro-rhetoric. This type of micro-rhetoric is often distinguished from the substance of the discourse, and the use of various stylistic features is often characterized as in some way obfuscating or making more complex than necessary the discernment of the content, to the point of accusing those who use various stylistic features of perhaps lacking an adequate argument and simply engaging in "rhetoric." This is a misleading characterization that merits correction, along with further exploration of the contribution of style to ancient rhetoric.

Another avenue of potential investigation is the relationship between the New Rhetoric and ancient rhetoric. From the advent of recent rhetorical analysis of the New Testament, there has been a tension between the New Rhetoric (by whatever name) and ancient rhetoric. As noted previously, ancient rhetoric draws upon especially the ancient rhetorical handbook tradition as encapsulating the principles by which ancient rhetors functioned—at least they served as textbooks or summaries of the kinds of things that ancient rhetors were taught in the course of their training. These handbooks differed according to the Greek or Latin rhetorical traditions, besides reflecting the personal orientations of their authors (see, e.g., the differences between Aristotle in his *Rhetoric* and Quintilian in his *Institutio oratoria*, differences reflecting both the Greek and Latin traditions and different orientations to such issues as invention). What might be called the New Rhetoric comes in a variety of forms, as already mentioned. Many of these, such as the literary-rhetorical interpretation of Burke (1973) or the New Rhetoric of Perelman and Olbrechts-Tyteca (1969), apply the categories of ancient rhetoric in contemporary contexts, including such venues as literary interpretation, the law court, and politics (see van Eemeren, ch. 52). In these instances, the ancients provide models, due to supposed similarities of context, of how to address contemporary "rhetorical" situations similar to those the ancients faced. All of these have found some resonance in New Testament studies. As noted already, perhaps the most well-developed of these is Robbins's (1996) socio-rhetorical criticism, which has been elaborated in a number of different ways by various practitioners. This category of rhetorical exposition attempts to position rhetoric within its social context, whether ancient or modern. Rhetoric is characterized by its socio-rhetorical position, and its exponence is classified according to various levels of texture, including inner texture, intertexture, social and cultural texture, and ideological texture (and possibly others). Each of these textures becomes increasingly abstract. Socio-rhetorical criticism has many similarities to types of discourse analysis, although it is defined almost exclusively without recognizing points of similarity and correlation—areas where discourse analysis might aid socio-rhetorical criticism in its interpretative task. Witherington (2009: 242–4) characterizes his commentaries on books of the

New Testament as socio-rhetorical, but he means something different by the term and is not practicing the kind of socio-rhetorical criticism that Robbins endorses.

A fourth consideration is the relationship between ancient rhetoric and modern discourse analysis and text linguistics. The linguists Robert de Beaugrande and Wolfgang Dressler (1981: 15) go further than simply recognizing the use of rhetoric and see a correlation between ancient rhetoric and modern discourse analysis. By this they mean that, for the ancients, rhetoric provided a useful conceptual framework for engaging in language analysis. Insofar as the ancients were literary-critically aware, they thought of such critical analysis by means of and through ancient rhetoric. However, de Beaugrande and Dressler also make clear that the modern correlative is certainly not ancient rhetoric, which was limited by the ancient conceptual framework that need no longer constrain the modern interpreter, nor is it modern rhetoric, which is an outgrowth of ancient rhetoric. As the modern equivalent of rhetoric, discourse analysis moves beyond ancient and even modern rhetoric by providing an interpretative matrix that avails itself of contemporary linguistic interpretative theory. Therefore, rather than being limited by the species, arrangement, invention, and even memory and delivery of ancient rhetoric, the modern discourse analyst focuses on how a text means in all its various dimensions. These include the features that constitute a text or give it texture, the content of the discourse and how this is transmitted through lexical and syntactic choice, and the indicated interpersonal dynamics conveyed through various grammatical means. As a result, from this perspective, those interested in the rhetorical features of ancient texts, rather than limiting their interpretative repertoire to the categories available to the ancients, should instead be cultivating their discourse-analytic abilities and making use of the most recent and wide and increasing range of contemporary linguistic thought. This goes beyond the simple means by which texts are labeled and described and even considers the social, cognitive, and cultural elements of linguistic expression.

A final area of rhetorical investigation is the relationship between formal and functional categories. At the end of the day, we are presented with various readings of the New Testament propounded by various self-styled rhetorical critics. In the course of the rhetorical identification of categories of arrangement (Gk. *taxis*; L. *dispositio*), some have noted that certain common patterns can be found between various discourse types and perhaps even across various cultural and temporal divides. For example, Jeffrey Reed (1997: 322–4) insightfully notes that epistolary structure has certain features in common with rhetorical structure. The question is how to view these similarities and hence how to account for them. Practitioners of rhetorical criticism such as those previously noted are inclined to examine the letter as an instance not of epistolary structure but of rhetorical structure—possibly with an epistolary prescript and salutation attached. In their eyes, that it is a letter is only incidental to its being rhetoric. However, there is another perspective on this issue. Those who recognize the functional value of rhetoric would contend, as has Reed, followed by others, that there are functional correlatives between rhetorical categories and other interpretative frameworks, such as epistolary analysis. Thus, common functions performed by the epistolary opening and the opening of a letter examined by other means are not based upon the author intentionally employing a rhetorical technique. Instead, they appear to involve a functional similarity—every work of writing, including literature, but much else as well, by definition must have an opening, middle, and closing. In fact, each writing must by virtue of being a text have such elements—even if they are not all letters or speeches. This means that there are bound to be functional similarities. As every work of writing must begin, so there will be typical functional categories that are shared by the openings of every written text, whether it is a letter or a speech or something else. The same is true to a large extent with the other two major parts of a written work, the middle and the close. There are only so many ways in which a written text may close, so endings will have functional similarities even if they represent different types of literature. Just because they share these functions does not mean that these different types of writing are necessarily the same. This is an illegitimate equation. In other words, just because a speech of the ancient world reached a close in a suitable and satisfactory way, and just because a Pauline letter reaches a suitable close, does not mean that an ancient speech is a Pauline letter or that a Pauline letter is an ancient speech—a mistake made by many New Testament rhetorical critics. However, this correlation provides the opportunity to explore cross-literary functional, structural, and other patterns.

Conclusion

Despite what has been argued by a number of New Testament rhetorical advocates, ancient rhetorical analysis does not enjoy a privileged place in the interpretative pantheon. As indicated already, it cannot be substantiated that the ancients at the time of the New Testament themselves practiced any form of sustained rhetorical criticism as it has been practiced in New Testament studies—apart from the use of various ancient rhetorical handbooks and perhaps other means to teach rhetoric to the privileged few in the grammar schools. Similarly, the New Testament authors were not trained rhetors, and the original hearers/readers, so far as we can tell, did not see themselves as rhetorical critics. Therefore, because it has no privileged place within the ancient world itself, the use of ancient rhetorical analysis to examine the books of the New Testament has no interpretative precedence and does not give the interpreter any privileged access to the original meanings of ancient texts. If Paul's letters are indeed letters, as they purport and appear to be, they should be examined first as ancient letters, however else they may be examined. Indeed, on the basis of the fact that ancient rhetoric was not used in such a way at the time of the writing of the New Testament and did not include the New Testament authors and readers/hearers, such interpretation may in fact distort ancient literary works like Paul's letters. One might argue further that such rhetorical criticism functions at a distinct disadvantage to other, more modern types of reading strategies because it has fixed upon ancient categories instead of progressing in its theoretical development, as has, for example, discourse analysis. However, one need not go this far to recognize that ancient rhetoric may still be employed as a means of textual analysis. It is a possible though not exclusive or privileged form of reading an ancient text. There is little doubt that rhetorical criticism of all types will continue to flourish. Nevertheless, we must recognize that rhetorical criticism does not necessarily arrive at a better or more authoritative or more authorially grounded understanding of books of the New Testament. Rhetorical criticism can at best provide another reading, to stand alongside others.

References

Betz, Hans Dieter. 1974–1975. "The Literary Composition and Function of Paul's Letter to the Galatians." *New Testament Studies* 21 no. 3: 353–379.

Betz, Hans Dieter. 1979. *Galatians.* Hermeneia Commentary Series. Philadelphia, PA: Fortress.

Burke, Kenneth. 1973. *The Philosophy of Literary Form: Studies in Symbolic Action.* 3rd ed. Berkeley: University of California Press.

de Beaugrande, Robert, and Wolfgang Dressler. 1981. *Introduction to Text Linguistics.* London: Longman.

Classen, Carl Joachim. 2000. *Rhetorical Criticism of the New Testament.* Wissenschaftliche Untersuchungen zum Neuen Testament 128. Tübingen: Mohr Siebeck.

Kennedy, George A. 1984. *New Testament Interpretation Through Rhetorical Criticism.* Chapel Hill: University of North Carolina Press.

Mitchell, Margaret M. 2000. *The Heavenly Trumpet: John Chrysostom and the Art of Pauline Interpretation.* Hermeneutische Untersuchungen zur Theologie 40. Tübingen: Mohr Siebeck.

Norden, Eduard. (1898) 1995. *Die antike Kunstprosa.* 2 vols. Stuttgart: Teubner.

Perelman, Chaïm, and Lucie Olbrechts-Tyteca. 1969. *The New Rhetoric: A Treatise on Argumentation.* Notre Dame, IN: Notre Dame University Press.

Porter, Stanley E. 1993. "The Theoretical Justification for Application of Rhetorical Categories to Pauline Epistolary Literature." In *Rhetoric and the New Testament: Essays from the 1992 Heidelberg Conference,* edited by Stanley E. Porter and Thomas H. Olbricht, 100–122. Sheffield: JSOT Press.

Porter, Stanley E. 1997. "Paul of Tarsus and His Letters." In *Handbook of Classical Rhetoric in the Hellenistic Period 330 B.C.–A.D. 400,* edited by Stanley E. Porter, 533–585. Leiden: Brill.

Porter, Stanley E. 2013. "Hellenistic Oratory and Paul of Tarsus." In *Continuity and Change: Oratory in the Hellenistic Period,* edited by Kathryn Tempest and Christos Kremmydas, 319–360. Oxford: Oxford University Press.

Porter, Stanley E., ed. 1997. *Handbook of Classical Rhetoric in the Hellenistic Period 330 B.C.–A.D. 400.* Leiden: Brill.

Reed, Jeffrey T. 1997. "Using Ancient Rhetorical Categories to Interpret Paul's Letters: A Question of Genre." In *Handbook of Classical Rhetoric in the Hellenistic Period 330 B.C.–A.D. 400,* edited by Stanley E. Porter, 292–324. Leiden: Brill.

Robbins, Vernon K. 1996. *The Tapestry of Early Christian Discourse: Rhetoric, Society and Ideology.* London: Routledge.

Rowe, Galen O. 1997. "Style." In *Handbook of Classical Rhetoric in the Hellenistic Period 330 B.C.–A.D. 400*, edited by Stanley E. Porter, 121–157. Leiden: Brill.

Wendland, Paul. 1912. *Die Hellenistisch-Römische Kultur, Die Urchristlichen Literaturformen.* 2nd and 3rd ed. Tübingen: Mohr Siebeck.

Witherington, Ben, III. 2009. *New Testament Rhetoric: An Introductory Guide to the Art of Persuasion in and of the New Testament.* Eugene, OR: Cascade.

CHAPTER 52

RHETORIC AND ARGUMENTATION

FRANS H. VAN EEMEREN

ARGUMENTATION THEORY

BECAUSE argumentation involves justifying our views to others, and we happen to do so virtually from the moment we get up in the morning until we have our last communication of the day, it is a social phenomenon everyone is familiar with. Argumentation is not only involved in our exchanges with family and friends but also can, for instance, be encountered in professional meetings, legal procedures, political debates, and international negotiations. The significance of argumentation for conducting our lives is therefore evident.

More often than not, the propositions that are justified by means of argumentation are evaluative or prescriptive rather than purely descriptive. If the truth of a statement can easily be established ("Albany is the capital of New York State"), giving persuasive arguments will generally not suffice because a definitive proof will be demanded. Argumentation is required when conclusive evidence cannot be easily provided and a justification is called for as to why a certain standpoint should be accepted on reasonable grounds. This is particularly the case when an evaluative view ("*Lost in Translation* is not a good movie") or a prescriptive view ("You should definitely lose a couple of pounds") is at issue.

The observation that argumentation is prototypically used when the acceptability of a standpoint on reasonable grounds is at stake and a binding verdict cannot be given played an important role in the rebirth of argumentation theory in the twentieth century. In their theoretical proposals for a renewed argumentation theory, Stephen Toulmin and Chaïm Perelman and Lucie Olbrechts-Tyteca strongly emphasized that argumentation, rather than logical proof of a standpoint, is an effort to make a standpoint in a reasonable way acceptable to people who are in doubt. They thus returned to a theoretical tradition of dealing with argumentation that started in antiquity, had been continued for a very long time, but had been abandoned in modern times. According to the views propounded by Toulmin and the "New Rhetoricians," the formal logical treatment of argumentation was to be replaced by a discipline with a broader and different scope. In their zeal to declare logic irrelevant to the study of argumentation, these authors may have somewhat overstated their case, but they certainly succeeded in bringing argumentation into the limelight again in its full magnitude.

Since argumentation can never be completely covered by approaching it from a single disciplinary angle, be it logic, linguistics, psychology, or any other discipline, argumentation theory is by definition a multidisciplinary or—if the required constituents can be joined together—interdisciplinary enterprise. It is an enterprise calling for the development of descriptive as well as normative insights. Because the various kinds of argumentative practices that are to be studied represent an empirical reality, descriptive research is necessary to make clear how exactly these practices work. But because argumentation theorists are also out to determine to what extent argumentative practices can stand the test of criticism, normative research is also required to reach well-considered judgments concerning the quality of argumentation. Ideally, the descriptive and the normative research carried out in the realm of argumentation theory should, of course, be attuned to each other.

Argumentation theorists aim to develop the theoretical instruments necessary for adequately describing and standardizing the various kinds of "moves" that are instrumental in the great variety of argumentative practices (see van Eemeren et al. 2012). In this endeavor they pay systematic attention to factors pertinent to the production of argumentative moves as well as to factors pertinent to their analysis and evaluation.

In analyzing argumentative discourse it is, for instance, important to realize that for a variety of reasons argumentative moves are in practice often performed in an implicit or even indirect way. "Shouldn't you bring along an umbrella? Or do you want to get wet?" may then be said instead of, "I think you should take an umbrella with you, because otherwise you will get wet." Such complications make it necessary that in the analysis a systematic reconstruction takes place of the argumentative moves that are made in the exchange concerned.

In evaluating argumentative discourse it is also important to realize that the argumentative moves that are made in a particular discourse do not always have to agree with the standards of soundness that need to be maintained in a reasonable exchange. If, for instance, in "You should reduce your intake of sweets, otherwise you will never lose weight" the person addressed in the argumentation cuts short the exchange by retorting, "Hear who is talking, potbelly!" then there is something wrong, because by giving this response the interlocutor is silenced as a discussion partner. His advice might well be valid, of course, however fat he himself is. In judging argumentative moves, reasonable moves are to be distinguished systematically from moves that are fallacious.

Separate Renaissances of Two Related Paradigms

Argumentation research started in ancient Greece and reached its apex in Aristotle's writings. In his treatment of dialectic and rhetoric Aristotle discussed primarily the use of syllogistic and other forms of reasoning in argumentation. In antiquity the term *dialectic* was used in various ways, pertaining to different kinds of theoretical projects, but Aristotle used it to refer to argumentative discourse in critical dialogues between the protagonist of a thesis and an antagonist who is to be convinced. The term rhetoric refers to the argumentative use of *logos* (along with *ēthos* and *pathos*) as a means of persuasion in political, legal, and ceremonial speeches.

Aristotle appears to have envisioned a division of labor between the dialectical and rhetorical perspectives on argumentation, the one complementing the other. According to Hanns Hohmann, Aristotle views it as "a coordinate relationship . . . emphasizing the parallels between the two fields" (2002: 43). Other classical and post-classical authors seem to envisage a competition between dialectic and rhetoric. In some cases the dialectical perspective is the preferred one, in other cases the rhetorical. Cicero, for example, puts rhetoric first by subordinating dialectical insights to rhetorical ones, while Boethius sees dialectic as crucial because it provides the required methods of inference. Michael Leff summarizes these developments as follows: "The historical record is one of constant change as the identity, function, structure, and mutual relationship [of the arts of dialectic and rhetoric] become issues of argumentative contestation" (2002: 53).

Eventually, the competition between dialectic and rhetoric leads, at the end of the Middle Ages, to the annexation of important parts of rhetoric by the dialecticians, most notably invention (*inventio*) and arrangement (*dispositio*)—simply by transferring them to dialectic. In this way rhetoric was reduced to the style (*elocutio*) and delivery (*actio*) of argumentative texts in the *oratio*. In the sixteenth century the development that had started with the medieval takeover of parts of rhetoric by dialectic culminates in Peter Ramus's division of the field of activity into two separate disciplines. Rhetoric becomes exclusively the domain of the humanities, while dialectic is included in the exact sciences. When the Ramist division of the field comes to be viewed as ideological, the dialectical and rhetorical views of argumentation are regarded as different paradigms representing entirely different, and incompatible, conceptions of argumentation (cf. Toulmin 2001).

In this way, dialecticians and rhetoricians have become part of different academic communities, each with its own specific infrastructure of scholarly societies, conferences, journals, and book series. As a consequence of their separate development, the distinct intellectual contexts in which they operate, and the ideological division between them, a yawning gap between dialectic and rhetoric has come into being that prevents a constructive exchange of ideas. According to the dialecticians, the rhetoricians' concentration on individual cases and their synthetic approach do not lead to systematic theorizing about argumentation. According to the rhetoricians, the generic, procedural, and often formal approach of the dialecticians, abstracting from vital characteristics of actual communication, does not result in worthwhile insights concerning argumentative practice. Even when both dialectic and rhetoric experienced modern renaissances that led to the resurgence of argumentation theory as a field of study, the two perspectives on argumentation remained completely isolated from each other.

Due to the reshaping of logic by mathematics around the turn of the twentieth century, the dialectical study of critical exchanges disappeared from sight for some time, not only outside but also inside formal logic. In the 1960s and 1970s, however, several developments sparked a resurgence of interest in dialectic (bearing in mind that modern dialectic is only in a general sense related to classical dialectic). What these developments have in common is the idea that dialectic involves having a regulated critical exchange aimed at systematically testing the tenability of a standpoint.

First, in Germany Paul Lorenzen and other members of the Erlangen School instigated a dialogical approach to logic. In this approach, logical derivations are viewed as critical dialogues in which a proponent defends a conclusion presented as a thesis against the critical doubts of an opponent who accepts certain premises as concessions (Lorenzen and Lorenz 1978). Second, in an epoch-making monograph, *Fallacies*, Charles Hamblin (1970) developed in Australia proposals for critical discussion procedures, which he named "formal dialectic." Subsequently, in the Netherlands, Else Barth and Erik Krabbe (1982) exploited both Lorenzen's and Hamblin's ideas in their study, *From Axiom to Dialogue*, to create a formal theory of argumentation, also referred to as formal dialectic.

Barth and Krabbe's formal dialectic consists of systems of procedural rules for critical dialogues aimed at determining whether a thesis can be maintained in the light of the concessions of a doubting opponent. The rules of formal dialectic lay down which discussion moves are allowed, when a thesis is successfully defended by the proponent, and when it is successfully attacked by the opponent (see Walton and Krabbe 1995). Inspired by the theoretical example of formal dialectic, Frans H. van Eemeren and Rob Grootendorst (2004) developed in the 1970s and 1980s their "pragma-dialectical" argumentation theory. The dialectical dimension is given shape in a model of a critical discussion that serves as the point of departure when dealing with argumentative discourse, the pragmatic dimension in a characterization of the argumentative moves made in the discourse as speech acts performed in natural language. The model of a critical discussion specifies which types of speech acts and discussion rules are instrumental in resolving a difference of opinion in a reasonable way.

Opting for a dialectical perspective means that the reasonableness of an argumentative exchange is made central: to be acceptable, argumentative moves need to comply with the standards of soundness applying to a critical discussion. This means that the point of departure is, in principle, normative (see Johnson 2000; Finocchiaro 2005). The possibility of nailing down the fallacies is generally seen as the litmus test of a dialectical procedure: if a dialectical procedure enables us to distinguish systematically between sound argumentative moves and fallacious moves, the procedure is considered dialecti-cally adequate. Exactly which standards will be applied may vary from one dialectical argumentation theory to the other, but dialecticians are likely to agree that the retort, "Hear who is talking, potbelly," given in response to the advice, "You should reduce your intake of sweets, otherwise you will never lose weight," is a variant of the ad hominem fallacy known as *tu quoque*—"you too!"

A major impetus to the revival of the study of argumentation from a rhetorical per-spective in Europe was given by Perelman and Olbrechts-Tyteca's monograph, *Traité de l'argumentation: La nouvelle rhétorique*, published in 1958, the same year that Toulmin published *The Uses of Argument*. After an English translation was published in 1969, the influence of the "New Rhetoric" extended to North America as well.

Just as in classical rhetoric, in the New Rhetoric the notion of audience plays a pivotal role. It is postulated that argumentation is always designed to have an effect on those for whom it is intended. Argumentation is *persuasive* if it succeeds in securing the approval of a "particular audience," consisting of a particular person or group, and *convincing* if it may lay claim to the approval of the "universal audience," consisting of all reasonable people. The discursive techniques used in persuading or convincing the audience must in all cases be attuned to the intended audience. The New Rhetoric is calculated to pro-vide a systematic survey of all elements in argumentative discourse that play a part in the discursive techniques used to bring about acceptance of the claims defended.

Perelman and Olbrechts-Tyteca (1969) present an overview of the various kinds of starting points—facts, truths, presumptions, values, value hierarchies, and loci—that, if they are acceptable to the audience, can be used as the point of departure of argu-mentation. They also discuss the argumentative schemes that can be employed to make standpoints acceptable to the audience on the basis of these starting points. If the use of a discursive technique succeeds in connecting an acceptable premise by means of a par-ticular argument scheme with the standpoint at issue, the acceptability of the premise concerned is transferred to the standpoint. The New Rhetoric distinguishes three types of argument schemes that can be employed in such associative discursive techniques: quasi-logical argument, argument based on the structure of reality, and argument estab-lishing the structure of reality. If, for instance, the standpoint that Paul will like cheese is defended by means of the argument that he is Dutch, the unexpressed premise that the Dutch like cheese points to the exploitation of a scheme of argumentation based on the structure of reality.

Alongside the associative techniques just discussed, Perelman and Olbrechts-Tyteca distinguish the technique of dissociation, which is used to give certain words a new content that agrees better with the argumentative purposes of the speaker or writer. The process of dissociation involves differentiating a concept from the concept it was originally part of and entails the introduction of a division. Such a division is, for instance, achieved in the following dissociation: "What you seem to think of as *de-Christianization* is in fact *secularization*."

The New Rhetoric is, in principle, a descriptive theory of argumentation. It does not provide, from a critical angle, standards of reasonableness to which arguers ought to adhere. According to Perelman, the New Rhetoric can be seen as an attempt at creating a framework that unites all forms of nonanalytic thinking directed toward convincing people in ways that lay claim to rationality (see van Eemeren et al. 2012, ch. 5).

Modern Rhetorical Approaches to Argumentation

Although in the course of time the rhetorical perspective on argumentation has been constantly redefined, starting in ancient Greece with the sophists, Plato, and Aristotle, the focus has always been on effective persuasion of an audience. In the same spirit as the New Rhetoric, modern rhetoricians also tend to concentrate on the effectiveness of argumentative discourse. However, following Aristotle's view, rhetoric is considered to concentrate not on examining the actual achievement of persuasive effects but on identifying the means of persuasion that may be effective in a given case.

Most definitions given in handbooks confirm that rhetoric is about communication as a way of influencing people. According to Herbert Simons, "Most neutrally, perhaps," rhetoric is "the study and practice of persuasion" (1990: 5). This does not mean, however, that rhetoric as it is currently practiced is always about argumentation. In *The Sage Handbook of Rhetorical Studies*, Jan Swearingen and Edward Schiappa observe that American rhetorical theories have extended their scope in the twentieth century "to the point that everything, or virtually everything, can be described as 'rhetorical'" (Lunsford, Wilson, and Eberly 2009: 2). Andrea Lunsford, Kirt Wilson, and Rosa Eberly therefore describe rhetoric as "a plastic art that moulds itself to varying times, places and situations" (xix).

Even when the term "argumentation" is used, in American rhetoric its meaning is often much broader than in argumentation theory. It may involve justifying not only a standpoint on reasonable grounds by giving reasons in its support but also any characteristic of communication that can have a persuasive effect on the audience. This more diffuse conception of argumentation may be a consequence of the influence of the Isocratean rhetorical tradition. The inclusion, next to *logos*, of *ēthos* and *pathos* in the rhetorical study of argumentation is also part of the explanation. The fact that the meaning of the words *argument* and *argumentation* in English is rather undetermined in pertinent respects compared to that of their counterparts in other European languages may also play a part in this broadening of scope.

Due perhaps to a combination of holding on to cultural tradition and a democratic ideology requiring every citizen to be capable of taking part in public debate, rhetoric has survived in the United States much more robustly than in Europe. Kenneth Burke's claim that "wherever there is persuasion, there is rhetoric—and wherever there is 'meaning,' there is 'persuasion'" (1969: 172) instigated an unprecedented broadening of the scope of rhetoric ("Big Rhetoric"). "Identification," for example, came to be regarded

FRANS H. VAN EEMEREN   667

as a rhetorical phenomenon. New angles of research were pursued, such as feminist rhetoric. Scholars such as Jürgen Habermas and Michel Foucault (who never labeled themselves in this way) were without much ado incorporated into rhetoric (Foss, Foss, and Trapp 1985). According to Schiappa, few American scholars would nowadays object to categorizing a narrative analysis of George W. Bush's discourse about the Persian Gulf War, a psychoanalytic reading of the movie *Aliens*, and an analysis of visual iconography in the advertisement of "Heroin Chic" under the rubric "rhetorical perspective on argumentative discourse" (2002: 67).

In spite of the dilution of rhetoric, in the past decades interesting rhetorical analyses of argumentative discourse have been made, also, or even particularly, in the United States. These analyses are usually grafted onto the classical and post-classical tradition. In some cases they are accompanied by an in-depth exposition of the rhetorical framework in which the analysis takes place. A case in point is Jeanne Fahnestock's (1999) study, *Rhetorical Figures in Science*. Fahnestock explains convincingly how structural options available in a language can lead to specific lines of argument. Concentrating on the linguistic constructions called figures of speech, which in her view epitomize lines of argument with great applicability and durability, she provides a well-grounded rhetorical analysis of the use of antithesis, *incrementum*, *gradatio*, antimetabole, *plokē*, and *polyptoton* in historical cases of scientific argumentative discourse.

Another American scholar who has contributed high-quality rhetorical analysis of argumentative discourse is Michael Leff. He explains that the Aristotelian classification of deliberative, forensic, and ceremonial oratory is not simply empirical but also "establishes logically proper functions for audiences in different contexts and implies normative standards of obligation connected with the activity of rhetoric itself" (Leff 2002: 55). In "Lincoln at Cooper Union," Leff and G. P. Mohrmann (1974) had already illustrated how such rhetorical insights can be exploited in the analysis of argumentative discourse. Making use of the rhetorical notions of enactment, embodiment, and evocation, Leff (2003) demonstrates, in his analysis of Martin Luther King, Jr.'s "Letter from Birmingham Jail," just how illuminating an analysis that methodically exploits rhetorical insights can be.

Remarkably thorough and sustained case-based analyses of public argumentative discourse in the modern American rhetorical tradition are carried out by David Zarefsky, who supplements classical rhetorical insights with modern rhetorical insights whenever this seems functional. In *President Johnson's War on Poverty*, for example, Zarefsky (1986) examines how public policy can be put in a strategic perspective by discursive means. He concentrates on Lyndon Johnson's efforts to promote his "Great Society" by declaring "unconditional war" on poverty. The central question is how Johnson's anti-poverty program as laid down in the Economic Opportunity Act first gained such strong support and fell so far later on. Instead of blaming the negative effect of the war in Vietnam for this, as others did, Zarefsky looks for the answer to this question in the discourse concerning the war on poverty.

Zarefsky's thesis is that the rhetorical choices ensuing from the decision to call the struggle for abolishing poverty a "war" were instrumental in obtaining the passage of the Economic Opportunity Act but also in bringing about its destruction. He focuses primarily on the executive branch's attempt to persuade Congress to initiate and sustain the program (see Campbell and Jamieson, ch. 50). The symbolic choice made by calling the anti-poverty policy a war, and the symbolic choices that go with it ("soldiers," "enemy," "battle plan"), suggest a view of the world that puts all measures proposed in a specific perspective. This is why these choices play an important role in the process of public persuasion: since the symbols used define the issues in a way that highlights some aspects of the issues while diminishing others, they "evoke support or opposition by virtue of their association with an audience's prior experience and belief" (Zarefsky 1986: 5). As Zarefsky explains, in the case of the "unconditional war on poverty" the rhetorical choices that were made stimulated by their symbolic value both short-term rhetorical success and long-term rhetorical failure.

RECONCILING THE RHETORICAL AND THE DIALECTICAL PERSPECTIVES

In the second half of the twentieth century the dialectical and the rhetorical approaches to argumentation have completely and independently of each other been brought to flourish again. In practice, the watershed between the dialectical perspective, which is mainly chosen by logicians in philosophy departments, and the rhetorical perspective, which has virtually become the prerogative of departments of (speech) communication, is almost absolute. One harmful consequence of this gap is that problems for which a contribution from both disciplines is required cannot be resolved. Since a full analysis and evaluation of argumentative discourse can be given only if both its effectiveness and its reasonableness are taken into account, it is of vital importance that rhetorical and dialectical insights are systematically linked together. Recently, some important steps have been taken in this direction.

Perhaps simply because of inertia, most dialecticians and rhetoricians seem inclined to maintain the status quo: dialecticians generally stick to their dialectical approach without paying much attention to rhetorical considerations and the same applies, *mutatis mutandis*, to rhetoricians. All the same, there are now some rhetorical and dialectical scholars who acknowledge that the relationship between the two perspectives deserves our attention. Key figures in argumentation theory such as Perelman certainly did not object to combining rhetorical and dialectical insights, but their own efforts usually remained limited to emphasizing that both disciplines play a part in theorizing about techniques of argument and employing such techniques to convince or persuade people.

Some rhetoricians are in favor of cooperation but are reluctant to allow too much space to the counterpart approach for fear of seeing their own approach be taken in. Hohmann, for one, is afraid that rhetoric might become the "handmaiden" (2002: 41) of dialectic if the two disciplines were theoretically in any way combined. Leff, on the other hand, does not share this remarkable lack of confidence in the power of survival of rhetoric. Holding on to the historical division of labor between rhetoric and dialectic, he sees clear advantages both to rhetoric and to dialectic in reestablishing the old ties. Leff imagines that rhetoric and dialectic can correct each other's "vices" (Leff 2003: 62). As far as rhetoric is concerned, "effective persuasion must be disciplined by dialectical rationality," in particular when it comes to the detection of fallacies (62). In turn, rhetoric could preserve dialectic from fruitless circularity and infinite regress. Because in rhetoric argumentation is studied as it is situated in the specific communicative and interactional context in which it takes place, the application of dialectical rules can be connected with concrete points of departure so that the danger that the discussion may get "bogged down" can be averted.

In their approach to argumentation some scholars already combine the use of rhetorical and dialectical insights. Christopher Tindale (2004), for one, considers—in a Ciceronian way—the rhetorical perspective to be primary and aims at integrating dialectical (and logical) insights into the theoretical framework of rhetoric. Along the lines of Plato, Socrates, and Aristotle, others think that to create a framework for a critical analysis of argumentative practice it is recommendable to start from a dialectical perspective. According to the pragma-dialecticians, the latter option, for methodological reasons, is also to be preferred because it makes it possible to include the application of rhetorical insights in a more general and systematic theoretical framework. As van Eemeren (2010) explains in *Strategic Maneuvering in Argumentative Discourse*, the introduction of the notion of strategic maneuvering allows for a functional integration of rhetorical insights into the pragma-dialectical theory of argumentation.

The need for strategic maneuvering in argumentative discourse arises from the argumentative predicament that in every argumentative move that is made, aiming for effectiveness and maintaining reasonableness may be presumed to go together (van Eemeren 2010: 40–1). Analytically, in all argumentative moves three aspects of strategic maneuvering can be distinguished, which are realized simultaneously in argumentative practice: a selection from the "topical potential" of moves available at a particular point in the discourse; an adaptation to "audience demand"; and a choice of "presentational design" (93–6). The strategic design of the discourse can be systematically taken into account in analysis and evaluation by methodically integrating rhetorical insights concerning the aiming for effectiveness with dialectical insights concerning the reasonableness of argumentative discourse. The strategic maneuvering that takes place in argumentative discourse is directed at maintaining the delicate balance between effectiveness and reasonableness. If the balance is distorted because one or more of the standards of reasonableness incorporated in the rules for critical discussion is violated, a fallacy has been committed and the strategic maneuvering "derails" (196–200).

In *Lincoln, Douglas, and Slavery*, Zarefsky's rhetorical study of the Lincoln–Douglas debates in 1858, he concludes that these debates should first of all be appreciated "for the mastery that they reflect of the strategy and tactics of argumentation" (1990: 246). With the help of the pragma-dialectical theory as extended for dealing methodically with strategic maneuvering, it can be made clear what exactly this strategic argumentative acting involves in terms of the simultaneous pursuit of effectiveness and the maintenance of reasonableness. Instead of considering the rhetorical dimension independently, it is in this approach intrinsically connected with the dialectical dimension. What is gained in this way is not only that in analyzing argumentative discourse rhetorical considerations concerning the effectiveness of argumentative moves are now systematically interwoven with dialectical considerations concerning reasonableness in resolving differences of opinion but also that a firmer theoretical basis is created for a critical appreciation of the argumentative quality of the discourse. By thus bringing general dialectical principles of reasonableness to bear in dealing rhetorically with the effectiveness of actual argumentative practices, we have provided an interpretation of the relationship between rhetoric and dialectic that may come close to what Aristotle envisioned when, in the first sentence of his *Rhetoric*, he called the two disciplines each other's counterparts.

References

Barth, Else, and Erik Krabbe. 1982. *From Axiom to Dialogue: A Philosophical Study of Logics and Argumentation*. Berlin: de Gruyter.

Burke, Kenneth. 1969. *A Rhetoric of Motives*. Berkeley: University of California Press.

Fahnestock, Jeanne. 1999. *Rhetorical Figures in Science*. New York: Oxford University Press.

Finocchiaro, Maurice. 2005. *Arguments about Arguments. Systematic, Critical, and Historical Essays in Logical Theory*. Cambridge: Cambridge University Press.

Foss, Sonja, Karen Foss, and Robert Trapp. 1985. *Contemporary Perspectives on Rhetoric*. Prospect Heights, IL: Waveland.

Hamblin, Charles. 1970. *Fallacies*. London: Methuen.

Hohmann, Hanns. 2002. "Rhetoric and Dialectic: Some Historical and Legal Perspectives." In *Dialectic and Rhetoric: The Warp and Woof of Argumentation Analysis*, edited by Frans H. van Eemeren and Peter Houtlosser, 53–64. Dordrecht: Kluwer Academic.

Johnson, Ralph. 2000. *Manifest Rationality. A Pragmatic Theory of Argument*. Mahwah, NJ: Lawrence Erlbaum.

Leff, Michael, and G. P. Mohrmann. 1974. "Lincoln at Cooper Union: A Rhetorical Analysis of the Text." *Quarterly Journal of Speech* 60: 346–358.

Leff, Michael. 2002. "The Relation between Dialectic and Rhetoric in a Classical and a Modern Perspective." In *Dialectic and Rhetoric: The Warp and Woof of Argumentation Analysis*, edited by Frans H. van Eemeren and Peter Houtlosser, 53–64.

Leff, Michael. 2003. "Rhetoric and Dialectic in Martin Luther King's 'Letter from Birmingham Jail.'" In *Anyone Who Has a View*, edited by Frans H. van Eemeren, Anthony Blair, Charles Willard, and Francisca Snoeck Henkemans, 255–268. Dordrecht: Kluwer Academic.

Lorenzen, Paul, and Kuno Lorenz. 1978. *Dialogische Logik*. Darmstadt: Wissenschaftliche Buchgesellschaft.

Lunsford, Andrea, Kirt Wilson, and Rosa Eberly. 2009. "Introduction: Rhetorics and Roadmaps." In *The Sage Handbook of Rhetorical Studies*, edited by Andrea Lunsford, Kirt Wilson, and Rosa Eberly, xi–xxix. Los Angeles, CA: SAGE.

Perelman, Chaïm. 1970. "The New Rhetoric: A Theory of Practical Reasoning." In *The Great Ideas Today*, Part 3, 273–312. Chicago, IL: Encyclopedia Britannica.

Perelman, Chaïm, and Lucie Olbrechts-Tyteca. 1969. *The New Rhetoric: A Treatise on Argumentation*. Notre Dame, IN: University of Notre Dame Press.

Schiappa, Edward. 2002. "Evaluating Argumentative Discourse from a Rhetorical Perspective: Defining 'Person' and 'Human Life' in Constitutional Disputes over Abortion." In *Dialectic and Rhetoric: The Warp and Woof of Argumentation Analysis*, edited by Frans H. van Eemeren and Peter Houtlosser, 5–80.

Simons, Herbert, ed. 1990. *The Rhetorical Turn: Invention and Persuasion in the Conduct of Inquiry*. Chicago, IL: University of Chicago Press.

Swearingen, C. J., and Edward Schiappa. 2009. "Historical Studies in Rhetoric: Revisionist Methods and New Directions." In *The Sage Handbook of Rhetorical Studies*, edited by Andrea Lunsford, Kirt Wilson, and Rosa Eberly, 1–13. Los Angeles, CA: SAGE.

Tindale, Christopher. 2004. *Rhetorical Argumentation: Principles of Theory and Practice*. London: SAGE.

Toulmin, Stephen. 2001. *Return to Reason*. Cambridge, MA: Harvard University Press.

Toulmin, Stephen. 1958. *The Uses of Argument*. Cambridge: Cambridge University Press.

van Eemeren, Frans H. 2010. *Strategic Maneuvering in Argumentative Discourse: Extending the Pragma-Dialectical Theory*. Amsterdam: John Benjamins.

van Eemeren, Frans H., and Rob Grootendorst. 2004. *A Systematic Theory of Argumentation: The Pragma-Dialectical Approach*. Cambridge: Cambridge University Press.

van Eemeren, Frans H., Bart Garssen, Erik Krabbe, Francisca Snoeck Henkemans, Bart Verheij, and Jean Wagemans. 2012. *Handbook of Argumentation Theory*. Dordrecht: Springer.

Walton, Douglas, and Erik Krabbe. 1995. *Commitment in Dialogue: Basic Concepts of Interpersonal Reasoning*. Albany: State University of New York Press.

Zarefsky, David. 1990. *Lincoln, Douglas and Slavery: In the Crucible of Public Debate*. Chicago, IL: University of Chicago Press.

Zarefsky, David. 1986. *President Johnson's War on Poverty: Rhetoric and History*. Tuscaloosa: University of Alabama Press.

CHAPTER 53

....

RHETORIC AND SEMIOTICS

....

THEO VAN LEEUWEN

INTRODUCTION

THIS chapter explores the relation between rhetoric and semiotics, focusing especially on social semiotics. While the Paris school of semiotics in the 1960s and early 1970s engaged explicitly and extensively with rhetoric (Bremond 1970; Barthes 1977), particularly in relation to the image, the Michael Halliday-inspired Sydney school of social semiotics that emerged in the 1990s did so only implicitly and tangentially. The key term was "grammar," the key pursuit the development of "grammars" of individual communicative modes such as images (O'Toole 1994; Kress and van Leeuwen 2006), color (van Leeuwen 2011), the voice and music (van Leeuwen 1999; West 2009), nonverbal communication (Martinec 2000; Kress et al. 2001), space (O'Toole 2004; Stenglin 2009), objects (Björkvall 2009), and animation (Leao 2013). Yet Halliday's systemic-functional grammar, which served as the model for these grammars, effectively did away with the traditional separation between grammar and rhetoric and its modern equivalents, the separation between *langue* (language itself) and *parole* (the way language is used), and between semantics, syntax, and pragmatics. It sees language, and by extension other semiotic modes, as resources for social action, and linguistic structures as realizing social practices, including their communicative goals and their attendant social relationships, and it insists, at every turn, on connecting *langue* and *parole*, semiotic resources and their uses.

This chapter therefore attempts to make the rhetorical aspect of social semiotics a little more explicit, looking in particular at the theory of genre as a theory of arrangement, or *dispositio*, to use the terminology of classical rhetoric. In contrast to the Paris school, which focused on rhetorical figures and hence on style (*elocutio*), social semiotic genre theory can be understood as a new approach to *dispositio*. In his introduction to a collection of papers on rhetoric, Claude Bremond observes that "of the four or five parts of traditional rhetoric, only *elocutio* will benefit from a reworking [*véritable reprise*]. It is too early to say whether *inventio*, *dispositio*, *actio*, and *memoria* have entirely disappeared from our intellectual horizon or whether they are only waiting their turn to reenter the arena" (1970: 2; trans. mine). But as Bremond was writing this, the beginnings of that reentering were already emerging in genre theory, for instance in William Labov and Joshua Waletzky's (1967) theory of narrative.

This chapter will place particular emphasis on visual rhetoric, not only because this has been my main area of interest for the past 25 years but also because images have, in the main, been studied for what they represent and connote rather than for the social (e.g., persuasive) work they do in the world, and it could be argued that they play an ever-increasing role in persuasive communication.

THE PARIS SCHOOL

Already in *Mythologies*, Roland Barthes defined rhetoric as the *form* of "bourgeois myths," as "a set of fixed, related, insistent figures, according to which the varied forms of the mythical signifier arrange themselves" (Barthes 1973: 150). He discusses seven of these figures. The figure of tautology, for instance, is interpreted as a "magical" authority argument, akin to the way one replies, "'Just because, that's all' to a child who keeps asking for explanations" (153; trans. modified). In his 1964 "Rhetoric of the Image" (in Barthes 1977), a classic study because of its treatment of text-image relations, Barthes focused on advertising, a key persuasive genre. Again he defines rhetoric as "the signifying aspect of ideology," now adding that it is comprised of a "set of connotators" (Barthes 1977: 49) and that the study of rhetoric should therefore focus on the classification of rhetorical figures, in other words, on *elocutio*. He speculates about the use of rhetorical figures in advertising, suggesting that

> it is possible now to foresee that one will find in it some of the figures formerly identified by the Ancients and the Classics: the tomato, for example [in the Panzani advertisement], signifies *Italianicity* by metonymy and in another advertisement the sequence of three scenes (coffee in beans, coffee in powder, coffee sipped in the cup) releases a certain logical relationship in the same way as an asyndeton. It is probable indeed that among the metabolas (or figures of the substitution of one signifier for another), it is metonymy which furnishes the images with the greatest number of its connotators, and that among the parataxes (or syntagmatic figures), it is asyndeton which predominates. (50)

Jacques Durand's "Rhetoric and the Advertising Image" (1970) is an exhaustive classification along these lines, with a wealth of both verbal and visual examples, but without Barthes's emphasis on rhetoric as the signifier of ideology. Durand shows, for instance, how visual metonyms can substitute not only the part for the whole, as in a Mercedes Benz ad showing the car's hood ornament instead of the car, but also the effect for the cause, as in an Arthur Martin ad in which a refrigerator is represented as a block of ice in the shape of a refrigerator, or the cause for the effect, as in a wool ad in which the wool is replaced by the sheep. Visual *litotes*, or understatements, are also possible, for instance by presenting a blank page to indicate the lack of change in a product (Volkswagen, 1962) or using the absence of an advertisement to promote a product, as in "No ad today . . . " (*Advertising Age*, 1966) and "If you do not yet have a Burroughs calculator, we offer you this page for your calculations" (Durand 1970: 87). In the more than 40 years since Durand's paper first appeared little has changed, and examples of the more than 70 visual rhetorical figures he discussed can still readily be found in contemporary advertisements.

Three things should perhaps be said about this approach. First, Barthes insists that rhetorical connotators are "scattered" throughout the text. Persuasion is not achieved through argument, through rhetorical convincing, but through scattered signs that trigger "myths," those complexes of "commonsense" ideas that constitute ideologies, rather than explicitly formulating them. This made the new rhetoric, as conceived of in the Paris school (see also the work of Groupe µ [1992]), a *traité des figures* concerned primarily with rhetoric as *elocutio* and separate from other contemporaneous ways of taking up the rhetorical tradition, such as exploring persuasive communication in mass communication research (e.g., Klapper 1960), argumentation theory (e.g., van Eemeren and Garssen 2009), or the hermeneutic tradition (e.g., Gadamer 1989).

Second, Barthes's approach does not deal directly with persuasion, or, in Hallidayan terms, with "interpersonal" meaning. The primary focus is on the way ideas, "bourgeois myths," are communicated, not on communicative strategies as such, despite the prevalence of direct address, imperatives, and so on in advertisements, and despite the fact that, by the time Barthes published these ideas, speech act theorists had already emphasized the performative role of language. Only Bremond (1970), in an article titled "Le rôle d'influenceur" ("The Role of the Persuader"), discussed rhetoric as the realization of persuasive strategies, such as hedonistic (seduction) strategies, ethical (obligation) strategies, or pragmatic (advice) strategies, all of which he links to specific rhetorical figures.

And third, even though Barthes clearly put rhetoric back on the agenda of semiotics, his approach continued the negative attitude toward rhetoric that had developed since the eighteenth century. Rhetoric, in Barthes's work, is less a noble art of persuasion than ideological manipulation in need of unmasking.

Elsewhere, there were attempts to use Charles Sanders Peirce's model of the sign to classify rhetorical figures (Podlewski 1982). As Winfried Nöth suggests, Peirce's work is in principle well suited to incorporating the idea of persuasion because his notion of "thirdness" deals with the way signs are "rendered effective" as interpretants (Nöth 1995: 343). Peirce describes rhetoric as "the study of the necessary conditions of the transmissions of meaning by signs from mind to mind, and from one state of mind to another," and as the study of "the formal conditions of the force of symbols, or their power of appealing to a mind" (343). This clearly suggests a semiotic approach that can tackle the issue of persuasion head-on.

SOCIAL SEMIOTICS

Social semiotics started with Halliday's theory of language as social semiotic, and before discussing the application of his approach to other semiotic modes, it is useful to return to these beginnings. In contrast to the Paris school semioticians, Halliday mentions rhetoric only in passing, relating it mainly to the uses of language, as when he refers to "the rhetorical concept of expository, didactic, persuasive, descriptive, and the like" (Halliday 1978: 43–5). He conceives of this as part of "mode," a contextual variable that also includes the channel, for instance whether language is spoken or written, and, if spoken, mediated or face to face, etc. On one hand, this maintains the separation between grammar and rhetoric, but on the other it also defines their relation, for Halliday's contextual variables relate directly to the "metafunctions" of language, in this case the textual function and, via these metafunctions, to specific grammatical and discourse systems, in this case to "the internal organization of each sentence as a thematic construct and the cohesive relation linking one sentence with another" (222–4).

The relation between rhetorical purpose and grammar was more fully articulated by another functional linguist, Robert Longacre (1974). In his theory of genre he distinguishes four genres on the basis of their rhetorical purpose: the narrative genre; the procedural ("how to do it" or "how it is done") genre; the expository genre, which describes, explains, and interprets the world; and the hortatory genre, which aims to influence conduct, to get people to feel or think or act in certain ways. Longacre (1971) claims universality for these rhetorical purposes and studies examples from various societies, correlating the rhetorical purposes of entertaining, instructing, explaining, and persuading to the linguistic features that typically manifest them, as shown in table 53.1:

Table 53.1 Longacre's discourse genres

	–prescriptive	+prescriptive
+chronological	*Narrative*	*Procedural*
	1st or 3rd person	Nonspecific person
	Actor-oriented	Goal-oriented
	Accomplished time (encoded as past or present)	Projected time (encoded as past, present, or future)
	Chronological linkage	Chronological linkage
–chronological	*Expository*	*Hortatory*
	Any person (usually 3rd)	2nd person
	Subject matter-oriented	Addressee-oriented
	Time not focal	Commands, suggestions (encoded as imperatives or "soft commands")
	Logical linkage	Logical linkage

This schema clearly links rhetorical purpose to grammatical choices, albeit, Longacre insists, "deep structure" choices. For instance, in a procedural text, time is always "projected" or oriented toward the future because the task that is being explained has not yet been performed by the listener or reader. But this need not be realized by the future tense. A procedural text, for example, may take the form of a "case story" or "best practice example." On the surface it will then have the features Longacre described as typical of narratives. But a closer look would show that all the stages of a particular process are included, so that the text can serve as instruction just as surely as a straightforwardly procedural text. Such texts will then combine the entertainment function of narrative with the instructional function of the procedural text. Paraphrasing Halliday's concept of "grammatical metaphor," we could call this "generic metaphor."

How should the link between rhetorical purpose and grammatical choice be theorized? In *Language as Social Semiotic*, Halliday insists that context "determines" and "predicts" linguistic choices, as when he argues, for example, that the "properties of the situation . . . collectively function as the determinants of text" (1978: 110; cf. 141–2). Yet his terminology, moving from terms like "code" and "rule" to terms like "choice," "option," and "selection," carries at least a suggestion of agency. Later approaches to social semiotics foreground agency. Sign makers and sign interpreters, rather than abstractions, determine how rhetorical purposes will be realized, whether they are constrained by contextual rules (which of course are also made and enforced by people) or not. As formulated by Gunther Kress and Theo van Leeuwen, "Representation is a process in which the makers of signs . . . seek to make a representation of some object or entity, whether physical or semiotic, and in which their interest in the object, at the point of making the representation, is a complex one, arising out of the cultural, social and psychological history of the sign-maker, and focused by the specific context in which the sign is produced" (2006: 6). The same applies, for instance, to Martin Reisigl and Ruth Wodak's "discourse-historical" approach, in which the concept of "strategy" is fundamental: "By strategy we mean a more or less intentional plan of practices (including discursive practices) adopted to achieve a particular social, political, psychological or linguistic goal" (2009: 94). Van Leeuwen (2005: 53–66) has emphasized that semiotic constraints are imposed by the rules or tacit conventions that apply in specific contexts, and that such rules are not hardwired in semiotic systems but differ in kind and in degree of institutionalization and prescriptiveness on a scale that ranges from implacable rules to the influence of role models or experts or best-practice examples, or even to near total creative freedom.

In his theory of grammatical metaphor, Halliday (1985) also engaged with rhetorical figures and explicitly used the term "rhetorical transference" to explain the processes of metaphor and metonymy, which he saw as "incongruent" realizations. Nominalizations, for instance, are incongruent because they represent something that is in fact a process (and would therefore be "congruently" realized by a verb or verbal group) as an object, realized by a noun or nominal group. However, he does not link such figures to ideology and views them as stylistic variants, even if they do "contribute something to the total meaning" (Halliday 1985: 322) in that, for instance, the "totally congruent" may sound "a bit flat" and the "totally incongruent" somewhat "artificial and contrived" (324). For critical linguistics and critical discourse analysts, on the other hand, such metaphors *are* ideological. Nominalization, for instance, allows interpretation and agent deletion and can therefore introduce bias and obscure responsibility, as in a well-known example from Tony Trew, where, in 1975, an editorial in a Rhodesian newspaper described an event in Salisbury (today's Harare) in which the police shot dead 13 demonstrators as "a political clash" that "led to death and injury" (1979: 106). This reinterprets the confrontation between unarmed demonstrators and the police as a "political clash" and avoids overtly blaming police officers for shooting unarmed citizens instead of protecting them.

Genre

In his discussions of mode, Halliday also introduced the concept of genre. While Halliday refers to it only briefly, genre theory subsequently became a major paradigm in social semiotics (Martin 1992: 546; Eggins 1994: 25). The text below, a magazine advice column, can serve to illustrate the main characteristics of this approach. The right-hand column labels the speech acts that make up the text:

I lied on my CV	*Revealing a problem (confession)*
↓	
Should I come clean with my boss?	*Appealing for help (question)*
↓	
Yes	*Providing a solution (answer)*
↓	
But be prepared for the possibility of losing your job if you have a scrupulous boss	*Issuing a caveat (warning)*
↓	
The bright side: you will gain her respect if you speak up and accept your mistake	*Predicting the result (prediction 1)*
↓	
And having got this burden off your chest will help you focus better on your work	*(Prediction 2)*

A genre consists of a series of "stages" that are given functional labels such as "revealing a problem" or "appealing for help" to indicate the communicative work done by each stage. These stages may consist of one or more of the same speech act, as in the "prediction" stage above. The sequence of stages as a whole realizes a particular strategy for achieving an overall communicative goal, in this case the solution of a problem. Because each stage is homogeneous in terms of the communicative acts it contains, it will also be relatively homogeneous in terms of the linguistic features that characterize it; for example, the "problem" stage of an advice column will have the linguistic characteristics typical of the confession (at least in its "deep structure"), using declarative mood, first person, past tense, and a verb that expresses what is, in the context, considered to be a deviant action or state. Finally, some stages are optional, not absolutely essential to the achievement of the rhetorical purpose. In the text above, for example, the second prediction could be left out. However, if a "problem–solution" strategy is chosen, the text must at least contain one problem and one solution. Conceived of in this way, genres may not be argumentative structures, and they may not always be focused on persuasion, but they do realize a beginning–middle–end structure designed to fulfill a rhetorical purpose, and as such they can be considered to be a social semiotic approach to *dispositio*.

Three things may be said about this approach. First, it conceives of *all* communication as strategic. Even in Labov and Waletzky's (1967) analysis of narrative, a forerunner of the social semiotic approach, the stages are strategic: an "abstract" to entice the listener, an "orientation" to ensure that the listener is oriented, "evaluations" to ensure attention is maintained, and so on.

Second, it again raises the issue of agency. Genres are understood as designed to do a certain communicative job and, as fit for purpose and ready for use, as a kind of technology. However, the logic of genre is not an abstract but a culturally and historically situated logic that reflects a dominant view of all communication as strategic that should at least be open to social critical questioning. Depending on context, agents may use genres as resources in less determined ways. To paraphrase Mikhail Bakhtin, analysis would then focus on "the possible generic sources" of a given sign maker or interpreter, on their "generic contacts," and on the "interrelationship of tradition and innovation" (1984: 157). And where determination, or something close to it, does occur, so that genres do become prescriptive templates, this, too, should be looked at, not just in terms of communicative efficiency and effectiveness but also critically, in terms of agency and power, especially in contemporary forms of online communication that not only do not allow deviation from the prescribed format but even make it technically impossible. It may not be an accident that the development of genre theory coincided with the development of such online templates and that in the 1980s engineers studied the structure of interactions as assiduously as did linguists.

And third, generic structures can be realized in different modes or combinations of modes. Certain stages may be realized visually, others verbally. Recipes (Eggins 1994) typically start with an "enticement," such as "A typical Balkan dish and a glorious way to serve the biggest, most succulent mushrooms you can find." Enticements can be, and very often are, realized by pictures that show the dishes in all their succulence. The choice will again depend on context but also leave a degree of freedom for the designer. Recipes in magazines more often feature visual enticements than recipes in books, for example, and there are cultural differences as well. As Radan Martinec (2003) has shown, in English recipes the "instructions" (e.g., "Stir in the grated cheddar cheese") are usually verbal, while in Japanese recipes they are often visual. And it is equally possible that a given stage can be realized by a combination of modes, for instance by a picture and text. But because pictures often have an immediate and emotive impact, they can play a crucial role in persuasive communication:

FIG. 53.1 Kitchener recruitment poster (1917)

The famous Kitchener poster (Figure 53.1) shows how an image may convey a more direct and hard-hitting message than the words that accompany it. The verbal text, though it uses direct address, makes an indirect appeal in the form of a statement. It is, in Halliday's terms, a grammatical metaphor that lexicalizes the demand rather than "congruently" using an imperative. But the visual realization of this statement, with its large and bold "YOU," is more direct and emphatic. And the image, with its pointed finger and penetrating, unsmiling gaze, is direct and personalized, made all the more compelling and authoritative by the military uniform and the forbidding Prussian moustache. Together these signifiers create a complexly modulated speech act, or rather a "multimodal act."

The persuasive potential of images and of visual signifiers in general, the "image acts" or "visual acts" they can realize ("problems," "enticements," "instructions"), has barely been studied, and because speech acts and visual acts are the building blocks of genres, both rhetoric and social semiotics will benefit from further work in this area.

The ability of images to create emotional impact also brings out their potential for *pathos*. But sweeping statements should be avoided here because the image is equally capable of instruction, or of factual exposition, especially where spatial or spatially conceived relations are concerned. Semiotic modes are not inherently emotional or rational. They are what people, in specific social and historical contexts, want and need them to be. For some time images have, in many contexts, served mainly as embellishment and illustration. Today, visualizations may form the core text, with the verbal providing only fragmented annotation or comment, not only in printed and electronic texts but also in the PowerPoint-assisted oral presentations that have now become such a dominant mode of public speech. The dispositional structure of this form of public speech has barely begun to be analyzed (Zhao, Djonov, and van Leeuwen 2014), although commentators have suggested that it is ill suited to the kind of protracted argumentative structures that were once at the heart of public oratory (Tufte 2003).

This chapter has shown that looking at social semiotics through the lens of rhetoric, and at rhetoric through the lens of social semiotics, can open new perspectives and a rethinking of accepted frameworks. Social semiotic genre theory is an *ars bene dicendi*, though one in which well-formedness is reinterpreted as strategic effectiveness. It can learn from the tradition of rhetoric that generic resources need not be described as bony-structured templates fit for purpose and ready for use but as resources that can be used creatively to suit the needs and interests prevailing in a given context and a given instance. Rhetoric, similarly, can benefit from the detailed grammars of different semiotic modes developed by social semiotics, which make it possible to link visual acts just as surely to their grammatical realizations as verbal acts, thus providing a solid foundation for multimodal text analysis. Rhetoric has always understood the importance of performance (*actio* or *pronuntiatio*), including what we now call nonverbal communication, but today's technologies have radically increased the range of resources available for the performance of persuasive communication. All these considerations clearly point to the need for a dialogue between rhetoric and social semiotics.

References

Bakhtin, Mikhail. 1984. *Problems of Dostoevsky's Poetics*. Translated by Caryl Emerson. Manchester: Manchester University Press.

Barthes, Roland. 1973. *Mythologies*. Translated by Annette Lavers. London: Paladin.

Barthes, Roland. 1977. *Image, Music, Text*. Translated by Stephen Heath. London: Fontana.

Björkvall, Anders. 2009. "Practical Function and Meaning: The Case of IKEA Tables." In *The Routledge Handbook of Multimodal Analysis*, edited by Carey Jewitt, 242–252. London: Routledge.

Bremond, Claude, ed. 1970. "Recherches rhétoriques." Special issue, *Communications* 16.

Durand, Jacques. 1970. "Rhétorique et image publicitaire." *Communications* 15: 70–93.

Eggins, Suzanne. 1994. *An Introduction to Systemic-Functional Grammar*. London: Pinter.

Gadamer, Hans-Georg. 1989. *Truth and Method*. London: Sheed & Ward.

Groupe μ. 1992. *Traité du signe visuel: Pour une rhétorique de l'image*. Paris: Seuil.

Halliday, Michael. 1985. *An Introduction to Functional Grammar*. London: Edward Arnold.

Halliday, Michael. 1978. *Language as Social Semiotic*. London: Edward Arnold.

Klapper, Joseph. 1960. *The Effects of Mass Communication: An Analysis of Research on the Effectiveness and Limitations of Mass Media in Influencing Opinions, Values, and Behavior of Their Audiences*. New York: Free Press.

Kress, Gunther, Carey Jewitt, Jon Ogborn, and Charalampos Tsatsarelis. 2001. *Multimodal Teaching and Learning: The Rhetorics of the Science Classroom*. London: Continuum.

Kress, Gunther, and Theo van Leeuwen. 2006. *Reading Images: The Grammar of Visual Design*. 2nd ed. London: Routledge.

Labov, William, and Joshua Waletzky. 1967. "Narrative Analysis: Oral Versions of Personal Experience." In *Essays on the Verbal and Visual Arts*, edited by June Helms, 12–44. Seattle: University of Washington Press.

Leao, Gisela. 2013. "A Systemic-Functional Approach to Animation in Film Opening Titles." PhD diss., University of Technology, Sydney.

Longacre, Robert, ed. 1971. *Philippine Discourse and Paragraph Studies in Memory of Betty McLachlin*. Canberra: Pacific Linguistics.

Longacre, Robert. 1974. "Narrative versus Other Discourse Genres." In *Advances in Tagmemics*, edited by Ruth M. Brend, 357–377. Amsterdam: North Holland.

Martin, James. 1992. *English Text: System and Structure*. Amsterdam: John Benjamins.

Martinec, Radan. 2000. "Types of Process in Action." *Semiotica* 130 no. 3/4: 243–268.

Martinec, Radan. 2003. "The Social Semiotics of Text and Image in Japanese and English Software Manuals and Other Procedures." *Social Semiotics* 13 no. 1: 43–71.

Nöth, Winfried. 1995. *Handbook of Semiotics*. Bloomington: Indiana University Press.

O'Toole, Michael. 1994. *The Language of Displayed Art*. London: Leicester University Press.

O'Toole, Michael. 2004. "*Opera Ludentes*: The Sydney Opera House at Work and Play." In *Multimodal Discourse Analysis*, edited by Kay L. O'Halloran, 11–27. London: Continuum.

Podlewski, Regina. 1982. *Rhetorik als pragmatisches System*. Hildesheim: Olms.

Reisigl, Martin, and Ruth Wodak. 2009. "The Discourse-Historical Approach." In *Methods of Critical Discourse Analysis*, edited by Ruth Wodak and Michael Meyer, 87–122. London: Sage.

Stenglin, Maree. 2009. "Space Odyssey: Toward a Social-Semiotic Model of 3D Space." *Visual Communication* 8 no. 1: 35–64.

Trew, Tony. 1979. "Theory and Ideology at Work." In *Language and Control*, edited by Roger Fowler, Bob Hodge, Gunther Kress, and Tony Trew, 94–117. London: Routledge.

Tufte, Edward. 2003. *The Cognitive Style of PowerPoint*. Cheshire, CT: Graphics.

van Eemeren, Frans H., and Bart Garssen. 2009. "Analysis and Evaluation of Argumentative Discourse." In *Discourse of Course: An Overview of Research in Discourse Studies*, edited by Jan Renkema, 171–181. Amsterdam: John Benjamins.

van Leeuwen, Theo. 1999. *Speech, Music, Sound*. London: Palgrave Macmillan.

van Leeuwen, Theo. 2005. *Introducing Social Semiotics*. London: Routledge.

van Leeuwen, Theo. 2011. *The Language of Colour: An Introduction*. London: Routledge.

West, Tore. 2009. "Music and Designed Sound." In *The Routledge Handbook of Multimodal Analysis*, edited by Carey Jewitt, 284–293. London: Routledge.

Zhao, Sumin, Emilia Djonov, and Theo van Leeuwen. 2014. "Semiotic Technology and Practice: A Multimodal Social Semiotic Approach to PowerPoint." *Text and Talk* 34 no. 3: 349–375.

CHAPTER 54

RHETORIC AND PSYCHOANALYSIS

GILBERT CHAITIN

The psychoanalyst is a rhetor. To continue to equivocate, I'll say that he *rhetifies*, which implies that he rectifies. *Rectus*, the Latin word, equivocates with rhetification.

—Jacques Lacan, "Une pratique de bavardage"

JACQUES LACAN'S LINGUISTIC UNCONSCIOUS

"THE unconscious . . . is structured like a language" (Lacan 1993: 166–7). With this dictum, Jacques Lacan cemented the relationship between rhetoric and psychoanalysis. In statements from the 1950s through the 1960s, Lacan attributed the rhetorical functions of persuasion, indirect expression of the ineffable, and use of tropes and figures to the unconscious as Sigmund Freud had described it.

Interest in the relationship between rhetoric and psychoanalysis began as early as 1936 with the publication of I. A. Richards's *The Philosophy of Rhetoric* and its theory that metaphor, as "the omnipresent principle of language" (1965: 135–6) (rather than a deviation from a norm), forms the basis of transference in everyday life and in psychoanalysis. In his *Philosophy of Literary Form* (1941), Kenneth Burke (1966: 7–8, 66) connected Freud's dream mechanisms of "displacement" (*Verschiebung*) and "condensation" (*Verdichtung*) with the use of language in poetry, a view he later qualified by arguing that such substitutive devices are not specific to dreams or other unconscious mechanisms but inherent properties of language. The same year Suzanne Langer published *Philosophy in a New Key* (1941), which develops a theory of symbolization that approaches symbolic logic and psychoanalysis as two aspects of the same phenomenon. Freud had shown that dreaming, rituals, and myths are all languages through which the mind constructs symbols and metaphors for human experiences. Building on Freud, Langer argues that metaphor is the principle of linguistic evolution, for "where a precise word is lacking," a speaker will resort to "logical analogy" (1980: 139)—in other words, metaphor—to find an expression for what she means.

Whether through his own reading or indirectly through French sources like Henri Delacroix's *Le langage et la pensée*, these ideas made their way into Lacan's theory uniting structural linguistics, traditional rhetoric, and Freud's primary processes, above all in texts like "The Function and Field of Speech and Language in Psychoanalysis" (1953), "The Instance of the Letter in the Unconscious, or Reason since Freud" (1957), *Freud's Papers on Technique* (1953–4), and *The Psychoses* (1955–6). In *Freud's Papers on Technique*, Lacan uses Langer's terminology to describe repression as the "lacking word" (see Chaitin 1996: 82–9). The function of psychoanalysis thus becomes providing the "missing signified" for the "knots" or "nodal points" (Lacan 2006a: 223) of meaning of which symptoms and other unconscious formations are constructed. Lacan later specifies that symptoms are metaphors of the subject, in which "a spark flies" between "the enigmatic signifier of sexual trauma and the term it comes to replace in a current signifying chain" (Lacan 1998: 431). Metaphor fixes the unknown meaning that must be unearthed in order to resolve the symptom (431). Indeed, "The entire behavior of hysterics and obsessionals is structured like a language ... [it represents] his or her entire history ... speech ... whose meaning remains unknown to the subject" (475; all translations from the French are mine).

Lacan gives the definitive explanation of his rhetorical theory of the structure of the unconscious in "The Instance of the Letter in the Unconscious" and in *The Psychoses*. After rereading Ferdinand de Saussure's *Course in General Linguistics* and reading Roman Jakobson's important article, "Two Aspects of Language and Two Types of Aphasic Disturbances" (1956), Lacan assimilated his ideas about the rhetoricity of the unconscious with the view that all language operates simultaneously on two "axes" (Jakobson) or "slopes" (Lacan): the syntagmatic, or axis of combinations, which Lacan equates with metonymy and Freud's displacement—replacing one element with another; and the paradigmatic, or axis of similarities, which Lacan equates with metaphor and Freud's condensation—representing several things by a single thing.

Although, as Lacan acknowledges (2006a: 426), Freud never claimed a linguistic basis for the unconscious, it is clear that his description of neurotic symptoms and other products of the unconscious as "substitute formations" (*Ersatzbildungen*) (Freud 1957b: 154–6) adheres to the broad definition of metaphor as substitution. In dreams, the "manifest content" (the dream as it appears to the dreamer) stands for a more or less hidden meaning, its "latent content" (the dream thoughts), by virtue of the operation of the primary process mechanisms of condensation, displacement, and graphic representation.

In the attempt to put psychoanalysis on a scientific footing, Lacan proclaimed three principles derived from what many then considered to be the new science of structural linguistics: the signifier takes precedence over the signified; signifiers are meaningless in themselves; and the primary processes of the unconscious (displacement and condensation), like all linguistic operations, take place along the two axes of connection and substitution corresponding to the rhetorical tropes of metonymy and metaphor. The most significant principle is perhaps the precedence of signifier over signified, which Lacan designated, in mathematical terms, by the "algorithm" S/s. While adopting the language of de Saussure's linguistics, calling meaning the "signified" (*signifié*) and words "signifiers" (*signifiants*), he followed his friend Claude Lévi-Strauss in reversing the traditional system of priority: "Symbols are more real than what they symbolise; the signifier precedes and determines the signified" (Lacan 1987: 37; quoted in Roudinesco 1997: 211; see also 485, n. 28). This is a radicalized form of the antirepresentational view of language Lacan had been asserting since the end of World War Two (2006a: 135–6, 228–9, 415, 1988: 238).

Not only is the order of the signifier prior to and fundamentally separate from that of the signified—the condition symbolized by the bar between the "S" and the "s" in Lacan's algorithm—but its elements (the sound images or combinations of phonemes) are in themselves meaningless, which is precisely why they can acquire all sorts of meanings, as his example of the many usages of the word "tree" in "The Instance of the Letter in the Unconscious" is meant to demonstrate.

As for the third principle, Lacan (2006a: 434) observes that in *The Interpretation of Dreams* Freud used the term "transference"—whose roots are equivalent to those of metaphor (*metaphoros, translatio*)—to indicate what is essentially a metaphorical process: in order to reach expression, an unconscious idea must get itself "covered" (Freud 1999: 367) by a preconscious idea, usually a harmless thought generated by an event occurring the previous day. In customary usage, the force of a metaphor depends on the interplay of the meanings of the terms invoked. Lacan (1998: 196) insists, however, that metaphor is first and foremost a relation among signifiers.

Freud (1999: 210–1) gave a similar explanation of the relation between dream thoughts and their representation in dream images: the manifest content of a dream is in fact a rebus, a kind of puzzle in which the function of the images is not to denote their referents, their meanings, but to evoke the phonemes that form their names. These sounds then function like the alphabet, or syllabary, of a writing system, in that the images can be juxtaposed to form the sounds of other words—those that constitute the dream thoughts. Dreams, then, are a form of writing, if one accepts the traditional notion of writing as a system of marks that stand for the sounds of spoken language, a relation of signifier to signifier as well as of signifier to signified. It is this notion of the dream as writing, of dream elements as marks indicating phonemes, that gives rise to Lacan's concept of the "letter" operative in the unconscious emphasized in "The Instance of the Letter in the Unconscious."

Lacan attempts to capture the transferential relations among signifiers and their effects on signification, which occur with varying degrees of complexity in all unconscious processes, in his formulas for metonymy and metaphor (Lacan 2006a: 428–9, 434):

$$f(S...S')S \cong S(-)s$$

As Lacan explains, albeit in rather obscure language, metonymy preserves the bar between the series of signifiers in an utterance and its signifieds. That is, it prevents tying any one signifier to a specific signified because in structural linguistics signifiers acquire their function only through their difference from the other members of the set (the language) and because the meaning of a series of signifiers becomes fixed only retrospectively, at the end of the utterance. In principle, this can occur only at infinity—in other words, never (428; see also Borch-Jacobsen 1991: 181–2). If we read the "—" to the right of the congruence sign as a minus sign as well as a bar, we can see that Lacan is claiming that metonymy (Freud's displacement) subtracts meaning. In fact, Lacan is simply repeating here Burke's remark that when the dream element "house" is used as a displacement, it is actually "house minus" ([1941] 1967: 277), that is, it stands for something other than a house.

As might be expected, Burke notes that condensation operates in the reverse direction, since the dream element then represents itself plus other meanings, "house plus" ([1941] 1967: 277). And Lacan's formula for metaphor, which he equates with condensation, does indeed contain the plus sign (Lacan 2006a: 434):

$$f\left(\frac{S'}{S}\right)S \cong S(+)s$$

The left side of the formula indicates that metaphor involves the substitution of one signifier for another; the right side demonstrates that this substitution produces a new meaning, a crossing of the bar that results in a plus of signification (42). Lacan repeatedly calls this plus a poetic or creative effect and asks rhetorically: "What need is there to talk of a reality which would sustain the so-called metaphorical usages? Every kind of usage, in a certain sense, is always metaphorical" because "the emergence of the symbol [i.e., of language] *creates*, literally, a new order of being in the relations between men" (1988: 238–9). With Jakobson, Lacan saw metaphor as the essence of poetry; with Richards (1965: 92) and Langer (1980: 141), and in keeping with his anti-mimetic conception of language, he viewed poetic power not as a bizarre or decorative deviation from a linguistic norm but as an extension of the creative capability inherent in language.

THE RHETORIC OF THE SUBJECT

As a psychoanalyst, Lacan was especially interested in one kind of chain of signifiers: sentences of the type, "I am . . . " or "You are . . . ," in which one or more attributes is predicated of a (grammatical) subject in an effort to define the latter. It is in these cases that the loss of meaning Lacan ascribes to metonymy becomes a "lack of being" (*manque d'être*) (Lacan 2006a: 428, 439), a term he later changed to *manque à être* ("want to be") to emphasize that this lack provokes desire, and, first of all, the desire to be. Metaphor, on the contrary, produces a "being that appears in a split second in the emptiness of the verb 'to be'" (432). Here the being brought into existence by the metaphoric plus of signification is the subject.

In this sense, the essence of metaphor is not, as tradition would have it, a matter of comparison or similarity but of identification (Lacan 1993: 218). In his seminar of June 16, 1954, Lacan had already noted that Freud's metaphoric transference is a two-step process: "The signifying material, be it phonematic, hieroglyphic, etc., is constituted out of forms which have forfeited their own meaning and are taken up again in a new organization, thanks to which another meaning finds a means of gaining expression" (1988: 245). He reiterates this view in "The Instance of the Letter in the Unconscious" (Lacan 2006a: 430, 431): metaphor is a process involving both the connection and substitution characteristic of the two axes of linguistic functioning and, according to Jakobson ([1956] 1971: 93), of all thought and symbolic operations.

Lacan illustrates this point with his analysis of Victor Hugo's metaphor in the poem, "Boaz Asleep": "His sheaf was neither miserly nor spiteful." Here the attributes (meanings) "miserly" and "spiteful" have clearly been transferred from the human Boaz to the natural sheaf. The first stage of this process is metonymic, in that it depends on the property of contiguity we know as predication: "The transference of the signified, so essential to human life, is possible only by virtue of the structure of the signifier" (Lacan 1993: 226). The attributes of spite and avarice have been separated from Boaz by virtue of the syntactic positionality of the French (or English) language, which allows any noun (or pronoun) to occupy the place of subject of the verb "to be," thus keeping it separate from, but referred to, the attributes placed as predicate adjectives or nominatives. Here, then, is the metonymic loss of meaning. These separable qualities are then, by virtue of the metonymic structure of the signifier, displaced and reattached to the noun "sheaf," which is thereby identified with Boaz (219).

In the second phase of the process, the metaphor gains its force only because the signifier "Boaz" remains latent, beneath the overt subject (i.e., condensed within it). The primary new meaning created by this substitution of one signifier for another, in the context of the entire poem and the myth upon which it is based, is that of paternity, the miracle that befalls Boaz as the result of his lack of miserliness and hatefulness (Lacan 2006a: 423). But the point Lacan (1993: 225–30) stresses repeatedly in his seminar on the psychoses is that it is only on the basis of the metonymic structure of the signifier, before any meaning, that metaphor becomes possible.

Lacan's assertion that metaphor is a matter of identification rather than analogy is therefore the equivalent of his contention that the signifier takes precedence over the signified. The force of both claims is that metaphor has a non-mimetic function and that this function is non-mimetic precisely because metaphor is a constructive process. The symbolic transfer of signifieds involved in metaphor somehow creates new meanings rather than comparing ones that already exist. To the extent that these new meanings open up a new identity, a new mode of being for the subject, metaphor will be the trope of tropes, the "trope of destiny" (1991a: 372), as Lacan calls it in his seminar on transference.

Lacan maintains that there is a homology between the two senses of transference in Freud, the early transfer of meaning and the later motive force of the psychoanalytic process. In both cases it is a matter of metaphor, that is, of the substitution of one signifier for another that brings into existence a new meaning; in the relation between analyst and analysand, the new meaning is that of love (Lacan 1991a: 53). From the start, the analysand is in the position of a beloved person, in that the analyst is there for the patient's good, to worry about and care for him or her. This "manifest effect," as Lacan calls it, results from the relation of demand established by the patient's conscious request to be relieved of his suffering, to be cured. Not basically different from the relation of any patient to a doctor, it is that of suggestion, which Freud and Lacan interpret as identification via the ego ideal. But in analysis there is also a latent effect that derives from the operation of the unconscious, namely, the fact that the analysand does not know the structure of his desire but imputes such knowledge to the analyst as the "subject supposed to know." In supposing that his *agalma*, as Lacan calls the unknown object of desire, is in the analyst, the analysand spontaneously assumes the position of a lover. Hence, the metaphor of substituting the position of the lover for that of the beloved is fulfilled by the conditions that preside over any psychoanalysis.

As with any metaphor, according to Lacan there is a creative aspect to transference (Lacan 1991a: 206–7). What the subject is trying to produce by means of repetition in the transference is the latent object of his or her true desire, in the present, of which he or she remains unconscious. For in Lacan's view it is precisely through this object that the subject can find his or her own individuality: "And it is insofar as [the object] is overvalued that it has the function of saving our dignity as subject, that is, of making of us something other than a subject submitted to the infinite sliding of the signifier . . . something unique, unappreciable, irreplaceable. . . . Individuality consists entirely in the privileged relation in which we culminate as subject in desire" (203). The ultimate goal of Lacanian psychoanalysis is thus to use transference in order to find the analysand's true desire and thereby to establish his or her dignity as an individual.

By the 1960s, then, Lacan had assimilated virtually every key psychoanalytic concept to a rhetorical function: desire (Freud's *Wunsch*), symptoms, dreams, lapses, jokes, repression, the unconscious, the primary processes of condensation and displacement, and transference love and its effects in the seeming dialogue of the psychoanalytic situation. At the same time, with this move all language has, in a sense, become rhetoric, so that in saying that the unconscious is structured like a language Lacan is asserting both that the unconscious is structured rhetorically and that all discourse has an unconscious, because rhetorical, component.

Against Rhetoric

By the end of the 1950s Lacan began to modify his understanding of the rhetoric of the subject and to reject the idea that the paternal metaphor was a genuine metalanguage. At that time he took as his mantra, "There is no Other of the Other" (Lacan 2006a: 688). In his seminar on *The Ethics of Psychoanalysis* (1959–60), he expressed the view that the

goal of desire is precisely to remain unsatisfied; metaphor and metonymy serve the pleasure principle as the means for avoiding, for occulting, the drive toward satisfaction,
what he now called *jouissance* (see Nobus 1998). There is a "central zone" that is "forbidden, because pleasure would be too intense there," and this is the "field of *jouissance*, of
bodily pleasure" (Lacan 2006b: 224). The metonymic motion along the chain of signifiers of the current symbolic system, substituting a series of objects for the lost original,
maternal object of desire, is now a wild goose chase that serves only to subjugate the
subject, to induce him or her to chase after the goods open to anyone in consumer society like slaves of capitalism (Miller 1990: 26; Lacan 1991b: 122–4). No longer the medium
for establishing the identity, the being of the subject, the symbolic has now become the
ultimate melting pot, the realm of the universal in which all are the same. Following
this logic to its conclusion, Lacan eventually would claim that the prohibition of the
mother, the incest taboo, was simply one metaphorization of the interdiction of the field
of intolerable *jouissance* and thus contingent on our historical and cultural epoch. As a
result, the Oedipus complex itself also becomes a contingent phenomenon appended to
this identification of the mother with the field of *jouissance* (Lacan 2006b: 277). Thus,
Lacan's use of "letters" as symbols is also at least quasi-mathematical: while it is true
that they do not authorize a mathematical operation, it is also true that, like algebraic
variables, S_1 and S_2 depart from the meaning they start out from, namely, the mother and
father or their substitutes, to take on many values.

In his seminar on *Transference* the year after *The Ethics of Psychoanalysis* seminar,
Lacan likewise altered his notion of the Other along the same lines, now asserting that
the Other, the symbolic order, is incomplete precisely because it lacks the signifier of
jouissance, and that Big Phi stands for this lack. This also implies that symptoms can no
longer be resolved completely by talking, since there is now something in them that is
outside the universalizing function of the field of signifiers: namely, the type of *jouissance* specific to the individual subject and represented by the a-object at the center of
the forbidden zone, which has now become the dwelling of the subject's particular identity and dignity (Lacan 1991a: 278; Miller 1994: 80–3). The exclusion of *jouissance* from
the Other is Freud's "primal repression" (*Urverdrängung*). Barred from the symbolic,
"The first effect of repression is that it [*jouissance*] speaks of something other. That is
the motive force [*ressort*] of metaphor" (Lacan 1975a: 57). In other words, metaphor, the
substitution of another signifier for the missing one of the *Urverdrängung*—of the other,
nonphallic *jouissance*—is now a force for repression rather than the source of healing, as
in the earlier theory of the 1950s. Now Lacan understands the function of the paternal
metaphor, of the Other and the unconscious structured like a language, to be the exclusion, the barring of the field of *jouissance* by the invocation of the phallus. There are
thus two types of *jouissance*: the tamed, phallic enjoyment and the intolerable *jouissance*
excluded from the Other (Lacan 1975a: 56–7, 2006b: 277).

In his last years, starting with his seminar on James Joyce titled *Le sinthome* (1975–6),
Lacan reinstated poetry and rhetoric as the key players in the psychoanalytic process.
At the heart of this turn were his changing and seemingly contradictory views on the

relation between *jouissance* and the signifier, that is, between the singularity, the uniqueness of the individual, and the symbolic, the set of signifiers that always have universalizable meanings.

In the Joyce seminar, Lacan (1976b: 8) states that the real, the realm of *jouissance*, both has *and* does not have a meaning/make sense (*sens*), and he plays on *jouissance*, forming it into "*J'ouis-sens*," "I hear meaning" (1976a: 16). In *Vers un significant nouveau*, his seminar of May 1977, he asserts that "the real takes shape [*se dessine*] as excluding meaning [*le sens*]" (Lacan 1977b: 9); then, a few lines later, he declares that "symptoms are real. They are even the only things that are truly real; that is, which preserve a meaning [*sens*] in the real. Indeed, it is for that reason the psychoanalyst can, if he's lucky, 'intervene symbolically to dissolve it in the real'" (9).

This new type of intervention will resemble the poetic process in that the analyst will play on the ambiguity of language (Lacan 1977c: 8). His only weapon against the symptom is "*l'équivoque*"—double meaning, equivocation—because *l'équivoque* is the only method of interpretation capable of liberating the *sinthome* (Lacan 1975b: 7). Lacan now translates the German for unconscious, *Unbewußt*, as *Une-bévue* (a blunder), playing on and distorting the sound of the word while referring to the lapses that signal the intervention of the Freudian unconscious. The new method is designed to respond to the blunders that signal the real unconscious. Jacques Alain Miller (2003: 39) asserts that this is the key to the later Lacan: the blunder, the lapse, before it is interpreted, before it is given a meaning, is the real unconscious.

Referring to Jakobson's writings on poetics, Lacan now argues that metaphor and metonymy contribute to interpretation only to the extent that they prepare the way for "something other" (1977d: 16) that unifies sound and meaning. The analyst has to surmount the two slopes of the signifier as a system of oppositions. Interpretation is no longer a matter of articulated logic, of mathematical formalization, as it was during his second phase ending with Seminar XX, *Encore* (1972–3). Now it is a manipulation of language rather than an insight into hidden meaning; its method is a knowing how (*savoir faire*) rather than a knowing that (*savoir*) (Lacan 1976c: 6–7). That is why he worked at the time with knots, which could be manipulated but for which there were no algorithms (Miller 2003: 37).

Lacan (1977d: 8) now accepted the formalist and structuralist view of poetic language as doing violence to the linguistic usages built up over the course of a language's historical development. By going against usage instead of creating new meanings, poetry produces a "new signifier" (Lacan 1977d: 11), language that avoids meaning, that creates a void of meaning, empty words (*le mot vide*). In this sense, poetry resembles wit in that it "crumples language up" (*le chiffonne*) a bit, "and it's in this crumpling up that its operative effect resides" (21).

Poetic interpretation thus uses the signifier to escape from the symbolic. In this way, according to Lacan, it resembles love. That is, while the new signifier has no meaning in the sense of accepted usage or dictionary meaning, it does have significance (*de la signification*) (Lacan 1977d: 11). Here Lacan presumably means that the poet, like the lover, aims toward the inexpressible uniqueness of the individual, the singularity that is "outside the limits of the Law," beyond the symbolic, in the terms Lacan used in *The Four Fundamental Concepts of Psychoanalysis* (1977a: 276).

In sum, in his first seminars of the 1950s, the aim of psychoanalysis was to create a new *signified*; in the middle period, the goal was mathematical *formalization*; and in Lacan's later teaching, starting from *Le sinthome*, the objective was to create a new *signifier* (see Miller 2003).

IDEOLOGICAL CRITIQUES

After the publication of *Écrits* in 1966, several prominent linguists, philosophers, and literary scholars criticized Lacan's rhetoric of the unconscious, claiming that he had misrepresented or misunderstood structural linguistics in that his arguments showed only that the primary processes are homologous to rhetorical tropes and figures, not that they are basic constituents of language, understood in terms of de Saussure's *langue* (Benveniste 1966; Todorov 1977; Lyotard 1989; Borch-Jacobsen 1991). This type of critique culminated in David Macey's (1988) saturation bombing of Lacan's linguistics in *Lacan in Contexts*. In fact, Lacan (1975a: 20–3) had already acknowledged this mistake when he coined the term *linguisterie* in December 1972: the signifiers he had in mind when asserting that the unconscious is structured like a language were not on the level of the word but on that of the sentence, the proverb, or other larger units.

Those who place the primary processes firmly in the camp of style rather than *langue* are implicitly struggling to purify the science of linguistics from any taint of poetry. Positivist readers of "The Instance of the Letter in the Unconscious" make this aim explicit, arguing that the tree passage is "an obviously 'poetical' deviation from the style of 'coherent arguments' which form the main thread of the essay. . . . To the extent that it threatens the discourse of truth, poetry thus appears as an infringement of the standards of professional ethics, and as a menace to the status of psychoanalysis as a scientific discipline" (Chaitin 1996: 15–6).

If to the positivists the tree passage appears to violate the proper separation of the frivolous from the scientific, for the deconstructionists, on the contrary, it represents an unwelcome reassertion of the primacy of truth over the play of language (see Chaitin 1996). In privileging metaphor over metonymy, Lacan is reinforcing the imprisoning effect of traditional fixed meaning instead of supporting the liberation they associate with the movement of *différance* (Lacoue-Labarthe and Nancy 1973: 78, 143). In fact, Jacques Derrida (1988: 184–5) argues that it is patriarchal truth, the priority of the paternal metaphor over the maternal and the feminine, that Lacan asserts. Feminist thinkers such as Luce Irigaray (1985: 109–10) have similarly argued that the priority Lacan assigns to metaphor has contributed to the subjugation of women.

Jane Gallop (1985: 128–9) observes, however, that in "The Instance of the Letter in the Unconscious" the greatest privilege of metaphor is its constant association with freedom, whereas metonymy is linked with servitude. At stake in the disputes with deconstruction and feminism here are thus radically divergent notions of liberty. For Lacan, the fixing of meaning via (the paternal) metaphor signified the establishment of freedom from enslavement to nature, as to the unknown desire of the Mother, by induction into the field of language and thus of culture.

Conclusion: The Psychoanalysis of Persuasion

From its inception, the rhetoric of meaning, of representation, has been developed to serve the larger purpose of persuasion, especially in the cultural fields of forensic and political argumentation, where freedom and coercion are at stake (see White 1982; Patterson 1990; Møller 1991). In psychoanalysis, these issues arise most directly in the operation of transference, as Lacan (2006a: 222) pointed out in "The Function and Field of Speech and Language in Psychoanalysis." In an interview with an anonymous psychoanalyst, Joachim Dyck (1989: 103) asks: Is transference a persuasive and thus rhetorical operation whose aim is to influence and even to coerce the analysand's acceptance of interpretations and eventually of action? Or does the analyst remain a totally disinterested, non-judgmental, "absolutely neutral" listener, thereby preserving and enhancing the analysand's freedom? The predictable conclusion is that while psychoanalysis ideally aims to establish a certain autonomy in the patient, in reality it also uses rhetoric to a certain extent.

Dyck's position is predicated on the belief in the existence of the person's "true self" (1989: 98), a belief not shared by the Lacanians Barbara Biesecker discusses in "Rhetorical Studies and the 'New' Psychoanalysis: What's the Real Problem? or Framing the Problem of the Real." Making use of the Lacanian concepts of the subject, the signifier, and the real, this "new psychoanalysis" produces rhetorical theory and criticism that is better equipped to account for the "affective and libidinal investments" (Biesecker 1998: 235) essential to ideological persuasion to "attitude and action" than the analysis of social, political, and cultural forces customary in rhetorical studies. Abandoning the humanistic notion of the self and the concomitant theory of ideology as false consciousness or "the illusory representation of reality," the "new" psychoanalysis "rerout[es] the question of symbolic actions and *their effects* through the dialectic of desire" (235), analyzing the pseudo-transcendent real excluded from the social symbolic, which does not exist but produces effects nevertheless. In short, this new psychoanalysis aims not simply at ideological critique but also at progressive political and social action. Lacanian analysis thus continues to give rise in the twenty-first century to rhetorical studies capable of accounting for the mobilization and manipulation of the affective components of political, social, and ethical ideologies, based on the concepts of the subject, *jouissance*, and the real operating in the dialectic of desire.

REFERENCES

Benveniste, Émile. 1966. *Problèmes de linguistique générale*. Paris: Gallimard.

Biesecker, Barbara A. 1998. "Rhetorical Studies and the 'New' Psychoanalysis: What's the Real Problem? or Framing the Problem of the Real." *Quarterly Journal of Speech* 84: 222–259.

Borch-Jacobsen, Mikkel. 1991. *Lacan, The Absolute Master*. Stanford, CA: Stanford University Press.

Burke, Kenneth. 1966. *Language as Symbolic Action*. Berkeley: University of California Press.

Burke, Kenneth. (1941) 1967. *The Philosophy of Literary Form*. Baton Rouge: Louisiana State University Press.

Chaitin, Gilbert D. 1996. *Rhetoric and Culture in Lacan*. Cambridge: Cambridge University Press.

Derrida, Jacques. 1988. "The Purveyor of Truth." In *The Purloined Poe*, edited by John P. Muller and William J. Richardson, 173–213. Baltimore, MA: Johns Hopkins University Press.

Dyck, Joachim. 1989. "Rhetoric and Psychoanalysis." *Rhetoric Society Quarterly* 19.2: 95–104.

Freud, Sigmund. 1957b. "The Unconscious." *Standard Edition*. Vol. 14. London: Hogarth.

Freud, Sigmund. 1999. *The Interpretation of Dreams*. Translated by Joyce Crick. New York: Oxford University Press.

Gallop, Jane. 1985. *Reading Lacan*. Ithaca, NY: Cornell University Press.

Irigaray, Luce. 1985. *This Sex Which Is Not One*. Ithaca, NY: Cornell University Press.

Jakobson, Roman. (1956) 1971. "Two Aspects of Language and Two Types of Aphasic Disturbances." In *Fundamentals of Language*, edited by Roman Jakobson and Morris Halle, 69–96. The Hague: Mouton.

Lacan, Jacques. 1966. *Écrits*. Paris: Le Seuil.

Lacan, Jacques. 1975a. *Le séminaire, Livre XX, Encore*. Paris: Le Seuil.

Lacan, Jacques. 1975b. *Le sinthome. Ornicar?* 6 (November 18): 3–11.

Lacan, Jacques. 1976a. *Ornicar?* 7 (January 13): 10–17.

Lacan, Jacques. 1976b. *Ornicar?* 10 (April 13): 5–12.

Lacan, Jacques. 1976c. "L'insu que sait de l'une-bévue s'aile à mourre." *Ornicar?* 12/13 (November 16): 4–16.

Lacan, Jacques. 1977a. *The Four Fundamental Concepts of Psychoanalysis*. Translated by Alan Sheridan. New York: Norton.

Lacan, Jacques. 1977b. *Ornicar?* 17/18 (May 10): 1–23.

Lacan, Jacques. 1977c. "Une pratique de bavardage." *Ornicar?* 19: 5–9.

Lacan, Jacques. 1977d. "Vers un significant nouveau." *Ornicar?* 17/18: 7–23.

Lacan, Jacques. 1988. *The Seminar of Jacques Lacan, Book I, Freud's Papers on Technique*. Translated by John Forrester. New York: Norton.

Lacan, Jacques. 1991a. *Le séminaire, Livre VIII, Le transfert*. Paris: Le Seuil.

Lacan, Jacques. 1991b. *Le séminaire, Livre XVII, L'envers de la psychanalyse*. Paris: Le Seuil.

Lacan, Jacques. 1993. *The Seminar of Jacques Lacan, Book III, The Psychoses*. Translated by Russell Grigg. New York: Norton.

Lacan, Jacques. 1998. *Le séminaire, Livre V, Les formations de l'inconscient*. Paris: Le Seuil.

Lacan, Jacques. 2006a. *Écrits*. Translated by Bruce Fink. New York: Norton.

Lacan, Jacques. 2006b. *Le séminaire, Livre XVI, D'un Autre à l'autre*. Paris: Le Seuil.

Lacoue-Labarthe, Philippe, and Jean-Luc Nancy. 1973. *Le titre de la lettre: une lecture de Lacan*. Paris: Éditions Galilée.

Langer, Suzanne K. 1980. *Philosophy in a New Key*. Cambridge, MA: Harvard University Press.

Lyotard, Jean-François. 1989. "The Dream-Work Does Not Think." In *The Lyotard Reader*, edited by Andrew Benjamin, 19–53. Padstow: Basil Blackwell.

Macey, David. 1988. *Lacan in Contexts*. London: Verso.

Miller, Jacques-Alain. 1990. "A Reading of Some Details in *Television* in Dialogue with the Audience." *Newsletter of the Freudian Field* 4.1/2: 4–30.

Miller, Jacques-Alain. 1994. "Extimité." In *Lacanian Theory of Discourse: Subject, Structure, and Society*, edited by Mark Bracher et al., 74–87. New York: New York University Press.

Miller, Jacques-Alain. 2003. "Lacan's Later Teaching." *Lacanian Ink* 21: 4–41.

Møller, Lis. 1991. *The Freudian Reading: Analytical and Fictional Constructions*. Philadelphia: University of Pennsylvania Press.

Nobus, Dany. 1998. *Key Concepts of Lacanian Psychoanalysis*. London: Rebus.

Patterson, Gordon. 1990. "Freud's Rhetoric: Persuasion and History in the 1909 Clark Lectures." *Metaphor and Symbolic Activity* 5.4: 215–233.

Richards, I. A. 1965. *The Philosophy of Rhetoric*. New York: Oxford University Press.

Roudinesco, Élisabeth. 1997. *Jacques Lacan*. New York: Columbia University Press.

Todorov, Tzvetan. 1977. *Théories du Symbole*. Paris: Le Seuil.

White, Hayden. 1982. *Tropics of Discourse*. Baltimore, MD: Johns Hopkins University Press.

CHAPTER 55

RHETORIC AND DECONSTRUCTION

PAUL ALLEN MILLER

> In a certain sense Socrates and the Sophists held the same position . . .
> Socrates actually struck at their very roots by carrying through their posi-
> tion, by destroying the halfness in which the Sophists set their minds at
> ease, so that Socrates by defeating the Sophists was thereby in a certain
> sense himself the greatest Sophist.
>
> —Søren Kierkegaard, *The Concept of Irony*

In "Plato's Pharmacy," Jacques Derrida demonstrates the way the ambivalent signifier *pharmakon*, meaning both poison and medicine, deconstructs the opposition
between speech and writing that subtends the *Phaedrus*. This opposition, he argues, is
based upon an even more fundamental opposition between internality and externality (Derrida 1981: 103). Speech is the reflection of truth because it emanates from the
inside and is directly present to consciousness. Writing, on the other hand, is secondary
and derivative, existing as an externalization of a prior moment of interiority, namely, of
thought as silent speech (Stoekl 1992: 201). The deconstruction of the priority of speech
over writing is a deconstruction of the priority of truth over its external and derivative
manipulation through formalized practices of speech and writing: rhetoric. Rhetoric is
associated throughout the Platonic corpus with the sophists and is generally opposed
to philosophy defined as the pursuit of truth. Derrida's deconstructive reading of the
opposition between speech and writing in the *Phaedrus* demonstrates that, in effect,
Plato himself deconstructs the opposition between rhetoric and philosophy by deploying philosophy's initial, constitutive trope—Socratic irony—as figured by the duplici-
tous *pharmakon*. The result is that rather than philosophy and rhetoric being mutually
exclusive alternatives, each becomes a moment within the other that can never be fully
sublimated. Philosophy, on this view, I contend, is less a policing of the borders of discourse than a series of persuasive interventions in the ongoing dialogue that constitutes
the movement of truth in time.

More precisely, in "Plato's Pharmacy" Derrida argues that writing as a *pharmakon* becomes the deconstructive hinge around which truth and philosophy are articulated in their opposition to sophistry and rhetoric. The *Phaedrus* thus becomes the site in which rhetoric and philosophy are constituted as opposed practices that nonetheless assume and depend on each other. This dialogue occupies a crucial position in the history of philosophy and rhetoric, and it is no accident that Cicero begins *De oratore* by having Scaevola say, "Why don't we imitate that Socrates who is in Plato's *Phaedrus*?" (*Cur non imitamur Socratem illum qui est in Phaedro Platonis?* [Cicero, *De oratore* 1.7.27]). The speakers then contend, first, that humans excel animals insofar as they come together in speech (1.8.32); second, that Plato only makes philosophy triumph over rhetoric in *Gorgias* because he is the superior orator (1.11.47); and finally, that the superior orator must be more desirous of the truth than contention (1.11.48). In short, according to Cicero's reading of the *Phaedrus*, the ideal orator is the pinnacle of human achievement precisely owing to his participation in rational discourse. The philosopher can assert his primacy over the rhetorician only insofar as he is himself the ideal orator, and in that capacity he must be the image of the wise man (*sophos*) of the philosophical tradition. Thus, while Derrida's concentration on the *pharmakon* deconstructs the opposition between rhetoric and philosophy, the simultaneous assertion and dismantling of this opposition is as old as the practices themselves and central to rhetoric's self-definition (Rorty 1989: 134).

In this chapter, I first look at Derrida's definition of the sophist and sophistry in "Plato's Pharmacy." I then examine Derrida's treatment of Socratic irony in relation to the problem of truth. Finally, I read a passage in *Phaedrus* that puts into question the possibility of truth as a form of presence rigorously separated from external repetition and hence from rhetorical manipulation. Over the course of these three movements, I outline a concept of ironic philosophy and rhetoric that does not allow them either to be thought separately or considered identical. Rather, it asks, in the manner of Cicero's Scaevola, *Cur non imitamur Socratem illum qui est in Phaedro Platonis?*

Rhetoric and Myth

While Plato's discussion of the sophists and the teaching of rhetoric is scattered throughout *Phaedrus*, the first reference to the *sophistai* occurs near the beginning. To Phaedrus's question as to whether he accepts the myth concerning Boreas's kidnapping of Oreithyia, Socrates responds that to distrust it would mean to accept the kind of rationalizing account offered by the sophists: "But if I were to disbelieve it, as do the wise [*hoi sophoi*], I would not be strange, but then acting like a sophist [*sophizomenos*] I would say that Boreas (the North Wind) took her over the nearby rock, while she was playing with Pharmaceia and thus she is said to have died with Boreas taking her" (Plato, *Phaedrus* 229c6–d1).[1] Socrates does not have time for such endless speculations (230a1–2). Instead, he follows the Delphic injunction to know himself and is completely occupied with determining whether he is a more tangled and covetous beast than Typhon, the son of a hundred-headed giant and father of the winds (Hesiod, *Theogony* 306), or a tamer and simpler animal who is not puffed up (*atyphos*) with pride. There is an elaborate play in this passage on Typhon as the father of Boreas. The name Typhon also means "delusion." Socrates has clearly not completely separated himself from sophistic practices of mythological exegesis and invention.[2] Instead, through an elaborate figure that involves taking the word as both the proper name of a mythological character and a common noun describing a mental state (delusion), he, as Kierkegaard notes, trumps the sophists at their own game in the same manner in which he trumps Lysias. His position is parasitic upon sophistic practices of rationalization and allegorization yet transcends their claims to power. Socrates does not explain myth in terms of a more fundamental reality but rather uses myth to problematize the practices of explanation that dominated both traditional thought (the poets, the oral tradition) and the brave new world of sophistic reason. Rather than decoding the myth of Boreas and Oreithyia, he ironically appropriates it. In short, Socrates does not simply reject sophistic rationalization but uses it to play within both the realm of myth (Typhon as the father of Boreas) and its sophistic rationalization (*typhon* as delusion), thereby creating a new form that is turned to the task of self-knowledge.

Nonetheless, that self and its truth do not exist separately from the realms of myth and rationalization and their accompanying delusions. Self-knowledge, as Derrida notes, proceeds through a form of externalization: "It is not perceived. Only interpreted, read, deciphered. A hermeneutics *assigns* intuition. An inscription, the *Delphikon gramma*, which is anything but an oracle, prescribes through its silent cipher; it signifies as one signifies an order—autoscopy and autognosis. The very activities that Socrates thinks can be contrasted to the hermeneutic adventure of myths, which he leaves to the sophists (229d)" (1981: 69).[3] The sophists are purveyors of an externalized rationality—a commodity (Plato, *Sophist* 223b–4d). As such, for Derrida, their knowledge is of a piece with what it purports to explain: myth as an externalization and repetition of thought, passed from one hearer to the next. Like the text of Lysias's speech Phaedrus carries under his cloak, sophistic knowledge travels from hand to hand. Sophistic knowledge is an object of exchange that must be contrasted with authentic knowledge of the self (Derrida 1981: 75; see Brisson and Pradeau 2007: 43–5).

From this point of view, myth is related to true knowledge in much the same fashion as writing. Each represents a seeming externality, as the sophist does in relation to the philosopher (Derrida 1981: 73, 103). These distinctions are quite classical. But Socrates is also a purveyor of myths on the grand scale, as in the great myth of the soul in his second speech and in the story of Thamus and Theuth, the Egyptian inventor of writing. It is in the latter myth that Thamus refers to writing as a *pharmakon* (Plato, *Phaedrus* 275a6), though the word has been haunting the dialogue from the moment Phaedrus mentions Pharmaceia. The *pharmakon* of writing is presaged by Pharmaceia (the poisoner), who seems to have been invented for this occasion. Writing, Thamus tells us, is not an aid to memory (*mnēmē*) but a mere reminder (*hypomnēmata*), an external supplement that threatens to supplant the internality of thought with the dead letter. Writing threatens to reduce the spontaneous and the self-present to the alienated, material, and external (cf. Miller 2008: 136–8).

Theuth, then, is not an inventor, the first finder or father of a discourse, but a divine bureaucrat (Nightingale 1995: 166). Like sophistic rhetoric, writing is a technocratic operation, a secondary manipulation of codified tools (Plato, *Phaedrus* 274e8–10; Derrida 1981: 86). None of this is out of character with his mythic identity. Traditionally, Theuth is son of Ra, the sun god. As the moon, he often plots and conspires to usurp Ra's throne. In some sources, Theuth conspires with Seth to overthrow Osiris (though in others he is instrumental in the healing of Horus). But in every case, he is the god of repetition. Theuth is never the thing itself but always signifies something else, always refers beyond himself, substituting for a lost original (Müller 1918: 33–4, 84–5, 90–1, 118, 126; Derrida 1981: 87–93). He is not unlike Phaedrus in carrying the speech of another. But Lysias, too, is a Theuth figure—a sophist or external manipulator of signs whose cynical lucubrations on love threaten to displace the thing itself.

In many ways, this relation between copy and original—and hence the problem of reference—is central to Platonic philosophy. It is at the heart of the critique of *mimēsis* in book 10 of the *Republic*. And while this indictment is problematized both in its immediate context (the myth of Er) and in the dialogue as a whole (a mimetic work in which Socrates plays all the parts [Szlezák 1999: 79–80]), it is most saliently called into question by the image of the sun in book 6. In this passage, Socrates uses the sun as a likeness or myth to discuss the Good, since its direct presentation is not possible. As Luc Brisson observes, myth in Plato is a form of semblance or *mimēsis* and thus susceptible to the same critique of usurping the authority of the original as writing, poetry, and rhetoric (Brisson 1998: 66, 69–70). At the same time, the Good in itself, which by definition knows no single instantiation, can be imitated only through the reproduction or recounting of a likeness (103–4).

In *Republic* 6 Glaucon asks Socrates to "go through" or "explain" (*dieltheis*) the good so that he might also understand the other virtues. Socrates replies that he would love to do so but is unable: "For those things, at least as they seem [*tou ge dokountos*] to me now, appear [*phainetai*] to go beyond the present undertaking. But now what appears [*phainetai*] to be the offspring of the good and most like it, I would like to say" (506d4–e5). We must be attentive to Plato's words here. The story of the sun will not tell us what the good is in itself, nor will it be a "going through" of the concept. Rather, it will be the recounting of an appearance of the way things seem to Socrates "now" via an offspring or a likeness. Plato takes pains to emphasize that we are dealing with a representation of the way the good seems at a certain point in space and time. In short, we are dealing with a myth, an imitation of an imitation (Derrida 1981: 82–4). We are dealing with an offspring whose father, as Socrates says of writing (Plato, *Phaedrus* 275e), is not there to vouchsafe his lineage.

But to what extent is the father ever present in the son? To what extent can Socrates guarantee the lineage of the myths he recounts, of Plato, or of the writings in which he appears? At what point can priority be guaranteed, and, if it cannot, where does repetition end and originality begin? This last question is precisely what is at stake in Derrida's argument on the reversibility of the relation between Socrates and Plato in *La carte postale* (1980: 27, 35, 54, 68, 141). If Socrates continues to play within the realm of myth and repetition, how can we differentiate him from a sophist, a manipulator of signs? Is such a distinction, as Cicero and Kierkegaard contend, fundamentally impossible? The answer to these questions is anything but straightforward. Nonetheless, it is precisely the impossibility, yet necessity, of making such distinctions of which Derrida and Plato's Socrates seek to remind us.

As Derrida (1993: 54–8) notes in *Khōra*, it is Socrates who ranges himself with the *genos mimetikōn* of poets and sophists. Moreover, if the sophist is defined as a man who appears (*phainetai*) to have the knowledge of many things (Plato, *Sophist* 232a1–2) but who is in fact merely the imitator (*mimētēs*) of the wise man (268c1), then for Socrates to be rigorously differentiated from the sophist he would have to deploy a knowledge that exists outside appearance and imitation, outside inscription and myth, and hence outside "the outside" itself (Derrida 1981: 106–7). But what Socrates provides us time and again is a likeness or myth, from the sun, the cave, and Er in the *Republic* to the final myth of *Gorgias* and the great speech in *Phaedrus*.

Myth is not a mere illustration or accidental ornament but a necessary supplement to the *logos* and dialectic (Robin [1933] 1966: xcvi; Zuckert 1996: 218). The archive of received semblances—myths, writing, speeches hidden under one's cloak—can never be completely dissociated from knowledge. Even the myths deployed by Socrates in his great speech on the immortality of the soul are derived from the poetic tradition, Pythagorean lore, the Eleusinian mysteries, and Egyptian mythology (Robin [1933] 1966: lxxix–xxxvii, 44, n. 1, 50, n. 3, 158–60; Thompson [1868] 1973: xxvi–vii, 43–74; Morgan 1992: 231–9; Heitsch 1993: 95, 98–107). As Harry Berger, Jr. argues, the great speech pretends "to be a spontaneous ecstatic outburst when it is actually a citational pastiche" (1994: 102).

But if Plato's Socratic myths derive from the archive, at what point do they, too, cease to represent the living "movement of truth" and become instead sophistic markers to be manipulated, counters on a game board (Derrida 1981: 109)? At what point does even memory, what Thamus cites as the opposite of writing's set of reminders, become just another form of externalization, a repetition and imitation? "A limitless memory would . . . be not memory but infinite self-presence. Memory . . . needs signs in order to recall the non-present, with which it is necessarily in relation. The movement of dialectics bears witness to this. Memory is thus contaminated by its first substitute: *hypomnēsis*. But what Plato *dreams* of is a memory with no sign. . . . A *mnēmē* with no *hypomnēsis*, no *pharmakon*" (109). Memory is therefore predicated on forgetting, on what must be *recalled*, on the movement of reference and hence of the sign and writing (Stoekl 1992: 202). As Freud (1965: 587–92) observes in *The Interpretation of Dreams*, consciousness itself would be impossible without repression: the unconscious, the voice of the other within the heart of identity, is the condition of possibility of self-awareness. Thus, even the boy whose sight provokes the memory of the beautiful in the soul is always a sign standing for a memory recalling a perception, a reference leading to a recollection of an imitation (Plato, *Phaedrus* 254b4–c4). As such, philosophy and rhetoric can never be rigorously distinguished; each must always be the reflection that threatens to turn into the other, *recto* and *verso* (Derrida 1981: 111–2; cf. 108). Socrates, in the end, is also Theuth (Derrida 1980: 59–60).

IRONY, RHETORIC, AND PHILOSOPHY

> Deconstruction is also a logic of the spectral and of haunting, of survival: neither present nor absent, neither living nor dead.
>
> —Derrida, "Résistances"

> And if there is a name for that which simultaneously brings together and separates the classical style [of philosophy] from the deconstructive, the least inappropriate would without doubt be irony.
>
> —Denis Kambouchner, "L'ironie et deconstruction"

To simply stop at the impossibility of distinguishing rhetoric from philosophy would be radically insufficient. Must there not, on some level, be a distinction between coercion, being "tamed by argument" (Plato, *Republic* 554d2), or engaging in mere repetition, and genuine assent, persuasion, a thought of one's own? The question, as always, is: How is that decision made, and to what end? If language itself functions by means of repetition, and repetition signifies a form of externality and hence the presence of the other in the same, then in what sense can a meaningful authenticity obtain, a claim to assent that is not an index of coercion? "Persuasive eloquence (*peithō*) is the power to break in, to carry off, to seduce internally, to ravish invisibly" (Derrida 1981: 116). Is there a form of persuasion that is not an invasion of the self by the other, whether wielded by the practitioner of Socratic refutation or the philosophically informed eloquence of Cicero?

One answer may be found in Socratic irony, as Derrida understands it. Irony is a moment of discursive turning. It seeks neither to establish a level of unbreachable internality nor to deny the difference between inside and outside, truth and repetition. Irony seeks instead to establish truth and authenticity as the moment of tropic turning (*tropos*) when one double-faced *pharmakon* encounters the next. As such, it depends on the very difference it calls into question:

> Irony does not consist in the dissolution of a sophistic charm or in the dismantling of an occult substance or power through analysis and questioning. It does not consist in undoing the charlatanesque confidence of a *pharmakeus* [magician, poisoner] from the vantage point of some obstinate instance of transparent reason or innocent *logos*. Socratic irony precipitates out one *pharmakon* by bringing it in contact with another *pharmakon*. Or rather, it reverses the *pharmakon*'s powers and turns *its* surface over—thus taking effect, being recorded and dated, in the act of classing the *pharmakon*, through the fact that the *pharmakon* properly consists in a certain

inconsistency, a certain impropriety, this nonidentity-with-itself always allowing it to be turned against itself. (Derrida 1972: 19)

Irony is precisely the trope by which the outside becomes the inside and vice versa. It is the turn by which Socrates becomes the wisest of men by knowing his own ignorance. But that self-knowledge can never be a settled fact, lest it become precisely a moment of sophistic externality, another counter moved on the game board of discursive combat (cf. Plato, *Republic* 487a10–e8). The salutary awareness of one's own inner lack can be proved only through the questioning of others, through leading them to recognize their ignorance, through the love of wisdom in the moment of tropic turning (Miller and Platter 2010: 160–1).

The self-knowledge of the Socratic philosopher, then, is always sought through engagement with the other (Derrida 1981: 121). For Plato and Derrida alike, philosophy begins at the moment of undecidability when the opposition between knowledge and ignorance, inside and outside, authenticity and imitation, first becomes possible. And philosophy ends when those distinctions become givens, figures in an argumentative game rather than self-questioning *pharmaka* that exhibit an infinite openness to their own turning (Blondell 2002: 42; Gasché 2002: 106, 115, 118; Hunter 2004: 86–7; cf. Derrida 1994: 21). That turning, if it is to retain its fidelity to truth, must question its own terms. It must mark the point at which the opposition on which it depends serves as a moment of constitutive opacity that points to the necessity of another terrain, a beyond of its own closure, and hence to the beginning of a knowledge that cannot be formulated by excluding its opposite (Gadamer 1991: 4–5; Courtine 2008: 26).

Thus, at the end of the *Greater Alcibiades* the question arises as to how one comes to know the self. If the self is the soul and the soul is not visible even to the mind's eye, then how is the call to self-knowledge not a bad joke? The answer, Socrates claims, is that one comes to know one's soul as it is reflected in the eyes and soul of the other. The practice of dialectic, the shared search for truth through question and answer, in the context of desire, becomes the way in which the self becomes visible through and as the other, the inside through and as the outside (Hadot 1995: 56–7, 103; Blondell 2002: 100):

SOCRATES.   I'm sure you've noticed that when a man looks into an eye his face appears in it, like in a mirror. We call this the "pupil," for it's a sort of miniature of the man who's looking.

ALCIBIADES.   You're right.

SOCRATES.   Then an eye will see itself if it observes an eye and looks at the best part of it, the part with which it can see.

ALCIBIADES.   So it seems.

SOCRATES.   But it won't see itself if it looks at anything else in a man, or anything else at all, unless it's similar to the eye.

ALCIBIADES.   You're right.

SOCRATES.   So if an eye is to see itself, it must look at an eye, and at that region of it in which the good activity of an eye actually occurs, and this, I presume, is seeing.

ALCIBIADES.   That's right.

SOCRATES.   Thus, if the soul, Alcibiades, is to know itself, it must look at a soul, and especially at that region in which what makes a soul good, wisdom, occurs, and at anything else similar to it. (Plato, *Greater Alcibiades* 132c–3b; trans. Hutchinson)

In this erotically charged moment, as Socrates and Alcibiades look into each other's eyes and into each other's soul, each sees himself in and through the other. In the same way, in *Phaedrus* the beloved, who receives the desire of the lover and reflects back his own beauty, begins to desire as well and in that desire sees himself in his lover as though in a mirror (255b7–d6). Self and other, then, are neither mutually exclusive nor meaningless terms. Rather, each is the object of knowledge only insofar as it is the predicate of the other, and truth lies not only in their difference but also in the ironic, tropic movement that defines their interrelation.

The structure of the ironic *pharmakon*, then, is never that of an either–or question but always that of a neither–nor/both–and statement (see Frank 2005: 5). A detour through time and difference, a moment of alienation, is precisely what makes authenticity possible:

> If the *pharmakon* is "ambivalent," it is because it constitutes the medium in which opposites are opposed, the movement and the play that links them among themselves, reverses them or makes one side cross over into the other (soul/body, good/evil, inside/outside, memory/forgetfulness, speech/writing, etc.). It is on the basis of this play or movement that the opposites or differences are stopped by Plato. The *pharmakon* is the movement, the locus, and the play: (the production of) difference. (Derrida 1981: 127)

Derrida in this passage betrays his own residually traditional reading of Plato in the assumption that the text of the *Phaedrus*, which deploys the ambivalences and ironies that he charts, tries to "stop" the currents it unleashes (Shankman 1994: 8). He conflates Platonism with the philosophy transmitted under that name (Ferrari 1987: 214; Berger 1994: 76, 114). In later texts, Derrida demonstrates that this is an oversimplification, that Platonism is but a moment in, or an abstraction from, the Platonic text whose ironic overdetermination deconstructs it (Alliez 1992: 226; Derrida 1993: 81–3; cf. Ferrari 1987: 207, 220; Halperin 1994: 62; Loraux 1996: 169).

In the end, the ironic production of truth functions in the opposite fashion to the logic of the *pharmakos* or "scapegoat" (the *pharmakon*'s etymological cousin). Where the *pharmakon* embodies the most fundamental ambiguities and thus serves as the ground of difference, the *pharmakos* represents the attempt to expel the other in the name of the same. Where the logic of the *pharmakon* is endlessly open, that of the *pharmakos* aspires to closure (Derrida 1981: 128–34; Stoekl 1992: 204). The *pharmakon* cannot but be ironic; the *pharmakos* aspires to the univocal. In this context, Plato's final ironic hyperbole in *Phaedrus*, namely, his advocacy of writing on the soul (278a3), is a gesture toward openness, toward a vision of the self that is not auto-entombed, toward a salutary internalization of the external.

The Inside ~~Is~~ the Outside

PHAEDRUS.   Who are they and where have you heard a better speech than this?

SOCRATES.   Now I really can't say. But it's clear I've heard them, whether they be
lovely Sappho or wise Anacreon or some prose writers. What sort of proof do
I offer in support? I have a strange fullness in my breast, divine Phaedrus, and
I perceive that I am able to say different things, which would not be worse, on this
same topic. I know well that I have not at all thought about these matters, being
conscious of my own ignorance. Indeed, I think, the only possibility left is that
I have been filled through my ears from the streams of others, like a pitcher. But on
account of a certain stupidity, I have forgotten this very thing, how and from whom
I heard them.

—Plato, *Phaedrus*

In many ways, this passage contains all the elements we have discussed concerning the
relation between rhetoric and philosophy in *Phaedrus* and "Plato's Pharmacy." I shall
conclude by offering a reading of it. Phaedrus's initial question is aimed at defending
Lysias's speech against the Socratic charge that it had not treated the matter of *ēros* in
depth (234e4–5a3) but instead merely repeated the same things time and again: "Who
are these speakers and where did you hear them?" (Plato, *Phaedrus* 235a3–b9). This is
both a challenge and an inquiry. If there are better speakers, Phaedrus would love to
hear them. Socrates, however, frustrates Phaedrus's request. He cannot remember
where he has heard them or who they were. We must ask: Is this a case of Socratic irony?
He has just cited "ancient and wise men and women" as his authorities (235b6). He must
have some idea who they are. Moreover, as the next clause makes clear, Sappho and
Anacreon, along with unnamed prose writers, loom large.

Socrates has been filled (*plēres, peplērōsthai*) with the words of others: poets and writers. These others, according to the ontology offered in *Republic* 10, are the imitators of
imitations, manipulators of externalities like the sophists, mythographers, and Theuth.
If we take his statement at face value, Socrates, as their secondary and self-described forgetful reporter, would thus be in an even more fallen state. Yet face value is hard to come
by. For one thing, in Socrates's second discourse the inspired poet participates in a form
of divine madness second only to that of priests and prophets (Plato, *Phaedrus* 245a1–8).
For another, we can accept the monologically negative reading of this passage only if we
disregard the irony of Socrates's claim that he does not know where or from whom he
has heard such speeches.

The proof that Socrates has heard these speeches is that he feels inspired—ready
to break out in speech, if not song. But since he "knows" that he is "without learning"
(*amathia*), then it must be the case that he has been filled from the streams of others.
That is, since Socrates knows that he is empty, his fullness must be external. And inasmuch as he knows that he knows nothing, then his knowledge must not be artificial,
factitious, an imitation of an imitation (like the *mathesis* of the sophists). Yet as the
Apology teaches, it is precisely because he knows that he knows nothing that Socrates is

the wisest of men (22e6–3c1). Moreover, in the *Symposium*, Socrates denies not only that wisdom can simply be poured from one individual into another (175d–e) but also that it can be exchanged, that Alcibiades can trade his favors for what Socrates hides within (218e–9b; Miller 2008: 121–32). Thus, if Socrates is ironic when he claims not to remember where he heard these speeches, are we also to assume he is ironic in his claim of ignorance or *amathia*? What would it mean for this claim to be ironic in light of the repeated assurances that Socrates "knows this well" and is "conscious" of this ignorance, especially when the claim itself is almost identical with the *Apology* as an explanation of the Delphic oracle? Does he know or not know? Is he full or empty? And if he is full, has he been filled from the streams of others, or, as in the case of the beloved who receives the stream of desire from the lover, does his own desire awaken and become a way of seeing himself through the other? The ironic tone makes a one-sided answer fundamentally impossible, even as it invites us to think beyond the antinomies in which it is couched (Rorty 1989: 73–4).

Perhaps, however, there is a simpler solution. Socrates does not offer a blanket claim here. It is local and specific and serves to preface his first speech, which he will renounce and then deliver his second speech as a recantation (*palinode*) in the manner of the poet Stesichorus (Plato, *Phaedrus* 242d12–3b7). Socrates's first speech is precisely an example of what should not be done, of bad speech. This is what happens when one is filled up with the words of another, with words from the outside, when one becomes a sophist or rhetorician. Yet, as we already hinted at by noting the precedent invoked for the second speech, Socrates's palinode also derives from a poet. It, too, floods in from the outside. It, too, depends on what is secondary and derivative. Indeed, in terms of Socrates's use of elements derived from the Mysteries, Pythagoreanism, and other sources, the second speech is also a tissue of citations. But if that is the case, then the passage we have been explicating, with its multiple layers of ironic displacement, claims, and counterclaims, applies every bit as much to the second speech as it does to the first. Indeed, on the most profound level, all language comes to us from the outside, poured through our ears from the streams of others. Even the *Republic*, which banishes poets from the ideal city, is filled with poetic citations.

Nevertheless, not all outsides are created equal. Socrates's first speech, like Lysias's before it, refers to an ontologically prior reality, to an outside that justifies the power the speaker seeks to wield. In much the same way, the sophistic explication of the myth of Boreas and Oreithyia seeks to ground it in a more fundamental level of signification. In Socrates's second speech, however, and in the larger Platonic practice of Socratic citationality, the practice of referring to the poets, to local myth, and to tales from Egypt seeks not to reproduce the sophistic claim to discursive power through the invocation of a determining reality but to turn that practice against itself, to refer to the act of referring per se, and thus to open reference to difference, to a critical realm whose relation to the immediate can only be ironic, can only dwell in the realm of the neither–nor/both–and.

Finally, if there is no original word, then at what point do we distinguish internal from external, philosophy as the pursuit of truth from rhetoric as the secondary manipulation of language? There are two answers to this question. The first is that we should not make such a distinction. The moment this distinction is made and the play of difference is arrested, words become dead letters, tokens to be moved on a playing board. The second answer is that we should acknowledge the infinite irony of this temporal play. Primary and secondary, inside and outside, are not terms with fixed meanings, but neither are they meaningless. Rather, only when Socrates ceases to ask questions, when he simply accepts being the wisest of men, does his proof become a sophistry and rhetoric the antithesis of philosophy. Likewise, only when deconstruction becomes a formalized procedure—rather than an event, an unveiling—does it, too, become just another style, another tropological routine (Courtine 2008: 20; Crépon 2008: 37).

NOTES

1. Unless otherwise specified, all translations are my own.
2. I refer here to "invention" in its ancient sense of coming upon something (*invenire*) that was already there but not yet found. Plato's Socrates, even when he "creates" myth, never invents them from whole cloth. As I show in my account of the second speech, his practice is *citational*.
3. This is in some ways an overly strict binary. Derrida's later problematization of the relationship between Plato and Socrates in *La carte postale* (1980) and of the contrast between *mythos* and *logos* in *Khōra* (1993) demonstrates that he, too, would later go beyond such stark oppositions.

REFERENCES

Alliez, Eric. 1992. "Ontologie et logographie. La pharmacie, Platon et le simulacre." In *Nos Grecs et leurs modernes*, edited by Barbara Cassin, 211–231. Paris: Seuil.

Berger, Jr., Harry. 1994. "*Phaedrus* and the Politics of Inscriptions." In *Plato and Postmodernism*, edited by Steven Shankman, 76–114. Glenside, PA: Aldine Press.

Blondell, Ruby. 2002. *The Play of Character in Plato's Dialogues*. Cambridge: Cambridge University Press.

Brisson, Luc. 1998. *Plato the Mythmaker*. Translated and edited by Gerard Nadaff. Chicago, IL: University of Chicago Press.

Brisson, Luc, and Jean-François Pradeau. 2007. *Dictionnaire Platon*. Paris: Ellipses.

Courtine, Jean-François. 2008. "L'ABC de la deconstruction." In *Derrida, la tradition de la philosophie*, edited by Marc Crépon and Frédéric Worms, 11–26. Paris: Galilée.

Crépon, Marc. 2008. "Déconstruction et traduction: Le passage à la philosophie." In *Derrida, la tradition de la philosophie*, edited by Marc Crépon and Frédéric Worms, 27–44. Paris: Galilée.

Derrida, Jacques. 1972. "La pharmacie de Platon." In *La dissémination*, 74–196. Paris: Seuil.

Derrida, Jacques. 1980. *La carte postale: de Socrate à Freud et au-delà*. Paris: Aubier-Flammarion.

Derrida, Jacques. 1981. "Plato's Pharmacy." In *Dissemination*, translated by Barbara Johnson, 61–171. Chicago, IL: University of Chicago Press.

Derrida, Jacques. 1993. *Khōra*. Paris: Galilée.

Derrida, Jacques. 1994. *Politiques de l'amitié, suivi de L'oreille de Heidegger*. Paris: Galilée.

Derrida, Jacques. (1992) 1996. "Résistances." In *Résistances de la psychanalyse*, 11–53. Paris: Galilée.

Ferrari, G. R. F. 1987. *Listening to the Cicadas: A Study of Plato's "Phaedrus."* Cambridge: Cambridge University Press.

Frank, Jill. 2005. *A Democracy of Distinction: Aristotle and the Work of Politics*. Chicago, IL: University of Chicago Press.

Freud, Sigmund. 1965. *The Interpretation of Dreams*. Translated by James Strachey. New York: Avon Books.

Gadamer, Hans-Georg. 1991. *Plato's Dialectical Ethics: Phenomenological Interpretations Relating to the "Philebus."* Translated by Robert M. Wallace. New Haven, CT: Yale University Press.

Gasché, Rodolphe. 2002. "L'expérience aporétique aux origines de la pensée. Platon, Heidegger, Derrida." *Etudes françaises* 38: 103–121.

Hadot, Pierre. 1995. *Qu'est-ce que la philosophie antique?* Paris: Gallimard.

Halperin, David M. 1994. "Plato and the Erotics of Narrativity." In *Plato and Postmodernism*, edited by Steven Shankman, 43–75. Glenside, PA: Aldine Press.

Heitsch, Ernst. 1993. *Phaidros*. Göttingen: Vandenhoeck & Ruprecht.

Hunter, Richard. 2004. *Plato's "Symposium."* Oxford: Oxford University Press.

Hutchinson, D. S., trans. 1997. "Alcibiades." In *Plato: Complete Works*, edited by John M. Cooper, associate editor D. S. Hutchinson, 557–595. Indianapolis, IN: Hackett.

Kambouchner, Denis. 2008. "L'ironie et deconstruction: Le problème des classiques." In *Derrida, la tradition de la philosophie*, edited by Marc Crépon and Frédéric Worms, 45–63. Paris: Galilée.

Kierkegaard, Søren. 1989. *The Concept of Irony with Continual Reference to Socrates: Notes of Schelling's Berlin Lectures*. Edited and translated by Howard V. Hong and Edna H. Hong. Princeton, NJ: Princeton University Press.

Loraux, Nicole. 1996. *Né de la terre: Mythe et politique à Athènes*. Paris: Seuil.

Miller, Paul Allen. 2008. *Postmodern Spiritual Practices: The Construction of the Subject and the Reception of Plato in Lacan, Derrida, and Foucault*. Columbus: Ohio State University Press.

Miller, Paul Allen, and Charles Platter. 2010. *Plato's "Apology of Socrates": A Commentary*. Norman: Oklahoma University Press.

Morgan, Michael L. 1992. "Plato and Greek Religion." In *The Cambridge Companion to Plato*, edited by Richard Kraut, 227–247. Cambridge: Cambridge University Press.

Müller, W. Max. 1918. "Egyptian." In *The Mythology of All Races*, vol. 12, edited by Louis Herbert Grey, 1–245. Boston, MA: Marshall Jones Company.

Nightingale, Andrea Wilson. 1995. *Genres in Dialogue: Plato and the Construct of Philosophy*. Cambridge: Cambridge University Press.

Robin, Léon. (1933) 1966. "Notice." In *Platon: Phèdre*, edited and translated by Léon Robin, vii–ccv. Paris: Société d'Edition "Les Belles Lettres."

Rorty, Richard. 1989. *Contingency, Irony, and Solidarity*. Cambridge: Cambridge University Press.

Shankman, Steven, ed. 1994. *Plato and Postmodernism*. Glenside, PA: Aldine Press.

Shankman, Steven, ed. 1994. "Plato and Postmodernism." In *Plato and Postmodernism*, edited by Steven Shankman, 3–28. Glenside, PA: Aldine Press.

Stoekl, Allan. 1992. *Agonies of the Intellectual: Commitment, Subjectivity and the Performative in the 20th Century French Tradition*. Lincoln: University of Nebraska Press.

Szlezák, Thomas. 1999. *Reading Plato*. Routledge: London.

Thompson, W. H. (1868) 1973. *The "Phaedrus" of Plato with English Notes and Dissertations*. New York: Arno Press.

Zuckert, Catherine H. 1996. *Postmodern Platos: Nietzsche, Heidegger, Gadamer, Strauss, Derrida*. Chicago, IL: University of Chicago Press.

CHAPTER 56

RHETORIC, COMPOSITION, DESIGN

DAVID KAUFER AND DANIELLE WETZEL

In this chapter, we explain "design" as a metaphor that allows us to make explicit the relationship between an author's language choices and a reader's experience of those choices. By design we mean four things. First, we mean forethought that superintends a vision relating initial conceptualizations to finished artifact. There is general agreement that design describes the "invention, planning, and realization of both tangible and intangible products, including all of the digital products that now exist alongside traditional analog products" (Buchanan 2001: 188). Designers in the ideal are obsessive about getting the small details right because they never lose sight of the big picture those details serve. Second, we mean a focus on the artifact not as an end in itself or a measure of abstractions (e.g., good writing) but as a producer of experience that informs and enlightens others. To paraphrase from Roger Rosenblatt's (2011) book title, why would anyone write "unless to move the human heart?" A design approach to writing features the reader's agency as well as the writer's. Third, we mean a knowledge access that enables writers to provide rationales for the decsions they make throughout the process, large and small. Students who believe that the secrets of good writing are locked inside the teacher's head fail to grasp their responsibilities and agency over the reading experience. And fourth, we mean attentiveness to the small actions of language and their repercussions on the reading experience. Such curiosity about and attentiveness to the consequences of small language choices for readers lays the foundation for the three aforementioned features of a design approach to writing.

While many teachers now implicitly or explicitly embrace design assumptions in their own writing pedagogy, these assumptions are seldom articulated. A primary aim of this chapter is to provide that articulation. We motivate that articulation in part through the straw man of alternative historical terms—rhetoric and composition. We do not mean to suggest that these terms are incompatible with design. We mean to say only that there are historical embodiments of both these notions that do not meet the criteria of design as enumerated above. In particular, although these embodiments may focus on sensitizing students to prescriptive violations of language, internal textual coherence, or even compliance with the goals of informing or persuading an audience, they do not necessarily present the language as an object of open-ended descriptive study in articulation with a reader's experience. A useful way to motivate the importance of design in writing education is thus to describe these nondesign embodiments of rhetoric and composition as historical polarities and then turn to design as the connective thread between the two.

Rhetoric

Rhetoric, with its beginnings in ancient Greece, concerned itself with education in the verbal arts for the citizen-orator to formulate and expound policies in the legislature (deliberative rhetoric), to attack others and defend oneself in the courtroom (forensic rhetoric), and to celebrate occasions of personal honor and collective solidarity (epideictic rhetoric). In *Rhetoric* Aristotle characterizes the art of rhetoric as the ability (*dynamis*) to find the available means of persuasion in any situation considered rhetorical. Deborah Brandt (1990: 59) describes the rhetorical art in a related way, noting that rhetorically astute speakers and writers had more than the linguistic skill to stick words together in pleasing ways—they had the skill to connect words in ways that made *audiences* stick together. In other words, they had what Kenneth Burke (1969: 20) describes in *A Rhetoric of Motives* as the capacity to pull together seemingly unconnected persons into a single force, headed in a single direction, through the "identification" (a Burkean "god-term") of common interest.

The special *dynamis* associated with Aristotelian rhetoric was later codified and subdivided by the Romans into the canons of invention (*inventio*), arrangement (*dispositio*), style (*elocutio*), memory (*memoria*), and delivery (*actio*) (see Quintilian, *Institutes of Oratory* 3.3). The characteristics of rhetorical discourse, classified under the canon of style, were understood to fluctuate with changing situations. Moreover, the ancient rhetorical situation was live oratory experienced by the audience in the unfolding moment. Therefore, audiences experienced speech not as "*a* means of influence but *the* means [in the moment]" (Jamieson 1988: 5). For these and probably other reasons, ancient Greek and Roman rhetoric exhibited little interest in how the overall design of a message shaped an audience's holistic experience.

Traditional rhetoric was not bereft of an investment in language. In his discussion of style in book 3 of the *Rhetoric*, Aristotle attends to matters of style and meter. Cicero, in *Orator* (82), discusses different stylistic registers (grand, medium, and low), and in his *Institutio oratoria* (book 3) Quintilian covers the identification of parts of speech, barbarisms, solecisms, foreign words, and figures and tropes. Students in the ancient tradition wrote language-identification exercises in speeches and texts. James Murphy notes that this "methodical treatment [of language] carried out on all kinds of texts for ten or a dozen years must surely have promoted a high degree of linguistic sensitivity in the students" (2001: 58). But an education for linguistic sensitivity to promote the ends of rhetoric is not the same as a *comprehensive* and *descriptive* study of language in the manner of the modern disciplines of theoretical and applied linguistics. Ancient rhetoric was mindful of the linguistic "surface" of discourse, the incessant and ambient contact and collisions (Hoey 1983) as words act and interact in combination before the ears or eyes of an audience. But rhetoric's mindfulness of language was more the traffic cop's interest in monitoring performance than the structural engineer's interest in understanding the principles by which changes in performance lead systematically to changes in what audiences experience. Students in the rhetorical tradition were interested in drilling into the language in speech and texts conditionally, when there was a clear alignment between language and the immediate rhetorical purpose. But this practical interest overlooks the deeper question as to how language, at its root, implements rhetorical purpose at all and across contexts. Some of these concerns about the implementation of purpose into expression were better addressed in the American tradition of composition.

COMPOSITION

Composition, as the North American institution we recognize today, had its beginnings in the nineteenth-century movement to mass produce the teaching of writing to immigrants wishing to compete on a level playing field of American meritocracy (Douglas 1976; Lerner 1996; Knoblauch and Matsuda 2008; Yancey 2009). Although there were and remain notable exceptions (Hill 1887; Kitzhaber 1963; Douglas 1976; Connors 1985; Stewart 1985), accommodating great variation, American composition has retained a dominant institutional mission within the academy of certifying a rite of linguistic passage for students in written expression. Writing of the transition from rhetoric to composition in late nineteenth-century education, Elizabethada Wright and Michael Halloran observe that "much of great value was lost in the evolution from the neoclassical rhetoric of the late eighteenth century to the composition course of the late nineteenth" (2001: 239).

The ancient rhetorical tradition responded to the high-minded possibility of elites rising to leadership. American composition responded to the harsh reality that fluency in written English was an essential milestone for the novice or immigrant in search of classroom success and employment. Despite wide variation and experimentation, composition's dominant focus on skills put writing situations in the service of language standards, inverting the rhetorical tradition that had put language in the service of situational problem solving. The rhetorical tradition left language in the tactical shadows of style; composition domesticated the situations of writing into uncomplicated "classroom genres" (the five-paragraph essay, for example) and emphasized the "correct" discursive forms required to "fill in" genre. Composition brought visibility to the textual surface through vocabulary lists, idioms, phrases, clauses, sentences, and paragraphs. Paragraphs, like blocks, could be stacked together to form an essay. They scaled from smaller structures (words) to larger ones (sentences, paragraphs, essays). The blocks were self-contained, and their principles of sound construction could be embodied in handbook standards covering the structural correctness of blocks at every level (in grammar, diction, usage, cohesion, and coherence). Based upon norms favoring sound construction, correctness became the goal of language education in composition.

But while norms of correctness scaled through the building blocks of text, they did not scale to nontextual representations of audience and situation. Correctness cannot predict comprehensibility (making sense to the reader), much less effectiveness (making compelling sense to the reader) (Williams 1981). Rules of correctness are conveniently easier to track than standards of comprehensibility and effectiveness. Rather than puzzling through and evaluating the quality of the student's meaning (many early composition teachers did not believe student writing could be meaningful), the composition teacher could mark structural violations of handbook prescriptions as a convenient surrogate for the student's ability to be understood or effective (Hawhee 1999). However, beyond convenience, there was a more profound reason within composition for elevating correctness above meaning. Correctness was a self-contained standard reinforced more by handbooks than by research on actual writers. And research was not the point because composition was not initially formulated as a research enterprise but a screening practice. As Kathleen Yancey writes, "Without a research base or a planned curriculum . . . composition tended to take on the colors of the time, primarily (1) its identification as a rudimentary skill and (2) its predominant role in the testing of students" (2009: 3).

The Rhetorical Turn within Composition

In the 1970s, strains of a rhetorical backlash entered composition, and they continue to this day. New priorities displaced the testing of students on "correct products" as the sine qua non of composition. Taking his lead from ancient rhetoric, Richard Young prioritized invention above grammar for writing instruction (Young, Becker, and Pike 1970: 9; see also Crowley 1996 for a history). From cognitive science, John Hayes and Linda Flower (1980) showed that expert writers make adequate products based on a deep foundation of widely varying but nonetheless systemic processes. Other researchers studied the harm done to writers when teachers focused exclusively on correctness at the expense of meaning (Bartholomae 1985; Rose 1985). And still others built systematic pedagogies on making meaning from lived experience (Elbow 1981), creating authentic rhetorical situations within writing classrooms (Petraglia 1998), or training students to become citizen critics (Eberly 2000). In the 1980s and 1990s, research turned toward the social (Miller 1984), sociocultural (Kaufer and Carley 1993), social-cognitive (Flower 1994), cognitive-historical (Geisler 1994), and sociohistorical (Russell 1995; Prior 1998) roots of effective writing. Finally, research in the first decade of the twenty-first century has explored the proliferating rhetorical contexts of digital writing, from weblogs ("blogs") to Facebook, MySpace, and Twitter networks (Takayoshi 1996; Bloom 2003) and the challenge of transferring what is taught in the writing classroom to workplace settings (Beaufort 2007: 9).

These reframings of composition exposed the gulf between the sterility of the stereotypical writing classroom and the rich motivating contexts of writing that lay beyond the classroom in physical and digital spaces. The collective significance of this research was to open up writing as a serious field of study beyond classroom screening. The collective limitation of this research, however, was that, despite some efforts to make classroom writing rhetorically authentic (Petraglia 1998; Eberly 2000), it tended to leave behind classroom pedagogy and assessment altogether. Furthermore, in keeping with the diminution of language and style in classical rhetoric in relation to invention, a side effect of the rhetorical turn in composition was the eclipse of close language instruction and analysis, leading Robert Connors (2000) to publish an article in *College Communication and Composition* with the provocative title, "The Erasure of the Sentence." Second-language writing research points to the necessity of explicit teaching of academic genre moves (Swales and Feak 2004) and even teaching about the cultural and geopolitical assumptions behind those moves (Canagarajah 2002). In his overview of composition, Richard Fulkerson (2005: 676) acknowledges how language is being taught in relation to teaching target academic genres, but he raises the enduring complaint that pedagogies dedicated to discourse analysis and genre tend to neglect process and invention for producing language to create experiences for readers. Unfortunately, this research has had little impact to date on the composition classroom and composition research. We say "unfortunately" because as new forms of digital writing keep evolving, the need for an approach to rhetoric that integrates rhetorical purpose, reader experience, process, and language choice becomes more acutely felt. In her manifesto on twenty-first-century writing, Yancey indicates that the most important tasks ahead lie in articulating new curricula and new models of teaching based on all the expanding contexts of composing "developing right before our eyes" (2009: 7). As these new contexts unfold, it is not clear how composition can account for new situations when it has yet to produce a theoretical framework for how language interfaces with audience experience in systematic ways.

DESIGN

Design represents a paradigm for reconciling the stereotyped polarities of rhetoric and composition. Increasingly, effective theories of pedagogy conducted under the name of rhetoric or composition are coming to embrace some combination of the four principles of design we enumerated at the beginning. Through the cultivation of forethought, an emphasis on reader experience, accountability for decision-making, and a sustained attention to the way words on the page construct worlds of experience for the reader, a design approach to writing makes available for systematic descriptive study the parts in an emerging text that can be seen, altered, and elaborated as a way of envisioning, altering, and elaborating the reader's experience. In the realm of visual design, these parts have standard names, such as repetition, symmetry, and emphasis. In the realm of writing, they include lexical, grammatical, pragmatic, and rhetorical features.

Because of its focus on public accountability for decision-making, a design approach to writing focuses on how students can be empowered to assess a text in process. It furthermore helps students call into question the line between self-sponsored and teacher-sponsored writing. Like all reflective practitioners (Schon 1984), designers must account for their actions as part of an overall design rationale (Gropius 1965).

Unlike some nondesign extremes of composition, which detach student authority from the testing process, design students evaluate themselves in the process of making artifacts. Students compose for themselves and for audiences but learn that, despite input from others, they alone are responsible for the decisions made. Richard Buchanan (2001) classifies the four arts of design as invention, judgment, developing-testing, and evaluating the final product. He likens these four arts to the ancient rhetorical canons—*inventio, dispositio, elocutio, memoria,* and *actio*—but notes a key difference: they must be taught and practiced concurrently rather than in "silos." This means that, from high concept to local expression, the student must monitor and account for the product's progression (see Buchanan 1985, 1992).

In the design studio, students must explain how well their compositional choices span the gulf between high concept and audience experience and must defend these choices publicly. Thus, design students, unlike traditional composition students, must self-sponsor not only their own drafts (prototypes) but also the public evaluation of their drafts. These forms of self-sponsored evaluation are built into the design studio process through the ritual of "critique." In critique sessions, design students mount their prototypes on the studio walls; they may also include in their display meta-level criticism of their decisions. This meta-criticism is part of an oral classroom genre known as the "design rationale," which ensures that students have taken ownership of both making and improving their own work. Students, teachers, and often visitors (without knowledge of the studio or the student) attend the critique and give feedback. But even more important than giving feedback on the student's prototype, they give feedback on the student's *rationale* and its capacity to support the prototype. The critique session is a design student's public defense about how she has managed to connect the larger goals for her artifact with her local choices for the artifact's surface. This defense requires students to explain intentions for communicating through the artifact to an audience. The audience at the critique responds only after hearing the student's public defense of the work. The teacher evaluates the student only after participating as audience member. In this way, the design student, like the composition student, is tested. But testing within composition omits the student's own input and identity in the process of making audience experience. Those calling for reform in composition rightly reject the current testing environment. However, the culprit is not necessarily testing but seeing testing as removed from the student's agency over the evaluation process.

Through the ritual of critique, design pedagogy makes composition choices visible. Because it is a shared communication space among the student, instructor, and other studio participants, the critique also frames the student's design artifact as a self-sponsored rather than teacher-sponsored, or even institution-sponsored, artifact. When the pedagogical emphasis rests upon articulating processes and materials of *making*, students must be equipped with a vocabulary and a space to explain that making.

Turning Composition Spaces into Design Spaces

We cannot turn writing classrooms into design studios by fiat, neologisms, buzzwords, or metaphor. Two problems must be considered for instruction in rhetoric and composition to embrace systematically the four aspects of design previously enumerated.

The first problem relates to students' prior knowledge. Top design schools are conservatories, selecting students based upon juried portfolio work. Such students typically begin their visual training at a young age and are tutored to "see" design on the page early in their development. Because they are trained over years to see their local actions and their consequences for viewers, they are prepared to learn how their actions shape audience experience in the college studio class. By contrast, students entering writing classrooms often have no extensive background in writing and have been placed in such classrooms for remedial purposes. They may not have been avid readers and so may not recognize textual patterns that shape reader experience. Alternatively, they may have been avid readers, but for content only, without stopping to reflect on and acquire control over the textual patterns that shaped the impact of that content. These latter students may have made themselves "well attuned" to looking *through* text for meaning but not well attuned to looking *at* text for the textual patterns that make meaning possible (Lanham 1993: 5). When students cannot *see* their actions on the page, they cannot take ownership of them as makers or as critics. They cannot judge what they cannot see. Consequently, the teacher remains the final judge, with students neither participating in nor taking ownership of evaluating their own texts.

A second and more fundamental problem is that the patterns of language representing production units that shape the reader experience at the point of utterance have yet to be given precise descriptions. The vocabulary of parts of speech (viz., noun, verb, adjective) and lexical syntax (viz., subject, verb, object, case, tense, aspect) were in the end not units intended to describe the interplay between words and reader experience.

To develop design spaces within the composition classroom, we need to do the hard intellectual work of developing theory that addresses these problems. More specifically, we need to theorize *what* writers should see in a text, *how* writers act on what can be seen, and how students can both visualize and understand the *aggregate effects* of their cumulative composing choices on the conventionalized experience of a reader.

For 15 years, David Kaufer and colleagues have worked sequentially on all three questions (Kaufer and Butler 1996, 2000; Kaufer et al. 2004a). The first question pertains to what writers should see in texts. Kaufer and Brian Butler (1996) studied the Lincoln–Douglas debates as a rhetorical paradigm for understanding how small language patterns (what can be seen in a text) could be extracted and isolated for study. Their theoretical approach was consistent with Paul Hopper's (2003) innovations in theoretical linguistics and Michael Hoey's (2005) parallel innovations in applied linguistics. Hopper's theory of grammaticalization claimed that grammar is not monolithic but is composed of loosely coupled word sequences whose coupling strengthens or weakens according to principles of usage. In the realm of applied linguistics, Hoey argues that word collocation and cueing (somewhat similar to Hopper's word sequences) provide a deeper clue about the organization of language than previously recognized. Anticipating these developments in linguistics, Kaufer and Butler (1996) showed how higher-level rhetorical interpretations of the debates can be explained through the local choices within the discourse.

The second question looks into *how* writers act on what can be seen. To learn what composing choices writers employed across a range of genres (from personal to public writing), Kaufer and Butler (2000) then studied student writers. They isolated seven fundamental writing skills as form–effect pairings that, through constellations of word clusters, shape predictable experiences for readers. The seven pairings require written moves that (1) make acquaintance with a reader from the first-person perspective (self-portrait); (2) make acquaintance with a reader from the third-person perspective (observer-portrait); (3) make the reader an eyewitness (scenic writing); (4) make the reader recall a world with the vividness of yesterday (oral history); (5) lead the reader through an information hierarchy motivated by the reader's curiosity about the subject (information writing); (6) lead the reader through a task with an "over the shoulder" guide (instruction writing); and (7) lead the reader through a decision space with enough alternative paths to convince the reader that relevant perspectives have been fairly portrayed (argument).

Over 10 years, students were studied on all seven challenges. They kept track of their local decisions at the sentence and paragraph levels and then described and evaluated their decisions publicly before being graded. This leads, finally, to the third issue: how students can visualize and understand the aggregate effects of their cumulative composing choices. This activity enabled the development of software (Kaufer et al. 2004b) that allowed Kaufer and colleagues to store, categorize, and visualize the composing choices (words or word strings) their students had isolated over 10 years of writing. Over the course of this decade, Kaufer and his colleagues classified and indexed over 40 million such composing patterns (Ishizaki and Kaufer 2011). Using an earlier version of this database of patterns, Jeff Collins (2003) assembled strong evidence that the composing choices isolated from student writing were visible in professional writing across a range of genres. Since 2003, this visualization software has been in classroom use so that students can receive immediate feedback on their composing choices when they write and thus learn, over time, to see their choices without the software.

The efforts of Kaufer and his colleagues are but one of many ways of turning composing spaces into design spaces. Given the complexity of texts, it is likely that visualization technologies that help students "see" their composing choices will be an important part of any solution. For example, if a student writes about himself for an internship application, how will he communicate competence to his reader? What composing choices signal competence? Visualization technologies can display a spectrum of linguistic options for communicating a variety of experiences (e.g., sadness, authority, or negation). And as visualization technologies proliferate and become increasingly easy and cost-effective to use, solutions will likely extend in many directions.

By helping students learn writing within a design perspective, we can encourage them to become more responsible agents of their texts and better able to appreciate that writers, consequential rhetoricians of the written word, are, through linguistic choice, designers of the reading experience. We can help them see that writers earn their stripes because they can make experiences that readers care about. As such, a design approach to writing brings together the non-textual consequentiality of rhetoric, the textual focus of composition, and a seriousness about developing theories of language that bridge the divide between the surface stream and the material contexts of readers. In this sense, a design approach to writing forges a new and promising alignment for twenty-first-century pedagogies.

References

Bartholomae, David. 1985. "Inventing the University." In *When a Writer Can't Write: Studies in Writer's Block and Other Composing Process Problems*, edited by Mike Rose, 134–165. New York: Guilford Press.

Beaufort, Anne. 2007. *College Writing and Beyond*. Logan: Utah State University Press.

Bloom, Lynn Z. 2003. "The Great Paradigm Shift and Its Legacy for the Twenty-First Century." In *Composition Studies in the New Millennium: Rereading the Past, Rewriting the Future*, edited by Lynn Z. Bloom, Donald A. Daiker, and Edward M. White, 31–48. Carbondale: Southern Illinois University Press.

Brandt, Deborah. 1990. *Literacy as Involvement*. Carbondale: Southern Illinois University Press.

Brandt, Deborah. 1998. "Sponsors of Literacy." *College Composition and Communication* 49 no. 2: 165–185.

Brereton, John C., ed. 1995. *The Origins of Composition Studies in the American College, 1875–1925: A Documentary History*. Pittsburgh, PA: University of Pittsburgh Press.

Buchanan, Richard. 1985. "Declaration by Design: Rhetoric, Argument, and Demonstration in Design Practice." *Design Issues* 2 no. 1: 4–22.

Buchanan, Richard. 1992. "Wicked Problems in Design Thinking." *Design Issues* 8 no. 2: 5–21.

Buchanan, Richard. 2001. "Design and the New Rhetoric: Productive Arts in the Philosophy of Culture." *Philosophy & Rhetoric* 34 no. 3: 183–206.

Burke, Kenneth. 1969. *A Rhetoric of Motives*. Berkeley, CA: University of California Press.

Canagarajah, Suresh. 2002. *Critical Academic Writing and Multilingual Students*. Ann Arbor: University of Michigan Press.

Collins, Jeff. 2003. "Variations in Written English Characterizing Authors' Rhetorical Language Choices Across Corpora of Published Texts." Ph.D. diss., Carnegie Mellon University.

Connors, Robert J. 1985. "Mechanical Correctness as a Focus in Composition Instruction." *College Composition and Communication* 36 no. 1: 61–72.

Connors, Robert J. 2000. "The Erasure of the Sentence." *College Composition and Communication* 52 no. 1: 96–128.

Crowley, Sharon. 1996. "Around 1971: Current-Traditional Rhetoric and Process Models of Composing." In *Composition in the Twenty-First Century: Crisis and Change*, edited by Lynn Z. Bloom, Donald A. Daiker, and Edward M. White, 64–74. Carbondale: Southern Illinois University Press.

Douglas, Wallace. 1976. "Rhetoric for the Meritocracy: The Creation of Composition at Harvard." In *English in America*, edited by Richard Ohmann, 97–132. Oxford: Oxford University Press.

Eberly, Rosa. 2000. *Citizen Critics: Literary Public Spheres*. Urbana: University of Illinois Press.

Elbow, Peter. 1981. *Writing with Power*. Oxford: Oxford University Press.

Flower, Linda. 1994. *The Construction of Negotiated Meaning: A Social Cognitive Theory of Writing*. Carbondale: Southern Illinois University Press.

Fulkerson, Richard. 2005. "Composition at the Turn of the Twenty-First Century." *College Composition and Communication* 56 no. 4: 654–687.

Geisler, Cheryl. 1994. *Academic Literacy and the Nature of Expertise*. Mahwah, NJ: Lawrence Erlbaum.

Gropius, Walter. 1965. *The New Architecture and the Bauhaus*. Cambridge, MA: MIT Press.

Hawhee, Debra. 1999. "Composition History and *The Harbrace College Handbook*." *College Composition and Communication* 50 no. 3: 504–523.

Hayes, John R., and Linda Flower. 1980. "Identifying the Organization of Writing Processes." In *Cognitive Processes in Writing: An Interdisciplinary Approach*, edited by Lee Gregg and Erwin Steinberg, 3–30. Hillsdale, NJ: Lawrence Erlbaum.

Hill, Adams Sherman. 1887. "English in Our Colleges." *Scribner's Magazine* 1: 507–512.

Hoey, Michael. 1983. *On the Surface of Discourse*. London: Unwin Hyman.

Hoey, Michael. 2005. *Lexical Priming: A New Theory of Words and Language*. New York: Routledge.

Hopper, Paul J., and Elizabeth Traugott. 2003. *Grammaticalization*. Cambridge: Cambridge University Press.

Ishizaki, Suguru, and David Kaufer. 2011. "Computer-Aided Rhetorical Analysis." In *Applied Natural Language Processing: Identification, Investigation and Resolution*, edited by Phillip M. McCarthy and Chutima Boonthum-Denecke, 276–296. Hershey, PA: IGI Global.

Jamieson, Kathleen Hall. 1988. *Eloquence in an Electronic Age: The Transformation of Political Speechmaking*. New York: Oxford University Press.

Kaufer, David S., and Brian S. Butler. 1996. *Rhetoric and the Arts of Design*. Mahwah, NJ: Lawrence Erlbaum.

Kaufer, David S., and Brian S. Butler. 2000. *Designing Interactive Worlds with Words: Principles of Writing as Representational Composition*. Mahwah, NJ: Lawrence Erlbaum.

Kaufer, David S., and Kathleen Carley. 1993. *Communication at a Distance: The Role of Print in Sociocultural Organization and Change*. Mahwah, NJ: Lawrence Erlbaum.

Kaufer, David S., Ananda Gunawardena, Aaron Tan, and Alexander Cheek. 2011. "Bringing Social Media to Writing Instruction: Classroom Salon." *Journal of Business and Technical Communication* 25 no. 3: 299–321.

Kaufer, David S., Suguru Ishizaki, Brian S. Butler, and Jeff Collins. 2004a. *The Power of Words: Unveiling the Speaker and Writer's Hidden Craft*. Mahwah, NJ: Lawrence Erlbaum.

Kaufer, David S., Suguru Ishizaki, Jeff Collins, and Pantelis Vlachos. 2004b. "Teaching Language Awareness in Rhetorical Choice Using IText and Visualization in Classroom Genre Assignments." *Journal of Business and Technical Communication* 18 no. 3: 361–402.

Kitzhaber, Albert R. 1963. *Themes, Theories, and Therapy: The Teaching of Writing in College*. New York: McGraw.

Knoblauch, Abby A., and Paul K. Matsuda. 2008. "First-Year Composition in Twentieth-Century U.S. Higher Education: An Historical Overview." In *Teaching Academic Writing*, edited by Patricia Friedrich, 3–25. New York: Continuum.

Lanham, Richard. 1993. *The Electronic Word: Democracy, Technology, and the Arts*. Chicago, IL: University of Chicago Press.

Lerner, Neal. 1996. "The Institutionalization of Required English." *Composition Studies* 24 no. 1–2: 44–60.

Miller, Carolyn R. 1984. "Genre as Social Action." *Quarterly Journal of Speech* 70: 151–167.

Murphy, James J. 2001. *A Short History of Writing Instruction: From Ancient Greece to Modern America*. Mahwah, NJ: Lawrence Erlbaum.

Petraglia, Joseph. 1998. *Reality by Design: The Rhetoric and Technology of Authenticity in Education*. Mahwah, NJ: Lawrence Erlbaum.

Prior, Paul A. 1998. *Writing/Disciplinarity: A Sociohistoric Account of Literate Activity in the Academy*. Mahwah, NJ: Lawrence Erlbaum.

Rose, Mike, ed. 1985. *When a Writer Can't Write: Studies in Writer's Block and Other Composing Process Problems*. New York: Guilford.

Rosenblatt, Roger. 2011. *Unless It Moves the Human Heart: The Craft and Art of Writing*. New York: Harper Collins.

Russell, David. 1995. "Activity Theory and Its Implications for Writing Instruction." In *Reconceiving Writing, Rethinking Writing Instruction*, edited by Joseph Petraglia, 51–78. Mahwah, NJ: Lawrence Erlbaum.

Schon, Donald. 1984. *The Reflective Practitioner: How Professionals Think in Action*. New York: Basic Books.

Stewart, Donald C. 1985. "The Status of Composition and Rhetoric in American Colleges, 1880–1902: An MLA Perspective." *College English* 47 no. 7: 734–746.

Swales, John M., and Christine B. Feak. 2004. *Academic Writing for Graduate Students: Essential Tasks and Skills*. Ann Arbor: University of Michigan Press.

Takayoshi, Pamela. 1996. "The Shape of Electronic Writing." *Computers and Composition* 13 no. 2: 235–241.

Williams, Joseph M. 1981. "The Phenomenology of Error." *College Composition and Communication* 32 no. 2: 152–168.

Wright, Elizabethada A., and Michael S. Halloran. 2001. "From Rhetoric to Composition: The Teaching of Writing in America to 1900." In *A Short History of Writing Instruction*, edited by James J. Murphy, 213–246. Davis, CA: Hermagoras Press.

Yancey, Kathleen Blake. 2009. "Writing in the 21st Century: A Report from the National Council of Teachers of English." National Council of Teachers of English. Accessed June 10, 2012. http://www.ncte.org/library/NCTEFiles/Press/Yancey_final.pdf

Young, Richard E., Alton L. Becker, and Kenneth L. Pike. 1970. *Rhetoric: Discovery and Change.* New York: Harcourt.

CHAPTER 57

RHETORIC AND SOCIAL EPISTEMOLOGY

LORRAINE CODE

> Knowledge is in the end based on acknowledgement.
> —Ludwig Wittgenstein, *On Certainty*

IN *Ecological Thinking* (2006) I read Rachel Carson's work, especially *Silent Spring* (1962), as an epistemological project situated within a tension that requires her to move back and forth between an instituted scientific orthodoxy and an attentive respect for particularity that is subversive of many of the constitutive assumptions of that very orthodoxy. For the modern Western "general public" and for the majority of practicing scientists and philosophers of science, scientific knowledge is paradigmatic knowledge, and "real" science is "hard" science: it is the model to which all knowledge worthy of the name aspires. It is governed, in its epistemic imaginary, by an allegiance to a deductive-nomological method whose purpose is to derive monolithic, universally valid, necessary, and sufficient conditions that will enable reliable manipulation, prediction, and control of the physical-natural world. Paying close attention to particularities amounts, under these regulative assumptions, to a descent into the contingencies of the everyday and the idiosyncratic: it stands in the way of achieving the objectivity in practice and epistemic certainty in product that are the goals of bona fide projects of inquiry. Hence, the method of working back and forth between "scientificity" and "secularity" that characterizes Carson's epistemic and rhetorical practice, together with the palpable traces of her literary accomplishments in her books and articles, takes the tension I have mentioned into something of an ironic register. Addressing her writings to both a general and a specialized audience allegedly "softens" her conclusions, subverts the rhetoric of scientific orthodoxy, and unsettles the aura of esotericism that surrounds modern science and analytic epistemology, whose power to confer or withhold the acknowledgment on which epistemic legitimacy depends derives from a founding gesture with which, as Lynette Hunter aptly observes, "neutral logic and pure language replaced 'rhetoric'" (Hunter 1999: 30). She continues: "[Science assumed] a rhetorical stance that denied that the rhetoric of social persuasion in historical context was needed, even denied that it existed.... Built upon the concept of the 'universal autonomous man,' able to communicate infinitely replicable experience [and] isolated from the social world, which might contaminate the purity or challenge the totality of explanation . . . *its rhetoric claims that there is no need for rhetoric*" (30–1; emphasis added) (see Walmsley, ch. 43; Doyle, ch. 59). Carson, writing for scientists, policymakers, and an "educated reading public" in a language that often leaves the rhetoric of "normal science" behind, thus forfeits a certain professional stature. Yet the result, for those prepared to go some of the distance with her, is to promote a more participatory, ecologically sensitive, democratic epistemology (and rhetoric) than the alleged purity of the hard-edged discourses of mastery can allow. The place she holds open for experiential—testimonial—evidence consolidates this claim while at once exacerbating the rhetorical tension and enhancing her work's social and political import.

Here I am reading Carson as a proto-social epistemologist even though she would not have identified herself as one. Social epistemology has come into its own as a specific domain of inquiry and analysis long after her death, but many of the ways her research practice departs from the prescriptions of "the epistemological tradition" are consonant with the aims and rhetorical positionings that have come to define social epistemology as a field of inquiry. Moreover, the respect Carson accords to testimony in knowledge-seeking, the part advocacy practices—practices, indeed, of "social persuasion"—play in her larger project, and the taken-for-granted acceptability of a level of affective engagement with the subject matters she investigates, undoubtedly vitiate the purity and disrupt the isolation from the social world presupposed by the strictures with which mainstream Anglo-American epistemologies have claimed hegemony (see Moss, ch. 34).

To set the stage for the inquiry I pursue in this chapter, consider the following passage from the editors' introduction to the volume, *Social Epistemology*:

> The epistemological enterprise—indeed, arguably philosophy more generally—has for much of its history . . . been cast along egocentric lines. Where a non-egocentric approach has been taken . . . the focus has been on individuals . . . interacting with their environment rather than on the significance of social interaction for an understanding of the nature and value of knowledge. . . . The only kind of social topic discussed at any length by mainstream epistemologists was that of testimony, and even then the issue tended to be largely understood from the perspective of the consumer of testimony rather than . . . the complex social web in which testimonial exchanges take place. (Haddock, Millar, and Pritchard 2010: ix)

Here, then, I am reading Carson as a social epistemologist before her time, for the challenge her research strategies and rhetorical practices pose to the hegemony of egocentric, asocial inquiry. Her respect for testimony as a source of evidence, hitherto summarily dismissed as merely subjective—akin to anecdote, opinion, or hearsay within the exclusions effected by a commitment to neutral language and pure

logic—presages the rhetorical and substantive shifts that have resulted in social epistemology's now being "firmly lodged at the very heart of a vibrant contemporary epistemological literature" (ix).

In short, social epistemology seeks to establish itself within and against the exclusionary strictures of an epistemological domain—an "ideal theory," to use Charles Mills's apt
words—whose borders and precepts are guarded by practices of principled disengage-
ment allegedly modeled upon, and normatively required of, bona fide scientific inquiry
(see Mills 2005: 164–84). In the instituted epistemic imaginary of the white, Western
world, such inquiry is commonly enacted in the figure of autonomous man (Castoriadis
1994, 1998). In what I have called "S-knows-that-p" epistemologies, the governing conviction is that claims to know accorded the honorific status "knowledge" will be such
that S could be any would-be knower, and p any putative object of knowledge (see Code
1995: 23–57). Hence, Hunter continues, "Both the new 'rhetoric' and the new communication of science mimic the autonomous individual of the liberal democratic state, isolated and capable of pure objective judgement, relying on his sight and his capacity for
precise, faultless, rational procedure" (1999: 31). In short, the rhetorical positioning of
autonomous man as a character ideal and emblematic figure in Anglo-American philosophy in general, and epistemology in particular, has played a constitutive part in shaping
the instituted social-epistemic imaginary of the white, Western/northern world, which
silently generates and upholds standards of epistemological and social-political-ethical
legitimacy.

It is also significant that in the epistemological tradition, where simple empirical knowledge claims are commonly presented in an "S-knows-that-p" rubric ("Sam
knows that the door is open"), the unquestioned assumption is that S could be anyone
at all, located in "standard observation conditions," and p could be any item at all, likewise located. Not only, then, are knowers and objects represented as substitutable for
one another, but an overarching assumption of human sameness tacitly but forcefully
governs the epistemological inquiry reliant on such practices. Such an assumption has
wide-ranging rhetorical and political implications, generated, often unreflectively, from
its self-presentation as ideal theory. Accompanied and informed by an overweening fear
of any position that smacks of relativism, prior to the emergence of naturalized epistemology and social epistemology, mainstream Anglo-American epistemologists worried that inquiry that would count such aspects of human diversity as sex, race, class,
embodiment, and situation among conditions for the production of knowledge would
amount to the first step onto a slippery slope leading directly into a pernicious relativism
and thereby would signal the death of "the epistemological project." Many still evince
such worries. Moreover, and perhaps less visibly to many practitioners, standard, allegedly "neutral" empirical examples—cups on tables, cats on mats, doors being opened—
assume the ubiquity of such basic objects as comprise the "everyday" in materially
replete societies, even though such objects cannot be so readily presumed to be matters of course in other places and for other populations. In short, the effects of taken-
for-granted human and material homogeneity generated from the putatively exemplary

location of autonomous man are far-reaching and often unjustly, even offensively, presumptuous, both in epistemology and in the wider world.

All of these caveats notwithstanding, autonomy does not in itself deserve unqualified critical condemnation. For reasons situated at the intersections of feminist, antiracist, postcolonial, and ecological thinking, its significance as a liberatory ideal is not easily gainsaid. Thus, for example, Jennifer Nedelsky's analysis of feminist reasons for aspiring to autonomy still claims persuasive salience. Noting how autonomy in its received articulations has carried within it "the individualism characteristic of liberalism"—a position inimical to much twentieth-century feminist theory—she insists that "the basic value of autonomy is ... central to feminism" (Nedelsky 1989: 7). It is analogously central in other "new social movements." Many feminists are justifiably disenchanted with liberal individualism, yet neither then nor now are feminists and other Others from autonomous man prepared to relinquish a belief in "freedom as a value" or to abandon "the notion of a human capacity for making one's own life and self" (8). The paradox, for Nedelsky, is that although "liberalism has been the source of our language of freedom and self-determination ... the values we cherish have come to us embedded in a theory that denies the reality we know: the centrality of relationships in constituting the self" (9). A capacity for self-determination, then, is semantically central to the idea(l) of autonomy in its instantiations as a release from heteronomy: a capacity for self-governance, for giving the law to oneself. Yet, owing to how this capacity has evolved—again semantically, rhetorically—into a hyperbolic, hard-edged isolation and insulation from "external" social and other ecological influences, the promise of the original idea(l) has been corrupted to yield a monstrous picture of a human self/subject closed against acknowledging the influences that have made him (and continue to make him) who or what he is, in both a positive and a negative sense.

Giving the moral law to oneself, acting in one's own name politically, and achieving knowledge by one's "own" efforts are of a piece with and perpetuate the stark individualism realized by a moral-political agent accountable principally, and often solely, to himself. This characterization may seem hyperbolic, but the rhetorical effects of the conceptions of autonomy that have evolved to inform the Western/northern social imaginary of the late twentieth- and early twenty-first centuries justify so stark a reading. Thus, whether despite or because of its putatively universal pertinence, "autonomy" in its autonomy-of-knowledge modalities restricts the purview of "proper" knowledge to autonomous knowledge claims made by infinitely replicable individual knowers, thereby positioning *social* epistemology uneasily alongside, or indeed in opposition to, epistemological orthodoxy. Clearly, it requires a curious sleight of hand to ignore, as Hunter observes, that the "social world always underlies scientific procedures and rhetoric, but by convention science operates as if it can take the social and contextual for granted" (1999: 32). Nor do the alleged gains in objectivity or neutrality warrant the contortions required to do so. These concerns are germane to thinking about epistemic responsibility, testimony, and advocacy, all of which are central issues for social epistemology in its nascent rhetoric but which, as I have noted, have been—and still frequently are—discredited or disdained in the epistemological mainstream for destroying epistemology's isolation from the social world where its purity is bound to be sullied. Social epistemology, then, has yet to claim a rhetoric of its own: to establish itself in rhetorical spaces carved out so as to exclude from "epistemology proper" practices of inquiry that eschew the possibility of achieving "a view from nowhere" or a "god's-eye view," some simulacrum of which has long been imagined to be a defining feature of objectivity, and hence the desideratum for conducting empirical observation worthy of informing properly—if ideally—objective knowledge. This fantasy of objectivity reaches its rhetorical apotheosis in Karl Popper's programmatic dictum that "knowledge in the objective sense is *knowledge without a knower*: it is *knowledge without a knowing subject*" (1979: 109), with its brief for the definitive veracity of knowledge claims uncontaminated by human thought, and thence closed to any prospect of naturalizing or, a fortiori, of socializing inquiry. Social epistemologists, in sharp contrast, seek evidence and derive conclusions from a conviction that, as Donna Haraway puts it, "the only way to find a larger vision is to be somewhere in particular" (1991: 196). Dislocated observation—were it even thinkable—could yield no knowledge of value for real knowers attempting to know responsibly and well in a real, diversely configured, and multiply populated world. Nor for social epistemologists is knowledge-seeking the solitary, solipsistic endeavor it is held to be, both descriptively and normatively, in mainstream Anglo-American epistemologies. In short, the hegemonic status of autonomous man and, by extension, of autonomy as a legitimating feature of credible knowledge production and verification, functions as a silently controlling presence in the ways it blocks or discredits a range of practices that have subsequently come to be definitive of social epistemology.

Appearing before social epistemology had claimed credibility as a viable epistemic project, yet still counted among its landmark texts, are two articles by John Hardwig—"Epistemic Dependence" (1985) and "The Role of Trust in Knowledge" (1991)—whose titles alone break with entrenched, rhetorically sustained presumptions about the autonomy of knowledge. Drawing on the report of a physics experiment in which 99 participants are listed as authors, and as interdependent throughout the processes of inquiry for results they could not have produced or verified for themselves, Hardwig argues convincingly for the centrality of trust—an echo of the *ēthos* and *fides* of rhetorical persuasion—in making the experiment's conclusions possible. For social epistemologists, his analyses opened the way toward claiming recognition of the implausibility of autonomy as a governing epistemic value, and toward understanding the significance of trust in the production of knowledge as such, beyond the confines of physical-natural science.

In short, I am suggesting that recognizing the part trust in its multiple modalities plays in making knowledge possible and in reclaiming the epistemological centrality of testimony functions as a bridge between the practices of formal, dislocated knowledge projects constitutive of the epistemologies of the Anglo-American mainstream and the central, if diverse, ingredients of social epistemology in its currently evolving instantiations. Trust is integral to giving, receiving, and relying on testimony. Trusting is "second-personal," social, epistemically responsive, and potentially responsible; it is required if epistemic justice is to be done and epistemic injustice is to be avoided or repaired. It cannot be given or received in epistemic interactions where "knowers" are accorded mere placeholder status, and it needs to inform epistemic negotiations where coercive assumptions about human sameness and the rhetoric that sustains them are explicitly eschewed. There could be no trust without a trusting subject!

Thus, in my view it is partly owing to the centrality it accords to testimony that social epistemology claims its title (see Code 2010): a practice made possible, in part, by the subtle yet far-reaching effects of linguistic and rhetorical shifts from impersonal, third-person propositional claims that "S knows that p" to the language of speakers and hearers. Such a shift toward a new rhetoric of social epistemology is well illustrated in Edward Craig's (1990) *Knowledge and the State of Nature* and Miranda Fricker's (2007) *Epistemic Injustice*. It is equally striking in the attention social epistemologists pay to extended examples of situated epistemic negotiation and to simple and complex knowledge-conveying exchanges between and among people in the real world.

Where reliance on the "S-knows-that-p" rubric enabled twentieth-century Anglo-American epistemologists to imagine they could transcend the vicissitudes of the world by determining formal, universal, a priori, necessary and sufficient conditions for "knowledge in general," Craig, as his title reference to the "state of nature" signals, returns to the world as the place where knowledge is made, conveyed, deliberated, and adjudicated. A distinction he draws is germane to the epistemic significance of this shift to an addressive mode: "There are informants, and there are sources of information. . . . Roughly, the distinction is between a person's telling me something and my being able to tell something from observation of him" (Craig 1990: 35). He thus focuses on practices of hearing and speaking as these are involved in engaging with people as informants. By contrast, treating people as sources of information involves a level of objectification not unlike what is involved in knowing the age of a tree by counting its rings (Craig's example). Yet it is in his attention to the informant as a source of knowledge that the innovative significance of this approach for social epistemology is apparent. This is no mere spectator theory but a communicative, rhetorical one, where people acquire knowledge from and with one another "as subjects with a common purpose, rather than as objects from which services, in this case true belief, can be extracted" (36). That said, most of Craig's analysis is of third-person and first-person knowledge (cf. 68): there is no discussion of "second persons"—of the complexities of addressing or attempting to reach agreement with a "you" (singular or plural) in recognizably social situations—beyond this mention of a common purpose. Hence a flavor of replicability remains. Craig focuses more on the consumer of testimony than on what Haddock, Millar, and Pritchard call the "complex social web in which testimonial exchanges take place" (2010: ix). In this respect his analyses are typical of much recent work on testimony, as is his neglect of the *politics* of testimony, of asymmetrical, power-infused social-epistemic positionings of speaker and hearer, or of the multiple ways treating people as sources of information could play into their vulnerability. Perhaps most urgently, he does not consider the strong possibility that dealing with people as informants can be expected to be as straightforward as he proposes only if speakers and listeners are situated on a level playing field, with equal expectations of claiming a place to speak, and of being heard and believed. Beyond simple exchanges of neutral information—if indeed there are exchanges of this kind—such ease of communication can never be presumed.

My interest in these thoughts is prompted, if somewhat incongruously, by recent Anglo-American work in the epistemology of testimony (Welbourne 1986, 2001; Coady 1992; Lackey and Sosa 2006). Yet, starting from a feminist-informed position, my purpose is to think away from places where its authors treat testimony merely as information-conveying one-liners reporting everyday "facts" as though into a void and toward thinking about the modalities of testimony where it functions as telling, as exposing, as involving modalities of power, vulnerability, and trust, and hence as being directed to specific interlocutors. Such elaborated testimony is enacted in narrating back and forth, creating relations between teller and hearer that in their political implications, whether benign or malign, exceed the pronouncements uttered on the putatively "level playing field" of which pre-social epistemologies are made. Following this line of thought thus requires moving away from a spectator mode of knowing toward an addressive, rhetorical mode such as is pivotal, for example, in Fricker's (2007) analyses and in her indebtedness to Craig (1990).

Fricker's writings on epistemic injustice are grounded in a careful reading of virtue epistemology and a broader engagement with a range of real-world implications of power, prejudice, stereotypes, credibility, situated knowledges, the ethical-epistemological complexities of trust, and some of the social conditions for conceiving or conferring the status of knower. Such issues animate the discussion throughout and are quintessentially social in their rhetoric and practice. Epistemic injustice can, in her analysis, be testimonial, hermeneutical, or an amalgam of the two, but in every case it is a source of harm to human beings as knowing subjects or as knowable. Working with a range of subtly analyzed examples, Fricker shows how would-be testifiers whose testimony is systemically misheard, misinterpreted, or heard through predetermined judgments of its credibility or lack thereof based on *who* the testifier is (female, black, disabled, old) are degraded and disenfranchised as putative members of a community of knowers: the incredulity enacted "can carry symbolic weight to the effect that the speaker is less than a full epistemic subject" (Fricker 2007: 145). With hermeneutic injustice, the issue has more to do with "a lacuna in the collective hermeneutical resource" (150) whose effect is to render certain experiences unintelligible. Among the most common examples are minority or oppressed-group experiences. Fricker's analysis of women's struggles to bring into common currency a language capable of analyzing and addressing sexual harassment aptly illustrates the point. In the absence of any available rhetorical space where their reports could claim a just hearing, their putative knowledge fails to achieve acknowledgment. Such analyses, which are among the touchstones of current social-epistemological theory, find no place in the benign rhetoric of "S-knows-that-*p*" epistemologies: human interchangeability cannot be taken for granted once the power differentials such events expose are taken into account.

This said, in view of the tenacity of the dominant rhetoric of impersonal objectivity it is worth recalling how the epistemology of testimony had to establish itself cautiously, by claiming initial rhetorical credibility as a minor variation on the "S-knows-that-*p*" orthodoxy. Thus, in Tony Coady's (1992) text, for example, monological, empirical knowledge claims conveyed from knower to knower are the putative and paradigmatic stuff of which testimonially conveyed knowledge was made, with the consequence that, despite the innovative and indeed landmark status of his text, the larger complexities of testimonial exchange went unaddressed. By contrast, my *Epistemic Responsibility* (1987), which initially was read as entering the discussion as a contributor to virtue epistemology, claimed a place only uneasily in the epistemology of the mainstream but is now often cited as a founding text in social epistemology. Diagnosing the marginalization of such works would require too lengthy a discussion, but significant among reasons for resistance were the compromises to the ideal of certainty entailed in granting epistemological credibility to theories for which the specificities of epistemic subjectivity were central.

Indeed, perhaps the most rhetorically outrageous consequence of a shift to social epistemology, for philosophers committed to epistemological orthodoxy, is the new-found pertinence—indeed, the urgency—of questions about epistemic subjectivity: about the identities and social-political positionings of the putative knowers. In the relatively closed rhetorical spaces of a rhetoric that "claims that there is no need for rhetoric" (recalling Hunter) it is difficult to carve out a place where subjectivity can be taken appropriately into account in the face of intransigent fears about the collapse of epistemology into subjectivism or relativism (an echo of the ancient philosophical critiques of the sophists). Autonomy discourse, as I have noted, perpetuates a rhetoric of human sameness and interchangeability that produces yet another obstacle for social epistemology to navigate in giving theoretical substance to its recognition that sameness cannot be presupposed in any epistemic inquiry. It goes without saying that the characteristics attributed to "autonomous man" are those imagined to be typical of a white, adult (but not old), able-bodied, educated, and propertied man in a materially replete society whose circumstances afford him access to the stuff of which knowledge is made. Once these constitutive assumptions have been exposed, questions about "whose *social* are we talking about?" inevitably claim a place in social epistemology. They have generated some of the most compelling, creative responses now occupying center stage in social epistemology and its emerging rhetoric, responses which continue to unsettle the old mainstream analytic rhetoric while offering more capacious analyses in its place.

Space permits addressing only two salient examples. In her contribution to a text aptly (rhetorically) titled *the center must not hold*, Susan Babbitt cites Charles Mills, who asks, "What is wrong with moral equality, autonomy, self-realization . . .?" While Mills takes the question to be a rhetorical one, Babbitt maintains that it is "not a rhetorical question: it is one with an answer. There *is* something wrong with moral equality, autonomy, self-realization, etc., when such concepts are defined in terms of popular (liberal) assumptions of Anglo-American philosophy" (Babbitt 2010: 173). She engages with the rhetorical implications of Carol Pateman's *indifference contract*, which has the effect—epistemologically, ethically, politically—of rendering 80 percent of the world's population *other*, indifferent to the concerns addressed at the putatively *white* center. Contrary to the founding assumptions of theories that aver no need for rhetoric, Babbitt argues that "Anglo-American philosophy may be wrong in some of its deepest, identifying commitments, particularly about the nature of human freedom" (188) and, by implication, about the rhetorical principles and values constitutive of its conceptions of knowledge, wisdom, and trust.

The thought that mainstream philosophy may be *wrong* connects, if obliquely, to a second rupture social epistemologists have brought about in the seamless rhetoric of the mainstream: the birth and creative contributions of what has come to be called *agnotology*. Drawing from the language of agnosticism, the term refers to the new epistemologies of ignorance in which analysis focuses on the conditions that generate and sustain ignorance, much as epistemology *tout court* has concentrated on determining conditions for achieving and sustaining knowledge (Sullivan and Tuana 2007; Proctor and Schiebinger 2008). At once social and political in its epistemological orientation, contributors to this body of work turn their attention to situations where ignorance, in various ways, retains a place as the underside of, or a counter discourse to, the discourse of knowledge, and to analyzing the exclusions established knowledge often tacitly, sometimes more explicitly, enacts. For example, Shannon Sullivan, asking why she knows so little about Puerto Rico, produces a genealogical analysis of the effects of her schooling in the United States, where a particular story about "Porto Rico" was promulgated as the "going wisdom," leaving those for whom it became the "true story" ignorant of the complex relations of coloniality that continue to infuse everyday American assumptions and moral-political judgments about how things are in Puerto Rico (Sullivan and Tuana 2007: 225).

In "The Power of Ignorance"—my contribution to the same volume—I address British colonialist ignorance of everyday life in India, despite the availability of James Mill's (1818) putatively definitive volume, *The History of British India*. Mill's self-avowed rhetorical positioning, on which he based his "knowledge" of India and from which he derived his colonial policies, was to discount any possibility that Indians might have been able to define and represent themselves. He worked from a conviction that Indians had no history of their own, no record of progress, and therefore no claim to be studied or engaged with as a civilized people whose resistance to being colonized called out for a respectful, knowledgeable response. Analogously, the *Agnotology* collection (Proctor and Schiebinger 2008) analyzes some of the ways doubt has systematically been cast on warnings about climate change and about the dangers of cigarette smoking by playing on a margin of uncertainty that responsible scientific inquiry must often avow, yet the authors record how that very uncertainty can generate "reasons" to continue promoting corporate interests and ecologically damaging practices (see McMurry, ch. 58).

I cite these two examples as a way of demonstrating that social epistemology's principal and overriding rhetorical departure from the epistemologies of the mainstream is to be found in its practice of eschewing "ideal theory" to work down on the ground, often with fairly extended empirical examples and situations, to determine how they can best be known and lived in their multiple ramifications. Ideal theories based, if implicitly, on assumptions of human and circumstantial sameness mask fundamental differences and inequalities, set them outside the purview of epistemological analysis, and truncate possibilities of social-political knowledge and understanding. A viable social epistemology—and its accompanying rhetoric—will refuse such idealizations.

FURTHER READING

Heidi Grasswick's (2006) article provides a fine overview of feminist contributions to social epistemology. *Social Epistemology*, a collection of essays edited by Adrian Haddock, Alan Millar, and Duncan Pritchard (2010), is currently the most up-to-date volume analyzing this phenomenon. Jennifer Lackey and Ernest Sosa's (2006) *The Epistemology of Testimony* is a fine collection of state-of-the-art analyses of testimony. Helen Longino's (1990) *Science as Social Knowledge* is a landmark text in the challenge it poses to the rational/social dichotomy, a critique she develops further in *The Fate of Knowledge* (2004). Frederick Schmitt's (1994) edited collection, *Socializing Epistemology: The Social Dimensions of Knowledge*, remains the most frequently cited landmark text in social epistemology.

REFERENCES

Babbitt, Susan. 2010. "Philosophy's Whiteness and the Loss of Wisdom." In *the center must not hold: White Women Philosophers on the Whiteness of Philosophy*, edited by George Yancy, 167–192. Plymouth: Lexington Books.

Carson, Rachel. 1962. *Silent Spring*. New York: Houghton Mifflin.

Castoriadis, Cornelius. 1994. "Radical Imagination and the Social Instituting Imaginary." In *Rethinking Imagination: Culture and Creativity*, edited by Gillian Robinson and John Rundell, 136–154. London: Routledge.

Castoriadis, Cornelius. 1998. *The Imaginary Institution of Society*. Translated by Kathleen Blamey. Cambridge, MA: MIT Press.

Coady, C. A. J. 1992. *Testimony: A Philosophical Study*. Oxford: Oxford University Press.

Code, Lorraine. 1987. *Epistemic Responsibility*. Hanover, NH: University Press of New England.

Code, Lorraine. 1995. *Rhetorical Spaces: Essays on (Gendered) Locations*. New York: Routledge.

Code, Lorraine. 2006. *Ecological Thinking: The Politics of Epistemic Location*. New York: Oxford University Press.

Code, Lorraine. 2010. "Testimony, Advocacy, Ignorance: Thinking Ecologically about Social Knowledge." In *Social Epistemology*, edited by Adrian Haddock, Alan Millar, and Duncan Pritchard, 29–50. Oxford: Oxford University Press.

Craig, Edward. 1990. *Knowledge and the State of Nature: An Essay in Conceptual Synthesis*. Oxford: Clarendon.

Fricker, Miranda. 2007. *Epistemic Injustice: Power and the Ethics of Knowing*. Oxford: Oxford University Press.

Grasswick, Heidi. 2006. "Feminist Social Epistemology." *Stanford Encyclopedia of Philosophy.* http://plato.stanford.edu/entries/feminist-social-epistemology/.

Haddock, Adrian, Alan Millar, and Duncan Pritchard, eds. 2010. *Social Epistemology.* Oxford: Oxford University Press.

Haraway, Donna. 1991. *Simians, Cyborgs, and Women: The Reinvention of Nature.* New York: Routledge.

Hardwig, John. 1985. "Epistemic Dependence." *Journal of Philosophy* 82 no. 7: 335–349.

Hardwig, John. 1991. "The Role of Trust in Knowledge." *Journal of Philosophy* 88 no. 12: 693–708.

Hunter, Lynette. 1999. *Critiques of Knowing: Situated Textualities in Science, Computing and the Arts.* London: Routledge.

Lackey, Jennifer, and Ernest Sosa, eds. 2006. *The Epistemology of Testimony.* Oxford: Clarendon.

Longino, Helen. 2004. *The Fate of Knowledge.* Princeton, NJ: Princeton University Press.

Longino, Helen. 1990. *Science as Social Knowledge.* Princeton, NJ: Princeton University Press.

Mill, James. 1818. *The History of British India.* London: Baldwin, Cradick, and Joy.

Mills, Charles W. 2005. "'Ideal Theory' as Ideology." *Hypatia: A Journal of Feminist Philosophy* 20 no. 3: 164–184.

Nedelsky, Jennifer. 1989. "Reconceiving Autonomy: Sources, Thoughts and Possibilities." *Yale Journal of Law and Feminism* 1 no. 1: 7–36.

Popper, Karl. 1979. *Objective Knowledge: An Evolutionary Approach.* Oxford: Clarendon.

Proctor, Robert N., and Londa Schiebinger, eds. 2008. *Agnotology: The Making and Unmaking of Ignorance.* Palo Alto, CA: Stanford University Press.

Schmitt, Frederick, ed. 1994. *Socializing Epistemology: The Social Dimensions of Knowledge.* Lanham, MD: Rowman and Littlefield Publishers.

Sullivan, Shannon, and Nancy Tuana, eds. 2007. *Race and Epistemologies of Ignorance.* Albany: State University of New York Press.

Welbourne, Michael. 1986. *The Community of Knowledge.* Aberdeen: Aberdeen University Press.

Welbourne, Michael. 2001. *Knowledge.* Montreal: McGill-Queen's University Press.

Wittgenstein, Ludwig. 1968. *On Certainty.* Edited by G. E. M. Anscombe and G. H. von Wright. Translated by Denis Paul and G. E. M. Anscombe. Oxford: Basil Blackwell.

CHAPTER 58

RHETORIC AND ENVIRONMENT

ANDREW MCMURRY

RHETORIC WITHOUT ENVIRONMENT

THE rhetorical study of environment is justifiably described as a crisis discipline, in that it emerges as an autoimmune response to human-generated emergencies in the biophysical world and, in particular, to the representational and discursive aspects of those emergencies. Robert Cox argues that, "like perturbations in biological systems, distortions, ineptitudes, and system pathologies occur in our communication about the environment" (2007: 10). In fact, one might argue that "environment" itself was born of a crisis of representation: it was a weakly anchored concept of little moment outside a small circle of biologists and conservationists before the signifieds to which it referred heaved wounded and bloodied into everybody's view (Luke 1999: 120–5). "Nature," the concept that environment nominally supersedes, bridges to older discourses on place, organism, and being that held currency when it could still be imagined that man occupied a privileged and separate reality and that his hand did not have a death grip on the throat of Earth. Environment is now rhetorically charged root to tip: its very nebulousness is proof that the biophysical Other will not be extricated, materially or symbolically, from humankind itself: "Of our environment, what we say is what we see" (Cantrill and Oravec 1995: 1).

Lawrence Coupe argues that Kenneth Burke was an eco-rhetorician *avant la lettre*, noting that "it may yet be acknowledged that his most important contribution lay in his foregrounding Earth itself as the ultimate setting of critical activity" (2001: 418). If Coupe is right, then Burke's forays into the "metabiological" would be an exception to the rule in rhetorical studies, which has been to recast environmental problems as rhetorical problems so that the salient participants are human agents alone. In other words, the nonsymbolic *scene*—with its immense assembly of nonhuman entities, including rocks, trees, rivers, clouds, birds, bacteria—must be elided from the picture in favor of exclusive attention to audience, argument, narrative, and other rhetorical features.

Thus, with the same obsessiveness as industrial civilization, fixated on reconfiguring the planet for human ends, rhetoric once imagined it could attend solely upon human "misunderstandings and their remedies" (Richards 1965: 3). Lacking terms (or motivation) to focalize extra-human factors, rhetoric could not easily step beyond its anthropocentric bailiwick—unlike, for example, modern ecology or classical physics, which displaced human agency to the peripheries of their notations, describing entire realms where the presence or absence of man was of no account. Rhetoric, it is safe to say, was foundationally antienvironment, though in that respect no different from the rest of the humanities and social sciences, which also "produced curiously disembodied interpretations of social systems that fail to grasp the degree to which man, no less than leafmold and toads, grows from the loam and tilth of his planet" (James 1973: xiv–v). Rhetoricians toeing the anthropocentric line might recognize and approve of the scholarly approach of Elizabeth Malone, who describes the orientation of her *Debating Climate Change* as follows: "This book revolves around what are, I believe, more interesting questions than whether climate change is actually happening . . . My focus is on how we talk to each other about . . . climate change" (2009: 2). That rhetoricians routinely consider how we talk about phenomena to be more interesting than the phenomena themselves is a perspective that no doubt contributes mightily to rhetoric's disrepute.

Yet rhetoricians and their colleagues in other language-centered approaches (environmental communication, ecocriticism, ecolinguistics, environmental philosophy) are certainly correct that "discourse about the environment plays a formidable role in shaping human interaction with nature" (Muir and Veenedall 1996: xiii). The vision of our species' unlimited growth and progress that so stirred the imagination of the Enlightenment is vitiated by human-induced climate change, resource depletion, ecosystem collapse, and toxification of soil, air, and water. Nevertheless, environmental rhetoric and its allies are up against the blind optimism that permeates the collective consciousness, whereby the profligate misuses of the planet become evidence for the social system's remarkable potency. "It is clear that the future is above all conceived of as the asylum of all uncertainties" (Abeles 2010: 35). Though widely ignored, the collapse is well underway, moving at variable speeds and scales across all of the planet's ecoregions. The pregnant question is this: When will the collapse attract the full attention of civilization's management class—before or after it is too late to do anything about it? In this late hour of Earth—and therefore of us—the most urgent task facing rhetoric scholars is to remedy rhetoric's own misunderstanding of its relationship with the environmental Real. Rhetorical studies of environment take place in the shadow of a rolling catastrophe.

There are two main regions of scholarship in rhetoric and environment: the practico-political and the ethico-epistemic. By no means mutually exclusive, the two nonetheless assemble their own preferred issues, genres, exemplars, and stakes. The practico-political deals with environmentally inflected controversies, communities, and social movements; it draws on the rhetorical heritage's time-tested methods and resources but adjusts or repurposes them in the service of the environmental commitments of its practitioners. Its aim, broadly speaking, is to reduce polarization among environmental persuaders and their constituencies, the better to influence ongoing debates, policies, and policy-making processes. The practico-political, where possible, intervenes directly in these matters by actively addressing appropriate stakeholders. By contrast, the ethico-epistemic concerns itself with the fundamental interplay between societies and their environments, not surprisingly taking communication as its central concept. Intensely curious about the "obstructions to perception" (Ayres 1999: 47) that cause us to underplay our planet's dimming prospects, the ethico-epistemic draws on a wide range of theoretical perspectives, and the environmentalist commitments of its practitioners may not be immediately obvious, given that its chief goal is to probe the fundamental, nearly inaccessible structures and thought-regimes of contemporary social systems, and that its chief work product is critique. One could say that the difference between the practico-political and ethico-epistemic strains is analogous to that between shallow and deep ecology, the first anchored in the world as we find it, the second steering for the world that might be.

This chapter seeks to reaffirm the importance of the practico-political strain as an organic extension of rhetorical studies and to make the case for the ethico-epistemic as the crucial seedbed of the field as it moves toward a study of what I will dub *rhetorical environmentality*, a cultural condition in which the thing-world is understood to exert rhetorical pressure.

THE PRACTICO-POLITICAL APPROACH

The basic alignments of rhetorical participants in the practico-political arena are easy to define, though, of course, boundaries shift as centers of political gravity advance or retreat with the times. Toward one pole lie environmentalists, concerned scientists, critics of industrial civilization, and a host of fellow travelers from across the political spectrum who argue that the current mode of human interaction with the planet is unsustainable; toward the other are mainstream economists and businesspeople, conservative politicians, boosters of technology, and (it must be admitted) the vast majority of the citizenry who assume that most environmental problems are manageable on a planet that, despite wear and tear, is still robust and bountiful. The former group expresses anxiety, sounds alarms, and calls for immediate action; the latter group ignores, resists, or temporizes. Sometimes these counterpositions refer to sound scientific principles (e.g., caution before conclusion, abundance of evidence), but frequently the "go slow" approach is obviously in the service of a "business as usual" mentality. A simpler way to understand the division is to say that declinists produce narratives of environmental depletion and ecosystem collapse, while exuberantists argue that there are actually few limits on resources (allowing for resource substitution) and Earth's ability to absorb the impact of humans, and that even if there are limits they are more than offset by the unlimited potential of the "ultimate resource": human ingenuity (Simon 1981: x). 50 years after Rachel Carson's *Silent Spring* (1964), 40 after Donella Meadows's *Limits to Growth* (1972), and 25 after the *Brundtland Report* (1987), no argument has truly punctured this "Promethean/cornucopian" bubble (Dryzek 2005: 51–2), which was summed up nicely by two of Carson's contemporaries, the resource economists Harold Barnett and Chandler Morse: "The finite limits of the globe, so real in their unqueried simplicity, lose definition under examination" (1963: 245). So while declinists call for the immediate relief of environmental stresses, exuberantists continue to stall, suggesting that any reckonings with biophysical challenges should be deferred to a future society that will meet them with superior wealth and technologies—a happy trajectory that, unsurprisingly, jibes perfectly with the expansionist designs of exuberantism.

The impediments to making a declinist case are many, but we can boil them down to two basic types of refutations: spatial and temporal. Spatial refutations build on the perception that existential threats are geographically distant and that the planet is vast; temporal refutations build on the perception that such threats are far in the future and that in any case we have heard doomsaying before. In the first category lies most of modern political economy, which hinges on an implicit refusal of spatial limits. This refusal rises from bedrock: modern societies must deal continually with inequalities and social divisions, and these are normally not repaired so much as rendered moot by the creation of wealth, that is, growth, which resolves conflict by "transforming non-economic issues into ones that could be solved by economic bargaining" (Ophuls and Boyan 1992: 237). In essence, growth is the universal balm, and leaders from right to left, Washington to Beijing, call for ever more of it. Thus, it is difficult for declinists to have their arguments accepted when, to paraphrase Upton Sinclair, social harmony depends on them not being accepted. This double bind helps explain why a major environmental leader like Al Gore has staked his credibility on the fallacy that there is no contradiction between economic growth and environmental health. While it might be unfair to accuse Gore of confirmation bias (that is, he adduces evidence only for the position he already espouses), he surely has judged that it would be ethotically fatal for him to claim otherwise (that is, he must never frame his environmentalism within the declinist camp). Nevertheless, the planet is finite, human demands on it are soaring, and growth cannot undo the destruction that growth itself is causing.

In addition to their gainsaying of economic growth, declinists face the widespread perception that environment is somehow external to human affairs in general and economic development in particular. *Homo sapiens*, after all, evolved to meet in-the-face threats like saber-toothed cats, snakes, and other violent humans, not toxic sludge, destabilized weather patterns, and soil erosion. More to the point, in advanced industrial societies the vast majority of citizens are urbanites, moving from one climate-controlled enclosure to another, cosseted against all manner of natural impingements—insects, weeds, wind. The ongoing calamities in the oceans, the forests, and the skies are exigencies that cannot be easily brought near to them. For example, declinists are challenged to make the case for taxing carbon when, first, in its objectionable form, carbon dioxide, it is odorless and invisible, and, second, climate change effects spurred by carbon are (so far) from the quotidian perspective glacially slow in their realization. Climate change is something of a concrete abstraction: we hear of it, but it appears to be happening mostly elsewhere, disconnected from everyday life. Ecologists speak of a "shifting baseline syndrome"; in popular parlance one refers to the "new normal." These terms can be usefully applied to our disconcertingly easy psycho-rhetorical adjustment to what ought to be perceived as environmental calamities. But Burke (1985: 17–8), with typical acuity, notes that the *rationalization* presumed to undergird such self-deception has to be understood not as the refusal of ugly truths (à la Sigmund Freud) but as the pure motive of those for whom there is literally no other orientational vocabulary. In other words, we do not repress environmental warning signs; it is more accurate to say we are simply incapable of bringing these distal events closer to us than our other, proximal priorities.

The second type of impediment to the declinist case is more classically rhetorical and speaks to our habituation to, and consequent faith in, the progress narrative. Since the invention of linear time, the allure of tomorrow was its potential to make up for the deficiencies of today: in the Christian era, a postlapsarian state of sin; in the secular era, a stunted and uneven humanism. The converse idea—that the future is a pale shadow of the past, that in the Ages of Man the Golden precedes the Bronze and the Iron, that there is nothing new under the sun—is premodern and downright pagan. The modern cultural disposition toward the future is that it promises at a minimum more of the same and in most cases an improved version of what exists now. Relatedly, the experience of all individuals is necessarily narrowed to their own precious cadence of days; it is no easy task to fold this compelling personal narrative into the deep time of geo-ecological upheaval. Everyone admits we should not ignore the dangers, but we are like the character Melissa in Ian McEwan's novel *Solar*: "To take [climate change] seriously would be to think about it all the time. Everything else shrank before it. And so like everyone she knew, she could not take it seriously, not completely. Daily life would not permit it" (2010: 165).

This progressivist sentiment exerts a powerful influence on debates about the preferable because it lays out its meaning along irreducible rhetorical continua: the *loci* of quantity and of quality, and the superiority of the later over the earlier (newness). Because the present world is demonstrably stocked with more artifacts, people, information, and options than the past, the future is easily projected as a rising curve of abundance. The same may be said for quality, in that modern history shows a clear record of technological and material improvement, so clear that even when the future arrives and the improvements are quickly routinized and forgotten (e.g., the labor-saving devices of the kitchen have produced time-saving benefits that are quickly eaten up by other demands elsewhere), the die has been cast for the next round of upgrades. Lastly, the rapid succession of new products, services, information, and creative works destabilizes the present, providing no fixed surface, as if we were perpetually slipping downstream toward the unreachable ocean of tomorrow. The modern social system, indeed, is powered by this constant production of difference; each fresh moment is extruded from the previous, newly obsolesced moment, with all its urgent baggage (gadgets, celebrity divorces, crimes, disasters), so that the pressing forward of time is given not just historical but material weight and momentum. The latest eco-catastrophic thriller from Hollywood (e.g., *The Day After Tomorrow*, *Children of Men*, *The Road*) rivets attention on the declinist theme—but only until the next release. What abides is not the theme of decline but the reassuring flow of entertainment products, confirming that tomorrow's spectacle of destruction is sure to be bigger and better than today's.

Between the politico-economic requirement for comforting growth talk and the rhetorico-cognitive preference for triumphalist historicism, it is difficult for warnings of ecological scarcity, environmental hazards, and the like to gain rhetorical traction. Together these two components of the exuberantist program portray a future in which progress and plenty will continue to put paid to Malthusian prophecies of regress and scarcity. Declinists enlist argumentative support from a variety of powerful discourses (economics, science, justice, religion, moral philosophy, and so on), but it is frustratingly difficult to put a dent in audiences' protective cognition. When it comes to framing the future, the slenderest optimism will beat a pessimistic vision every time, for as Richard Weaver notes, "the 'optimists' have the current rhetoric on their side even while the 'pessimists' have the proof. The modern world has a terrific momentum in the direction in which it is going, and many of the words of our everyday vocabulary are terms implicit with approval of modern tendencies" ([1964] 1995: 5).

Not surprisingly, then, rhetorical analyses of the practico-political arena often become absorbed in discovering and unpacking this same formal antagonism between decline and exuberance, usually in play in every environmental disputation, as the following passages exemplify: "By constructing an audience of people 'who cannot be moved to action by an appeal to beauty, or a plea for mercy,' and then by indulging rather than attempting to reconstitute that audience, Ehrlich has created an essentially egocentric appeal, one that has failed to move an audience motivated primarily by a homocentric or ecocentric ethic" (Waddell 1998: 68); "As long as the owl only offers a choice of life with the environment or liberty with the timber industry, it will prevent resolution and remain a problem in its own right" (Moore 1998: 159); "Although each new voice adds to the discordance of an already boisterous debate, U.S. environmentalism rings hollow if it silences the rancher who is rooted in the land" (Peterson and Horton 1998: 190). Each of these passages (all drawn from conclusions to essays in the important volume, *Landmark Essays on Rhetoric and the Environment* [1998]) epitomizes what the authors argue in their respective essays: that the win-lose, up-down approach to environmental debate is counterproductive (no matter that a given result favors the exuberantists or the declinists) because it only furthers the climate of audience polarization and deadlock. What is required instead is rhetorical mediation of the symbolic collisions that exacerbate—and may even create—the conflict about the underlying environmental exigence. In short, rhetoric can help do for environmental disputes what it has done elsewhere: foster recognition of shared values and common interests with a view to integrating divergent visions of the future into mutually satisfying narratives and plans of action. As Jimmie Killingsworth and Jacqueline Palmer put it in their field-pioneering book, *Ecospeak*, "If we find ourselves in a Babel of discourse communities, each with its own characteristic language, epistemological outlook and agenda for action, there remains in rhetorical inquiry a need, a mission, a hope for a generally accessible narrative, the story of how human action reconciles conflicting demands in the search for the good life . . . rhetorical criticism urges continued development of the story of human cooperation" (1992: 20–1). And if, as I have suggested, so many of these conflicting demands involve a struggle between declinist and exuberantist "terministic screens," the goal for practico-political rhetoricians must be to find or create points of overlapping urgency so that the good life is visible to both parties.

THE ETHICO-EPISTEMIC APPROACH

In the practico-political mode, then, rhetorical analysis and instruction address environmental imbroglios using a familiar suite of tactics: diverse audiences are profiled and reconstituted, sources of mutual incomprehension are uncovered and repaired, suitable *topoi* are located and revivified. Narratives and tropes emerge to inspire and motivate. Technical evidence is explained to the hoi polloi. From improved communication, communities of shared value are built; responsive legislatures enact laws to reflect these values; state, corporate, and individual practices conform; and the environment is preserved and protected.

Or not. The open question is: Are the root causes of environmental decline truly amenable to standard rhetorical tactics? There are good reasons to be unsatisfied with the kinds of solutions rhetoric can provide, first among them the fact that the exigencies we are dealing with do not generally disappear simply because disputants reach agreements. A rhetorically sound process with a satisfying result (say, an achieved consensus between environmentalists and ranchers about wolf reintroduction) does not mean the actual environmental exigence has been removed; in fact, it has only been deferred to some later moment when sheep killings by the wolves again threaten the latter's extirpation. Or it may be that the environmental gain—here, a more diverse ecosystem complete with its top predator—is in part or in whole undermined by the broader degradation of the ecoregion through expanded ranching, gold mining, natural gas drilling, or climate change. Even the best-case scenario (e.g., a proactive, transparent consultative process that avoids a potential dispute and heads off environmental damage before it even happens) cannot mitigate the overarching reality, which is that environmentalists are engaged in rearguard actions behind a crumbling front. The mainstream discourse of balance (as in the political candidate's aphorism that "we must seek balance between environmental and economic goals" or the mass media's habit of "balancing" every worrisome environmental datum with a cornucopian sop) means precisely that there is to be no balance: incremental environmental victories here will be swallowed up by developmental victories elsewhere (Patterson and Lee 1997). In global industrial civilization, practico-political resolutions of environmental disputes are almost always provisional: any putative gain may be instantly erased when human priorities change. Thus, proposals to revoke long-held moratoria on offshore drilling can emerge from even a nominally pro-environment administration (Broder 2010).

Debates about environmental issues serve to remind us that rhetoric sees only what it sees, that it functions—as practice and theory—largely within the self-delimiting domain of agent-to-agent interaction, sorting among the symbols, images, and myths that are meaningful within human social systems. But while nothing human is alien to rhetoric, environment is not human. Moreover, despite being produced by humans, social systems are not human either. Their operations do not depend on the intentionality of individuals, no matter how rhetorically astute they are (Luhmann 1989). Thus, even a president using the bully pulpit to change the "dialogue" in America about wealth, poverty, health, or environment can do little to actually shift the operations of the social system. The economic subsystem, for example, continues to grind against Earth: that is its prime directive, a straightforward process of turning nature into commodity and then waste. Presidential rhetoric under such conditions becomes linguistic disaster management: mollifying victims of an oil spill or scapegoating CEOs whose companies are technically behind it, making the sow's ear of the extractive economy into the silk purse of jobs and progress (Peterson 2004). The rhetoric of politicians, environmentalists, celebrities, or scientists can do little to halt or redirect the operations of transnational logging companies turning rain forests into palm plantations or factory trawlers strip-mining the oceans for protein. The demands made upon the planet by humans are not symbolic demands; they are real, they are vast, and they continue despite what anyone says—or could possibly say—about them. Thus rhetorical inquiry that restricts itself to the language moves of persons or groups trying to motivate, denounce, justify or otherwise channel the symbolic flow within the interstices of the social system is literally missing the forest for the trees.

"Now we come to the region of *ecospeak*, where public divisions are petrified, conflicts are prolonged and solutions are deferred by a failure to criticize deeply the terms and conditions of the environmental dilemma" (Killingsworth and Palmer 1992: 8). What drives ethico-epistemic rhetorical inquiry is the need to break through the hoary narratives, encrusted metaphors, and other mental detritus of our destructive modernity. The challenge for even those who "offer sustainable development as a substitute for progress" is an "examination of the symbolic interactions that contribute to our current environmental problems yet fail to equip us to deal with them" (Peterson 1997: 33). I will not rehearse here any of the replacement orientations that have been offered. Suffice it to say that any one of them would be preferable to the exuberantist fantasy that has styled biophysical reality as a vast, free smorgasbord upon which humans are encouraged to gorge.

The ethico-epistemic strain of rhetorical studies thus prompts a deeper evaluation of the obstacles to lasting environmental progress and sustainable society. Most environmental rhetoricians know that practico-political analyses at some point must grapple with the social-systemic hardwiring that limits every tentative gain. When we speak of the ethico-epistemic we are concerned with the most intransigent of those social-systemic functions, alluded to above, that emerged during modernity, when the current stance toward the environment was formed and consolidated. These functions include but are not restricted to the economic, which turns the world and all its contents, including humans, into profits and losses; the juridical, which resolves all legal questions around humans and their rights and properties; the political, which provides no representation to nonhuman agents; the religious, which styles Earth as the creator's gift to humans alone; and the educational, which is primarily abstract and delocalized. According to Niklas Luhmann (1989), all communication is filtered through these function systems, each of which is an environment to the others. The natural environment itself does not communicate at all; it can only stimulate the social systems to produce communications about it. Burke (1984: 7), following Thorstein Veblen, would have agreed that these function systems display a trained incapacity, in that they follow through on their singular programming no matter the cost to environment or to themselves. We need not search far to find examples of the insane rationality of our social systems. Tuna overfishing leads to higher price for tuna, which in turn makes tuna fishing more lucrative. Fossil-fuel emissions lead to the melting of the Arctic ice cap, which opens the Arctic to petroleum exploration, which leads to more fossil-fuel emissions. And so on.

A simple way to understand the problematic is to consider the enormously important ideological differences between the West and the Soviet Union. Then consider that despite these differences—and the very real effects they had upon the organization of mass society and life-possibilities of individuals—the centrally planned economy of the Soviet Union depended as much on the processing of environment as did the free market economies of the West. Given that all modern economies operate by reducing environmental complexity so as to build up their own internal complexity, the question becomes (and it is one that rhetorical inquiry must develop a response to): How can ethical imperatives toward environment gain purchase on this metabolically insatiable function system?

RHETORICAL ENVIRONMENTALITY

What I have outlined above leads to the conclusion that we observe two broad temperaments in rhetoricians concerned about environment. The first is more or less deliberative, belonging to those who believe rhetoric should solve problems: What in the discursive record and the communicational potentialities of humankind can be deployed to help it survive its disastrous tenancy on Earth? The second is a less sanguine perspective that is more or less forensic: If, as they suspect, humankind has exceeded the planet's capacity to support its population and activities, what have been the chief discursive and rhetorical contributions to our impending collapse? The difference here, to a cynic, is that between hope and fatalism, the one group seeking scope for future actions, buoyed by a vision of the virtuous life and the "good man speaking well" (*vir bonus, dicendi peritus*), the other determining the cold facts of a murderous deed already done by a murderous ape.

A more searching view, however, would set aside hope and despair and simply acknowledge that the difference here is between humanism and ecology: the former is a body of thought that claims humans have special powers and rights when it comes to the lifeworld; the latter is a science of the lifeworld that says humans are subject to the same biophysical laws as any other species. The special bias of the humanist rhetorician is the same bias of all humanists: that her subject, man, is improvable, and that the sources of such improvement may be defined and cultivated by rhetoric, the study of communicational cooperation and reconciliation. The special bias of the ecological rhetorician is that *Homo sapiens* is one species among many, with no monopoly on survival. In that view, it is not at all clear that rhetoric can be anything more than a descriptive knowledge.

Still, in our desperate moments we would all probably prefer to view our discipline in the optative mood. Even the pessimists hope in the end that we are more than coroners of a doomed primate, and that our inquiries and interventions into the communicational vagaries of the systems of modern society can somehow effect changes in their programming. But for hope to flourish rhetoric must begin to acknowledge rhetoric's own embeddedness in the scene, which is not so much a setting or place but the substrate of rhetorical possibility. We already have a good way to imagine what that might mean. John Bender and David Wellbery coin the term "rhetoricality" to indicate the notion that contemporary culture is perfused by rhetoric, which is not to be understood as a separate phenomenon or distinct activity. Rhetoric constitutes modern thought and culture, manifesting the "groundless, infinitely ramifying character of discourse in the modern world . . . Rhetoric is no longer the title of a doctrine and a practice, nor a form of cultural memory; it becomes instead something like the condition of our existence" (Bender and Wellbery 1990: 25).

But we must insist that our all-penetrating rhetoricality is itself conditioned by an even more pervasive *environmentality*. The nonsymbolic, the environmental Real, the thing-world—all that we have hitherto understood as nonparticipating and nonpersuasive—must come to be part and parcel of rhetorical culture. At a minimum, we will require the following: critique of our overwhelmingly anthropocentric rhetorical tradition; theorization of the environmental conditioning of all rhetorical situations; and, finally, exploration of the rhetorical capacities of nonhumans.

FURTHER READING

DeLuca (1999) is an influential study of social movement politics and rhetoric that will also be of interest to scholars of visual culture. Garrard (2004) remains the best introduction to studies of literature and environment; the book is structured by rhetorical analyses of the key tropes that inform contemporary environmental perception. Brendon (2011) studies the problems and issues that emerge as modern science grapples with the environmentally damaging effects of its own powerful metaphors. Senecah (2004) is a wide-ranging collection of insightful essays on such topics as systems approaches to environmental communication, women's narratives, public policy, and presidential campaigns. Modern environmentalism begins with Rachel Carson's (1964) *Silent Spring*, and the essays in Waddell (2000) explore and extend her work into contemporary debates about language, rhetoric, activism, and politics.

REFERENCES

Abeles, Marc. 2010. *The Politics of Survival*. Translated by Julie Kleinman. Durham, NC: Duke University Press.

Ayres, Ed. 1999. *God's Last Offer*. New York: Four Walls Eight Windows.

Barnett, Harold, and Chandler Morse. 1963. *Scarcity and Growth: The Economics of Natural Resource Availability*. Baltimore: Johns Hopkins University Press.

Bender, John, and David Wellbery. 1990. *The Ends of Rhetoric: History, Theory, Practice*. Stanford, CA: Stanford University Press.

Broder, John. 2010. "Obama to Open Offshore Areas to Oil Drilling for First Time." *New York Times*, March 31, New York ed.

Burke, Kenneth. 1984. *Permanence and Change*. Berkeley: University of California Press.

Cantrill, James, and Christine Oravec. 1995. *The Symbolic Earth*. Lexington: University of Kentucky Press.

Carson, Rachel. 1964. *Silent Spring*. London: Hamish Hamilton.

Cox, Robert. 2007. "Nature's 'Crisis Disciplines': Does Environmental Communication Have an Ethical Duty?" *Environmental Communication* 1 no. 1: 5–20.

Coupe, Lawrence. 2001. "Kenneth Burke: Pioneer of Ecocriticism." *Journal of American Studies* 35 no. 3: 413–431.

DeLuca, Kevin M. 1999. *Image Politics: The New Rhetoric of Environmental Activism*. New York: Guilford.

Dryzek, John. 2005. *The Politics of the Earth: Environmental Discourses*. 2nd ed. Oxford: Oxford University Press.

Garrard, Greg. 2004. *Ecocriticism*. New York: Routledge.

James, Bernard. 1973. *The Death of Progress*. New York: Knopf.

Killingsworth, M. Jimmie, and Jacqueline S. Palmer. 1992. *Ecospeak: Rhetoric and Environmental Politics in America*. Carbondale: Southern Illinois University Press.

Luhmann, Niklas. 1989. *Ecological Communication*. Translated by John Bednarz. Chicago, IL: University of Chicago Press.

Luke, Timothy W. 1999. *Capitalism, Democracy, and Ecology*. Urbana: University of Illinois Press.

Malone, Elizabeth L. 2009. *Debating Climate Change: Pathways Through Argument to Agreement*. London: Earthscan.

McEwan, Ian. 2010. *Solar*. New York: Anchor.

Meadows, Donella H., et al. 1972. *The Limits to Growth: A Report for the Club of Rome's Project on the Predicament of Mankind*. New York: Universe.

Moore, Mark P. 1998. "Constructing Irreconcilable Conflict: The Function of Synecdoche in the Spotted Owl Controversy." In *Landmark Essays on Rhetoric and the Environment*, edited by Craig Waddell, 145–163. Mahwah, NJ: Lawrence Erlbaum.

Muir, Star, and Thomas Veenendall. 1996. *Earthtalk: Communication Empowerment for Environmental Action*. Westport, CT: Praeger.

Ophuls, William, and A. Stephen Boyan. 1992. *Ecology and the Politics of Scarcity Revisited.* New York: W.H. Freeman.

Patterson, Robert, and Ronald Lee. 1997. "The Environmental Rhetoric of 'Balance': A Case Study of Regulatory Discourse and the Colonization of the Public." *Technical Communication Quarterly* 6 no. 1: 25–40.

Peterson, Tarla Rai. 1997. *Sharing the Earth: The Rhetoric of Sustainable Development.* Columbia: University of South Carolina Press.

Peterson, Tarla Rai, ed. 2004. *Green Talk in the White House.* College Station: Texas A&M Press.

Peterson, Tarla Rai, and Cristi Choat Horton. 1998. "Rooted in the Soil: How Understanding the Perspectives of Landowners Can Enhance the Management of Environmental Disputes." In *Landmark Essays on Rhetoric and the Environment*, edited by Craig Waddell, 165–194. Mahwah, NJ: Lawrence Erlbaum.

Richards, I. A. 1965. *The Philosophy of Rhetoric.* London: Oxford University Press.

Senecah, Susan. 2004. *The Environmental Communication Yearbook.* Vol. 1. Mahwah, NJ: Lawrence Erlbaum.

Simon, Julian. 1981. *The Ultimate Resource.* Princeton, NJ: Princeton University Press.

Waddell, Craig. 1998. "Perils of a Modern Cassandra: Rhetorical Aspects of Public Indifference to the Population Explosion." In *Landmark Essays on Rhetoric and the Environment*, edited by Craig Waddell, 55–73. Mahwah, NJ: Lawrence Erlbaum.

Waddell, Craig, ed. 2000. *And No Birds Sing: Rhetorical Analyses of Rachel Carson's "Silent Spring."* Carbondale: Southern Illinois University Press.

Weaver, Richard M. (1964) 1995. *Visions of Order.* Wilmington, DE: Intercollegiate Studies Institute Books.

CHAPTER 59

RHETORIC AND SCIENCE

RICHARD DOYLE

> It should be obvious to anyone that what we as subjects can know about
> the cosmos depends to a large degree on our starting point, and this goes
> back to who we are. Of course it is also true that the tools and methods we
> employ in our investigations determine what we will discover, just as the
> mesh of the net determines—in Eddington's famous analogy—what kind
> of fish we will pull from the sea. Nonetheless, more than anything else, the
> investigator himself is the net.
>
> —William C. Chittick, *The Self-Disclosure of God*

IN the beginning, two question marks, with some exclamation points thrown
in: Rhetoric?! Science?! When paired together, the terms "rhetoric" and "science" might
appear as oxymorons, but this cultural understanding of scientific knowledge as the
antithesis of rhetoric can be sustained only as long as we ignore the *practice* of science.
Rhetoric, as the domain of probabilistic and relative knowledge (if not downright deception), appears antithetical to science. Science tends to be widely accepted as the sine qua
non of absolute authority and truth in the secular world. That is, until we attempt to
actually *do* science.

In fact, one of the historical mutations that is perhaps most characteristic of the rhetoric of science in the modern and postmodern periods has been the eternal *return of
the problem of rhetoric for science* (Latour and Woolgar 1979; Bazerman 1988; Gross
1990; Moss 1993; Fahnestock 1999; Doyle 1997, 2011). Although our cultural ideals of
science suggest that it should "speak for itself," in practice the creation, circulation,
and transformation of scientific knowledge demand that we use all available means
of persuasion (as Aristotle puts it): language, images, gestures, diagrams, simulations.
A DNA sequencer makes a sequence glow with luciferase, signaling the presence of a
gene to a researcher; the Hubble telescope relays images of the glorious pillars of creation, which become the focus of a 3D IMAX movie; a disabled astrophysicist speaks
through a computer-enabled adjunct; minds increasingly wander in response to a
massive production of information; and all focus our attention on the transduction

of the asymptotically eternal truth of the scientific quest with the contingent, finite, and momentary aspect of truth available to any particular human audience at any particular time within the "realm of rhetoric" (Perelman 1982). As technological evolution and, as I shall suggest, thermodynamics, push us to ever expanding rhetorical practices and contexts, this return of the repressed of rhetoric in science becomes increasingly acute.

This very need science has for rhetoric presents an experiential, but continuously navigated, tension between "objectivity" and the conditions of communication exchange and interpretation (see Moss, ch. 34). In other words, the objectivity claimed for scientific statements, or the independence of any particular result from any particular subject making a claim, conflicts with the specificity and peculiarities of a scientific report composed for some necessarily particular audience, namely, *the collective formation of subjectivities for whom and to whom the practice of science exists*. Rhetorical practices are part of a suite of techniques fundamental to scientific inquiry, from the electron microscope (a technique of characterization) to the *Gedankenexperiment* (a technique of imagination) (cf. Rotman 1993). Given the rather fortunate proliferation of ecologies of information technology as well as techniques of DIY (do it yourself) science, science is increasingly practiced outside of the official domain of universities, government labs, and research and development sectors. The question of the specificity and objectivity of any particular act of scientific communication becomes particularly acute as both the practitioners and audiences of scientific communication become pluralized, globalized, transformed, diversified, and leaked.

When we go about doing science, we find that it entails doing what Belgian bioethicist Gilbert Hottois (1981) dubbed "technoscience." This neologism, coined to label a new, or newly perceived, aspect of reality, conjoins "science" and "technology"—precisely because the practice of science cannot be disentangled from the use of technologies or the contexts of cultural authority and persuasion that attend those technologies. In Hottois's field of bioethics, this is particularly obvious. The very topics of bioethics, such as stem cell research, organ donation scarcity, and abortion policy, are irreducibly entangled with the practices of tissue culture (cell culture technologies, the 3D printing of flesh), pharmaceutical technologies (immunosuppressants), and visualization technologies (ultrasound) that give rise to, alter, and sometimes transform perspectives on and the experience of living systems.

Writing is one of the oldest, most powerful and invisible technologies of science. Writing, and the patterns of writing (rhetorical tropes, figures, and schemes), enables the production, circulation, and refutation of scientific knowledge (Fahnestock 1999). Furthermore, these forms and structures of discourse provide us with perhaps the largest domain for the rhetorical analysis of technoscience's entanglement between the quest for knowledge and its tools. Yet the very transformations of information technologies alluded to previously suggest that this domain is about to be—or already has been—dwarfed by *technologies of attention* (smartphones, tablets, brain-activated headsets) for which writing remains a necessary but insufficient model. Hence in this heuristic account I shall offer a more general description of the rhetoric of science with which we can both model the transformations currently underway and also map new modalities of scientific knowledge production not yet imagined.

And what we must imagine is that scientific knowledge production is itself already dependent on a new order of *being* that even now evolves beyond the archetype of *human* and toward what V. I. Vernadsky (1945) dubbed the "noösphere." Vernadsky, an early-twentieth-century geochemist and mineralogist, offered "noösphere" as a map for articulating the transformative power of differences of attention on the Earth. While cosmic evolution saw the Earth forming first as a mineral lithosphere, thermodynamics—the tug on chemical reactions to dissipate the solar energy continuously bombarding the Earth—likely pushed the chemistry of this mineral planet toward life, as living systems emerged as dissipative structures for the effective degradation of heat energy. Spreading, entropy pushed chemical systems into biosis, and 3.5 billion years ago bacteria appeared and began exchanging information in acts of "quorum sensing" (Fuqua et al. 1994), observed and modeled 3.5 billion years later through the medium of human attention. With the emergence of the exchange of information as an attribute of living systems, or biosemiosis, the noösphere came into being. As organisms evolved to manipulate the attention of other organisms, rhetoric was born (on this "proto-rhetoric" see Kennedy 1998: 9–29). Angiosperms, or flowering plants, tuned their attention-gathering capacities toward trans-species communication about 150 million years ago, and pollinators (such as ourselves) and flowering plants have been interacting and coevolving ever since (on the *colores rhetorici* of plants, see Kennedy 1998 and Kull 2001). While the biosphere is currently undergoing massive extinction events, in part due to the proliferation of conscious beings such as ourselves, the noösphere evolves with each passing moment, those moments themselves measured by an atomic clock of unparalleled accuracy in Boulder, Colorado and signaled all over the planet via radio-wave time stamps.

As a contribution to a handbook that seeks to circulate a form of knowledge as an act of collective, open-source exchange that is mindful of this noöspheric evolution, "rhetoric of science" is here heuristically defined as the study of and training in those entropic as well as tropic features of the system of attention gradients in which scientific knowledge circulates, emerges, actualizes, and transforms. Now any such definition will have to define "entropic" as well as "tropic." Here it gets a little more complicated because entropy itself refers to multiple implications of the second law of thermodynamics. In technical usage, entropy signifies: (1) the requirement that isolated systems not in equilibrium increase their level of microscopic disorder over time (Clausius and Hirst 1867); (2) a measurement of the uncertainty or "surprise value" of any given string of symbols (Shannon 1949: 19); and (3) the tendency of information and energy to spread (Lambert 2011: 67). Of these three aspects of entropy labeled by strings of symbols, the chemist Frank Lambert has pointed out that aspect (3) is the most general, encompassing both the uncertainty that develops as symbols travel into different contexts in the ongoing processes of information dispersion (2) and the apparent increase of "disorder" from the perspective of local scales (1) (such as ourselves). System scientist Stanley Salthe's model of a "specification hierarchy" could represent the relation between these three aspects of entropy as follows: "[Tendency of energy and information to spread [capacity to measure surprise value of a string of symbols [vector toward increasing disorder in closed systems]]]" (Salthe and Fuhrman 2005: 295).

This chapter will map the emergence and future of scientific communication along these three nested attributes of entropy, providing both a thermodynamic and a semiotic framework for participating in the ongoing "reinvention of discovery" augured by the rapid dispersion of knowledge and the means of sharing it—e.g., computer networks, open-source softwares, smartphones, free online education, social media, and the practices of *communitas* they all can enable and upon which they depend. The term entropy itself will serve as a key example because it is such an excellent instance of itself: it reveals aspects of processes that serve both to extend and to expand communication even as the content and meaning of any given communication become dispersed. (For example, the tracking of phone conversations by the NSA is enabled by the same technologies that practically ensure the leakage of this information.) Salthe models this in terms of the capacity of increased information to act as a constraint as well as a message:

> Dissipative structures continually incorporate new *informational constraints*, although the rate of incorporation eventually slows down. Almost any form with a variable configuration might be an informational constraint; such variability is "information carrying capacity" or "informational entropy." *Information* here has the sense of "reduction of uncertainty": we are uncertain which of its possible configurations the given form will take, until one is actually taken; this step being generally irreversible, the form now represents a *constraint* on further variability. (Salthe and Fuhrman 2005: 305)

Salthe's insight here helps remind us that information exchange entails *irreversible* processes that constrain as well as enable "dissipative structures." Coined by Ilya Prigogine (1980), this term describes phenomena that emerge to effectively dissipate energy, from tornadoes that mitigate the heat of the American Midwest to rain forests that cool the Upper Amazon. The effect of this, according to Salthe's analysis, is that dissipative structures would insert new information that could disrupt internal communications, causing lags and delays in responses to environmental changes. As Salthe and Fuhrman argue, "The second major effect of inserting new information into an already definitive system would be to enhance or further over-determine those of its habitual behaviors that have already become inertial, thereby diminishing its flexibility of response to perturbations. This effect is pathological in many kinds of senescent systems when combined with their reduced energy-specific (per unit mass) throughput" (306) (see Zotin 1972; Aoki 1991). Salthe calls this diminished flexibility "systemic rigidity," which can be a paradoxical effect of increased information.

Here I want to apply Salthe's model of "infodynamics" to the ongoing production of knowledge characteristic of scientific practice. This recourse to the language of thermodynamics allows for a very general model for the rhetoric of science because it is rooted in fundamental aspects of rhetorical practice and science. Yet comprehending the irreducible scale of scientific practice—the cosmic rules, as it were, for scientific knowledge production, any time, anywhere—demands that we attend to the concomitant substrate of uncertainty as well as the rigidity that Salthe's model suggests is essential to scientific practice. That is, when we look closely we will see that it is uncertainty, rather than authority, that lies at the basis of scientific practice because uncertainty is associated with the irreversible arrival of new information that can both "tear apart" existing habitual modes of thought (paradigms and their rigidity) and undermine already inertial models, such as the subject–object paradigm itself (Kuhn 1962). When the context is appropriate, I will suggest that the very substrate of this uncertainty and this rigidity is our collective ecological experience of subjectivity. That is, any arrival of new information implicitly and necessarily asks: For whom does this information arrive? This implicit and necessary query bundled with any and all infodynamic events carries with it the return of the repressed of consciousness that has so effectively generated the wide-ranging interventions into and invention of an objective world capable of being manipulated—by whom?

In addition to the generality that thermodynamic models afford, they allow us to focus on a specifically cultural aspect of the rhetoric of science during the modern and postmodern periods. C. P. Snow's (in)famous "Two Cultures" lecture focused precisely on thermodynamics as the demographic principle of selection by which to differentiate "traditional" and "scientific" cultures:

> A good many times I have been present at gatherings of people who, by the standards of the traditional culture, are thought highly educated and who have with considerable gusto been expressing their incredulity at the illiteracy of scientists. Once or twice I have been provoked and have asked the company how many of them could describe the Second Law of Thermodynamics. The response was cold: it was also negative. Yet I was asking something which is the scientific equivalent of: *Have you read a work of Shakespeare's?* (1961: 16)

But as we have shifted from the use of typewriters to networks of computers, we are all, whatever our disciplines, perhaps coming to know a bit more, implicitly or explicitly, about the second law of thermodynamics and its infodynamic implications. Clearly, as means for exchanging and transforming information themselves disperse—a kind of second-order technological entropy wherein entropy feeds back onto itself to amplify and accelerate the means of information dispersal—new forms of identity (Rotman 1993) and new forms of scientific practice itself are coming into being. In short, the very means for producing, gathering, sorting, and storing information enable new forms of losing, destroying, and decontextualizing information. And these transformations in the very nature of information in turn transform knowledge and subjectivity through and for *us*. But what exactly are we becoming?

As the apparently irreducible horizon of scientific practice, human subjectivity is the domain where these three aspects of entropy manifest persistently and clearly in the history of scientific discourse. While Thomas Sprat (1734) wrote of the need of the Royal Society to banish "eloquence" in favor of the free and "plain" circulation of knowledge, most scholars in the history of rhetoric and science acknowledge that this banishment was merely a heuristic solution to the division between the subjective experience of knowledge production and its circulation as a putatively objective phenomenon (see Walmsley, ch. 43; Code, ch. 57). As many scholars and scientists have noted, "subjects" and "objects" are themselves maps that are increasingly inadequate to a deeply interconnected reality. After sketching out a heuristic model for the rhetoric of science, I will suggest the efficacy of an alternative model of what computer scientist Ted Nelson calls "intertwingularity" (1974: 45), or the nonlocal yet intensely specific interconnection of everything, and then conclude with some suggestions for transformations in human subjectivity—what rhetoric often terms "ethos"—for the future of scientific efficacy and increased human happiness in an intertwingled reality.

THERMOSEMIOSIS

On the thermodynamic front, the rhetoric of science can be seen, not surprisingly, as operating according to the constitutive constraints governing all systems. As such, rhetoric in the scientific context constantly seeks methods for the transmission of more information with less energy. With more information being exchanged about more for less time and attention, the rhetoric of science encounters the fundamental thermodynamic, cosmic limit of information transfer as hypothesized by computer scientist Rolf Landauer in 1961. According to Landauer (1961), by thermodynamic necessity, information exchange should also be considered an energetic dispersal. Stewart Brand famously noted that "information wants to be free" (1989: 202), exemplifying Lambert's third aspect of thermodynamics: information leaks, it spreads. And this may be so precisely because it costs too much to erase it. "We can show, or at least very strongly suggest," notes Landauer, "that information processing is inevitably accompanied by a certain minimum amount of heat generation" (1961: 183).

In other words, when we shed light, metaphorically speaking, we also yield heat—thermodynamically speaking. Landauer's principle has since been experimentally verified, demonstrating that "entropy of the environment increases by a finite amount" (Bérut et al. 2012: 187) even for the most concise and insightful sequence of signs. Even *erasing* mistaken information, such as the notion that the meaning of "entropy" is itself stable across contexts, entails the dispersal of some minimum amount of energy to inform any given audience. On a quest for dispersal, these entropic inclinations of the cosmos, or the tendency of energy and knowledge to spread, cultivate shorthand attractors of attention that point away from that which goes without saying to highlight what does not go without saying, and these modes of compression themselves create new forms of uncertainty in their dependence upon unstated and often forgotten premises. Tropes—organized patterns of rhetoric such as metaphor, metonymy, and synecdoche—emerge to capture our attention with fewer symbols, and in capturing our attention the forgetting of other domains of attention inevitably ensues. New information, such as the notion of a "genetic code," enters the system, enabling new paths of research and obscuring others. Hence, the dialectic of entropy involves both the dissipation or spreading of energy and information on the thermodynamic scale (more being said with smaller and smaller but irreducible amounts of energy) and new forms of uncertainty (less being said more often, more knowledge making any subsequent search more difficult, increased information storage enabling new instances of catastrophic loss, the dispersal of shorthand increasing misinformation).

THE THERMODYNAMICS OF BABEL'S SEMIOTIC SUCCESS

This thermodynamic aspect of semiosis as a symptom of rather than rejoinder to the dispersal of energy enjoined by the second law of thermodynamics is concisely allegorized in a perhaps unlikely location: the account of Babel in Genesis 11. While "Babel" is perhaps most famous for its ironic increase of the dispersal of meaning, its very name indicates the paradoxical and simultaneous success of two meanings of the term entropy—as an increase in disorder (Clausius and Hirst 1867) and an increase in information (Shannon 1949). Indeed, this biblical allegory of entropy suggests that this characteristic of new information to both enable and constrain further communication is a fundamental attribute of all ecologies of discourse.

Genesis 11:1 describes a linguistic ecology with extremely minimal drift of meaning. "And the whole earth was of one language, and of one speech." Strictly speaking, reading in a literalist vein, such a scenario entails not only one language but one speech act itself, as if Elohim's "Let there be light" and John 1:1's "In the beginning was the Word" named a single eternal speech act unfolding to itself —God talking to itself. In such a context, which is necessarily addressed not to the world of matter but to the consciousness of a reader or a listener (in rhetorical terms, an audience), there would literally be no new information, only the unfolding of already existing order immanent to reality, what physicist David Bohm has dubbed the "implicate order" (2002: 186). Note that this world of consciousness unfolding to and for itself suggests not a transcendental theology but an immanent one: the "one speech" of Elohim incorporates both the emergence of light itself and the discussion of light by humans ("and God said, let there be light").

But Genesis 11 quickly leaves the realm of pure consciousness at one with itself engaged in acts of self creation and begins making bricks:

> And it came to pass, as they journeyed from the east, that they found a plain in the land of Shinar; and they dwelt there. And they said one to another, Go to, let us make brick, and burn them thoroughly. And they had brick for stone, and slime had they for mortar. And they said, Go to, let us build us a city and a tower, whose top may

reach unto heaven; and let us make us a name, lest we be scattered abroad upon the face of the whole earth. (Genesis 11:2–4)

Note the importance of thermodynamic expenditure to the account: "Let us make brick, and burn them thoroughly." In order to locate the fuel for this semiotic fire, a fire that would "make us a name," a separation must already take place—the perception and marking of an energy gradient, a differential of exergy between one aspect of reality and another, such as that between dry and wet wood, oak and pine. Is this gradient difference—hot or not—the very *telos* of consciousness that would become divided from itself and, eventually, aware of itself in ecological devastation?

Of one language, they began to travel. Were they perhaps restless? Was there energy to be dissipated, even squandered? Applying heat, creating division (abstraction and separation from mud is a fundamental component of bricks), the division continues: "Let us make us a name." It is this making of a name that itself generates a separation, a decontextualization: this new speech becomes transmitted by a tower in the sky. Indeed this tower in the sky is the creation of the first sign separate from this one speech: the making of a name.

This making of a name is, allegorically speaking, a dispersal into multiple modes of speech for which Babel is now indeed famed and named: Babel translates the Hebrew word *balal*, which means "jumble." Making a name through recourse to the separation, compression, and burning of earth into bricks, what had been one speech becomes multiple. This phenomenon of *thermosemiosis*—the thermodynamic inclination of signs to disperse—is then narrated as the act of a God separated from his people, the making of another name:

> And the LORD said, Behold, the people is one, and they have all one language; and this they begin to do: and now nothing will be restrained from them, which they have imagined to do.
> Go to, let us go down, and there confound their language, that they may not understand one another's speech.
> So the LORD scattered them abroad from thence upon the face of all the earth: and they left off to build the city.
> Therefore is the name of it called Babel; because the LORD did there confound the language of all the earth: and from thence did the LORD scatter them abroad upon the face of all the earth. (Genesis 11)

Thus, a successful, even famous name was in fact created. Yet the name heralds not the monumental marking of a territory but the very scattering dispersal the burning of bricks had been intended to avoid. This thermodynamic expenditure of semiurgy (the creation of signs) exemplifies what French philosophers Gilles Deleuze and Félix Guattari (1987) characterize as "territorialization" and "deterritorialization." The avoidance of entropy, or the dispersal of a people and the subsequent uncertainty of their name or identity, necessarily creates yet more dispersal even as it coins a sign that comes to meaningfully name the dispersal essential to communication. In this context, the apparently self-evident existence of a "self" or "I" becomes legible as a compression device for building a name for the self. While contemporary neuroscience represents the ongoing activity of the biological brain as highly distributed and even dispersed, the "narrative mind" (Farb et al. 2007) conjoins all of these distinct processes as an "I" separate from the world.

I THINK, THEREFORE NOÖSPHERE IS

It is precisely the jumbled inconsistency between the names, usages, and implications of words such as entropy and information that becomes vital to what philosopher and rhetoric of science pioneer Paul Feyerabend calls the "invention of alternatives" (Feyerabend 1993: 29). He describes this phenomenon as "the development of alternative hypotheses that contradict well-confirmed theories and/or well-established experimental results" (29). Feyerabend implicitly connects the role of these "asignifying" rhetorics—rhetorics that seem to say something but actually function to contest Salthe's "systemic rigidity" (Salthe and Fuhrman 2005: 306), sometimes induced by new information—to an evolutionary model of scientific knowledge production emerging from a gorgeously diverse "ocean" of truths:

> Knowledge so conceived is not a series of self-consistent theories that converges toward an ideal view; it is not a gradual approach to the truth. It is rather an ever increasing ocean of mutually incompatible alternatives, each single theory, each fairy-tale, each myth that is part of the collection forcing the others into greater articulation and all of them contributing, via this process of competition, to the development of our consciousness. (Feyerabend 1993: 21)

Feyerabend here describes a "skaldic" process of knowledge production through which mutually incompatible and even entropic claims compete for audience attention and the status of current scientific truth. Easwaran Eknath (1987) notes that skaldic rhetorics, a term used to describe early Scandinavian poetry contests, are more generally applicable to competitive contexts of discourse production continually threatened by the entrainment into Salthe's systemic rigidity and its ensuing subjective correlative: boredom. Charles Darwin (1876: 368), writing in the mid-nineteenth century, noted that it is precisely these sorts of contests (agons) that frequently determine mating choice among songbirds, and Fernando Nottebohm (2005) has mapped neurogenesis emerging from juvenile birdsong practice. In short, in competition for the most beautiful song, young male birds sing their brains larger, and, on a larger scale, Feyerabend is pointing to the development of human consciousness through the contesting of competing and necessarily incompatible claims on that beauty, truth.

Feyerabend points here to the history of science as the Darwinian evolution of a larger category: the rhetoric of science. Here the "development of our consciousness" (Feyerabend 1993: 21) becomes a kind of ideal obstacle course for honing our individual and collective consciousness. Thinking alongside Darwin, Isaac Newton, or Lynn Margulis, we force ourselves to articulate their findings and conclusions with our own subjective experience of the world. And when we do so, we do so neither subjectively nor objectively in any rigorous sense of either term. Instead, the development of consciousness named by Feyerabend takes place on the evolutionary scale, in a dissipative structure on a larger scale than ourselves—the noösphere, defined here as "the collective, cumulative and emergent effects of attention gradients on the biosphere." This definition satisfies our feeling for the "rigor" of scientific practice. We have to participate to understand, and our contribution must withstand the attraction of alternatives while also recognizing that our participation takes place in an infrastructure of discourses that function on "gradients" or differentials of attention that are not usually subject to individual control but which are instead an outcome of collective intelligence even as they take place entirely, for each of us, within subjective experience.

Who participates in these discourses, and what is the status of their claims to truth? The fact of our nonnegotiable experience of subjectivity suggests that we cannot simply wave away subjectivity in search of objectivity; nor do we have norms for the transmission of distinct subjective states to distinct subjective states that would allow for the sorting of true and false, useful and useless alternatives, in a fashion that essentially and necessarily respects the singularity of the participants in "communicative rationality" (Habermas). Can the noösphere—the collective entity that has, for example, yielded the open-source operating system Linux—provide us with the mechanisms of selection with which to collectively sort out good science from junk science while overcoming the repeated attempts to erase the distinctive import of subjectivity?

As a priori distinct instances of conscious experience, the antimony between the subjectivity of each and every researcher and the goal of objective knowledge independent of any of them was articulated by Immanuel Kant (1781) in the *Critique of Pure Reason*. Working with what he called "pure apperception," he pondered the conditions of possibility (the "transcendental" conditions) of thought itself. Kant posited the necessary existence of what he called a "transcendental unity of self-consciousness" for thought to exist:

> I call it pure apperception, to distinguish it from empirical apperception, or, again, original apperception, because it is that self-consciousness which, while generating the representation "I think" (a representation which must be capable of accompanying all other representations, and which in all consciousness is one and the same), cannot itself be accompanied by any further representation. The unity of this apperception I likewise entitle the transcendental unity of self-consciousness, in order to indicate the possibility of a priori knowledge arising from it. For the manifold representations, which are given in an intuition, would not be one and all my

representations, if they did not all belong to one self-consciousness. As my representations (even if I am not conscious of them as such) they must conform to the condition under which alone they can stand together in one universal self-consciousness, because otherwise they would not all without exception belong to me. (Ch. 2 §16)

Intriguingly, however, given the insights of neuroscience, evolutionary biology, and, indeed, thermodynamics, it is increasingly difficult to sustain the idea that when "I think," these thoughts in fact "belong" to myself, even if—as is likely and perhaps necessary—Kant looked precisely to his "own" subjective experience in order to glimpse pure apperception in the act of "his" thought beholding itself. The work of Benjamin Libet (1999), for example, suggests that "our" intentions are latecomers to "our" actions: the readiness potentials in my brain are already firing well before "I" even begin to intend typing the next word (which happened to be "word"). So too does our status as organisms in what Lynn Margulis and Dorion Sagan (1991) call the "long embrace" with bacteria, which highlights the continual contact our nucleated cells enjoy with the biosphere, make us wonder if even "our" bodies are our own or instead sites of intertwingled living systems dissipating energy, and of which we are only beginning to become conscious. Entropy itself suggests that however and in whatever fashion such universal self-consciousness was encoded, it would not be by me, or by you, but would instead be the *outcome* by which a string of symbols (or its molecular analogue) maintained informational content in the short run even as new information arrived. Thermodynamics, as William S. Burroughs puts it, "wins at a crawl" (1966: 164).

Still, if Kant's attempt to unify instances of subjective experience by means of the transcendental unity of a subject whose thoughts and actions are her "own" is put into radical disarray, what of the larger-scale domain where science actually occurs? If we can no longer really assert that "I think" without inquiring into the distributed, even ubiquitous nature of this "I," we can follow the source of these "I" thoughts in our own experience by turning our attention onto itself. And when we do so, we see not only the local, contingent, and constantly shifting nature of our own experience—this and that—but also the condition of possibility of any experience whatsoever, what the mathematician and philosopher Franklin Merrell-Wolff calls "consciousness without an object" (1973: 69). First-person investigators of diverse traditions report that when following this path of inquiry—uncannily proximate to and yet distant from Kant's—they find a larger-scale structure for which "noösphere" is not such a poor name. Twentieth-century researchers into this experience chose the perhaps unfortunate name of "ego death" for this perception of a larger-scale structure in which our apparently local, fleeting subjectivity is embedded:

During the mystical experience when the experiencer has lost individuality and become part of a Reality-Greater-than-Self, paradoxically, something of the self remains to record the experience in memory. One of the greatest fears about human death is that personal individual existence and memory will be gone forever. Yet having passed through psychological ego death in the mystical experience, a person still preserves enough self-consciousness so that at least part of the individual memory is not lost. (Pahnke 1969: 16)

In the context of this "Reality-Greater-than-Self" as a layer of consciousness from which anything like pure apperception might occur, it is not "I think" but "the noösphere thinks" that might be the best experimental protocol for the collective investigation of this subject of science. For when we do science we do it subjectively and collectively, and it is perhaps here that we must look for Kant's condition of possibility of all thought. And as technologies for focusing and recording states of attention proliferate, sharing our subjective experiences becomes a mode of communication that is not between subjects but *about them* as social media asymptotically approach the impossible but alluring "sharing" of subjective states. And newer technologies—such as NeuroSky's headset that enables users to interact with computer applications directly with focused attention—make clear that the *telos* of information technologies themselves tugs us toward overcoming the apparent division between ourselves and the lifeworld we inhabit through the medium of attention.

Yet while the reciprocity of an intersubjective sphere of understanding seems hopelessly naive in the light of this deconstruction and distribution of identity, where subjective states are the object of a collective thermodynamic tug toward dispersal, collective science indeed happens anyway, *as if* it emerged from subjects. But perhaps it does not happen to *us*. Recent research on long-term meditation suggests that "mind wandering"—the movement from gradients of attention to gradients of attention without focus—decreases among long-term meditators, and that this decrease correlates with a dwindling or even disappearance of the "I thought" or ego and an increase in happiness for whoever remains, just as "something of the self remains to record the experience in memory" (Pahnke 1969: 16) in ego death. In *Civilization and Its Discontents*, Sigmund Freud (1962) famously described the "oceanic feeling" as a kind of "threat" to the ego, but this research, along with research on problem solving with psychedelics in the 1950s and 1960s, suggests that it is precisely in ego death that anything worthy of the name "idea" actually emerges and can be shared. The Royal Society and the rhetorical practices that followed wished to efface subjectivity in order to yield objectivity through the "modest witness," but the "I" thought remained sufficiently intact to cultivate a system of intellectual property that links subjective ownership to the necessarily collective act of knowledge production—Salthe's "systemic rigidity" indeed (see Walmsley, ch. 43). But perhaps in the stilling of the mind in meditation or awe, linked to the self-aware collective production of knowledge enacted in open-source software development but available to all forms of inquiry, we more effectively dwindle the "I" in its performativity. And perhaps when the noösphere thinks, it selects, in the Darwinian sense, under pressure to dissipate ever greater amounts of energy. By decoupling our thoughts from that powerful rhetorical stratagem, "I," we may not so much efface subjectivity as enable experimental access to the transcendental aspects of subjective experience beyond the specific signifier "I," as each of us, here and now, experiments with the ecological condition of all thought: the noösphere, the thinking stratum of the planet, yielding more knowledge and more uncertainty as the abatement of energy bombarding the Earth from the sun continues.

References

Aoki, Ichiro. 1991. "Entropy Principle for Human Development, Growth and Aging." *Journal of Theoretical Biology* 150 no. 2: 215–223.

Bazerman, Charles. 1988. *Shaping Written Knowledge: The Genre and Activity of the Experimental Article in Science*. Madison: University of Wisconsin Press.

Bérut, Antoine, et al. 2012. "Experimental Verification of Landauer's Principle Linking Information and Thermodynamics." *Nature* 483 no. 7388: 187–190. doi:10.1038/nature10872.

Bohm, David. 2002. *Wholeness and the Implicate Order*. London: Routledge.

Brand, Stewart. 1989. *The Media Lab: Inventing the Future at MIT*. New York: Penguin.

Burroughs, William S. 1966. *The Soft Machine*. New York: Grove.

Chittick, William C. 1998. *The Self-Disclosure of God: Principles of Ibn al-'Arabi's Cosmology*. Albany: SUNY Press.

Clausius, Rudolf, and Thomas Archer Hirst. 1867. *The Mechanical Theory of Heat with Its Applications to the Steam-Engine and to the Physical Properties of Bodies*. London: J. Van Voorst.

Darwin, Charles. 1876. *The Descent of Man, and Selection in Relation to Sex*. New York: D. Appleton.

Deleuze, Gilles, and Félix Guattari. 1987. *A Thousand Plateaus: Capitalism and Schizophrenia*. Minneapolis: University of Minnesota Press.

Doyle, Richard. 1997. *On Beyond Living: Rhetorical Transformations of the Life Sciences*. Redwood City, CA: Stanford University Press.

Doyle, Richard. 2011. *Darwin's Pharmacy: Sex, Plants, and the Evolution of the Noösphere*. Seattle: University of Washington Press.

Eknath, Easwaran, and Michael Nagler, eds. 1987. *The Upanishads*. Petaluma, CA: Nilgiri.

Fahnestock, Jeanne. 1999. *Rhetorical Figures in Science*. Washington, DC: Catholic University of America Press.

Farb, Norman A. S., et al. 2007. "Attending to the Present: Mindfulness Meditation Reveals Distinct Neural Modes of Self-Reference." *Social Cognitive and Affective Neuroscience* 2 no. 4: 313–322. doi:10.1093/scan/nsm030.

Freud, Sigmund. 1962. *Civilization and Its Discontents*. New York: W.W. Norton.

Feyerabend, Paul K. 1993. *Against Method*. New York: Verso.

Fuqua, W. C., S. C. Winans, and E. P. Greenberg. 1994. "Quorum Sensing in Bacteria: The LuxR-LuxI Family of Cell Density-Responsive Transcriptional Regulators." *Journal of Bacteriology* 176 no. 2: 269–275.

Genesis. Bible Hub. Accessed September 6, 2013. http://biblehub.com/genesis/11-1.htm.

Gross, Alan. 1990. *The Rhetoric of Science*. Cambridge, MA: Harvard University Press.

Hottois, Gilbert. 1981. *Pour une métaphilosophie du langage*. Paris: J. Vrin.

Kant, Immanuel. 1781. *Critique of Pure Reason*. Marxists Internet Archive. Accessed September 6, 2013. http://www.marxists.org/reference/subject/ethics/kant/reason/ch02.htm.

Kennedy, George. 1998. *Comparative Rhetoric: An Historical and Cross-Cultural Introduction*. New York: Oxford University Press.

Kuhn, Thomas. 1962. *The Structure of Scientific Revolutions*. Chicago, IL: University of Chicago Press.

Kull, Kalevi. 2001. "A Note on Biorhetorics." *Sign Systems Studies* 29 no. 2: 693–704.

Landauer, Rolf. 1961. "Irreversibility and Heat Generation in the Computing Process." *IBM Journal of Research and Development* 5 no. 3: 183–191.

Lambert, Frank. 2011. "The Conceptual Meaning of Thermodynamic Entropy in the 21st Century." *International Research Journal of Pure and Applied Chemistry* 1 no. 3: 65–68.

Latour, Bruno, and Steve Woolgar. 1979. *Laboratory Life: The Social Construction of Scientific Facts*. Beverly Hills, CA: Sage.

Libet, Benjamin. 1999. "Do We Have Free Will?" *Journal of Consciousness Studies* 6 nos. 8–9: 47–57.

Margulis, Lynn, and Dorion Sagan. 1991. *Mystery Dance: On the Evolution of Human Sexuality*. New York: Summit.

Merrell-Wolff, Franklin. 1973. *The Philosophy of Consciousness without an Object: Reflections on the Nature of Transcendental Consciousness*. New York: Julian.

Moss, Jean Dietz. 1993. *Novelties in the Heavens: Rhetoric and Science in the Copernican Question*. Chicago, IL: University of Chicago Press.

Nelson, Ted. 1974. *Computer Lib: Dream Machines*. Chicago, IL: Hugo.

Norman, A. S., et al. 2007. "Attending to the Present: Mindfulness Meditation Reveals Distinct Neural Modes of Self-Reference." *Social Cognitive and Affective Neuroscience* 2 no. 4: 313–322. doi:10.1093/scan/nsm030.

Nottebohm, Fernando. 2005. "The Neural Basis of Birdsong." *PLoS Biology* 3 no. 5. doi:10.1371/journal.pbio.0030164.

Pahnke, Walter N. 1969. "The Psychedelic Mystical Experience in the Human Encounter with Death." *Harvard Theological Review* 62 no. 2: 1–21.

Perelman, Chaïm. 1982. *The Realm of Rhetoric*. Notre Dame, IN: University of Notre Dame Press.

Prigogine, Ilya. 1980. *From Being to Becoming: Time and Complexity in the Physical Sciences*. San Francisco, CA: W. H. Freeman.

Rotman, Brian. 1993. *Ad Infinitum: The Ghost in Turing's Machine; Taking God out of Mathematics and Putting the Body Back In*. Stanford, CA: Stanford University Press.

Salthe, Stanley N., and Gary Fuhrman. 2005. "The Cosmic Bellows: The Big Bang and the Second Law." *Cosmos and History* 1 no. 2: 295–318.

Shannon, Claude Elwood. 1949. *The Mathematical Theory of Communication*. Urbana: University of Illinois Press.

Snow, C. P. 1961. "The Two Cultures and the Scientific Revolution." In *The Rede Lecture*, 1–58. New York: Cambridge University Press.

Sprat, Thomas. 1734. *The History of the Royal Society of London: For the Improving of Natural Knowledge*. 4th ed. London: J. Knapton et al.

Vernadsky, W. I. 1945. "The Biosphere and the Noösphere." *American Scientist* 33 no. 1: 1–12.

Zotin, A. I. 1972. *Thermodynamic Aspects of Development Biology*. New York: S. Karger.

CHAPTER 60

RHETORIC AND DIGITAL MEDIA

IAN BOGOST AND ELIZABETH LOSH

CRITICS of computational media can often be seen as being allied with one of two genealogies, that of Marshall McLuhan or that of Friedrich Kittler. McLuhan famously declared that "the medium is the message" (1964: 7) and expanded the range of cultural messages worth celebrating to include media that might seem to resist interpretation, such as lighting and clothing. McLuhan also distinguished between "hot" media, such as film, which supposedly provide an audience experience of deep immersion through sequential, linear, and logical arrangements, and "cool" media, such as comics, which require perception of abstract patterning and a simultaneous decoding of all parts. Like Vannevar Bush, who viewed the computer largely as a storage and retrieval device, McLuhan saw the computer as a "research and communication instrument" (1995: 295) and compared it to print genres like the encyclopedia or print storage systems like the library.

If McLuhan (1962, 1964, 1992) considered media to be "extensions of man," Kittler saw technology as having certain autonomous operations. Once computer programs were written and pathways were etched upon silicon chips, there were logics of progression at work independent of human agency. For Kittler, media are not simple vessels for extending the human body. Kittler argues that specific technological devices, such as the typewriter, the gramophone, or the film camera, shape human expression, and that the computer operates similarly, although computer code functions very differently from human language. He examines how media record, store, and display information as part of the larger history of technology. Along with Vilém Flusser, Kittler is often seen as a key figure in contemporary German media theory, one whose approach focuses on the workings of an increasingly automated and technical world rather than the agency of human beings who interact with technologies and media merely as tools.

Many critics would argue that an understanding of rhetoric in relation to the procedural systems of computational media has an even longer history that dates back to the birth of computer science in the mid-twentieth century. For example, in Claude

Shannon's famous 1949 text on information theory, *The Mathematical Theory of Communication*, the introduction by Warren Weaver includes a meditation on how "propaganda theory" operates, and imagines how audiences in the Soviet Union might understand the persuasive functions of a US newsreel. (The fact that the title of Shannon's work had gone from "A Mathematical Theory" to "The Mathematical Theory" speaks to his own understanding of making effective claims to expertise.) By 1965, Robert Abelson and J. Douglas Carroll were speculating about "computer simulation of individual belief systems" in the journal *American Behavioral Scientist* and positing how an "ideology machine" could be constructed that reduced the premises of political arguments to if–then statements. In 1966 Joseph Weizenbaum built the ELIZA computer program, which mimicked patient interchanges with a Rogerian therapist by using a logic of repetition and open-ended questions as a template for scripting outputs from inputs. In 1968 J. C. R. Licklider and Robert W. Taylor wrote the influential essay, "The Computer as a Communication Device," which predicted that people would soon be able to communicate more effectively through a machine than face to face.

In the 1970s came the rise of what Peter Lunenfeld has called "The Aquarians," a group of technological utopians that included Douglas Engelbart, Alan Kay, and Ivan Sutherland. Lunenfeld (2011) argues that these technologists promoted a *Kindercult* that emphasized the early education of children with computers as a way to promote human creativity and to bridge the gap between a specific culture of scientific and mathematical rationality and the rest of humanity. The same period spawned the influential manifestos of Ted Nelson about the liberatory potential of hypertext and how computers could serve as "dream machines" (1974: 1); Nelson's self-published pamphlets influenced early microcomputer designers at Xerox PARC and Apple, among others. In his attempts at software development, Nelson's ideas about possible alternatives to the design of hyperlinked HTML pages or the traditional desktop computer never proved to be practical for the mainstream market. Despite this failure in practice, Nelson's importance in theory is difficult to minimize, and his work has been cited as inspiration for Tim Berners-Lee's design for the World Wide Web.

Although some rhetoricians were aware that the paradigm of media theory was changing in the post-McLuhan era, relatively few viewed the computer as a device for communicating as well as for calculating until the 1990s. The term "digital rhetoric" can be traced to Richard Lanham and his seminal essay on the subject, "Digital Rhetoric: Theory, Practice, and Property" (1992), which later appeared as "Digital Rhetoric and the Digital Arts" (1995). Lanham's essay focuses on one central question: "What happens when the text moves from page to screen?" and suggests that the fact that texts have become "unfixed and interactive" (1995: 31) undermines already decaying traditional canons of knowledge while also creating exciting new possibilities along with the rise of electronic information. At the time Lanham was writing, he was part of a larger debate about the "death" of print literature, although Lanham's specific interest in rhetorics of digital media dated back to the early 1980s and his attendance at gatherings of computer graphics specialists at the SIGGRAPH conference and his involvement with early experiments with publishing in new multimedia digital formats. While Lanham challenged the idea that rhetoric should be located exclusively in humanities disciplines, he also described "digital rhetoric" primarily through the verbal and visual features that would be familiar to his fellow humanists (see Lanham 1995).

Jay David Bolter and Richard Grusin could similarly be seen as conservative figures because they situated new forms of digital "remediation"—how "digital forms both borrow from and seek to surpass earlier forms" (1999: 171)—in a longer lineage of conventional rhetorical history, albeit one that included branching multimodal media in its cultural narrative, such as illuminated manuscripts, stained glass windows, and comic books. While Bolter and Grusin emphasized the importance of visual as well as verbal rhetoric, they also deemphasized the importance of computer algorithms and other rule-based systems and flattened the potential dimension of computational rhetoric to the reconfiguration of existing methods of symbolization.

Instead of focusing on the technical specifics of code and platforms, earlier digital rhetoricians in the 1990s frequently analyzed how new digital genres for the screen, particularly hypertext fiction, were composed by authors and received by audiences. Much of this criticism also responded to at least one of two trends in rhetorical study during the 1980s and 1990s: the rise of deconstruction and poststructuralism more generally and the elevation of pre-Socratic rhetoric, especially by feminist theorists. The work of Gregory Ulmer, Victor Vitanza, Stuart Moulthrop, and George Landow could be seen as typifying the poststructuralist turn in rhetorical study, while the work of Kathleen Welch (1999) might be seen as representative of the feminist pre-Socratic one.

In his classic and frequently upgraded book, *Hypertext*, which later appeared as *Hypertext 2.0* and *Hypertext 3.0* (1991, 1997, 2006), Landow navigates the pathways through which electronic documents link to each other and makes generalizations about how the reader makes choices among competing texts and alternative logical paths. Landow sees a cultural convergence taking place in which software development and poststructuralist theory are producing similar texts, and he frequently cites the work of Michel Foucault, Roland Barthes, and Jacques Derrida (along with that of Ulmer) as a way to understand seemingly nonlinear texts created for the screen. Yet Landow asserts that the poststructuralist reader is still oriented through a "rhetoric of arrivals and departures" and suggests that hypertext conventions could be codified into what he calls "a rhetoric and stylistics of writing for e-space" (1999).

Welch's 1999 book, *Electric Rhetoric*, also cites Ulmer as it rejects the Aristotelian/Platonic/Socratic model of rhetoric as fundamental and proposes Isocrates as the better classical rhetorician through which to understand the current media age. Isocrates, she argues, did not rely on the rigid, mutually exclusive, binary opposition of writing to speaking, and could be seen as both a sophist and a precursor to postmodernism for whom the word *logos* represented a "flux of language, thought, and action" rather than a master logic of structured hierarchies and a taxonomy of parts to wholes.

Although this small cadre of rhetoricians was exhilarated by the advent of new media, many other new media critics tended to devalue the importance of the legacy of classical rhetoric if their work was devoted to radical paradigm shifts in communication. For example, in *The Language of New Media* software theorist Lev Manovich concludes that "digital rhetoric" was probably insignificant if not obsolescent:

> Traditionally, texts encoded human knowledge and memory, instructed, inspired, convinced, and seduced their readers to adopt new ideas, new ways of interpreting the world, new ideologies. . . . While it is probably possible to invent a new rhetoric of hypermedia that will use hyperlinking not to distract the reader from the argument (as is often the case today), but rather to further convince her of an argument's validity, the sheer existence and popularity of hyperlinking exemplifies the continuing decline of the field of rhetoric in the modern era. (2001: 76)

Ironically, by the 2009 annual conference of the College Art Association, Manovich was celebrating the power of what he called "database rhetorics" for furthering strong digital arguments about politics and policy with massive and heterogeneous collections of evidence.

Scholars of mass media and social psychology also began taking an interest in computation media and considering how they might influence both individual human actors and specific segments of the population. Because computational media could narrowcast personalized content and schedule reinforcing stimuli with more precision based on user feedback, computational media promised to capture more cognitive attention in more user environments than even television had, and moral panics about excessive use and digital "addiction" soon became part of the larger cultural conversation. Those such as B. J. Fogg (2002) of the "persuasive technologies" movement argue that the aim of such technologies should be to persuade rather than coerce. They locate the new field of "captology" in the traditional frameworks of classical rhetoric in general and Aristotle in particular. With the rise of ubiquitous computing technologies, the emphasis of Fogg's persuasive technologies movement has perhaps shifted from the screen to the sensor, as "smart" environments cue users to avoid risk, conserve energy, exercise, and promote other forms of public health and safety.

High-profile technocrats championing digital inclusion and the adoption of new technologies tended to approach the rhetorical tradition somewhat differently as a framework for thinking about traditional technologies of memory, recording, display, replication, and dissemination in comparison to digital ones. For example, the ancient method of rhetorical training known as the "palace of memory" or "theater of memory" technique has been an important point of reference. In *Being Digital* Nicholas Negroponte argues that memory structures that survive from classical antiquity serve as valuable models for "navigating three-dimensional space to store and retrieve information" (1996: 107). Plato's anxieties about writing or the theater (and his debates with Aristotle about new media technologies) were frequently cited in discussions about digital culture by both cyberutopians and cyberdystopians and became an important touchstone for Nicholas Carr's *The Shallows* (2010).

With the invention of web browsing software in the 1990s, new forms of Internet-based communication such as blogs, wikis, vlogs (video blogs), and online video games began to flourish and thus also spurred new forms of rhetorical criticism in response. When Patricia Roberts-Miller created a blog supposedly written by her dog that was popular with rhetoricians, it suggested that there were many new questions about identities, roles, subjectivities, and voices to be asked with Web 2.0 technologies. The once relatively small movement in rhetoric and composition, in which scholars had networked through one journal, *Computers and Composition*, and one conference, *Computers and Writing*, since the 1980s, suddenly grew in complexity and size as new journals, conferences, mailing lists, and groups on social media sites shared information and showcased debate. Laura Gurak (2001), Barbara Warnick (2007), Jonathan Alexander (2006), and John Logie (2006) published books about the rhetorical dimensions of new forms of online behavior and new media literacies, and some scholars, such as Cheryl Ball and Virginia Kuhn, intentionally eschewed print publication in order to argue for the greater rhetorical richness of writing that is not dependent on the limitations of the printed page. The collaborative nature of digital genres such as wikis and blogs also appealed to specialists in writing with multiple authors, such as Andrea Lunsford and Lisa Ede. Increased access to once-forbidden types of texts, such as pornography, was explored by John Durham Peters, who argues that the advent of pornography that is "privately viewed, digital, networked, virtual in sociability, and based as much in image as text" (2011: 158) challenges traditional definitions of obscenity. Even the senior rhetorician Gerald Graff was defending the practices of digital youth against critics like Mark Bauerlein, author of *The Dumbest Generation* (2009), in the fall 2008 President's Column in the Newsletter of the Modern Language Association.

Rhetoricians also became more concerned with copyright policy after the passage of the Digital Millennium Copyright Act by the US Congress in 1998. Just as their students were expanding their creative experimentation with these new genres, it seemed that many kinds of new digital behaviors were being prohibited, particularly since exemptions from the law's antiduplication regulations were only granted initially for film and media studies professors. Because rhetoric and composition was not judged to be a protected field, and many writing studies faculty did not have regular professorial appointments, many felt that the language of the law would bar the fair use of digital materials in learning environments in ways that would hamper instruction in digital literacy. In 2005 Martha Vicinus and Carolyn Eisner organized the Originality, Imitation, and Plagiarism conference at the University of Michigan, which invited a number of popular "copyleft" and free culture advocates, who became participants in an influential subsequent publication (Vicinus and Eisner 2009). Writing faculty such as Martine Courant Rife testified before Congress, pleading for revisions to the law, and the intellectual property caucuses and working groups of a number of professional associations sought to challenge the law. While algorithms to detect plagiarism came into wider use, and many campuses adopted proprietary technologies such Turnitin, some free culture advocates like Rebecca Moore Howard (1995, 2005) championed the importance of Internet "patchwriting" and encouraged multicampus research efforts, including the Citation Project, to explore the developmental function of online borrowing as writers imitate and evolve their own styles.

However, before the publication of Ian Bogost's *Persuasive Games: The Expressive Power of Videogames* in 2007, rhetoricians—like new media scholars—often overlooked theories from discourses of computer science and the role of what Bogost calls "procedural rhetoric," which he characterizes as "the art of persuasion through rule-based representations and interactions rather than spoken word, writing, images, or moving pictures" (Bogost 2007: ix). According to Bogost, such persuasion is "tied to the core affordances of the computer: computers run processes, they execute calculations and rule-based symbolic manipulations" (ix). For Bogost, playing computer games can spur understanding of procedural rhetoric because players can infer the structures of underlying rules.

Bogost cites the work of James Paul Gee (2003), who had become an influential figure in understanding the rhetoric of games, which Gee characterized as an important model for comprehending literacy, discourse, and expertise. Gee argues that games often contain messages that require play to decode. For example, he famously argued that the mechanic of play in *Tomb Raider* actually encourages the student Lara Croft to defy the professor who seems to be a didactic source of authority in the beginning. *Persuasive Games* appeared near the height of a heated debate in computational media criticism between the so-called narratologists, led by Janet Murray and Henry Jenkins, and the so-called ludologists, led by Espen Aarseth and Gonzalo Frasca. Murray (1997) argued that interactive media have lasting cultural value because such media represent an ongoing commitment to storytelling that deeply engages audiences, and that the narrative function of new media as a relationship between teller and tale is primary. In contrast, Aarseth insisted that such media are much more like games than stories, and that they are structured primarily by rules rather than by plots. Aarseth also asserted that games have a rich cultural history that should not be undervalued, and that game studies as a formal scholarly discipline has a place in the academy as well.

Bogost later allied himself with speculative realism, a school of philosophical thought very different from the positions of either Murray or Aarseth, but one that matched his own understanding of how "unit operations" function when software programs are actually executed. Bogost adopts a stand in favor of what he calls "object-oriented ontology" (OOO), a metaphysical movement that rejects the privileging of human existence over the existence of nonhuman objects and follows the antianthropocentric teachings of Bruno Latour (as read by Graham Harman [2009]). Other rhetoricians were also drawn to OOO, some of whom examined objects of study in the rhetorical tradition related to complex systems like the environment or politics rather than computational media, as did Bogost and, later, Alex Reid (2007), author of *The Two Virtuals: New Media and Composition*. Romanticist Timothy Morton (2011) has argued that the canon of rhetoric related to delivery (Gk. *hypokrisis*; L. *actio*), for example, invites an engagement with the discrete components of the physical world, whether it be the pebbles in the mouth of Demosthenes, the parts of a modern amplification system with a microphone, or the components of a contemporary computer chip.

Since publishing *Persuasive Games*, Bogost has become embroiled in a number of disputes with advocates of "gamification" who reduce procedural rhetoric to a schema that focuses on simple correlations between the motivation of participants to participate in play and how rewards are either gratified or delayed. The gamification movement in business, education, and other sectors of the economy and culture has also spurred a backlash from critics of digital labor, who argue that the paradigm of recreation and voluntary engagement hides the way that gamification schemes compel compliance with rule-based systems in which it may be more difficult for users to gain an advantage than in traditional games.

The work of defining digital rhetoric has continued throughout the twenty-first century. Elizabeth Losh's (2009) *Virtualpolitik* took issue with Bogost's claim that rhetoric was more about persuasion than occasion, though she was one of the first rhetoricians to accept his procedural rhetoric framework and the importance of examining technical affordances and constraints. She defines digital rhetoric as existing on four levels: (1) the conventions of new digital genres that are used for everyday discourse, as well as for special occasions, in average people's lives; (2) public rhetoric, often in the form of political messages from government institutions, which is represented or recorded through digital technology and disseminated via electronic distributed networks; (3) the emerging scholarly discipline concerned with the rhetorical interpretation of computer-generated media as objects of study; and (4) mathematical theories of communication from the field of information science, many of which attempt to quantify the amount of uncertainty in a given linguistic exchange or the likely paths through which messages travel. Losh argues that naive positions that laud efficiency in communication as a primary goal actually show a failure to understand the actual writings of early pioneers of telecommunication and cybernetics like Shannon and Wiener, who understood the value of seemingly inefficient message redundancy and the use of multiple channels.

Despite the utility of procedural rhetoric as an analytical and design tool, Bogost later embraced Losh's account of public rhetoric as an apt description of many, and perhaps even most, computational rhetoric practices in the first decade of the new millennium. In particular, both the positive and negative characterizations of software and video games by the government in the public media primarily serve to associate public works with (or dissociate them from) functional aspects of that medium, irrespective of how any actual examples are put to use. For example, as part of First Lady Michelle Obama's "Let's Move!" campaign to end childhood obesity, the White House ran a contest inviting submissions of "apps for healthy kids." As Losh's theory of public computational rhetoric predicts, the actual quality, accuracy, or utility of the resulting programs have much less rhetorical effect than the fact that the contest itself existed and associated the White House with the positive features of the "app economy." Likewise, when Vice President Joe Biden assembled a gun control task force in the wake of the Sandy Hook massacre of 2012, his invitation of media industry representatives, including members of the video game industry, placed that medium in the position of potential wrongdoer not by virtue of what behavior video games do or do not elicit but by making the industry a participant in talks in the first place. This gesture had the political effect of allowing Biden to appear to be addressing all possible concerns, not just that of firearm access and manufacturing, even if his task force really hoped to impose controls on the latter from the start. In both these cases, the procedural rhetoric of specific software programs, applications, and games is less rhetorically relevant than the public positioning of those forms in the media.

In his encyclopedic account of digital rhetoric, Douglas Eyman (2013) contests a number of the central claims in Losh's *Virtualpolitik*, while still characterizing it as an important precursor in the attempt to write a global theory to characterize the field. Eyman is particularly vexed by Losh's appropriation of information theory, on the grounds that she is repeating the mistakes of Tiziana Terranova, who fetishizes the quantitative character of information at the expense of rhetoric, though Eyman agrees with Losh and Bogost that technological theories may well add complexity and depth to the field of digital rhetoric. Like N. Katherine Hayles, whose account of posthumanism tells the "story" of "how information lost its body" (1999: 4), Losh was interested in recovering the Latin understanding of the *forma* as being analogous to a "last, mold, or stamp" closely tied to investments in material substrates, and regretted possible misreadings of her work.

Eyman (2013) devotes a section of his introduction to "computational rhetoric," which incorporates theories from artificial intelligence about argument and computation and relies on the development of argumentation schema and computational methods to address and process informal logic and persuasion. Eyman specifically cites Floriana Grasso's (2002) "Towards Computational Rhetoric" and Crosswhite et al.'s (2004) "Computational Models of Rhetorical Argument" as examples of efforts to use rhetoric to design the programming of artificial intelligence systems. Eyman insists that the main drawback to the computational rhetoric approach is its reliance on formal argumentation schemas, which reveals a tendency to reduce rhetoric to argument, which he considers to be just as incomplete as reducing rhetoric to ornamentation. Eyman also asserts that representing complex systems purely algorithmically makes it too easy to ignore material connections.

By the time of Eyman's critique, Noah Wardrip-Fruin (2009) had revisited Abelson and Weizenbaum in his work on "expressive processing" that challenged older models of hypertext rhetoric. He also had worked with Pat Harrigan to create the *First Person* (2006), *Second Person* (2007), and *Third Person* (2009) series of edited collections about the relationship between identity, subjectivity, and playable systems. In addition to his work on "procedural literacy," Wardrip-Fruin's colleague Michael Mateas developed what he calls "rhetoric engines" in creating AI systems to stage virtual dramas or create interactive multimedia textbooks.

Yet as issues involving computational rhetoric become more mainstream in rhetorical studies, new critics have argued that this rhetoric may be constituted too narrowly. Cynthia Selfe has led a group advocating for the importance of auditory rhetorics and the need to avoid privileging the visual over other kinds of interactions involving human perception with computational media that record, store, and display/play information. Her 2009 call to action, "The Movement of Air, the Breath of Meaning: Aurality and Multimodal Composing," was particularly influential. Rhetorician Jentery Sayers (2010) has asserted that a similar bias against considering the sound file as an object of study also operates in archival projects in the digital humanities.

Other scholars argue that digital rhetoric has become too focused on first-world rhetorical practices and personal electronics that privilege individual freedom and a self separate from social agency. François Bar (Sey et al. 2013) led an international team of researchers studying public computing on a multiyear odyssey that seemed to show that private ownership of consumer electronics without social interaction with "infomediaries" is not the first choice of many residents in the Global South. Genevieve Bell and Paul Dourish (2011) note that technological visions about infrastructure and ubiquitous computing were shaped by ideologies and assumptions that could not be assumed to be natural or universal. However, subaltern computational practices were not idealized either. Nishant Shah and Sunil Abraham (2009) note the presence of digital vigilantism in China and India and the problems with assuming that Pierre Lévy's model of collective intelligence would always hold true. Wendy Chun (2009) analyzed Internet rumors in South Korea. Sam Gregory, the head of WITNESS, a video sharing web archive for citizen journalism captured with mobile devices, challenged celebratory narratives about the digital rhetoric of remix culture by emphasizing the importance of privacy, consent, and verification in cases involving human rights abuse and the value of traditional ethics developed in fields such as documentary filmmaking, ethnography, and international law. Political activists working to promote civil society in the developing world argued that people's technological preferences in vehicles of rhetorical expression are not always for devices that require extensive infrastructure and consequently risk surveillance by the authorities. For example, Tad Hirsch, creator of Freedom Fone, developed an open-source software system that enables person-to-person broadcast without relying on the Internet. Among self-described rhetoricians, Gustav Verhulsdonck and Marohang Limbu (2014) have challenged the Anglo-American biases of discourses around digital literacy and called for a broader approach to the field.

Questions about the necessary expertise for effective rhetorical instruction have also risen to the forefront as digital rhetoric becomes a recognizable academic field. The discipline of digital design is increasingly important for rhetorical studies; graphic designers such as Ellen Lupton spoke to rhetoricians, and rhetoricians such as Anne Frances Wysocki participated in design communities. xtine burrough redesigned the basic Bauhaus course developed in Weimar Germany for the Adobe Creative Suite. When Annette Vee, Mark Marino, Mark Sample, Dave Parry, Karl Stolley, Carl Whithaus, Jim Brown, and many other digital rhetoricians made the argument for explicitly teaching students to write lines of code in specific computer languages, many pedagogues responded with anxiety about issues of access and competency. Melanie Yergeau and Paul Heilker (2011) also feared that disability issues around cultures of difference and affective comfort would be ignored.

The work of defining "digital rhetoric" continues as members of the Digital Rhetoric Collaborative attempt to separate—as well as integrate—rhetorics *within* computation from rhetorics *about* computation. Understanding how particular rhetorical operations may be inscribed in the processes of computation is important to these stakeholders, but so is positioning themselves as public rhetors in the growing body of commentary about new forms of literacies and new types of computer-mediated engagement with machines and other human beings.

This is not necessarily a victory for rhetoric and computation. While earlier forms of rhetoric might seem less rhetorical, in the sense that they are less about making themselves appear valuable or important and more about inventing and carrying out processes of communication, persuasion, and expression, the truth is that computational rhetorics arose at a time when it had become difficult to ascend beyond appearances in public rhetoric. Stated differently, computational rhetorics that deeply and earnestly engage with the unique representational features of hardware and software have a hard time overcoming the popularity and conventions of more familiar forms of inscription: writing, speech, and images. In part, this is because the computer as a medium is mostly used as an extension of these prior forms of inscription; it is primarily used as a networked terminal for creating and distributing text, images, and video via websites, blogs, apps, and other online services. In this sense, today's computer age is really a continuation of the prior triumph of writing and images.

Rhetoric still has much to offer computation as a field and today's computational culture. Traditionally, rhetoric has thrived by breaking down forms of representation and signification into component techniques, both through the formal activity of identification and cataloging and through the expository activity of practice and pedagogy. By digging deeper into the computational foundations of software and hardware systems and elucidating those systems as participants in meaning creation as much as engineering practice, rhetoric has the potential to offer a complement or "counterpart" (*antistrophos*) to computer science and engineering.

FURTHER READING

In addition to the well-known works of Marshall McLuhan, those interested in the material properties of media in general and digital media in particular should consult the works of Friedrich Kittler in greater detail: *Discourse Networks 1800/1900* (1990), *Gramophone, Film, Typewriter* (1999), and *Optical Media* (2009). Vilém Flusser's *Into the Universe of Technical Images* (2011) is also helpful for understanding contemporary German theories of computational media. Historically speaking, the "father of cybernetics" Norbert Wiener's book, *Cybernetics* (1965), and his introductory article, "Men, Machines, and the World About" (1954), complement Vannevar Bush's 1945 article, "As We May Think," a speculation about the informational uses of computational devices. Those interested in the origins of hypertext and the World Wide Web should consult Ted Nelson's (1965) "A File Structure for the Complex, the Changing, and the Indeterminate" as well as web inventor Tim Berners-Lee's (2000) autobiographical *Weaving the Web*. Alan Kay and Adele Goldberg's (1977) classic article, "Personal Dynamic Media," accompanies Licklider and Nelson as an influential text of the early days of the personal computer. For a one-stop dip into many of these readings and others, consult *The New Media Reader* (Wardrip-Fruin and Montfort 2003). For more on the relationships between computer hardware and software, consult books in the MIT Press's Software Studies and Platform Studies book series, especially Wardrip-Fruin's (2009) *Expressive Processing* and Bogost and Montfort's (2009) *Racing the Beam*, as well as Erkki Huhtamo and Jussi Parikka's (2011) *Media Archaeology*.

REFERENCES

Abelson, Robert, and J. Douglas Carroll. 1965. "Computer Simulation of Individual Belief Systems." *American Behavioral Scientist* 7 no. 9: 24–30.

Alexander, Jonathan. 2006. *Digital Youth: Emerging Literacies on the World Wide Web.* Cresskill, NJ: Hampton.

Bauerlein, Mark. 2009. *The Dumbest Generation: How the Digital Age Stupefies Young Americans and Jeopardizes Our Future.* New York: Tarcher.

Bell, Genevieve, and Paul Dourish. 2011. *Divining a Digital Future: Mess and Mythology in Ubiquitous Computing.* Cambridge, MA: MIT Press.

Berners-Lee, Tim. 2000. *Weaving the Web.* New York: Harper.

Bogost, Ian. 2007. *Persuasive Games: The Expressive Power of Videogames.* Cambridge, MA: MIT Press.

Bolter, Jay, and Richard Grusin. 1999. *Remediation: Understanding New Media.* Cambridge, MA: MIT Press.

Bush, Vannevar. 1945. "As We May Think." *Atlantic Monthly*, July.

Carr, Nicholas. 2010. *The Shallows: What the Internet Is Doing to Our Brains.* New York: W. W. Norton.

Chun, Wendy Hui Kyong. 2009. "The Internet: In Theory, in Crisis." Keynote address at the Association of Internet Researchers Annual Conference.

Crosswhite, Jim, John Fox, Chris Reed, Theodore Scaltsas, and Simone Stumpf. 2004. "Computational Models of Rhetorical Argument." In *Argumentation Machines: New Frontiers in Argument and Computation*, edited by Chris Reed and Timothy J. Normans, 175–209. Dordrecht: Kluwer Academic Publishers.

Eyman, Douglas. 2013. *Digital Rhetoric: Theory, Method, Practice.* Ann Arbor: University of Michigan Press.

Flusser, Vilém. 2011. *Into the Universe of Technical Images.* Minneapolis: University of Minnesota Press.

Fogg, B. J. 2002. *Persuasive Technology: Using Computers to Change What We Think and Do.* New York: Morgan Kaufmann.

Gee, James Paul. 2003. *What Video Games Have to Teach Us About Learning and Literacy.* London: Palgrave.

Grasso, Floriana. 2002. "Towards Computational Rhetoric." *Informal Logic* 22 no. 3: 195–229.

Gurak, Laura J. 2001. *Cyberliteracy: Navigating the Internet with Awareness.* New Haven, CT: Yale University Press.

Harman, Graham. 2009. *Prince of Networks: Bruno Latour and Metaphysics.* Victoria, Australia: Re.press.

Hayles, N. Katherine. 1999. *How We Became Posthuman: Virtual Bodies in Cybernetics, Literature, and Informatics.* Chicago, IL: University of Chicago Press.

Howard, Rebecca Moore. 1995. "Plagiarisms, Authorships, and the Academic Death Penalty." *College English* 57 no. 7: 708–736.

Howard, Rebecca Moore. 2005. "Plagiarism: What Should a Teacher Do?" In *Guiding Students from Cheating and Plagiarism to Honesty and Integrity: Strategies for Change*, edited by Ann Lathrop and Kathleen Foss, 174. Westport, CT: Libraries Unlimited.

Huhtamo, Erkki, and Jussi Parikka. 2011. *Media Archaeology: Approaches, Applications, and Implications*. Berkeley: University of California Press.

Kay, Alan, and Adele Goldberg. 1977. "Personal Dynamic Media." *Computer* 10 no. 3: 31–41.

Kittler, Friedrich A. 1990. *Discourse Networks 1800/1900*. Stanford, CA: Stanford University Press.

Kittler, Friedrich A. 1999. *Gramophone, Film, Typewriter*. Stanford, CA: Stanford University Press.

Kittler, Friedrich A. 2009. *Optical Media*. New York: Polity.

Landow, George P. 1991. *Hypertext: The Convergence of Contemporary Critical Theory and Technology*. Baltimore, MD: Johns Hopkins University Press.

Landow, George P. 1997. *Hypertext 2.0: The Convergence of Contemporary Critical Theory and Technology*. Baltimore, MD: Johns Hopkins University Press.

Landow, George P. 1999. *A Rhetoric and Stylistics of Writing for E-Space*. Aarhus: Department of Aesthetics, University of Aarhus.

Landow, George P. 2006. *Hypertext 3.0: Critical Theory and New Media in an Era of Globalization*. Baltimore, MD: Johns Hopkins University Press.

Lanham, Richard. 1992. "Digital Rhetoric: Theory, Practice, and Property." In *Literacy Online: The Promise (and Peril) of Reading and Writing with Computers*, edited by Myron C. Tuman, 221–243. Pittsburgh, PA: University of Pittsburgh Press.

Lanham, Richard. 1995. *The Electronic Word: Democracy, Technology, and the Arts*. Chicago, IL: University of Chicago Press.

Licklider, J. C. R., and Robert W. Taylor. 1968. "The Computer as a Communication Device." *Science and Technology* 76: 21–31.

Logie, John. 2006. *Peers, Pirates, and Persuasion: Rhetoric in the Peer-to-Peer Debates*. West Lafayette, IN: Parlor.

Losh, Elizabeth. 2009. *Virtualpolitik: An Electronic History of Government Media-Making in a Time of War, Scandal, Disaster, Miscommunication, and Mistakes*. Cambridge, MA: MIT Press.

Lunenfeld, Peter. 2011. *The Secret War between Downloading and Uploading: Tales of the Computer as Culture Machine*. Cambridge, MA: MIT Press.

Manovich, Lev. 2001. *The Language of New Media*. Cambridge, MA: MIT Press.

McLuhan, Marshall. 1962. *The Gutenberg Galaxy: The Making of Typographic Man*. Toronto: University of Toronto Press.

McLuhan, Marshall. 1964. *Understanding Media: The Extensions of Man*. Toronto: University of Toronto Press.

McLuhan, Marshall. 1992. *The Global Village: Transformations in World Life and Media in the 21st Century*. New York: Oxford University Press.

McLuhan, Marshall. 1995. "*Playboy* Interview." In *Essential McLuhan*, edited by Eric McLuhan and Frank Zingrone, 233–269. Toronto: University of Toronto Press.

Monfort, Nick, and Ian Bogost. 2009. *Racing the Beam*. Cambridge, MA: MIT Press.

Morton, Timothy. 2011. "Sublime Objects." *Speculations* 2: 254–274.

Murray, Janet. 1997. *Hamlet on the Holodeck*. Cambridge, MA: MIT Press.

Negroponte, Nicholas. 1996. *Being Digital*. New York: Vintage.

Nelson, Theodor H. 1965. "A File Structure for the Complex, the Changing, and the Indeterminate." In *Association for Computing Machinery: Proceedings of the 20th National Conference*, edited by Lewis Winner, 84–100. New York: Lewis Winner.

Nelson, Theodor H. 1974. *Computer Lib/Dream Machines*. Chicago, IL: Nelson.

Peters, John Durham. 2011. "Preludes to a Theory of Obscenity." In *Obscenity and the Limits of Liberalism*, edited by Loren Glass and Charles Francis Williams, 146–166. Columbus: Ohio State University Press.

Reid, Alexander. 2007. *The Two Virtuals: New Media and Composition*. Anderson, SC: Parlor.

Sayers, Jentery. 2010. "Integrating Digital Audio Composition into Humanities Courses." *ProfHacker* (blog), *The Chronicle of Higher Education*. May 25. http://chronicle.com/blogs/profhacker/integrating-digital-audio-composition-into-humanities-courses.

Selfe, Cynthia L. 2009. "The Movement of Air, the Breath of Meaning: Aurality and Multimodal Composing." *College Composition and Communication* 60 no. 4: 616–663.

Sey, Araba, Chris Coward, François Bar, George Sciadas, Chris Rothschild, and Lucas Koepke. 2013. *Connecting People for Development: Why Public Access ICTs Matter*. Seattle: Technology and Social Change Group, University of Washington Information School. http://www.globalimpactstudy.org/report/.

Shah, Nishant, and Sunil Abraham. 2009. *Digital Natives with a Cause? A Knowledge Survey and Framework*. The Hague: Humanist Institute for Cooperation with Developing Countries.

Shannon, Claude. 1949. *The Mathematical Theory of Communication*. Champaign: University of Illinois Press.

Verhulsdonck, Gustav, and Marohang Limbu. 2014. *Digital Rhetoric and Global Literacies: Communication Modes and Digital Practices in the Networked World*. Hershey, PA: Information Science Reference.

Vicinus, Martha, and Caroline Eisner, eds. 2009. *Originality, Imitation, and Plagiarism: Teaching Writing in the Digital Age*. Ann Arbor: University of Michigan Press.

Wardrip-Fruin, Noah. 2009. *Expressive Processing*. Cambridge, MA: MIT Press.

Wardrip-Fruin, Noah, and Pat Harrigan, eds. 2007. *Second Person: Role-Playing and Story in Games and Playable Media*. Cambridge, MA: MIT Press.

Wardrip-Fruin, Noah, and Pat Harrigan. 2009. *Third Person: Authoring and Exploring Vast Narratives*. Cambridge, MA: MIT Press.

Wardrip-Fruin, Noah, and Nick Montfort. 2003. *The New Media Reader*. Cambridge, MA: MIT Press.

Warnick, Barbara. 2007. *Rhetoric Online: Persuasion and Politics on the World Wide Web*. New York: Peter Lang.

Welch, Kathleen. 1999. *Electric Rhetoric: Classical Rhetoric, Oralism, and a New Literacy*. Cambridge, MA: MIT Press.

Wiener, Norbert. 1954. "Men, Machines, and the World About." In *Medicine and Science*, edited by I. Galderston, 13–28. New York: International Universities Press.

Wiener, Norbert. 1965. *Cybernetics*. Cambridge, MA: MIT Press.

Yergeau, Melanie, and Paul Heilker. 2011. "Autism and Rhetoric." *College English* 73 no. 5: 485–497.

Glossary of Greek and Latin Rhetorical Terms[1]

....

A

Abominatio (L. "loathing"; *rejectio, detestatio*; Gk. *bdelygmia, apodioxis*). An expression of disgust or hatred: "What, drawn, and talk of peace? I hate the word / as I hate hell, all Montagues, and thee" (William Shakespeare, *Romeo and Juliet* 1.1.69–70). See *apodioxis*.

Abusio (L. "misuse"; Gk. *catachrēsis*; Eng. "the Figure of Abuse" [Putt. = Puttenham 2007]). The use of words outside their proper context, common usage, or standard grammatical function: "I fear 'tis *deepest winter* in Lord Timon's *purse*" (*Timon of Athens* 3.4.15).

Accumulatio (L. "piling up"; *frequentatio*). Assembling the main points of an argument and restating them for emphasis.

Accusatio (L. "accusation," "charge," "formal indictment"; *criminis reprehensio*; Gk. *catēgoria*). Leveling a charge or accusation. See *catēgoria*.

Accusatio Concertativa*, *Accusatio Adversa (L. "counteraccusation," "countercharge"; *translatio in adversarium, tu quoque* ["you too!"]; Gk. *anticatēgoria*). Turning a charge back against an accuser: "[HERMIONE]. For Polixenes, / With whom I am accused, I do confess / *I loved him* as in honour he required; . . . with a love even such, / . . . *as yourself commanded*" (*The Winter's Tale* 3.2.59–64). See *anticatēgoria*.

Acervatio. See *polysyndeton*.

Acrylogia. See *improprietas*.

Actio (L. "activity," "delivery"; *pronuntiatio*; Gk. *hypokrisis*). The physical delivery or performance of a speech by means of voice, facial expression, gesture, and motion ("graceful regulation of voice [*vocis*], countenance [*vultus*], and gesture [*gestus*]" [*Rhetorica ad Herennium* 1.3]). The last of the five parts of rhetoric (Gk. *rhētorikēs merē*; L. *rhetorices partes*). See *dispositio, elocutio, inventio, memoria*.

Adagium (L. "proverb"; *sententia, maxim*; Gk. *apothegm, gnōmē*). A pithy expression of traditional lore or wisdom: "Honest plain words best pierce the ear of grief" (*Love's Labours Lost* 5.2.746).

Adfectus. See *pathopoēia*.

Adhortatio. See *protrope*.

Adianoeta (Gk. "unintelligible"). An expression that carries an implicit, often ironic, meaning that differs from its explicit meaning: "This councillor / Is now most still, most secret and most *grave* [dead]" (*Hamlet* 3.4.211–2). See *allegoria*.

Adjectio. See *anaphora*.

Admiratio (L. "wonder," "astonishment"; Gk. *thaumasmos*). An exclamation of wonder: "Admired Miranda! / Indeed the top of admiration, worth / What's dearest to the world" (*The Tempest* 3.1.37–9).

Admonitio (L. "reminder," "warning," "reproof"; Gk. *paraenesis*). A warning of impending evil: "Welcome destruction, blood and massacre. / I see, as in a map, the end of all" (*King Richard III* 2.4.54–5).

Adnominatio. See *parōnomasia*.

Adumbratio. See *hypotypōsis*.

Adynaton (Gk. "powerless"; L. *impossibilia*). A confession of one's inability to express oneself adequately: "For I have neither wit, nor words, nor worth, / Action, nor utterance, nor the power of speech / To stir men's blood. I only speak right on" (*Julius Caesar* 3.2.214–6).

Aenos (Gk. "tale," "story," "saying"). A riddling fable, often with a moral lesson: "I loved you ever—but it is no matter. / Let Hercules himself do what he may, / The cat will mew and dog will have his day" (*Hamlet* 5.1.279–81).

Aetiologia (Gk. "giving a cause"; *apodeixis*; L. *redditio causae, raciocinatio*; Eng. "the Tell Cause" [Putt.]). Providing a cause or reason for a claim or statement: "Let them be well / used, for they are the abstract and brief chronicles of / the time" (*Hamlet* 2.2.461–3).

Affectus (L. "mood," "feeling," "emotion"). In Roman rhetorical theory, the seat of the emotions and passions (*adfectibus*), held to be located in the liver: "This wins him, liver and all!" (*Twelfth Night* 2.5.94). See *pathos, pathopoēia*.

Affectus Expressio. See *pathopoēia*.

Agōn (Gk. "contest," "battle," "gathering"). Competitive struggle, especially in legal, political, and epideictic rhetoric.

Aischrologia, Aeschrologia (Gk. "foul speaking"; *cacemphaton*; L. *scurra, turpis loquutio*). Abusive language or foul, scurrilous joking: "Prick the / woman's tailor: well, Master Shallow; deep, / Master Shallow" (*King Henry IV Part 2* 3.2.158–60).

Allēgoria (Gk. "speaking otherwise than one seems to speak"; L. *inversio, permutatio, continua metaphora* [Quintilian]; Eng. "the False Semblant" [Putt.]). Mode of figurative speech in which a metaphor is sustained throughout a discourse, often to express a secret meaning. See *adianoeta*.

Alloiosis (Gk. "change," "alteration"; L. *mutatio*). Highlighting differences by dividing a subject into alternatives: "Ah ha, my lord, this prince is not an Edward. / He is not lulling on a lewd love-bed, / But on his knees at meditation; / Not dallying with a brace of courtesans, / But meditating with two deep divines; / Not sleeping, to engross his idle body, / But praying, to enrich his watchful soul" (*King Richard III* 3.7.70–6).

Allusio. See *parōnomasia*.

Ambiguitas, Ambiguum. See *amphibolia*.

Amphibolia (Gk. "ambiguity"; L. *ambiguitas, ambiguum*; Eng. "the Figure of Sence Incertaine" [Putt.]). An ambiguity or obscurity of meaning: "Fair is foul, and foul is fair" (*Macbeth* 1.1.11).

Amplificatio (L. "enlargement," "expansion"; *dilatio*). Expanding on a subject by means of repetition, enumeration, elaboration, etc.: "I will be master of what is mine own. / She is my goods, my chattels; she is my house, / My household-stuff, my field, my barn, / My horse, my ox, my ass, my anything" (*The Taming of the Shrew* 3.2.230–3).

Anabasis. See *climax*.

Anadiplōsis (Gk. "doubling back," "redoubling"; L. *duplicatio, reduplicatio*; Eng. "the Redouble" [Putt.]). Repetition of the last word or phrase of a line, clause, or sentence at the beginning of the next one: "She being none of *your flesh and blood, your flesh and blood* has not offended the king" (*The Winter's Tale* 4.4.696–7).

Anamnēsis (Gk. "remembrance"; L. *recordatio*). Recollection of past events, ideas, or persons: "I was never so berhymed since Pythagoras' time / that I was an Irish rat, which I can hardly remember" (*As You Like It* 3.2.172–3).

Anaphora (Gk. "carrying back"; *epembasis*; L. *adjectio, repetitio*). Repetition of the same word or phrase at the beginning of successive clauses: "Mad world! Mad kings! Mad composition!" (*King John* 2.2.361). See *antistrophē*.

Anastrophē (Gk. "turning back"; *parallage, syncatēgorema*; L. *inversio, perversio, reversio*). A departure from normal word order for the sake of emphasis, often by reversing the position of two words: "Taffeta phrases, *silken terms precise*, / Three-piled hyperboles, spruce affectation, / *Figures pedantical*: these summer flies / Have blown me full of maggot ostentation" (*Love's Labours Lost* 5.2.406–9).

Anatomy (Gk. "cutting up," "dissection"; Fr. blazon). Analysis of an issue into its constituent parts; vivid, point-by-point description, usually of a person: "I'll be sworn thou art— / Thy tongue, thy face, thy limbs, actions, and spirit / Do give thee fivefold blazon" (*Twelfth Night* 1.5.283–5). See *effictio*.

Animorum Motus. The emotions. See *affectus, pathos*.

Antanaclasis (Gk. "reflect," "bend back"; *anaclasis*; L. *refractio, reciprocatio*; Eng. "the Rebound" [Putt.]). Repetition of a word or phrase whose meaning changes in the second instance: "She speaks, and 'tis such *sense* / That my *sense breeds* with it" (*Measure for Measure* 2.2.142–3).

Anthypophora. See *hypophora*.

Anticatēgoria (Gk. "countercharge"). Counteraccusation against an adversary in a law case.

Antilogiae (Gk. "against speaking," "strife," "contradiction"; L. *argumentum in utramque partem*). Advancing opposed speeches on the same topic, an art developed by Protagoras, Gorgias, Antiphon, and other sophists. See *dissoi logoi*.

Antimetabolē (Gk. "turning about"; L. *commutatio, permutatio*; Eng. "the Counterchange" [Putt.]). Repetition of words in reverse order in successive clauses, thus forming an ABBA pattern: "Madam, I swear I use no art at all. / That he's mad, 'tis true, 'tis true *'tis pity*, / And pity *'tis* 'tis true: a foolish figure!" (*Hamlet* 2.2.96–8).

Antinomy (Gk. "opposition of law"). In forensic rhetoric, a conflict or ambiguity in the law. See *scriptum et sententia/voluntas*.

Antiphora. See *hypophora*.

Antirrhēsis (Gk. "refutation," "counterstatement"). Rejecting an opinion or argument because of its insignificance or wickedness: "These are old fond paradoxes to make / fools laugh i' th'alehouse. What miserable praise hast / thou for her that's foul and foolish?" (*Othello* 2.1.138–40). See *apodioxis*.

Antistrēphon (Gk. "turning against"; L. *conversio, reciproca*). A retort or counterargument that turns an adversary's argument back against them: "[CLARENCE]. Take heed, for He holds vengeance in His hand, / To hurl upon their heads that break his law / [SECOND MURDERER]. And that same vengeance doth He hurl on thee / For false forswearing and for murder too" (*King Richard III* 1.4.198–201).

Antistrophē (Gk. "turning about"; *epiphora, epistrophē*; L. *conversio*; Eng. "the Counterturne" [Putt.]). Repetition of a word or words at the end of successive clauses, sentences, or verses: "Why then the world and all that's in't is nothing, / The covering sky is nothing, Bohemia nothing, / My wife is nothing, nor nothing have these nothings, / If this be nothing" (*The Winter's Tale* 1.2.290–3).

Antonomasia. See *periphrasis.*

Apodeixis (Gk. "proof," "demonstration"; *apodixis*). Proving a claim by referring to common knowledge or general experience: "But 'tis a common proof / That lowliness is young ambition's ladder / Whereto the climber upward turns his face" (*Julius Caesar* 2.1.21–3).

Apodioxis (Gk. "driving away"; *antirrhēsis*; L. *abominatio, detestatio, rejectio*). Scornful rejection of an argument as false, impertinent, or groundless. See *abominatio, antirrhēsis.*

Apologue. See *fabula.*

Apophasis. See *expeditio.*

Aporia (Gk. "impasse," "being at a loss"; *diaporesis*; L. *dubitatio*; Eng. "the Doubtfull" [Putt.]). Deliberating as if in doubt about an issue or course of action: "To be, or not to be—that is the question; / Whether 'tis nobler in the mind to suffer / The slings and arrows of outrageous fortune / Or to take arms against a sea of troubles / And by opposing end them" (*Hamlet* 3.1.57–9).

Apostrophē (Gk. "turning away"; L. *aversio*; Eng. "the Turne Tale" [Putt.]). Turning one's speech from one audience to another, most often to address an abstraction, inanimate object, or absent person: "*Come, seeling Night,* / Scarf up the tender eye of pitiful Day, / And, with thy bloody and invisible hand, / Cancel, and tear to pieces, that great bond / Which keeps me pale!" (*Macbeth* 3.2.46–9).

Apothegm. See *adagium.*

Argumentatio (L. *confirmatio, probatio*; Gk. *pistis, agōnes, apodeixis*). Section of the speech that furnishes proof for its claims. One of the basic parts (Gk. *logou merē*; L. *orationis partes*) of the classical oration. See *confutatio, divisio, exordium, narratio, partitio, peroratio, refutatio.*

Argumentum ad Baculum (L. "staff," "cudgel"). Argument based on the threat of force.

Argumentum ad Hominem (L. "man"). Argument based on a person's character.

Argumentum ad Misericordiam (L. "pity"). Argument based on the appeal to pity.

Argumentum ad Populum (L. "crowd"). Argument based on the appeal to popular opinion.

Argumentum ad Verecundiam (L. "awe," "reverence," "shame"). Argument based on the appeal to respect for authority.

Argumentum ex Concessis (L. "concession"). Argument based on an adversary's own premises.

Argumentum in Utramque Partem (L. "on either side"). See *antilogiae, dissoi logoi.*

Ars Dictaminis (L. "dictation"). The medieval art of prose composition, including letter writing (*ars epistolica*).

Ars Inveniendi. See *inventio.*

Ars Memoria. See *memoria.*

Ars Poetriae (L. "art of poetry"). The medieval art of writing poetry and epideictic speeches.

Ars Precandi (L. "art of praying"). The medieval art of prayer.

Ars Predicandi (L. "art of preaching"). The medieval art of preaching.

Articulus. See *asyndeton.*

Artistic Proofs (Gk. *entechnoi pisteis*). In Aristotle, proofs or means of persuasion derived from the techniques and principles of rhetoric as an art (*technē*), as opposed to contracts, witnesses, evidence gained by torture, etc. See *inartistic proofs.*

Asianism. Florid, ornamented style popular in the Greek-speaking cities of Asia Minor, especially during the Second Sophistic (100–300 CE). See *Atticism.*

Asyndeton (Gk. "unconnected," "unbound"; L. *articulus, dissolutio, dialyton*; Eng. "Loose Language" [Putt.]). Omission of conjunctions between words, phrases, and clauses: "Are all thy conquests, glories, triumphs, spoils, / Shrunk to this little measure?" (*Julius Caesar* 3.1.149–50). See *zeugma*.

Atticism. Spare, unadorned style modeled on the Attic orators of classical Greece. See *Asianism*.

Aversio. See *apostrophē*.

B

Barbarismos, Barbarolexis (Gk. "acting like a foreigner"). Employing nonstandard or foreign words, often out of affectation; mispronouncing a word through ignorance: "Neighbour *vocatur* / 'nebour,' neigh abbreviated 'ne'. This is abhominable, / which he would call 'abominable.' It insinuateth me of / insanie. *Ne intelligis, domine?*" (*Love's Labours Lost* 5.1.22–5).

Bdelygmia. See *abominatio*.

Benedictio. See *eulogia*.

Blazon. See *effictio, anatomy*.

Bomphiologia (Gk. "booming speech"; L. *verborum bombus*; Eng. "great gasying wordes" [Sherry, *A Treatise of Schemes and Tropes* [1550]). Bombastic, often bragging speech: "Farewell the plumed troop and the big wars / That makes ambition virtue! O, farewell, / Farewell the neighing steed and the shrill trump, / The spirit-stirring drum, th'ear-piercing fife, / The royal banner, and all quality, / Pride, pomp and circumstance of glorious war!" (*Othello* 3.3.352–7).

Brachylogia (Gk. "short speech"; L. *articulus*; Eng. "the Cutted Comma" [Putt.]). Brevity of speech or writing, often achieved by omitting conjunctions between words: "The courtier's, soldier's, scholar's eye, tongue, sword" (*Hamlet* 3.1.150).

C

Cacemphaton. See *aischrologia*.

Captatio Benevolentiae. Section of a speech or composition (usually in the *exordium*) designed to capture the good will of an audience: "Most potent, grave, and reverend signiors, / My very noble and approved good masters: / . . . Rude am I in my speech / And little blessed with the soft phrase of peace" (*Othello* 1.3.77–8, 82–3).

Carmina (L. "song," "verse"). Ritualized songs, prayers, and magical formulas in pre-literate Roman law and religion.

Catachrēsis. See *abusio*.

Cataplexis (Gk. "striking down"). Threat of punishment, misfortune, or disaster: "If you outstay the time, upon mine honour / And in the greatness of my word, you die" (*As You Like It* 1.3.85–6).

Catēgoria (Gk. "accusation"; L. *accusatio*). Accusation in a law case; openly criticizing a person's wickedness: "Judge me the world if 'tis not gross in sense / That thou hast practised on her with foul charms, / Abused her delicate youth with drugs or minerals / That weakens motion" (*Othello* 1.2.29–32). See *anticatēgoria*.

Catena (L. "chain"). Commentary on classic texts linked to the first words of a sentence or paragraph, thus forming a chain.

Causa. See *hypothesis*.

Charientismus (Gk. "graceful jest"; L. *graciosa nugutio*; Eng. "the Privy Nip" [Putt.]). Parrying harsh words by answering with an appeasing mock: "[LEONTES]. Give me the boy. I am glad you did not / nurse him. / Though he does bear some signs of me, yet you / Have too much blood in him. / [HERMIONE]. *What is this? Sport?*" (*The Winter's Tale* 2.1.56–8).

Chorographia (Gk. "description of a country"; Eng. "the Counterfeit of Place" [Putt.]). Vivid description of a place or nation.

Chreia (Gk. "useful"). An instructive anecdote, saying, or maxim: "To mourn a mischief that is past and gone / Is the next way to draw new mischief on" (*Othello* 1.3.205–6). One of the 14 *progymnasmata*.

Chrōma. See *colores.*

Chronographia (Gk. "time writing," "description of time"; Eng. "the Counterfeit of Time" [Putt.]). Description of a historical period or particular time: "[In Christmas season] the nights are wholesome, then no planets strike, / No fairy takes, nor witch hath power to charm, / So hallowed and so gracious is that time" (*Hamlet* 1.1.161–3).

Circumlocutio. See *periphrasis.*

Circumstantiae (Gk. *peristaseis, peristaka moria*; L. *negotium, circumstantiae partes*). In forensic rhetoric, the circumstances surrounding a case, including (1) person (Gk. *prosōpon*; L. *persona*): Who? (2) act (Gk. *pragma*; L. *actum*): What? (3) place (Gk. *topos*; L. *locus*): Where? (4) time (Gk. *chronos*; L. *tempus*): When? (5) cause (Gk. *aitia on*; L. *causa*): Why? "Why should he call her whore? who keeps her / company? / What place? what time? what form? what likelihood?" (*Othello* 4.2.138–40).

Climax (Gk. "ladder"; *anabasis, auxesis*; L. *gradatio, incrementum*; Eng. "the Clyming Figure" [Putt.]). The arrangement of words, phrases, or clauses in order of increasing (or decreasing) importance: "Sweet clown, sweeter fool, / sweetest lady!" (*Love's Labours Lost* 4.3.15–6).

Colometry. The study of rhythmical units (Gk. *cōla*) and their patterns in prose and poetry.

Cōlon. See *membrum.*

Colores (L. "colors"; *colores rhetorici*; Gk. *chrōma*). Tropes, figures, and ornaments that add stylistic luster to a composition; in forensic rhetoric (and declamation), the slant, gloss, or interpretation given to a case or series of events: "I love no colours, and without all *colour* / Of base insinuating flattery / I pluck this white rose with Plantagenet" (*King Henry VI Part 1* 2.4.34–6).

Commiseratio (L. "compassion," "pity"). The arousing of pity and sympathy: "Floods of tears will drown my oratory / And break my utterance even in the time / When it should move ye to attend me most, / And force you to commiseration" (*Titus Andronicus* 5.3.89–92).

Commoratio (L. "dwelling on a point"; Eng. "the Figure of Abode" [Putt.]). Dwelling on or repeating a strong argument: "But Brutus says, he [Julius Caesar] was ambitious, / And Brutus is an honourable man. / . . . And Brutus is an honourable man / . . . And sure he is an honourable man" (*Julius Caesar* 3.2.87–100).

Commutatio. See *antimetabolē.*

Compar. See *isocōlon.*

Complexio. See *symplokē.*

Compositio (L. "putting together"; Gk. *synthesis*). The arrangement of words and arguments; structure of a discourse. See *dispositio.*

Concessio (L. *permissio, confessio*; Gk. *epitrope, paromologia*). Conceding a point in order to prove a more important one: "Nay, do not pause; for I did kill King Henry, / But 'twas thy beauty that provoked me. / Nay, now dispatch; 'twas I that stabbed young Edward, / But 'twas thy heavenly face that set me on" (*King Richard III* 1.2.182–6).

Conciliare. See *officia oratoris.*

Conclusio (Gk. *epilogos*; L. *peroratio*). The final section of a composition (epilogue).

Conduplicatio. See * plokē.*

Conexum. See *symplokē.*

Confessio. See *concessio.*

Confirmatio. See *argumentatio.*

Confutatio (L. "refutation"; *refutatio*). Part of a composition that anticipates and refutes possible counterarguments: "And what's he then that says I play the villain? / When this advice is free I give and honest, / Probal to thinking and indeed the course / To win the Moor again?" (*Othello* 2.3.331–4).

Constitutiones (Gk. *zētamata logika*). Issues that give rise to controversy in a judicial case. See *circumstantiae, scriptum et sententia/voluntas, stasis.*

Contio (L. "meeting," "assembly"). In Latin oratory, a speech delivered at public meetings (*contiones*).

Controversiae. In Roman declamatory training, exercises requiring students to compose and perform imaginary forensic speeches. See *suasoriae.*

Conversio. Composition exercise in altering sentences to find the best formulation.

Copia (L. "copy," "abundance"). Abundance and variety of words (*verborum*) and ideas (*rerum*): "This is a gift that I have … / a foolish extravagant spirit, full of forms, figures, / shapes, objects, ideas, apprehensions, motions, / revolutions … begot in the ventricle of memory" (*Love's Labours Lost* 4.2.65–8).

Criminis Reprehensio. See *accusatio.*

Cursus Honorum (L. "course of honors"). The career path for Roman politicians, usually leading from *quaestor* to *praetor* to *consul.*

D

Declamatio (Gk. *meletē,* "practice," "exercise"). In Roman oratory and education, the practice of composing and performing fictitious speeches on topics in forensic rhetoric (*controversiae*) and deliberative rhetoric (*suasoriae*). See *controversiae, suasoriae.*

Decorum (L. "propriety"; Gk. *to prēpon*). Adapting a composition to suit the subject matter, audience, and occasion. See *kairos.*

Definitio. See *horismos.*

Delectare (L. "delight"). See *officia oratoris.*

Deliberative Rhetoric (Gk. *genos symbouleutikon*; L. *genus deliberativum*). Rhetoric designed to persuade a deliberative body to choose or reject a future course of action; one of the three principal genres of ancient rhetoric. See *epideictic rhetoric, forensic rhetoric.*

Demonstratio (L. *descriptio, hypotyposis*; Gk. *enargeia*). Vivid, lively description: "'Tis not your inky brows, your black silk hair, / Your bugle eyeballs, nor your cheek of cream, / That can entame my spirits to your worship" (*As You Like It* 3.5.47–9).

Denominatio. See *metonymy.*

Descriptio. See *demonstratio.*

Detestatio. See *abominatio.*

Diairesis. See *distributio.*

Dialogismos (Gk. "dialogue," "conversation"; L. *sermocinatio*; Eng. "the Right Reasoner" [Putt.]). Speaking in another person's character as part of a dialogue with oneself.

Dialysis (Gk. "separation"; L. *divisio*; Eng. "the Dismembrer" [Putt.]). Advancing either–or arguments that lead to a conclusion: "Your sense pursues not mine: *either* you are ignorant, / Or seem so craftily; and that's not good" (*Measure For Measure* 2.4.74–5).

Dialyton. See *asyndeton.*

Dianoias Schēmata. See *figures of thought.*

Dicendi Genera. See *stylistic genres.*

Dictatores (L. "dictate"). In the Middle Ages, teachers of letter writing; more generally, those skilled in rhetoric.

Diēgēsis. See *narratio.*

Dilatio. See *amplificatio.*

Dispositio (Gk. *taxis*). Arrangement, the art of distributing words (*verborum*) and arguments (*res*); the second task of the orator. See *actio, elocutio, inventio, memoria.*

Dissoi Logoi (Gk. "twofold arguments"; L. *argumentum in utramque partem*). Opposing arguments on the same topic or question. See *antilogiae.*

Dissolutio. See *asyndeton.*

Distributio (L. *divisio*; Gk. *merismōs*; Eng. "the Distributor" [Putt.]). Division of a topic or subject into parts: "Divide me like a bribe buck, each a *haunch*: I will / keep my *sides* to myself, my *shoulders* for the fellow of this / walk, and my *horns* I bequeath your husbands" (*The Merry Wives of Windsor* 5.5.21–3).

Divisio. Section of a composition that sets forth the agreed-upon points. See *confutatio, exordium, narratio, partitio, peroratio, refutatio.*

Docere. See *officia oratoris.*

Doxa (Gk. "belief," "opinion"; L. *opinio*). Belief or opinion, often contrasted (after Plato) with scientific knowledge (*epistēmē*). See *endoxa.*

Dubitatio. See *aporia.*

Duplicatio. See *anadiplōsis.*

E

Effictio (L. "fashioning"; Fr. *blazon*). Vivid, systematic description of a person's appearance. See *anatomy.*

Ekphrasis (Gk. "description"). Vivid visual description of a person, place, object, or experience: "Methoughts I saw a thousand fearful wracks, / A thousand men that fishes gnawed upon, / Wedges of gold, great anchors, heaps of pearl, / Inestimable stones, unvalued jewels, / All scattered in the bottom of the sea" (*King Richard III* 1.4.24–8).

Elenchus (Gk. "refutation," "testing"). Refutation by means of logical (or quasi-logical) reasoning: "I say unto / thee, I bid thy master cut out the gown, but I did not bid / him cut it to pieces. / Ergo, thou liest" (*The Taming of the Shrew* 4.3.127–9).

Elocutio (L. "speak out," "eloquence"; Gk. *lexis*). Style, the art of expressing and embellishing ideas and arguments with appropriate language; the third of the five tasks (*rhētoros erga*) of the orator. See *actio, Asianism, Atticism, dispositio, inventio, memoria, stylistic virtues.*

Elocutionis Virtutes. See *stylistic virtues.*

Enargeia. See *demonstratio.*

Endoxa (Gk. "beliefs," "opinions"). In rhetoric and dialectic, probable premises based on commonly held opinions. See *doxa.*

Energeia (Gk. "activity," "vigor"). Vigor and energy of expression: "Do your offices, do your / offices: Master Fang and Master Snare, do me, do me, do me your offices" (*King Henry IV Part 1* 2.1.39–40).

Enkyklios Paideia (Gk. "cycle of learning"). Ancient Greek ideal of a well-rounded education encompassing many fields.

Enthymēmē (Gk. "a thought," "a consideration"; L. *conclusio*). A rhetorical syllogism based on probable, often implied or unspoken, premises: "What, do you tremble? Are you all afraid?

/ Alas, I blame you not, for you are mortal, / And mortal eyes cannot endure the devil" (*King Richard III* 1.2.43–5).

Epainos (Gk. "praise"). In epideictic rhetoric, praise of a subject's general character, as opposed to blame (*psogos*): "I did infer your lineaments. . . . / Laid open all your victories in Scotland, / Your discipline in war, wisdom in peace, / Your bounty, virtue, fair humility; / Indeed, left nothing fitting for your purpose / Untouched or slightly handled in discourse" (*King Richard III* 3.7.12–9).

Epanalēpsis (Gk. "resumption," "repetition"; L. *repetitio*; Eng. "Eccho Sound," "the Slowe Return" [Putt.]). Repetition of an initial word or phrase at the end of the same clause or sentence: "*Blood* hath bought *blood*, and *blows* have answered *blows*" (*King John* 2.1.329).

Epideictic Rhetoric (Gk. *genos epideiktikon, panēgyrikon*; L. *genus demonstrativum*). Rhetoric designed for display (*epideixis*) and public ceremony, often involving praise and blame; for Aristotle, one of the three principal genres of rhetoric. See *deliberative rhetoric, forensic rhetoric*.

Epilogos. See *peroratio*.

Epimone (Gk. "tarrying upon"; Eng. "the Love Burden" [Putt.]). Frequent repetition of a phrase or question to dwell on a point: "Lest I revenge. / What, *myself* upon *myself*? / Alack, I love *myself*. Wherefore? For any good / That I *myself* have done unto *myself*?" (*King Richard III* 5.3.186–9). See *commoratio*.

Epiphora. See *anastrophē*.

Epistrophē. See *anastrophē*.

Epitaphios Logos. An ancient Greek funeral speech.

Epitropē (Gk. "a turning upon"; L. *concessio, permissio*). See *concessio*.

Epizeuxis (Gk. "fastening together"; L. *geminatio, iteratio*; Eng. "Cuckoo-Spell" [Putt.]). Repetition of words with no intervening words: "Never, never, never, never, never" (*King Lear* 5.3.306–7).

Eristics (from Gk. *eris*, "strife," "conflict"). In Plato, the sophistic practice of disputation (*eristikē*) that seeks victory without regard for truth.

Erōtēma (Gk. "questioning"; L. *interrogatio*; Eng. "the Questioner" [Putt.]). To affirm or deny a point by asking a question that does not invite a response (the "rhetorical question"): "I live with bread like you, feel want, / Taste grief, need friends. Subjected thus, / *How can you say to me I am a king?*" (*King Richard II* 3.2.175–7).

Ēthopoēia (Gk. "character making"; L. *moralis confictio*). Portrayal of character; *progymnasma* or composition (and performance) exercise in which students impersonate a thing or person, real or fictional, usually employing direct speech: "[BOTTOM AS PYRAMUS]. Thus die I, thus, thus, thus! / Now am I dead, / Now am I fled; / My soul is in the sky. / Tongue, lose thy light; / Moon take thy flight! / Now die, die, die, die, die" (*A Midsummer Night's Dream* 5.1.289–95). See *pathopoēia, prosōpopoēia*.

Ēthos (Gk. "character," "disposition"; L. *mores oratoris*). Persuasive appeal based on the speaker's character, especially as it is established in the speech: "I come not, friends, to steal away your hearts. / I am no orator, as Brutus is, / But, as you know me all, a plain blunt man / That love my friend" (*Julius Caesar* 3.2.209–12). One of Aristotle's three principal sources of persuasion. See *logos, pathos*.

Eucharistia (Gk. "thanksgiving"; L. *gratiarum actio*). Giving thanks for benefits received: "I thank my god for my humility" (*King Richard III* 2.1.77).

Euche (Gk. "vow," "prayer"; L. *promissio, votum*). A vow to keep a promise: "And thy commandment all alone shall live / Within the book and volume of my brain / Unmixed with baser matter" (*Hamlet* 1.5.102–4).

Eulogia (Gk. "speaking well of"; L. *benedictio*). Praising or blessing persons, places, or things: "He hath achieved a maid / That paragons description and wild fame; / One that excels the quirks of blazoning pens" (*Othello* 2.1.61–3).

Evidentia. See *hypotypōsis*.

Exemplum (L. "specimen," "sample"; Gk. *paradeigma*). An example used to support or illustrate an argument: "Grace is grace, despite of all controversy; / as for example, thou thyself art a wicked villain, despite of all / grace" (*Measure for Measure* 1.2.23–5).

Exordium (L. "beginning"; Gk. *prooimion*). The first part of a classical oration, which announces the topic and secures the attention and good will of an audience: "Friends, Romans, countrymen, lend me your ears: / I come to bury Caesar, not to praise him" (*Julius Caesar* 3.2.74–5). See *confutatio, divisio, exordium, narratio, partitio, peroratio, refutatio*.

Expeditio (L. "a freeing from difficulties"; *enumeratio*; Gk. *apophasis*; Eng. "the Speedie Dispatcher" [Putt.]). Rejecting all but one of several alternatives that have been enumerated.

Expositio. See *procthesis*.

F

Fabula (L. "discourse," "story," "narrative"; Gk. *apologue*). A fictitious narrative, often designed to illustrate a moral.

Facetia (L. "amusing remark," "joke," "witticism"). A witty or humorous remark: "It is the wittiest partition [an actor playing a wall/a rhetorical *partitio*] that ever I did hear discourse, my lord" (*A Midsummer Night's Dream* 5.1.165). See *partitio*.

Figurae Verborum. See *figures of speech*.

Figures of Speech (Gk. *lēxeos schēmata*, "word figures"; L. *exornationes verborum* [*Rhetorica ad Herennium*], *figurae verborum, figurae elocutionis*). Figures that operate at the level of the linguistic means of expression (*verborum*), such as metaphor, metonymy, etc. See *figures of thought*.

Figures of Thought (Gk. *dianoias schēmata*, "thought figures"; L. *exornationes sententiarum* [*Rhetorica ad Herennium*], *figurae sententiae, sensus figurae*). Figures that operate at the level of conceptual content (*sententia*), such as irony, allegory, etc. It is notoriously difficult to distinguish figures of thought (content) from figures of speech (style). See *figures of speech*.

Finitio. See *horismos*.

Flectere. See *officia oratoris*.

Forensic Rhetoric (Gk. *genos dikanikon*; L. *genus judiciale*). Legal rhetoric concerned with accusing or defending a past act; for Aristotle, one of the three principal genres of ancient rhetoric. See *deliberative rhetoric, epideictic rhetoric*.

Frequentatio. See *accumulatio*.

G

Geminatio. See *epizeuxis*.

Genos Dikanikon. See *forensic rhetoric*.

Genus Judiciale. See *forensic rhetoric*.

Gnōmē (Gk. "thought," "judgment," "opinion"; L. *sententia, adagium*). A brief, pithy statement of a general truth: "An honest tale speeds best being plainly told" (*King Richard III* 4.4.358). See *adagium*.

Graciosa Nugutio. See *charientismus*.

Gradatio. See *climax*.

Grammaticus. A professional teacher of grammar, language, and literature at the first stage of Roman education.

Gratiarum Actio. See *eucharistia*.

H

Hermeneutics (Gk. *hermēneuein*, "to interpret," "to translate"). The art of textual interpretation, especially of the Bible.

Heuresis. See *inventio*.

Homoiotēleuton (Gk. "like ending"; L. *similiter desinens*; Eng. "the Figure of Like Loose" [Putt.]). A series of words, phrases, or sentences with the same or similar endings: "The best actors in the world, either for / tragedy, comedy, history, pastoral, pastoral-comical, / historical-pastoral, scene individable" (*Hamlet* 2.2.333–5).

Horismos (Gk. "boundary," "definition"; L. *definitio, finitio*; Eng. "the Definer by Difference" [Putt.]). A brief, clear, pithy definition.

Humiliatio. See *tapinosis*.

Hypallage. See *metonymy*.

Hyperbaton (Gk. "overstepping"; L. *transgressio*). Violating conventional word order, often to achieve emphasis: "Yet I'll not shed her blood / Nor scar that *whiter skin of hers than snow* / And smooth as monumental alabaster" (*Othello* 5.2.3–5).

Hypokrisis. See *actio*.

Hypophora (Gk. "carrying under"; *antiphora, anthypophora*; L. *subjectio, rogatio*; Eng. "the Figure of Response" [Putt.]). A figure in which one asks and then immediately answers one's own questions, often as a way to refute potential objections: "What is honour? A / word. What is in that word 'honour'? What is that / 'honour'? Air" (*King Henry IV Part 1* 5.1.133–5).

Hypothesis (Gk. "subject under discussion"; L. *causa*). In rhetorical training, debating a particular or definite case ("Should I marry?"), as opposed to a *thesis*, a general or indefinite case ("Is marriage good?").

Hypotypōsis (Gk. "sketch," "outline," "pattern"; L. *demonstratio, evidentia, adumbratio*; Eng. "the Counterfeit Representation" [Putt.]). Lively, vivid description of a scene, thing, event, or action: "[GHOST]. I could a tale unfold whose lightest word / Would harrow up thy soul, freeze thy young blood, / Make thy two eyes like stars start from their spheres, / Thy knotted and combined locks to part / And each particular hair to stand on end / Like quills upon the fretful porcupine" (*Hamlet* 1.5.15–20).

Hysteron Prōteron (Gk. "the latter [put as] the former"; L. *prepostera loquutio*; Eng. "the Preposterous" [Putt.]). Inversion of logical or temporal order that puts the conclusion before the premise ("arsee versee"): "May not an ass know when the cart draws the horse?" (*King Lear* 1.4.215).

I

Icon (Gk. *eikōn*, "likeness," "image," "portrait"; Eng. "Resemblance by Portrait" [Putt.]). A figure that portrays the likeness of a person by means of imagery: "All furnished, all in arms / All plumed like ostriches, that with the wind / Baited like eagles having lately bathed, / Glittering in golden coats, like images. . . . / I saw young Harry [King Henry IV] . . ." (*King Henry IV Part 1* 4.1.96–101).

Idioi Topoi (Gk. "special topics, places"). See *topoi*.

Impossibilia. See *adynaton*.

Improprietas (L. "impropriety"; Gk. *acrylogia*; Fr. *mal à propos*, "ill-suited"). Improper or inappropriate use of words, especially words that sound similar but signify different things: "Our watch, sir, have indeed / *comprehended* [apprehended] two *auspicious* [suspicious] persons" (*Much Ado About Nothing* 3.5.40–1).

Inartistic Proofs (Gk. *atechnoi pisteis*). In Aristotle, proofs that do not employ the art of rhetoric, such as witnesses, contracts, and "tortures" (*basanoi*), as opposed to artistic or "artificial" proofs (*entechnoi pisteis*). See *artistic proofs*.

Ingenium (L. "nature," "talent," "genius"). In Roman oratory, natural talent or genius, as opposed to art (*ars*).

Interpretatio. See *synonymia*.

Interrogatio. See *erōtēma*.

Inventio (L. *invenire*, "to find"; Gk. *heuresis*). Invention, the art of discovering words and arguments, often by using the system of *topoi*. The first of the five tasks of rhetoric. See *actio*, *dispositio*, *elocutio*, *memoria*, *topoi*.

Inversio. See *allēgoria*.

Isocōlon (Gk. "of equal members or clauses"; L. *compar*, *parison*; Eng. "the Figure of Even" [Putt.]). A series of similarly structured clauses or members (*membra*, *cōla*) of the same length: "Was ever woman in this humour wooed? / Was ever woman in this humour won?" (*King Richard III* 1.2.230–1).

Iteratio. See *epizeuxis*.

J

Judicatio. See *stasis*.

Jus Jurandum. See *orcos*.

K

Kairos (Gk. "proper time"; L. *occasio*, *tempus speciale*). The opportune moment for speech and action, determined by grasping the exigencies of time, place, audience, and circumstances.

Koinoi Topoi. See *topoi*.

L

Lamentatio. See *threnos*.

Laudatio. See *panegyric*.

Leges Contrariae (L. "contrary laws"; Gk. *antinomia*). In forensic rhetoric, a dispute arising from the inconsistency between one law or written document and another.

Lexeos Schēmata. See *figures of speech*.

Lexis. See *elocutio*.

Licentia. See *parrhēsia*.

Litōtēs (Gk. "simple," "plain," "small"; L. *diminutio*; Eng. "the Moderateur" [Putt.]). Understatement.

Loci, *Loci Communes* (L. "common places"). See *topoi*.

Logographos (Gk. "speech writer"). In ancient Greece, a speech writer (logographer) who composed legal speeches to be memorized and delivered by a client before a jury.

Logos (Gk. "word," "speech," "thought," "reason"). A mode of persuasion that employs logic and reasoning; for Aristotle, one of the three principal sources of persuasion. See *ēthos*, *pathos*.

M

Martyria (Gk. "testimony," "evidence"; L. *testatio*). Confirming something by referring to one's own experience: "Before my God, I might not this believe / Without the sensible and true avouch / Of mine own eyes" (*Hamlet* 1.1.55–7).

Meiōsis. See *tapinosis*.

Membrum (L. "part," "section"; *membrum orationis*; Gk. *cōlon*). Section or member of a discourse roughly equivalent to a clause.

Membrum Orationis. See *membrum*.

Memoria (L. "memory"; *ars memoria*; Gk. *mnēmē*). The art of memorizing and recalling words and subject matter for invention, style, and delivery, often employing visual images (L. *imagines*) projected onto mental places (L. *loci*). The fourth of the five tasks (*rhētoros erga*) of the rhetor. See *actio, dispositio, elocutio, inventio*.

Mempsis (Gk. "blame," "reproach"; L. *querimonia*). An expression of complaint and a demand for help: "For God's / sake, pity my case! The spite of man prevaileth against me. O / Lord, have mercy upon me!" (*King Henry VI Part 2* 1.3.220–2).

Merismōs (Gk. "division"; *diairesis*; L. *distributio*; Eng. "the Distributor" [Putt.]). See *distributio*.

Metabasis (Gk. "transition," "change"; L. *transitio*). A transitional statement explaining what has happened and what will follow.

Metalēpsis (Gk. "alternation," "succession"; L. *transumptio*; Eng. "the Far Fetched" [Putt.]). Reference to something by means of another thing remotely related to it, often through an implied substitution of terms or tenuous ("far fetched") causal relationship: "Over thy *wounds* now do I prophesy / (Which like *dumb mouths do ope their ruby lips* / To beg the voice and utterance of my tongue) / A curse shall light upon the limbs of men" (*Julius Caesar* 3.1.260–2).

Metaphor (from Gk. *metaphērein*, "to carry over"; L. *metaphora, translatio*; Eng. "the Figure of Transsporte" [Putt.]). A figure of speech in which a name, word, or phrase is transferred to an object or action different from, but analogous to, that to which it is literally applicable: "All the world's a stage, / And all the men and women merely players" (*As You Like It* 2.7.140–1).

Metastasis (Gk. "removal," "change"; L. *transmotionem*; Eng. "the Flitting Figure or the Remove" [Putt.]). Denying arguments and then turning them back on an adversary.

Metonymy (Gk. "change of name"; L. *hypallage, denominatio, transmutatio*; Eng. "the Misnamer" [Putt.]). A figure of speech that refers to something or someone by naming one of its attributes: "*Bell, book, and candle* [excommunication] will not drive me back / When gold and silver becks me to come on" (*King John* 3.3.12–3).

Modus Inveniendi. In Augustinian hermeneutics, the means of discovering the meaning of Scripture, often involving allegorical exegesis. See *modus proferendi*.

Modus Proferendi. In Augustinian homiletics, the means of expressing the ideas discovered in Scripture. See *modus inveniendi*.

Moralis Confictio. See *ēthopoēia*.

Mores Oratoris. See *ēthos*.

Movere. See *officia oratoris*.

Mutatio. See *alloiosis*.

N

Narratio (L. "narration"; Gk. *prothesis, diēgēsis*). Section of a speech that provides a narrative overview of the facts of the case; a declamation exercise (*progymnasma*) that requires the student to tell a story (see *progymnasmata*). See *argumentatio, confutatio, divisio, exordium, partitio, peroratio, refutatio*.

Negotium. See *circumstantiae*.

Nōema (Gk. "thought," "idea"; Eng. "the Figure of Close Conceit" [Putt.]). Deliberately obscure and subtle speech. See *skotison*.

Nominis Communio. See *synonymia*.

O

Occasio. See *kairos.*

Occultatio (L. "concealment," "insinuation"). See *paralipsis.*

Officia Oratoris (L. "duties of the orator"). In Latin rhetorical theory, the duties ("offices") of the orator, which include to instruct (*docere*), to prove (*probare*), to delight (*delectare*), to conciliate (*conciliare*), and to move and bend (*movere, flectere*).

Ominatio. See *admonitio.*

Opinio. See *doxa, endoxa.*

Orcos (Gk. "oath"; L. *jus jurandum*). Swearing a statement to be true: "I am the master of my speeches, and would undergo / what's spoken, I swear" (*Cymbeline* 1.4.124–5).

Ordo Artificialis (L. "artistic order"). Arrangement of a speech or narrative in artistic fashion, often starting in the middle of things (*in medias res*) rather than from the beginning.

Ordo Naturalis (L. "natural order"). Arrangement of a speech or narrative in chronological order from beginning to end.

P

Paideia (Gk. "child rearing," "education"). The Greek system of education for boys.

Panegyric (Gk. "speech for a public assembly," "eulogy," "praise"; L. *laudatio*). Speech in praise of a person, place, or thing: "This superficial tale / Is but a preface of her worthy praise; / The chief perfections of that lovely dame— / Had I sufficient skill to utter them— / Would make a volume of enticing lines / Able to ravish any dull conceit" (*King Henry VI Part 1* 5.4.105). One of the principal genres of epideictic rhetoric (*genos panēgyrikon*).

Parabola (Gk. "throwing beside"; Eng. "Resemblance Mystical" [Putt.]). A parable that draws parallels between two dissimilar things to illustrate a moral lesson.

Paradeigma (Gk. "model," "example"). See *exemplum.*

Paraenesis. See *admonitio.*

Paragmenon. See *polyptoton.*

Paralipsis (Gk. "a leaving to one side"; L. *occultatio, preteritio*; Eng. "the Passager" [Putt.]). Drawing attention to something while pretending to pass it over: "I fear I wrong the honourable men / Whose daggers have stabbed Caesar: I do fear it" (*Julius Caesar* 3.2.152–3).

Parallage. See *anastrophē.*

Parataxis. See *asyndeton.*

Parison. See *isocōlon.*

Paromologia (Gk. "partial agreement"; L. *concessio, confessio*; Eng. "the Figure of Admittance" [Putt.]). See *concessio.*

Parōnomasia (Gk. "altering slightly in naming"; L. *allusio, adnominatio*; Eng. "the Nicknamer" [Putt.]). Wordplay that uses words that sound alike (homophones) but differ in meaning ("punning"): "An *ass's nole* [donkey's head] I fixed on his head" (*A Midsummer Night's Dream* 3.2.17).

Parrhēsia (Gk. "free-spokenness," "frankness"; L. *licentia*; Eng. "the Licentious" [Putt.]). Candid, fearless speech: "[KING LEONTES]. I'll ha' thee burnt. / [PAULINA]. I care not. / It is an heretic that makes the fire, / Not she which burns in't. I'll not call you tyrant, but . . ." (*The Winter's Tale* 2.3.112–4).

Partitio (L. "division"; *divisio, propositio*; Gk. *prothesis, prokataskeuē*). Section of a discourse that surveys the points to be made; one of the six parts of the classical oration. See *argumentatio, confutatio, divisio, exordium, narratio, peroratio, refutatio.*

Passio. See *pathos*.

Pathopoëia (Gk. "arousing of feeling"; *adfectus, affectus expressio*). General term for exciting the emotions, passions, and affects: "Call up her father, / Rouse him, make after him, poison his delight" (*Othello* 1.1.67–8).

Pathos (Gk. "suffering," "emotion," "feeling"; L. *passio*). Emotion; an appeal to the emotions, passions, and affects (*adfectibus*): "I never longed to hear a word till now. / Say 'pardon,' King; let pity teach thee how. / The word is short, but not so short as sweet" (*King Richard II* 5.3.114–6). In Aristotle, one of the three principal sources of persuasion. See *ēthos, logos*.

Peithō (Gk. "persuasion"). The Greek goddess of persuasion.

Periphrasis (Gk. "speaking around," "circumlocution"; L. *antonomasia, circumlocutio*; Eng. "the Figure of Ambage" [Putt.]). Talking around something, often by using descriptive phrases instead of names: "[KING CLAUDIUS]. Therefore *our sometime sister*, now our queen, / Th'imperial jointress of this warlike state, / Have we as 'twere with a defeated joy, / With one auspicious and one dropping eye, / With mirth in funeral and with dirge in marriage, / In equal scale weighing delight and dole / *Taken to wife*" (*Hamlet* 1.2.8–14).

Peristaseis. See *circumsantiae*.

Permissio. See *concessio*.

Permutatio. See *allēgoria, antimetabolē*.

Peroratio (Gk. *epilogos*; L. *conclusio*). The conclusion of a speech. See *argumentatio, confutatio, divisio, exordium, narratio, partitio, refutatio*.

Personae Confictio. See *prosōpopoëia*.

Perversio. See *anastrophē*.

Phronēsis (Gk. "thinking," "practical wisdom"; L. *prudentia*). The faculty of judgment or practical wisdom.

Pisteis. See *artistic proofs*.

Plokē (Gk. "plaiting"; L. *conduplicatio*; Eng. "the Doubler," "the Swift Repeat" [Putt.]). Repetition of a single word for emphasis or effect: "Why brand they us / With base? With baseness? Bastardy? Base, base?" (*King Lear* 1.2.9–10). See *antanaclasis, polyptoton*.

Polyptoton (Gk. "using the same word in many cases"; *paragmenon*; L. *adnominatio, traductio*; Eng. "the Tranlacer" [Putt.]). Repetition of the same root word with different endings: "That we find out the cause of this effect— / Or rather say the cause of this *defect*, / For this effect *defective* comes by cause. / Thus it *remains*, and the *remainder* thus" (*Hamlet* 2.2.101–4).

Polysyndeton (Gk. "using many conjunctions"; L. *acervatio*; Eng. "the Couple Clause" [Putt.]). Employing many conjunctions between clauses: "*And* in her bosom I'll unclasp my heart / *And* take her hearing prisoner with the force / *And* strong encounter of my amorous tale" (*Much Ado About Nothing* 1.1.271–3). See *asyndeton*.

Praemunitio (L. "strengthening beforehand"). Fortifying oneself in advance of an attack: "Go on, go on. / Thou canst not speak too much. I have deserved / All tongues to talk their bitterest" (*The Winter's Tale* 3.3.213–4).

Praesumptio. See *procatalēpsis*.

Pragmatographia (Gk. "description of an action"; L. *descriptio*; Eng. "the Counterfeit Action" [Putt.]). Vivid description of an action: "All but mariners / Plunged in the foaming brine and quit the vessel; / Then all afire with me, the King's son, Ferdinand, / With hair up-staring (then like reeds, not hair), / Was the first man that leapt, cried 'Hell is empty'" (*The Tempest* 1.2.210–4).

Precatio (L. "prayer"). See *ars precandi, euche*.

Prēpon (Gk. "what is fitting"). See *decorum*.

Prepostera Loquutio. See *hysteron prōteron*.

Preteritio (L. "passing over"). See *paralipsis*.

Probare. See *officia oratoris*.

Probatio. See *argumentatio*.

Procatalēpsis (Gk. "a seizing in advance"; L. *prolēpsis, praesumptio*; Eng. "the Presumptuous" [Putt.]). Refuting anticipated objections and counterarguments: "Perhaps thou wilt object my holy oath. / To keep that oath were more impiety / Than Jephthah, when he sacrificed his daughter" (*King Henry VI Part 3* 5.1.92–4).

Procthesis (Gk. "introduction," "prefatory account"; L. *expositio*). Providing reasons and circumstances to justify what has been said or done: "As I *slew my best lover for the / good of Rome*, I have the same dagger for myself when it shall / please my country to need my death" (*Julius Caesar* 3.2.41–3).

Progymnasmata (Gk. "preparatory exercises"; L. *praeexercitamina*). The sequence of 14 composition (and performance) exercises at the core of Hellenistic and Roman rhetorical training: (1) fable (Gk. *mythos*); (2) narrative (Gk. *diēgēma*); (3) anecdote (Gk. *chreia*); (4) proverb (Gk. *gnōmē*); (5) refutation (Gk. *anaskeuē*); (6) confirmation (Gk. *kataskeuē*); (7) commonplace (Gk. *koinos topos*); (8) encomium (Gk. *enkōmion*); (9) vituperation (Gk. *psogos*); (10) comparison (Gk. *synkrisis*); (11) impersonation (Gk. *ēthopoēia, prosōpopoēia*); (12) description (Gk. *ekphrasis*); (13) theme or thesis (Gk. *thesis*); (14) proposal of a law (Gk. *nomou eisphora*).

Prokataskeuē. See *partitio*.

Prolēpsis (Gk. "a preconception"). See *procatalēpsis*.

Promissio. See *euche*.

Pronuntiatio. See *actio*.

Propositio. See *partitio*.

Prosopographia (Gk. "face," "character"; *prosographia*; Eng. "the Counterfeit Countenance" [Putt.]). Vivid description of the face or appearance of an imaginary or fictional person: "The counterfeit presentment of two brothers: / See what a grace was seated on this brow, / Hyperion's curls, the front of Jove himself, / An eye like Mars to threaten and command" (*Hamlet* 3.4.51–5).

Prosōpopoēia (Gk. "character making"; L. *conformatio, sermocinatio, personae confictio*; Eng. "Counterfeit in Personation" [Putt.]). Figure in which an inanimate object or imaginary, absent, or dead person is represented as speaking or acting (impersonation): "In this same interlude it doth befall / That I, one Snout by name, present a wall; / And such a wall, as I would have you think, / That had in it a crannied hole or chink . . ." (*A Midsummer Night's Dream* 5.1.154–7). See *ēthopoēia*.

Prothesis. See *partitio*.

Protrope (Gk. "exhortation"; L. *adhortatio*). An exhortation to act that employs threats or promises: "Then in God's name, march. / True hope is swift and flies with swallow's wings: / Kings it makes gods, and meaner creatures kings" (*King Richard III* 5.3.22–4).

Psogos. See *epainos*.

Psychagōgia (Gk. "soul-leading"). In Plato's *Phaedrus*, Socrates's definition of rhetoric as the "leading of souls."

Pysma (Gk. "question"; L. *quaesitio, quaesitum*). Posing a series of questions: "How dares / Thy harsh rude tongue sound this unpleasing news? / What Eve, what serpent hath suggested thee / To make a second fall of cursed man? / Why dost thou say King Richard is deposed?" (*King Richard II* 3.4.74–7).

Q

Quaesitio, **Quaesitum**. See *pysma*.

Querimonia. See *mempsis*.

R

Raciocinatio. See *aetiologia*.

Reciproca. See *antistrēphon*.

Reciprocatio. See *antanaclasis*.

Recordatio. See *anamnēsis*.

Redditio Causae. See *aetiologia*.

Refractio. See *antanaclasis*.

Refutatio (L. *confutatio, reprehensio*; Gk. *lysis*). Part of a speech that refutes possible objections and counterarguments; one of the basic elements of the classical oration. See *argumentatio, confutatio, divisio, exordium, narratio, partitio, peroratio*.

Rejectio. See *abominatio*.

Repetitio. See *anaphora*.

Reprehensio (L. "blame," "refutation"). Rebuttal of an argument.

Reversio. See *anastrophē*.

Rhetoric (from Gk. *rhētorikē*, "art of speaking"; L. *rhetorica*). The art of effective expression, argument, and persuasion in speech, writing, and other media.

Rogatio. See *hypophora*.

S

Sardismus. See *soraismus*.

Schēma (Gk. "form," "figure"). Any kind of artful form or pattern of words.

Schēmatismos (Gk. "giving form"). Concealing a meaning by using figurative language ("figured speech"). See *allegoria, significatio*.

Scriptum et Sententia/Voluntas (L. "letter and intention"). In Roman legal rhetoric, the letter or literal meaning (*scriptum*) of a law as opposed to its sense, spirit, or authorial intention (*sententia, voluntas*): "The bloody book of law / You shall yourself read, in the bitter letter, / After your own sense" (*Othello* 1.3.68–70).

Scurra. See *aischrologia*.

Sententia (L. "judgment," "opinion," "thought"). See *adagium*.

Sermocinatio. See *dialogismos*.

Significatio (L. "sign," "emphasis"; Eng. "the Reinforcer" [Putt.]). To imply more than is actually stated: "[KING CLAUDIUS]. How is it that the clouds still hang on you? / [HAMLET]. Not so, my lord, I am too much i' th' sun [not your *son*/under royal surveillance]" (*Hamlet* 1.2.66–7).

Similiter Desinens. See *homoiotēleuton*.

Skesis. See *paronomasia*.

Skotison (Gk. "darkened"). Deliberate obscurity of meaning: "[ROSALINE]. What's your dark meaning, mouse, of this light word? / [KATHARINE]. A light condition in a beauty dark. / [ROSALINE]. We need more light to find your meaning out" (*Love's Labours Lost* 5.2.19–21).

Soraismus (Gk. "heaping up"; *cumulatio, sardismus*; Eng. "Mingle-Mangle" [Putt.]). Mingling different languages artlessly or with affectation. See *barbarismos*.

Stasis (Gk. "discord," "standing"; L. *status, constitutio*). A procedure for determining the decisive issue (Gk. *krinōmenon*; L. *judicatio*) under dispute in legal cases by posing a series of questions, including: (1) the question of fact: "Did it happen? [L. *An sit?*]" (Gk. *stokhasmos*; L. *status conjecturalis*); (2) the question of definition: "What happened? [L. *Quid sit?*]" (Gk. *horos, horismos*; L. *status definitiva, proprietas*); (3) the question of quality: "What is the quality of the act? [L. *Quale sit?*]" (Gk. *poiōtes*; L. *status generalis, qualitas*); and (4) the question of jurisdiction: "Is this the right court to decide this issue?" (Gk. *metalēpsis*; L. *status translativa, translatio*).

Stylistic Genres (Gk. *logou charaktēres*; L. *dicendi genera*). The three principal genres or levels of style, including plain (L. *humile, extenuatum*), moderate (L. *modicum, temperatum*), and elevated (L. *grande, gravis, sublime*).

Stylistic Virtues (Gk. *lexeos aretai*; L. *elocutionis virtutes*). The qualities of good style, including (1) correctness (Gk. *Hellenismos*; L. *Latinitas*); (2) clarity (Gk. *saphēneia*; L. *perspicuitas*); (3) appropriateness (Gk. *to prēpon*; L. *decorum, aptum*); and (4) ornamentation (Gk. *kataskeuē*; L. *ornatus*).

Suasoriae. In Roman declamatory training, exercises requiring students to compose and perform imaginary deliberative speeches. See *controversiae*.

Subjectio. See *hypophora*.

Symplokē (Gk. "intertwining"; L. *complexio, conexum*). Repetition of the same word or phrase at the beginning and the end of successive clauses or sentences: "*Thou hadst* an Edward, till a Richard *killed him*. / *Thou hadst* a Richard, till a Richard *killed him*" (*King Richard III* 4.4.42–3). See *plokē*.

Syncatēgorema. See *anastrophē*.

Synecdoche (Gk. "understanding one thing in terms of another"; L. *intellectio, pars pro toto*; Eng. "the Figure of Quick Conceit" [Putt.]). Substitution of part for whole, species for genus, or vice versa: "Take thy *face* hence" (*Macbeth* 5.3.18).

Synonymia (L. "naming alike"; *nominis communio, interpretatio*; Eng. "the Figure of Store" [Putt.]). Amplification by means of words or phrases with the same or similar meaning (synonyms): "'Sleep no more! / Macbeth does murther Sleep,'—the innocent Sleep; / Sleep, that knits up the ravell'd sleeve of care, / The death of each day's life, sore labour's bath, / Balm of hurt minds, great Nature's second course, / Chief nourisher in life's feast" (*Macbeth* 2.2.34–9).

Synthesis. See *compositio*.

Synthroesmus. See *accumulatio*.

T

Tapinosis (Gk. "reduction," "humiliation"; L. *humiliatio*; Eng. "the Abaser" [Putt.]). Giving a name to something that minimizes its importance: "Get you gone, you dwarf; / You minimus, of hindering knot-grass made; / You bead, you acorn" (*A Midsummer Night's Dream* 3.2.328–9).

Taxis (Gk. "arrangement," "order"). See *dispositio*.

Testatio (L. "a bearing witness"). See *martyria*.

Thaumasmos (Gk. "wondering," "marveling"). See *admiratio*.

Thesis. See *hypothesis*.

Threnos (Gk. "dirge"; L. *humiliatio*). A lamentation: "Tell thou the lamentable tale of me / And send the hearers weeping to their beds. / For why the senseless brands will sympathize / The heavy accent of thy moving tongue / And in compassion weep the fire out; / And some will mourn in ashes, some coal-black, / For the deposing of a rightful king" (*King Richard II* 5.1.44–50).

Topographia (Gk. "description of place"; Eng. "the Counterfeit Place"). Description of a place: "Wherein of antres vast and deserts idle, / Rough quarries, rocks and hills whose heads touch heaven / . . . And of the cannibals that each other eat, / The Anthropophagi, and men whose heads / Do grow beneath their shoulders" (*Othello* 1.3.141–6).

Topoi (Gk. "place"; L. *topica, loci, loci communes*). Basic categories and lines of argument ("places") that help the orator discover, arrange, and memorize material for a speech, such as definition (Gk. *horos*; L. *finitio*), division (Gk. *diairesis*; L. *divisio, partitio*), comparison (Gk. *parathesis*; L. *comparatio*), etc.: "And in his brain, / which is as dry as the remainder biscuit / After a voyage, he hath *strange places* crammed / With observation, the which he vents / In mangled forms" (*As You Like It* 2.7.38–42). Aristotle distinguished between topics of invention common to many fields (*koinoi topoi*, "common topics") and those useful in specialized areas of knowledge (*idioi topoi*, "special topics").

Topothesia (Gk. "description of a place"; L. *loci positio*). Description of an imaginary place. See *topographia*.

Traductio. See *polyptoton*.

Transgressio. See *hyperbaton*.

Transitio. See *metabasis*.

Translatio. See *metaphor*.

Transmutatio. See *metonymy*.

Transumptio. See *metalēpsis*.

Tria Genera Causarum (L. "three kinds of cause"). The three principal genres of rhetorical theory and practice in ancient Greek and Roman rhetoric, comprising judicial (forensic) rhetoric, political (deliberative) rhetoric, and epideictic (ceremonial) rhetoric. See *deliberative rhetoric, epideictic rhetoric, forensic rhetoric*.

Trope (Gk. "a turn"). A word or phrase that turns from its literal meaning toward a figurative one, as with metaphor, metonymy, etc.

V

Verborum Bombus. See *bomphiologia*.

Votum. See *euche*.

Z

Zētamata Logika. See *constitutiones*.

Zeugma (Gk. "yoking together"; L. *adnexio, junctio*; Eng. "the Single Supply" [Putt.]). A form of ellipsis in which one word, usually a verb, controls two or more parts of a sentence: "A husband and a son thou *ow'st* to me; / —And thou a kingdom; —all of you, allegiance" (*King Richard III* 1.3.169–70).

NOTE

1. "Writers," observes Quintilian, "have given special names to all the figures, but variously and as it pleased them" (*Institutio oratoria* 9.3.54). In light of Quintilian's warning, this glossary of basic Greek and Latin rhetorical terms aims above all at clarity, economy, and simplicity. It is designed for readers approaching rhetoric for the first time, and its definitions should serve as points of departure for further exploration of the philological labyrinths of the *lexicon rhetoricae*. The glossary draws on three indispensable resources for the study of tropes, figures, and rhetorical terminology in general: Richard Lanham's *A Handlist of Rhetorical*

Terms (Berkeley: University of California Press, 1990); Gideon O. Burton's *Silva Rhetoricae* (http://rhetoric.byu.edu/); and George Puttenham's 1589 *The Art of English Poesy*, edited by Wayne A. Rebhorn and Frank Whigham (Ithaca, NY: Cornell University Press, 2007). Advanced students and scholars are directed to Heinrich Lausberg's *Handbook of Literary Rhetoric*, edited by David E. Orton and R. Dean Anderson (Leiden: Brill, [1960] 1998), and the *Historisches Wörterbuch der Rhetorik*, edited by Gert Ueding et al. (Tübingen: Niemeyer, 1996). Quotations from William Shakespeare are drawn from the *Arden Shakespeare* (Third Series) and *The Norton Shakespeare*, edited by Stephen Greenblatt (New York: W.W. Norton, 1997).

Index